EXPLORE NIGERIA
12 KEY FACTS

by Rosie Nanz

12 STORY LIBRARY

www.12StoryLibrary.com

12-Story Library is an imprint of Bookstaves.

Photographs ©: peeterv/iStockphoto, cover, 1; Terry Whalebone/CC2.0, 4; Fabian Plock/ Shutterstock.com, 5; roseshutterstock25/Shutterstock.com, 6; Tetyana Dotsenko/ Shutterstock.com, 7; Kit Korzun/Shutterstock.com, 7; Oliver S/Shutterstock.com, 8; Daderot/CC, 8; Chatham House/CC2.0, 10; Orhan Cam/Shutterstock.com, 11; vanhurck/ Shutterstock.com, 12; roseshutterstock25/Shutterstock.com, 13; SIM USA/CC2.0, 14; bmszealand/Shutterstock.com, 15; DFID - UK Department for International Development/ CC2.0, 16; UNIDO/CC2.0, 17; Atfie Sahid/Shutterstock.com, 18; Jordi C/Shutterstock. com, 19; Jordi C/Shutterstock.com, 20; Atfie Sahid/Shutterstock.com, 21; tinglee1631/ Shutterstock.com, 22; The New Niger/Shutterstock.com, 22; Lorimer Images/Shutterstock. com, 23; John Wollwerth/Shutterstock.com, 24; Sosialistisk Ungdom (SU)/CC2.0, 25; Omnivisuals/Shutterstock.com, 26; Vlad1988/Shutterstock.com, 27; Julinzy/Shutterstock. com, 28; Nannucci/iStockphoto, 29

ISBN
978-1-63235-558-4 (hardcover)
978-1-63235-675-8 (ebook)

Library of Congress Control Number: 2018940813

Printed in the United States of America
Mankato, MN
June 2018

About the Cover

Zuma Rock, a popular tourist destination in central Nigeria, is 2,379 feet high (725 m).

Access free, up-to-date content on this topic plus a full digital version of this book. Scan the QR code on page 31 or use your school's login at 12StoryLibrary.com.

Table of Contents

1

Nigeria Is a Land of Rivers and Savannas

Nigeria is a country on the western coast of Africa. It shares borders with Niger to the north, Chad and Cameroon to the east, and Benin to the west. Its coast lies along the Gulf of Guinea in the Atlantic Ocean. The country has almost 500 miles (800 km) of coastline.

Nigeria has a total area of 356,669 square miles (923,768 sq km). It is larger than the US state of Texas. Because of its size, it is often called the Giant of Africa. Nigeria also has more people than any other country in Africa.

Many rivers and creeks flow through Nigeria. The two main rivers are the Niger and the Benue. They meet, form a Y, and turn into the Niger Delta. It is the third-largest delta in the world. The delta leads into the Gulf of Guinea.

The southern lowlands are along Nigeria's coast. Further north are huge grassy plains called savannas. Some stretch as far as the eye can

Logs are floated down the Niger River to sawmills to be processed for export.

2,600
**Length in miles
(4,184 km) of the Niger,
the third-longest
river in Africa.**

- Nigeria is on the west coast of Africa.
- It shares borders with four other nations.
- It is called the Giant of Africa.
- The geography is diverse.

THE MOUNTAIN OF DEATH

Chappal Waddi is a mountain near Nigeria's border with Cameroon. Rising 7,936 feet (2,419 m), it is the highest peak in Nigeria. Another name for the mountain is Gangirwal. This means "the mountain of death." According to legend, the keeper of the mountain sleeps at its base. He has a bad temper. Climbers who wake him will suffer disaster.

Most of Nigeria's jungles are in the Niger Delta.

see. The central region has hills and plateaus. There are extinct volcanoes and lava flows. Nigeria also has swamps, jungles, and deserts. Its geography is very diverse.

The Environment Varies

Nigeria has three main regions. The coast is swampy and wet. The interior is tropical. The north is dry grasslands. Although the environment changes, it is hot everywhere. Temperatures are usually around 90 degrees (32°C). Humidity is high.

Nigeria has a rainy season and a dry season. In the north, it rains for three to four months. The dry season starts in October. A trade wind called the Harmattan brings fine sands from the Sahara Desert. The air gets hazy. The dust is harsh on the skin. It causes respiratory and other health problems.

Nigeria has many environmental challenges. Rapid urbanization has led to pollution. Forests have been destroyed for the fast-growing population. The soil has been over-farmed. This causes it to lose nutrients crops need to grow. Nigeria is rich in oil, but oil spills are common.

Nigeria is home to a large variety of animals. There are more than 274 species of mammals. Many are endangered due to hunting

The Harmattan winds are harsh on livestock, and can last for three months in northern Nigeria.

and deforestation. One of the most endangered animals is the white-throated guenon, a type of monkey. These are hunted for their fur. Two famous Nigerian animals are the lion and the gorilla. Elephants, rhinos, antelopes, and hyenas are found in the savannas. The forests and swamps have leopards, snakes, and hippos. Various species of wild cats live all over the country.

The Cross River gorilla and white-throated guenon monkey are endangered in Nigeria.

200–300
Population of critically endangered Cross River gorillas.

- Northern Nigeria is dry and southern Nigeria is wet.
- Harmattan winds from the northeast make the air dusty.
- Deforestation, pollution, and over-farming are major environmental concerns.

THINK ABOUT IT

Pick an endangered animal you care about. Research online to learn more about it. Why is the animal endangered? What organizations work to save endangered animals?

Nigeria's History Includes Slavery

Nigeria's history reaches back thousands of years. The Nok civilization is the oldest known organized society in Nigeria. They lived in central Nigeria near the Jos Plateau. A Nok settlement discovered in 1928 is at least 3,000 years old. Many terra-cotta sculptures and other artifacts have been found.

By 1000 CE, Nigeria was made up of kingdoms. Some early kingdoms were the Hausa States, the Jukin States, and the Yoruba States. By 1200 CE, the Hausa people in the north were living in walled towns that were busy centers of trade.

In 1472, the Portuguese arrived on the Nigerian coast. They set up trading posts for goods and enslaved many people. Other European nations followed. By the eighteenth century, the British took over from the Portuguese as leaders of the slave trade. From the 1700s to the 1800s, millions of Nigerians were enslaved and sent to the Americas. Great Britain banned the slave trade in 1807.

Nok sculptures were found in caves high in the Jos Plateau.

By 1906, the British ruled most of Nigeria. In 1960, Nigeria gained its independence. It became a republic with a central government. In 1966, the military took over. There was a long period of conflict and unrest. A new constitution was written in 1999. It set up a new government that is still in place today.

But Nigeria has many troubles. These have included ethnic violence and religious violence. Starting in 2009, a militant Islamic group called Boko Haram has tried to take over the country. Thousands of Nigerian people have been killed in terrorist attacks. Millions have had to flee their homes.

36

States in Nigeria today.

- Nigeria was once divided into kingdoms.
- Europeans sold enslaved Nigerians for hundreds of years.
- The British ruled Nigeria until 1960.
- Nigeria has many troubles today.

TIMELINE

500 BCE: Nok civilization thrives.

1472: Portuguese come to Nigeria.

1807: Britain bans the slave trade.

1906: British control most of Nigeria.

1960: Nigeria gains independence from Britain.

1966: The Nigerian military takes control.

1999: New constitution is put in place.

2009: The Islamic group Boko Haram starts a campaign of violence.

The Government Is a Republic

Nigeria's government is similar to the one in the United States. It is a federal republic. A constitution outlines how the government works. A president is elected for four-year terms. This person is the head of state and chief executive. As of 2018, the president is Muhammadu Buhari. The president chooses a vice president and cabinet members. Nigeria also has a House of Representatives and a Senate. They have the power to create and pass laws.

All citizens over age 18 can vote. To be a Nigerian citizen, a person must have at least one parent or grandparent who was born in Nigeria.

The Nigerian legal system follows codes of law.

These codes help guide decisions. The first is customary law. It is based on tradition and community values. Another is Sharia law, or Islamic law. Rules are developed from religious beliefs. Other laws have been inherited from the time of British rule. The laws are enforced by courts and the police. The Nigerian Police Force is led by an inspector general of police. This person is appointed by the president.

Muhammadu Buhari was elected president in 2015.

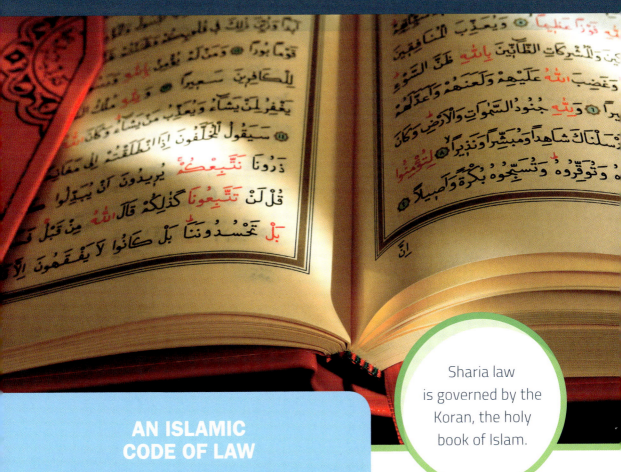

Sharia law is governed by the Koran, the holy book of Islam.

AN ISLAMIC CODE OF LAW

Sharia law governs Muslim life. Sharia means "the path." It comes from two sources. One is the Koran, the Islamic sacred book. It also comes from fatwas. These are rulings by Islamic scholars. Sharia law is a code for living. It describes how Muslims should behave toward themselves, their family, and their neighbors. The goal is to live life according to God's (Allah's) wishes. Sharia law is an important part of Nigeria's justice system.

7

Deputy inspectors of police in the Nigerian Police Force.

- People elect a president to lead the government.
- The House of Representatives and Senate make laws.
- Laws are based on tradition, religion, and British influence.

Nigeria's Economy Depends on Oil

Nigeria has one of the largest economies in Africa. Its Gross Domestic Product (GDP) was $395 billion in 2017. This is the total value of all goods a country produces. Nigeria's economy is ranked 29th in the world.

Nigeria is rich in oil. First discovered in 1956, oil is Nigeria's largest export. Oil helped Nigeria become one of the fastest-growing economies in the world. In recent years, this growth has slowed. Some reasons are lower oil prices and political unrest in the country. Corruption in the government has stood in the way of improving the nation's health, education, and infrastructure. More than half of Nigeria's people live in poverty.

Agriculture is on the rise. Nigerians are producing more crops. The government doesn't want the country to depend on imported food. Many food imports have been banned. It is illegal to import pork, beef, noodles, frozen

An oil rig and cargo ship near the port city of Lagos, the main outlet for Nigeria's exports.

Nigeria is working to increase rice production so it does not have to rely on imports.

poultry, and cocoa butter. The goal of these bans is to get more Nigerians back to farming. Today 60 percent of Nigerians work in farming.

Farmers grow rice, yams, plantains, ginger, and nuts. Many more food products are grown to feed the fast-growing population.

Nigeria exports cocoa beans, wood, machinery, manufactured items, and chemicals. In 2017, Nigeria had a good year. The value of what it exported was higher than the value of what it imported.

2.7 million
Barrels of crude oil produced in Nigeria per day in 2018.

- Nigeria has one of Africa's largest economies.
- Oil is its largest export.
- Some food imports are banned.
- Farming is becoming a focus for employment and food.

More Children Need Education

Nigeria's population is growing very quickly. By 2050, Nigeria will be the third most populous country in the world. Services like education have a hard time keeping up.

In 1999, Nigeria's government created a Universal Basic Education program. Children get six years of primary school and three years of secondary school for free. But there are extra costs. Parents have to buy uniforms and learning materials.

Poor families can't afford them. So 40 percent of children between ages of 6 and 11 don't go to school. Children from poor families often drop out. The Nigerian government believes they have the most out-of-school children in the world.

Also, there is a gender gap. More boys than girls attend school. Girls are often taken out of school because they are expected to help at home. In 2015, 69 percent of males over age 15 were literate. But only 46 percent of females were literate.

Girls are not given the same opportunities as boys to receive an education.

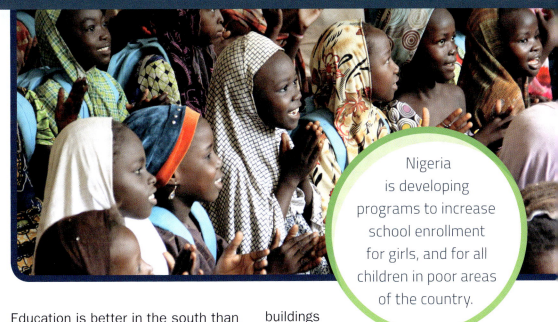

Nigeria is developing programs to increase school enrollment for girls, and for all children in poor areas of the country.

Education is better in the south than in the north. More people in the north are poor. There are not enough teachers and schools. Many school buildings need repairs. School supplies are scarce.

Nigeria has a large higher education system. The country has more than 80 federal and state universities. There are many private universities as well.

1948
Year Nigeria's first college, the University of Ibadan, was founded.

- The Universal Basic Education program gives children nine years of free schooling.
- 40 percent of school-age children don't go to primary school.
- More boys than girls go to school.
- More teachers and schools are needed.

THINK ABOUT IT

When children can't or don't go to school, what are the consequences? How does their lack of education affect their lives? How does it affect their community and country? Research online to learn more.

Scientific Research Is Key to the Future

Nigeria has several organizations that do scientific research. They focus on engineering, medicine, genetics, microbiology, and geography.

Nigeria is looking to its youth to develop technologies that will modernize the country.

The Federal Ministry of Science and Technology (FMST) has 25 research institutes. They research things like forestry, livestock, marine sciences, and horticulture. Dr. Ogbonnaya Onu is minister of the FMST. The Technology Orientation Center helps entrepreneurs work together with researchers and investors. New technologies can help modernize Nigeria.

The Nigerian Academy of Science works on science and innovation. Its experts advise the government on matters of science. Many scientists are trained there.

One priority is bringing technology to the people of Nigeria. The FMST is working with Intel and Microsoft. More Nigerians need computers. In 2014, fewer than 10 percent of Nigerian households had a

Dr. Ogbonnaya Onu meets with China's Li Yong, director general of the United Nations Industrial Development Organization.

computer. The Computers for All Nigerians Initiative (CANI) plans to increase that percentage. It wants to make computers more affordable for Nigerians. When more people have access to computers, economic and social opportunity should rise.

The government also supports investment in solar, hydro, and wind energy. These are sustainable sources of energy. More innovation will create jobs, reduce poverty, and help the economy. The goal is to make economic and social progress happen more quickly.

40
Percent of Nigerian college students studying science and engineering.

- The Federal Ministry of Science and Technology has 25 research institutes.
- Bringing technology to the people is a priority.
- Less than 10 percent of Nigerians have a computer.
- Solar, hydro, and wind energy are important for Nigeria's future economy.

The Infrastructure Needs Work

Nigeria has many roads, railroads, and airports. It has communication networks. But the systems are not in good repair.

Telephone lines have been in cities since the 1970s. But they are not reliable. Most people use cell phones.

TV and radio networks exist throughout the country. Every state has at least one TV or radio station. Radio broadcasts are a main source of information. They are affordable

26
Airports in Nigeria.

- Most people in Nigeria use cell phones instead of landlines.
- The railroads and roads are poorly maintained.
- Public transportation is very popular.

Trains in most states have been neglected and are in poor condition.

and don't need much power. In 2016, 86 million Nigerians were using the internet. That is nearly half the population.

Nigeria has a vast railroad network. There are more than 2,200 miles (3,540 km) of railways. But the railroads have been neglected. They are no longer a useful source of transportation.

The roads in Nigeria are poorly kept. Most are unpaved. Traffic is heavy and there are many accidents.

Motor parks are found in almost every settlement. A motor park is a crowded hub for public transportation. People go there to find rides. Minibuses and bush taxis are used for travel over longer distances. A bush taxi is usually a car, often a station wagon. For shorter distances within towns or cities, people take okadas.

Waterways were once a primary mode of transportation. Today the Niger and Benue rivers are mainly used to ship goods. The coastal city of Lagos is an important port city.

Okadas are an affordable but risky form of transportation in towns and cities.

GETTING AROUND TOWN

Many Nigerians get around cities and town on okadas. These are like taxis, but instead of cars, they are motorcycles. Okadas are also called *achabas, inagas,* and sometimes just "going." They can easily cut through traffic, people, and busy streets. Taking an okada can be a wild ride. The Nigerian government has banned them in some places.

19

The Population Is Young

Nigeria is the seventh most populous country in the world. As of 2018, nearly 195 million people live there. Most are under the age of 24.

Nigeria has more than 250 ethnic groups. The largest are the Hausa, Fulani, Yoruba, and Igbo. Each has its own language and traditions. Together they make up almost 70 percent of the population.

English is the official language of Nigeria. But there are hundreds of other indigenous languages. Society is generally male-dominated. Property and wealth are typically

43 percent of the population is under the age of 14.

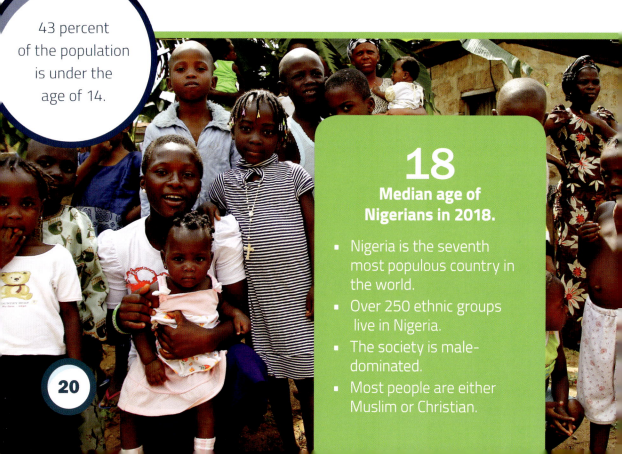

18

Median age of Nigerians in 2018.

- Nigeria is the seventh most populous country in the world.
- Over 250 ethnic groups live in Nigeria.
- The society is male-dominated.
- Most people are either Muslim or Christian.

The National Mosque in Abuja is one of the largest in Nigeria.

passed down to sons. It is difficult for women to inherit money or become independent. Their traditional role is to maintain the home. They also raise the children.

The constitution grants all Nigerians religious freedom. Approximately half of the population is Muslim. The other half is Christian. Some people practice indigenous religions. There are few of these. The north has a high concentration of Muslims. The southern states are majority Christian.

NAIJA: A NEW NIGERIA

The youth of Nigeria are unhappy with the old and corrupt ways of their country. They have come up with a new word, *Naija*. It means many things. It is about loving the country and feeling frustrated. It is a way to tell the world that change is coming. Naija is about breaking away from the past and moving toward a better future.

Nigerians Love to Eat and Celebrate

Cassava is a good source of dietary fiber and vitamins.

use various grains to cook cereal. Soups and stews are common. Food is often flavored with onions or chilies. Tropical fruits thrive in Nigeria. People enjoy mangoes, bananas, pineapples, and oranges.

Muslims in Nigeria hold Islamic festivals. These often celebrate the life of the prophet Muhammad. Christians observe Christmas and Easter. Nigeria's Independence Day is October First. Another national holiday is Workers' Day, which recognizes working people. The Osun-Osogbo Festival is held at the end of the rainy season. People

Food is central to Nigerian culture. It is an important part of ceremonies and everyday life. The dishes people eat depend on where they live. Corn and cassava, a starchy root, are staples in the southern regions. These are ground into flour and used to make dough. Northern people

Fried rice and fish is a popular Nigerian meal.

100,000

Approximate number of people who attend the Osun-Osogbo Festival each year.

- Nigerians celebrate many holidays and festivals.
- Grains, vegetables, and fruits are common foods in Nigeria.
- Nigerians create popular music and art forms inspired by their heritage.

A POPULAR NIGERIAN SNACK

Foods fried in coconut or palm oil are common in Nigeria. One popular dish is called *puff puff.* It is a snack similar to donut holes. Flour is mixed with sugar, water, yeast, and nutmeg to make a dough. This is made into small balls and fried in oil. The treat is common at parties and gatherings.

celebrate Osun, the Yoruba goddess of fertility. This festival attracts people from around the world.

The arts are alive and well in Nigeria. Juju music is popular. It involves percussion instruments and electric guitars. Artists make pottery and wood carvings of spiritual figures. The figures represent the earth, sea, water, fire, and thunder. Nigerians find inspiration for art in their rich heritage.

Men perform traditional dances as part of Nigeria's Independence Day celebration.

Health Care in Nigeria Needs Improvement

The Nigerian government doesn't spend much money on health care. Most people don't get proper treatment. There are hospitals and clinics in most towns. But they are understaffed. There is a shortage of vaccines. These are needed to prevent diseases. Antibiotics and medical supplies are limited.

Some diseases are more common in the densely populated cities. Waste disposal is a serious problem. Trash is dumped on streets and highways. Sewage lines are often blocked.

Conditions are unsanitary. The risk of infection is very high.

Nigerians face other public health threats. Cholera and tuberculosis are common diseases. The leading causes of death are lower respiratory infections (LRIs), malaria, and HIV/AIDS. In 2016, 3.2 million people in Nigeria were living with HIV.

The average life expectancy of a Nigerian person is 55 years. Frequent oil spills in the Niger Delta area have contaminated the

Pollution and inadequate sewage systems contribute to health issues for many Nigerians.

Oil spills from broken pipelines and illegal refineries cause environmental damage and health issues in the Niger Delta.

environment and affected local communities. Infant deaths are twice as high in those areas. Still, the birth rate in the country is more than twice as high as the death rate. Approximately 20,000 babies are born every day.

$217

Average amount per person the Nigerian government spends on health care each year.

- Nigeria's health care system does not have enough staff, supplies, and medicine.
- Lower respiratory infections are common.
- Malaria and HIV/AIDS are leading health concerns.
- The average life expectancy is 55 years.

THINK ABOUT IT

Diseases can vary from one place to another. What are some health concerns where you live? What do people in your area do to stay healthy?

Cities Are Hubs of Life

Most Nigerians live in cities. Many people leave their rural homes to find work. More than 21 million people are believed to live in Lagos.

Cities in Nigeria are overcrowded. Most of the people who live there are poor. Some 64 percent of Nigerians live in poverty. They can't afford homes or apartments. So shantytowns form. People build homes from whatever they can find. They use scrap metal, wood, or cardboard. There is no running water or electricity. Federal housing programs in Nigeria are working on building homes for low- and middle-income people.

Living conditions are very different for wealthy Nigerians. Some live in Western-style homes. Others have expensive apartments or mansions in gated communities. Houses in rural areas often have mud walls. Roofs are made of palm leaves and grass mats. In wet regions of the

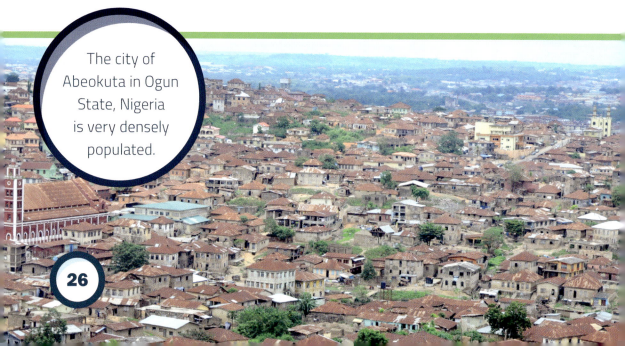

The city of Abeokuta in Ogun State, Nigeria is very densely populated.

Nigerian fans enjoy supporting their football team.

country, wood and bamboo homes are built on stilts.

Less than half of the population has electricity. Two-thirds of the country's energy comes from thermal plants. They burn natural gas and coal to create electricity. The rest of Nigeria's energy comes from hydroelectric plants. This type of electricity is produced by the power of dams. People use firewood and charcoal in their homes for heating and cooking.

Despite their varied living styles, Nigerians share similar interests. People across the country enjoy recreation and hobbies. Some of these activities are music, dance, and making pottery. Nigerians love to visit friends and family to share meals.

Soccer is the most popular sport. The Nigerians call it football. The country has a national football team. Dambe Boxing is a traditional sport. It is centuries old.

5

Average size of a Nigerian family.

- The poverty rate in Nigeria is high.
- Nigerians live in vastly different kinds of homes.
- Most people don't have electricity in their homes.
- Nigerians enjoy music, dance, and soccer.

Nigeria at a Glance

Population in 2018: 195,875,237

Area: 356,669 square miles (923,768 sq km)

Capital: Abuja

Largest Cities: Lagos, Kano, Ibadan, Benin City

Flag:

National Language: English

Currency: Nigerian Naira

What people who live in Nigeria are called: Nigerians

Where in the World?

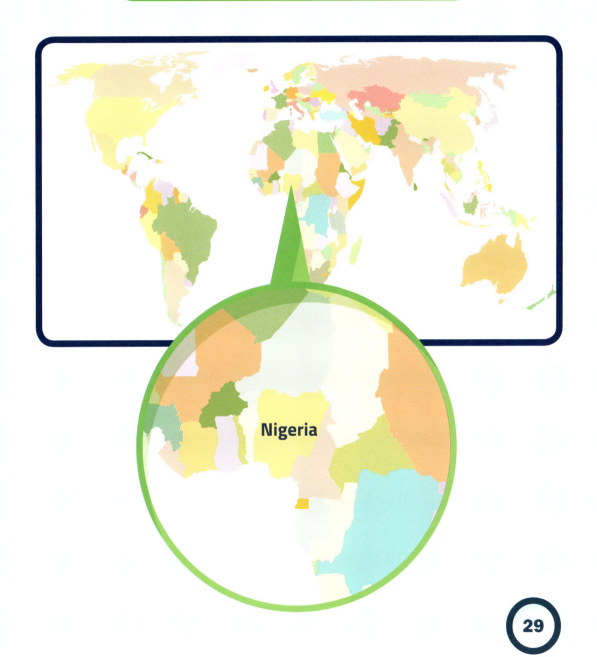

Nigeria

Glossary

cassava

The starchy root of a plant found in the tropics.

constitution

A set of rules and principles that guide how a country, state, or other organization works.

delta

The area where sediment is deposited at the mouth of a river or where rivers meet.

entrepreneur

Someone who sets up a new business.

hydro energy

Power generated by the force of flowing water. Also called hydroelectricity.

infrastructure

Structures and systems required by a society, including transportation and communications networks.

literate

Able to read and write.

populous

Having a large population.

plantain

A fruit similar to a banana, usually cooked before eating.

republic

Form of government where power is given to representatives of the people.

savanna

A grassy plain in a tropical or subtropical region.

For More Information

Books

Kovacs, Vic. *Life As a Nigerian American*. One Nation for All: Immigrants in the United States. New York: Powerkids Press, 2018.

Cantor, Rachel Anne. *Nigeria.* Countries We Come From. New York: Bearport Publishing, 2017.

Klepeis, Alicia. *Nigeria.* Exploring World Cultures, New York: Cavendish Square, 2016.

Thoennes, Kristen. *Nigeria.* Countries of the World, North Mankato, MN: Capstone Press, 2016.

Visit 12StoryLibrary.com

Scan the code or use your school's login at **12StoryLibrary.com** for recent updates about this topic and a full digital version of this book. Enjoy free access to:

- Digital ebook
- Breaking news updates
- Live content feeds
- Videos, interactive maps, and graphics
- Additional web resources

Note to educators: Visit 12StoryLibrary.com/register to sign up for free premium website access. Enjoy live content plus a full digital version of every 12-Story Library book you own for every student at your school.

Index

About the Author

Rosie Nanz is a graduate of St. Olaf College with degrees in English and American Studies. She enjoys researching and writing on many topics for kids. Nanz lives in southern California with her family and two corgis, Hubble and Kepler.

WHO'S WHO

IN

THEOLOGY AND SCIENCE

1996 Edition

WHO'S WHO

── IN ──

THEOLOGY AND SCIENCE

1996 Edition

*An International Biographical and Bibliographical
Guide to Individuals and Organizations
Interested in the Interaction
of Theology and Science*

Compiled and Edited by

The John Templeton Foundation

CONTINUUM • NEW YORK

1996

The Continuum Publishing Company

370 Lexington Avenue

New York, NY 10017 USA

Copyright © 1996, The John Templeton Foundation

Printed in the United States of America

Library of Congress Cataloging-in-Publication Data

Who's Who in Theology and Science: An international biographical and bibliographical guide
  to individuals and organizations interested in the interaction of theology and science /
  compiled and edited by the John Templeton Foundation.
    p. cm.
  Includes indexes.
  ISBN 0-8264-0874-5
  1. Religion and science—Bio-bibliography. 2. Theologians—Biography—Dictionaries.
  3. Scientists—Biography—Dictionaries.
  I. Templeton Foundation.
  Bl240.2.w514 1996
  291.1175—dc20   95-39201
                                                                        CIP

Contents

Introduction

by John M. Templeton

This directory is an international biographical and bibliographical guide to individuals and organizations interested in the interaction of science and theology. It is hoped that its publication will provide a stimulus to communication between individuals and organizations in the field and between the scientific and theological communities generally. Most (but not all) of those included see science and theology as related, complementary avenues of truth, and seek in some sense an integration of the ideas and concepts of these two spheres of research, often recognizing that the God of Creation is the source of both the natural and the spiritual.

This is the second edition of *Who's Who in Theology and Science.* The first edition was published in 1992. As before, the preparation of this directory has been subsidized by the Templeton Foundation, which has as a major goal the encouragement of further research and publication of the continual discoveries by natural scientists of the creative and purposive activities of God. Furthermore, it emphasizes that the pace of this discovery has been accelerating, revealing a God infinitely greater than our minds can conceive, yet intimate and inseparable in His relationship to human creatures and the rest of the universe. For a more detailed discussion of the views of the Foundation, you may wish to read the statement entitled "Theology of Humility" which is included as an addendum at the end of the book.

It should be noted that the Foundation's views concerning the strong interpenetration of theology and science are not shared by everyone, or perhaps even a majority of those included in this Directory. Indeed, there is considerable variation in the degree of interaction between theology and science acknowledged by those listed in this compilation. For some scientists and theologians, the two are seen as complementary. Explanations in terms of scientific laws and in terms of divine activity are not rival answers to the same question. Yet they are talking about the same things, as complementary accounts, presenting different aspects of the same event which in its full nature cannot be described adequately by either alone. Some have cautioned that this should be the limit of our integration — that neither science nor theology should be interpreted in terms of the other. In particular, concern has been expressed that we not seek scientific support for our theological constructions. For example, the late Donald MacKay, neurophysiologist at the University of Keele, cautioned that scientific quantum indeterminacy should not be interpreted as evidence for a theological notion of "free will."

A second group of those for whom theology and science interact go beyond the idea of complementary descriptions. Many have been impressed with Michael Polanyi's philosophy of personal knowledge, which frames scientific truth-gathering in the context of a personal act of knowing and a commitment to an external reality yet largely unseen. In this setting, science and religious faith are seen to have surprisingly similar features. One lesson to be learned, according to theoretical chemist Walter Thorson, could be immensely practical for theory-building. He points out that one part of the personal aspect of knowing, the appreciation of elements of a theory which might collectively be called beauty, has a real power to evoke creative vision in the scientist.

Theologian Thomas Torrance has also argued for a greater interaction between theology and science, emphasizing the deep significance of theological elements such as the Incarnation, and creation *ex nihilo* for our appreciation of the natural world, and proposing that any unified view of the cosmos must transcend the artificial dichotomy between the traditional categories of the "how" of science and the "why" of theology. Furthermore, even ethics is implicated because of the obligation of science to maximize order in the world.

Again from the theological perspective, the late Harold Nebelsick has emphasized the importance of continual dialogue between scientists and theologians with a willingness on the part of each to modify concepts and interpretations in either area in response to new developments. Anything else is hardly reasonable. For example, for the scientific community to seal off scientific concepts from the language of faith is to encourage the doing of science as if God had nothing to do with the cosmos. From the standpoint of our limited understanding of the universe, this choice would be impoverishing.

Physician Lewis Thomas has said that the greatest of all the accomplishments of twentieth-century science has been the discovery of human ignorance. Indeed, our expectation is that rather than obtaining a complete scientific picture of reality, we will instead be increasingly overwhelmed by the awesome immensity and complexity of the cosmos. With such a prospect, it seems we need to search diligently for theological correlates. There is no threat of a "God of the Gaps" here — we are finding with every scientific breakthrough that there are a hundred new questions to be explored. Every explanation is accompanied by multiplied mysteries.

But still the sum total of what we have learned from science is staggering! It has revealed a new world — dynamic, ever-changing and diversifying, profound in its economy and its complexity. Indeed, some theologians and scientists see tremendous possibilities for our future understanding of ourselves and our Creator through an integration of these new scientific findings with time-honored religious traditions, a new "theology of science." Perhaps one of the most futuristic of such thinkers is Ralph Wendell Burhoe, who sees the revelations of science as a gold mine for theology, leading to the revitalization and universalization of religion by providing clear evidence for an essential relationship between human values and the cosmic scheme of things.

It may be that we shall see the beginning of a new age of "experimental theology," where studies will reveal that there are spiritual laws which operate in the spiritual realm just as natural laws function in the physical realm. Indeed, we may be on the threshold of a great new Reformation! What is called for is a new spirit of humility in both scientific and theological communities: scientists humble enough to admit that the unseen is vastly greater than the seen, and theologians humble enough to admit that their ideas and interpretations of God's nature and activity may be far too small and circumscribed for the vast universe which we only just begin to perceive.

There are great rewards for the kinds of integration being carried out by the scholars and organizations listed in this Directory. It is our fond hope that these workers will be joined by a host of others. In fact, we are aware that the present compilation is far from complete, and we welcome input from others who have heretofore escaped our notice. Inquiries and suggestions may be sent to the John Templeton Foundation, 3 Radnor Corporate Center, Suite 230, 100 Matsonford Road, Radnor, PA U.S.A.

Preface

Who's Who in Theology and Science is intended as a reference tool for use in a burgeoning but still rather nebulous field. This preface seeks to establish a context for understanding what the book is about, how it came to be, and how it may be used most effectively.

Perhaps the best way to describe the book is to call it a "User's Guide" to the people, organizations, and journals currently active in the dialogue between science and theology. To that end it contains four directories and a set of five indexes. Directories A and B, combined, have entries gleaned from the responses of 1086 individuals (up from 971 in the 1992 edition) from most of the United States and 39 other countries. Directories C and D, in turn, contain descriptions of 73 institutions, organizations, journals and newsletters, plus name-and-address-only listings for 49 more. Something of the international scope of the publication can be gauged from the fact that 35% of the individuals, and almost 32% of the organizations, are located outside the United States of America.

Many of the individual listings from the 1992 edition have been greatly expanded, with significantly more contact, background, and bibliographic information included. Most original entries are at least twice as long as they were in the 1992 edition, and some are three or more times as long. New listings include, where possible, the same greater range of information.

The first three indexes provide alphabetical, geographical, and subject listings of all individuals (with extensive cross-referencing), while an index of organizations and another of journals and newsletters completes the work.

Of course, it is not a simple matter to give a succinct description of just what this "field" is that the book purports to be about. We have called it "theology and science," while others might prefer to talk of "religion/spirituality and science/technology" or "faith/belief and science." In its specific use in this book, the phrase "theology and science" should be understood as a general rubric that can be fairly clearly specified at its center, while remaining rather general at the edges. Thus, while for most people the notion of "theology and science" might conjure up the image of a physicist and a theologian discussing the meaning, appropriateness, and range of the so-called "anthropic principle" or a version of the theory of "complementarity," it is no less applicable to the case of the psychologist who, drawing on Kierkegaard, Bohr and Polanyi, seeks to articulate an integrative under-standing of the workings of the human spirit and the Divine Spirit in experiences of human creativity and transformation. Likewise, issues such as ethics and technology, religious experience and rationality, spirituality and ecology, and so on, can also be considered to fall within the same broad rubric.

Many different types of people have been included in this work. A majority of them are, or have been, part of the academic world, and most of the journals and organizations have largely academic constituencies. On the other hand, the fields of ministry, medicine, commerce, industry, and government are also well represented. A full list of the fields of study/professional fields of those included can be found at the beginning of the index section.

The character of the book has been shaped from its inception by the desire to tap into the *current network* of those actively engaged in the dialogue between theology and science in its many forms. Thus, instead of starting with an electronic database search in libraries and periodical indexes (proce-dures now available to most individual researchers anyway) the approach that was adopted was to start with a core list of well-known individuals and organizations drawn up by a few prominent figures in the field. These individuals and organizations were contacted, requesting biographical and bibliographical information as well as asking for recommendations of others whom they thought should be contacted. Then, by soliciting further refer-ences from these new names, the network spread out further and further. It should be added that the process was also supplemented with names gathered from well-known institutions and journals active in the field. The main strength of this "from centers to margins" procedure was that it enabled us: (a) to get a sense of the center (i.e. those who were repeatedly recommended); (b) to spread the nct wider than would otherwise have been possible (i.e. particularly by tapping into networks in other countries); and (c) to be in a position to make a judgment as to when one was approaching a certain level of comprehensiveness (i.e. from a sense of diminishing returns). Of course, the limitations of this procedure are also clear. Despite our best efforts, important individuals or even whole networks can be missed altogether. For example, while many individuals in the social sciences have been included, we clearly cannot claim to have included everyone working in sociology, cultural anthropology, psychology, etc., who might have an interest in religion. The main purpose for this book, however, is to try to provide you with a starting point for developing or expanding your own networks.

Using *Who's Who in Theology and Science*

Directories A and B, which make up the bulk of the book, each consist of an alphabetical listing of entries on specific individuals. Directory A gives biographical and selected bibliographical information on individuals who have written and published in the specific field of theology and science. Directory B gives biographical information on those with an active interest in theology and science, who have not yet published in the field. It should be noted that many of the individuals in Directory B are highly distinguished scholars with extensive bibliographies in their own areas of expertise. Furthermore, the bibliographies that are included in Directory A list only items relevant to the field of theology and science, and are in some cases highly selective due to space restrictions.

In contrast to the typical *Who's Who* which focuses on an individual's distinctions and accomplishments, our primary purpose has been to facilitate the ongoing dialogue between science and theology. The criterion used in deciding which information to include was above all its relevance and "usefulness" to the dialogue. In no case could a complete *curriculum vitae* be included, nor could a rigid consistency be maintained. Our goal has simply been to include as much that was directly relevant as possible, and enough general biographical data for an adequate overall assessment of the person's work, interests and accomplishments.

In all but a very exceptional cases the data used comes directly from the individuals concerned. This was generally supplied in the form of a completed questionnaire, and/or an accompanying *curriculum vitae*. It should be clearly understood that the individuals appearing in the book are those who *responded* to our request for information. This means, of course, that we know of many whom we would like to have included, but could not, for lack of information. It also means that the quantity, quality and significance of the information may vary widely from entry to entry. No editorial attempt was made to evaluate the entries, but we always tried to give sufficient information so that the reader would be in a position to do so. Once the information was processed, the typeset entry was returned to the individual for checking and proofing. Unfortunately, not all of these proofs were returned to us. A few entries from the 1992 edition remain unchanged in this edition because we did not receive updated information from some individuals. In all cases we have depended on the individuals themselves for the accuracy of the given data. As a general principle, the *absence* of information should be always be treated with some circumspection. This is specially true in the case of bibliographical information, languages spoken, honors, awards and memberships.

Here is a brief summary of some other details that might be pertinent to the use of the directories:

• With regard to Publications in Directory A, we have had to be particularly selective. Please keep in mind that we were limited by space to ten publications per entry. If the individual indicated which publications were most significant, we have listed those. Otherwise, we have simply listed the ten most recent ones.

• If possible, we have supplied telephone, fax, e-mail, and/or telex numbers. For US numbers, we follow the standard form *(Area Code) xxx-xxxx*. The form used for other countries was left as it was given to us (which sometimes included international country and area codes, and at other times did not).

• Where we had access to the full bibliography of an individual, we have tried to give some idea of its size, scope and range in a brief note before the list of relevant publications. The absence of such a note simply means that we did not have such information at hand.

• For the sake of clarity (particularly in an international setting) we have chosen to use a minimum of abbreviation. However, we have consistently abbreviated US States (see list on page xvii-xviii). Titles, Degrees and abbreviations for Catholic Orders have not been standardized, but follow the practices used in various parts of the world. If the author used abbreviations of which we were not sure, they were included as given.

Directory C consists of an alphabetical listing of descriptions of 60 institutions, organizations and other more informal groups which are active in the interface between theology and science, plus name-and-address-only listings for 40 more. Directory D gives an account of 13 journals or other regular publications whose major focus falls in the area of theology and science, plus name-and-address-only listings for 9 more.

Using the information submitted to us by organizations and journals, we tried to convey as much information as we could that would be useful in giving an overall grasp of the nature and goals of each organization or journal.

Five indexes have been included at the back of the book, and a description of how to use them appears on page 619.

It is always somewhat unnerving to realize that despite the enormous efforts put into completing a project such as this, it will inevitably be outdated before it is even published. But this is simply an occupational hazard that has to be faced. A more substantive concern is the awareness that a project of this nature can never be truly finished. Even as we go to press, we discover other individuals and organizations that we would have liked to have seen included. But the temptation must be resisted in the hope that an "incomplete word" will be better than no word at all.

Acknowledgments to the 1992 Edition: The original edition was initiated by the late Harold Nebelsick of Louisville Presbyterian Theological Seminary and the Center of Theological Inquiry in Princeton, New Jersey, and was completed by John Webster of Princeton Theological Seminary. Others who helped with the massive project include Dr. James F. Armstrong, Professor Roland M. Frye of CTI, Professor Daniel W. Hardy of CTI, Dr. Robert L. Herrmann, Lance Hickerson, Patricia Grier, Jennifer Jones, Kate Le Van, the late Dr. James I. McCord of CTI, Eileen Moffett, Melissa K. Nebelsick, the late Dr. W. Jim Neidhardt, Annegrete Sauter, Professor Gerhard Sauter, Frances D. Schapperle of the John Templeton Foundation, Lynn Schroeder of the Winthrop Publishing Company, Professor Thomas F. Torrance, and Cheryl Webster.

Acknowledgments to the 1996 Edition: The second edition is the work of Scott Ames of Harvard University and Robert L Herrmann, Trustee of the Templeton Foundation, with the editorial assistance of Patricia Ames of Publication Management Resources, Ipswich, MA. Others who helped complete this enormous undertaking include Donna Ames, Ann F. Droppers, Mary K. Fagan, Mary X. Fagan, Judith Marchand of the Templeton Foundation, Susanne R. McCarron, and Beth Welin.

Alphabetization & Abbreviation

The alphabetical practices used include the following:

• Individuals are listed according to surname, and where surnames are identical according to the first names. Suffixes such as Jr., II, etc. are ignored for alphabetization purposes.

• Surnames beginning with De, Des, Del, Du, Mac, Mc, Saint, St., Van, etc., however capitalized or spaced, are listed with the prefix preceding the name, and arranged in strict alphabetical order (ignoring spaces). The only exception to this rule is with surnames beginning with Von or von, in which case we follow the standard German practice of listing them as follows: Weizsäcker, Carl Friedrich von

• Organizations and journals are listed alphabetically, and any leading article (i.e. "the") is ignored.

The list of standard U.S.A. state abbreviations used throughout the book is as follows:

AK	Alaska	HI	Hawaii
AL	Alabama	IA	Iowa
AR	Arkansas	ID	Idaho
AZ	Arizona	IL	Illinois
CA	California	IN	Indiana
CO	Colorado	KS	Kansas
CT	Connecticut	KY	Kentucky
DC	Washington, D.C.	LA	Louisiana
DE	Delaware	MA	Massachusetts
FL	Florida	MD	Maryland
GA	Georgia	ME	Maine

Alphabetization & Abbreviation

MI	Michigan	OR	Oregon
MN	Minnesota	PA	Pennsylvania
MO	Missouri	RI	Rhode Island
MS	Mississippi	SC	South Carolina
MT	Montana	SD	South Dakota
NC	North Carolina	TN	Tennessee
ND	North Dakota	TX	Texas
NE	Nebraska	UT	Utah
NH	New Hampshire	VA	Virginia
NJ	New Jersey	VT	Vermont
NM	New Mexico	WA	Washington
NV	Nevada	WI	Wisconsin
NY	New York	WV	West Virginia
OH	Ohio	WY	Wyoming
OK	Oklahoma		

Directory A

Individuals Publishing in the Field

Ajakaiye, Deborah Enilo

Present Position and Address: Professor of Physics and Dean for Faculty of Natural Sciences (since 1986) University of Jos, Private Mail Bag 2084, Jos, Nigeria **Work Phone:** 073-55930/55931-4 Ext. 25 **Home Phone:** 073-52910/53786 **Cables:** Unijos Jos **Education:** B.S. Physics (1962), University of London; M.S. (1964), University of Birmingham, UK; Ph.D. Ahmadu Bello University (1970), Nigeria. **Selected Congresses and Conferences:** Participated at the World Council of Churches Conference on "Faith, Science and the Future," (July 12-24, 1979) in Boston, MA; Was also a participant at the Lutheran Church in America and the Lutheran World Federation sponsored global consultation on "The New Scientific World: What Difference Does It Make for the Churches," in Lanarca, Cyprus (November 1987) **Previous Positions:** Assistant Lecturer in Physics (1964-65), University of Ibadan, Nigeria; Lecturer (1965-1972)/Senior Lecturer (1972-75)/Reader (1975-77)/Head of Department (1975-1986)/Professor (1977-86), Department of Physics, Ahmadu Bello University, Zaria, Nigeria; Research Associate (July-September, 1972-1975), Earth Physics Branch, Department of Energy, Mines and Resources, Ottawa, Canada; Research Associate (July-September, 1980-1982), Precambrian Center, University of Manitoba, Winnipeg, Canada **Selected Memberships:** Fellow (1980), Nigerian Academy of Sciences; Fellow (1980), Science Association of Nigeria; Fellow (1982), Nigerian Mining and Geosciences Society; Fellow (1983), Geological Society of Africa; Fellow (1984), Association of Exploration Geophysicists, India; Fellow (1984), Institute of Physics, London; Honorary Fellow (1986), Geological Society of London; Church and Society Commission, World Council of Churches; President, African Christian Intellectuals Fellowship. **Discipline:** Geophysics **Related Interests:** Theology and Science in the African Context. **Current Research:** Gravimetric, magnetic, seismic refraction investigations for geodynamic and tectonic studies; The interpretation of aeromagnetic surveys; Geophysical prospecting for minerals and groundwater.

Selected Publications: The bibliography lists 2 books and 46 published articles in refereed journals, together with many other papers and lectures.

_____. "Developed or Developing: Science from Different Perspectives." Paper presented at the international congress on 'Concern about Science', Amsterdam, Netherlands (1980).
_____. "The Future of Science and Technology, Concerns of the Third World." *Anticipation* 28 (1980): 65-67. Paper presented, WCC meeting in Geneva Switzerland.
_____. T. King. "First World. Third World: Uses and Abuses of Science." *Christianity and Crises* 40 (1980): 298-303.
_____. "Cultural Implications of the Uses and Abuses of Science and Technology in Nigeria." Paper presented at the International Symposium on the Cultural Implications of Science Education, Zaria, Nigeria 1983.
_____. "Faith-Science Debate Group Report: Africa." In *The New Faith-Science Debate: Probing Cosmology, Technology and Theology*, ed. John M. Mangum. Minneapolis: Augsburg Fortress Press, 1989.

Albright, Carol Rausch *(formerly Carol Rausch Gorski)*

Present Position and Address: Executive Editor (since 1989), *Zygon: Journal of Religion and Science*; Associate for Programs (since 1988), Chicago Center for Religion and Science, 1100 E. 55th Street, Chicago, IL; Self-employed publishing consultant (since 1975) (Home) 5415 South Hyde Park Blvd., Chicago, IL 60615-5819 USA **Work Phone:** (312) 256-0767 **Work Fax:** (312) 256-0682 **Home Phone:** (312) 667-5342 **Home Fax:** (312) 667-9123 **Date of Birth:** March 20, 1936 **Languages:** English **Education:** B.A. (1956), Augustana College, Rock Island, IL **Previous Positions:** Director, Lutheran Campus Ministry (1958-1961); National Executive Committee (1960-1961), Lutheran Campus Ministry; Assistant Editor (1970-75), World Book encyclopedia **Editorial Work:** Editorial Consultant to the Faculty (1986-90), Lutheran School of Theology at Chicago and McCormick Seminary; Editorial Coordinator (1983-93), *"Doctor I've Read..."* **Honors:** Phi Beta Kappa **Selected Memberships:** Secretary, Center for Advanced Study in Religion and Science; Institute on Religion in an Age of Science; The Chicago Group; American Theological Society; Lutheran Church in America **Discipline:** Publishing **Related Areas of Interest:** Neuroscience and theology; Medicine; Theology of Wolfhart Pannenberg; Constructive process theology.

Selected Publications: She is the editor of over 100 books, the sole author of a medical newsletter for 10 years, co-editor of one book and co-author of another.

_____ and J. Haugen, Eds. *Laying Theological Claim to Scientific Understanding: Wolfhart Pannenberg and Scientists in Dialogue.* LaSalle, IL:Open Court. In Press.
James Ashbook and_____. *Rediscovering The Soul.* (Working title for a book on the relationships between theology and neuroscience.) In preparation.

Albright, John R.

Present Position and Address: Professor of Physics and Head of the Department of Chemistry and Physics (since 1995), Purdue University Calumet, Hammond, IN 46323-2094 USA (Home) 5415 South Hyde Park Blvd., Chicago, IL 60615-5819 **Work Phone:** (219) 989-2284 **Work Fax:** (219) 989-2771 **Home Phone:** (312) 667-5342 **Home Fax:** (312) 667-9123 **Date of Birth:** June 10, 1937 **Languages Spoken:** English, German, French, Spanish **Education:** A.B. (1959), Susquehanna University; M.S. (1961)/Ph.D. (1964), University of Wisconsin - Madison **Postgraduate Studies:** Wisconsin Alumni Research Foundation Fellowship (1959-61) **Previous Positions:** Associate Professor (1970-1978)/Professor of Physics (1978-95)/Associate Chair, Department of Physics, Florida State University, Tallahassee, FL 32306-3016, USA; Senior Fellow (1976), Science Research Council of Great Britain; Assistant Professor (1963-70)/Associate Professor (1970-78)/Associate Chair (1980-85), Department of Physics, Florida State University **Awards:** President's Teaching Award (1980), Florida State University; Florida State University Teaching Incentive Award (1994); Templeton Science & Religion Model Course Award (1994); Templeton Foundation Science & Religion Course Award (1995) **Selected Memberships:** American Physical Society; American Association of Physics Teachers; Evangelical Lutheran Church in America; Center for Advanced Study in Religion and Science; Institute for Religion in an Age of Science, (IRAS) **Discipline:** Physics **Related Interests:** Nonlinear Dynamics; Chaos; Determinism and Causality; Modern Physics; Quantum Mechanics; Teaching of Science and Religion.

Selected Publications: Numerous papers on experimental high-energy physics.

_____, H. Semat. *Introduction to Atomic and Nuclear Physics.* 5th ed. Holt, Rinehart & Winston, 1972.
_____. "Concerning the Visual Acuity of Quark Hunters." *Synthese* 50, 147 (1982).
_____. Biography of P. A. M. Dirac (still in preparation. This biography has the blessing of Dirac's family, especially his widow).

_____. "Science and Faith." *Insights* 3, 17 (1991).
_____. "The End of the World: A Scientific View of Christian Eschatology." *Dialog* 30, 279 (1991).
_____. "God and the Pattern of Nature: A Physicist Considers Cosmology." *The Christian Century* 109, 711. (1992). A condensed version has been published in *The Catholic Digest* January 1993.
_____, "Undergraduate Course in Science and Religion: REL 3169." *Council of Societies for the Study of Religion Bulletin* 23, 91 (1994).

Allen, Diogenes

Present Position and Address: Stuart Professor of Philosophy (since 1981), Princeton Theological Seminary, CN 821, Princeton, NJ 08542, USA; (Home) 133 Cedar Lane, Princeton, NJ 08540, USA **Date of Birth:** October 17, 1932 **Education:** B.A. (1954), University of Kentucky; Princeton University (1954-1955); B.A. Honours, Rhodes Scholar (1957)/M.A. (1961), Oxford University; B.D. (1959)/M.A. (1962)/Ph.D. (1965), Yale University **Previous Positions:** Assistant Professor (1964-66)/Associate Professor (1966-1967), York University, Toronto; Associate Professor (1967-74)/Professor of Philosophy (1974-81), Princeton Theological Seminary (PTS); Chair, Theology Department (1977-1979, 1988-1989), PTS; Visiting Professor (Spring 1978), Drew University; Visiting Professor (Fall 1980), University of Notre Dame **Selected Memberships:** American Theological Society; Executive board, Society of Christian Philosophers; Leibniz Gesellschaft; Executive board, American Weil Society; Association étude pensées S. Weil; American Philosophical Association; Canadian Philosophical Association; Advisory Committee, Center of Theological Inquiry, Princeton **Discipline:** Philosophy **Related Interests:** Cosmology and Theology; Quantum Physics and Theology; Evolutionary Theory and Theology.

Selected Publications: The bibliography lists 13 major books and 50 articles.

_____. "Natural Evil and the Love of God." *Religious Studies* (December 1980).
_____. "Suffering at the Hands of Nature." *Theology Today* (July 1980).
_____. *Mechanical Explanations and the Ultimate Origin of the Universe According to Leibniz.* Weisbaden, Germany: Franz Steiner Verlag, 1983.
_____. "Nature as a Witness to God's Existence and Goodness." *Faith and Philosophy* (January 1984).
_____. "From vis viva to Primary Force." *Studia Leibnitiana* 25 (1984).
_____. *Philosophy for Understanding Theology.* Atlanta: John Knox Press, 1985.
_____. "The Issues Posed by the Order of the Universe." In *Proceedings of the V Leibnitz Kongress*, 1988.
_____. *Christian Belief in a Postmodern World: the Full Wealth of Conviction.* Atlanta: John Knox Press, 1989.
_____. *Quest: The Search for Meaning Through Christ.* New York: Walker and Co., 1990.
_____, Eric Springstead. *Nature, Spirit, and Community: Issues in the Thought of Simone Weil.* Albany, NY: SUNY Press, 1994.

Allert, Gebhard

Present Position and Address: Department of Psychotherapy, University of Ulm Hochstrasse 8, D-89081 Ulm, Germany **Work Phone:** 0731-5025667 **Fax:** 07315025662 **E-Mail:** Allert@sip medizin.uni-ulm.de **Date of Birth:** January 6, 1955 **Languages Spoken:** German, English, French **Education:** Study of Theology and Medicine at Tübingen, Liège(B), Paris, Bonn and Heidelberg; Licenced as a Physician (1983); Doctor of Medicine degree (1985); Doctoral work in Theology at Heidelberg (since 1985). **Postgraduate Studies:** Visiting fellow (1988-90), Kennedy Institute of Ethics, Georgetown University, Washington DC **Selected Memberships:** Akademie für Ethik in der Medizin, Göttingen; European Society for Philosophy of Medicine and Health Care, Maastricht, Netherlands; Philosophy Group of the Royal College of Psychiatrists, London; Hastings Center, Hastings on Hudson, NY; Kennedy Institute of Ethics, Washington, DC. **Discipline:** Medicine, Psychotherapy, Psychosomatics; Theology: Pastoral Care and Counseling **Related Interests:** Psycho-

therapy - Psychoanalysis, Psychosomatics; Medical Ethics: Teaching and Training in medical eth-
ics/bioethics; Ethical questions in the field of Psychotherapy, Psycho-Oncology, Human Genetics and
Reproductive Medicine **Current Research:** Interdisciplinary Dialogue: Science and Religion.

Selected Publications:

_____. "Theologie und Naturwissenschaft im Dialog," *Evangelische Kommentare* 21 (May 1988): 251-2.
_____. "Medizinische Ethik lernen und lehren. Ein Bericht über Aus- und Weiterbildungsprogramme in medizinis-
cher Ethik - bioethics - in den USA." *Sonderbeilage Medizinische Ethik* Nr. 30, Ärzteblatt Baden-Württemberg
(January 1989).
_____. "Reproduktionsmedizin und Gentechnologie in der Diskussion." *Evangelische Kommentare* 22 (March
1989): 29-30.
_____. "Das Selbstbestimmungsrecht und der Schutz der Betroffenen sind das Mass. Bioethik in den USA - eine
kurzgefasste Übersicht." *Deutsches Ärzteblatt - Ärztliche Mitteilungen* 86 (1989): 3780-84.
_____. "Sterben und Tod: Ethische Überlegungen am Ende des menschlichen Lebens." *Schleswig-Holsteinisches
Ärzteblatt* 43 (January 1990): 52-4.
_____. "Die aktuelle Diskussion um ein neues Pflegeversicherungssystem - politische, soziale und ethische
Aspekte." *Mensch, Medizin, Gesellschaft* 17 (1992): 47-53.
_____. "Health Care for the Elderly and People Needing Long-Term Care." *Journal of Health Care, Medicine and
Community* (Hiresaki, Japan) 2, (December 1992).
_____. G. Sponholz, H. Baitsch, M. Kautenberger. "Consensus Formation in Genetic Counseling: a Complex
Process." In *Ten Have, H.A.M.J.; Sass, H-M: Consensus Formation in Healthcare Ethics.* Dordrecht: Kluwer, 1993.

Alley, James W. *(Deceased)*

Former Position and Address: Director (since 1973), Department of Human Resources, Division of
Public Health, 878 Peachtree Street, NE Room 201, Atlanta, GA 30309, USA **Education:** B.A. (*cum
laude*, 1955), University of Buffalo NY; M.D. (1959), State University of New York College of
Medicine -Syracuse; M.P.H. (1961-62), Harvard University School of Public Health; Resident in
Preventive Medicine (1969), Johns Hopkins University School of Hygiene and Public Health **Honor-
ary Degrees:** Honorary Sc.D. (1969), Marquette School of Medicine - Milwaukee, WI **Previous
Positions:** Missionary (1965-72), United Methodist Church Board of Missions - Bolivia **Discipline:**
Public Health **Related Interests:** Public Health and Missions; Church/Family and Community Health;
Ethics and Public Health.

Selected Publications:

_____. "A Framework for Applying Ethical Theory to Public Health Practice." *Family and Community Health*
(May 1987).
_____. "Social Transformation Model: Human Development and Disease Patterns." *SRI International Business
Intelligence Program* (June 1987).

Alston, William P.

Present Position and Address: Professor of Philosophy (since 1980) Syracuse University, Syracuse,
NY 13244-1170, USA **Work Phone:** (315) 443-5815 **Date of Birth:** November 29, 1921 **Education:**
B.M. (*magna cum laude*, 1942), Centenary College; Ph.D. Philosophy (1951), University of Chicago
Honorary Degrees: Doc. Hum. Litt. (1988), Church Divinity School of the Pacific; Chancellor's
Award for Exceptional Academic Achievement, Syracuse University (1990) **Previous Positions:**
Instructor (1949-52)/Assistant (1952-56)/Associate (1956-61)/Professor (1961-71)/Acting Chairman
(1961-64)/Director of Graduate Studies (1966-71), Department of Philosophy, University of Michigan;
Professor of Philosophy (1971-76)/Acting Chairman (1972-73), Douglass College - Rutgers Univer-
sity; Professor of Philosophy (1976-80)/Chairman (1977-79), University of Illinois at Urbana-Cham-

paign; Member (1968-78)/Chairman (1972-78), Board of Examiners in Philosophy for Educational Testing Service; Associate Adviser Member, Centre Superiore di Logica e Scienze Comparate; Evaluation of programs in Philosophy at the State University of NY (1972, 1976), University of Maryland (1982), Wayne State University (1984), Indiana University (1985), Ohio State University (1986), University of Wisconsin, (1986); Leader of delegation of American Philosophers on visit to USSR (1987); Consultant to Philosophy Department (1987-89), University of Florida; Member of 8 year project sponsored by Vatican Observatory on God's Actions in the World in the Light of Modern Science. **Editorial Work:** Editor (1982-1990), *Faith and Philosophy, Philosophy Research Archives*, (1974-77); Editorial Board of the *Journal for the Theory of Social Behavior* (since 1972), *Monist* (1968-88), *Nous* (since 1966), *American Philosophical Quarterly* (1963-68,1983-86) **Selected Memberships:** Previous President, American Philosophical Association; Previous President, Society of Christian Philosophers; Previous President, Society for Philosophy of Psychology **Discipline:** Philosophy **Related Interests:** Philosophical Theology; Theory of Knowledge; Epistemology of Religious Experience; Speech Acts and Linguistic Meaning; Divine Action in the light of Contemporary Science.

Selected Publications: His bibliography lists 6 books, over 80 articles, and 20 reviews.

_____. "Perceiving God." *Journal Philosophy* 83, 11 (November 1986): 655-65.
_____. "Religious Diversity and the Perceptual Knowledge of God." *Faith and Philosophy* 5 (October 1988): 433-48.
_____. "Referring to God." *International Journal of Philosophy of Religion* 24 (1988): 113-28.
_____. "The Perception of God." *Philosophical Topics* 16 (Fall 1988).
_____. *Divine Nature and Human Language*. Ithaca NY: Cornell University Press, 1989. Most of his articles in the area of philosophical theology are collected in this book.
_____. "How to Think About Divine Action." In *Divine Action*, ed. B. Hebblethwaite and E. Henderson. Edinburgh: T. & T. Clark, 1990.
_____. *Perceiving God*. Cornell University Press, 1991.
_____. "The Inductive Argument from Evil and the Human Cognitive Condition." *Philosophical Perspectives*. 5. (1991).
_____. "Divine Action, Human Freedom, and the Laws of Nature." In *Quantum Cosmology and the Laws of Nature: Scientific Perspectives on Divine Action*, ed. R.J. Russell, N. Murphy, and C.J. Isham. Vatican City State: Vatican Observatory Publications, 1993.
_____. "Divine Action: Shadow or Substance?" In *The God Who Acts: Philosophical and Theological Explorations*, ed. F. Tracy. Pennsylvania State University Press, 1994.

Altner, Günter

Present Position and Address: Professor ordinarius, Universität Koblenz-Landau Abt. Koblenz Weinbrennerstrasse 61, 6900 Heidelberg, Germany **Date of Birth:** September 20, 1936 **Education:** Doctorate in Biology; Doctorate in Theology **Previous Positions:** Student leader for Theology-Science 'border questions' (1968-71), Evangelischen Akademie Mülheim/Ruhr; Professor of Human-Biology (1971-73), Pädagogische Hochschule Schwäbisch Gmünd; Scientific Consultant (1973-76), Forschungsstätte der Evangelischen Studiengemeinschaft Heidelberg für Grenzfragen im Bereich Naturwissenschaften und Ökologie; Professor of Evangelical Theology (since 1977), Erziehungswissenschaftliche Hochschule Rheinland-Pfalz **Selected Memberships:** Mitbegründung (1977), Institut für angewandte Ökologie e.V. (Öko-Institut), Freiburg, Mitarbeit im Vorstand; Mitglied (1979-82), Enquête-Kommission "Zukünftige Kernenergiepolitik" des Deutschen Bundestages Gründung (1982), Günter-Altner-Stiftung gemeinnützige GmbH, Heidelberg. Förderung ökologisch und friedenspolitisch relevanter Forschungsvorhaben **Discipline:** Theology; Biology **Related Interests:** Darwinism; Creation; Ecology and Theology.

Selected Publications:

_____. *Schöpfung am Abgrund - Die Theologie vor der Umweltfrage.* Neukirchen: Neukirchener Verlag, 1974 and 1978.

_____. *Der Darwinismus - Die Geschichte einer Theorie.* Darmstadt: Buchgesellschaft, 1981.

_____, editor. *Die Welt als offenes System - Eine Kontroverse um das Werk von Ilya Prigogine.* Frankfurt: Fischer Taschenbuch Verlag, 1986.

_____. *Die Überlebenskrise in der Gegenwart - Ansätze zum Dialog mit der Natur in Naturwissenschaft und Theologie.* Darmstadt: Wissenschaftliche Buchgesellschaft, 1987.

_____. *Die grosse Kollision - Mensch und Natur.* Graz/Wien: Verlag Styria, 1987.

_____. *Leben auf Bestellung? - Das gefährliche Dilemma der Gentechnologie.* Freiburg: Herder Verlag, 1988.

_____, W. Krauth, I. Lünzer, and H. Vogtmann, eds. Gentechnik und Landwirtschaft - Folgen für Umwelt und Lebensmittelerzeugung. Karlsruhe: Verlag C. F. Müller, 1988.

_____, editor. *Ökologische Theologie - Perspektiven zur Orientierung.* Stuttgart: Kreuz Verlag, 1989.

_____. *Naturvergessenheit - Grundlagen einer umfasseden Bioethik.* Darmstadt: Wissenschaftliche Buchgesellschaft, 1991.

_____. *Über Leben - Von der Kraft der Furcht.* Dusseldorf: Patmos Verlag, 1992.

Ambrose, Edmund Jack

Present Position and Address: Professor Emeritus, University of London, The Mill House, Westfield, Nr. Hastings, East Sussex TN35 4SU, UK **Date of Birth:** February 3, 1914 **Languages Spoken:** English, French, German **Education:** B.A./M.A., University of Cambridge; D.Sc., University of London **Awards and Honors:** Emeritus Member, International Society for (Biological) Differentiation; Commemorative Medal for Leprosy Research, Paris; Ordre de St. Jean de Malte, 750th Anniversary of St. Elizabeth of Hungary **Previous Positions:** Chester Beatty Institute (Cancer Research); Senior Lecturer (1954)/Reader (1960)/Professor and Head of Department of Cell Biology (1965-1975), University of London; Chairman, Scientific Advisory Committee; Tota Memorial Cancer Hospital and Research Institute (1964-1974), Bombay, India; Cofounder and Advisor (1975), Foundation for Medical Research (Leprosy) Bombay, India; Development of a Rehabilitation Center for Leprosy patients in association with Tear Fund and Leprosy Mission; Retired Diocesan Reader, Chichester Diocese, UK **Discipline:** Cell Biology **Related Interests:** General interest in Third World Problems both Spiritual and Medical.

Selected Publications: Extensive bibliography lists various research publications and books in the fields of cancer and leprosy research, and a university textbook on cell biology.

_____. *The Nature and Origin of the Biological World.* UK: Ellis Horwood Chichester; New York: J. Wiley, 1982.

_____. "The Mirror of Creation." In *Theology and Science at the Frontier of Knowledge*, ser. ed. T. F. Torrance. Edinburgh UK: Scottish Academic Press, 1990.

_____. *Eternal Life.* In press.

Ammerman, Nancy Tatom

Present Position and Address: Associate Professor of Sociology of Religion (since September 1990), Adjunct Professor of Sociology Candler School of Theology, Emory University, Atlanta GA 30322, USA **Home Phone:** (609) 683-4231 **E-Mail:** THEONA@EMORY.EDU **Date of Birth:** November 29, 1950 **Education:** B.A. American History/Sociology (*summa cum laude*, 1972), Southwest Baptist University, Bolivar MO; M.A. Sociology (1977), University of Louisville; Ph.D. Sociology (1983), Yale University. **Selected Lectures:** H. Paul Douglas Lecture, Religious Research Association, October 1993; Sociology of Religion lecture series, Loyola University of Chicago, October 1992 **Awards and Honors:** Graduate Dean's Citation (1977); 1992 Distinguished Book Award, Society for the Scientific Study of Religion **Previous Positions:** Teaching Fellow at Universities of Louisville

(1976-77)/Yale (1978-80); Acting Instructor (1981-82), Yale University; Lecturer (1983), Princeton University; Adjunct Assistant Professor (1983), Columbia University; Assistant Professor of Sociology of Religion, Candler School of Theology/Adjunct Assistant Professor of Sociology (1984-90), Emory University **Concurrent Positions:** Visiting Scholar, Center for the Study of American Religion, Princeton University (1993-94) **Editorial Work:** Editorial Referee for *Journal for the Scientific Study of Religion/Review of Religious Research/Sociological Analysis* **Administrative Experience:** Director, Baptist Studies Program, (since 1991); Director, Center for Religious Research, (since 1985) **Selected Memberships:** Member and Chair of the Fichter Grant Committee, Association for the Sociology of Religion; Member and Chair of the Nominating Committee, Religious Research Association; Society for the Scientific Study of Religion; Southern Sociological Society; American Sociological Association; Board of Directors, Louisville Institute for the Study of Protestantism and American Culture; Executive Committee of The Fundamentalism Project of the American Academy of Arts and Sciences. **Discipline:** Sociology, including the Sociology of Religion **Related Interests:** Social Sources of Christian Fundamentalism; the use of Scientific Methodology in the Study of Religion. **Current Research:** Principal Investigator, "Congregations in Changing Communities," funded by the Lily Endowment, Institute for the Study of Economic Culture, Boston University; Congregational Studies Project Team

Selected Publications: Her Curriculum Vitae lists 6 publications, 20 articles, and 23 book reviews.

_____. "Fundamentalism: Bastion of Traditionalism in the Modern World." Chap. in *Religion and the Sociology of Knowledge*, ed. B. W. Hargrove. New York: Edward Mellen, 1984.
_____. *Bible Believers: Fundamentalists in the Modern World*. New Brunswick, NJ: Rutgers University Press, 1987.
_____. "Southern Baptist and the New Christian Right." *Review of Religious Research* (forthcoming).
_____. Jackie W. Ammerman. *A Directory of Data on the Changing Relationship Among Work, Family, and Religion.* Center for Religious Research, Emory University. 1990.
_____. editor. *Southern Baptists Observed: Multiple Perspectives on a Changing Denomination.* University of Tennessee Press, Knoxville. 1993.
_____. "Priests and Prophets." In *Proclaiming the Baptist Vision: Priesthood of All Believers*, ed. Walter B. Shurden. Macon, GA: Smyth and Helwys, 1993.
_____. "SBC Moderates and the making of a Post-Modern Denomination." *Christian Century* 110, 26 (1993): 896-9.

Amrhein, Eva Maria

Present Position and Address: Teaching and Spiritual Formation (since 1988), Schoenstatt International Center, Waukesha, WI, USA; Berg Schoenstatt 1, D-5414 Vallendar, Germany **Work Phone:** 49-261-6404249 **Date of Birth:** September 21, 1933 **Languages Spoken:** English, German, Spanish **Education:** Ph.D. Physics (1963), University of Wuerzburg, Germany; Habilitation "Venia Legendi," Physics (1969), University of Marburg, Germany **Previous Positions:** University of Marburg (until 1971), American Foundation for Biological Research, Madison, WI; University of Missouri - Rolla (1971-73); University of Puerto Rico, Mayaguez (1985-88); Theological Instructing of Laity (1974-83), Schoenstatt International Center at Waukesha WI/Vallendar in Germany (since 1988) **Selected Memberships:** Secular Institute - Schoenstatt Sisters of Mary; ITEST; Physical Societies **Discipline:** Physics; Theology **Related Interests:** Spirituality for Scientists; Theology and Science/Technology/Society.

Selected Publications:

_____. "Aspects of a Theology of Technology." In *Etica Profesional para la Ingenieria*, ed. E. Lugo. Lib. Universal, 1985.
_____. *The Vineyard. Scientists in the Church*. St. Louis MO: ITEST Faith/Science Press, 1992.

Anch, A. Michael

Present Position and Address: Associate Professor of Psychology (since 1989), St. Louis University, 221 N. Grand, St. Louis, MO 63103, USA **Work Phone:** (314) 977-2300 **Home Phone:** (314) 256-8553 **Date of Birth:** June 9, 1945 **Education:** B.A. (1967), Rockhurst College; M.S. (1970)/Ph.D. Physiological Psychology (1971), St. Louis University; M.Div. (1989), University of Toronto (Regis College) **Previous Positions:** Director (1973-76), Sleep Laboratory and Assistant Professor of Psychiatry; Baylor College of Medicine; Assistant Professor (1978-81), Department of Internal Medicine, University of Texas Medical Branch **Selected Memberships:** Association of Professional Sleep Societies; ITEST; Sigma Xi; Society for Neuroscience; New York Academy of Sciences **Discipline:** Physiological Psychology; Sleep Research; Theology **Related Interests:** Lonergan studies; The Relationship between Religion and Science.

Selected Publications: His bibliography lists 28 publications and 33 abstracts and presentations, most of which are in the area of sleep physiology.

_____, C. J. Chiasson. "Models and Modelling in Spiritual Development: Toward a New Concept in Spiritual Developmental Theory." *Toronto Journal of Theology* 4, 2 (1988): 218-35.
_____. *Sleep: A Scientific Perspective*. N.p., n.d.

Anderson, Odin W.

Present Position and Address: Professor of Sociology, University of Wisconsin - Madison 2105 Kendall Avenue, Madison, WI 53705, USA **Work Phone:** (608) 262-2133 **Home Phone:** (608) 233-6055 **Date of Birth:** July 5, 1914 **Education:** B.A. in Sociology (1938), University of Wisconsin - Madison; B.A. Library Science (1940)/Ph.D. in Sociology (1948), University of Michigan (1948) **Previous Positions:** University of Chicago (1962-80) **Selected Memberships:** Subcommittee of Religion and Science (1962-80), University of Chicago; Committee on Bioethics, University of Wisconsin, Madison **Discipline:** Sociology **Related Interests:** Bio-ethical problems; Health Service Organizations.

Selected Publications: His bibliography lists 123 entries.

_____. "The Sociologist and Medicine: Generalizations from a Teaching and Research Experience in a Medical School." *Social Forces* 31 (October 1952): 38-42.
_____, Gerald Gordon and Sue Marquis. "Organization for Scientific Productivity: Research in the Sociology of Science." *The American Behavioral Scientist* 5, 4 (December 1961): 35-7.
_____, Gerald Gordon and Sue Marquis. "Structural Constraints Under the Freedom of the Scientist." *The American Behavioral Scientist* (September 1962).
_____, Gerald Gordon and Sue Marquis. "Freedom and Control in Four Types of Scientific Settings." *The American Behavioral Scientist* (December 1962).
_____. Gerald Gordon, Henry P. Brehm, and Sue Marquis. *Disease, the Individual, and Society*. New Haven, Connecticut: College and University Press, 1968.
_____. Milovy S. Seacat. "Behavioral Science Research in the Health Field: A Statement of Problems and Priorities." *Social Problems* 6, 3 (Winter 1969): 268-71.
_____. "Vital Organ Transplants and Mutual Obligations." *Wisconsin Medical Journal* (April 1991): 158.

Apczynski, John V.

Present Position and Address: Professor, St. Bonaventure University, NY; Box 12, St. Bonaventure, NY 14778, USA **Work Phone:** (716) 375-2298 **E-Mail:** APCZYNSKI @ SBU.EDU **Date of Birth:** August 25, 1942 **Education:** Ph.D. (1972), McGill University, Montreal **Previous Positions:** Assistant/Associate/Full Professor in Theology (since 1970), St. Bonaventure University, NY **Selected**

Memberships: American Academy of Religion; Society for the Scientific Study of Religion; Polanyi Society **Discipline:** Fundamental Theology and Systematic Theology **Related Interests:** Epistemological implications of Philosophy of Science for Theological Foundations.

Selected Publications:

_____. *Doers of the Word: Toward a Foundational Theology Based on the Thought of Michael Polanyi*. Missoula, MT: Scholar's Press, 1977.
_____. "Truth in Religion." *Zygon* 17 (1982): 49-73.

Armogathe, Jean-Robert

Present Position and Address: Directeur d'études (since 1989), Ecole pratique des hautes études (5é section), Sorbonne, Paris; 6 Rue Guynemer 75006, Paris, France **Work Phone:** (331) 43254171 **Date of Birth:** July 6, 1947 **Education:** Ecole Normale Supérieure (1967); Docteur en Sciences Religieuses (1970), Ecole Pratique des Hautes études (Sciences Religieuses); Agrégé (1971); Docteur en Philosophie (1972), Ordonné Prêtre (1976), Paris **Postgraduate Studies:** Martin Luther University, Halle Wittenberg; Collegio Borromeo Pavia, Italy; Trinity College, Oxford, (1983-84) **Honorary Degrees:** All Souls College, Oxford (1985-86) **Discipline:** History of Ideas; History of Science; Philosophy **Related Interests:** Sixteenth through eighteenth centuries, History of Science/Ideas and its relation to Theology.

Selected Publications: His bibliography lists 14 books, over 230 papers or articles, and over 200 reviews.

_____. "Concepts théologiques et pensée scientifique en Europe au 17e siécle: 1. J. A. Comenius." *Annuaire Ecole Pratiquer des Hautes Études (Sciences Religieuses)* 5, Conférence EPHE (1979-80).
_____. *Postface à Science, Histoire, Epistémologie: pour une pratique pluridisciplinaire*. Paris, 1980.
_____. "Concepts théologiques et pensée scientifique au 17e siécle (suite): 2. Caramuel, Pascal et Maignan." *Annuaire EPHE* 5, Conférence EPHE (1980-81).
_____. "Concepts théologiques et pensée scientifique en Europe au 17e siècle (suite): 3. Leibniz et la recherche de la catholicité." *Annuaire EPHE* 5, Conférence EPHE (1981-82).
_____. "Concepts théologiques et pensée scientifique au 17e s. (suite): 4. Leibniz, de la dynamique à la théodicée." *Annuaire EPHE* 5, Conférence EPHE (1983-84).
_____, et al. "Descartes." Chap. 14 in *A Critical Bibliography of French Literature*, ed. H. G. Hall. 3A Syracuse, NY: 1983.
_____. "1. Autour de Galilée: la cosmologie du cardinal Bellarmin (1542-1621); 2. Concepts théologiques et pensée scientifique (suite): Leibniz, de la dynamique à la théodicée (1692-1710)." *Annuaire EPHE* 5, Conférence EPHE (1983-84).
_____. "1. Vie spirituelle et vérité des sciences: le Père Marin Mersenne (1588-1648) et origines de l'Académie des Sciences. 2: Leibniz et Bayle: les animaux-machines." *Annuaire EPHE* 5, Conférence EPHE (1984-85).
_____. "Histoire et philosophie des sciences." *History of European Ideas* 7 (1986): 3-7.
_____. "Genetics and the Rights of Man." *National Catholic Register* (Los Angeles), 62:34:24 (1986): 7-9.

Armstrong, John Reginald

Present Position and Address: Honorary Assistant (Deacon), St. Philip the Evangelist Anglican Church (since 1985) B1, 4515 Varsity Drive N.W., Calgary, Alberta, T3A OZ8, Canada. **Date of Birth:** February 3, 1947 **Education:** B.S.. (1969), University of Alberta; Diploma in Christian Studies (1972), Regent College; M.Div. (1975), Wycliffe College, Toronto School of Theology **Previous Positions:** Geologist (1976-81), Canadian Stratigraphic Service; Geologist (1981-87), Gas Supply Department, Alberta, and Southern Gas Company Ltd., Calgary; Lab Assistant (Summer 1990), Vertebrate Paleontology, Tyrrell Museum of Paleontology, Drumheller, Alberta **Selected Memberships:** Canadian Society of Petroleum Geologists; National Center for Science Education; Canadian Scientific and Christian Affiliation; Affiliation of Christian Geologists; National Association of Geology Teachers (until 1990); American Scientific Affiliation **Discipline:** Minister; Geologist **Related Interests:** History of Science and Biblical Interpretation; Earth Science; Evolution and Creation.

Selected Publications: His bibliography also lists many book reviews in *Perspectives on Science and Christian Faith* and elsewhere.

_____. "The Evolution of Creationism." *Earth Sciences History Journal.* 7, 2 (1988): 151-8.
_____. "Seeking Ancient Paths." *Perspectives on Science and Christian Faith (PSCF)* (March 1989). Paluxy River investigations, Glen Rose, Texas.
_____. "Rediscovering John Ray." *(PSCF)* (June 1989).
_____. "William Buckland in Retrospect." *(PSCF)* (March 1990): 34-38.

Artigas, Mariano

Present Position and Address: Professor of Philosophy of Nature and Philosophy of Science (since 1986) Universidad de Navarra, 31080 Pamplona, Spain **Work Phone:** SP (948) 10.56.00 **Date of Birth:** December 15, 1938 **Languages Spoken:** Spanish, English, Italian **Education:** Licenciado Physics (1960), University of Barcelona, Spain; Doctorate in Philosophy (1963), Pontifical University of the Lateran, Rome; Doctorate in Physics (1968)/Doctorate in Philosophy (1979), University of Barcelona, Spain **Selected Congresses and Conferences:** Academie Internationale de philosophie des sciences (1980, 81, 85, 86, 87, 89, 90, 92); Faculty of Theology St. Vincent (1984); Episcopal Commission on the Doctrine of Faith of the Spanish Conference of Bishops (1985); Societe Suisse de Logique et Philosophie des Sciences (1987, 88); Conference on Science and Creation (1987); Wethersfield Institute; 3rd World Congress of Christian Philosophy (1989); European Conferences on Science and Theology (1990-94); I Congreso Internacional de Filosofia, Bogota (1990) **Previous Positions:** Professor of Philosophy of Nature and Epistemology (1968-1972), University of Barcelona; Professor through Ordinary Professor (since 1966), Studium Generale of the Prelature of Opus dei in Spain; Professor of Theology (1973-1978), Institute of University Studies; Guest Professor (1987)/Extraordinary Professor of Philosophy of Nature and Philosophy of Science (since 1988), Ateneo Romano della Santa Croce -Rome; Professor (1986-1988)/Full Professor (since 1988), Dean of Ecclesiastical Faculty of Philosophy, University of Navarra, Pamplona, Spain; Guest Professor (1985, 1990), Universidad de la Sabana, Colombia; Guest Professor (1989), Universidad de Piura, Peru; Guest Professor (1990), Universidad Nacional Mayor, San Marcos, Peru; Guest Professor (1990), Universidad de Los Andes, Santiago, Chile; Guest Professor, Universidad Panamericana, Mexico (1991); Guest professor (1994), Facoltà di Teologia di Lugano, Switzerland. Correspondent member, Academie Internationale de Philosophie des Sciences; European Society for the Study of Science and Theology **Discipline:** Physics; Philosophy **Related Interests:** Christianity and Philosophy; Philosophy of Science/Theology; Science and Creation; Teleology.

Selected Publications: His bibliography lists 10 books, 25 articles and collective contributions, and over 100 review articles.

_____. *Las fronteras del evolucionismo* (The frontiers of evolution), Preface by Sir John Eccles. Madrid, Spain: Editorial Palabra, 1984, 85, 86, 91. Translated into Italian and Portugese, 1993.
_____. *Filosofia de la ciencia experimental* (Philosophy of empirical science). Pamplona, Spain: Ediciones Universidad de Navarra, 1989, 92.
_____. *Ciencia, razon y fe* (Science, reason and faith). Preface by E. Agazzi, President of the Académie Internationale de Philosophie des Sciences, Brussels. Madrid, Spain: Editorial Palabra, 1984, 85, 92.
_____. *La Inteligibilidad de la naturaleza* (The intelligibility of nature). Pamplona: Ediciones Universidad de Navarra, 1992.

_____. "Three Levels of Interaction between Science and Philosophy." In *Intelligibility in Science,* ed. C. Dillworth. Amsterdam: Rodopi, 1992.

_____. "Emergence and Reduction in Morphogenetic Theories." In *Philosophy and the Origin and evolution of the Universe*, ed. E. Agazzi and A. Cordero. Dordrecht: Kluwer, 1991.

_____. "Scientific Creativity and Human Singularity." In *The Science and Theology of Information*, ed. C. Wasserman, R. Kirby, and B. Rordorff. Geneve: Labor et Fides, 1992.

_____. *El hombre a la luz de la ciencia (Man Under the Light of Science)*. Madrid: Editorial Palabra, 1992.

_____. *Ciencia y Fe: nuevas perspectivas* (Science and faith, new perspectives). Pamplona: Ediciones Universidad de Navarra, 1992.

_____. *El desatio de la racionalidad* (The challenge of rationality). Pamplona: Ediciones n Universidad Navarra, 1994.

Ashbrook, James B.

Present Position and Address: Former Professor and Senior Scholar in Religion and Personality, Garrett-Evangelical Theological Seminary; Advisory Member, Graduate Faculty, Northwestern University, Evanston, IL; Garrett-Evangelical Theological Seminary, 2121 Sheridan Road, Evanston, IL 60201, USA **Work Phone:** (708) 866-3985 **Date of Birth:** November 1, 1925 **Education:** B.A. (1947), Denison University; B.D. (1950), Colgate Rochester Divinity School; Union Theological Seminary and William Alanson White Institute of Psychiatry (1954-55), New York City; M.A., Psychology (1962)/Ph.D., Psychology (1964), Ohio State University; Pastoral Counselor Intern (1954-55), American Foundation for Religion and Psychiatry, NYC; Training and Supervision (1955-60), Columbus Psychiatric Out-patient Clinic, Columbus, OH **Postgraduate Studies:** Postdoctoral Fellow (1971-73), Department of Psychology, University of Rochester, NY **Honorary Degrees:** Honorary Doctor of Law (1976), Denison University **Awards and Honors:** Recognized as "A Pioneer" by the American Association of Pastoral Counselors and by The Alumni/ae Association of the Institutes of Religion and Health, NYC (1987); Distinguished Contribution Award (1990), American Association of Pastoral Counselors **Previous Positions:** Chaplain/Pastor (1948-60), Rochester, NY and Granville, OH; Associate Professor/Professor of Pastoral Theology (1960-69), Colgate Rochester Divinity School, NY; Professor of Psychology and Theology (1969-81), Colgate Rochester/Bexley Hall/Crozer Theological Seminary, NY **Other Academic Experience:** Sabbatical study in Neuroscience with Dr. Garth Thomas (1976-77), Center for Brain Research, University of Rochester Medical School, NY **Selected Memberships:** American Psychological Association (1965-present); American Association of Pastoral Counselors, diplomate (1964-present); American Academy of Religion (Sections: Person, Culture and Religion; Science and Theology); Institute on Religion in an Age of Science; Center for Religion and Science, The Lutheran School of Theology, Chicago; Society of Pastoral Theology; Society for the Scientific Study of Religion **Discipline:** Theology; Psychology; Psychiatry **Related Interests:** The Brain and Belief; Mind and Theology.

Selected Publications: His bibliography lists 12 books..

_____. *Christianity for Pious Skeptics*. Abingdon Press, 1977.

_____. *The Human Mind and The Mind of God: Theological Promise in Brain Research*. University Press of America, 1984.

_____. *Paul Tillich In Conversation*. Bristol, IN: Wyndham Hall Press, 1988.

_____. *The Brain and Belief: Faith in the Light of Brain Research*. Bristol, IN: Wyndham Hall Press, 1988.

_____, editor. *Brain, Culture, and the Human Spirit: Essays from the Perspective of Emergent Evolution*. Lanham, MD: University Press of America, 1993.

_____. "Making Sense of Soul and Sabbath: Brain Processes and the Making of Meaning." *Zygon* 27, 1 (March): 31-49.

_____. *Minding the Soul: Pastoral Counseling as Remembering Who We Are*. Minneapolis, MN: Fortress Press, 1994.

Ashley, Benedict M.

Present Position and Address: Senior Professor of Moral Theology (since 1988), Pontifical Pope John Paul II Institute for Studies on Marriage and Family, 487 Michigan Avenue, N.E., Washington, DC 20017, USA **Date of Birth:** May 3, 1915 **Education:** Undergraduate and M.A. Comparative Literature (1937), University of Chicago; Ph.D. Political Science (1941), University of Notre Dame; S.T.Lr./Ph.D. Philosophy, Aquinas Institute; Master of Sacred Theology (1979), University of St. Thomas Aquinas, Rome **Previous Positions:** Instructor (1952)/Professor (1957-69), Philosophy, Aquinas Institute, River Forest, IL; Professor of Moral Theology (1969-72), Institute of Religion and Human Development, Texas Medical Center, Houston TX; Professor of Moral Theology (1969-81), Aquinas Institute of Theology, Dubuque, IA, and at St. Louis (1981-88); Part-time or short period teaching at University of Notre Dame, Xavier College, St. Mary's College in New Orleans, St. Xavier College in Chicago, St. Mary's of the Lake Seminary in Mundelein, IL and in Houston, TX, Kenrich Seminary in St. Louis **Consultancies:** Dubuque Archdiocesan Medical-Morals Committee (1975-79); Senior Fellow of Pope John XXIII Center for Medical-Moral Research and Education, St. Louis and Braintree (since 1975); Consultant for Pastoral Research and Practices (1981-86); National Catholic Bishops Conference; Committee on Doctrine (since 1988), National Catholic Conference **Editorial Work:** *Listening*; *Dominican Sources* **Administrative Experience:** Director of the Albertus Magnus Lyceum for Philosophy of Science (1958-63); President of Aquinas Institute, Dubuque, IA and River Forest, IL (1962-69, 1972-75); Director of the Provincial Self Study of the Central Dominican Province (1968); First President of the Midwest Association of Theological Schools (1966-68); Founding Member of the Board of the Association of Chicago Theological Schools (1967) **Discipline:** Moral Theology; Political Science; Theology; Philosophy **Related Interests:** Medical Ethics; Ethics and Society; Science and Religion; Methodology; Change and Process (as it relates to Evolution); Cosmic Community in Plotinus, Aquinas Whitehead.

Selected Publications: His bibliography lists over 10 books, more than 40 articles and many papers and addresses..

_____. *Theologies of the Body: Humanist and Christian.* St. Louis: Pope John Center, 1985.
_____. "Theology and the Mind-Body Problem." *Mind and Brain.* St. Louis: Institute for the Encounter of Theology, Science, and Technology, 1985.
_____. *Ethics of Health Care.* n.p., 1986.
_____. "Genetic Engineering." *Annual Thomist Colloquium.* Washington, 1986.
_____. "Theological Mind Today." *Bishops' and Scientists' Dialogue of the NCCB.* 1987.
_____. "The Church's Message to Artists and Scientists." Keynote Address for Annual Convention of the Fellowship of Catholic Scholars, San Francisco. August 25, 1987.
_____. "Science and Religion." Eight Columns for *The National Catholic Register.* (1987).
_____. Kevin D. O'Rourke. *Health Care Ethics: A Theological Analysis.* 3rd ed. n.p., 1987. Textbook edition, *Ethics of Health Care.* n.p. n.d..
_____. "A Christian Perspective on Scientific Medicine." Keynote address for Giornate di studio e di riflessione in occasione del 120 Anniversario della fondazione dell' Ospedale Pedicatrico Bambino Gesu, Rome, November 28-29, 1989.
_____. "Dominion or Stewardship." A paper to be delivered at the International Study Group in Bioethics, International Federation of Catholic Universities, Brussels, March 29-31, 1990. To be published in *Catholic Studies Bulletin.*

Personal Notes: Became Catholic in 1938, Dominican Order in 1941, ordained a priest in 1948.

Atkinson, David John

Present Position and Address: Canon Chancellor of Southwark Cathedral, London; (Work) Southwark Cathedral, London SE1 9DA; (Home) 7 Temple West Mews, London SE11 4TJ **Work Phone:**

071-403-8686 **Home Phone:** 071-735-5924 **Date of Birth:** September 5, 1943 **Education:** B.S.. Chemistry (1965), King's College/Ph.D. Organic Chemistry (1969)/Certificate in Student Counselling (1979), University of London; Bristol Diploma in Theology (1970)/M.Lit., "The Theological Method of T. F. Torrance" (1973), Trinity College, Bristol; M.A. Special Resolution (1984), Oxford University; Ordained as deacon (1972); priest (1973), Society of Ordained Scientists **Previous Positions:** Chaplain and Fellow (1977-93), Corpus Christi College, Oxford; Member of the Faculty of Theology (1984-93), University of Oxford; Visiting Lecturer (1983-93), Pastoral Theology, Wycliffe Hall, Oxford; Teacher of Chemistry and Religious Studies (1968-69), Maidstone Technical High School for Boys; Curate of St. Peter's parish, Halliwell, Bolton (1972-74)/St. John's Harborne, Birmingham (1974-77); Librarian (1977-80), Latimer House, Oxford; Visiting Lecturer/Lecturer in Christian Ethics at Oxford Diocese NSM Training Course (1978, 1981)/London Bible College (1980-83)/Fuller Theological Seminary, Pasadena (1983); Counsellor, University Counselling Service, Trinity Term (1981); Theological Consultant (1980-87), Care and Counsel; Northrup Visiting Professor in Religion (Spring 1986), Hope College, Michigan **Discipline:** Theology, Counselling and Organic Chemistry.

Selected Publications:

_____. *The Values of Science*. Grove, 1980.
_____. *Life and Death*. Oxford University Press, 1985. A school textbook in the Oxford series on Christianity and Science.
_____. "Barth on Creation." A response to Professor W. A. Whitehead, read at the Barth Conference, Oxford, 1986.
_____. "Perspectives on Embryo Research." Paper presented at Hope College, Michigan as the Northrup Lecture (1986).
_____. "Some Theological Perspectives on the Human Embryo." Chap. in *Embryos and Ethics*, ed. N. M. de S. Cameron. Rutherford House, 1987.
_____. *Pastoral Ethics in Practice*. Eastbourne: Monarch, 1989; reprint, *Pastoral Ethics*. Lynx, 1994.

Augros, Robert M.

Present Position and Address: Philosophy Department (since 1969) St. Anselm College, Manchester, NH 03102, USA **Work Phone:** (603) 641-7065 **Languages Spoken:** English, French **Education:** B.A. Philosophy (1965), St. Mary's College, CA; Ph.L. Philosophy (1967)/Ph.D. Philosophy (avec trés grande distinction, 1974), Laval University, Quebec, Canada **Previous Positions:** English Department (1966-68), University of Laval; Philosophy Department (1968-69), University of San Francisco; **Discipline:** Philosophy **Related Interests:** Researching special topics related to Ethics, Biology, Neuroscience, and the impact of Science on Intellectual Life. Coauthoring books that document the changed intellectual outlook that accompanies the scientific revolutions of the twentieth century. **Current Research:** Teaching courses in ethics, nature and human beings, scientific world views, and seminars in liberal studies.

Selected Publications:

_____. George Stanciu. *The New Story of Science*. Regnery/Gateway, 1984; The Bantam New Age edition, December 1986. Also available in French and Japanese.
_____. "Role of the Philosopher Today in Relation to Modern Science." Paper presented at the regional meeting of the Society for Aristotelian Studies (August 1985).
_____. George Stanciu. "Systematic Differentiation: A New Evolutionary Synthesis." *Biology Forum* (Winter 1986).
_____. George Stanciu. *The New Biology: Discovering the Wisdom in Nature*. New Science Library. Shambhala/Random House, March 1987.

Aurenche, Christian

Present Position and Address: Doctor responsible for the Centre de Promotion la Santé de Tokombéré (since 1975) B.P. 74 Maroua, Cameroun **Fax:** Maroua, Cameroun - 29.22.44 **Date of Birth:** May 1, 1940 **Languages Spoken:** French, English **Education:** Doctorat d'etat en médecine (1964), Faculté de Médecine, Paris; Licence en theologie (1971), Faculte de Theologie, Institut Catholique de Paris **Awards and Honors:** Prize (1988), SASAKAWA **Previous Positions:** Doctor of Medicine (1964-70), Central African Republic (R.C.A.); Chaplain (1970-75), d'Université á Paris; Consultant (1970-75), P. Gentilini of Paris **Discipline:** Public Health and Development (Priest and Doctor) **Related Areas of Interest:** Relationship between faith and health, and faith and development; global vision for development.

Selected Publication

_____. *Sous l'arbe fairé*. Le Cerf, 1989.

Austin, William H.

Present Position and Address: Professor of Philosophy (since 1980), University of Houston; Department of Philosophy, University of Houston, Houston, TX 77204-3785, USA **Work Phone:** (713) 743-3207 **E-Mail:** WAUSTIN@UH.EDU **Date of Birth:** April 10, 1936 **Education:** B.A. Mathematics (1957), Wesleyan University; B.D. (1960), Yale Divinity School; Ph.D. Philosophy of Religion (1966), Yale University **Awards and Honors:** Council on Philosophical Studies grant for Summer Institute in Philosophy of Science (1967); National Endowment for the Humanities Fellowship (1972-73) **Previous Positions:** Assistant in Instruction in Mathematics (1958-61), Yale University; Instructor (1964-67)/Assistant Professor of Philosophy (1967-73), Rice University; Associate Professor of Philosophy (1974-80), University of Houston; Visiting Scholar (Spring 1973), Program in History and Philosophy of Science, Cambridge University; Research Fellow in the Department of Religious Studies (Fall 1983), University of Lancaster **Selected Memberships:** Philosophy of Science Association; American Academy of Religion **Discipline:** Philosophy **Related Interests:** Philosophy of Evolutionary Biology; Probability, Decision Theory, and Rational Belief; Ethics of Belief and Inquiry; Historical Interplay of Natural Science and Theology.

Selected Publications:

_____. *Waves, Particles, and Paradoxes*. Rice University Studies 53, 2 (1967).
_____. *The Relevance of Natural Science to Theology*. London: Macmillan; New York: Barnes & Noble, 1967.
_____. "Complementarity and Theological Paradox." *Zygon* 2 (1967): 365-81.
_____. "Isaac Newton on Science and Religion." *Journal of the History of Ideas* 31 (1970): 521-42.
_____. "Paradigms, Rationality, and Partial Communication." *Journal for General Philosophy of Science* 3 (1972): 203-18.
_____. "Are Religious Beliefs 'Enabling Mechanisms for Survival'? (on E. O. Wilson)." *Zygon* 15 (1980): 193-201.
_____. "Theology and Natural Science: Beyond the Truce?." *The Thomist* 48 (1984): 433-49.
_____. "Rational Credibility and Causal Explanations of Belief." *Neue Zeitschrift für Systematische Theologie und Religionsphilosophie* 26 (1984): 116-33.
_____. "Evolutionary Explanations of Religion and Morality: Explaining Religion Away?" In *Evolution and Creation*, ed. Ernan McMullin. Notre Dame: University of Notre Dame Press, 1985.
_____. "Sociobiology and Post-Axial Religion." Paper presented at Conference on Science, Technology, and Religious Ideas, Kentucky State University, April 1993.

Ayala, Francisco J.

Present Position and Address: Donald Bren Professor of Biological Sciences, Department of Ecology and Evolutionary Biology and Professor of Philosophy, University of California - Irvine, Irvine, CA 92717, USA **Concurrent Positions:** President, American Association for the Advancement of Science **Work Phone:** (714) 824-8293 **Fax:** (714) 824-2474 **Date of Birth:** March 12, 1934 **Languages Spoken:** Spanish, English, French, Italian **Education:** M.A. (1963)/Ph.D. (1964), Columbia University, New York **Honorary Degrees:** Doctor Honoris Causa, Universidad de Leon (1982)/Universidad de Barcelona (1986)/Universidad de Madrid (1986)/Agricultural University of Athens (1991); College of France Medal (1979); Fulbright Fellow (1979, 81); Guggenheim Fellow (1977-78) **Awards and Honors:** Gold Mendel Medal, Czech Republic Academy of Sciences (1994) **Previous Positions:** Research Associate (1964-65)/Assistant Professor (1967-71), Rockefeller University, NYC; Assistant Professor (1965-67), Providence College, RI; Associate Professor of Genetics (1971-74)/Professor of Genetics (1974-87)/Director of the Institute of Ecology (1977-81)/Chairman and Associate Dean, Division of Environmental Studies (1977-81), University of California - Davis; Distinguished Professor of Biological Sciences (1987-89)/Affiliated Faculty Member of Department of Philosophy (since 1989), University of California - Irvine **Editorial Work:** *Contention*; Cambridge Studies in Evolutionary Biology; *Evolucion Biologica*; *Biology and Philosophy*; *History and Philosophy of Life Sciences*; *Arbor*; *Acta Zoologia Mexicana*; *Molecular Biology and Evolution*; *Oxford Surveys in Evolutionary Biology*; *Journal of Molecular Evolution*; *Brazilian Journal of Ethics* **Selected Memberships:** Center for Theology and the Natural Sciences, CA; Member (1981-82), National Academy of Sciences Committee on Creationism; Foreign Member, Royal Academy of Sciences of Spain; Foreign Member, Russian Academy of Sciences; American Society of Naturalists; Genetics Society of America; Ecological Society of America; American Genetics Society; American Institute of Biological Studies; Charter Member, Molecular Biology and Evolution Society; National Academy of Sciences; American Academy of Arts and Sciences; American Philosophical Society **Discipline:** Biological Sciences; Genetics; Philosophy of Science **Related Interests:** Religious freedom; Ethics in Science; Evolutionary Biology; Epistemology; Philosophy of Science.

Selected Publications: He is author of more than 550 articles and 8 books, and editor of 3 other books.

_____. *Studies in the Philosophy of Biology.* London: Macmillan; Berkeley: University of California, 1974.
_____. *Molecular Evolution.* Sunderland, MA: Sinajer Associates, 1976.
_____. *Evolving: The Theory and Processes of Organic Evolution.* Menlo Park, CA: Benjamin/Cummings, 1979.
_____. *Population and Evolutionary Genetics: A Primer.* Menlo Park, CA: Benjamin/Cummings, 1982.
_____. *Modern Genetics.* 2nd ed. Menlo Park, CA: Benjamin/Cummings, 1984.

Bag, A. K.

Present Position and Address: Deputy Executive Secretary and Head (since 1990), History of Science Division, Indian National Science Academy, Bahadur Shah Zafar Marg, New Delhi-110002, India **Date of Birth:** January 11, 1937 **Education:** M.S.. Mathematics (1960)/Ph.D. History of Mathematics (1969), Calcutta University **Previous Positions:** Junior/Senior Research Fellow (-1971); Mathematics Lecturer (-1977); Project Coordinator (-1982) for History of Science program **Editorial Work:** Associate Editor, *Indian Journal of History of Science* **Selected Memberships:** Member-Secretary, Indian National Commission for History of Science; Member-Secretary National Committee International Union for History and Philosophy of Science; Elected Member, International Academy of History of Science (Paris, 1989); Member, The Asiatic Society, Calcutta **Discipline:** History of Indian Mathematics and Astronomy; History of Science from both National and International perspective **Related Interests:** Ancient science from earliest times to the 12th Century; 18th Century Science and Technology.

Selected Publications: 75 articles (over and above a large number of review articles) have been published in various Journals in India and abroad, in such areas as history of mathematics, history of astronomy, and on science and technology in general.

_____, S. N. Sen and S. R. Sarma. *A Bibliography of Sanskrit Works on Astronomy and Mathematics*. Indian National Science Academy, 1966.
_____. *Mathematics in Ancient and Medieval India*. Varanasi: Chowkhamba Orientalia, 1979.
_____, S. N. Sen. *The Sulbasutras. The Altar geometry*. Indian National Science Academy, 1983.
_____. *Science and Civilization in India - Harappan Period*. New Delhi: Navrang, 1985.
_____, G. Swarup and K. S. Shukla, eds. *History of Oriental Astronomy*. Cambridge University Press, 1987.
_____, et al, eds. *General Ideas of Methodology, Astronomy, Mathematics and Physical Concepts*, vol. 1. *Medicine, Technology, Arts and Crafts, architecture and Music*, vol. 2 of *Interaction between Indian and Central Asian Science and technology in Medieval Times*. Indo-Soviet Joint Monograph Series. New Delhi: Indian National Science Academy, 1990.
_____, editor. *History of Technology in India, From Antiquity to 1200 A.D.* New Delhi: Indian National Science Academy, in press.

Balslev, Anindita Niyogi

Present Position and Address: Fellow (since 1990), Indian Institute of Advanced Study, Simla 22 Harris Road, Charlottesville, VA 22901, USA **Date of Birth:** July 1, 1940 **Education:** BA Hons in Philosophy (1960)/ MA in Philosophy (1962), Calcutta University; Ph.D. (1968), Doctoral d'Université (mention trés honorable) at University of Paris; Thesis: "Une etude comparée de quelques themes philosophiques proposes par le Bouddhisme et l'Existentialisme" **Previous Positions:** Lecturer (1969-71), Department of Religious Studies, Canisius College, Buffalo, NY; Lecturer (1973), California State College, Dominguez Hills; Lecturer (1974-75), Theological Faculty, Aarhus University,

Denmark; Research Fellow (1976-1978), Danish Research Council for the Humanities **Selected Memberships:** Institute on Religion in an Age of Science; Council of the International Society for the Study of Time; International Board of Advisors for Center for Advanced Research in Phenomenology **Discipline:** Philosophy and Religion **Related Interests:** Cosmology and Soteriology; Time in Philosophy, Theology and Science; Encounter of Religions.

Selected Publications:

_____. *A Study of Time in Indian Philosophy*. Wiesbaden, Germany: Otto Harrassowitz, 1983.
_____. *Religious Tolerance or Acceptance*? Calcutta: Ramakrishna Mission Institute of Cultural Publications, 1987.
_____. J. N. Mohanty, eds. *Religion and Time* (to be published).

Balswick, Jack Orville

Present Position and Address: Professor of Sociology and Family Development/Director of Research for Marriage and Family Ministries (since 1982), Fuller Theological Seminary, Pasadena, CA 91182-3600, USA **Work Phone:** (818) 584-5334 **Home Phone:** (818) 791-4075 **Education:** B.A. (1960), Chico State College, CA; M.A. (1962)/Ph.D. (1967), University of Iowa **Postgraduate Studies:** Trinity Divinity School (1967-69) **Previous Positions:** Assistant Professor (1967), Wisconsin State University - Oshkosh; Assistant (1968-71)/Associate (1972-78)/Professor (1978-82), University of Georgia **Editorial Work:** Associate Editor (1975-80), *Review of Religious Research* **Selected Memberships:** Society for the Scientific Study of Religion, (has presented 9 papers from 1971-present); Board of Directors (1978), Religious Research Association; American Sociological Association **Discipline:** Sociology, Family Development and Theology **Related Interests:** Scientific Models of Society; Society and Theology.

Selected Publications: He has published 10 books, 2 monographs and over 50 articles.

_____, Dawn Ward. "The Nature of Man and Scientific Models of Society." *Journal of the American Scientific Affiliation (JASA)* 28, 4 (December 1976): 181-5.
_____, Dawn Ward. "Responsibility in 1984." *(JASA)* 33, 1 (March 1981): 24-9.
_____, Jack Balswick. "Towards a Social Theology of Punishment." Perspectives on Science and Christian Faith 41, 4 (1989).

Bame, Michael

Present Position and Address: Dean (since 1983), Faculty of Protestant Theology, PO Box 4011, Yaoundé, Republic of Cameroon **Date of Birth:** November 27, 1947 **Education:** B.D. Hons in Theology (1972), Faculté de Théologie; Th.M. (1974), Princeton Theological Seminary; Ph.D. (1978), King's College, Aberdeen **Previous Positions:** Secretary (1983)/Professor (1985)/Treasurer of Conference of Theological Institutions in Africa (1984-1989) **Discipline:** Dogmatics **Related Areas of Interest:** Parapsychology; anthropology; horticulture; eco-theology; architecture.

Selected Publications:

_____. Le Notre Père. Strassbourg: Navpresse, 1985.
_____. "Jesus Christ est-il reellement mort?" Flambeau 1(1993): 7-26.
_____. Death and Life Eternal. Nairobi: ACC Publications, 1994.
_____. Le Vie Chrétien face à la Puissances du Mal. Yaounde: CLE, 1995.

Banco, Eugene C.

Present Position and Address: Professor of Religion (since 1968), Department of Religion, Emory University, Atlanta, GA 30322; (Home) 968 Castle Falls Drive, Atlanta, GA 30329, USA **Home Phone:** (404) 634-9111 **Date of Birth:** May 5, 1930 **Education:** B.A. Humanities (1954)/M.A. Philosophy (1955), Gonzaga University; S.T.L. Theology (1962), College St. Albert de Louvain in Belgium; Ph.D. Religion (1966), Columbia University **Previous Positions:** Assistant Professor of Religion and Founder/Director, Center for the Study of Contemporary Values (1966-68), University of Santa Clara; Founder and President of Society of Priests for a Free Ministry (1969-71); International European Correspondent (1958-62)/Assistant Editor (1963-66), *America*; Visiting Professorships - San Francisco (1966, 68)/Stanford (1969)/Santa Clara/California at Davis (1973, 75)/California State University, Sacramento (1974-75) **Selected Memberships:** American Academy of Religion; Federation of Christian Ministries; Amnesty International **Discipline:** Religion **Related Interests:** Religion and Ecology.

Selected Publications:

_____. "Psychospirituality: The Ecological Matrix." In *An Ecology of the Spirit*, ed. Michael Barnes. University Press of America, 1994.

Banner, Michael Charles

Present Position and Address: Dean and Fellow (since 1988), Peterhouse, Cambridge, CB2 1RD, UK **Date of Birth:** April 19, 1961 **Education:** B.A. (1983)/M.A. (1985)/D. Phil. (1986), Balliol College, Oxford University **Previous Positions:** Bampton Fellow (1985-1988), St. Peter's College, Oxford **Discipline:** Philosophy **Related Interests:** Philosophy of Science and Religion.

Selected Publications:

_____. *The Justification of Science and the Rationality of Religious Belief.* Oxford University Press, 1990.

Barbour, Ian G.

Present Position and Address: Professor Emeritus, Department of Religion, Carleton College, Northfield, MN 55057, USA **Work Phone:** (507) 645-5723 **Date of Birth:** October 5, 1923 **Education:** B.S. (1943), Swarthmore; M.S. Physics (1946), Duke University; Ph.D. Physics (1950), University of Chicago; B.D. Theology (1956), Yale University **Awards and Honors:** Fulbright Fellowship (1967-69); National Endowment for the Humanities Fellowship (1976-77); Fellow of the National Humanities Center (1980-81); Guggenheim Fellowship (1967-68) **Previous Positions:** Assistant/Associate Professor (1949-53), Chair for the Department of Physics, Kalamazoo College; Assistant/Associate Professor/Chairman (1955-73), Department of Religion, Carleton College; Visiting Professor of Science, Theology and Human Values (1973-74), Purdue University; Professor of Religion and Physics/Director of Program in Science, Ethics and Public Policy (1974-89)/Winifred and Atherton Bean Professor of Science, Technology and Society (1981-86), Carleton College **Editorial Work:** Editorial Board of *Process Studies; Zygon; Research in Philosophy and Technology* **Selected Memberships:** Advisory Board (1975-86), *Ethics and Values in Science and Technology*, National Science Foundation **Discipline:** Theology, Physics and Philosophy **Related Interests:** Science, Technology, Environment, Ethics and Religion.

Selected Publications: His bibliography lists 12 books and over 44 articles directly relevant to the topic, including the following.

_____. *Christianity and the Scientist.* New York: Association Press, 1960.

_____. *Issues in Science and Religion.* Englewood Cliffs, N.J. Prentice Hall, 1966. British edition, London: SCM Press, 1968. Paperback edition, New York: Harper Torchbook, 1971. Spanish translation, Guevara, Spain: Sal Terrae, 1971. Chinese translation,. Sichuan: People's Publishing House, 1993.

_____, editor. *Science and Religion: New Perspectives on the Dialogue.* New York: Harper & Row, 1968. British edition, London: SCM Press, 1968.

_____. *Science and Secularity: The Ethics of Technology.* New York: Harper & Row, 1970. Spanish translation, Buenos Aires, Argentina: Editorial La Aurora, 1971.

_____. *Myths, Models and Paradigms.* New York: Harper & Row, 1974. British edition, London: SCM Press, 1974. Polish translation, Krakow: Znak, 1984.

_____. *Technology, Environment and Human Values.* New York: Praeger, 1980.

_____. *Religion in an Age of Science, Gifford Lectures for 1989-90.* San Francisco: Harper & Row, 1990. British edition, London: SCM Press, 1990.

_____. *Ethics in an Age of Technology, Gifford Lectures for 1990-91.* San Francisco: Harper Collins, 1993. British edition, London: SCM Press, 1993.

Barclay, Oliver Rainsford

Present Position and Address: International Secretary, Christians in Science, 8A Southland Road, Leicester, LE2 3RJ UK **Work Phone:** (0116) 2705538 **Date of Birth:** February 22, 1919 **Education:** B.A. Natural Sciences (1942)/Ph.D. Zoology (1945), Cambridge University. **Postgraduate Studies:** Postdoctoral Research and Teacher (1945-46), Zoology Department, Cambridge University **Selected Memberships:** Secretary (1944-1988), Research Scientists' Christian Fellowship (now Christians in Science) **Discipline:** Zoology **Related Interests:** Science and Faith; Apologetics; Applied Theology.

Selected Publications: Note that he has been editor of *Science and Christian Belief*, a journal published by Christians In Science since 1989. He has also published numerous articles and booklets, two of which are listed below.

_____. *Reasons for Faith.* UK: InterVarsity Press, 1974.

_____. *Developing a Christian Mind.* UK: InterVarsity Press, 1984. Published in the United States as *The Intellect and Beyond.* Zondervan, 1985.

Bargatzky, Thomas

Present Position and Address: Professor of Anthropology, University of Bayreuth Kulturwissenschaftliche Fakultät, Geschwister-Scholl-Platz 3, 8580 Bayreuth, Germany **Date of Birth:** September 13, 1946 **Languages Spoken:** German, English, French, Italian **Education:** Dr. phil. Anthropology (*magna cum laude*, 1977), University of Hamburg; Dr. phil. habil. Anthropology (1988), University of Munich **Field Work:** 15 months in West Samoa, supported by grants from the German National Research Foundation **Previous Positions:** Tutor (1976), Institute for Mesoamerican Studies, University of Hamburg; Assistant Lecturer/Lecturer/Tenured Lecturer (1979-present), Anthropology, Institute of Anthropology and African Studies, University of Munich; Privatdozent - Dr.Phil. Habil. (1988-present), Philosophical Faculty, University of Munich; Visiting Professor of Anthropology (Summer 1989), Department of Anthropology, Institute of South Asian Studies, University of Heidelberg; Visiting Professor of Anthropology, Institute of Anthropology, University of Tübingen **Selected Memberships:** Board of Directors (since 1990), International Society for the Study of Human Ideas on Ultimate Reality and Meaning (URAM), Toronto, Canada **Discipline:** Social and Cultural Anthropology **Related Interests:** History of liturgical forms, ritual, Augustinus' distinction between civitas terrena and civitas Dei.

Selected Publications: The bibliography lists 31 publications, plus 4 more currently in press.

_____. "Das Phänomen der Religion aus ethnologischer Sicht: Ein Beitrag zum Dialog mit der Religionsphiloso-phie." *Saeculum* 35, 3, 4. Jahrgang (1984): 372-80.

_____. *Einführung in die Ethnologie. Eine Kultur- und Sozialanthropologie.* Hamburg: Helmut Buske, 1985.

_____. *Einführung in die Kulturökologie. Umwelt, Kultur und Gesellschaft.* Berlin: Dietrich Reimer, 1986.

_____. "On Adaptation and Equilibrium: A Critique of Biological Analogies in Cultural Anthropology." *Zeitschrift für Ethnologie* 111, 2 (1986): 193-203.

Barker, Eileen

Present Position and Address: Professor of Sociology (with special reference to the study of religion), London School of Economics; Chair of Board of Governors (since 1988), INFORM (Information Network Focus On Religious Movements); (Work) Department of Sociology, London School of Economics, Houghton Street, London WC2A 2AE, England; (Home) 29A Crawford Avenue, Wembley, Middx, HA0 2HY, England **Work Phone:** (0171) 955 7289 **Date of Birth:** April 21, 1938 **Education:** Cheltenham Ladies' College (1950-1955); Voice and Drama Teaching Diploma with distinction (1955-1957), Webber Douglas School of Singing and Dramatic Art; Extra-mural Diploma in Social History and Modern Britain (1965-67), Ealing Technical College and Regent Street Polytechnic; B.S.. Honors, Sociology, 1st Class with Distinction, (1970)/Ph.D. Sociology, London School of Economics. **Awards and Honors:** Gold Medalist for best performance (1955), Webber Douglas School of Singing and Dramatic Art; First non-American to receive the Society for the Scientific Study of Religion's annual Distinguished Book Award for *The Making of A Moonie* (1985); Fulbright Scholarship, to teach and research in the USA (Fall 1987) **Previous Positions:** Lecturer/Senior Lecturer/Reader, Sociology, London School of Economics (LSE); Dean of Undergraduate Studies (1982-86), LSE; Vice-Dean of the Faculty of Economics (1986-90), University of London; Visiting Professor (Fall 1987), Department of Religious Studies, University of California - Santa Barbara; Visiting Professor (Summer 1988), Department of Sociology, University of New England, Australia **Selected Memberships:** Convener (1976-1981)/Chair (1985-1990), Sociology of Religion Study Group, British Sociological Association; Executive Council Member (1981-1984)/President (1991-1993), Society for the Scientific Study of Religion (SSSR); Executive Committee (1985- 1989), Conference Internationale de Sociologie des Religiones; Vice President (1985-93), Religious Research Committee, International Sociological Association; Executive Committee (1987-91), Association for the Sociology of Religion **Discipline:** Sociology **Related Interests:** Relationship between Science and Religion in Contemporary Society; New Religious Movements; Religion in Europe; Armenians in Diaspora.

Selected Publications: Her bibliography lists 8 books and over 130 articles. She has also reviewed over 250 books..

_____. "DNA in the Age of Aquarius." *Theology* (November 1978): 463-6.

_____. "In The Beginning: The Battle of Creationist Science Against Evolutionism." In *On the Margins of Science*, ed. Roy Wallis, 179-200. Keele University Press, 1979.

_____. "Science and Theology: Diverse Resolutions of an Interdisciplinary Gap by the New Priesthood of Science." *Interdisciplinary Science Reviews*, 5, 4 (December 1980): 281-91.

_____. "Science as Theology: The Theological Functioning of Western Science." In *The Sciences and Theology in the Twentieth Century*, ed. A. R. Peacocke, 262-80. London: Oriel Press; Indiana: University of Notre Dame, 1981.

_____. "The Conversion of Conversion: A Sociological Anti-Reductionist Perspective." In *Reductionism in Academic Disciplines*, ed. Arthur R. Peacocke, 58-75. Giuldford, Surrey: SHRE and NFER-Nelson, 1985.

_____. "Let There Be Light: Scientific Creationism in the Twentieth Century." In *Darwinism and Divinity: Essays in Evolution and Religious Belief*, ed. John R. Durant, 181-204. Oxford: Martin Roberts, 1985.

_____. "Does it Matter How We Got Here? Dangers Perceived in Literalism and Evolutionism." *Zygon* 22, 2 (June 1987): 213-25.

_____. "A Marriage through Divorce: Relationships between Science and Values." In *Synthesis of Science and Religion: Critical Essays and Dialogues*, ed. T. D. Singh, 130-9. San Francisco and Bombay: Bhaktivedanta Institute, 1988.

_____. *The Making of a Moonie: Brainwashing or Choice?* Oxford: Basil Blackwell, 1984. Reprint, Aldershot, Hampshire: Gregg Revivals, 1993.

_____, et al, eds. *Secularization, Rationalism and Sectarianism.* Oxford University Press, 1993.

Barkman, Paul F.

Present Position and Address: Practicing Clinical Psychology (since 1971), Twentynine Palms, California Psychological Corporation, 6476 Adobe Road, Twentynine Palms, CA 92277, USA **Date of Birth:** June 1, 1921 **Education:** A.B. Psychology and Education (1943), Bethel College, North Newton, KS; M.A. Mental Hygiene and Vocational Guidance (1946), New York University, NYC; M.Div., New York Theological Seminary; Ph.D. Human Relations Studies (1959), New York University **Postgraduate Studies:** Postdoctoral Internship in Clinical Psychology (1960-61), Grant County Mental Health Clinic, Marion, IN; Postdoctoral Internship in Clinical Psychology (Summer 1961), Traverse City State Hospital, MI; Postdoctoral Fellowship in Clinical Child Psychology (1963-64), Reiss-Davis Clinic for Child Guidance, Los Angeles; Psychoanalysis, 700 hours under Newell Schmalzreid and Alfred Goldberg **Previous Positions:** Pastor of various churches (1942-62); Superintendent of Grace Children's Home (1946-1955), Henderson, NE; Associate Professor/Head of the Psychology Department (1956-63), Taylor University, Upland, IN; Associate Professor of Psychology (1964-1970), Fuller Theological Seminary, CA **Licences:** Psychologist #PT 002912 (California); Marriage, Family and Child Counselor #MK 004976 (California) **Selected Memberships:** American Psychological Association, Divisions 1, 12 and 30; California Psychological Association; American Scientific Affiliation; California Association of Marriage and Family Therapists **Discipline:** Clinical Psychology with specialty in Child Psychology; Psychological Testing; Minister of Religion **Related Interests:** The relation of Theology to Psychology.

Selected Publications:

_____. "The Relationship of Personality Modes to Religious Experience and Behavior." *Journal of the American Scientific Affiliation* 20, 1 (March 1968). Reprint in *Current Perspectives in the Psychology of Religion*, ed. H. Newton Maloney. Grand Rapids, MI: Eerdmans Publishing Company, 1977.

_____. *Man in Conflict.* Grand Rapids, MI: Zondervan Publishing House, 1965.

_____. "The Relationship of Theology to Psychology." Paper presented at the 7th World Mennonite Conference, Kitchener, Ontario, Canada (1972).

Personal Notes: Ordained Clergyman, American Baptist Churches of the Pacific Southwest.

Barnes, Michael H.

Present Position and Address: Professor of Religious Studies, University of Dayton, Dayton, OH 45469, USA **Education:** Ph.D. in Religious Studies (1976), Marquette University. **Selected Memberships:** American Academy of Religion; College Theological Society; CTSA; Society for the Scientific Study of Religion **Discipline:** Philosophical Theology **Related Interests:** Cultural Evolution; Method of Science; Method of Theology **Current Research:** The history of major shifts in thought-styles (cognitive techniques) in religion and science in Western civilization.

Selected Publications:

_____. "Faith and Imagination in Science and Religion." *Theology Today* 40 (April 1983):15-24.

_____. "Creationism as a Rejection of Responsibility." In *Fundamentalism Today*, ed. Marla Selvidege. Brethren Press, 1984.

_____. *In the Presence of Mystery*. Twenty-Third Publications, 1984. An introduction to the study of religion, based on Robert Bellah's sociological and anthropological theory of religious evolution.
_____. "Religion and Science, Focusing the Light of Imagination." *Word and World* 5 (Summer 1985):240-7.
_____. "Creationism." Supplement article for *The New Catholic Encyclopedia* 18 (1989).
_____. "The Method of Science: a Reply to Susan Kwilecki." *Journal for the Scientific Study of Religion* (Fall 1989).
_____. "Primitive Religious Thought and the Evolution of Religion." *Religion* 22 (1992): 21-46.

Barnhouse, Ruth Tiffany

Present Position and Address: Psychiatrist in private practice (since 1956), 5956 Sherry Lane, Suite 1221, Dallas TX 75225, USA **Work Phone:** (214) 987-0792 **Fax:** (214) 987-0796 **Education:** M.D. (1950), Columbia University NYC; Boston Psychoanalytic Institute (1966), Resident in Psychiatry, McLean Hospital (1953-55)/Massachussetts General Hospital (1955-56) **Previous Positions:** Acting Director Children's Unit (1956-57), Metropolitan State Hospital; Staff Psychiatrist (1958-59), Southard Clinic, Boston; Attending Psychiatrist (1959-78), McLean Hospital, Belmont; Invited Lecturer and Supervisor (1971-74), Weston College of Theology; Seminar Leader in Psychiatry (1972-75), Harvard Divinity School; Visiting Lecturer in Pastoral Theology (1975-76), Weston College of Theology; Adjunct Professor of Pastoral Theology (1978-80), Virginia Theological Seminary; Adjunct Professor of Psychology (1979), Loyola College; Courtesy Staff (1979-80), Sibley Memorial Hospital; Professor of Psychiatry and Pastoral Care (1980-89), Perkins School of Theology **Selected Memberships:** Scientific Associate, American Academy of Psychoanalysis; American Academy of Religion; American Association for the Advancement of Science; Life Fellow, American Psychiatric Association; Conference of Anglican Theologians; International Physicians for Prevention of Nuclear War; President, The Isthmus Institute; Massachussetts Medical Society; New York Academy of Science; Physicians for Social Responsibility **Discipline:** Psychiatry; Theology **Related Interests:** Psychiatry/Psychology and Theology/Religion; Science and Religion in dialogue.

Selected Publications: Her bibliography list 4 books and 27 other publications.

_____. "Psychiatry and Religion: Partners or Strangers." Paper presented at the American Academy of Psychoanalysis, December 1981.
_____. "Science and Religion: A New Conversation." *Anglican Theological Review* 71, 1 (Winter 1989).

Personal Notes: Mother of 7 children.

Barrow, John D.

Present Position and Address: Professor (since 1989), Astronomy Centre, University of Sussex Astronomy Centre, University of Sussex, Falmer, Brighton BN1 9QH, UK **Work Phone:** (0273) 678574 **Fax:** (0273) 678097 **E-Mail/Telex:** 877159 UNISEX G **Date of Birth:** November 29, 1952 **Education:** B.S.. Hons. in Mathematics, 1st Class Honours (1974), Van Mildert College, University of Durham; D.Phil. Astrophysics, Thesis title: "Non-Uniform Cosmological Models," (1977), Magdalen College and Department of Astrophysics, University of Oxford **Lectures Presented:** Gifford Lecturer (1988), University of Glasgow; Scott Memorial Lecturer (1989); Collingwood Lecturer (1990); Sigma — Tau — Latzera Lecturer (1991); George Darwin Lecturer, Royal Astronomical Society (1992); Spinoza Lecturer (1993); BBV Spanish Lectures **Awards and Honors:** Samuel Locker Award Winner (1989); Nuffield Fellow (1986); Leverhulme Royal Society Fellow (1992); PPARC Senior Research Fellow (1994) **Previous Positions:** Lindeman Fellow, Berkeley Astronomy Department (1977-78), University of California; Christ Church and Department of Astrophysics (1978-80), Oxford University; Miller Fellow, Berkeley Physics Department (1980-81), University of California; Lecturer (1981-88)/Senior Lecturer (1988-1989)/Professor (since 1989)/Director (1989-1990), Astronomy Center, University of Sussex **Selected Memberships:** Fellow, Royal Astronomical Society; Member of Commission 47, International Astronomical Union; Founding Member, Centre International de Recherche Transdisciplinaire; Member L'Academie Internationale de Philosophie des Sciences **Discipline:** Astrophysics **Related Interests:** Cosmology; Gravitation; Particle Physics; The Anthropic Cosmological Principle; Interdisciplinary Learning; History and Philosophy of Science.

Selected Publications: His bibliography lists 200 highly relevant published articles in the field of astrophysics and cosmology.

_____. J. Silk. *The Left Hand of Creation: the Origin and Evolution of the Expanding Universe.* New York: Basic Books 1983; 2nd ed. Oxford and New York: Oxford University Press, 1994.
_____. Frank J. Tipler. *L'Homme et le Cosmos.* Paris: Radio France Imago, 1984. (In French).
_____. Frank J. Tipler. *The Anthropic Cosmological Principle.* Oxford and New York: Oxford University Press, 1988.
_____. *The World Within the World.* Oxford and New York: Oxford University Press, 1988.
_____. *Theories of Everything: the Quest for Ultimate Explanation.* Oxford and New York: Oxford University Press, 1991.
_____. *Pi In The Sky: Counting, Thinking, and Being.* Oxford and New York: Oxford University Press, 1992.
_____. *Perche il mondo e matematico?* Rome: Laterza, 1992.
_____. *The Origin of the Universe.* New York: Basic Books, 1994.
_____. *The Artful Universe.* Oxford and New York: Oxford University Press, 1995.

Bartek, Edward J.

Present Position and Address: Philosophy and Psychology Instructor (Since 1975), Manchester Community College, 68 Walnut Street, East Hartford, CT 06108, USA **Date of Birth:** November 25, 1921 **Education:** B.A. (1952)/M.Ed. (1953), University of Hartford **Previous Positions:** General Education Department Head (1953-1975); Courses taught: Philosophy, Philosophy of Religion, Philosophy of History, Ethics, Psychology; Institute on Religion in an Age of Science; American Philosophical Association; International Society for Comparative Study of Civilizations; Association for the Study of Dreams; Connecticut Poetry Society **Discipline:** Philosophy and Psychology **Related Interests:** Seeking a "Grand Unifying Theory" to Encompass all Disciplines by the Same few Ultimate Principles and Structures. Encompasses all Relevant Areas.

Selected Publications

_____. *The Mind of Future Man.* East Hartford, 1965.
_____. *Ultimate Philosophy:* Trinityism. East Hartford, 1968.
_____. *Unifying Principles of the Mind.* East Hartford, 1969.
_____. *Ultimate Principles: Theology.* East Hartford, 1987.
_____. *Ultimate Principles. A Grand Unifying Theory Pending.* East Hartford, 1987.
_____. Trinitarian Philosophy. A Grand Unifying Theory Pending. East Hartford, 1988.
_____. Trinitarian Psychology. East Hartford, 1988.
_____. Trinitarian Philosophy of History. East Hartford, 1988.
_____. Universal Trinitarian Ethics. East Hartford, 1988.
_____. Trinityism Applied. East Hartford. East Hartford, 1990.

Bartholomew, Gilbert A.

Address: P.O. Box 150, Lion's Bay, BC, V0N 2E0, Canada **Date of Birth:** April 8, 1922 **Education:** B.A. (1943), University of British Columbia; Ph.D. (1948), McGill University **Previous Positions:** Scientist (1948-83)/Head Neutron Physics Branch (1962-71)/Director Physics Division(1971-83), Atomic Energy of Canada Ltd (A.E.C.L.) **Selected Memberships:** Fellow, Royal Society of Canada;

Fellow, American Physical Society; Fellow, American Association for Advancement of Science; Science and Technology Seminar, Association for Bahai Studies (ABS) **Discipline:** Nuclear Physics **Related Interests:** Harmony of Religion and Science.

Selected Publications: Over 100 scientific titles in scientific journals and A.E.C.L. reports including several review articles in neutron capture, gamma rays, neutron physics, low-energy nuclear physics, and advanced systems for nuclear power.

_____. "Harmony of Science and Religion: A Complementarity Perspective." *Journal of Bahai Studies* 1, 3 (1989).

Bassett, Rodney L.

Present Position and Address: Professor of Psychology, Roberts Wesleyan College, Rochester, NY 14624 **Phone:** (716) 594-6468 **Date of Birth:** June 22, 1951 **Languages Spoken:** English **Honors:** Award for Teaching Excellence, Robert Wesleyan College; Award for Professional Accomplishment, Robert Wesleyan College **Memberships:** American Psychological Association, Christian Association for Psychological Studies, Society for Personality and Social Psychology, Society for the Scientific Study of Religion **Discipline:** Psychology **Relevant Areas of Interest:** Psychology of Religion **Current Project:** Integrating Psychology and Christianity in the area of emotions; Sexual Attitude among Religious Populations.

Selected Publications:

_____, Basinger, D. & Livermore, P. "Lying in the Laboratory: Deception in Human Research from Psychological, Philosophical, and Theological Perspectives." *Journal of the American Scientific Affiliation* 34 (1982): 201-212.
_____, Hill, P.C., Hart, C., Mathewson, K., & Perry, K. "Helping Christians Reclaim Some Abandoned Emotions: The ACE Model of Emotion." *Journal of Psychology and Theology* 21 (1993): 165-173.
_____, Sadler, R.D., Kobischen, E.E., Skiff, D.M., Merrill, I.J., Atwater, B.J., & Livermore, P.W. "The Shepherd Scale: Separating the Sheep from the Goats." *Journal of Psychology and Theology* 9 (1981): 335-351.

Batson, C. Daniel

Present Position and Address: Professor of Psychology (since 1981), Department of Psychology, University of Kansas, Lawrence, KS 66045 **Date of Birth:** March 15, 1943 **Education:** Studied at Davidson College (1960-61)/Yale University (Psychology, 1961-62); B.S. Psychology (1964), University of Tennessee; B.D. Religious Education (1967)/Ph.D. Religious Education (*summa cum laude*, 1971), Princeton Theological Seminary; M.A.(1971)/Ph.D. Psychology (1972), Princeton University **Previous Positions:** Assistant Professor of Psychology (1972-76), University of Kansas; Associate Professor (1976-81), University of Kansas; Visiting Scholar (Spring 1979), Oxford University UK; Visiting Professor (1983-84), University of Texas; Visiting Scholar (Spring 1987, 91-92), University of Georgia; Visiting Fellow (Spring 1987), Princeton University; Director, Graduate Program in Social Psychology (1984-87, 92-), University of Kansas **Discipline:** Psychology and Religious Education **Related Interests:** Psychology of Religion; Religious Experience and Social Psychology; Sociobiology and Religion; Social and Moral Values; Ethics.

Selected Publications: His bibliography lists over 80 publications, with 20 papers in psychology, 7 papers in religion, and many book reviews.

Darley, J. M., C. D. Batson. "From Jerusalem to Jericho." *Journal of Personality and Social Psychology* 27 (1973): 100-8.
_____. "Rational Processing or Rationalization? *Journal of Personality and Social Psychology* 32 (1975): 176-84.
_____. W. L. Ventis. *The Religious Experience: A Social-Psychological Perspective.* New York: Oxford University Press, 1982.

_____, K. C. Oleson, J. L. Weeks, S. P. Healy, P. J. Jennings, and T. Brown. "Religious Prosocial Motivation: Is it Altruistic or Egoistic?" *Journal of Personality and Social Psychology* 57 (1989): 873-84.

_____, J. D. Flory. "Goal-Relevant Cognition Associated individuals High on Intrinsic, end Religion." *Journal for the Scientific Study of Religion* 29 (1990): 346-60.

_____. "Good Samaritans. . .or Priests and Levites?: Using William James as a Guide in the Study of Religious Prosocial Motivation." *Personality and Social Psychology Bulletin* 16 (1990): 758-68.

_____, P. A. Schoenrade. "Validity Concerns." Part 1. "Reliability Concerns." Part 2 of "Measuring Religion as Quest." *Journal for the Scientific Study of Religion* 30 (1991): 416-29; 430-47.

_____, P. Schoenrade, and W. L. Ventis. *Religion and the Individual: A Social-Psychological Perspective*. New York: Oxford University Press, 1993.

_____, C. T. Burris. "Personal Religion: Depressant or Stimulant of Prejudice and Discrimination?" In *The Psychology of Prejudice: The Ontario Symposium, Vol. 7*, ed. M. P. Zanna and J. M. Olson. Hillsdale, NJ: Erlbaum, in press.

Beck, Horst Waldemar

Present Position and Address: Professor for Interdisciplinary Theology (since 1985), Evangelical Theological Faculty, Leuven, Belgium; Professor for Philosophy of Science (since 1991), Gustav-Siewerth University, Weilheim, Germany; Sommerhalde 6, D-72270 Baiersbronn, Germany **Work Phone:** (0) 7442-7653 **Date of Birth:** September 1, 1933 **Education:** Diploma Engineering (1958)/Dr. Engineering (1964), University of Stuttgart; Dr. Theology (1971), University of Basel, Switzerland; Dr. theol. habil (licence for Academic teaching), University of Basel, Switzerland (1972) **Previous Positions:** Lecturer, Systematic Theology (1972), University of Basel, Switzerland; Lecturer Philosophy of Science (1981-93), University of Karlsruhe, Germany; VDI, Association for German Engineers; Wort und Wissen (Word and Knowledge), German-speaking Europe **Discipline:** Traffic Engineering; Philosophy of Science; Systematic Theology **Related Interests:** Philosophy of Science; Interdisciplinary Theology.

Selected Publications: Bibliography lists a large number of German publications in the field of theology and science, of which only a representative few are listed below.

_____. *Die Welt als Modell. Gegen den Mythos vom geschlossenen Weltbild*. Wuppertal: Theol. Verlag Rolf Brockhaus, 1973.

_____. *Götzendämmerung in den Wissenschaften. Karl Heim als Prophet und Pionier*. Wuppertal: Theol. Verlag Rolf Brockhaus, 1974.

_____. *Biologie und Weltanschauung. Gott der Schöpfer und Vollender und die Evolutionskonzepte des Menschen*. Wort und Wissen Bd.1. Neuhausen: Hänssler Verlag, 1979.

_____. *Schritte über Grenzen zwischen Technik und Theologie*. Teil 1: Der Mensch im System. Perspektiven einer kybernetischen Kultur (Wort und Wissen Bd. 6 (1)); Teil 2: Schöpfung und Vollendung. Perspektiven einer Theologie der Natur. Wort und Wissen Bd. 6 (2), Neuhausen: Hanssler Verlag, 1979.

_____. "Die Dialogsituation zwischen Theologie und Naturwissenschaft." In *Wer ist Gott? Bericht und Dokumentation von der 2. Studienkonferenz des AfeTH*, ed. H. Burkhardt. Giessen/Wuppertal: Theol. Verlagsgemeinschaft Brunnen/Brockhaus, 1982.

_____. "Biblische Universalität und Wissenschaft." In *Grundriss Interdisziplinärer Theologie*. Neuhausen-Stuttgart, 1987.

_____. "A Biblically Oriented Science Concept in the Postmodern Society." In *Christianity Facing the 21st Century*. International symposium on Christian culture and theology. Seoul: Soong Sil University Press, 1989.

_____. "The Ecological Crisis and Christian Doctrine on the Creation." In *Christianity Facing the 21st Century*. International symposium on Christian culture and theology. Seoul: Soong Sil University Press, 1989.

_____. *Christian Belief in Creation Within the Context of Modern Science*. Baiersbronn-Röt: Institut für Interdisziplinäre Theologie und Naturphilosophie, 1993.

_____. *Biblische Universalität und Wissenschaft. Interdisziplinäre Theologie im Horizont Trinitarischer Schöpfungslehre*. Weilheim-Bierbronnen: Gustav-Siewerth-Akademie, 1994.

Beck, Malcolm Nestor

Present Position and Address: Retired; 35 Ambrose Street, Charlottetown, Prince Edward Island, C1A 3P3, Canada **Home Phone:** (902) 894-3544 **Education:** Prince of Wales College, Charlottetown (1942-44), P.E.I.; Mount Allison University (1944-45), Sackville, New Brunswick; M.D./C.M., McGill University (1945-49), Montreal, Quebec; Medical Internship (1949-50), Metropolitan General Hospital, Windsor, Ontario **Postgraduate Studies:** Fellowship (earned degree, 1956), Royal College of Physicians and Surgeons, Canada; Residency in Psychiatry (1952-54), Dalhousie University, Halifax, NS; Residency in Child Psychiatry (1954-55), Medical College of Virginia and Memorial Guidance Clinic, Richmond, VA **Awards and Honors:** Centennial Medal of Canada (1967); Queen Elizabeth Medal (1977) **Previous Positions:** General Practitioner (1950-52), St. Peters, P.E.I.; Director of Child Psychiatry (1955-70)/Director of Mental Health(1970-73), Department of Health, Province of Prince Edward Island; Private Practice of Child Psychiatry (1973-93); Lecturer, Maritime Christian College; sometime Lecturer, Cincinnati Christian Seminary; Consultant, Psychiatrist Department of Veteran's Affairs; Psychiatrist, Private Practice of Medicine **Selected Memberships:** Elder, Central Christian Church; President of APPA/CPA/P.E.I. Medical Society; Member or Chairman of various committees and associations in the Medical and Psychiatric fields **Discipline:** Psychiatry **Related Interests:** Medical Ethics; Christ and Psychiatry; Mental Retardation.

Selected Publications: His bibliography lists 26 publications.

_____. "Faith." *Christian Standard* 53, 15 (Cincinnati, April 13, 1968).
_____. "Christ and Psychiatry." Presidential Address, *Canadian Psychiatric Association Journal* 18, 5 (1973).
_____. "The Myth of the Self-Sufficient Man." *Christianity Today* 12, 24 (September 23, 1977).
_____. "Eugenic Abortion: an ethical critique." *Canadian Medical Association Journal* 143, 3 (1990): 181-6.

Becker, Gerhold K.

Present Position and Address: Professor (Personal Chair, Philosophy and Religion; since 1991), Department of Religion and Philosophy, Hong Kong Baptist University; Founding Director, Centre for Applied Ethics, 224 Waterloo Road, Kowloon, Hong Kong **Date of Birth:** July 22, 1943 **Education:** Licentiate in Philosophy (*magna cum laude*, 1969), Hochschule für Philosophie, München; Licentiate in Theology (*summa cum laude*, 1973), Philosophisch-Theologische Hochschule, Frankfurt; Doctorate in Philosophy (*summa cum laude*, 1979), Ludwig-Maximilians-Universität, München; Lecturer (1975-80)/Assistant Professor (1980-86), Ludwig-Maximilians-Universität, München; Senior Lecturer (1986-88), Principal Lecturer (1988-91), Reader (1991), Hong Kong Baptist College **Discipline:** Theology; Religious Studies; Philosophy **Related Interests:** Religious Studies; Philosophy of Religion; Philosophy; History of Ideas; Ethics; Applied Ethics.

Selected Publications: His Bibliography lists 4 books, 7 chapters, and 17 major articles.

_____. *Theologie in der Gegenwart. Tendenzen und Perspektiven*. Regensburg: Pustet Verlag, 1978.
_____. *Neuzeitliche Subjektivität und Religiosität. Die religionsphilosophische Bedeutung von Heraufkunft und Wesen der Neuzeit im Denken Ernst Troeltschs*. Regensburg: Pustet Verlag, 1982.
_____. *Die Ursymbole in den Religionen*. Graz: Styria Verlag, 1987.
_____. "In Search for the Ultimate. Reflections on Methodology in URAM Research and Asian Studies." *Ultimate Reality and Meaning. Interdisciplinary Studies in the Philosophy of Understanding* 15, 1 (1992): 77-88.
_____. "Divinization of Nature in Early Modern Thought. In *The Invention of Nature*, ed. Thomas Bargatzky and Rolf Kuschel, 47-61. Frankfurt/Berlin/New York: Peter Lang Verlag, 1993.
_____. "Unity and University. The Neo-humanist Perspective in the Age of Post-Modernism." *International Philosophical Quarterly* 34, 2 (1994): 177-89.
_____. "Manipulating Nature: The Challenge of Biotechnology to the Traditional Concept of Nature." *Studies of Science and Theology* 3 (1995). In press.

Becker, Thomas

Present Position and Address: Chief Journalist of the Journal, *Caritas* (Charities) Kirchstr. 26g, D-7800 Freiburg I. Br., Germany **Concurrent Positions:** Editor (since 1989), *Caritas* **Date of Birth:** May 8, 1957 **Languages Spoken:** German, English, French **Education:** State examinations in Theology and Biology (1981), Albert-Ludwigs-Universität; Dr. theol. (1986), Freiburg **Previous Positions:** Research Assistant (1982-87), Institute for Systematic Theology, Freiburg **Selected Memberships:** Arbeitsgemeinschaften für Evolution, Menschheitszukunft und Sinnfragen (AGEMUS) **Discipline:** Biology, Theology **Related Interests:** Biology, Theology, Creationism; Teilhard de Chardin; Sociobiology; Natural Theology.

Selected Publications:

_____. *Geist und Materie in den ersten Schriften Teilhard de Chardins.* Freiburg: Herder, 1987.
_____. Review of *A Brief History of Time,* by Stephen Hawking. *Zygon* 24 (1989): 491-4.

Becker, Werner

Present Position and Address: Professor (since 1987), University Giessen, Zentrum für Philosophie und Grundlagen der Wissenschaft der Justus-Liebig-Universität; Otto-Behaghel Str. 10/C, II. OG D-6300, Giessen, Germany; (Home) Im Lech 16, 61350 Bad Homburg, Germany **Date of Birth:** February 21, 1937 **Languages Spoken:** German, English **Education:** Dr. phil. University of Frankfurt **Previous Positions:** Professor (1971-86), University of Frankfurt **Selected Memberships:** Allgemeine Gesellschaft für Philosophie in Deutschland; Institut International de Philosophie Politique in Paris **Discipline:** Political Philosophy and Ethics **Related Interests:** Political Philosophy.

Selected Publications: His Bibliography lists some 10 books in philosophy, 3 coauthored books, and 64 articles.

_____. K. Hübner. *Objektivität in den Natur- und Geisteswissenschaften.* Hamburg, 1976.
_____. "The Function of Reason in Western Philosophy, especially Political Philosophy." In *The Search of Absolute Values: Harmony among Sciences.* New York: Eccles, 1977.
_____. "Der Gegensatz zwischen wissenschaftlichem und politischem Ethos." In *Der Mensch und die Wissenschaft vom Menschen.* Innsbruck, 1981.
_____. "Das Versagen der rationalen Weltbildfunktion und die politische Legitimation der Wissenschaften." In *Zur Kritik der wissenschaftlichen Rationalität*, ed. H. Lenk. Festschrift für Kurt Hübner. Freiburg/München: Alber, 1987.

Begzos, Marios

Present Position and Address: Assistant Professor of Philosophy of Religion - with special reference to Science-Theology Dialogue (since 1986), University of Athens, Ilissia, Athens Dilou 1, GR-14562 Kifissia, Athens, Greece **Date of Birth:** November 27, 1951 **Languages Spoken:** German, English, French **Education:** B.Th (1973), Faculty of Theology, University of Athens; D.Th "Philosophy of Religion in W. Heisenberg's Thought" (1985), University of Athens **Postgraduate Studies:** Postgraduate studies in Ecumenical Theology (1973-74), University of Geneva; Philosophy, Evangelical and Catholic Theology (1979-81), University of Tübingen **Previous Positions:** Editor (1972-74), students periodical in the faculty of theology, University of Athens; Assistant to Prof. N. Nissiotis (1974-85), Faculty of Theology, University of Athens; Member of editorial committee of Greek Theological Periodical *Synaxis* in Athens (1982-85); Moderator of Workshop for Theology (1985-86), Goulandris-Horn-Foundation, Athens **Selected Memberships:** Treasurer, Greek Philosophical Society **Discipline:** Philosophy of Religion; Science and Religion in Debate **Relevant Areas of Interest:** Christian Faith and Natural Sciences in Eastern Orthodox Perspective; Philosophy of Physics/Religion; Technology and Theology; W. Heisenberg.

Selected Publications: Most of his 14 publications are in this area.

_____. "Dialectical Physics and Eschatological Theology. The Contemporary Dialogue between Theology and Science on the Basis of Werner Heisenberg's Thought." D.Th. Thesis under the supervision of Prof. N. Nissiotis, University of Athens (1985).

_____. "Between Apologetics and Apocalyptics. Christian Faith and Natural Sciences in an Eastern Orthodox Perspective." *Synaxis* 5, 17 (1986): 35-51.

_____. "From Separation to Relation. Faith and Science." In *Approaches to the Life and Thought of A. Tarkovsky.* Athens: Domus-Books, 1987.

_____. "The Dialectics of Nature in Werner Heisenberg's Thought." In *Dialectics, Proceedings of the Third Conference of Modern Greek Philosophy*, Athens, 1988.

_____. "Technology and Theology. Facing the Freedom of Man Today." *Exodos* 3 (1988): 7-10.

_____. "Philosophy of Physics and Philosophy of Religion." In *Diakonia*, Honorary Volume for B. Stoyianos. Thessaloniki: University of Thessaloniki, Faculty of Theology, 1988.

_____. *Essays in the Philosophy of Religion. Metamodernism and Eschatology, Collected Articles and Unpublished Studies.* Athens: Grigoris Publishing House, 1988.

_____. "Religion und Dualismus in der modernen Naturphilosophie." *Skepsis* 2 (1991): 143-150.

_____. "Sein und Zeit bei W. Heisenberg." *Platen* 44 (1992): 110-115. Also published as *Let es ido W. Heisenbergnel.* (Hungary) Theologiai Szemle 35 (1992): 116-17.

_____. *Eastern Ethics and Western Technology.* Athens: Grigoris Publishing House, 1993.

Personal Note: "I am the first Eastern Orthodox Theologian in Greece to deal with this subject in a comprehensive way. Due to my work, the subject 'Christian Faith and Natural Science' has now been introduced for the first time (1985) into the curriculum of studies in the Faculty of Theology of the University of Athens. This was first proposed by my teacher, the late, P. Nissiotis. In other Eastern Orthodox Educational centers there is still no mention of this as a subject."

Beinert, Wolfgang

Present Position and Address: Ordinary Professor for Dogmatics and History of Dogmatics, Kath.-Theologie Fakultät, University of Regensburg, Postf. 397, D 8400 Regensburg, Germany **Date of Birth:** March 4, 1933 **Education:** lic. phil.; Dr. theol.; Dr. theol. habil. **Selected Memberships:** The following scientific councils - Johann Adam Mochler-Institute, Paderborn, Germany; Catholic Academy of Bavaria, Munich, Germany; Pontifical Academia Mariana, Rome, Italy; Fondazione Ambrosiana Paolo VI, Milano, Italy **Discipline:** Dogmatics and History of Dogmatics (Roman-Catholic) **Related Interests:** Fundamental Dogmatics; Ecclesiology; Mariology; and Theological Anthropology.

Selected Publications: His bibliography lists ca. 800 publications. Over and above his major works in the area of Catholic dogmatics, here are a few smaller publications that have a more direct bearing on the relationship between theology and science.

_____. "Theologie als Wissenschaft und geistliches Leben." *Schottenarchiv* 70, 1 (1970): 21-4.

_____. *Christus und der Kosmos.* Freiburg, 1973.

_____. "Christus und der Kosmos. Perspektiven zu einer Theologie der Schöpfung." Paper presented at a theological seminary. Herder, 1974.

_____. "Theologie als Wissenschaft. Eine Anfrage an Thomas aus der Sicht heutiger Theologie." *Kath. Akademie Schwerte, Themen u. Termine.* October 1974/March 1975.

_____. "Ich glaube an Gott - den Schöpfer des Himmels und der Erde. Schöpfungsglaube heute." *Theol.-prakt. Quartalschrift* 124 (1976): 313-24.

_____. "Die Verantwortung des Christen für die Zukunft des Kosmos." *Catholica* 31 (1977): 1-16.

Bennema, P.

Present Position and Address: Faculteit der Natuurwetenschappen, Katholieke Universiteit, Toernooiveld, Nijmegen 6525 ED, Nederlands (Home) Heilige Stoel 6016, 6601 SW Wijchen, Netherlands **Work Phone:** (080) 653070 **Fax:** (080) 55 34 50 **E-mail/Telex:** 48228 winat nl **Date of Birth:** December 15, 1932 **Education:** Drs. Degree (1959), Free University, Amsterdam; Dr. Degree Crystal Growth (1965), University of Delft **Previous Positions:** Visiting Assistant Professor (1967-69), North Carolina Chapel Hill; Reader (1969-76), University of Delft; Reader through Professor (since 1976), Solid State Chemistry - Crystal Growth, University of Nijmegen **Discipline:** Solid State Chemistry and Crystal Growth **Related Interests:** Science, Philosophy, Religion/Theology and Art **Current Research:** Currently working on a book in Dutch on Science, Philosophy of Science, Sociology and Religion.

Selected Publications: His bibliography lists about 150 technical articles, most in the field of solid-state chemistry and crystal growth.

_____. "Schepping: een spoor van de geheel andere (Creation: a trace of the totally other)." *Tijdschr. Geestelijk Leven* 42 (1986): 403-19.
_____. "Natuurwetenschap en religie, Het heil van de natuurwetenschap, Uitgeverij Gooi en Sticht." *Baarn* (1993), 34-57.

Benner, David G.

Present Position and Address: Professor of Psychology (since 1988), Redeemer College, 777 Highway # 53 East, Ancaster, Ontario L9K 1J4, Canada **Concurrent Positions:** Chief Psychologist, Child and Adolescent Services of Hamilton; Adjunct Professor of Psychology and Christianity (since 1990), University of Toronto **Work Phone:** Canada (905) 648-2131 **Date of Birth:** February 9, 1947 **Languages Spoken:** English **Education:** B.A. Psychology (Honors, 1970), McMaster University; M.A. Clinical Psychology (1971)/Ph.D. Clinical Psychology (1972), York University **Postgraduate Studies:** Postdoctoral Studies (1979-80), Chicago Institute of Psychoanalysis **Certifications:** Licensed Psychologist - Ontario #857 (1973)/Illinois #072-002435 (1979) **Previous Positions:** Consulting Psychologist: Hershey Medical School PA (1971-73); Davenport Boy's Home in Toronto (1972-75); Percy and Associates, Windsor (1972-76); Canadian Department of National Defense (1972-78); St. Mary's General Hospital in North Bay Ontario (1973-76); Metro Toronto Youth Services (1973-77); Christian Horizons of Waterloo (1974-81); Child and Adolescent Services of Hamilton Ontario (since 1989); Associate Professor of Psychology and Director of Counselling Services (1976-78), Ontario Theological Seminary/Ontario Bible College of Toronto; Professor of Psychology (1978-88), Wheaton College; Clinical Director (1985-88), Institute for Eating Disorders, Ltd. **Editorial Work:** Associate Editor (1984-88)/Book Review Editor (1988-92), *Journal of Psychology and Christianity*; Contributing Editor (1984-92), *Journal of Psychology and Theology*; Editor for Pastoral Psychology section (since 1986), *The Best in Theology of Christianity Today, Inc.*; Series Editor (since 1986), of *Psychology and Christianity* book series and Coeditor of *Christian Explorations in Psychology* book series both published by Baker Book House; Member of Editorial Committee (1988-90), *Journal of Clinical Theology*; Assistant director of Publications, (1989-91), the Pascal Center for Advanced Studies in Faith and Science, Redeemer College **Administrative Experience:** Member of the Board (since 1987), Pastoral Counseling Institute, Atlanta, GA **Selected Memberships:** International Society for the Study of Multiple Personality and Dissociation; Ontario Psychological Association **Discipline:** Psychology **Related areas of Interests:** Psychology of Religion.

Selected Publications: Bibliography lists 28 professional publications.

_____. "The Incarnation as a Metaphor for Psychotherapy." *Journal of Psychology and Theology* 11, 4 (1983): 287-94.
_____, editor. *Baker Encyclopedia of Psychology.* Grand Rapids: Baker Book House, 1985.
_____, editor. *Psychotherapy in Christian Perspective.* Grand Rapids: Baker Book House, 1987.
_____. *Psychotherapy and the Spiritual Quest.* Grand Rapids: Baker Book House, 1988.
_____, editor. *Psychology and Religion.* Grand Rapids: Baker Book House, 1988.
_____. "Toward a Psychology of Spirituality: Implications for Personality and Psychotherapy." *Journal of Psychology and Christianity* 8, 1 (1989): 19-30.
_____. *Healing Emotional Wounds.* Grand Rapids: Baker Book House, 1990.
_____. *Strategic Pastoral Counseling.* Grand Rapids: Baker Book House, 1992.
_____. "The Functions of Faith: Religious Psychodynamics in Multiple Personality Disorder." In *Object Relations Theory and Religion: Clinical Applications*, ed. M. Finn and J. Gardner. Westport, CT: Praeger, 1992.

Benson, Purnell H.

Present Position and Address: Professor Emeritus (since 1984), Rutgers University; Consulting in Marketing Research (since 1960); 21 Maple Avenue, Madison, NJ 07946, USA **Date of Birth:** November 10, 1913 **Education:** A.B. (1935), Princeton University; M.A. (1936), Harvard University; Ph.D. (1952), University of Chicago **Previous Positions:** Adjunct Professor (1984-1986), New York University; Visiting Professor (1984-1986), Columbia University; Professor of Marketing (1967-1984), Rutgers University **Selected Memberships:** Fellow, American Psychological Association; Fellow, American Scientific Affiliation; Christian Association for Psychological Studies; Operations Research Society of America **Discipline:** Psychology; Sociology; Economics **Related Interests:** Psychology of Religion; Psychology of Christian Faith; Analysis of Stock Market Behavior.

Selected Publications:

_____. *Religion in Contemporary Culture.* Harpers, 1960.
_____. "New Testament Concepts for a Sociopsychological Model of Personality Development." In *Spiritual Wellbeing: Sociological Perspectives*, ed. D. O. Moberg. University Press of America, 1979.
_____. "Psychology in the Gospel of John." Paper presented at Eastern Convention of Christian Association for Psychological Studies, 1987. Circulated by the author.
_____. "Model for Jesus' Teachings About Altruistic Living in Relation to Personal Well-Being." *Journal of Psychology and Christianity* 9, 1 (1990): 56-69.

Benvenuto, Edoardo

Present Position and Address: Dean of the Faculty of Architecture, University of Genoa, Italy; Corso Firenze 26 - 3, I-16136, Genoa, Italy **Date of Birth:** December 11, 1940 **Languages Spoken:** Italian, English, French, German **Education:** Ph.D. Dynamics of Structures (1970), University of Genoa, Italy **Previous Positions:** Assistant (1966-74)/Full Professor (1975-present), Structural Mechanics; Professor (1970-74) in charge of Science of Structures at the Faculty of Chemical Engineering; Professor (1977-80), Contemporary Philosophy at Faculty of Theology, all at the University of Genoa **Editorial Work:** Coeditor, *Bailamme* (Italian Journal of Theology); Coeditor, *Palladio* (International Journal of History of Architecture and Construction) **Selected Memberships:** Accademia Ligure di Scienze e Lettere; Associazione Teologica Italiana (A.T.I.); Advisory Board, Meccanica (International Journal of Theoretical and Applied Mechanics) **Discipline:** "Scienza delle Costruzioni" (i.e. Mechanics of Solids and Structures); History of Mechanics; Theology and Epistemology **Related Interests:** Theoretical Mechanics; History of Mechanics; Epistemology; Epistemological Problems of Theology.

Selected Publications: His bibliography lists 63 theological papers.

_____. "La scienza fra incerti confini e domanda su Dio (Science between uncertain bounds and theological questions)." *Il Regno* 6 (1984).
_____. "Bi-logica e Teologia (Bi-logic and Theology)." *Archivio di Psicologia Neurologia e Psicologia* (Universita Cattolica di Milano), 3-4 (1984): 387-404.
_____. "Il dialogo con la scienza (Dialogue between theology and science)." *Asprenas* 34 (1987): 38-51.
_____. "Teologia e Scienze della Natura (Theology and Natural Sciences)." *Atti del XIII Congresso A.T.I.* Brescia: Italian Association of Theology, 1989.
_____. "Moderne metamorfosi nei concetti di Natura e di Storia (Modern Metamorphoses in the concepts of Nature and History)." *Rassegna di Teologia*, 33 (1992): 483-500.
_____. "Instante filosofiche nella moderna cosmologia scientifica (Philosophical instances of the modern scientific cosmology), *La creatione e l'uomo,* Padova: Edizioni Messaggero, 1992.
_____. *L'uomo, la tecnica e Dio (Man, Technology and God)*, Bologna: Edizioni Dehoniane, 1994.
_____. *Teologia e Scienza* (Theology and science). Queriniana, Brescia, in press.

Berg, Myles Renver

Present Position and Address: President, Berg Enterprises, 52 Mariannia Ln., Atherton, CA 94027, USA **Work Phone:** (415) 326-1452 **Fax Number:** Manual on same # **Date of Birth:** September 6, 1932 **Languages Spoken:** English, some German, Spanish **Awards and Honors:** Engineer of the Year, Lockheed Corp. **Previous Positions:** Technical Consultant, Lockheed Corporation, Missiles and Space Company; Manager, Advanced Technology, Lockheed Corporation , Probe Systems, MIT/Lincoln Laboratory; TSC Corporation and Aerospace Corporation; Project Manager, SRI international **Selected Memberships:** American Scientific Affiliation **Discipline:** Engineering; Physics and Mathematics **Related Areas of Interest:** Advanced Technologies; System Engineering; Integration of God's Word and God's World **Current Areas of Research:** Parallels and Differences between Jesus and Satan; Cosmology and Genesis 1 and 2; The Three Dimensions of Body, Soul, and Spirit; Contrast between Secular and Sacred.

Selected Publications: His bibliography contains 52 articles used in Bible studies by the Menlo Park Presbyterian Church. Essentially all of his scientific work has been classified.

_____. "Genesis 1 and 2: In the Beginning God Created the Heaven and the Earth." Menlo Presbyterian Church, October 28, 1993.
_____. "Was There Death before the Fall of Adam and Eve?" Menlo Presbyterian Church, January 5, 1994.
_____. "God's Activities in the World." Menlo Presbyterian Church, January 24, 1994.
_____. "What Would Have Happened If . . .?" Menlo Presbyterian Church, February 18, 1994.
_____. "The Three Dimensions of the Bible." Menlo Presbyterian Church, March 16, 1994.

Bergh, Bob

Present Position and Address: College of Natural and Agricultural Sciences, Department of Botany and Plant Sciences University of California, Riverside, CA 92521-1024, USA **Work Phone:** (714) 684-7979 **Fax:** (714) 787-4437 **E-Mail/Telex:** 676427 IPM 45 CA **Date of Birth:** January 30, 1925 **Education:** B.S.A., M.S.., Ph.D. **Previous Positions:** 35 years, University of California, Riverside **Discipline:** Genetics **Related Interests:** Creation and Evolution; Human Heredity and Evolution.

Selected Publications:

_____. "Theories, Facts, and Presuppositions." *Creation/Evolution Newsletter* 5, 4 (1985): 6.
_____. "Biological Evolution and Extremist Critics." *Creation/Evolution Newsletter* 6, 2 (1986): 20.

Bergman, Jerry

Present Position and Address: Tenured faculty teaching Biology, Physics and Chemistry (since 1986), Northwest College 321 Iuka, Montpelier, OH 43543, USA **Date of Birth:** May 30, 1946 **Education:** AA Biology and Psychology (1967), Oakland Community College; B.S.. General Science, Biology and Psychology (1969)/Certified (1970)/M.Ed. Psychology and Counseling (1971)/Ph.D. Psychology Evaluation, Measurement (1976), Wayne State University; M.A. Social Psychology (1986), Bowling Green State University; Ph.D. Human Biology (1992), Columbia Pacific University **Previous Positions:** Measurement and General Psychology (1973-80), Bowling Green State University; Statistics, Computer Science and Mathematics (1980-86), University of Toledo; Visiting Lecturer at Oakland Community College, Spring Arbor College, and Defiance College **Selected Memberships:** 30 professional organizations including American Chemical Society; American Association for the Advancement of Science; American Scientific Affiliation **Discipline:** Biology; Physics; Chemistry; Psychology **Related Interests:** The interface between hard sciences and philosophy/theology. Other areas of interest are evolutionary thought/and the rise of racism and Nazism; and the problems of natural selection, vestigial organs, and creation-evolution controversies in general.

Selected Publications: His bibliography lists over 400 articles and 30 books and monographs.

_____. *Teaching About the Creation/Evolution Controversy.* Bloomington, IN: Phi Delta Kappa Education Foundation, 1979.
_____. "Censorship in Academia; The Case of Richard H. Bube." *Contrast* 9, 3 (1990): 1-2.
_____. "A Brief History of the Eugenics Movement." *CEN Tech. J.* 5, 2 (1991).
_____. "Eugenics and the Development of Nazi Race Policy." *Perspective on Science and Christian Faith* 44, 2 (1992): 109-23.
_____. *The Creation/Evolution Controversy: A Bibliographic Guide from 1839 to the Present.* New York: Garland Publishing, 1993.
_____. "Censorship in Secular Science; The Mims Case." *Journal of the American Scientific Affiliation* 45, 1 (1993): 37-43.
_____. "A Brief History of the Modern Creation Movement." *Contra Mundum* no. 6 (1993): 36-47.
_____. "The History of *Hesperopithecus, Haroldcookii Hominidae.*" *CRSQ* 30, 1 (1993):27-34.
_____. "Panspermia—The Theory That Life Came From Outer Space." *CEN. Tech. Journal* 7, 1 (1993): 82-7.
_____. "A Brief History of the Theory of Spontaneous Generation." *CEN Tech. Journal* 7, 1 (1993): 73-81.

Berry, Robert James

Present Position and Address: Professor of Genetics (since 1978), Department of Biology, University College London, Gower Street, London WC1E 6BT, UK **Date of Birth:** October 26, 1934 **Education:** M.A. Natural Sciences (1959), Cambridge; Ph.D. Genetics (1959), London; D.Sc. (1976); FI Biology (1974), FRSE (1981) **Previous Positions:** Lecturer/Reader/Professor (1962-78), Royal Free Hospital School of Medicine, London **Selected Memberships:** Chairman (1968-88)/President (since 1993), Christians in Science (formerly Research Scientists Christian Fellowship); Board of Social Responsibility, General Synod of the Church of England; Chairman, Environmental Issues Network, Council of Churches of Britain and Ireland **Discipline:** Genetics/Population and Evolutionary Biology **Related Interests:** Environmental and Biomedical Ethics; Evolution and Creation.

Selected Publications: His bibliography lists over 150 publications, most of which are in his discipline. A number of publications though, deal with the science/theology dialogue.

_____. *Environmental Ethics and Conservation Action.* London: Nature Conservancy Council, 1982.
_____. "Genes and Morals." In *Behavioral Science - a Christian Perspective*, ed. M. A. Jeeves. Inter-Varsity Press, 1984.
_____. "I believe in God . . . Maker of heaven and earth." In *When Christians Disagree: Creation and Evolution*, ed. D. C. Burke. Leicester: IVP, 1985.

_____. *Response to the Warnock Committee Report, General Synod of the Church of England*. Personal Origins. London: CIO, 1985.
_____. "Evolution and Creation: Origin of Man." *Epworth Review* 13 (1986): 74-85.
_____. "What to Believe about Miracles." *Nature London* 322 (1986): 321-2.
_____. "Our Responsibility for the Living Environment." Working Party Report. London: CIO, 1986.
_____. "The Theology of DNA." *Anvil* 4 (1987): 39-49.
_____. *God and Evolution*. Sevenoaks: Hodder & Stoughton, 1988.
_____, editor. *Real Science, Real Faith*. Eastbourne: Monarch, 1991.

Berry, Thomas

Present Position and Address: Founder and Director (since 1970), Riverdale Center of Religious Research 5801 Palisade Avenue, Riverdale, NY 10471, USA **Date of Birth:** November 9, 1914 **Languages Spoken:** English, Chinese; Sanskrit **Education:** Ph.D. History (1949), Catholic University of America **Previous Positions:** Assistant Professor (1956-60), Institute of Asian Studies - Seton Hall University; Associate Professor (1960-66), Center for Asian Studies - Saint John's University; Taught at summer Program on History of Religions (1972-74), University of San Diego; Adjunct Professor (Fall 1973, 74), Religion Department, Drew University/Barnard College; Associate Professor of History of Religions (1966-79), Fordham University **Other Academic Experience:** Travels: China and Japan (1948 for 1 year); North Africa and Palestine (Summer 1954); Philippines (Summer 1982, 84) **Selected Memberships:** President (1975-87) and member, American Teilhard Association **Discipline:** History, including History of Religions **Related Interests:** Teilhard studies; Cosmology of Religion; Ecology.

Selected Publications: His bibliography lists 4 books and 70 selected articles and presentations including several to the Teilhard Association.

_____. "Teilhard in the Ecological Age." *Teilhard Studies* 7 (Fall 1982).
_____. "Technology and the Healing of the Earth." Paper presented at LeHigh University October 1985. Teilhard Studies 14 (Fall 1985).
_____. The Cosmology of Religions." Paper presented at the College Theology Society meeting in Los Angeles, May 1988.
_____. *The Dream of the Earth*. San Francisco: Sierra Club Books, 1988.
_____. "The Gaia Theory: Its Religious Implications." Paper presented at Isthmus Institute in Dallas, April 1990.
_____. "To Honor the Earth:" Foreword to *To Honor the Earth*. MacLean-Carr, Spring 1990.

Bertsch, Hans

Present Position and Address: Biology and Geography Instructor (since 1981), National University, 8 Executive Circle, Irvine, CA 92714, USA; (Home) 640 The Village #203, Redondo Beach, CA 90277, USA **Home Phone:** (213) 372-4436 **Date of Birth:** November 2, 1944 **Languages Spoken:** English, Spanish **Education:** B.A. Philosophy (*cum laude*, 1967), San Luis Rey College, CA; B.Th. Theology (1971), Franciscan School of Theology - Berkeley; Ph.D. Zoology (1976), University of California - Berkeley **Previous Positions:** Assistant Professor (1976-78), Chaminade University of Honolulu, Hawaii; Chairman/Curator (1978-80), Department of Marine Invertebrates, San Diego Natural History Museum; Professor (1981-83), Ciencias Marinas, Mexico/Investigator (1981-83), Instituto de Investigaciones Oceanologicas, Universidad Autonoma de Baja California, Ensenada, Mexico; Extensive subtidal and intertidal research in numerous southern California locations (1978-present) **Editorial Work:** On five editorial boards **Selected Memberships:** American Association for the Advancement of Science; President (1988-89), Western Society of Malacologists; Society of Systematic Zoology; Sigma XI **Discipline:** Biology (especially zoology). Also studied in Theology and Philosophy **Related Interests:** Philosophy of Science; Natural History and Natural Theology; "Creation" as Revelation.

Selected Publications: His bibliography lists over 50 scientific articles, 9 anthropological contributions, and more than 60 papers, articles, translations and reviews.

_____. "Ecology and St. Francis." *Way* 28, 8 (1970): 3-9.
_____. "Mollusks in the Ancient Civilizations and Religions of the Near East: Part I." *The Tabulata* 4, 3 (1971): 19-22.
_____. "Mollusks in the ancient civilizations and religions of the Near East: Part II." *The Tabulata* 4, 4 (1971): 20-22. Reprint, Levantina, Israel Malacological Society, Vol. 9 (1977): 85-69; and Vol. 10 (1977): 95-8.

Birch, L. Charles

Present Position and Address: Emeritus Professor (since 1983), University of Sydney, Sydney, Australia; (Home) 5A/73 Yarranabbe Road, Darling Point, NSW 2027, Australia **Education:** B.Agr.Sc. (1939), University of Melbourne; M.S. (1941)/D.Sc. (1948), University of Adelaide, Australia **Awards and Honors:** Fellow (1961), Australian Academy of Science; Fellow (1980), American Association for the Advancement of Science; Member (1974), Club of Rome; Honorary Life Fellow, British Ecological Society; Honorary Life Member, Ecological Society of America; Eminent Ecologist Award (1988); Templeton Prize, (1990) **Previous Positions:** Visiting Professor of Biology, Columbia University (1953)/Minnesota (1957)/Sao Paulo (1955)/University of California - Berkeley (1960); Professor of Biology (1958-83), University of Sydney **Selected Memberships:** Center for Process Studies, Claremont, CA; American Center for a Post Modern World, Santa Barbara, CA; World Council of Churches **Discipline:** Population Biology. Science and Religion **Related Interests:** Process Theology.

Selected Publications: His bibliography lists 9 books, and 60 publications on Science, Religion and Human Existence.

_____. *Nature and God.* The Westminster Press, 1965.
_____. "Chance, Necessity, and Purpose." In *Studies in the Philosophy of Biologe*, ed. F. Ayala and T. Dobzhansky. London: Macmillan, 1974.
_____. "Can Evolution be Accounted for Solely in Terms of Mechanical Causation." In *Mind in Nature*, ed. John B. Cobb and David R. Griffin. Washington: The University Press of America, 1975.
_____. John B. Cobb. *The Liberation of Life: from Cell to Community.* Cambridge University Press, 1981. Reprint, Denton, TX: Environmental Ethics Books, 1990.
_____. "The Post Modern Challenge to Biology." In *Essays Toward a Post-Modern World: the Reenchantment of Science: Post Modern Proposals*, ed. David Ray Griffin. State University of New York Press, 1988.
_____. "The Scientific Environmental Crisis: Where Do Churches Stand?" *Ecumenical Review* 40 (1988): 185-93.
_____. "Chance and Purpose and Darwinism." In *The Philosophy of Charles Hartshorne*, ed. E. Hahn. Library of Living Philosophers. La Salle, IL: Open Court, 1990.
_____. *A Purpose for Everything: Religion in a Postmodern Worldview.* Mystic, CT: Twenty-Third Publications, 1990.
_____. "Process Thought: Its Value and Meaning To Me." *Process Studies* 19, 4 1990: 129.
_____. *Regaining Compassion: For Humanity and Nature.* St. Louis: Chalice Press, 1993.
_____, W. Eaken and J. B. McDaniel, eds. *Liberating Life: Contemporary Approvals to Ecological Theology.* Maryknoll, 1990.

Bishop, Robert C.

Present Position and Address: Research Scientist (since 1989), Austin Research Associates Austin Research Associates, 1101 Capital of Texas Highway South, B-210, Austin, TX 78746, USA **Date of Birth:** November 21, 1961 **Education:** B.S. Physics (1984)/M.A. Physics (1986), University of Texas - Austin, Ph.D. Physics student, University of Texas - Austin **Awards and Honors:** Awarded a NASA Office of Space Science and Applications Graduate Fellowship for the 1989-91 academic years **Previous Positions:** Research Assistant (1982-86), Center for Relativity Theory, University of Texas

- Austin; Research Scientist (1984-1989), Science Applications International Corporation, Austin, TX **Selected Memberships:** American Physical Society; American Association for the Advancement of Science; American Astronomical Society; Ruling Elder (1987), Presbyterian Church in America **Discipline:** Theoretical Physics **Related Interests:** Science, Theology and Philosophy.

Selected Publications:

_____. "A Comparison of the Enterprise of Science with the Enterprise of Theology." *Zygon* (submitted to *Zygon*, 27 February 1989).
_____. Review of *Science and Creation*, by Stanley L. Jaki (1986). *Journal of Interdisciplinary Studies*. 2 (1990).

Blake, Deborah D.

Present Position and Address: Assistant Professor (since 1988), Department of Religious Studies, Regis College, W. 50th Avenue and Lowell Blvd., Denver, CO 80221, USA; (Home) 662 Sunnyside Street, Louisville, CO 80027, USA **Work Phone:** (303) 458-4972 **Home Phone:** (303) 665-2705 **Date of Birth:** March 4, 1951 **Education:** B.A. Biological Sciences (1974), University of California - Santa Barbara; Standard Teaching Credential (1979), Biological Sciences/Physical Sciences, State of California; M.T.S. Theological Studies (1981), Franciscan School of Theology, Berkeley CA; Ph.D. Ethics (1989), Graduate Theological Union, Berkeley, CA **Selected Memberships:** American Academy of Religion; Society of Christian Ethics; Catholic Theological Society of America **Discipline:** Theological and Philosophical Ethics **Related Interests:** Issues of Cultural Diversity in Healthcare Ethics; Incorporating Ethical Issues into Secondary Science Curriculum (curriculum and teacher training); Theological and Ethical Issues Raised by the Human Genome Initiative.

Selected Publications:

_____, Karen Lebacqz. "Safe Sex or Love Lost: AIDS Crisis and Christian Sexual Ethics." Religious Education Journal 83, 2 (1988): 201-10.
_____. "Ethics of Possibility: Biotechnology for the 90's." *The Catholic World* 234, 1403 (1991): 234-7.
_____. "Societal Issues in the Classroom: Why Don't We Call Them Ethical?" In *Proceedings Supplement: National Biotechnology Education Sharing Conference*. Madison, WI: University of Wisconsin, Madison, 1991.
_____. Review of *Genetics, Creation and Creationism*, by Lloyd Bailey. *U.S. Catholic* (accepted August 1993 for future issue).
_____. "Revolution, Revision or Reversal: Genetics-Ethics Curriculum." *Science and Education* (Accepted for review, May 1993).
_____. "Infertile Couples: Psychological Needs, Social Responsibilities." Chap. in *Infertility: A Crossroad of Faith and Technology*, Catholic Studies in Bio-ethics subseries of the *Philosophy and Medicine* series. Kluwer Publishers, 1994.

Blankenburg, Wolfgang

Present Position and Address: Professor/Director (since 1979), Clinic for Psychiatry, University of Marburg, Rudolf-Bultmann-Strasse 8, 3550 Marburg (Lahn), Germany; (Home) Am Hasselhof 11, D-3550 Marburg, Germany **Date of Birth:** May 5, 1928 **Discipline:** Psychiatry and Philosophy (was taught philosophy by Heidegger in Freiburg) **Related Interests:** Psychiatry, Psychotherapy, Psychopathology; Philosophy (Phenomenology); Religious Problems.

Selected Publications: Over 120 publications, mostly in the area of his discipline.

_____. "Ethnopsychiatrie im Inland. Zur Kultur- und Subkulturbezogenheit psychisch Kranker." In *George Devereux zum 75. Geburtstag. Eine Festschrift*, ed. D. Friessem and E. Schroder. Braunschweig-Wiesbaden: Vieweg & Sohn, 1984.

_____. "Prolegomena to a Psychopathology of Freedom." In *The Changing Reality of Modern Man*, ed. D. Kruger. Cape Town: Wetton; Johannesburg: Juta & Co. Ltd., 1984.
_____. "Autonomie- und Heteronomie-Konzepte in ihrer Bedeutung für die psychiatrische Praxis." In *Psychopathologie und Praxis*, ed. W. Janzarik. Stuttgart: Enke, 1985.
_____. "The Dialectics of 'Freedom' and 'Unfreedom' in the Psychiatric View." In *Analecta Husserliana*, ed. A. Tymieniecka, vol. 22, 409-23. N.p., 1987.

Blasi, Paolo

Present Position and Address: Full Professor (since 1983), Department of Physics, University of Florence, Largo Enrico Fermi no. 2 (Arcetri) - 50125, Florence, Italy; Rector (since 1991), University of Florence; (Home) Via Vecchia Fiesolana no. 30 - 50014 Fiesole (Florence), Italy **Work Phone:** 0039-55-2757211 **Date of Birth:** November 2, 1940 **Education:** doctorate in Physics (1963), University of Florence, Italy **Previous Positions:** Director (1979-82), Istituto Nazionale di Fisica Nucleare I.N.F.N.; Director (1983-88), Department of Physics, University of Florence, Italy; Member of the Executive Committee (1988-91), I.N.F.N.; President, Scientific and Technological Commission for Industrial Research in the South of Italy **Selected Memberships:** *Nova Spes* (International Foundation - a periodical of cultural information) **Discipline:** Nuclear Physics; Experimental Physics; Applied Physics **Related Areas of Interest:** Science and Humanity; Environmental Problems.

Selected Publications: His bibliography lists over 70 scientific articles in international reviews.

_____. *Nova Spes*, letter 7 (1986). English ed.
_____. "Man - Environment and Development: Towards a Global Approach." 1988.
_____. "The Dimension of Knowledge as the Basis of a New Culture Aimed at the Integral Recomposition of Man." N.d.

Bloemendal, Michael

Present Position and Address: Senior Research fellow (since 1994), Department of Protein and Molecular Biology, Royal Free Hospital School of Medicine, Rowland Hill Street, London NW3 2PF, UK; (Home) 27 Vincent Court, Bell Lane, London NW4 2AN, UK **Work Phone:** (71) 5485382/5757 **Date of Birth:** November 1, 1955 **Languages Spoken:** Dutch, English, Hebrew **Education:** B.S.. (1977)/M.S.. (1980)/ Ph.D. (1985), Free University, Amsterdam **Postgraduate Studies:** Postdoctorate (1985-87), Hebrew University, Jerusalem **Awards and Honors:** Christiaan and Constateyn Huygens Fellowship **Previous Positions:** Spiritual leader (1978-85), Jewish community, Rotterdam, The Netherlands; Spiritual leader (1987-91), Jewish community of Bussum, The Netherlands; Lecturer, oral Law, The Netherlands, Israelites Seminarian **Discipline:** Biophysical and Analytical Chemistry **Related Interests:** The Structure of Proteins and the Influence of the Surroundings on it; Judaism, Its Theory and Application to Daily Life.

Selected Publications: His bibliography lists about 40 works, mostly dealing with Chemistry.

_____. "Science and Religion, the Jewish Position." In *One World, Changing Perspectives on Reality*, ed. J. Fennema and I. Paul. Dordrecht: Kluwer Academic Publ., 1990: 47-60.
_____. *The Jewish Attitude Towards Nature, Studies in Science and Theology.* 1994.

Bloom, John A.

Present Position and Address: Director, Bloomsbury Research Corporation (since 1980); Computer software and hardware Consultant (since 1986); 60 West Broad Street, Hatfield, PA 19440, USA **Work Phone:** (215) 362-8062 **Previous Positions:** Teaching/Research Assistant (1974-80)/Postdoctoral

Research Associate (Summers 1981-82), Cornell University; Lecturer in Physics (1984-1989), Ursinus College, Collegeville, PA **Selected Memberships:** American Scientific Affiliation; Biophysical Society; Fellow, Interdisciplinary Biblical Research Institute of Hatfield **Discipline:** Physics; Biblical Studies; Computer Consulting; Ancient Near Eastern Studies **Related Interests:** Interdisciplinary Fields: Ancient Technologies and Science (medicine and mathematics); Ancient Document Preservation via Optical Disk Technology; Use of Computer Image Enhancement Techniques in the Study of Ancient Cuniform and Papyrus/Vellum Documents **Current Research:** In Biblical Studies: The comparative study of creation myths and of prophetic phenomena; Exegetical/historical problems in Israelite prehistory and history through the First Temple period.

Selected Publications: His bibliography lists 5 publications.

_____. "Finding Truth in Religion: Is There a Factual Basis?" *Interdisciplinary Biblical Research Institute Research Report* 26 (1985).

Böckman, Peter Wilhelm

Present Position and Address: Full Professor of Religion (since 1975), University of Trondheim, Department of Religion, N - 7055 Dragvoll, Norway **Date of Birth:** May 14, 1927 **Languages Spoken:** Norwegian, English, German **Education:** Cand. Theology (1953)/Venia Docendi (1969), University of Oslo; Master of Sacred Theology (1961), Union Theological Seminary NYC **Previous Positions:** Research Scholar (1956-59,62-63)/Assistant Professor (1964-67)/Associate Professor (1967-75), University of Oslo, Norway **Discipline:** Ethics; Theology; Philosophy of Religion **Related Interests:** Christianity and Science; Christianity and other Religions; Ecumenics; Social Ethics; Luther Research.

Selected Publications:

_____. *Liv — Fellesskap — Tjeneste. En Kristen Etikk* (Life — community — service. A Christian ethics). 4th ed. (Oslo, 1981).
_____, editor. *Kristendom og Naturvitenskap* (Christianity and science). University of Trondheim, 1981.
_____. "Tragedien om Kristendommen og Utviklingsteorien (The Tragedy about Christianity and the theory of evolution)." In *Evolusjonsteorien*, ed. N. Chr. Stenseth and T. Lie. Oslo, 1984.
_____. *Two Approaches and One Reality. On Religion and the Perception of Cosmos.* Mimeographed, Trondheim, 1986.
_____. *On the Possibility of a Unified Cosmology.* Mimeographed, Trondheim, 1988.
_____, editor. *Hvem er Gud? En Droftelse av Gudsbetrepet* (Who is God? A discourse on the concept of God). Trondheim, 1986.
_____, editor. *Bibelske Temaer I Litteratur, film og Teater.* (Biblical themes in literature, films, and theater). Trondheim, 1989.
_____. *Den Norske Kirke — Historisk og Aktuelt* (The church in Norway — In history and today). Trondheim, 1989.
_____, editor. *Kristendommen og Religionene* (Christianity and the religions). Trondheim, 1989.
_____, editor. *Naturvitenskap og Kristendom* (Science and Christianity). Trondheim, 1993.

Bohon, Robert L.

Present Position and Address: Retired (since 1989), as Director, Analytical and Properties Research Laboratory, Corporate Research Laboratories, 3M Company, St. Paul, MN 5960 Hobe Lane, White Bear Lake, MN 55110, USA **Home Phone:** (612) 426-4698 **Date of Birth:** July 20, 1925 **Languages Spoken:** English, German **Education:** B.S. Chemical Engineering (1946), University of Illinois; Ph.D. Physical Chemistry (1950), University of Illinois **Previous Positions:** Head of Infrared Laboratory (1950-56), Anderson Physical Laboratory, Champaign, IL; 3M Company: Senior Chemist (1956-64), Supervisor (1964-68), Manager (1969-85), Lab Director (1985-1989) **Selected Memberships:** Fellow,

American Scientific Affiliation; Chairman (1977-78), Environmental Task Force, Health and Environmental Effects Subcommittee, MCA; Member (1978-80), Expert Group A, Physical Chemistry, OECD Chemicals Testing Program; Member (1975-85), Minnesota Section Exhibits Chairman (1975), American Chemical Society; Moderator, Woodbury Baptist Church (1966); Joint Religious Legislative Coalition (JRLC), Task Force on Corporate Social Responsibility (1976); Moderator, Mid-American Baptist Churches (1980-82) **Discipline:** Chemistry and Research Management **Related Interests:** Chemicals and the Environment and Ethics; Science confronts Christian Youth.

Selected Publications: His bibliography lists 17 technical, and 3 non-technical works.

_____. "The Industrial Scientist: Money, Time and Achievement." *Journal of the American Scientific Affiliation* 14, 3 (September 1962).
_____. "Science Confronts Christian Youth." *Baptist Leader* (March 1966).

Bolt, Martin

Present Position and Address: Professor of Psychology (since 1978), Department of Psychology, Calvin College, Grand Rapids, MI 49546 USA **Work Phone:** (616) 957-6396 **Home Phone:** (616) 364-9020 **Date of Birth:** August 12, 1944 **Education:** A.B. Psychology (1966), Calvin College; M.A. Psychology (1967)/Ph.D. Psychology (1969), Michigan State University, East Lansing **Previous Positions:** Lecturer in Astronomy (part-time, 1965-66), Grand Rapids Planetarium; Research Assistant (1969-70), Michigan State University; Counseling Psychologist (1971-74), Veterans Administration Hospital - Battle Creek MI; Assistant/Associate Professor of Psychology (1970-78), Calvin College **Discipline:** Psychology **Related Interests:** Applications of Social Psychology to the Christian Community; Psychology and its relation to Religion.

Selected Publications: His bibliography lists 28 articles and papers.

_____. A. Shoemaker and M. Bolt. "Perceived Christian Values and the Rokeach Value Survey." *Journal of Psychology and Theology* 5 (1977): 139-42.
_____. "Religious Orientation, Belief in a Just World, and Prosocial Behavior." Paper presented at the 90th Annual Convention of the American Psychological Association, Washington, DC, 1982.
_____. D. G. Myers. *The Human Connection.* Downers Grove, IL: InterVarsity Press, 1984. Applications of Social Psychology to the Christian Community.

Bolyki, János

Present Position and Address: Professor for New Testament (since 1983), Budapesti Református Theologiai Akadémia, 1092 Budapest, Raday Utca 28, H-1092, Hungary **Date of Birth:** June 11, 1931 **Languages Spoken:** Hungarian, German, English **Education:** I. and II. Ministerial Exam (1954-55), Reformed Theological Academy, Budapest; Consultation Exam for Entering Doctoral Program (1971); Doctor's Degree (1979) in Church History/Science and Theology **Previous Positions:** Lecturer, New Testament (1982)/Dean (1989), Reformed Theological Academy, Budapest **Selected Memberships:** Collegium Doctorum in the Reformed Church of Hungary; European Society for the Study of Science and Theology; Societas Novi Testamenti Studiorum **Discipline:** Church History; Ideas of Science and Theology; New Testament **Related Interests:** Theological Models about the Connection of Science and Christian Faith; The Role of the Reformed Church in the Cultural History of Hungary; Christological-Complementary Model for the Connection between Science and Faith **Current Research:** The Problem of Complementarity; The New Testament and the Ancient View of Nature.

Selected Publications: His bibliography lists 20 contributions to this field.

_____. "The Questions of Sciences in the History of Theology in the 20th Century." (in Hungarian). Dissertation, Study Department of the Synod of the Hun.
_____. "Chardin - From Three Sides." *Theológiai Szemle* (Theological review) 14 (1971): 98-9.
_____. "The Responsibility of a Christian Atomic-Physicist. Carl Friedrich von Weizsäcker's Message on Nature and Man." *Theológiai Szemle* 15 (1972):. 23-8.

Bonting, Sjoerd L.

Present Position and Address: Anglican Chaplain (since 1993), Specreyse 12, 7471 TH Goor, The Netherlands **Work Phone:** 31-5470-60947 **Date of Birth:** October 6, 1924 **Languages Spoken:** Dutch, English, German, French **Education:** B.S.. Chemistry (1944)/M.S.. Biochemistry (*cum laude*, 1950)/Ph.D. Biochemistry (1952), University of Amsterdam; intermed. B.D. (1958), University of London **Awards and Honors:** NIH postdoctoral fellowship (1952-1954); Fight for Sight Citation (1961, 1962); Arthur S. Flemming Award (1964); Heinz Karger Prize (1964), Basel; Pro Mundi Beneficis Award (1975), Brazil; Citation by Archbishop of Canterbury (1985) **Previous Positions:** Instructor (1947-1949), Department of Analytic Chemistry, University of Amsterdam; Biochemist (1950-1952), Netherlands Institute of Nutrition; Instructor (1950-1952), Department of Biochemistry, University of Amsterdam; Research Associate (1952-1955), Department of Physiology, Iowa State University; Assistant Professor, Department of Physiological Chemistry, University of Minnesota, Minneapolis; Assistant Professor (1956-1960), Department of Biological Chemistry, University of Illinois - Chicago; Head, Section of Cell Biology (1960-1965), National Institute of Health, Bethesda, MD; Visiting Scientist (1964-1965), Institute of Animal Physiology, Babraham, Cambridge, UK; Professor and Chair (1965-1985), Department of Biochemistry, University of Nijmegen, the Netherlands; Scientific Consultant (1985-93), NASA Ames Research Center, Moffett Field, CA; Anglican Chaplain (1965-1985), Nijmegen; Assistant Priest (1985-1990), St. Thomas' Episcopal Church, Sunnyvale, CA; Assistant Priest (1990-93), St. Mark's Episcopal Church, Palo Alto, CA **Editorial Work:** Editorial Boards of six scientific journals **Selected Memberships:** Fellow, American Association for the Advancement of Science; American Society of Biological Chemists; International Society for Eye Research (vice-president 1978-1984); American Society for Cell Biology; Federation of European Biochemistry Societies (councilor 1979-1982); Jewish-Christian Consultation on Creation and Evolution (1977), Zürich; Muslim-Christian Consultation on Faith, Science and Technology, Beirut, Lebanon (1977); Member, Diocesan Committee on Ministry to High Tech Society (1986-88); Member, Diocesan Committee on Medical Ethics, (1989-90) **Discipline:** Biochemistry, Biology, Chemistry, Theology **Related Interests:** Evolution and Creation; Medical Ethics; Science and Faith; Technology and Faith.

Selected Publications: His scientific bibliography includes 367 papers, 13 reviews and chapters, and 5 books; his religious publications include 2 books, 1 chapter, and 16 papers.

_____. "De Taal van het Leven (The language of life: DNA and logos)." In *Geloof bij Kenterend Getij* (Faith at changing tide), ed. H. van der Linde and H. A. M. Fiolet. Romen, Roermond, 1967.
_____. *Evolutie en Scheppingsgeloof* (Evolution and creation). Ambo, Baarn, 1978.
_____. *Word and World*. Sunnyvale, 1989.

Boon, Rudolf

Present Position and Address: University Professor in Liturgical Science, Free University, Amsterdam, The Netherlands; Kromboomssloot 63, 1011 GS, Amsterdam, The Netherlands **Work Phone:** 020-274805/256523 **Date of Birth:** February 4, 1920 **Languages Spoken:** Dutch, English, German

Education: University of Amsterdam (1940-43); Doctor Theologiae (1947), University of Utrecht; Master of Theol. Science (1949), Union Theological Seminary, NY; Mansfield College Oxford (1950); New College Edinburgh (1950-51) **Previous Positions:** Pastor; Teacher in the History of Church and Christian Culture **Selected Memberships:** ATOMIUM (Society for the Investigation of the Relations between Religion/Theology and Science), Enschede University; v.d. Leeuw-Stichting (Society for the Study of the Relations between Culture and Christian Faith), Amsterdam Ecumenical Society for the Study of the problems about 'Faith and Order's Hertogenbosch **Discipline:** Theology; Philosophy; History of Culture **Related Interests:** Historical background of Secularization in the Western Culture; Religion and Science in the Age of Reason; Ecclesiology and Mariology; The relation between Judaism and Christianity; Cultural History of the Reformed Tradition.

Selected Publications:

_____. *The Relations between Judaism and Christianity.* Amsterdam: v.d. Leeuw-Stichting, 1970; 3rd edition 1989.
_____. *The Rise of West European Atheism.* Kampen: KOK, 1976. A research of the historical sources.
_____. *An Anthropological Survey: The Human Being in Scripture and Philosophy.* Amsterdam: Free University Press, 1978.
_____. *Myth and Secularization.* Amsterdam: Free University Press, 1979.
_____. *Hebrew Revival in the Christian Church.* Kampen: KOK, 1983.
_____. *Ecclesiology and Mariology.* Amsterdam: v.d. Leeuw-Stichting, 1988.
_____. *Antiquitas graeco-romana et dignitas israelitica.* Free University Press, 1989. A treatise about secularization as an uprooting factor in the West European culture.
_____. *On Secularization: The Way to a Culture of Alienation.* Amsterdam: Free University Bookstore, 1990.
_____. *The Ensemble of Science and Religion.* Amsterdam: Free University Bookstore, 1990. Natural Science and Theology in the Age of Reason.

Bouma III, Hessel

Present Position and Address: Professor of Biology (since 1978), Calvin College, 3201 Burton Street SE, Grand Rapids, MI 49546, USA **Date of Birth:** September 16, 1950 **Education:** A.B. (1972), Calvin College; Ph.D. (1975), University of Texas Medical Branch **Postgraduate Studies:** Postdoctoral Fellow (1975-78), University of California - San Diego **Previous Positions:** Calvin Fellow and Coordinator (1985-86), Calvin Center for Christian Scholarship (on topic: "Christian Faith, Health, and Medical Practice") **Selected Memberships:** American Scientific Affiliation; Associate, Hastings Center; Associate, Christian Community Health Fellowship **Discipline:** Biology; Human Genetics **Related Interests:** Biomedical Ethics.

Selected Publications:

_____, D. Diekema, E. Langerak, T. Rottman, and A. Verhey. *Christian Faith, Health, and Medical Practice.* Eerdmans, 1989.

Bourne, Malcolm C.

Present Position and Address: Professor of Food Science and Technology (since 1974), NYS Agricultural Experiment Station, Cornell University, Geneva, NY 14456, USA **Work Phone:** (315) 787-2278 **Fax Number:** (315) 787-2397 **E-Mail:** malcolm-bourne@cornell.edu **Date of Birth:** May 18, 1926 **Languages Spoken:** English **Education:** Diploma of Industrial Chemistry (1947), University of South Australia; B.S.. Chemistry (1948), University of Adelaide, Australia; M.S. Food Science (1961)/Ph.D. Agricultural Chemistry (1962), University of California - Davis **Congresses and Conferences:** Chairman, National Academy of Sciences team visiting China for conference on losses in horticultural crops (November 1984) **Lectures Presented:** Institute of Food Technologists, national Scientific Lecturer (1967-68/84-87); Lectures in food rheology in Moscow and Leningrad (June 1983),

Guest of USSR Ministry of Higher and Secondary Education **Awards and Honors:** Phi Kappa Phi (1961); Honorary Life Member of Philippine Association of Food Technologists; International Award of Institute of Food Technologists (1992); Scott Blair Award of American Association of Cereal Chemists (1993) **Previous Positions:** Chief Chemist (1948-58), Brookers (Australia) Limited; Research Assistant (1958-62), University of California - Davis; Assistant through Associate Professor (1962-73), Cornell University **Editorial Positions:** Editor, *Journal of Texture Studies* **Other Academic Experience:** Member, Committee on International Relations of the Institute of Food Technologists (1976-81/86- 91), Chair (1990-91); Member, US National Academy of Sciences steering committee on the world food loss problem (1976-78); also served on other NAS committees **Selected Memberships:** American Chemical Society; Fellow, Institute of Food Technologists; American Association for the Advancement of Science; Fellow, Society for Food Science and Technology ; American Association of Cereal Chemists; New York Academy of Science **Discipline:** Chemistry **Related Areas of Interest:** Food Science and Technology; World Food Problem; Food Rheology **Current Areas of Research:** Texture and Rheology of Foods; Fruit, Vegetable and Legume Processing Technologies; International Transfer of Food Technology; Post Harvest Food Systems.

Selected Publications: His bibliography contains 1 book, 2 edited books, 26 chapters in books, 111 papers in refereed journals and 124 other publications.

_____. *Postharvest Food Losses - The Neglected Dimension in Increasing the World Food Supply.* New York: Cornell University International Mimeograph No. 53, 1976.
_____. "Graduate Education Needs for Students from Less-Developed Countries." *Food Technology* 34, 1 (1980): 50-5.
_____. "Creativity Assessment in Basic Research." *Food Technology* 36, 9 (1982): 67-72.
_____, Yin Zonglun and F. W. Liu, eds. *Postharvest Food Losses in Fruits and Vegetables.* Washington, DC: National Academy of Sciences Press, 1986.
_____. "Applications of Chemical Kinetic Theory to the Rate of Thermal Softening of Vegetable Tissue." Chap. 9 in *Quality Factors of Fruits and Vegetables. Chemistry and Technology*, American Chemical Society Symposium Series No. 405, ed. J. J. Jen, 98-110. Washington, DC, 1989.
_____. "Water Activity: Food Texture." In *Encyclopedia of Food Science and Technology*, ed. Y. H. Hui, 2801-15. New York: John Wiley & Sons, 1992.
_____. "Texture Measurement in Finished Baked Goods." Chap. 6 in *Advances in Baking Technology*, ed. B. S. Kamel and C. E. Stauffer, 134-51. London: Blackie Academic and Professional, 1993.
_____, W. Ptasnik, translators. "Food Science in the Former Soviet Union," by Dr. V. V. Krasnikov. NYS Agricultural Experiment Special Report No. 66. 1993.
_____. *Food Texture and Viscosity. Concept and Measurement.* New York: Academic Press, 1982. Reprint, 1994.

Boyd, Sir Robert Lewis Fullerton

Present Position and Address: Professor Emeritus of Physics (since 1983); Fellow, University College London (since 1989); (Home) "Roseneath", 41 Church Street, Littlehampton, West Sussex, BN17 5PU, UK **Date of Birth:** October 19, 1922 **Education:** ACGI and Hons.BSc Engineering (1943), Imperial College London; Ph.D. Engineering (1949), University College, London UCL **Selected Lectures:** Prize lectures: Appleton Lecture (1976) at Institution of Electrical Engineers/Bakerian Lecture (1978) at Royal Society/Halley Lecture (1981) at University of Oxford **Previous Positions:** Experimental Officer (1943-46), Admiralty Mining Establishment; Research Assistant/Research Fellow (1946-50, Department of Mathematics/Research Fellow through Professor (1950-83), Department Physics, UCL; Professor of Astronomy (1961-67), Royal Institution; Founding Director (1965-83), Mullard Space Science Laboratory UCL **Selected Memberships:** Fellow (1969), Royal Society; Commander of the Order of the British Empire (1972); Hon. DSc. (1979), Heriot Watt University; Knight Bachelor (1983); Member, Christians in Science; Fellow/Vice President (1964-66), Royal

Astronomical Society; President (1965-76), Victoria Institute; Chairman (1983-90), London Bible College **Discipline:** Physics - Astronomy **Related Interests:** Science and Faith.

Selected Publications:

_____. "The Why and the How." BBC broadcast (1953). Published in *The Listener* and by Lutterworth Press and later slightly adapted as *What Questions can Science Answer?* Inter-Varsity Fellowship.

_____. "The Universe Around Us." BBC broadcast (1953). Published (and later reprinted) in *Where Faith and Science Meet.* Inter-Varsity Press, 1953, 1966.

_____. "Faith in this Space Age." The Second Rendle Short Memorial Lecture (1963) at the University of Bristol. Published in *Faith and Thought* 93, 1.

_____. *Can God be Known?* Inter-Varsity Press, 1967 and 1970. Also in Japanese 1973.

_____. "A Physicist Thinks It Through." In *Why I Am Still A Christian.* Grand Rapids: Zondervan, 1971.

_____. "The Space Sciences." In *Horizons of Science.* New York: Harper & Row, 1978.

_____. "Creation of the Cosmos," Part I: "Space and Time," and Part II: "Creating." *Faith and Thought* 109, 1 (1982), and 109, 2 (1982).

_____. "Creation." A poem in *The Expository Times. 101, 2 (1989).*

_____. "Non in Tempore sed cum Tempore." Real Science, Real Faith. Eastbourne: Monarch 1992.

Bradley, Walter L.

Present Position and Address: Full Professor and former Head of Mechanical Engineering (since 1976), Texas A & M University, 1302 Augustine Circle, College Station, TX 77840, USA **Date of Birth:** December 27, 1943 **Education:** B.S. Engineering Science (1965)/Ph.D. Materials Science (1968), University of Texas - Austin **Previous Positions:** Assistant/Associate Professor (1968-76), Metallurgical Engineering, Colorado School of Mines; Associate/Full Professor (1976-present), Mechanical Engineering, Texas A & M University; Fellow (since 1985), American Scientific Affiliation; Fellow (since 1991), American Society for Materials **Discipline:** Materials Science - Polymer Science, Composite Materials **Related Interests:** Christianity and Science in the area of origins; Scientific apologetics on the existence of God.

Selected Publications:

_____, Roger Olsen. "The Trustworthiness of Scripture in Areas Relating to Nature Science." In Hermeneutics, Inerrancy and the Bible, ed. Earl D. Radmacher and Robert D. Preus. Zondervan, Academic Books, 1983.

_____, Charles Thaxton, Walter Bradley, and Roger Olsen. The Mystery of Life's Origin: Reassessing Current Theories. Philosophical Library, 1984.

_____, Randy Kok, John Taylor and Walter Bradley. "A Statistical Examination of Self Ordering of Amino Acids in Proteins." Origin of Life and Evolution of Biosphere 18 (1988): 135-42.

_____. "Thermodynamics and the Origin of Life." Perspectives on Science and Christian Faith 40, 2 (June 1988).

Brand, Raymond H.

Present Position and Address: Professor of Biology Emeritus, Wheaton College; Wheaton, IL 60187, USA **Concurrent Positions:** Research Associate, The Morton Arboretum, Lisle, IL 60532, USA **Date of Birth:** September 22, 1928 **Education:** B.A. Zoology (1950), Wheaton College; M.S. Biological Sciences (1951)/Ph.D. Animal Ecology (1955), University of Michigan **Postgraduate Studies:** Postdoctoral studies (1958-60), Universities of Wisconsin and Chicago **Previous Positions:** Assistant Professor (1955-57)/Associate Professor (1957-59), Westmont College; Chairman of Biology Department (1955-59), Westmont College; Acting Chairman (1957-59), Division of Science/Chairman (1966-68), Biology Division, Associated Colleges of Chicago Area (17 Colleges); Associate Director (1969), Summer Institute in Radiobiology, Argonne National Laboratory; Chairman, Division of Science (1968-71)/Department of Biology (1973-78), Wheaton College **Consulting Experience:**

Sheaffer and Roland Company (1975-78); Bauer Engineering Company (1974-75); Certified Senior Ecologist by Ecological Society of American (1990-95) **Selected Memberships:** Ecological Society of America; American Institute of Biological Sciences; American Association for the Advancement of Science; Sigma Xi; President, American Scientific Affiliation (1995) **Discipline:** Biology **Related Interests:** Being a Biologist and a Christian; Science and Christian Faith; Ecology and Ethics; Environmental Stewardship.

Selected Publications:

_____, John R. Sheaffer. *Whatever Happened to Eden?* Wheaton IL: Tyndale House Publishers, 1980.
_____. "At the Point of Need." *Perspectives on Science and Christian Faith* 39, 1 (March 1987): 2-8.
_____, Fred Van Dyke, Joseph Shelton, David Mahan. *Creation Redeemed: A Biblical Basis of Environmental Ethics.* Nashville, TN: Star Song Publishers, 1995.

Branson, Roy

Present Position and Address: Senior Research Fellow (since 1973), Kennedy Institute of Ethics Georgetown University, Washington, DC 20057, USA **Education:** B.A. English Literature (1959), Atlantic Union College MA; M.A. English Literature (1961), University of Chicago; M.A. Religion (1961), Andrews University, MI; Ph.D. Religious Ethics (1968), Harvard University **Selected Congresses and Conferences:** Delegate to discuss religion and bioethics (1979), Academy of Social Sciences and Academy of Medicine, Beijing, People's Republic of China **Previous Positions:** Associate Professor of Christian Ethics (1967-73), Andrews University; President (1970-72), Association of Adventist Forums; Consultant (1974-78), Encyclopedia of Bioethics; Acting Director of the Center for Bioethics (Summers, 1975-78), Kennedy Institute of Ethics; Consultant to Center for Christian Bioethics (1983-84)/Visiting Professor (Spring 1990), Loma Linda University; **Editorial Work:** Coeditor (1975-80)/Editor (since 1980) of *Spectrum*, an interdisciplinary journal **Selected Memberships:** Executive Committee (1968-72, since 1975), Association of Adventist Forums; Program Council (since 1989), Washington Institute of Ethics Relevant Organizations: Board Member (since 1990), Loma Linda University Ethics Center **Discipline:** Ethics **Related Interests:** Biomedical Ethics.

Selected Publications: His bibliography lists 4 books and 50 articles and chapters in books.

_____. "The Secularization of American Medicine." *Hastings Center Studies.* 1, 2 (1973): 17-29. Reprint, *On Moral Medicine: Theological Perspectives in Medical Ethics*, ed. Stephen E. Lammers and Allen Verhey. Grand Rapids: William B. Eerdmans, 1987.
_____. "Vocational Schizophrenia and the God of Creation." *Spectrum* 5, 4 (1973): 51-7.
_____. "The Doctor as High Priest." *Intellectual Digest* (January 1974): 60-1.
_____. "Bioethics: What Is It?" Review article in *Christianity Today.* 19, 2 (October 25, 1974): 36-40.
_____. "Bioethics: Individual and Social — The Scope of a Consulting Profession and Academic Discipline." *Journal of Religious Ethics* 3, 1 (Spring 1975): 111-39.
_____. *Ethics and Health Policy*, ed. Robert Veatch. Boston: Ballinger Press, 1976.
_____. Review of *Genetic Engineering: Threat or Promise?*, by Lawrence E. Karp. *American Society for Microbiology News* 43, 3 (March 1977): 172-3.
_____. "Theories of Justice and Health Care." In *Encyclopedia of Bioethics*, Vol. 2, ed. Warren T. Reich. New York: Free Press, Macmillan, 1978.
_____. Review of *Bioethics*, Thomas A. Shannon, editor. In *Religious Studies Review*, 4, 2 (April 1978): 143-4.
_____. "The Demand for a New Ethical Vision." In *A New Ethical Vision*, ed. James Walters. Loma Linda, CA: Loma Linda University, 1989.

Bratton, Susan P.

Present Position and Address: Coordinator of US National Park Service, Cooperative Park Studies Unit, Institute of Ecology, University of Georgia, Athens, GA 30602, USA **Concurrent Positions:** Professor of Environmental Ethics (since 1985), AuSable Trails Environmental Institute, Mancelona, MI **Date of Birth:** October 11, 1948 **Languages Spoken:** English, German **Education:** A.B. Biology (*cum laude*, 1970), Barnard College, Columbia University; Ph.D. Ecology (1975), Cornell University; 1 year certificate in Biblical Studies (1982), Liberty Bible College, Pensacola FL; M.A. Theology/Ethics (1987), Fuller Theological Seminary **Previous Positions:** Laboratory Assistant of General Biology (1969-70), Columbia University; Teaching Assistant in Ecology (1972-75), Cornell University NY; Coordinator (1976-79), Uplands Field Research Laboratory - Great Smoky Mountains National Park; Adjunct Assistant Professor of Graduate Program in Ecology (1979-82), University of Tennessee - Knoxville; Instructor (since 1977), US National Park Service; Adjunct Research Associate at Institute of Ecology/Adjunct Associate Professor of Environmental Ethics/Adjunct Associate Professor of Forest Resources (since 1982), University of Georgia **Discipline:** Ecology; Environmental Ethics **Related Interests:** Environmental Ethics, Land Ethics; Bioethics.

Selected Publications: Her bibliography lists over 30 works on theoretical and applied ecology, over 20 on the management of parks, wilderness and nature reserves and over 15 on environmental ethics, as well as many abstracts and technical reports.

_____. Review of *The Spirit of the Earth: A Theology of the Land*, by N. J. Ramsey. *Environmental Ethics* 7 (1985): 283-5.
_____. "Manager Reflects on New Environmental Ethics Program at University of Georgia." *Restoration and Management Notes* 4, 1 (1986): 53-75.
_____. "Teaching Environmental Ethics from a Theological Perspective." *Religious Education* 85, 1 (1990): 25-33.
_____. "A Fierce Green Fire Dying: Christian Land Ethics and Wild Nature." In book awaiting publisher's final approval. ed. C. DeWitt.

Breed, David R.

Present Position and Address: President and Consultant, Maximum Entropy, Inc. (consultant for electronics and computer applications) 5218 S. Dorchester Ave., # 3, Chicago IL 60615, USA **Work Phone:** (312) 288-7411 **Date of Birth:** February 13, 1945 **Education:** B.A. Physics/Mathematics (1967), Knox College IL; Ordained Pastor (1971), Lutheran Church in America; M.Div. (1972), Lutheran School of Theology, Chicago; Studies in Psychology (all but thesis completed, 1974-77), Illinois State University; Th.M. (1982)/Th.D. (1988), Lutheran School of Theology, Chicago **Previous Positions:** Pastor (1971-74), Christ Evangelical Lutheran Church, Dryville, PA; Director of Psychology Laboratories (1976-77), Department of Psychology, Illinois State University; Systems Engineer (1977-79), Bloomington Broadcasting Corporation; Instructor in Applied Computer Science (1979-80), Illinois State University **Selected Memberships:** American Academy of Religion - Theology and Science Group; Center for Theology and the Natural Sciences; Chicago Center for Religion and Science; History of Science Society; Council member (1980-86)/Editor of newsletter (1980-87)/1982 Summer Conference Program Cochair, Institute on Religion in an Age of Science (IRAS); Council for a Parliament of the World's Religions **Discipline:** Relationship of Religion and Science **Related Interests:** Interpretation of Religion in Terms of Scientific Concepts and Theories; Interpretation of the Religious Significance of Scientific Concepts, Theories, and Data; Ethical Problems raised by the Sciences and Technology; Philosophical Systems of Hegel and Whitehead; Works of Ralph Burhoe.

Selected Publications:

_____, Karl E. Peters. Introductory editorial to the issue "Order and Disorder: Thermodynamics, Creation, and Values." *Zygon* 19 (December 1984): 389-93.

_____. Review of *The Gospel from Outer Space,* by Robert Short. *Zygon* 20 (March 1985): 95-6.

_____. Review of *The Evolution of Darwin's Religious Views* by Frank Burch Brown. *Journal of Religion* 69 (October 1989): 556-7.

_____. "Ralph Wendell Burhoe: His Life and Thought (a four-part series)." *Zygon*: Part I, 25 (September 1990): 323-51; Part II, 25 (December 1990); Part III, 26 (March 1991); Part IV, 26 (June 1991).

Breed, James Lincoln

Present Position and Address: Pastor (since 1982) 1st Presbyterian Church, 307 South Tremont Street, Kewanee, IL 61443, USA **Concurrent Position:** Adjunct Professor of Philosophy, Black Hawk College-East Campus, Kewanee, IL, USA **Date of Birth:** September 1, 1944 **Education:** B.S. Mathematics (*cum laude,* 1966), University of Dubuque, IA; M.Div. (*summa cum laude,* 1970)/S.T.M. Old Testament (*summa cum laude,* 1971), University of Dubuque Theological Seminary; Ph.D. Historical Theology (1980), Aquinas Institute, St. Louis, MO **Previous Positions:** Pastor (1971-79), Garden Plain and Spring Valley Presbyterian Churches, Fulton, IL; Pastor (1979-82), Wequiock and Robinsonville Presbyterian Churches, Green Bay, WI **Selected Memberships:** Institute on Religion in an Age of Science (IRAS); American Society of Church History; Presbyterian Association of Science, Technology, and the Christian Faith **Discipline:** Pastoral Ministry; Historical Theology **Related Areas of Interest:** Relevant Area of Interest: Creation and cosmology.

Selected Publication:

_____. Articles on "John Cotton," "Cotton Mather," "David Brainard," "Increase Mather," and the "Mayflower Compact." In *Encyclopedia of the Reformed Faith*, ed. Donald K. McKim. Louisville, KY: Westminster Press, 1992.

Bregman, Lucy

Present Position and Address: Associate Professor of Religion, Religion Department, Temple University, Philadelphia PA 19122, USA; (Home) 238 McClellan Street, Philadelphia, PA 19148, USA **Work Phone:** (215) 204-7252 **Home Phone:** (215) 467-1541 **Date of Birth:** December 18, 1944 **Education:** B.A. (1966), Brown University; Studied at Harvard Divinity School (1966-67); M.A. Religion (1970)/Ph.D. Religion and Psychological Studies (1973), University of Chicago Divinity School **Previous Positions:** Assistant Professor (1972-74), Religious Studies Department of Indiana University - Bloomington, IN **Selected Memberships:** American Academy of Religion; Society for the Scientific Study of Religion; Association for Death Education and Counseling; The Liturgical Conference; Associate, American Psychological Association, Div. 36 (Psychologists Interested in Religious Issues) **Discipline:** Religious Studies - Religion; Psychology **Related Interests:** Psychological and Theological understandings of Death **Current Research:** The study of autobiographical narratives dealing with illness, death, and grief. The culmination of this study will be a book, co-authored with Dr. Sara Thiermann, entitled *First Person Mortal.*

Selected Publications: Her bibliography lists 3 books, 27 articles, and 14 book reviews.

_____. "The Interpreter/Experiencer Split: Three Models in the Psychology of Religion." *Journal of the American Academy of Religion* 46 (June 1978): 116-49. Abstract, Supplement.

_____. *The Rediscovery of Inner Experience.* Chicago: Nelson-Hall, 1982. Dealing with popular psychologies' "religiousness".

_____. "Three Psycho-Mythologies of Death: Becker, Hillman and Lifton." *Journal of the American Academy of Religion* 52 (September 1984): 461-79.

_____. "Death and its Denial: Definitions and Perspectives from Depth Psychology and Christian Thought." *Thought* 61 (March 1986): 306-20.

_____. *Through the Landscape of Faith*. Philadelphia: Westminster Press, 1986. Deals with life-maps and psychologies of faith development.

_____. "Baptism as Death and Birth: A Psychological Interpretation of its Imagery." *Journal of Ritual Studies* 1, 2 (1987): 27-41.

_____. *Death in the Midst of Life: Perspectives on Death form Christianity and Depth Psychology*. Grand Rapids: Barker Book House, 1992.

Brooke, John Hedley

Present Position and Address: Professor, History of Science, Department of History, University of Lancaster, Lancaster LA1 4YG, UK **Work Phone:** 0524-592513 **Fax:** 0524-846102 **Date of Birth:** May 20, 1944 **Education:** M.A./Ph.D. (1968), University of Cambridge UK **Previous Positions:** Research Fellow (1968)/Visiting Fellow (1975), Fitzwilliam College, Cambridge; Tutorial Fellow (1968-69), University of Sussex; Lecturer/Senior Lecturer (since 1970)/Principal of Bowland College (1980-84), University of Lancaster UK **Editorial Work:** Editor, *The British Journal for the History of Science* (1988-93) **Selected Memberships:** Member, Royal Society National Committee for History of Science; Former Treasurer and Council Member, British Society for History of Science; Council member, Society for History of Alchemy and Chemistry; Committee member, Historical Studies Group of Royal Society of Chemistry; Member of several research networks on "Science and Religion" including the Science and Theology Consultation at Princeton **Discipline:** History and Philosophy of Science **Related Interests:** Philosophical Aspects of Organic Chemistry and the Life-sciences; History of Natural Theology; the Darwinian Revolution etc. **Current Research:** Due to give the Gifford Lectures, jointly with Professor N. Cantor at Glasgow University in 1995.

Selected Publications: His bibliography lists more than 30 publications, most of which have a direct bearing on the field.

_____. *New Interactions between Theology and Natural Science*. London: Open University Press, 1974.

_____. *The Crisis of Evolution*. London: Open University Press, 1974.

_____. "Natural Theology and the Plurality of Worlds: Observations on the Brewster-Whewell Debate." *Annals of Science*. 34 (1977): 221-86.

_____. "The Natural Theology of the Geologists: Some Theological Strata." In Images of the Earth, ed. L. Jordanova and R. Porter. British Society for the History of Science, Monograph 1. Chalfont St. Giles, 1979.

_____. "The Relations between Darwin's Science and his Religion." In Darwinism and Divinity, ed. J. R. Durant. Oxford: Blackwell, 1985.

_____. "The God of Isaac Newton." In Let Newton Be, ed. J. Fauvel, R. Flood, M. Shortland and R. Wilson. Oxford: Oxford University Press, 1988.

_____. "Science and the Fortunes of Natural Theology." Zygon 24 (1989): 3-22.

_____. "Science and Religion." In A Companion to the History of Modern Science, ed. G. Cantor, J. Christie, J. Hodge, and R. Olby. London: Routledge, 1989.

_____. *Science and Religion: Some Historical Perspectives*. Cambridge: Cambridge University Press, 1991.

_____. "Natural Law in the Natural Sciences: The Origins of Modern Atheism?" *Science and Christian Belief*. 4 (1992): 83-103.

Brown, Robert Hanbury

Present Position and Address: Professor Emeritus of Physics (since 1981), Sydney University, Australia White Cottage, Penton Mewsey, Andover, SP11 0RQ, UK **Date of Birth:** August 31, 1916 **Education:** B.S.. (1934)/D.I.C. (1936), University of London, UK; D.Sc. (1960), Manchester **Honor-**

ary Degrees: Hon. D.Sc. (1984), Monash, Sydney **Awards and Honors:** Holweck Prize (French Physical Society, 1959); Eddington Medal from Royal Astronomical Society (1968); Lyle Medal of Australian Academy of Science (1970); Britannica Medal (1971); Hughes Medal (Royal Society of London, 1971); Flinders Medal (Australian Academy of Science 1982); Michelson Medal (Franklin Institute, 1982); Anzaas Medal (1984); Companion of the Order of Australia (1986) **Previous Positions:** Professor of Radio Astronomy (1949-64), Manchester; Professor of Physics (1964-81), Sydney **Selected Memberships:** Honorary Fellow, Indian National Science Academy/Indian Academy of Science/Canadian Astronomical Society/Optical Society of Australia; President (1982-85), International Astronomical Union **Discipline:** Physics - Astronomy **Related Interests:** The Nature of Science; Science and Faith; Cosmology; Science and Culture.

Selected Publications: His bibliography lists 62 technical articles, 5 books and 45 general articles.

_____. *Man and the Stars*. Oxford: Oxford University Press, 1978.
_____. "Does God Play Dice?" In *Chance in Nature*, ed. P. A. P. Moran. Canberra: Australian Academy of Science, 1979.
_____. "Science and Faith." *Current Affairs Bulletin* (University of Sydney), 56, 7 (1979): 12-14.
_____. "The Nature of Science." *The Ecumenical Review* (World Council of Churches, Geneva). 31, 4 (1979): 352-63.
_____. "The Nature of Science." *Zygon* 14, 3 (1979): 201-15.
_____. "What is Science?" In *Faith and Science in an Unjust World*. Geneva: World Council of Churches, 1980.
_____. "La Nature de Science." In *Science sans Conscience*. Geneva: Labor et Fides, 1980.
_____. "Das Wessen der Wissenschaft." *Die Zeichender Zeit* 5 (Berlin, 1980): 164-74.
_____. "Concern about the Control of Science." In *Proceedings*, Academic Congress "Concern about Science," October 1980. Amsterdam: Free University, 1982.
_____. "Faith and Works." Address to Laser and Optical Conference, 28 August 1985 Curzon Hall, Sydney. *Australian Physicist*, 22: 306-8.

Brown, Warren S.

Present Position and Address: Adjunct Professor (since 1982), Department of Psychiatry and Biobehavioral Sciences, UCLA School of Medicine, Los Angeles CA 90024; Professor of Psychology (since 1982), Fuller Graduate School of Psychology, 180 N. Oakland Ave. Pasadena, CA 91182; (Home) 2309 Paloma Street, Pasadena, CA 91104, USA **Work Phone:** (818) 584-5525 **Home Phone:** (818) 798-3081 **Fax:** (818) 584-9630 **E-Mail:** WSBROWN @ FULLERPSYC.EDU **Date of Birth:** September 8, 1944 **Education:** B.A. Psychology/Religion (*magna cum laude*, 1966), Point Loma College; M.A. (1968)/Ph.D. (1971), Experimental Psychology (Physiological), University of Southern California **Previous Positions:** N.I.M.H. Trainee (1966-70), University of Southern California; Postdoctoral Trainee (1971-73), Brain Research Institute UCLA; Department of Psychiatry (1973-present), UCLA School of Medicine; Visiting Scholar (1986), Department of Communication and Neuroscience, University of Keele UK **Discipline:** Neuropsychology/Psychophysiology **Related Interests:** Brain and Epistemology; Brain Pathology and Religious Experience; Spirituality and Mind-Brain-Immune Interactions (psychoneuroimmunology).

Selected Publications: His bibliography lists over 50 scientific publications, over 60 scientific abstracts and 7 general articles, besides many presentations and addresses.

_____. D. Vogt and W. S. Brown. "Bottom-line Morality." *Christianity Today* (March 1988).
_____. "Memory," "Psychosurgery," "Brain Research," "Biological Dimensions of Personality and Behavior." In *The Dictionary of Pastoral Care and Counselling*, ed. H. N. Malony. (in press).
_____. C. Castano. "Conversion. Cognition, and Neuropsychology." In *Handbook of Conversion*, ed. H.N. Maloney and S. Southland. Birmingham, AL, Religious Education Press, 1992.

Browning, Don S.

Present Position and Address: Alexander Campbell Professor of Ethics and the Social Sciences (since 1981), The Divinity School, University of Chicago; Chicago, IL 60637 **Work Phone:** (312) 702-8275 **Home Phone:** (312) 935-9252 **Date of Birth:** January 13, 1934 **Education:** A.B. (1956), Central Methodist College; B.D. (1959), M.A. (1962), Ph.D. (1964), Divinity School, University of Chicago **Honorary Degrees:** Honorary Doctor of Divinity, Central College (1984), Christian Theological Seminary (1990) **Awards and Honors:** Guggenheim Fellowship (1975-76); Fellow, Center of Theological Inquiry (1990) **Previous Positions:** Assistant Professor (1963-65), Pastoral Theology, The Graduate Seminary, Phillips University; Instructor/Assistant (1965-68)/Associate (1968-77)/Full Professor (1977-81), Divinity School, University of Chicago **Selected Memberships:** American Academy of Religion; Society for Christian Ethics; Society for the Scientific Study of Religion; Institute on Religion in an Age of Science; President (1991-pres.), International Academy of Practical Theology **Discipline:** Religion and Social Sciences; Theological Ethics; Practical Theology **Related Interests:** Relation of Theology to Social Sciences, Psychology of Religion.

Selected Publications:

_____. *Atonement and Psychotherapy*. Westminster, 1966.
_____. *Generative Man*. Westminster, 1973.
_____. *Pluralism and Personality: William James and Some Contemporary Cultures of Psychology*. Backnell, 1990.
_____. *Religious Thought and the Modern Psychologies*. Fortress Press, 1987.
_____, editor. *Religious and Ethical Factors in Psychiatric Practice*. Nelson Hall, 1990.
_____. *A Fundamental Practical Theology: Descriptive and Strategic Proposals*. Fortress Press, 1991.

Brück, Hermann Alexander

Present Position and Address: Professor Emeritus, University of Edinburgh UK; Craigower, Penicuik, Midlothian EH26 9LA, UK **Date of Birth:** August 15, 1905 **Education:** Augusta Gymnasium, Charlottenburg; Universities of Bonn, Kiel, Munich, and Cambridge. D.Phil., University of Munich; Ph.D., University of Cambridge **Awards and Honors:** CBE (1966); Hon. D.Sc. NUI (1972)/St. Andrews (1973) **Previous Positions:** Astronomer (1928), Potsdam Astrophysical Observatory; Lecturer (1935), Berlin University; Research Associate (1936), Vatican Observatory, Castel Gandolfo; Assistant Observer (1937), Solar Physics Observatory, Cambridge; Assistant Director (1946), Cambridge Observatory; Director (1947-57), Dunsink Observatory; Professor of Astronomy (1947-57), Dublin Institute for Advanced Studies; Astronomer Royal for Scotland and Regius Professor of Astronomy (1957-75)/Dean of Faculty of Science (1968-70), University of Edinburgh **Selected Memberships:** Member (1971-84), Board of Governors, Armagh Observatory NI; MRIA (1948); FRSE (1958); Member (1955), Pontifical Academy of Sciences, Rome; Member (1955), Academy of Sciences, Mainz **Discipline:** Astronomy and Astrophysics **Related Interests:** History and Philosophy of Science.

Selected Publications: His bibliography lists some 100 papers and articles.

_____. "P. Angelo Secchi, S.J. (1818-1878)." *Specola Vaticana, Ricerche Astronomiche* 9 (1979). International Astronomical Union Colloquium 47.
_____. "Astrophysical Cosmology." In *Proceedings of the 1981 Study Week of the Pontifical Academy of Sciences*, ed. G. V. Coyne and M. S. Longair. Vatican Press, 1982.
_____. *The Story of Astronomy in Edinburgh*. Edinburgh University Press, 1983.
_____, M. T. Bruck. *The Peripatetic Astronomer, The Life of Charles Piazzi Smyth*. Philadelphia: Adam Hilger, 1988.

Brugger, Hans Rudolf

Present Position and Address: Part-time worker with Vereinigte Bibelgruppen VBG (= IVF Switzer-land), especially among Christians in science. Garglasweg 39, CH-7220 Schiers, Switzerland **Date of Birth:** August 1, 1928 **Languages Spoken:** German, English, French **Education:** M.S.. (1954)/Ph.D. (1961), Swiss Federal Institute of Technology, Zurich **Previous Positions:** Research Assistant (1961-63), Rutgers University, New Brunswick, NJ; Guest Scientist (1961-63), Brookhaven National Lab; Taught Physics and Mathematics (1969-94), Evangelische Mittelschule Schiers, Switzerland **Selected Memberships:** American Scientific Affiliation; Vereinigte Bibelgruppen - IFV Switzerland; Karl-Heim-Society, Einshausen, Germany; Swiss Astronomical Society; Swiss Physical Society **Discipline:** Crystal Physics (1953-54); Neutron Physics (1954-61); Elementary Particle Physics (1961-63); Astronomy (since 1970) **Relevant Areas of Interest:** Creation and Evolution. Specifically the Relations between the Biblical Account of the Creation of the World and the Scientific Concepts of Evolution in Cosmology (Big Bang); Astronomy (evolution of galaxies and stars); Geohistory (age of solar system and earth).

Selected Publications: He has written several articles in Christian periodicals and books, and given numerous talks on this topic. Many book reviews.

_____. "The History of Creation: Is the Earth a Young Planet?" *Reformatio* (March 1982): 160-75.
_____. "Geology or Creationism?" *C + B, Chemistry and Biology* (September 1985).
_____. "Creation or Evolution in Cosmology and Geosciences." *Offenes Wort* (June 1986).
_____. "The Universe - This Marvelous Creation." *Bausteine* (July 1989).
_____. "The History of the Earth in Biblical and Scientific View." *Bulletin Groupes Bibliques Universitaires* (December 1994).
_____. "Age Determinations in Geology and Astronomy." *Schöpfung und Evolution, Porta-Studie* 6 (Spring 1995).

Brun, Rudolf B.

Present Position and Address: Professor of Biology (since 1978), Texas Christian University, Biology Department, Box 32916, Fort Worth, TX 76129, USA **Work Phone:** (817) 921-7165 **Date of Birth:** March 4, 1938 **Languages Spoken:** German, English, French **Education:** Ph.D. Biology (1968), University of Basel, Switzerland; Postdoctoral training in developmental biology (Fall 1868-70), University of Geneva, Switzerland **Previous Positions:** Teaching/Research Assistant (1965-68), University of Basel; Senior Teaching Assistant (1969-77), University of Geneva; Invited Assistant Professor (1977-78), Embryology and Developmental Genetics, Indiana State University **Discipline:** Biology **Related Interests:** Science; Aesthetics; Theology.

Selected Publications: His bibliography lists over 25 articles as well as many papers and presentations in his field.

_____. "Evolution und Christentum." *Communio, Internationale Katholische Zeitschrift* 13 (1984): 518-523.
_____. "Schöpfungslehre und Herrlichkeit." *Communio, Internationale Katholische Zeitschrift* 21 (1992)349-60.
_____. "Integrating Evolution: A Contribution to the Christian Doctrine of Creation." *Zygon* 29 (1994): 275-96

Brungs, Robert

Present Position and Address: Director (since 1968), ITEST (Institute for Theological Encounter with Science and Technology), 221 N. Grand Blvd, St. Louis, MO 63103, USA; Adjunct Professor (since 1984), Department of Physics, Saint Louis University, St. Louis, MO **Date of Birth:** July 7, 1931 **Education:** A.B. (1955), Bellarmine College, Plattsburgh NY; Ph.L. (1956), Fordham University

NY; Ph.D. Physics (1962), St. Louis University, MO; S.T.B. (1963)/S.T.L. (1965), Woodstock College, Woodstock MD; Ordination to Priesthood (1964), Woodstock PA; Final Vows (1967), Society of Jesus **Previous Positions:** Assistant Professor Dogmatic and Systematic Theology (1971-75)/Associate Professor of Department of Theological Studies (1975-83), Divinity School, Saint Louis University; Assistant (1970-75)/Associate (1975-84)/Adjunct Professor (since 1984), Department of Physics, Saint Louis University, MO; Invited participant (September 1972), International Conference on the Physical Nature of Matter, Institute of Theoretical Physics, Trieste, Italy; Participant (July 1979), World Council of Churches Conference on "Science, Technology, and the Future," MIT, MA; Consultant (since 1973), Committee on Science, Technology, and Human Values, National Council of Catholic Bishops; Liaison (since 1977), Bishops' Committee on Science, Technology, and Human Values: Archdiocese of Saint Louis **Selected Memberships:** Member of Board of Advisors, Institute on Religion in an Age of Science (IRAS)/Center for Advanced Study in Religion and Science (CASIRAS); Member of Editorial Advisory Board, *Zygon* **Discipline:** Theology and Physics **Related Interests:** Role of Christians in Science; Implications for Christian Belief from Scientific Development.

Selected Publications: His bibliography lists 2 books, over 30 compilations/editorials, over 50 articles and reviews and over 300 talks most of which are in this area.

_____. "The Science-Faith Controversy: Is the Old Conflict Being Revived?" *Atheism and Dialogue* 19, 1 (1984): 37-49.
_____. "The Church and Science." *Atheism and Dialogue* 19, 2 (1984): 144-50.
_____. "Toward a Theology of Health Care." *Review for Religious* 45, 1 (January/February 1986): 24-44.
_____. "Brain Research/Human Consciousness." In *Compiled proceedings of the ITEST Workshop* (March 1986).
_____. "Creating the New Man: Advances in Bio-technology." *The Canadian Catholic Review* 5 (June 1987): 204-13.
_____. *You See the Lights Breaking Upon Us: Doctrinal Perspectives on Biological Advance.* ITEST Faith/Science Press, 1989.
_____. "Biology and the Future: A Doctrinal Agenda." *Theological Studies* 50 (1989): 698-717.
_____. "Science — Democracy — Christianity." *Thought* 64 (December 1989): 377-98.
_____. "The Catholic Faith: A Covenantal Approach." Chapter 11 in *Transfiguration: Elements of Science and Christian Faith*, ed. Marianne Postiglione. ITEST Faith/Science Press, 1993): 245-78.
_____, editor. *Secularism Versus Biblical Secularity.* ITEST Faith/Science Press, 1994.

Bube, Richard H.

Present Position and Address: Professor of Materials Science and Electrical Engineering (from 1964, Emeritus in 1992), Stanford University, CA, USA 753 Mayfield Avenue, Stanford, CA 94305, USA **Work Phone:** (415) 723-2535 **Fax:** (415) 725-4034 **E-Mail:** bube @ leland.stanford.edu **Date of Birth:** August 10, 1927 **Education:** Sc.B. Physics (1946), Brown University, RI; M.A. Physics (1948)/Ph.D. (1950), Princeton University **Selected Lectures:** Joint Conference of the American Scientific Affiliation and the Research Scientists Christian Fellowship on Science and Christian Faith (1965, 1985), Oxford University, UK; Adjunct Professor of Theology and Science, Fuller Theological Seminary (1974/Fuller Extension Program (1983); Faculty, Regent College (1976), Vancouver, BC; Staley Distinguished Christian Scholar Lecturer (9 Lecture Tours, 1975-90 at 8 Colleges); Templeton Lecturer (1992) Stanford University; Faculty, New College Berkeley (1993) **Previous Positions:** Senior Member of Technical Staff (1948-62), Group Manager of Research in Photoelectronic Materials, RCA Lab, Princeton; Associate Professor (1962-64)/Professor (since 1964)/Department Chairman (1975-86)/Associate Chairman (1990-91)/Professor Emeritus (since 1992), Materials Science and Electrical Engineering, Stanford University **Editorial Work:** Editor (1969-83), *Journal of American Scientific Affiliation*; Associate Editor (1969-83), *Annual Review of Materials Science*; Editorial Advisory Board (since 1975), *Solid-State Electronics*; Editorial Board (since 1992), *Christians in Science* **Selected Memberships:** Fellow, American Physical Society; Fellow, American Association for the Advancement of Science; Fellow/Executive Council (1964-68)/Vice President (1967)/President (1968)/Founder of San Francisco Bay Section (1963), American Scientific Affiliation; Life Member, American Society for Engineering Education **Discipline:** Materials Physics **Related Interests:** Science and Christian Faith/Theology/Whole Person.

Selected Publications: His bibliography lists 9 books (4 relating science and Christian faith), 261 scientific research papers and 37 survey and review papers on the photoelectronic properties of solids; 136 papers on science and Christian faith; 5 book reviews of scientific books; 180 reviews of science/Christianity books; and 3 patents on photo conducting materials and devices. Lectures on science and Christianity have been given on the campuses of 60 Colleges and Universities since 1962.

_____. "Science and the Whole Person." a 22 part series of extended papers, *Journal of the American Scientific Affiliation* (1976-1983).
_____. "Probing the Mystery of Being Human." In *The Sanctity of Life Conference*, June 1987, ed. D. A. Fraser. Princeton: Princeton University Press, 1988.
_____. "Science and Christianity." In the *International Standard Bible Encyclopedia*. Vol. IV, ed. G. W. Bromiley. Grand Rapids: Wm. B. Eerdman's, 1988.
_____. "Crises of Conscience for Christians in Science." *Perspectives in Science and Christian Faith* 41, 11 (1989).
_____. "'So You Want to Be a Science Professor!' The Education Business: Things My Mother Never Told Me." *Perspectives in Science and Christian Faith* 41, 143 (1989).
_____. "Of Dominoes, Slippery Slopes, Thin Edges of Wedges, and Camels' Noses in Tents: Pitfalls in Christian Ethical Consistency." *Perspectives in Science and Christian Faith* 42, 162 (1990).
_____. "Penetrating the Word Maze." An 11 part series of brief papers, *Perspectives in Science and Christian Faith* (1988-1990).
_____. "How Can a Scientist be a Christian in Today's World?" In *Can Scientists Believe? Some Examples of the Attitude of Scientists to Religion*, ed. Sir Nevill Mott. London: James and James, 1991.
_____. "The Future of the American Scientific Affiliation: Challenges and Pitfalls." *Perspectives in Science and Christian Faith* 43, 273 (1991).
_____. "Seven Patterns for Relating Science and Theology." In *Man and Creation: Perspectives on Science and Theology*, ed. M. Baumann. Hillsdale, MI: Hillsdale College Press, 1993.

Buckley, Michael J.

Present Position and Address: Professor of Systematic Theology, Department of Theology, University of Notre Dame, Notre Dame, IN 46556, USA **Work Phone:** (219) 239-7811 **Date of Birth:** October 12, 1931 **Languages Spoken:** English, Greek, Latin, French, German, Italian **Education:** B.A. Philosophy (1955), Gonzaga University; Ph.L. Philosophy (1956), Pontifical Faculty of St. Michael's; M.A. Philosophy (1956), Gonzaga University; S.T.L. Theology (1963), Pontifical University of Alma; S.T.M. Theology (1963), University of Santa Clara **Awards and Honors:** ATS Award for Theological Scholarship and Research (1978) **Previous Positions:** Language Instructor (English, Latin, Greek, 1956-59), Bellarmine College Prepatory, San Jose, CA; Visiting Lecturer (1967-68), University of Chicago; Assistant Professor, Philosophy (1968-69), Gonzaga University; Assistant Professor (1969-71)/Rector (1969-73)/Associate Professor of Philosophy (1971-86), The Jesuit School of Theology at Berkeley, Graduate Theological Union; Visiting Professor (1973-1975), Pontifical Gregorian University, Rome; Visiting Scholar (1981), University of Santa Clara; Bannan Scholar in Residence (1982-83), University of Santa Clara; Professor of Systematic Theology (1986-1990), The Jesuit School of Theology at Berkeley, Graduate Theological Union **Editorial Work:** Member of the Editorial Advisory Board (1978-present), *Theological Inquiries* (Paulist Press); Editorial Consultant (1980-present), *Theological Studies* **Selected Memberships:** Board of Directors, Center for Theology and the Natural Sciences; Executive Director (as of 1988), Committee on Doctrine and Committee on Pastoral Research and Practices, National Conference of Catholic Bishops, Washington DC Systematic

Theology and Philosophy **Discipline:** Social Justice as Christian Humanism; Philosophy and Religion; Atheism.

Selected Publications: His bibliography lists 3 books, over 40 articles and 5 book reviews.

_____. "Philosophy and the Liberal Arts." *Perspectives, A Journal of General and Liberal Studies* (University of Michigan) 3, 1 (1971): 18-31.
_____. "The Catholic University as Pluralistic Forum." *Thought* (Fordham University Quarterly) 46, 181 (1971): 200-12.
_____. *Motion and Motion's God: Thematic Variations in Aristotle, Cicero, Newton and Hegel.* Princeton University Press, 1971.
_____. "The University and the Concern for Justice: The Search for a New Humanism." *Thought* 57, 225 (June 1983): 219-233.
_____. *At the Origins of Modern Atheism.* New Haven: Yale University Press, 1987.
_____. "The Newtonian Settlement and the Origins of Atheism." In *Physics, Philosophy, and Theology: A Common Quest for Understanding*, ed. Robert J. Russell, William R. Stoeger, and George V. Coyne. Vatican City State: Vatican Observatory, 1988; Notre Dame University Press, 1989.
_____. "God in the Project of Newtonian Mechanics." In *Proceedings of the Cracow Conference, May 25-28, 1987,* ed. G. V. Coyne, M. Heller, and J. Zycinski. Città del Vaticano: Specula Vaticana, 1988.

Budenholzer, Frank

Present Position and Address: Vice President, Fu Jen Catholic University, Taiwan; Catholic Priest; Department of Chemistry, Fu Jen Catholic University, Hsinchuang 242, Taipei, Taiwan **Work Phone:** (02) 902-0904 **Fax Number:** 886-2-901-4749 **Date of Birth:** August 21, 1945 **Languages Spoken:** English, Mandarin Chinese **Education:** B.A. Philosophy (1967), Divine Word College, Epworth, IA; B.S. Chemistry, De Paul University, Chicago (1969); M.A. Theology, Catholic Theological Union, Chicago (1972); Ph.D. Physical Chemistry (1977), University of Illinois, Chicago **Previous Positions:** Associate Professor of Chemistry (1980-84)/Professor of Chemistry (1984-present), Fu Jen Catholic University, Taiwan **Selected Memberships:** Catholic Priest (Societas Verbi Divini) ordained 1972; Institute on Religion in an Age of Science; American Physical Society; American Chemical Society; Chinese Chemical Society - Taipei **Discipline:** Physical Chemistry - molecular collision dynamics **Related Interests:** Scientific and Theological Methodology; Religion and Science in China, especially in the late Ching and Republican era.

Selected Publications: His bibliography lists over 24 articles.

_____. "Science and Religion: Seeking a Common Horizon." *Zygon* 19 (1984): 351-368.
_____. "Some Observations on the Origin of Conflicts Between Science and Religion in Modern China." In *The Impact of Science and Technology on Christian Higher Education in Asia, Proceedings of the 1986 Workshop sponsored by the Association of Christian Colleges and Universities in Asia.* Taiwan: Chung Yuan Christian University, 1986.
_____, Schang-Shing P. Chou. "Science, Technology, and Religion in Taiwan China." *Atheism and Dialogue* (Vatican City) 24-2 (1989). Reprint, *ITEST Bulletin* 20, 4 (Fall 1989).

Buehler, David A.

Present Position and Address: Bioethics Coordinator, Charlton Memorial Hospital, Fall River, MA; Editor, Tischrede Software, No. Dartmouth, MA. Phone: (508) 994-7907 FAX: (508) 679-7144 **E-Mail:** sources@aol.com **Date of Birth:** December 31, 1944 **Languages Spoken:** English, German **Education:** A.B. (1967) Wittenberg University; M.A. (1968) Reed College; M.Div (1972) Harvard Divinity School **Previous Positions:** Science Teacher (1968-69), Katonah Elem. School, Katonah, NY; Vicar (1972-73), First Lutheran Church, W. Haven, CT; Chaplain-Resident (1978-80), Yale-New Haven

Medical Center **Honors:** CAMCON Prize for software innovation (National Council of Churches), 1987 **Memberships:** American Association for the Advancement of Science; American Society of Law, Medicine and Ethics; Apple Programmers & Developers Association; Fellow, The College of Chaplains; Clinical Member, Association for Clinical Pastoral Education; Associate Member, The Hastings Center; Founding Member, International Bioethics Institute; Mind/Body Medical Institute; Charter Member, Center for Health, Faith and Ethics; Society for Health and Human Values **Discipline:** Theology and Ethics; Computer Science **Relevant Areas of Interest:** Cosmology, complexity, chaos theory **Current projects:** Developing CD-ROM on science and religion.

Selected Publications:

____. "Call to Care and Cure." *Specialized Pastoral Care Journal* 4 (1981):27-30.
____. *Health and Healing in the Bible*. Philadelphia: Parish Life Press, 1985.
____. "Challenge to Critical Care Nursing: Informed Consent and the Elderly." *Critical Care Nursing Clinics of N. America* 2 No. 3 (9/90): 461-71.
____. "Consenso informato e ruolo del nursing." *Medicina e Morale* 2 (Rome 1991): 367-8.
____. "Computerizing Chaplaincy." Chapter 8. *Chaplaincy Services in Contemporary Health Care*, ed. L. Burton. Chicago: American Hospital Association, 1992.
____. "Organ Ethics." *Cambridge Quarterly of Healthcare Ethics* 1,4 (UK, 1993): 355-60.
____. "Medical Futility." *Cambridge Quarterly of Healthcare Ethics* 2,2 (UK, 1993): 225-27.
____. "Euthanasia & Physician-Assisted Suicide." *Cambridge Quarterly of Healthcare Ethics* 2,1 (UK, 1993): 77-80.
____. "From Cells to Selves." *Cambridge Quarterly of Healthcare Ethics* 2,3 (UK, 1993): 327-30.
____. "A Small, Good Thing: Anencephalic Organ Donation." *Cambridge Quarterly of Healthcare Ethics* 2, 1 (UK, 1993): 81-87.

Bulka, Reuven P.

Present Position and Address: Rabbi (since 1967), Congregation Machzikei Hadas, Ottawa, Ontario, Canada; Center for the Study of Psychology and Judaism, 1747 Featherston Drive, Ottawa, Ontario K1H 6P4 Canada **Languages Spoken:** English, Hebrew, Yiddish **Education:** B.A. Philosophy (1965), City University NY; M.A. Logotherapy (1969)/Ph.D. Logotherapy of Viktor E. Frankl (1971), University of Ottawa **Previous Positions:** Associate Rabbi (1965-67), Congregation K'Hal Adas Yeshurun, Bronx, NY; Chairman of the Jewish Community Council Sub-Committee for the Jewish Studies Program (1973-76), Carleton University; Regular columnist for *Ottawa Citizen* (1974-78, 1988-present); Founder of Ottawa Jewish Community Eruv and operator of Eruv Hotline; Advisor of Judaic Studies Program (since 1986), Hillel Academy; Chairman of Hebrew Curriculum Committee of Ottawa Talmud Torah Board (1972-74, 86-89); Jewish Chaplain at Children's Hospital of Eastern Ontario **Media Work:** Hosted TV series "Quest" (1974-80), "About Ourselves" (1980-88), and "In Good Faith" (since 1988), on CJOH **Selected Memberships:** Executive, League for Human Rights of B'nai Brith Canada; National Religious Affairs Committee of the Canadian Jewish Congress; Ontario Government Advisory Council for Multiculturalism and Citizenship (1986-88); American Psychological Association; Founder (1976), Centre for the Study of Psychology and Judaism **Discipline:** Rabbi; Philosophy and Psychology **Related Interests:** Logotherapy and Judaism; Environmental Ethics; Psychology and Judaism; Mysticism and Medicine.

Selected Publications: His bibliography lists over 90 works.

_____. *The Quest for Ultimate Meaning: Principles and Applications of Logotherapy*. NY: Philosophical Library, 1979.
_____. *The Jewish Pleasure Principle*. NY: Human Sciences Press, 1986.
_____. *Individual, Family, Community: Judeo-Psychological Perspectives*. Oakville, Ontario, Canada, 1989.

Burhoe, Ralph Wendell

Present Position and Address: Acting Director, Center for Advanced Study in Religion and Science (CASIRAS), 1524 E. 59th Street, Chicago IL 60637, USA **Concurrent Positions:** Honorary President (since 1960) of IRAS **Work Phone:** (312) 643-5131 **Date of Birth:** June 21, 1911 **Honorary Degrees:** D.Sc. (1975), Meadville/Lombard School of Theology affiliated with University of Chicago; DHL (1977), Rollins College **Awards and Honors:** 1st American recipient of the Templeton Prize for Progress in Religion; 1st recipient (1984) of the Distinguished Achievement Award in Recognition of Outstanding Contributions to Understanding the Relationship between Religion and Science **Previous Positions:** Professor of Theology and the Sciences (1964-74)/Professor Emeritus (since 1974), Meadville/Lombard School of Theology; Editor and Publisher of *Zygon* (1974-79); Volunteer leader of seminars on religion and science and thesis-advisor at the Lutheran School of Theology at Chicago **Editorial Positions:** Founding Editor of *Zygon* and member of its joint publication board **Selected Memberships:** Fellow (1965), American Academy of Arts and Sciences; Fellow (1964), American Academy of Religion; The American Association for the Advancement of Science; American Theological Society; Chicago Center for Advanced Study in Religion and Science; Institute Academic Fellow (1987), Institute on Religion in an Age of Science; Society for the Scientific Study of Religion; Fellow, World Academy of Arts and Sciences (1962) **Discipline:** Theology and Science **Related Interests:** Translating Traditional Religious Values into the Language of the Sciences thus Making the Basic Elements of Much of Traditional Christian Theology Intelligible and Credible Today.

Selected Publications:

_____. *Evolution and Man's Progress*. Columbia University Press, 1962.
_____. *Science and Human Values in the Twenty First Century*. Westminster Press, 1971.
_____. *Towards a Scientific Theology* (out of print. May be available from *Zygon* editorial office, Rollins College, Winter Park, FL 32789, USA).
_____. "War, Peace, and Religion's Biocultural Evolution." *Zygon* (December 1988).

Burke, Derek C.

Present Position and Address: Vice-Chancellor (since 1987) University of East Anglia, Norwich, Norfolk NR4 7TJ, UK **Work Phone:** 01603-456161 **Fax:** 01603-58553 **E-Mail:** d.c.burke@uea.ac.uk **Date of Birth:** February 13, 1930 **Education:** B.S.. Chemistry (1950), University of Birmingham; Ph.D. Chemistry (1953), University of Birmingham **Postgraduate Studies:** Research Fellow (1953-55), Yale University **Honorary Degrees:** LLD (1982), University of Aberdeen **Previous Positions:** Scientist (1955-60), National Institute for Medical Research, London; Lecturer/Senior Lecturer (1960-69), Department of Biochemistry, University of Aberdeen; Professor (1969-82), Biological Sciences, University of Warwick; Vice President and Scientific Director (1982-86), Allelix, Toronto **Selected Memberships:** European Molecular Biology Organization (1980); President (1987-90), Society of General Microbiology **Discipline:** Molecular Biology **Related Interests:** Molecular Biology of Interferon and Animal Viruses; Creation and Evolution.

Selected Publications: Numerous scientific papers on interferon and animal viruses.

_____, editor and contributor. *Creation and Evolution*. IVP, 1985.

Burke, Thomas J.

Present Position and Address: Associate Professor (since 1988)/Division Head (since 1984), Hillsdale College, Hillsdale, MI 49292, USA; (Home) 5120 State Road, Hillsdale, MI 49242, USA;. **Work Phone:** (517) 437-7341 **Date of Birth:** December 25, 1943 **Education:** B.A. (1965), Baylor

University; M.Div. (1969), Evangelical Divinity School; Ph.D. (1978), Garrett-Evangelical Seminary, Northwestern University; M.A. Philosophy (1983)/Ph.D. (1989), Michigan State University **Previous Positions:** Assistant Professor of Religion and Philosophy (1982-88), Hillsdale College **Editorial Work:** Editor, *Man and Mind: A Christian Theory of Personality* **Selected Memberships:** American Scientific Affiliation; Society of Christian Philosophers **Discipline:** Religion: History of Theology and Systematics; Philosophy: Philosophy of Mind, Philosophy of Science, Epistemology **Related Interests:** Philosophy of Science, Philosophy of Mind; Doctrine of Creation.

Selected Publications:

_____. "The Mind-Body Problem: Scientific or Philosophic?" *Journal of the American Scientific Affiliation* 36, 1 (1984).
_____. "Psychology, Theology, and Liberal Arts: Towards the Unity of Knowledge." *Man and Mind: A Christian Theory of Personality*. Hillsdale College Press, 1987.

Burneko, Guy C.

Present Position and Address: Assistant Professor of Humanities (since 1988), interdisciplinary and intercultural graduate and undergraduate courses in Comparative Literature and Philosophy, "Integration", Pacific Rim Studies, Alaska Pacific University, 4101 University Drive, #536, Anchorage, AK 99508, USA **Work Phone:** (907) 344-8365 **Date of Birth:** November 14, 1946 **Languages Spoken:** English, French, some Chinese (Putonghua) **Education:** B.A. English (1968), Fordham University, Bronx, NY; M.A. English (1971), University of Alaska, Fairbanks, Alaska; Ph.D. Interdisciplinary Studies (1981), Graduate Institute of the Liberal Arts, Emory University, Atlanta, GA **Postgraduate Studies:** National Endowment for the Humanities fellowship in "Chinese Literature in an Interlingual Context," (Summer 1985), Stanford University **Previous Positions:** Instructor in Literature, Composition, Interdisciplinary Humanities (1972-74), Kuskokwim Community College, University of Alaska; (1981-83), Liaoning Teachers' University, Dalian, China; Assistant Professor (1983-84), Department of English and Humanities, Mohawk Valley Community College, Utica, NY; English Instructor (1984-85), Syracuse University, NY; Adjunct Assistant Professor (1985-86), Humanities Program/Philosophy Department, University of North Carolina - Asheville; Visiting Assistant Professor (1986-87), Interdisciplinary Liberal Studies, Emory University; Assistant Professor (1987-88), Adult Degree Program: Interdisciplinary Humanities and Liberal Studies, Mary Baldwin College, VA **Selected Memberships:** International Jean Gebser Society; Association for Integrative Studies; Founder, Asheville, NC Noetics Group **Discipline:** Interdisciplinary Liberal Studies/Humanities **Related Interests:** Symbolic Anthropology; Philosophy of Science; History of Consciousness; Philosophical Hermeneutics; Archetypal Psychology; Taoist Philosophy; Theory of Literature; Interdisciplinary Writing and Critical Thought; Chaos Theory; Post-structuralism; Intercultural Noetics; Evolution of Consciousness.

Selected Publications: His bibliography lists 14 publications and papers.

_____. "Chuang Tzu's Existential Hermeneutics." *Journal of Chinese Philosophy* 13, 4 (1986).
_____. "Interdisciplinary, Transdisciplinary, and Intercultural Post-Modern Noetics and Guerilla Hermeneutics." *International Synergy* 3, 1 (1988).
_____. "Interdisciplinary, Transdisciplinary, and Intercultural Education." Paper presented at the National Conference on Interdisciplinary Baccalaureate Education, University of South Carolina, Columbia, SC, March 7, 1988.

Burnham, Frederic B.

Present Position and Address: Director (since 1984), Trinity Institute, 74 Trinity Place, New York, NY 10006, USA; (Home) 311 Greenwich St., New York, NY 10013, USA **Date of Birth:** July 21,

1938 **Education:** A.B. (1960), Harvard College; B.D. (1963), The Episcopal Theological School; Certificate in History and Philosophy of Science (1963-64), Cambridge University; Ph.D. History of Science (1970), The Johns Hopkins University; D.D. (1985), Hobart and William Smith Colleges **Previous Positions:** Instructor (1968-70)/Assistant Professor (1970-78), Department of History, Wayne State University; Assistant Dean for Graduate Studies (1970-75), Graduate Division, Wayne State University; President (1978-84), The Association of Episcopal Colleges, New York **Discipline:** History and Philosophy of Science **Related Interests:** Christianity in a Postmodern World; Theology and Science in a Postmodern World; American Values; Teleology and the Plurality of Worlds; Chaos and Complexity: A Postmodern Paradigm for the Church.

Selected Publications:

_____. "Teleology and the Plurality of Worlds." Papers presented at American Historical Association, July 1982, 1983, 1984.
_____. "American Values: The Last Twenty Years." Lecture series given at Wesleyan University, February 20-23, 1983.
_____. Review of *God and the New Physics* by Paul Davies. *Religion and Intellectual Life* 2, 1 (1984).
_____. "A Reply to Arthur Peacocke's Critical Realism." *Religion and Intellectual Life* 2 (November 1985).
_____. "Science and Religion: A Personal Overview." Paper presented at John E. Hines Lectures, The Diocese of Newark, December 4, 1985.
_____, producer. Living the Christian Story in a Postmodern World. Harper and Row, 1989. (Video)
_____, editor. Postmodern Theology. Harper and Row, 1989.
_____, editor. Love, The Foundation of Hope. Harper and Row, 1988.
_____. "The Bible and Contemporary Science." Religion and Intellectual Life 6 (Spring/Summer 1989).
_____. "Maker of Heaven and Earth: A Perspective of Contemporary Science" Horizons in Biblical Theology. 12, 12 (1990).

Busse, Richard Paul

Present Position and Address: Associate Faculty, Indiana University - Northwest; Founding Associate (since 1988), Chicago Center for Religion and Science (CCRS); (Home) 1706 Calumet Avenue, Valparaiso, IN 46383, USA **Work Phone:** (312) 753-0670 **Home Phone:** (219) 464-7278 **Date of Birth:** June 4, 1950 **Education:** B.A. Philosophy (1972), Valparaiso University; M.T.S. (1975)/Th.M. Process Philosophy and Theology, Nature of Religious Language (1979)/Th.D Systematic Theology (1984), all at the Lutheran School of Theology - Chicago (LSTC) **Previous Positions:** Owner-operator during Summers (since 1974), Fried Vegetable Concessions; Instructor in Philosophy (1983)/Lecturer/Assistant Professor in Theology (1983-88), LSTC **Editorial Work:** Editor of *CCRS Newsletter, Insights,* LSTC; Editor of *Bulletin for the Council of Societies for the Study of Religion,* Macon, GA **Selected Memberships:** Center for Process Studies; American Academy of Religion; Institute on Religion in an Age of Science; Chicago Center for Science and Religion; Christ Lutheran Church **Discipline:** Philosophy and Theology **Related Interests:** Has taught classes and been project leader in topics such as "Ethics and Morality"; "From Kant to Nietzsche"; "Is God a Creationist"; "Creation - Issues in Science and Theology"; "The Problem of Language in Science and Religion."

Selected Publications:

_____. "Science, Religion and Theissen's Hermeneutics of Mutation." Paper presented at the Annual Spring Seminar on Science and Religion sponsored by the Center for the Advanced Study in Science and Religion, LSTC (May 5, 1986).
_____. "Science, Religion and Christmas Star Programs." Paper presented at the 23rd Annual Conference of the Great Lakes Planetarium Association Merrillville, IN, October 19, 1987.
_____. "The Life and Work of Ralph Burhoe." Seminar on Science and Religion at LSTC April/May 1988.
_____. "Why the Church Should Pay Attention to Science." Paper presented at Northwest Indiana Conference of Pastors, ELCA, May 1988.

Buswell III, James O.

Present Position and Address: Vice President for Academic Affairs and Professor of Anthropology, The William Carey International University, 1539 E. Howard Street, Pasadena, CA 91104 **Phone:** (818) 797-1200, **Fax:** (818) 398-2111 **Date of Birth:** January 12, 1922 **Languages Spoken:** English **Education:** Wheaton College, B.A. Anthropology (1948); University of Pennsylvania, M.A. Anthropology and Linguistics (1952); St. Louis University, Ph.D. Anthropology-Sociology, (1972) **Previous Positions:** Various teaching positions in NY and ILL; Assistant Professor of Anthropology, St. John's University, Jamaica, NY (1967-73); Professor of Anthropology and Sociology, Trinity College, Deerfield, ILL (1973-75); Professor of Anthropology, Wheaton College, Wheaton, IL (1974-79); William Carey International University, Pasadena, CA, Dean of Graduate Studies; Professor of Anthropology (1980-89), Vice President for Academic Affairs (1989-present) **Honors:** Wheaton College Scholastic Honors Society **Memberships:** American Scientific Affiliation (President 1978), American Anthropological Association, Royal Anthropological Institute, American Ethnological Society, American Society of Missiology, Society for Applied Anthropology, Trans World Radio (Board of Directors), Navajo Gospel Mission (Board of Directors), Emmanual Bible College (Board of Directors). **Discipline:** Anthropology **Relevant Areas of Interest:** North American Indians, esp. S.E.; Evolution/Creation interface; Applied (Missionary) Anthropology.

Selected Publications: His bibliography contains one book and 63 published articles, as well as nearly 100 book reviews.

____. "Is There an Alternative to Organic Evolution?" *The Gordon Review* V No. 1 (1959): 2-13 (Presented at the Graduate Seminar, Dept. of Anthropology, University of Chicago, 2/18/57)
____. "A Creationist Interpretation of Prehistoric Man." In *Evolution and Christian Thought Today*, ed. Russell L. Mixter. Grand Rapids: Wm. B. Eerdmans (1959): 165-189.
____. "The Origin of Man and the Bio-Cultural Gap." *Journal of the American Scientific Affiliation* 13 No. 2 (1961): 47-55.
____. "Man's Antiquity and Fall." *Christianity Today* IX No. 12 (March 1965): 22.
____. "Genesis, the Neolithic Age, and the Antiquity of Adam." *Faith and Thought* 96, No.1 (1967): 3-23.
____. "Anthropology and the Nature of Man." *Journal of the Evangelical Theological Society* XIII, Part IV (Fall 1970): 219-227.
____. "Contextualization: Theory, Tradition, and Method." In *Theology and Mission*, ed. David Hesselgrave. Grand Rapids: Wm. B. Eerdmans (1978): 87-111, 124-127.
____. "Conn on Functionalism and Presupposition in Missionary Anthropology." In E*ternal Word and changing Worlds: Theology, Anthropology, and Mission in Trialogue*, Harvie M. Conn. Grand Rapids: Zondervan (1984). TJ Vol. 7, No. 2: 69-95.
____. "Anthropological Appraisal and Missionary Response." In *Current Concerns of Anthropologists and Missionaries*, ed. Karl Franklin. Dallas: IMC Publication No. 22: 67-79.
____. "Toward a Christian Metaanthropology." *Journal of Interdisciplinary Studies* I, Nos.1,2 (1989): 2-44.

Buttiglione, Rocco

Present Position and Address: Chair for Ethics and Philosophy of Politics, Economics and Society Internationale Akademie für Philosophie, Obergass 75, FL-9494 Schaan, Fürstentum, Liechtenstein **Date of Birth:** June 6, 1948 **Languages Spoken:** German, English, Spanish, Portuguese, French, Polish **Education:** Doctor of Law (1970), Rome, La Sapienza; Assistant/Ordinarus Professor **Previous Positions:** Associate Professor for Political Philosophy, University of Urbino; Ordinarus Professor for Political Philosophy, University of Teramo **Selected Memberships:** Consuletore (1984-89), Pontifical Commission Justice and Peace, Vatican City, Rome **Discipline:** Social and Political Philosophy.

Selected Publications:

_____. *Dialettica e Nostalgia* (Dialectics and nostalgia). Milan: Jaca Book, 1978.

_____. *Metafisica della Conoscenza e Politica* (Metaphysics of knowledge and politics). Bologna: CSEO, 1986.

Byers, David M.

Present Position and Address: Staff to the Committee on Science and Human Values, National Conference of Catholic Bishops, 3211 Fourth Street NE, Washington, DC 20017, USA **Work Phone:** (202) 541-3011 **Date of Birth:** October 28, 1941 **Education:** B.A. English (1963), Assumption College; M.A. English (1966), Seton Hall University; Ph.D. English (1973), University of Minnesota **Selected Memberships:** American Association for the Advancement of Science; ITEST; Cosmos and Creation; Center for Theology and the Natural Sciences Administrative position for Catholic Bishops **Discipline:** Religion and Science.

Selected Publications:

_____. "The Common Ground of Science and Religion." *America* (January 7, 1984).
_____. "Religion, Science, and the Search for Wisdom." *Bulletin of the Institute for Theological Encounter with Science and Technology* (May 1985).
_____, editor. *Religion, Science, and the Search for Wisdom: Proceedings of a Conference on Religion and Science.* Washington, DC: National Conference of Catholic Bishops, 1987.
_____. "Science and Religion: Not on Speaking Terms." *Columbia* (1994).
_____. "Pace Galileo: The Present and Future of Religion/Science Dialogue." *America* (1994).

Byrne, Patrick H.

Present Position and Address: Associate Professor of Philosophy (since 1983); Boston College, Chestnut Hill, MA 02167, USA; (Home) 70 Johnswood Rd., Roslindale, MA 02131, USA **Date of Birth:** May 16, 1947 **Education:** B.S. Physics (1969)/M.A. Philosophy (1972), Boston College; Ph.D. Philosophy (1978), SUNY - Stony Brook **Previous Positions:** Instructor (1976-78/Assistant Professor (1978-83), Boston College **Selected Memberships:** P. Teilhard de Chardin Center for Theology and Natural Science; American Philosophical Association; Philosophy of Science Association **Discipline:** Philosophy **Related Interests:** Science and Religion; Ethics and Social Ethics; Works of Bernard Lonergan, H. Bergson, A. N. Whitehead.

Selected Publications: His bibliography lists 18 publications and 18 presented papers.

_____. "God and the Statistical Universe." *Zygon* 16 (1981): 345-63.
_____. "On Taking Responsibility for the Indeterminate Future." In *Phenomenology and the Understanding of Human Destiny, Volume I,* ed. S. Skousgaard. Current Continental Research (1981).
_____. "The Thomist Sources of Lonergan's Dynamic World View." *The Thomist* 46 (1982): 108-45.
_____. "The Significance of Voegelin's Work for the Philosophy of Science." In *The Beginning and the Beyond,* ed. Fred Lawrence. Chico CA: Scholar's Press, 1984.
_____. "Normative Science and Cover Story: Re-opening the Horizon of Modern Science to Ethical and Religious Thought." Paper presented at Perspectives Faculty Seminar, June 1984.
_____. "Is Evolution Continuous or Discontinuous?" Paper presented at Concordia University, March 11, 1985.
_____. "Mystery and Mathematical Infinity." *Lonergan Workshop* 7 (1988).
_____. "Lonergan's Insight and the Retrieval of Natural Law." *Lonergan Workshop* 8 (1990).

C

Cahill, Lisa Sowle

Present Position and Address: Professor of Theology (since 1989), Theology Department, Boston College, Chestnut Hill, MA 02167 USA **Work Phone:** (617) 552-3880 or 3890 **Date of Birth:** March 27, 1948 **Education:** B.A. (1970), University of Santa Clara; M.A. Christian Theology (1973)/Ph.D. Christian Theology (1976), University of Chicago Divinity School **Previous Positions:** Instructor in Theology (1976), Concordia College, Moorhead, MN; Assistant Professor (1976-82)/Associate Professor (1982-1989)/Director of Graduate Programs in Theology (1985-87), Boston College; Visiting scholar (Fall 1986), International Study Group on Science and Theology/Reproductive Biology, Kennedy Institute of Ethics, Georgetown University **Editorial Work:** Editorial Board and Board of Directors, *Journal of Medicine and Philosophy* **Selected Memberships:** American Academy of Religion, Ethics Program Committee (1981-83); Society of Christian Ethics (Board of Directors, 1982-86); Catholic Theological Society of America (Chair, Moral Theology Steering Committee, 1984-87/Vice President 1990-91 President 1992-93, Past President 1993-94); March of Dimes Advisory Board; National Advisory Board on Ethics in Reproduction **Discipline:** Theology and Ethics **Related Interests:** Method in Theological Ethics, especially Roman Catholic Natural Law Methodology, and the use of Scripture in Christian Ethics; Sexual Ethics; Medical Ethics; History of Christian Ethics.

Selected Publications: Her bibliography lists 5 books, and over 50 articles and chapters. Editing a special issue of *Theology and Bioethics* on "Playing God in Biomedicine" to appear in Feb. 1995.

_____. "Ethical Issues in Medicine: Catholic, Lutheran, and Reformed Perspectives." *Second Opinion* 2 (1986).
_____. "Sanctity of Life, Quality of Life, and Social Justice." *Theological Studies* 48 (1987): 105-123.
_____, Thomas A. Shannon. *Religion and Artificial Reproduction: Inquiry into the Vatican Instruction on Human Life.* Crossroad Press, 1988.
_____. "The Ethics of Surrogate Motherhood: Biology, Freedom, and Moral Obligation." In *Surrogate Motherhood: Politics and Privacy*, ed. Larry Gostin. Indiana University Press, 1990.
_____. "Can Theology have a Role in 'Public' Bioethical Discourse?" *Hastings Center Report* (July 1990).
_____, editor. "Theology and Bioethics." A special edition of the *Journal of Medicine and Philosophy*, June 1992.
_____. *The Embryo and Fetus: New Moral Contexts.* N.p. March 1993.

Cain, Dallas E.

Present Position and Address: Retired from General Electric Company (1943-1982); 18 Edmel Road, Scotia, NY 12302, USA **Work Phone:** (518) 399-1833 **Education:** BSEE (1943), West Virginia University **Selected Memberships:** Victoria Institute, London; Friend, Interdisciplinary Biblical Research Institute, Hatfield, PA; American Scientific Affiliation **Discipline:** Electrical Engineering **Related Interests:** Genesis 1.

Selected Publications:

_____. "Let There Be Light, Spectrum of Creation Theories." *Eternity Magazine* 33, 5 (Philadelphia, 1982).
_____. *Creation and Capron's Explanatory Interpretation: A Literature Search*. Report No. 27. Hatfield, PA: Interdisciplinary Biblical Research Institute.
_____. "Translating Genesis One In the Light of Modern Scientific Findings." In preparation.

Cantor, Geoffrey

Present Position and Address: Professor of the History of Science in the Division of History and Philosophy of Science, Philosophy Department, University of Leeds, Leeds LS2 9JT, UK **Work Phone:** +44 (0113) 33269 **Fax:** +44 (0113) 333265 **Date of Birth:** May 10, 1943 **Education:** B.S.. (1964)/Ph.D. (1968), University of London. **Previous Positions:** Lecturer (1970-72), Hendon College of Technology; Research Fellow (1972), Institute for Advanced Studies in the Humanities, Edinburgh University; Lecturer/Professor (1973-present), University of Leeds; Visiting Professor (1979-80), University of California - Los Angeles; Gifford Fellow (1988), Glasgow University **Discipline:** History and Philosophy of Science **Related Interests:** Relation between Natural Philosophy (physics) and Religion, 18th-20th Centuries.

Selected Publications:

_____. "The Theological Significance of Ethers." In *Conceptions of Ether*, ed. G. N. Cantor and M. J. S. Hodge. Cambridge University Press, 1981.
_____. *Optics after Newton: Theories of Light in Britain and Ireland*. Manchester: University Press, 1983.
_____. "Berkeley's Analyst Revisited." *Isis* 75 (1984): 668-83.
_____. "Light and Enlightenment: An Exploration of Mid-eighteenth Century Modes of Discourse." In *The Discourse of Light from the Middle Ages to the Enlightenment*, ed. D. C. Lindberg and G. N. Cantor. William Andrews Clark Memorial Library, 1985.
_____. "Reading the Book of Nature: The Relation between Faraday's Religion and his Science." In *Faraday Rediscovered*, ed. D. Gooding and F. James. Macmillan, 1985.
_____. *Michael Faraday, Sandemnian and Scientist: A Study of Science and Religion in the Nineteenth Century*. Macmillan, 1991.
_____. "Dissent and Radicalism? : The Example of the Sandemnians." *Enlightenment and Dissent* 10 (1991): 3-20.

Cantore, Enrico

Present Position and Address: Adjunct Professor at Fordham University, New York; Christian Brothers East Harlem, 125 E. 103rd Street, New York, NY 10029, USA **Work Phone:** (212) 427-5928 **Languages Spoken:** English, Italian, German, French, Latin **Education:** Doctorate in Physics (1955), State University of Turin; Doctorate in Philosophy (1966), Gregorian University of Rome; M. Theol. (1959), Jesuit Theologate Northern Italy **Postgraduate Studies:** Postgraduate research in the History and Philosophy of Science, University of Chicago and the Max-Planck-Institut für Physik - München **Previous Positions:** Participated in the preparation and execution of the Non-Governmental Organizations Forum of the United Nations Conference on Science and Technology for Development (Vienna, August 19-31, 1979); Member of the Jesuit Order and a Catholic Priest; Taught at the Gregorian University, Rome; Director of World Institute for Scientific Humanism, Fordham University at Lincoln Center **Discipline:** A philosophical reflection on science studied in its historical, psychological, sociological and religious contexts. Goal: Seeking to update traditional humanism in order to meet the needs of our scientific age. The final goal is global development, the universal and effective fostering of human dignity. **Related Interests:** Significance of science, pure and applied, for human dignity and the common good; pursuing dialogue with prominent scientist-humanists, among others Werner Heisenberg and Jean Piaget. The religious inspiration is the firm conviction that "the glory of God is the human being fully alive" (Saint Iranaeus). Currently engaged in a multi-year writing project entitled *Christ-Wisdom and Science: Fostering Human Dignity in the Third Millennium.*

Selected Publications: His bibliography lists 3 related books and 23 related articles.

_____. *Atomic Order: An Introduction to the Philosophy of Microphysics.* Cambridge, MA: The M.I.T. Press, 1969; paperback edition: M.I.T. Press, 1977.
_____. "Humanistic Significance of Science: Some Methodological Considerations." *Philosophy of Science* 38 (1971): 395-412.
_____. *Scientific Man: The Humanistic Significance of Science.* New York: Institute for Scientific Humanism Publications, 1977.
_____. "Science as an Experience of the Absolute: Religious and Moral Implications of Research, The Search for Absolute Values in a Changing World." In *Proceedings of the 6th International Conference on the Unity of the Sciences, San Francisco, November 1977.* New York: International Cultural Foundation, 1978.
_____. "Science for Human Dignity: A Christian Leadership Task." *Homiletic and Pastoral Review* (June 1982): 47-53.
_____. "Galileo, Scientist and Believer." *Atheism and Dialogue* 19, 1 (1984): 31-7.

Carey, Patrick W.

Present Position and Address: Associate Professor of Religious Studies and Chair; Theology Department, Marquette University, Coughlin Hall, Milwaukee, WI 53233 **Work Phone:** (414) 288-7170 **Fax Number:** (414) 288-5548 **Date of Birth:** July 2, 1940 **Languages Spoken:** French, German, Latin **Education:** BA Philosophy (1962), St. John's University; M.Div. Theology (1966), St. John's Seminary, MN; S.T.M. American Religions (1971), Union Theological Seminary, NY; Ph.D. Theology (1975), Fordham University **Field Work:** Study of American Protestant and Catholic Religious Life and Thought **Congresses and Conferences:** Annual Meeting of the Organization of American Historians (1981), Detroit, MI; Annual Convention of the College Theology Society (1985), Salve Regina College, RI; Conference on Knowledge and Belief (1990), Woodrow Wilson International Center for Scholars (Smithsonian Institute), Washington, DC; Wingspread Center Conference (1993), Racine, WI **Lectures Presented:** Faculty Symposiums (1976-77), Jersey City, NJ and Northfield, MN and Symposium on Catholic Studies, Notre Dame; Special Meeting of American Catholic Historical Association (1984), Villanova University; Lutheran-Catholic-Anglican Milwaukee dialogue (1987), Our Saviour's Lutheran Church, Milwaukee, WI; Aquinas Lecture (1988), Ohio Dominican College, Columbus, OH; American Catholic Historical Association, Spring Meeting (1988), St. Mary's College, Moraga, CA; College Theology Society (1988), Marymount University, CA; St. Sebastian's Adult Education (1989), Milwaukee, WI; Participant and chair (1991), one session at College Theology Society Annual Meeting, Chicago, IL **Awards and Honors:** Full Tuition Scholarship (1972-75), Fordham University; (1978), Notre Dame Cushwa Travel Grant; Summer Faculty Fellowship Grants (1979, 1985), Marquette University; Award for manuscript ((1985), University of Notre Dame Cushwa Center; Marquette Religious Commitment Fund Grant and Mellon Fund Grant for Team-taught courses (1990); Milwaukee Archdiocesan Fund for a National Conference to be held at Marquette University, August 1995 (1994) **Previous Positions:** Assistant Professor (1975-76), St. Peter's College; Assistant Professor (1976), Elizabeth Seton College; Assistant Professor (1976-77), Carleton College; Assistant Professor (1077-78), Gustavus Adolphus; Assistant Professor through Chair (since 1978), Theology Department, Marquette University **Selected Memberships:** American Academy of Religion; American Society of Church History; American Catholic Historical Association; American Catholic Historical Society of Philadelphia; United States Catholic Historical Society; College Theology Society; Catholic Theological Society of America **Discipline:** Historical Theology **Related Areas of Interest:** American Protestant and Catholic Religious Life and Thought **Current Areas of Research:** A Comprehensive History of American Catholic Theological Thought; Biographical Dictionary of Theologians.

Selected Publications: His bibliography contains 6 books, over 20 articles, over 15 contributions to books and about 30 book reviews.

_____. *American Catholic Religious Thought.* New Jersey: Paulist Press, 1987.
_____. *People, Priests and Prelates: Ecclesiastical Democracy and the Tensions of Trusteeism.* Notre Dame, IN: University of Notre Dame Press, 1987.
_____. *Marquette Theology: A History.* Privately printed and distributed at Marquette University, 1987.
_____. "American Catholics and the First Amendment: 1776-1840." *The Pennsylvania Magazine of History and Biography* 113 (July 1989): 323-45.
_____. "Lay Catholic Leadership in the United States." *U.S. Catholic Historian* (Summer 1990): 10-20.
_____. *Orestes A Brownson: Selected Writings.* New Jersey: Paulist Press, 1991.
_____. *The Roman Catholics.* Westport, CT: Greenwood Press, 1993.
_____. *The Roman Catholics in America.* Westport, CT: Praeger, 1994.
_____. "Orestes A. Brownson on Tradition and Traditionalism." In *The Quadrilog: Tradition and the Future of Ecumenism,* ed. Kenneth Hagen, 162-88. St. John's MN: The Liturgical Press, 1994.
_____. "American Protestantism in Catholic Perspective." In *New Directions in American Religious History: The Protestant Experience,* ed. Harry Stout. New York: Cambridge University Press, in press.

Carvallo, Marc E.

Present Position and Address: Lecturer in Philosophy of Religion (since 1979), State University of Groningen, The Netherlands Department of Philosophy of Religion, State University of Groningen, Nieuwe Kijk in 't Jatstraat 104, 9712 SL Groningen, The Netherlands **Work Phone:** 050-635571 **Fax:** 050-636200 **Date of Birth:** April 7, 1934 **Languages Spoken:** Indonesian, Latin, German, Dutch, English **Education:** B.A. Science of Education (1964), Catholic University of Indonesia; M.A. Philosophy of Educational Sciences (1972), Catholic University of Nijmegen, The Netherlands; Ph.D. Philosophy of System/Science (1994), University of Twente, The Netherlands **Previous Positions:** Assistant lecturer (1965-67), Theoretical Pedagogics and Developmental Psychology, Teacher's College, Flores; Lecturer (1974-78), Anthropology and Metasciences of Education, Teachers College, Tilburg, The Netherlands; Lecturer (1975-78), History and Philosophy of Education, State University of Groningen **Selected Memberships:** International Sociological Association; International Society for Systems Sciences; International Federation for Systems Research; Dutch Society for Philosophy of Religion; New York Academy of Sciences; Australasian Society for Cognitive Science **Discipline:** Philosophy of Systems/Science; Philosophy of Religion **Related Interests:** Philosophy of Education; Theory and Research in Alienation; Philosophy of Quantum Physics; Cognitive Science.

Selected Publications: His bibliography contains 45 entries.

_____, editor. *Nature, Cognition, and System.* Vol. 1. Dordrecht/Boston/London: Kluwer Academic Publishers, 1988.
_____. *Converging the Two Time-Arrows, Nature, Cognition, and System.* Vol. 1 Dordrecht/Boston/London: Kluwer Academic Publishers, 1988.
_____. "Selftranscendence and Symmetrybreak. Some Notes on Cognition and Self-Organization in Erich Jantsch's Theory of Natural Systems." In *Nature, Cognition, and System,* 253-77. Vol. 1. Dordrecht: Kluwer Academic Publishers, 1988.
_____. "David Bohm and Cognitive Science." In Proceedings of the European Congress on Systems Science, 1071-1089. Lausanne, Switzerland: 1989.
_____. "A Corollary to an Expanding Chapter in the Philosophy of Religion." In Proceedings of the 12th International Congress on Cybernetics, ed. J. Ramaekers, 578-91. Association Internationale de Cybernetique Press, Namurs. 1990.
_____. "Systems Science and the Observing Systems." In Systemica VIII: Mutual Uses of Cybernetics and Science, ed. G. de Zeeuw and R. Glanville. Amsterdam: Thesis Publishers, 1991.
_____. "What is System Science: Definition One." In Cybernetics and Applies Systems, ed. C.V. Negoita, 43-93. Basel: Marcel Dekker, Inc., 1992.

_____, editor. Nature, Cognition, and System, Volume II. Dordrecht: Kluwer Academic Publishers, 1992.
_____. "A Brief Prolegomenon to the Principle of Metaphoricity." In *Nature, Cognition, and System*. Vol. 2. Dordrecht: Kluwer Academic Publishers, 1992.
_____. "First Steps to the Anthropic Paradigm." In *Ethical Management of Science as a System*, ed. R. Packham. Hawkesbury: The University of Western Sydney Press, 1993.

Casebolt, James R.

Present Position and Address: Assistant Professor of Psychology (since 1993), Danville Community College, 1008 S. Main Street, Danville, VA 24541-4004, USA; (Home) 230 Crestwood Drive, Danville, VA 24541, USA **Work Phone:** (804) 797-8511 **Home Phone:** (804) 797-3158 **E-Mail:** Bitnet, DCCASEJ@VCCSCENT **Date of Birth:** May 29, 1967 **Languages Spoken:** English **Education:** B.A. Psychology (*Summa cum laude*, 1989), Alderson-Broaddus College, Philippi, WV; M.A. (1992)/Ph.D. (1994), Psychology, University of North Carolina, Chapel Hill, NC **Congresses and Conferences:** Invited speaker at symposium on "Religious Orientation: Where Have We Been, Where Are We Going?" American Psychological Association Annual Convention, August 16, 1992, Washington, DC **Awards and Honors:** Alderson-Broaddus College Social Science Academic Award (1989); Alderson-Broaddus College Edna Pickett Winter Humanities Writing Award (1990); National Science Foundation Graduate Fellowship Honorable Mention (1990) **Previous Positions:** Teaching Assistant (1989-93), University of North Carolina, Chapel Hill, NC **Media Work:** Feature story on Holiday Depression, Danville *Register & Bee* (1993); Feature story on Older Drivers, Danville *Register & Bee* (1994); Feature on Video Games and Aggression in Children, WFET Television (1994) **Editorial Positions:** Staff: *Representative Research in Social Psychology* (1989-93), University of North Carolina - Chapel Hill; Ad-Hoc Reviewer: "Religious Influences on Personal and Societal Will-being," a prospectus for the *Journal of Social Issues* (1993) **Other Academic Experience:** Academic Committee Service at DCC (since 1993), Instruction Subcommittee for Institutional Self-Study; Curriculum and Instruction Planning Group Action Team; Assessment Committee for Education Curriculum (since December 1993) **Selected Memberships:** Teaching of Psychology (Div. 2); Society for the Psychological Study of Social Issues (Div. 6); Society of Personality and Social Psychology (Div. 9); Psychology of Religion (Div. 36); Peace Psychology (Div. 48); American Psychological Society; Religious Research Association; Society for the Scientific Study of Religion; American Psychological Association; Virginia Academy of Science **Discipline:** Social Psychology **Related Areas of Interest:** Post-empiricist Approaches to Social Theory; Political Participation; Minority Influence, Social Innovation, and Creativity; Theories of Interpersonal Relationships as Heuristic Models of the God-Believer Relationship **Current Areas of Research:** Terror management and derogatory attribution of AIDS victims; Reconnoitering the enemy: Self-inoculation, reactance, and selective exposure; Test-wiseness of traditional versus non-traditional community college students.

Selected Publications:

_____. "The Role of Religious Behavior in Decision-Making and Problem-Solving: Reliance on God." Paper presented at the Society for the Scientific Study of Religion/Religious Research Association Annual Meeting, November 11, 1990, Virginia Beach, VA.
_____. "Complexity of Beliefs and Values: Individual and Social Context." Discussant at the Society for the Scientific Study of Religion/Religious Research Association Annual Meeting, November 8, 1991, Pittsburgh, PA.
_____. "The Structure and Measurement of Humanistic Beliefs." Paper presented at the Society for the Scientific Study of Religion/Religious Research Association Annual Meeting, November 10, 1991, Pittsburgh, PA.

Casey, Thomas Michael

Present Position and Address: Chairperson, Department of Religious Studies, Merrimack College, North Andover, MA 01845, USA **Work Phone:** (508) 837-5188 **Home Phone:** (508) 685-6002 **Date of Birth:** May 30, 1939 **Languages Spoken:** English **Previous Positions:** Assistant Professor, Villanova University; Academic Vice President, Merrimack College, North Andover, MA **Selected Memberships:** College Theology Society; Society for the Scientific Study of Religion **Discipline:** Religious Studies; Psychology of Religion **Related Areas of Interest:** Religious Fundamentalism; Authority and Authoritarianism in Roman Catholicism **Current Areas of Research:** The problem of credibility within Roman Catholicism.

Selected Publications: His bibliography contains 1 book, 4 published articles and 2 book reviews.

_____. *Meaning in Myth*. Sheed and Ward, 1989.
_____. "Mariology and Christology." In *Death Comes for the Archbishop*. Willa Cather Pioneer Memorial Newsletter (Fall 1991).
_____. "Catholic Moral Theology: The Need for Reform." *Professional Approaches for Christian Educators* (January 1991).

Cauthen, W. Kenneth

Present Position and Address: John Price Crozer Griffith Professor of Theology Emeritus, Colgate Rochester Divinity School, Crozer Theological Seminary, 1100 South Goodman Street, Rochester, NY 14620; (Home) 46 Azalea Rd., Rochester, NY 14620, USA **Work Phone:** (716) 271-1320 **Home Phone:** (716) 461-9435 **Date of Birth:** March 10, 1930 **Education:** A.B. (1950), Mercer University; B.D. (1953), Yale Divinity School; M.A. (1955), Emory University; Ph.D. Theology (1959), Vanderbilt University **Postgraduate Experience:** Fellow (1966-67), Center for Advanced Studies in Theology and the Sciences, Chicago **Previous Positions:** Pastor (1953-55), Locust Grove Baptist Church, GA; Professor of Christian Ethics (1957-61), Mercer University; Professor of Theology (1961-present), Crozer Theological Seminary **Editorial Work:** Editorial Advisory Board, *Zygon* **Selected Memberships:** Board of Directors, Center for Advanced Studies in the Integration of Religion with the Sciences; Council Member, Institute on Religion in an Age of Science; World Future Society; American Academy of Religion **Discipline:** Theology **Related Interests:** Philosophy of Science; Science and the Concept of God and Nature.

Selected Publications: The bibliography lists 9 books, and over 30 articles and papers.

_____. "Science and Theology: From Orthodoxy to Neo-orthodoxy." *Zygon* (September 1966): 256-74.
_____. "Process and Purpose." *Zygon* (June 1968): 183-204.
_____. "The Case for Christian Biopolitics." *The Christian Century* (November 19, 1969): 1481-3.
_____. *Science, Secularization and God*. Nashville: Abingdon Press, 1969.
_____. "The Churches and the Future: A Utopian Proposal." *Zygon* (December 1971): 311-29.
_____. "Imaging the Future: New Visions and New Responsibilities." *Zygon* (September 1985): 321-39.
_____. *Theological Biology: A Case Study for a new Modernism*. Lewiston: The Edwin Mellen Press, 1991.

Chadha, N. K.

Present Position and Address: Assistant Professor (since 1981), Department of Psychology, University of Delhi, Delhi - 110007, India **Date of Birth:** April 16, 1952 **Education:** B.S.. (1972), Punjab University; M.S.. Mathematics (1974)/M.A. Philosophy (1976)/M.A. Psychology (1978)/M.Phil. Psychology (1979)/Ph.D. Psychology (1981), Delhi University **Discipline:** Psychology **Related Interests:** Reincarnation; ESP; Aging and Drug Abuse and Organizational Behavior.

Selected Publications: His bibliography lists 4 research articles.

_____, G. Gulati. "Anthropology and Parapsychology: A Convergence." *Spectra of Anthropological Progress* 9 (1987): 71-7.

Challice, Cyril Eugene

Present Position and Address: Professor Emeritus (since 1991), Physics Department, University of Calgary, 2500 University Drive N.W., Calgary, Alberta T2N 1N4, Canada; (Home) Box 659, Bragg Creek, Alberta T0L OKO, Canada **Concurrent Positions:** Coordinator of Inter-University Exchanges (1991 - present) **Date of Birth:** January 17, 1926 **Languages Spoken:** English, French **Education:** B.S.. Physics (1947)/Ph.D. Physics (1950)/D.Sc. Biophysics (1975), Imperial College, University of London **Previous Positions:** Biophysicist (1949-52), National Institute for Medical Research - London; Biophysicist (1952-57), Wright-Fleming Institute, London; Assistant Lecturer (1954-57), St. Mary's Hospital Medical School, London; Visiting Scientist (1956), Institute of Arthritis and Metabolic Diseases; Assistant Professor (1957-59)/Administrative Officer (1957-63)/Associate Professor (1959-63)/Professor (1963-91)/Department Head (1963-71), Physics Department, University of Calgary; Vice-Dean (1973-76), Faculty of Arts and Science, University of Calgary; Visiting Scientist (summers 1958, 59), New York State Department of Health, Albany, NY; Ordained Deacon (1980)/Priest (1981) and licensed as honorary assistant to Bishop at Cathedral Church of the Redeemer; Appointed Canon Residentiary (1987); Honorary Assistant, St. Mark's Episcopal Church, Calgary (1991 - present) **Selected Memberships:** Fellow (1959), New York Academy of Sciences; Fellow (1981), American Association for the Advancement of Science; Associate (1949)/Fellow (1956)/Chartered Physicist (1986), Institute of Physics; Alberta Society of Professional Engineers; Canadian Association of Physicists; Biophysical Society; American Society of Cell Biology; Sigma XI; Royal Institution of Great Britain; Society of Ordained Scientists **Discipline:** Biophysics; Ordained Priest **Related Interests:** Extension of Scientific Inquiry to Consider a Purpose, and Emphasis of this Element in Christian Theology.

Selected Publications:

_____. "Science and Religion." *Cathedral Parish Magazine* 62, 1 (Calgary, Alberta, 1965): 8.
_____. *The Challenge of Scientific Thought to Christian Theology*. Saskatoon, Saskatchewan: Rotunda, 1966.
_____. "Moral Questions Raised by Developing Science and Technology." In *Calgary Inter-Faith Community Action Committee, Proceedings of Inter-Faith Banff "Good Life Conference on Population, Biomedical Technology and Ethics,"* October 1973 ed. H. Zentner, 4-6. Calgary.
_____. "Atomic Energy"/"Nuclear Warfare." Two entries In *Encyclopedia of Biblical and Christian Ethics*, ed, R. K. Harrison and T. Nelson, 29-32, 279-81. Nashville Tennessee, 1987: .

Chase, Gene Barry

Present Position and Address: Professor of Mathematics and Computer Science (since 1985), Messiah College, Department of Mathematical Sciences, Messiah College, Grantham, PA 17027, USA; (Home) 115 Slover Road, Mechanicsburg, PA 17055, USA **Work Phone:** (717) 766-2511 **Home Phone:** (717) 766-7904 **Fax:** (717) 691-6002 **E-Mail:** chase@mcis.messiah.edu **Date of Birth:** November 22, 1943 **Education:** S.B. Mathematics (1965), Massachusetts Institute of Technology; M.A. Mathematical Logic (1970)/Ph.D. Mathematics Education, Curriculum and Instruction (1979), Cornell University; Summer Institute of Linguistics (Summers 1974-76): Gordon College (1974), University of Washington (1975), University of North Dakota (1976) **Previous Positions:** Grumman Aircraft Engineering Corporation (Summers 1961-65); Instructor in Mathematics, Houghton College (1966-67) and Wells College (1969-70); Computer consulting, Tangram VII firm (1971-1972);

Teaching Assistant (1965-73), Cornell University; Linguistic teacher, University of Washington (Summer 1979); Systems analyst/programmer (1982-83, and 1987-88), Summer Institute of Linguistics; Assistant (1973-79)/Associate Professor (1979-81), Mathematics, Messiah College; Associate (1981-85), Mathematics and Computer Science, Messiah College, PA **Selected Memberships:** American Association for Artificial Intelligence; Association for Computing Machinery; Association of Christians in the Mathematical Sciences **Discipline:** Mathematics and Computer Science **Related Interests:** Christianity and Mathematics; Artificial Intelligence.

Selected Publications: His bibliography lists over 35 publications or papers.

_____. "Skolem's paradox and the predestination/free-will discussion, A Christian Perspective on the Foundations of Mathematics." *Proceedings* (April 28-30, 1977).
_____, *Calvin Jongsma. Bibliography of Christianity and Mathematics: 1910-1983.* Dordt College Press, 1983.
_____. "Complementarity as a Christian philosophy of mathematics." In *The Reality of Christian Learning: Strategies for Faith-Discipline Integration*, ed. Harold Heie and David Wolfe. Eerdmans, 1987.
_____, editor. *A Seventh Conference on Mathematics from a Christian Perspective. Proceedings of the Biennial Conference of the Association of Christians in the Mathematical Sciences held at Messiah College, May 31- June 2, 1989.* Wheaton College Press, 1990.
_____. "How Has Christian Theology Furthered Mathematics." In *An Eighth Conference on Mathematics from a Christian Perspective - Proceedings of the biennial conference of the Association for Christians in the Mathematical Sciences held at Wheaton College, May 29 - June 1, 1991*, ed. Robert L. Brabenec. Revision to appear 1995, *Proceedings of the Conference on Science and Belief, August 1992, Redeemer College*, ed. Jitse van der Meer.
_____. "Programming Languages for Artificial Intelligence." In *Magill's Survey of Science: Physical Science*, 1943-1950. Salem Press, 1992.

Childs, Brian H.

Present Position and Address: Assistant Professor of Community Health (since 1985), Emory University School of Medicine, Atlanta, Georgia; Professor of Pastoral Theology Chair (since 1990), Practical Theology Area, Columbia Theological Seminary, Decatur, GA 30031; (Home) 433 Mimosa Drive, Decatur, GA 30030; (Work) Columbia Theological Seminary, Decatur, GA 30031, USA **Concurrent Positions:** Theologian in Residence, Project in Ethics and Interdisciplinary Care (1990-1991), Georgia Baptist Medical Center **Work Phone:** (404) 378-8821 **Home Phone:** (404) 371-8141 **Date of Birth:** January 25, 1947 **Education:** B.A. Philosophy (1969), Maryville College; M.Div. New Testament (1972)/Th.M. New Testament (1973)/Ph.D. (*cum laude*, 1981), Princeton Theological Seminary **Postgraduate Studies:** Non-Degree Programs: Certificate in Family Psychotherapy (1974-1976), Trinity Counseling Service/Nathan W. Ackerman Family Institute **Field Work:** Pastoral Counseling Training Program (1974-1977), Trinity Counseling Service; Basic Quarter C.P.E. (Summer 1973), Medical Center at Princeton **Previous Positions:** Project in Thanatology (1977-81); Supervisor - S.T.M. in Pastoral Care (1979-1981), New York Theological Seminary; Director, Advanced Pastoral Studies (1981-1985), Trinity Counseling Service; Lecturer in Pastoral Theology (1983-1985), Princeton Theological Seminary; Adjunct Professor of Pastoral Theology and Codirector of Th.M. in Pastoral Counseling (1984-1985), New Brunswick Theological Seminary; Visiting Guest Professor of Pastoral Theology (1984-1985), Moravian Theological Seminary, Bethlehem PA; Associate Professor of Pastoral Theology (1985-1990), Columbia Theological Seminary, Decatur GA **Editorial Work:** Current Editorial Boards: *The Journal of Pastoral Care, The Journal of Medical Humanities, Bioethics Forum;* Manuscript Consultant, Hospital and Community Psychiatry **Selected Memberships:** Founding member (June 1985), The Society for Pastoral Theology; Clinical member, American Association of Marriage and Family Therapists; Charter member, American Family Therapy Association; Association for Clinical Pastoral Education; Society for Health and Human Values; Institute on Religion in an Age of Science; American Academy of Religion; Fellow, Institute for Medicine and the Humanities (The National Endowment for the Humanities), (1991-92); Fellow, The Center for Medicine, Literature, and the Health Care Professions, Seminar in Narrative Bioethics (1993) **Discipline:** Clinical and Pastoral Counseling, Family Therapy and Community Health **Related Areas of Interest:** Religion and Human Psychology; Bioethics.

Selected Publications:

_____. "The Possible Connection Between Prayer and Private Speech." *Pastoral Psychology* (Autumn 1983).

_____, Seward Hiltner. "Religious Pathology Vs. Genuine Spiritual Experience." In *The Continuing Education Library*. Belle Meade, NJ: The Carrier Foundation, 1984.

_____. "Experience." In *Dictionary of Pastoral Care and Counseling*, ed. Rodney J. Hunter. Abingdon Press, 1990.

_____. "Homosexuality, Contemporary Theological Ethics, and AIDS." *Bioethics Forum* 9, 2 (1993).

_____. "Writing Into the Lives of Patients." *Report from the Center* (The Center for Medicine, Literature, and the Health Care Professions) 2, 1 (1993).

_____, David Waanders. *The Treasure of Earthen Vessels: Exploration in Theological Anthropology.* Westminster/John Knox Press, 1994.

_____. "In Life and Death We Belong to God: Physician Assisted Suicide and Euthanasia." A Study Document of General Assembly, Presbyterian Church (USA), 1994.

Chirico-Rosenberg, Donna

Present Position and Address: Lecturer in Psychology, York College, CUNY, 94 - 20 Guy Brewer Boulevard, Jamaica, NY 11451, USA **Work Phone:** (718) 262-2687 **E-Mail:** rosenberg@ycvax.york.cuny.edu **Date of Birth:** February 26, 1956 **Languages Spoken:** English, French **Education:** B.A. Psychology (1979), York College, CUNY; M.S. Counseling (1980), Fordham University Graduate School of Education at Lincoln Center, NYC **Field Work:** Research in the Himalayan Province of Ladakh, India which was formerly a part of Tibet **Awards and Honors:** Phi Delta Kappa, Fordham University; Psi Chi, York College; *Who's Who Among Italian Americans*; *Italian American Scholars and Professionals in Universities and Colleges: New York, New Jersey and Connecticut* **Previous Positions:** Music Teacher (1980-81), St. Nicholas of Tolentine Elementary School; Psychometrician (1980-82), Institute for Behavioral Change; Psychometrician (1980-84), Brooklyn Therapy and Counseling Service; Consulting Psychologist/Special Projects Coordinator (1989-91), School of Law at Queens College, Community Advocacy Center, CUNY, NY; Adjunct Lecturer in Psychology (1980-91), York College, CUNY, NY **Editorial Positions:** Editorial Consultant, McGraw Hill Book Company/College Division (1987-90); Book Reviewer, *Journal for the Scientific Study of Religion*; Editor, *The Legal Awareness Bulletin* **Administrative Experience:** Jewish Student Union and the Jewish Campus Life Fund, Inc, Columbia University Jewish Office (1991- 93) **Selected Memberships:** Society for the Scientific Study of Religion; American - Italian Historical Association **Discipline:** Psychology **Related Areas of Interest:** Religious Development; Moral/Ethical Development **Current Areas of Research:** Cross - Cultural Study of Religious Affiliation; Level of Involvement and Ethical Behavior.

Selected Publications: Her bibliography contains 3 published articles and 12 papers presented.

_____, Uwe P. Gielen, Stuart Dick, Sidney Rosenberg and Frank Cheafettelli. "Naturalistic Observation of Sex and Race Difference in Visual Interaction." *International Journal of Group Tension* 1-4, (1979): 211-27.

_____, Uwe P. Gielen. *A Helping Hand for the Psychology Major: The Student Handbook. Teaching of Psychology* 7, 4 (1980).

_____. "Cross - Cultural Aspects of Aging: Socio-Moral and Religious Thinking in Buddhist Ladakh." Paper presented at the Institute for Cross - Cultural and Cross - Ethnic Studies, Molloy College, March 20, 1982.

_____. "Development of Socio - Moral and Religious Thinking in Buddhist Ladakh." Paper presented at the Divisional Colloquium, Teacher's College - Columbia University, October 16, 1982.

_____. "Buddhist Ladakh: Psychological Portrait of a Nonviolent Culture." Paper presented at the annual conference of the Society for Cross - Cultural Research, Washington, DC, February 21, 1983. Cited in "Cross -

Cultural Universality of Social - Moral Development: A Critical Review of Kohlbergian Research," by John R. Snarey. *Psychological Bulletin* 97, 2 (1985): 202-32.

_____. "Jungian Perspectives in Buddhist Symbolism." Paper presented at the Ethical Cultural Society of Queens, January 20, 1985.

_____. "The Status of Women in Eastern Religions." Paper presented as part of National Women's History Month festivities; sponsored by the Women's Center of York College, March 26, 1991.

_____. "Reauthorizing the Older Americans Act." Panel Moderator, presented as part of the Preventive Law Community Fair Day; Sponsored by the CUNY School of Law, May 3, 1991.

_____, Uwe P. Gielen. "Traditional Buddhist Ladakh and the Ethos of Peace." *International Journal of Group Tensions* 23, 1 (1993).

Clark, Kelly James

Present Position and Address: Associate Professor of Philosophy, Calvin College Department of Philosophy, Calvin College, Grand Rapids, MI 49546, USA **Work Phone:** (616) 957-6421 **Date of Birth:** March 3, 1956 **Education:** B.A. (with honors) Philosophy and Religious Studies (1978), Michigan State University; M.A. (with honors) Humanities (1980), Western Kentucky University; M.A. History and Philosophy of Science (1983), University of Notre Dame; Ph.D. Philosophy (1985), University of Notre Dame **Awards and Honors:** Recipient of CAPHE Grant for research on Spanish Common Sense Philosophy in Spain (Summer 1988) **Previous Positions:** Teaching Assistant (1982-83/84-85), University of Notre Dame; Lecturer, Gordon College's European Seminar (Summers 1986,87); Assistant Professor of Philosophy (1985-1989), Gordon College **Discipline:** Philosophy. Areas of specialization are Epistemology and Philosophy of Religion. Areas of competence are Philosophy of Science and History of Science.

Selected Publications: His bibliography lists 3 books and 12 articles and papers.

_____. "Probabilistic Confirmation Theory and the Existence of God." Ph.D. diss., written under Alvin Plantinga, University of Notre Dame, 1985.

_____. "The Religious and Philosophical Views of Sir William Herschel." *Astronomy Quarterly* 6, 21 (1988): 27-43.

_____. "The Explanatory Power of Theism." *International Journal for Philosophy of Religion* 25 (1989): 129-46.

_____. "Proofs of God's Existence." *The Journal of Religion* 69, 1 (1989): 59-84.

_____. "Spanish Common Sense Philosophy: Jaime Balmes' Critique of Cartesian Foundationalism." *History of Philosophy Quarterly* 7, 2 (1990): 207-26.

_____. Return to Reason. Grand Rapids: Eerdmans, 1990.

_____, editor. Our Knowledge of God: Essays on Natural and Philosophical Theology. Dordrecht, The Netherlands: Kluwer Academic Publishers, 1992.

_____, editor. Philosophers Who Believe. Downers Grove, Il: InterVarsity Press, 1993.

Clarke, Christopher James Seaton

Present Position and Address: Professor of Applied Mathematics, University of Southampton, UK; Faculty of Mathematical Studies, University of Southampton, Southampton SO17 1BJ, UK **Work Phone:** +44 703 593685 **Date of Birth:** February 22, 1946 **Languages Spoken:** English, German **Education:** B.A. (first class), mathematics (1966)/Part III (with distinction) mathematics tripos (1967)/Ph.D., research under D. W. Sciama, "Global aspects of general relativity" (1970), Christ's College, University of Cambridge **Postgraduate Studies:** Postdoctoral junior research fellow **Previous Positions:** Lecturer in Mathematics (1974-85)/Senior Lecturer (1985-86), University of York **Editorial Work:** Editorial board until 1983, J. Phys. A; Editorial board (1988-92), Classical and Quantum Gravity **Selected Memberships:** Scientific and Medical Network; Member, Church of

England **Discipline:** Quantum Theory, Cosmology, Creation Centered Spirituality **Current Research:** Shock waves in general relativity; Numerical Relativity; Physics of Consciousness.

Selected Publications: His bibliography lists over 50 papers or articles.

_____. "Eternal Life." *Theoria to Theory* 8 (1974): 317-32.
_____. "On Physics and Mysticism." *Theoria to Theory* 14 (1981): 333-7.
_____, F. de Felice. *Relativity on Curved Manifolds*. Cambridge University Press: 1992.
_____. *Space Time Singularities*. Cambridge University Press: 1994.
Nunn, C. M. H., Christopher J. S. Clarke, and B. H. Blott. "Collapse of a Quantum Field May Affect Consciousness." *Journal of Consciousness Studies* 1 (1994): 127-39.

Clayton, Philip

Present Position and Address: Assistant Professor (since 1988), Philosophy Department, Williams College, Williamstown, MA 01267, USA; (Home) 51 Stetson Court, Williamstown, MA 01267, USA **Work Phone:** (413) 597-2138 **Home Phone:** (413) 458-9314 **Date of Birth:** April 3, 1956 **Education:** B.A. Philosophy (1978), Westmont College; M.A. Theology (1980), Fuller Seminary; Studied philosophy and theology, University of Munich (1981-83); M.A. (1984)/M.Phil (1985)/Ph.D. (1986), Philosophy and Religious Studies (1984-1986), Yale University **Awards and Honors:** Senior Fulbright Professor (1990-1991), University of Munich, Germany **Previous Positions:** Teaching Assistant (1984-85), Yale University; Visiting Assistant Professor (Spring 1986), Haverford College **Discipline:** Areas of specialization are Metaphysics (Contemporary Analytic and History of), and Philosophy of Religion. Areas of competence are History of (Modern) Philosophy, Epistemology, Hermenutics, Philosophy of Science (especially Social Science), Contemporary Continental Philosophy.

Selected Publications: His bibliography lists 3 books, and 19 articles, papers or translations.

_____. "Imre Lakatos and Theological Method." Paper presented in the Theology and Religious Reflection Section, American Academy of Religion annual meeting, Chicago November 22, 1988.
_____, Carl Braaten, eds. *The Theology of Wolfhart Pannenberg: Twelve American Critiques*. Minneapolis: Augsburg Press, 1988.
_____. *Explanation from Physics to Theology: An Essay in Rationality and Religion*. New Haven: Yale University Press, 1989.
_____. "Disciplining Relativism and Truth." *Zygon* 24, 3 (1989): 315-34.
_____. "Religious Truth and Scientific Truth." In *Phenomenology of the Truth Proper to Religion: An Anthology*, ed. Daniel Guerrière. Albany, NY: SUNY Press, 1990.
_____. "Toward a Pluralistic Metaphysics: Models of God in Early Modern Philosophy." (in progress)

Clifton, Robert K.

Present Position and Address: Assistant Professor in Philosophy of Science, Department of Philosophy, Talbot College, University of Western Ontario, London, Ontario, Canada **Work Phone:** (519) 661-3453, ext 5750 **Fax:** (519) 661-3922 **E-Mail:** RCLIFTON@UWOVAX.UWO.CA **Date of Birth:** July 11, 1964 **Education:** Hons.B.Sc. Theoretical Physics (1982-86), University of Waterloo; Ph.D. Philosophy of Physics (1991), Cambridge University **Selected Memberships:** Member (1986), The Canadian Scientific and Christian Affiliation; Member (1987), The Philosophy of Science Association; Member (1987), The British Society for the Philosophy of Science; Fellow (1987), The Cambridge Philosophical Society; Member (1988), The Royal Institute of Philosophy; Member (1988), The American Philosophical Association **Discipline:** History and Philosophy of Science **Related Interests:** Modern Physics; Philosophy of Religion.

Selected Publications:

_____, M. G. Regehr. "Toward a Sound Perspective on Modern Physics: Capra's Popularization of Mysticism and Theological Approaches Re-Examined." *Zygon* 25 (1989): 73-104.

_____, M. G. Regehr. "Capra on Eastern Mysticism and Modern Physics: A Critique." *Science and Christian Belief* 1 (1989): 53-74.

_____. "Discussion Review: The Anthropic Cosmological Principle." *Science and Christian Belief* 1 (1990): 41-6.

_____. "Discussion Review: J. Leslie's Universes." *Philosophical Quarterly* (1991).

Cloots, André

Present Position and Address: Associate Professor in Philosophy, Katholieke Universiteit Leuven, Belgium Hoger Instituut voor Wijsbegeerte, Kard. Mercierplein 2 B-3000 Leuven, Belgium **Date of Birth:** November 22, 1948 **Languages Spoken:** Dutch, English, French **Education:** M.A. Philosophy (1972)/Ph.D. Philosophy (1978), Katholieke Universiteit Leuven, Belgium. **Postgraduate Studies:** Fellowships: CRB-Fellowship (1975), Belgian American Educational Foundation **Discipline:** Metaphysics, Philosophical Theology, Philosophy of Science **Related Interests:** Process philosophy; Evolutionary Theory; the Relations between Philosophy, Religion and Science.

Selected Publications:

_____. "The Poet of the World, The Affirmation of God in Whitehead's Philosophy." *Louvain Studies* 7, 2 (1978): 91-101.

_____. "De vraag naar het Ultieme in de proces-filosofie (The quest of the ultimate in process philosophy)." *Tijdschrift voor Filosofie* 42, 1 (1980): 48-74.

_____. "De vossen en de goden. Rede en cultuur in het denken van Whitehead (Reason and culture in the thought of Whitehead)." *Wijsgerig Perspectief op Maatschappij en Wetenschap* 25, 4 (1984-5): 114-18.

_____, J. Van der Veken. "Can the God of Process-Thought be Redeemed?" In *Charles Hartshorne's Concept of God, Philosophical and Theological Responses*, ed. S. Sia. Dordrecht: Kluwer Academic Publishers, 1990.

_____, ed. *Whitehead en de Religie (Whitehead and Religion)*. Leuven: Peeters, 1990.

_____. "Een Huis Waarin de Geest Kan Wonen. Over Metafysica Vandaag (A house in which the spirit can live. On Metaphysics Today)." In *Existentie en zin - Geloof en Utopie,* ed L. Braeckmans, P. Reynaert. Leuven: Acco, 1991.

_____. ed. God en de Wetenschap. Gerard Bodifee en Christoffel Waelkens in Samenspraak met Andre Cloots (God and science)." *Kultuurleven*. 59, 5. 1992.

_____. "Snijdt het Kosmologische Argument Nog Hout (Is the cosmological argument still valid)?" *Collationes* 24, 2 (1994): 133-55.

Cobb, Jr., John B.

Present Position and Address: Professor of Theology (since 1958), School of Theology at Claremont, CA; School of Theology at Claremont, 1009 N. College Avenue, Claremont, CA 91711, USA **Date of Birth:** February 9, 1925 **Education:** (1941-43), Emory at Oxford, GA; (1943), University of Michigan; M.A. (1949)/Ph.D. Systematic Theology (1952), University of Chicago **Honorary Degrees:** D. Theology (1967), University of Mainz; D.Litt. (1971), Emory University **Previous Positions:** Teacher (1950-53), Young Harris College; Assistant Professor (1953-58), Emory University **Selected Memberships:** Director, Center for Process Studies; Member Advisory Board, Center for Theology and the Natural Sciences **Discipline:** Systematic Theology **Related Interests:** Whitehead's philosophy; Ecology; Theology and the Sciences.

Selected Publications:

_____. *Is It Too Late? A Theology of Ecology.* New York: Bruce, 1972.

_____, David Griffin. *Mind in Nature: Essays in the Interface of Science and Philosophy*. University Press of America, 1977. Primarily on evolutionary theory.

_____, Charles Birch. *The Liberation of Life: from the Cell to the Community*. Cambridge University Press, 1982.

_____. "Whitehead and Natural Philosophy." In *Whitehead and the Idea of Progress*, ed. Harold Holz and Wolf-Gazo. Freiburg/München: Karl Alber Verlag, 1984.

_____. "Bohm and Time." In *Physics and the Ultimate Significance of Time*, ed. David Griffin. Albany: SUNY, 1986.

_____. "Bohm's Challenge to Faith in Our Time." In *Beyond Mechanism*, ed. David Schindler. Lanham, MD: University Press of America, 1986.

_____. "A Christian View of Biodiversity." In *Biodiversity*, ed. E. O. Wilson. Washington, DC: National Academy Press, 1988.

Cohen, Ernest B.

Present Position and Address: Technical Director (since 1975), Technical Industries Prediction Service (TIPS), Upper Darby, PA; 525 Midvale Avenue, Upper Darby, PA 19082, USA **Date of Birth:** June 16, 1932 **Education:** A.B. Mathematics and Physics (1953)/M.A. Psychology and Industrial Engineering (1955), Cornell University; M.S. Engineering, Computers (1965)/Ph.D. Systems Engineering and Operations Research (1969), University of Pennsylvania **Previous Positions:** Systems Engineer (1962-79), General Electric Company, Space Divisions, Philadelphia, PA; Senior Management Scientist/Operations Research Analyst (1970-73), Atlantic-Richfield Company, Philadelphia, PA; Consulting Engineer (1973-75), United Engineers and Constructors, Inc., Philadelphia, PA; Scientific Advisor to Congressman Robert W. Edgar (1974-86); Department of Environmental Protection, State of New Jersey, Trenton (1976-79); Delaware Valley Citizen's League (1981), Transportation Study Group; Associate Professor of Electrical Engineering (1982-83), Wilkes College, PA; Developing the Family-Community Movement, an experimental project in synthesizing a sub-culture for the world of modern technology **Other Academic Experience:** Registered Professional Engineer (PA and NJ); Institute of Electrical and Electronic Engineers (IEEE) **Selected Memberships:** American Association for the Advancement of Sciences (AAAS); Philadelphia Futurists; Mayor's Science and Technology Advisory Council (M-STAC), Chair of subcommittee on Abandoned Housing; Seventh Congressional District Energy Advisory Committee, Chair of subcommittee on Coal, Nuclear, and the Environment; Temple Israel of Upper Darby; Beverly Hills Civic Association, board member **Discipline:** Engineering, Technology and Community **Related Interests:** Goals and Interests: Synthesizing a better society for the age of technology and limited resources by applying social science with the implicit assumption that the Creator would like us humans to serve as stewards for Planet Earth (the cofounder of Kehillat Mishpakhot, meaning "Community of Families"); The Role of Religion in Family-community; Meta-religious Concepts; Ethics and Technology; Guided Evolution; Systems Approach to Social Ethics.

Selected Publications: His bibliography lists 25 papers and publications.

_____. "Ethics and Technology." *Reconstructionist* 36, 6 (1970).

_____. "The Tower of Babel Revisited." *Reconstructionist* 37, 10 (1972).

_____. "A Systems Approach to Social Ethics." *Reconstructionist* 40, 3 (1974).

_____. *Reduction in Force*. Unpublished novel dealing with the social consequences of technology (1976).

_____. "Guided Evolution." Paper presented to the Philadelphia Futurists (1980).

Cole-Turner, Ronald

Present Position and Address: Associate Professor of Theology, Memphis Theological Seminary, 168 East Parkway South, Memphis, TN 38104, USA **Work Phone:** (901) 458-8232 **Home Phone:** (901) 684-1963 **Fax Number:** (901) 452-4051 **Date of Birth:** December 22, 1948 **Languages Spoken:**

English **Awards and Honors:** Winner (1992), John Templeton Foundation Call for Papers in the Theology of Humility; Award of Honorable Mention (second Place) for excellence in religious journalism (1992), Associated Church Press for "Theological Care in a Technological Context" (1991) **Previous Positions:** Pastor (1974-77), First Congregational Church, Fulton, NY; Pastor (1979-82), Malden Road United Church of Christ, Syracuse, NY; Campus Minister (1982-85), Michigan Technological University; Assistant through Associate Professor (since 1985), Memphis Theological Seminary, Memphis, TN **Selected Memberships:** American Association for the Advancement of Science; American Academy of Religion; Center for Theology and the Natural Sciences; Institute on Religion in an Age of Science **Discipline:** Systematic Theology; Theological Ethics **Related Areas of Interest:** Theological Implications of Human Genetics and Neuroscience; Relating the Institutional Church to Science and Technology **Current Areas of Research:** Theological and Pastoral Implications of Prenatal Genetic Screening; Theological Implications of Neuroscience and Psychopharmacology.

Selected Publications:

_____. "Is Genetic Engineering Co-Creation?" *Theology Today* 44 (October 1987): 338-49.
_____. "Genetic Engineering: Our Role in Creation." In *The New Faith - Science Debate*, ed. John M. Mangum. Minneapolis: Fortress Press, 1989. Originally presented at an international consultation convened by the Lutheran Church in America, Larnaca, Cyprus, December, 1987.
_____. "Science, Technology and the Education of Religious Professionals." Paper presented at the American Association for the Advancement of Science, New Orleans, February, 1990. *Bulletin of the Center for Theology and the Natural Sciences* (Winter 1991).
_____. "Genetics and the Church." *Prism* 6, 1 (1991): 53-61.
_____. "Just War and the Gulf War." *Memphis Theological Seminary Journal* 29 (1992).
_____. *An Unavoidable Challenge: Our Church in the Midst of Science and Technology.* Cleveland, OH: United Church Board for Homeland Ministries, 1992. A position paper circulated throughout the United Church of Christ in January, 1992.
_____. "Religion and the Human Genome." *Journal of Religion and Health* 31, 2 (1992): 161-73.
_____. *The New Genesis: Theology and the Genetic Revolution.* Louisville, KY: Westminster/John Knox Press, 1993.
_____. "Genetics and the Pastor." *Dialog* 33, 1 (1994): 49-53.
_____. "The Genetics of Moral Agency." In *The Genetic Frontier: Ethics, Law, and Policy*, ed. Mark S. Frankel and Robert H. Teich. Washington, DC: AAAS, 1994.

Collins, Gary R.

Present Position and Address: Executive Director (since 1991), American Association of Christian Counselors, 20720 N. Meadows Ct., Kildeer, IL 60047, USA **Date of Birth:** October 22, 1934 **Education:** B.A. (1956), McMaster University; M.A. Psychology (1958), University of Toronto; Ph.D. Clinical Psychology (1963), Purdue University. Other Selected Courses: University of London; Western Baptist Seminary **Previous Positions:** Teaching Assistant (1956-58), University of Toronto; Instructor in Psychology (1958-59), University of Maryland Overseas; Teaching Assistant (1959-62), Purdue University; Predoctoral Clinical Psychology Internship (1962-63), University of Oregon Medical School; Counselor, Portland State University (1963-64); Associate Professor of Psychology/Chairman (1964-68), Bethel College, St. Paul, MN; Professor of Pastoral Psychology (1968-69), Conwell School of Theology; Division Chairman(1969-83)/Professor of Psychology (1969-89), Trinity Evangelical Divinity School; Professor of Psychology (1989-90), Liberty University, Lynchburg, VA **Editorial Work:** Editor, *Christian Counseling Today*; Contributing Editor: *Journal of Psychology and Theology*; *Journal of the American Scientific Affiliation* **Selected Memberships:** American Psychological Association; American Scientific Affiliation (National President 1974) **Discipline:** Clinical Psychology **Related Interests:** Counseling Psychology; The integration of Psychology and Theology.

Selected Publications: He has published over 125 articles and 40 books, and is general editor of Word, Inc. "Resources for Christian Counseling" - A series of 30 professional counseling books, published between 1986-90; "Christian Counselor's Library" - A series of 35 cassette tapes with written materials to aid counselors; "Christian Counseling Newsletter" - A monthly newsletter with a current circulation of about 6,000. Books include

_____. *The Rebuilding of Psychology: An Integration of Psychology and Theology.* Tyndale, 1977.
_____. *Christian Counseling: A Comprehensive Guide.* Rev. Ed. Word, 1988.
_____. The Biblical Basis of Christian Counselors for People Helpers. NavPress. 1993.

Colzani, Gianni

Present Position and Address: Lecturer (since 1983), Catholic University of Milan, Via E. Kant 8, 20151 Milano, Italy **Concurrent Positions:** Professor of Theoretical Theology (since 1964), Seminary of Milan (since 1978), Istituto Superiore di Scienze Religiose of Milan (since 1988), Instituto Pastorale Lombardo of Milan: (since 1988), Theological University of Florence (since 1992) **Work Phone:** 02/33401641 **Fax:** 02/33401641 **Date of Birth:** July 31, 1940 **Languages Spoken:** Italian, English, French, German **Education:** Bachelorship (1962); Licenza (1964); Doctor of Divinity (1971), Pontificia Facultas Theologica Mediolanensis, Italy **Previous Positions:** Theological Seminary of the Pontifical Institute for Foreign Missions (1987-92) **Discipline:** Theoretical Theology **Related Interests:** Theological Anthropology; Ecclesiological, Eschatological Reflection.

Selected Publications: His bibliography lists 7 books and several articles.

_____. Antropologia Teologica. L'uomo Paradosso e Mistero. Edizioni Dehoniane. Bologna, 1988.
_____. Antropologia Cristiana. Il dono e La Responsabilita. Ed. Primme. Casale Monferrato. 1991.
_____. "L'immagine Del Sacerdote." In Italia Cattolica Fede e Pratica Religiosa Negli Anni Novanta, ed. Vallecchi, 240-52. Firenze. 1991.
_____. "Recenti Manuali di Antropologia Teologica di Lingua Italiana e Tedesca." Vivens Homo. 3 (1992):391-407.

Combs, Allan L.

Present Position and Address: Professor (since 1982), Department of Psychology, University of North Carolina - Asheville, One University Heights, Asheville, NC 28804-3299, USA **Education:** B.S. Psychology (1964), Ohio State University; MRC Counseling (1967), University of Florida; M.S. Psychology (1969)/Ph.D. Biopsychology (1974), University of Georgia **Previous Positions:** Earlham College (1972-1973); Missouri Southern State College (1973-1982) **Selected Memberships:** Association of Transpersonal Psychology; Hermetic Academy; Washington Evolutionary Systems Society; General Evolution Research Group Society for Chaos Theory in Psychology **Discipline:** Psychology **Related Interests:** Myth, Science, Transpersonal Psychology, Philosophy of Science, Hermeneutics, Systems Theory, Evolution.

Selected Publications: His bibliography lists 7 books, 8 chapters, and over 40 articles and papers. He is book review editor of *World Futures: The Journal of General Evolution.*

_____. *The Radiance of Being: Chaos, Evolution, and Consciousness.* Floris Books 1993-94.
_____, E. Laszlo and C. Vilmos. *The Evolution of Cognitive Maps: New Paradigms for the Twenty First Century.* Philadelphia: Gordon and Breach, 1993.
_____, ed. *Cooperation: Beyond the Age of Competition.* Philadelphia: Gordon and Breach, 1992.
_____, M. Holland. *Synchronicity: Science, Myth and the Trickster.* New York: Paragon House, 1990.

Conrad, Constance C.

Present Position and Address: Professor of Preventive Medicine and Community Health (since 1978); Department of Community Health, Emory University School of Medicine, 1599 Clifton Road N.E., Atlanta, GA 30329, USA; Clinical Professor of Community Health and Preventive Medicine (since 1988), Morehouse School of Medicine, Atlanta, GA; (Home) 1069 Burton Drive N.E., Atlanta, GA 30329, USA **Work Phone:** (404) 727-7805 **Home Phone:** (404) 636-3902 **Date of Birth:** June 30, 1936 **Education:** M.D. (1961), School of Medicine, George Washington University, Washington, DC; M.P.H. (1965), School of Public Health, Harvard University. Currently busy with M.T.S., Candler School of Theology, Atlanta, GA **Awards and Honors:** Myki Mobley Award (1990), Candler School of Theology **Previous Positions:** Physician in Nigeria in various capacities (1962-64); Family Planning (1966-73), Emory University Family Planning Program, Atlanta, GA; Associate Director through Director (1974-82), Master of Community Health Program, Emory University School of Medicine; Clinical Instructor through Assistant Professor, OB/GYN (1966-75)/Assistant Professor (1974-78), Preventive Medicine and Community Health, Emory University School of Medicine, Atlanta, GA; Symposium Coordinator (1988-89), for National Church Leaders Conference on Health, Carter Center of Emory University; Planning Committee, Intensive Colloquy on Ethics for Religious Leaders (1990), University of Virginia **Selected Memberships:** American/Georgia Public Health Associations; Fellow, American College of Preventive Medicine; Association of Teachers of Preventive Medicine; American Medical Writers' Association **Discipline:** Preventive Medicine and Public Health **Related Interests:** Developing a dual degree program (Master of Public Health/Master of Theological Studies) that will bring together competency in Health Science and Theology; Policy and Ethical Issues Relating to the Church and Public Health; Collecting Models of Church-based, Health Related Programs and Activities.

Selected Publications: Her bibliography lists 38 articles and 4 exhibits..

_____. "Biomedical Ethics: Unique Issues for Preventive Medicine - Introduction." *Biomedical Ethics: Unique Issues for Preventive Medicine* (1982).
_____, M. Stoto, M. L. Straf, C. Conrad, and T. P. Stossel. "Ethics and Policy in Scientific Publication." *Abstracts of Addresses, ASM News* 55 (1989): 2-3.

Cook, Sir Alan Hugh

Present Position and Address: Professor Emeritus of Natural Philosophy (since 1990), Cambridge, UK; Master of Selwyn College, Cambridge, UK, (to 1993); 8 Wootton Way, Cambridge CB3 9LX, UK **Date of Birth:** December 2, 1922 **Education:** B.A. (1943)/M.A. (1947)/Ph.D. (1950)/Sc.D. (1967), Corpus Christi College, Cambridge, UK **Awards and Honors:** Knight Bachelor (1988); Institute of Physics: CV Boys Prize; Charles Chree Medal and Prize (1993) **Previous Positions:** Senior Principal Scientific Officer (1952-1966), National Physical Laboratory; Superintendent (1966-1969), Division of Quantum Metrology, National Physical Laboratory, UK; Professor of Geophysics (1969-1972), University of Edinburgh; Professor of Natural Philosophy (1972-1990), University of Cambridge; Visiting Fellow (1965-66), JT Institute of Astrophysics, University of Colorado; Visiting Professor (1981-82), University of California; Member (Fall 1993), Center for Theological Inquiry, Princeton, NJ **Selected Memberships:** Fellow Royal Society (FRS); Fellow Royal Society of Edinburgh (FRSE); Past President, Royal Astronomical Society; Socio Straniero, Academy Naz. Lincei (Rome); F. Inst. P.; Explorer's Club of New York **Discipline:** Physics; Geophysics, Astronomy **Related Interests:** History and Philosophy of Science.

Selected Publications: His bibliography lists many articles on physics, Earth science, and history of science. He lists eight books as follows:.

_____. *Gravity and the Earth.* 1969.
_____. *Interference of Electromagnetic Waves.* 1971.
_____. *Physics of the Earth and Plants.* 1973.
_____. *Celestial Masers.* 1977.
_____. *Interiors of the Plants.* 1980.
_____. *The Motion of the Moon.* 1988.
_____, Y.T. Chen. *Gravitational Experiments in the Laboratory.* 1993.
_____. *The Observational Foundations of Physics.* N.p., 1994.

Copenhaver, Brian P.

Present Position and Address: Provost, College of Letters and Sciences/Professor, History and Philosophy (since 1988), University of California - Riverside, Los Angeles, CA 92521, USA **Date of Birth:** December 21, 1942 **Languages Spoken:** English, French **Education:** A.B. (1964), Loyola College, Baltimore; M.A. (1966), Creighton University; Fulbright Scholar (1968-69), Université de Lyon, France; Ph.D. (1970), University of Kansas. **Previous Positions:** Assistant Instructor (1966-70), University of Kansas; Assistant (1971-74)/Associate Professor of General Studies (1975-77)/Professor of Liberal Studies (1978-81)/Director of Honors Program (1974-80)/Associate Dean, College of Arts and Sciences (1977-81), Western Washington University; Professor of History/Dean of College of Arts and Sciences (1981-88), Oakland University **Selected Memberships:** History of Science Society; American Society for Church History; Society for the History of Alchemy and Chemistry; Sigma Xi **Discipline:** History and Philosophy **Related Interests:** History of Science, with Particular Interest in 16-17th Century Focus on Occultism, Hermeticism and Magic and Their Relationship to the Rise of Modern Science, Philosophy and Theology.

Selected Publications: His bibliography lists 6 books, 28 articles, 23 reviews and 25 papers.

_____. *Symphorien Champier and the Reception of the Occultist Tradition in Renaissance France.* The Hague: Mouton, 1978.
_____. Essay Review of *Hermeticism and the Scientific Revolution* by R. S. Westman and J. E. McGuire. *Annals of Science* 35 (1978): 527-31.
_____. "William Mewe's Pseudomagia and the Reputation of the Occultist Tradition in Early Seventeenth Century England." In *Acta Conventus Neo-Latini Turonensis*, ed. J. C. Margolin. Paris: 1980.
_____. "Jewish Theologies of Space in the Scientific Revolution: Henry More, Joseph Raphson, Isaac Newton and their Predecessors." *Annals of Science* 37 (1980): 193-214.
_____. "Science and Philosophy in Early Modern Europe: The Historiographical Significance of the Work of Charles B. Schmitt." *Annals of Science* 44 (1987): 507-17.
_____. *Hermetica, A New English Translation of the Greek Corpus Hermeticum and the Latin Asciepius.* Cambridge University Press. 1992.
_____, C. Schmidt. *Renaissance Philosophy.* Oxford University Press. 1992.
_____. "Natural Magic, Hermetism and Occultism in Early Modern Science." In *Reappraisals of the Scientific Revolution*, ed. David Lindberg and Robert Westman. Westman, Cambridge University Press, forthcoming.

Copestake, David R.

Present Position and Address: Retired on health grounds 22 Meadow View, Banbury, Oxon, OX16 9SR, UK **Date of Birth:** March 12, 1940 **Education:** B.D. (1963)/B.A. Psychology (1980), University of London; M.Phil. (1967), University of Leeds **Previous Positions:** Industry (5 years); Methodist minister (10 years); Director and founder, the Friends of Jesus (youth care organization) **Selected Memberships:** Institute on Religion in an Age of Science; Society Scientific Study of Religion

Discipline: Theology; Psychology **Related Areas of Interest:** Psychology and Modern Theology and their Relation to Science **Current Research:** "I am now running a project, "Christian Faith for the Scientific Age," mainly to produce literature. My student contact in London is my eldest son Stephen Westey Copestake.

Selected Publications:

_____, H. Newton Maloney. "Adverse Effects of Charismatic Experiences: A Reconsideration." *Journal of Psychology and Christianity* 12, 3 (1993): 236-44.

Corbally, Christopher J.

Present Position and Address: Research Astronomer of the Vatican Observatory (since 1983), Vatican City State; Vice Director of VORG, Tucson, AZ; Vatican Observatory Research Group, Steward Observatory, University of Arizona, Tucson, AZ 85721, USA **Work Phone:** (602) 621-3225 **Fax:** (602) 621-1532 **E-Mail:** CORBALLY@AS.ARIZONA.EDU **Date of Birth:** January 24, 1946 **Education:** Licentiate, Philosophy (1968), Heythrop Pontifical Athenaeum, Oxon, UK; B.Sc.Hons Physics (1971), Bristol University; M.S.. Astronomy (1972), Sussex University; B.D.Hons Theology (1976), Heythrop College, London University; Ph.D. Astronomy (1983), University of Toronto, Canada **Selected Memberships:** Council member (1985-91), Institute on Religion in an Age of Science **Discipline:** Astronomy **Related Interests:** General Interrelation of Theology and Science (i.e. methodology, cosmology).

Selected Publications:

_____. "A Model for the Relation of Science and Theology." Diploma diss, Heythrop College, 1977.
_____. "Science and Faith: An Astronomer's Perspective." *America* 170, 12 (1994): 22.

Corsi, Pietro

Present Position and Address: Associate Professor (since 1987), History of Science, Department of Philosophy, University of Cassino, Italy 30, Via di San Giuseppe, 50122 Firenze, Italy **Work Phone:** (55) 241755 **Date of Birth:** July 20, 1948 **Languages Spoken:** Italian, English, French **Education:** The Scuola Normale Superiore (1967-1973), Pisa; Italian Doctorate (1971), "Epistemology and History of Science in France, from Henri Poincaré to Alexandre Koyré," University of Pisa; D.Phil., History of Science (1980), Department of History, Oxford University **Previous Positions:** Research Officer (1976-78, 1979-80), The Wellcome Unit for the History of Medicine, Oxford University; Senior Research Officer (1978-79, 1981-83), Faculty of Philosophy, University of Pisa; Senior Research Fellow (1980-81), King's College Research Center, The King's College, Cambridge, UK; Assistant Professor, Department of the History of Science (1983-87), Harvard University; Professeur Associé (Spring 1986/Fall 1988), Ecole des Hautes Etudes en Sciences Sociales, Maison des Sciences de l'Homme, Paris; Scientific secretary (1987-present), Exhibition "Images of the Mind: From the Art of Memory to the Frontiers of Neurosciences," Istituto e Museo di Storia della Scienza, Florence, April-July 1989 **Editorial Work:** Book Review Editor (1987-present), *Nuncius. Annali di Storia della Scienza*, Istituto e Museo di Storia della Scienza, Florence **Discipline:** History of Science, History of Philosophy **Related Interests:** 19th Century Scientific and Theological Discussions.

Selected Publications: His bibliography lists 5 books, 4 translations/editions, 30 articles, and 14 essays and reviews.

_____. "Darwin on Man," essay-review of *Darwin on Man: A Psychological Study of Scientific Creativity*, by H. E. Gruber and P. H. Barrett. *Annals of Science*, 32 (1975): 583-586. London: Wildwood House, 1974.

_____. Essay-review of *The Crisis of Evolution* by J. H. Brooke and A. Richardson. In *Annals of Science* 33 (1976): 490-493. Bletchley: The Open University Press, 1974.

_____, P. J. Weindling. *History of Science, History of Philosophy and the History of Theology, Information Sources in the History of Science and Medicine.* London: Butterworth & Co., 1983.

_____. "'Lamarckiens' et 'Darwiniens' à Tourin (1812-1894)." In *De Darwin au darwinisime. Science et idéologie*, ed Y. Conry. Paris: Vrin, 1983.

_____. "Recent Studies on French Reactions to Darwin" and "Recent Studies on Italian Reactions to Darwin." In *The Darwinian Heritage*, ed. D. Kohn. Wellington and Princeton: Nova Pacifica and Princeton University Press, 1985.

_____. Essay-review of *Darwin's Metaphor Nature's Place in Victorian Culture* by R. M. Young. In *Nuncius, Annali di Storia della Scienza.* 1, 2 (1986): 139-146. Cambridge: Cambridge University Press, 1985.

_____. Further Letters of Darwin, essay-review of *The Correspondence of Charles Darwin*, eds. F. Burkhart and S. Smith. *Science* 236 (1987):988-9.

Cotter, Graham

Present Position and Address: Retired Priest, Diocese Toronto; R.R.2 Warkworth, Ontario K0K 3K0 Canada **Home Phone:** (705) 924-2492 **Date of Birth:** January 12, 1925 **Education:** B.A. (1946)/M.A. (1947)/Ph.D. (1952), University of Toronto; L.Th. Trinity College, Toronto (1958); Proctor fellow (1982-83), Episcopal Divinity School, Cambridge, MA **Postgraduate Studies:** Retirement Sabbatical, Graduate Theological Union, Berkeley, CA (1989-90), Study with CTNS and Religion and the Arts **Previous Positions:** Lecturer in English (1948-49), University of Manitoba; Lecturer in English (1952-58), University of Toronto; Diocesan Administrator in Social Service (1958-65); Parish Priest (1965-88), Diocese of Toronto **Selected Memberships:** Center for Theology and Natural Sciences (CTNS), subscriber, The Pascal Centre; Associate, American Scientific Affiliation and Canadian Scientific and Christian Affiliation **Discipline:** Theology; English Language and Literature; Philosophy of Science; Liturgical Drama and Liturgical Dance.

Selected Publications:

_____. "The Quantum Christ." Paper presented at Center for Theology and the Natural Sciences, Berkeley, California, April 1989. Manuscript in progress for publication.

_____. "Touchstone Words in Faith and Physics: Authority and Power, Nonseparability and Locality." Chap 4 in "The Quantum Christ." Paper resented at the annual meeting of the Canadian Scientific and Christian Affiliation, University of Toronto, October 29, 1994.

_____. "Charles Williams' Influence on My Spiritual Growth." Paper presented to the C. S. Lewis Society, Toronto, Canada, November 23, 1994. *Pilgrimage* (In press).

Count, Earl W.

Present Position and Address: Writing and publishing. Retired Professor; 2616 Saklan Indian Drive 2, Walnut Creek, CA 94595, USA **Concurrent Positions:** Various positions as Visiting Professor (1968-present); Book Committee, The Key Reporter (1959-present) **Date of Birth:** October 22, 1899 **Education:** A.B. (1922), Williams College (Phi Beta Kappa); B.D. (1926), Garrett Theological Seminary; Ph.D. Anthropology (1936), University of California - Berkeley **Awards and Honors:** N.I.H. Grant; Wenner-Gren Foundation for Anthropological Research; Litt. D. (*honoris causa*) (1990), Purdue University **Previous Positions:** Instructor/Associate Professor, Biology/Zoology (1928-37), San José State University; Assistant/Associate Professor of Anatomy (1937-46), NY Medical College; Research Associate (1946-47), Wenner-Gren Foundation for Anthropological Research; Professor of Anthropology (Founder of Department; 1947-68), Hamilton College; Book Committee (Phi Beta Kappa) **Editorial Work:** Editorial Board of *Homo* **Selected Memberships:** Fellow, American Anthropological Association; Fellow, American Association for the Advancement of Science; Sigma XI

Discipline: Anthropology; Episcopal Clergyman, non-parochial **Related Interests:** Vertebrate Evolution; Mythology; Culture-History. His professional interest (since 1926) has ranged from zoology through comparative and human anatomy to anthropology.

Selected Publications: His bibliography lists over 40 publications, most of which are articles in scientific journals.

_____. "Church and Science." *Anglican Theological Review* 22, 2 (1941): 154-72.
_____. *4000 Years of Christmas*. Henry Schuman, 1948.
_____. "The Twilight of Science. I: Age of Dinosaurs?" *The Educational Forum* 12, 2 (1948): 199-207.
_____. "The Twilight of Science. II: But Science is a Humanity." *The Educational Forum* 12, 3 (1948): 299-310.
_____, Raymond Hoche-Mong. "God and Man-science." To be published.
_____. The Mind Body Problem: Towards a Science of Man. In process.

Coyne, George V.

Present Position and Address: Director of the Vatican Observatory (since 1978); The Vatican Observatory, Specola Vaticana, V-00120, Citta del Vaticano, Rome, Italy **Date of Birth:** January 19, 1933 **Languages Spoken:** English, Italian, Spanish **Education:** A.B. Mathematics (1958), Fordham University; Ph.D. Astronomy (1962), Georgetown University **Previous Positions:** Summer Research (1963), Harvard University; Summer Lecturer NSF Institute (1964), University of Scranton; Summer Visiting Research Professor (1965)/Visiting Assistant Professor (1966-67, 1968-69)/Assistant Professor (1970-76)/Senior Research Fellow (1976-80)/Director (1977-78), Lunar and Planetary Lab, University of Arizona; Visiting Astronomer (1967-68)/Astronomer (1969-77), Vatican Observatory; Coinvestigator (1969), OAO-2 Guest Observer Program; Lecturer (1976-80), Department of Astronomy, University of Arizona; Associate Director (1978-79)/Acting Director and Head (1979-80), University of Arizona Observatories **Selected Memberships:** International Astronomical Union; American Astronomical Society; Astronomical Society of the Pacific; American Physical Society; Optical Society of America **Discipline:** Astronomy **Related Interests:** As director of the Specola Vaticana, is currently helping to organize the series of conferences under the general theme "God's Action in the Universe."

Selected Publications:

_____, R. J. Russell and W. R. Stoeger, eds. *Physics, Philosophy and Theology: A Common Quest for Understanding*. Vatican City State: Vatican Observatory, 1988; Notre Dame, IN: University of Notre Dame Press, 1989.
_____. "Some Theological Reflections on the Anthropic Principle." In *The Anthropic Principle*, ed. F. Bertola and V. Curi. Cambridge University Press, 1989.
_____. "Il Principio Antropico nella Scienza Cosmologica." *Civilta Cattolica* 3, 16 (1989).
_____, editor. *John Paul II on Science and Religion: The New View from Rome*. University of Notre Dame Press, 1990.
_____. "Implicazioni Filosofiche e Teologiche delle Nuove Cosmologie." *Civilta Cattolica* 4, 343 (1992).
_____. "Philosophical and Theological Implications of the New Cosmologies." In *Science ed Etica alle Soglie del Terzo Millenio*. Rome: Societa Italiana di Fesica, 1993.
_____. "The Role of Theology and Philosophy in Cosmology." In *Apres Galilee, Science et Foi: Noveau Dialogue*, ed. Cardinal Paul Poupard. Paris: Desclee, 1993, in press.

Cramer, John Allen

Present Position and Address: Associate Professor of Physics (since 1982), Oglethorpe University; 2778 Winding Lane, Atlanta, GA 30319, USA **Work Phone:** (404) 457-1157 **Date of Birth:** June 25, 1943 **Education:** B.S. Physics (1965), Wheaton College; M.S. Physics (1968), Ohio University; Ph.D. Physics (1975), Texas A & M University **Previous Positions:** Physics Instructor (1968-71), Wheaton

College, IL; Assistant Professor of Physics (1980-82), The King's College, Briarcliff Manor, NY; Assistant Professor (1980-82), Physics, Oglethorpe University **Selected Memberships:** American Scientific Affiliation **Discipline:** Physics **Related Interests:** All areas where Science and Christian Faith Interact.

Selected Publications:

_____. "The Clockwork Image Controversy." *Journal of the American Scientific Affiliation (JASA)* 28, 3 (1970): 123-5.
_____. "General Evolution and the Second Law of Thermodynamics." *JASA* 23, 1 (March 1971): 20-1.
_____. "Science, Scientism and Christianity: The Ideas of D.M. MacKay." *JASA* 37, 3 (1985): 142-8.
_____. "Miracles and David Hume." *JASA* 40, 3 (1988): 131-7.

Crippen, Timothy

Present Position and Address: Associate Professor (since 1988) and Department Chair (since 1991), Department of Sociology and Anthropology, Mary Washington College, Fredericksburg, VA 22401-5358, USA; (Home) 8639 Ivy Mint Ct., Springfield, VA 22153, USA **Work Phone:** (703) 899-4896 **Home Phone:** (703) 455-8467 **Date of Birth:** June 1, 1952 **Education:** A.B. Sociology (1974), Indiana University at Fort Wayne; M.A. Sociology (1976)/Ph.D. Sociology (1982), University of Texas - Austin **Previous Positions:** Teaching Assistant (1976-1979)/Assistant Instructor (1978-1982), University of Texas -Austin; Assistant Professor (1982-88), Mary Washington College **Selected Memberships:** American Sociological Association; Association for the Sociology of Religion; Association for Politics and the Life Sciences; European Sociobiological Society; Society for the Scientific Study of Religion; Southern Sociological Society; Southwestern Social Science Association. **Discipline:** Sociology **Related Interests:** Political Sociology; Religion; Social Evolution; Sociological Theory; Stratification/Social Mobility.

Selected Publications: His bibliography lists 9 articles, 6 reviews, and 10 papers.

_____. "Old and New Gods in the Modern World: Toward a Theory of Religious Transformation." *Social Forces* 67 (December 1988): 316-36.
_____, Richard Machalek. "The Evolutionary Foundations of the Religious Life." In *International Review of Sociology.* 3 New Series (December 1990).
_____. "Further Notes on Religious Transformation." Social Forces 71 (September 1992): 219-23.
_____. "An Evolutionary Critique of Cultural Analysis in Sociology." Human Nature 3 (Fall 1992): 379-412.

Crombie, Alistair Cameron

Present Position and Address: Honorary Fellow (since 1994), Retired Fellow (since 1983), Trinity College, Oxford Orchardlea, Boars Hill, Oxford OX1 5DF, UK **Work Phone:** (0865) 735692 **Date of Birth:** November 4, 1915 **Languages Spoken:** English, French, Italian, German **Education:** B.S.. (1938), Melbourne University; Ph.D. Zoology (1942), Cambridge University; M.A. (1954), Oxford University **Honorary Degrees:** Hon. D. Litt. (1979), Durham University; Docteur honoris causa (1993), Université de Paris X **Awards and Honors:** Galileo Prize (1969); Member (1972), Academia Leopoldina; Fellow (1990), British Academy; Alexander van Humboldt Research Award (1994); Member (1994), Pontifical Academy of Science **Previous Positions:** Lecturer, History and Philosophy of Science (1946-53), University College, London; Lecturer, History of Science (1953-83), Oxford University; Fellow (1969-83), Trinity College; Professeur Associé (1982, 83), Université de Paris I; Kennedy Professor, Renaissance/History of Science (1982-85), Smith College, MA; Directeur Associé (1989), Ecole des Hautes Etudes, Paris **Selected Memberships:** British Society for the History of Science; History of Science Society; International Academy of History of Science; Royal Historical

Society; British Academy **Discipline:** History of Science **Related Interests:** History of Scientific Thought in Relation to Intellectual Context, Including Theology.

Selected Publications:

_____. Scientific Change. Heinemann Educational Books, 1963.
_____. Robert Grosseteste and the Origins of Experimental Science, 1100-1700. 3d ed. Oxford: Clarendon Press, 1971.
_____. Augustine to Galileo: Medieval and Early Modern Science. 4th ed. Harvard University Press, 1979.
_____. *Science, Optics and Music in Medieval and Early Modern Thought.* London: Hambledon Press, 1990.
_____. *Styles of Scientific Thinking in the European Tradition.* London: G. Duckworth, 1994.
_____. *Science, Art and Nature in Medieval and Modern Thought.* London: Hambledon Press, 1995.

Crosby, Donald Allen

Present Position and Address: Professor of Philosophy, Department of Philosophy, Colorado State University, Fort Collins, CO 80523, USA; (Home) 3517 Canadian Parkway, Fort Collins, CO 80524, USA **Home Phone:** (970) 493-5125 **Date of Birth:** April 7, 1932 **Education:** B.A. Classical Languages (1953), Davidson College, NC; B.D. (1956)/Th.M. American Church History (1959), Princeton Theological Seminary; Ph.D. Religion (1963), with emphasis on Philosophy of Religion and Ethics, Columbia University, NY **Postgraduate Studies:** Postdoctoral Research Fellow (1971-72), Yale University **Awards and Honors:** Honors Professor (1981), National Endowment for the Humanities Summer Institute on "Concepts of Nature and God" (June-July 1987); Burlington Northern Faculty Achievement Award (1989) **Previous Positions:** Minister (1956-59), Christiana Presbyterian Church, Delaware; Assistant Minister (1959-61), First Congregational Church on the Green, Norwalk, CT; Assistant Professor of Philosophy and Religion, Center College of Kentucky, Danville, KY (1962-65); Visiting Professor, Iliff School of Theology, Denver, CO; Assistant/Associate/Full Professor of Philosophy (1965-present), Colorado State University, Fort Collins **Selected Memberships:** American Philosophical Association; American Academy of Religion; Society for the Study of Process Philosophies; Society for Philosophy of Religion; Highlands Institute for American Religious Thought; North American Society for Social Philosophy; Society for the Study of Human Ideas on Ultimate Reality and Meaning **Discipline:** Philosophy **Related Interests:** Process Metaphysics; Philosophy of Religion; History of Western Philosophy; Philosophy and Religion of Nature; Existentialism.

Selected Publications: His bibliography lists 3 books, 29 articles, 9 reviews and numerous papers.

_____. "Religion and Solitariness." In *Explorations in Whitehead's Philosophy*, ed. Lewis Ford and George Kline. New York: Fordham University Press, 1983.
_____, Ron G. Williams. "Creative Problem-Solving in Physics, Philosophy, and Painting: Three Case Studies." In *Creativity and the Imagination*, Vol. 3 of *Studies in Science and Culture*, ed. Mark Amsler. Newark, DE: University of Delaware Press, 1987.
_____. *The Specter of the Absurd: Sources and Criticisms of Modern Nihilism.* Albany, NY: State University of New York Press, 1988.
_____. "Whitehead's God and the Dilemma of Pure Responsibility." In *God, Values, and Empiricism*, ed. Larry Axel and Creighton Peden. Mercer, GA: Mercer University Press, 1989.
_____. "From God to Nature: A Personal Odyssey." *Religious Humanism* 25, 3 (1991): 107-116.
_____. "God as Ground of Value: A Neo-Whiteheadian Revision." *American Journal of Theology and Philosophy* 13, 1 (1992): 37-52.
_____. "Toward a Psychology That is Radically Empirical: Recapturing the Vision of William James." In *The Legacy of William James*, ed. Margaret E. Donnelly. Washington, DC: American Psychological Association, 1992.
_____. "Was William James a Closet Nihilist?" *Ultimate Reality and Meaning* 16, 1-2 (1993): 141-148.
_____. "The Ultimacy of Nature: An Essay on Physidecy." *American Journal of Theology and Philosophy* 14, 3 (1993): 2-14.
_____. "Einstein on Religion." *Midwest Quarterly* 35, 2 (1994).

Crosby, John F.

Present Position and Address: Full Professor of Philosophy (since 1990) University of Steubenville, Steubenville, OH 43952, USA **Date of Birth:** November 5, 1944 **Languages Spoken:** English, German, Italian **Education:** B.A. (*cum laude*, 1966), Georgetown University; Ph.D. Philosophy (1970), University of Salzburg, Austria **Previous Positions:** Assistant (1970-84)/Associate Professor of Philosophy (1984-88), University of Dallas; Visiting Professor: University of Salzburg (Spring 1972)/John Paul II Institute for Studies on Marriage and Family (Spring 1983-present), Lateran University of Rome/International Academy of Philosophy (1987-90), Principality of Liechtenstein **Editorial Work:** Founding editor, and presently associate editor of the international journal of philosophy, *Aletheia* **Selected Memberships:** Member, American Catholic Philosophical Association; Fellowship of Catholic Scholars **Discipline:** Philosophy **Related Interests:** Philosophy of the Person, Ethics, and Religion.

Selected Publications: His bibliography lists 6 translations, 11 book reviews, over 40 articles and one major book on personhood.

_____. "Essay on Teilhard de Chardin's philosophy of religion." In *Der Fels* (April 1971): 110-2.
_____. "Refutation of Skepticism and General Relativism." In *Rehabilitierung der Philosophie*, ed. Schwarz, 103-22. Regensburg: Habbel, 1974.
_____. "Evolutionism and the Ontology of the Human Person: Critique of the Marxist Theory of the Emergence of Man." *Review of Politics* 38 (April 1976): 208-43.
_____. "The Idea of Value and the Reform of the Traditional Metaphysics of Bonum." *Aletheia* 1, 2 (1978): 221-336.

Crowe, Michael J.

Present Position and Address: Professor (since 1973), Program of Liberal Studies and Graduate Program in History and Philosophy of Science, University of Notre Dame, Notre Dame, IN 46556, USA **Work Phone:** (219) 631-6212 **Home Phone:** (219) 272-3426 **Date of Birth:** March 18, 1936 **Languages Spoken:** English **Awards and Honors:** Jean Scott Prize; Phi Beta Kappa; Woodrow Wilson Fellow, *Who's Who in the Midwest* **Previous Positions:** Instructor (1961-65)/ Assistant Professor (1965-68), Program of Liberal Studies/Director (1966-67), College Honors Program/Acting Chairman (1967-68)/Associate Professor (1968-73), Program of Liberal Studies/Chairman (1968-73), Program of Liberal Studies and Graduate Program in History and Philosophy of Science, University of Notre Dame **Selected Memberships:** History of Science Society; Midwest History of Science Society; History of Astronomy Division of the American Astronomical Society **Discipline:** History of Science **Related Areas of Interest:** History of Astronomy; Physics and Mathematics, 1750-1910; Science and Religion **Current Areas of Research:** Calendar of the correspondence of Sir John Herschel.

Selected Publications: His total bibliography includes 5 books (1 authored and 1 edited), and about 57 articles and book reviews.

_____. *The Extraterrestrial Life Debate, 1750-1900: The Idea of a Plurality of Worlds from Kant to Lowell.* Cambridge: Cambridge University Press, 1986.
_____. *Theories of the World from Ptolemy to Copernicus.* New York: Dover, 1990.
_____. *A History of Vector Analysis: The Evolution of the Idea of a Vectorial System.* Notre Dame, IN: University of Notre Dame Press, 1967. Reprint, New York: Dover, 1994.
_____. *Modern Theories of the Universe from Herschel to Hubble.* New York: Dover, 1994.

Curry, John F.

Present Position and Address: Associate Professor (since 1988), Duke University Medical Center, Box 3313, Durham, NC 27710, USA; (Home) 3303 Pinafore Drive, Durham, NC 27705, USA **Concurrent Positions:** Associate Professor (since 1991), Duke University Department of Psychology; Director of Psychological Services (1984-present), McDowell Ward, Inpatient Adolescent Psychiatry Unit, Duke Hospital **Work Phone:** (919) 684-3092 **Home Phone:** (919) 489-5974 **Date of Birth:** October 11, 1947 **Education:** B.A. Philosophy (*summa cum laude*, 1970), Villanova University, PA; M.A. Psychology (1972)/Ph.D. Clinical Psychology (1978), Catholic University of America, Washington, DC; M.A. Theology (1983), Washington Theological Union, MD **Certification:** National Register of Health Service Providers in Psychology; Licensed Practicing Psychologist, NC; Diplomate in Clinical Psychology, American Board of Professional Psychology **Previous Positions:** Psychology teacher (1970-72), Archbishop Carroll High School, Washington, DC; Psychology teacher (1972-73), Suitland Senior High School, Prince Georges County, MD; Staff Psychologist (1978-79)/Chief Psychologist (1980-83), Durham Community Guidance Clinic, Duke University Medical Center; Clinical Instructor (1977-78)/Associate Instructor (1978-79)/Assistant Professor (1980-88), Division of Medical Psychology, Department of Psychiatry, Duke University Medical Center **Selected Memberships:** American Psychological Association; Association for the Advancement of Psychology; Society for Research in Child and Adolescent Psychopathology; Catholic Theological Society of America; Society for Personality Assessment; American Group Psychotherapy Association **Discipline:** Clinical Psychology **Related Interests:** Relationship between applied Psychology, particularly Psychotherapy, and Religion; Normal Adolescent Development and Religion.

Selected Publications: His bibliography lists over 50 papers, presentations and publications.

_____. "Christian Humanism and Psychotherapy: A Response to Bergin's Antitheses." *Zygon* 22 (1987): 339-54.

D'Ambrosio, Ubiratan

Present Position and Address: Professor of Mathematics (since 1972), Universidade Estadual de Campinas; Coordinator (since 1987), Research Institutes of Sáo Paulo State Secretary of Health; President (since 1987), Sociedade para Integracào das Ciências e das Tradicóes; Rua Peixoto Gomide 1772 op 83, 01409 Sáo Paulo, SP, Brazil **Work Phone:** 55-11-280.0266 **Date of Birth:** December 8, 1932 **Languages Spoken:** Portuguese, English, Spanish, French, Italian **Education:** "Bacharel" (1954)/"Licenciado" (1955)/Doctorate (1963), all in Mathematics, University of Sáo Paulo; Visiting Fellow (1961-62), University of Genova, Italy **Previous Positions:** Research Associate Professor (1964-65), Brown University; Assistant Professor of Mathematics (1965-66), SUNY - Buffalo; Associate Professor of Mathematics (1966-68), University of Rhode Island; Associate Professor of Mathematics and Director of Graduate Studies in Mathematics and the Natural Sciences (1968-72), SUNY - Buffalo; Professor of Mathematics (1972-present) and Director (1972-80), Institute of Mathematics, Statistics and Computer Sciences of UNICAMP; "Ida Beam" Distinguished Visiting Professor (Spring 1981), The University of Iowa; Director (1974-83), Multi-national Project for the Improvement of Science Education, joint OAS-Brazilian Ministry of Education Program; Chief (1980-81), Unit for the Improvement of Educational Systems of the Organization of American States; General Coordinator of the Institutes (1982-86)/Prò-Rector for University Development (1986-1990), UNICAMP; Visiting Professor of Mathematics (1987), University of Illinois - Chicago; Secretary (1983-87)/Vice President (1987-89), The Sociedade Brasileira de Historia da Ciencia **Selected Memberships:** Member (1986-present), Sáo Paulo State Council of Education; Founding Member, Academia de Ciencias do Estado de Sáo Paulo; Elected Fellow, Institute of Mathematics and its Applications; Elected Fellow, American Association for the Advancement of Science (AAAS); Founding Member, Council of the Latin American Society for the History of Science and Technology; Founding Member, Society for the Integration of Sciences and Traditions **Discipline:** History of Science; Mathematics; Philosophy; Social Sciences **Related Areas of Interest:** History of Science; History of Ideas, with a Heavy Interest in the Historical Understanding of the Several Cases of Approximation/Separation of Religious and Scientific Ideas.

Selected Publications:

_____. "A Methodology for Ethnoscience: the Need for Alternative Epistemologies." *Theoria* I, 3 (Segunda Epoca, 1985): 397-409.
_____. "Some Reflections on the Western Mode of Thought on Science and on Education." In *Science and the Boundaries of Knowledge: The Prologue of our Cultural Past, Final Report of a Symposium in 1986.* Paris: UNESCO/CINI Foundation, 1987.
_____. "Socio-Cultural Influences in the Transmission of Scientific Knowledge and Alternative Methodologies." In *Cross Cultural Diffusion of Sciences: Latin America, Cuadernos de Quipu no. 2.* Mexico: Sociedad Latinoamericana de Historia de las Ciencias y la Tec.
_____, editor. *Anais do II Congreso Latinoamericano de Historia da Ciência da Tecnologia.* Wrote chapter "Do Misticismo ä Mistificacao." Sáo Paulo: Nova Stella, 1989.

d'Aquili, Eugene G.

Present Position and Address: Clinical Associate Professor of Psychiatry (since 1979), University of Pennsylvania Medical School; Vice President (since 1986), Institute for Cognitive and Behavioral Therapies, Presbyterian-University of Pennsylvania Medical Center; Private Practice in Psychiatry (since 1974); (Home) "Salus House", 609 Newtown Road, Berwyn, PA 19312, USA; (Work) Suite 1503, 2400 Chestnut Street, Philadelphia, PA 19103, USA; Department of Psychiatry, Hospital, University of Pennsylvania, 3400 Spruce Street, Philadelphia, PA 19104, USA **Date of Birth:** June 4, 1940 **Education:** A.B. Philosophy and Science (*magna cum laude*, 1962), Villanova University; M.D. (1966) University of Pennsylvania Medical School; M.A. Anthropology (1979), University of Pennsylvania; Ph.D. Anthropology (1988), Columbia Pacific University **Postgraduate Studies:** Postgraduate Training and Fellowships: Research Trainee (1963-66), Institute of Neurological Sciences, University of Pennsylvania; Mixed Medicine-Psychiatry Internship (1966-67), University of Kansas **Awards and Honors:** Academic Fellow Award, Institute on Religion in an Age of Science **Previous Positions:** Instructor (1972-73)/Assistant Professor (1973-79), University of Pennsylvania Medical School; Acting Director (1979-80)/Medical Director (1980-85), Center for Cognitive Therapy and the Mood Clinic, Department of Psychiatry, University of Pennsylvania **Editorial Work:** Member of board of Editors (1975-present), *Zygon*; Member of the board of Editors (1986-present), *Journal of Ritual Studies* **Selected Memberships:** Center for the Advanced Study of Religion and Science, University of Chicago; American Psychiatric Association; American Anthropological Association; American Association for the Advancement of Science; Institute on Religion in an Age of Science **Discipline:** Psychiatry and Anthropology **Related Interests:** The interrelationship of Psychiatry, Neurophysiology, and Religion.

Selected Publications: His bibliography lists 11 original papers, 4 books, and 3 articles.

_____. *The Biopsychological Determinants of Culture*. Reading MA: Addison-Wesley Molular Publications, 1972.
_____. *Charles Laughlin. Biogenetic Structuralism*. New York: Columbia University Press, 1974.
_____. "The Biopsychological Determinants of Religious Ritual Behavior." *Zygon* 10, 1 (1975): 32-58.
_____. *The Spectrum of Ritual: A Biological Structural Analysis*. New York: Columbia University Press, 1979.
_____. "The Neurobiological Bases of Myth and Concepts of Deity." *Zygon* 13, 4 (1979): 257-75.
_____. "Senses of Reality in Science and Religion." *Zygon* 17, 4 (1982): 361-84.
_____. Hans Mol. *The Regulation of Physical and Mental Systems: Systems Theory of the Philosophy of Science*. Lewiston: Edwin Mellen Press, 1990.
_____, Charles Laughlin, John Mc Manus and E. G. D'Aquili. *Brain Symbol and Experience*. Boston: Shambhala Press, New Science Library, 1990.

da Cruz, Eduardo Rodrigues

Present Position and Address: Assistant Professor (since 1979), Departamento de Teologia, Pontificia Universidade Catolica de S. Paulo, Rua Monte Alegre, 984 - Caixa Postal 7982, CEP 05014, São Paulo, Brazil **Home Phone:** (11) 65-5599 **Fax:** (11) 871-1416 **E-Mail** IROZJO@PUC001.PUCSP.ANSP.BR **Date of Birth:** September 29, 1950 **Education:** B.S. Physics (1973)/M.S.. Experimental Nuclear Physics (1978), University of São Paulo; M.Div. (1980), Fac. Teologia N. Sa. Assuncao, São Paulo; Th.M. (1985)/Th.D. Systematic Theology - Religion and Science Program (1987), Lutheran School of Theology at Chicago, IL **Selected Congresses and Conferences:** "The Dilemma Between Theological Concreteness and Scientific Speculation on Cosmology" presented at the annual meeting of The American Association for the Advancement of Science, Boston, February 14, 1993; On the Relevance of Paul Tillich's concept of Ontological Life and its Ambiguity" presented, at the International Paul Tillich Conference, New Harmony, IN, June 17-20, 1993 **Previous Positions:** Assistant Professor (1979-present), Pontificia Universidade Catolica de São Paulo, Brazil **Discipline:** Systematic Theology **Related Interests:** Theology of Scientific Activity; Philosophy and History of Science

Current Research: The meaning of the Ambiguity and the soteriological character of modern science in the thought of Langdon Gilkey, and the messianic character of post-war efforts to promote science for development.

Selected Publications:

_____. "The Ambivalence of Science: A Theological Study Informed by the Thought of Paul Tillich and the Latin American Situation." Th.D. diss., Lutheran School of Theology at Chicago 1987.

_____. Review of *Evolution as a Religion: Strange Hopes and Stranger Fears*, by Mary Midgley. London and New York: Methuen, 1986. *Zygon* 24, 2 (1989): 275-8.

_____. "Science and Culture Revisisted." *Insights: The Magazine of the Chicago Center for Religion and Science* 5, 1 (1993).

Daecke, Sigurd

Present Position and Address: Professor (since 1980), Evangelische Theologie (Systematic Theology), Rheinisch-Westfälische Technische Hochschule Aachen (University of Technology), Dienstgebäude, Ahornstrasse 55, D52074 Aachen, (Home) Flandrische Strasse 36, D-52076 Aachen, Germany **Work Phone:** (0241) 80-3558 **Home Phone:** (0241) 61234 **Date of Birth:** November 22, 1932 **Languages Spoken:** German, English, French **Education:** Dr. theol. (1967), Hamburg; Professor (1972), Aachen **Awards and Honors:** Strassburg-Preis (1967) **Previous Positions:** Pastor (1959-67); Professor (1972-80), Päd. Hochschule Aachen **Editorial Work:** Editor (1967-70)/Editor-in-Chief (1970-72), *Evangelische Kommentare* **Related Interests:** Systematic Theology. **Current Research:** Theology and Science; Theology and Ecology; Ethics of Science and Technology.

Selected Publications: His bibliography lists over 120 publications and papers almost all of which are relevant to this topic.

_____. "Anthropozentrik oder Eigenwert der Natur?" In *Ökologische Theologie*, ed. G. Altner. Stuttgart, 1989.

_____, editor. *Kann man Gott aus der Natur erkennen*? Freiburg: Herder, 1990. Also wrote Introduction and chapter "Naturliche Theologie im Gesprach zwischen Naturphilosophie und Worttheologie."

_____, editor. *Albert Einstein: Worte in Zeit und Raum*. Freiburg: Herder , 1991. Also wrote Introduction.

_____, editor. *Naturwissenschaft und Religion*. Mannheim: BI Wissenschaftsverlag, 1993. Also wrote Introduction and chapter "Naturwissenschaft als sicherer Weg zu Gott? Die neue Begegnung von Wissenschaft und Religion."

_____, editor. *Verantwortung in der Technik, Ethische Aspekte der Ingenieurwissenschaften*. Mannheim: BI Wissenschaftverlag, 1993. Also wrote Introduction and three of the chapters.

_____, editor. *Gut und Bose in der biologischen und kulturellen Evolution*. Wissenschaftliche Verlagsgesellschaft, 1994. Also wrote Introduction and chapter "Evolutionare contra christliche Ethik? Die Frage nach Gut und Bose in einer sich wandelnden Welt."

_____. "Theologie der Natur als 'naturliche' Theologie? Interdisziplinare und okologische Uberlegungen mit Tillichs Hilfe." In *Natural Theology versus Theology of Nature*, ed. Gert Hummel. Berlin: De Gruyter, 1994.

_____. "Eigeninteresse des Menschen - Eigenwart der Natur." *Uneversitas, Zeitschrift für Wissenschaft, Kunst, und Kultur* (1994).

_____. "Altruismus oder langfristiger Egoismus? Zur Frage der Begrundung einer Unweltethik." In *Mensch - Unwelt*, ed. H.P. Klocking. Acta Avademiae Scientarium. Akademie Gemeinnutziger Wissenschaften zu Erfurt, 1994.

_____. "Der Mensch als Nitschopfer und Mitzerstorer. Ethische Uberlegungen zur Gentechnologie und Reproduktionsmedizin." In *Baer and Modern Biology*, ed. Toomas Sutt. *Golia Baerina* v 6 (Tartu/Estonia) 1994.

Dalferth, Ingolf Ulrich

Present Position and Address: Ordinarius für Systematische Theologie, Dogmengeschichte und Symbolik (since 1995), University of Zürich, Switzerland; Professor für Systematische Theologie und Religionsphilosophie (since 1990), University of Frankfurt am Main, Germany; (Home) Veilchenstr.

9, D-7400 Tübingen, Germany **Date of Birth:** July 9, 1948 **Languages Spoken:** German, English, French **Education:** Evang.-Theol. Seminar, Schöntal und Urach (1964-67); Theologie und Philosophie (1968-1969), Universität Tübingen/Evang. Stift; Theology, Philosophy and Linguistics (1969-70), University of Edinburgh; Certificate de Langue Française (1970), Paris University; Theology and Philosophy (1971-72), Tübingen; Theology, Philosophy, and Linguistics (1972-74), University of Cambridge; Philosophy and English (1975), Tübingen. Arbitur (1967); Promotion (1977); Habilitation (1982); Zweite Evang.-theol. Dienstprüfung der Evang. Landeskirche Württemberg (1987) **Previous Positions:** Vicar (1974-79), Hagelloch/Tübingen; University of Tübingen (1974-80, 1986-90); Lecturer (1981-82), Durham University, UK; Lecturer (1987-89), Cambridge University; Visiting Professor (1988), Uppsala University, Sweden **Discipline:** Theology; Philosophy **Related Interests:** Rationality and Theology; Philosophy of Religions; Theology and Philosophy; Systematic Theology; Methodology.

Selected Publications: His curriculum vitae lists over 60 entries.

_____. *Sprachlogik des Glaubens*. Munich: Chr. Kaiser, 1974.
_____. *Religiöse Rede von Gott*. Munich: Chr. Kaiser, 1981.
_____. *Existenz Gottes und christlicher Glaube*. Munich: Chr. Kaiser, 1984.
_____. "Theologischer Realismus und realistische Theologie bei Karl Barth." *Evangelische Theologie* 46 (1986): 402-422.
_____. "Wissenschaftliche Theologie und kirchliche Lehre." *Zeitschrift für Theologie und Kirche (ZThK)* 85 (1988): 98-128.
_____. *Theology and Philosophy*. Oxford: Basil Blackwell, 1988.
_____. *Kombinatorische Theologie. Probleme theologischer Rationalität*. Freiburg: Herder, 1991.
_____. *Gott. Philosophisch - theologische Denkversuche*. Tübingen: J. C. B. Mohr (Paul Siebeck), 1992.
_____. *Jenseits von Mythos und Logos. Drechristologische Transformation der Theologie*. Freiburg: Herder, 1993.
_____. *Der anferweckte gekrenzigte*. Tübingen: J. C. B. Mohr (Paul Siebeck), 1994.

Dallaporta, Nicolo

Address: via Carducci 26, 35123 Padova, Italy **Work Phone:** (0039) 49 8802660 **Date of Birth:** October 28, 1910 **Languages Spoken:** Italian, French, English, German, Greek **Education:** Laurea in Fisica (Masters Degree, 1932), University of Bologna **Awards and Honors:** Premio Presidente Republica Rome (1967) **Previous Positions:** Assistant Professor of Physics (1934-47), Universities of Catania/Turin/Padua; Full Professor of Theoretical Physics (1947-70)/ Theoretical Astrophysics (1970-79), University of Padua; Full Professor of Theoretical Astrophysics (1979-85), ISAS Trieste; Has also participated in several conferences around the theme "Faith and Science" **Discipline:** Cosmic Rays (Particle Physics); Stellar Evolution (Cosmology) **Related Areas of Interest:** Metaphysics - Eastern religions; Christianity - Connections between Faith and Science.

Selected Publications: He has also written several short publications (mostly in Italian).

_____. *Alcune Note di Cosmologia: Commentarii*. Pontificia Academia Scientiarum 3, 32 (1990).
_____. *Cristianesimo e Mondi tradizionali*. Piovan Editori, Abano Terme, 1991.

Dally, Andreas Michael

Present Position and Address: Director of Studies, Evangelische Akademie Loccum, Postfach 2158, 31545 Rehburg-Loccum, Germany **Phone:** 05766/81-108 **Fax:** 05766/81-128 **Date of Birth:** June 24, 1958 **Languages Spoken:** German, English, French **Education:** Kaiserslautern (Diplom 1985), Montpellier (Ph.D. 1988), Bayreuth and Düsseldorf (research assistant) **Memberships:** The Institute of Applied Ecology (Freiburg i. Brsg) **Discipline:** Biology **Relevant Areas of Interest:** Ecology, Biology, Genetics, Ethical and Philosophical Implications of Science and Technology.

Selected Publications:

_____, S. de Chadarevian, R. Kollek. "Experimente mit der Evolution." Öko-Institut e.V., Freiburg i. Brsg., Werkstatt-Reihe, 1991. (On long-term risks of genetic engineering.)

_____, H. Weidner, H. Fietkau, editors. *Mediation als politischer und sozialer Proteß* Loccumer Protokolle, Evangelishche Akademim Loccum, 1994.

Davies, Paul Charles William

Present Position and Address: Professor of Natural Philosophy (since 1993), Department of Physics and Mathematical Physics, University of Adelaide, Adelaide, South Australia 5005 **Work Phone:** (08) 303 5685 **Date of Birth:** April 22, 1946 **Education:** B.S.. Physics (First Class, 1967)/Ph.D. in Theoretical Physics (1970), University College of London. **Selected Lectures:** Has given lectures at international conferences, and special lectures including the " Annual Teilhard de Chardin Lecture," London (April 1988) **Previous Positions:** Research Fellow (1970-72), Institute of Theoretical Astronomy, University of Cambridge; Lecturer in Applied Mathematics (1972-80), King's College, University of London; Professor of Theoretical Physics (1980-90) and Head of Department of Theoretical Physics (1980-87), University of Newcastle upon Tyne; Professor of Mathematical Physics (1990-93), University of Adelaide **Media Work/Radio:** about 100 BBC Radio 3 documentaries, i.e. " The Ghost in the Atom" and "Desperately Seeking Superstrings," and contributions to Open University productions and programs in the USA, Canada, South Africa, Australia, and New Zealand **Media Work/T.V.** about 40 BBC and commercial TV programs on science and philosophy including one on quantum theory **Editorial Work:** Consultant for *Nature* and *The Economist*, and editor for Cambridge University Press; written several hundred articles world-wide on a wide range of topics varying from Sexism in Science to the Origin of the Universe **Selected Memberships:** Fellow, Institute of Physics and Australian Institute of Physics; Fellow, World Academy of Arts and Sciences; Board of Advisors, Isthmus Institute, USA; Honorary Fellow, Indian Astronomical Society. **Discipline:** Theoretical Physics. Career started in Atomic Astrophysics but moved to Particle Physics and Cosmology **Related Interests:** Nature of Time and its Relation to the Evolution of the Universe - in Recent Years this Theme has Broadened to Include Chaotic and Self-organizing Systems and the Relation Between Physics and Biology; Philosophical Problems of Modern Physics - Mind Body Problem, Paradoxes of Quantum Measurement and of Time Reversal, Relationship of the Observer to the Physical World, Problem of the Ultimate Origin and Fate of the Universe, Possibility of a Completely Unified Theory of Fundamental Physics; God and the new Physics **Current Research:** Most of research output in area of quantum field theory in curved spacetime. Has discovered and investigated a number of quantum effects associated with black holes and the very early stages of the big bang (helped develop the thermodynamic theory of black holes). Current projects include work in areas of quantum gravity, gravitational entropy, physics of complexity and foundations of quantum mechanics.

Selected Publications: His bibliography lists over 20 books, 107 technical articles and 8 recently presented papers, many of which are relevant to this subject.

_____. *The Search for Gravity Waves*. Cambridge University Press, 1980.
_____. "The Anthropic Principle and the Early Universe." *Mercury* 10, 66 (1981).
_____. *The Edge of Infinity*. UK: J.M. Dent, 1981; USA: Simon & Schuster, 1981; UK: Penguin 1993, paperback.
_____. *The Accidental Universe*. Cambridge University Press, 1982.
_____. *God and the New Physics*. Simon & Schuster, 1983.
_____, D. Birrell. *Quantum Fields in Curved Space*. Cambridge University Press.
_____. *The Mind of God*. Simon & Schuster, 1992.
_____. *The Last Three Minutes*. Basic Books, 1994.
_____. *About Time*. Simon & Schuster, 1995.
_____. *Are We Alone*. Basic Books, 1995.

Davis, Edward B.

Present Position and Address: Associate Professor, Department of Natural Sciences, Messiah College, Grantham, PA 17027, USA; (Home) 23 S. Seasons Dr., Dillsburg, PA 17019, USA **Work Phone:** (717) 766-2511 **Home Phone:** (717) 432-8315 **E-Mail:** tdavis @ mcis.messiah.edu **Date of Birth:** August 5, 1953 **Education:** B.S. Physics (1975), Drexel University, Philadelphia; Ph.D. History and Philosophy of Science (1984), Indiana University **Previous Positions:** Research Assistant (1972-74), National Radio Astronomy Observatory, Charlottesville, VA; Teaching Assistant (1975-76), Department of Physics and Atmospheric Science, Drexel University; Teacher (1976-79), Secondary Science and Mathematics; Associate Instructor (1980-83), Department of Mathematics, Indiana University - Bloomington; Visiting Assistant Professor (1984-85), Departments of History and Philosophy, Vanderbilt University, Nashville; Assistant (1985-90)/Associate Professor of Science and History (1990-present), Messiah College, Grantham; Mellon Fellow in the Humanities, (1991-92), University of Pennsylvania, Philadelphia **Selected Memberships:** American Scientific Affiliation; History of Science Society **Discipline:** History of Science **Related Interests:** Robert Boyle; Creationism; Theology and Science since 1600.

Selected Publications: His bibliography lists 21 publications, and 20 papers and presentations.

_____. "Newcomb's Problem and Divine Foreknowledge." *Journal of the American Scientific Affiliation* 36, 1 (1984): 9-12.
_____. "Creation, Contingency, and Early Modern Science: The Impact of Voluntaristic Theology on 17th-Century Natural Philosophy." Ph.D. diss., Indiana University, August 1984.
_____. "Newton's Rejection of the 'Newtonian World View'." *Fides et Historia* 22, 2 (1990): 6-20. Reprint, *Science and Christian Belief* 3, 2 (1991): 103-27.
_____. "God, Man, and Nature: The Problem of Creation in Cartesian Thought." *Scottish Journal of Theology* 44, 3 (1991): 325-48.
_____. "A Whale of a Tale." *Perspectives on Science and Christian Belief* 43, 4 (1991): 224-37.
_____. "Parcare Nominibus: Boyle, Hooke, and the Rhetorical Interpretation of Descartes." In *Robert Boyle Reconsidered*, ed. Michael Hunter, 157-75. Cambridge University Press, Cambridge, 1994.
_____. "The Anonymous Works of Robert Boyle and the Reasons Why a Protestant Should not Turn Papist (1687)." Journal of the History of Ideas 55 (1994): 611-29.
_____, editor. "The Anti-Evolution Pamphlets of Harry Rimmer," vol. 6 in the Series, *Creationism in Twentieth Century America*, general editor, Ronald L. Numbers. New York: Garland Publishing, 1995.
_____. "Rationalism, Volunteerism, and Seventeenth-Century Science." In *Science and Belief: Proceedings of the First International Pascal Centre Conference, August 11-15, 1992*, ed. Jitse van der Meer. 2 vols., 1995.
_____, Michael Hunter, editors. *The Works of Robert Boyle.* 15 vols., The Pickering Masters Series, Pickering and Chatto, London (Forthcoming, 1999).

Davis, Marjorie Hall

Present Position and Address: Adjunct Staff, (Since 1989), Pastoral Counseling Center of West Hartford; (Home), 30 Barn Door Hills Rd., Granby, CT 06035, USA **Home Phone:** (203) 653-3304 **Date of Birth:** April 19, 1932 **Education:** A.B. (1954)/M.S. (1958), Cornell University; M.Div. (1984), Yale University **Previous Positions:** Adjunct Faculty (1979-83), Hartford Seminary; Interim Minister of Outreach (1985-86), First Congregational Church, Granby, CT; Interim Associate Minister (1986-87), Immanuel Congregational Church, Hartford; Interim Minister (1989-90), First Church in Harland, Congregational, East Hartland, CT; Intern (1985-88), Pastoral Counseling Center of West Hartford **Selected Memberships:** Immediate Past-President, Institute on Religion in an Age of Science; Council of the Institute of Religion in an Age of Science (IRAS) (1981-Pres.); Board Member, Association for Case Teaching; American Association for the Advancement of Science; Center for Theology and the Natural Sciences, Berkeley; Science and Technology Working Group member, United Church of Christ; Member, American Association of Pastoral Counselors **Discipline:** Pastoral

Theology and Counseling; Pastoral ministry **Related Interests:** Science (biochemistry) and Religion and their Relation.

Selected Publications: Her bibliography lists 3 publications in the area of Biochemistry, and 2 in the area of science and religion.

_____, Robert A. Evans, and G. Douglass Lewis. *Explorations in Faith*. Alban Institute Inc., 1981.
_____. "Beliefs of a Christian Minister in Light of Contemporary Science." *Zygon* 22, 3 (1987): 361-76.
_____. "A Matter of Statistics." *Journal for Case Teaching* 4 (Fall 1992): 115-22.

Deason, Gary Bruce

Present Position and Address: Senior Tutor of the Paracollege (since 1987), and Associate Professor of Religion (since 1985), Philosophy and History, St. Olaf College, Northfield, MN 55057, USA; (Home) 414 East 4th Street, Northfield, MN 55057, USA **Work Phone:** (507) 663-3175 **Home Phone:** (507) 663-1469 **Date of Birth:** October 25, 1945 **Education:** B.A. Chemistry/Mathematics (1967), University of Texas - Austin; M.Div. Philosophy/Theology (1971), Princeton Theological Seminary (PTS), NJ; Ph.D. Theology, History of Science (1977), PTS in conjunction with Program in History and Philosophy of Science **Previous Positions:** Teaching Fellow (1973-75), Departments of History and Theology, PTS; Lecturer (Winter 1977), General Studies Program, NY University; Lecturer (Winter 1977), Department of Social Science, Polytechnic Institute of NY; Instructor (1978), Department of Religion, St. Olaf College, Northfield, MN; Adjunct Assistant Professor of Philosophy (1978), Carleton College, Northfield; Andrew W. Mellon Assistant Professor of Philosophy and Humanities (1978-80), Vanderbilt University, Nashville; Assistant Professor of Religion (1980-85), Philosophy and History, and Tutor (1980-87)/Senior Tutor (1987-present) in the Paracollege, St. Olaf College, Northfield, MN **Selected Memberships:** History of Science Society; American Historical Association; Project on Science, Religion, and Public Policy, Humphrey Institute, University of Minnesota, Minneapolis, MN (1986-87) **Discipline:** Religion, Philosophy and History **Related Interests:** Reformation and Scientific Revolution; Concepts of Nature and Environmental Attitudes.

Selected Publications: His bibliography lists 10 publications and 21 papers, almost all of which are relevant to this area.

_____. "The Philosophy of a Lord Chancellor: Religion, Politics and Science in the Work of Francis Bacon." Doctoral dissertation supervised by C. C. Gillispie, Department of History, Princeton University and E. A. Dowey, Departments of History and Theology, Princeton University.
_____. Review of *The Essential Tension*, by Thomas Kuhn. *The Christian Century* 95, 40: 1183-5.
_____. Review of *The Road of Science and the Ways of God*, by Stanley Jaki. In *Isis: Journal of the History of Science Society* 71, 257 (June 1980): 315-16.
_____. Review of *Paradigms and Revolutions: Appraisals and Applications of Thomas Kuhn's Philosophy of Science*, ed. Gary Gutting. *Theology Today* 38, 2 (N.d.): 275.
_____. "The Protestant Reformation and the Rise of Science." *Scottish Journal of Theology* 38 (Fall 1985): 221-240.
_____. "Protestantism and Science: A Critique of the Merton Thesis." *Bulletin of the Center for Religion and the Natural Sciences*. Paper presented at Graduate Theological Union (Spring 1986).
_____. "Reformation Theology and the Mechanistic Conception of Nature." In *God and Nature: Historical Essays on the Encounter between Christianity and Science*, ed. David Lindberg and Ronald Numbers. University of California Press, 1986.
_____. Review of *Francis Bacon's Natural Philosophy: A New Source*, by Graham Rhess. *Isis* 77 (September 1987).
_____. "John Wilkins and Galileo Galilei: Copernicanism and Biblical Interpretation in the Protestant and Catholic Traditions." In *The Nature of Reform: Essays in Honor of E. A. Dowey*. Philadelphia: Westminster Press, 1989.

de Beauregard, O. Costa

Present Position and Address: Retired from C. N. R. S. (France); (Home) 76 Rue Murger, 77780 Bourron, France **Home Phone:** 64459013 **Fax:** 64459013 **Date of Birth:** November 6, 1911 **Education:** Ph.D. Physics (1943), Paris; Ph.D. Epistemology (1963), Paris **Previous Positions:** Laboratoire de Physique Théorique, Institut Henri Poincaré **Selected Memberships:** New York Academy of Sciences; International Society Study of Time; Acad. Intern. de Philosophie des Sciences; American Physical Society; Ste. Francaise de Mathématiques **Discipline:** Theoretical Physics and Epistemology.

Selected Publications:

_____. *Precis of Special Relativity*. Academic Press, 1967.
_____. *Time, The Physical Magnitude*. Reidel, 1987.

DeHaan, Robert F.

Present Position and Address: Retired; 826 E. Haines Street, Philadelphia, PA 19138-1702, USA **Home Phone:** (215) 848-4836 **Date of Birth:** May 14, 1925 **Languages Spoken:** English **Previous Positions:** Director, Gifted Child Program, University of Chicago, Quincy Youth Development Community; Chair, Department of Psychology, Hope College, Holland, MI; Director, GLCA Programmed Instruction Project; Director, GLCA Urban Seminar Program, Philadelphia, PA; Director, Chicago Metropolitan Center; Director, Lincoln University Master's of Human Services Program **Selected Memberships:** American Scientific Affiliation; American Association for the Advancement of Science; New York Academy of Science **Discipline:** Developmental Psychology **Related Areas of Interest:** Urban Education **Current Areas of Research:** "Development as a Large Scale Historical Process and its Relation to Evolutionary." Manuscript, in process.

Selected Publications: His bibliography contains 7 books mostly on gifted children and 3 articles.

_____, Robert J. Hauighust. *Educating Gifted Children*. N.p., 1956. Rev. ed., 1960.
_____, Jack Kough. *Identifying and Educating Gifted Children*. 4 vols. N.p., 1956-60.
_____. *For Parents of Gifted Children*. N.p., 1961.
_____. *Come Unto Me* (devotional). N.p., 1964.

de Knijff, Henri Wijnandus

Present Position and Address: Professor of the Dutch Reformed Church, Theology Faculty University of Utrecht, Heidelberglaan 2, P.O. Box 80105, 3508TC, Utrecht; M.H. Trompstraat 5, 3572XS, Utrecht, The Netherlands **Date of Birth:** June 23, 1931 **Languages Spoken:** Dutch, English, German, French **Education:** Theol. Dr. (1970), University of Leiden, The Netherlands; Theol. Dr. L. C. Collegium Theol. (1988), Debrecen, Hungary **Awards and Honors:** Prize Mallinckrodt (1975) for dissertation **Selected Memberships:** European Conference of Science and Theology; Wissensch. Ges. für Theologie; International Ref. Theol. Institute; ATOMIUM, working group in Religion and Science **Discipline:** Systematic Theology **Related Interests:** Religion and Science; Sexual Ethics; Hermeneutics.

Selected Publications:

_____. "Een nieuwe fase in het gesprek tussen geloof en natuurwetenschap (A new phase in the discussion between faith and natural science)." *Kerk en Theologie* 25, 4 (1974).
_____. "De verantwoordelijkheid voor het milieu als vraagstuk van de christelyke ethiek." *Kerk en Theologie* 32, 4 (1981). On Environmental Ethics.
_____. *Teksten over Geloof en Natuurwetenschappen* (Texts on faith and natural science), Translated texts of G. Altner, G. Liedke, T. F. Torrance, et al. with an Introduction by H. W. de Knijff. Delft, 1989.

_____. *Sleutel en Slot, Beknopte geschiedenis van de Bÿbelse hermeneutiek* (History of Biblical Hermeneutics, with special reference to the scientific world-view). Kampen, 1991.

Del Re, Giuseppe

Present Position and Address: Professor of Theoretical Chemistry (since 1969), University of Naples, Italy via della Giuliana 58, I-00195, Roma, Italy **Work Phone:** +39-6-3743109 **Fax:** +39-6-39730607 **Date of Birth:** April 4, 1932 **Languages Spoken:** Italian, English, French, Spanish **Education:** B.A. Humanities (1949), Liceo Michelangelo, Florence; Ph.D. Physics (1953), University of Florence; Ph.D. Chemistry (1957), University of Naples; Habilitation Theoretical Chemistry (1963), University of Rome **Awards and Honors:** Full Member, International Academy Philosophy of Science (1986); Full Member, European Academy for Environmental Problems (Tübingen) (1988) **Previous Positions:** Assistant (1954-59), Institute of Organic Chemistry, University of Naples; Associate Professor of Theoretical Chemistry (1962-70), University of Naples **Editorial Work:** Editor of two books of the Pontifical Academy of Science **Selected Memberships:** Italian Physical Society; Italian Chemical Society; Italian Society for the Philosophy of Science **Discipline:** Theoretical Chemistry **Related Interests:** Foundations of Science and cultural status of Science, with emphasis on the problem of Realism; Science and Theology.

Selected Publications: As of 1993 he had published 163 works, which included 2 books and about 25 papers of a cultural nature. Has translated into Italian for the Vatican Publishing House 7 fundamental essays on science and theology by T.F. Torrance.

_____. "The Aquinas vs. Epistemological Criticism. A Case for Philosophy in Science." *Phil. in Sci.* 2 (1986): 15-27.
_____. "Cause, Chance, and the State-Space Approach." In *Probability in the Sciences*, ed. E. Agazzi. Dordrecht: Kluwer Academic Publishers, 1988.
_____. "Science-Faith or Scientism-Religion? The Example of Teilhard de Chardin." *Il Futuro dell'uomo* (Florence), 15 (1988): 5-22.
_____. "The Crisis of the Foundations of Science." *Sapienza*. (Naples) 44 (1991): 51-5.
_____. "Meaning as an ingredient of Physical Reality." *La Nuova Critica* (Rome) Nuova Serie 1-2 (19-20) (1992): 41-50.
_____. "The Case for Finalism in Science." In *Intelligibility in Science*, ed. C. Dillworth. The Poznan Studies in the Philosophy of Science and the Humanities Amsterdam: Rodopi, 1992.
_____, editor. "Brain Research and the Mind-Body Problem: Epistemological and Metaphysical Issues." In *Proceedings of a round-table discussion held at the Pontifical Academy of Science on* (25 October 1988). Vatican City: Pont Acad. Sci., 1992.
_____. "Being and Truth as Foundations of Science." Introduction to *T.F. Torrance: Senso del Divino e Scienza Moderna (7 essays translated by Giuseppe Del Re and M.T. Benedetti)*. Vatican City: Libreria Editrice Vaticana, 1992.
_____, M. Sela, ed. "Complexity in Physics, Chemistry, and Biology." *Proceedings of the Plenary Session of the Pontifical Academy of Sciences, October 1992*. Vatican City: Pont. Acad. Sci., 1994.

Deuser, Hermann

Present Position and Address: Professor of Systematic Theology, University of Giessen Ringstrasse 2, D-35460, Staufenberg-Treis, Germany **Fax:** 0641-702-9562 **Date of Birth:** February 19, 1946 **Languages Spoken:** German, English, Danish **Education:** Dr. theol. (1974), (Habilitation, 1981), University of Tübingen **Previous Positions:** Professor, University of Wuppertal **Discipline:** Systematic Theology **Related Interests:** Science and Religion; Philosophy of Religion; Semiotics; Metaphysics; Creation and Evolution; Kierkegaard Research.

Selected Publications:

_____. *Kierkegaard - Die Philosophie der religiosen Den Nobelles.* Darmstadt 1985.
_____. "Schöpfung und Zufall. C. S. Peirce' 'Tychismus'." In *Gottes Zukunft - Zukunft der Welt, Festschrift for J. Moltmann.* (München, 1986): 298-309.
_____. "Schöpfung und Evolution. Versuch einer theologischen Orientierung." *Hochschul-Kolloquium 2* (hg. v. Rektor der Bergischen Universität - Gesamthochschule Wuppertal, 1987): 33-45.
_____. "'Determinism or Meaninglessness': Science and Religion." In *Free Will and Determinism*, ed. V. Mortensen and R. C. Sorensen. Aarhus University Press, 1987.
_____. "Christianity - Sign Among Signs?" *The Journal of Speculative Philosophy* 7, 4 (1993): 286-97.
_____. *Gott: Geist und Natur - Theologische Konsequenzen aus Charles S. Peirce' Religionsphilosophie.* Berlin/New York, 1993.
_____, editor. *Charles S. Peirce: Religionsphilosophische Schriften.* Hamburg, 1995.

DeWitt, Calvin B.

Present Position and Address: Professor of Environmental Studies (since 1972), University of Wisconsin - Madison, 550 North Park St., Madison, WI 53706, USA; (Summers) Director (since 1980), Au Sable Institute of Environmental Studies, 7526 Sunset Trail N.E., Mancelona, MI 49659; (Home) 2508 Lalor Road, Route 1, Oregon, WI 53575, USA **Work Phone:** (608) 222-1139 **Fax:** (608) 255-0950 **Date of Birth:** November 7, 1935 **Education:** B.A. Biology (1957), Calvin College; M.A. Biology (1958)/Ph.D. Zoology (1963), University of Michigan **Awards and Honors:** FUNEP 500 Award (Friends of the United Nations Environmental Program). Granted in recognition for the design and implementation of Au Sable Institute - an institute for the integration of environmental science and theology (1987) **Previous Positions:** Teaching Fellow (1962), Cellular Physiology/Lecturer (1963), Zoology, University of Michigan - Ann Arbor; Assistant (1963-66)/Associate (1966-69)/Professor of Biology (1969-71), University of Michigan - Dearborn; Honorary Fellow in Zoology (1970), University of Wisconsin-Madison; Fellow (1977-78), Calvin Center for Christian Scholarship (Christian Stewardship and Natural Resources), Calvin College **Editorial Work:** Corresponding/Consulting Editor (since 1993), *Christianity Today* **Selected Memberships:** American Association for the Advancement of Science; Sigma Xi; Scientific Research Society; Phi Sigma; Biological Honorary Society; Society of Wetland Scientists; Member (1988-90), Vice (1986-88)/Chair (1990-92) Board of Directors, North American Conference on Christianity and Ecology, Colorado Springs; Founding Member and Chair, American Society of the Green Cross (U.S.A.) (since 1992); Religion and Science Group of the Center for Theological Inquiry, Princeton (since 1993) **Discipline:** Biology, Environmental Science, Christian Environmental Ethics **Related Interests:** Judeo-Christian Environmental Ethics; Land Stewardship; Wetland Ecology; Food and Hunger Issues; Environmental Physiology, Ecosystems Analysis.

Selected Publications: His bibliography lists 39 works under the subject Ecology, Theology, and Stewardship; 8 under the topic World Food Problem and Development; 10 under Physiological Ecology and 14 under Wetland Ecosystems.

_____. "Seven Degradations of Creation." *Perspectives* 4, 2 (1989): 4-8.
_____. "Ecological Issues and our Spiritual Roots." *Chrisitan Living* (1989) 36, 10: 14-18.
_____, editor. *The Environment and the Christian.* Grand Rapids: Baker Book House, 1991.
_____, Peter A. DeVos, Vernon Ehlers, Eugene Dykema, and Loren Wilkenson. *Earthkeeping in the Nineties.* Grand Rapids: Eerdman's Publishing, 1991.
_____. "The Church's Role in Environmental Action." *Word & World* 11, 2(1991): 180-5.
_____. "Creation's Care and Keeping: A Reformed Perspective." *Theological Forum* (Reformed Ecumenical Council) 19, 4 (1991): 1-7.
_____. "Responding Creatively to Creation and Its Degradation." *Theology, News and Notes* (Fuller Theological Seminary, Pasadena) 15-19.

_____, Ghillean T. Prance, eds.. *Missionary Earthkeeping*. Macon, GA: Mercer University Press, 1992.
_____. "God's Love for the World and Creation's Environmental Challenge to Evangelical Christianity." *Evangelical Review of Theology* 17, 2 (1993):134-49.
_____. "A Scientist's Theological Reflection on Creation." *Transformation* 10, 2:12-16.

Di Bernardo, Giuliano

Present Position and Address: Chair, Philosophy of Science, University of Trento, Italy; (Home) Via Mesiano 15-38050 Povo, Trento, Italy **Languages Spoken:** Italian, English **Education:** Diploma of Sociology (1966) **Previous Positions:** Director of Department of Philosophy (1982-85)/Vice-Chancellor (1985-87), University of Trento **Selected Memberships:** Life member, Académie Internationale de Philosophie des Sciences; Italian Society of Philosophy; Italian Society of Logic and Philosophy of Sciences; Coordinator of the Research Doctorate in Philosophy of Science; Master, Lodge Zamboni-de Rolandis in Bol **Discipline:** Philosophy of Science and Scholar of the Social Sciences and Deontic Logic **Related Interests:** Philosophical foundation of the Social Sciences; Author of the *Philosophy of Freemasonry* (translated into English and German).

Selected Publications: Bibliography lists 5 books and 16 articles.

_____. "Linguaggio, scienza e sociologia (Language, science and sociology)." *Sociologia* 3 (1969): 173-98.
_____. "Previsione e profezia nelle scienze sociali (Prediction and prophecy in the social sciences)." *Sociologia* 4 (1970): 73-99.
_____. "Thetic and Prohairetic Normative Systems." *Poznan Studies in the Philosophy of Sciences and the Humanities* 3 (1979): 87-118.
_____. "Il problema della razionalità nelle scienze sociali (The problem of rationality in the social sciences)." In *Simplicité et complexité*, ed. E. Morin. Milano: Mondadori, 1988.
_____. *Normative Structures of the Social World*. Amsterdam: Rodopi, 1988.

Dillenberger, John

Present Position and Address: Emeritus Professor of Historical Theology (since 1983), Graduate Theological Union, Berkeley; (Home) 727 Gelston Place, El Cerrito, CA 94530 **Work Phone:** (510) 528-2041 **Fax:** (510) 528-3228 **Date of Birth:** July 11, 1918 **Education:** B.A. (1940), Elmhurst College; B.D. (1943), Union Theological Seminary, NY; Ph.D. (1948), Columbia University; Ordained (1943), United Church of Christ **Honorary Degrees:** D.D. - University of Vermont (1957)/Elmhurst College (1959); S.T.D. - Ch. Divinity School Pacific (1965)/Ripon College (1966); L.H.D. - University of San Francisco (1966) **Previous Positions:** Chaplain Corps (1943-46), USNR; Instructor in Religion (1948-49), Princeton University; Assistant (1949-52)/Associate Professor of Religion (1952-54), Columbia University; Associate Professor of Theology (1954-57)/Parkman Professor of Theology (1957-58), Harvard University Divinity School; Ellen S. James Professor of Systematic and Historical Theology (1958-62), Graduate School and Seminary, Drew University; Professor of Historical Theology and Dean of Graduate Studies (1962-64), San Francisco Theological Seminary; President and Dean (1962-72)/Professor of Historical Theology (1962-78), Graduate Theological Union, Berkeley; Research Scholar (1973-74), Nat. Museum of American Art, Smithsonian Institution; President (1978-83), Hartford Seminary **Selected Memberships:** Fellow, Society for Values in Higher Education; Society of Arts, Religion and Contemporary Culture; Vice President (1985)/President (1987), American Academy of Religion **Discipline:** Historical Theology **Related Interests:** Art and Modern Culture; History of Science.

Selected Publications:

_____. *Protestant Thought and Natural Science. A Historical Interpretation*. Westport: Greenwood Press, 1960; University of Notre Dame Press, 1988.

_____. *The Visual Arts and Christianity in America.* New York: Crossroad Publishing, 1989.

Dilworth, Craig

Present Position and Address: Reader (docent) in Theoretical Philosophy (since 1989), Uppsala University, Department of Philosophy, Villavägen 5, S-752 36 Uppsala, Sweden **Concurrent Position:** Reader (docent) in Philosophy (1986-present), Åbo Akademi, Finland; Visiting Senior Member (1986-present), Linacre College, University of Oxford **Date of Birth:** August 24, 1949 **Languages Spoken:** English, Swedish, French **Education:** B.A. Sociology (1970)/B.A. Sociology with Honors (1973)/M.A. Philosophy (1977), Carleton University, Ottawa, Canada; Filosofie doktor, Theoretical Philosophy (1981), Uppsala University, Sweden **Previous Positions:** Lecturer in Theoretical Philosophy (1977-80), Uppsala University **Editorial Work:** Assistant Editor (1979-present), *Epistemologia* **Selected Memberships:** Corresponding Member, International Academy of Philosophy of Science **Discipline:** Theoretical Philosophy **Related Interests:** Philosophy of Science; Metaphysics; Environmental Studies.

Selected Publications: His bibliography lists 50 entries.

_____. Scientific Progress (Synthese Library, Vol. 153), Doctoral thesis. Dordrecht: Reidel, 1st edition 1981; 2nd edition 1986, 3rd edition 1994.
_____, editor. *Idealization IV: Intelligibility in Science.* Atlanta: Rodopi, 1982.
_____. *The Metaphysics of Science.* Dordrecht: Kluwer, 1995.

Dobbs, Betty Jo Teeter

Present Position and Address: Professor of History (since 1986), Harris Hall, Northwestern University, Evanston, IL 60208, USA **Home Phone:** (919) 967-0716 **Date of Birth:** October 19, 1930 **Education:** B.A. Chemistry (1951), Hendrix College, Conway, AR; M.A. Psychology (1953), University of Arkansas -Fayetteville; Ph.D. History (1974), University of North Carolina - Chapel Hill **Previous Positions:** Assistant (1975-76)/Associate (1976-86), Professor of History, Northwestern University, Evanston **Selected Memberships:** History of Science Society **Discipline:** History of Science **Related Interests:** Religion and Theology in the Scientific Revolution of the 17th Century.

Selected Publications:

_____. "Isaac Newton and Humanist Values in Science." In The *Humanist as Citizen: Essays on the Uses of the Humanities*, ed. John Agresto and Peter Riesenberg. Chapel Hill: University of North Carolina Press and National Humanities Center, 1981: 25-36.
_____. "Newton and Stoicism." *Southern Journal of Philosophy* 23 Supplement (1985): 109-123. Deals with Newton's belief in a fiery apocalypse.
_____. "Alchemische Kosmogonie und arianische Theologie bei Isaac Newton." *Wolfenbütteler Forschungen* 32 (1986): 137-50.
_____. "Newton's Commentary on The Emerald Tablet of Hermes Trismegistus: Its Scientific and Theological Significance." In *Hermeticism and the Renaissance, Intellectual History and the Occult in Early Modern Europe*, ed. I. Merkel and A. G. Debus. Washington: The Folger Shakespeare Library; London/Toronto: Associated University Presses, 1988.
_____. "Newton's Alchemy and his 'Active Principle' of Gravitation." In *Newton's Scientific and Philosophical Legacy, International Archives of the History of Ideas*, ed. P. B. Scheuer and G. Debrock. Dordrecht/Boston/London: Kluwer Academic Publishers.
_____. Alchemical Death and Resurrection: The Significance of Alchemy in the Age of Newton. Washington DC: Smithsonian Institution Libraries, 1990.
_____. "Newton as Alchemist and Theologian." In Upon the Shoulders of Giants: Newton and Halley 1686-1986, ed. Norman J. W. Thrower. Berkeley/Los Angeles: University of California Press, in press.

_____. "The Unity of Truth: An Integrated View of Newton's Work." In Proceedings of the University of Maryland-Smithsonian Institution Celebration of the Tercentenary of the Publication of Newton's Principia. Smithsonian Institution Press, in press.
_____. The Janus Faces of Genius: The Role of Alchemy in Newton's Thought. Cambridge University Press, in press. Deals with Newton's effort to restore true religion.
_____. "From the Secrecy of Alchemy to the Openness of Chemistry." In Solomon's House Revisited: Proceedings of Nobel Symposium 75, in press. Deals with the place of alchemy in the Protestant Reformation.

Dodson, Edward O.

Present Position and Address: Professor Emeritus (since 1981), University of Ottawa, Canada; 15 Laval Road, Aylmer, Québec J9H 1C4 Canada **Work Phone:** (819) 684-4200 **Date of Birth:** April 26, 1916 **Languages Spoken:** English, French **Education:** A.B. (1939), Carleton College, Northfield, MN; Ph.D. in Cytology and Genetics (1947), University of California - Berkeley **Previous Positions:** Lecturer in Zoology (1945), University of California - Los Angeles; Instructor in Biology (1946-47), Dominican College of San Rafael, CA; Instructor in Biology (1947-49)/Assistant Professor (1949-52)/Associate Professor (1952-57), University of Notre Dame, IN; Associate Professor (1957-59)/Full Professor (1959-81), University of Ottawa; Professeur invité (1961), Université de Montréal; Visiting Research Professor (1964-65), Roswell Park Memorial Institute, Buffalo, NY; Professeur invité (1971-72), Foundation Teilhard de Chardin, Paris; Visiting Professor (1979), Stazione Zoologica, Naples, Italy/Laboratoire Arago, Banyuls-sur-Mer, France/Station biologique d'Arcachon, France/Station biologique de Roscoff, France **Selected Memberships:** Phi Beta Kappa; Sigma Xi; Fellow, American Association for the Advancement of Science; Genetics Society of America; Genetics Society of Canada; Society for the Study of Evolution; ACFAS; Member (1980-83), Committee on Evolution Education of the National Association of Biology Teachers (USA) **Discipline:** Cytology and Genetics **Related Interests:** Genetics, evolutionary biology.

Selected Publications: His bibliography lists over 70 publications, and 40 papers and reports presented.

_____. "Evolution/Creation Debate." *BioScience* 30 (1980): 220-1.
_____. "Was Teilhard de Chardin a Co-Conspirator at Piltdown?" *Natural History* 90:6 (1981): 16-21; Rev. version, *The Teilhard Review* 16:3 (1981): 16-21.
_____. "Mendel, Teilhard de Chardin, and Pastushnyi." *Analecta Augustiniana* 45 (1982): 321-8.
_____. "The Relevance of Teilhardian Synthesis Today." Seminar on Visionaries of Peace, United Nations, NYC (21 September 1983), *Humanity's Quest for Unity*, 166-68. Wassenaar, The Netherlands: Miranada, Zonneveld, L. 1985.
_____. *The Phenomenon of Man Revisited: A Biological Viewpoint on Teilhard de Chardin*. New York: Columbia University Press, 1984.
_____. *Teilhard and Mendel: Parallels and Contrasts*. Teilhard Studies no. 12 . White Plains, NY: American Teilhard Association for the Future of Man, 1984.
_____. "Harpur and Parthenogenesis." *Canadian Catholic Review* 4, 11 (December 1986): 21-24.
_____, George F. Howe. *Creation or Evolution: Correspondence on the Current Controversy*. University of Ottawa Press, 1990.
_____. "The Teilhardian Synthesis, Lamarkism, and Orthogenesis." Teilhard Studies no. 29. White Plains, NY: American Teilhard Association, 1993.

Downing, Barry H.

Present Position and Address: Senior Pastor (since 1971), Northminster Presbyterian Church, Box 8655, Endwell, NY 13760, USA; (Home) 3663 Rath Avenue, Endwell, NY 13760 **Date of Birth:** October 14, 1938 **Education:** B.A. Physics (1960), Hartwick College; B.D. Theology (1963), Princeton Theological Seminary; Ph.D. (1966), University of Edinburgh - New College (Specialized in relation between Theology and Natural Science under Professor John McIntyre and Professor T. F. Torrance) **Previous Positions:** Assistant (1967-71), Northminster Presbyterian Church **Discipline:** UFOs and Christian Theology **Related Interests:** Cosmology; Space Travel; UFOs; Government Secrecy.

Selected Publications:

_____. "UFOLOGY, Religion and Deception." *Mufon UFO Journal* (February 1977).
_____. *The Bible and Flying Saucers.* New York: Berkley Books, 1989.

Drago, Antonino

Present Position and Address: Associate Professor of History of Physics (since 1986), University of Naples, Dipartimento di Scienze Fisiche, Universita' di Napoli, Mostra D'Oltremare, Pad. 19, 80125, Napoli, Italy **Work Phone:** (081) 725-3417 **E-mail:** adrago@na.infn.it **Date of Birth:** May 5, 1938 **Languages Spoken:** Italian, English, French **Education:** M.D. Physics (1961), University of Pisa, Italy **Previous Positions:** 'Assistente' of Theory Information (1973-1985), University of Naples **Selected Memberships:** IFOR - ARK Community **Discipline:** History of Physics **Related Interests:** Non-violence; Ecumenism; Apocalypse.

Selected Publications:

_____, editor. *di G. Lanza del Vasto: Lezioni di Vita.* Firenze: Libr. Ed. Fiornetina, 1976.
_____. "Guerra, scienziati e morale." *Rassegna di Teologia* 26 (1986): 149-63.
_____. "A Characterization of the Newtonian Paradigm." In *Newton's Scientific and Philosophical Legacy*, ed. P. B. Scheurer and G. Debrock, 239-52. Kluwer Academic Press, 1988.
_____. "Gioacchino da Fiore, teologo meridionale." *Il Tetto* 27, 157 (1990): 83-103.
_____. "Scienza: Parola o silenzio di dio?" In AA.VV. *Parola e silenzio di Dio*, Ed., 300-18. Dehoniane, Roma, 1991.
_____. *Le Due Opzioni. Per Una Storia Popolare Della Scienza*, Ed. La Meridiana, Molfetta (BA), 1991.
_____. "The Alternative Content of Thermodynamics." In *Thermodynamics: History and Philosophy. Facts, Trends and Debates*, ed. K. Martinas, L. Ropolyi, and P. Szegedi, 329-45. Singapore: World Scientific, 1991.
_____. "Is Goedel's Incompleteness theorem a Consequence of the Two Kinds of Organization of a Scientific Theory?" In *First International Symposium on Goedel's Theorems*, ed. Z. W. K. Wolkowski, 107-35. Singapore: World Scientific, 1993.
_____. "The Challenge of Infinitesimal Analysis to Adam's Language." In *Leibniz and Adam*, ed. M. Dascal and E. Yakira, 219-27.
_____. "Leibniz' *Scientia Generalis* Re-interpreted and Accomplished by Means of Modern Scientific Theories." In *Atti Convegno Soc; It. Logica e Filos*, ed. C. Cellucci. Lucca: Scienza, 1993.

Drees, Willem B.

Present Position and Address: Research worker, Bezinningscentrum, Vrije Universiteit, De Boelelaan 1115, 1081 HV, Amsterdam, The Netherlands; (Home) Hertog Hendriklaan 11, 3743 DL Baarn, The Netherlands **Work Phone:** (011-31-20) 444-5675 **Home Phone:** (011-31-21) 542-4223 **Fax:** (011-31-20) 444-5680 **Date of Birth:** April 20, 1954 **Languages Spoken:** Dutch, English, German, French **Education:** Candidate Physics (1973)/Doctorandus in Theoretical Physics (1977), University of Utrecht; Candidate Theology (*cum laude*, 1984)/Doctorandus Theology/Philosophy of Religion (*cum laude*, 1985)/Doctorate of Theology (*cum laude*, 1989), University of Groningen **Previous Positions:** High-school teacher (1977-85); Research worker, Department of Theology (1985-86)/paid by National Science Foundation (1986-89), University of Groningen; Visiting scholar (Fall 1987), Center for Theology and National Sciences, Berkeley, CA; Visiting Scholar (1988), Chicago Center for Religion and Science, Chicago, IL **Selected Memberships:** Associate, Chicago Center for Religion and

Science; Member, ATOMIUM; Member, Council of the European Society for the Study of Science and Theology; Member, Center of Theology and the Natural Sciences; Member, Institute on Religion in an Age of Science **Discipline:** Systematic Theology and Philosophy of Religion, especially in relation to Science (Physics and Cosmology) **Related Interests:** Theology and Astrophysical Cosmology and Physics; Methods in Religion and Science; Holism and Christianity.

Selected Publications:

_____. "Theologie over buitenaardse personen (Theology concerning Extraterrestrials)." *Tijdschrift voor Theologie* 27 (1987): 259-76.

_____. "Interpretation of 'The Wave Function of the Universe'." *International Journal of Theoretical Physics* 26 (1987): 939-42.

_____. "Beyond the Limitations of the Big Bang Theory: Cosmology and Theological Reflection." *CTNS Bulletin* 8, 1 (Winter 1988): 1-15.

_____. *Beyond the Big Bang: Quantum Cosmologies and God.* La Salle, IL: Open Court, 1990.

_____. "Theology and Cosmology Beyond the Big Bang Theory." In *Science and Religion: One World - Changing Perspectives on Reality*, ed. Jan Fennema and Iain Paul. Dordrecht: Kluwer Academic Publishers, 1990.

_____. "Extraterrestrial Persons." In *Concepts of Person in Religion and Thought*, ed. H. G. Kippenberg, Y. B Kuiper and A. F. Sander. Berlin: Mouton de Gruyter, 1990.

Drozdek, Adam

Present Position and Address: Associate Professor of Computer Science, Duquesne University, Pittsburgh, PA 15282, USA **Work Phone:** (412) 396-5897 **Date of Birth:** January 1, 1951 **Languages Spoken:** English, Polish, Russian **Selected Memberships:** American Scientific Affiliation; Association for Computing Machinery **Discipline:** Computer Science **Related Areas of Interest:** Philosophy; Theology; Mathematics **Current Areas of Research:** Infinity in Western Thought; Philosophical Problems of Computer Science.

Selected Publications: His bibliography contains 2 books and 20 papers.

_____. "Interlingua in Machine Translation." In *The Proceedings CSC, '89. Louisville, KY, 1989.*

_____. "Programmabilism: A New Reductionism." *Epistemologia* 13 (1990).

_____. "Pecunia not olet?" *Journal of Information Ethics* 1 (1992).

_____. "Moral Dimension of Man and Artificial Intelligence." *AI & Society* 6, 3 (1992).

_____. "Computers and the Mind-Body Problem: On Ontological and Epistemological Dualism. *Idealistic Studies* 23, 1 (1993).

_____. "The Infinite and the Finite." *Perspectives on Science and Christian Faith* 45, 3 (1993).

_____. "Awe and Arrogance in Science." *The Midwest Quarterly* 35, 2 (1994).

_____. "Semantics of Programming Languages and the Theory of Truth." *Epistemologia* 16 (1993).

_____. "The Possibility of Computers Becoming Persons." *Social Epistemology* 8 (1994).

_____. *Data Structures in C.* Boston: PWS (1995).

Duchrow, Ulrich

Present Position and Address: Professor of Systematic Theology (since 1984), University of Heidelberg; Regional Director of Mission and Ecumenism in the Protestant Church in Baden (since 1979), Regionalstelle für Mission und Ökumene, Regionalbeauftragter, Ulrich Duchrow, Hegenichstrasse 22, 6900 Heidelberg, Germany **Date of Birth:** June 13, 1935 **Languages Spoken:** German, English, French **Education:** Studies in Theology and Philosophy (1955-60), Universities of Tübingen/Heidelberg/Zurich and Basel; Ordained Pastor (1964), Evangelische Landeskirche in Baden; Doctorate in Theology (1963), University of Heidelberg **Selected Congresses and Conferences:** Delegate at Vancouver Assembly of WCC (1983) and Consultant of WCC (since 1986); SODEPAX, IAMS, AACC

Selected Lectures: Lecturer and guest Professor in various countries throughout the world **Previous Positions:** Study Secretary Forschungsstätte der Evangelischen Studiengemeinschaft (F.E.ST.), Heidelberg (1963-70)/Assistant Professor of Systematic Theology (since 1968); Director (1970-77) of newly integrated Department of Studies of the Lutheran World Federation; Guest Professor at Ecumenical Institute, Bossey/Geneva, (1977-78); Assistant Pastor in Denzlingen/Freiburg (1978-79) **Editorial Work:** Editorial Board of *Pastoraltheologie* (since 1966)/*Junge Kirche* (since 1985) **Other Academic Experience:** Ecumenical Initiative: "Kairos Europe 1992" **Discipline:** Theology **Related Interests:** Church and Society; Theology and Philosophy.

Selected Publications: His bibliography lists 10 monographs, 19 edited books and other documents, 3 brochures, and over 100 articles.

_____. *Lutheran Churches, Salt or Mirror of Society? Case Studies on the Theory and Practice of the Two Kingdoms Doctrine*. Geneva: Lutheran World Foundation, 1977.
_____. *Conflict over the Ecumenical Movement. Confessing Christ Today in the Universal Church*, trans. David Lewis. Geneva: World Council of Churches, 1981.
_____. "Friede, Gerechtigkeit und Befreiung der Schöpfung (konziliarer Prozess)." In *Ökologische Theologie. Perspektiven zur Orientierung*, ed. G. Altner. Stuttgart: Kreuz Verlag, 1989.
_____. "Political and Economic Wellbeing and Justice: A Global View." In *Studies in Christian Ethics*. Political Ethics, (Edinburgh) 3, 1 (1990): 61ff.
_____, G. Eisenbürger, and J. Hippler. *Total War against the Poor. Confidential Documents of the 17th Conference of American Armies*. New York: New York Circus Publications, 1990. Also in German.
_____, C. Springe. "Beyond the Death of Socialism. Visions from Germany on Alternatives to Capitalism." In *Occasional Papers #19*, ed. Archer, K.. Manchester: The William Temple Foundation, 1991.
_____. *Justice, Dictionary of the Ecumenical Movement*. Geneva, 1991.
_____. *Europe in the World System 1492-1992, Is Justice Possible?* Geneva: WCC Publications, 1992. Also in German, Spanish, and Swedish.
_____. *Ecumenical Perspectives on South Africa's Economic Future in the Context of the New-Liberal Transnational Capitalist System. Towards a Code of Investment, Ethics for South Africa's International Economic Relations*. Johannesburg: South African Council of Churches, 1992.

Dufner, Andrew J.

Present Position and Address: Coordinator, Jesuit Religious Retreat Center, The Nestucca Sanctuary, Pacific City, OR 97135, USA **Date of Birth:** November 9, 1932 **Education:** B.S. Physics (1954), Gonzaga University, Spokane, WA; Studies in Ascetical Theology and Humanities (1954-57), Francis Xavier Jesuit Novitiate, Sheridan, OR; Ph.L. Philosophy (1960)/Ph.D. Physics (1964), St. Louis University, MO; S.T.M., S.T.L. Theology (1968) Alma College of Santa Clara University, Los Gatos, CA, and ordained as a Catholic Priest (1987) **Selected Lectures:** Lectured on various topics in Theology and Science, Theological Faculty of Louvain, Belgium (1970); Ecological Ethics (1972), Pastoral Conference of the Pacific School of Religion, Berkeley; Seminar on Religion and Conservation Ethics, Conference on Ethics and Environment: Social Policy for the 1980's (January 1975), Ministry of Ecology and University Extension of the University of California - Berkeley **Previous Positions:** Staff (1965-69), Theoretical Division, Stanford Linear Accelerator Center, Stanford, CA; Assistant Professor (1969), Physics and Theology, Seattle University; Visiting Professor (1969-70), University of Louvain, Leuven, Belgium; Dean (1971-79)/Associate Professor (1971-81), Theology and Science, Jesuit School of Theology - Berkeley; Guest Researcher, Theoretical Division, Lawrence Berkeley Laboratory; J. K. Russell Fellow in Religion and Science (1981-83), Center for Theology and the Natural Sciences, Berkeley, CA; Visiting Associate Professor of Physics and Theology (1983-87), Seattle University, WA **Media Work:** Interview on "Ecology and Religion," (October 1980), National Public Radio series, Minding the Earth **Selected Memberships:** American Physical Society; Federation of American Scientists; Union of Concerned Scientists, Board of Directors, Center for Theology and the Natural Sciences, Graduate Theological Union, Berkeley (1981-83) and Advisory Board (since 1990); "Spirituality of Ecology" (February 1989), LARCO Ecumenical Retreat, Los Angeles **Discipline:** Theology, Philosophy and Physics **Related Interests:** Issues in Theology and Ecology; Issues in Science and Religion and their interaction; Logical Principles and Theological Methodology; Physics and Creation; Science, Technology and Values; Ecological Spirituality.

Selected Publications:

_____. "Logical Principles and Theological Methodology." *Kalidowina* (University of Louvain) 2, 3, 33 (1969-70).
_____. "Computers and the Kingdom of God." In the *Report of the Conference on Computers: Altering the Human Image and Society*. University of California at Berkeley, January 1982.
_____, Robert J. Russell. "Foundations in Physics for Revising the Christian Creation Tradition." Chapter 8 in *Cry of the Environment: Rebuilding the Christian Creation Tradition*, ed. Philip N. Joranson and Ken Butigan. Santa Fe, NM: Bear & Co., 1985.
_____. "Andy Dufner: Physicist - Theologian." Chap. 22 in *Charged Bodies: A Portrait of Silicon Valley, The World's Premier High Technology Community*, ed. Thomas Mahon. New American Library and Signet Pub., 1985.
_____. "The Ignatian Spiritual Exercises and the New World View." *The Way Supplement 76: Person and Society in the Ignatian Exercises*. London, Spring 1993.

Dundon, Stanislaus J.

Present Position and Address: Member of Statewide Public Advisory Committee for Sustainable Agriculture, Agricultural Issues Center, University of California - Davis, CA 95616; Professor (since 1970), Philosophy Department, California Polytechnic State University, San Luis Obispo, CA 93407; (Home) 626 B Street, Davis, CA 95616, USA **Date of Birth:** July 18, 1935 **Languages Spoken:** English, Latin, French, German, Spanish **Education:** Catholic University (1954); B.A. Philosophy (1958), Carmelite College of Philosophy, Hubertus, WI; B.A. Theology (1962), Carmelite College of Theology, Washington, DC; M.A. Philosophy/History of Science (1965), Institute for the Philosophy of Science, St. John's University, NY (including study at Boston College and Marquette University in Physics and Mathematics); Ph.D. Philosophy and Physics (1972), St. John's University (including study at Boston College and University of California - Berkeley in Philosophy of Nature and History of Science) **Previous Positions:** Lectured in Philosophy (1966-69), University of Santa Clara; Lecturer, Philosophy, Ethics, Science and Society, History of Science and Technology, and World Religions (1970-present)/Associate Dean (1973-74), School of Communicative Arts and Humanities, California Polytechnic State University; Lecturer, History of Science/Agricultural Sciences (1981-82), University of Maryland, College Park; Director (1983-85), Human Values in Agriculture, Interdisciplinary Academic Improvement Program **Discipline:** Philosophy; History of Science; Interdisciplinary learning; Sustainable Agriculture **Related Interests:** Professional Ethics in Agriculture/Engineering.

Selected Publications: His bibliography lists over 40 papers and publications.

_____. "The 'Moral' Factor in Innovative Research." In *The Agricultural Scientific Enterprise: A System in Transition*, ed. Lawrence Busch and William Lacy. Westview Press, 1986.
_____. "Sources of Consensus First Principles in Agriculture Ethics." Chap. in *Readings in Agricultural Ethics*, ed. Charles Blatz. University of Idaho Press, 1988.

Durant, John Robert

Present Position and Address: Professor of Public Understanding of Science (since 1993), Imperial College - London; Head of Science Communications (since 1989), Science Museum, London 5W7 2DD, UK **Date of Birth:** July 8, 1950 **Education:** M.A. Natural Sciences (1972)/Ph.D. History of Science (1977), Cambridge University **Previous Positions:** Staff Tutor in Biological Sciences (1983-1989), Department for External Studies, University of Oxford **Discipline:** Biology; History of Science;

Social Studies of Science **Related Interests:** History of relationship of Science and Religion; Evolution and Religious Belief.

Selected Publications:

_____. "Darwinism and Divinity: A Century of Debate." In *Darwinism and Divinity Essays on Evolution and Religious Belief*, ed. J. R. Durant. Basil Blackwell, 1985.

_____. "The Ascent of Nature in Darwin's Descent of Man." In *The Darwinian Heritage*, ed. D. Kohn. Princeton University Press, 1985.

_____. "A Critical-Historical Perspective on the Argument about Evolution and Creation." In *Evolution and Creation: A European Perspective*, ed. S. Andersen and A. R. Peacocke. Aarhus University Press, 1987.

_____. "Charles Darwin and the Problem of Organic Diversity." In *Man Masters Nature: 25 Centuries of Science*, ed. R. Porter. BBC Books, 1987.

_____. "Evolution, Ideology and World View: Darwinian Religion in the Twentieth Century." In *The Humanity of Evolution: Essays in Honour of John Greene*, ed. J. R. Moore. Cambridge University Press.

Durbin, Jr., William A.

Present Position and Address: Ph.D. Candidate, Duke University, Durham, NC 27706; Free-lance Writer; 308 Oakridge Road, Cary, NC 27511, USA **Work Phone:** (919) 481-2782 **E-Mail:** bdurb@acpub.duke.edu **Date of Birth:** March 18, 1949 **Awards and Honors:** Story of the Year (1985), CBN News; Award of Excellence, Religion in Media (1984, 85) **Media Work:** Television News Producer and Writer, CBN News, Christian Broadcasting Network (1979-85) **Editorial Positions:** Contributing Editor, *The Pascal Centre Notebook* (since 1992) **Selected Memberships:** American Scientific Affiliation; Institute for Theological Encounter with Science and Technology **Discipline:** History of Religious Thought **Related Areas of Interest:** Science and Religion; Religion in America; Philosophy of Science **Current Areas of Research:** Twentieth Century Physics and New Age Metaphysics.

Selected Publications:

_____. "A Scientist Caught Between Two Faiths." Interview with Physicist Robert Jastrow. *Christianity Today* (August 6, 1982): 14-19.

_____. "Ramifications of Artificial Intelligence." *Christianity Today* (April 4, 1986). News report of Yale Conference.

_____. "The Return of the God Hypothesis." *Christianity Today* (April 3, 1987): 22-3.

_____. "Philosopher's Lament." Review of *Death of the Soul: From Desecrates to the Computer*, by William Barrett. *Christianity Today* (April 3, 1987): 31.

_____. "Should Christians Oppose Genetic Engineering?" *Christianity Today* (September 4, 1987): 54-5. News report on ASA Conference.

_____. "What Kind of God from Science?" Review of *Cosmic Joy and Local Pain*, by Harold J. Marowitz. *Christianity Today* (May 13, 1988: 58-9.

_____. "How It All Began." Forum on Science and Creation. *Christianity Today* (August 12, 1988): 31-41.

_____. "Frameworks for Reconciliation." *The Pascal Centre Notebook* (Fall 1992): 1-4. Essay Relating Three Philosophies of Science and Religion.

_____. Review of *The Knight's Move: The Relational Logic of the Spirit in Theology and Science*, by James E. Loder and W. Jim Neidhardt. *Journal on Interdisciplinary Studies* 5 (1993): 193-5.

Dye, David L.

Present Position and Address: Consulting Faculty, National Institute for Occupational Safety and Health (NIOSH)/USC Institute of Safety and Systems Management (1990-present); 12825 South East 45th Pl, Bellevue, WA 98006, USA **Date of Birth:** August 5, 1925 **Education:** B.S. Electrical Engineering (1945)/Ph.D. Physics (1952), University of Washington Selected **Conferences and**

Congresses: Also has been Conference Speaker on Science/Christianity issues InterVarsity Christian Fellowship/College groups/Church Camps **Previous Positions:** Instructor (1951-53), AFSWC, Albuquerque, NM (in Nuclear Weapons Physics)/US Navy Electronics School, Treasure Island (Radar); Development of 70 MeV Synchrotron for Cancer Therapy (1954-55), Radiological Lab/Instructor (1958-59), Radiology Department, University of California Medical Center; Head of Physics Department (1955-58), Gordon College, Rawalpindi, West Pakistan; Senior Scientist, TREES (1968-70), AF Special Weapons Center, Kirtland, AFB, NM; Instructor (1975-76), Nuclear Engineering Department, University of Washington; Research Engineer (1959-62)/Chief of Radiation Effects (1963-67)/Survivability Task Group (1967-68, 70-73)/Environmental and Radiation Hazards (1974-76)/Nuclear Science Computing (1976-81); Radar Countermeasures, Free Electron Laser development (1981-90), The Boeing Company (Retired, 1990); Lecturer, Netherlands Institute for Radiation Technology (1988), Amsterdam **Selected Memberships:** American Association for the Advancement of Science; American Scientific Affiliation; American Physical Society; Institute Electronic/Electrical Engineers **Discipline:** Radiological Physics **Related Interests:** A Comprehensive, Consistent Christian World View.

Selected Publications: The bibliography lists 35 technical, unclassified and open literature, and 3 non-technical works.

_____. *Faith and the Physical World - A Comprehensive View*. Grand Rapids, MI: W. B. Eerdmans, 1967 and 1971 but now out of print.
_____. "Another letter from Screwtape." *Christianity Today* (1976).
_____. "Environmental Issues Under the Lens of A Christian World View." American Scientific Affiliation meeting paper, August 1993.

Dyson, Freeman J.

Present Position and Address: Professor Emeritus (since 1994), School of Natural Sciences, Institute for Advanced Study, Princeton, NJ 08540, USA; (Home) 105 Battle Rd. Circle, Princeton, NJ 08540, USA **Date of Birth:** December 15, 1923 **Education:** B.A. (1945), Cambridge University UK **Previous Positions:** Operations Researcher (1943-45), RAF Bomber Command; Fellow (1946-49), Trinity College, Cambridge University, UK; Commonwealth Fellow, Cornell University (1947-49) and Princeton; Professor of Physics (1951-53), Cornell University; Author; Professor (1953-94), School of Natural Sciences, Institute for Advanced Study, Princeton, NJ **Selected Memberships:** Fellow, Royal Society of London; Member, American Physical Society; National Academy of Sciences **Discipline:** Physics **Related Interests:** Ethics and Science (i.e. arms control).

Selected Publications:

_____. *Disturbing the Universe*. Harper and Row, 1979.
_____. *Weapons and Hope*. Harper and Row, 1984.
_____. *Infinite in All Directions*. 1985 Gifford Lectures given at Aberdeen. Harper & Row, 1988.
_____. *From Eros to Gaia*. Pantheon Books, 1992, Penguin Books, 1993.

Eaves, Lindon John

Present Position and Address: Priest-in-residence, Episcopal Church of the Holy Comforter, Richmond; Department of Human Genetics, Medical College of Virginia, Box 3, MCV Station, Richmond, VA 23298-0003, USA; (Home) 10312 Maremont Place, Richmond, VA 23233, USA **Work Phone:** (804) 371-8754 **Home Phone:** (804) 741-0094 **Date of Birth:** September 23, 1944 **Education:** B.S.. Genetics (with Honors, Class I, 1966)/Ph.D. Genetics (1970), University of Birmingham; Student of Theology (1966-68), Cuddesdon College, Oxford, UK (recipient of Justin Banbury Prize in Theology); Ordained as Priest (1969), Church of England, Birmingham; M.A.(1979) University of Oxford; D.Sc. Genetics, University of Birmingham for collected works on "Application of Biometrical Genetics to Human Behavior" **Previous Positions:** Research Fellow in Genetics (1970-78), Birmingham University; University Lecturer, Department of Experimental Psychology, University of Oxford; Distinguished Professor (1981)/Professor of Psychiatry (1988), Department of Human Genetics, Medical College of Virginia, Richmond **Selected Memberships:** President (1991), Behavior Genetics Association **Discipline:** Genetics; Behavioral Genetics; Statistical Genetics; Ordained Episcopal Priest **Related Interests:** Theology and Biology.

Selected Publications: His bibliography lists 65 published papers, 10 books or chapters, 8 reviews, 32 abstracts. Most of these are in the field of genetics and human behavior.

_____. "Religion and Values: A Model System for the Impact of Genes and Culture." Invited GTE lecture and seminar series. CCRSO, University of Chicago, January 1989.
_____. "Spirit, Content and Method in Science and Religion: The Theological Perspective of a Geneticist." *Zygon* (1989).

Eccles, Sir John C.

Address: CH 6646 Contra (TI), Switzerland Date of Birth: January 27, 1903 Education: M.D. (1925), University of Melbourne, Australia; B.A. (1927)/M.A. (1927)/D.Phil. (1929), a Rhodes Scholar - Oxford University, UK **Honorary Degrees:** 18 Honorary Doctorates worldwide **Awards and Honors:** Fellow, Royal Society and Royal Medal (1940); Knight Bachelor (1958); Nobel Prize for Medicine/Physiology (1963); Mitglied Deutsche Academie Naturforschung and Cothenius Medal (1963); Foreign Member, Max-Planck-Institut für biophysikalische Chemie - Göttingen (1973); Order of the Rising Sun (Gold and Silver Stars, 1986), Japan; Companion of the Order of Australia, A.C. (1990) **Selected Memberships:** Honorary National Academy of Sciences; American Academy of Art and Sciences; American Philosophical Society; American College of Physicians; Academy dei Lincei; Pontifical Academy; Royal Belgian Academy; Indian Academy of Science **Discipline:** Physiology **Related Interests:** Neuroscience: The Brain; Evolution of the Brain. Miracle of Existence as Human Persons devoted to Truth, Love and Beauty.

Selected Publications: Over 500 scientific publications and 15 published books.

_____, Karl Popper. *The Self and its Brain*. Springer, 1977. Also in German, Italian, and Spanish.
_____. *The Human Mystery*. Springer, 1979. Also in German, Italian, and French.
_____. *The Human Psyche*. Springer, 1980. Also in German, Italian, and Spanish.
_____, D. Robinson. *The Wonder of Being Human*. Macmillan, 1984. Also in German, and Italian.
_____. *Evolution of the Brain: Creation of the Self*. Routledge, 1989. Also in German, Italian, Spanish, French, and Japanese.
_____. *How the Self Controls its Brain*. Springer Verlag, 1993. Also in German, Italian, French, Spanish, and Japanese.

Eckstrom, Vance L.

Present Position and Address: Academic Dean (since 1993), Bethany College, 421 N. First Street, Lindsborg, KS 67456, USA **Date of Birth:** March 14, 1931 **Education:** B.A. (1952), Gustavus Adolphus College; M.Div. (1956), Lutheran School of Theology at Chicago; M.A. (1966), San Jose State University; Th.D. (1971), Graduate Theological Union, Berkeley **Previous Positions:** Assistant Professor (1970-75), University of Portland, OR; Assistant Professor (1975-82), University of Santa Clara; Assistant Professor through Professor (1982-92), Bethany College **Discipline:** Theology **Related Interests:** Mind/Brain; Freedom/Determinism; Social Effects of Technology.

Selected Publications:

_____. "Science and Technology in the Religious Studies Classroom." *Institute for Theological Encounter with Science and Technology (ITEST) Newsletter* 2, 4 (October 1980): 2-8.

Eder, Gernot

Present Position and Address: Full Professor for Nuclear Physics (since 1971), Technical University of Vienna, Wiedner Hauptstrasse 8-10/142, A-1040 Wien, Austria; Director (since 1971), Atominstitut der Österreichischen Universitäten; (Home) Czartoryskigasse 46, A-1180 Wien, Austria **Date of Birth:** May 9, 1929 **Education:** Dr. phil. Mathematics and Physics (1951), University of Vienna **Previous Positions:** Max-Planck-Institut für Physik - Göttingen, with Professor W. Heisenberg (1953-55)/Niels-Bohr-Institut in Kopenhagen (1955-56); Lecturer (Universitätsdozent), (1957-63)//Honorary Professor of Theoretical Physics (1968), University of Vienna; Full Professor (1963-71), Theoretical Physics, University of Giessen, Germany **Discipline:** Theoretical Physics **Related Interests:** Philosophy of Science; Relation between Science and Theology.

Selected Publications: His bibliography lists 62 scientific articles, 4 books, 2 chapters, and more than 40 general works, 25 of which the author recommends as relevant to this topic.

_____. *Benimm dich, lieber Christ*. Johannesverlag, Einsiedeln, 1955.
_____. "Anfang und Ende der Welt in der Sicht der heutigen Physik." *Weltgespräch* 1, 3 Freiburg: Herder, 1967.
_____. "Eschatologie und Gegenwart aus naturwissenschaftlicher Sicht." *Bibel und Liturgie* 48, 4 (1975): 223-32.
_____. "Gott als Ordnungsprinzip." Review of *Gibt es Gott?* by J. Rosenthal. Literas, 25-8. Wien, 1982.
_____. "Religionspädagogische Aspekte heutigen Denkformen." *Christl. pädagog. Bl.* 98, 1 (1985): 51-8.
_____. "Einsicht als Resonanzphänomen." In *Grammatik des Glaubens*, ed. H. Bogensberger and R. Kögerler. In *Forum St. Stephan* vol. 2. Niederösterr. Pressehaus St. Pölten, 1985.
_____. "Thesen zur Diskussion Naturwissenschaft-Theologie. Am Beispiel des Schöpfungsbegriffs." *Diakonia* 17, 4 (1986): 246-50.
_____. "Wie ein Physiker über Gott denken kann." In *Forum St. Stephan*, ed. H. Bogensberger and W. Zauner, vol. 4, 9-33. Niederösterr. Pressehaus St. Pölten, 1987.

Ehlers, Vernon J.

Present Position and Address: State Senator (since 1985) (Chair - Natural Resources and Environmental Affairs Committee), 32nd District, Kent County, State Capitol, Lansing, MI 48913, USA **Work Phone:** (517) 373-1801 **Date of Birth:** February 6, 1934 **Education:** A.B. Physics (1956), Calvin College MI; Ph.D. Physics (1960), University of California - Berkeley **Postgraduate Studies:** NATO Postdoctoral Research Fellow (1961-62), University of Heidelberg, Germany **Previous Positions:** Teaching and Research Assistant (1956-60)/Lecturer in Physics (1960-66), University of California - Berkeley; Research Physicist (1960-66), Lawrence Radiation Laboratory, Berkeley, CA; Professor of Physics (1966-83), Calvin College; NFS Science Faculty Fellow (1971-72), Laboratory Astrophysics, University of Colorado; Fellow (1977-78), Calvin Center for Christian Scholarship, Calvin College; State Representative (1983-85), State of Michigan **Selected Memberships:** Member, American Scientific Affiliation; Very active in church and civic affairs, and has served on numerous church boards and councils, including national committees; Served on Christian Reformed Synodical Task Force on World Hunger California Christian College Association Board of Trustees; West Michigan Environmental Action Council/Environmental Protection Foundation **Discipline:** Senator; Physics **Related Interests:** Theology/Philosophy of Environmental Science; Energy problems, World hunger, Science and the Citizen, the Christian's responsibility to the Environment.

Selected Publications: His bibliography lists 3 books, 19 journal articles and several popular articles.

_____, coauthor with other Fellows of Calvin Center for Christian Scholarship. *Earthkeeping: Christian Stewardship of Natural Resources*. Grand Rapids, MI: Eerdmans, 1980.

Ehrenfeld, David W.

Present Position and Address: Professor of Biology (since 1974), Department of Natural Resources, Cook College, Rutgers University, New Brunswick, NJ 08903, USA **Work Phone:** (908) 932-9553 **Date of Birth:** January 15, 1938 **Education:** B.A. (1959), Harvard College; M.D. (1963), Harvard Medical School; Ph.D. Zoology (1967), University of Florida **Previous Positions:** Assistant to Associate Professor of Biological Sciences (1967-74), Barnard College, Columbia University **Editorial Work:** Founding Editor (since 1987), *Conservation Biology*; Member Editorial Board, *Environmental Ethics* **Selected Memberships:** Fellow, American Association for the Advancement of Science; Member of Board of Directors, E. F. Schumacher Society; Trustee, Educational Foundation of America **Discipline:** Biology; Ecology; Environmental Philosophy; Conservation **Related Interests:** Judaism and the Environment; Religious Attitudes towards the Environment; Technology; Environmental Philosophy.

Selected Publications:

_____. *The Arrogance of Humanism*. Oxford University Press, 1978, 1981.
_____, Philip J. Bentley. "Judaism and the Practice of Stewardship." *Judaism* 34, 3 (1985): 301-11.
_____. "The Roots of Prophecy: Orwell and Nature." *The Hudson Review* 38, 2 (1985): 193-213.
_____. "The Lesson of the Tower." *The Hudson Review* 38, 3 (1986): 367-81. About the social/environmental implications of space technology.
_____. *Beginning Again: People and Nature in the New Millennium*. Oxford University Press, 1993.

Eiff, August Wilhelm von

Present Position and Address: Professor Emeritus/Director Medical University Clinic, Bonn, Germany; Holder of a Grant studying Ethical problems on AIDS (1988-90, 90-present); Consultant to Ministry for Environment in Berlin (since 1975); (Work) Medical University Clinic, Am Paulshof 30,

53127 Bonn 4, Germany; (Home) Haager Weg 18a, D-53127 Bonn 4, Germany **Concurrent Positions:** Consultant (since 1988) of Instituto Scientifico San Rafaele, Milan **Work Phone:** 0228-285587 **Date of Birth:** August 15, 1921 **Languages Spoken:** German, English **Education:** Study of Medicine in Marburg-/Frankfurt/Heidelberg/Tübingen; State examination for doctorate (1945), Tübingen; Habilitation (1956), University of Bonn **Awards and Honors:** Bundesverdienstkreuz 1. class (1988); Hippokrates medal (1988); Romano Guardini Price (1992); Verdienst Order des Lauder Nordrhein-Westphalen (1994) **Previous Positions:** Associate Professor (1961)/Professor (1973), University of Bonn; House Physician (1945-47), Medical Clinic, University of Frankfurt; Assistant of Hans Schaefer at the Physiological Institute (1949-52), University of Heidelberg; Consultant to Concilium (1974-85)/German Bishop Conference (1960-64) **Selected Memberships:** A member of several German and International Medical Associations and Inter-disciplinary Research Institutes i.e. Interdisciplinary Institute of Görres Society; Nova Spes; E.I.U.C.; Kirche und Wissenschaft **Discipline:** Internal Medicine **Related Interests:** Science and Theology; Ethics in Medicine.

Selected Publications: He has written more than 300 publications about stress, autonomic nervous system, hyper-tension, AIDS, and ethical problems in medicine.

_____. "Medicine for the Promotion and the Respect of the Psychological and Physical Integrity of Human Beings." XV World Congress of the International Federation of Catholic Medical Association, Rome, Abstracts, 1982.
_____. "Instructions on the Prevention of AIDS." International AIDS Congress, Vatican, 1989.
_____. "The Specific Being of Men and Women." World Congress of FIAMC, 1990.
_____. "Criteri per la pratica medica o la ricerca di base circa la possibilità di influenzare gli istireti readarali." *Scienza id Etica mella Centralis dell' Domo* (Marland, 1990).
_____. "Ethische Probleme in der Immeren Medizin." *Schreigerinle Medizin* (Wochenschriff, 1992).
_____. "Verantwortung für den menschliche Leben." *Düsseldorf* 2 (1992).

Eigen, Manfred

Present Position and Address: Director (since 1964), Max-Planck-Institut für biophysikalische Chemie, Am Fassberg 11, D-37077 Göttingen, Germany **Date of Birth:** May 9, 1927 **Languages Spoken:** German, English **Education:** Studied Physics and Chemistry; Dr. rer. nat. Physical Chemistry (1951) **Honorary Degrees:** Honorary Doctorates from Washington University, St. Louis, MO (1966)/Harvard University (1966)/University of Chicago (1966)/ University of Nottingham (1968)/Hebrew University (1973)/University of Hull, UK (1976/University of Bristol (1978)/Debrecen (1982)/Techinschen Universität in München (1983)/Bielefeld (1985)/Utah State University (1990) **Awards and Honors:** Nobel Prize for Chemistry (1967); Otto-Hahn-Preis für Chemie und Physik (1962) **Previous Positions:** Scientific Researcher (1951-53), Institut für physikalische Chemie der Universität Göttingen; Assistant (1953)/Scientific Member (1958-62)/Leader of Section of Chemical Kinetics (1962-64), Max-Planck-Institut für physikalische Chemie; Andrew D. White Professor at Large (since 1965), Cornell University **Selected Memberships:** Fellow, Royal Society of Arts, London; Royal Society of Chemistry, London; USSR Academy of Sciences; Indian Chemical Society; Fellow, Royal Society of Edinburgh; Fellow, Royal Society of Scotland; Royal Danish Academy of Sciences; American Association of Biological Chemists; American Academy of Arts and Sciences; Päpstlichen Akademie der Wissenschaften, Rome **Discipline:** Biochemistry; Chemistry; Cosmology **Related Interests:** Origin and evolution of life **Current Research:** Mechanisms of biochemical reactions (enzyme kinetics, code reading, biopolymerization, sequential kinetics); Molecular self-organization (Origin and evolution of life - theory and experiments).

Selected Publications: Over 200 published papers.

_____, Peter Schuster. *The Hypercycle, A Principle of Natural Self-Organization.* Berlin: Springer-Verlag, 1979.
_____, Ruthild Windler. *Laws of the Game - How the Principles of Nature Govern Chance.* New York: Alfred A. Knopf, 1981.

Elgee, Neil J.

Present Position and Address: Clinical Professor of Medicine Emeritus (since 1993), University of Washington, Seattle, WA 91895, USA; President, Ernest Becker Foundation (since 1993) Private Practice of Medicine (retired 1993), 3621 72nd Ave. SE, Mercer Island, WA 98040, USA **Date of Birth:** April 3, 1926 **Education:** B.S.. (1946), University of New Brunswick; M.D. (1950), University of Rochester, NY **Awards and Honors:** Honors and Master, American College of Physicians **Previous Positions:** Intern (1950-51), Peter Bent Brigham Hospital, Boston, MA; Assistant Resident in Medicine (1951-52), Strong Memorial Hospital, Rochester, NY; Research Fellow in Endocrinology (1952-54), University of Washington, Seattle; Chief Resident in Medicine (1954-55), University of Washington, King County Hospital, Seattle **Selected Memberships:** Institute of Medicine of the National Academy of Sciences **Discipline:** Medicine **Related Interests:** Ernest Becker's writings; Ethics and war.

Selected Publications: His bibliography lists 17 medical works, and 9 general articles.

_____. "Freud and Kierkegaard: A Synthesis. Psychodynamics Come to Life." *Forum on Medicine* (December 1977): 46-9. Rev. Ed. *Bulletin of King County Medical Society* (June 1979).
_____. "Health Belief Systems and War's Madness: A Clinical Look at Ernest Becker's Psychology of War." *Pharos* 52 (Winter 1989): 27-32.
_____. "Norman Cousins' Sick Laughter Redux." *Arch Intern Med* 150 (August 1990): 1588.
_____. "Treasuring Old Age: Second Thoughts on Setting Limits." *Bulletin of the King County Medical Society*, 16 (February 1992).
_____. "Laughing at Breast Cancer: A Commentary." *Pharos* 56 (Winter 1993): 31-3.

Elkins, Thomas Edward

Present Position and Address: Professor and Chair (since 1992), Department of Obstetrics and Gynecology, Louisiana State University, School of Medicine/New Orleans, 1542 Tulane Avenue, Room 550, New Orleans, LA 70112 **Concurrent Positions:** Adjunct Professor (since 1993), Department of Tropical Medicine, Tulane University School of Public Health and Tropical Medicine, New Orleans, LA **Work Phone:** (504) 568-8663 **Fax Number:** (504) 568-5140 **Date of Birth:** December 23, 1949 **Languages Spoken:** English **Education:** BA (*Magna cum laude* 1972), Baylor University, Waco, TX; MD (with honors 1975), Baylor College of Medicine, Houston, TX; MA Religion (1984), Harding University Graduate School, Memphis, TN **Postgraduate Experience:** Internship (1976-80), Rotating Family Practice Internship; Residency (1977-80), Obstetrics and Gynecology, Naval Regional Medical Center, Portsmouth, VA **Awards and Honors:** *Who's Who in American Colleges and Universities* (1984); Citizen of the Year (1987), Washtenaw Country Association for Retarded Citizens; First Prize for Audiovisual Programs (1989), The American College of Obstetricians and Gynecologists, with E. J. McGuire and M. Kozminski, for "Vesico-Vaginal Fistula Repair with Interposition of Labial Fat Pad Graft" **Previous Positions:** Clinical Instructor, (1980-83)/Assistant Professor (1983-85), Department of Obstetrics and Gynecology, University of Tennessee College of Medicine/Memphis; Assistant Professor (1985-87)/Associate Professor (1987-92) Chief, Division of Gynecology, Department of Obstetrics and Gynecology, University of Michigan Medical School, Ann Arbor, MI **Editorial Experience:** Editorial Board: *International Journal of Gynecology and Obstetrics*, *American Journal of Obstetrics and Gynecology*; Special Reviewer, *Obstetrics and Gynecology* **Selected Memberships:** Fellow, American College of Obstetricians and Gynecologists; American Medical Association; Baptist Medical and Dental Fellowship; American Society of Law and Medicine; National Down Syndrome Congress; Society for Health and Human Values; Uro-Gynecology Society; American Association on Mental Deficiency; Washtenaw County OB/GYN Society; American Association for Maternal and Neonatal Health; Christian Medical and Dental Society; American Colposcopy Society; North American Society for Pediatric and Adolescent Gynecology; Michigan Association for Retarded citizens; Society for Gynecologic Surgeons; Central Association of Obstetrics and Gynecology; American Professors of Gynecology and Obstetrics; Jacobs Institute of Women's Health Society; Greater New Orleans OB-GYN Society; Norman Miller Society **Discipline:** Obstetrics and Gynecology **Related Areas of Interest:** Ethics in Medicine.

Selected Publications: His bibliography contains 90 articles, 43 books, chapters in books and monographs and 19 other publications.

_____, S. G. McNeeley and T. Tabb. "A New Era in Contraceptive Counseling for Early Adolescents." *Sexually Active Teenagers* 1 (1987): 19-22.
_____, D. Brown. "The Meaning of Prayer: A Christian Physician's Experience." *Journal of Religion and Health* 26, 4 (1987): 286-99.
_____, D. Brown. "A Physician's Study of Human Suffering and God Consciousness in the Sermons of Friedrich Schleiermacher." *Journal of Religious Studies* 13, 1 (1987): 1-14.
_____, D. Brown. Restoring the Covenant." *Christian Medicine Society Journal,* 18, 2 (1987): 17-20.
_____, D. Brown. "Baby Doe and the Concept of Grace." *Christian Medical Society Journal* 18, 3 (1987): 5-9.
_____, D. Brown. *Faith for Troubled.* Nashville, TN: Times Broadman Press, 1988.
_____. *On the Need for More Careful Consideration by Gynecologists of Sex Education Programs in Public Schools.* Stafford, VA: American Life League, Inc., 1989. Monograph.
_____. "Ethics at the Edges of Life: Euthanasia. Life in the Balance." In *Proceedings of the 1989 Christian Life Commission Seminar,* 41-8. Nashville, TN: Christian Life Commission of the Southern Baptist Convention , 1989.
_____. "Ethical Issues in Obstetrics and Gynecology." In Precis IV: An Update in Obstetrics and Gynecology, 67-71. Washington, DC: The American College of Obstetricians and Gynecologists, 1990.
_____. "The Body Spiritual. How Do I Love Me." Christianity Today (1993): 24.

Ellens, J. Harold

Present Position and Address: Psychotherapist in private practice (since 1965); Executive Director Emeritus, Christian Association for Psychological Studies International (CAPS), 26705 Farmington Road, Farmington Hills, MI 48334, USA **Work Phone:** (810) 477-1350 **Home Phone:** (810) 474-0514 **Date of Birth:** July 16, 1932 **Education:** B.A. Philosophy/Psychology (1953), Calvin College; M.Div. Biblical Studies and Pastoral Theology (1956), Calvin Seminary; Th.M. Biblical Studies and Pastoral Theology (1965), Princeton Theological Seminary; Graduate (1965), Cranbrook Institute for Advanced Pastoral Studies; Ph.D. Communication Psychology (1970), Wayne State University **Previous Positions:** Pastoral work (1956-78/84-85); Lecturer in Pastoral Psychology (1967-70), Calvin Theological Seminary; Professor of Communication Psychology (1970-77), Oakland University; Visiting Professor of Pastoral Theology/Psychology (1977-78), Princeton Seminary; Adjunct Professor of Pastoral Theology in D.Min. Extension Program (1979-90), Drew University; Executive Director (1974-88, now Emeritus), Christian Association for Psychological Studies, International (CAPS) **Editorial Work:** Founder and Editor in Chief (1974-88, now Emeritus), Journal of Psychology and Christianity **Selected Memberships:** American Academy of Religion; Society for the Scientific Study of Religion **Discipline:** Psychology and Judeo-Christian Theology **Related Interests:** During the last 20 years, interest has focused on the scientific interface of theology and the social sciences, particularly psychology - based on specialization in theological and psychological anthropology, and its relationship to personality theory and development.

Selected Publications: Bibliography lists 26 major publications and mentions 104 professional journal articles.

_____, William Donaldson. Research in Mental Health and Religious Behavior. Atlanta: PSI/Georgia State University, 1976.
_____. God's Grace and Human Health. Nashville: Abingdon, 1982.
_____. *Pyschotheology: Key Issues.* Johannesburg, South Africa: University of South Africa Press, 1987.

_____, David Benner. *Psychology and Religion*, ed. David G. Brenner. Grand Rapids: Baker Book House, 1988.
_____, Malham Wakin. *Moral Obligation and the Military*. Washington: National Defense University Press, 1988.
_____, LeRoy Aden and David Benner. *Christian Perspectives on Human Development*. Grand Rapids: Baker Press, 1990.
_____, LeRoy Aden and David Benner. *Counseling and the Human Predicament*. Grand Rapids, MI: Baker Press, 1989.
_____, LeRoy Aden. *Turning Points in Pastoral Care*. Grand Rapids, MI: Baker Press, 1990.
_____, LeRoy Aden. *The Church and Pastoral Care*. Grand Rapids, MI: Baker Press, 1988.
_____, David Benner. *Christian Counseling and Psychotherapy*. Grand Rapids, MI: Baker Press, 1987.

Ellis, George F. R.

Present Position and Address: Professor (since 1990), Applied Mathematics Department, University of Cape Town, Rondebosch 7700, Cape Town, South Africa **Work Phone:** +27-21-650-2339/2340 **Fax:** University of Cape Town, 27-21-6502334 **E-Mail:** Ellis@maths.uct.ac.za **Date of Birth:** August 11, 1939 **Languages Spoken:** English, German, Italian **Education:** B.S.. Hons. (1960), University of Cape Town; Ph.D. (1964), Cambridge University **Previous Positions:** Lecturer (1968-73), Cambridge University; Professor (1973-88, 1990-present), Cape Town University; Professor (1988-90), SISSA, Trieste, Italy **Discipline:** Cosmology and Relativity Theory **Related Interests:** Cosmology and Theology.

Selected Publications:

_____. "Critique: The Church and the Scientific Community." In *John Paul II on Science and Religion: Twenty Reflections on the New View from Rome*, ed. R. J. Russell. California: Center for Theology and the Natural Sciences, 1990.
_____. "Major Themes in the Relation between Philosophy and Cosmology." *Mem Ital Ast Soc* 62 (1991): 553-605.
_____. "The Theology of the Anthropic Principal." In *Quantum Cosmology and the Laws of Nature*, ed. R.J. Russell, N. Murphy, and C.J. Isham. Vatican Observatory, (1993): 367-406.
_____. *Before the Beginning*. London: Bowerdean Press/Marion Boyers, 1993.
_____. "Ordinary and Extraordinary Divine Action: The Nexus of Intervention." Paper presented at CTNS/Vatican Observatory Conference, Berkeley. August 1993.
_____. "God and the Universe: Venosis as the Foundation of Being." *CTNS Bulletin* 14, 2 (1994): 1-14.

Emerton, Norma Elizabeth

Present Position and Address: Freelancer, 34 Gough Way, Cambridge CB3 9LN, UK **Work Phone:** (0223) 63219 **Date of Birth:** May 21, 1932 **Education:** B.A. (1953)/M.A. (1957), Oxford University; Ph.D. (1975), Cambridge University **Awards and Honors:** Phi Beta Kappa Prize for best science book (1985) **Previous Positions:** Freelancing; Teaching on a part-time basis, History and Philosophy of Science Department, Cambridge University UK **Discipline:** History of Science **Related Interests:** Relation between Scientific Theory and Theology before 1800 in the Areas of Creation, Cosmology and Earth Science.

Selected Publications:

_____. *The Scientific Reinterpretation of Form*. Cornell University Press, 1984. This deals with the use of philosophical concept of form in chemical and crystallographic theory before 1800 - Phi Beta Kappa prize winner.
_____. "The Argument from Design in Early Modern Theology." *Science and Christian Belief* 1, 2 (1989).

Engels, Eve-Marie

Present Position and Address: Prof. Dr., FB Erziehungswissenschaft/Humanwissenschaft (Philosophie), Universität - GhK Kassel Nora-Platiel Strasse 1, D-34127 Kassel, Germany **Date of Birth:** February 23, 1951 **Languages Spoken:** German, English, French **Education:** (Dr. phil.) Promotion in Philosophie (1981)/Habilitation in Philosophie (Priv.-Doz., 1988), Bochum. **Discipline:** Epistemology; Philosophy and History of Biology; Philosophical Ethics.

Selected Publications: Her bibliography lists some 30 entries in the fields of epistemology, philosophy and history of biology and philosophical ethics.

_____. *Die Teleologie des Lebendigen. Kritische Überlegungen zur Neuformulierung des Teleologieproblems in der angloamerikanischen Wissenschaftstheorie. Eine historisch-systematische Untersuchung* (Teleology of Life. Critical Reflections on the New Formulation of the Problem of Teleology in Anglo-American Philosophy of Science. A Historical-Systematical Inquiry). Berlin: Duncker & Humblot 1982. Enlarged and revised, Dissertation, philosophy.
_____. *Erkenntnis als Anpassung? Eine Studie zur Evolutionären Erkenntnistheorie* (Knowledge as Adaptation? A Study in Evolutionary Epistemology). Frankfurt: Suhrkamp, 1989.
_____. "Herbert Spencers Moralwissenschaft - Ethik oder Sozialtechnologie? Zur Frage des naturalistischen Fehlschlusses bei Herbert Spencer" (Herbert Spencer's Moral Science - Ethics or Social Technology? The Question of Naturalistic Fallacy in Herbert Spencer). In *Evolution und Ethik*, ed. Kurt Bayertz. Stuttgart: Reclam, 1993.
_____. "Georg Edward Moores Argument der 'naturalistic fallacy' in seiner Relevanz für das Verhältnis von philosophischer Ethik und empirischen Wissenschaften" (George Edward Moore's Argument of the 'naturalistic fallacy' in its Relevance for the Relationship between Philosophical Ethics and Empirical Sciences). In *Ethische Norm und empirische Hypothese*, eds. Lutz H. Eckensberger and Ullrich Gähde. Frankfurt: Suhrkamp, 1993.

Erbrich, Paul

Present Position and Address: Professor at the Hochschule für Philosophie (der Jesuiten), Kaulbachstrasse 33, D-80539, München, Germany **Date of Birth:** February 23, 1928 **Languages Spoken:** German, English, French **Education:** Master in Theology (1957), Enghien; Ph.D. in Biology (1965), Vienna, Austria **Previous Positions:** College Teacher (at a "gymnasium" in Austria) **Selected Memberships:** Member of the Jesuit Order since 1947 **Discipline:** Natural Philosophy; Philosophy of Science **Related Interests:** Evolution and Creation; Bioethics; Human Ecology.

Selected Publications:

_____. "Evolution und Schöpfung." *Schweizer Rundschau* 70, 3 (1971): 157-80.
_____. "Kritische Evolutionstheorie." *Theologie und Philosophie* 58 (April 1983): 556-65.
_____. "On the Probability of the Emergence of a Protein with a Particular Function." *Acta Biotheoretica* 34 (1985): 53-80.
_____. "Technik - Chance oder Verhängnis." *Technische Rundschau* 79, 46 (1987): 8-15.
_____. *Zufall, eine naturwissenschaftlich-philosophische Untersuchung*. Stuttgart: Verlag W. Kohlhammer 1988.
_____. "Weltweite Umweltproblematik." In *Soziales Denken in einer zerissenen Welt*, eds. J. Müller und W. Kerber. Freiberg I. Br. Herder, 1991.

Erdmann, Erika

Present Position and Address: Publisher of the quarterly *Humankind Advancing: Toward more Farsighted, Responsible Attitudes*; Retired Library Research Assistant (1981-1990), of Professor Dr. Roger W. Sperry, Nobel Laureate. This work involved the study, condensation, and discussion with him of all relevant publications in science, philosophy, psychology, etc. and their relation to his own writing and thinking. R.R.1, Lockeport, N.S., BOT 1LO, Canada **Work Phone:** (902) 656-2085 **Date of Birth:** January 16, 1919 **Education:** Hon. B.A. Physiological Psychology (1971), Sir-George-William's University, Montreal; M.A. Interdisciplinary Studies (1985)/D.Phil. (1987), Columbia Pacific University, San Francisco **Previous Positions:** Research Assistant (1938-42), Thermodynamics, Altenkirch, Berlin; Research Assistant in Physiological Psychology for Dr. Roy Wise (1971-72), Sir-George-William's University; Library Assistant (1973-77)/Head Librarian (1977-81), Shelburne Library **Selected Memberships:** Institute on Religion in an Age of Science; International Advisory Council for the World Culture Project; World Future Society **Discipline:** Independent scholar - interdisciplinary studies **Related Interests:** Closing the Chasm Between Facts and Values; Global Ethic; Responsibility for Future Generations.

Selected Publications:

_____. *Realism and Human Values.* New York: Vantage Press, 1978.
_____. *In Search of Values for Human Survival.* Ann Arbor: University Microfilms International, 1988. Ph.D. diss., Columbia Pacific University, 1987.
_____. *Challenge to Humanity: Values for Survival and Progress.* Dundas, Ontario: Peace Research Institute-Dundas, 1989.
_____, David Stover. *Beyond a World Divided/ Human Values in the Brain - Mind Science of Roger Sperry.* Boston: Shambhala Press, 1991.
_____. "Values Needed for Survival." In Hopes and Fears/The Human Future, ed. H. Newcombe. Toronto: Science for Peace/Samuel Stevens, 1992.

Euvé, François

Present Position and Address: Professor in Institut Catholique de Paris Centre d'Etudes Russes, 15 rue Porto-Riche, F 92190 Meudon, France **Work Phone:** 46 26 13 38 **Date of Birth:** August 9, 1954 **Languages Spoken:** French, English, Russian **Education:** Agrégation, Physics (1976), Paris; Ecole Normale Supérieure (1973-1977), Paris; Licence, Philosophy (1987); Maitrise, Theology (1989) **Discipline:** Theology and Philosophy **Related Interests:** Epistemology; Theology.

Selected Publications:

_____. "Science et Foi: un nouveau dialogue." Cahiers pour Croire Aujourd'hui (April 1988).

Evans, Abigail Rian

Present Position and Address: Director of Health Ministries, National Capital Presbytery Health Ministries and Research Fellow, Kennedy Institute of Ethics, Georgetown University, Washington, DC, USA; 6120 North Kings Highway, Alexandria, VA 22303, USA **Work Phone:** (703) 768-3097 **Languages Spoken:** English, Portuguese, Spanish, German **Education:** Diploma in Brazilian Language and Culture (1960), Campinas, Brazil; Graduate Studies in Theology (1964-66), University of Basel, Switzerland; M.Div. (1968), Princeton Theological Seminary; Ordained as a Presbyterian Minister (1969); Independent Study in Ethics (1984), Corpus Christi College, Oxford University **Awards and Honors:** Who's Who in East; Who's Who International Leaders; Who's Who International Women **Previous Positions:** Pioneer missionary (1959-64), United Presbyterian Church, Brasil; Instructor in Liturgy and Church History (1966-67), Campinas Theological Seminary, Brasil; Pastor and Community Organizer in various USA churches (1968-84); Chaplain (1971-76), Columbia University; Assoc. Synod Executive (1976-79); Director of New Programs and Senior Staff Associate (1984-88), Kennedy Institute of Ethics, Georgetown University **Selected Memberships:** Some Task Force on Science, Values, and Technology, Washington Council of Churches (1984-85) Society for Health and Human Values (since 1983); Board of Governors, Washington Theological Consortium; Ethics Consultant, National Institutes of Health **Discipline:** Philosophy/Bioethics; Theology **Related**

Interests: Bioethics and the Christian Faith/Public Policy; Ethical Theory; Relations between Medicine and Theology; Science and Religion; Women's Issues; Addiction, AIDS, Aging, Genetics.

Selected Publications: Bibliography lists some 22 published, or soon to be published, items.

_____. "Moving Toward Wholeness: A Ministry of Healing where Medicine and Theology Meet." In *Bereavement of the Physical Disability: Recommitment to Life, Health and Function*, ed. Downey, Riedel and Kutscher. Arno Press, 1982.
_____. *Genesis, Procreation, or Reproduction: Cosmology and Ethics*. Pittsburgh: Carnegie Mellon Press, 1989.
_____. Review of *Genethics: The Clash Between the New Genetics and Human Values,* by Suzuki, David and Peter Knudtson. *Princeton Seminary Bulletin* (Spring 1990).

Evans, C. Stephen

Present Position and Address: Professor of Philosophy (since 1986)/Curator of the Howard and Edna Hong Kierkegaard Library; Department of Philosophy, 502 Holland Hall, St. Olaf College, Northfield, MN 55057, USA **Work Phone:** (507) 663-3170 **Education:** B.A. Philosophy (1969), Wheaton College IL; M.Phil (1971)/Ph.D. Philosophy (1974), Yale University **Previous Positions:** Assistant Professor of Philosophy (1972-74), Trinity College, IL; Visiting Associate Professor of Philosophy (1980-81), Western Kentucky University; Assistant through Professor of Philosophy (1974-84)/Professor of Psychology (1982-84), Wheaton College; Associate Professor (1984-86), St. Olaf College **Editorial Work:** *Faith and Philosophy; Kierkegaardiana*; International Kierkegaard Commentary series; *Journal of Psychology and Theology* **Selected Memberships:** Member/Executive Committee (1986-89), Society of Christian Philosophers; American Academy of Religion; Kierkegaard Society, USA/Denmark; Society for Values in Higher Education; Society for Phenomenology and Existential Philosophy **Discipline:** Philosophy of Religion; Philosophy of the Human Sciences; Phenomenology and Existentialism; Philosophical Psychology **Related Interests:** Religion and Philosophy/Psychology/Human Sciences.

Selected Publications: The bibliography includes 7 books, 27 articles, 19 book reviews. He is also the general editor of the Contours of Christian Philosophy series, published by InterVarsity Press.

_____. "Christian Perspectives on the Sciences of Man." *Christian Scholar's Review* 6, 2 and 3. N.d.
_____. "Must Psychoanalysis Embrace Determinism? Or Can a Psychoanalyst be a Libertarian?" *Psychoanalysis and Contemporary Thought* 7, 3 (1984).
_____. *Preserving the Person: A Look at the Human Sciences*. InterVarsity Press: 1977; Reprint, Baker Press, 1982.
_____. *Wisdom and Humanness in Psychology*. Baker Books, 1989.

Everest, F. Alton

Present Position and Address: Registered Consulting Engineer in Acoustics (since 1973), retired; (Home) 2661 Tallant Rd. #619, Santa Barbara, CA 93105, USA **Home Phone:** (805) 682-6551 **Fax:** (805) 687-3386 **Date of Birth:** November 22, 1909 **Education:** B.S.. EE (1932), Oregon State University; E.E. Degree (1936), Stanford University; 3 semesters in Physics (1946-48), UCLA **Awards and Honors:** Hon. D. Sc. (1959), Wheaton College **Previous Positions:** Television Engineer (1936), Don Lee Broadcasting System; Instructor/Assistant Professor of Electrical Engineering (1936-41), Oregon State University; Section Chief, Underwater Sound Research (1941-45), Division of War Research, University of California; Cofounder/Director of Science and Prod., science films (1945-70, retired), Moody Institute of Science; Senior Lecturer (1970-73), Communication Department, Hong Kong Baptist College **Editorial Work:** Editor of the *American Scientific Affiliation Newsletter* for 10 years **Selected Memberships:** Acoustical Society of America; Inst. of Electrical and Electronic

Engineers; Cofounder(1941), President (1941-50), American Scientific Affiliation **Discipline:** Acoustical Engineering **Related Interests:** Modern Science/Technology and Christian Faith.

Selected Publications: His bibliography includes 9 books in the field of audio engineering and about 50 papers in professional journals and technical magazines.

_____, editor. *Modern Science and Christian Faith*. Chicago: Van Kampen Press, 1948, 1950.

Ewald, Günter

Present Position and Address: Professor of Mathematics, University of Bochum, Germany; Aeskulapweg 7, 4630 Bochum 1, Germany **Date of Birth:** April 1, 1929 **Languages Spoken:** German, English **Education:** Studies in Mathematics/Physics/Chemistry/Philosophy (1948-54); Dr. rer. nat. (1954), University of Mainz, Germany; Habilitation, University of Mainz (1960) **Previous Positions:** Assistant Professor of Mathematics (1957-58), Michigan State University/University of Southern California, LA (1960-62); Rektor (1973-75), University Bochum, Germany; Präsidium Deutscher Ev. Kirchentag (1974-88) **Selected Memberships:** Deutsche Mathematikervereinigung; Hamburger Mathematische Gesellschaft; Bund der Religiösen Sozialisten Deutschlands **Discipline:** Mathematics **Related Interests:** Science and Theology; Artificial Intelligence; Religious Socialism.

Selected Publications: Not including publications in Mathematics and others specialized fields.

_____, B. Klappert, and H. Demmer. *Das Ungewöhnliche. Wunder im Blick von Naturwissenschaft, Theologie und Gemeinde*. Wuppertal: Aussaat Verlag, 1969.
_____. *Der Mensch als Geschöpf und kybernetische Maschine*. R. Brockhaus, 1971.
_____. "Bemerkungen zum Begriff von Raum und Zeit in der Physik." *Gott-Geist-Materie. Theologie und Naturwissenschaft im Gespräch*. Hamburg: Lutherisches Verlagshaus, 1980.
_____. "Apokalyptik und Rüstungswettlauf." *Erziehen heute* 36 (1986): 2-11.
_____. "Naturwissenschaft und christlicher Glaube: Kosmischer oder kritischer Weg aus der Krise?" *Materialdienst der Ev. Zentralstelle für Weltanschauungsfragen* 49 (1986): 92-101.
_____. "Geist und Materie - religiöses Denken und Reden in einer naturwissenschaftlich geprägten Welt." In *Naturwissenschaft und Glaube*, ed. H. A. Müller. Scherz-Verlag, 1988.
_____. "Computer - intelligente Technik oder techniache Gutelligeuz?" *Materialdieust der EZW* 52 (1989): 289-98.
_____. "Sind wir ant dern Wege zu einer Computer - Kultur?" *Herrenalber Protobolle* 85 (1992): 7-22.
_____. *Naturwissenschaftliche und religiöse Ideologien*. EZW-Texte Inpulse III (1993).
_____. "Gottesglaule in einer naturwisseuschaftlich geprligten Welt." *Materialdieust der EZW* 57 (1994): 1-10.

Faber, Roger J.

Present Position and Address: Professor of Physics (since 1972), Lake Forest College, Lake Forest, IL 60045; (Home) 608 Smith Ave., Lake Bluff, IL 60044, USA **Work Phone:** (708) 735-5166 **Home Phone:** (708) 234-7135 **Date of Birth:** October 4, 1931 **Education:** A.B. (1953), Calvin College; Ph.D. (1957), Michigan State University **Previous Positions:** Research Instructor (1957-58)/Assistant Professor of Chemistry (Summer 1959), Michigan State University; Instructor through Associate Professor (1958-64), Calvin College; Assistant/Associate Professor of Physics (1965-72), Lake Forest College; Consultant (1967-70), Argonne National Laboratory; Research Associate (1973-74/80-81), Department of Philosophy, Boston University (sabbaticals) **Selected Memberships:** Philosophy of Science Association; American Association for the Advancement of Science; American Physical Society; American Association of Physics Teachers **Discipline:** Physics **Related Interests:** Quantum Theory; Mind/Body Issue; Reductionism.

Selected Publications: His bibliography lists 7 publications.

_____. "Feedback, Selection, and Function: A Reductionistic Account of Goal Orientation." In *Methodology, Metaphysics and the History of Science*, ed. R. S. Cohen and M. Wartofsky. Dordrecht: D. Reidel, 1984.
_____. *Clockwork Garden: On the Mechanistic Reduction of Living Things*. Amherst, MA: The University of Massachusetts Press, 1986.

Facchini, Fiorenzo

Present Position and Address: Professor of Anthropology (since 1971), Department of Biology, Unità di Antropologia via F. Selmi, 1, 40126 Bologna, Italy **Work Phone:** (051) 35.42.01 **Fax:** (051) 35.41.91 **Date of Birth:** November 9, 1929 **Education:** Bachelor in Theology (1951); Doctorate in Natural Sciences (1957); Libero Docente in Antropologia (1968) **Selected Memberships:** Academy of Sciences of Bologna (Italy) **Discipline:** Anthropology **Related Interests:** Paleoanthropology; Human Biology; Evolution.

Selected Publications:

_____. "Divaricazione tra etica e scienza. Possibilità e presupposti per un incontro e un dialogo." In *Corso di Bioetica*, ed. E. Sgreccia. Milano: Angeli, 1986.
_____. "The Roots of Ethics. An Anthropological Approach." *Human Evolution*, 6, 5-6 (1991): 461-8.
_____. *Premesse per una Paleoatropologia culturale*. Milano: Jaca Book, 1992.
_____, M. Gimbutas, J. K. Kozlowski, and B. Vandermeersch. *La religiosità nella preistoria*. Milano: Jaca Book, 1991.
_____. "Le origini dell'uomo: le ragioni della scienza e della fede." *Sette e Religioni* 4, 1 (1991): 621-47.
_____, di a. Beltran e A. Broglio. *Paleoantropologia e Preistoria. Dizionario enciclopedico* Milano: Jaca Book, 1993.
_____. "La culture dans le rapport homme-milieu." *Revue des questions scientifiques* 162, 3 (1991): 271-88.
_____. *Il cammino dell'evoluzione umana*. Milano: Jaca Book, 1985. 2d. ed., 1994.

_____. "Vita e salute delle future generazioni. Il ruolo dell'equilibrio ambientale. problemi ed esigenze di ordine etico." *Atti del XX Congresso Nazionale AMCI*, 8-10 dic. 1994. (In press).
_____. *Evoluzione, Uomo e ambiente. Lineamenti di Antropologia.* Torino: UTET, 1988. 2d. ed., 1995.

Fagg, Lawrence W.

Present Position and Address: Research Professor in Physics (since 1977), Physics Department, Catholic University of America; Washington, DC 20054, USA; (Home) 905 Canterburg Road, Stephens City, VA 22655, USA **Work Phone:** (202) 319-5326 **Date of Birth:** October 10, 1923 **Education:** B.S. Military Engineering (1945), US Military Academy; M.S. Physics (1947), University of Maryland; M.A. Physics (1948), University of Illinois; Ph.D. Physics (1953), Johns Hopkins University; M.A. Religion (1981), George Washington University **Awards and Honors:** Fellow, American Physical Society; Navy Meritorious Civilian Service Award **Previous Positions:** US Naval Research Laboratory (1953-58); Atlantic Research Corporation (1958-63); Naval Research Laboratory (1963-76) **Selected Memberships:** International Society for the Study of Time; Former Vice President, Institute on Religion in an Age of Science; Center for Theology and the Natural Sciences; Fellow, American Physical Society **Discipline:** Nuclear Physics; Religion **Related Interests:** Time in Science and Religion.

Selected Publications: His bibliography lists 70 articles in professional journals of physics.

_____. *Two Faces of Time.* Theosophical Publishing House, 1985. A book comparing religious and physical concepts of time.
_____. *The Becoming of Time.* Under consideration by Oxford University Press.

Falla Jr., William S.

Present Position and Address: Chaplain; Assistant Professor of Religion (since 1983), Department of Philosophy/Religion, Cedar Crest College, 100 College Drive, Allentown, PA 18104-6196, USA **Date of Birth:** September 6, 1942 **Education:** B.A. Chemistry (1964), Harpur College (SUNY - Binghamton); M.S. Geology (1967), Pennsylvania State University; M.Div. (1976), UTS, Dayton; Th.M. (1980), Lutheran School of Theology at Chicago **Selected Memberships:** Sigma Xi; Institute on Religion in an Age of Science; Center for Theology and the Natural Sciences; History of Science Society; Philosophy of Science Association **Discipline:** Constructive Theology **Related Interests:** Science and Religion; History of Science; Philosophy of Science; Women Issues in Science and Religion.

Selected Publications:

_____. "Effects of Use of Scientific Models as Basis for Theological Systems: Evolution." Th.M. thesis, Lutheran School of Theology at Chicago, 1980.
_____. "Theology, Science and a New Environmental Ethic." *EcoSpirit* (Fall 1986).

Farnsworth, Kirk E.

Present Position and Address: Vice President/Executive Director (since 1985), CRISTA Counseling Service (A Division of CRISTA Ministries), 19303 Fremont Avenue North, Seattle, WA 98133, USA; Adjunct Professor (since 1988), Fuller Theological Seminary - Seattle extension; (Home) 8088 N.E. Bayberry Lane, Kingston, WA 98346, USA **Date of Birth:** February 16, 1940 **Education:** B.S. Industrial Psychology/Minor in Economics (1962)/M.S. Counseling Psychology (1966)/Ph.D. Counseling Psychology (1968), Iowa State University, Ames **Previous Positions:** Staff of Counseling and Testing Center/Associate Professor of Psychology, University of New Hampshire (1968-75); Associate

Professor of Psychology/Director of Counseling (1975-79)/Professor of Psychology and Chairperson (1979-83), Trinity College, Deerfield, IL; Professor of Psychology (1983-85), Wheaton College, IL **Selected Memberships:** American Psychological Association: divisions 2, 17, 24, 29 and 36 (Psychologists Interested in Religious Issues); Fellow, American Scientific Affiliation; Christian Association for Psychological Studies; Psi Chi; Sigma Xi. **Discipline:** Counseling Psychology **Related Interests:** Integrating Psychology and Christianity in Counseling and Management.

Selected Publications:

_____. "Application of Scaling Techniques to the Evaluation of Counseling Outcomes." *Psychological Bulletin* 66 (1966): 81-93.

_____. "Christian Psychotherapy and the Culture of Professionalism." *Journal of Psychology and Theology* 8 (1980): 115-21.

_____. W. H. Lawhead. *Life Planning: A Christian Approach to Careers.* Downers Grove, IL: InterVarsity, 1981.

_____. *Integrating Psychology and Theology: Elbows Together but Hearts Apart.* Washington, DC: University Press of America, 1981.

_____. *Wholehearted Integration: Harmonizing Psychology and Christianity Through Word and Deed.* Grand Rapids, MI: Baker Book House, 1985.

_____. "Furthering the Kingdom in Psychology." Chap. 4 in *The Making of a Christian Mind: A Christian World View and the Academic Enterprise*, ed. A. Holmes. Downers Grove, IL: InterVarsity 1985.

_____. "Consumerism," "Interest Measurement," "Phenomenological Psychology," " Phenomenological Therapy," and "Vocational Counseling." In *Baker Encyclopedia of Psychology*, ed. D.G. Benner. Grand Rapids: Baker Book House, 1985.

_____. "Understanding Religious Experience and Putting It to the Test." *Journal of Psychology and Christianity* 9 (1990): 56-64.

_____. "On an Equal Footing." Chap. 6 in *Storying Ourselves: A Narrative Perspective on Christians in Psychology*, ed. D.J. Lee. Grand Rapids: Baker Books, 1993.

Fasching, Darrell J.

Present Position and Address: Professor of Religious Studies (since 1989) and Chair (since 1993)/Courtesy Professor of Philosophy (since 1988), University of South Florida, Tampa, FL 33620, USA; (Home) 15811 Cottontail Place, Tampa, FL 33624, USA **Work Phone:** (813) 972-2221 **Home Phone:** (813) 963-2968 **Fax:** (813) 962-1499 **Education:** B.A. Philosophy (1968), University of Minnesota; M.A. Religious Studies (1971)/Ph.D. Religious Studies (1978), Syracuse University **Previous Positions:** Program Director (1971-75)/Assistant Dean (1975-80), Hendricks Chapel, Syracuse University; Assistant Professor of Religious Studies (1980-82), Le Moyne College, Syracuse NY; Assistant Professor (1982-85)/Associate Professor (1985-1989) of Religious Studies/Director of Graduate Religious Studies (1984-1989)/Associate Dean, College of Arts and Sciences (1991-93), University of South Florida, Tampa; Affiliate Professor of Comprehensive Medicine (since 1983), College of Medicine, University of South Florida **Discipline:** Religious Studies and Philosophy **Related Interests:** Ethics, Technology and Public Policy; Comparative Religious Ethics; Post-Holocaust Theological Ethics.

Selected Publications:

_____. "Technology as Utopian Technique of the Human." *Soundings* 60, 2 (Summer 1980).

_____. *The Thought of Jacques Ellul.* New York and Toronto: Edwin Mellen Press, 1981.

_____. "Theology and Technology." In *The New Handbook of Christian Theology.* Abingdon Press, 1991.

_____. *Narrative Theology After Auschwitz: From Alienation to Ethics.* Minneapolis: Fortress Press, 1992.

_____. *The Ethical Challenge of Auschwitz and Hiroshima: Apocalypse or Utopia?* Albany, NY: SUNY Press, 1993.

Fayter, The Rev. Paul

Present Position and Address: Currently a Ph.D. candidate (expected 1994-95), University of Toronto; Lecturer in Science and Humanities (since 1988), York University, 228 Varnier College, York University 4700 Keele St., North York, Ontario, M3J 1P3, Canada; Pastor, Echo Place United Church, Brantford, Ontario, Canada **Date of Birth:** December 23, 1953 **Languages Spoken:** English, French **Education:** B.A. (Hons. 1977)/M.A. (1980), University of Toronto; Certificate in Bioethics (1980), Centre de Bioéthique, Institut de Recherches Cliniques de Montreal; M.Div. Victoria University (1991) **Previous Positions:** Lecturer in History of Science, Institute for the History and Philosophy of Science and Technology, University of Toronto (1987-91); Associate Minister (1984-86), St. James United Church, Parry Sound **Selected Memberships:** Canadian Society for History and Philosophy of Science; Canadian Scientific and Christian Affiliation; Victorian Studies Association; History of Science Society; Center for Theology and the Natural Sciences; North American Conference on Christianity and Ecology; British Society for History of Science; Christians in Science; Victoria Institute of Great Britain; International Society for History, Philosophy, and Social Studies of Biology; United Church of Canada; Society for the History of Natural History **Discipline:** Social History of Science and Theology (especially 19th and 20th Century natural theology, Darwinism) **Related Interests:** Cosmology, Evolutionary Biology, and Theology; Social History of Science and Medicine; Environmental, Biomedical, and Sexual Ethics; Science Fiction and Religion **Current Research:** "Interplanetary Darwinism," (on religious and political meanings of late Victorian mars).

Selected Publications: Two major projects, a bibliographic work on natural theology and evolution, and a book on "Varieties of Theistic Evolution in the 19th and 20th centuries" are still in their initial stages. Various newspaper articles, letters to the editors, resolutions, articles, sermons, prayers, poems, etc. in secular and church publications. Various reviews of books on religion and science, and history of science..

_____. "Scientific Creationism and its Critics." *Journal of the American Scientific Affiliation* 37 (June 1985): 104-8.
_____. "Senses of the Natural World." *Forest Conservation and History* 34 (April 1990): 85-92. Discusses nature as world, environment, creation in history of science and environmental philosophy.
_____. "God and Modern Cosmology." Appendix in *The Voice of Earth*, ed. Theodore Roszak. New York: Simon and Schuster, 1992.
_____. "Creator Spirit," and eleven other hymns. In *Worship for all Seasons*, ed. Thomas Harding, Vol. 1. Toronto: UCPH, 1993.
_____. "Post-Darwinian Natural Theology: Nature and its Ideological Uses in Victorian Scientific Naturalism, 1860-1900." Thesis almost complete.

Feifel, Herman

Present Position and Address: Emeritus Clinical Professor of Psychiatry and the Behavioral Sciences, University of Southern California School of Medicine, Los Angeles; (Home) 360 South Burnside Avenue, #10M, Los Angeles, CA 90036, USA **Home Phone:** (213) 935-0065 **Date of Birth:** November 4, 1915 **Languages Spoken:** English, French, Hebrew **Education:** B.A. Psychology (1935), City College of New York; M.A. Psychology (1939), Columbia University, NYC; Ph.D. Psychology (1948), Columbia University, NYC **Honorary Degrees:** Dr. of Humane Letters (1984), University of Judaism **Awards and Honors:** Distinguished Professional Contributions to Knowledge Award, American Psychological Association (1988); Distinguished Contributions to Research in Clinical Psychology Award, American Psychological Association, Clinical Psychology Division (1989) **Previous Positions:** Research Psychologist, Personnel Research Section, Adjunct General's Office, Washington, DC (1946-1949); Supervisory Clinical Psychologist (1950-54), Winter VA Hospital, Topeka, KS; Research and Clinical Psychologist (1954-59), VA Mental Hygiene Clinic, Los Angeles,

CA; Research Associate (1956-58), Department of Medicine, City of Hope Medical Center Duarte, CA; Visiting Senior Research Scientist (1960), Research Center for Mental Health, New York University; Chief Psychologist (1960-91), VA Outpatient Clinic, Los Angeles, CA **Selected Memberships:** Fellow, American Psychological Association; Fellow, American Psychological Society; Fellow, Academy of Religion and Mental Health; Fellow, Society for the Scientific Study of Religion; Sigma Xi; International Work Group on Dying, Death, and Bereavement **Discipline:** Psychology **Related Areas of Interest:** Dying, Death, and Bereavement; Coping with Old Age and Illness; Religion and Psychology; Ethics; Philosophy of Science **Current Areas of Research:** Coping with Illness, Old Age, and Death.

Selected Publications: His bibliography contains 2 books, 18 book chapters, and 100 published research articles, book reviews, commentaries, etc.

_____. "Ego Structure and Mental Deterioration." Journal of Personality 20 (1951): 188-98.
_____. "Relationships between Religion and Mental Health." American Psychologist 13 (1958): 565-6.
_____, editor. The Meaning of Death. New York: McGraw-Hill, 1959.
_____. "Philosophy Reconsidered." In The Science of Philosophy: Critical Reflections, ed. D. P. Schultz, 30-5. New York: Appleton-Century-Crofts, 1970.
_____. "Relation of Religious Conviction to Fear of Death in Healthy and Terminally Ill Populations." Journal for the Scientific Study of Religion 13 (1974): 353-60.
_____. "Death and Dying in Modern America." *Death Education: An International Journal* 1 (1975): 5-14.
_____, editor. *New Meanings of Death*. New York: McGraw-Hill, 1977.
_____, S. Strack, and V. T. Nagy. "Coping Strategies and Correlative Features of Medically Ill Patients." *Psychosomatic Medicine* 49 (1987): 616-25.
_____, S. Strack. "Coping with Conflict Situations: Middle-aged and Elderly Men." *Psychology and Aging* 4 (1989): 26-33.
_____. "Psychology and Death: Meaningful Rediscovery." *American Psychologist* 45 (1990): 537-43.

Felt, James W.

Present Position and Address: Professor of Philosophy (since 1965), Santa Clara University, Santa Clara, CA 95053, USA **Date of Birth:** January 4, 1926 **Languages Spoken:** English, German **Education:** B.A. (1957), Alma College - now the Jesuit School of Theology, Berkeley; M.S. Physics (1961)/Ph.D. Philosophy (1965), Saint Louis University **Previous Positions:** Visiting Professor (Spring 1971), Institute of European Studies, Vienna/Gonzaga University, Spokane (Fall 1976); Founder of annual Philosophy Conference at Santa Clara University; Founding editor, *Logos: Philosophic Issues in Christian Perspective* **Selected Memberships:** Past president (1981-82), Jesuit Philosophical Association, USA **Discipline:** Philosophy; Physics **Related Interests:** Metaphysics; Process Philosophy; Philosophy of Nature.

Selected Publications:

_____. "Mach's Principle Revisited." *Laval Théologique et Philosophique* 20 (1964): 35-49.
_____. "Whitehead and the Bifurcation of Nature." *The Modern Schoolman* 45, 4 (1968): 285-98.
_____. "The Temporality of Divine Freedom." *Process Studies* 4, 4 (1974): 252-62.
_____, William A. Barker, Karel L. De Bouvère. S.C.J., Dean R. Fowler. "Alfred North Whitehead." In *Dictionary of Scientific Biography*, vol. 14. Scribner's Sons, 1975.
_____. "Impossible Worlds." *International Philosophical Quarterly* 23, 3 (1983): 251-65.
_____. "God's Choice: Reflections on Evil in a Created World." *Faith and Philosophy* 1, 4 (1984): 370-7.
_____. "Fatalism and Truth About the Future." *The Thomist* 56, 2 (1992).
_____. *Making Sense of Your Freedon: Philosophy for the perplexed*. Cornell University Press, 1994.

Fennema, Jan W. R.

Present Position and Address: Researcher (since 1986), Nederlandse Organisatie voor Wetenschappelijk Onderzoek (Dutch Organization for Scientific Research), Universiteit Twente, Postbus 217, NL-7500 AE Enschede, The Netherlands; (Home) Marterlaan 42, NL 1216 EX Hilversum, The Netherlands **Work Phone:** 31-35-213125 **Fax:** University of Twente: 31-53-356 695 **Date of Birth:** June 18, 1929 **Languages Spoken:** Dutch, English, German, French, and Spanish **Education:** Final Examinations in Physics (1956)/Thesis for doctorate (1967), Vrije Universiteit, Amsterdam **Previous Positions:** Part-time teacher, Grammar schools and Professional medicine schools (1957-1983); Researcher (1960-1986), Stichting voor Fundamenteel Onderzoek der Materie (Foundation for Fundamental Research on Matter) **Discipline:** Physics and Philosophy **Related Interests:** Science and Humanity/Religion; Criticism of the present Scientific Method.

Selected Publications: A list of published materials indicates some 42 articles in the field of science and religion.

_____. "Vision unitaire du monde et choc d'altérité." *Revue des Questiones Scientifiques* 161, 2 (1990): 151-63.

_____. "'Give Me Where to Stand', and I Will Move the Earth'; on the So-Called Foundations of Physics." In *Proceedings of the 8th International Congress of Logic, Methodology and Philosophy of Science, Moscow, 1987. Abstracts* 2: 34-7.

_____. "Contingency and Lawfulness: Conditions for Encounter." *Symposium Microphysical Reality and Quantum Formalism.* Dordrecht: Kluwer Academic Publishers, 1988.

_____. "An Encounter Between Science and Religion." In *Science and religion: One World — Changing Perspectives on Reality.* Second European Conference on Science and Religion, ed. Jan Fennema and Iain Paul. Dordrecht: Kluwer Academic Publishers, 1990.

_____. "Qetiv und Qere, die natürliche Theologie als Gottessuche." *Evangelische Theologie* 53, 2 (1993): 157-74. Also Published in *Grenz-Überschreitung, Festschrift zum 70. Geburtstag von Manfred Büttner,* ed. Heyno Kattensted. Bochum: Universitätsverlag Dr. N. Brockmeyer, 1991.

_____. "'The Law ... Written in Our Heart': On the Balance Between Solidarity and Autonomy." In *The Influence of the Frankfurt School on Contemporary Theology, Critical Theory and the Future of Religion, Dubrovnik Papers in Honor of Rudolf J. Siebert,* ed. James Reimer. Lewiston/Queenston/Lampeter: The Edwin Mellen Press, 1992.

_____. "L'ouverture de l'homme et du monde." In *Actes Séminaire Réna 7,* ed. Jean de Lagarde and Xavier Sallantin. Enveitg (Pyr.Or.): Fondation Béna, 1994.

_____. "über die Beziehung der Theologie zu den Wissenschaften: zwischen Isolierung und Vereinnahmung?" Forthcoming.

_____. "Peniel, That is, Man 'Transcending' Horizontal and Vertical Transcendence." Forthcoming, 1996.

_____. "Science and Religion. An Observation Regarding the Contribution of Science to the Debate." In *Studies of Science and Theology,* Vol. 4. N.p., 1996. Also published in *Debreceni Szemle* 3 (1993).

Ferré, Frederick

Present Position and Address: Research Professor of Philosophy (since 1988), Department of Philosophy at Peabody Hall, Faculty of Environmental Ethics, University of Georgia, Athens, GA 30602; (Home) 275 Davis Estates Road, Athens, GA 30606, USA. **Work Phone:** (706) 542-2823 **Fax:** (706) 542-2839 **E-Mail:** FFERRE@UGA.CC.UGA.EDU **Date of Birth:** March 23, 1933 **Education:** Oberlin College (1950-51); A.B. History (*summa cum laude*, 1954), Boston University; M.A. Philosophy of History (1955), Vanderbilt University; Theological Studies (1955-56), Vanderbilt University Divinity School; Ph.D. Philosophy of Religion (1959), University of St. Andrews, Scotland **Previous Positions:** Visiting Assistant Professor of Philosophy (1958-59), Vanderbilt University; Assistant Professor of Religion (1959-62), Mount Holyoke College; Associate (1962-67)/Professor (1967-70)/Charles A. Dana Professor Philosophy (1970-80), Dickinson College; Professor/Head, Department of Philosophy and Religion (1980-88), University of Georgia; Chair (1984-91), Faculty of Environmental Ethics, University of Georgia **Editorial Work:** General editor (1986-94), *Research in Philoso-*

phy and Technology; Editorial boards: 8 journals including *American Journal of Theology and Philosophy; Environmental Ethics; Journal of Religion; Philosophical Forum; American Philosophical Quarterly* **Selected Memberships:** American Philosophical Association; American Theological Society; Philosophy of Science Association; Society for Christian Philosophers; Society for Philosophy of Religion **Discipline:** Philosophy of Religion/Philosophy of Technology **Related Interests:** Ethics, Metaphysics, Religion and Environment; Science and Religion; The Post-Modern World.

Selected Publications: His bibliography lists 6 books he has authored, plus 12 more of which he was the editor, 38 chapters, and over 50 articles, over 45 book reviews and over 80 papers and presentations.

_____. *Language, Logic, and God.* New York: Harper and Brothers, 1961. Reprint, Greenwood Press, 1976. Paper edition, Midway Editions, University of Chicago Press: 1981.
_____. "Explanation in Science and Theology." Chap. 2 in *Earth Might be Fair, Reflections on Ethics, Religion, and Ecology*, ed. Ian G. Barbour. Englewood Cliffs, NJ: Prentice-Hall, 1972.
_____. *Shaping the Future: Resources for the Post-Modern World.* New York: Harper and Row, 1976.
_____. "Science, Religion, and Experience." In *Experience, Reason, and God*, ed. Eugene Thomas Long. Vol. 8 of *Studies in Philosophy and the History of Philosophy*. Washington: The Catholic University of America Press, 1980.
_____. "Einstein on Religion and Science." *American Journal of Theology and Philosophy.* 1, 1 (January 1980): 21-8.
_____. "Religious World Modelling and Postmodern Science." *Journal of Religion* 62, 3 (July 1982): 261-71.
_____. *Philosophy of Technology.* Englewood Cliffs, N.J. Prentice-Hall Publishing Company, Inc., 1988.
_____. *Hellfire and Lightning Rods: Liberating Science, Technology, and Religion.* Maryknoll, NY: Orbis Books, 1993.

Feucht, Dennis L.

Present Position and Address: Engineer (since 1988), Innovatia Laboratories; (Home) 5275 Crown Street, West Linn, OR 97068, USA **Date of Birth:** October 6, 1950 **Education:** B.S.E.E. Computer Science (1972), Oregon State University **Awards and Honors:** Vincent Bendix Design Award (1st place internationally), Institute of Electrical and Electronic Engineers (IEEE) **Previous Positions:** Tektronix Inc. (1969-85); Synektron Corporation (1985-88) **Selected Memberships:** Fellow, American Scientific Affiliation **Discipline:** Robotics, Electronics, Artificial Intelligence **Related Interests:** Mind/Body relationship; Artificial Intelligence and its Implications.

Selected Publications:

_____. "Logical Indeterminacy, Levels of Meaning, and Mystery." *Journal of the American Scientific Affiliation (JASA)* 29, 4 (1977).
_____. "Some Implications of Artificial Intelligence Research." *JASA* 34, 2 (1982).
_____. "The Mind-Brain Problem and Knowledge Representation in Artificial Intelligence." *JASA* 38, 4 (1986).

Fiddes, Victor H.

Present Position and Address: Retired minister of the United Church of Canada. Ordained in 1941 and retired in 1982; 5841 Bellevue Terrace, Niagara Falls, Ontario, L2G 4G4 Canada **Home Phone:** (416) 374-3578 **Date of Birth:** July 21, 1916 **Education:** B.A. (1938)/M.Div. (1941), Queen's University, Kingston Ontario; M.Th. (1953), School of Graduate Studies, University of Toronto **Honorary Degrees:** Doctor of Divinity (honoris causa, 1969), Queen's University **Previous Positions:** Pastorates include Lundy's Lane United Church, Niagara Falls (1952-62); Queen Mary Road United Church, Montreal (1962-69); Westminster United Church, Regina, Saskatchewan (1969-73); St. James United Church, Montreal (1973-82) **Selected Memberships:** Chairman, National Committee on Church Architecture, The United Church of Canada (20 years) **Discipline:** Christian Faith - Theology;

Preaching; Church Architecture; Natural Science **Related Interests:** Lay interest in Ecclesiastical Architecture and Natural Science.

Selected Publications:

_____. *Science and the Gospel.* Vol. 7 of *Theology and Science at the Frontiers of Knowledge,* series ed. T. F. Torrance. Edinburgh: Scottish Academic Press, 1988.

Finney, Joseph Claude Jeans

Present Position and Address: President, American Institute of Higher Studies (since 1991); 11561 Spur Road, Monterey, CA 93940-6621, USA. **Date of Birth:** March 18, 1927 **Education:** B.A. Chemistry (1946), Vanderbilt; Graduate Studies in Philosophy (1946-1947), University of Notre Dame; M.D. (1949), Harvard University; Graduate Studies in Biology (1950-53), University of California - Berkeley; Ph.D. in Psychology (1959), Stanford University; LL.B. in Law (1972); Graduate Studies in Theology (1975-79), Liberal Catholic Institute of Studies; Ordained as Priest (1979) **Previous Positions:** Taught Psychology/Psychiatry, University of Illinois (1956-60)/ University of Hawaii (1960-63)/University of Kentucky (1963-77)/Loyola University of Chicago (1980-83); Colonel, US Army (1983-87); National Secretary (1987-1991), The Synod of Liberal Catholic Priests in the United States **Selected Memberships:** Catholic Theological Society of America; S.S.S.R.; R.R.A; American Psychological Association; American Psychiatric Association; American Anthropological Association; Chairman (1976-80), American Bar Association Committee on Law and Mental Health; Vice-Chairman (1980-82), American Bar Association Committee on Medicine and Law; Linguistic Society of America **Discipline:** Psychology; Psychiatry; Ordained Priest **Related Interests:** Scientific study of Religion **Current Research:** Several research projects in behavioral sciences, including a study of religion in Polynesia.

Selected Publications: His bibliography includes over 80 professional papers and 1 book.

_____. *Culture Change, Mental Health and Poverty.* University of Kentucky Press, 1969; Simon and Schuster, 1970.
_____. "The Story of Lusi, A Nanumangan Legend." *Rongorongo Studies* (1992): 3-13, 50-61.

Fischer, Dick

Address: 6623 Williamsburg Blvd., Arlington, VA 22213, USA **Work Phone:** (703) 533-1809 **Date of Birth:** January 29, 1939 **Education:** B.S./B.A. (1961), University of Missouri; Graduate Studies (1975-76), Troy State University; Presently working on M.T.S., Evangelical Theological Seminary **Selected Memberships:** American Scientific Affiliation; American Association for the Advancement of Science; Faith and Science Fellowship (local) **Discipline:** Theology **Related Interests:** Resolution of Theological/Scientific Conflict Concerning Human Origins.

Selected Publications:

_____. "The Days of Creation: Hours or Eons?" *Perspectives on Science and Christian Faith* 42, 1 (March 1990): 15-22.

Fischer, Robert B.

Present Position and Address: Provost and Distinguished Professor Emeritus (since 1989), Biola University; (Home) 30238 Via Victoria, Rancho Palos Verdes, CA 90275, USA **Date of Birth:** October 24, 1920 **Education:** B.S. (1942), Wheaton College IL; Ph.D. (1946), University of Illinois **Previous**

Positions: Research Chemist (1944-46), Manhattan Project, University of Chicago; Instructor of Chemistry (1946-48), University of Illinois; Professor (1948-63), Indiana University; Dean of School of Science (1963-79 and Emeritus), California State University; Provost and Senior Vice President (1979-88), Biola University **Selected Memberships:** American Scientific Affiliation (national president 1966-67) **Discipline:** Chemistry **Related Interests:** Science and Society; Science and Theology; Biblical Hermeneutics.

Selected Publications: His bibliography includes over 70 research articles, several textbooks on chemistry and 2 general books.

_____. *Science, Man and Society.* Philadelphia: W.B. Saunders Co., 1971, 1975.
_____. *God Did It, But How?* Grand Rapids: Zondervan, 1981.

Fleming, Fraser Fergusson

Present Position and Address: Associate Professor of Chemistry (since 1992), Duquesne University, Pittsburgh, PA 97331, USA **Work Phone:** (503) 737-6765 **Fax Number:** (503) 737-2062 **E-Mail:** fleming@duq3.duq.cc.edu **Date of Birth:** March 20, 1964 **Education:** B.S.. (Honors, 1986), Massey University, Palmerston North, New Zealand; Ph.D. (1990), University of British Columbia, Vancouver, Canada **Postgraduate Experience:** Postdoctoral research with Professor E. Piers, Oregon State University **Awards and Honors:** Massey Scholar (1985), New Zealand; Izaak Walton Killam Predoctoral Fellowship (1986-90), Canada; Shirtcliffe Scholarship (1986-89), New Zealand **Selected Memberships:** American Chemical Society; American Scientific Affiliation **Discipline:** Chemistry.

Selected Publications:

_____, E. Piers. "Total Synthesis of the trans-Clerodane Diterpenoid (±) Stephalic Acid." *J.C.S. Chem. Comm* (1989): 1665-7.
_____, E. Piers. "Conversion of Enol Trifluoromethanesulphonates into α, β-Unsaturated Nitriles." *J.C.S. Chem. Comm.* (1989): 756-7.
_____, E. Piers, and B. W. A. Yeung. "Bifunctional Conjunctive Reagents: 5-chloro-2-lithio-1-pentene and Related Substances. A Methylenecyclohexane Annulation Methol." *Canadian Journal of Chemistry* 71 (1993): 280-6.
_____, J. D. White, N. J. Green. "Tin (IV)-Catalysed Lactonization of ω-Hydroxy Trifluoroethyl Esters." *Tetrahedron Lett.* 34 (1993): 3515.
_____, J. T. Hovermale, J. D. White, and M. Craig. "Improved Labeling Methods for $C9\text{-}^{2}H$-Retronecine." *Heterocycles* 38 (1994): 135.

Fokker, Adriaan D.

Address: Kruislaan 17, 3721 AL Bilthoven, The Netherlands **Work Phone:** 30-285610 **Date of Birth:** July 18, 1926 **Languages Spoken:** Dutch, English, German **Education:** Ph.D. Astronomy (1960), Utrecht University **Previous Positions:** Assistant Professor of Astronomy (1962-87), Utrecht University Observatory **Selected Memberships:** Dutch Astronomical Society **Discipline:** Astronomy **Related Interests:** Impact of Astronomical Knowledge on World-view; Implications of Astro-knowledge for "Belief."

Selected Publications:

_____. "The Play that is Going on in the Cosmic Scenery." Paper presented at the 2nd European Conference on Science and Religion; March 10-13, 1988. Abstract in *Science and Religion: One World - Changing Perspectives on Reality*, ed. Jan Fennema and Iain Paul. Dordrecht: Kluwer Academic Publishers, 1990.
_____. "Ecologische theologie?" *De Ronde Tafel.* no. 15 (February 1987). English translation available.
_____. "A Philosophical Approach to the Extraterrestrial Life Issue." Paper presented at the 3rd International Symposium on Bioastronomy, June 18-23, 1990.

_____. "Natuurwetenschap en religieus bewustzijn" (Natural science and religious consciousness.). *In de marge.* 2, 2 (1993): 18-23. Amsterdam: Center for Reflection, Free University of Amsterdam.
_____. "Onze visie op de werkelijkheid" (Our vision on reality). In *Religieus junanisme als levens — en wereldbeschouwing.* The Hague: Religious humanistic circle "Modern Bread," 1993.
_____. "Ons zicht op de natuur" (Our sight on nature). *Barchembladen.* 37 (1993): 7-12.
_____. *Gespreks - stof,* 4th ed. Free Faith Community NPB, 1993. English translation, "*Topics for discussion, a guide for conversations.*" Available.
_____. "Reflecties over onze kennis betreffende het heelal" (Reflections on our Knowledge Concerning the Universe). *Parodos* (Periodical of International for Philosophy, the Netherlands) 39 (May 1994).
_____. "Reflections on the Anthropic Principle and on the Issue of Extraterrestrial Life." (in Chech) Lecture presented for the European Cultural Club, Prague. *Riše huězd* 74 (December 1993).

Force, James E.

Present Position and Address: Department of Philosophy; University of Kentucky, Lexington, KY 40506-0027, USA **Date of Birth:** August 3, 1947 **Education:** B.A. (1969), University of Colorado; M.A. (1975)/Ph.D. (1977), Washington University, St Louis. **Previous Positions:** Research Professor (1987-88), University of Kentucky **Selected Memberships:** History of Science Society; American Society for 18th Century Studies; Hume Society **Discipline:** Philosophy **Related Interests:** Theology and Science in the Early Modern Period, e.g. in the thought of Isaac Newton, and in that of David Hume.

Selected Publications:

_____. "Hume and the Relation of Science to Religion Among Certain Members of the Royal Society." *Journal of the History of Ideas* 45, 4 (1984): 517-36.
_____. *William Whiston, Honest Newtonian.* Cambridge: Cambridge University Press, 1985.
_____. "Hume's Interest in Newton and Science." *Hume Studies* 13, 2 (1987): 166-216.
_____. "Newton's 'Sleeping Argument' and the Newtonian Synthesis of Science and Religion." In *Upon the Shoulders of Giants: Newton and Halley, 1686-1986,* ed. Norman J. W. Thrower. Berkeley and Los Angeles: University of California Press, 1989.
_____. "The Origins of Modern Atheism." *Journal of the History of Ideas* 50, 1 (1989): 153-62.
_____. Richard H. Popkin. *Essays on the Context, Nature, and Influence of Isaac Newton's Theology.* Dordrecht: Martinus Nijhoff, 1990.

Ford, Charles E.

Present Position and Address: Director of Computer Science (since 1986); Associate Professor (since 1979), Department of Mathematics and Computer Science, Saint Louis University, 221 North Grand Boulevard, Saint Louis, MO 63103, USA **Date of Birth:** July 8, 1941 **Education:** B.S. Mathematics (1963), University of Chicago; Ph.D. Mathematics (1968), University of Oregon **Postgraduate Studies:** Postdoctoral Fellow (1968-69), University of Toronto **Selected Congresses and Conferences:** International Congress of the History of Science (August 1989), Germany; Organized conference on Artificial Intelligence for Theologians and Scientists **Selected Lectures:** Gave 4 talks at annual meetings of the mathematical societies (1988, 90, 92, 94), on the religious background of the Moscow School of Mathematics **Previous Positions:** Assistant Professor (1969-75), Washington University; Assistant Professor (1976-79)/Director of Computer Certificate Program (since 1978), Saint Louis University **Selected Memberships:** ITEST; Association of Christians in the Mathematical Sciences **Discipline:** Science and Theology in Modern Europe; Christian roots of Modern Russian Science/Mathematics.

Selected Publications:

_____. "Dmitrii Egorov: Mathematics and Religion in Moscow." *The Mathematical Intelligencer* 13, 2 (1991): 24-30.
_____. "Luther, Bonhoeffer and Revolution." *Lutheran Forum* 25, 4 (1991): 24-8.
_____. "Father Pavel Florensky and Modern Soviet Mathematics." *Bulletin of the Institute for Theological Encounter with Science ant Technology* 23, 2 (1992): 3-9.
_____. Dietrich Bonhoeffer, the Resistance and the Two Kingdoms." *Lutheran Forum* 27, 3 (1993): 28-34.
_____, Sergei S. Demidov. "N. N. Luzin and the Affair of the 'National Fascist Center.'" In *Festschrift for Joseph Scriba*. Academic Press, in press.

Forster, Peter R.

Present Position and Address: Senior Tutor (since 1983), St. John's College, University of Durham, South Bailey, Durham, DH1 3RJ, UK **Work Phone:** Telephone: 091-3743574 **Education:** B.A. Chemistry Class I (1973), Merton College, Oxford; B.D. Systematic Theology Class I (1977)/Ph.D. Patristic Doctrine of Creation (1986), Edinburgh University UK **Selected Memberships:** Science and Religion Forum, UK **Discipline:** Systematic and Historical Theology **Related Interests:** General Interest in Doctrine of Creation, Linked with Scientific Aspects.

Selected Publications:

_____. "Providence and Prayer." In *Belief in Science and in Christian Life*, ed. T. F. Torrance. Edinburgh, 1980.

Foster, Mark A.

Present Position and Address: Assistant Professor of Sociology (since 1989), Macon College, Macon, GA; (Home) 248 Tom Hill Sr. Blvd., Suite 434, Macon, GA 31210-1815, USA; (June-August) 133 Barbara Lane, Levittown, NY 11756, USA **Home Phone:** (912) 742-5795 **Fax:** Holiday No. (516) 796-127 **Date of Birth:** February 27, 1956 **Education:** A.A. English (1976), Nassau Community College, S.U.N.Y.; A.B.J. Journalism (1978), University of Georgia; M.A. Sociology (1981), Long Island University; Ph.D. Sociology (1984), Mississippi State University **Previous Positions:** Assistant Professor of Sociology and Acting Chair (1985), Department of Sociology, Caldwell College, NJ; Assistant Professor of Sociology (1985-1989)/ Chair, Department of Social and Behavioral Sciences (1986-88), Clinch Valley College, University of Virginia **Selected Memberships:** American Sociological Association; Institute on Religion in an Age of Science **Discipline:** Sociology **Related Interests:** Hermeneutics and Transcendence; Structural Paradigm in the Human Sciences; Certain Religious movements in Society.

Selected Publications:

_____. "The Structural Paradigm in the Human Sciences: Ethnomethodology, Ethnoscience, and Neurolinguistic Programming." Paper presented as part of the Faculty Colloquium series at Clinch Valley College, University of Virginia, Spring 1987.
_____. "The Conditions of Reality: An Examination of Baha'i Cosmology." Paper presented at the annual meeting of the Institute on Religion in an Age of Science, Star Island, New Hampshire, 1988.

Fowler, III, James W.

Present Position and Address: Charles Howard Candler Professor of Theology and Human Development and Director, Center for Faith Development, Candler School of Theology, Emory University, Bishops Hall 3A, Atlanta, GA 30322, USA; (Home) 2740 Janellen Drive NE, Atlanta GA 30345, USA **Date of Birth:** October 12, 1940 **Education:** B.A. History (Honors, 1962), Duke University; B.D.

Theology and Ethics (*magna cum laude*, 1965), Drew University; Ph.D. Religion and Society (1971), Harvard University **Postgraduate Studies:** Postdoctoral study (1973), Center for Moral Development, Harvard Graduate School of Education **Previous Positions:** Youth minister (1962-64), United Methodist Church; Associate Director (1968-69), Interpreters' House, Lake Junaluska; Director of Continuing Education/Lecturer (1969-71)/Assistant Professor and Chairman (1971-74), Department of Applied Theology, Harvard Divinity School; Associate Professor of Applied Theology (1974-76), Director of Research Project on Faith and Moral Development, Harvard Divinity School; Associate Professor of Theology and Human Development (1976-77), Boston College; Associate Professor (1977-80)/Professor (1980-87) of Theology and Human Development; Over 30 lectureships, 8 visiting professorships and institutes **Editorial Work:** Editorial board, *Zygon* **Selected Memberships:** Society for Values in Higher Education; Religious Education Association; American Academy of Religion; Association of Professors and Researchers in Religious Education Board of Directors, National Catholic Reporter **Discipline:** Religion and Society; Theology and Ethics; Religious Education **Related Interests:** Stages of Faith - Psychology of Human Development; Morality in Society; Sexism in Religion; Theology and Psychology; Faith Development and the Transforming Moment.

Selected Publications: His bibliography lists 10 books, over 50 articles, 10 reviews and 5 interviews.

_____. "H. Richard Niebuhr as Philosopher." *The Journal of Religion* 57, 3 (1977): 307-13.
_____. "Moral Stages and the Development of Faith." In *Kohlberg and Moral Basic Issues in Philosophy, Psychology, Religion, and Education*, ed. Brenda M. Mapel. Notre Dame IN: Religious Education Press, 1980.
_____. *Stages of Faith: The Psychology of Human Development and the Quest for Meaning*. San Francisco: Harper and Row, 1981. Also available in Korean, Portuguese and German.
_____. "Pluralism, Particularity, and Paideia." *Journal of Law and Religion* (April 1985).
_____. "Religion and Clinical Issues: An Interview with Theologian James Fowler." Interview by Edward Shafranske for *Psychologists Interested in Religious Issues*, Newsletter Division 36, American Psychological Association 11, 2 (1986): 1-4.
_____. *Responsible Selfhood: An Interdisciplinary Approach to Ethics Education*. (J. Fowler supervised editing and writing done by John Shippee and Linda Johnson.) Orange County Public Schools, 1988.
_____. "Character, Conscience, and the Education of the Public." In *Proceedings of a conference on moral education*. University of Notre Dame Press, Spring 1990.
_____. "H. Richard Niebuhr." In *Twentieth Century Thinkers*, ed. Elmer Borklund. London: St. James Press, forthcoming.

Fowler, Thomas B.

Present Position and Address: Principal Engineer (since 1987), MITRE Corporation; Associate Professor/Lecturer (since 1986), George Washington University, 1571 44th Street, NW, Washington, DC 20007, USA **Concurrent Positions:** Adjunct Professor, Christendom College (since 1992) **Work Phone:** (703) 883-7912 **Home Phone:** (202) 342-8794 **Fax:** (202) 298-0495 **E-Mail:** tfowler @ mitre.org **Date of Birth:** January 30, 1947 **Languages Spoken:** French, English, Spanish **Education:** B.A. (1969)/B.S. (1972), University of Maryland; M.S. (1973), Columbia University; Sc.D. (1986), George Washington University **Previous Positions:** Member of Technical Staff (1973-82), MITRE Corporation; Assistant Professor and Coordinator of Math/Science program (1982-87), Christendom College **Selected Memberships:** American Association for the Advancement of Science; American Physical Society; American Mathematical Society; Institute of Electrical and Electronics Engineers; Phi Beta Kappa **Discipline:** Systems Theory/Systems Engineering **Related Interests:** Philosophy of Science; Evolution; Systems Theory and Complexity Theory and the Limits they Impose on the Behavior of Things.

Selected Publications:

_____. "Thermodynamics and Evolution: Contradiction, Constraint, or Cooperation?" *Faith and Reason* 10, 2 (1984): 101-48.

_____. "Gilson on Aristotle and Darwin." *Faith and Reason* 10, 4 (1984): 327-32.

_____. "Order Out of Chaos." *Faith and Reason* 11, 1 and 2 (1985): 145-55.

_____. "A Time Domain Solution Approach to Model Reduction." *IEEE Trans. on Circuits and Systems* 35, 8 (1988): 1020-24.

_____. "Molecular Biology and Evolution: The Crisis and the Challenge." A paper presented at the Consultation on Theology and Science, Burlingame, California (1988). Rev. *Faith and Reason* 19, 2/3 (1993): 167-80.

_____. "Application of Stochastic Control Techniques to Chaotic Nonlinear Systems." *IEEE Trans. Automatic Control* 34, 2 (1989): 201-5.

_____. "Is Society Controllable?" *Faith and Reason* 18, 4 (1992): 387-43.

_____. "The International Narcotics Trade: Can it be Stopped by Interdiction?" *Journal of Policy Modeling* (forthcoming).

_____. "Science and Western Civilization." In *Cultural Conservatism: Theory and Practice*, ed. W. Lind and W. Marshner. Washington, DC: Free Congress Foundation, 1991.

_____. "El Gran Cambio de Paradigma: Xavier Zubiri Y Las Revolucion Cientifica, 1890-1990." Presented at Congreso Internacional Xavier Zubiri, Madrid, July 1993. "The Great Paradigm Shift: Xavier Zubiri and the Scientific Revolution, 1890-1990. *Faith and Reason* 20, 2 (1994): 163-98.

Frair, Wayne

Present Position and Address: Professor Emeritus of Biology; 34 Piping Rock Dr. Ossining, NY 10562, USA **Date of Birth:** May 23, 1926 **Education:** A.B. Zoology (1950), Houghton College; B.S. Zoology (1951), Wheaton College; M.A. Embryology (1955), University of Massachusetts; Ph.D. Serology (1962), Rutgers State University **Previous Positions:** Instructor through Professor (since 1955), King's College **Selected Memberships:** Fellow, American Association for the Advancement of Science; Fellow, American Scientific Affiliation; Fellow Victoria Institute; Fellow and President, Creation Research Society; American Physiological Society; American Institute of Biological Sciences; The Herpetologists League; American Society of Zoologists; The American Physiological Society **Discipline:** Biology **Related Interests:** Turtle Systematics (Origins); Science and Creation/Evolution, Christianity and Science; Scientific Possibilities for Original Kinds; Purpose and Chance.

Selected Publications:

_____. "Purpose and Chance." *Alternatives* 1, 2 (1973):14.

_____. "The Heart of Creation." *Creation Research Society Quarterly* 14, 1 (1975): 61-2.

_____. P. Davis. *A Case for Creation*. 3rd ed. Chicago, IL: Moody Press, 1983.

_____. "A Positive Creationist Approach Utilizing Biochemistry." In *Science at the Crossroads: Observation or Speculation*. Papers of the 1983 BSA National Creation Conference. Richfield MN: Onesimus Publishing, 1985.

_____. "Use of Proteins and DNA for Understanding Relationships Among Organisms." In *The Origin and Destiny of Life Lecture Abstracts from the 1987 National Creation Conference: August 2-5; Seattle, WA*. Seattle Pacific University, n.d.

_____. "The Narnia Experience." *Bible Science Newsletter* 26, 10 (1988).

_____. "Australopithecines: Relationship to Man?" *Creation Research Social Quarterly* 25 (1988): 151-3.

_____. "Second Response to Robert C. Newman." In *Evangelical Affirmations*, ed. K.S. Kantzer and C.F.H. Henry. Grand Rapids: Zondervan Publishing House, 1990.

_____. "Original Kinds and Turtle Phylogeny." *Creation Research Society Quarterly* 28, 1 (1991): 21-4.

_____. "Additional Information on the Freiberg Human Skull Composed of Coal." *Creation Research Society Quarterly* 30, 1 (1993): 36-9.

Frecska, Ede

Present Position and Address: Senior Fellow, Mount Sinai Medical School, New York; 273 Winsor Ave., Brightwaters, NY 11718 **Date of Birth:** May 6, 1953 **Languages Spoken:** Hungarian, English **Education:** MD (1977), Hungary; M.A. Psychology (1986), Hungary **Discipline:** Psychiatry and Psychopharmacology **Related Interests:** Psychobiology of Religious and Transcendental Experiences.

Selected Publications:

_____, Zsuzsanna Kulcsar. "Social Bonding in the Modulation of the Physiology of Ritual Trance." *Ethos* 17 (1989): 70-89.

Freire-Maia, Newton

Present Position and Address: Emeritus Professor (since 1987), Department of Genetics, Federal University of Parana, Caixa Postal 19071, 81531-990 Curitiba, PR, Brazil **Date of Birth:** June 29, 1918 **Languages Spoken:** Portuguese, English, French, Spanish **Education:** Dentistry (1945); General Biology (1946-48), University of Sao Paulo; Fellowship (1956-57), Rockefeller Foundation, University of Michigan; Doctor in Natural Sciences (1960) **Awards and Honors:** Medal, National Council for Scientific and Technological Development, Brazil; National Genetics Prize, Brazil; Award from the National Foundation for Ectodermal Dysplasias **Previous Positions:** Full Professor (1969-87), Federal University of Parana; Scientist (1970-71), World Health Organization **Selected Memberships:** Brazilian Society of Genetics (former President); Brazilian Society for the Advancement of Science (former vice-president; now honorary president) **Discipline:** Human Genetics; Biological Evolution **Related Interests:** Science and Religion; Evolution and Creation.

Selected Publications: He has written 5 papers and 14 books on this topic.

_____. *Criacão e evolução: Deus, o acaso e a necessidade.* Petropolis: Vozes, 1984.
_____. *Teoria da evolução: de Darwin àteoria sintética.* Itatiaia: Belo Horizonte/São Paulo: EDUSP, 1988.

Frey, Christofer

Present Position and Address: Professor (since 1981), Ruhr-Universität Bochum, Evangelisch Theologische Fakultät, D-44780 Bochum. private: Hebeler Weg 7, 44388 Dortmund, Germany **Work Phone:** 0234-700-2506 **Date of Birth:** April 7, 1938 **Languages Spoken:** German, English, French **Education:** Studies in Theology/Philosophy/Sociology at Berlin, Tübingen, Chicago, Göttingen, Heidelberg, Paris. 1st Theologie Prüfung (1964); 2nd Theologie Prüfung (1968); Promotion (Dr. theol., 1967) Heidelberg; Habilitation (1972), Heidelberg **Previous Positions:** Pastor (1967-69); Professor (1969-78), Heidelberg; Professor (1978-80), Erlangen **Selected Memberships:** Societas Ethica; Wiss. Gesellschaft für Theologie **Discipline:** Systematic Theology with special emphasis on Ethics and Social Ethics **Related Interests:** Social Ethics; Systematic Theology and Philosophy and Sociology; Creation Theology.

Selected Publications: He has published more than 100 articles in German and English, most of which are relevant to this field.

_____. *Mysterium der Kirche - Öffnung zur Welt.* (Mystery of the church - opening towards the world. A study of French reform-Catholicism) Göttingen: Vandenhoeck & Ruprecht, 1969.
_____. *Reflexion und Zeit.* (Reflection and time. A study of the problem of subjectivity and theology in Hegel's thought.) Gütersloh: Gütersloher Verlagshaus Gerd Mohn, 1973.

_____. *Arbeitsbuch Anthropologie.* (Study book "Anthropology." A manual for teachers and ministers introducing into the theological and secular teaching of man.) Stuttgart: Kreuz-Verlag, 1979.
_____. *Die Theologie Karl Barth.* Eine Einführung. Frankfurt am Main: Athenäum, 1988.
_____, M. Hoffman. *Die Ethik des Protestantismus.* (A historical survey of the development of Protestant ethics, also translated into Polish.) Gütersloh: Gütersloher Verlagshaus, 1989.
_____. *Theologische Ethik.* (A study book for students.) Neukirchen: Neukirchener Verlag, 1990.
_____. *Dogmatik, Studienbuch.* (A study guide which introduces the problems and methods of dogmatics.) 3rd ed. Gütersloh: Gütersloher Verlagshaus, 1993.

Frye, Roland Mushat

Present Position and Address: Professor Emeritus (since 1983), English Department, University of Pennsylvania, Philadelphia, PA 19104-6273; 226 West Valley Road, Strafford-Wayne, PA 19087, USA **Date of Birth:** July 3, 1921 **Education:** A.B. (1943)/Ph.D. (1952), Princeton University; Special student in theology at Princeton Theological Seminary (1950-52) **Previous Positions:** Emory University (1952-61); Folger Shakespeare Library (1961-65); University of Pennsylvania (1965-83) **Selected Memberships:** Member, Institute of Advanced Study, Princeton; Chairman of the Board of Trustees, Center of Theological Inquiry, Princeton; American Philosophical Society; American Academy of Arts and Sciences **Discipline:** Literature and Theology **Related Interests:** The Religious Case against Creation-Science.

Selected Publications:

_____. "The Two Books of God: Scripture and Nature." *Theology Today* 39 (1982): 260-6.
_____. *Is God A Creationist: The Religious Case Against Creation-Science.* Scribner's, 1983.
_____. "So-Called 'Creation-Science' and Mainstream Christian Responses." *Proceedings of the American Philosophical Society* 127 (1983): 61-70.
_____. *The Religious Case Against Creation-Science, Report No. 1.* Princeton: Center of Theological Inquiry, 1983.

G

Gaál, Botond

Present Position and Address: Professor of Systematic Theology, Reformed College of Debrecen; Scientific Secretary (since 1993), Regional Committee of the Hungarian Academy of Sciences in Debrecen; Debrecen, Kálvin tér 16, 4044, Hungary **Date of Birth:** March 27, 1946 **Languages Spoken:** Hungarian, English **Education:** Diploma Mathematics/Physics (1970), University of Sciences, Debrecen; Theological Doctor's Degree (1985), Reformed Theological Academy, Debrecen **Selected Congresses and Conferences:** Has given many lectures at conferences in Hungary and abroad dealing with the relation between Theology and Science; Has also presented lectures at conferences abroad on the pioneering contribution of Hungarian Reformed Theologians and Pastors to the various branches of learning, especially the natural sciences; The International Association of Christian Education (Rüschlikon, Switzerland 1986); The 14th Dialogue of Christians and Marxists (1987); The Second European Conference on Religion and Science (1988) **Previous Positions:** Deputy Principal (1977-87)/Principal (1987-91), Reformed College; Headmaster (1982-87), Reformed Secondary School; Dean (1988-89), Theological Academy; Minister of Reformed Church (1976), Reformed Theological Academy, Debrecen **Editorial Work:** Edited the *Year Book* (since 1982) dealing with the cultivation of learning in the Debrecen College of the Reformed Church - collections of relevant papers by teachers, professors, and professing Christians **Selected Memberships:** Advisor member, Central Committee of International Association for Christian Education; Member, "Doctorum Collegium," Reformed Church in Hungary **Discipline:** Theology **Related Interests:** Theology and Science.

Selected Publications: Founder, and Editor (since 1982), of a series of Year Books on the cultivation of learning in the Debrecen College of the Reformed Church in Hungary.

_____. "Space, Time and the Word." Thesis for Doctor of Theology degree. Debrecen, 1985.
_____. *The Cultivation and Instruction of Natural Sciences in the Reformed College of Debrecen.* Debrecen, Hungary: 1988. Published on the occasion of the 450th anniversary of the Reformed College.
_____. "Higher Dimensions in Thinking - The Benefit of the Thoughts of Michael Polanyi in Theology." *Protestant Journal of Theology* (Hungary, 1991).
_____, Laszló Vegh. "The Holy Scriptures and the Anthropic Cosmological Principle." *Protestant Journal of Theology* (Hungary, 1991).
_____. "The Faith of a Great Scientist - A Methodology of the Exact Sciences and the Role of the Trinity in the Thoughts of James Clerk Maxwell." *Protestant Journal of Theology* (Hungary, 1992).

Gaede, S. D.

Present Position and Address: Provost (since 1993), Gordon College, 255 Grapevine Rd. Wenham, MA 01984, USA **Work Phone:** (508) 927-2300, Ext. 4206 **Date of Birth:** November 1, 1946 **Education:** B.A. Sociology/History (1969), Westmont College; M.A. Sociology (1971), California State University - Northridge; Ph.D. Sociology (1974) Vanderbilt University **Previous Positions:**

Instructor of Sociology (1971-72) University of Tennessee - Nashville; Vanderbilt Fellow (1972-73) Vanderbilt University; Assistant Professor of Sociology (1974), Houghton College; Assistant through Professor of Sociology (1974 - present))/Dean of Students (1977-81)/Chair of Division of Social and Behavioral Sciences (1982-84)/Chair of Department of Sociology and Social Work (1987-93), Gordon College **Selected Memberships:** American Sociological Association; Society for the Scientific Study of Religion; Association for the Sociology of Religion **Discipline:** Sociology **Related Interests:** Social Theory; Sociology of Religion; Philosophy of Science.

Selected Publications: His bibliography lists 6 books, 12 published articles, and 18 professional papers and presentations.

_____. "A Question of Legitimacy: On the Right to Approach Sociology from a Christian Perspective." Paper presented at the National Endowment for the Humanities/Christian College Coalition faculty workshop on "Christianity and Social Theory," Covenant College, April 13, 1983.
_____. " How the Social Sciences May Contribute to Christian Thinking." Paper presented at the conference on "The Task of Evangelical Higher Education," Institute for the Study of American Evangelicals, The Billy Graham Center, Wheaton College, May 1985.
_____. *Where Gods May Dwell: On Understanding the Human Condition.* Grand Rapids: "Academie Books", Zondervan, 1985.
_____. "The Problem of Truth." In Making Sense of Modern Times: Peter L. Berger and the Vision of Interpretive Sociology, ed. James D. Hunter and Stephen Ainley. London: Routledge and Keagan Paul, 1987.

Galleni, Lodovico

Present Position and Address: Professor of General Zoology, Faculty of Agricultural Sciences (since 1987), University of Pisa; Via San Michele degli Scalzi 2, I 56124 Pisa, Italy; (Home) Via A. Cesalpino 7, I 56124 Pisa, Italy **Work Phone:** 050-578154 **Date of Birth:** December 29, 1947 **Languages Spoken:** Italian, English **Education:** Laurea in Scienze Naturali (1970), University of Pisa **Previous Positions:** Assistente di Zoologia (1975-77), Facoltà di Scienze M.F.N.; Professore di Zoologia generale (1977-87), Facoltà di Scienze; Invited Professor Instituto Superiore Di Scienze Religiose (Pisa) (1992), Studio Teologico Florentino (Fierenze) (1993) **Editorial Work:** Editor (1983-92) Co-Editor (since 1993), *Il Futuro dell'Uomo*, an Italian Journal on Pierre Teilhard de Chardin and the relationships between Science and Theology; Member, Editorial Board (since 1987), *Antropologia e Psicologia*, Pisa University's Journal for the teacher of religious disciplines; Member, Consulting Committee (since 1993) *Nuova Secondaria*, a journal for the high school teacher **Selected Memberships:** European Society for the Study of Science and Theology (ESSST); European Society for Evolutionary Biology (ESEB) **Discipline:** General Zoology **Related Interests:** Experimental Areas - Chromosomal evolution of animals/Mechanisms of speciation in animals; Historical Areas - Scientific papers of Pierre Teilhard de Chardin/Impact on Theology of evolutionary theories; Theoretical Area - Evolutionary Theories.

Selected Publications: His bibliography lists 10 published works since 1986.

_____. "I meccanismi dell'evoluzione e il loro impatto sui rapporti tra scienza e teologia." *Il Futuro dell'Uomo* 14, 3-4 (1987): 33-63.
_____. "Storia della teoria dell'evoluzione." In *L'origine dell'Uomo*, ed. A. G. Manno and F. Fedele. Dehoniane, Napoli, 1987.
_____. "P. Teilhard de Chardin e l'evoluzione umana." In *L'origine dell'Uomo*, ed. A. G. Manno and F. Fedele. Dehoniane Napoli, 1987.
_____. "Alle radici dell'etica ambientale: proposte per una linea di ricerca in prospettiva teilhardiana." *Il Futuro dell'Uomo* 15, 1 (1988): 45-54.
_____. "I programmi di ricerca scientifica e la teoria dell'evoluzione." *Il Futuro dell'Uomo* 16, 1 (1989): 85-92.
_____. "I meccanismi di speciazionetra pluralismo teorico e finalismo." *Il Futuro dell'Umo* 17, 2 (1990):43-59.

_____. "Il Concetto di specie dalle origini fino all'inizio della scienza moderna." *Il Futuro dell'Umo* 19, 1 (1992): 69-86.
_____. *Scienza e Teologia. Proposte per una sintesi feconda.* Queriniana: Brescia, 1992.
_____. "Evoluzionismo ed etica." *A/P Antropologia e Psicologia* 9, 1,2 (1992): 12-15.
_____. "Relationships Between Scientific Analysis and the World View of Pierre Teilhard de Chardin." *Zygon* 27, 2 (1992): 153-66.

Ganguli, H. C.

Present Position and Address: President (since 1988)/Research Director (since 1989), Psychological Center for Comparative Mysticism, F 8/13 Model Town, Delhi - 110009, India **Work Phone:** 011-722-6080 New Delhi **Date of Birth:** November 25, 1924 **Education:** D.Phil/D.Litt, University of Calcutta **Postdoctoral Studies**: Department of Psychology at Illinois/Ohio State Universities and Counseling at Minnesota University **Awards and Honors:** Sandoz Award of the Indian Psychiatric Society; Swami Pranavananda Psychology National Award; Platinum Jubilee Lecture Award of the Indian Science Congress/its President in Psychology **Previous Positions:** Founder/Head and Professor of Psychology, University of Delhi (1963-89) **Selected Memberships:** Fellow, Indian National Science Academy; President, Indian Psychological Association **Discipline:** Psychology **Related Interests:** Work Ethics; Mental Health; Sexual Behavior and Sexual Ethics; Moral Values and Meditation; Yoga.

Selected Publications: His bibliography lists 6 books, 3 chapters, 9 special reports and 70 papers.

_____. "Religion and Population Explosion, Numen, Supplement, XV, 1969." Chap. in *Religious Pluralism and World Community; Interfaith and Intercultural Communication*, ed. E. J. Jurji. Leiden: E. J. Brill, 1969.
_____. "Values, Moral Education and Social Studies." Chap. 8 in *UNESCO Handbook for the Teaching of Social Studies*. London: Croom Helm; UNESCO: Paris, 1981.
_____. "Meditation Program and Modern Youth: Dynamics of Initiation." *Human Relations* 15, 10 (1982): 903-26.
_____. *Structure and Process of Organization.* New Delhi: Allied Publishers, 1983.
_____. "On a Moral Order." Platinum Jubilee Lecture of the Indian Science Congress Association, 1989.
_____. "Development of a Moral Order: Some Considerations." *Indian Journal of Social Work* 50, 3 (Bombay, 1989).

Gay, Volney P.

Present Position and Address: Graduate Director, Program in Religion and Psychology (since 1993), Professor of Anthropology (since 1990)/Psychiatry (since 1989)/Religious Studies (since 1989), Departments of Religion/Psychiatry, Box 1581, Station B, Vanderbilt University, Nashville, TN 37235, USA; (Home) 3910 General Bates Drive, Nashville, TN 37204, USA **Work Phone:** (615) 322-4884 or 6341 **Home Phone:** (615) 297-4145 **Education:** B.A. Philosophy (1970), Reed College, Portland, OR; M.A. Religion and Psychology (1973)/Ph.D. Religion and Psychology (1976), University of Chicago; Graduate, Clinical training in psychoanalysis (1982-90), St. Louis Psychoanalytic Institute; Graduate Fellow in Psychotherapy, (1973-75), Center for Religion and Psychotherapy in Chicago; Certified in Adult Psychoanalysis, American Psychoanalytic Association (1990) **Awards and Honors:** Outstanding Teacher, Department of Psychology (1993); Heinz Hartmann Award for 1994, New York Psychoanalytic Institute (1993) **Previous Positions:** Acting Chair (1984), Department of Religious Studies; Cross-appointed as Associate Professor (1985), Department of Psychiatry, Vanderbilt University **Editorial Work:** Reader and expert reviewer for *Journal of American Academy of Religion/Journal for the Scientific Study of Religion/Journal of Ritual Studies/Journal of Pastoral Psychology.* Book manuscript reviewer for - monograph Series, American Academy of Religion **Selected Memberships:** American Academy of Religion; American Association of University Professors; American Psychoanalytic Association; American Psychological Association; Committee for the Advancement of Psychoanalytic Education; Psychosocial Interpretations in Religion; Society for the Scientific Study of Religion; Ritual Studies Group, American Academy of Religion **Discipline:** Psychology; Psychoanalysis and Religion; Psychology and Religion; Psychoanalytic Anthropology **Related Interests:** Science, Psychology and Religion.

Selected Publications: His bibliography lists 4 books, 22 published articles and over 20 unpublished works.

_____. "Reductionism and Redundancy in the Analysis of Religious Forms." *Zygon* 13, 2 (1978): 169-83.
_____. *Reading Freud: Neurosis, Psychology, Religion, Series on the Study of Religion.* American Academy of Religion, 1983.
_____. *Reading Jung: Science, Psychology and Religion, Series on the Study of Religion.* American Academy of Religion, 1984.
_____. *Understanding the Occult: Fragmentation and Repair of the Self.* Fortress Press, 1989.
_____. *Freud on Sublimation: Reconsiderations.* Albany, NY: State University of New York Press, 1992.
_____. "Interpretation Interminable: Agonistic in Psychoanalysis." In *Agonistics: Arenas of Creative Contest*, ed. J. Lugnstrum and E. Sauer. Albany, NY: State University of New York Press, N.d..
_____. "Ritual and Psychotherapy: Similarities and Differences." In *Ritual and Ritual Cure*, ed. V. DeMartinis and M. Aune. Albany, NY: State University of New York Press, N.d..
_____. "Religious Autobiography, Psychoanalysis, and Suicide." In *Religious Autobiography.* Oakville, Ont. Mosaic Press, N.d..

Geisler, Norman L.

Present Position and Address: Dean of Liberty Center for Research, Liberty University, Lynchburg, VA 24506 USA **Work Phone:** (804) 582-2140 **Date of Birth:** September 21, 1932 **Education:** (1950-55), William Tyndale College; (1956-57), University of Detroit; B.A. Philosophy (1958)/M.A. Theology (1960), Wheaton College; (1964), William Tyndale College; Ph.D. Philosophy (1970), Loyola University - Chicago **Previous Positions:** Various pastoral positions (1952-63); Assistant Professor of Bible and Apologetics (1963-66), Detroit Bible College; Assistant Professor of Bible and Philosophy (1967-69)/Associate Professor of Philosophy (1970-71)/Chairman of Philosophy of Religion (1970-79), Trinity Evangelical Divinity School; Professor of Systematic Theology (1979-89), Dallas Theological Seminary; Traveled and lectured in 50 states in USA and 20 countries on 6 continents; Lead expert witness for the defense in the "Scopes II" creation/evolution trial in Arkansas (1981) **Media Work:** Featured on nationally televised news and quoted in *Time* magazine and participated in many debates **Selected Memberships:** Evangelical Theological Society; American Philosophical Society; Evangelical Philosophical Society; American Scientific Affiliation American Theological Society; American Academy of Religion **Discipline:** Philosophy and Theology/Ethics. He is an author, lecturer and professor **Related Interests:** Philosophy; Origin Science; Contemporary Humanism; Ethics.

Selected Publications: Author of over 20 books and 100 articles.

_____. *The Creator in the Courtroom - Scopes II.* Baker Book House, 1982.
_____. *Is Man the Measure?* Baker Book House, 1983.
_____. *Cosmos: Carl Sagan's Religion for the Scientific Mind.* Quest Publications, 1983.
_____. *Origin Science.* Baker Book House, 1987.

Gelwick, Richard

Present Position and Address: Chair (since 1989)/Associate Professor of Medical Humanities and Behavioral Science, University of New England College of Osteopathic Medicine, Biddeford, ME 04005, USA **Work Phone:** (207) 283-0171 **Home Phone:** (207) 725-7975 **Fax:** (207) 283-3249 **Date**

of Birth: March 9, 1931 **Education:** B.A. (1952), Southern Methodist University, Dallas; (M.Div.)/B.D. (1956), Yale University; Th.D. (1965), Pacific School of Religion and Graduate Theological Union, Berkeley **Postgraduate Studies:** Postdoctoral studies as a visiting scholar (1982), Union Theological Seminary NY/Associate (1973-74) at Clare Hall, Cambridge University, UK; Postdoctoral Fellowship for Cross-Disciplinary Study on Molecular Biology and its implications for Religion and Philosophy; Fellowship for study of Philosophy of Sciences in an Archaeological excavation in Israel **Selected Congresses and Conferences:** Invited Participant, Academie Internationale Des Sciences Religieuses; Invited Papers, discussant and participant at International Conferences on the Unity of the Sciences **Previous Positions:** Assistant Professor of Religion (1956-58), Washington and Lee University; Director of Religious Activities (1958-60), Oberlin College; Visiting Lecturer (1965-66), Pacific School of Religion; Assistant Professor of Religion (1966-67), Chapman College; Adjunct Professor of Polanyi Studies (1970-71), Dayton University; Division Chair (1971-73)/Chair (1967-1988), Religion and Philosophy Department, Stephens College; Faculty Status (1973-74), Cambridge University **Editorial Work:** Chief Bibliographer of Polanyi's literary opera; Coordinator of the Polanyi Society and editor of its journal; Referee for *Zygon* **Selected Memberships:** American Philosophical Association; Society for Health and Human Values; American Academy of Religion; Center for Theology and the Natural Sciences **Discipline:** Religion and Philosophy; Philosophy and History of Science; Interdisciplinary teaching and leadership. **Relevant Areas of Interest:** Religion in Higher Education; Science and Religion; Post-critical Thought of Physical Chemist and Philosopher Michael Polanyi; Philosophy and Religion; Women's Studies; Medical Ethics.

Selected Publications: His bibliography lists 4 books and monographs, 8 chapters in books, 12 articles in journals and over 20 addresses, papers and programs organized.

_____. *Collected Articles and Papers of Michael Polanyi.* Pacific School of Religion. Graduate Theological Union Library Microfilm, 1963.
_____. *Credere Aude: Michael Polanyi's Theory of Knowledge and its Implications for Christian Theology.* University of Michigan, 1965.
_____. "A Bibliography of Michael Polanyi's Social and Philosophical Writings." In *Intellect and Hope*, ed. T. A. Langford and W. H. Poteat. Duke University Press, 1968.
_____. "Discovery and Theology." *Scottish Journal of Theology* 28 (1975): 301-22.
_____. *The Way of Discovery: An Introduction to the Thought of Michael Polanyi.* Oxford University Press, 1977; published in Japanese as *Maikeru Porani No Sekai.* Taga Shuppan, 1982.
_____. "Science and Reality, Religion and God: A Reply to Prosch." *Zygon* 17 (1982): 25-39.
_____. *Michael Polanyi's Conspectus of Knowing," Absolute Values and the New Cultural Revolution.* International Cultural Foundation, 1986.
_____. "Transformations and Convergences in the Frame of Knowledge: Explorations in the Interrelations of Scientific and Theological Enterprise." A review of a work by T. F. Torrance. *Journal of the American Academy of Religion* 54 (1986): 198.
_____. "Michael Polanyi and the Philosophy of Medicine." *Tradition and Discovery* 18, 3 (1992).

Germine, Mark

Present Position and Address: Research Psychiatrist, Clinical Neuroscience Research Unit, Department of Psychiatry, Yale University School of Medicine, New Haven, CT 06510 USA **Date of Birth:** December 18, 1954 **Education:** B.A. Geology (1975)/M.S. Geology (1981), Rutgers University; M.D. (1988), New Jersey Medical School **Previous Positions:** Research Professor (1988-89), Geology Department, Rutgers University **Selected Memberships:** American Association for the Advancement of Science; American Medical Society; American Psychiatric Association **Discipline:** Geology; Neurology; Psychiatry **Related Interests:** Evolution; Mind; Creativity.

Selected Publications:

_____. "On Creation and the Mind in Science and Religion." *Zygon* (under review).

Giannoni, Paolo

Present Position and Address: Professor in Studio Teologico Fiorentino (Florence, since 1961); Professor (since 1988), University of Urbino, I 50027, Strada in Chianti, Firenze, Italy **Date of Birth:** June 28, 1935 **Languages Spoken:** Italian, French **Education:** Licentia in S. Theologia (1960)/Doctoratus in S. Theologia (1969), Pontificia Universitas Gregoriana, Rome; Corso per la laurea, Philosophy, University of Florence **Selected Memberships:** Member (since 1987), Central Committee ATI (Theological Italian Society); Seminar on "Language and Theology" (1980, in Florence); Symposium for "Florence European Cultural Capital (Florence, 1987) "Matter, Evolution, and Hope," (Florence, 1982); "Theology and Science" (Florence, 1987); Chairman of section on "Theology and Science" of XIII meeting of ATI (Frescia, 1989). **Discipline:** Theology of Creation/Anthropology; Popular Religion and Piety **Related Interests:** Theology and Science; Popular Religion; Anthropology; Theology and Language.

Selected Publications:

_____. "Cattolicesimo (Catholicism)," (On creation and theological anthropology). In *Enciclopedia delle Religioni* 1 Firenze: c/o Vallecchi, 1970.
_____. "La Dottrina Cristiana sulla creazione nel confronto con la cultura del 1900" (Christian doctrine on creation in comparison with the culture of the twentieth century). *Il futuro dell'Uomo* (Firenze, 1982).
_____. "Note di metodologia relative al rapporto tra teologia e scienza" (Methodological notes concerning the relationship between theology and science). *Il futuro dell'Uomo* (Firenze, 1983).
_____. Article. In *Schöpfungslehre*, ed. A. Ganoczy. Düsseldorf, Germany: Patamos Verlag; Breseia, Italy: c/o Queriniana, 1985.
_____. "Energia umana, principialità trinitaria" (Human energy, trinitarian principle). *Il futuro dell'Uomo* (Firenze, 1985).

Giberson, Karl Willard

Present Position and Address: Professor of Physics, Eastern Nazarene College, 23 E. Elm Ave, Quincy, MA 02170 **Phone:** (617) 745-3541, **Fax:** (617) 745-3590 **Date of Birth:** May 13, 1957 **Languages Spoken:** English, Some French **Honors:** Dissertation received Wilson Award; Who's Who in Science and Technology; Sigma Xi **Memberships:** American Scientific Affiliation; National Center for Science Education **Discipline:** Physics **Relevant Areas of Interest:** History of Science, Philosophy, Creation/Evolution **Current Project:** Creation/Evolution debate, Anthropic Principle

Selected Publications:

_____, Chu Cheng, Denning, F.B., Tittel, F.K. "Tunable Single Mode Operation of a CW Color Center Laser in the Near Infrared." *Applied Optics* 21 (1982):172
_____, Hammond, M.S., Hart, M.W., Lynn J.G., & Dunning, F.B. "Optical Pumping with a Frequency Modulated Multimode Dye Laser." *Optics Letters* (1985).
Chu Cheng, Giberson, K.W., Harrison, A.R., Tillet, F.K., Dunning, F.B., & Walters, G.K., "Measurement of the Spin Polarization of an Optically Pumped Ensemble of He (2^3S) Atoms." *Review of Scientific Instruments* 53 No.9 (1982).
Gray, L.G., Giberson, K.W., Chu Cheng, Kieffer, R.S., Dunning, F.B. & Walters, G.K. "Intense Source of Spin-Polarized Electrons Using Laser-Induced Optical Pumping." *Review of Scientific Instruments* 54 No.3 (1983).
_____, Jeys, T.H. and Dunning, F.B. "Generation of Tunable CW Radiation Near 875 Nanometers." *Applied Optics* 22 No.18 (1983).

____. "What has Jerusalem to say to Boston? Is There a Christian Philosophy of Science?" *Christian Scholar's Review* (December 1993).
____. "The Finely Tuned Universe: Handiwork of God or Scientific Mystery?" *Christian Scholar's Review* (December 1992).
____. "Scientists Find Strong Evidence for the Big Bang." Salem Press, 1993 (In Magill's Survey of Science: *Great Events from Physics*).
____. *Worlds Apart: The Unholy War Between Religion and Science* Beacon Hill Press of Kansas City, 1993.

Gibson, Arthur

Present Position and Address: Chairman/founder of European Maritime Security Council International Functions, Inc., 30 Lovell Road, Cambridge CB4 2QR, UK **Date of Birth:** April 12, 1943 **Education:** A school drop-out at the age of 15, was self-taught/nightschool, until accepted by Cambridge University; B.A. Hons, (1973)/M.A. Hons, (1977), University of Cambridge; Student barrister (since 1975), Grays's Inn, London **Postgraduate Studies:** Honorary Fellow, European Maritime Security Council **Awards and Honors:** Schneider Stiftung Peace Prize (1975), Hamburg, for a research dissertation on international law and politics; Philosophy and Religion Poetry book *Boundless Function* - subject of International Poetry Competition judged by Sir Frank Kermode (1989) **Previous Positions:** His unusual career has included teaching philosophy, law, ancient languages, archaeology, theology, cosmology, linguistics and English literature for 18 university Colleges and faculties in Cambridge (since 1980); From 1983-85 he lectured on the Cambridge Tripos Course, "Creation, cosmology and aspects of modern physics," and in 1984 was awarded the Cambridge University Burney Prize grant to lecture in Philosophy of Religion and Creativity at Lund University, Swed; Cambridge University Proctor (1984-89); Sometime Cambridge University Lecturer in Divinity (since 1983); Director of Studies in Philosophy (since 1984), Jesus College, Pembroke College, Downing College, Lucy Cavendish College, Cambridge University; Supervisor of Trinity College, Cambridge **Other Academic Experience:** Sometime ex officio member of the University of Cambridge (since 1984); Adviser to a number of international law enforcement and intelligence agencies concerning organized crime and terrorism; Adviser on international crises particularly regarding USA, Middle East, Eastern Europe and Africa in government and corporate domains **Discipline:** Philosophy; Poetry; Astrophysical Cosmology; International Relations in security and intelligence analysis; Application of these subjects to links between Theology and Science **Related Interests:** See under "Discipline:"; Also Philosophy of Religion; Cosmology; Evolutionary Theory; Philosophy of Physics; Aesthetics in Science **Current Research:** Trying to lay a foundation informed by theology and methods drawn from Science to resolve problems and develop new insights i.e. pharmaceutical ethics, specialties in logic and proof to problems of terrorism and organized crime.

Selected Publications: His bibliography lists 5 books and over 100 articles dealing with a large variety of subjects.

_____. *Biblical Semantic Logic: A Preliminary Analysis*. Oxford: Basil Blackwell, 1981.
_____. *Boundless Function*. Newcastle upon Tone: Bloodaxe Books, 1987. The application of philosophical and scientific linguistics to creative literary areas.
_____. *Divining Cosmology* (in press).

Gilbert, Thomas L.

Present Position and Address: Codirector, Chicago Center for Religion and Science; Adjunct Professor of Religion and Science Studies, Lutheran School of Theology at Chicago; (Home) 11919 Ford Road, Palos Park, IL 60464, USA **Work Phone:** (312) 753-0775 **Fax Number:** (312) 753-0682 **Date of Birth:** November 24, 1922 **Languages Spoken:** English **Previous Positions:** Senior Physicist,

Argonne National Laboratory **Selected Memberships:** American Physical Society; American Association for the Advancement of Science; American Theological Society (Midwest); Institute for Religion in an Age of Science; Center for Advanced Study in Religion and Science; Institute for the Study of Ultimate Reality and Meaning; Sigma Xi; Tau Beta Pi **Discipline:** Physics **Related Areas of Interest:** Issues and Questions Concerning the Relationship of Religion and Science, and More Generally, Commonalties and Differences in Conceptual Frameworks **Current Areas of Research:** The Epic of Creation: Scientific and Religious Perspectives on Our Origins.

Selected Publications: His bibliography contains over 40 scientific articles (mainly chemical physics) in refereed journals, about 20 other articles and government reports (mainly environmental risk analysis), and 3 articles in religion and science.

_____. "The Quest for Ultimate Reality and Meaning: A Scientist's View." In vol. 6 of *Ultimate Reality and Meaning: Interdisciplinary Studies in the Philosophy of Understanding*, 270-83. N.p., 1983.
_____. "What is the Role of Science in the Dialogue Proposed by William Klink?" *Zygon* 27, 2 (1992): 211-21.
_____. "Testing the Truth of the Noble Lie." *Zygon* 29, 2 (1994).

Gilkey, Langdon

Present Position and Address: Shailer Mathews Professor of Theology Emeritus (since 1989), Divinity School, University of Chicago Divinity School, Chicago, IL 60637, USA; (Home) 123 Cameron Lane Charlottesville VA 22903 **Date of Birth:** February 9, 1919 **Languages Spoken:** English, Dutch **Education:** A.B. (1940), Harvard University; A.M. (1949)/Ph.D. Theology (1954), Union Theological Seminary/Columbia University **Concurrent Position:** Kenny Distinguished Visiting Professor, Georgetown University, Washington, D.C.; Visiting Professor of Theology, Dept. of Religious Studies, University of Virginia, Charlottesville, VA **Awards and Honors:** Fulbright Scholar, Jesus College, Cambridge (1950-51); Guggenheim Fellowship (1960-61), Munich, Germany, and Rome (1965-66); AATS Subsidy Grant, Amsterdam, The Netherlands (1970-71); Fellowship, Japan Society for the Promotion of Science, Kyoto, Japan (1975); Fulbright Teaching Fellow, Theological Faculty, Catholic University of Nijmegon, The Netherlands (1979) **Previous Positions:** Instructor in English (1940-41), Yenching University, China; Instructor in Theology (1949-50), Union Theological Seminary, New York; Lecturer in Religion (1951-54), Vassar College, New York; Professor of Theology (1954-62), Vanderbilt University, TN; Professor of Theology (1963-78), University of Chicago Divinity School, IL Shailer Mathews Professor of Theology (1978-89), University of Chicago Divinity School, IL **Memberships:** Previous President of American Academy of Religion; American Academy of Arts and Sciences, New York Academy of Science **Discipline:** Theology and the Philosophy of Religion **Related Interests:** Theology and Science (have had an interest in and written in this area since 1959; Religion and Science; Buddhism and Christianity.

Selected Publications: His bibliography lists 11 books, 29 chapters, 20 articles, and 18 book reviews.

_____. *Nature, Reality and The Sacred*. Minneapolis: Fortress Press, 1993
_____. *Gilkey on Tillich*. New York: Crossroads, 1990.
_____. *Maker of Heaven and Earth*. New York: Doubleday and Company, 1959; Reprint Landham, MD: University Press of America, 1985.
_____. "Darwin and Christian Thought." *The Christian Century* 87, 1 (1960: 7-11; Reprint, *Science and Religion*, ed. Ian Barbour. New York: Harper and Row, Harper Forum Books, 1968.
_____. "Cosmology, Ontology, and the Travail of Biblical Language." *The Journal of Religion* 41, 3 (1961): 194-205. Reprint, *Concordia Theological Monthly* 33, 3 (1962): 143-154.
_____. *Religion and the Scientific Future*. New York: Harper and Row, 1970; London SCM Press, 1970; Reprint, Macon, GA: Mercer University Press, 1981.
_____. "Religious Dimensions of Scientific Inquiry." *Journal of Religion* 50, 2 (1970): 245-67. Reprint of Chapter 2 of *Religion and the Scientific Future*.

_____. "Religion and the Technological Future." *Criterion* 13, 3 (1974).
_____. "The Structure of Academic Revolutions." In *The Nature of Scientific Discovery*, ed. Owen Gingerich. Washington, D.C.: Smithsonian Institution Press, 1975.
_____. "The Religions Dimensions of a Scientific Culture." In *Being Human in a Technological Age*, ed. R. M. Borchert and D. Steward. Athens, OH: Ohio University Press, 1979.

Gill, Anthony J.

Present Position and Address: Assistant Professor, Department of Political Science, DO-30, University of Washington, Seattle, WA 98195, USA **Work Phone:** (206) 543-2780 **Fax Number:** (206) 685-2146 **Languages Spoken:** Spanish **Selected Memberships:** American Political Science Association; Latin American Studies Association **Discipline:** Political Science **Related Areas of Interest:** Church-State Relations; Rational Choice **Current Areas of Research:** Catholic Political Strategy in Latin America; Church-State Relations in Latin America.

Selected Publications:

_____. "Rendering Unto Caesar?: Religious Competition and Catholic Political Strategy in Latin America, 1962-1979." *American Journal of Political Science* (1994)

Gillespie, Neal C.

Present Position and Address: Emeritus Professor of History (since 1991), 1049 Clifton Rd. N.E., Atlanta, GA 30307-1227, USA **Work Phone:** (404) 377-3562 **Date of Birth:** March 9, 1933 **Education:** B.A. (1959), Emory University; M.A. (1961)/Ph.D. History (1964), Duke University **Previous Positions:** Assistant (1963-67)/Associate Professor (1967-72)/Professor (1972-91), Georgia State University **Selected Memberships:** Fellow, American Council of Learned Societies; History of Science Society; British Society for the History of Science; American Society of Church History **Discipline:** History; History of Science. Specializations in United States Intellectual History and History of Science; 19th & 20th Cent. **Related Interests:** Natural Theology in British and American Science.

Selected Publications:

_____. *The Collapse of Orthodoxy: The Intellectual Ordeal of George Frederick Holmes*. Charlottesville: University Press of Virginia, 1972.
_____. "The Duke of Argyll, Evolutionary Anthropology and the Art of Scientific Controversy." *Isis* 68 (1977).
_____. *Charles Darwin and the Problem of Creation*. Chicago: University of Chicago Press, 1979.
_____. "Preparing for Darwin: Conchology and Natural Theology in Anglo-American Natural History." *Studies in History of Biology* 7 (1984).
_____. "Natural History, Natural Theology and Social Order: John Ray and the 'Newtonian Ideology'." *Journal of the History of Biology* 20 (1987).
_____. "The Interface of Natural Theology and Science in the Ethology of W. H. Thorpe." *Journal of the History of Biology* 23 (1990).
_____. "Divine Design and the Industrial Revolution: William Paley's Abortive Reform of Natural Theology." *Isis* 81 (1990).
_____. Review of *The Post-Darwinian Controversies: A Study of the Protestant Struggle to Come to Terms With Darwin in Great Britain and America, 1870-1900*, by James R. Moore. *Zygon* 20, 3 (1985): 349-52.

Gingerich, Owen

Present Position and Address: Senior Astronomer (since 1986), Smithsonian Astrophysical Observatory; Professor of Astronomy and of the History of Science (since 1969), Harvard University, Cambridge, MA 02138, USA **Work Phone:** (617) 495-7216 **Fax:** (617) 496-7564 **E-Mail:** ginger@cfa.harvard.edu **Date of Birth:** March 24, 1930 **Education:** A.B. (1951), Goshen College; A.M. (1953)/Ph.D. (1962), Harvard University **Selected Lectures:** George Darwin Lecturer (1971), Royal Astronomical Society; Gross memorial Lecture (1993), Valparaiso University; First Dwight Lecture in Christian Thought ((1982), University of Pennsylvania; McNair Lecture (1983), University of North Carolina; First Helen Sawyer Hogg Lecture (1985), Canadian Astronomical Society **Previous Positions:** Director (1955-58), American University Observatory of Beirut; Assistant Professor of Astronomy (1957-58), American University of Beirut; Lecturer (1958-59), Wellesley College; Lecturer (1960-68)/Associate Professor (1968-69)/Professor (since 1969), Harvard University; Astrophysicist (1962-86), Smithsonian Astrophysical Observatory **Editorial Work:** Associate Editor for Reviews (since 1975), *Journal for the History of Astronomy*; Chairman of Editorial Advisory Board (since 1972), *General History of Astronomy*; Associate Editor, *Dictionary of American History Supplement*; Advisory Board, *The History of Science and Religion in the Western Tradition* **Selected Memberships:** US National Committee for the International Astronomical Union (Chairman: 1981-83/Member: 1981-90); Vice President (1982-85)/ Councilor (since 1994), American Philosophical Society; Member, International Academy of the History of Science; Fellow, American Association for the Advancement of Science; American Astronomical Society; American Scientific Affiliation; History of Science Society; International Astronomical Union; Royal Astronomical Society/Society Club; Advisory Board, Center of Theological Inquiry; American Academy of Arts and Sciences; Hon. Member, Royal Astronomical Society of Canada; Advisory Board, Center for Humility Theology of John Templeton Foundation **Discipline:** Astrophysics and History of Science **Related Interests:** Creation and modern cosmogony; Theology and Science; Theology and Science in the History of Science.

Selected Publications: The complete bibliography lists 20 books edited, translated, or written by the author, over 150 technical or research articles, over 200 educational, encyclopedia or popular articles, and 100 reviews. One of the astrophysics papers has been cited over 500 times.

_____. "The censorship of Copernicus' De revolutionibus." *Annali dell'Istituto e Museo di Storia della Scienza di Firenze*. 6, 2 (1981): 44-61.
_____. "The Galileo Affair." *Scientific American* 246 (August 1982): 118-27.
_____. "Kepler's Anguish and Hawking's Query: Reflections on Natural Theology" and "Response to Mortimer Adler." In *Great Ideas Today*, ed. M.J. Adler and J. Van Doren. Chicago: Encyclopedia Britannica, 1992.
_____. "Let there be Light: Modern Cosmogony and Biblical Creation." In *Is God a Creationist?*, ed. Roland M. Frye, 119-37. New York: Charles Scribner's Sons, 1983; rev. In *The World Treasury of Physics, Astronomy, and Mathematics*, ed. Timothy Ferris. Boston: Little, Brown, and Company, 1993.
_____. "Dare a Scientist Believe in Design." In *Evidence of Design*, ed. Robert Herrmann and John Templeton. N.p., n.d..
_____. "Where in the World is God?" In *Man and Creation, Perspectives on Science and Theology*, ed. Michael Bauman and Lissa Roche, 209-29. Hillsdale, MI: Hillsdale College Press, 1993.
_____. "Hypothesis, Proof, and the Censors: How Galileo Changed the Rules of Science." In *Proceedings of the International Symposium "Tribute to Galileo in Padua."* Trieste: Edizioni Lint.
_____. "Space, Time, and Beyond: Reflections on the Place of God in the Cosmos." Paper presented at the Valparaiso University, Gross Memorial Lecture, 1993.
_____. "Is There a Role for Natural Theology Today?" In *Proceedings of the Otago Symposium on Science and Theology*.

Glassman, Robert B.

Present Position and Address: Professor (since 1984) and Chairperson (since 1990), Department of Psychology, Lake Forest College, Lake Forest, IL 60045, USA **Work Phone:** (708) 735-5257 **Fax:** (708) 735-6291 **Date of Birth:** February 14, 1941 **Education:** A.B. (1962), Columbia University; Ph.D. (1967), University of Pennsylvania **Postgraduate Studies:** Postdoctoral (1967-69), Center for Brain Research, University of Rochester **Previous Positions:** Faculty (1969-84), Department of Psychology, Lake Forest College **Selected Memberships:** Chicago Center for Religion and Science; Society for Neuroscience; American Psychological Society; Sigma XI **Discipline:** Physiological Psychology **Related Interests:** The Mind/Brain Issue; Brain Evolution; Ethology; Sociobiology; Memory and Cognitive Science; Touch and Movement; Artificial Intelligence; Neural Networks; Science Education; History of Issues of Science, Secularism, and Religion.

Selected Publications:

_____. "An Evolutionary Hypothesis about Teaching and Proselytizing Behaviors." *Zygon* 15, 2 (1980): 133-54.
_____. Review of "Free Will Has a Neural Substrate: Critique of Joseph F. Rychlak's Discovering Free Will and Personal Responsibility." *Zygon* 18, 1 (1983): 67-82.
_____. "Let All of Us Praise our Component Parts." *Zygon* 18, 4 (1983): 443-6. (Response to Joseph F. Rychlak's "Commentary: Free Will as Transcending the Unidirectional Neural Substrate" on pp. 439-442, which in turn, was a response to the Review article listed above).
_____. E.W. Packel, and D.L. Brown. "Greenbeards and Kindred Spirits: A preliminary mathematical model of altruism toward non-kin who bear similarities to the giver." *Ethology and Sociobiology* 7 (1986): 107-15.
_____. "Insights on Aggression." *Insights/The Magazine of the Chicago Center for Religion and Science.* 3, 1 (1991): 15-16.
_____. "'Cognitive Theism': Proposed Sources of Accommodation between Secularism and Religion for Continuing Evolution of Civilization." *MS.* (Under review).
_____, K. J. Garvey. "Spatial Working Memory Capacity of Adult Humans, Inferred from performance in a large 17-Arm radial maze is 9.4 places." *Society for Neuroscience Abstracts* 19, 1 (1993): 790/323.3.

Goldsmith, W. (Walter) Mack

Present Position and Address: Clinical Psychologist; 112 E. Fairmont Avenue, Suite B, Modesto, CA 95359, USA **Concurrent Positions:** Professor of Psychology, Emeritus (since 1991), California State University-Stanislaus **Work Phone:** (209) 522-6188 **Fax Number:** (209) 571-8476 **Date of Birth:** October 4, 1934 **Languages Spoken:** English, Some German **Education:** A.B. (1957), Ripon College; Ph.D. (1966), Cornell University **Congresses and Conferences:** Invited participant to conventions: Eastern Psychological Association; Western Psychological Association; CAPS; CAPS-West; American Psychological Association; Society for the Scientific Study of Religion; Association for Behavior Analysis **Previous Positions:** Assistant Professor (1954-66), St. Olaf College; Assistant Professor through Professor, Emeritus (1966-1991), Department of Psychology, California State University-Stanislaus; Visiting Scholar (1970, 71), University of Wisconsin-Milwaukee; Honorary Visiting Scholar (1974-75), Regent College; Visiting Scholar (1974-75), Religion Department, University of British Columbia; Visiting Professor of Psychology (part-time, Spring 1990), Rosemead Graduate School of Psychology, Biola University, La Mirada, CA **Editorial Positions:** Contributing editor (since 1981), *Journal of Psychology and Theology*; Editorial Consultant (since 1977), *Journal for the Scientific Study of Religion*; Associate Editor (since 1990), *Review of Religious Research* **Selected Memberships:** American Psychological Association; American Scientific Affiliation; Christian Association for Psychological Studies; Society for the Scientific Study of Religion; Religious Research Association; Psi Chi (National Honorary Society for Psychology) **Discipline:** Psychology **Related Areas of Interest:** Psychology of Religion; Clinical Psychology; Experimental Psychology (Perception) **Current Areas of Research:** Several in Psychology of Religion - Why Ministers are Fired.

Selected Publications: His bibliography contains more than 40 professional papers, articles, and reviews. In addition to regular editorial work for three journals, he has served as a guest reviewer for several other academic journals and has done textbook reviews.

_____, B. Spilka, and G. Comp. "Faith and Behavior: Religion in Introductory Psychology Texts of the 1950s and 1970s." *Teaching of Psychology* 8 (1981): 158-60.

_____, B. N. Ekhardt. "Personality Factors of Men and Women Pastoral Candidates." Part 2 of "Sex Role Preferences." *Journal of Psychology and Theology* 12 (1984): 211-21.

_____. Review of *Representations: Philosophical Essays on the Foundations of Cognitive Science*, ed. J. Fodor. *Journal of Psychology and Theology* 12 (1984): 146.

_____. Review of *Americans and the Unconscious*, by R. C. Fuller. *Review of Religious Research* 29 (1988): 333-4.

_____, K. L. Seil. "Concerns About Professional Counseling: An Exploration of Five Factors and the Role of Christian Orthodoxy." *Journal of Psychology and Christianity* 7, 3 (1988): 5-21. Also presented as a paper to a CAPS-West Convention.

_____. "Through a Glass Darkly, But Face to Face: Comments on Psychology and Theology Eyeing One Another." *Journal of Psychology and Theology* 17 (1989): 385-93.

_____. "Investigative Inquiry: Response 1." *Journal of Psychology and Theology* 18 (1990): 179-80.

_____, D. J. Wistow, and J. A. Wakefield. "The Relationship Between Personality, Health Symptoms and Disease." *Personality and Individual Differences* 11 (1990): 717-23.

_____, B. K. Hansen. "Boundary Areas of Religious Clients' Values: Target for Therapy." *Journal of Psychology and Christianity* 10 (1991): 224-36. A version of this paper was presented to the June 23, 1990 CAPS-West Convention held in Vancouver, BC. Reprint, chap. 6 of *Psychotherapy and Religious Values*, ed. E. L. Worthinton, Jr. Grand Rapids, MI: Baker Book House, 1993.

_____. Review of *A Psychology of Ultimate Concern: Erik H. Erikson's Contribution to the Psychology of Religion*, by H. Zock. *Review of Religious Research* 33 (1991): 95-6.

Glódz, Malgorzata

Present Position and Address: Adjunct (since 1977), working in research in Physics, Institute of Physics of the Polish Academy of Sciences, Warsaw, Poland; (Work) Al. Lotników 32/46, 02-668 Warszawa, Poland; (Home) ul. Mokotowska 51/53 m. 12, 00-542 Warszawa, Poland **Date of Birth:** April 28, 1946 **Languages Spoken:** Polish, English, Russian, French **Education:** M.Sc. Physics (1969), Warsaw University, Poland; Ph.D. Physics (1976), Institute of Physics, Polish Academy of Sciences, Warsaw **Discipline:** Physics - Laser Spectroscopy **Related Interests:** Philosophy of Science; Science and Religion, mainly Physics and Christian Faith.

Selected Publications:

_____. M. Heller. "Poza granicami fizyki (Beyond physics)." In *Drogi My l cych* (Roots of the thinkers), ed. M. Heller and J. Zycinski. Kraków: Polskie Towarzystwo Teologiczne, 1983.

_____. "Ruch - sposób wszelkiego istnienia (Motion - the way everything exists)." *Prezgl d Powszechny* 9, 757 (1984): 350-65. Critical treatment of the principles of the mechanistic system of Holbach.

_____. "Zagadka substancji wszechrzeczy I cz owieka (Mystery of the substance of existence and of man)." Part I: *Prezgl d Powszechny* 6, 754 (1984): 397-408; Part II, *Prezgl d Powszechny* 7/8, 755/756 (1984): 112-22.

_____. "Nauka I Religia (Science and religion)." *Prezgl d Powszechny* 10, 806 (1988):145-50.

_____. "Beyond the Alternative: Divorce or Methodological Chaos." *Studia Interdyscyplinarne* 2 PAT Kraków (1988): 3-7. Text of contribution to the Conference in Enschede, in English.

_____. "Uwagi o wspó zale no ci eksperymentu I zmatematyzownej teorii (Remarks on interrelations between experiment and mathematized theory)." In *Matematyczno Przyrody* (Is the world mathematical?), ed. M. Heller, J. Zycinski, and A. Michalik, 84-92. Kraków: PAT, 1990. Proceedings of the conference of the same title held in Kraków, May 12-13, 1989.

Golshani, Mehdi

Present Position and Address: Professor of Physics (since 1985), Sharif University of Technology, P.O. Box 11365-8639, Tehran, Iran **Languages Spoken:** Persian, English, Arabic **Education:** B.S. (1960), Tehran University, Iran; Ph.D. Physics (1970), University of California - Berkeley **Previous Positions:** Assistant (1970)/Associate Professor of Physics (1979), Sharif University of Technology, Tehran **Selected Memberships:** American Physical Society; American Association of Physics Teachers; ASPEN (Asian Physics Education Network); Philosophy of Science Association (Michigan State University); Senior associate member of the International Center for Theoretical Physics **Discipline:** Physics **Related Interests:** Philosophy; Philosophy of Science; Theology.

Selected Publications: Besides the works below, he also wrote 4 articles in Persian about Einstein's, Heisenberg's and Bohr's Philosophy of Science, published in *The Iranian Journal of Physics*.

_____. "Science and the Muslim Ummah." *Al-Tawhid Journal* 1, 1 (1983).
_____. *The Holy Qur'an and the Sciences of Nature*. Tehran: I. P. O., 1986.
_____. "The Scientific Dimension of the Qur'an." *Al-Tawhid Journal* 5, 1 (1987).
_____. "Philosophy of Science from the Qur'anic Perspective." In *Toward Islamization of Disciplines*. Herndon, VA: International Institute of Islamic Thought, 1989.
_____. "Physical Reality in Contemporary Physics." Paper presented to the Symposium on the Foundations of Modern Physics, Joensuu, Finland, 1990.
_____, M. J. Khalili. *The English Translation of the Holy Qur'an*. Vol. 1. Tehran: I. P. O., 1992. Vol. 2 , in press.
_____. "The Significance of Physical Science in Islamic Outlook and the Need for a Scientific Renaissance in Islamic Polity." *Islamic Thought & Scientific Creativity* 5, 1 (1994).
_____. "Have Physicists Been Able to Dispense with Philosophy?" In *Physical Interpretations of Relativity Theory*. London: British Society for the Philosophy of Science, 1994.
_____. "God and Contemporary Physicists." In *Proceedings of the International Conference on Science in Islamic Polity in the Twenty-first Century*. Islamabad: COMSTECH, 1995.
_____. "The Sciences of Nature in the Islamic Perspective." *Studies of Science and Theology* 3 (1995) or 4 (1996).

Goodenough, Ward H.

Present Position and Address: Emeritus University Professor (since 1989), School of Arts and Sciences, Department of Anthropology, University of Pennsylvania, 325 University Museum, 33rd and Spruce Streets, Philadelphia, PA 19104-6398, USA **Date of Birth:** May 30, 1919 **Education:** A.B. (1940), Cornell University; Ph.D. (1949), Yale University **Field Work:** Ethnographic studies in Truk (1947, 64-65), Gilbert Islands (1951), Papua New Guinea (1951, 54) **Previous Positions:** Instructor in Anthropology (1948-49), University of Wisconsin; Assistant (1949-54)/Associate (1954-62)/Professor (1962-80)/University Professor (1980-89)/Department Chairman (1976-82), Department of Anthropology, University of Pennsylvania - Philadelphia; Visiting lecturer/professor at Cornell University, Swarthmore College, Bryn Mawr College, University of Hawaii, University of Wisconsin, Yale University, Colorado College, University of Rochester, St. Patrick's College, Maynooth, Ireland **Editorial Work:** Editor (1966-70), *American Anthropologist*; Editorial Board of *Science* **Selected Memberships:** National Academy of Sciences (1971); American Philosophical Society (1973); American Academy of Arts and Sciences (1975); Fellow, Center for Advanced Study in the Behavioral Sciences (1957-58); Fellow, American Anthropological Association (editor 1966-70); American Association for the Advancement of Science (Vice President/Section Chairman/Board of Directors (1972-75); Royal Anthropological Institute; Institute on Religion in an Age of Science (council 1985-1992, President 1987-89) **Discipline:** Anthropology **Related Interests:** Anthropology and Religion; Ethics.

Selected Publications: His bibliography lists over 150 publications since 1944.

_____. "Human Purpose in Life." *Zygon* 1 (1966): 217-29.
_____. "Right and Wrong in Human Evolution." *Zygon* 2 (1967): 59-76.
_____. "Toward an Anthropologically Useful Definition of Religion." In *Changing Perspectives in the Scientific Study of Religion*, ed. A. W. Eister. New York: John Wiley, 1974.
_____. "On Describing Religion in Truk: An Anthropological Dilemma." *Proceedings of the American Philosophical Society* 125 (1981): 411-15.
_____. "Consequences of Social Living, Language, and Culture for Conflict and Its Management." *Zygon* 18 (1983): 415-424.
_____. Self-Maintenance as a Religious Concern." *Zygon* 23 (1988): 117-28.
_____. "Concern with Social Identity and Personal Worth as a Source of Social Turbulence." *Proceedings of the American Philosophical Society* 134 (1990): 328-34.
_____. "Evolution of the Human Capacity for Beliefs." *American Anthropologist* 92 (1990): 579-612.
_____. "Belief, Practice, and Religion." *Zygon* 27 (1992): 187-295.

Gorsuch, Richard L.

Present Position and Address: Professor of Psychology and Director of Research/Evaluation and Training, Graduate School of Psychology, Fuller Theological Seminary, 180 N. Oakland Ave., Pasadena, CA 91101 USA **Work Phone:** (818) 584-5527 **Fax:** (818) 584-9630 **Date of Birth:** May 14, 1937 **Languages Spoken:** English **Previous Positions**: Associate Professor/Professor of Social Work and Psychology, University of Texas at Arlington (1975-79); Associate Professor, Institute of Behavioral Research, Texas Christian University (1973-75); Kennedy Associate Professor of Psychology, George Peabody College for Teachers (1970-73); Kennedy Assistant Professor of Psychology, the Kennedy Center for Research on Education and Human Development, George Peabody College for Teachers (1968-70); Assistant Professor of Psychology, Vanderbilt University and Director of Statistical Consultation, Vanderbilt Computer Center, (1966-68); Instructor, Vanderbilt University (1965-66) **Honors:** Fellow, American Psychological Association, Div. 5 & Div. 36; Fellow, Society for the Scientific Study of Religion; Fellow, Western Psychological Association; Diplomate, Board of Assessment Psychology (newly established), William James Award, APA Div. 36, 1986 **Selected Memberships**: American Psychological Association, Div. 8; American Men and Women of Science; American Psychological Association accreditation site visitor for programs in counseling, clinical, and school psychology; President, American Psychological Association Div. 36 (1990-91); Member, Council of Representatives, American Psychological Association, (1984-85, 1989-90); Religious Research Association; Society of Multivariate Experimental Psychology; **Discipline:** Social Psychology; Ordained Minister **Related Areas of Interest:** Psychology of Religion; Churches and Conflict **Current Areas of Research:** Religion and Substance Abuse; Applying a Two-Dimension Conflict Model to Churches and Denominations; the Relationship of Beliefs and Values to Behavior.

Selected Publications: His bibliography includes 4 books, 114 published articles, 68 unpublished articles, 20 book reviews, and 17 reports.

_____. "A Two Theory Approach to Religious Conflict." Paper presented at the Second International Congress on Discrimination, Prejudice, and Conflict, Jerusalem. July 1994.
_____. "Assessing Spiritual Variables in Alcoholics Anonymous Evaluation." In B.S. McCrady and W.R. Millers (Eds.) *Research on Alcoholics Anonymous: Opportunities and Alternatives.* Piscataway, NJ: Rutgers Center of Alcohol Studies. In press.
_____. *Factor Analysis.* (3rd ed.) Hillsdale, NJ: Lawrence Erlbaum. 1983.
_____. "Measurement in Psychology of Religion Revisited." *Journal of Psychology and Christianity,* 9(2), 82-92 1990.
_____. "Toward Motivational Theories of Intrinsic Religious Commitment." *Journal for the Scientific Study of Religion.* 33 (4), 315-325. 1994.

_____. "Toward motivational theories of intrinsic religious commitment." *Journal for the Scientific Study of Religion,* 33(4), 315-325. 1994.

McPherson, S. & Gorsuch, R.L. "Intrinsic/extrinsic measurement: I/E-revised and single item scales." *Journal for the Scientific Study of Religion,* 28, 348-354. 1989.

_____. "Psychology of Religion." *Annual Review of Psychology,* 39, 1988, pp. 201-221.

_____. "Religion and Drug Abuse." *Journal of Social Issues.* In press.

_____. "Pitfalls and Possibilities in Processing People: A Psychometric Perspective." In *Clergy Assessment and Career Development,* R.A. Hunt, J.E. Hinkle, Jr., & H.N. Malony (Eds.) Nashville: Abingdon. 1990, pp. 55-60.

_____. "Religion and Prejudice: Lessons Not Learned from the Past." *The International Journal for the Psychology of Religion,* 3 (1), 20-31. 1993.

Gracely, Brett W.

Present Position and Address: Water Resources Engineer, Ted Zorich and Associates, Inc:7333 W. Jefferson Ave., Suite 210, Lakewood, CO 80235, USA (Home) 4385 Comanche Drive, #2, Boulder, CO 80303-3618, USA **Work Phone:** (303) 980-0030 **Work Fax:** (303) 980-0126 **Home Phone:** (303) 499-6252 **Home Fax:** (303) 279-5525 **Date of Birth:** February 21, 1966 **Education:** US Naval Construction Training Center, Engineering Aide, Honor Graduate, 1985; Westmont College, B.S., Engineering Physics, *cum laude,* 1990; University of California/Berkeley, MS, Civil (Water Resources) Engineering, 1992. **Awards and Honors:** ODK National Honor Society **Previous Positions:** Civil Engineer Intern, US Forest Service, Santa Barbara, CA; Environmental Engineer, SAIC, Pleasanton, CA **Selected Memberships:** American Society of Civil Engineers; American Geophysical Union; American Scientific Affiliation; Association of Groundwater Scientists and Engineers **Discipline:** Civil and Water Resources Engineering **Related Areas of Interest:** Hydrology; Hydraulic Engineering; Water Resources Planning and Management **Current Areas of Research:** The Significance of Water in Transformative Old and New Testament Events.

Selected Publications:

_____, W. A. Hoppes. *LLNL Site 300 Groundwater Monitoring Program. Quarterly Report, April - June, 1991.* Livermore, CA: Lawrence Livermore National Laboratory, 1991. UCAR - 10191 - 91 - 2.

_____, W. W. Schwartz. *Engineering Evaluation of the Sewer Diversion Facility.* Livermore, CA: Lawrence Livermore National Laboratory, 1992. UCRL - 1D - 107444.

_____, W. W. Schwartz, and D. A. Gracely. *Engineering Assessment and Certification of Integrity of the 177 - R1 Tank System.* Livermore, CA: Lawrence Livermore National Laboratory, University of California, 1992. UCRL -1D - 110440.

_____. *A Hydraulic Feasibility Study for a Combined - Use Recreation and Aquaculture Lake.* University of California - Berkeley, 1992.

_____, Dona Lierle. "Earth Science Terrain Modeling Systems Hep Consultancy Generate Feasibility Studies and Analyze Contamination Data." *Pollution Engineering* (July 1994).

Grant, Theodore F.

Present Position and Address: Pastoral Consultant (Clinical Psychology, since 1964), St. Patrick's Episcopal Church, Washington, DC; Consultant, Washington VA Hospital; Presenter, College of Preachers, Washington, DC; Parish I Cathedral House 7C, 3217 Wisconsin Avenue N.W., Washington, DC 20016; (Home) 4928 Sentinel Drive #402, Bethesda, MD 20816, USA **Concurrent Positions:** Independent Practice of Psychotherapy (since 1968) **Work Phone:** (202) 966-3217 **Home Phone:** (301) 229-1938 **Date of Birth:** May 18, 1930 **Education:** B.A. (1952), Dartmouth College; M.A. (1960), The New School for Social Research; Ph.D. (1964), University of North Carolina **Previous Positions:** Assistant Professor (1964-65), Virginia Commonwealth University; Staff Psychologist (1965-67), Washington VA Hospital; Director of Training (1967-68), Fairfax-FC MHC; **Licenses:**

Psychologist, District of Columbia; Clinical Psychology, Virginia Board of Medicine **Selected Memberships:** American Academy of Psychotherapists; Fellow, Virginia Academy of Clinical Psychologists; Associate, Holy Cross Fathers, West Park, NY; Episcopal Church **Discipline:** Clinical Psychology **Related Interests:** Selection and Training of Priests; Mental Health of the Clergy; Clinical and Pastoral Consultation; Psychotherapy.

Selected Publications:

_____. "The Three Temptations of Christ." *Voices* (The Art and Science of Psychotherapy) 8, 3 (1972).
_____. "Integrating the Psychotherapist with His or Her Assumptions . . . ." *Voices* 24, 2 (1988).

Green, Thomas F.

Present Position and Address: Professor of Education (since 1966)/Margaret O. Slocum Professor (since 1980), Syracuse University, 263 Huntington Hall, Syracuse, NY 13244, USA; (Home) Box 100, Pompey, NY 13138, USA **Work Phone:** (315) 423-3343 **Home Phone:** (315) 677-9935 **Date of Birth:** February 8, 1927 **Education:** B.A. Philosophy and Government (1948)/M.A. Philosophy (1949), University of Nebraska; Ph.D. Philosophy (1952), Cornell University **Previous Positions:** Instructor (1952-55), School of Mines and Technology, Rapid City SD; Assistant Professor of Humanities (1955-58)/Assistant through Associate Professor of Education (1958-64), Michigan State University; Associate Professor (1964-66), Syracuse University; Director (1967-69)/Codirector (1970-73), Educational Policy Research Center, Syracuse University Research Corporation, NY; Some Relevant Experience: United States delegate to World Conference on Teaching and Theology (1960), University of Strasbourg; Sabbatical Year as Senior Research Fellow (1961-62), Princeton Theological Seminary; J. Richard Street Lecturer at Syracuse University (1966), on "Education and Pluralism: Ideal and Reality"; Lecturer (1986), Provost Series on Ethics and Higher Education, Duke University **Selected Memberships:** American Philosophical Association; American Educational Research Association; Philosophy of Education Society **Discipline:** Philosophy; Education **Related Interests:** Ethics and Society; Learning and Liberalism; Education and Theology **Current Research:** "In progress is a set of fifteen to twenty informal and personal explorations of theological and biblical topics in *Letters to Larry*. The question of the book is 'How might a relatively corrupt, deeply secular person rationally assess the claims of the Christian and Hebrew traditions upon life? There is no projected completion date as yet. This is a labor of love in the most literal sense."

Selected Publications:

_____. "Authority and the Office of the Teacher," "Education and the Theory of Man," and "The Nature of Wonder." In *Essays in Education and Theology*, ed. Marjorie Reves. Geneva: World Student Christian Federation, 1965.
_____. "The Formation of Conscience in an Age of Technology, a monograph. The John Dewey Lecture 1984." Syracuse University Printing Services, 1984. Reprint *The American Journal of Education* (1985).

Greenhow, Donald Eric Fraser

Present Position and Address: Associate Professor of Anesthesia, University of Pennsylvania, 3400 Spruce Street, Philadelphia, PA 19104, USA **Work Phone:** (610) 662-3749 or (610) 647-3789 **Fax Number:** (610) 651-2848 **Date of Birth:** December 4, 1931 **Languages Spoken:** English **Previous Positions:** District Vice-Moderator (3 Years), Presbytery of Philadelphia, PCUSA; Chairman (8+ Years), Two Committees of Presbytery of Philadelphia, PCUSA; Member, Board of Trustees (2 Years), Society of Cardiovascular Anesthesiologists; Member and Secretary (1976-80), Medical Faculty Senate, University of Pennsylvania **Selected Memberships:** Christian Medical and Dental Society; American Society of Anesthesiologists; Society for Education in Anesthesia; Society of Cardiovascular

Anesthesiologists; International Anesthesia Research Society; American Scientific Affiliation; American Association for the Advancement of Science **Discipline:** Anesthesia **Related Areas of Interest:** Anesthesia; Research in Education, Specifically the Definition and Measurement of Competence.

Selected Publications: His bibliography contains 1 book, chapters in 4 books and 15 published articles.

_____. *Towards an Operational Definition of Competence.* Ph.D. diss., University of Michigan - Ann Arbor, 1991. UMI - Ann Arbor, 1991.

Gregersen, Niels Henrik

Present Position and Address: Associate Professor, Institute of Systematic Theology (since 1989), Aarhus University, Denmark Bedervej 72, 8320 Maarslet, DK - Denmark **Work Phone:** (+45) 89422274 **Home Phone:** (+45) 86297070 **Fax:** (45) 86 13 04 90 **E-Mail:** nhg.teologi.aau.dk **Date of Birth:** June 16, 1956 **Languages Spoken:** Danish, English, and German **Education:** M.A. Theology (1983)/Ph.D. (1987), University of Copenhagen **Previous Positions:** Lecturer in Philosophy (1983), University of Copenhagen; Assistant Professor in Ethics and Philosophy of Religion (1986-1989), Aarhus University, Denmark **Selected Memberships:** Forum Theology - Science, Aarhus University; ESSSAT; IRAS **Discipline:** Dogmatics, Philosophy of Religion; Ethics; Philosophy of Biology; General Systems Theory.

Selected Publications:

_____. "Freedom and Evolution. Systems Theoretical and Theological Perspectives." In *Free Will and Determinism*, ed. V. Mortensen and R. C. Sorenson. Aarhus University Press, 1987.
_____. *Teologi og kultur. Protestantismen mellem isolation og assimilation I det 19. og 20. Aarhundrede* (Theology and culture. Protestantism between isolation and assimilation in the 19th and 20th Centuries). *Acta Jutlandica* 64, series 15. Aarhus University Press, 1987.
_____. *Gud og universet. W. Pannenbergs religionsfilosofi (God and the universe.* W. Pannenberg's philosophy of religion). Gad Inc., 1989.
_____. "Vender den naturlige teologi tilbage?" (Return of natural theologies?). In *Religion og religiøsitet*, ed. Johs. Aagaard. ANIS, Inc., 1991.
_____. "Goethe versus Newton? Goethe versus Darwin?" *Praesteforeningens Blad* 24 (1990): 516-25.
_____. "Gud og tilfaeldigheden - et teologisk forsøg med indeterminismen." In *Kaos og kausalitet. Om Kaosteorien og dens betydning for filosofi og teologi* (Chaos and causality. On chaos theory and its implications for philosophy and theology), ed. N. H. Gregersen and Aksel Wiin Nielsen, 151-230. Aarhus University Press, 1992.
_____, editor. *Naturvidenskab og livssyn* (Science and philosophy of life). Munksgaard Inc., 1993. 2d. ed., 1994.
_____. "Theology in a Neo-Darwinian World." *Studia Theologica* 2 (1994): 43-68.
_____. "Providence in an Indeterministic world." *CTNS Bulletin* 14, 1 (1994): 16-31.

Gregorios, Paulos Mar

Present Position and Address: Metropolitan of Delhi, Orthodox Syrian Church of the East; New Delhi, 110 062, India; Orthodox Seminary, P. B. 98, Kottayam, Kerala - 686 001, India **Work Phone:** (011) 6436417; 6474975 (personal) **Home Phone:** (0841) 3526 or 3650 **Date of Birth:** August 9, 1922 **Education:** B.A. (1952), Goshen College, IN, USA; Oklahoma University (Summer 1951) and Union Theological Seminary (summers 1951, 52); M.Div. (1954), Princeton Theological Seminary; S.T.M. (1960), Yale University; Doctoral Research (1960-61), Oxford University/Gregory of Nyssa Institute of Münster, Germany; D.Th. (1975), Serampore University **Honorary Degrees:** D.Th. (honoris causa), Leningrad Theological Academy/Lutheran Theological Academy, Budapest, Hungary/Jan Hus Faculty, Prague/Orthodox Faculty, Czechoslovakia **Awards and Honors:** Certificate of Merit for Distinguished Service and Inspired Leadership of World Church by Dictionary of International Biography; Distinguished Leaders **Previous Positions:** Journalist in India (1937-42); Secretary of Public Library (1939-42), Tripunithura, India; Indian Post and Telegraph (1942-47); Teacher (1947-50), Secondary Schools in Ethiopia; Moderator of Church and Society (1975-83); Fellow at Indian Institute of Advanced Study in Shimla (1987, 1990); Visiting Fellow (1986, 88), Princeton Theological Seminary; Observer (1963-65), II Vatican Council; Member of Joint Working Group of Roman Catholic Church and the WCC (1963-75), Faith and Order Commission (1968-75); Senate of Kerala University (1972-76)/Serampore University (1970-74, 84-93); Hein Memorial Lecturer in USA (1968); MIT; Distinguished Visiting Professor (1981), College of Wooster; General President, Indian Philosophical Congress (1990); Member, Council for Research in Values and Philosophy, Washington, DC; President of World Council of Churches (WCC), Geneva (1983-91) **Editorial Experience:** Editor and Contributor: *Science and Our Future* (Madras, 1978); *Koptisches Christentum* (Stuttgart, 1973); *Die Syrischen Kirchen in Indien* (Stuttgart, 1974); *Burning Issues* (Kottayam, 1977) **Selected Memberships:** Societas Liturgica; Gregory of Nyssa Society; Indian Philosophical Congress; International Societies for Metaphysics/Neoplatonic Studies ; Fellow, International Biographical Association; Association of Christian Philosophers of India; India International Center, New Delhi; Indian Institute of World Culture, Bangalore **Discipline:** Theology; Administration **Related Interests:** Cosmology; Philosophy of Science; Metaphysics; Science, Society and Religion; Science, Technology and Society; Religion and World Peace and Justice.

Selected Publications: His bibliography lists 14 books and 5 chapters. He has also written dozens of articles and contributed to many symposia.

_____. *The Joy of Freedom*. New York: Associated Press, 1967.

_____. *Truth Without Tradition?* Tirupati: S. V. University, 1978.
_____. *The Human Presence*. Geneva: WCC, 1978, 1979; Indian Edition - Madras: C. L. S., 1980; USA Edition - New York: Amity House, 1987.
_____. *Science for Sane Societies*. Madras, 1980; NY: Paragon, 1987.
_____. *Enlightenment - East and West*. Shimla: Indian Institute of Advanced Study, 1989.
_____. *The Freedom of Man*. Philadelphia: Westminster, 1972.
_____. *The Meaning of Diakonia*. Geneva: WCC, 1988.
_____. *Cosmic Man*. Delhi, 1980; New York: Paragon, 1988.
_____. *A Light Too Bright*. New York: SUNY, 1992.

Gregory, Frederick

Present Position and Address: Professor and Chair of Department of History (since 1991), University of Florida, 4131 Turlington Hall, Gainesville, FL 32611, USA **Work Phone:** (904) 392-0271 **Home Phone:** (904) 377-6762 **Date of Birth:** December 3, 1942 **Education:** B.S. (1965), Wheaton College; B.D. (1968), Gordon-Conwell Theological Seminary; M.A. (1970), University of Wisconsin; Ph.D. (1973), Harvard University **Previous Positions:** Instructor in Mathematics (1965-68), Gordon College; Assistant Professor of Mathematics and History of Science (1973-78), Eisenhower College; Assistant Professor of Physical Sciences (1978-79)/Associate Professor of History (1980-91), University of Florida **Selected Memberships:** Vice-President and President Elect, History of Science Society **Discipline:** History, with special emphasis on History of Science **Related Interests:** A Historical Investigation of the interrelationships between Science, Philosophy, and Theology.

Selected Publications: His bibliography lists over 50 publications including book reviews, and 9 papers and 5 TV commentaries, much of which is relevant to the current dialogue between Science and Theology.

_____. *Scientific Materialism in Nineteenth Century Germany*. Dordrecht and Boston: D. Reidel Publishing Company, 1977.

_____. "Scientific vs. Dialectical Materialism: A Clash of Ideologies in Nineteenth Century German Radicalism." *Isis* 68 (1977): 206-23.

_____. "Darwin and the Creationists." TV conversation (WUFT-TV, 1981).

_____. "The Boundary Between Science and Religion, Wissen, Glaube, and Ahnung in the Thought of J. F. Fries." Paper presented at American Society of Church History Annual Meeting, Denver, March 1984.

_____. "The Impact of Darwinian Evolution on Protestant Theology in the Nineteenth Century." In *God and Nature*, ed. D. C. Lindberg and R. L. Numbers. Berkeley: University of California Press, 1986.

_____. Introduction to *Knowledge, Belief, and Aesthetic Sense*, by Jakob Fries. Translated by Kent Richter. Düsseldorf: Dinter Verlag, 1989.

_____. "Theology and the Sciences in the German Romantic Period." In *Romanticism and the Sciences*. Cambridge: Cambridge University Press, 1990.

_____. *Nature Lost: Religion and Natural Science in Nineteenth Century Germany*. Cambridge, MA: Harvard University Press, 1992.

_____. "Darwin and the German Theologians." In *World Views and Scientific Discipline Formation*, ed. William Woodward and Robert Cohen. Amsterdam: Kluwer Publications, 1991.

_____. "Theologians, Science, and Theories of Truth in Nineteenth-Century Germany." In *The Invention of Physical Science*, eds. Mary Jo Nye, Joan Richards, and Roger Stuewer. Amsterdam: Kluwer Publications, 1992.

Griffin, David Ray

Present Position and Address: Executive Director (since 1973), Center for Process Studies; Professor of Religion, Claremont Graduate School; Professor of Philosophy of Religion and Theology, School of Theology at Claremont, 1325 North College Avenue, Claremont, CA 91711-3199, USA **Date of Birth:** August 8, 1939 **Education:** B.A. (1962), Northwest Christian College; M.A. (1963), University of Oregon; School of Theology at Claremont (1963-64); Johannes Gutenberg University (1965-66); Claremont Graduate School (1966-68); Ph.D. (1970), Claremont Graduate School **Previous Positions:** Assistant Professor of Theology (1968-73), University of Dayton **Discipline:** Philosophy of Religion and Theology **Related Interests:** Process Theology; Postmodern Theology.

Selected Publications: His bibliography lists 10 books, 10 edited works, over 85 articles, and 13 book reviews. Much of his work deals with process philosophy and theology.

_____. "Introduction: Time and the Fallacy of Misplaced Concreteness," and "Bohm and Whitehead on Wholeness, Freedom, Causality, and Time." In *Physics and the Ultimate Significance of Time: Bohm, Prigogine, and Process Philosophy*, ed. David Ray Griffin. SUNY, 1986.

_____. *God and Religion in the Postmodern World*. SUNY, 1988. Note chapters "Evolution and Postmodern Theism" and "Postmodern Animism and Life after Death" (the latter deals with parapsychology).

_____. "Introduction: The Reenchantment of Science," and "Of Minds and Molecules: Postmodern Medicine in a Psychosomatic Universe." In *The Reenchantment of Science: Postmodern Proposals*, ed. David Ray Griffin. SUNY, 1988.

_____. "On Ian Barbour's *Issues in Science and Religion*: A Review Essay." *Zygon* 23 (1988).

_____. "The Restless Universe: A Postmodern Vision." In *The Restless Earth: Nobel Conference 24*, ed. Keith J. Carlson. Harper & Row, 1990.

_____. "Professing Theology in the State University." In *Theology and the University*, ed. David Ray Griffin and Joseph C. Hough. SUNY, 1990.

_____. "Green Spirituality: A Postmodern Convergence of Science and Religion." *Journal of Theology* (United Theological Seminary) 1992.

_____. "Hartshorne, God, and Relativity Physics." *Process Studies* 21 (Summer, 1992).

_____. "Parapsychology and Philosophy: A Whiteheadian Postmodern Perspective." *The Journal of the American Society for Physical Research* 87 (July 1993).

_____. "Whitehead's Deeply Ecological Worldview." *Worldviews and Ecology: The Bucknell Review* 37, 2 (1993).

Griffiths, Robert B.

Present Position and Address: Professor of Physics (since 1969), Carnegie-Mellon University, Pittsburgh, PA 15213, USA **Work Phone:** (412) 268-2765 **Fax:** (412) 681-0648 **E-Mail:** (Internet): rgrif + @ cmu.edu **Date of Birth:** February 25, 1937 **Education:** A.B. Physics (1957), Princeton University; M.S. Physics (1958)/Ph.D. Physics with Mathematics minor (1962), Stanford University. **Postgraduate Studies:** Postdoctoral fellow (1962-64), University of California at San Diego **Previous Positions:** Assistant (1964-67)/Associate Professor of Physics (1967-69), Carnegie-Mellon University **Selected Memberships:** Member, National Academy of Sciences; Fellow, American Physical Society; Fellow, American Scientific Affiliation **Discipline:** Physics **Related Interests:** The Statistical Mechanics and Thermodynamics of Phase Transitions, Especially Critical Points; the Mathematical Foundations of Statistical Mechanics; the Theory of Magnetism; the Relation of Physical Science and Christian Theology; the Interpretation and Philosophical Implications of Quantum Theory.

Selected Publications: His bibliography lists 110 publications.

_____. "Is Theology a Science?" *Journal of the American Scientific Affiliation* 32 (1980): 169.
_____. "Consistent Histories and the Interpretation of Quantum Mechanics." *Journal of Statistical Physics* 36 (1984): 219.
_____. "Correlations in Separated Quantum Systems. : A Consistent History Analysis of the EPR Problem." *American Journal of Physics* 55 (1987): 11.
_____. "Consistent Interpretation of Quantum Mechanics Using Quantum Trajectories." *Phys. Rev. Lett.* 70 (1993): 2201-4.

Grizzle, Raymond Edward

Present Position and Address: Assistant Professor of Environmental Science, Randall Environmental Science Center, Taylor University, Upland, IN 46989, USA **Work Phone:** (317) 998-2751 **Fax Number:** (317) 998-4910 **Date of Birth:** July 6, 1950 **Languages Spoken:** English **Previous Positions:** Research Scientist (1987-89), University of New Hampshire; Assistant Professor of Biology (1989-92), Livingston University; Assistant Professor of Biology (1992-94), Campbell University, Buies Creek, NC **Selected Memberships:** American Institute of Biological Sciences; American Scientific Affiliation; Ecological Society of America; Estuarine Research Federation; National Shellfisheries Association; Society for Ecological Restoration **Discipline:** Environmental Science; Biology **Related Areas of Interest:** Science/Theology Interactions; Environmental Ethics **Current Areas of Research:** Human Needs in Environmental Ethics; History of Science/Theology Interactions; Restoration of Coastal Habitats.

Selected Publications: His total bibliography includes 19 published papers; 5 deal with science/theology interactions or environmental ethics.

_____. "Some Comments on the 'Godless' Nature of Darwinian Evolution, and a Plea to the Philosophers Among Us." *Perspectives on Science and Christian Faith* (*PSCF*) 44 (1992): 175-7.
_____. "A Conceptual Model Relating Theology and Science." *PSCF* 45 (1993): 222-8.
_____, M. G. Cogdill. "Subduing the Earth While Tending the Garden: A Proposal for a More Balanced Environmental Ethic." *Faculty Dialogue* (Winter 1993/94): 73-81.
_____. "Environmentalism Should Include Human Ecological Needs." *BioScience* (1994).
_____. "Darwin, Darwinism, and Religion." Review of *The Darwinian Paradigm*, by Michael Ruse. *BioScience* (1994).

Gromacki, Robert Glenn

Present Position and Address: Distinguished Professor of Bible and Greek; Cedarville College, Cedarville, OH 45314 **Work Phone:** (513) 766-5155 **Fax Number:** (513) 766-2760 **Date of Birth:** September 20, 1933 **Language Spoken:** English **Education:** Th.B. (1956), Baptist Bible Seminary; Th.M. (1960), Dallas Theological Seminary; Th.D. Theology (1966), Grace Theological Seminary **Postgraduate Experience:** Institute of Holy Land Studies (1982), Jerusalem, Israel **Lectures Presented:** Five Thomas F. Staley Distinguished Lectureships (1972, 81, 86, 89 [2]) **Awards and Honors:** Distinguished Educator Award (1975), Cedarville College Alumni Association; Faculty Member of the Year (1976), Cedarville College; Alumni Outstanding Service Award (1985), Baptist Bible College; First Faculty Member to become a Distinguished Professor (1993), Cedarville College **Selected Memberships:** Evangelical Theological Society; Creation Research Society; Near East Archaeological Society **Discipline:** Theology; New Testament Book Studies; New Testament Greek **Related Areas of Interest:** Pastoring Churches; Travel to Israel **Current Areas of Research:** New Testament Book Commentaries.

Selected Publications: His total bibliography contains 15 books, over 80 published articles, and foreign translations of 4 books in Portuguese, German, Spanish, and Bengali.

_____. *The Modern Tongues Movement.* Presbyterian and Reformed Publishing Co., 1967.
_____. *New Testament Survey.* Baker Book House, 1974.
_____. *Are These the Last Days?* Regular Baptist Press, 1975.
_____. *Called to be Saints.* 1 Corinthians. Baker Book House, 1977.
_____. *Stand Firm in the Faith.* 2 Corinthians. Baker Book House, 1978.
_____. *Stand Fast in Liberty.* Galatians. Baker Book House, 1979.
_____. *Stand United in Joy.* Philippians. Baker Book House, 1980.
_____. *Stand Perfect in Wisdom.* Colossians. Baker Book House, 1981.
_____. *The Virgin Birth: Doctrine of Deity.* Baker Book House, 1981.
_____. *Salvation is Forever.* Regular Baptist Press, 1989.

Gruenwald, Oskar

Present Position and Address: Cofounder and President (since 1983), Institute for Interdisciplinary Research, Santa Monica, 2828 3rd Street #11, Santa Monica, CA 90405, USA **Concurrent Positions:** Consultant: Institute for Advanced Philosophic Research, Boulder, CO (since 1977); Democracy International Committee to Aid Democratic Dissidents in Yugoslavia, Washington, DC (since 1980); Public Research, Syndicated, Claremont, CA (since 1982) **Work Phone:** (310) 396-0517 **Date of Birth:** October 5, 1941 **Languages Spoken:** English, German, French, Serbo-Croatian, and Hungarian **Education:** A.A. (1964), Pasadena City College; B.A. (1966), University of California - Berkeley; M.A. (1967)/Ph.D. (1972), Claremont Graduate School **Previous Positions:** International Economist (1967-68), US Treasury Department, Washington, DC; Visiting Research Associate (1971-72), Social Sciences Research Center, University of Erlangen-Nurnberg, Germany; Lecturer (1972-73), Government and Economics, Pepperdine University, Malibu/Santa Monica College (1973-76); Independent Research and Writing (1976-83), Santa Monica, CA **Editorial Work:** Freedom House Exchange, NY (since 1985); *Slavic Review,* University of Texas - Austin (since 1986); Institute for the Study of International Problems, Switzerland (since 1988) **Selected Memberships:** Founder (since 1983), International Christian Studies Association (ICSA); Coordinator, ICSA Quadrennial World Congresses (since 1984); American Scientific Affiliation; American Association for the Advancement of Slavic Studies; American Philosophical Association; Nominated to Delta Tau Kappa (1975, 1991), the International Social Science Honor Society **Discipline:** Author and Consultant - Interdisciplinary Studies and Research; Political Science; Philosophy of Science and Religion **Related Interests:** Interdisciplinary and Interfaith Dialogue.

Selected Publications: Articles in many scholarly journals and chapters of books. Editor (since 1983), *ICSA Newsletter* (International Christian Studies Association). Editor (since 1989), *Journal of Interdisciplinary Studies - An International Journal of Interdisciplinary and Interfaith Dialogue.*

_____. *The Yugoslav Search for Man: Marxist Humanism in Contemporary Yugoslavia.* South Hadley, MA: J. F. Bergin, 1983.
_____, Karen Rosenblum-Cole, eds. *Human Rights in Yugoslavia.* New York: Irvington Publishers, 1986.

Grzegorczyk, Andrzej

Present Position and Address: Professor (since 1973), Instytut Filozofii I Socjologii, Polskiej Akademii Nauk, Nowy Swiat 72, Palac Staszica, 00-330 Warszawa, Poland; (Home) Filtrowa 67 m. 77, 02055 Warszawa, Poland **Date of Birth:** August 22, 1922 **Languages Spoken:** Polish, English, French **Education:** Ph.D. (1950), University of Warsaw **Previous Positions:** Professor (1960-1973), Institute of Mathematics, Polish Academy of Science **Selected Memberships:** International Institute of Philosophy **Discipline:** Philosophy and Mathematics - Logic; Ethics **Related Interests:** Structure of the Human Being and his Moral Comportment. "God provided human beings with freedom. He only repairs what we have spoilt, and continually gives us new chances for better choices."

Selected Publications: Has written many articles and a few books in logic. In the area of ethics he has written 7 books in Polish as well as many articles.

_____. *Filozofia czasu proby*, (The philosophy of the time of ordeal). Warsaw: PAX, 1983.
_____. *Moralitety*. Warsaw: PAX, 1986.
_____. *Etyka w doswiadczeniu wewnetrznym*, (Ethics in inner experience). Warsaw: PAX, 1989.
_____. *Zycie jako wyzwanie*, (Life as a challenge). Warsaw: IFIS PAN 1993.

Gumlich, Hans-Eckhart

Present Position and Address: Professor of Physics, Emeritus, Technische Universität Berlin, Institut für Festkörperphysik, Sekr. PN 4-1, Hardenbergstrasse 36, D-14197 Berlin; (Home) Tribergerstrasse 3, D-1000 Berlin 33 (Wilmersdorf), Germany **Work Phone:** 030-8213350 **Date of Birth:** March 10, 1926 **Languages Spoken:** German, English, French **Education:** Dipl. Ing (1953)/Dr. Ing (1958), Technische Universität, Berlin **Previous Positions:** Fritz Haber Institut der Max-Planck-Gesellschaft (1959-1969); Université de Paris (1953-54); University of Delaware (1962-1963) **Selected Memberships:** German Physical Society; Evangelische Akademikerschaft **Discipline:** Solid State Physics **Related Interests:** Physics; Physics and Society; Physics and Theology.

Selected Publications:

_____. "Time among Physicists." *Radius* (Zeitschrift der Evangelischen Akademikerschaft in Deutschland, September 1987).
_____. "Physics: The Uncertainty continues." *Radius* (January 1989).
_____. "Limits of Research in Physics." In *Science and Transcendence*, ed. G. Abel, 29-48. Tub Dokumentation 60 (1992).

Haas Jr., John W.

Present Position and Address: Head of Department of Chemistry/Professor of Chemistry (since 1967)Gordon College, Grapevine Road, Wenham, MA 01984, USA **Work Phone:** (508) 927-2300 ext. 4387 **Date of Birth:** February 19, 1930 **Education:** B.S. Chemistry/Geology minor (1953), The King's College; M.S. Chemistry (1955)/Ph.D. (1957), University of Delaware **Postgraduate Studies:** Postdoctoral Study in the History of Science (Summer 1987), Ian Ramsey Centre, Christ Church College, Oxford **Previous Positions:** Associate Professor of Chemistry (1957-61), Grove City College; Associate Professor (1961-67), Gordon College; Visiting Professor of Chemistry (Summer 1980-82), Boston University; Visiting Professor of Chemistry (Summer 1983), Tufts University; History of Science Research Grant (1986-88) to travel Europe and the Near-East for discussions with leading people researching various areas of integration of Christian thought and science **Editorial Experience:** Editor (since 1989), *Perspectives on Science and Christian Faith* **Selected Memberships:** Fellow, American Scientific Affiliation (Council member 1972-77/President 1976); American Chemical Society; History of Science Society **Discipline:** Chemistry; History of Science **Related Interests:** Science and Christian Faith; Complementarity and Christian Thought; The influence of John Wesley and the Wesleyans on 18th and 19th Century science.

Selected Publications:

_____, "Complementarity and Christian Thought - An Assessment." Part 1, "The Classical Complementarity of Niels Bohr." *JASA* 35 (1983), 145-157. Part 2, "Logical Complementarity." *JASA* 35 (1983), 203-209.

_____, "Integrity in Science - a Christian Response." *JASA* 38 (1986): 204-206.

_____, "Relativity and Christian Thought: The Early Response." *Perspectives on Science and Christian Faith* 40 (1988), 10-18.

_____, "Arthur Peacocke's New Biology: New Wine in Old Bottles." *Science and Christian Belief* 1 (1989): 161.

_____, "Science and Christian Faith in Western Europe: A Personal View." *Perspectives on Science and Christian Faith* 42 (1990) : 39-43.

_____, Irvin Moon, F. Alton Everest and Will Houghton. "Early Links Between the Moody Bible Institute and the American Scientific Affiliation." *Perspectives on Science and Christian Faith* 43 (1991): 249-258.

_____, "Donald Macrimmen MacKay (1924-1987): A View From the Other Side of the Atlantic." *Perspectives on Science and Christian Faith* 44 (1992): 55-60.

_____, "John Wesley's 18th Century Views on Science and Christianity: An Examination of the Charge of Antiscience." *Church History* 63 (1994): 318-392.

_____, George V Coyneand Karl Schmitz-Moorman, eds. "The Changing Face of American Evangelicals Toward Evolution." *Origins, Time and Complexity, Part II: Studies in Science and Theology* (1994): 262-268.

_____, "Eighteenth Century Evangelical Responses to Science: John Wesley's Enduring Legacy." *Science and Christian Belief* 6 (1994): 83-102.

Habgood, John S.

Present Position and Address: The Most Reverend John Habgood, Archbishop of York (since 1983); Bishopthorpe Palace, Bishopthorpe, York YO2 1QE, UK **Work Phone:** 0904 707021 **Date of Birth:** June 23, 1927 **Education:** B.A. (1948)/M.A. and Ph.D. (1952), King's College, Cambridge UK **Honorary Degrees:** Honorary Doctor of Divinity degrees from Durham/Cambridge/Aberdeen/Huron, Hull **Awards and Honors:** Privy Councillor; Honorary Fellow, King's College **Previous Positions:** Demonstrator in Pharmacology (1950-53), Cambridge; Vice-Principal (1956-62), Westcott House, Cambridge; Rector (1962-67), St. John's Church, Jedburgh; Principal (1967-73), Queen's College, Birmingham; Bishop of Durham (1973-83) **Selected Memberships:** Founder, member, Council for Science and Society; Council member, Worldwide Fund for Nature; Moderator, Church and Society, World Council of Churches **Discipline:** Physiology and Pharmacology and subsequently Theology **Related Interests:** Philosophy and the Social Implications of Science.

Selected Publications: Numerous articles and reviews listed up to 1983 in a biography entitled Living with Paradox by J. S. Peart-Binns.

_____, Religion and Science. Hodder and Stoughton, 1964.
_____, A Working Faith. Darton, Longman and Todd, 1980.
_____, Church and Nation in a Secular Age. Darton, Longman and Todd, 1983.
_____, Confessions of a Conservative Liberal. S.P.C.K., 1988.
_____, *Making Sense*. S.P.C.K., 1993.

Hafner, Hermann Friedrich

Present Position and Address: Secretary of the Karl-Heim-Gesellschaft, Unter den Eichen 13, D-35041 Marburg, Germany **Work /Home Phone:** 06421 / 83129 **Date of Birth:** November 18, 1939 **Languages Spoken:** German, some English, some French **Education:** Abitur (1959); Studied Prot. Theology at Tübingen, Göttingen, Mainz and Heidelberg (12 Semesters); First (1965)/Second (1967) theol. Examination at the Ev. Oberkirchenrat at Karlsruhe; Studies in Philosophy of Science (1980-1988), University of Marburg **Previous Positions:** Pastor (1967-70), Mannheim; Assistant to the chair of Protestant Theology at the Education Faculty (1970-74), University of Würzburg; Private work (1974-76); Theological Secretary (1976-80, 88-92), Pfarrer-Gebetsbruderschaft, Marburg **Selected Memberships:** Karl-Heim-Gesellschaft, Marburg; Fachgruppe Naturwissenschaftler der (Study Group of Natural Scientists of the) Studentenmission in Deutschland (SMD), Marburg; American Scientific Affiliation; European Society for the Study of Science and Theology (ESSSAT) **Discipline:** Systematic Theology **Related Interests:** Doctrine of God; Doctrine of Creation; Theological and other Concepts of Reality; Epistemology; Philosophy of Science; Questions between Theology and the Sciences (including historical).

Selected Publications: His bibliography lists 24 works plus he has published 50 book reviews since 1963.

_____. Translation of T. F. Torrance as "Grundlegende Aufgaben in Theologie und Wissenschaft" (Fundamental issues in theology and science). *Evangelium und Wissenschaft* (Rundbrief der Karl-Heim-Gesellschaft) 13 (1985): 4-22.
_____. "Naturwissenschaft und Menschenbild" (Science and the image of man). *Evangelium und Wissenschaft* 13 (1985): 23-28.
_____, Edith Gutsche, eds. "Im Vorfeld wissenschaftlicher Theorien. Vor- und außerwissenschaftliche Motive der Theoriebildung am Beispiel Albert Einsteins" (Scientific theories in the making: pre- and extrascientific motifs in the formation of theories - Albert Einstein for example). *Porta-Studien No. 14* . 2d ed. Marburg: Studentenmission in Deutschland (SMD), 1988.

_____. "Christliches Wahrheitszeugnis als Cantus firmus im Chor der Wissenschaften. Ein Tagungsbericht" (Christian Witness for Truth as Cantus Firmus in the Choir of the Sciences. Report on a Conference). *Theologische Beiträge* 17 (1986): 154-9.

_____. "Scheidung hin, Versöhnung her - gibt es ein Evangelium für Wissenschaften? Von der wahren Beziehung zwischen Evangelium und Wissenschaft" (Neither divorce nor reconciliation: is there a gospel for the sciences? On the real relation between gospel and science). *Evangelium und Wissenschaft* (Rundbrief der Karl-Heim-Gesellschaft) 24 (1992): 14-33.

_____, Edith Gutsche, eds. "Descartes und das neuzeitliche Denken. Anfragen an die Grundlagen naturwissenschaftlicher Weltbilder" (Descartes and the thought of modern age. Questions on the basic principles of scientific conceptions of the world). *Porta-Studien* Nr. 13. 2d ed . Marburg: Studentenmission in Deutschland (SMD), 1993.

_____. "Faktenwahrheit und kerygmatische Wahrheit. Einige Umrisse zum Problem" (Factual truth and kerygmatic truth: some outlines of the problem). In Das Problem der kerygmatischen Wahrheit, ed. Martin Petzolt, 24-9. Symposion des Instituts für wissenschaftstheoretische Grundlagenforschung im Deutschen Institut ür Bildung und Wissen vom 14. bis 16. September 1992 in Paderborn. Wuppertal/Paderborn, 1993.

_____. "Glaube, systematisch-theologisch" (Faith). "Glauben und Denken" (Faith and thought). "Natur" (Nature). Naturwissenschaft und Theologie" (Science and theology). "Wahrheit" (Truth). Evangelisches Lexikon für Theologie und Gemeinde 2 and 3 (Wuppertal 1993/94).

_____, Edith Gutsche and Peter C. Hägele, eds. "Zur Diskussion um Schöpfung und Evolution. Gesichtspunkte und Materialien zum Gespräch" (On the discussion about creation and evolution: aspects and materials for a dialogue). Porta-Studien No. 6. 4th ed. Marburg: Studentenmission in Deutschland (SMD), 1995.

Haikola, Lars T. J.

Present Position and Address: Associate Professor (since 1986), Philosophy of Religion Teologiska Institutionen, Lunds Universitet, Allhelgona Kyrkogata 8, S-22362, Lund, Sweden **Work Phone:** +46 46 10 90 53 **Date of Birth:** December 10, 1947 **Languages Spoken:** Swedish, English, German **Education:** M.A. (1971)/M.Theol. (1976)/Dr. Theol. (1977), Dept. of Theology, Lund University **Previous Positions:** Assistant Professor (1978-85), Lund University, Sweden; **Selected Memberships:** European Society for the Study of Science and Theology; European Conference on Philosophy of Religion **Discipline:** Philosophy of Religion **Related Interests:** Science and Religion; Ecosophy; Religious Language.

Selected Publications: His bibliography lists 8 publications.

_____. "Teleologisk renässans I kosmologin (Teleological renaissance in cosmology)." I Mystik och verklighet (1987). (En festskrift till Hans Hof bokförlaget Asak).

_____. "Natursyner och natursynder. En kritisk analys av ekosofin mot en biblisk bakgrund" (Views of nature and sins of nature. A critical analysis of ecosophy at a biblical background) *Religio* 18: Lund, 1985.

_____. "Vad är kunskap? (What is knowledge?)" in *Naturvetenskap och religion (Science and religion)* Lund: Teologiska institutionen, 1989.

_____, "Religion, naturvetenskap och människans behov av kosmologi (Religion, science and man's need of cosmology)" in *Naturvetenskap och religion (Science and religion)* Lund: Teologiska institutionen, 1989.

_____, "Behöver vetenskapen Gud? (Does science need God?)" "Mellan himmel och jord (Between sky and earth)" *Religio* Nr. 35 Lund, 1991.

_____, *Skapelse och försyn* I ljuset av modern vetenskap (Creation and providence in the light of modern science). Lund: Svensk Teologisk Kvartalskrift, 1991.

_____, "Har naturen egenvärde? (Does nature have an intrinsic value?)" Platonsällskapets skriftserie: Lund 1993.

_____, Livs åskådning, etik ock ekologi (Ideology, ethics and ecology) Klippan: Föreningen lärare i religionskunskap årsbok, 1993.

_____, "Naturvetenskapen - en ifrågasatt världsbildsskapare (Science - a questioned creator of world-views)" Vär Lösen Nr. 5-6 1993, ågång 84.

_____, "Tro och vetande (Faith and knowledge)" *Religion och livsfrågor* Nr. 3, Lund 1993.

Hallberg, Fred W.

Present Position and Address: Associate Professor of Philosophy and Humanities (since 1969), Department of Philosophy and Religion, University of Northern Iowa, Cedar Falls, IA 50614 (Home) 630 Main Street, Box 323, Janesville, IA 50647, USA **Date of Birth:** August 15, 1935 **Education:** B.A. (1958)/M.A. (1963)/Ph.D. Philosophy (1969), University of Minnesota; M.S. Psychology (1977), Iowa State University **Previous Positions:** Instructor (1966-67) in Humanities, University of Minnesota; Assistant Professor of Philosophy and Humanities (1967-69), University of Northern Iowa **Discipline:** Philosophy and Psychology **Related Interests:** Philosophy of Psychology; Philosophy of Science; Religion and Science.

Selected Publications:

_____. "Barrow and Tipler's 'The Anthropic Cosmological Principle.'" *Zygon* (June 1988). A critique of their attempt to revive de Chardin's theology in *The Phenomenon of Man.*

Hancock, Jr., Monte F.

Present Position and Address: Chief Scientist, Director Research and Development, CSI Inc. (1987-pres.)406 Dartmouth Ave. W., Melbourne, FL 32901, USA **Work Phone:** (407) 676-2923 **Fax:** (407) 676-2355 **Date of Birth:** November 14, 1953 **Languages Spoken:** English, Koiné Greek **Awards and Honors:** *Who's Who in the South and Southwest, Who's Who of Emerging Leaders in America, Who's Who Among Young American Professionals,* Outstanding Young Men of America, Certificate of Merit, FPEA (1990) **Previous Positions:** New Covenant Fellowship Church: Ordained Elder, Assoc. Choir Director, Soloist (1988-pres.); Founder and Director, Young People's Research Project (1989-pres.); Rollins College: Adjunct Faculty, Mathematics/Computer Science (1985-pres); Chairman, Florida Parent Educators Association (1990-pres.); Board of Directors, Home Education Foundation (1991-pres.); Advanced Engineer, HRB Singer Corp (1979-82); Assoc. Principal Engineer, Harris Corp (1982-87); Adjunct Faculty, Pennsylvania State University (1981-82) **Selected Memberships:** Associate member, American Scientific Affiliation (1974-pres.) **Discipline:** Applied Mathematics **Related Interests:** Artificial intelligence, machine learning, pattern classification, foundations of mathematics and the philosophy of religion **Current Research:** Radial basis functions, Wavelet multi-resolution decomposition, trainable turing machines and knowledge-based systems, non-deterministic algorithms.

Selected Publications: Bibliography contains 8 published articles, a tape series, a training video, and 3 conference proceeding abstracts.

_____. "Hyper-speed Waveform Processing Using Radial Basis Functions." Air Force Technical Application Center Sensor Technical Conf. Proc. May 1994.
_____. "Solving Hard Problems Using Machines That Learn." *Brevard Technical Journal* 1, 6.
_____. "Solving Big Classification Problems with Small Neural Networks." Technical & Business Engineering Symposium Proc. TABES 91-316A, 1991.
_____. "Doppler Radar Processing Neural Network Experiment." Air Force Technical Application Center Sensor Technical Conf. Proc. Nov. 1989.
_____. *Establishing Home School Support Groups in Florida.* Florida Parent Educators Assoc., 1989.

Handspickel, Meredith Brook

Present Position and Address: Professor of Pastoral Theology and Evangelism, Andover Newton Theological School, 210 Herrick Road, Newton Centre, MA 02159, USA **Work Phone:** (617) 964-1100, ext. 233 **Fax Number:** (617) 965-9756 **Date of Birth:** June 25, 1932 **Languages Spoken:**

German **Awards and Honors:** Phi Beta Kappa; Danforth Fellow **Previous Positions:** Member of the Secretariat for Faith and Order, World Council of Churches, Geneva, Switzerland **Selected Memberships:** AAUP; AAAS; SVHE; AAR **Discipline:** Systematic Theology **Related Areas of Interest:** Philosophy of Science **Current Areas of Research:** Religious origins of Empirical Science.

Selected Publications: Her total bibliography contains about 20 articles.

_____. "Toward a Post-Liberal Apologetics." *Journal of the Academy for Evangelism in Theological Education* 7 (1991-92).
_____. "Intimations of Transcendence: Some Developments in the Relationship between Science and Religion." *Centre for Theology and Natural Sciences Bulletin* 12, 4 (1992).
_____. "Evangelizing Liberalism." *First Things* 36 (October 1993).

Hanford, Jack T.

Present Position and Address: Professor of Philosophy and Religion (since 1970), Department of Humanities, Ferris State University, Big Rapids, MI 49307, USA **Education:** A.B. (1952), Albion College; M.Div. (1959), Garrett Theological Seminary; M.A. (1961), Northwestern University; Th.D. (1974), Iliff School of Theology/University, Denver **Postgraduate Studies:** Participant in four workshops on Medical Ethics with Hastings Center (1975-79); Workshop on Moral Development with Lawrence Kohlberg at Harvard (1977); Institute on Health Care Ethics (Summer 1983), University of Kentucky; Visiting Fellow (Summer 1987), Princeton University **Previous Positions:** Pastor and Teacher (1959-60), Depauw University, IN; Pastor and Instructor (1962-68), University of Northern Iowa; Visiting Professor (1984-85), Medical Humanities Program, Michigan State University **Selected Memberships:** American Philosophical Association; American Academy of Religion; Society for the Scientific Study of Religion; Association of Moral Education Teaching Philosophy; Society for Creative Philosophy; Philosophy of Science **Discipline:** Philosophy and Religion; Biomedical Ethics **Related Interests:** Psychology of Religion; Moral Reasoning in Bioethics; Moral Development (Kohlberg); Scientific Study of Religion.

Selected Publications: Has also refereed articles for *The Journal for the Scientific Study of Religion* and *The Journal of Interdisciplinary Studies*.

_____. "A Synoptic Approach: Resolving Problems in Empirical and Phenomenological Approaches to the Psychology of Religion." *Journal for the Scientific Study of Religion* (September 1975).
_____. "Moral Reasoning in a Bioethics Course." *Faculty Research Report in Religious Education* 76, 4 (July 1981).
_____. Review of *Philosophy of Moral Development* by Kohlbergs. (Harper) *Journal for the Scientific Study of Religion* (December 1982).

Hankins, Thomas L.

Present Position and Address: Professor of History (since 1975), Department of History, DP-20, University of Washington, Seattle, WA 98195, USA **Work Phone:** (206) 543-5695 **Date of Birth:** October 9, 1933 **Education:** B.S. Physics (1956), Yale University; M.A.T. Education (1958), Harvard University; Ph.D. History (1964), Cornell University **Previous Positions:** Instructor (1956-60), Phillips Academy, Andover; Assistant (1964-69)/Associate (1969-75), University of Washington **Editorial Work:** Advisory Editor, *Isis* (1976-80)/*Historical Studies in the Physical Sciences* (1975-79, 83-present)/*Eighteenth Century Studies* (1983-86); Contributing editor *Osiris* (since 1984) **Selected Memberships:** Secretary (1980-82)/Chairman (1982-85), US National Committee (National Academy of Sciences) for the International Union of the History and Philosophy of Science; Various offices in History of Science Society (since 1971) **Discipline:** History; Education **Related Interests:** Areas of Specialization: History of Science; History of the Enlightenment; Scientific Biography.

Selected Publications:

_____. *Jean d'Alembert: Science and the Enlightenment.* Oxford Clarendon Press, 1970.
_____. "D'Alembert and the Great Chain of Being." In *12th Congres International d'histoire des Sciences, Paris, 1968. Actes 2B.* Paris: Albert Blanchard, 1971.
_____. Essay review of *Seeing through the Enlightenment. Isis* 73 (1982): 274-9.
_____. *Science and Enlightenment.* Cambridge University Press, 1985.

Hannon, Ralph H.

Present Position and Address: Professor of Chemistry (since 1970), Department of Chemistry, Kishwaukee College, Malta, IL 60150; (Home) 101 Charter Street, DeKalb, IL 60115, USA **Date of Birth:** October 22, 1941 **Education:** B.S. Education (1963), Eastern Illinois University; M.S. (1967)/Ph.D. (1972), Northern Illinois University **Selected Memberships:** The Theosophical Society of America **Discipline:** Chemistry; Physics; Mathematics **Related Interests:** Science; Theosophy; Mysticism.

Selected Publications:

_____. "How Can Theosophy Reach Out to Contemporary Science." *The Theosophical Research Journal* 3, 1 (1986).
_____. "H. P. Blavatsky and Contemporary Science." *The Quest* (1988). This is a quarterly journal of Philosophy, Science, Religion and the Arts.

Happel, Stephen

Present Position and Address: Associate Professor, Religion and Culture (since 1983)/Chair (since 1994), Department of Religion and Religious Education, School of Religious Studies, The Catholic University of America, Washington, DC 20064, USA **Work Phone:** (202) 319-5700 **Fax:** (202) 319-5704 **E-Mail:** happel@cua.edu **Date of Birth:** August 18, 1944 **Languages Spoken:** English, French, German **Education:** M.A. English (*summa cum laude*, 1969), Indiana University; Ph.D. Religious Studies (*summa cum laude*, 1977)/S.T.D. Theology (*summa cum laude*, 1979), University of Louvain - KUL **Previous Positions:** Instructor (1973-77), Department of Theology, Catholic University of America; Associate Professor (1978-83), St. Meinrad School of Theology; Visiting Professorships, University of Notre Dame (1984)/Boston College (1986); Flannery Professor of Theology, Gonzaga University (1992-3) **Selected Memberships:** Modern Language Association; American Academy of Religion; American Society for Aesthetics; Society for Science and Literature **Discipline:** Interpretation Theory; Role of Imagination in Cognition and Religious Knowing; Religion and Culture **Related Areas of Interest:** The Role of Imagination in the Construction of Scientific Arguments **Current Research:** The Psychologization of Dramatic and Religious Narratives in Nineteenth Century Literature.

Selected Publications:

_____. *Coleridge's Religious Imagination.* In *Institut für Anglistik und Amerikanistik, Romantic Reassessment No. 100,* ed. James Hogg. Salzburg, Austria: Universität Salzburg, 1983.
_____. "Religious Rhetoric and the Language of Theological Foundations." In *Religion and Culture,* ed. Timothy P. Fallon and Philip Boo Riley. Albany, NY: SUNY Press, 1987.
_____. "Metaphors and Time Asymmetry: Cosmologies in Physics and Christian Meanings." In *Quantum Cosmology and the Laws of Nature: Scientific Perspectives on Divine Action,* ed. Robert John Russell, Nancey Murphy, and C.J. Isham. Vatican City State: Vatican Observatory Publications, 1993.

_____. "The Postmodernity of Judas: Religious Narrative and the Deconstruction of Time." In *Postmodernism, Literature, and the Future of Theology*, ed. David Jasper. London: Macmillan, 1993.

_____. "Divine Providence and Instrumentality: Metaphors for Time in Self-Organizing Systems and Divine Action." In *Chaos, Complexity, and Self Organization: Perspectives on Divine Action*, ed. Nancey Murphy, Robert John Russell, and Arthur Peacocke. Forthcoming.

Hardy, Daniel W.

Present Position and Address: Director (since 1990), Center of Theological Inquiry, 50 Stockton Street, Princeton, NJ 08540, USA **Work Phone:** (609) 683-4797 **Fax:** (609) 683-4030 **Date of Birth:** November 9, 1930 **Languages Spoken:** English, French, German **Education:** B.A. (1952), Haverford College; S.T.B. (1955)/S.T.M. (1963), General Theological Seminary, NY **Postgraduate Studies:** (1961-1965), St. John's College, Oxford University. Ordained Deacon (1955), Priest (1956), Episcopal Church. Parish Minister (1955-59), Christ Church, Greenwich, CT; Lecturer in Modern Theological Thought (1965-75)/Senior Lecturer (1975-86), University of Birmingham, UK; Van Mildert Professor of Divinity (1986-90), University of Durham; Residentiary Canon (1986-90), Durham Cathedral; President, Society for the Study of Theology, UK; American Academy of Religion; American Theological Association **Discipline:** Systematic Theology; Modern Theology **Related Interests:** Doctrines of God; Creation; Church.

Selected Publications: Below are listed some of his recent publications.

_____, D. F. Ford. *Jubilate: Theology in Praise*. Darton, Longman and Todd, 1984.
_____, D. F. Ford. *Praising and Knowing God*. Westminster Press, 1985.
_____. "Science, Rationality and Theology." In *Keeping the Faith*, ed. G. Wainwright. SPCK, 1987; Fortress Press, 1988.
_____. "T. F. Torrance" and "British Theology through Philosophy." In *The Modern Theologians*, ed D. F. Ford, Vols. 1 and 2. Blackwell, 1989.
_____, C. E. Gunton, eds. *On Being the Church*. T. & T. Clark, 1989. Contributed the following: "Created and Redeemed Sociality."
_____, P. S. Sedgwick, eds. *The Weight of Glory: Essays for Peter Baelz*. T & T Clark, 1991. Contributed the following: "God and the Form of Society," and "The Strategy of Liberalism."
_____. "The Future of Theology in a Complex World." "The Spirit of God in Creation and Reconciliation." Chaps. in *Christ and Context: The Confrontation of Christ and Culture*, ed. H. Regan and A. J. Torrance. T. & T. Clark, 1993.

Harper, Charles L.

Present Position and Address: Balliol College, Oxford OX1 4JD, UK **Date of Birth:** December 29, 1958 **Education:** B.S.E. Civil/Geological Engineering (*cum laude*, 1980), Princeton University; London Institute for Contemporary Christianity (Spring Semester, 1982); D.Phil. Earth Science (1987), Balliol College, Oxford; Dip. Theol. (1988), Wycliffe Hall, Oxford **Discipline:** Geochronology; Cosmochronology; Cosmology; Theory of Time; Interpretation of Quantum Mechanics **Related Interests:** Looking from the standpoint of a Scientist at Apologetics, the Doctrine of Creation, Theodicy, the Problem of Evil, the Theology of Freedom, and Fundamentalism.

Selected Publications:

_____, A. N. Halliday and T. E. Krogh. "The Geology of Space-Time." *Terra Cognita* 6, 2 (1986).
_____. "Geochronology, Time-Asymmetry and the Foundations of Quantum Mechanics." *Lunar and Planetary Science* 18 (1987): 384ff.
_____. "On the Nature of Time in Cosmological Perspective." Ph.D. diss. (examined at Oxford University, 1988).
_____. "New Applications of Geochronological Measurements to the Unification Programme in Physics and Cosmology." *Chemical Geology* 70, 1-2 (1988): 25ff.

Harré, Rom

Present Position and Address: Adjunct Professor of Philosophy of Science (since 1975), SUNY - Binghamton University Lecturer (since 1960), Linacre College, Oxford OX1 3JA, UK; Professor of Psychology, Georgetown University, Washington, DC, USA **Date of Birth:** December 18, 1927 **Education:** B.Sc. (1948)/M.A. (1953), New Zealand; B.Phil. (1956), Oxford University **Honorary Degrees:** Hon. D.Sc. (Brussels, 1986); Hon. Pol. Doc. (Helsinki, 1986), Royden B. Davis Professor, (Georgetown, 1993) **Previous Positions:** Lecturer (1956-60), Leicester University **Concurrent Positions:** Professor, Psychology Department, Georgetown University, Washington, DC **Discipline:** Philosophy of Science; Discursive Psychology **Related Interests:** Metaphysics and Rhetoric of Science; Theoretical Psychology

Selected Publications:

_____. *Great Scientific Experiments.* Phaidon Press and Oxford University Press, 1982. US Edition, 1983.
_____. *Personal Being.* Blackwell and Harvard University Press, 1983.
_____. *Varieties of Realism.* Blackwell, 1986.
_____, P. Mühlhäusler. *Pronouns and People.* Blackwell, 1990.
_____. *Laws of Nature.* Duckworth, 1993.

Harrington, Donald S.

Present Position and Address: Minister Emeritus, Community Church of New York, Unitarian Universalist, 40 E. 35th Street, New York, NY 10016; (Work) 10 Park Ave., Apt. 16K, New York, NY 10016, USA **Work Phone:** (212) 725-3011 **Date of Birth:** July 11, 1914 **Education:** A.B. (1936), Antioch College, University of Chicago; B.D. (1938), Meadville-Lombard Theological School, Chicago; S.T.D. (1959), Starr King School for Ministry, Berkeley, CA; D.D. (1964), Meadville-Lombard Theological School, Chicago; D.D. Ecumenical Theological Faculty of the Babes-Bolyai University, Cluj-Kolozsvar, Romania **Previous Positions:** Minister, First Unitarian Church, Hobart, IN (1936-38)/Peoples Liberal Church, Chicago (1939-44); Founding Minister, Beverly Unitarian Church, Chicago (1942-44); Minister (1944-82), The Community Church of New York **Selected Memberships:** Institute on Religion in an Age of Science; President, Center for Advanced Study in Religion and Science; State Chairman, Liberal Party of NY State (1965-85) Founding Chair, American Comm. on Africa; Past President, World Federalists Association; Chair, Council on International and Public Affairs **Discipline:** Pastoral Ministry; Biblical Studies; Science and Religion; Process Theology **Related Interests:** Religion and Science; Religion and Politics.

Selected Publications:

_____. *Religion In An Age of Science.* Beacon Press.
_____. *Modern Humanity In Search of a Myth.* Zygon Press.
_____. *Outstretched Wings of the Spirit.* Unitarian Universalist Association Press.
_____. *As We Remember Him: Jesus as Viewed by His Own People.* Beacon Press.

Harris, E. Lynn

Present Position and Address: Assistant Professor (since 1970), University of Illinois - Chicago; Box 412, Wheaton, IL 60189-0412, USA **Work Phone:** (708) 393-1034 **Languages Spoken:** French, German, Swedish, Biblical Greek, Hebrew **Education:** A.B. English/Philosophy/A.M., University of Chicago; 2 years of Graduate studies in English literature, Northwestern University; M.Div. Biblical Studies (1975), Northern Baptist Theological Seminary; D.Min. (1978), Chicago Theological Seminary; Ph.D. Religion/Religious Education (1980), New York University **Previous Positions:** Part-time

Instructor (1983-1986), College of DuPage, IL and Indiana University; Assistant Professor (1965-1967), Chicago City College **Discipline:** Biblical Studies; Religious Studies; English Literature; Imagery Research including Psychological Studies; Minister **Related Areas of Interest:** Jungian Psychology; Asian Religions; Imagery Research in Religious Studies/literature; Mystic Spirituality - Visions.

Selected Publications:

_____. "Current Imagery Research, Especially Involving Biblical Materials." Paper presented at the International Meeting, Society of Biblical Literature, Copenhagen, Denmark, August, 1989.

_____. Review of *The Song of Songs: A New Translation and Interpretation*, by Marcia Falk. San Francisco: Harper and Row, 1990. Christianity and Literature 40, 3 (1991).

_____. *The Mystic Spirituality of A. W. Tozer, A Twentieth Century American Protestant*. San Francisco; Lewiston, NY: Mellen Press, May 1992.

_____. "A. W. Tozer's Mystical Perspective on Ultimate Reality." *Ultimate Reality and Meaning, Interdisciplinary Studies in the Philosophy of Understanding* (forthcoming).

Hart, John

Present Position and Address: Professor of Theology (since 1985), Carroll College, Helena, MT 59625(Home) 521 Clarke Street, Helena, MT 59601, USA **Work Phone:** (406) 447-4335 **Home Phone:** (406) 449-6912 **Date of Birth:** October 5, 1943 **Languages Spoken:** English, Spanish **Education:** B.A. Spanish (1966), Marist College, Poughkeepsie, NY; S.T.M. Church and Community (1972)/M.Phil. Christian Ethics (1976)/Ph.D. Christian Ethics (1978), Union Theological Seminary, NY **Postgraduate Studies:** Postdoctoral study (Summer 1986), Harvard Divinity School; Graduate studies: Psychology (1968-69), New York University; Spanish/Latin American History and Literature (1966), Universidad Nacional Autónoma de México; Economics (1973-74), New School for Social Research, NY **Previous Positions:** Various positions in teaching Language, Religion, Christian Ethics from 1966-77; Director of Planning and Community Development (1977-78), City of San Juan, TX; Visiting Assistant Professor of Religion (1978-79), Howard University School of Religion, Washington, DC; Director of the Heartland Project (1979-81); Assistant Professor of Religious Studies (1981-82), Mount Marty College; Associate Professor of Religious Studies (1983-85), College of Great Falls, MT; **Media Work:** Involved in producing and scriptwriting media productions on Environmental Ethics; Computer based course on Ethics, Technology, and Sustainable Development (William C. Norris Institute, 1994) **Discipline:** Christian Ethics **Related Interests:** Theology and Ecology; Economic Ethics; Environmental Ethics; Ethics and Technology; Native American Spirituality.

Selected Publications:

_____. *The Spirit of the Earth - A Theology of the Land*. Ramsey, NJ: Paulist Press, 1984.

_____. "Crisis on the Land: Agribusiness vs. Agriculture." *Christianity and Crisis* (1985).

_____. "Land, Theology and the Future." In *Theology of the Land*, eds. B. F. Evans and G. D. Cusack. Collegeville, MN: The Liturgical Press, 1987.

_____. "New Vision, New Project, New Creation." *Catholic World* (July-August 1990).

_____. "Jubilee and New Jubilee: Values and Visions for the Land." In *Ethics and Agriculture*, ed. Charles V. Blatz. Moscow, ID: University of Idaho Press, 1991.

_____. "Para um Jubileu Novo." In *A Teologia se Fez Terra*, ed. Alfredo Ferro Medina. São Leopoldo, Brazil: Editora Sinodal, 1991.

_____. "Report from the Earth Summit." *New World Outlook* (1992).

_____. "Indigenous Voices from the Earth Summit." *New World Outlook* (1993).

_____. "Indigenous Lands, Rights and Nature." *Christianity and Crisis* (1993).

_____. "Orchids, Eagles, and Natural Rights." *Horizons* (1994).

Hartzell, Karl Drew

Present Position and Address: Retired (1971), Administrative Officer, State University of New York (SUNY) - Stony Brook; 8 Shore Drive, Setauket, NY 11733, USA **Work Phone:** (516) 751-3554 **Date of Birth:** January 17, 1906 **Education:** A.M. (1928)/Ph.D. (1934), Harvard University; Ph.B. (cum laude, 1927), Wesleyan University, CT; Sabbatical leave (1969-70) to study evolution, structure, and function of values; social ethics; philosophy of religion - Visiting scholar (1969), Union Theological Seminary; Research Fellow (1970), Yale Divinity School. **Previous Positions:** Associate Professor of Economics and Social Science (1935-40), Georgia School of Technology; Visiting Professor of History (summers 1937-39), Emory University; Associate Professor of Social Studies (1940-47), New York State College - Geneseo; Admin. Officer (1947-50), Brookhaven National Laboratory; Director of Educational Services (1950-52), Associated Universities Inc.; Dean (1952-56), Cornell College, IO; Dean (1956-62), Bucknell University; Chief Administrative Officer (1962-65)/Administrative Officer, President's Office (1965-71), SUNY - Stony Brook, NY; Consultant and Librarian (1971-74), Institute for Advanced Studies of World Religions **Selected Memberships:** American Association for the Advancement of the Humanities; American Association for the Advancement of Science; American Society of Christian Ethics; Institute for Society, Ethics and the Life Sciences (The Hastings Center); Phi Beta Kappa; Society for Values in Higher Education **Related Interests:** Human Valuation; American Values; Evolution, Structure and Function of Values.

Selected Publications:

_____. *A Philosophy for Science Teaching.* Bucknell University Press, 1957.
_____, Coeditor. *The Study of Religion on the Campus of Today.* Association of American Colleges, Washington, DC, 1967.

Hartzler, H. Harold

Present Position and Address: Emeritus Professor (since 1976), Mankato State University, 901 College Avenue, Goshen, IN 46526, USA **Date of Birth:** April 7, 1908 **Education:** A.B. (1930), Juniata College; Ph.D. Physics (1934), Rutgers University **Postgraduate Studies:** Pennsylvania State University/University of Michigan/University of Arizona; Fellow in Astronomy, University of Arizona **Previous Positions:** Professor of Mathematics and Physics/Dean of Men (1935-37), Elizabethtown College; Assistant through Professor of Mathematics (1937-58), Goshen College; Professor of Mathematics (1945-46), Bluffton College; Associate/Professor of Physics (1958-64), Professor of Mathematics and Astronomy (1964-76), Mankato State College **Selected Memberships:** Secretary-Treasurer (1951-55)/President (1955-60)/Executive-Secretary (1961-72)/Member (currently), American Scientific Affiliation; American Astronomical Society; American Physical Society; American Mathematical Society; Creation Research Society **Discipline:** Mathematics; Physics; Astronomy **Related Interests:** How Science can increase Faith in God; Science and Religion.

Selected Publications:

_____. "The American Scientific Affiliation History and Purposes." JASA 7, 3 (1955).
_____. "The Relationship between the American Scientific Affiliation and the Creation Research Society." *JASA* 35, 2 (June 1983).
_____. "Forty years with ASA." *JASA* 37, 2 (June 1985).

Hasel, Frank Michael

Present Position and Address: Ph.D. Candidate; 550 Maplewood Ct. F-68, Berrien Springs, MI 49103, USA **Work Phone:** (616) 471-6847 **Fax Number:** (616) 471-6166 **Date of Birth:** May 13,

1962 **Languages Spoken:** German, English **Education:** M.A. Thesis (1989), Andrews University, "The Concept of the Divine Wrath in the Church Dogmatics of Karl Barth" **Awards and Honors:** Theta Alpha Kappa **Previous Positions:** Minister (1985-88), Seventh-Day Adventist Church **Administrative Experience:** President of Seminary Doctoral Club (1991-92), Theological Seminary, Andrews University **Selected Memberships:** Coordinating Director (1990-91), Mid-West Chapter of the Adventist Theological Society; Christians in Science; Society of Christian Philosophers; Society of Biblical Literature; Karl Barth Society of North America **Discipline:** Systematic Theology **Related Areas of Interest:** Fundamental Theology (Fundamental Theologie); Integration of Faith and Science; Possibilities of Contemporary Apologetics **Current Areas of Research:** The Role of Scripture in Contemporary Systematic Theology.

Selected Publications: His bibliography contains 7 published articles.

_____. "Scientific Revolution: An Analysis and Evaluation of Thomas Kuhn's Concept of Paradigm and Paradigm Change for Theology." *Journal of the Adventist Theological Society* 2, 2 (1991): 160-77. Reprint, in *Christ in the Classroom: Adventist Approaches to the Integration of Faith and Learning*, ed. Humberto M. Rasi, vol. 8, 115-32. Silver Spring, MD: Institute for Christian Teaching, 1993.
_____. "Thomas Kuhn's Revolution: A New Way of Looking at Science." *College and University Dialogue* 4, 2 (1992): 11-13. Reprint, in *Christ in The Classroom: Adventist Approaches to the Integration of Faith and Learning*, ed. Humberto M. Rasi, vol. 8, 133-5. Silver Spring, MD: Institute for Christian Teaching, 1993.
_____. "Theology and the Role of Reason." *Journal of the Adventist Theological Society* 4, 2 (1993): 172-98.
_____. "The Christological Analogy of Scripture in Karl Barth." *Theologische Zeitschrift* 49 (Forthcoming).

Haught, John F.

Present Position and Address: Professor of Theology (since 1984)/Chair (since 1990)Department of Theology, Georgetown University, Washington, DC 20057, USA **Work Phone:** (202) 687-6119 **Home Phone:** (703) 528-8092 **Date of Birth:** November 12, 1942 **Education:** B.A. (1964), St. Mary's Seminary and University; M.A. (1968)/Ph.D. (1970), The Catholic University of America **Other Academic Experience:** Some Relevant Courses Taught: Modern Theologies of Evolution; Science, Myth and Religion; Theology after Freud; Chaos and Cosmos; Theology and Existentialism; A World in Process; Theological Method **Selected Memberships:** American Academy of Religion **Discipline:** Theology **Related Interests:** Cosmology; Theology and Modern Science; Environmental Ethics; God and Evolution.

Selected Publications: His bibliography lists 20 papers, 8 books, 14 articles and 35 book reviews many of which are relevant to this dialogue.

_____. Review article of books on science and religion. *Commonweal* (1986): 669-670.
_____. "The Emergent Environment and the Problem of Cosmic Purpose." *Environmental Ethics* 8 (1986): 139-150.
_____. "God in Modern Science." *The New Catholic Encyclopedia* 18 (Fall 1987).
_____. "Is Human Life only Chemistry?" *Current* (1987): 4-7.
_____. "The Informed Universe and the Existence of God." *Existence of God*, eds. John R. Jacobson and R. L. Mitchell. Lewiston/Queenston, Lampeter: Edwin Mellen Press, (1988): 223-244.
_____. *The Promise of Nature: Ecology and Cosmic Purpose*. New York: Paulist Press, 1993.
_____. *Mystery and Promise: A Theology of Revelation*. Collegeville: Liturgical Press, 1993.
_____. "Chaos, Complexity, and Theology." *Teilhard Studies* (1994).
_____. "Religious and Cosmic Homelessness." In *Liberating Life*, eds. Charles Birch, et. al.. Maryknoll: Ortis Press, 1990.
_____. "Dipolar Theism: Psychological Considerations." *Process Studies* 4 (1976): 43-50.

Hay, David

Present Position and Address: Senior Lecturer (since 1990), Centre for the Study of Humlan Relations (Home) 39 The Strand, Attenborough, Notts. NG9 6AU, UK **Concurrent Positions:** Director (since 1975), Religious Experience and Education Project, Nottingham University, Nottingham NG 72RD, UK **Date of Birth:** June 23, 1935 **Education:** B.Sc. (1958), Aberdeen University; M.Sc. (1962)/Ph.D. (1988), Nottingham University **Previous Positions:** Director (1985-1989), Alister Hardy Research Centre, Oxford; Chairman of Council, Alister Hardy Research Centre, Westminster College, Oxford, UK **Discipline:** Zoology; Scientific Study of Religious Experience **Related Interests:** The Interfaces between Biology and Theology, Sociology and Theology, and Psychology and Theology.

Selected Publications:

_____. "Suspicion of the Spiritual: Teaching Religious Education in a World of Secular Experience." *British Journal of Religious Education* 7 (1985).
_____. "Secular Society/Religious Meanings: A Contemporary Paradox." *Review of Religious Research* 26 (1985).
_____. *Exploring Inner Space: Scientists and Religious Experience*. 2d ed. Oxford: Mowbrays, 1987.
_____. *Religious Experience Today: Studying the Facts*. Oxford: Mowbrays, 1990.
_____. "The Bearing of Empirical Studies of Religious Experience on Education." *Research Papers in Education* 5 (1990).
_____. "'The Biology of God': What is the Current Status of Hardy's Hypothesis?" *International Journal for the Psychology of Religion* 4 (1994).

Hayward, Jeremy

Present Position and Address: Trustee, The Naropa Institute, Boulder, CO; Associate Editor (since 1982), New Science Library/Shambhala Publications, Site 9 Box 15 RR#7, Armdale, NS B3L 4R7, Canada **Date of Birth:** July 19, 1940 **Education:** B.A. Mathematics/Physics (1961)/Ph.D. Nuclear Physics (1965), Trinity College, Cambridge University, UK **Selected Congresses and Conferences:** Recent conferences he has attended are "Nature, Man and Life" (The 7th Kyoto Symposium on Religious Philosophy. Kyoto. March 1989) **Previous Positions:** Research Assistant (1965), Laboratory of Molecular Biology, Cambridge, UK; Research Associate, Massachusetts Institute of Technology (1965-68)/Tufts University Medical School (1968-69); Staff (1971-74), Karme-Choling Buddhist Contemplative Center, Vermont; Vice President and Cofounder and Faculty and Academic Chairman, The Naropa Institute (since 1974) **Discipline:** Nuclear Physics; Philosophy of Science; Tibetan Buddhism **Related Interests:** Science and Buddhism; Religious Philosophy **Current Research:** "Mind and Life" (Dialogues between Cognitive Scientists and the Dalai Lama, Dharmsala, 1987). He has written papers on nuclear physics, biology, education and religious philosophy.

Selected Publications:

_____. *Perceiving Ordinary Magic: Science and Intuitive Wisdom*. New Science Library, Shambhala Publications, 1984.
_____. *Shifting Worlds, Changing Minds: Where the Sciences and Buddhism Meet*. New Science Library, Shambhala Publications, 1987.

Hazard, Evan Brandao

Present Position and Address: Professor of Biology Emeritus, Bemidji State University, 1500 Birchmont Drive NE, Bemidji, MN 56601-2699, USA **Work Phone:** (218) 755-2920 **Fax:** (218) 755-4107 **Date of Birth:** November 17, 1929 **Languages Spoken:** English **Awards and Honors:** Sigma Xi, Phi Kappa Phi **Previous Positions:** 1st Lt., USAF (1951-53); Teaching Asst. in Zoology, University of Michigan, Ann Arbor (1957-58); Biology Faculty, BSU: Asst.. Prof (1958-62), Assoc.

Prof (1962-65), Professor (1965-94); Head, Div. of Science and Math (1969-71); Visiting Biologist, Garrett-Evangelical Theological Seminary, Evanston, IL (Jan-Mar 1993) **Selected Memberships:** United Methodist Church, AAAS, American Society of Mammalogists, Society for the Study of Evolution, Am. Inst. Biol. Sci., National Association of Biology Teachers; Association of Midwest College Biology Teachers, Minn Acad. Sci., N.D. Nat. Sci. Soc., Wildlife Society; Association for Religion and Intellectual Life **Discipline:** Zoology; Mammalogy, Evolutionary Biology **Related Interests:** Role of science in liberal education; science (esp. evol. biol.) in relation to theology **Current Research:** Helping students, clergy, and lay people integrate their faith with a scientific worldview, possibly a book on this from a teacher's (rather than primarily a researcher's) perspective.

Selected Publications: Bibliography comprises of one book, nine professional articles and notes, three contributions to compilations, several newspaper articles.

_____. *The Mammals of Minnesota*. University of Minnesota Press, 1982.
_____. "The Chronological Distribution and Subgeneric Status of *Citellus Rexroadensis*" *Journal of Mammalogy* 42 (1961):477-483.
_____. "Evolution vs. Creationism." *American Biology Teacher* 55 (1993): 328-329.
_____. "T. C. Mits and the Utility of Science." *Journal of the Minnesota Academy of Science* (1975).
_____. "Pairing of Evolution with Humanism Disputed" *The Pioneer* (3 October 1993).

Hazelett, Samuel Richard

Present Position and Address: Research Engineer, Hazelett Strip-Casting Corp., 217 Lakeshore Drive, P.O. Box 8, Colchester, VT 05446, USA **Work Phone:** (802) 658-1238 or -1237 **Fax Number:** (802) 863-1523 **Date of Birth:** July 24, 1923 **Languages Spoken:** Some German **Previous Positions:** Design Engineer, Baldwin Locomotive Works (1943, 1946-51) **Selected Memberships:** Association for Religion and Intellectual Life; Temple Sinai, So. Burlington, VT **Discipline:** Philosophy; Mechanical Engineering **Current Areas of Research:** Currently working on manuscript: "Find God through Your Intellect: Our Roots in Judiac Civilization. "

Selected Publications: His bibliography lists 2 books, 6 articles, 14 US patents, most of them as joint inventor.

_____, Dean Turner, eds. *The Einstein Myth and the Ives Papers*. Old Greenwich, CT: Devin-Adair Co., 1979.
_____. "Public Management of Private Employment Volume," with comments by Albert G. Hart. *American Economic Review* 47 (1957): 136-48. Portions reprinted in *Solutions to Unemployment*, ed. David C. Colander. New York: Harcourt Brace Jovanovich, 1981.
_____, Dean Turner. *Benevolent Living: Tracing the Roots of Motivation to God*. Pasadena, CA: Hope Publishing House, 1990.

Hazen, Craig J.

Present Position and Address: Editor-at-Large (since 1986), *Paradigms*, A Journal of Religious Studies; Currently a Ph.D. candidate Religious Studies, University of California - Santa Barbara, CA 93106; (Home) 795 Juniper Walk #B, Goleta, CA 93117, USA Concurrent Positions: Computer Consultant (since 1981); University Teaching Assistant (since 1988), University of California - Santa Barbara **Home Phone:** (805) 685-9020 **Date of Birth:** June 20, 1959 **Languages Spoken:** English, French, German **Education:** B.A. Biological Sciences (1981), California State University - Fullerton; Certificat (1982), Human Rights, Institut International Des Droits De L'Homme/Law and Theology, International Institute for Law and Theology, University of Strasbourg, France; Law, Theology, Human Rights (1981-83), Simon Greenleaf School of Law, Orange County, CA; M.A. Religious Studies (1989), University of California - Santa Barbara **Previous Positions:** Laboratory Instructor and

Research Director in Physiology (1978-81), California State University - Fullerton; College Instructor in Speed Reading (1982-84), North Orange County Community College, Fullerton; High School Teacher in Biology/Chemistry/Computer Science (1981-86), Rosary High School, Fullerton **Selected Memberships:** American Academy of Religion; American Association for the Advancement of Science; American Scientific Affiliation; The Center for Theology and the Natural Sciences; History of Science Society; Society for the Scientific Study of Religion **Discipline:** Biology; Religious Studies **Related Interests:** The Interaction of Religion and Science in America.

Selected Publications:

_____. "The Puzzling Success of the Institute for Creation Research: The Fundamentalist Fission and Fusion of Religion and Science." Paper presented at the University of California Colloquium Lecture Series, May 1988.

_____. "Science as Theological Absolute: Science and the Origin of Metaphysical Religion in Antebellum America." In *Science and Religion/Wissenschaft und Religion: Abhandlungen zur Geschichte der Geowissenschaften und Religion-Unwelt-Forschung*, ed. Änne Bäumer and Manfred Büttner. Bochum: Universitätsverlag, Dr. N. Brockmeyer, 1989.

_____. "The Interaction of Science and Religion, a Bibliography." In process.

Heaney, John J.

Present Position and Address: Professor of Theology (since 1958), Fordham University, Bronx, NY 10458, USA; (Home) 9 Heathcote Road, Yonkers, NY 10710, USA **Date of Birth:** December 7, 1925 **Education:** M.A. Philosophy (1950), Boston College; S.T.L. (1957), Woodstock College; S.T.D. (1963), Institut Catholique, Paris **Selected Memberships:** Catholic Theological Society of America; American Society for Psychical Research; Person and Society Group of the American Academy of Religion **Discipline:** Fundamental Theology **Related Interests:** Fundamental Theology; Parapsychology; Psychology of Religion.

Selected Publications: His bibliography lists 5 books and 10 articles.

_____. "Catholic Hermeneutics." *Continuum* (Winter-Spring 1969): 106-20.

_____, editor. *Psyche and Spirit. Readings in Psychology and Religion, An Annotated Bibliography*. New York: Paulist Press, 1973. Also author of 88 of the 310 pages.

_____. *The Sacred and the Psychic. Parapsychology and Christian Theology*. New York: Paulist Press, 1984.

_____. *Psyche and Spirit II*. New York: Paulist Press, 1984. This is a totally changed work. Authored 120 of the 252 pages and the full bibliography.

_____. "Modernism." In *New Catholic Encyclopedia*, Vol. 9.

Hearn, Walter Russell

Present Position and Address: Self-employed writer and editor (since 1972); Adjunct Professor of Christianity and Science, New College for Advanced Christian Studies, Berkeley, CA; 762 Arlington Avenue, Berkeley, CA 94707, USA **Work Phone:** (510) 527-3056 **Date of Birth:** February 20, 1926 **Languages Spoken:** English, some Spanish **Education:** B.A. (Honors in Chemistry, 1948), Rice University; Ph.D. Biochemistry (1951), University of Illinois **Selected Congresses and Conferences:** Participated in international conference on Christian Philosophy of Science in Oxford (1965) **Previous Positions:** Instructor in Biochemistry (1951-52), Yale University School of Medicine; Assistant Professor of Biochemistry (1952-55), Baylor University College of Medicine; Associate Professor of Biochemistry (1955-71), Iowa State University; Served as Visiting Biologist to Colleges for the American Institute of Biological Sciences (1961-66); Reviewer for Science Books of the AAAS (1965-71); N.I.H. Research Associate/Fellow/Professor (1968-69, 1972-73), University of California - Berkeley; Served on Committee for Integrity in Science Education of ASA (since 1984) **Editorial Work:** Editor of *ASA Newsletter* (1969-1993); Editor of *Search: Scientists Who Serve God* (1988-92);

Consulting Editor of *Perspectives on Science and Christian Faith* **Selected Memberships:** Center for Theology and the Natural Sciences, Berkeley; American Chemical Society; Fellow, American Association for the Advancement of Science; Fellow, American Scientific Affiliation; Sigma Xi; Phi Sigma; Phi Lambda Upsilon; Phi Beta Kappa; Gamma Sigma Delta **Discipline:** Biochemistry; Editor and Writer **Related Interests:** Christianity and Science.

Selected Publications: Author and coauthor of over 20 scientific papers on amino acid and peptide chemistry, hypothalamic hormones and bacterial metabolism. Author of several hundred articles, reviews, poems and chapters.

_____. "The Origin of Life." In *Evolution and Christian Thought Today*, ed. R. L. Mixter. Eerdmans, 1959: 53-70.
_____. "Biological Science." In *The Encounter between Christianity and Science*, ed. R. H. Bube. Eerdmans, 1968: 199-223.
_____. "A Biochemist Shares His Faith." In *Why I Am Still a Christian*, ed. E. M. Blaiklock. Zondervan, 1971: 65-80.
_____. "Chemistry." In *Christ and the Modern Mind*, ed. R. W. Smith. IVP, 1972: 273-284.
_____. "Whole People and Half Truths." In *The Scientist and Ethical Decision*, ed. C. Hatfield. IVP, 1973: 83-96.
_____, D. Price, and J. L. Wiester. *Teaching Science in a Climate of Controversy*. Ipswich, MA: Committee for Integrity in Science Education, American Scientific Affiliation, 1986, 1987, revision, 1989, 1993.
_____, D. Price and J. L. Wiester. "Science and Something Else: Religious Aspects of the NAS Booklet, 'Science and Creationism'" *Perspectives on Science and Christian Faith* 42, 2 (June 1990): 115-18.
_____. "Science, Selves, and Stories." *CTNS Bulletin* 11, 2 (Spring 1991).
_____. "The Future of the Planet: Signs of Harvest." *Radix* 20, 1 (Fall 1991):3-7, 23-24, 26-31.
_____. "Scientific Gamesmanship." *Perspectives on Science and Christian Faith* 44, 2 (June 1992): 138-9.

Heckenlively, Donald B.

Present Position and Address: Vice President for Academic Affairs/Professor of Biology, Hillsdale College, Hillsdale, MI 49242; (Home)34 State Street, Apt. 33A, Hillsdale, MI 49242, USA **Home Phone:** (517) 437-4615 **Date of Birth:** September 18, 1941 **Education:** B.A. Zoology/Chemistry minor (1963), University of Denver; M.S. Biology (1965), New Mexico State University (Coursework emphasized ecology and evolutionary biology); Ph.D. Zoology (1974), University of Michigan **Postgraduate Studies:** Postgraduate workshops and courses in Computers **Previous Positions:** Teaching Fellow (1965-71), Department of Zoology, University of Michigan; Assistant Professor through Full Professor (since 1971), Biology Department, Hillsdale College **Selected Memberships:** American Scientific Affiliation; Sigma Xi, Beta, Beta, Beta; Member of Choir (since 1990), Holy Trinity Parish Anglican Church **Discipline:** Biology; Computers **Related Interests:** Ecology and Theology, specifically Ecology/Evolutionary Biology and Creationism.

Selected Publications:

_____. "Coming to Grips with Darwin by R. F. Baum." *The Intercollegiate Review* 12, 1: 59-62 (letter).
_____. "Scientists Who Keep the Faith." In *Man and Creation, Perspectives on Science and Theology*, ed. Michael Bauman, 231-46. Hillsdale, MI: Hillsdale College Press, 1993.

Hedman, Bruce A.

Present Position and Address: Pastor (since 1988), Abington Congregational Church, Abington, CT; Associate Professor (since 1988), Department of Mathematics, University of Connecticut, 85 Lawler Road, West Hartford, CT 06117; (Home) 18 Charter Oak Square, Mansfield Center, CT 06250, USA **Work Phone:** (203) 456-8733 **Date of Birth:** November 30, 1953 **Languages Spoken:** English, German **Education:** B.S. Mathematics (1974), University of Washington, Seattle; M.A. (1976)/Ph.D. Mathematics (1979), Princeton University; M.Div. Preaching (1980), Princeton Theological Seminary.

Ordained by United Presbyterian Church - USA (July 1980) **Previous Positions:** Pastor (1980-81), Calvary Presbyterian Church, Philadelphia; Assistant Professor (1981-82), St. Andrews Presbyterian College in Laurinburg, NC; Assistant Professor (1982-88), University of Connecticut, W. Hartford **Selected Memberships:** Mathematical Association of America; New York Academy of Sciences; American Scientific Affiliation; Evangelical Theological Society **Discipline:** Minister; Mathematics (specializing in combinatorics, graph theory, history and philosophy of mathematics) **Related Interests:** The influence of Mathematics on Philosophy and Religion **Current Research:** The religious impact of the revolution in modern Cosmology; Infinity in Mathematics and Theology.

Selected Publications:

_____. "Mathematics in Western Civilization." 200 page unpublished paper tracing the influence of Mathematics upon Philosophy and Religion.
_____. "The New Dialogue Between Science and Faith." Paper Presented at CT Biblical Witness Fellowship of United Church of Christ, First Congregational Church of North Branford (February 1, 1986).
_____. "The Clash of Worldviews: Culture, Mathematics, and the Church in the 4th, 18th, and 20th Centuries." Papers presented at Faculty Seminars, Westover School, Middlebury, CT (October 1, 24, 31, 1989).
_____. "Mathematics, Cosmology, and the Contingent Universe." *Perspectives on Science and Christian Faith* 41, 2 (1989): 99-103.
_____. "Cantor's Concept of Infinity: Implications of Infinity for Contingence." *Perspectives on Science and Christian Faith* 45, 1 (1993): 8-16. Awarded Templeton Prize for Humility Theology.

Heelan, Patrick A.

Present Position and Address: Professor of Philosophy (since 1970), State University of New York (SUNY) - Stony Brook, NY 11794, USA (Home) 6 Park Street, Setauket, NY 11733, USA **Work Phone:** (516) 632-7564 **Home Phone:** (516) 751-7617 **Education:** B.A./M.A. Mathematics and Physics (1st Class hons., 1948), National University, Dublin, Ireland; Lic. Phil. (1954), St. Stanislaus College, Tullamore; S.T.L. Theology (1959), Milltown Park, Dublin; Ph.D. Geophysics (1952), St. Louis University, MO; Ph.D.. **Previous Positions:** Research Associate Theoretical Physics (1964-65)/Cosmic Physics (1964-65), Dublin Institute for Advanced Studies; Visiting Fellow in High Energy Physics (1960-62), Fordham University, NY/Palmer Laboratory, Princeton University; Summer Fellowships at Stanford University/University of Colorado; Lecturer in Mathematical Physics (1964-65); Assistant and Associate Professor of Philosophy (1965-70)/Codirector of Honors Program and member of College Council (1969-70), Fordham University, NY; Visiting Professor of Physics (1968-69), Boston University; Invited lecturer (Denver, 1974) to International Colloquium on Cosmology, History and Theology; Chairman of Philosophy Department (1970-74)/Joint Professor of Humanities and Social Sciences at the Health Sciences Center (1972-75)/Vice President for Liberal Studies and Dean of Arts and Sciences (1975-79)/Acting Chair of Department of Religious Studies; NSF Senior Fellow and Visiting Fellow (1983), Center for the Philosophy of Science, University of Pittsburgh **Editorial Work:** Editorial board of SUNY Press; *American Philosophical Quarterly*; *Journal of Social and Biological Structures*; the former *Maincurrents in Modern Thought*; Editorial Consultant of 7 Scientific and Philosophical Journals and over 6 presses **Selected Memberships:** Center for Religious Studies, SUNY (since 1980); Fellow, New York Academy of Sciences; Sigma Xi; Philosophy of Science Association; History of Science Society; Society for the Social Study of Science; Society for Phenomenological and Existential Philosophy American Catholic Philosophical Association (on executive committee 1972-75); Society for Health and Human Values; Centro Superiore di Logica Scienze Comparate; American Association for the Advancement of Science **Discipline:** Philosophy; Geophysics; Theology **Related Interests:** Science and Religion/Christianity; Cosmology and Christianity.

Selected Publications:

_____. "God, the Universe, and the Secular City." In *The Sacred and the Secular*, ed. Michael Taylor. Prentice-Hall, 1968.

_____. "The Search for Perfect Science in the West." *Thought* 43 (1968): 165-186; Reprint *Fifty Years of Thought*, ed. J. O'Neill. Fordham, 1978.

_____. "Nature and its Transformations." *Theological Studies* 33 (1972): 486-502; Translated into Hungarian.

_____. "Quantum Relativity and the Cosmic Observer." In *Cosmology, History and Theology*, ed. W. Yourgrau and A. Breck. Plenum, 1977.

_____. "Purpose in the Universe." In *Encyclopedia of Bioethics*, ed. W. Reich. Washington DC: Kennedy Institute, 1979.

_____. "Comments on Alex Comfort's 'Demonic and Historical Models in Biology'." *Journal of Social Biological Structure* 3 (1980): 217-8.

_____. "Space as God's Presence." *Journal of Dharma* 8 (1983): 63-86; Also in *Religious Experience and Scientific Paradigms*. Stony Brook: Institute for Advanced Studies of World Religions, 1985. Also in *The World and I*. (May 1986): 607-23.

_____. "A Heideggerian Meditation on Science and Art." In *Hermeneutic Phenomenology*, ed. J. J. Kockelnams. Washington DC and Pittsburgh: University Press of American and CARP, 1988.

_____. Review of *Hermeneutics vs. Science*, ed. by J. M. Connolly and T. Keutner, University of Notre Dame Press, 1988. *Review of Metaphysics* 43 (1989): 615-6.

Hefner, Philip

Present Position and Address: Professor of Systematic Theology (since 1969), Lutheran School of Theology at Chicago, 1100 East 55th Street, Chicago, IL 60615-5199, USA **Work Phone:** (312) 753-0700 **Date of Birth:** December 10, 1932 **Languages Spoken:** English, German **Education:** B.A. (*summa cum laude*, 1954), Midland Lutheran College; Studied at Tübingen University, Germany (1954-55); B.D. (1959), Chicago Lutheran Theological Seminary; M.A. (1961)/Ph.D. (with distinction, 1962), University of Chicago; L.H.D. (1982), Midland Lutheran College **Selected Congresses and Conferences:** Chair for Summer 1984 Conference, Institute on Religion in an Age of Science, "Recent Developments in Neurobiology: Do They Matter for Religion, the Social Sciences and the Humanities?" **Selected Lectures:** Over 50 lectureships. Religion and Science Forum of Great Britain, Durham (1983); Nobel Lecturer, Gustavus Adolphus College (1987) **Awards and Honors:** Distinguished Visiting Scholar, Oklahoma Scholar-Leader Enrichment Program, University of Oklahoma (1991) **Previous Positions:** Director of Graduate Studies (1978-1987), Lutheran School of Theology at Chicago; Organizer and Chair (1986-1988), Theology and Science Group, American Academy of Religion; **Concurrent Positions:** Editor of *Zygon: Journal of Religion and Science* (since 1990); Director of Chicago Center for Religion and Science **Discipline:** Systematic Theology **Related Interests:** Teilhard; Creation and Evolution; Science and Theology in the 19th and 20th Centuries; Constructive Theology.

Selected Publications: He is author of more than 100 articles and 17 books.

_____, K. Haselden, eds. *Changing Man: The Threat and the Promise*. Doubleday, 1968.
_____. *The Promise of Teilhard*. Lippincott, 1970.
_____. *Three Essays by Albrecht Ritschl*. Fortress, 1972.
_____. *Defining America: A Christian Critique of the American Dream*. Fortress, 1974.
_____. *Belonging and Alienation*. Center for Scientific Study of Religion, 1976.
_____. "Creation" and "Church." In Christian Dogmatics, eds. Carl Braaten and Robert Jenson.
_____. *The Human Factor: Evolution, Culture, Religion*. Fortress, 1993.

Heller, Michael

Present Position and Address: Catholic Priest; Professor of Philosophy (since 1972), Pontifical Academy of Theology; Lecturer in Philosophy of Science and Logic (since 1965), Theological Institute in Tarnów; Adjoint member (since 1981), Vatican Astronomical Observatory; ul. Powstańców Warszawy 13/94, 33-110, Tarnów, Poland **Date of Birth:** March 12, 1936 **Languages Spoken:** Polish, English, French, Italian, Russian **Education:** M.A. Philosophy (1965)/Ph.D. Relativistic Cosmology (1966)/Docent Degree (for assistant Professorship) (1969), Catholic University of Lublin; Professorship (1985), Pontifical Academy of Theology - Kraków **Previous Positions:** Visiting Professor (1977, 1982), Catholic University of Louvain **Other Academic Experience:** Research Visits: Oxford; Leicester; Ruhr; Catholic University of America, and others **Selected Memberships:** Pontifical Academy of Science; International Astronomical Union; European Physical Society; International Society for the Study of Time; Center for Theology and Natural Science, Berkeley; Polish Theological/Physical/Astronomical Societies; Scientific Society of the Catholic University of Lublin **Discipline:** Philosophy; Cosmology **Related Interests:** General Relativity and Relativistic Cosmology; History and Philosophy of Science (especially cosmology); Science and Theology Problem.

Selected Publications: His selected bibliography lists 60 papers in Theory of Relativity and Relativistic Cosmology, and over 100 in Philosophy/History of Science and others, and over 20 books.

_____, O. Godart. "Les Relations entre la Science et la Foi chez Georges Lemaitre," *Commentarii Pontificia Academia Scientiarum* 3, 21: 1-12.

_____. "On Creation without Anthropomorphisms." In *The Human Person and Philosophy in the Contemporary World*, ed. J. M. Zycinski. Proceedings of the Meeting of the World Union of Catholic Philosophical Societies. Kraków: The Pontifical Faculty of Theology, 1980.

_____. *Wszechswiat I Slowo*. Znak: Kraków, 1981.

_____, J. Zycinski. *Drogi Myslacych, Polskie Towarzystwo Teologiczne*. Kraków, 1983, 2d ed. 1985.

_____, V. Coyne, M. Heller, and J. Zycinski. *The Galileo Affair: A Meeting of Faith and Science*. Proceedings of the Cracow Conference, May 24-27, 1984. Specola Vaticana, Citta del Vaticano, 1985.

_____. *The World and the Word - Between Science and Religion*. Tucson: Pachart, 1986.

_____. "Scientific Rationality and Christian Logos." In *Physics, Philosophy and Theology: A Common Quest for Understanding*, ed. R. J. Russell, W. R. Stoeger, and G. V. Coyne. Vatican City State: Vatican Observatory, 1988; Notre Dame, IN: University of Notre Dame Press, 1989.

Hemminger, Hansjörg

Present Position and Address: Science Referent (since 1985, scientific investigation of the world view aspects of the sciences), Evangelische Zentralstelle für Weltanschauungsfragen, Hölderlinplatz 2A, D-7000 Stuttgart 1, Germany **Date of Birth:** October 9, 1948 **Languages Spoken:** German, English **Education:** Diploma in Biology (1972)/Dr. rer. nat. (1975)/Dr. habil. (1983), University of Freiburg **Previous Positions:** Assistant Professor in Behavioral Biology and Human Behavior, University of Freiburg, Germany **Selected Memberships:** Ethologische Gesellschaft **Discipline:** Behavioral Biology; Human Ethology; Knowledge Theory **Related Interests:** Relation between Biological and Christian Anthropology.

Selected Publications:

_____. *Der Mensch - Eine Marionette der Evolution?* Frankfurt, 1983.

_____. "Evolution als Existenzdeutung." *Evangelische Zentralstelle für Weltanschauungsfragen* 48 (Stuttgart, 1985).

_____. "Über Glaube und Zweifel." In *Rückkehr der Zauberer*, ed. Hansiörg Hemminger. Reinbek, 1987.

_____. "Die Suche nach Realität in der Naturwissenschaft und im Glauben." *Kerygma und Dogma* 33 (Göttingen, 1987).

_____. "Naturwissenschaft und neue Mythen in der Psychotherapie." *Glaube und Aberglaube in der Medizin.* Karlsruhe: n.p., 1988.

_____. "Dialog Glaube - Naturwissenschaft." *Evangelische Zentralstelle für Weltanschauungsfragen.* Stuttgart: n.p., 1988.

Henry, Carl F. H.

Present Position and Address: Visiting Professor, Trinity Evangelical Divinity School; (Home) 3824 North 37th Street, Arlington, VA 22207, USA **Date of Birth:** January 22, 1913 **Education:** B.A. (1938), /M.A. (1940), Wheaton College, IL; B.D. (1941)/Th.D. (1942), Northern Baptist Theological Seminary, Chicago; Ph.D. (1949), Boston University; Ordained to Ministry by Baptist Church (1941) **Honorary Degrees:** Seattle-Pacific College (1963); Houghton College (1973); Northwestern College (1979); Gordon-Conwell Theological Seminary (1984); Hillsdale College (1989) **Previous Positions:** Assistant through Professor (1942-47), Northern Baptist Theological Seminary; Acting Dean (1947)/Professor (1947-56)/Peyton lecturer (1963)/Visiting Professor (1980), Fuller Theological Seminary; Visiting Professor of Theology at Wheaton College, Gordon Divinity School, Columbia Bible College, Japan School of Theology, Trinity Evangelical Divinity School, Denver Conservative Baptist Seminary, Eastern Baptist Theological Seminary; Distinguished Visiting Professor at Hillsdale College, Calvin Theological Seminary and many engagements overseas and on radio **Selected Memberships:** Society for the Scientific Study of Religion; AAAS; American Society Christian Ethics; American Academy of Religion; Evangelical Theological Society; Society of Christian Philosophers; Board of Directors for the Institute of Advanced Christian Studies (1976-79) **Discipline:** Theology **Related Interests:** Science, Philosophy, Theology and Ethics.

Selected Publications: His Bibliography lists over 34 books.

_____. *God, Revelation and Authority in Six Volumes.* Waco, TX: Word Books, 1976-1983. Relevant sections include Vol. 1 chapters 4, 5, 10, 12; Vol. 2 chapters 8, 9; and Vol. 6 chapters 1, and 5-8.

_____, editor. *Horizons of Science.* New York: Harper & Row, 1978.

_____. *Toward a Recovery of Christian Belief.* Westchester, IL: Crossway Books, 1990.

Henry, James P.

Present Position and Address: Professor of Medicine (since 1986), Drew Medical School; Research Professor of Psychiatry (since 1981), Department of Psychiatry, School of Medicine, Loma Linda University, Loma Linda, CA 92350, USA **Date of Birth:** July 12, 1914 **Education:** B.A. Natural Science (1933)/M.B., B.Ch Medicine (1938)/M.D. Medicine (1952), Cambridge University, UK; Ph.D. Experimental Medicine (1952), McGill University, Canada **Honorary Degrees:** Honorary Doctorate (1981), University of Bordeaux, France **Awards and Honors:** Carl Ludwig Medal (German Heart Association) - Distinguished Scientific Achievement (with Otto Gauer); Award from the American Heart Association (1976) **Previous Positions:** Banting Research Fellow (1941-43), McGill University; Fellow in Biology (1943), California Institute of Technology, Pasadena; Assistant and Associate Professor (1943-47), Physiology, University of Southern California; Chief (1947-56), Acceleration and Stress Physiology Section of Aerospace Medicine, Wright-Patterson AFB; Director of Bioscience (1956-59), European Office, USAF/ARDC, Brussels, Belgium; Chief (1959-63), Manned Spacecraft Center, NASA; Professor of Physiology (1963-81), School of Medicine, University of Southern California **Selected Memberships:** Fellow (since 1981), Institute for Advanced Study in Gerontology and Geriatrics, University of Southern California; American Physiological Society (since 1948); Fellow, Int. College Psychosomatic Medicine **Discipline:** Experimental Medicine; Psychiatry; Biomedicine

Selected Publications:

_____. "Religious Experience, Archetypes, and the Neurophysiology of Emotion." *Zygon* 21 (1986): 47-74.
_____. Review of *Aldous Huxley and Eastern Wisdom* by B. Chakoo. *Zygon* 23 (1988): 98-102.
_____. The Archetypes of Power and Intimacy and the Aging Process. In *Theories of Aging*, eds J.E. Birren and V. Bengtson. New York: Springer, 1988.
_____. "Psychological and Physiological Responses to Stress: The Right Hemisphere and the Hypothalamo-Pituitary-Adrenal Axis, An Inquiry into Problems of Human Bonding." *Integration of Physiologic and Behavioral Science* 28 (1993): 368-86.
_____, P.M. Stephens. *Stress, Health, and the Social Environment: A Sociobiologic Approach to Medicine*. New York: Springer Verlag, 1977.
_____. *Instincts, Archetypes, and Symbols: An Approach to the Psysiology of Religious Experience*. Dayton, OH: College Press.

Hernandez, Edwin Ivan

Present Position and Address: Assistant Professor of Sociology, Behavioral Science Department, Andrews University, Berrien Springs, MI 49104, USA **Work Phone:** (616) 471-3159 **Home Phone:** (616) 471-7308 **Fax Number:** (616) 471-3108 **E-Mail:** edwinh@andrews.edu **Date of Birth:** May 1, 1960 **Languages Spoken:** English, Spanish **Education:** B.A. Theology with Educational Emphasis (1982), Loma Linda University, CA; M.Div. (1985), Andrews University; M.A. Sociology (1987)/Ph.D. Sociology (1989), University of Notre Dame **Congresses and Conferences:** He has presented papers at the annual meetings and symposiums of the following professional societies: Andrews Society for Religious Studies; PARAL Symposium; Society for the Scientific Study of Religion; Religious Research Association; Adventist Health System Sunbelt Mission Conference; Hispanic Consultation in the Religion Division of the Lilly Endowment; American Sociological Association; Panel presentation, Andrews Scholars Society Meetings **Lectures Presented:** "American Dream or Nightmare: The Challenge of Diversity"; "Dare to Make a Difference: A Call for Visionary Leadership," National Association of Students at Catholic Colleges and Universities (1993); "Hung Between Two Worlds: The Experience of Second Generation Hispanics," Annual John Osborne Lectureship **Awards and Honors:** Volunteer of the Year Award (1990-91); Phi Kappa Phi (1993); Research/Creative Activity Award (1993), Andrews University; Excellence in Teaching-noncontinuous category (1994), Andrews University **Previous Positions:** Teacher Assistant to Dr. Richard Rice, Professor of Systematic Theology (1980-82), Loma Linda University; Associate Pastor for Youth Ministry (1982-83), Elmshaven Church, Northern California Conference of Seventh-day Adventists; Research Assistant (1983-84), Institute of Church Ministry, Andrews University; Associate Director for the Human Relations Center (1984-85), Institute of Church Ministry, Andrews University; Research Assistant (1985-86), Social Science Training and Research Laboratory, University of Notre Dame; Research Assistant/ Computer Analyst (1986-88), University of Notre Dame Study of Catholic Parish Life research team; Teaching Fellow (1988-89), Department of Sociology, University of Notre Dame; Director of Pastoral Care and Bioethics (1989-91), Hialeah Hospital, Hialeah, FL; Faculty member (summer 1993), Youth Theology Institute, Candler School of Theology, Emory University, Atlanta, GA **Selected Memberships:** Society for the Scientific Study of Religion; The Religious Research Association; Association for the Sociology of Religion; American Sociological Association; Asociación para la Educación Teológica Hispana **Discipline:** Sociology **Current Areas of Research:** 1. Research Participant in the "Hispanic Protestantism Project" at Perkins School of Theology — a project funded by the Lilly Endowment, Inc. (1994-1997); 2. Principle Investigator of "The Future of Hispanic Graduate Theological Education," a Study on Successful Strategies for Access, Retention, and Development of Hispanic Religious Leaders and Scholars — a project funded by the Pew Charitable Trusts. (October 1, 1994-July 1995)

Selected Publications: His bibliography contains 1 coauthored book, 14 authored or coauthored published articles and reports, 2 book reviews, and 3 publications in progress.

_____, Evelyn R. Barritt, Linda S. Quick, and Sonya R. Albury. "Life and Death Decisions: A Special Study of Community Values. Vols 1 and 2. Reports. Miami, FL: Heath Council of South Florida, 1991.

_____, Roger L. Dudley, and Sara M. K. Terian. "Conservative Christians and American Politics: The Case of Seventh-Day Adventists." *Research in the Social Scientific Study of Religion* 4 (1992).

_____, Roger L. Dudley. *Citizens of Two Worlds: Religion and Politics Among American Seventh-Day Adventists.* Berrien Spring, MI: Andrews University Press, 1992.

_____, Roger L. Dudley, and Sara M. K. Terian. "Religiosity and Public Issues Among Seventh-day Adventists." *Review of Religious Research* 33, 4 (1992).

_____, Roger L. Dudley. "Do Adventist Voters Lean Left or Right?" *Spectrum* (A Journal of the Association of Adventist Forums) 23, 3 (1993).

_____. "Sobreviviendo la Adolescencia de sus Hijos." *Revista Adventista* (Enero-Marzo, 1994).

_____. "Recapturing the Prophetic Imagination." *Adventist Review* (February 17, 1994).

_____, Duane C. McBride, Clyde B. McCoy, Dale D. Chitwood, James F. Inciardi, and Patricia M. Mutch. "Religious Influence and Churches/Temples as Sources of AIDS Information for Street Injection Drug Users." *Review for Religious Research* (Forthcoming).

_____. "Hung Between Two Worlds: Towards Hispanic Youth Ministry." Chap. in *Youth Ministry Today*, ed. Bailey Gellespie. Riverside, CA: La Sierra University Press, forthcoming.

_____. "Rediscovering a Prophetic Imagination." *Adventist Review* (Forthcoming).

Herrmann, Robert A.

Present Position and Address: Professor of Mathematics (since 1987), US Naval Academy, 572 Holloway Rd., Annapolis, MD 21402-5002, USA **Work Phone:** (410) 293-6717 **Date of Birth:** April 29, 1934 **Education:** B.A. Mathematics (1963), Johns Hopkins University; M.A. (1968)/Ph.D. Mathematics (1973), American University **Previous Positions:** Assistant (1968-81)/Associate Professor of Mathematics (1981-87), US Naval Academy **Selected Memberships:** Sigma Xi; Creation Research Society; Mathematical Association of America; American Mathematical Society; Director, Institute for Mathematics and Philosophy **Discipline:** Mathematics; Philosophy **Related Interests:** Mathematically generating models for philosophical concepts and cosmologies which help explain and solve certain perplexing and longstanding problems. These **Current Research:** models and concepts are used to clarify natural system behavior, to rationally explain or solve controversies.

Selected Publications: associated with both scientific and philosophic systems and to give further insight into their conceptual content. The models must meet the general restriction that their content be consistent with and thus not contradict the fundamental concepts of Christianity.

_____. "The Reasonableness of Metaphysical Evidence." *Journal of American Scientific Affiliation* 34, 1 (1982):12-23.

_____. "Language and Science." *C.R.S. Quarterly* 22, 3 (1985): 128-137.

_____. *Nature: The Supreme Logician, I.* Annapolis and London: IMP Press (1986).

_____. "Developmental Paradigms." *C.R.S. Quarterly* 22, 4 (1986): 189-198.

_____. "Nonstandard Consequences Operators." *Kobe Journal of Mathematics* 4, 1 (1987): 1-14.

_____. "Physics is Legislated by a Cosmogony." *Speculations in Science and Technology* 11, 1 (1988):17-24.

_____. "The Scientific Existence of a Higher Intelligence." *C.R.S. Quarterly* 30, 4 (1994): 218-22.

Herrmann, Robert L.

Present Position and Address: Adjunct Professor of Chemistry (since 1982), Chairman of Premedical Program, Gordon College, 255 Grapevine Road, Wenham, MA 01984, USA; (Home) 12 Spillers Lane, Ipswich, MA 01938, USA **Work Phone:** (508) 927 2300, ext. 4029 **Home Phone:** (508) 356-4238

Date of Birth: July 17, 1928 **Education:** B.S. Chemistry (1951), Purdue University; Ph.D. Biochemistry (1956), Michigan State University **Previous Positions:** Research (1956-59), Department of Biology, MIT, Cambridge, MA; Assistant (1959-65)/Associate Professor (1965-76), Boston University School of Medicine; Consultant in Biochemistry (1964-76), V.A. Hospital, Bedford; Professor and Chairman (1976-81), Department of Biochemistry/Associate Dean for Biomedical Sciences (1977-79), Oral Roberts University Schools of Medicine and Dentistry; ; Executive Director (1981-94), American Scientific Affiliation, Ipswich, MA **Editorial Work:** Editorial Board (1984-87), Christian University Press; Editor, *Progress in Theology* **Selected Memberships:** Fellow (1965), American Association for the Advancement of Science; President (1968), Boston University Chapter of Sigma Xi; President (1981), American Scientific Affiliation; Board of Trustees (since 1986), Templeton Foundation; Board of Trustees (1988-95), Southeastern Massachusetts University; Board of Trustees, National Institute of Health Care Research; American Society for Biochemistry and Molecular Biology; American Chemical Society; Christian Medical and Dental Society; Institute for Society, Ethics and the Life Sciences; Victoria Institute of Noetic Sciences **Discipline:** Biochemistry **Related Interests:** Biomedical Ethics; Philosophy of Science; Science and Theology.

Selected Publications:

_____. "Human Engineering and the Church." *JASA* 28 (1976), pp. 59-62.

_____. "Taking Vows in Two Priesthoods, Scientific and Christian." *Yale Journal of Biology and Medicine* 49 (1976): 455-9.

_____. "Dominion or Papier-Mache," Response to D. M. MacKay's paper "Biblical Perspectives on Human Engineering." In *Modifying Man: Implications and Ethics*, ed. C. W. Ellison. Washington DC: University Press of America, 1978.

_____. "Molecular Biology in the Dock." In *Horizons of Science: Christian Scholars Speak Out,* ed. C. F. H. Henry. New York: Harper & Row, 1978.

_____. "The Tension Between Scientific Objectivity and Values." In *Whole Person Medicine, An International Symposium*, ed. D. Allen, L. Bird, and R. Herrmann. Downer's Grove, IL: InterVarsity Press, 1980.

_____. "Christian Perspectives on Genetic Engineering." In *Life in the Balance*, ed. J. C. Hefey. Wheaton IL: Victor Books, 1980.

_____, John M. Templeton. *The God Who Would Be Known: Revelations of the Divine in Contemporary Science.* Harper and Row, 1989.

_____. *Genetic Engineering - A Teaching Module*. Washington, DC: Council of Independent Colleges, 1990.

_____. "Religion." In *Looking Forward: The Next Forty Years*, ed. John M. Templeton, 197-217. New York: Giniger/Harper Business, 1993.

_____, John M. Templeton. *Is God the Only Reality?: Science Only Points to a Deeper Reality.* New York: Continuum Publishing, 1994.

Hesse, Mary Brenda

Present Position and Address: Emeritus Professor of Philosophy of Science, Cambridge University, Free School Lane, Cambridge CB2 RH, UK **Date of Birth:** October 15, 1924 **Education:** B.Sc. Special Mathematics (1st Class, 1945)/Ph.D. (1948)/M.Sc. in History and Philosophy of Science (1950), University of London **Honorary Degrees:** Honorary D.Litt (1986), University of Hull; D.Sc. (1987), University of Guelph **Previous Positions:** Demonstrator in Mathematics (1945-47), Imperial College; Assistant Lecturer in Mathematics (1947-51), University of London; Lecturer in Mathematics (1951-55), University of Leeds; Lecturer in History and Philosophy of Science (1955-59), University College, London; Lecturer (1960-68)/Reader (1968-75)/Professor (1975-85)/Stanton Lecturer (1977-80), Philosophy of Science, University of Cambridge; Fellow (1966-92)/Vice President (1976-80)/Emeritus Fellow (since 1994), Wolfson College, Cambridge; Visiting Professor in Philosophy, Yale University (1962-63)/University of Minnesota (1966)/University of Chicago (1968)/University of Notre Dame (1972); Joint Gifford Lecturer (1983), University of Edinburgh **Editorial Work:** Editor, *British Journal* *for the Philosophy of Science* (1965-69); Editorial board member, *Isis* (1971-85)/*Philosophical Studies* (1972-85)/*Studies in the History and Philosophy of Science* (since 1968)/*Philosophy of Science* (1976-1989) **Selected Memberships:** Fellow (since 1971)/Member of Council (1979-81), British Academy **Discipline:** Philosophy of Science; Physics; Mathematics **Related Interests:** Issues in the History and Philosophy of Science that impinge on the understanding of Religion and Theology.

Selected Publications:

_____. *Science and the Human Imagination: Aspects of the History and Logic of Physical Science*. London: N.p., 1954.
_____. "Miracles and the Laws of Nature." In *Miracles*, ed. C. F. D. Moule. London, 1965: 33-42.
_____. "Lonergan and Method in the Natural Sciences." In *Looking at Lonergan's Method*, ed. P. Corcoran. Dublin, 1975: 59-72.
_____. "Criteria of Truth in Science and Theology." *Religious Studies* 11 (1976): 385-400.
_____. "Retrospect." In *The Sciences and Theology in the 20th Century*, ed. A. R. Peacocke. University of Notre Dame Press, 1981.
_____. "Cosmology as Myth." *Concilium* 6 (1983): 49-54.
_____, M. A. Arbib. *The Construction of Reality, The Gifford Lectures at the University of Edinburgh*. Cambridge University Press, 1987.
_____. "Science Beyond Realism and Relativism." In *Cognitive Relativism and Social Science*, eds. D. Raven, L. Van Vucht Tijssen and J. de Wolf. New Brunswick, NJ: N.p., 1992.
_____. "Physics, Philosophy and Myth." In *Physics, Philosophy, and Theology: A Common Quest for Understanding*, ed. R. J. Russell, W. R. Stoeger and G. V. Coyne. Notre Dame, IN: University of Notre Dame Press, 1989.
_____. "Religion, Science and Symbolism." In *Religious Pluralism*, ed. I. Hamnett. 1990.

Hickernell, Fred S.

Present Position and Address: Technical Staff Member, Motorola Government and Systems Technology Group, 8201 E. McDowell, Scottsdale, AZ 85252 **Work Phone:** (602) 441-2923 **Fax:** (602) 441-7714 **E-Mail:** p04564@email.mot.com **Date of Birth:** January 16, 1932 **Languages Spoken:** English **Awards and Honors:** Engineering Award, IEEE(1969); NASA Certificate of Recognition (1974); American Baptist Layman of the Year for Arizona (1979); Dan Noble Fellow, Motorola (1988); Motorola Quality CEO Awards (1989 & 1990) **Previous Positions:** Weather Officer, US Air Force (1953-57); Teaching Assistant, Arizona State University (1957-58); Engineer, Goodyear Aerospace (1958-60); Faculty Associate, Arizona State University (1981-83); Visiting Professor, University of Arizona (1985-87); Adjunct Professor, University of Arizona (1987 to date); Motorola, Various groups and divisions (1960 to date) **Selected Memberships:** American Scientific Affiliation (President, 1994); Institute of Electrical and Electronic Engineers; American Physical Society; American Vacuum Society; American Meteorological Society **Discipline:** Acoustic and optical microelectronics **Related Interests:** Microwave acoustics, surface acoustic waves, integrated optics, vacuum thin films **Current Research:** The surface acoustic wave characterization of dielectric and piezoelectric films for acoustoelectronic applications.

Selected Publications: 85 published articles, 130 presentations at conferences, 9 patents.

_____, N. G. Sakiotis. "An Electroacoustic Amplifier with Net Electrical Gain." *Proc. of the IEEE*, 52, 194 (1964).
_____, W. R. Gayton. "The Elastic Constants of Single Crystal Indium Phosphide." Journal of Applied Physics 37, 462 (1966).

Hiebert, Erwin Nick

Present Position and Address: Professor Emeritus of History of Science (since 1989), Harvard University, Science Center 235, Cambridge, MA 02138, USA; (Home) 40 Payson Road, Belmont, MA 02178, USA **Work Phone:** (617) 495-0325 **Date of Birth:** May 27, 1919 **Languages Spoken:** English, German **Education:** A.B. Chemistry and Mathematics (1941), Bethel College, North Newton, KS; A.M. Chemistry and Physics (1943), University of Kansas, Lawrence; M.Sc. Physical Chemistry (1949), University of Chicago; Ph.D. Physical Chemistry, History of Science (1954), University of Wisconsin **Previous Positions:** Visiting Scholar (1961-62, 68-69), School of Historical Studies, Institute for Advanced Studies in Princeton; Visiting Scholar (Fall 1978-79, Summer 1979), Zentrum für interdiziplinäre Forschung der Universität Bielefeld; Visiting Research Scholar (summers 1980/81, January 1982, 1984-85) Churchill College, Cambridge University; Research Chemist (1943-46), Standard Oil Company, IN; Assistant to Chief of Scientific Branch (1946-47), War Department General Staff, Pentagon, Washington, DC; Research Physical Chemist (1947-50), Institute for the Study of Metals, University of Chicago; Assistant Professor of Chemistry (1952-55), San Francisco State College; Assistant (1957-60)/Associate (1960-63)/Full Professor (1963-70) of History of Science, University of Wisconsin; Instructor (1955-57)/Professor (since 1970)/Chairman of History of Science Department (1977-84), Harvard University; Participated in Summer Institute on "History and Philosophy of Science" in East Berlin (17 June - 5 July, 1988), sponsored by the Humboldt University of Berlin **Selected Memberships:** American Physical Society; History of Science Society (American); British Society for the History of Science **Discipline:** History of Science; Physical Chemistry **Related Interests:** Historical and philosophical examination of modern scientists' perspectives on religious belief/unbelief in relation to the sciences. Focus on modes of achieving reciprocity between and accommodation of the scientists' religion to their science, and vice versa. **Major Teaching and Research Areas:** History and philosophy of the physical sciences and thought since 1800 with major current emphasis on 20th century studies. Special areas are thermodynamics, physical chemistry and chemical physics, structure of matter, nuclear physics and chemistry, science and Marxist thought, and interaction between scientists and philosophers of science.

Selected Publications:

_____. "The Uses and Abuses of Thermodynamics in Religion." *Daedalus* 95 (1966): 1046-1080.
_____. "The Integration of Revealed Religion and Scientific Materialism in the Thought of Joseph Priestley." In *J. Priestley: Scientist, Theologian and Metaphysician*, ed. L. Kieft and B. R. Willeford Jr.. London: Associated University Presses, 1980.
_____. "Einstein's Image of Himself as a Philosopher of Science." Chapter 9 in *Transformation and Tradition in the Sciences, Essays in Honor of I. Bernard Cohen.* Cambridge University Press, 1984.
_____. "The Influence of Mach's Thought on Science." *Philosophia Naturalis* 21 (1984): 598-615.
_____. "Modern Physics and Christian Faith." In *God and Nature*, ed. R. Numbers and D. Lindberg. University of California Press, 1986.
_____. "The Scientist as Philosopher of Science." *Schriftenreihe für Geschichte der Naturwissenschaften Technik und Medizin* 24 (1987): 7-17.
_____. "The Role of Experiment and Theory in the Development of Nuclear Physics in the Early 1930's." In *Theory and Experiment*, ed. D. Batens and J. P van Bendegem. Dordrecht: Reidel, 1987.

Hiebert, Paul G.

Present Position and Address: Professor of Anthropology and South Asian Studies, and Chair of the Department of Missions and Evangelism; Director of the Ph.D. in Intellectual Studies; Trinity Evangelical Divinity School, 2065 Half Day Road, Deerfield, IL 60015, USA; (Home) 3524 Old Mill Road, Highland Park, IL 60035, USA **Work Phone:** (708) 317-5429 **Date of Birth:** November 13, 1932 **Languages Spoken:** English, Telugu **Education:** B.A. Mathematics and History (1954), Tabor

College; M.A. (1957), Mennonite Brethren Biblical Seminary; M.A. Anthropology (1959)/Ph.D. Anthropology (1967), University of Minnesota **Previous Positions:** Missionary (1960-65), Mennonite Brethren Board of Missions and Services, Principal of Bethany Bible School and College in India; Assistant (1966-71)/Associate Professor (1971-72) of Anthropology, Kansas State University, Manhattan, KS; Associate Professor of Anthropology and South Asia Studies (1972-77), University of Washington, Seattle; Fulbright Professor of Anthropology, Osmania University, Hyderabad, India (1974-1975); Associate Professor of Anthropology and South Asia Studies (1977-79)/Professor (1979-1990). Fuller Theological Seminary, Faculty of the Haggai Institute in Singapore (since 1981); Visiting Professor of Missions in India (1982, 1985) **Selected Memberships:** Fellow (since 1971), American Anthropological Association; American Society of Missiology; Association of South Asian Studies; Evangelical Missiological Society **Discipline:** Anthropology of Religion; Epistemology; Indian Cultures and Hinduism; Urban Anthropology **Related Interests:** Long term interest in theology and science is in area of epistemology as it springs out of looking at different cultures and trying to sort out how we deal with cultural difference.

Selected Publications:

_____. *Cultural Anthropology*, 2d ed.. Grand Rapids: Baker Book House, 1983.
_____. "Epistemological Foundations for Science and Theology." *TSF Bulletin* 8, 4 (1985): 5-10.
_____. "The Missiological Implications of an Epistemological Shift." *TSF Bulletin* 8, 4 (1985): 6-11.
_____. *Anthropological Insights for Missionaries*. Grand Rapids: Baker Book House, 1985.
_____. "Critical Contextualization." *International Bulletin* 11, 3 (1987): 104-112.
_____. "Beyond Anti-Colonialism to Globalism." *Missiology: An International Review* 19, 3 (1991): 263-282.
_____. "Conversion in Hinduism and Buddhism." In *Handbook of Religious Conversion*, ed. H. Newton Malone and Samuel Southard. Birmingham, AL: Religious Education Press, 1992.
_____. "Popular Religions." In *Toward the Twenty-First Century in Christian Mission*, ed. James M. Phillips and Robert T. Coote. Grand Rapids, MI: William B. Eerdmans Publishing Company, 1993.
_____. *Kondura: Structure and Integration in a South Indian Village*. Minneapolis, MN: University of Minnesota Press.
_____. *Anthropological Reflections on Missiological Issues*. Grand Rapids, MI: Baker Book House, 1994.

Hilhorst, Medard T.

Present Position and Address: Associate Professor in Medical and Applied Ethics, Erasmus Universiteit Rotterdam, Postbus 1738, 3000 DR Rotterdam, The Netherlands; (Home) Kantoorgracht 9, 2611 PE Delft, The Netherlands **Work Phone:** 010-4087842 **Home Phone:** 015-136260 **Languages Spoken:** Dutch, English **Education:** B.Sc. Electronics (1972)/M.Sc. Applied Mathematics (1974), Twente Universiteit; M.D. Theology (1982)/Ph.D. Ethics (1987), Amsterdam **Field Work:** Research in ethics. Together with Dr. T. Meijknecht, initiated the Technology Profession and Faith Foundation, aimed at assisting those in technical professions to integrate their faith and their lives. **Previous Positions:** Protestant student Chaplain for the Dutch Reformed Church (1982-90), Delft University of Technology **Selected memberships:** , National Committee on Aids Prevention; Committee on Tuberculosis of the Dutch Health Council; Several other Medical Ethical Committees; Secretary, Dutch Society of Ethicists **Discipline:** Ethics; Theology **Related Interests:** (Medical) Professional Ethics; Ethical (Medical) Technology Assessment.

Selected Publications:

_____. *Responsible for Future Generations? A Moral Approach to Social Questions: Population Size, Nuclear Energy, Natural Resources and Genetics* (in Dutch). Kampen, 1987.

Hill, David R.

Present Position and Address: Professor Emeritus of Computer Science and Faculty Professor of Psychology, University of Calgary, 2500 University Drive, Calgary, ALB T2N 1N4, Canada **Work Phone:** (403) 220-5561 **Date of Birth:** May 8, 1937 **Languages Spoken:** English, French **Education:** B.A. Engineering (1961), University of Cambridge; M.Sc. Human Factors and Artificial Intelligence (1963), Loughborough University; P.Eng. (1988), Association of Professional Engineers, Geologists and Geophysicists of Alberta **Previous Positions:** Qualified Pilot, Royal Air Force (1956-58); Flight Test Engineer (1961-62), Shorts in Belfast; Research Engineer and Project Leader (1963-67), Standard Telecommunication Labs, UK; Assistant through Full Professor (since 1967)/Acting Head of Dept. of Computer Science (1980-81), University of Calgary; Company Director (since 1984), various companies: Microelectronics Centre in Edmonton (1986-89), currently Trillium Sound Research, Inc.; Visiting Lecturer and Fellow (1974-1975), Essex University, UK **Editorial Work:** Coeditor of *International Journal of Man-Machine Studies* (Academic Press)/Associate Editor (since 1993) **Discipline:** Computer Science, Psychology, and Engineering **Related Interests:** Theology and Philosophy

Selected Publications:

_____. "The Human as an Information Processor." Man-Machine Systems Laboratory Report, Department of Computer Science, University of Calgary. Paper first presented at University of Calgary Humanities Institute Conference, April 1984: "Images of Humanity - The implication of contemporary developments and discoveries in science for the uniqueness of the human being.

Hillar, Marian

Present Position and Address: Professor of Molecular Biology, Biochemistry, and Philosophy (since 1981), Dept. of Biological Sciences, Texas Southern University, Houston, TX 77004, USA; (Home) 9330 Bankside, Houston, TX 77031, USA **Work Phone:** (713) 527-7990 **Home Phone:** (713) 777-0374 **Date of Birth:** March 22, 1938 **Languages Spoken:** English, French, Greek, Italian, Polish, Portuguese, Russian, Spanish **Education:** Secondary School (preparatory for the University, equivalent of B.S./B.A. (1952-56), Bromberg, Poland; M.D. (*summa cum laude*, 1962)/Ph.D. Biochemistry (studies in biochemistry, history of philosophy, history of medicine, languages and history of french literature (1962-66); University Medical School of Danzig **Postgraduate Studies:** University of Danzig/Jagellonian University, Cracow (1964-65) **Selected Congresses and Conferences:** Attended conference on "A Philosophical Problem about Religious Belief," Center for Thomistic Studies, University of St. Thomas in Houston, January 16, 1989; Conference at the Center for Classical Studies at Rice University on "Gnostic Religion and Christianity," (March 14, 1989); Conference on "The Encounter of Religions in China." (April 1-3, 1989) **Previous Positions:** Instructor through Assistant Professor (1958-69), Dept. of Biochemistry, University Medical School of Danzig; Senior Research Associate (1969-70)/Adjunct Assistant Professor in Myocardial Biology (1971-75), Baylor College of Medicine, Houston, TX; Assistant through Professor of Molecular Biology and Biochemistry and Philosophy (1971), Texas Southern University; Visiting Professor, University of Camerino, Italy (1983) **Selected Memberships:** Biophysical Society; Biochemical Society (London); American Association for the Advancement of Science; American Humanist Association Alliance Francaise; Polish Institute of Arts and Sciences of America; Institute on Religion in an Age of Science; Society for the Advancement of American Philosophy **Discipline:** Biochemistry; History of Philosophy **Related Interests:** History of Western and Eastern Philosophy; History of Ideologies and Religious Thought; History of Science and Medicine; New Testament and Early Christianity .

Selected Publications: Over and above lectures, papers and seminars, the bibliography lists 4 books, 100 articles, 50 abstracts or presentations and 9 book reviews, in the areas of molecular biology, biochemistry, philosophy and religion.

_____. "Philosophical Aspects of Hippocratic Medicine." Seminar presented to the American Humanist Association, Houston Chapter, Houston, October 16, 1986.
_____. "Liberation Theology: Universalism and Human Realization." Paper presented to the 11th Annual Intercultural Communication Conference, Texas Southern University, April 7-8, 1988.
_____. "Evolution: Two Perspectives." Seminar presented at Dept. of Biological Sciences, Texas Southern University, October 10, 1988.
_____. "Bringing Philosophies Together." Workshop at National Humanist Conference, San Jose, CA, April 21-23, 1989.
_____. "The Justification of Morals in The Philosophy of Thomas Aquinas." In *Ethics and Humanism*, ed. M. Hillar and H. R. Leuchtag, 19-33. Houston: Humanists of Houston, 1992.
_____. "Liberation Theology: Religious Response to Social Problems." In *Humanism and Social Issues*, ed. M. Hillar and H. R. Leuchtag, 35-52. Houston: Humanists of Houston, 1993.

Hillery Jr., George A.

Present Position and Address: Professor Emeritus of Sociology (since 1995), Virginia Polytechnic and State University, Blacksburg, VA 24061, USA **Date of Birth:** May 21, 1927 **Languages Spoken:** English, German **Education:** Studied Anthropology (1948), University of New Mexico. B.A. Anthropology and Geography (1949)/M.A. Sociology and Anthropology (1951)/Ph.D. Sociology and Anthropology (1954), Louisiana State University **Postgraduate Studies:** Postdoctoral fellow (1959-60), Dept. of Sociology and Anthropology, University of Florida; Research (1964-66), University of Kentucky; Ford Foundation Fellow (1969-70) **Previous Positions:** Assistant Professor (1954-55), University of Georgia, Atlanta Division; Assistant Professor (1955-58), College of William and Mary; Assistant Professor of Sociology (1958-59), George Washington University; Visiting Professor (1959, and Summer 1957), Louisiana State University; /(1967), East Carolina University/(1969), University of West Florida/(1986), Xavier University, Philippines; Assistant (1960-63)/Associate Professor of Sociology (1963-68), University of Kentucky; Associate Professor (1968-69)/Professor of Sociology (1969-71), University of Iowa; Professor of Sociology (1971-94), Virginia Polytechnic and State University **Editorial Work:** Associate Editor (1980-84), *Review for Religious Research*; Consulting Editor (1982-84)/Honorary Senior Editor (since 1984), *Quarterly Journal of Ideology*; Editorial Review Board and Publications Committee (1968-71), Rural Sociological Society **Selected Memberships:** Coordinator (1972-1992), Christian Sociological Society; Member and previously visiting scientist, American Sociological Association; Member of Advisory Board (since 1981), Association of Christian Scholars Phi Kappa Phi (International); Alpha Kappa Delta (Sociology); Delta Phi Alpha (German Language) **Discipline:** Sociology; Community, Theory, Social Anthropology **Related Interests:** The Christian and Community/Society; Sociology and Theology.

Selected Publications: His bibliography lists 3 books, and over 40 articles and book chapters.

_____. "A Christian Perspective on Sociology." In *A Reader in Sociology: Christian Perspectives*, eds. C. P. De Santo, Calvin Redekop and William Smith-Hinds. Scottdale, PA: Herald Press, 1980.
_____. "Triangulation in Religious Research: A Sociological Approach to the Study of Monasteries." *Review of Religious Research* 23, 1 (1981): 22-34.
_____. "Gemeinschaft Verstehen: A Theory of the Middle Range." Presidential address read before the Southern Sociological Society. *Social Forces* 63, 2 (December 1984): 307-334.
_____. *The Monastery: A Study in Freedom, Love and Community*. Westport CT: Praeger Publications, 1992.

Hird, John Francis

Present Position and Address: Consulting Management Engineer/ Episcopal Priest; Pastoral Team, St. Martha's Episcopal Church, Bethany Beach and St. Martin's - In - The - Field Episcopal Church, Selbyville, DE; Board of Directors, Beebe Medical Center, Lewes, DE; 1002 - N Edgewater House, Sea Colony, Bethany Beach, DE 19930, USA **Concurrent Positions:** Chairman, Long-range and Strategic Planning, Beebe Medical Center, Lewes, DE; President, Interfaith Housing, Sussex County, DE; Codirector SAFE (Science and Faith Exchange), Sussex County, DE **Work Phone:** (302) 539-3210 **Fax:** (302) 539-3208 **E-Mail:** Compuserve, 72652, 2725 **Date of Birth:** January 9, 1923 **Languages Spoken:** Some Spanish **Previous Positions:** Retired, Senior Staff Engineer, Western Electric Company; Special Assistant to the President, Standard Fruit & Steamship Company, New Orleans, LA; Quality Control Manager, Taco Heaters, Inc., Cranston, RI; Rector or Vicar of several Episcopal Churches in MD and DE **Selected Memberships:** Fellow, American Society for Quality Control; Fellow, American Association for the Advancement of Science; American Scientific Affiliation; Society of Ordained Scientists (Anglican) **Discipline:** Tropical Agriculture; Statistical Quality Control Engineering; Manufacturing Engineering; Organizational Development **Related Areas of Interest:** Science and Theology; Health Care Issues **Current Areas of Research:** Development of Educational Materials for Middle School Age Children on Faith and Science Issues.

Selected Publications: His bibliography contains many articles in various professional and trade magazines in the USA, Europe, and Japan on quality assurance, statistical quality control and human resource development.

_____, contributing author. *Statistical Quality Control Handbook*. Western Electric (Japanese ed.), 1965.
_____. *Behavior in Organizations*. Brown & Little, 1975.
_____, W. Edward Deming. *Out of the Crisis*. Cambridge, MA:
M.I.T./CAES, 1986.
Personal Notes: He is an Episcopal Priest involved in applied industrial theology, faith and science issues, creative work systems and concepts, such as synergy in the work place.

Hodges, Bert H.

Present Position and Address: Professor of Psychology (since 1983), Gordon College, Wenham, MA 01984, USA; (Home) 8 Mineral Street, Ipswich, MA 01938, USA **Work Phone:** (508) 927-2300 ext. 4404 **Home Phone:** (508) 356-9424 **Date of Birth:** July 7, 1946 **Education:** B.A. (1968), Wheaton College; M.A. Social Psychology (1971)/Ph.D. Social Psychology (1972), Vanderbilt University **Previous Positions:** Assistant (1972-76)/Associate (1976-83) Professor of Psychology, Gordon College; Visiting professor, University of California at Santa Barbara (1977), University of Southampton, UK (1993) **Selected Memberships:** American Psychological Association; Eastern Psychological Association; New England Social Psychological Association; International Society of Ecological Psychology **Discipline:** Social Psychology **Related Interests:** Cognitive and Social Psychology and Values; Philosophy of Science.

Selected Publications: His bibliography lists over 20 works.

_____. "Information Processing and Related Models of Perception: Giving Body to our Notion of Mind." In *Proceedings of the 3rd Symposium on the Christian and Science: The Mind-Body Problem*. Calvin College, 1975.
_____. "Toward a Model of Psychological Man and His Science." *Christian Scholar's Review* 6 (1976): 3-18.
_____. "Perception, Relativity, and Knowing and Doing the Truth." In *Psychology and the Christian Faith*, ed. S. Jones. Grand Rapids MI: Baker, 1986.
_____. "Perception is Relative and Veridical: Ecological and Biblical Perspectives on Knowing and Doing the Truth." In *The Reality of Christian Learning*, ed. H. Heie and D. Wolfe. Grand Rapids, MI: Eerdmans, 1987.

_____. "Ecological Perspectives on Realism, Idealism, and Perceptual Warrant." Paper presented at American Psychological Association, New Orleans, 1989.
_____, R.M. Baron. "Social and physical affordances: the value of negotiation." Paper presented to the meetings of the American Psychological Association. Boston, 1990.
_____, R.. Baron. "Values as constraints on affordances" Perceiving and acting properly." Journal for the Theory of Social Behaviour. 22:3 (1992), 263-294.
_____. "Faith-learning integration: Appreciating the integrity of a shopworn phrase." *Faculty Dialogue.* 22 (1994): 95+-106.
_____. "Beyond goals: Values in am postmodern world of affordances." Paper presented at the International Conference on Perception and Action. Marseilles: 1995.
_____, J. E. Martin. *Vision, Values, Virtues: Appreciating Cognitive Psychology.* Grand Rapids: Baker, in progress.

Hodgson, Peter E.

Present Position and Address: Head (since 1958), Nuclear Physics Theoretical Group, Nuclear Physics Laboratory, Oxford, UK Senior Research Fellow (since 1962), Corpus Christi College, Oxford OX1 4JF, UK **Date of Birth:** November 27, 1928 **Education:** B.Sc. (1948)/Ph.D. Nuclear Physics (1951)/D.Sc. Nuclear Physics (1966), University of London **Previous Positions:** Lecturer in Physics (1958), University of Reading **Selected Memberships:** Science and Religion Forum (editor of Reviews); Secretariat for Scientific Questions (Pax Romana); Farmington Institute **Discipline:** Nuclear Physics **Related Interests:** History and Philosophy of Science; Theology and Science.

Selected Publications: His bibliography lists 6 books and many articles on nuclear physics.

_____. *Nuclear Physics in Peace and War.* Hawthorn Books, 1961.
_____. *World Energy Needs and Resources.* Grove Books on Ethics No. 44, 1981. (Booklet).
_____. "The Christian Origin of Science." *Farmington Paper:* 4 (1982).
_____. *Our Nuclear Future.* Christian Journals Ltd, 1983.
_____. "Science and Creation." *Farmington Paper: 17* (1984).
_____. "After Chernobyl." *Farmington Paper: 22* (1987).
_____, J.R. Lucas. *Spacetime and Electromagnetism.* Oxford University Press, 1990.
_____. *Christianity and Science.* Oxford University Press, 1990.

Hoge, Dean Richard

Present Position and Address: Professor of Sociology, The Catholic University of America, Washington, DC 20064, USA **Work Phone:** (202) 319-5999 **Home Phone:** (301) 589-4407 **Date of Birth:** May 27, 1937 **Languages Spoken:** English, German **Education:** B.D. (1964), Harvard Divinity School **Awards and Honors:** Best Professional Book, Catholic Press Association, for *The Future of Catholic Leadership.* Sheed and Ward, 1987 **Previous Positions:** Assistant Professor of Christianity and Society (1969-74), Princeton Theological Seminary; Associate Professor/Professor (since 1974), The Catholic University of America **Selected Memberships:** Society for the Scientific Study of Religion; Religious Research Association; Southern Sociological Society; International Council for the Sociology of Religion **Discipline:** Sociology **Related Areas of Interest:** Sociology of American Churches; Sociology of the Clergy; Theology and Ecology; Religion of Intellectuals **Current Areas of Research:** Currently working on a large five-denomination empirical study of factors in giving to churches, funded by the Lilly Endowment.

Selected Publications: His publications include 9 books and about 70 articles.

_____, David A. Roozen, eds. *Understanding Church Growth and Decline, 1950-1978.* New York: Pilgrim Press, 1979.
_____. *The Future of Catholic Leadership: Responses to the Priest Shortage.* Kansas City: Sheed and Ward, 1987.

_____, Jackson W. Carroll, and Francis K. Sheets. *Patterns of Parish Leadership: Cost and Effectiveness in Four Denominations*. Kansas City: Sheed and Ward, 1988.

_____, William V. D'Antonio, James D. Davidson, and Ruth A. Wallace. *American Catholic Laity in a Changing Church*. Kansas City: Sheed and Ward, 1989.

_____, Eugene F. Hemrick. *A Survey of Priests Ordained Five to Nine Years*. Paperback. Washington, DC: American Catholic Educational Association, 1991.

_____, Douglas L. Griffin. *Research on Factors Influencing Giving to Religious Bodies*. Ringbound. Indianapolis: Ecumenical Center for Stewardship Studies, 1992.

_____, Benton Johnson and Donald A. Luidens. "Mainline Churches: The Real Reason for Decline." *First Things* 31 (March 1993): 13-18.

_____, Benton Johnson and Donald A. Luidens. *Vanishing Boundaries: The Religion of Mainline Protestant Baby Boomers*. Louisville: Westminster/John Knox, 1994.

Personal Notes: Presbyterian Layperson.

Hogenhuis, C. T.

Present Position and Address: Scientific Worker (since 1988), Multidisciplinair Centrum voor Kerk en Samenleving (MCKS) P.B. 19, 3970 AA Driebergen, Netherlands **Date of Birth:** October 25, 1960 **Education:** Doctorandus in Physics (1988), State University of Utrecht, Netherlands **Discipline:** Physics **Related Areas of Interest:** Technology Dynamics and Ethics of Science and Technology; Church and Society.

Selected Publications:

_____. *What Moves Us?* (in Dutch). Delft, Netherlands: Eburon, 1991.
_____. *Professional Codes and Moral Responsibility in Science and Technology* (in Dutch). Driebergen, The Netherlands: Netherlands Ministry of Science and Education/Multidisciplinary Center for Church and Society, 1993.

Holmes, Arthur F.

Present Position and Address: Emeritus Professor of Philosophy and Chairman of Department of Philosophy, Wheaton College, Wheaton, IL 60187-5593, USA **Date of Birth:** March 15, 1924 **Languages Spoken:** English, French **Education:** B.A. (1950)/M.A. Theology (1952), Wheaton College; Ph.D. Philosophy (1957), Northwestern University **Previous Positions:** Instructor through Full Professor (1951-94), Wheaton College; Summer Teaching at University of Pacific/Garrett Theological Seminary/Regent College/Seattle Pacific University; National Coordinator of "Ethics Across the Curriculum Project" (1985-88), Christian College Consortium **Editorial Work:** Editorial Board (1976-1986), Christian University Press; Contributing Editor, *The Reformed Journal*; Editorial Consultant (1984-86), *Faith and Philosophy*; Editorial Consultant, *History of Philosophy Quarterly* **Selected Memberships:** Board of Directors (1976-80)/Treasurer (1977-80, 81-85, 87-90, Institute for Advanced Christian Studies; Member, American Philosophical Association; Illinois Philosophy Association; Executive Committee (1978-82,92-present), and member, Society of Christian Philosophers **Discipline:** Philosophy **Related Interests:** Philosophy and Theology/History of Philosophy.

Selected Publications: His bibliography lists 7 books, 12 chapters and articles in 11 journals including *Journals of Philosophy/Religion/American Scientific Affiliation, Faith and Philosophy, Christianity Today,* and *The Reformed Journal*.

_____. *Christianity and Philosophy*. InterVarsity Press, 1960; British edition, 1964; Rev. ed. *Philosophy: A Christian Perspective*. 1975, British edition, 1976.
_____. *Christian Philosophy in the 20th Century*. Craig Pressman, 1969.
_____. *Faith Seeks Understanding*. Eerdmans, 1971. Latin American Translation, 1979.

_____. *All Truth is God's Truth*. Eerdmans, 1977; British edition, 1979; InterVarsity Press, 1983.
_____. *Contours of a World View*. Eerdmans, 1983.
_____. *Ethics*. InterVarsity Press, 1984.
_____. *Shaping Character*. Eerdman's, 1991.
_____, editor. *War and Christian Ethics*. Baker, 1975.

Hood, Randall

Present Position and Address: Bell Industries, 3917 Via Solano, Palos Verdes, CA 90274, USA **Work Phone:** (800) 289-2355, ext. 5843 **Date of Birth:** December 24, 1956 **Education:** B.A. (1979), California Polytechnic State University **Selected Memberships:** *Zygon*; Institute on Religion in an Age of Science; Chicago Center for Religion and Science **Discipline:** Sociobiology and Theology as an avocation **Related Interests:** Sociobiology and Theology; Science as a Religion based on Altruism.

Selected Publications:

_____. *The Genetic Function and Nature of Literature*. San Luis Obispo: Cal Poly University, 1979.
_____. *Opiate of the Few*. Los Angeles: Mariners Press, 1988.

Hood, Thomas Charles

Present Position and Address: Executive Officer, Society for the Study of Social Problems, (since 1990); Professor, Department of Sociology, University of Tennessee - Knoxville, TN 37996-0490; (Home) 3508 Blow Drive, Knoxville, TN 37920, USA **Work Phone:** (615) 974-7012 **Home Phone:** (615) 577-1131 **Date of Birth:** April 27, 1938 **Education:** B.A. (highest honors, 1960), Michigan State University; M.A. (1964)/Ph.D. (1969), Duke University **Postgraduate Studies:** Scholar Diplomat Seminar on Science/Technology (March 1973), Washington, DC **Previous Positions:** Research Investigator for various projects (since 1967) funded by organizations including Tennessee Department of Transportation (1973-80, 88-89); Martin Marietta (1984-85, 88-90) and others; Instructor to Professor (1965-present, tenured 1971), University of Tennessee; Visiting Associate Professor (Winter 1978), Western Michigan University, Kalamazoo; Acting Department Head (1983-84), Department Head (1984-91), Department of Sociology, University of Tennessee - Knoxville; Principal Investigator in Research "Technical Assistance in Hazard and Disaster Management" (1989-91), Martin Marietta Energy Division, Oak Ridge National Laboratory, TN **Selected Memberships:** Executive Council (1983-84), Membership Committee (1985-88), Association for the Sociology of Religion; American Sociological Association; Society for the Scientific Study of Religion; Christian Sociological Society; President (1994 - 95), Southern Sociological Society **Discipline:** Sociology and Anthropology **Related Interests:** Ethics and Technology/Society.

Selected Publications: His bibliography lists 22 publications, 8 technical reports, and 8 manuscripts.

_____, Arnett Elliott and Jack Holmes. "The Working Scientist as a Political Participant." *Journal of Politics* 34 (May 1972): 399-427.
_____, Arnett Elliott and Thomas C. Hood. *Autonomy Versus Social Responsibility in the Regulation of Research Activities: The Case of the Natural Sciences*. Manuscript.
_____, K. D. van Liere and Leslie Daniels. *Nuclear Issues: The Technical and Institutional Dimensions. Technical Report*. Oak Ridge: Oak Ridge National Laboratory, 1986.
_____. "Environmental Justice in Contemporary America." Manuscript.

Horvath, Tibor

Present Position and Address: Professor of Systematic Theology (since 1962), Regis College, 15 Saint Mary Street, Toronto, ONT M4Y 2R5, Canada **Date of Birth:** July 28, 1927 **Concurrent Position:** Founder and first Headmaster (1994-95), Fényi Gyula Miskolci Jezsuita Gimnázium (High School), Miskolc, Hungary **Languages Spoken:** English, Hungarian, German, Spanish, French, Italian, Latin **Education:** Philosophical Studies M.A. and L. Phil. Aloysianum, Szeged, Hungary (1948)/University of Innsbruck (1949)/Aloysianum Chieri, Italy (1949-51)/College Philosophique, St. Albert, University of Leuven, Belgium (1952-54). Theological Studies: Facultad Teologica, Granada, Spain, (1954, S.T.L. 1958)/Universita Gregoriana, Rome, Italy (S.T.D. 1960-62) **Postgraduate Studies:** Information Science, Computer Science, Anthropology, all at University of Chicago (1970) **Field Studies:** Germany (1959-60) **Previous Positions:** Visiting Professor of Theology (1967-69), St. Paul's University, Ottawa **Editorial Work:** Founder and Editor of the journal *Ultimate Reality and Meaning, Interdisciplinary Studies in the Philosophy of Understanding* (University of Toronto Press, since 1978) **Administrative Experience:** Editor of Newsletter of the Institute for Encyclopedia of Human Ideas on Ultimate Reality and Meaning **Selected Memberships:** Founder and first President (since 1978), International Society for the Study of Human Ideas on Ultimate Reality and Meaning; Institute for Ultimate Reality and Meaning; Founder and Director (since 1978), Association of Concern for Ultimate Reality and Meaning **Discipline:** Theology and Philosophy; Interdisciplinary Studies **Related Interests:** Concept of Time; Learning and Scientific Discovery; Academic Disciplines, Science, Physics etc. as various intentionality-types or strata of human conscience; activity of forming axioms, concepts of ultimate realities and meanings.

Selected Publications:

_____. *Faith Under Scrutiny.* Notre Dame IN: Fides, 1975.
_____. "Revelation, Combat of Culture-Types, Thermodynamics. A Fundamental Theological Analysis of Crisis Event." In *Traditio-Krisis-Renovtio aus theologischer Sicht*, ed. J. Jaspert and R. Mohr. Festschrift Winfried Zeller, 65. Marburg: N.G. Verlag, (1976).
_____. "The Structure of Scientific Discovery and Man's Ultimate Reality and Meaning." *Ultimate Reality and Meaning* 3 (1980):144-163.
_____. "A New Notion of Time." *Science et Esprit* 40 (1988): 35-55.
_____. *Eschatology: Eternity and Eternal Life, Speculative Theology and Science in Discourse.* Waterloo, Ontario: Wilfrid Laurier University Press, 1993.

Houghton, John T.

Present Position and Address: Chairman, Royal Commission on Environmental Pollution (since 1992); (Home) Brynhyfryd, Aberdyfi, Gwynedd LL35 OSN, UK **Date of Birth:** December 30, 1931 **Education:** B.A. Physics (1951)/M.A. (1955)/D.Phil. Physics (1955), Oxford University **Previous Positions:** Director-General (1983-1991) Meteorological Office, UK; Professor of Atmospheric Physics (1976-83), Oxford University; Director (1979-83), Appleton Laboratory, Science and Engineering Research Council **Selected Memberships:** Fellow, Royal Society of London; Vice President, World Meteorological Organization (1987-91); Chairman, Scientific Assessment, Intergovernmental Panel on Climate Change (1988-) **Discipline:** Physics; Meteorology **Related Interests:** Comparative Study of the Methods of Science and Theology; Science and God's World; Miracles; Environmental issues.

Selected Publications: He has written a number of books and scientific papers in his field.

_____. *Does God Play Dice?* UK: InterVarsity Press, 1988; USA: Zondervan, 1989.
_____. *Global Warming: The Complete Briefing.* UK, Lion, 1994.
_____. *The Search for God, Can Science Help?* UK: Lion, 1995, in press.

Howe, George Franklin

Present Position and Address: Professor (since 1968) and Previously Chairman, Division of Natural Sciences and Mathematics, The Master's College, 21726 W. Placerita, Canyon Road, Santa Clarita, CA 91322-1200, USA; (Home) 24635 Apple Street, Newhall, CA 91321-2614, USA **Date of Birth:** November 15, 1931 **Education:** B.S. Botany (high honors, 1953), Wheaton College, IL; M.Sc. Botany (1956)/Ph.D. Botany (1959), Ohio State University **Postgraduate Studies:** Botany (1961), Washington State University; Desert Biology (1963), Arizona State University; Radiation Biology (1965-66), Cornell University, NY **Previous Positions:** Fellow (1957-59), Ohio State University; Instructor (1958), Ohio State University; Instructor through Associate Professor (1959-1968), Westmont College, Santa Barbara, CA; Lecturer in Allergy (1974-1976), Veterans' Hospital in Long Beach, CA **Editorial Work:** Editor of *Creation Research Society Quarterlies* (1969-73), Currently Associate Editor **Selected Memberships:** Vice President (1967-68, 83-85)/President (1977-83)/Director (since 1983) Creation Research Society **Discipline:** Biology and Botany **Related Interests:** Natural Sciences and Creation/Faith; Medical Science and Ethics

Selected Publications:

_____. "Cells, the Amazing Abode of Life." In *Behind the Dim Unknown*, ed. J. C. Monsma. New York: C. P. Putnam's Sons, 1966.
_____, H. Nicholas and G. F. Howe. "The Problem of Abortion." *Moody Monthly* (September 1971): 35-37.
_____. "Chance, Probability and the Will of God." *Biblical Research Monthly (BRM)* 36, 7 (August 1971): 11-13.
_____. "Miracles and the Study of Origins." *BRM* 37, 10 (1972): 3-6.
_____. "The Biological Macroevolutionary Origins Model is not a 'Scientific Theory'." Paper presented at Southern California Academy of Sciences meeting (7 May 1981).
_____. "Like all other Origins Models, Macroevolutionism Is Based on Faith." Paper presented at annual meeting of Southern California Academy of Sciences (May 1983).
_____. "Man of Science: Man of Faith." *BRM* 39, 3: 6-8.

Hübner, Jürgen

Present Position and Address: Professor of Systematic Theology (since 1978)/Science and Theology Referent, Forschungsstätte der Evangelischen Studiengemeinschaft (F.E.ST.) Schmeilweg 5, D-69118 Heidelberg, Germany; (Home) Silcherstrasse 2, D-69256 Mauer bei Heidelberg, Germany. **Date of Birth:** August 30, 1932 **Languages Spoken:** German, English, French **Education:** Study of biology and theology; Theologische Prüfung (1960/62), Evangelisches Konsistorium, Berlin-Brandenburg; Doktorprüfung (1965), Universität Zürich; Ordination (1966), Berlin-Spandau-Klosterfelde; Habilitation (1972), Universität Heidelberg **Previous Positions:** Assistant (1969-70), Institut für Hermeneutik in Tübingen; Studies leader (1970-77), Evangelische Akademie Baden; Lecturer through Professor (since 1972), Systematische Theologie, Heidelberg **Selected Memberships:** Wissenschaftliche Gesellschaft für Theologie; Kepler-Gesellschaft; Societas Ethica; Kuratorium der Evangelischen Zentralstelle für Weltanschauungsfragen; The Science and Religion Forum at Cambridge and Oxford; The Hastings Center, Institute of Society, Ethics and Life Sciences, Hastings-on-Hudson, NY; Institute for Theological Encounter with Science and Technology (ITEST); Institute on Religion in an Age of Science (IRAS); European Society for the Study of Science and Theology (ESSSAT) **Discipline:** Systematic Theology **Related Interests:** The Theology/Science dialogue; Bioethics.

Selected Publications:

_____. "Evolution als Frage an die Theologie." *Zeitwende* 42 (1971): 296-306.
_____. "Biologie und christlicher Glaube. Konfrontation und Dialog." In *Bücherei für Erwachsenenbildung 2*, ed. W. Böhme. Gütersloh: Gütersloher Verlagshaus, 1973.

_____. "Die Theologie Johannes Keplers zwischen Orthodoxie und Naturwissenschaft." In *Beiträge zur Historischen Theologie 50*, ed. G. Ebeling. Tübingen, 1975. Habilitationsschrift.

_____. "Kepler's Praise of the Creator," and "Natural Science as Praise of the Creator." In *Vistas in Astronomy 18*, ed. A. Beer and P. Beer. Oxford/New York, 1975.

_____. "Naturwissenschaft und Theologie zwischen Objektivität und gesellschaftlicher Verantwortung." *Ökumenische Rundschau* 29 (1980): 61-74.

_____. "Wissenschaft, Glaube und Ethik. Über die Voraussetzung christlich-ethischer Urteilsbildung im Blick auf die moderne Medizin." *Evangelische Theologie* 41 (1981): 507-524.

_____. "Die Welt als Gottes Schöpfung ehren. Zum Verhältnis von Theologie und Naturwissenschaft heute." München: Chr. Kaiser, 1982.

_____. "In-vitro-Fertilization im Horizont moderner Biotechnologie. Evangelisch-theologische Aspekte und Perspektiven." *Societas Ethica (Jahresbericht, 1985)*. English translation: "Bioethics: The Paradigm of In vitro fertilization." Palermo.

_____. *Die neue Verantwortung für das Leben. Ethik im Zeitalter von Gentechnologie und Umweltkrise*. Müncher: Chr. Kaiser, 1986.

_____. "Eschatologische Rechenschaft, Kosmologische Weltoriontierung und die Artikulation von Hoffunng." In *Die Zukunft der Erlösung. Zur neueren Diskussion um die Eschatologie*, ed. K. Stock, 147-75. Gütersioh: Chr. Kaiser, 1994.

Hugenberger, Gordon P.

Present Position and Address: Associate Professor of Old Testament, Gordon-Conwell Theological Seminary, So. Hamilton, MA 01936, USA **Work Phone:** (508) 468-7111 **Date of Birth:** October 6, 1948 **Languages Spoken:** English **Selected Memberships:** American Scientific Affiliation; Society of Biblical Literature; Tyndale Fellowship; Institute of Biblical Research **Discipline:** Old Testament **Related Areas of Interest:** Old Testament; Biblical Theology; Hebrew; Akkadian **Current Areas of Research:** Commentary on Judges.

Selected Publications: His bibliography contains 1 book and 11 articles.

_____. *Marriage as a Covenant. A Study of Biblical Law and Ethics Governing Marriage, Developed from the Perspective of Malachi*. Supplements to *Vetus Testamentum*. Leiden/New York/Köln: E. J. Brill, 1994.

Hughes, Cecil Forrest

Address: 63480 La Brisa Drive, Joshua Tree, CA 92252-3376, USA **Home Phone:** (619) 366-9213 **Date of Birth:** April 4, 1913 **Related Areas of Interest:** Apologetics; Theology and all branches of Science.

Selected Publications: He has written 5 books, 1 published book, and articles in the local newspaper, refuting some statements by two atheists.

_____. *Eternal Absolutes*. N.p., N.d.
_____. "He Was, He Is and He Forever Shall Be." Unpublished manuscript.

Hull, John M.

Present Position and Address: Professor of Religious Education, Dean of Faculty of Education and Continuing Studies (since 1990), University of Birmingham, Edgbaston, Birmingham B15 2TT, UK **Date of Birth:** April 22, 1935 **Education:** B.A. (1956)/Dip. Ed. (1957)/B.Ed. Psychology and Philosophy of Education (1959), University of Melbourne; B.A. Theology Tripos (1962)/M.A. Theology Tripos part III, Cambridge University; Ph.D. Magic, Exorcism and Miracle in the 1st Christian Century (1970), University of Birmingham **Previous Positions:** Assistant Master (1957-59),

Caulfield Grammar School, Melbourne; Head of Religious Education Department (1962-66), Selhurst Grammar School for Boys, Surrey; Lecturer in Divinity (1966-68), Westhill College of Education, Birmingham; Lecturer in Religious Education (1968-78)/Senior Lecturer (1978-86)/Professor of Religious Education (since 1989), University of Birmingham; Founded International Seminar for Religious Education and Values (1977); International lectures in Ireland, New Zealand, Australia, Germany, Canada, USA, Holland, Sweden, Italy, Gibraltar, Estonia and Denmark **Media Work:** Participated in 10 T.V. broadcasts **Editorial Experience:** Former Editor, *British Journal of Religious Education* **Selected Memberships**: United Reformed Church - Birmingham; Church of England **Current Research:** At University of Birmingham: History, philosophy and character of school assembly; Laid foundations of theology of education as a discipline within educational studies; Problems of adult religious learning with special reference to theology, psychoanalysis, sociology, and ideology studies; impact of modernity and capitalism upon adult life cycle and religious attitudes.

Selected Publications:

_____. *Studies in Religion and Education*. Falmer Press, 1984.
_____, editor. "Science, Technology and Religious Education." *British Journal of Religious Education* (Autumn 1990).
_____. *What Prevents Christian Adults from Learning?* Philadelphia: Trinity Press International, 1991.
_____. *God-Talk with Young Children: Notes for Parents and Teachers*. Philadelphia: Trinity Press International, 1991.
_____. *Touching the Rock: An Experience of Blindness*. New York: Random House Vintage Books, 1992. Also in Dutch, Italian, German, Spanish with others forthcoming.
_____. "Human Development and Capitalist Society." In *Stages of Faith and Religious Development, Implications for Church, Education and Society*, ed. James W. Fowler, Karl Ernst Nipkow, and Friedrich Schweitzer. London: SCM Press, 1992.
_____. "Christian Education in a Capitalist Society: Money and God." In *Essentials of Christian Community, Essays in Honour of Daniel W. Hardy*, ed. David Ford and Dennis L. Stamps. Edinburgh: T. & T, Clark, 1995.

Humbert, Jean

Present Position and Address: Retired Biologist and Geologist 198, rue Houdan, F-92330 Sceaux, France **Date of Birth:** April 7, 1911 **Education:** Agrégé de l'Université (1939) **Discipline:** Biology; Geology **Related Interests:** Creation and Evolution.

Selected Publications:

_____. *Creation, Evolution - Faut il trancher?* Editions SATOR - 11 route de Pontoise F95540, Mery-sur Oise, France, 1990.

Hummel, Charles E.

Present Position and Address: Retired Director of Faculty Ministry, InterVarsity Christian Fellowship, 17 Worcester Street, Grafton, MA 01519, USA **Work Phone:** (617) 839-4343 **Date of Birth:** August, 8 1923 **Education:** B.E. (1943), Yale University; M.S. (1949), Massachusetts Institute of Technology; M.A. (1961), Wheaton College, IL **Previous Positions:** Chemical Engineering Technologist (1949-50); Field Director (1950-65), InterVarsity Christian Fellowship; President (1965-75), Barrington College (introducing a unique interdisciplinary study program); Director of Faculty Ministry (1975-1990), InterVarsity Christian Fellowship **Selected Memberships:** Executive Council/President (1988), American Scientific Affiliation **Discipline:** Chemical Engineering; Biblical Literature - New Testament **Related Interests:** History and Philosophy of Science.

Selected Publications:

_____. "The Natural Sciences." In *Christ and the Modern Mind*, ed. R. W. Smith. InterVarsity Press, 1972.
_____. *The Galileo Connection: Resolving Conflicts Between Science and the Bible*. InterVarsity Press, 1986.

Humphreys, Colin John

Present Position and Address: Professor of Materials Science (since 1990), Head of the Department of Materials Science and Metallurgy, University of Cambridge, Pembroke Street, Cambridge CB2 3QZ, UK; (Home) 8 Diamond Close, Cambridge CB2 2AU, UK **Work Phone:** 0223 334457 **Home Phone:** 0223 65725 **Fax:** 0223 334437 **E-mail/Telex:** 81240 CAMSPL G **Date of Birth:** May 24, 1941 **Education:** B.Sc. Physics (1st Class, 1963), Imperial College, London; M.A. (1968), Oxford; Ph.D. (1968), Cambridge **Awards and Honors:** Medal of the Royal Society of Arts; Rosenhain Medal and Prize; Reginald Mitchell Memorial Lecture and Medal; D.K.C. MacDonald Memorial Lecturer (1988-1992) **Previous Positions:** Senior Research Fellow (1974-1985), Jesus College, Oxford; University Lecturer (1980-1985), Department of Metallurgy and Science of Materials, Oxford; Henry Bell Wortley Professor of Materials Engineering (1985-1989), University of Liverpool, UK; Overseas Appointments for Summer or Spring: Consultant, United States Steel Co., USA (1969)/Bell Lab., Murray Hill USA (1979)/Materials Research Lab., University of Illinois (1983); Visiting Professor, Arizona State University (1979)/University of Kuwait (1983)/Department of Metallurgy, University of Illinois (1984, 85, 86); Invited to present papers internationally in USA, Australia, Norway, Germany, Israel, Holland, Tunisia, France, Japan, China, Taiwan, Sweden, Denmark and Italy **Editorial Work:** Editorial Board Member: *Monographs on the Physics and Chemistry of Materials*; *Applied Physics Reviews*; *Journal of the Physics and Chemistry of Solids*; *Reports on Progress in Physics*; *Micron*; *Journal of Microscopy and Analysis* **Other Academic Experience:** Patent: Electron beam cutting of 20 Å holes and lines **Selected Memberships:** ; Member (1988-1992), Council of Science and Engineering Research Council; Vice-President, Institute of Materials; Professional Institutions: C.Eng., F.R.M.S., F.I.M., F.Inst.P. **Discipline:** Materials Science **Related Interests:** Biblical Chronology; Creation and Evolution **Current Research:** Ongoing work in the field: dating the Exodus, the date of Joseph, the date and nature of the Last Supper.

Selected Publications: Numerous scientific papers on materials science and electron microscopy.

_____, W. G. Waddington. "Dating the Crucifixion." *Nature* 306, 5945 (1983): 743-6.
_____, W. G. Waddington. "The Date of the Crucifixion." *Journal American Scientists* 37 (1985): 2-10.
_____. *Creation and Evolution*. Oxford University Press, 1985, Chinese translation, 1988.
_____, W. G. Waddington. "Astronomy and the Date of the Crucifixion." In *Chronos, Kairos, Christos, Festschrift to Jack Finegan*, ed. J. Vardaman and E. M. Yamauchi, 165-81. Eisenbrauns, 1989.
_____. "The Star of Bethleham - a Comet in 5 BC - and the Date of the Birth of Christ." *Quarterly Journal of the Royal Astronomical Society* 32 (1991): 389-407.
_____. "The Star of Bethleham - a Comet in 5 BC - and the Date of the Birth of Christ." *Tyndale Bulletin* 43, 1 (1992): 31-56.
_____, W. G. Waddington. "The Jewish Calendar, a Lunar Eclipse and the Date of Christ's Crucifixion." *Tyndale Bullatin* 43, 2 (1992): 331-51.

Hunt, Mary E.

Present Position and Address: Co-director, Women's Alliance for Theology, Ethics and Ritual, 8035 13th Street, Suites 1 & 3, Silver Spring, MD 20910, USA **Work Phone:** (301) 589-2509 **Home Phone:** (301) 589-1292 **Fax:** (301) 589-3150 **E-Mail:** mary.hunt@his.com **Date of Birth:** June 1, 1951 **Languages Spoken:** English, Spanish **Education:** B.A. (1972) Marquette University, Milwaukee, WI; M. Theological Studies (1974) Harvard Divinity School, Cambridge, MA; M. Div. (1979) Jesuit School of Theology, Berkeley, CA; Ph.D. (1980) Graduate Theological Union, Berkeley, CA **Awards and Honors:** Danforth Fellowship Competition; Who's Who in American Colleges and Universities; Ms. Magazine "Eighty Women to Watch in the Eighties"; Isaac Hecker Award; Women's Ordination Conference Prophetic Figure Award; Crossroad Women's Studies Prize **Previous Positions:** Library Assistant (1978-80), Graduate Theological Union Library, Berkeley, CA; Frontier Internship in Mission (1980-82), Buenos Aires, Argentina: Visiting Professor of Theology, ISEDET (ecumenical seminary); Co-director, Women's Project, Centro de Estudios Cristianos; Collaborator, Servicio Paz y Justicia; Visiting Assistant Professor of Religion (1986-87), Colgate University, Hamilton, NY **Editorial Work:** Board Member: *Journal of Feminist Studies in Religion*; *Continuum*; Women's Advisory Committee, *Concilium* **Selected Memberships:** Board of Directors: Institute for the Study of Christianity and Sexuality (London); Catholics for a Free Choice; American Academy of Religion; Phi Sigma Tau; Alpha Sigma Nu **Discipline:** Theology and Ethics **Related Interests:** Feminist theology; reproductive ethics **Current Research:** Feminist ethical methodologies to see how they can be applied to a range of issues such as reproductive choice, professional boundaries, etc..

Selected Publications: One book, edited one book, co-edited one book, written chapters in a dozen books, and published scores of articles.

_____, Rosino Gibellini, eds.. *La sfida del femminismo alla teologia* (The Challenge of Feminism to Theology). Brescia, Italy: Queriniana, 1980.
_____. "Abortion in a Just Society." *Conscience* 9, 4 (1988): 9-12.
_____. "Reproductive Ethics in a Technological Age." In *The Public Health Nurse Consultant Role and the Contemporary Health Care Delivery System*. Newark, DE: University of Delaware, College of Nursing, 1989.
_____. "Ethics on Ice: Soul-Chilling Dilemmas in New Reproductive Technologies." *Conscience* 10, 5 (Sept/Oct, 1989): 1-6, 23-24.
_____, Anne McGrew Bennett. *From Woman-Pain to Woman-Vision: Writings in Feminist Theology*, ed. Mary E. Hunt. Minneapolis: Fortress Press, 1989.
_____. *Fierce Tenderness: A Feminist Theology of Friendship*. New York: Crossroad, 1990.
_____. "Packaging Feminism for the Abortion Debate." *Conscience* 12, 4 (1991): 1, 3-9.

Huntemann, Georg

Present Position and Address: Professor of Theology and Philosophy, FETA Basel/Evangelisch-Theologische Fakultät Leuven, Barlachweg 21, 2800 Bremen 33, Germany **Date of Birth:** June 10, 1929 **Languages Spoken:** German, English, Dutch **Education:** Dr. phil. (1953), University of Erlangen; Dr. theol. (1957), University of Bern; Pastoral Examination and Ordination (1957), Bremische Evangelische Kirche. **Previous Positions:** Pastor in Bremen (1957-1986); Professor of FETA (since 1970), Basel; Professor of ETF (since 1985), Leuven Belgium **Discipline:** Theology; Ethics; Apologetics; Philosophy **Related Interests:** "I am a Reformed fundamentalist fighting against modernism in Theology and Society."

Selected Publications: 25 books listed in Bibliography. Most deal with theology and aspects of modern culture.

_____. *Provozierte Theologie in technischer Welt*. 1968.

Hutch, Richard A.

Present Position and Address: Reader (since 1991), Department of Studies in Religion, University of Queensland, Australia 4072 **Date of Birth:** September 11, 1945 **Education:** B.A. (1967), Gettysburg College; B.D. (1970), Yale University; M.A. Religion and Psychological Studies (1971)/Ph.D. Religion and Psychological Studies (1974), University of Chicago **Previous Positions:** Assistant Professor

(1974-78), Southern Illinois University, Carbondale, IL; Lecturer and Senior Lecturer (since 1978), Department of Studies in Religion, University of Queensland, Australia **Selected Memberships:** Society for the Scientific Study of Religion; Australian Association for the Study of Religions; American Academy of Religion **Discipline:** Religion and Psychological Studies; Biography **Related Interests:** Psychology/Psychiatry, Biography and Religion **Current Research:** Leadership in World Religions; Biographical Studies; Psychology of Religion.

Selected Publications: His bibliography lists some 59 publications.

_____. "A Psychological Consideration of Transcendence." In *Ways of Transcendence*, ed. E. Dowdy. Adelaide: Australian Association for the Study of Religions, 1981: 127-147.

_____. "An Essay on Psychotherapy and Religion." *Journal of Religion and Health* 22 (1983): 7-18.

_____. "An Approach to Consciousness Studies: Experiential Religion." *Australian Journal of Transpersonal Psychology* 4, 2 (July 1984): 177-201.

_____. "Lacan in a Nut(shell) House: Psychiatry and Religion Under One Roof." *Australian Religion Studies Review* 2, 2 (August 1989): 20-24.

_____. "Uncanny Experience in Psychoanalytical Perspective." In *Exploring the Paranormal: Different Perspectives on Belief and Experience*, eds. G. K. Zollschan, J. F. Schumaker and G. F. Walsh. London: Prism Press, 1989: 150-163.

_____. "Religious Leadership: Personality, History, and Sacred Authority." In *Toronto Studies in Religion Series*, Vol. 10, gen. ed. Donald Wiebe. New York: Peter Lang, Inc., 1990.

_____. "Biography as a Reliquary." *Soundings: An Interdisciplinary Journal* 76, 4 (Winter, 1993): 459-477.

Hyers, Conrad

Present Position and Address: Professor of Religion (since 1977), Gustavus Adolphus College, St. Peter, MN 56082, USA **Work Phone:** (507) 931-1062 **Date of Birth:** July 31, 1933 **Languages Spoken:** English, Japanese **Education:** B.A. (1954), Carson-Newman College; B.D. (1958), Eastern Theological Seminary; Th.M. (1959)/Ph.D. Mythologies of Creation and Fall (1965), Princeton Theological Seminary **Previous Positions:** Assistant and Associate Professor of Religion (1966-77), Beloit College; Associate through Full Professor of Religion (since 1977), Gustavus Adolphus College **Selected Memberships:** American Scientific Affiliation; American Academy of Religion **Discipline:** Comparative Religion; Philosophy of Religion **Related Interests:** Creation/Evolution; Mythologies of Creation/Origin.

Selected Publications:

_____. "Ambivalent Man and His Ambiguous Moon." *The Christian Century* (1969). On the ambiguity of scientific and technological advances.

_____. "Prometheus and the Problem of Progress." *Theology Today* (1980).

_____. "Comedy and Creation." *Theology Today* (1982).

_____. "Biblical Literalism: Constricting the Cosmic Dance." *The Christian Century* (1982).

_____. "Biblical Literalism and Creationism." Chapter in *Is God a Creationist?*, ed. Roland M. Frye. Scribners, 1983.

_____. *The Meaning of Creation: Genesis and Modern Science*. John Knox, 1984.

_____. "Genesis Knows Nothing of Scientific Creationism." *Creation/Evolution Journal* 17 (1984).

_____. "Dinosaur Religion: Interpreting and Misinterpreting the Creation Accounts." *Journal of the American Scientific Affiliation* (1984).

_____. "Cosmogony, Yes; Science, No: The Narrative Form of Genesis 1." *Journal of the American Scientific Affiliation* (1984).

_____. The Fall and Rise of Creationism." *The Christian Century* (1985).

I

Ice, Jackson Lee

Present Position and Address: Professor (since 1974), Department of Religion, Florida State University Tallahassee, FL 32306-1029, USA **Education:** A.B. (1945), University of Pittsburgh; M.Div. (1948), Colgate-Rochester Divinity School; Ph.D. (1955), Harvard University **Previous Positions:** Lecturer (1953-54), Tufts College, Medford, MA; Assistant (1955-63)/Associate (1963-74), Florida State University **Selected Memberships:** American Philosophical Association; Society for Philosophy of Religion; Southern Association for Philosophy and Psychology; American Academy of Religion **Discipline:** Religion - Philosophy of Religion; Religion and Science; Religion and the Arts; Contemporary Religious Thought **Related Interests:** Philosophy - Ethics; Aesthetics; Existential Phenomenology.

Selected Publications: His bibliography lists 3 books and 17 articles.

_____. "The Ecological Crisis: Radical Monotheism versus Ethical Pantheism." *Religion in Life* 44, 2 (Spring 1975): 203-211.
_____. "The Impact of Schweitzer's Radical Christianity." *Uniquest* Berkeley, CA: 1975.

Ice, Rodney D.

Present Position and Address: Principal Research Scientist, Manager, Office of Radiation Safety, Georgia Institute of Technology, 78 Beverly Road, Atlanta, GA 30309, USA **Work Phone:** (404) 894-3621 **Home Phone:** (404) 876-5897 **Date of Birth:** April 24, 1937 **Languages Spoken:** English **Awards and Honors:** Purdue Old Master **Previous Positions:** Assistant through Associate Professor, Temple University; Associate through Professor, University of Michigan; Dean/Professor, University of Oklahoma; Vice President for Research, Eagle - Picher Industries **Other Academic Experience:** Board Certified Health Physicist; Registered Pharmacist **Selected Memberships:** American Association for the Advancement of Science; Society of Nuclear Medicine; Health Physics Society; American Nuclear Society; American Pharmaceutical Association; American Scientific Affiliation **Discipline:** Health Physics **Related Areas of Interest:** Radiopharmaceutical Design; Development and Dosimetry; Radioprotectants; Boron Neutron Capture Therapy **Current Areas of Research:** Mixed Field Radiation Dosimetry Radioprotectants; Boron Neutron Capture Therapy; Radiopharmaceuticals.

Selected Publications: His total bibliography contains 10 book chapters, 1 book edited, 82 published articles, 120 published abstracts of presentations.

_____, G. R. Basmadjian, K. R. Hetzel and W.H. Beierwaltes. "Synthesis of a New Adrenal Scanning Agent." *Journal of Labeled Compounds* 11 (1975): 427-34.
_____, C. E. Hotte and G. L. Flynn. "Radiolysis of Iodohipporan." *Journal of Labeled Compounds and Radiopharmaceuticals* 17 (1980): 715-25.
_____, P. G. Grussing, et al. "Development of Pharmacy's First Specialty Certification Examination." *American Journal of Pharmaceutical Education* 47 (1983): 11-18.

Ingram, David J. E.

Present Position and Address: Retired Vice-Chancellor (since 1994), University of Kent at Canterbury, The Registry, The University, Canterbury, Kent CT2 7NZ, UK; (Home), Cordwainers Cottage, Maundown, Wireziscombe, Somerset TA4 2BU, UK **Date of Birth:** April 6, 1927 **Education:** 1st Class Honours in Physics (1948)/M.A. and D.Phil. (1951), Oxford University **Postgraduate Studies:** Fellowship at Kings College, London and Roehampton Institute of Higher Education **Honorary Degrees:** Hon.D.Sc. (Clermond-Ferrand) Keele; Hon.D.Sc., Kent **Previous Positions:** Lecturer/Reader (1952-59), Department of Electronics, University of Southampton; Professor of Physics/Head of Department (1959-73) and Deputy Vice-Chancellor (1964, 68-71), University of Keele; Principal (1973-80), Chelsea College, University of London; Vice-Chancellor (1980-94), University of Kent, Canterbury, Kent, UK **Selected Memberships:** Member of governing body, Society for Promoting Christian Knowledge; Vice President, Universities and Colleges Christian Fellowship; Member, Higher Education Foundation **Discipline:** Physics (including research in Microwave Physics) **Related Interests:** Teaching of science to non-scientists; The interaction of science and religion.

Selected Publications: His bibliography lists 5 books in the fields of Radio and Microwave Spectroscopy, Radiation and Quantum Physics, and Electron Spin Resonance and its applications. Over 100 scientific articles have been published.

_____. Contribution to *Christianity in a Mechanistic Universe*, ed. D. MacKay. InterVarsity Press.

Ingram, Larry C.

Present Position and Address: Professor (since 1980), Department of Sociology and Anthropology, University of Tennessee - Martin, TN 38238, USA; (Home) 115 Ramer Street, Martin, TN 38237, USA **Work Phone:** (901) 587-7515 **Home Phone:** (901) 587-4066 **Date of Birth:** October 24, 1941 **Education:** B.A. Sociology (with honors 1965), Texas Wesleyan College; M.A. Sociology (1966), Texas Christian University; Ph.D. Sociology (1971), University of Tennessee **Previous Positions:** Instructor (1966-67), Lamar University; Instructor (1967-68/68-70), University of Tennessee - Knoxville; Adjunct Associate Professor through Professor (1973-86), Memphis State University; Assistant through Full Professor (1971-present), University of Tennessee at Martin **Selected Memberships:** American Sociological Association; Society for the Scientific Study of Religion; Religious Research Association; Association for the Sociology of Religion; Christian Sociological Society; Southern Sociological Society **Discipline:** Sociology **Related Interests:** Sociology of Religion/Religion and Society; Social and Formal Organization; Sociological Theory; Self and Society.

Selected Publications:

_____. "Teaching the Sociology of Religion: The Student's Religious Autobiography." *Teaching Sociology* 6 (January 1979): 161-172.

_____. "Sectarian Colleges and Academic Freedom." *Review of Religious Research* 27 (June 1986): 300-314.

_____. "Evangelism as Frame Intrusion: Observations on Witnessing in Public Places." *Journal for Scientific Study of Religion* 28 (March 1989): 17-26.

_____, Ann Carol King. "Organizational Mission as Source of Vulnerability: Comparing Attitudes of Trustees and Professors in Southern Baptist Colleges." *Review of Religious Research* Forthcoming.

_____. "Fundamentalism on Campus: A Frame Analysis of Protest Over a Classroom Showing of "The Last Temptation of Christ." *Case Analysis* 3, 1 (1992): 11-28.

Isaak, Paul John

Present Position and Address: Chairperson (since 1987), Usakos Circuit; Secretary (since 1987), Paulinum Faculty, Paulinum Seminary; Permanent Appointment at the University of Namibia; (Home) P.O. Box 60618, Katutura, Windhoek, Namibia **Concurrent Positions:** Lecturer in Systematic Theology and Ethics, Paulinum Lutheran Seminary, Otjimbingue, Namibia (1979-91) **Work Phone:** (061) 307-2180 **Home Phone:** (061) 213110 **Fax:** (061) 307-2444 **Date of Birth:** September 30, 1947 **Education:** Diploma in Theology (1972), Paulinum Seminary, Namibia; Master in Theology (1978), Pacific Lutheran Theological Seminary; Master in Theology (1985)/Th.D. (1987), Lutheran School of Theology at Chicago **Awards and Honors:** Scholarship from Lutheran World Federation, 1975, 1983, 1985 **Previous Positions:** Pastor of Bethanien Lutheran Church in Bethanien, Namibia (1972-75); Vice Principal of Paulinum Seminary, (1979-81); Principal of Paulinum Seminary, (1981-83); Dean of the Western Region of the Evangelical Lutheran Church in the Republic of Namibia (1980-83); Chairperson of the Synod of the ELCRN (1991); Lecturer in Systematic Theology and Ethics, (1990-91); Lecturer of Religious Studies and Morality and Biblical Studies at the University of Namibia (1992) **Administrative Experience:** Chair; National Theological Committee of ELCRN and National Committee on Mission in Cities of the ELCRN; Secretary; National Stewardship Committee of the ELCRN, African Association for Liturgy, Arts, and Music **Selected Memberships:** SWAPO, Joint Board of Theology in Southern Africa; Lutheran World Federation: Theological Education in Africa, National Scholarship Committee of the ELCRN, Curriculum Panel for Religious and Moral Education - Ministry of Education and Culture General Meeting of the CCN, and Non-Formal Education Committee of the CCN. **Discipline:** Systematic Theology **Related Interests:** Black Theology; Liberation Theology; Church, Development and Science.

Selected Publications:

_____. "Anthropology and Ethics in The Theology of Karl Barth: An African Lutheran Perspective." Th.D. Dissertation (Lutheran School of Theology at Chicago, 1987).
_____. *Religious and Moral Education.* Winhoek: UNAM Press, 1991.
_____. "Church and Development in the context of Reconciliation and Nation Building: The Namibian Experience." In *Church and Development: an Interdisciplinary Approach*, ed. R. Koelenberg. Institute for Theological and Interdisciplinary Research of the Ecumenical Foundation of Southern Africa, 1992.
_____. *Religion and Morality.* Windhoek: UNAM Press, 1993.

Isak, Rainer

Present Position and Address: Studienleiter (Dr. Theology, since 1990), Katholische Akademie der Erzdiözese Freiburg, Alfred Holler Weg 8, D-79540 Lörrach, Germany **Date of Birth:** May 25, 1958 **Languages Spoken:** German, English **Education:** Study of Theology (Roman Catholic), Philosophy and Biology (1979-85), Albert-Ludwigs-Universität, Freiburg **Previous Positions:** Science Assistant, Institut für systematische Theologie, Arbeitsbereich Dogmatik der Universität Freiburg **Selected Memberships:** AGEMUS e.v. (Arbeitsgemeinschaften Evolution, Menschheitszukunft und Sinnfragen) Kreuzkopfsteige 1a, 79100 Freiburg **Discipline:** Theology; Philosophy; Biology **Related Interests:** Biology and Theology in dialogue (Is there an aim in evolution?).

Selected Publications:

_____. "Zufall oder Plan? Der Mensch im Licht der Evolution." *Religion heute* (1987): 223-7.
_____. "Gespräch zwischen Naturwissenschaft und Theologie." *Freiburger Forum* (June 1, 1988).
_____. *Evolution ohne Ziel? Ein interdisziplinärer Forschungsbeitrag.* Freiburg I. Br. 1992.
_____, editor. *Wir und die Fremden: Entstehung und Abbau von Ängsten.* Freiburg I. Br. Verlag der Katholischen Akademie, 1993.
_____, editor. *Sicherheit: Ein mißbrauchtes Bedürfnis.* Freiburg I. Br. Verlag der Katholischen Akademie, 1994.

_____, editor. *Gottes Handeln in der Welt: Woran Naturwissenschaftler glauben, nicht glauben können*. Freiburg I. Br. Verlag der Katholischen Akademie, 1995.

Isham, Christopher J.

Present Position and Address: Professor of Theoretical Physics (since 1982), Blackett Laboratory, Imperial College, South Kensington, London SW7 2BZ, UK **Date of Birth:** April 28, 1944 **Education:** B.Sc. Physics Hons. (1966)/Ph.D. Theoretical Physics (1969), University of London **Previous Positions:** Lecturer in Theoretical Physics (1969-73); Reader in Applied Mathematics (1973-76), King's College, London; Reader in Theoretical Physics (1976-82), Imperial College **Selected Memberships:** Chairman, Science and Religion Forum; Member, Guild of Pastoral Psychology **Discipline:** Theoretical Physics **Related Interests:** Quantum Gravity and the Early Universe; Philosophical Aspects of Modern Theoretical Physics; Work of C. G. Jung.

Selected Publications: Almost all publications are in the professional field of theoretical physics.

_____. "Creation of the Universe as a Quantum Tunnelling Process." In *Physics, Philosophy, and Theology: A Common Quest for Understanding*, eds. Robert J. Russell, William R. Stoeger, and George V. Coyne. Vatican City State: Vatican Observatory, 1988; Notre Dame, IN: University of Notre Dame Press, 1989.

J

Jackson, Wes

Present Position and Address: Codirector (since 1976), The Land Institute, 2440 E. Water Well Road, Salina, KS 67401, USA **Work Phone:** (913) 823-8967 **Date of Birth:** June 15, 1936 **Education:** B.A. Biology (1958), Kansas Wesleyan University; M.A. Botany (1960), University of Kansas; Ph.D. Genetics (1967), North Carolina State University; NASA Fellow (1964-67) **Previous Positions:** High School Biology Teacher (1960-62); Instructor and Assistant Professor of Biology (1967-71)/Professor (1973-76), California State University - Sacramento **Selected Memberships:** Audubon Society; American Association for the Advancement of Science; Ecological Society of America; American Institute of Biological Sciences **Discipline:** Biology; Genetics **Related Interests:** Environmental Ethics; Ecology - Use of the Land and Stewardship.

Selected Publications:

_____. *Man and the Environment*. (An anthology). First edition published in 1971 was first environmental reader. This book has been adopted in more than 500 Colleges and Universities, 1979.
_____, W. Berry and B. Colman, eds. *Meeting the Expectations of the Land*. North Point Press, January 1985.
_____. *New Roots for Agriculture*. 2d ed. University of Nebraska Press, 1985.
_____. *Altars of Unhewn Stone*. North Point Press, 1987.

Jain, Devaki

Present Position and Address: Director (since 1975), Institute of Social Studies Trust, S.M.M. Theatre Crafts Museum 5, Deen Dayal Upadhyay Marg, New Delhi - 110002, India; "Tharanga", 10th Cross, Rajmahal Vilas Extension, Bangalore - 560080, India **Date of Birth:** June 11, 1933 **Languages Spoken:** English, Hindi, Tamil and Kannada **Education:** B.A. Mathematics/Economics/English Literature (1953), Mysore University; Diploma in Social Science (1955-56), Ruskin College, Oxford; B.A. Hons PPE (1962), Oxford; Harvard International Seminar (Summer 1958) **Previous Positions:** Research Assistant (1956); Research Associate (1957-59), Indian Co-operative Union; Lecturer in Economics (1963-69), University of Delhi; Completed the volume on Indian Women for the Publications Division, Government of India - released by India as its book for Women's Year (1974) **Discipline:** Social Sciences with special stress on Women's Issues **Related Interests:** Faith and Women; Ethics and Society; Economic development of developing countries; Women and identity.

Selected Publications: Most of her work deals with development, social issues and women.

_____, ed. *Indian Women*. New Delhi: Publications Division, Government of India, Patiala House, Tilak Marg, New Delhi 110 001, 1974.
_____. *Women's Quest for Power: Five Indian Case Studies*. New Delhi: Vikas Publication, 1980.
_____, N. Banerjee. *Tyranny of the Household*. New Delhi: Vikas Publication, 1985.
_____. *Speaking of Faith*. New Delhi: Kali for Women, N-84, Panchsila Park, New Delhi, 1986.

_____. "Healing the Wounds of Development." Curriculum requirements paper presented at the Conference on World-wide Education for Women: Progress, Prospects and Agenda for the Future in South Hadley (November 1987).
_____. "Alliances and Ethics: in Retrospect." Paper presented at Inter Action Forum: New Beginnings, New Approaches: North - South Partnership, Philadelphia (1988).

Jaki, Stanley L.

Present Position and Address: Benedictine Priest; Distinguished University Professor, History and Philosophy of Physics, Seton Hall University, South Orange, NJ 07079, USA PO Box 167, Princeton, NJ 08542, USA **Work Phone:** (609) 896-3979 **Languages Spoken:** Hungarian, English, French, Italian, German **Education:** Doctorate in Systematic Theology (1950), Pontifical Athenaeum of Sant' Anselmo in Rome; Doctorate in Nuclear Physics (Terrestrial Radioactivity, 1957), Fordham University **Postgraduate Studies:** Postdoctoral studies in History and Philosophy of Science (1960-62), Princeton University **Selected Conferences and Congresses:** Invited lecturer at 22 conferences worldwide, including "Conference on Science and Religion" (Star Island, 1968); "International Conference on Cosmology, History of Science, and Theology" (University of Denver, 1974); International Congress on Business and Ethics: (Nijenrode, Netherlands, 1979); "Science and Islamic Polity" (Islamabad, Pakistan, 1983); Environmental Crises" (Vatican City, 1990); Physics and Religion: (University of Madrid, 1990) **Selected Lectures:** Lectures world-wide at over 50 USA Universities and over 20 overseas; Invited Lecturer at "Man and His Environment," a symposium sponsored by the Pontifical Academy of Science (May 1990); Invited Lecturer at the International Symposium, "The Inspiration of Astronomical Phenomena." Castelgandolfo, Italy **Awards and Honors:** Lecomte du Nouy Prize (1970); Templeton Prize for Progress in Religion (1987) **Previous Positions:** Lecturer in Theology (1951-1954), St. Vincent's Archabbey and Major Seminary, Latrobe, PA; Gifford lecturer (1974-1976), Edinburgh University; Professor (since 1968), Seton Hall University **Selected Memberships:** Sigma Xi; History of Science Society; Olbers Gesellschaft, Bremen; Hellenic Society for Humanistic Studies, Athens; Académie Nationale des Sciences, Belles-Lettres et Arts de Bordeaux; Pontifical Academy of Sciences, Vatican **Related Interests:** Priest; Theology; History and Philosophy of Physics **Current Research:** Origin of Science and Theology; Cosmological Argument; Scientific Methodology.

Selected Publications: His bibliography lists over 25 relevant publications. Also listed are translations into English of cosmological works of Giordano Bruno, J. H. Lambert, and I. Kant.

_____. *The Road of Science and the Ways to God, The Gifford Lectures, University of Edinburgh, 1974-75 and 1975-76.* University of Chicago Press, Scottish Academic Press, 1978 and 1981. Also in Italian translation.
_____. *The Origin of Science and the Science of Its Origin, Fremantle Lectures, Balliol College, Oxford, 1977.* Scottish Academic Press; Regnery Gateway, 1978.
_____. *Cosmos and Creator. Scottish Academic Press, 1979; Regnery Gateway, 1980.*
_____. *Angels, Apes and Men.* Sherwood Sugden, 1982.
_____. *The Savior of Science.* Wethersfield Institute Lectures, New York, 1987. Scottish Academic Press; Regnery Gateway, 1988.
_____. *God and the Cosmologists,* Farmington Institute Lectures, Oxford, 1988. Scottish Academic Press; Regnery Gateway, 1989.
_____. The Purpose of It All. Farmington Institute Lectures, Oxford, 1990. Scottish Academic Press, Regnery Gateway, 1991.
_____. *Genesis 1 Through the Ages.* Wethersfield Institute Lectures, New York, 1992. Wethersfield Institute, 1992.
_____. *Universe and Creed.* Père Marquette Lecture, 1992. Marquette University: Marquette University Press, 1992.
_____. *Is There a Universe?* Forwood Lectures, Liverpool University, 1992. Wethersfield Institute: Liverpool University Press, 1993.

Jasso, Guillermina

Present Position and Address: Professor of Sociology, Department of Sociology, New York University, 269 Mercer Street, 4th floor, New York, NY 10003-6687, USA **Work Phone:** (212) 998-8368 **Fax Number:** (212) 995-4140 **E-Mail:** jasso@acfcluster.nyu.edu **Date of Birth:** July 22, 1942 **Languages Spoken:** English; Spanish **Education:** Ph.D. Social Relations (1974), Johns Hopkins University **Awards and Honors:** Distinguished Alumni Lecture (1987), University of Notre Dame; Johns Hopkins Society of Scholars (1994), Johns Hopkins University **Previous Positions:** Assistant Professor (1974-77). Barnard and Columbia; Special Assistant to the Commissioner (1977-79), U.S. Immigration Service; Director of Research (1979-80), U.S. Select Commission on Immigration Policy; Assistant Professor (1980-82), University of Michigan; Associate through Full Professor (1982-87), University of Minnesota; Professor (1987-91), University of Iowa **Selected Memberships:** American Sociological Association; American Statistical Association; Econometrics Society; Population Association of America **Discipline:** Sociology **Related Areas of Interest:** Mathematical Theory of Human Behavior; Insights About Human Behavior in the Writings of Saints and of Moral Theologians **Current Areas of Research:** Constructing a Justice Index with Links to Inequality and Democracy; Writing a book on Comparison Theory, with Predictions for a Wide Range of Behavioral and Social Phenomena.

Selected Publications: His bibliography contains 1 book, 40 articles and 9 book reviews.

_____. "On the Justice of Earnings: A New Specification of the Justice Evaluation Function." *American Journal of Sociology* 83 (1978): 1398-1419.
_____. "A New Theory of Distributive Justice." *American Sociological Review* 45 (1980): 3-32.
_____. "Choosing a Good: Models Based on the Theory of the Distributive- Justice Force." *Advances in Group Processes: Theory and Research* 4 (1987): 67-108.
_____. "Principles of Theoretical Analysis." *Sociological Theory* 6 (1988): 1-20.
_____. "Self-Interest, Distributive Justice, and the Income Distribution: A Theoretical Fragment Based on St. Anselm's Postulate." *Social Justice Research* 3 (1989): 251-76.
_____. "Cloister and Society: Analyzing the Public Benefit of Monastic and Mendicant Institutions." *Journal of Mathematical Sociology* 16 (1991): 109-36.
_____. "Analyzing Conflict Severity: Predictions of Distributive-Justice Theory for the Two-Subgroup Case." *Social Justice Research* 6 (1993): 357-82.
_____. "Building the Theory of Comparison Processes: Construction of Postulates and Derivation of Predictions." In *Theoretical Research Programs: Studies in the Growth of Theory*, ed. J. Berger and M. Zelditch, Jr., 212-64. Stanford, CA: Stanford University Press, 1993.
_____. "Choice and Emotion in Comparison Theory." *Rationality and Society* 5 (1993): 231-74.
_____. "Using Abell's Narrative Method to Build a Theory: The Case of the Theory of Distributive Justice and Its Generalization to the Theory of Comparison Processes." *Journal of Mathematical Sociology* 18 (1993): 219-51.

Jeeves, Malcolm A.

Present Position and Address: Professor of Psychology (since 1969)/Honorary Research Professor (since 1993), University of St. Andrews, Psychological Laboratory, St. Andrews, Fife, Scotland KY1 6 9JU **Date of Birth:** November 16, 1926 **Education:** B.A. (1951)/M.A. (1954)/Ph.D. (1957), Cambridge University **Honorary Degrees:** Honorary Doctor of Science (1993), Edinburgh University **Awards and Honors:** Gregg Bury Prize, Philosophy of Religion, University of Cambridge; Kenneth Craik Award, Research in Physiological Psychology, University of Cambridge; Hon.D.Sc., Edinburgh University; National Honors: Commander to the British Empire (C.B.E.)(1992), services to Psychology **Previous Positions:** Research (1951-56), University of Cambridge; Fellow (1953-54), Harvard; Lecturer in Psychology (1956-59), University of Leeds; Professor/Head of Department of Psychology (1959-69), University of Adelaide, Australia; Vice Principal (1981-85), University of St. Andrews **Selected Memberships:** Fellow, Royal Society of Edinburgh; Fellow, British Psychological

Society; Member, Christians in Sci Neuropsychology **Discipline:** General relationship between Science and Christian Faith with a special interest in the relationship between Psychology and Christian Belief.

Selected Publications:

_____. *Where Science and Faith Meet*. UK: InterVarsity Press, 1952.
_____. *The Scientific Enterprise and Christian Faith*. UK: Tyndale Press, 1968.
_____. *Psychology and Christianity - The View Both Ways*. UK: InterVarsity Press, 1976.
_____, R. J. Berry and D. Atkinson. *Free to be Different*. Marshall, 1984.
_____, D. Myers. *Psychology through the Eyes of Faith*. Harper & Row, 1987.
_____. *Mind Fields: Reflections on the Science of Mind and Brain*. Aust. Lancu/UK: Apolles/USA: Baker, 1994.

Jenkins, Eric Neil

Present Position and Address: The Reverend Canon Emeritus, Jenkins 51 Oulton Road, Childwall, Liverpool L16 8NP, UK **Work Phone:** (051) 929-2469 **Date of Birth:** January 24, 1923 **Education:** B.Sc. (1943)/M.Sc. Chemistry (1947), University of Wales; General Ordination Examination (1962), Wycliffe Hall, Oxford **Selected Lectures:** Occasional lecturer for WEA/University Extension on Science and Ethics, Nuclear power/weapons **Previous Positions:** Research Fellow (1946-47)/Assistant Lecturer (1947-50), University of Wales; Research in Chemistry, UK Atomic Energy Authority (1950-60)/Harwell Analytical/Radiochemistry/Wycliffe Hall (1960-62), Oxford; Parish Priest of Church of England (1962-73); Science Advisor to Diocese of Liverpool (1973-88); Hon. Canon of Liverpool Cathedral (1980-88); World Council of Churches - Church and Society (1977-87); Medical Ethicist (1983-89), Merseyside Hospitals Board Committee **Selected Memberships:** Science and Religion Forum; Victoria Institute, London; Society of Ordained Scientists **Discipline:** Chemistry - Analytical and Radio; Pastoral Theology and Ethics **Related Interests:** Faith and Science; Science and Religion in the Parish. Concern is to develop "spirituality" relevant to the "received science story."

Selected Publications:

_____. "Fruit of the Atom." *Third Way Magazine* (London, 1977): 13-15.
_____. "Faith, Science and the Future." *Third Way Magazine* (London, 1979): 14-16.
_____. *Radioactivity: A Science in its Historical and Social Context*. London: Wykeham Publications, 1979.
_____. "Encounters in Faith and Science." *Crucible Magazine* (London, 1980): 110-115.
_____. "Science and Religion in the Parishes." *Church Times* (London, 15 February 1985).
_____. *Twisting the Dragon's Tail: Radioactivity, 1896-1996*. London: Reed Reference Books, 1995.

Jervis, R. E.

Present Position and Address: Professor of Applied Chemistry, Chemical Engineering Department, University of Toronto, Toronto M5S 1A4, Canada **Date of Birth:** May 21, 1927 **Languages Spoken:** English, some Japanese, and French **Education:** B.A. Physics and Chemistry (1949)/M.A. Physical Chemistry (1950)/Ph.D. Physical Chemistry (1952), University of Toronto **Selected Congresses and Conferences:** Co-organizer of major Canadian Conference on Ethical issues in Nuclear energy, environment and bio-engineering called "Shaping the Future" held at Chalk River, Ontario Nuclear Research Center (1977) **Previous Positions:** Associate Research Officer (1952-58), Chalk River Nuclear Laboratories, Atomic Energy of Canada; Assistant through Full Professor (since 1958), University of Toronto; Visiting Professor of Radio Chemistry, Universities of Tokyo (1965-66)/Cambridge (1978)/National University Malaysia (1979); Associate Dean (Research and Advanced Studies), Faculty Applied Science and Engineering (1974-78)/Chairman of Research (1981-85), University of Toronto **Selected Memberships:** Canadian Scientific and Christian Affiliation; Inter-Varsity Christian

Fellowship/Faculty Christian Fellowship; Fellow, Royal Society of Canada; Chemical Society for Canada **Discipline:** Nuclear and Radio Chemistry. Nuclear methods of Trace Analysis applied to Chemical, Biomedical, environmental and energy-producing systems **Related Interests:** Moral and ethical issues of nuclear energy.

Selected Publications:

_____. "Can Truth be Rightly Sub-divided? - The Dangers of Specialization." *IVCF Graduate Journal, Crux* 5, 1 (1967): 21-26.
_____. "Moral and Ethical Issues of Nuclear Energy." Paper presented to South Ontario Chapter of Canadian Christian and Scientific Affiliation (1987).

Johnson, Delmer A.

Present Position and Address: Pastor (since 1981), Rocky Mountain Conference of Seventh-day Adventists, 512 Cantril #12, Castle Rock, CO 80104, USA **Date of Birth:** August 3, 1955 **Education:** B.A. (1978), Union College; M.Div. (1982), SDA Theological Seminary, Andrews University MI **Previous Positions:** Associate Pastor (1981), Denver First; Pastor (1981-84), Evanston and Afron, Wyoming **Selected Memberships:** Chapter President, Denver Association of Adventist Forums; President, Evanston Ministerial Association **Discipline:** Theology **Related Interests:** Eschatology; Physics; Artificial Intelligence; Geology; Psychology.

Selected Publications:

_____. "By the Campfire: Red Giants, White Dwarfs, Black Holes - And God. " *Spectrum* 20, 1 (October 1989): 29-39.

Johnson, Doyle Paul

Present Position and Address: Professor and Chairperson (since 1990) Department of Sociology, Texas Technical University, Lubbock, TX 79409, USA **Work Phone:** (806) 742-2400 **Date of Birth:** March 12, 1941 **Education:** B.A. (1965)/M.A. (1967)/Ph.D. Sociology (1969), University of Illinois **Previous Positions:** Research Assistant (1966)/Associate (1967-69), University of Illinois; Adjunct Assistant Professor (Sociology of Religion Seminar), New College, Sarasota, FL; Graduate Program Coordinator for University of South Florida's M.A. program (1973-76/81-85); Assistant (1969-77)/Associate Professor (1977-90), Department of Sociology, University of South Florida **Editorial Work:** Associate (1980-90)/Editor (since 1990), *Review of Religious Research*; Manuscript reviewer for *Journal for the Scientific Study of Religion* **Other Academic Experience:** Chairperson for session on "Religion as a Social Problem: Jonestown and the Cults," Association for the Sociology of Religion/Society for the Scientific Study of Social Problems (Boston, August 24-27, 1979); Chairperson and discussant for session on "Mechanisms of Power," Society for the Scientific Study of Religion annual meeting in Baltimore, MD (October 30, 1981) **Selected Memberships:** American Sociological Association; Religious Research Association; Society for the Scientific Study of Religion; Association for the Sociology of Religion **Discipline:** Sociology **Related Interests:** Religion in Society.

Selected Publications: His bibliography lists 4 books, and 33 journal articles and reports.

_____. "Religious Commitment, Social Distance and Authoritarianism." *Review of Religious Research* 18, 2 (Winter 1977): 99-113.
_____. "Dilemmas of Charismatic Leadership: The Case of the People's Temple." *Sociological Analysis* 40, 4 (1979): 315-323.

_____. "The Brain-Mind Relation, Religious Evolution, and Forms of Consciousness." *Sociological Analysis* 49, 1 (1988): 52-65.
_____. "Subjective and Social Dimensions of Religiosity and Loneliness among the Well Elderly." *Review of Religious Research* 31, 1 (1989): 3-15.

Johnson, Rodney W.

Present Position and Address: Director of Civil Space Programs (since 1986), SRS Technologies, Washington Operations, 1500 Wilson Blvd., Suite 800, P.O. Box 12707, Arlington, VA 22209-2415; (Home) 5701 Mossrock Drive, Rockville, MD 20852, USA **Work Phone:** (703) 522-5588 **Date of Birth:** October 4, 1925 **Languages Spoken:** English and German **Education:** B.S. (1950)/M.S. (1954), Civil Engineering, University of Minnesota; Ph.D. Geophysics/Engineering Science (1962), Purdue University **Awards and Honors:** NASA Achievement Award (1985); Who's Who in Government (1977, 1979) **Previous Positions:** Director of Advanced Studies (1966-79), OSTS/Headquarters, NASA; Senior System Engineer (1980), General Dynamics, NASA; Senior Project Manager (1980-83), General Electric; Deputy Division Manager of Space Technology Division (1983-86), ANSER **Discipline:** Space Technology; Space Systems **Related Interests:** Space Exploration; Origin of Life; Christian Ethics.

Selected Publications: His bibliography lists more than 24 publications mainly in the field of space exploration.

_____. "Science and Religion in Space Exploration." *Journal of the American Scientific Affiliation* (June 1967).
_____. "Space Exploration." In *Our Society in Turmoil*, ed. G. Collin. (1970): 233-252.
_____. "The Pots and the Bowls." Unpublished paper, 1980. Follow-up to the author's three articles in *Voice Magazine* (February 1963; July-August 1964; and June 1967) discussing the spiritual and theological implications of space exploration.

Johnson, Walter Colin

Present Position and Address: Private Practice in Psychiatry (since 1962), Courtesy Visiting Staff (since 1970), Bournewood Hospital, 300 South Street, Brookline, MA 02167, USA; 132 Pine Street, Hanover, MA 02339, USA **Date of Birth:** October 1, 1921 **Education:** M.B.B.S. (Medical Degree, 1944), University of London; Massachusetts/Connecticut license (medicine, 1959) **Selected Memberships:** American Scientific Affiliation; American Psychiatric Association; Massachusetts Medical Society **Discipline:** Psychiatry **Related Interests:** Bible; Comparative religion; Relationship of Science to Bible; Nature of man - mind/body problem; apologetics.

Selected Publications:

_____. "Only a Machine or Also A Living Soul?" *Journal of the American Scientific Affiliation (JASA)* (December 1970).
_____. "Depression: Biochemical Abnormality or Spiritual Backsliding?" *JASA* (March 1980).
_____. "Demon Possession and Mental Illness." *JASA* (September 1982).

Jones, D. Gareth

Present Position and Address: Chairman and Professor of Anatomy and Structural Biology (since 1983) Department of Anatomy and Structural Biology, University of Otago, P.O. Box 913, Dunedin, New Zealand **Date of Birth:** August 28, 1940 **Education:** B.Sc. Hons. in Anatomy (1961), University College, London; M.B.B.S. (1965), University College Hospital Medical School of London; D.Sc. (1977), University of Western Australia **Previous Positions:** Lecturer (1965-70), Department of

Anatomy, University College of London; Senior Lecturer (1970-76)/Associate Professor (1977-83), Department of Anatomy, University of Western Australia **Selected Memberships:** Fellow (1985)/Member, American Scientific Affiliation; Fellow (1987)/Member, Institute of Biology; Christians in Science, UK; Hastings Center; Institute of Medical Ethics; World Literary Academy; Institute on Religion in an Age of Science **Discipline:** Anatomy; Medical Ethics **Related Interests:** Biomedical Ethics; Brain and Human Responsibility; Creation and Evolution.

Selected Publications: His bibliography lists 9 books, 15 chapters in books, and 59 articles in the area of biomedical ethics. Two books, 3 chapters in books, and 7 articles in the field of evolution.

_____. *Issues in Biomedical Ethics*. Zadok Institute Reading Guide. Canberra, 1989.
_____. "Brain, Birth, and Personal Identity." *Journal of Medical Ethics* 15 (1989): 173-178.
_____. "Fetal Neural Transplantation: Placing the Ethical Debate within the Context of Society's use of Human Material." *Bioethics* 5 (1991): 23-43.
_____. "Non-existence and its Relevance for Medical Ethics and Genetic Technology." *Perspectives on Science and Christian Faith* 43 (1991): 75-81.
_____. "Fetal Neural Transplantation: Placing the Ethical Debate within the Context of Society's use of Human Material." *Bioethics* 5 (1991): 23-43.
_____. "The Human Embryo: From Oblivion to Meaningful Life." *Science and Christian Belief* 6 (1994): 3-19.
_____. "Gene Therapy: A Glimpse into the Future." *Faith and Freedom* 3, 1 (1994): 4-8.
_____. "Manipulating Human Life: The Ambiguous Interface between Science and Theology." *Colloquium* 26 (1994): 17-31.
_____. *Coping with Controversy*. Dunedin: Vision Publication, 1994.
_____, B. Telfer. "Before I was an Embryo, I was a Pre-embryo: or was I?" *Bioethics* 9 (1995): 32-49.

Jones, James W.

Present Position and Address: Licensed Clinical Psychologist; Professor (since 1990), Department of Religion, Faculty of Arts and Sciences, Rutgers University, P.O. Box 270, New Brunswick, NJ 08903-0270 **Work Phone:** (201) 932-9641 **Date of Birth:** January 23, 1943 **Education:** B.A. (1964), Earlham College, Richmond, IN; M.Div. (1967), Episcopal Theological School, Cambridge, MA; Ph.D. Religious Studies (1970), Brown University, Providence, RI; Certificate in Family Therapy (1979), Department of Psychiatry, University of Pennsylvania **Previous Positions:** Instructor (1968-69), Department of Religious Studies, Brown University RI; Instructor (1970-71), Department of Religion, Macalester College, St. Paul, MN; Assistant (1971-75)/Associate Professor (1975-90), Department of Religion, Rutgers College, Rutgers University **Selected Memberships:** American Academy of Religion (Member working group of AAR on psycho-social interpretations of theology); Clinical Member, American Association for Marriage and Family Therapy and New Jersey Association for Marriage and Family Therapy; American Psychological Association **Discipline:** Clinical Psychology; Religious Studies **Related Interests:** Philosophy of Religion/Science; Religion and the Social and Natural Sciences; Religion and Psychology.

Selected Publications: His bibliography lists 18 entries.

_____. *The Texture of Knowledge: An Essay on Religion and Science*. Lanham, MD: University Press of America, 1981.
_____. "The Delicate Dialectic: Religion and Psychology in the Modern World." *Cross Currents* 32 (1982): 143-153.
_____. *The Redemption of Matter: Towards the Rapprochement of Science and Religion*. Lanham, MD: University Press of America, 1984.
_____. "Personality and Epistemology: Cognitive Social Learning Theory as a Philosophy of Science." *Zygon* (March 1989).
_____. *Contemporary Psychoanalysis and Religion*. New Haven: Yale University Press, 1990.

Jones, Stanton Louis

Present Position and Address: Chairman/Professor (since 1981); Department of Psychology, Wheaton College, Wheaton, IL 60187, USA **Concurrent Positions:** Private practice in Individual and Marital Psychotherapy (since 1981) **Work Phone:** (708) 752-5762 **Education:** B.S. Psychology (1976), Texas A & M University; M.A. and Ph.D. Clinical Psychology (APA Approved, 1976-81), Arizona State University, Tempe; Internship (APA approved 1980-81), University of Mississippi Medical Center and Veteran's Administration Medical Center, Jackson **Previous Positions:** Research Consultant (1976-80), St. Lukes Medical Center - Alcoholism Treatment Program; Psychology Resident (1980-81), University of Mississippi **Selected Memberships:** American Psychological Association; Association for the Advancement of Behavior Therapy; Christian Association for Psychological Studies **Discipline:** Clinical Psychology **Related Interests:** Psychology and Christian Faith; Science and Religion; Human Sexuality.

Selected Publications: His bibliography lists over 21 entries.

_____, R. Butman. *Modern Psychotherapies: A Comprehensive Christian Appraisal*. Downer's Grove IL: InterVarsity, March 1991.
_____, D. Workman. "Homosexuality: The behavioral sciences and the Church." *Journal of Psychology and Theology* 17, 4 (1989): 213-25.
_____, editor. *Psychology and the Christian Faith: An introductory reader*. Grand Rapids, MI: Baker Books, 1986.
_____, E. Watson and T. Wolfram. "Results of the Rech Conference Survey on Religious Faith and Professional Psychology." *Journal of Psychology and Theology* 20, 2 (1992).
_____. "A Constructive Relationship for Religion with the Science and Profession of Psychology: Perhaps the Boldest Model Yet." *American Psychologist* 49, 3 (1994).

Juergensmeyer, Mark

Present Position and Address: Professor of Sociology and Chair, Global Peace and Security Program, University of California, Santa Barbara, CA 93106 USA **Education:** B.A. (1962), University of Illinois; M.Div. (1965), Union Theological Seminary, NYC; M.A.(1968)/Ph.D. Political Science (1974), University of California - Berkeley **Previous Positions:** Project Director (1972-74), Center for South/Southeast Asia Studies, University of California - Berkeley; Co-founder and Assoc. Director (1974-80), Center for Ethics and Social Policy/Professor, Ethics and the Phenomenology of Religions/Director of Programs in Comparative Religion, Graduate Theological Union; Codirector (1979-84) Berkeley/Harvard Program in Comparative Values; Codirector (since 1985), Berkeley-Chicago-Harvard Project in Comparative Religion; Director (1987) NEH Summer Institute on Comparative Religion; Coordinator, Religious Studies Program, University of California — Berkeley; Consultant on Ethics to Wells Fargo Bank, Levi Strauss Co., and General Motors Co. ; Dean, School of Hawaiian, Asian and Pacific Studies, 1890 East-West Road, 309 Moore Hall, University of Hawaii, Honolulu, HI 96822 (1989-93) **Media Work:** Consultant on Comparative Religion and Indian Politics for several news organizations (including NY Times, Washington Post, CBS News, and ABC Nightline), over 50 appearances on radio and TV **Editorial Work:** General Editor of: *Berkeley Religious Studies Series*; *Comparative Studies in Religion and Society* (published by the University of California Press); *Union Seminary Quarterly Review* (1963-65). Editorial Board of: *The Journal of Ethics and Animals*; *Religion*; *The Journal of Religion and Society* **Selected Memberships:** Chairman (1983-85) of the Nominating Committee/President (1983-84), American Academy of Religion; Chairman (1984-85), selection committee for grants in religious studies, Fulbright Program; Chairman (1976-80), Asia Bureau (PBS and National Public Radio based at KQED, San Francisco) **Discipline:** Ethics, Phenomenology of Religions, Comparative Religion **Related Interests:** Comparative Ethics; Asian Religions and Society.

Selected Publications: Author of 10 books, with chapters in over 50 books and encyclopedias (including *Theology and Bioethics*), and author of over 100 articles, reviews, and monographs (including *The Journal of Science and Religion*, and *Zygon*).

_____. *The New Cold War: Religious Nationalism Confronts the Secular State.* University of California Press, 1993.
_____. *Religion as Social Vision.* University of California Press, 1982.
_____, coeditor. *A Bibliographical Guide to the Comparative Study of Ethics.* Cambridge University Press, 1988.
_____. *Radhasoami Reality: The Logic of a Modern Faith.* N.p. 1991.

Kahoe, Richard Dean

Present Position and Address: Clinical Psychologist, Alternative Care Center, 1020 Texas Avenue, Woodward, OK 73801, USA; President, manna forty, inc., Rte. 1, Box 548, Sharon, OK 73857, USA **Work Phone:** (405) 256-2400 **Home Phone:** (405) 995-4906 **Fax Number:** (405) 256-5777 **Date of Birth:** November 27, 1935 **Languages Spoken:** English **Awards and Honors:** Numerous Who's Who type listings; NIMH Clinical Psychology Fellow (1962-64; 1965-66), Peabody College **Previous Positions:** Dean of Men and Assistant Professor of Psychology (1966-67), Southwest Baptist College, Bolivar, MO; Dean of Students and Associate Professor (1967-71), Southwest Baptist College, Bolivar, MO; Chair and Associate Professor of Psychology (1971-77), Georgetown College, Georgetown, KY; Staff Psychologist (1977-87), Christian Haven Homes, Wheatfield, IN; Private Practice and Adjunct Professor (1987-90), Southwest Baptist University, Bolivar, MO **Editorial Positions:** Editor/Publisher of *manna*, Literary - Professional Quarterly in Nature, Science, and Religion **Administrative Experience:** Administrator and Clinical Director (1990-91), manna forty Group Home, Dunnegan, MO **Selected Memberships:** President (1986-87), Division 36 (Psychology of Religion) of American Psychological Association; Society for the Scientific Study of Religion (since 1974) **Discipline:** Clinical Psychology **Related Areas of Interest:** Psychology of Religion; Inter- Relationships of Religion, Psychology, and Nature Experiences.

Selected Publications: His bibliography contains 2 books, 6 chapters, 13 journal articles, 6 journal short reports or comments, 5 book reviews, 10 encyclopedia articles, 5 other professional documents, and at least 9 lay articles on professional and/or religious topics.

_____. "Personality and Achievement Correlates of Intrinsic and Extrinsic Religious Orientations." *Journal of Personality and Social Psychology* (June 1974).

_____. "The Psychology and Theology of Sexism." *Journal of Psychology and Theology* (Fall 1974).

_____. "A Search for Mental Health." *Journal of Psychology and Theology* (Fall 1975).

_____. "The Fear of Death and Religious Attitudes and Behaviors." *Journal for the Scientific Study of Religion* (December 1975).

_____. "Religious Conservatism in a Quasi-Longitudinal Perspective." *Journal of Psychology and Theology* (Winter 1977).

_____. "A Developmental Perspective on Religious Orientation Dimensions." *Journal of Religion and Health* (Spring 1981).

_____, Mary Jo Meadow. *Psychology of Religion: Religion in Individual Lives.* Harper & Row, 1984.

_____. "The Development of Intrinsic and Extrinsic Religious Orientations." *Journal for the Scientific Study of Religion* (December 1985).

_____. "Social Science of Gender Differences: Ideological Battleground." *Religious Studies Review* (July 1985).

_____. *Songs of Soul and Psyche.* Northwest Oklahoman Press, 1993. Collected Original Poems, mostly on Psychology/Science/Religious Topics.

Kaiser, Christopher B.

Present Position and Address: Professor of Historical and Systematic Theology (since 1988), Western Theological Seminary, Holland, MI 49423 USA; (Home) 246 Norwood Avenue, Holland, MI 49424 USA **Work Phone:** (616) 392-8555 **Education:** A.B. Physics and General Studies (*cum laude*, 1963), Harvard University; Ph.D. Astro-Geophysics (1968), University of Colorado; M.Div. (*summa cum laude*, 1971), Gordon-Conwell Theological Seminary; Ph.D. Christian Dogmatics and Divinity (Thesis: "The Logic of Complementarity in Science and Theology," 1974), University of Edinburgh **Previous Positions:** Research Assistant on solar convection (1965), Sacramento Peak Observatory; Graduate Research Assistant on infrared radiation of interplanetary dust (1966-67), National Center for Atmospheric Research; Lecturer in Physics (1968-71), Gordon College; Computer Scientist (1975-76), QEI Inc, Bedford, MA; Lecturer in Christian Dogmatics (1973-75), University of Edinburgh; Visiting Professor (sabbatical replacement for M. E. Osterhaven, 1976-77)/Assistant (1977-82)/Associate (1982-88)/Full (since 1988) Professor of Historical and Systematic Theology, Western Theological Seminary; Resident Member (Spring 1984, 87), Center of Theological Inquiry, Princeton, NJ (research on the interaction of science and theology in the Renaissance and the 18th century) **Selected Memberships:** Ordained Minister in the Reformed Church in America; American Scientific Affiliation; Institute for a Theological Encounter with Science and Technology; ELCA Work Group on Science and Theology; Society for the History of Technology **Discipline:** Historical and Systematic Theology **Related Interests:** History of Science; Philosophy of Quantum Theory. **Current Research:** Training students for Christian ministry in a world dominated by science and technology. Special interest in the historical development of science as a source of theological issues and insights for today. His theological focus in on the doctrines of God, Creation, and Christology.

Selected Publications: His bibliography lists 7 publications in historical studies in theology and science; 3 publications in astrophysics; 16 publications in modern science, theology and society; and 12 unpublished lectures on science, theology and society.

_____. "Some Recent Developments in the Sciences and Their Relevance for Christian Theology." *Reformed Review* 29 (Spring 1976): 148-155.
_____. "Niels Bohr and Michael Polanyi: Some Interesting Parallels." *Convivium* 9 (Winter 1979-80)" 13-23.
_____. "A Scientists's View of the Universe." *Crux* 15 (1979): 162-171.
_____. "The Early Christian Critique of Greek Science." *Patristic and Byzantine Review* 1 (1982): 211-216.
_____. "Calvin, Copernicus, and Castellio." *Calvin Theological Journal* 21 (April 1986): 5-31.
_____. "The Early Christian Belief in Creation: Background for the Origins and Assessment of Modern Western Science." *Horizons in Biblical Theology* 9 (1987): 1-30.
_____. "How Can a Theological Understanding of Humanity Enrich Artificial Intelligence Work." *Asbury Theological Journal* 44 (1989): 61-75.
_____. *Creation and the History of Science, History of Christian Theology Series*, ed. P. D. L. Avis. Grand Rapids MI: William B. Eerdmans, 1991.
_____. "The Creationist Tradition in the History of Science." *Perspectives in Science and Christian Faith* 45 (1993): 80-89.
_____. "Humanity as the Exegete of Creation with Reference to the Work of Natural Scientists." *Horizons in Biblical Theology* 14 (1992): 112-28.

Kaita, Robert

Present Position and Address: Principal Research Physicist, Princeton University, Plasma Physics Laboratory, P.O. Box 451, Princeton, NJ 08543, USA **Work Phone:** (609) 243-3275 **Fax Number:** (609) 243- 3266 **E-Mail:** kaita@pppl.gov **Date of Birth:** September 2, 1952 **Languages Spoken:** English **Lectures Presented:** Lectured to numerous church and student groups on Science and Theology **Selected Memberships:** American Association for the Advancement of Science; American

Physical Society; American Scientific Affiliation; Sigma Xi - the Scientific Research Society **Discipline:** Plasma Physics **Related Areas of Interest:** Experimental Research in Controlled Thermonuclear Fusion; Relationship between Science (primarily physical science) and the Christian Faith **Current Areas of Research:** Development of advanced concepts for the "tokamak" type of magnetic confinement for thermonuclear fusion plasmas.

Selected Publications: His bibliography contains over 150 published articles in nuclear and plasma physics.

_____. Review of *Darwin on Trial*, by Phillip E. Johnson. *The Crucible* 2, 2 (1992): 27-9.
_____. "Obstacles and Opportunities in Science for Christian Witness." *Perspectives on Science and Christian Faith* 45, 2 (1993): 112-15.

Kanagy, Sherman P.

Present Position and Address: Assistant Professor of Physics (since 1984), Mathematics and Physics Department Purdue, University North Central, 1401 S. US 421, Westville, IN 46391-9528 USA **Work Phone:** (219) 785-5320 **Education:** B.S. Astronomy (1970), Case Institute of Technology, Cleveland OH; M.S. (1972)/Ph.D. (1977), Astronomy, University of Illinois, Urbana-Champaign **Previous Positions:** Visiting Lecturer in Physical Science (1977-79)/Assistant Professor of Physics (1980-81), University of Illinois, Urbana; Assistant Professor of Philosophy (1980-81)/Assistant Professor of Physics (1979-82), Illinois State University; Instructor (1982) Eureka College/Lincoln College; Assistant Professor of Physics (1982-84), Planetarium/Observatory Director, Valparaiso University, IN; Adjunct Professor of Geology (1985)/Physics (1984-85), Indiana University Northwest, IN **Selected Memberships:** Fellow (1988), American Scientific Affiliation; American Astronomical Society; American Association for the Advancement of Science **Discipline:** Astronomy **Related Interests:** Astronomy, Science and Theology.

Selected Publications:

_____. *The Religion-Science Controversy: the Use and Abuse of Science in the Defense of Religion.* Proceedings of the Religion/Science Conference held October 5, 1985 at Purdue University North Central, with a bibliography on "Science, Christianity, and Pseudoscience." Westville, IN: Purdue University North Central, 1986.
_____. "Is Scientific Evidence Relevant to Justifying Religious Claims?" In *The Religion-Science Controversy: the Use and Abuse of Science in the Defense of Religion.* Westville, IN: Purdue University North Central, 1986.
_____. "Religion and Pseudoscience in Christmas Star Shows." *The Planetarian* 16, 4 (October 1987): 12-20.
_____. *A Defense of the Appropriateness of the Star of Bethlehem as a Topic in Science Education.* Proceedings of the 24th Annual GLPA Conference. Ohio: Great Lakes Planetarium Association, 1989.
_____. *Are Christmas Star Programs in Secular Planetariums Akin to Creation Science in the Public Schools?* Proceedings of the 25th Annual GLPA Conference (Illinois: Great Lakes Planetarium Association, 1990), pp. 69-75.
_____. K. D. Boa, The Star of the Magi: Scientific, Educational, and Theological Issues (in progress).
_____. K. D. Boa, Astrology: Scientific, Philosophical, and Theological Issues (in progress)..
_____. *The Relationship of Science and Religion*, Manuscript of 175 pages.

Kang, Phee Seng (alias Jiang, Pisheng)

Present Position and Address: Lecturer in Theology and Philosophy (since 1988) Department of Religion and Philosophy, Hong Kong Baptist College, 224 Waterloo Road, Kowloon, Hong Kong. **Date of Birth:** November 20,1950 **Languages Spoken:** English, Chinese, German **Education:** Military - Officer Cadet School (1973-74), Singapore Armed Forces Training Institute and School of Manpower (Spring 1987, Spring 1988), Singapore Armed Forces. B.Sc. Mathematics and Physics (1972)/B.Sc. (Hons) Mathematics (1973), University of Singapore **Awards and Honors:** King William Scholarship (1980-82)/Bruce and Fraser Scholarship (1980-82), University of Aberdeen; Tien-Tao

Exegetical Award (1979), China Graduate School of Theology **Previous Positions:** Tutor in Mathematics (1972-73), University of Singapore; Instructor in Officer Cadet School (1974-75), Singapore Armed Forces Training Institute; Resident Faculty Member (1984-87), Southeast Asia Graduate School of Theology, Singapore; Lecturer (1984-86), Trinity Theological College, Singapore; Brigade Staff Officer (1988)/Battalion Staff Officer (1985-87), Singapore Armed Forces; Division Manager (1986-88)/Chairman of Management Committee (1987-88), Phillip Securities and Phillip Commodities, Singapore; Computer Systems Analyst (1975-76), Ministry of Finance, Singapore **Selected Memberships:** Institute of Studies on Religion and Society, Singapore; Chinese Theological Society, Hong Kong; Hong Kong Philosophy Society; Lam Chi Fung Memorial Symposium Committee **Discipline:** Philosophy; Theology; Mathematics/Physics **Related Interests:** Scientific and Theological Epistemologies; Concepts of Time and Space in Historical, Scientific and Theological Inquiries. **Current Research:** Theological Reflections on Man as Shaped by Today's Economic and Financial Systems; Issues in Ethics.

Selected Publications: His bibliography lists 6 papers and manuscripts.

_____. "The Epistemological Significance of 'Homoousion' in the Theology of Thomas Forsyth Torrance." Accepted for publication in 1991 by *Scottish Journal of Theology* (Edinburgh).

Karkalits, Jr., Olin Carroll

Present Position and Address: Dean, College of Engineering and Technology, McNeese State University, P.O. Box 91860, Lake Charles, LA 70609-1860, USA **Work Phone:** (318) 475-5876 **Home Phone:** (818) 475-5286 **Date of Birth:** May 31, 1916 **Awards and Honors:** *Who's Who in the South and Southwest*; Fellow, American Scientific Affiliation; Fellow, American Institute of Chemical Engineers **Previous Positions:** Assistant Director of Engineering (1966-72), Petro-Tex Corp., Houston, TX; Manager of Research (1956-66); Supervisor of Process Evaluation (1956), FMC Corp.; Group Leader in Process Development (1948-56), American Cyanimid Corp., Bound Brook, NJ; Instructor in Chemical Engineering (1945-48), University of Michigan, Ann Arbor **Selected Memberships:** American Scientific Affiliation; American Institute of Chemical Engineers; National Society of Professional Engineers; Geothermal Research Society **Discipline:** Chemical Engineering **Related Interests:** Interaction Between Science and Christianity **Current Research:** Paper now in preparation for publication, *A Christian Approach Toward Harmony with Science.*

Selected Publications: His bibliography contains 12 patents, 6 articles on geothermal energy, and two essays on religion and science.

_____. "Naturalism Must Bow to Theism." In *Evidences of God in an Expanding Universe*, ed. Monsma. New York: G. Putnam and Sons, 1958.

Keilholz, Peggy J.

Present Position and Address: Clinical Therapist (since 1989) of Provident Counselling, (Home) 9700 Cisco Drive, St. Louis, MO 63123, USA **Date of Birth:** August 8, 1945 **Education:** A.B. Biology (1968), Fontbonne College, St. Louis; M.A. Religion and Education (1977), St. Louis University; M.S.W. (1984), Washington University, St. Louis **Previous Positions:** Technician (1968-73), Missouri Water Pollution Board; Assistant Director (1973-76)/Executive Director (1976-81), Missouri Catholic Conference; Caseworker (1984-85), Catholic Social Service; Therapist (1985-89), Catholic Family Service **Selected Memberships:** Institute for Theological Encounter with Science and Technology **Discipline:** Clinical Therapy **Related Interests:** Environment Issues; Impact of Science/Technology on individuals; Ethics and Science/Technology.

Selected Publications:

_____, editor. *ITEST Summary 1968-83.* ITEST, 1988. Presents contemporary issues in Science/Technology and Theology as reflected in 15 years of ITEST-sponsored conferences and workshops.

Kelly, William L.

Present Position and Address: Director, Medical Devices, Medisorb Technologies International, 1081 Markley Road, Cincinnati, OH 45230 USA **Work Phone:** (513) 624-6426 **Fax:** (513) 489-7244 **Date of Birth:** March 24, 1940 **Previous Positions:** Division Director, Wellman, Inc.; National Marketing Director, Wellman, Inc.; Commercial Development Manager, Ashland Chemical; Automotive Specialist, Dupont Company **Selected Memberships:** Society of Plastics Engineers; Society of Biomaterials **Discipline:** Organic Chemistry; Plastics **Related Areas of Interest:** Plastics, Resorbable Biomaterials, Science and Theology **Current Areas of Research**: Resorbable Biopolymers.

Selected Publications:

_____. "Human Rights: A Basis for Christian Action, or A Trap for the Unwary?" Paper presented at the American Scientific Affiliation's 33rd Annual Meeting, held at Hope College on August 11-14, 1978.

Kerze, Michael A.

Present Position and Address: Director of the Chapel and InterFaith Center, Occidental College, 1600 Campus Road, Los Angeles, CA 90041, USA **Work Phone:** (213) 259-2621 **Fax Number:** (213) 259-2958 **E-Mail:** kerze@Oxy.edu **Date of Birth:** July 20, 1948 **Languages Spoken:** English **Previous Positions:** Visiting Professor, Department of Theology, Loyola Marymount University; Assistant Professor, Department of Religious Studies, California State University - Northridge **Selected Memberships:** American Academy of Religion; University and College Ombudsperson Association **Discipline:** History of Religions; History of Science **Related Areas of Interest:** Experiment and Ritual; Interreligious Dialogue **Current Areas of Research:** Sixteenth and Seventeenth Century Religious Justification of Experimental Science.

Selected Publications: His bibliography contains 6 published articles.

_____. "Religious Origins of the Binary Number System." In *A Common Vision,* ed. George Derfer. N.p., 1987.
_____. "Euchid." "Ptolemy." "Copernicus." "Binary Number." In *The Encyclopedia of Religions*, ed. Mircea Eliade. N.p., 1987.
_____, Ven. Karuna Dharma. *An Early Journey: The Los Angeles Buddhist, Roman Catholic Dialogue.* N.p., 1991.

Key, Thomas D. S.

Present Position and Address: Instructor of Biology, Minds Community College, Raymond, MS; Pastor of Springridge Bible Church, Raymond, MS; Pastor of Springridge Bible Church, Raymond, MS; PO Box 1152, Raymond, MS 39154-1152, USA **Work Phone:** (601) 857-5035 **Date of Birth:** August 4, 1928 **Education:** B.A. (1952)/M.A. (1952), Southern Methodist University; ED.D. Biology (1969), Ball State University; M.R.E. (1983)/Th.D. (1986), Antioch Seminary **Previous Positions:** Science Education Consultant (since 1968); Developmental Advisor, Wesley College (since 1989) **Selected Memberships:** American Scientific Affiliation **Discipline:** Biology - science education, ecology, sensory physiology; Bible - Nature Illustrations, Apologetics, Hermeneutics **Related Interests:** Apologetics; Bible/Nature Illustrations; Cosmology; Hermeneutics.

Selected Publications:

_____, coauthor. *Darwin and Christian Thought Today.* Revell Publishing, 1969.

_____, coauthor. "Levitical Dietary Laws in the Light of Modern Biology." *Journal of the American Scientific Affiliation* 25, 2 (1973).

_____. "A Biologist Examines the Book of Mormon." *Journal of the American Scientific Affiliation* 37, 2 (June 1985).

_____. "Does the Canopy Theory Hold Water?" *Journal of the American Scientific Affiliation* 37, 4 (December 1985).

King Jr., Morton B.

Present Position and Address: Professor of Sociology, Emeritus, Southern Methodist University, 401 East 8th. Street, Georgetown, TX 78626, USA **Work Phone:** (512) 863-7108 **Date of Birth:** March 24, 1913 **Languages Spoken:** English **Awards and Honors:** Phi Beta Kappa **Previous Positions:** Case Visitor (1934-35), Davidson Co. Welfare Commission; Assistant Professor of Sociology (1934-41)/Chair (1946-56), University of Mississippi; Associate Professor of Sociology (1941-43), Mississippi State College; Private DEML to 2nd. Ll. AGD. (1943-46), U.S. Army; Visiting Professor of Sociology (Summer 1951), University of North Carolina - Chapel Hill; Visiting Professor of Sociology (Summer 1953), Michigan State University; Lecturer (Summer 1968), University of Utrect, The Netherlands; Visiting Lecturer in Sociology (1957-58), Northwestern University; Department of Sociology (1956-79), Chair of Department (1960-64; 69-71; 75-77), Southern Methodist University **Selected Memberships:** Fellow, American Sociological Association; American Association for the Advancement of Science; President, Southern Sociological Society (1954-55); President, Association for the Scientific Study of Religion: S.W. (1967-68) **Discipline:** Sociology **Related Areas of Interest:** The Epistemology and Ontology of Applying Quantitative Research Procedures to the Study of Human Behaviors, including Religious Behavior - Overt and Covert.

Selected Publications: He has authored and/or coauthored 8 books and monographs, about 25 articles and book chapters.

_____. "Some Comments on Concepts." *Social Forces* 34, 1 (1955): 1-4.

_____, Richard A. Hunt. "The Intrinsic - Extrinsic Concept: Review and Evaluation." *Journal of the Association for the Scientific Study of Religion (JSSR)* 10, 4 (1971): 340-56.

_____. "Response to Blaylock." *ASA Footnotes* 1, 3 (1973): 7.

_____, Richard A. Hunt. "Moral Man and Immoral Science?" *Sociological Analysis* 35, 4 (1974): 240-50.

_____, Richard A. Hunt. "Religious Dimensions: Entities or Constructs?" *Sociological Focus* 8, 1 (1975): 57-63.

_____, Richard A. Hunt. "Measuring the Religious Variable: Final Comment." *JSSR* 27, 4 (1990): 531-5.

_____. "Is Scientific Study of Religion Possible?" *JSSR* 30, 1 (1991): 108-13.

_____. "One Message." A Poem. In *Poetry and Prose*, by Morton Brandon King. Georgetown, TX: JSK Publication, 1993.

Kirkpatrick, Lee Alan

Present Position and Address: Visiting Assistant Professor, Department of Psychology University of South Carolina, Columbia, SC 29208, USA **Work Phone:** (803) 777-6294 **Date of Birth:** November 22, 1958 **Education:** B.S. Psychology and Philosophy (*magna cum laude*, 1980) Lynchburg College; M.A. General/Experimental Psychology (1983), University of Texas - El Paso; Ph.D. Social Psychology, Psychology of Religion (1988), University of Denver **Previous Positions:** Research Associate (since 1988), Colorado Mental Health Systems Evaluation Project, University of Denver **Editorial Work:** Reviewer (since 1986), *Journal for the Scientific Study of Religion*; Reviewer for D. Moberg and M. Lynn (1987), *Research in the Social Scientific Study of Religion*, Vol. 1; Reviewer (since 1989),

Journal of Social and Personal Relationships **Selected Memberships:** Rocky Mountain Regional Director (since 1987)/Program Committee (1989-90)/Program Chair (1990-91), American Psychological Association **Discipline:** Psychology (including the Psychology of Religion) **Related Interests:** Psychology and Religion; The Psychology of Religion.

Selected Publications:

_____, B. Spilka, P. Shaver and L. A. Kirkpatrick. "General Attribution Theory for the Psychology of Religion." *Journal for the Scientific Study of Religion* 24 (1985): 1-20.

_____, R. W. Hood, G. Hartz. "Fundamentalist Religion Conceptualized in Terms of Rokeach's Theory of the Open and Closed Mind: A Theoretical Model and its Implications for Mental Health." *Research in the Social Scientific Study of Religion* 3 Greenwich, CT: JAI Press, in process.

Klaaren, Eugene M.

Present Position and Address: Associate Professor of Religion, Wesleyan University, Middletown, CT 06457, USA. **Work Phone:** (203) 347-9411 ext. 2659 **Date of Birth:** August 9, 1937 **Education:** M.A. (1960), Emory; Ph.D. (Thesis: "Belief in Creation and the Rise of Modern Natural Science . . .," 1970), Harvard University **Previous Positions:** Lecturer/Assistant/Associate Professor of Religion (since 1968)/Chairman of Religion Department (1981-83, 94-95), Wesleyan University; Visiting Lecturer, Systematic Theology (1976), Fuller Theological Seminary **Selected Memberships:** American Academy of Religion; Fellow, Society for Values in Higher Education; Biblical Theologians Discussion Group; New Haven Theological Discussion Group; Society for Philosophy and Technology **Discipline:** Theology and Philosophy **Related Interests:** Wide-ranging interest in Theology, Modern Science and Technological Culture, with particular focus on a contemporary Theology of Creation in America and South Africa.

Selected Publications: His bibliography contains 10 books, theses, articles, and critical reviews; 5 book reviews, and 30 lectures and papers. The following works are in process: "Towards a Contemporary Theology of Creation;" "The Genesis Song: A Reading of Genesis 1;" "Christian Rituals and the Decline of Common Belief;" "Studies in Contemporary African Theologies of Creation."

_____. "Belief in Creation and the Rise of Modern Natural Science." Ph.D., Religion, Harvard University, 1970.

_____. *Religious Origins of Modern Science.* Grand Rapids: Eerdmans, 1977; University Press of America, 1985.

_____. "Creation and the World of Science by A. R. Peacocke." *Zygon* 16:2 (June 1981): 191-194.

_____. "An Ambitious Program," (critical review of T. F. Torrance's *Christian Theology and Scientific Culture,* Oxford, 1981; and H. Nebelsick's *Theology and Science in Mutual Modification,* Oxford, 1981). *Reformed Journal* 32, 11 (November 1982): 24-26.

_____. "A Discussion of Deason's 'Protestant Theology and the Rise of Modern Science'." *CTNS (Center for Theology and the Natural Sciences) Bulletin* 7, 2 (1987): 13-18.

_____. "Creation and Community." *Religion and Intellectual Life* 5, 2 (1988): 82-95.

Klaus, Hanna

Present Position and Address: Director (since 1980), Natural Family Planning Center of Washington DC Inc., 8514 Bradmoor Drive, Bethesda, MD 20817-3810 Box 30239, Bethesda, MD 20824-0239, USA **Date of Birth:** January 27, 1928 **Education:** B.A. (1948), University of Louisville, KY; M.D. (1950), University of Louisville School of Medicine; Full-time Research, Natural Family Planning - Ovulation Method in USA and overseas (1977-78) **Postgraduate Studies:** Assistant Resident (1951-53), Pathology, Massachusetts General Hospital, Boston; Assistant and Associate Resident (1953-56), OB/GYN, Washington University School of Medicine, St. Louis; Assistant - Surgery (1956-57), Peter Bent Brigham Hospital; Clinical Assistant - Surgery Harvard Medical School, Trainee (1956-57), National Cancer Institute **Previous Positions:** Chief (1961-66), Department of Obstetrics and Gynecology and at times Acting Medical Director, Holy Family Hospital - Rawalpindi, Pakistan; Director (1966-68), Department of Obstetrics, Holy Family Hospital - Dhaka, Bangladesh; Instructor (1969-70), Department of OB/GYN, Washington University/Barnes Hospital; Assistant Professor (1970-75), OB/GYN, St. Louis University Medical Center/Associate Section Head, Department of OB/GYN, St. Louis City Hospital; Director (1975-77), Department of OB, St. Francis Hospital - Wichita, KS; Associate Professor (1978-80)/Associate Clinical Professor (since 1980), OB/GYN, George Washington University Medical Center, Washington, DC **Selected Memberships:** Society of Catholic Medical Missionaries (since 1957); Fellowship of Catholic Scholars (since 1977) **Discipline:** Medicine; Obstetrics; Gynecology; Catholic Sister **Related Interests:** Ethics and Medicine; Adolescent Sexuality and Fertility; Natural Family Planning; Theology of the Body.

Selected Publications:

_____. "Medical Cop Out?" *America* 133, 4 (August 16, 1975): 68-70.
_____. "Three Years Experience in Teaching the Billings Method." In *Theological Aspect of Human Sexuality*. San Rafael: ITEST, 1976.
_____. "The Power, Glory and Limitations of the Human Body's Sexuality (as viewed by an Obstetrician)." *ITEST workshop: Contribution of Mariology to Contemporary Christian Anthropology* (January 14-17, 1982). Published as "The Virgin Mary and the Human Body," *Fidelity* 3,3 (February, 1984).
_____. "Laboratory Generation of Human Life II." *Fellowship of Catholic Scholars Newsletter* 9, 3 (June 1986).
_____. "The Importance of Being a Bodily Person." *Fidelity* 8, 5 (1989): 15-18.
_____. "Body Theology: The Road to Chastity." *Seminarians for Life International Newsletter* 2, 1 (February 1990).
_____. "The Existential Isolation of Contraception." *Linacre Quarterly* 59, 4: 329-32.

Klotz, John W.

Present Position and Address: Professor (since 1974), Concordia Seminary, 801 De Mun Avenue, Saint Louis, MO 63105 (Home) 6417 San Bonita, Clayton, MO 63105, USA **Work Phone:** (314) 721-6402 **Date of Birth:** January 10, 1918 **Education:** M.S. (1940), University of Pittsburgh; M.Div. (1941), Concordia Seminary - St. Louis; Ph.D. (1947), University of Pittsburgh **Awards and Honors:** Honors: D.D. (1985), Concordia Theological Seminary - Fort Wayne **Previous Positions:** Instructor (1941-43), Concordia College - Bronxville, NY; Instructor (1943-45), Bethany Lutheran College, Mankato, MN; Associate and Full Professor (1945-59), Concordia College - River Forest, IL; Professor (1959-74), Concordia Senior College - Ft. Wayne, IN **Other Academic Experience:** American Association for the Advancement of Science; Nature Conservancy; Hastings Center Genetics, Ecology, Theology **Discipline:** Evolution; Environmental Problems; Medical Ethics.

Selected Publications:

_____. *Genes, Genesis and Evolution*. Concordia Publishing House, 1955, 1970.
_____. *Modern Science in the Christian Life*. Concordia Publishing House, 1959.
_____. *The Challenge of the Space Age*. Concordia Publishing House, 1961.
_____. *Ecology Crisis*. Concordia Publishing House, 1971.

Knapp, Andreas

Present Position and Address: Studentenpfarrer (since 1988), Universität Freiburg, Goethestrasse 40, D-7800 Freiburg I. Br., Germany **Work Phone:** (0049) 761-701893 **Date of Birth:** June 8, 1958 **Education:** Abitur (1977); Vordiplom in Theologie (1979), Freiburg; Baccalaureat in Theologie (1982)/Lizentiat in Moraltheologie (1985)/Dr. theol. (1988), University Gregoriana, Rome **Previous Positions:** Kaplan in Blankenloch, Karlsruhe (1988) **Discipline:** Moral Theology **Related Interests:** Bioethics; Fundamental Morality; The dialogue between Theology and Science.

Selected Publications:

_____. *Biologie und Moral*. Stuttgart, 1986.

_____. "Biologisches Menschenbild und Moral" *Scheidewege* 17 (1987/88): 120-141.

_____. "Grenzen des naturwissenschaftlichen Weltbildes, aufgezeigt am Beispiel der 'Evolutionären Erkenntnis-theorie'." *Die Welt - Produkt des Zufalls oder Gottes Schöpfung, Hg. von der Akademie der Diözese Rottenburg-Stuttgart*. Stuttgart: N.p., 1988.

_____. "Soziobiologie und christliche Moral." In *Internationale Katholische Zeitschrift* 17 (1988).

_____. "Leben ist mehr als Überleben. Von den Grenzen des Versuchs, alle Phänomene des Lebendigen als 'Anpassungen' zu erklären." In *Entwicklung. Interdisziplinäre Aspekte zur Evolutionsfrage*, ed. W. H. Arnold. Stuttgart: Urachhaus, 1989.

_____. *Soziobiologie und Moraltheologie. Kritik der ethischen Folgerungen moderner Biologie*. Weinheim: Acta Humaniora, 1989.

Knapp II, John Allen

Present Position and Address: Professor of English (since 1976), State University of New York (SUNY) - Oswego, NY 13126, USA; (Home) RR 10, Box 1037, Germar Drive, Oswego, NY 13126, USA **Date of Birth:** September 9, 1940 **Education:** A.B. Psychology (1963), Wheaton College; M.A.T. General Science (1968), Michigan State University; Ph.D. Science Education (1972), Western Michigan University; Biblical Studies and Literature (Wheaton College and Conservative Baptist Theological Seminary **Previous Positions:** Volunteer teacher in Liberia (1963-64), US Peace Corps; High School Chemistry Teacher, Louisa, VA (1965-67); Assistant/Associate Professor of Science Education (1972-76)/Associate and Full Professor of English (since 1976), SUNY - Oswego **Selected Memberships:** American Scientific Affiliation; former member and editor of School Science and Mathematics Association **Discipline:** English (especially children's literature, Ancient and Medieval Literature); Science Education and General Science; Psychology **Related Interests:** Children's Fiction/Science Textbook writing (Silver Burdett for 8 years); Censorship and Children's Literature; Creation and Evolution; the Bible and Science; Science Education for Children - specifically Creationism **Current Research:** "I am a creationist who believes that Genesis reports reliable and sequential history, though obviously not in modern scientific language, that the 'days' of creation were, in fact, great periods of time."

Selected Publications: He has published more than 200 books, articles, poems, newspaper columns, etc.

_____, part of a team. *Science: Understanding Your Environment*. Silver Burdett, 1978-85. Textbooks for Grades 3-6.

_____. "Ten Commandments for teaching Elementary Science." *The Education Digest* 47, 3 (1981): 50-52.

_____. "A Response to R. W. French's 'Teaching the Bible as Literature'." *College English* 45, 7 (1983).

_____. *The Burgomaster's Rain*. Ephemeron Press, 1990.

_____. *A Pillar of Pepper*. David C. Cook, 1982.

Knight, Christopher C.

Present Position and Address: Chaplain, Fellow and Director of Studies in Theology (since 1987), Sidney Sussex College, Cambridge, CB2 3HU, England **Date of Birth:** January 11, 1952 **Education:** B.Sc. Physics (1973), University of Exeter; Ph.D. Astrophysics (1977), University of Manchester; B.Th. Theology (1983), University of Southampton **Discipline:** Theology; Astrophysics **Related Interests:** Natural Theology; Theological Language; Psychological Aspects of Religious Belief.

Selected Publications: Many papers in Ecclesiastical History and General Theology.

_____. "Hysteria and Myth: The Psychology of the Resurrection Appearances." *Modern Churchman* 31, 2 (1989): 38ff.

Knight, David Marcus

Present Position and Address: Professor (since 1991) , Philosophy Department, University of Durham, 50 Old Elvet, Durham DH1 3HN, UK **Date of Birth:** November 30, 1936 **Education:** B.A. Chemistry (1961)/Diploma in History of Science (1962)/M.A. (1964)/D.Phil. History of Science (1964), Oxford University, UK **Previous Positions:** Lecturer (1964)/Senior Lecturer (1975)/Reader (1988), History of Science, University of Durham **Editorial Work:** Editor (1982-88), *British Journal for History of Science;* Currently general editor of the *New Series, Blackwell Science Biographies;* Editorial Board, *Annals of Science* **Selected Memberships:** President (1994-96), British Society for History of Science **Discipline:** History of Science **Related Interests:** Science and Religion in the 19th Century.

Selected Publications:

_____. *Natural Science Books in English 1600-1900.* Batsford, 1972; 1989. Chapter and Bibliography on Natural Theology.
_____. *The Age of Science.* Blackwell, 1986; new edition 1988. Science and Scientism in the 19th century.
_____. *Companion to the Physical Sciences.* Routledge, 1989. Discussion of Miracle, Religion, Values - a bedside book on the History of Science.
_____. "Experiment, Observation, Theory - and the Spirits." *Durham University Journal* (1990): 55-8. Psychical Research.
_____. *Ideas in Chemistry.* Rutgers, 1992. Chapter on Occult Science.
_____. *Humphry Davy: Science and Power.* Blackwell, 1992. Chapter on his religious ideas.

Knight, Douglas A.

Present Position and Address: Professor of Hebrew Bible (since 1986), Vanderbilt University Divinity School, Nashville, TN 37240; (Home) 2106 19th Avenue South, Nashville, TN 37212, USA **Work Phone:** (615) 343-5008 **Home Phone:** (615) 292-6078 **Date of Birth:** May 1, 1943 **Languages Spoken:** English, German, Norwegian **Education:** B.A. Philosophy (1965), Ottawa University; M.Div. Biblical Studies (*cum laude*, 1968), California Baptist Theological Seminary; Advanced study in Theology (1967), University of Oslo, Norway; Dr. Theol. (*magna cum laude*, 1973), Georg-August-Universität Göttingen, Germany **Previous Positions:** Research Assistant (1970-72), Georg-August-Universität; Adjunct Professor of Old Testament (1973), American Baptist Seminary of the West, CA; Assistant (1973)/Associate (1978), Vanderbilt University Divinity School and Graduate Department of Religion; Visiting Professorships: University of Montana (1977)/The Iliff School of Theology, Denver (1980)/The Hebrew University of Jerusalem (1981-82)/Ecumenical Institute for Theological Research, Jerusalem (1981-82) **Editorial Work:** General Editor, *The Bible and Its Modern Interpreters* in 3 volumes; Coeditor of *Issues in Religion and Theology Series;* Editor of *The Library of Ancient Israel Series* **Selected Memberships:** American Academy of Religion **Discipline:** Hebrew Bible and Ancient Near Eastern Studies **Related Interests:** Ancient Cosmologies; Ethics of Ancient Israel.

Selected Publications: His bibliography lists 6 books, 19 articles, 19 edited works, and 5 translations most of which are in the area of Old Testament.

_____. "Cosmogony and Order in the Hebrew Tradition." In *Cosmogony and Ethical Order: New Studies in Comparative Ethics*, ed. R. W. Lovin and F. E. Reynold. Chicago and London: The University of Chicago Press, 1985.

_____. "Cosmology;" "Ethics in the Old Testament." In *Mercer Dictionary of the Bible*, ed. Watson E. Mill. Macon: Mercer University Press, 1990.

_____. "Ancient Israelite Cosmology: Images and Evaluations." In *The Church and Contemporary Cosmology: Proceedings of the Consultation on the Church and Contemporary Cosmology*, ed. J. B. Miller and K. E. McCall. Pittsburgh: Carnegie Mellon University, 1990.

Knight, James Allen

Present Position and Address: Professor of Psychiatry and Humanities in Medicine (since 1992), Texas A & M University, College of Medicine, College Station, TX 77843-1114, USA; (Home) 2110 Chippendale, College Station, TX 77845-5581, USA **Work Phone:** (409) 847-8650 or (409) 696-4231 **Fax Number:** (409) 845-6509 **Date of Birth:** October 20, 1918 **Languages Spoken:** English **Education:** A.B. (1941), Wofford College, Spartanburg, SC; B.D./M.Div. (1944), Duke University Divinity School, NC; M.D. (1952), Vanderbilt University School of Medicine, TN; M.P.H. (1962), Tulane University School of Medicine, LA; C.J. Jung Institute, Zurich, Switzerland (summer 1961), training in Jungian Psychology and Religion; Center for Training in Community Psychiatry, University of California - Berkeley (summer 1962), didactic and field training in Community Psychiatry **Awards and Honors:** The John P. McGovern Award Lecture in the Medical Humanities (1983), University of Texas Medical Branch; Annual Award of the Society for Health and Human Values, "for creative and dedicated leadership in the furtherance of human values in medical education"; Michael J. McCulloch Memorial Award of the Delta Society, "for outstanding contributions in furthering the human-companion animal bond" **Previous Positions:** Medical Director (1954-55), American Cyanamid Company, New Orleans, LA; Assistant (1955-57)/Instructor of Psychiatry (1957-58), Tulane University School of Medicine, LA; Assistant Professor of Psychiatry (1958-61)/Assistant Dean (1960-61), Baylor University College of Medicine; Associate Professor of Psychiatry and Preventive Medicine/Director of Section on Community Psychiatry (1961-63), School of Medicine and School of Public Health, Tulane University, LA; Director of the Program in Psychiatry and Religion/Professor of Psychiatry and Religion (1963-64), Union Theological Seminary, NY; Associate Dean and Director of Admissions/Professor of Psychiatry (1964-74), School of Medicine and Public Health, Tulane University, LA; Dean and Professor of Psychiatry (1974-77), Texas A & M University, TX; Professor of Psychiatry and Medical Ethics (1978-91, Emeritus since 1991), Louisiana State University **Editorial Positions:** Member of Editorial Board: *Annals of Allergy*; *Current Concepts in Psychiatry*; *Journal of Clinical Psychiatry*; *Journal of Religion in Psychotherapy*; *Pastoral Psychology Journal* **Other Academic Experience:** Specialty Certification: American Board of Psychiatry and Neurology (1960); Ordained Clergyman (Methodist) **Selected Memberships:** American Academy of Psychoanalysis; American Osler Society; American Psychiatric Association; Delta Society—Human-Companion Animal Bond; Group for the Advancement of Psychiatry (GAP); Institutes of Religion and Health; President Elect (1982-83)/President (1983-84), Society for Health and Human Values; Society for the Scientific Study of Religion **Discipline:** Psychiatrist; Ministry **Related Areas of Interest:** Psychiatry and Religion; Ethical and Value Issues in Medicine; Self-destructive Behaviors; The Human-Companion Animal Bond **Current Areas of Research:** Biblical stories and Psychiatric insights; Ethical issues in Geriatric care; Divided loyalties in mental health care.

Selected Publications: His bibliography contains 9 books and 102 published articles.

_____. *A Psychiatrist Looks at Religion and Health*. New York: Abingdon Press, 1964.
_____. *For the Love of Money: Human Behavior and Money*. Philadelphia, PA: J. B. Lippincott, 1968.
_____. *Conscience and Guilt*. New York: Appleton-Century-Crofts, 1969.
_____. *Medical Student: Doctor in the Making*. New York: Appleton-Century-Crofts, 1973.
_____. *Doctor-To-Be: Coping with the Trials and Triumphs of Medical School*. New York: Appleton-Century-Crofts, 1981.

_____. "The Spiritual as a Creative Force in the Person." *Journal of the American Academy of Psychoanalysis* 15, 3 (1987): 365-82.

_____. "Judging Competence: When the Psychiatrist Need, or Need Not, be Involved." In *Competency — A Study of Informal Competency Determinations in Primary Care*, ed. Mary Ann Gardell Cutter and Earl E. Shelp, 3-28. Dordrecht, The Netherlands: Kluwer Academic Publishers, 1991.

_____. "The Suffering of Suicide: The Victim and Family Considered." In *The Hidden Dimension of Illness: Human Suffering*, ed. Patricia L. Starck and John P. McGovern, 245-68. New York: National League for Nursing Press, 1992.

_____. "Would Sir William Osler Have Liked a Jazz Funeral New Orleans Style?" *The Journal of Medical Humanities* 13, 4 (1992): 247-52.

_____. "Ethics of Care in Caring for the Elderly." *Southern Medical Journal* 87, 9 (1994):909-17.

Knobloch, Irving William

Present Position and Address: Professor Emeritus (since 1976), Michigan State University (Home) 6104 Brookhaven, E. Lansing, MI 48823, USA **Date of Birth:** March 1, 1907 **Education:** B.A. (1930)/M.A. (1932), SUNY - Buffalo; Ph.D. (1942), Iowa State University **Previous Positions:** Assistant through Professor (1945-76), Michigan State University **Selected Memberships:** American Scientific Affiliation **Discipline:** Biology; Botany **Related Interests:** Areas of conflict between Christianity and Modern Science.

Selected Publications:

_____. "The Development of Life." *Christian Life* 17 (1956): 18-21.

_____. "Rank Materialism Will Not Do." In *The Evidence for God in an Expanding Universe*, ed. John Monsma. New York: C. P. Putnam's Sons, 1958.

_____. "The Role of Hybridization in Speciation and Evolution." In *Evolution and Christian Thought Today*, ed. Russell Mixter. Eerdmans, 1959.

_____. *Livable Planets Are Hard to Find*. Self Published, 1994.

Koelega, D. G. A.

Present Position and Address: Project Secretary for the "Technology, Ethics and the Future" project, Multidisciplinary Centre for Church and Society (MCKS), Postbus 19, 3970 AA Driebergen, Netherlands. Also working at the Free University of Amsterdam, Institute for Ethics (since May 1990), De Boelelaan 1105, 1081 HV Amsterdam, Holland **Date of Birth:** July 20, 1957 **Languages Spoken:** Dutch, English, German **Education:** M.Theol. (1984), State University, Leiden **Selected Memberships:** World Council of Churches (WCC) - Government Organizations **Discipline:** Theology; Philosophy **Related Interests:** Science, Technology, Theology and Social Science, Ethics.

Selected Publications:

_____, editor. Verantwoord werken aan technologie (Responsible working at technology). MCKS Publication, 1987.

_____, editor. Zorgen voor verantwoorde technologie (Caring for responsible technology). MCKS Publication, 1988.

_____, editor. *De Ingenieur Buitenspel? Over maatschappelijke verantwoordelijkheid in technische en natuurwetenschappelijke beroepen* (The engineer offsides? Social responsibility in technical and scientific professions). The Hague: Boekencentrum, 1989.

_____. *Verantwoorde technologie. Wat kunnen wÿ er zelf aan doen?* (Responsible technology. What can we do to make it?). Toerusting, Zoetermeer: Boekencentrum, 1993.

Koenig, Harold G.

Present Position and Address: Assistant Professor of Psychiatry and Medicine (since 1993), Box 3400, Duke University Medical Center, Durham, NC 27710; (Home) 415 Clarion Drive, Duham, NC 27705 **Concurrent Positions:** Director of Psychiatric Services (since 1992), Geriatric Evaluation and Treatment Clinic, Duke University Medical Center; Senior Fellow (since 1992), Center for the Study of Aging and Human Development, Duke University Medical Center; Director, Program on Religion, Aging, and Health, Center for Aging, Duke University Medical Center (since 1994) **Work Phone:** (919) 684-2647 or 8111, ID# 5106 **Home Phone:** (919) 383-6002 **Date of Birth:** December 25, 1951 **Education:** B.S. (1974), Stanford University; RN (1980), San Joaquin Delta College; MD (1982), University of California School of Medicine/San Francisco; M.Sc. (1989), Division of Biometry, Duke University **Postgraduate Experience:** Family Medicine Residency (1982-85), University of Missouri/Columbia; Geriatric Medicine Fellow (1986-89), Duke University Center for Aging and GRECC VA Medical Center; Residency in Psychiatry (1989-92), Duke University **Congresses and Conferences:** Keynote Address, American Society on Aging, Annual Conference on Religion and Aging, San Francisco, CA, April, 1990; Two presentations and panel discussion leader, Clergy/Healthcare Professionals Conference, Eastern Maine Medical Center, Bangor, ME; Presented three lectures, Southern Medical Society annual conference, Hilton Head, SC, March 18-20, 1994; Invited speaker, Conference on Health Promotion and Disease Prevention in the Elderly, UC Berkeley Center on Aging, Berkeley, CA, May 6, 1994; Participant, North Carolina Bar Association Conference on Ethical Issues and Medicine, Debate issue on Physician-Assisted Suicide with former president of NC Hemlock Society, Greenville, NC, September 14, 1994 **Lectures Presented:** NIMH sponsored BART Lecture series (1992-93); PGY-II Lecture Series on Geriatric Psychiatry (1993); PGY-III Lecture Series on Geriatric Psychiatry (1993); Duke Pastoral Care program, Geriatric lecture, Chaplain students **Awards and Honors:** Fellow Award (1990-92), American Association for Geriatric Psychiatry (AAGP); Research Award (1991-92), Counsel on Ministries in a Special Setting (COMISS); NIMH Clinical Mental Health Academic Award (1993) **Previous Positions:** Assistant Professor, (1985-86), Division of Geriatrics, Department of Family Practice, Southern Illinois University; Clinical Assistant Professor (1992-93), Division of Geriatric Psychiatry, Department of Psychiatry, Duke University Medical Center **Media Work:** "Depression in the Elderly," Health Program, WRAL, October 1993; "Religion, Aging and Health," National Public Radio, taped May 20, 1994; "Depression," Family and Health Program, WTVD, October, 1994 **Editorial Experience:** Journal Reviewer: *Journal of the American Medical Association, Journal of Gerontology,* Social Sciences Section, *Journal of Gerontology,* Psychological Sciences Section, *Journal of the American Geriatrics Society, Journal of General Internal Medicine, Psychosomatics, Western Journal of Medicine, International Journal of Geriatric Psychiatry, International Journal of Psychiatry in Medicine, American Journal of Geriatric Psychiatry, Journal of Personality Disorders, Journal of Geriatric Psychiatry and Neurology, The Gerontologist;* Editorial Boards: *International Journal of Psychiatry in Medicine, Journal of Religious Gerontology;* Consulting Coeditor, *Association of Medicine & Psychiatry Newsletter* **Discipline:** Geriatric Medicine; Psychiatry; Biometry.

Selected Publications: His bibliography contains 3 books, 15 book chapters, 71 articles, and numerous invited presentations.

_____, M. Smiley and J. Gonzales. *Religion, Health, and Aging.* Westport, CT: Greenwood Press, 1988.
_____. "Religion and Prevention of Illness in Later Life." In *Prevention in Human Services*, vol. 10, ed. K. Pargament, K. Manton, and R. Hess, 69-89. New York: Haworth Press, 1991.
_____. "Religion and Mental Health in Later Life." In *Religion and Mental Health*, ed. J. F. Schumacher, 177-88. London: Oxford Press, 1992.
_____, M. Hover, J. L. Travis, and L. B. Bearon. "Pastoral Research in a Hospital Setting: A Case Study." *Journal of Pastoral Care* 46 (1992): 283-90.

_____. "Religion and Hope in the Disabled Elder." In *Religious Factors in Aging and Health*, ed. J. Levin, 18-52. Newbury Park, CA: Sage Publications, 1993.

_____, S. Ford, L.K. George, D. G. Blazer, and K. G. Meador. "Religion and Anxiety Disorder: An Examination and Comparison of Associations in Young, Middle-aged, and Elderly Adults." *Journal of Anxiety Disorders* 7 (1993): 321-42.

_____. *Aging and God: Spiritual Paths to Mental Health in Midlife and Later Years*. New York: Haworth Press, 1994

Koenigsberger, Dorothy

Present Position and Address: Historian and Writer (until 1988), Hatfield Polytechnic, The Cedar Tree, 116 Waterfall Road, London, N14 7JN, England **Phone:** (081) 886-6416 **Date of Birth:** August 10, 1938 **Languages Spoken:** English, French **Education:** B.A. (*cum laude*, 1960), Brooklyn College CUNY; Ph.D. History (1969), University of Nottingham **Previous Positions:** Eastern District High School Teacher, NYC (1960-61); Lecturer in History (1969-71), Wells College; Research and Teaching Fellow (1971-72), Cornell University; Lecturer in History of Education (1975), Polytechnic of North London; Lecturer through Principal Lecturer (1976-83)/Reader in Intellectual History (since 1983)/Director of Research and Postgraduate Studies in Humanities (1984-88), Hatfield Polytechnic **Selected Memberships:** Institute of Historical Research; American Historical Association; Fellow, Royal Historical Society; Modern Humanities Research Association; American Society for Reformation Research; Society of Renaissance Studies **Discipline:** History; History of Education; History of Science/Religion **Related Interests:** Music, Arts, Natural History.

Selected Publications: Her bibliography lists 5 publications, also reviews for European History Quarterly, History of European Ideas, Technology and Culture.

_____. "Universality, The Universe and Nicholas of Cusa's Untastable Foretaste of Wisdom." *European History Quarterly* 17, 1 (January 1987).

Kohn, David

Present Position and Address: Oxnam Professor of Science and Society (since 1988), Drew University, Nineteenth Century Studies, Graduate School, Madison, NJ 07940, USA **Date of Birth:** January 25, 1941 **Education:** B.S. Biology (1965), Queens College, City University of New York (CUNY); Ph.D. History of Science (1976), University of Massachusetts - Amherst **Previous Positions:** Assistant through Professor of History of Science (since 1983), Drew University **Selected Memberships:** History of Science Society; Sigma Xi; Associate Member (since 1985), Darwin College, Cambridge **Discipline:** History of Science **Related Interests:** Darwin; Victorian Science and Religion.

Selected Publications:

_____. "Theories to Work by: Rejected Theories, Reproduction, and Darwin's Path to Natural Selection." *Studies in History of Biology* 4 (1980).

_____. "On the Origin of the Principle of Diversity." *Science* 213 (1981): 1105-1108.

_____. "New Light on the 'Foundations' of the Origin of Species." *Journal of the History of Biology* 15 (1982): 421-444.

_____, editor. *The Darwinian Heritage*. Princeton University Press, 1985.

_____, M. J. S. Hodge. "Darwin's Principle of Divergence as Internal Dialogue," and "The Immediate Origins of Natural Selection." In *The Darwinian Heritage*. Princeton: Princeton University Press, 1985.

_____, P. Barrett, P. Gautrey, S. Herbert and S. Smith, eds. *Charles Darwin's Notebooks (1936-44): Geology, Transmutation of Species, Metaphysical Enquiries, British Museum of Natural History.* Cornell University Press, and Cambridge University Press, 1987.

_____. "Darwin's Ambiguity: Tree, Secularization of Biological Meaning." British Journal History of Science (to be published).

Koltermann, Rainer

Present Position and Address: Professor of Zoology (since 1976), University of Mainz; Professor of Philosophy of Nature (since 1975), Philosophisch-Theologische Hochschule Sankt Georgen, Frankfurt Offenbacher Landstrasse 224, D-60599 Frankfurt/M, Germany. **Date of Birth:** March 18, 1931 **Languages Spoken:** German, English, Spanish **Education:** lic. phil. (1958), Hochschule für Philosophie, Berchmanskolleg, München; Lic. theol. (1962), Philosophisch-Theologische Hochschule Sankt Georgen, Frankfurt; Dr. phil. nat., Biology, Anthropology and Chemistry (1969), Wolfgang Goethe-Universität, Frankfurt; Research Assistant (1969-75), Universities of Frankfurt and Würzburg; Dr. rer. nat. habil. (1975) **Selected Memberships:** German Zoological Society; Participant in European Congresses on Science and Religion: Philosophy, Theology, Biology, Anthropology and Chemistry **Discipline:** Evolutionary theory and creation with specific reference to investigations into the memory of bees, and comparative animal and human behavior.

Selected Publications:

_____. "Ethische Grundsätze zu Tierversuchen." Pharma-Technologie Journal, Momo-Script 3 (1983, Anhang): 1-3.
_____. "Grenzen biologischer Aussagen und ihr Überstieg in Philosophie und Theologie - aufgezeigt am Beispiel von Evolution und Schöpfung." Information (Mitteilungsblatt für die kathol. Schulen in freier Trägerschaft in den Diözesen Fulda, Limburg und Mainz no. 1 (1983): 15-25.
_____. "Das Phänomen Leben: Zufall, Entwicklung, Schöpfung? (Die wissenschaftlich-biologische Erforschung des Menschen und der christlich Glaube)." K.F.S. im Erzbistum Köln. Lehrer-Fortbildungsreihe 60 (1984): 1-59.
_____. "Schöpfung in Evolution." Lebendiges Zeugnis 41 (H.1, 1986): 52-67.
_____. "Entwicklung/Evolution." In Lexikon der Religionen, ed. F. König and H. Waldenfel. Freiburg, Wien: Herder, 1987.
_____. "Vom Urknall an in Gottes Hand." In Kontexte, Forum Religion, ed. W. Trutwin. Düsseldorf: Patmos, 1987.
_____. "Reviews on more Recent Treatises about Natural Philosophy and Evolutionary Epistemology." Entomologia Generalis 13 (1988): 125-135.
_____. "The Concept of Evolution and its Reception in Philosophy and Theology." In *Science and Religion: One World — Changing Perspectives on Reality*, ed. Jan Fennema and Iain Paul. The Second European Conference on Science and Religion. Netherlands, Twene, 1988.
_____. *Grundzüge der modernen Naturphilosophie. Ein kritischer Gesamtentwurf.* Frankfurt: Knecht, 1994.

Korsmeyer, Jerry D.

Present Position and Address: Retired Physicist, 132 Highland Drive, McMurray, PA 15317 **Phone:** (412) 941-9431 **E-Mail:** 74160,3177@compuserve.com **Date of Birth:** December 5, 1930 **Languages Spoken:** English **Previous Positions Held:** Supervisor (1963-66) Experimental Physics Operations and Analyses, Light Water Breeder Reactor Project, Bettis Laboratory; Managing Irradiations Project Analyses (1969-72) Bettis Laboratory; Manager of Nuclear Analyses (1972-74) Nimitz-Class Aircraft Carrier, Bettis Laboratory; Manager of Reactor Engineering (1974-84) Nimitz-Class Aircraft Carrier, Bettis Laboratory; Consultant on Reactor Performance Analysis (1984-89) Bettis Laboratory, West Mifflin, PA **Honors:** Sigma Ix, Sigma Pi Sigma **Memberships:** American Nuclear Society, American Academy of Religion, Catholic Theological Society of America, Center for Process Studies, Center for Theology and the Natural Science **Discipline:** Nuclear Physics, Theology **Relevant Areas of Interest:** Process Theology, Theology and Science, and Fundamental Theology **Current Projects:** Research for a book on a Theology of Evolution, Abstracting articles for the journal *Process Studies*

Selected Publications: Most of his scientific papers are U.S. government classified information.

_____, S. Glickstein, P. Lehmann, L. Wheat, S. Milani, G. Smith and S. Weiss. "Thermal Disadvantage Factors in Uranium-Thorium Seed-Blanket Assemblies." *Nuclear Science and Engineering* 30(1967).

_____, H. Raab and S. Milani. "Uranium-233 Thorium Seed-Blanket Experimental Program." Transactions of the American Nuclear Society (1966).

_____, S. Milani and Staff. "Non-Asymptotic Lattice Parameters in a "Dry" UO2 Blanket." Transactions of the American Nuclear Society (1963).

_____. "A Resonance Model for Revelation." *Process Studies* 6 No.3 (Fall 1976): 195-96.

Koteskey, Ronald L.

Present Position and Address: Professor of Psychology (since 1977), Asbury College, Wilmore, KY 40390, USA; (Home) 122 Lowry Lane, Wilmore, KY 40390, USA **Work Phone:** (606) 858-3511 ext. 224 **Home Phone:** (606) 858-3436 **Date of Birth:** March 15, 1942 **Education:** A.B. (1963), Asbury College; M.A. (1966)/Ph.D. (1967), Wayne State University **Previous Positions:** Greenville College; Assistant through Associate Professor of Psychology (1967-70); Associate Professor through Professor (1970-present)/Acting Chairman (1972-73), Asbury College **Selected Memberships:** American Psychological Association; Midwestern Psychological Association; Kentucky Psychological Association; Christian Association for Psychological Studies; American Scientific Affiliation; Society for the Scientific Study of Religion **Discipline:** Psychology (the learning process); Mathematics and Statistics (minor) **Related Interests:** Integration of Psychology and Christianity; Development of Adolescence.

Selected Publications:

_____. "Behavioral Psychology in Christian Perspective." *Journal of American Scientific Affiliation (JASA)* 24 (1972): 144-147.

_____. "An Integration of Statistics and Christianity." *Journal of Psychology and Theology (JPT)* 3 (1975): 195-201. Also published as "The Integration of Statistics and Christianity in the Classroom." *CAPS Bulletin* 2 (1976): 17-21.

_____. "Toward the Development of a Christian Psychology: Learning and Cognitive Processes." *JPT* 6 (1978): 254-265.

_____. "Toward the Development of a Christian Psychology: Developmental Psychology." *CAPS Bulletin* 4, 4 (1978): 1-4.

_____. "Toward the Development of a Christian Psychology: Motivation." *JPT* 7 (1979): 3-12.

_____. "Toward the Development of a Christian Psychology: Personality." *JPT* 7 (1979): 92-104.

_____. "Toward the Development of a Christian Psychology: Adjustment and Maladjustment." *JPT* 7 (1979): 176-186.

_____. *Psychology from a Christian Perspective*. Nashville, TN: Abingdon, 1980.

_____. "Toward the Development of a Christian Psychology: Comparative and Physiological Psychology." *JASA* 32 (1980): 64ff.

_____. "Toward the Development of a Christian Psychology: Social Psychology." *JASA* 32 (1980): 224-230.

Kovel, Joel

Present Position and Address: Alger Hiss Professor of Social Studies (since 1988), Bard College, Anandale on Hudson, NY 12504, USA; (Home) Box 89, Willow, NY 12495, USA **Home Phone:** (914) 679-2756 **Date of Birth:** August 27, 1936 **Languages Spoken:** English, Spanish **Education:** B.S. (*summa cum laude*, 1957), Yale University; M.D. (1961), Columbia University; Resident Psychiatry (1962-65), Albert Einstein College of Medicine, Bronx Municipal Hospital Center; Graduate of Psychoanalytic Institute (1977), Downstate Medical Center, Brooklyn, NY **Previous Positions:** Instructor of Psychiatry (1967-69)/Director of Undergraduate Medical Education in Psychiatry (1968-71)/Assistant (1969-74)/Associate (1974-79)/Professor of Psychiatry (1979-85)/Director of

Residency; Training (1977-83), Albert Einstein College of Medicine; Adjunct Professor of Anthropology (1980-85), Graduate Faculty, New School for Social Research, NYC; Visiting Professor of Political Science and Communications (1986-87), University of California - San Diego **Selected Memberships:** Institute for Media Analysis **Discipline:** Psychoanalysis; Society/Politics and Anthropology; Critical Theory **Related Interests:** Society and Religion; Psychology/Psychiatry and Religion.

Selected Publications: His bibliography lists 8 books, 55 articles, and 30 reviews among other things.

_____. *The Radical Spirit: Essays in Psychoanalysis and Society.* London: Free Association Books, 1988.
_____. "On the Notion of Human Nature: A Contribution Towards a Philosophical Anthropology." In *Hermeneutical Approaches to Psychology*, ed. S. Messer, L. Sass, and R. Woolfolk. New Brunswick: Rutgers University Press, 1988.
_____. "Beyond the Future of an Illusion: Further Reflections on Freud and Religion." *Psychoanalytic Review* 77 (1990): 69-88.
_____. *History and Spirit.* Boston: Beacon Press, 1991.
_____. *Red Hunting in the Promised Land.* New York: Basic Books, 1994.

Kracher, Alfred

Present Position and Address: Assistant Scientist (since 1983), Geological Sciences, 253 Science 1, Iowa State University, Ames, IA 50011-3212, USA **Work Phone:** (515) 294-5439 **Fax Number:** (515) 294-6049 **E-Mail:** akracher@iastate.edu **Date of Birth:** September 21, 1945 **Languages Spoken:** English, German **Previous Positions:** Research Assistant (1972-74), University of Vienna, Austria; Research Assistant (1974-76), Museum of Natural History, Vienna, Austria; Staff Scientist (1976-80), Museum of Natural History, Vienna, Austria; Research Associate (1981-82), University of New Mexico **Selected Memberships:** American Geophysical Union; Meteoritical Society; Geochemical Society; European Society for the Study of Science and Theology; Philosophy of Science Association **Discipline:** Geochemistry; Theory of Science **Related Areas of Interest:** Science and Myth - Social Implications of the Philosophy of Science **Current Areas of Research:** Scientific Content of Origin Narratives.

Selected Publications: His bibliography contains about 35 scientific papers, 6 articles on science, culture, and religion, contributions to newspapers, and numerous conference abstracts.

_____. "The Unity of Creativity and Its Significance to Science and Social Progress." In *Essays on Creativity and Science*, ed. Diana Macintyre DeLuca, 81-8. Honolulu, HI, 1986.
_____. "Coming Home to the World." *Chrysalis* 5 (1990): 129-32.
_____. "A Scientist's View from Coyote's Rock." *Chrysalis* 7 (1992): 73-7.
_____. "Nutcracker and Computer - The Prophetic Vision of E. T. A. Hoffmann." *Humanities and Technology Association Review* 12 (1993): 1-11.
_____. "The Concept of Creation as Epistemological Critique." *Studies in Science and Theology* 2 (1994):174-81.
_____. "Evolutionary History and the 'Symbolism of Evil'." *Studies in Science and Theology* (in press).

Kraft, R. Wayne

Present Position and Address: Professor Emeritus (since 1989), Lehigh University, Bethlehem, PA 18015, USA; (Home) 645 Biery's Bridge Rd., Bethlehem, PA 18017, USA **Date of Birth:** January 14, 1925 **Languages Spoken:** English **Education:** B.S. Metallurgical Engineering (1948), Lehigh University; M.S. (1956)/Ph.D. Metallurgical Engineering (1958), University of Michigan **Honorary Degrees:** Honorary Doctorate of Humanities (1984), Allentown College of St. Francis de Sales **Previous Positions:** Professor of Materials Science and Engineering, Lehigh University in Bethlehem, PA **Selected Memberships:** Society for General Systems Research; American Teilhard Association for the Future of Man; Institute for Theological Encounter of Science and Theology; Institute on

Religion in an Age of Science; *Zygon*; Fellow, American Association for the Advancement of Science **Discipline:** Physical Metallurgy (Solidification, X-ray diffraction); Systems Philosophy - Teilhardian thought **Related Interests:** Permanent Deacon, Roman Catholic diocese of Allentown, PA. Teilhard studies.

Selected Publications

_____. *A Reason to Hope: A Synthesis of Teilhard de Chardin's Vision and Systems Thinking*. Salinas CA: Intersystems Publishers, 1984.
_____. *Love As Energy, Teilhard Studies No. 19*. Chambersburg PA: Anima Books, 1988.

Krolzik, Udo

Present Position and Address: Director of Ev. Johanneswerk e.v. Schildescher Str. 101, 33611 Bielefeld, Germany **Date of Birth:** March 25, 1948 **Languages Spoken:** German, English **Education:** Master of Theology (1976)/Doctor of Theology (1984), University of Hamburg **Awards and Honors:** Henry Miller Prize (1973), University of Edinburgh **Previous Positions:** Assistant Professor (1976-87), University of Hamburg; Minister of the Lutheran Church (1987-93), Hamburg, Germany **Selected Memberships:** Secretary, International Working Group on the Geography of Belief Systems; Chairman, Working Group on Ecological Theology in Germany; Secretary, Working Group on the History of Physicotheology in Germany **Discipline:** Minister; Social Ethics and Church History **Related Interests:** Christian Ethics and Genetic Engineering; History of the Relationship of Theology and Science.

Selected Publications: His bibliography lists 3 books, and over 20 chapters and articles.

_____. *Umweltkrise - Folge des Christentums?* Stuttgart/Berlin, 1st edition 1979; 2nd edition 1980. Sections also republished in Werkbuch Umwelt, ed. E. Knöpfel. Wuppertal, 1984; and in Verantwortung für die Schöpfung, ed. E. Knöpfel. Paderborn, u.a., 1987.
_____. "Das physikotheologische Naturverständnis und sein Einfluss auf das naturwissenschaftliche Denken im 18. Jahrhundert." *Medizinhistorisches Journal* 15 (1980): 90-102.
_____. "Zum Einfluss der Theologie auf das geographische Denken zu Beginn des 18. Jahrhunderts." In Zur Entwicklung der Geographie vom Mittelalter bis zu Carl Ritter, ed. Manfred Büttner. Paderborn u.a., 1982.
_____. *Ökologische Probleme und das Naturverständnis des christlichen Abendlandes, Information Nr. 87*. Stuttgart: Evangelische Zentralstelle für Weltanschauungsfragen, 1983. Sections also published in Verantwortung für die Schöpfung, ed. E. Knöpfel. Paderborn, u.a., 1987.
_____. "Christliche Wurzeln der neuzeitlichen mechanistischen Naturwissenschaften und ihres Naturbegriffes." In "All Geschöpf is Zung' und Mund," ed. Heimo Reinitzer. *Beiträge aus dem Grenzbereich von Naturkunde und Theologie, Vestigia Bibliae 6* Hamburg, 1984.
_____. "Technik als Kultivierung der Schöpfung. Theologie und Technik im 18. Jahrhundert." *Die Technikgeschichte als Vorbild moderner Technik, Schriften der Georg-Agricola-Gessellschaft* 12 (1986): 119-126.
_____. "Natur zwischen Dogma, Mystik und Wissenschaft." *Materialdienst der EZW 51. Jg.* (1988): 129-140.
_____. *Säkularisierung der Natur. Providentia-Dei-Lehre und Naturbegriff der Frühaufklärung*. Neukirchen-Vluyn, 1988.
_____. "Kultivierung der Schöpfung. Zur Bewertung der Naturbearbeitung durch den Menschen in Theologie und Kirche vom 12. bis zum 18. Jahrhundert." In *Mensch und Umwelt in der Geschichte*, ed. Jörg Calliess, Jörn Rüsen, Meinfried Striegnitz. (1989).

Kropf, Richard W.

Present Position and Address: Writer (since 1981) in Northern Michigan, R.D. Box 629, Johannesburg, MI 49751-9622, USA **Work Phone:** (517) 732-9580 **Date of Birth:** January 9, 1932 **Education:** B.A. (1954), Sacred Heart Seminary - Detroit; S.T.B. (1958), Catholic University of America; M.Th. (1969), University of Ottawa; S.Th.L. (1969), St. Paul University; Ph.D. Theology (1973), University of Ottawa; S.Th.D. (1980), St. Paul University **Previous Positions:** Instructor in Philosophy and Religion (1972-75), Lansing Community College; Associate Professor in Religion (1974-75), Olivet College; Adjunct Assistant Professor of Religion and Chaplain (1976-78), Mercy College of Detroit; Instructor in Philosophy and Psychology (1977-78), Madonna College; Instructor in Philosophy (Spring 1979), St. Mary's College, Orchard Lake; Lecturer in Theology (1979-80), St. John's Provincial Seminary; Retired in 1981 **Selected Memberships:** Catholic Theological Society of America; American Teilhard Association **Discipline:** Systematic and Philosophical Theology **Related Interests:** Theology and Evolutionary Science; Psychology of Religion.

Selected Publications

_____. *Teilhard, Scripture, and Revelation.* Fairleigh Dickinson/Association of University Presses, 1980.
_____. *Evil and Evolution: A Theodicy.* Fairleigh Dickinson/Association of University Presses, 1984.
_____. *Faith: Security and Risk: The Dynamics of Spiritual Growth.* Paulist Press, 1990.

Külling, Samuel

Present Position and Address: Founder and Rector (since 1970), Free Evangelical Theological Academy, Basel, Switzerland (a state-independent academic seminary); Founder and Rector, Séminaire Libre de Théologie à Genève (Seminary f Mühlestiegrain 50, CH-4125, Riehen, Basel, Switzerland **Date of Birth:** January 9, 1924 **Languages Spoken:** German, French, English, Dutch **Education:** Studies in Theology, University of Bern (1945-51)/University of Edinburgh (1952-53); Studies in Jerusalem (1959-60); Free University in Amsterdam, Netherlands (1960-64); Dr. theol. (1964) **Previous Positions:** Pastor (1953-59)> Reformed Evangelical Church of Switzerland; Theology teacher (1964-70), Bible Seminary of St. Chrischona; Professor of Old Testament (since 1965), Vaux-s.Seine, Paris **Selected Memberships:** President, Bibelbund of the ICBI; Editor (since 1980), Fundamentum (Evangelical Quarterly of the Free Evangelical Theological Academy, Basel) **Discipline:** Old Testament; Semitic Languages **Related Interests:** Creation and Science, Pentateuch. **Selected Publications**

_____. *Der Schöpfungsbericht und naturwissenschaftliche Fragen.* Riehen/CH, 1976.

Kupke, Donald Walter

Present Position and Address: Professor of Biochemistry and Biophysics (since 1966), School of Medicine, University of Virginia, Charlottesville, VA 22908, USA **Date of Birth:** March 16, 1922 **Education:** A.B. (1947), Valparaiso University; M.S. (1949)/Ph.D. Biochemistry (1952), Stanford University; Postdoctoral studies (1952-55), Carlsberg in Copenhagen/Uppsala University **Previous Positions:** Staff (1955-56), Carnegie Institute, Washington; Assistant (1957-63)/Associate Professor of Biochemistry (1963-66)/Chairman of Department (1964-66), University of Virginia **Selected Memberships:** American Association for the Advancement of Science; American Chemical Society Biophysical Society; Protein Society; American Society of Biological Chemists; Sigma Xi. Also a member of the Lutheran Church (Missouri Synod) **Discipline:** Biophysics and Biochemistry **Related Interests:** Biomacromolecules and the role of water in living systems. (Dilettante) Cosmology; Philosophy and History of Science; The 6-day timespan and the perception of time in Genesis 1.

Selected Publications: His bibliography lists numerous scientific papers (research) and reviews in a variety of journals dealing primarily with structure and function of proteins and other macromolecules.

_____. "Science and the Scriptures after 200 Years." *The Lutheran Witness* S.E. District Edition (1976): 3-4.
_____. "Change in Time: Special Relativity and Genesis One." *Academy: Lutherans in Profession* 33 (1976): 12-24.

_____. "A Young Versus an Old Creation: A Reconciliation?" *Journal of American Scientific Affiliation* 31 (1979): 60-61.

Küppers, Bernd-Olaf

Present Position and Address: Professor of Philosophy, Institüt für Philosophie, Universität Jena, Zwätzengasse 9, D-07743 Jena, Germany **Date of Birth:** June 10, 1944 **Languages Spoken:** German, English **Education:** Studied Physics at the Universities of Bonn and Göttingen **Previous Positions:** Max-Planck-Institut für biophysikalische Chemie, Göttingen (1971-1993); Universitt Heidelberg, Lecturer of Philosophy (1992-93); Special Visiting Professor, Japan (1993); Lecturer of Philosophy (1979-84), University of Göttingen **Discipline:** Philosophy of Science **Related Interests:** Molecular Biology of Evolution; Physics, Chemistry and Biology.

Selected Publications: His bibliography lists over 60 scientific publications including the following books.

_____. *Molecular Theory of Evolution*. Heidelberg: Springer Verlag, 1983, 1985.
_____, editor. *Leben = Physik + Chemie?* Munich: Piper Verlag, 1987, 1990.
_____, editor. *Ordnung aus dem Chaos*. Munich: Piper Verlag, 1987, 1988, 1991.
_____. *Information and the Origins of Life*. Cambridge MA: MIT Press, 1990.
_____. *Natur als Organismus*. Frankfurt: Klostermann Verlag, 1991.

LaBar, Martin

Present Position and Address: Chairman of Science (since 1964), Central Wesleyan College, Central, SC 29630; (Home) 319 Gilstrap Dr., Liberty, SC 29657, USA **Work Phone:** (803) 639-2453 **Home Phone:** (803) 843-9194 **Date of Birth:** May 15, 1938 **Education:** B.A. Biology/Chemistry/Physics (1958), Wisconsin State University, Superior, WI; M.S. Genetics (1963)/Ph.D. Genetics and Zoology (1965), University of Wisconsin - Madison **Previous Positions:** Research Assistant (1958-64), University of Wisconsin; Sabbatical (1982-83), Bryan College, Dayton, TN **Selected Memberships:** The Wesleyan Church (since 1959), member, Task Force on Public Morals and Social Reform (1988-92); American Scientific Affiliation; American Association for Advancement of Science; Animal Behavior Society; Ecological Society of America; Biology Task Force, Christian College Coalition (1984-88) **Discipline:** Zoology; Genetics **Related Interests:** Bioethics, including medical (especially genetic engineering) and environmental; Philosophy of Science; Computers and Mathematics.

Selected Publications: His curriculum vitae lists 13 relevant articles, 2 contributions to Science books, and 26 book reviews in the field.

_____. "Ecology and the Bible." *Wesleyan Advocate* (1972).
_____. "Reversing the 2nd Law." *Wesleyan Advocate* (1980).
_____. "Genetic Engineering: Good, Bad or Indifferent." *Wesleyan Advocate* (1981).
_____. "A World is Not Made to Last Forever: The Bioethics of C. S. Lewis." *Journal of the American Scientific Affiliation* 35 (1983): 104-107.
_____. "Earth, Age of," and "Origin of the Universe." In *Evangelical Dictionary of Theology*, ed. Walter Elwell. Grand Rapids: Baker, 1984.
_____. "The Pros and Cons of Human Cloning." *Thought* 59, 234 (1984): 319-333.
_____. "A Biblical Perspective on Nonhuman Organisms: Values, Moral Considerability, and Moral Agency." In *Religion and Environmental Crisis*. Athens: University of Georgia, 1986.
_____. "Celebrate the Diversity of God's Creation." *Wesleyan Advocate* 145, 329 (1987).

Laeyendecker, L.

Present Position and Address: Marskramersbaan 16, 3981 TK Bunnik, The Netherlands **Date of Birth:** April 18, 1930 **Languages Spoken:** Dutch, English, German **Education:** High school (1947); Philosophy and Theology (Augustinian Order, 1951-58)/Sociology - including Sociology of Religion (1958-64)/Ph.D. (1967), University of Amsterdam, Netherlands **Previous Positions:** Director (1989-92) of the Multidisciplinair Centrum voor Kerk en Samenleving (MCKS), a Multidisciplinary Center for Church and Society; Assistant Professor in Sociology (1964-69)/ Associate Professor in Sociology (1969-1973), University of Amsterdam; Full Professor (1973-1989), University of Leyden; Church Experience: Member of various (advisory) committees of the Roman Catholic Church in The Netherlands; Chairman of the board of the Catholic Institute of social research **Selected Memberships:**

Fellow, Netherlands Institute for Advanced Study in the Humanities and the Social Sciences; Member, Academy of Science of Holland; Member of the Royal Netherlands Academy of Arts and Sciences **Discipline:** Sociology - including Sociology of Religion **Related Interests:** Sociological theory; Sociology of Religion and Culture; Sociology of Science; Historical Sociology.

Selected Publications: Numerous articles on sociology, sociology of religion and cultural sociology. (Titles below are translations from Dutch).

_____. *Religion and Conflict*. Ph.D. thesis, Meppel, 1967.
_____, K. Dobbelaere, eds. *Religion, Church and Society*. Rotterdam, 1974.
_____, W. F. van Stegeren. *Strategies of Social Change*. Meppel, 1978.
_____. *Order, Change and Inequality*. Meppel, 1981.
_____. *Social Change*. Meppel, 1984.
_____, W. J. Berger. *Choice as a Necessity*. Baarn, 1984.
_____, O. Schreuder, eds. *Religion and Politics*. Kampen, 1985.
_____. *Does Progress Really Help*? Baarn, 1986.
_____. *Who Controls the Charisma? Salvation and Power in the Roman Catholic Church*. Amsterdam, 1993.
_____. *Culture in Danger. Essays on Modernity, Science and Religion*. Kampen, 1994.

LaFargue, Michael

Present Position and Address: Lecturer (since 1983), Study of Religion, University of Massachusetts - Boston, Boston, MA 02125 USA **Work Phone:** (617) 287-5720 **Home Phone:** (617) 731-6886 **Date of Birth:** June 5, 1939 **Languages Spoken:** English, Spanish **Education:** B.A. Scholastic Philosophy (1962)/Graduate Studies in Catholic Theology (1962-66), Immaculate Conception College, Oconomowoc, WI; Doctoral Candidate in Biblical Studies (1967-69), Graduate Theological Union, Berkeley, CA; Th.D. New Testament Studies (1977), Harvard Divinity School **Previous Positions:** Teaching Assistant (1969), Church Divinity School of the Pacific, Berkeley; Lecturer (1969), College of the Holy Names, Oakland, CA; Teaching Fellow (1972), Harvard College; Lecturer (1972-82), Cambridge and Boston Centers for Adult Education; Lecturer (1978-82), University of Massachusetts - Boston; Visiting Assistant Professor (1982-83), Wheaton College **Selected Memberships:** American Academy of Religion **Discipline:** Religious Studies **Related Interests:** Philosophy of Mathematics and Science; Early History of Science; Theological Method; Demythologizing.

Selected Publications

_____. "Objectivity in Morals and Science: Are Values 'Creations of the Human Mind'?" Paper given at a faculty seminar on "Science, Values, and Technology." (University of Massachusetts, April 1986).
_____. "Radically Pluralist, Thoroughly Cultural, A New Theory of Religions." *Journal of the American Academy of Religion* 60, 4 (1992): 693-715. Contains sections on Philosophy of Mathematics and of Science.
_____. *Tao and Method: A Reasoned Approach to Tao Te Ching*. Albany, NY: SUNY Press, 1994.

Landsberg, Peter T.

Present Position and Address: Professor of Applied Mathematics (since 1973); Emeritus Professor since 1988), University of Southampton, Southampton SO9 5NH, England, UK **Work Phone:** (0703) 593681 **E-mail:** ptl@maths.soton.ac.uk **Date of Birth:** August 8, 1922 **Education:** M.Sc (1949)/Ph.D. and D.I.C. (1949)/D.Sc. (1966), University of London **Previous Positions:** Lecturer in Natural Philosophy (1950-59), University of Aberdeen, UK; Professor of Applied Mathematics and Mathematical Physics (1959-72), University College, Cardiff, Wales; Professor of Applied Mathematics (1973-87), University of Southampton, UK; Visiting Professor (1982-87), University of Florida, Gainesville **Administrative Experience:** Dean of Faculty of Science (1966-68)/Deputy Principal (1969-71), University College, Cardiff, Wales **Selected Memberships:** Royal Society of Edinburgh (since 1971); Institute of Physics; Institute of Mathematics and its Applications **Discipline:** Mathematics and Physics **Related Interests:** Philosophy of Science and Religion; Thermodynamics and Cosmology.

Selected Publications: His curriculum vitae lists some 6 books and over 330 research papers in the fields of solid state theory, thermodynamics and statistical mechanics, and in relativity theory and cosmology.

_____. "Does Quantum Mechanics Exclude Life?" *Nature* 203 (1964): 928; and 205 (1965): 306.

_____, D. A. Evans. "Free Will in a Mechanistic Universe?" *British Journal of Philosophy of Science* 21 (1970): 343ff; and 23 (1972): 236ff.

_____. "Gambling on God." *Mind* 80, New Series, No. 317 (January 1971): 100-104.

_____, ed. and contributor. *The Enigma of Time.* Bristol: Adam Hilger, 1982, 1984.

_____. "Entropy and the Unity of Knowledge II." *Journal of Non-Equilibrium Thermodynamics* 12 (1987): 45.

_____. "The Search for Completeness." *Nature and Systems* 3 (1981): 236-242.

_____. "Components of Probabilistic Support." *Philosophy of Science* 55 (1988): 402ff.

_____. "Problems of Explanation in Physics." In *Beyond Belief: Randomness, Prediction, and Explanation in Science*, eds. J.L. Casti and A. Karlquist. Boca Raton, FL: CRC Press, 1991.

_____. "From Entropy to God?" In *Thermodynamics: History and Philosophy; Facts, Trends, and Debates*, eds. K Martinas, L. Ropolyi, and P. Szegedi. Singapore: World Scientific, 1991.

Lantum, Noni Daniel

Present Position and Address: Professor of Community Health (Public Health, since 1970), University Centre for Health Sciences, CUSS University of Yaounde, BP 1364, Yaounde, Cameroon **Concurrent Positions:** External Examiner and Examiner for Medicine Examinations (since 1975); 6 National Development Commissions **Date of Birth:** September 13, 1934 **Languages Spoken:** English, French, Lamnso **Education:** M.B.B.S. London (Doctor of Medicine, 1962), University of Ibadan, Nigeria; D.T.M.& H. Diploma in Tropical Medicine and Hygiene (1965), University of Liverpool, UK; M.P.H. Public Health (1969)/Dr. P.H. (Doctor of Public Health, 1970), University of Tulane **Selected Congresses and Conferences:** Participated in over 50 International Conferences and Workshops (since 1970) **Previous Positions:** Medical officer of 3 Hospitals (1965-68); Research Associate (1969-70), Faculty of Tulane School of Public Health and Tropical Medicine; Professor of Community Health (since 1970)/Coordinator of First Year U.C.H.S. Programme of Studies (1971-72)/Coordinator of Public Health Unit (1972-81)/Head of Department of Human Ecology (1973-75)/Head of Department of Health Education and Behavioral Sciences (since 1975)/Vice Dean (Deputy Director) of University Centre for Health Sciences (1978-86), (CUSS) University of Yaounde; Médecin/Chef Service (1972-74), Dispensaire, Grand Messa; Ford Foundation Research Fellow (1972-85); Ford Foundation and World Health Organization short-term consultant in Traditional Medicine and Community Medicine etc. (since 1973); President (1975-87), Anglophone Parish for Catholics, Yaounde **Editorial Work:** Editor, *Nso News Journal*, (1958-62)/*Patriot* (1959-62), Ibadan University **Administrative Experience:** Consultant to FAO, CDC, Save the Children, GURC/USAID, UNICEF/Cameroon, World Bank, UNECA, W.H.O. (since 1975) **Other Academic Experience:** Chairman (since 1988), of Sub-Committee of Experts charged to conduct the Feasability Study for the creation of the Catholic University of Cameroon, Yaounde **Discipline:** Medicine and Public Health **Related Interests:** Religion and Society; Religion and Medicine/Public Health.

Selected Publications: His bibliography lists over 50 scientific publications, 5 publications for educational reforms, over 25 in the humanities and arts and 5 on religion.

_____. "What is Community Medicine in 1979?" *Le Cameroun Médical Revue, Trimestrielle des Sciences de la Santé du Cameroun* 2, 1 (1980).

_____. Recent Advances in the Healing Ministry of the Catholic Church in Cameroon - A Contribution to Primary Health Care. University of Yaounde, Cameroon: Public Health Unit, UCHS/CUSS, March 1984.

_____. "A Reflection on the Commitment of the Christian Intellectual in the Church and in the City According to the Address of Pope John Paul II at the Yaounde Conference Centre on 13th August 1985." Keynote address to National Congress of MICA, Mvolye May 11, 1987. Cameroon Panorama (September/October, November/December, 1987).

_____. "The Relevance of Religious Education on our Materialistic World." Paper presented at St. Augustine's College for their Silver Jubilee Celebrations - Kumbo (April 1989).

_____. Traditional Medicine-Men of Cameroon: The Case of BUI Division. Yaounde: Public Health Unit, University of Yaounde, 1985.

_____. Traditional Medicine-Men of Centre Province of Cameroon. Yaounde: University of Yaounde, 1989.

_____. Dr. Bernard Nsokika Fonlon (1924-1986) Is Now A Legend. NSA History Publication 3. Kumbo Town, Cameroon: NSO History Society Publications, 1988.

_____. Dr. Bernard Nsokika Fonlon: An Intellectual in Politics (Gown and Throne). Yaounde: UCHS, 1992.

_____. Professor Bernard Nsokika Fonlon — The Luminary or Saint in the University Campus? N.p., 1989.

_____. Our Heritage (History of the Anglophone Parish for Catholics in Yaounde, 1961-65). Yaounde: Mimeo, 1991.

Larson, David Bruce

Present Position and Address: President; National Institute for Healthcare Research, 6110 Executive Blvd., Suite 680, Rockville, MD 20852; (Home) 998 Farm Haven Drive, Rockville, MD 20852 **Concurrent Positions:** Adjunct Professor (since 1994), Department of Preventative Medicine and Biometrics, Uniformed Services University of Health Sciences, Bethesda, MD; Adjunct Professor (since 1994) Dept of Psychiatry and Behavioral sciences, Northerwestern University Medical School; Adjunct Associate Professor (since 1991), Department of Psychiatry, Duke University **Work Phone:** (301) 984-7162 **Home Phone:** (301) 231-8677 **Fax Number:** (301) 984-8143 **Date of Birth:** March 13, 1947 **Languages Spoken:** English **Education:** B. S. Humanities and Technology (1969), Drexel University; M.D. (1973), Temple University Medical School; Rotating Internship (1973-74), MacNeal Memorial Hospital, Berwin, IL; Resident in Psychiatry (1974-77), Duke University Medical Center; M. S. Public Health in Epidemiology (1982), University of North Carolina/Chapel Hill **Postgraduate Experience:** Psychosomatics Teaching Fellow (1975-77), Department of Psychiatry, Duke University; Postdoctoral Fellow in the Behavioral Sciences, (1976-78), Duke University; Chief Resident in Psychiatry, Duke University (1977-79); Clinical Fellowship in Geropsychiatry (1979-81), Duke University Medical Center; National Institute of Mental Health Epidemiology Fellow (1982-83), University of North Carolina, The School of Public Health/Chapel Hill; National Institute of Mental Health Epidemiology Fellow (1983-85), Clinical Services Research Branch, Division of Biometry and Epidemiology, Rockville, MD **Congresses and Conferences:** Dr. Larson has been an invited participant to many conferences and workshops including, National Research forum on Family Issues: The White House Conference on Families, April, 1980, Washington, DC; Duke University Medical Center Conference on the Therapeutic Usefulness of Faith, March, 1981, Durham, NC; Co-Coordinator, Section on Research, International Congress on Christian Counselling, November, 1988, Atlanta, GA; Coordinator, First NIMH Research Development Workshop in C-L Psychiatry, September, 1984, Rockville, MD; Consortium on Consultation-Liaison Psychiatry, Brooks Lodge, June, 1989, Kalamazoo, MI; Co-Coordinator, Mental Health Services for Children and Adolescents in Primary Care Settings: A Research Conference, Yale University, June, 1989, New Haven, CT; Chair, Fourth Annual NIMH International Research Conference on the Classification and Treatment of Mental Disorders in General Medical Settings, June 11-12, 1990, Bethesda, MD; Coolfont: Public Health Service Conference Plan for the Prevention and Control of AIDS and the AIDS Virus, Committee on Patient Care and Health Services Delivery, June, 1986, Berkeley Springs, WV **Lectures Presented:** The following represent only a few scholarly lectures: The Steinhart Lectures (1993), University of Nebraska/Lincoln; **Awards and Honors:** Five Commissioned Corps Commendation Awards (1989, 90 [2], 91,93); Who's

Who in the East (1988); Dictionary of International Biography (1989); Personalities of America (1989); Who's Who in America (since 1990); Community Leaders of America (1990); *Who's Who of Emerging Leaders in America* (1990); *Who's Who Among Human Services Professionals* (1990); American Medical Association Physician Recognition Award in CME and the American Psychiatric Association CME Award (1982, 85, 88, 91,94) **Previous Positions:** Clinical Associate (1979-80)/Clinical Assistant Professor (1980-81)/Assistant Professor (1981-90)/Adjunct Associate Professor (1990-91), Department of Psychiatry, Duke University; Assistant Director (1979-82)/Acting Director (1979-80), Department of Psychiatry, Durham County General Hospital, Milieu/Family Oriented Inpatient Psychiatry Unit, Durham, NC; Research Psychiatrist (1985-91), Rockville, MD/Section Chief (1988-91)/Senior Analyst (1993-94), Office of the Secretary, Department of Health and Human Services, Washington, D.C.; Senior Researcher (1993-94),The Office of the Director/President (since 1994), Bethesda, MD, National Institute for Healthcare Research **Selected Memberships:** American Medical Association; Southern Medical Association; American Psychiatric Association; Southern Psychiatric Association; Society for Psychotherapy Research; Christian Medical and Dental Society; Association of Voluntary Action Scholars; Society for the Scientific Study of Religion; American Society for Psychiatric Oncology/AIDS; Christian Association for Psychological Studies; American Association of Marital and Family Therapy; American Association for the Advancement of Science **Discipline:** Medicine; Psychiatry; Administration.

Selected Publications: His total bibliography contains 93 journal publications, 40 monographs, invited reviews, and book chapters, 14 letters to the editor, 9 books, bibliographies, and national reports, 12 research papers submitted for journal review, and 7 unpublished manuscripts.

_____, A. H. Hohmann, L. Z. Kessler, J. H. Boyd, K. Meador, and E. McSherry. "The Couch and The Cloth: The Need for Linkage." *Hospital and Community Psychiatry* 39, 10 (1988): 1064-9.

_____, M. J. Donahue, J. S. Lyons, P. L. Benson, E. M. Pattison, E. L. Worthington, Jr., and D. G. Blazer. "Religious Affiliation in Mental Health Research Samples Vs. U. S. National Samples." *Journal of Nervous and Mental Disease* 177, 2 (1989): 109-11.

_____, H. G. Koenig, B. H. Kaplan, R. F. Greenberg, E. Logue, and H. A. Tyroler. "The Impact of Importance of Religion and Frequency of Church Attendance On Blood Pressure Status." *Journal of Religion and Health* 28, 4 (1989): 265-78.

_____, D. R. Williams, R. E. Buckler, R. C. Heckman, and C. M. Pyle. "Religion and Psychological Distress in a Community Sample." *Social Science and Medicine* 32, 11 (1991): 1257-62.

_____, K. A. Sherrill, J. S. Lyons, F. C. Craigie, Jr., S. B. Thielman, M. A. Greenwold, and S. S. Larson. "Associations Between Dimensions of Religious Commitment." *American Journal of Psychiatry* and the *Archives of General Psychiatry: 1978-1989. American Journal of Psychiatry* 149, 4 (1992): 557-9.

_____, S. B. Thielman, M. A. Greenwold, J. S. Lyons, S. G. Post, K. A. Sherrill, S. S. Larson, and G. G. Wood. Religious Content in the *Diagnostic and Statistical Manual, Third Edition-Revised (DSM-III-R)* Appendix C: The Glossary of Technical Terms. *American Journal of Psychiatry* 150, 12 (1993): 1884-5.

_____, L. G. Kessler, B. J. Burns, H. A. Pincus, J. L. Houpt, S. Fiester, and L. Chaitkin. "The Research Development Workshop: The Case of NIMH and C-L Psychiatry." *Hospital and Community Psychiatry* 38, 10 (1987): 1106-10.

_____, S. S. Larson. *The Forgotten Factor in Physical and Mental Health: What Does the Research Show?* Rockville, MD: National Institute for Healthcare Research; Philadelphia, PA: The John Templeton Foundation, 1992.

_____, D. A. Mathews and C. P. Barry. *An Annotated Bibliography of Clinical Research on Spiritual Subjects.* Vol. 1 of *The Faith Factor.* Rockville, MD: National Institute for Healthcare Research; Philadelphia, PA: The John Templeton Foundation, 1993.

_____. *An Annotated Bibliography of Systematic Reviews and Clinical Research on Spiritual Subjects.* Vol. 2 of *The Faith Factor.* Rockville, MD: National Institute for Healthcare Research; Philadelphia, PA: The John Templeton Foundation, 1993.

Larson, Duane H.

Present Position and Address: Associate Professor of Systematic Theology, Lutheran Theological Seminary at Gettysburg, 61 NW Confederate Ave, Gettysburg, PA 17325 Phone: (717) 334-6286, **Fax:** (717) 334-3469 **Date of Birth**: December 13, 1952 **Languages Spoken:** English, German **Education:** B.A. (1975) Pacific Lutheran University, Tacoma; M.Div. (1979) Luther-Northwestern Theological Seminary, St. Paul; Ph.D. (1993) Graduate Theological Union, Berkeley, CA **Previous Positions Held:** Teaching Assistant (1976-79) Luther Northwestern Seminary; Instructor (1981-82) Center for Theological Study, CA; Associate Pastor (1979-84) St. Andrew's Lutheran Church, San Diego, CA; Pastor (1984-88) Christ the Victor Lutheran Church, Fairfax, CA; Pastor (1988-93) St. Andrew's Lutheran Church, San Mateo, CA **Memberships:** Center for Theology and Natural Science; American Academy of Religion; The Karl Barth Society **Discipline:** Systematic Theology **Relevant Areas of Interest:** Doctrine of the Trinity, Cosmology, the Idea of 'Nature' in Luther's Thought, Doctrines of Creation, Providence, etc. **Current Projects:** Extension of the Doctrine of the Trinity as a Research Program; "Reality" and the Doctrine of Justification; the Eucharist

Selected Publications:

____. "Arthur Peacocke, Anselm, Atonement." *CTNS Bulletin* (June 1986)
____. "Book Review of Joseph Bracken, S.J. *Society and Spirit*." *CTNS Bulletin* (June 1992)
____. "The Trinity and Time's Flow." *Dialog* 33 (Winter, 1994): 62-70.
____. *Times of the Trinity.* New York: Peter Lang, 1995.

Larson, Edward J.

Present Position and Address: Associate Professor of Law and History (since 1987), Department of History and School of Law, University of Georgia, LeConte Hall, Athens, GA 30602, USA **Date of Birth:** September 21, 1953 **Education:** B.A. History (honors, 1974), Williams College; J.D. (honors, 1979), Harvard Law School; M.A. (1976)/Ph.D. History of Science (1984), University of Wisconsin **Previous Positions:** Analyst (1974-76), Wisconsin State Senate, Madison, WI; Counsel (1981-82), Washington State House of Representatives, Olympia; Attorney (1979-82), Davis, Wright and Tremaine, Seattle, WA; Associate Counsel (1983-86), Committee on Education and Labor, US Congress; Counsel (1986-87), Office of Educational Research and Improvement, United States Department of Education **Selected Memberships:** History of Science Society (since 1984); Washington State Bar Association (since 1979) **Discipline:** Law and History - including History of Science **Related Interests:** Creation-Evolution Controversy/Scientific Creationism; Medical Ethics; Church and State/Law.

Selected Publications

____. "Before the Crusade: Evolution in American Secondary Education before 1920." *Journal of the History of Biology* 20, 1 (1987): 89-114.
____, coauthor. *Euthanasia: Spiritual, Medical and Legal Issues in Terminal Health Care.* Portland: Multnomah, 1988.
____. *Trial and Error: The American Controversy over Creation and Evolution.* New York: Oxford University Press, 1989. Expanded paper-back edition. (Previously released in 1985).
____. "We the People: Constitutional Challenges to Textbooks." *Educational Policy* 3, 2 (1989): 137-151.
____. "Personhood: Current Legal Views." *Second Opinion* 14, 2 (1990): 40-53.
____. "Human Gene Therapy and the Law: An Introduction to the Literature." *Emory Law Review* 39, 3 (1990): 855-874.
____. *Sex, Race, and Science: Eugenics in the Deep South.* Baltimore, MD: Johns Hopkins University Press, 1994.
____. "The Rhetoric of Eugenics: Expert Authority and the Mental Deficiency Bill." *British Journal for the History of Science.* 24 (1991): 45-60.

Larson, Laurence A.

Present Position and Address: Professor of Botany (since 1963), Ohio University, Athens, OH 45702, USA **Date of Birth:** March 17, 1930 **Education:** B.S. (1956), Ohio University; M.S. (1959), University of Tennessee; Ph.D. Botany (1963), Purdue University, IN **Selected Congresses and Conferences:** Ethical Issues (1974), Miami University; Medical Ethics (1976), Georgetown University/Dartmouth Medical School; Institute for Philosophical Ethics (1978) Georgetown University; Ethics in Science Workshop (1980) Vassar College, NY; Conference on Ultimate Reality and Meaning (1985), Institute on Science and Religion, Toronto; Creation/Evolution Workshop (1987), Dayton, OH **Previous Positions:** Radar Mechanic (1951-52), US Army; Oceanographer (1956-57), US Department of Defense, Washington D.C.; Instructor in Botany (1959), University of Tennessee; Research Assistant (1959-63), Purdue University; Assistant (1963-68)/Associate (1968-75) Professor, Ohio University **Selected Memberships:** Fellow (1976), Society for Health and Human Values; Institute of Society, Ethics and the Life Sciences; Institute on Religion in an Age of Science; Kennedy Institute for the Study of Human Reproduction and Bioethics; American Institute Biological Science; *Zygon* **Discipline:** Botany; Plant Physiology; Biological Education **Related Interests:** Interdisciplinary Course Development; The Biology, Art and Poetry of the Human Life Cycle; Methods of Investigation in Science and Art; Ethics in Science; Science and Creation.

Selected Publications: His bibliography lists 8 journal publications, 10 laboratory manuals and study guides and 9 reviews of books, films and video tapes.

_____. "The Use of Fine Arts in Elucidating Ethical Issues." Paper presented at the Ethics in Science Conference - Vassar College (12 June 1980).
_____. "Changing World, Changing Church." unpublished paper.
_____. "Ohio University Course List of Courses dealing with Human Values in Science and Technology." unpublished paper.
_____. Review of *Science and Creation* edited by R. W. Hanson. *Science Books and Films* 22, 2 (1986): 82.
_____. Review of *Religion from Science* by R. B. Cattell. *Science Books and Films* 23, 5 (1988).

Larzelere, Robert Earl

Present Position and Address: Director of Residential Research, Father Flanagan's Boys' Home, Youth Care Bldg., 13603 W. Flanagan Blvd., Boys Town, NE 68010 Phone: (402) 498-1936 **Fax:** (402) 498-1125 **Date of Birth:** April 3, 1945 **Languages Spoken:** English **Previous Positions Held:** Assistant Professor and Head of Psychology Dept. (1977-79) Bryan College, Dayton, TN; Post-Doctoral Fellow (1979-80) Family Violence Research Program, University of New Hampshire, Durham, NH; Assistant Professor of Psychology (1980-82) Western Baptist Seminary, Portland, OR; Senior Post-Doctoral Fellow (1988-89) Oregon Social Learning Center, Eugene, OR; Associate Professor and Director of Research (1982-90) Rosemead School of Psychology, Biola University, La Mirada, CA **Honors:** NIMH Pre-Doctoral Fellow (1976-77); NUMH Post-Doctoral Fellow (1979-80, 1988-89) **Memberships:** American Psychology Association; Society for Research in Child Development; National Council on Family Relations; Association for Advancement of Behavior Therapy; American Professional Society on the Abuse of Children; American Scientific Affiliation; Christian Association of Psychology; International Society for Traumatic Stress Studies **Discipline:** Psychology **Relevant Areas of Interest:** Parental discipline of young children; Evaluation of treatment for child sex abuse; Integration of psychology and theology; Research methodology and statistics **Current Project:** Parental discipline of young children; Evaluation of treatment for child sex abuse; Predictive validity of a suicide predication scale; Methods to increase feedback from clinical research for therapists

Selected Publications:

____ and Mulaik, S. A. "Single-sample Tests for Many Correlations." *Psychological Bulletin* 84 (1977): 557-569.
____. "The Task Ahead: Six Levels of Integration of Christianity and Psychology." *Journal of Psychology and Theology* 8 (1980): 3-11 (Reprinted in *Psychology and Christianity: Integrative Readings*, eds. J. R. Fleck & J. D. Carter. Nashville: Abingdon, 1981.)
____ and Breashears, G. "The Authority of Scripture and the Unity of Revelation: A Response to Crabb." *Journal of Psychology and Theology* 9 (1981): 312-317
____. "Dyadic Trust and Generalized Trust of Secular-vs. Christian-College Students." *Journal of Psychology and Theology* 12 (1984): 119-124
____ & Skeen, J. H. "The Method of Multiple Hypotheses: A Neglected Research Strategy in Family Studies." *Journal of Family Issues* 5 (1984): 474-492
____ & Klein, D. M. "Methodology." In *Handbook of Marriage and the Family*, eds. M. B. Sussman & S. K. Steinmetz. New York: Plenum Press: 125-155.
____ & Paterson, G. R. "Parental Management: Mediator of the Effect of Socioeconomic Status on Early Delinquency." *Criminology* 28 (1990): 301-324.
____. "Empirically Justified Uses of Spanking: Toward a Discriminating View of Corporal Punishment." *Journal of Psychology and Theology* 21 No. 2 (1993): 142-147.
____. "Should use of Corporal Punishment by Parents be Considered Abusive? No." In *Children and Adolescents: Controversial Issues*, eds. E. Gambrill & M. Mason. Newbury Park, CA: Sage, 1994.

Lategan, Bernard C.

Present Position and Address: Dean of Faculty of Arts (since 1991); Head (since 1988), Centre for Contextual Hermeneutics/Professor of Biblical Studies and Department Head (since 1978), University of Stellenbosch, Stellenbosch 7600, South Africa **Date of Birth:** June 8, 1938 **Languages Spoken:** English, Afrikaans, German, French, and Dutch **Education:** B.A., major in Greek (*cum laude*, 1958)/M.A., major in Greek (*cum laude*, 1962), University of Orange Free State; Candidate in Theology (*cum laude*, 1963)/Licenciate in Theology (*cum laude*, 1967), University of Stellenbosch; Th.D. New Testament (1967), Johannes Calvijn Academie, Kampen, The Netherlands **Previous Positions:** Minister (1968-69), Dutch Reformed Church, George; Professor of New Testament (1969-77), University of Western Cape; Editor and publisher (1980-90), Scriptura - Journal of Biblical Studies; Professor of New Testament (1982), Georg-August University, Göttingen **Other Academic Experience:** With the assistance of several grants, including the Alexander von Humboldt Stipend (1976-87), research was undertaken between 1971-1987 at Institute for Antiquity and Christianity, Claremont, CA; University of Tübingen; University of Munich; University of Chicago; University of Göttingen; University of Münster **Selected Memberships:** South African Academy of Arts and Sciences; HSRC Investigation into Research Methodology/Investigation into Intergroup Relations; South African Academy of Religion; Studiorum Novi Testamenti Studies **Discipline:** Biblical Studies and Hermeneutics **Related Interests:** Linguistics, Exegesis, Literary Theory, Contextual Hermeneutics.

Selected Publications: His bibliography lists 28 monographs and collective works, 42 articles and 18 papers read at international conferences. Most of his work is in the area of Biblical Studies and Hermeneutics.

____. "Current Issues in the Hermeneutical Debate." *Neotestamentica* 18 (1984): 1-17.
____, W. S. Vorster. *Text and Reality, Aspects of Reference in Biblical Texts*. Philadelphia: Fortress, 1985.
____, editor. *The Reader and Beyond, Theory and Practice in South African Reader-oriented Studies*. Pretoria: HSRC, 1990.

Laughlin, Charles D.

Present Position and Address: Professor of Anthropology (since 1984), Department of Sociology-Anthropology, Carleton University, Ottawa, Ontario, Canada K1S 5B6 **Date of Birth:** July 25, 1938 **Education:** B.A. (1966), San Francisco State College; M.A. (1968)/Ph.D. Anthropology (1972), University of Oregon **Postgraduate Studies:** Senior Postdoctoral Fellow (1973-74), Institute of Neurological Sciences, University of Pennsylvania **Previous Positions:** Assistant Professor of Anthropology (1970-74)/Associate Professor (1974-76), State University of New York (SUNY) - Oswego; Associate Professor (1976-84) Carleton University, Ottawa, Ontario **Editorial Work:** Editor: *Pre- and Perinatal Psychology Journal/Neuroanthropology Network Newsletter, Anthropology of Consciousness* **Selected Memberships:** Canadian Anthropological Society; American Anthropological Association; Association for the Study of Play; Pre- and Perinatal Psychology Association of North America; Society for the Anthropology of Consciousness; International Consciousness Research Laboratories **Discipline:** Anthropology; Neuroanthropology; Pre- and perinatal Anthropology **Related Interests:** Symbolism, brain and culture, transpersonal experience, ritual evocation of experience, universal structures of religious experience.

Selected Publications: His bibliography lists 9 books, 36 articles.

_____, Eugene d'Aquili. *Biogenetic Structuralism.* Columbia University Press, 1974.
_____, Eugene d'Aquili. "The Biopsychological Determinants of Religious Ritual Behaviour." *Zygon* 10, 1 (1975): 32-58.
_____, E. G. d'Aquili and J. McManus. *The Spectrum of Ritual.* Columbia University Press, 1979.
_____, R. Rubinstein and J. McManus. *Science as Cognitive Process: Toward an Empirical Philosophy of Science.* Philadelphia: University of Pennsylvania Press, 1984.
_____, G. F. MacDonald, J. McManus and J. Cove. "Mirrors, Portals and Multiple Realities." *Zygon* 23, 4 (1988): 39-64.
_____, J. McManus and E. G. d'Aquili. *Brain, Symbol and Experience: Toward a Neurophenomonology of Consciousness.* New Science Library. New York: Columbia University Press, 1990.
_____, J. McManus and J. Shearer. "The Function of Dreaming in the Cycles of Cognition." In *The Function of Dreaming,* ed. A. Morritt, et al.. Albany: SUNY Press, 1990.
_____. "Pre- and Perinatal Brain Development and Enculturation: A Biogenetic Structural Approach." *Human Nature* 2, 3 (1991): 171-213.
_____. "Fuzziness and Phenomenonlogy in Ethnological Research: Insights from Fuzzy Set Theory." *Journal of Anthropological Research* 49, 1 (1993): 17-37.
_____. "Transpersonal Anthropology, Then and Now." *Transpersonal Review* 1, 1 (1993).

Laurikainen, Kalervo Vihtori

Present Position and Address: Retired (1978), but still lecturing in History and Philosophy of Science, Research Institute for Theoretical Physics, University of Helsinki, Siltavuorenpenger 20C, SF-00170 Helsinki, Finland (Home) Kelotie 4, SF-01820 Klaukkala, Finland **Date of Birth:** January 6, 1916 **Languages Spoken:** Finnish, Swedish, English, German **Education:** Ph.Mag. Philosophy (1940)/Ph.D. Physics (1950), University of Helsinki **Selected Congresses and Conferences:** Chairman of the organizing committees for several international conferences arranged in North-Karelia **Previous Positions:** Lecturer (1946-56), Institute of Technology, Turku, Finland; Associate Professor of Physics (1956-60), University of Turku; Department Head and Professor of Nuclear and Elementary Particle Physics (1960-78)/Head (1961-78), Computing Bureau of Department of Nuclear Physics, University of Helsinki; Rector (Summers 1966-69), North-Karelian Summer University **Selected Memberships:** Administrative Board Member (1960-70), NORDITA (Nordic Institute for Theoretical Atomic Physics); Chairman of Administrative Board of Research Institute for Theoretical Physics (1965-75); Chairman (1968-75), Particle Physics (CERN) Committee, Academy of Finland; Member

(1974) Academia Scientiarum Fennica; Honorary Member and past President, Finnish Physical Society; Honorary Member, MAOL (Association of Teachers of Mathematical Sciences **Discipline:** Originally Mathematics; then Theoretical Physics; now Philosophy of Science **Related Interests:** Natural Philosophy, based on modern Physics; Relations between Science and Religion.

Selected Publications: Most of his books and articles are in Finnish, dealing with fundamental problems of modern Physics.

_____. *Todellisuus ja elämä* (Reality and Life). Helsinki: WSOY, 1980.
_____. *Fyysikon tie* (The Way of a Physicist). Helsinki: MFKA Publishing Company, 1982.
_____. *Luonto puhuu Luojastaan* (Nature Speaks of Its Creator). Kirjapaja, 1983.
_____. *Tieteem giljotiini* (The Guillotine of Science). Helsinki: Otava, 1987.
_____. *Beyond the Atom. The Philosophical Thought of Wolfgang Pauli*. Heidelberg: Springer-Verlag, 1988.
_____. "Wolfgang Pauli's Conception of Reality." In *Symposium on the Foundations of Modern Physics, 1987: The Copenhagen Interpretation 60 Years after the Como Lecture*, ed. P. Lahti and P. Mittelstaedt. Singapore: World Scientific, 1988.
_____. "Ontological Implications of Complementarity." *Preprint Series in Theoretical Physics, HU-TFT-88-2* (1988).
_____. "Atoms and Consciousness as Complementary Elements of Reality." *European Journal of Physics*. Abingdon: IOP Publishing Ltd. and The European Physical Society, 1990.
_____. "Quantum Physics, Philosophy, and the Image of God." *Zygon: Journal of Religion and Science* (in print).
_____. "Ontological Implications of Complementarity." In *Nature, Cognition, and System*, ed. M. E. Carvallo. Dordrecht: Kluwer, in process.

Legrain, Michel

Present Position and Address: Professor of Canon Law (since 1965)/Professor of Theology and Science of Religion (since 1972), á l'Institut Catholique de Paris 24 rue Cassette, 75006 Paris, France **Work Phone:** 42 22 76 00 **Date of Birth:** January 5, 1929 **Education:** Licence de théologie (1957), Gregorian University, Rome; Doctorate in Canon Law (1965), á l'Institut Catholique de Paris **Previous Positions:** Professor of Moral Theology, Pastoral Care and Canon Law (1960-74), au Séminaire des Pères du Saint-Esprit à Chevilly-Larue **Discipline:** Canon Law and Ethics **Related Areas of Interest:** Theology and culture.

Selected Publications:

_____. *Le corps humain, du soupçon á l'évangélisation*. Centurion, 1987, 1993.
_____. *Mariage chrétien, modèle unique*? Des questions vinues d'Afrique. Chalet, 1978.
_____. *Questions autour du mariage, permanences et mutations*. Salvator, 1987, 1994.
_____. *Les divorcés remariés, dossier de réflexion*. Centurion, 1987, 1994.
_____. *Aujord'hui le mariage*? Mame, 1988.
_____. *Remariage et communautés chrétiennes*. Salvator, 1991.
_____. *Le Père Adolphe Jeanjean*. Cerf, 1994.

Lejeune, Jérôme Jean Louis Marie

Present Position and Address: Professor of Fundamental Genetics (since 1964), Faculty of Medicine, Paris (Faculté de Médecine Necker-Enfants Malades); Consultant/Researcher in Human Genetics (since 1952), Hôpital des Enfants Malad Institut de Progenèse, Université de Paris, 45, rue des Saints-Pères, 75270 Paris, Cedex 06, France **Work Phone:** 42 86 21 25 **Date of Birth:** June 13, 1926 **Languages Spoken:** French and English **Education:** Doctor of Medicine (1951), Faculté de Médecine de Paris; Doctorate in the Natural Sciences - Genetics/Biochemistry (1960), Facultédes Sciences de Paris **Honorary Degrees:** Docteur Honoris Causa de l'Université Dusseldorf (1973)/Navarre

(1974)/Buenos Aires (1981)/Puebla (1986) **Awards and Honors:** Kennedy Prize (1962); Prix Cognacq - Jay, Paris (1963); William Allen Memorial Award (1964); Feltrinelli Prize, Rome (1984) **Previous Positions:** Researcher (1952-64), C.N.R.S. Paris; Participated in International Conferences worldwide and presented his findings at many renowned Universities world-wide (since 1958) **Selected Memberships:** Pontifical Academy of Sciences, Rome; Academie Sciences Morales and Politiques, Paris; Academie de Medecine, Paris; American Academy of Arts and Sciences, Boston **Discipline:** Human Genetics **Related Interests:** Human Nature and Destiny.

Selected Publications: The full bibliography lists over 390 works, most of which are in the area of human genetics.

_____. "Adam et Eve ou le monogénisme." *Nouvelle Revue Théologique* 90 (1968): 191-96.
_____. "On the Nature of Man." The WIlliam Allan Memorial Award Lecture at the American Society of Human Genetics (October 1969). *American Journal of Human Genetics* 22 (1970): 121-28.
_____. "Réflexions sur le début de l'tre humaine." Acad. Sci. mor. et politiques. *Medecine de France* 247 (October 1973).
_____. "Le message de vie." Presentation at Synod (1974).
_____. "Test-tube Babies are Babies." *Studies in Medicine, Law and Ethics.* London: SPUC, 1984.
_____. "Faith and Science in Religion, Science and the Search for Wisdom. In *Bishops Committee on Human Values, National Conference of Catholic Bishops* (September, 1986): 136-164.
_____. "Psychologie de l'intelligence." *La Revue des Deux Mondes* (May 1987).
_____. "To Heal or Kill — That is the Question." In *Scarce Medical Resources and Justice.* Braintree: Pope John Center, 1987.
_____. "La Science seule ne pout pas sauver le monde." *Osservatore Romano* (October 20, 1987).
_____. *L'Enciente concentrationnaire.* Vol. 1 Paris: Rayard edit, 1990.

Leming, Michael Richard

Present Position and Address: Chairperson and Professor (since 1975), Department of Sociology, Saint Olaf College, Northfield, MN 55057, USA **Work Phone:** (507) 663-3134 **Home Phone:** (507) 645-6237 **Date of Birth:** January 16, 1949 **Education:** A.B. (*cum laude*, 1970), Westmont College; M.A. (1971), Marquette University; Ph.D. (1975), University of Utah **Selected Congresses and Conferences:** Presented over 40 papers at academic societies and professional conferences including most of the annual meetings of the Society for the Scientific Study of Religion/Midwest Sociological Society/Association of Christians Teaching Sociology **Previous Positions:** Research Associate (1970-71), National Liberty Foundation of Valley Forge PA; Assistant Professor of Sociology (1974-75), Weber State College; Founder and Director (1981-84,86), St. Olaf College Social Research Center **Discipline:** Sociology **Related Interests:** Sociology of Family, Sociology of Religion, Research Ethics, and the Sociology of Death and Dying.

Selected Publications: The full bibliography lists 3 books, 2 instructor's manuals and 16 journal articles.

_____. "How Does Religion Inform my Sociology and Sociology my Religion?" *Newsletter - Christian Sociological Society* 8, 15 (June 1981): 10-11.
_____, George E. Dickinson. *Understanding Dying, Death, and Bereavement* Holt, Rinehart, and Winston Publishers, 1985; 2d ed. 1990.
_____,. Raymond DeVries and Brendan Furnish, ed. *The Sociological Perspective: an Introduction to a Value-Committed Approach.* Zondervan Publishers, 1988. A collection of original essays on the relationship of faith and learning within the discipline of learning.
_____, George E. Dickinson. *Understanding Families: Continuity, Diversity, and Change* Allyn and Bacon Publishers, 1990.

Lenz, Hermann

Present Position and Address: Retired Psychiatrist/Professor at Linz/Regensburg Universities, Bischofstrasse 3/1, A4020 Linz, Austria **Date of Birth:** November 9, 1912 **Languages Spoken:** German, English **Education:** M.D. Psychiatry (1937), University of Vienna. Promotion (1937), University of Vienna **Previous Positions:** Chief of the hospital (1959-78), Barmh. Brüder, Linz; Lecturer (1944-45), University of Würzburg, Germany; Lecturer (1962-69)/a.o. Professor (1974), University of Vienna; Professor (1969-79), University of Linz; Professor (1973-74), University of Regensburg, Germany **Discipline:** Psychiatry **Related Interests:** Psychopathology, delusion, faith.

Selected Publications: He has written over 130 publications in his field, 10 of which are in the area of Science and Theology.

_____. "Glaube und Wahn." *Zeitschrift für Neurologie und Psychiatrie* 41 (1973): 341-359.
_____. "Vergleiche zwischen Glauben und Wahn." *Archiv für Religionspsychologie* 11 (1975).
_____. *Wahnsinn, das Irrationale im Wahngeschehen.* Wien: Herder, 1976.
_____. "Glauben und Wahn." A chapter in *Wahn, Wirklichkeit, Religion* Karlsruhe: Tron, 1978.
_____. "Element of the Irrational in the Course of Delusion." *Confinia Psychiatrica* 22 (1979): 183-190.
_____. "Belief and Delusion, Common Origin and Different Course." *Zygon* 18 (1983): 112-138.
_____. "Das verlorene Selbst." *Fundamenta psychiatrica* (1987): 23-42.
_____. *Die psychokulturelle Evolution.* Supplementum der WiKliWo 186. Wein: Jahrgang Springer Verlag, 1991.
_____. *Vergleichende Entwicklung der Selbst.* Hamburg: Verlag Dr. Kovac, 1994.

Leslie, John

Present Position and Address: Professor (since 1982), Department of Philosophy, University of Guelph, Guelph, Ontario N1G 2W1, Canada **Concurrent Positions:** Advisory Board of the Pachart Foundation (since 1987), which publishes journals and occasional books in astronomy and allied areas **Work Phone:** (519) 824-4120 ext. 3885 **Home Phone:** (519) 821-2133 **Date of Birth:** August 2, 1940 **Languages Spoken:** English, French, German **Education:** B.A. Philosophy and Psychology (1962)/M.A. Philosophy and Psychology (1967)/M.Litt. Philosophy (1968), Oxford University **Postgraduate Studies:** Fellowship, Canada Council Research Grant (1973-74), to work on book in metaphysics and philosophy of religion (*Value and Existence*); Fellowship (1981-82), Social Sciences and Humanities Research Council Research Grant (1973 - 74), to work on *Argument from Design* and its relationship to modern cosmology **Previous Positions:** Copywriter (1962), Advertising, McCann-Erickson, London; Vice-Chairman/Chairman (1977-80), Guelph-McMaster Joint Ph.D. Programme; Visiting Professor of Religious Studies (1986), University of Calgary; Visiting Fellow (1987), Research Department of Philosophy, Australian National University; Visiting Professor (January - April 1993), Institut d'Astrophysique, Université de Liège, funded by Belgium's Fonds National de la Recherche Scientifique **Selected Memberships:** Canadian Philosophical Association; American Philosophical Association; Philosophy of Science Association **Discipline:** Philosophy **Related Interests:** Metaphysics; Philosophy of Religion; Philosophy of Science; Philosophy of Mind; Ethics; Neoplatonism; Cosmological and Design.

Selected Publications: His full bibliography lists 3 books, 12 chapters in books and 32 articles, besides many book reviews, papers and contributions presented at other universities and conferences.

_____. "The Scientific Weight of Anthropic and Teleological Principles." In *Current Issues in Teleology*, ed. N. Rescher. Lanham: University Press of America, 1986.
_____. "Anthropic Explanations in Cosmology." In *PSA 1986: Volume One, Proceedings of the 1986 Biennial Meeting of the Philosophy of Science Association*, ed. A. Fine and P. Machamer. Ann Arbor, MI: Edwards Brothers, 1986.

_____. "Probabilistic Phase Transitions and the Anthropic Principle." In *Origin and Early History of the Universe, Proceedings of the 26th Liège International Astrophysical Colloquium*, ed. J. Demaret. Liège: Presses of University of Liège, 1987.

_____. "The Prerequisites of Life in Our Universe." In *Newton and the New Direction in Science*, ed. G. V. Coyne, J. Zycinski and M. Heller. Citta del Vaticano, 1988. Reprint, *Truth* (Fall 1990), a Journal of Religion, in an issue on the *Cosmological and Design Arguments*, ed. W.L. Craig.

_____. "How to Draw Conclusions from a Fine-Tuned Universe." In *Physics, Philosophy, and Theology: A Common Quest for Understanding*, ed. Robert J. Russell, William R. Stoeger, and George V. Coyne. Vatican City State: Vatican Observatory, 1988; Notre Dame, IN: University of Notre Dame Press, 1989.

_____. *Physical Cosmology and Philosophy, Philosophical Topics Series*, gen. ed. Paul Edwards. New York: Macmillan Company, 1989.

_____. *Universes*. New York and London: Routledge, 1989. Much on Anthropic Principle, Argument from Design and Neoplatonist theology.

_____. " A Spinozistic Vision of God." *Religious Studies* 34, 2 (1993): 277-86.

Levitt, J. Peter Fletcher

Present Position and Address: Methodist Minister in Chester, UK **Home Phone:** (0244) 321950 **Date of Birth:** October 31, 1953 **Education:** B.Sc. Applied Physics (1975), University of Durham; Ph.D. Physics (1979), Cambridge University; M.Phil. Theology (1989), University of Leeds **Previous Positions:** Methodist Minister in an Ecumenical Appointment as Town Centre Chaplain, Telford, UK; Methodist Minister (1982-89), Whitehaven Circuit **Selected Memberships:** Society of Ordained Scientists; Founder, ACTUSET (Applied Christian Theology Unit for Scientists, Engineers and Technologists) **Discipline:** Theology; Physics **Related Interests:** The encouragement of Scientists, Engineers and Technologists to reflect theologically on their activities within the natural world viewed as part of the Christian God's Creation.

Selected Publications

_____. "Interpreting the Christian Doctrine of Creation: An Investigation of the Thinking of Scientists, Engineers and Technologists in Contemporary Britain." Unpublished M.Phil. thesis, University of Leeds, UK (1989).

Lewthwaite, Gordon R.

Present Position and Address: Professor Emeritus of Geography, California State University - Northridge, 18111 Nordhoff Street - GEOG, Northridge, CA 91330, USA; (Home) 18908 Liggett Street, Northridge CA 91324-2844, USA **Work Phone:** (818) 349-5308 **Date of Birth:** August 12, 1925 **Education:** B.A. (1947)/M.A. History (1949), University of Canterbury, Christchurch, New Zealand; M.A. Geography (1950), University of Auckland, New Zealand; Ph.D. Geography (1956), University of Wisconsin - Madison, USA **Field Work:** New Zealand, Australia, some Pacific Islands, USA **Previous Positions:** Teacher (1950)> Gisborne High School, New Zealand; Lecturer in Geography (1955-59), University of Auckland; Secretary (1955-1959), Auckland Branch, New Zealand Geographical Society; Assistant Editor (1955-1959), New Zealand Geographer; Participated in Symposium on the Mapping of the Pacific at Pacific Science Congress (1961), Honolulu; Assistant (1959-62)/Associate (1962-65)/Full Professor (1965-92), Department of Geography, California State University - Northridge, CA; Visiting Professor at Universities of Hawaii (summer 1964)/British Columbia (1966-67)/Newcastle, Australia (1973)/Auckland, New Zealand (1980) **Editorial Positions:** Consulting editor of *Journal of the American Scientific Affiliation* **Selected Memberships:** American Scientific Affiliation; Biblical Geographers Interest Group (Association of American Geographers) **Discipline:** Geography and History **Related Interests:** Cultural-Historical Geography; Agricultural Geography; Southwest Pacific, and the Middle East; History of Geographic Thought; Historical Geography of the Holy Land.

Selected Publications

_____. "Naturalism, Mechanism, and the Nature of Social Science." *Journal of the American Scientific Affiliation (JASA)* 22, 4 (December 1970): 141-145.
_____. "The Shrunken World of Marxism." *HIS* (November 1971): 16-19.
_____. "A Geographer Addresses the Question." In *Why I am Still a Christian*, ed. E. M. Blaiklock. Grand Rapids, MI: Zondervan Press, 1971: 109-123.
_____. "Geography: A Christian View." In *Christ and the Modern Mind: Essays in the Liberal Arts*, ed. R. W. Smith. Downers Grove: Inter-Varsity Press, 1972.
_____. "Christian Faith and Higher Education." *JASA* 31, 1 (March 1979): 33-36.
_____. "The Geographical Horizons of the Early Israelites: the Table of Nations Revisited." *The California Geographer* 27 (1987): 39-74.
_____. "Via Maris and King's Highway: Ancient Routeways and Biblical History." *Historical Geography* 18, 1 (1988): 1-7.

Liedke, Gerhard

Present Position and Address: Pastor of the Congregation of Handschuhsheim, Handschuhsheimer Landstrasse 52, 69121 Heidelberg 1, Germany **Date of Birth:** December 18, 1937 **Languages Spoken:** German, English **Education:** Theologische Examina (1962 and 1964 in Heidelberg and Karlsruhe); Promotion zum Dr. theol. (1968), Heidelberg **Previous Positions:** Environmental Representative (1982-89), Evang. Landesk. in Baden, Der Umweltbeauftragte; Research Assistant to Prof. Georg Picht (1964-67), University of Heidelberg; Guest Researcher (1968-69), Nuclear Research Center at Karlsruhe; Research Fellow (1971-78), Forschungsstätte der Evangelischen Studiengemeinschaft (F.E.ST.), Heidelberg **Selected Memberships:** F.E.ST **Discipline:** Theology including the relation between natural science and theology/Environmental Studies (Umweltwissenschaften) **Related Interests:** Theology of Creation.

Selected Publications

_____, H. Aichelin, eds. *Naturwissenschaft und Theologie, Texte und Kommentare, Reihe "grenzgespräche"* 6 Neukirchen, 1974.
_____. "Kernenergie und Schöpfungsauftrag." In *Alternative Möglichkeiten für die Energiepolitik*, ed. W. Lienemann, U. Ratsch, A. Schuke, F. Solms. Vol. 1 Heidelberg: Materialien zum Gutachten, 1977.
_____, C. Buddeberg, D. Langmaack, E. Leinert and E. Reccius, eds. *Baustelle Gottesdienst. Das gottesdienstliche Mahl in der wissenschaftlich-technischen Welt*. Heidelberg: Erfahrungsbericht einer Arbeitsgruppe, 1978.
_____. "Science, Power and God." In *Proceedings of the Conference - Concern about Science - Amsterdam, 1982*, ed. J. Buit. Vrije Universiteit, 1982.
_____. "Bis die Schöpfung zurückkehrt." In *Wie grün darf die Zukunft sein?: Naturbewusstsein in der Umweltkrise, Reihe Zeitzeichen 1*, ed. Hermann Timm. Gütersloh, 1987).
_____. *Im Bauch des Fisches, Ökologische Theologie*, 5th ed. Stuttgart: Kreuz-Verlag, 1988.
_____. "Verminderung der Gewalt gegen die Schöpfung." In *Ökologische Ethik, Schriftenreihe der Katholischen Akademie der Erzdiözese*, ed. K. Bayerts. Freiburg, 1988.
_____, U. Duchrow. *Shalom. Biblical Perspectives on Creation Justice and Peace*. Geneva: WCC Publications, 1989.
_____. "The Challenge of the Church to Science and Theology." In The New Faith-Science Debate, ed. John M. Mangum. Minneapolis, MN: Fortress Press, 1989.
_____. "Tier-Ethik" - Biblische Perspektiven. In Gefährten und Feinde des Memschen, Bernd Janowski, (Hrsg.), 199-213. Neukirchen-Vluyn, 1993.

Lifton, Robert Jay

Present Position and Address: Lecturer in Psychiatry/Senior Researcher in Nuclear Psychology (since 1982), Harvard University; Distinguished Professor of Psychiatry and Psychology (since 1985),

The City University of New York, John Jay College of Criminal Justice, 899 Tenth Avenue, Suite 434, New York, NY 10019, USA **Date of Birth:** May 16, 1926 **Education:** Pre-Med (1942-44), Cornell University; M.D. (1948), New York Medical College; Intern (1948-49), Jewish Hospital of Brooklyn, New York; Resident in Psychiatry (1949-51), State University Medical Center, New York; Candidate (1957-60), Boston Psychoanalytic **Honorary Degrees:** Hon. D.Sc. Lawrence University (1971)/Merrimack College (1973)/University of Vermont (1984); Hon. Doctor of Law (1984), Iona College; Hon. D. of Humane Letters: Wilmington College (1975)/New York Medical College (1977)/Marlboro College (1983)/Maryville College (1983)/University of New Haven (1987); Honorary D. of Social Sciences (1989), Amerika-Institut der Universität München, Germany; has received many awards for work on Hiroshima and Nuclear Psychology research, Nazi doctors and the Holocaust **Previous Positions:** Associate in Psychiatry (1956-60), Massachusetts General Hospital, Boston; Research Associate in Psychiatry (1956-61), Harvard Medical School, and Associate in East Asian Studies, Harvard University; Associate in Psychiatry (since 1961), Yale-New Haven Hospital; Associate (1961-67)/Full (1967-85) Professor of Psychiatry, Yale University School of Medicine; Member of Council on East Asian Studies (1964-75), Yale University; Psychiatrist (First Lieutenant to Captain) in the Military (1951-53); Research Associate in Psychiatry (1960-61), Tokyo University; Vis Lec Social Psychiatry, Tulane University (1963)/East Asian Studies, University of Michigan (1964)/Berry Lectureship in Psychology and Religion, University of Hawaii (1972); Also Visiting Lecturer or Fellow: University of Kentucky/Duquesne University/Max-Planck-Institute for Psychiatry and Psychotherapy - Munich/Cornell University/Menninger Clinic/Macalester College/Duke University/Woodrow Wilson School of Princeton University. Participant (1988) in Space Bridge, Global Classroom Project, Joint Program with Tufts University and Moscow State University. Lectured (1989) at the Peace Lecture Series at Bethel College, and Peace Symposium at 52nd Annual Convention of Japanese Psychological Association, Hiroshima **Editorial Work:** Editorial Boards of Suicide and Life-threatening Behavior (since 1974); The American Journal of Drug and Alcohol Abuse (since 1975); Psychohistory Review (since 1977); *Brunner/Mazel Psychosocial Stress Series, Journal of Traumatic Stress* (since 1978); *Zygon* (since 1981) **Selected Memberships:** Fellow, American Psychiatric Association; Physicians for Social Responsibility; International Society of Political Psychology; International Physicians for the Prevention of Nuclear War; American Academy of Psychoanalysis; Association for Asian Studies **Discipline:** Psychiatry; Psychology; Medicine; Philosophy **Related Interests:** Ethics in a Nuclear Age; Psychology/Philosophy /Society within the context of a Nuclear Age: "Brainwashing" and Religion: Survival and Meaning **Current Research:** Psychological behavior in extreme situations, including holocaust and war with special emphasis on the psychology of the survivor and on posttraumatic effects. Psychological components of mass killing (i.e. Auschwitz and Nazi doctors in general); Psychiatric and Psychological theory - especially concerning an evolving model or paradigm of symbolization of life and death; general psychological aspects of war and peace and of attitudes concerning nuclear weapons; psychological dimensions of individual, social, and historical change (specific studies of Japanese youth and innovative young American professionals); Methods and concepts in Psychological study of historical problems; Contemporary psychological styles ("Protean" experimentation and constricted cult behavior); Psychology of totalism or "Ideological Totalism" (specific study of Chinese "thought" or "brainwashing").

Selected Publications: His bibliography lists 16 published books, 6 edited books, 72 published original reports, 74 reviews and articles and 5 film-related works.

_____. *The Nazi Doctors: Medical Killing and the Psychology of Genocide*. New York: Basic Books, 1986. Winner of the 1987 Los Angeles Times Book Prize for History; recipient of the 1987 National Jewish Book Award - Holocaust; awarded the Lisl and Leo Eitinger Award for 1988, Oslo, Norway.

Lindberg, David C.

Present Position and Address: Hilldale Professor of History of Science (since 1993), 4143 Helen White Hall, The University of Wisconsin - Madison, WI 53706, USA **Date of Birth:** November 15, 1935 **Education:** B.S. Physics (1957), Wheaton College; M.S. Physics (1959), Northwestern University; Ph.D. History and Philosophy of Science (1965), Indiana University. **Honorary Degrees:** Guggenheim Fellowship (1977-78); Fellow (elected 1984), Medieval Academy of America **Previous Positions:** Assistant Professor of History (1965-67), University of Michigan; Assistant through Full Professor of History of Science (since 1967)/Hilldale Professor (since 1993), University of Wisconsin - Madison **Editorial Positions:** Advisory editor or editorial board member for *Isis/Osiris/British Journal for the History of Science* **Selected Memberships:** Member (1970-71), School of Historical Studies, Institute for Advanced Study, Princeton; Member (elected 1986), International Academy of the History of Science; President, History of Science Society, 1994-5; History of Science Society; Renaissance Society of America; British Society for the History of Science **Discipline:** History of Science **Related Interests:** Science and Christianity from the patristic period to the 17th century.

Selected Publications

_____. *Theories of Vision from al-Kindi to Kepler*. University of Chicago Press, 1976.
_____, ed. *Science in the Middle Ages*. University of Chicago Press, 1978.
_____, R. L. Numbers, eds. *God and Nature: Historical Essays on the Encounter between Science and Christianity*. University of California Press, 1986.
_____. "Science and the Early Church." In *God and Nature*. University of California Press, 1986: 19-48.
_____, R. L. Numbers. "Beyond War and Peace: A Reappraisal of the Encounter between Christianity and Science." *Church History* 55 (1986): 338-354.
_____. "Science as Handmaiden: Roger Bacon and the Patristic Tradition." Isis 78 (1987): 518-536.
_____. The Beginnings of Western Science: The European Scientific Tradition in Philosophical, Religious, and Industrial Context, 600 B.C. to A.D. 1500. Chicago: University of Chicago Press, 1992.
_____. "Medieval Science and Its Religious Context." Osiris 10 (1995).

Lindquist, Stanley E.

Present Position and Address: Professor Emeritus (since 1988), California State University - Fresno; Private Practice in Clinical Psychology (since 1950), 5142 N. College, Fresno, CA 93704, USA **Date of Birth:** November 9, 1917 **Education:** B.A. Education-Music (1940), California State College; Ph.D. Psychological - Clinical, Physiological and Experimental Concentration (1950), University of Chicago; 1 year Graduate Study in Europe in various Universities and Hospitals (1961-62) **Honorary Degrees:** Litt.D. (Hon, 1974), Trinity College **Previous Positions:** Assistant Professor (1946-53)/Dean and Chairman (1950-53), Pastoral Counseling Concentration, Trinity College and Seminary, Chicago; Various Administrative roles/Professor of Psychology (1953-88), California State University - Fresno; Founder and President Emeritus, Link Care Foundation **Selected Memberships:** Sigma Xi; Kappa Delta Pi; Psi Chi; American Psychological Association; Former Psychologist/Editor and past President, American Scientific Affiliation; Christian Association for Psychological Studies; CAPS West; California Psychological Association **Discipline:** Psychology **Related Interests:** Science and Faith.

Selected Publications: His bibliography lists 4 books and 34 articles and papers.

_____. "Psychology and Religion." In The Encounter Between Christianity and Science, ed. Richard Beebe. Grand Rapids: Eerdman, 1968.
_____. "Psychotherapy, Ethics and Faith." Journal of the American Scientific Affiliation (September 1978).
_____. "Psychotherapy, Ethics and Faith." In *Making Whole Persons: Ethical Issues in Biology and Medicine*, ed. R. L. Hermann. American Scientific Affiliation Press, 1980.

Link, Christian

Present Position and Address: Professor of Theology (since 1993), Ruhr Universität Bochum; Rittershaus, Strasse 7, D-44803, Bochum, Germany **Work Phone:** 0049 234 352754 **Date of Birth:** July 12, 1938 **Languages Spoken:** German, English **Education:** Study of Physics (1958-61), Erlangen, Tübingen; Studies in Theology (1961-65), Heidelberg, Göttingen; Dr. theol. and habilitation (1970, 1976), University of Heidelberg **Previous Positions:** Vorstand der Ges. für Evangelische Theologie; Mitarbeiter der Forschungsstätte der Evangelischen Studiengemeinschaft (F.E.ST.), Heidelberg; Leiter der Karl-Barth-Konferenzen, Leuenberg-Schweiz; Professor of Theology (since 1979), Bern University **Selected Memberships:** F.E.ST.; Wiss. Ges. für Theologie **Discipline:** Theology; Physics **Related Interests:** Theology of Creation; Calvin Research; Ecclesiology and Ecumenics **Current Research:** The Theme and Problem of the Divine Providence.

Selected Publications

_____. "Die Erfahrung der Welt als Schöpfung (The World Experienced as Creation)." In *Anthropologie als Thema von psychosomatischer Medizin und Theologie*, ed. M. von Rad. Stuttgart, 1974.

_____. "Die Erfahrung der Schöpfung. Zum Gespräch zwischen Theologie und Naturwissenschaft (The Experience of Creation)." *EvKom* 8 (1975): 193-196.

_____. "La crise écologique et l'éthique theologique (The Ecological Crisis and Theological Ethics)." *Revue d'Histoire et de Phil. Religieuse* 61 (1981): 147-160.

_____. "Gott - in der Welt verborgen (God - Hidden in the World)." *Naturwissenschaft und Theologie*, ed. H. Aichelin and G. Liedke. (4. Aufl., 1981): 168-77.

_____. "Schwierigkeiten des kosmologischen Redens von Gott (Difficulties in Speaking of God in Terms of Cosmology)." In *Offene Systeme II*, ed. K. Maurin, u.a.. Stuttgart: N.p., 1981.

_____. "Barths Anfragen an die Wissenschaft (Barth's Inquiries About Science)." *Zeitschrift für Dial. Theol.* 3 (1987): 65-87.

_____. "'Physik'/'Anthropologie'/'Theorie der Naturwissenschaften' (Introductions to the sections on Physics/Anthropology/Theory of Science)." In *Der Dialog zwischen Theologie und Naturwissenschaft, Ein bibliographischer Bericht*, ed. J. Hübner. München: Chr. Kaiser Verlag, 1987.

_____. "Rights of the Creation - Theological Perspectives." In *Rights of the Future Generations - Rights of Nature, Studies from the World Alliance of Reformed Churches, No. 19*, ed. L. Vischer. Geneva: N.p., 1990.

_____. "Schöpfung (Creation - Confronted by Scientific Inquiries and Interpretations)." In *Handbuch Syst. Theol.* 7, 2 (Gütersloh, 1991): 400-454.

Lipinski, Boguslaw

Present Position and Address: Director of Laboratories (since 1982), Boston Cardiovascular Health Center; Director (since 1987), H.S. Research Laboratory, 1101 Beacon Street, Boston, MA 02146, USA (Home) 97 Beaumont Avenue, Newton, MA 02160, USA **Work Phone:** (617) 739-0730 **Home Phone:** (617) 527-1395 **Date of Birth:** July 21, 1933 **Languages Spoken:** Polish, English **Education:** M.S. Chemistry (1955), Warsaw University; Ph.D. Biochemistry (1962), Institute of Nuclear Research, Warsaw; D.Sc. Biochemistry (1971), University of Lodz **Postgraduate Studies:** Predoctoral Fellow (1958-59), McMaster University, Hamilton, Canada; Postdoctoral Fellow (1964-65), Northwestern University, Evanston, IL, USA **Previous Positions:** Research Assistant, Serum and Vaccines Laboratories (1955-56); Research Associate (1956-67), Institute of Nuclear Research, Warsaw; Assistant Professor (1967-69), School of Medicine, Bialystok, Poland; Chairman (1969-71), Department of Biochemistry, Postgraduate School of Medicine, Warsaw, Poland; Visiting (1971-73)/Assistant Professor (1973-81), Tufts University School of Medicine; Associate Director (1976-82), Vascular Laboratory, St. Elizabeth's Hospital, Boston; Visiting Associate Professor (1986-87), Thrombosis Center, Temple University School of Medicine, Philadelphia, PA **Selected Memberships:** Polish Biochemical Society; President (1980-84), Society for Bioelectricity; American Heart Association;

International Society for Thrombosis and Hemostasis **Discipline:** Biochemistry **Related Interests:** Unorthodox Medicine; Faith Healing.

Selected Publications

_____. "Wrong Science and Right Science." A letter written to *Nature* 331, 14 (January 1988): 129.
_____. "Unknown Type of Radiation Recorded in Medjugorje, Yugoslavia, in Association with Apparitions of Our Lady." Unpublished paper.
_____. "The Paradox of Health." *New England Journal of Medicine* 319, 6 (August 11, 1988): 378.

Livingstone, David Noel

Present Position and Address: Professor (since 1993) , The Queen's University of Belfast, School of Geosciences, Belfast, BT7 1NN, Northern Ireland **Work Phone:** (0232) 335145 **Date of Birth:** March 15, 1953 **Education:** B.A. honours (1975)/Dip. Ed. (1976)/Ph.D. (1982)/Research Fellow on Economic and Social Science Research Council Project (1982-84), The Queen's University of Belfast **Previous Positions:** Lecturer (1989-91)/Demonstrator in Geography (1979-82)/Research Officer and Curator of Maps (1984-88)/ Reader (1991-93), The Queen's University of Belfast **Administrative Experience:** Founder and joint secretary (1981-84)/Committee Member (since 1984), Institute of British Geographers' Study Group on the History and Philosophy of Geography; Member, Royal Irish Academy's National Committee for the History and Philosophy of Science **Selected Memberships:** British Society for the History of Science; History of Science Society; Institute of British Geographers; Member of the International Union of the History and Philosophy of Science and the International Geographical Union, Commission on the History of Geographical Thought; National Committee for the History and Philosophy of Science; Royal Irish Academy **Discipline:** Geoscience **Related Interests:** Areas of Interest: History of geography, geology and anthropology. Historical relations between science and religion; Darwinism.

Selected Publications

_____. "Preadamites: The History of an Idea from Heresy to Orthodoxy." *Scottish Journal of Theology* 40 (1987): 41-66.
_____. "Farewell to Arms: Reflections on the Encounter between Science and Faith." In *Christian Faith and Practice in the Modern World*, ed. M. A. Noll and D.F. Wells. Grand Rapids: Eerdmans, 1988.
_____. "Changing Scientific Concepts." *Christian Scholar's Review* 17 (1988): 361-380.
_____. "Science, Magic, and Religion: a Contextual Reassessment of Geography in the 16th and 17th Centuries." *History of Science* 26 (1988): 269-294.
_____. "Evolution, Eschatology, and the Privatization of Providence." *Science and Christian Belief* 2 (1990): 117-130.
_____. *The Preadamite Theory and the Marriage of Science and Religion*. American Philosophical Society, 1991.
_____. *The Geographical Tradition: Episodes in the History of a Contested Enterprise*. Blackwell, 1991.
_____. "Darwinism and Calvinism. The Belfast-Princeton Connection." *Isis* 83 (1992): 408-28.
_____. "Science and Religion: Toreword to the Historical Geography of an Encounter." *Journal of Historical Geography* 20 (1994): 367-83.
_____, Mark A. Nell, eds. *Charles Hodge, What is Darwinism? And Other Writings on Science and Religion*. Grand Rapids, MI: Baker, 1994.

Loder, James Edwin

Present Position and Address: Mary D. Synnott Professor of the Philosophy of Christian Education (since 1982), Department of Practical Theology, Princeton Theological Seminary, CN 821, Princeton, NJ 08542, USA; (Home) 74 Mercer Street, Princeton, NJ 08540, USA **Date of Birth:** December 5, 1931 **Education:** B.A. (1953), Carleton College, MN; B.D. (1957), Princeton Theological Seminary;

Th.M. (with distinction, 1958), Harvard Divinity School; Clinical Training (1958-59), Massachusetts Mental Health Clinic, Boston; Ph.D. History and Philosophy of Religion (1962), Harvard University Graduate School of Arts and Science **Postgraduate Studies:** Danforth Grant in Theology and Psychiatric Theory (1961-62), Menninger Foundation, Topeka, KS; American Association of Theological Schools Research Fellowship (1968-69), Institute Jean J. Rousseau, Geneva; Fellowship (1980-81, 85-86), Center of Theological Inquiry; Visiting Fellow (Spring, 1980), Oxford University; Visiting Scholar (1985-86), Harvard University **Previous Positions:** Minister at Hope Chapel (1957-58), Lakewood, NJ; Minister at North Christian Church (1959-60), Fall River, MA; Instructor (1962)/Assistant (1965)/Associate (1967)/Full Professor (1979), Christian Education, Princeton Theological Seminary; Guest Professor (1966), Drew Theological Seminary, Madison, NJ **Selected Memberships:** Center of Theological Inquiry, Princeton; American Scientific Affiliation **Discipline:** Psychology; Theology; Philosophy of Christian Education **Related Interests:** Epistemology in theology and science; Anthropology in theological perspective. Runs a regular Ph.D. seminar (since 1987), "Theology and Human Science."

Selected Publications

_____. *Religious Pathology and Christian Faith.* Westminster, 1965.
_____. *The Transforming Moment: Understanding Convictional Experiences.* Harper & Row, 1982; 2d ed., Helmers & Howard, 1989.
_____. *The Knight's Move: Kierkegaard and Modern Science.* Helmers & Howard, forthcoming.

Lovell, Sir Bernard

Present Position and Address: Professor Emeritus, University of Manchester; Director (until 1981), Nuffield Radio Astronomy Laboratories, Jodrell Bank, University of Manchester, Macclesfield, Cheshire, SK11 9DN; (Home) The Quinta, Swettenham, Cheshire, UK **Work Phone:** Lower Withington 01477-571321 **Home Phone:** 01477-571254 **Fax Number:** 01477 571618 **Education:** B.Sc. (1934)/Ph.D. (1936), University of Bristol **Honorary Degrees:** Hon. LLD, Edinburgh University (1961)/Calgary University (1966); Hon. D.Sc., Leicester (1961)/Leeds (1966)/London (1967)/Bath (1967)/Bristol (1970)/DUniv. Stirling (1974)/DUniv. Surrey (1975) **Honors and Awards:** Order of the British Empire (1946); Fellow of the Royal Society (1955); Knighted (1961); Hon. FIEE (1967); Hon. FInstP (1976); Duddell Medal (1954); Royal Medal (1960); Daniel and Florence Guggenheim International Aeronautics Award (1961); Order du Mérite pour la Recherche et l'Invention (1962); Churchill Gold Medal (1964); Gold Medal (1981), Royal Astronomical Society; Rutherford Memorial Lecturer, Royal Society (1984) **Previous Positions:** Assistant Lecturer in Physics (1936-39), University of Manchester; Telecommunication Research Establishment (1939-45), University of Manchester and Jodrell Bank Experimental Station (now Nuffield Radio Astronomy Laboratories), Cheshire; Lecturer (1945)/Senior Lecturer (1947)/Reader (1949) in Physics/Reith Lecturer (1958)/Professor of Radio Astronomy (1951), University of Manchester; Montague Burton Professor of International Relations (1973), University of Edinburgh **Selected Memberships:** SRC (1965-70); American Philosophical Society (since 1974); President (1969-71), Royal Astronomical Society; Vice President (1970-76), International Astronomical Union; President (1975-76), British Association; President (1976-89), Guild of Church Musicians; Hon. Fellow (1964), Society of Engineers; Honorary Foreign Member (1955), American Academy of Arts and Sciences; Honorary Life member (1960), New York Academy; Honorary Member (1962), Royal Swedish Academy; Royal Northern College of Music (1962); Manchester Literary and Philosophical Society (1988) **Discipline:** Physics, Astronomy **Related Interests:** Cosmology; Creation and Science.

Selected Publications

_____. *The Individual and the Universe*. Oxford University Press, and Harper & Row, 1959. The 1958 BBC Reith Lectures.

_____. *The Impact of Modern Astronomy on the Problems of the Origin of Life and the Cosmos*. Oregon State System of Higher Education Booklet, 1963. Condon Lecturer, Oregon 1962.

_____. "A University Sermon." *University of Edinburgh Journal* (Autumn 1963). A sermon presented in St. Giles Cathedral, Edinburgh.

_____. *In the Centre of Immensities*. Harper & Row, 1978.

_____. "Creation." *Theology* 80 (1980): 359ff. Address presented in St. Ann's Church, Manchester.

_____. *Emerging Cosmology*. Columbia University Press, 1981; Praeger, 1985.

_____. "Reverence for Life and the Cosmos." *Albert Schweitzer International Symposium, St. John's College*. Cambridge, 1983.

_____. "Reason and Belief in Cosmology." *Nuova civilta delle Machine Anno* IV (1986): 101ff.

_____. *Astronomer by Chance*. Basic Books, 1989. Autobiography.

Löw, Reinhard

Present Position and Address: Director (since 1987), Forschungsinstitut für Philosophie Hannover, Kirchliche Stiftung des öffentlichen Rechts, Cerppen Strasse 26, 30169 Hannover, Germany **Work Phone:** (0511) 164-0920 **Date of Birth:** February 15, 1949 **Languages Spoken:** German, English, Italian **Education:** Staatsexamen Pharmazie (1973)/Dr. rer. nat (1977)/Dr. phil. in Philosophie (1979)/ Dr. phil. habil. in Philosophie (1983), Ludwig-Maximilians-Universität, München **Awards and Honors:** Partington prize for History of Chemistry, London (1978); Letamendi-Forns-Stiftung (Barcelona) Prize for Anthropology **Previous Positions:** Assistant Professor of Philosophy (1977-84), Ludwig-Maximilians-Universität, München; Full Professor of Philosophy (1984-87), Universität München **Selected Memberships:** President (1987)/Member (1979-82), CIVITAS; Vice President (1983-87), Gesellschaft zur Förderung von Wissenschaft und Kunst; Member, editorial board, *Scheidewege* (Jahresschrift für skeptisches, since 1982)/*Communio* (International Catholic Journal, since 1987) **Discipline:** Philosophy; History of Science; Ethics of Science and Technology **Related Interests:** Philosophy of nature; Bioethics; Philosophy of politics

Selected Publications

_____, R. Spaemann. *Die Frage WOZU? Geschichte und Wiederentdeckung des teleologischen Denkens*. München: Piper-Verlag, 1981, 1985, 1987, 1991. Japanese translation available. English and French translations in progress.

_____. Wahrheit und Evolution." *Communio* 16, 4 (1987): 314-9.

_____. Ordnung der Wirklichkeit. Werner Heisenberg in seinen philosophischen Schriften." *Universitas* 42, 11 (1987): 1167-76.

_____. "Wozu Philosophie? Die Relevanz der Philosophie für die Biowissenschaften." *Artz und Christ*. 33 (1987): 3-13.

_____. "Die Unverzichtbarkeit des Naturbegriffs für die Moraltheologie." In *Weisheit Gottes- Weisheit der Welt*, ed. W. Baier. J. Card., Ratzinger, St. Ottilien: EOS-Verlag, 1987.

_____. "Evolutionismus und Wirklichkeit." In *Schöpfung*. Freiburg: Informationszentrum Berufe in der Kirche, 1988.

_____. "Evolution und Theorie - Philosophische Probleme des Evolutionismus" In *Entwicklung - interdisziplinäre Aspekte zur Evolutionsfrage*, ed. W. Arnold. Stuttgart: Urachhaus, 1989.

_____. "Wenn Gottes Weltmaschine steckenbleibt. Traktat über die moralischen und ethischen Verhaltensnormen für den Umgang mit Katastrophen." *Die Welt* 94, 22 (23 April 1989).

_____. *Bioethic. Philosophisch-Theologische Beiträge zu einen brisanten Thema*. Köln: Communio Verlag, 1990.

_____. *Nietzsche - Sophist und Erzieher*. Dienheim: Acta Humauiora, 1990.

Lucas, J. R.

Present Position and Address: Fellow and Tutor, College (since 1960) Oxford OX1 4JD, UK **Work Phone:** Oxford 276 321 **Date of Birth:** June 18, 1929 **Education:** B.A. (1951)/M.A. (1954), Winchester/Balliol College, Oxford University **Postgraduate Studies:** Junior Research Fellow (1953-56), Merton College; Fellow and Assistant Tutor (1956-59), Corpus Christi College, Cambridge; Jane Eliza Procter Visiting Fellow (1957-58), Princeton University; Leverhulme Research Fellow (1959-60), Leeds University; Gifford Lecturer (1971-73), University of Edinburgh; Margaret Harris Lecturer (1981), University of Dundee **Selected Memberships:** Archbishops' Commission on Christian Doctrine (1967-76); Fellow of the British Academy (1988) **Discipline:** Philosophy **Related Interests:** Time, Space, Causality and Theology.

Selected Publications

_____. *The Freedom of the Will*. Oxford: OUP, 1970.
_____. *A Treatise on Time and Space*. London: Methuen, 1973.
_____. *Essays on Freedom and Grace*. London: SPCK, 1976.
_____. *Space, Time and Causality*. Oxford: OUP, 1985.
_____. *The Future*. Oxford: Blackwell, 1989.
_____. *Space, Time and Electromagnetism*. Oxford: OUP, 1990.

Lumsden, Charles J.

Present Position and Address: Professor of Medicine (since 1991), Department of Medicine, Room 7313, Medical Sciences Building, University of Toronto, Ontario M5S 1A8, Canada **Work Phone:** (416) 978-7178 **Date of Birth:** April 9, 1949 **Education:** B.Sc. Mathematics, Physics (1972)/M.Sc. Theoretical Physics (1974)/Ph.D. Theoretical Physics (1978), University of Toronto **Postgraduate Studies:** Postdoctoral Fellow (1979-82), Department of Biology, Harvard University **Previous Positions:** Lecturer in Biophysics (1975-78), University of Toronto; Associate Professor, Department of Medicine, University of Toronto, 1983-90 **Selected Memberships:** Editorial Board, *Journal of Social and Biological Structures*; American Physical Society; Society for Mathematical Biology; Biophysical Society **Discipline:** Physics; Biology (including Membrane Biology); Biophysics **Related Interests:** Sociobiology and Religion; Mathematical Theology; The Origin of the Mind.

Selected Publications

_____, E. O. Wilson. *Genes, Mind and Culture: the Coevolutionary Process*. Cambridge: Harvard University Press, 1981.
_____, E. O. Wilson. *Promethean Fire: Reflections on the Origin of Mind*. Cambridge: Harvard University Press, 1983.
_____, C. S. Findlay and C. J. Lumsden. *The Creative Mind: Toward an Evolutionary Theory of Discovery and Innovation*. London: Academic Press, 1988.
_____. "Sociobiology, God, and Understanding." *Zygon* 24, 1 (March 1989).
_____. *Satan: An Informal Sociobiology of Transcendent Evil*. Forthcoming.
_____. *The Sociobiology of Michelangelo and His Art*. Forthcoming.

ℳ

Maatman, Russell W.

Present Position and Address: Emeritus Professor of Chemistry (since 1990), Dordt College, Sioux Center, IA 51250, USA; (Home) 401 Fifth Avenue SE, Sioux Center, IA 51250, USA **Date of Birth:** November 7, 1923 **Education:** A.B. (1946) Calvin College; Ph.D. Chemistry (1950), Michigan State University **Previous Positions:** Assistant Professor of Chemistry (1949-51), De Pauw University; Senior Research Chemist (1951-58), Mobil Oil Company; Associate Professor of Chemistry (1958-63), University of Mississippi; Professor of Chemistry (1963-90), Dordt College **Selected Memberships:** Fellow, American Scientific Affiliation; American Chemical Society **Discipline:** Chemistry **Related Areas of Interest:** The Origins Debate; The Unity in all Creation; Teaching Chemistry as a Gift of God.

Selected Publications:

_____. *The Bible, Natural Science, and Evolution*. Grand Rapids: Reformed Fellowship, 1970. Reprint, Dordt College Press. Translations: Korean, Russian and Ukrainian.
_____. "Christian Education Through Science Studies." Calvin College Monograph Series. *Contrasting Christian Approaches to Teaching the Sciences*, ed. D. Oppewal. Grand Rapids: Calvin College, 1971.
_____. *The Unity in Creation*. Sioux Center: Dordt College Press, 1978.
_____. Editorial. "Symposium: Unity in Creation?" *Journal of the American Scientific Affiliation (JASA)* 35 (March 1983): 1.
_____. *Chemistry, a Gift of God*. Written under the auspices of the Dordt Studies Institute. It could also be classified as a syllabus, 1985.
_____. "Chemistry, a Gift of God." *JASA* 38 (December 1986): 232ff.
_____. *Natural Sciences and Christian Faith - Scientific contributions of the PU for CHE; Series J, Potchefstroom Studies in Christian Scholarship, Series J3, no. 17*. Potchefstroom University for CHE, Potchefstroom, RSA, 1986.
_____. "The Origins Debate." Parts 1, 2, 3. *Pro Rege* (the Dordt College faculty quarterly) 14 and 15 (March, June, September 1986): 2ff; 9ff; 22ff.
_____. *Natural Science and Two Themes in Human History. Wetenskaplike Bydraes of Potchefstroom University for Christian Higher Education:*. Series F, Institute for Reformational Studies; Series F, IRS-study pamphlets; Study Pamphlet, no. 239. Potchefstroom University for Christian Higher Education:, Potchefstroom 2520, RSA, 1987.; ISBN 0 86990 963 0.
_____. *The Impact of Evolutionary Theory: A Christian View*. Sioux Center: Dordt College Press, 1993.

MacCready, Paul B.

Present Position and Address: Scientist, Lecturer, Businessman (father of human-powered flight, including the Gossamer Condor now at the Smithsonian Air and Space Museum, Washington, DC). Designer, inventor, founder and President of AeroVironment Inc. (since 1971), 222 E. Huntington Dr., Monrovia, CA 91016, USA Work **Phone:** (818) 357-9983 **Education:** B.A. Physics (1947), Yale University; M.S. Physics (1948)/Ph.D. Aeronautics (1952), California Institute of Technology **Honorary Degrees:** Four honorary degrees (including Yale University) **Awards and Honors:** Kremer

Awards (1977, 1979); The Collier Trophy (1979); The Engineer of the Century Gold Medal (1980); Inventor of the Year (1981); The 1982 Lindbergh Award; Guggenheim Medal (1987) **Previous Positions:** Founder (1952), Meteorology Research Inc. **Selected Memberships:** National Academy of Engineering; American Academy of Arts and Sciences; Fellow, American Institute of Aeronautics and Astronautics; American Meteorological Society Committee for the Scientific Investigation of Claims of the Paranormal; International President, International Human-Powered Vehicle Association; Humanist Laureate, Academy of Humanism **Discipline:** Aeronautics; Physics; Business; Humanism **Related Areas of Interest:** Responsible Science and Humanism; Cosmology; Responsible Science Education; Science and Ethics; Creation and Evolution.

Selected Publications:

_____. "An Evolutionary Perspective." *Free Inquiry* (Spring 1987): 20-1.
_____. "Technology in Perspective and Under Control." *Engineering and Science* (Fall 1987): 23-7.
_____. "The Gell-Mann Approach, and Thoughts on the Human Future." Paper presented at the Murray Gell-Mann 60th Birthday Symposium in Pasadena, CA, January 28, 1989. To be published.

Personal Notes: Among the pioneering vehicles created by AeroVironment are the Gossamer Condor (1977), making the first sustained, controlled human-powered flight, the Gossamer Albatross (1979), the Solar Challenger (with DuPont, 1981), flying from Paris to England powered by sunlight, and with General Motors, the GM Sunraycer (1987), a solar-powered car, and the Impact, a battery-powered car.

MacKay, David B.

Present Position and Address: Professor of Marketing and Geography, School of Business, Indiana University, Bloomington, IN 47405, USA **Work Phone:** (812) 855-1164 **Fax Number:** (812) 855-8679 **E-Mail:** Mackay@ucs.Indiana.edu **Date of Birth:** May 1, 1944 **Languages Spoken:** English **Previous Positions:** Visiting Professor, University of Pittsburgh, PA; Visiting Professor, Norges Handelshøyskole, Bergen, Norway **Selected Memberships:** American Marketing Association; Association of American Geographers; Psychometrics Society; Association for Computing Machinery **Discipline:** Marketing; Geography; Cognitive Science **Related Areas of Interest:** Decision Making; Consumer Behavior **Current Areas of Research:** Consensual Decision Making; Neural Networks; Density Estimation.

Selected Publications: His bibliography contains over 60 articles and chapters in 6 books.

_____. "Probabilistic Multidimensional Scaling: An Auisotropic Model for Distance Judgments." *Journal of Mathematical Psychology* 33 (June 1989): 187-205.
_____, Cornelia Dröge. "Extensions and Applications of Probabilistic Perceptual Maps." *International Journal of Research in Marketing* 7 (1990): 265-82.

Maciel, Paulo Frederico do Rêgo

Address: Rua Mandacaru, 738 Apipucos, Recife (52071) PE, Brazil **Date of Birth:** April 15, 1924 **Languages Spoken:** French, English, Spanish **Education:** B.A. (1939)/Law School (1946), Federal University Pernambuco **Postgraduate Experience:** Postgraduate in Economics (1954), University of Paris **Previous Positions:** Director of IJNPS (1955-1957); Teacher (1957-1960), Catholic University of Pernambuco; Finance Secretary of Pernambuco (1960-1962); President of the State Bank of Pernambuco (1962); President of the National Institute of Sugar and Alcohol (1964-1966); Federal Representative (1967-1970); Rector of the Federal University of Pernambuco (1975-1979) **Selected Memberships:** Letter's Academy of Pernambuco; Institute on Religion in an Age of Science **Disci-**

pline: Economics and Philosophy **Related Areas of Interest:** The Mind and Body Relations - Brain and Belief; Philosophy of Social Sciences.

Selected Publications:

_____. *The Sacred in the Arts, Science and Philosophy.* Federal University of Pernambuco, 1978.

Macy, Joanna R.

Present Position and Address: Adjunct Professor, Starr King School of Ministry, Berkeley, and California Institute of Integral Studies, San Francisco, CA; 1306 Bay View Place, Berkeley, CA 94708, USA **Date of Birth:** May 2, 1929 **Education:** B.A. (1950), Wellesley College; Ph.D. (1978), Syracuse University **Discipline:** Buddhism; General Systems Theory **Related Areas of Interest:** Environmental and Social Ethics in Buddhism and Systems Theory.

Selected Publications:

_____. *Interdependence: Mutual Causality in Early Buddhist Teachings and General Systems Theory.* Ph. D. diss., Syracuse University, 1978. Ann Arbor: University Microfilms, 1978.
_____. *Mutual Causality in Buddhism and General Systems Theory.* New York: SUNY Press, 1991.
_____. "The Ecological Self: Shift in Identity and Ground for Right Action." In *Essays Toward a Post Modern World.* New York: SUNY Press, in press.

Magnuson, Norris A.

Present Position and Address: Professor of Church History and Director of the Resource Center, Bethel Theological Seminary, 3949 Bethel Drive, New Brighton, MN 55112, USA **Work Phone:** (612) 638-6183 **Fax Number:** (612) 638-6006 **Date of Birth:** June 15, 1932 **Awards and Honors:** Social Science Research Council Stipend (1954); Graduate Student Tuition Scholarship, University of Minnesota (1961-63); Lilly Endowment Fellowship, American Theological Library Association (1964-65); Research Fellow, Institute for Advanced Christian Studies (1968-69) **Selected Memberships:** Conference on Faith and History; American Theological Library Association; Minnesota Theological Library Association **Discipline:** Religious History and Theological Librarianship **Related Areas of Interest:** American Social and Intellectual History **Current Areas of Research:** Revivals, renewal and social concern with special reference to Swedish Baptists in the US; Swedish Baptist general Conference; Bethel College and Seminary history.

Selected Publications: His total bibliography contains 6 books, 3 revised editions, and more than 40 published articles (including articles of varying lengths in encyclopedias and dictionaries).

_____, David O. Moberg. "Current Trends in Evangelism." *Journal of Pastoral Care* (Spring 1956).
_____. "Revivalism and Social Reform." In *American Festival of Evangelism Notebooks.* Washington, DC: American Festival of Evangelism, 1981.
_____. *Missionsskolan: The History of an Immigrant Theological School; Bethel Theological Seminary, 1871-1891.* St. Paul, MN: Bethel Theological Seminary, 1982.
_____. "Social Service and the Churches, 1865-1930." In *Eerdmans' Handbook to Christianity in America.* Grand Rapids, MI: Eerdmans, 1983.
_____, editor. *"Proclaim the Good News": Essays in Honor of Gordon G. Johnson.* Arlington Heights, IL: Harvest, 1986.
_____. "Along Kingdom Highways - American Baptist and Swedish Baptists in a Common Mission: An Introductory Essay." *American Baptist Quarterly* 6 (September 1987).
_____. *How We Grew: Swedish Baptists in America.* Arlington Heights, IL: Harvest Publications, 1976. Rev. eds. 1985, 88.

_____, William Travis. *American Evangelicalism: An Annotated Bibliography*. West Cornwall, CT: Locust Hill Press, 1990.
_____. *Salvation in the Slums: Evangelical Social Work, 1865-1920*. American Theological Library Association Monograph Series. Metuchen, NJ: Scarecrow Press, 1977. Reprint, Baker Book House, 1990.

Mailloux, Noël

Present Position and Address: Professor Emeritus, Department of Psychology, University of Montreal, Canada; 2715 Cote St. Catherine Road, Montreal, PQ H3T 1B6, Canada **Concurrent Positions:** President and Director of Research Program (since 1950), Research Center on Human Relations. Scientific Committee, Quaderni di Criminologia Clinica **Date of Birth:** December 25, 1909 **Languages Spoken:** French, English, Italian, German **Education:** B.A. (1930), University of Montreal; Ph.D. Psychology (1934)/S.Th.L. Theology (1938), Angelicum Rome, Italy. Ordained Priest (1937), Dominican Order; Research Fellow (1939), Department of Psychology, University of Cincinnati; Diplomate in Clinical Psychology (1948), the American Board of Examiners in Professional Psychology **Previous Positions:** Professor of Experimental Psychology (1939-1942), Faculty of Philosophy and Theology of the Dominican Order, Ottawa; Founder/Head of Department of Psychology (1942-1957, 1969-1973)/Vice-Dean of Faculty of Philosophy (1960-69), University of Montreal; Founder and Director (1943-1974), of Scientific and Professional Services "Centre d'Orientation," Montreal Center for Problem Children **Editorial Positions:** Chief Editor, *Contributions a l'Etude des Sciences de l'Homme* and 7 other journals **Selected Memberships:** American Psychological Association; American Catholic Psychological Association; Fellow, American Sociological Association; International Catholic Association for Medico-Psychological Studies; Academy of Religion and Mental Health; International Union of Religion and Mental Health; International Union of Psychological Science (1954-77); Fellow, Canadian Psychological Association; Fellow, Royal Society of Canada; elected to the council (1964-66), Society for the Scientific Study of Religion **Discipline:** Psychology; Catholic Priest **Related Areas of Interest:** Psychology and Religion/Ethics/Moral Values; Religion, Science and Mental Health.

Selected Publications:

_____. "The Joint Role of Religion, Behavioral Sciences and Medicine in Regard to Mental Health." In *Academy of Religion and Mental Health: Religion, Science and Mental Health, Proceedings of the 1st Academy Symposium on Interdiscipline Responsibility for Mental Health - Religious and Scientific Concern, 1957*, 63-75. New York University Press, 1959.
_____. "Modern Psychology and Moral Values." In *The Nature of Man in Theological and Psychological Perspective*, ed. S. Doniger, 97-104. New York: Harper and Brothers, 1962.

Mallove, Eugene F.

Present Position and Address: Engineer-Author, Starbound Engineering; 171 Woodhill-Hooksett Road, Bow, NH 03304, USA **Concurrent Positions:** Freelance Science writer (since 1982), *MIT Technology Review* and *The Washington Post*; freelance writer (since 1987), science features for magazines and newspapers **Date of Birth:** June 9, 1947 **Education:** S.B. Aero/Astro Engineering (1969)/S.M. Aero/Astro Engineering (1970), MIT; Sc.D. Environmental Health Sciences (1975), Harvard University **Previous Positions:** Chief Science Writer (1987-1991), MIT news office; Lecturer in Science Journalism, Department of Humanities, MIT; Worked in Industry from (1970-85), Hughes Research Laboratories/Harvard University Air Cleaning Laboratory/Analytic Sciences Co./Northrop Precision Products Division/Jaycor, Systems Engineering Division/Astronomy New England, Inc.; MIT Lincoln Laboratory (1983-85) **Media Work:** International science writer and broadcaster at Voice of America *Science Notebook*, 5 minute daily program (1985-87) and *New Horizons*, 20 Minute weekly program (1985-87) **Selected Memberships:** Institute on Religion in an Age of Science; American Institute for Aeronautic and Astronautics; Fellow, British Interplanetary Society; American Association for the Advancement of Science **Discipline:** Science Writing; Cosmology; Cosmobiology **Related Areas of Interest:** Cosmology; The Search for Extraterrestrial Intelligence (SETI); The relation between the two above; Cold Fusion R+D.

Selected Publications:

_____. *The Quickening Universe: Cosmic Evolution and Human Destiny.* New York: St. Martin's Press, 1987.
_____. *The Starflight Handbook: A Pioneer's Guide to Interstellar Travel.* New York: John Wiley & Sons, 1989.
_____. *Fire From Ice: Searching for the Truth Behind the Cold Fusion Furor.* New York: John Wiley & Sons, 1991.

Malony, H. Newton

Present Position and Address: Senior Professor of Psychology, Fuller Theological Seminary, 180 N. Oakland Avenue, Pasadena, CA 91182, USA **Concurrent Positions:** Private Practice of Clinical Psychology (since 1969), Pasadena **Work Phone:** (818) 584-5528 **Date of Birth:** May 17, 1931 **Education:** B.A. (1952), Birmingham-Southern College; M.Div. (1955), Yale Divinity School; M.A. (1961)/Ph.D. Clinical Psychology (1964), George Peabody College of Vanderbilt University **Postgraduate Experience:** Further Study - William Alanson White Institute of Psychiatry, Psychology and Psychoanalysis; Emory University; Vanderbilt University; Harvard University **Previous Positions:** Pastor of local churches (Methodist and Interdenominational, 1954-59), AL and NY; Adjunct Professor in Clinical Psychology (1964-65), University of Kentucky; Director of Psychology (1964-65), Frankfort State Hospital, KY; Consultant in Clinical Psychology (1966-69), McMinn Mental Health Center; Professor of Psychology/Chairman of Psychology and Sociology Dept./Director of Counseling Service, Tennessee Wesleyan College; Associate Professor/Director of Church Consultation Service, Graduate School of Psychology, Fuller Theological Seminary **Editorial Positions:** Contributing Editor of 7 journals including *Journal of the American Scientific Affiliation*; *Journal for the Scientific Study of Religion*; *Journal of Psychology and Theology* **Selected Memberships:** Past Council Member, Society for the Scientific Study of Religion; Christian Association for Psychological Studies; Fellow, American Psychological Association, Past President, Psychologists Interested in Religious Issues; American Scientific Affiliation **Discipline:** Clinical Psychology; Minister **Related Areas of Interest:** The integration of Religion and the Social/Behavioral Sciences.

Selected Publications:

_____, Gary R. Collins. *Psychology and Theology: Prospects for Integration.* Nashville, TN: Abingdon Press, 1980.
_____, Hendrika Vande Kemp. *Psychology and Religion: A Bibliography of Historical Bases for Psychotheological Integration.* Millwood, NY: Kraus-Thomson Organization Limited, 1984.
_____, Christopher Rosik, eds. *The 1983 Travis Papers in the Integration of Psychology and Theology.* Pasadena: Integration Press, 1986.
_____. *Integration Musings: Thoughts on Being a Christian Professional.* Pasadena: Integration Press, 1986.
_____, editor. *Is There a Shrink in the Lord's House? How Psychologists can Help the Church.* Pasadena: Integration Press, 1987.
_____, B. Spilka, eds. *Religion in Psychodynamic Perspective: The Contributions of Paul W. Pruyser.* New York: Oxford University Press, 1991.
_____, editor. *Psychology of Religion: Personalities, Problems, Possibilities.* Grand Rapids: Baker Book House, 1991.
_____. *Relaxation for Christians.* New York: Ballantine, 1992.
_____, S. Southard, eds. *Handbook on Conversion.* Birmingham, AL: Religious Education Press, 1992.
_____. *The Psychology of Religion for Ministry.* Baltimore: Paulist Press, 1993.

Manenschijn, Gerrit

Present Position and Address: Full Professor of Ethics (since 1988), Theological University of Kampen, Holland; Parmentierlaan 29, 1185 CV Amstelveen, The Netherlands **Date of Birth:** November 11, 1931 **Languages Spoken:** Dutch, English, German **Education:** M.A. Theology (1972)/Ph.D. Theology (1979), Free University of Amsterdam, The Netherlands **Congresses and Conferences:** The European Conference of Science and Theology **Previous Positions:** Lecturer of Theology (1973), Free University of Amsterdam **Selected Memberships:** Societas Ethica (European Conference on Ethics); Vereniging van ethici in Nedeland (Association of Moral Philosophers in the Netherlands) **Discipline:** Ethics and Theology **Related Areas of Interest:** Economics, Political Philosophy, Science and their relationship to Theology and Ethics.

Selected Publications:

_____. *Moraal en Eigenbelang bij Thomas Hobbes en Adam Smith* (Morality and self-interest in the works of Thomas Hobbes and Adam Smith, summaries in English and Germany). Amsterdam: Rodopi, 1979.

_____. "Reasoning in Science and Ethics." In *Science Education and Ethical Values*, ed. D. Gosling and B. Musschenga, 37-54. Geneva: WCC Publications; Washington, DC: Georgetown University Press, 1985.

_____. "Evolution and Ethics." In *Evolution and Creation*, ed. S. Andersen and A. Peacocke" 85-103. Aarhus, Denmark: Aarhus University Press, 1987.

_____. *Geplunderde Aarde, Getergde Hemel. Ontwerp voor Een Christelijke Milieu-ethiek* ("Earth plundered, heaven provoked." Introduction to Christian environmental ethics). Baarn: Ten Have, 1988.

Manganello, James A.

Present Position and Address: President, Charis Psychological Services, 3 Militia Drive, Lexington, MA 02173; The Liberty Tree Medical Center, Danvers, MA 01923, USA **Work Phone:** (617) 863-0350 or (508) 532-0664 **Fax Number:** (617) 674-2450 or (508) 774-1591 **Date of Birth:** November 30, 1944 **Languages Spoken:** English, Italian **Awards and Honors:** Pi Lambda Theta Honor Society; Listed in *Who's Who in the East* **Previous Positions:** President, Health Integration Services, Peabody, MA; Clinical Fellow in Psychology (Psychiatry), Massachusetts General Hospital/Harvard Medical School, Boston, MA; Consulting Psychologist, Westwood Lodge Hospital, Westwood, MA; Intern in Clinical Psychology, Massachusetts General Hospital/Harvard Medical School, Boston, MA **Selected Memberships:** Fellow, American Orthopsychiatric Association; American Scientific Affiliation; American College of Healthcare Executives **Discipline:** Clinical Psychology **Related Areas of Interest:** Integration of Faith and Theology **Current Areas of Research:** Communication Skills: Understanding Diversity in the Local Church.

Selected Publications: His total bibliography contains 4 articles and 2 monographs.

_____. *An Investigation of Fear of Death, Denial and Belief in Afterlife with its Effect on Empathy with Terminally Ill Patients*. Ph.D. diss., Boston University, 1977. Abstract in Dissertation Abstracts, Boston University, 1977.

_____. *Communication Skills: A Practical Manual*. Boston, MA: Higher Education: Research, 1978.

_____, Janet Lanahan. *A Competency Based Training Manual for Health Care Workers*. Boston, MA: Higher Education: Research, 1979.

Mangum, John M.

Present Position and Address: Consultant on Science and Theology (since 1988), Division for Global Mission, Evangelical Lutheran Church in America, 8765 West Higgins Rd, Chicago, IL 60631, USA; P.O. Box 188, Henryville, PA 18332, USA **Date of Birth:** December 18, 1920 **Education:** B.A. (1942), Lenoir Rhyne College, Hickory, NC; M.S.T. (1945), Philadelphia Lutheran Seminary; M.S. (1948), Columbia University **Honorary Degrees:** D.L. (1963), Lenoir Rhyne College **Previous Positions:**

Director for Planning (1968-87), Division for World Mission and Ecumenism, Lutheran Church in America **Editorial Positions:** Editor of 4 Lutheran publications (1946-89) **Discipline:** Theology; Journalism; Administration **Related Areas of Interest:** Liturgical and Homiletical Materials for the Church in an age of Science/Technology; Formation of regional networks of Scientists/Theologians in Asia, Africa, Latin America.

Selected Publications:

_____. *The New Faith-Science Debate: Probing Cosmology, Technology, Theology.* Minneapolis: Augsburg Fortress; Geneva: World Council of Churches, 1989.

Marc, Alexandre

Present Position and Address: Founding Advisor; Centre International de Formation Européenne, 327 avenue du Maréchal-Leclerc, F-06140 Vence, France **Work Phone:** 93-58 64 28 **Date of Birth:** January 19, 1904 **Languages Spoken:** French, English, German, Russian **Education:** Diplôme Ecole des Sc. Pol. (1947), Paris **Previous Positions:** Board of Directors, Centre Européen de la Culture; Honorary Vice President, World Association of World Federalists; Professor, l'Institut Európen des Hautes Etudes et au College Universitaite d'Etudes Fédéralistes; Research Fellow, Center for the Study of Federalism, Temple University, Philadelphia, PA; Research Fellow, Jerusalem Institute for Federal Studies; Honorary President of l'union Européenne Fédéraliste et Membre du Conseil du Mouvement Fédéraliste Européen; Permanent Consultant to Centre International de Formation Européenne **Discipline:** Philosophy; Politics **Related Areas of Interest:** European Federalism; Dialectic and the New Humanity; Integrative thought.

Selected Publications:

_____. "Le christianisme et la révolution spirituelle." *Revue Esprit no* 6 (1 March 1933).
_____. *De La Methodologie a La Dialectique.* Paris: Presses d'Europe, 1970.
_____. "Dialogue avec la Science." Extract from *l'Europe en formation* 273 (1988).

Margulis, Lynn (formerly Lynn Alexander Sagan)

Present Position and Address: Distinguished University Professor (since 1988), Biology Department, University of Massachusetts - Amherst, MA 01003, USA; 20 Triangle Street, Amherst, MA 01002, USA **Work Phone:** (413) 545-3244 **Date of Birth:** March 5, 1938 **Languages Spoken:** English, Spanish, French **Education:** A.B. (1957), The College, University of Chicago; M.Sc. joint degree in Zoology and Genetics (1960), University of Wisconsin; Ph.D. Genetics (1965), University of California - Berkeley **Honorary Degrees:** Hon. D. Sc. - Southeastern Massachusetts University (1989)/Westfield State College (1989) **Lectures Presented:** Invited lecturer world-wide **Previous Positions:** Research Associate (1963-64)/Lecturer in Biology (1963-65), Brandeis University; Consultant and staff member (1963-67), Elementary Science Study, Educational Services Incorporated; Biology Coordination (1965-66), Brandeis University Peace Corps - Columbia Project; Adjunct Assistant Professor (1966-67)/Assistant Professor (1967-71)/Associate (1971-77)/Professor of Biology (1977-1986)/University Professor of Biology (1986-88), Boston University **Selected Memberships:** American Association for the Advancement of Science; American Museum of Natural History; Catalan Society for Biology; International Society for the Study of the Origin of Life (ISSOL); Marine Biological Laboratory; Sigma Xi; Cofounder, Society for Evolutionary Protistology **Discipline:** Biology; Genetics **Related Areas of Interest:** Cell Motility; Global Ecology; Symbiosis and Evolution.

Selected Publications: Her bibliography lists over 100 articles, over 60 books and chapters published and 17 in press and 2 in preparation.

_____, D. Sagan. "The Gaian Perspective of Ecology." *The Ecologist* 13 (1983): 160-7.

_____, D. Sagan. *Microcosmos: Four Billion Years of Evolution From Our Bacterial Ancestors*. New York: Summit Books, 1986; Paperback, 1988. Translated into French, Italian and Danish.

_____. "Early Life: The Microbes have Priority." In *Gaia - A Way of Knowing*, ed. W. I. Thompson, 98-109. Great Barrington, MA: Lindisfarne Press, 1987.

_____. "Jim Lovelock's Gaia" and also with D. Sagan "Gaia and Biospheres." In *Gaia, the Thesis, the Mechanisms and the Implications*, ed. P. Bunyard and E. Goldsmith, 50-65, 237-42. Cornwall, UK: Wadebridge Ecological Centre, Worthyvale Manor, 1988.

_____. "Gaia and Geognosy." In *Global Ecology: Towards a Science of the Biosphere*, ed. M. B. Rambler, L. Margulis and R. Fester, 1-30. Boston, MA: Academic Press, 1989.

_____, D. Sagan. *Mystery Dance: On the Evolution of Human Sexuality*. New York: Simon & Schuster, 1991.

_____. *Symbiosis in Cell Evolution*. New York: W. H. Freeman Co., 1993.

_____, D. Sagan. *What is Life?* New York: Simon & Schuster, 1995.

_____. "Big Trouble in Biology: Physiological Autopoiesis vs. Mechanistic Neodarwinism." In *Reality Club*, ed. Brockman, vol. 2. NJ: Prentice-Hall, in press.

Martin, Daniel

Present Position and Address: Retired lecturer in Mathematics (1980), University of Glasgow; Cygnetbank, 27 Clyde Street, Carluke, Lanarkshire, Scotland ML8 5BA, UK **Date of Birth:** April 16, 1915 **Education:** M.A. (1936)/B.Sc. (1937)/Ph.D. (1948), University of Glasgow **Awards and Honors:** FIMA (around 1950); FRSE (1962) **Previous Positions:** Lecturer in Mathematics (1938-1947), Royal Technical College, Glasgow (now University of Strathclyde); Lecturer/Senior Lecturer in Mathematics (1947-1980), University of Glasgow **Discipline:** Mathematics of Theoretical Physics **Related Areas of Interest:** The Relevance of Modern Physics to Theology.

Selected Publications:

_____. *Manifold Theory: An Introduction for Mathematical Physicists*. Ellis Horwood, 1991.

Martin, David Alfred

Present Position and Address: Retired Professor of Sociology (since 1989), London School of Economics; 174 St. John's Road, Woking Surrey GU21 1PQ, UK **Date of Birth:** June 30, 1929 **Education:** Westminster College of Education (1950-52); Primary School Teacher Training (1959); B.Sc. Sociology (1959), London (external); Ph.D. (1964), London University **Congresses and Conferences:** President (1975-1983), International Conference of the Sociology of Religion; President (1976-78), Science and Religion Forum; Chairman (preliminary stages 1981), H.E.F. Conference on Reductionism and Personhood in the Life Sciences **Previous Positions:** Lecturer (1962-67)/Reader (1967-71)/Full Professor (1971-88), London School of Economics; Elizabeth Scurlock Professor (1986-89), Southern Methodist University, Dallas **Editorial Positions:** Editorial Advisory Committee (since 1985), *Encyclopedia Britannica* **Selected Memberships:** London Society for the Study of Religion (since 1972); Co-director (1965-69), Socio-Religious Research Services; President (1976-1981), Religion section of the British Sociological Association; Chairman (1979-1986), Religion and Society Unit, University (1979-86), Religion and Society Unit, University of Kent **Discipline:** Sociology **Related Areas of Interest:** Sociology and Theology.

Selected Publications:

_____. "The Status of the Human Person in the Behavioral Sciences." In *Technology and Social Justice*, ed. R. Preston, 237-65. World Council of Churches, 1971. Reprinted in part in *Christian* (October 1973).
_____. "Ethical Comment and Political Decision." In *Duty and Discernment*, ed. G. Dunstan. S.C.M. Press, 1974. First published in *Theology* (October 1973).
_____. "The Sociological Mode and the Theological Vocabulary." In *Sociology and Theology*, ed. D. Martin, W. S. F. Pickering and J. Orme-Mills. Brighton: Harvester Press, 1980.
_____, J. Orme Mills, O. P. Mills and W. S. F. Pickering, eds. *Sociology and Theology: Alliance and Conflict*. Brighton: Harvester Press, 1980.
_____. "Comparing Different Maps of the Same Ground." In *The Sciences and Theology in the Twentieth Century*. Stockfield, UK: Oriel Press, 1982.
_____. "Theological Roots of Sociology." *The Times Higher Education: Supplement* (October 25, 1985).

Martin, Helen Elizabeth

Present Position and Address: Science Teacher (1967), Unionville High School, Unionville, PA 19375, USA; (Home) 329 Lamborntown Road, West Grove, PA 19390, USA **Date of Birth:** February 19, 1945 **Education:** B.A. Mathematics (1967), The King's College, Briarcliff Manor, NY; M.Ed. Physical Science (1970), West Chester University, PA **Postgraduate Experience:** Spent time studying Sir Isaac Newton's unpublished theological manuscripts in England, Israel, Massachusetts and California (1978-87). Additional studies at West Chester University/The Goethe Institute, Freiburg, Germany/Oxford University **Lectures Presented:** International Lecturer for the National Science Teachers Association (1987)/Association for Science Education, UK **Awards and Honors:** Appointed by Carnegie Corporation and Charter member of National Board for Professional Teaching Standards; Named 1987 Alumna of the Year, The King's College; Challenger 7 Fellowship Award for Innovation in Educational Technology, *Business Week* (1991); NOAA Award, outstanding Satellite Educator, US Department of Commerce **Selected Memberships:** History of Science Society; Fellow, American Scientific Affiliation; American Association for the Advancement of Science **Discipline:** Mathematics and Science **Related Areas of Interest:** Sir Isaac Newton's unpublished Theological Manuscripts; The Biblical and Biological imperative of Meditation.

Selected Publications:

_____. "Meditation - A Requirement." *Journal of the American Scientific Affiliation* (June 1979). Based on a presentation of "Meditation - A Biological and Biblical Requirement," at ASA 1977 Annual meeting, Wheaton, IL.
_____. "Junior Meteorologists on Cloud Nine." *The Christian Reader* (March/April 1988).

Martin, James P.

Present Position and Address: Professor Emeritus (since 1988), Vancouver School of Theology, 6000 Iona Drive, Vancouver, BC V6T1L4, Canada **Date of Birth:** February 12, 1923 **Education:** B.A.Sc. Chemical Engineering (1946), University of British Columbia; B.D. (1950)/Th.M. (1951)/Ph.D. (1958), Princeton Theological Seminary **Previous Positions:** Instructor (1954-58)/Assistant Professor of New Testament (1958-62), Princeton Theological Seminary; Associate Professor through Professor of Biblical Interpretation (1962-72), Union Theological Seminary - Virginia; Principal and Professor (1972-83)/Professor (1983-88) of Biblical Interpretation, Vancouver School of Theology **Discipline:** Biblical Interpretation and Hermeneutics **Related Areas of Interest:** Hermeneutics and Philosophy of Science and Scientific Culture; Theology in a Scientific Culture (taught this course for 2 years); Moving towards a Post-critical Paradigm.

Selected Publications:

_____. "Cosmic Christ and Cosmic Redemption." *Affirmation* 1, 2 (1967). Inaugural address given at Union Theological Seminary - Virginia.
_____. "Toward a Post-Critical Paradigm." *New Testament Studies* 33 (1987): 370-85.

Marty, Martin E.

Present Position and Address: Fairfax M. Cone Distinguished Service Professor (since 1978), The Divinity School, University of Chicago, 1025 East 58th Street, Chicago, IL 60637, USA; George B. Caldwell Senior Scholar in Residence, The Park Ridge Center for the Study of Health, Faith, and Ethics, 211 E. Ontario, Suite 800, Chicago, IL 60611, USA **Concurrent Positions:** Professor, History of Modern Christianity (since 1963), The Divinity School, History Department, the committee on the History of Culture, University of Chicago **Date of Birth:** February 5, 1928 **Education:** M.Div. (1952), Concordia Seminary; S.T.M. (1954), Lutheran School of Theology at Chicago; Ph.D. American Religious and Intellectual History (1956), University of Chicago; Ordained to Ministry by Lutheran Church (1952) **Honorary Degrees:** Thiel College, Thomas More College, Marian College, West Virginia Wesleyan College, Colorado College, Providence College, Willamette University, St. Olaf College, DePaul University, Bethany Seminary, Wabash College, Muhlenberg College, Capital University, University of Southern California, Valparaiso University, Christ Seminary, Maryville College, North Park College, Keuka College, Bethany Seminary, Wittenberg University, Rosary College, Rockford College, Virginia Theological Seminary, Hamilton College, Loyola University, University of Notre Dame, Roanoke College, Mercer University, IL, Wesleyan, Roosevelt University, Aquinas College, Franklin College, No. Michigan University, Muskingum College, Coe College, Lehigh University, Hebrew Union College, St. Xavier College, Colgate University, Governors State University, Mt. Union, Texas Lutheran, Whittier College, Aurora University, Baker, University of Nebraska, California Lutheran, Hope College; Northwestern College; George Fox College; Drake University; Centre College **Pastoral Positions:** Washington (1950-51)/River Forest, IL (1952-56)/Elk Grove Village, IL (1956-1963) **Editorial Positions:** Senior Editor, *Christian Century*; Coeditor, *Church History* (since 1963); Editor, *Context* (since 1969); editor, *Second Opinion* **Selected Memberships:** Elected member, American Philosophical Society; Fellow, American Academy of Arts and Sciences; Past President, Society of American Historians; Past President, American Society of Church History; Past President, American Catholic History Association; Past President, American Antiquarian Society; Past President, American Academy of Religion; Past President, Park Ridge Center, An Institute for the Study of Health, Faith and Ethics **Discipline:** Religion (Educator, Editor) **Related Areas of Interest:** Historical Aspects of Theology/Science Dialogue; Relation of Religion to Modern Medicine.

Selected Publications

_____. "Religion, Theology, Church, and Bioethics." *The Journal of Medicine and Philosophy* 17 (1992): 273-89.

Masani, Pesi R.

Present Position and Address: University Professor Emeritus of Mathematics (since 1989), University of Pittsburgh, Pittsburgh, PA 15260, USA; (Home) 401 Shady Avenue, Apt. 603D, Pittsburgh, PA 15206, USA **Work Phone:** (412) 624-8378 **Date of Birth:** August 1, 1919 **Education:** B.Sc. (1940), The University of Bombay; M.A. (1942)/Ph.D. (1946), Harvard University **Awards and Honors:** Fulbright-Hays Senior Scholar (Summer 1977), State University of Tbilisi, USSR; Alexander von Humboldt Senior Visiting Scientist (1979-80), Germany **Previous Positions:** Professor and Head of Mathematics Department (1949-1959), Institute of Science, Bombay; Professor of Mathematics (1960-1972), Indiana University, Bloomington; Professor of Mathematics (1972)/University Professor of Mathematics (1973-1989), University of Pittsburgh **Selected Memberships:** American Mathematical Society; Mathematical Association of America; IRAS **Discipline:** Mathematics **Related Areas of Interest:** Scientific Methodology and Cybernetics; Problem of Evil; Marxism; Liberation Theology.

Selected Publications:

_____. "The Common Ground of Marxism and Religion." *Journal of Ecumenical Studies* (1979).
_____. "Humanization as De-Alienation." *Alternatives* (1981).
_____. "The Thermodynamic and Phylogenetic Foundations of Human Wickedness." *Zygon* (1985).
_____. "The Illusion that Materialism Promotes Science." *CAREE Christian-Marxist Encounter Newsletter* (1986).
_____. "The Tenuous Linkage of Marxism and Materialism." *CAREE Christian-Marxist Encounter Newsletter* (1989).

Mason, John Martin

Present Position and Address: Retired Clergy (since 1974), The Evangelical Lutheran Church in America (ELCA); 2536 Seabury Avenue, Minneapolis, MN 55406, USA **Home Phone:** (612) 729-5495 **Date of Birth:** January 29, 1909 **Languages Spoken:** English; Studies Latin, Greek, Hebrew, German, French, Norwegian **Awards and Honors:** The Award of Honor - The American Association of Homes for the Aging (1970); The Distinguished Alumnus Award - St. Olaf College, Northfield, MN (1972); The Doctor of Humane Letters Award, Luther College, Decorah, IA (1973) **Previous Positions:** Dean of Religion (1938-44), Waldorf College, Forest City, IA; The Parish Ministry (1934-38; 1944-54); Director of the Department of Services for the Aging (1954-74), The Evangelical Lutheran Church (ELCA) **Selected Memberships:** The Planetary Society **Discipline:** Theology **Related Areas of Interest:** Science **Current Areas of Research:** The Neanderthal Problem - To indicate that the Neanderthal People were definitely in the direct line of descent to the human family and closer to the *Homo sapiens* people chronologically than the African *Homo sapiens* of the Near East 90,000 years before the present - even though they were less advanced physically.

Selected Publications:

_____. *The Universe and the Creator-God.* New York: The Carlton Press, 1990. May be available from author.
_____. "The Human Family and the Creator-God." Unpublished manuscript.
_____. "The Universe and the Creator-God." Paper prepared for delivery to the adult forum of the University Lutheran Church of Hope.
Personal Notes: Nine articles have been published for distribution to Congregational groups, "In Behalf of Credibility," "Energy - What Is It?," "Think On These Things," "The Universe and the Creator - God," "The Human Family and the Biblical Family - A Reconciliation," "The Rehabilitation of Charles Darwin," "The Neanderthal Problem," "The Image of God - In His Likeness," "Thoughts on Quantum Mechanics." A tenth article in preparation, in which I intend to show that the Human family was in existence long before the time of Adam is titled "When Did Adam Live?"

Matsen, Fredrick A. (Al)

Present Position and Address: Professor of Chemistry and Physics; University of Texas, Austin, TX 78701 **Date of Birth:** July 26, 1913 **Education:** B.S., Wisconsin; Ph.D. Princeton University **Awards and Honors:** Guggenheim Fellow; Fellow, International Institute of Quantum Molecular Dynamics; Fellow, American Physical Society **Discipline:** Theories of Matter **Current Areas of Research:** Superconductivity; Modern Religious Existentialism.

Selected Publications: His bibliography contains 4 books and 200 papers.

_____, R. Paunz. *Unitary Group in Quantum Chemistry.* Elsevier, 1986.
_____. "The Electro Magnetic Higgs Boson." *Review Modern Physics* (Forthcoming).

Matthews, Dale A.

Present Position and Address: Associate Professor of Medicine, Georgetown University School of Medicine, 6 PHC, 3800 Reservoir Road NW, Washington, DC 20007, USA; (Home), 8447 Holly Leaf Drive, McLean, VA 22102, USA **Concurrent Positions:** Staff Physician, Georgetown University Medical Center; Research Fellow, National Institute for Healthcare Research, Rockville, MD; Regional Consultant, Bayer (formerly Miles) Institute for Health Care Communication, New Haven, CT **Work Phone:** (202) 687-6403 **Home Phone:** (703) 903-9458 **Fax Number:** (202) 687-5208 **Date of Birth:** January 12, 1954 **Languages Spoken:** French **Education:** BA Romance Languages and Special Program in European Civilization (*cum laude*, 1976), Princeton University, Princeton, NJ; MD (1980), Duke University School of Medicine **Postgraduate Experience:** Internship and Residency in Internal Medicine (1980-83), University of Connecticut School of Medicine, Farmington, CT; Robert Wood Johnson Clinical Scholars Program and Clinical Fellowship in Internal Medicine (1983-85), Yale University School of Medicine, New Haven, CT **Congresses and Conferences:** More than 30 presentations at competitive national academic medical meetings in the US, including, the Society for General Internal Medicine, American Federation for Clinical Research, and American Psychiatric Association; International presentations include the International Conference on Doctor-Patient Communication in London, ONT, Canada (1986), The Canadian Society of Internal Medicine in Edmonton, ALB (1989), and the Medical Association of the Bahamas (1989); Presentations on Christianity and medicine include the Paul Tournier Institute of the Christian Medical and Dental Society (1990, 92), and meetings of the Connecticut Valley (1984, 93) and Buffalo (1993) chapters of the Christian Medical and Dental Society **Lectures Presented:** Over 75 lectures at numerous medical schools, hospitals, and continuing medical Education meetings throughout the United States on numerous topics, including the spiritual dimension of medicine, doctor-patient communication, chronic fatigue, and psychiatric illness in primary care medicine **Awards and Honors:** King's Fund College Scholar (London, UK), (1979), Duke University; Trent Award in the History of Medicine (1980), Duke University; Diplomate of National Board of Medical Examiners (June 10, 1982); Diplomate in Internal Medicine, American Board of Internal Medicine, (September 14, 1983); Lee B. Lusted Prize (Honorable Mention, 1985), Society for Medical Decision-Making; George Morris Piersol Teaching and Research Scholarship (1989-92), American College of Physicians; Fellowship (1993), American College of Physicians (FACP) **Previous Positions:** Instructor (1983-85), Yale University School of Medicine, New Haven, CT; Staff Physician (1983-85), Yale-New Haven Hospital; Assistant Professor of Medicine (1985-91), University of Connecticut School of Medicine, Farmington, CT; Staff Physician (1985-91), John Dempsey Hospital, Farmington, CT and Department of Veterans Affairs Medical Center, Newington, CT; Chief of Internal Medicine (1991-93), Minirth-Meier and Byrd Clinic; Founder and Director (1991-93) National Center for Chronic Fatigue, Arlington, VA; Staff Physician (1991-93), Northern Virginia Doctors Hospital, Arlington, VA and Psychiatric Institute of Washington **Media Work:** National Television Appearances: Oprah Winfrey Show, Larry King Live, Good Morning America, The Other Side; Featured in National Newspapers: *New York Times, Washington Post, USA Today* **Editorial Positions:** Review Board: *Journal of Clinical Epidemiology, Annals of Internal Medicine, Journal of General Internal Medicine, Hastings Center Report, The Physician and Sportsmedicine,* and *Psychosomatics, Pediatrics, and Biological Psychiatry*; Editorial Board (1989-92), *Medical Encounter* **Selected Memberships:** Board of Directors (1990-93), Paul Tournier Institute, Christian Medical and Dental Society; Board of Advisors (1991-), Humility Theology Information Center of the John Templeton Foundation; Co-chair, Mood and Anxiety Disorders Subcommittee for DSM-IV (Diagnostic and Statistical Manual): Primary Care Version, American Psychiatric Association (1991-), Primary Care Evaluation of Mental Disorders Project (1991-2); Member, (1994-), National Board of Medical Examiners, Step 1, Behavioral Science Committee **Discipline:** Internal Medicine.

Selected Publications: His bibliography contains 3 books, 3 book chapters, 35 scientific articles, 45 research abstracts, 8 letters to the editor, and 1 teaching videotape.

_____, W. H. Sledge, and P. B. Lieberman. "Evaluation of Intern Performance by Medical Inpatients." *American Journal of Medicine* 83 (1987): 938-44.

Suchman, A. L., Dale Matthews. "What Makes the Doctor-Patient Relationship Therapeutic: Exploring the Connexional Dimension of Patient Care." *Annals of Internal Medicine* 108 (1988): 125-30.

_____, A. R. Feinstein. " 'Review of Systems' for the Personal Aspects of Medical Care." *American Journal of Medical Science* 295 (1988): 159-71.

_____, A. R. Feinstein. "A New Instrument for Patients' Ratings of Physician Performance in the Hospital Setting." *Journal of General Internal Medicine* 4 (1989): 14-22.

_____. "The Secret of Patient Care." *Society of General Internal Medicine News* 12, 6 (1989): 1-6.

_____, P. Manu, and T. J. Lane. "Evaluation and Management of Patients with Chronic Fatigue." *American Journal of Medical Science* 302 (1991): 269-77.

_____, A.L. Suchman, and W. T. Branch. "Making Connections: Enhancing the Therapeutic Potential of Patient-Clinician Relationships." *Annals of Internal Medicine* 118 (1993): 973-77.

_____, D. B. Larson, and C. M. Barry. *The Faith Factor: An Annotated Bibliography of Clinical Research on Spiritual Subjects.* Arlington, VA: National Institute for Health Care Research, 1993.

_____, D. B. Larson. *The Faith Factor: An Annotated Bibliography of Clinical Research on Spiritual Subjects, Vol. III.* Rockville, MD: National Institute for Health Care Research, 1995.

_____. "On Being a Christian Physician." *Christian Medical and Dental Society Journal* 26, 2 (1995).

May, Hans

Present Position and Address: Academic Director (since 1978), Evangelische Akademie Loccum, Postfach 2158, 31545 Rehburg-Loccum, Germany **Work Phone:** 05766/81-100 **Fax Number:** 05766/81-128 **Date of Birth:** January 29, 1931 **Languages Spoken:** German, English **Education:** Studies in Münster, Basel, Heidelberg, Göttingen; Dr. h.c. (1990), Thiel College **Editorial Positions:** Editor, *Lutherische Monatshefte* **Selected Memberships:** ökumenische Vereinigung der Akademien und Laienzentren in Europa; Kuratorium der "Hanns-Lilje-Stiftung"; Chair, Leiterkreises der Evangelischen Akademien in Deutschland; Board of Directors, Vesper International, Vesper Society, San Francisco **Discipline:** Systematic Theology **Related Areas of Interest:** Theology and Science; Religion and Society.

Selected Publications:

_____. "Die Krise der technischen Rationalität. Thesen zur Erarbeitung eines neuen Integrationsmodells für gemeinsames technisch-naturwissenschaftliches Selbstverständnis der Gesellschaft." *Ökologisches Konzepte* 16: 5-13 (Kaiserslautern 1982). Reprint, in *Strategien mettlerer Technologie*, ed. K. W. Kieffer u.a., 372-80. Karlsruhe, 1988.

_____. "Für ein neues Orientierungssystem. Die Aufgaben Evangelischer Akademien heute." *Lutherische Monatshefte* 22 (1983): 362-6.

_____. *Warum Meditation? Unbeabsichtigte Nebenfolgen der Moderne als Anfrage an die Frömmigkeit der Kirche.* Hannover: Lutherhaus Verlag, 1987. Vorlagen H. 46/47.

_____. "Auf dem Weg zu einer neuen Orientierung? Zum Begriff des Paradigmenwechsels." *Lutherische Monatshefte* 27 (1988): 320-5.

_____, editor. "Kooperation und Wettbewerb. Zu Ethik und Biologie memshlichen Sozialverhaltens." *Loccumer Protokolle* 75 (1988). Loccum: Evangelische Akademie, 1989, 2.Aufl. 1992.

May, John Y.

Present Position and Address: Academic Coordinator (1982-90), Dwight Lecture in Christian Thought held annually at the University of Pennsylvania campus; 556 Austin Avenue, Pittsburgh, PA

15243, USA **Education:** B.A. Lehigh University; M.A. University of Pittsburgh **Discipline:** Philosophy **Related Areas of Interest:** Christianity and Science.

Selected Publications:

_____. "Christianity and Science: A Reappraisal." Parts. 1 and 2. *Evangelical Journal* (Fall 1987 and Spring 1988). Reprints available in booklet form.

Maziarz, Edward Anthony

Present Position and Address: Professor Emeritus, Philosophy, Philosophy Department, Loyola University, 6525 N. Sheridan Road, Chicago, IL 60626 USA; (Home) 1033 W. Loyola # 1007, Chicago, IL 60626 USA **Work Phone:** (312) 274-3000 **Home Phone:** (312) 262-4888 **Date of Birth:** March 6, 1915 **Languages Spoken:** English, Polish, French, some German **Education:** B.S./M.A. Mathematics/Physics; M.A./Ph.D. Philosophy **Congresses and Conferences:** Chair, Loyola Centennial Symposium, "Current Evolution of Man's Sense of Values" (1969-70) **Awards and Honors:** *Who's Who in America*; *Who's Who in Religion*; *Directory of American Scholars*; Phi Eta Sigma; National Vice President and President (1959-61), Delta Epsilon Sigma; Fellowship (1962), First NSF Institute on History and Philosophy of Sciences and Mathematics **Previous Positions:** Instructor in Philosophy (1941-42), Marian College, Fond Du Lac, WI; Instructor through Professor (1942-64)/Academic Dean (1955-63), St. Joseph's College, Rensselaer, IN; Professor of Philosophy (1964-66)/Chair (1964-66), Calument College Self-Study, Calumet College, E. Chicago, IN; Professor of Philosophy (1966-84)/Honors Program Director (1972-74)/Chair (1969-70), Loyola Centennial Symposium, Loyola University **Editorial Positions:** Associate Editor and Cofounder, *Philosophy*; Associate Editor (1969-92), *Philosophia Mathematica* **Selected Memberships:** AAR; AAAS; ACPA; AMS; APA; Association for Symbolic Logic; History of Science Society; Philosophy of Science Association; SSSR **Discipline:** Theology; Philosophy; Mathematics/Physics **Related Areas of Interest:** Inter- and Cross-disciplinary Interests **Current Areas of Research:** A. One project now being readied for publication as book, tries to link notions of possible world theorizing; Mythologizing and Ecumenical movements as hopes for new world futures. B. Cutting across disciplines to search for a "plurality of selves" as unifying framework for peace movements. C. Book of Meditations American Style for US citizens.

Selected Publications: His bibliography shows 8 books, 25 articles plus numerous contributions to various encyclopedias; 17 book reviews and much unpublished material and works in progress.

_____, translator. *A Short History of Philosophy*, by F. J. Thonnard. Desclee, 1960.
_____, Thomas Greenwood. *Greek Mathematical Philosophy*. Newman, 1968.
_____, Edmund F. Byrne. *Human Being and Being Human: Man's Philosophies of Man*. Appleton-Century Crofts, 1969.
_____. "Sciences and Myths as Symbolic Structures." *A.C.P.A. Proc.* 45 (1971): 58-66.
_____. "A Proposal for Metatheology." *Zygon* 7 (1972): 125-34.
_____. "The Individual in Dialogic Involution." *Phil. Forum* (De Kalb, IL, 1972): 285-317.
_____. "Meta-Mathematics and Metatheology: An Inquiry." *Phil. Math.* 12 (1975): 87-123.
_____. *Value, and Values in Evolution*. Gordon & Breach, 1979.
_____. "Polyarchy: A Social/Political Philosophy for the Future." *Phil. Res. and Analysis* 7, 6 (1979): 18-20.
_____. *You: Become a Full Person*. Shaman Books, 1983.

McCone, R. Clyde

Present Position and Address: Retired Professor of Anthropology and Linguistics, 1901 Snowden Avenue, Long Beach, CA 90815, USA **Date of Birth:** September 30, 1915 **Education:** B.A. Religion (1946), Wessington Springs College; M.S. Sociology (1956), South Dakota State College; Ph.D.

Anthropology/Linguistics (1961), Michigan State University **Honors and Awards:** Elected member of Phi Kappa Phi Honor Society - South Dakota State University (1955); Elected to Alpha Kappa Delta National Sociology Honor Society - Michigan State University (1958) **Previous Positions:** Various Pastoral positions (1941-1953); Graduate Teaching and Research Assistant (1954-56)/Instructor in Sociology (1956-57), South Dakota State College; Graduate Teaching and Research Assistant (1956-60)/Instructor (1960-61), Michigan State University; Assistant to Full Professor (1961-1986), California State University - Long Beach **Relevant Courses Taught:** Science and the Bible; How to Teach Creation; Anthropology and the Bible; Biblical Archaeology; Linguistics and Meaning **Selected Memberships:** Ordained Elder, Wesleyan Church; Evangelical Theological Society; Fellow, American Scientific Affiliation; American Anthropological Association **Discipline:** Anthropology; Linguistics; Religion **Current Areas of Research:** In preparation for publication: "Historical Integrity and Divine Inerrancy in the Scriptures," dealing with Science and the Spiritual in the Study of Creation Expansion; rewriting of *Culture and Controversy, An Investigation of the Tongues of Pentecost*, a book which was published by Dorrance in 1978.

Selected Publications:

_____. "The Phenomena of Pentecost." *Journal of the American Scientific Affiliation* (*JASA*) (September 1971): 83-8.
_____. "Origins of Civilization: Archaeological Data and Problems of Evolutionary Explanation." In *Symposium on Creation IV*, ed. D. W. Patten, 123-3. Grand Rapids: Baker Book House, 1972.
_____. "Three Levels of Anthropological Objection to Evolution." *Creation Research Quarterly* 9 (1973): 204-10.
_____. "Man and His World." *Science and Scripture* 3 (1973): 27-8.
_____. "Toward an Applied Anthropology of Beliefs." *JASA* 32 (1980): 247-9.
_____. "Essay on the Length of the Days of Creation," ed. R. Youngblood. In *The Genesis Debate*. Nashville, TN: Thomas Nelson, 1986.
_____. "The Day the Sun and the Moon Stood Still." In *Bible Life*. Kansas City, MO: Beacon Hill Press, 1989.

McDargh, John

Present Position and Address: Associate Professor (1986), Boston College, Department of Theology, Chestnut Hill, MA 02167, USA; (Home) 50 Florence St., Roslindale, MA 02131, USA **Work Phone:** (617) 323-5388 **Date of Birth:** September 5, 1948 **Education:** B.A. English Literature (1970), Emory University; Ph.D. Religion/Social Sciences and Ethics (1980), Harvard University **Previous Positions:** Chief (1970-74), Office Procurement Division, United States Coast Guard, Department of Transportation, Washington, DC; Teaching Fellow (1976)/Lecturer in Psychology and Prayer (1978-79), Harvard University **Editorial Positions:** Newsletter Editor, *Person Culture and Religion* (affiliated scholarly society of the AAR) **Selected Memberships:** Executive Committee, Religion and Social Sciences Division, American Academy of Religion; Steering Committee for affiliated scholarly society of the AAR; Associate member of Division 36 (Psychologists Interested in Religious Issues) and 39 (Psychoanalysis), American Psychological Association; College Theology Society; Society for the Scientific Study of Religion; Society for Values in Higher Education: **Discipline:** Psychology and Religion **Related Areas of Interest:** Psychology of Religious Development; Christian Spirituality and Theological Anthropology; Modern Psychoanalytic Theory and the Social Scientific Study of Religion; Moral Development and Ethics.

Selected Publications:

_____. *Psychoanalytic Object Relations Theory and the Study of Religion: On Faith and the Imaging of God.* Washington, DC: University Press of America, 1983.
_____. "Theological Uses of Psychology: A Retrospective and Prospective." *Horizons* 12, 2 (1985): 247-64.
_____. "Theology and Psychoanalysis." In *Dictionary of Pastoral Care and Counseling*, ed. Rodney Hunter et al. Nashville, TN: Abingdon Press, 1990.

_____. "Growing Up in a Nuclear Age: The Psychological Challenges and Spiritual Possibilities." In *Dawning Darkness: Religious Studies and the Nuclear Age*, ed. E. Linenthal and I. Chernus. New York: SUNY Press, forthcoming.

McDonald, Harry S.

Present Position and Address: Professor and Program Coordinator, Department of Biology, Box 13003, SFA Stations, Stephen F. Austin State University, Nacogdoches, TX 75962, USA **Work Phone:** (409) 468-2316 **Home Phone:** (409) 564-2698 **Fax:** (409) 468-1226 **E-Mail:** f_mcdonald@titan.sfasu.edu **Date of Birth:** September 24, 1930 **Languages Spoken:** English **Postgraduate Experience:** NIH Postdoctoral Fellow (1958-60), University of California-Los Angeles **Awards and Honors:** Stephen F. Austin State University Distinguished Professor (1971) **Previous Positions:** Assistant through Associate Professor (1960-65), St. John's University, NY **Selected Memberships:** American Association for the Advancement of Science; Sigma Xi; American Scientific Affiliation; Human Anatomy and Physiology Society **Discipline:** Comparative Animal Physiology **Related Areas of Interest:** Compatibility of Science and Religion; The "Mind-body" Problem; Incompatibility of Free Will and "Proof" of God's Existence; Nature of the Shroud of Turin.

Selected Publications: His bibliography contains 1 book chapter and about 10 published articles, all related to animal physiology.

_____. "Methods for the Physiological Study of Reptiles." In *Biology of the Reptilia*, ed. Carl Gans and William Dawson, vol. 5, 19-126. New York: Academic Press, 1976.

McFague, Sallie

Present Position and Address: Carpenter Professor of Theology Divinity School, Vanderbilt University, Nashville, TN 37240, USA **Work Phone:** (615) 322-2776 **Fax:** (615) 343-9957 **Date of Birth:** May 25, 1933 **Languages Spoken:** English **Education:** B. A. (1955), Smith College; B.D. (1959), Yale University Divinity School; Ph.D. (1964), Yale University **Honorary Degrees:** Litt. D. (1977), Smith College **Selected Congresses and Conferences:** Vatican Observatory Conference on Science, Philosophy, and Theology, Rome, Italy, (Sept. 1987); Conference on Consciousness and the Physical World, Isthmus Institute, Dallas, TX (April, 1988); Consultation on Theology of Nature and a Theocentric Ethics, World Council of Churches, Annecy, France (Sept. 1988); Symposium on Spirit and Nature, Middlebury College, (Sept. 1990) **Awards and Honors:** 1988 American Academy of Religion Award for Excellence on books in the Field for "Models of God" (Fortress Press, 1987); Howie Branscomb Distinguished Professor, Vanderbilt University, 1989-90 **Previous Positions:** Dean (1975-9), Vanderbilt Divinity School; Visiting Professor (Fall 1990), Harvard Divinity School **Editorial Work:** Editor (1967-75), *Soundings: An Interdisciplinary Journal*; Editorial Consultant, *Science/Theology Series* **Selected Memberships:** Advisor, Center for Respect for Life and the Environment, Washington, DC; Member, Advisory Board, The Center for Theology and the Natural Sciences, Berkeley, CA **Discipline:** Theology **Related Interests:** Theology of Nature; Feminist Theologies; Ecology and Theology **Current Research:** Christian Attitudes Toward the Natural World.

Selected Publications: Her bibliography includes 5 books and over 50 articles.

_____. *The Body of God: An Ecological Theology*. N.p. 1993.
_____. *Models of God, Theology for an Ecological, Nuclear Age*. N.p. 1987.
_____. *Metaphorical Theology: Models of God in Religious Language*. N.p. 1982.

McIntyre, John A.

Present Position and Address: Professor of Physics (since 1963), Texas A & M University, College Station, TX 77843-4242, USA **Work Phone:** (409) 845-8624 **Date of Birth:** June 2, 1920 **Education:** B.S. Electrical Engineering (*summa cum laude* , 1943), University of Washington; M.A./Ph.D. Physics (1950), Princeton University **Previous Positions:** Instructor in Electrical Engineering (1943-44), Carnegie Institute of Technology; Radio Engineer (1944-45), Westinghouse Corporation; Research Associate (1950-57), High Energy Physics Laboratory, Stanford University; Assistant Professor (1957-60)/Associate Professor (1960-63), Department of Physics, Yale University; Associate Director for Research (1965-70), Cyclotron Institute **Selected Memberships:** Sigma Xi; Tau Beta Pi; Fellow, American Physical Society; American Association for the Advancement of Science; American Association of University Professors; President and Council, American Scientific Affiliation **Discipline:** Physics **Related Areas of Interest:** The Relation between Science and Christianity.

Selected Publications: His bibliography lists 48 refereed articles in journals and 63 talks.

_____. "A Physicist Believes." *HIS Magazine* (June 1961). Reprint, in *Chinese Christians Today* 2, 2 (1963): 6-7. Trans. into Chinese by Micah Leo. *Power*, Part 7 (May 19, 1963): 1-3. *The Wesleyan Methodist* (September 2, 1964).
_____. "The Scientist and His Faith." *Journal of the American Scientific Affiliation* (*JASA*) 17 (1965): 100-4.
_____. "The Appeal of Christianity to a Scientist." *Christianity Today* (March 15, 1968): 6-8.
_____. "The Relationship between the Bible and Science." *JASA* 21 (1969): 118ff.
_____. Review of *Mathematical Challenges to the Neo-Darwinian Interpretation of Evolution*, ed. Paul S. Moorhead and Martin M. Kaplan. Philadelphia: Wister Institute, 1967. *JASA* 24 (1972): 70-2.
_____. "Is the Scientist for Hire?" In *The Scientist and The Ethical Decision*, ed. Charles Hatfield, 57-67. Downers Grove, IL: InterVarsity, 1973.
_____, Richard H. Bube. "What is a Christian's Responsibility as a Scientist?" *JASA* 27 (1975): 98-104.
_____. "Creation Science." Letter to the Editor. *Academe* (September-October 1982): 5.
_____. "Calls of Ivy." *Christianity Today* (November 5, 1990): 31-4.
_____. "It's Time to Rejoin the Scientific Establishment." *JASA* 44 (1992): 124-7.

McKenna, John E.

Present Position and Address: Adjunct Professor of Theology, Azusa Pacific University, Graduate Department of Theology; 542 N. Marengo # 6, Pasadena, CA 91101, USA **Work Phone:** (818) 449-3165 **Date of Birth:** October 30, 1935 **Education:** A.B. Physical Chemistry (1957), Princeton University; Creative Writing (1967-71), San Francisco State College; Certificate (1974-76), Christian Associates Bible Training Center, Dallas, TX; M.Div. (1979)/Ph.D. Theology (1987), Fuller Theological Seminary **Previous Positions:** US Army Security Agency (1958-1961); Laguna Outreach Ministry (1972-1974), Laguna Beach, CA; Intern (1976-79), Centrum of Hollywood, CA; Christian **Education:** (1979-87) at various churches in Pasadena, CA; Adjunct Professor in Issues in Science and Religion (1986), Fuller Theological Seminary; Adjunct Professor of Hebrew and Old Testament (1983-91), Fuller Theological Seminary; Adjunct Professor of Hebrew and Old Testament, International Theological Seminary, Altadena, CA **Selected Memberships:** American Scientific Affiliation; Society of Biblical Literature **Discipline:** Theology; Physical Chemistry **Related Areas of Interest:** Scientific Theology and Old Testament; Theology in the Context of Scientific Change.

Selected Publications:

_____. "Intimations of Contingency: A Response to Arthur Peacocke." *Religion and Intellectual Life* (Summer 1986): 118-20.
_____. "Christian Theology and Scientific Culture." *Studia Biblica et Theologia* 14, 2 (1986): 133-43.
_____. "The Life-Setting of the 'The Arbiter' by John Philoponos, a 6th Century Alexandrian Scientist." Ph.D. diss., Fuller Theological Seminary, June 1987.
_____. Review of *The God Who Would Be Known. Perspectives on Science and Christian Faith* (*PSCF*) (June 1991).

_____. "Hebel in Ecclesiastes." *SJT* 45, 1 (1992): 19-28.
_____. "The Concept of Nature." Chap. 7 in *The Aubiter*, by John Philoponos. The Pascal Center Conference, Redeemer College, 1992.

McMullen, Emerson Thomas

Present Position and Address: Visiting Assistant Professor (since 1989), Department of History of Science, University of Oklahoma, 601 Elm Street, Rm. 621, Norman, OK 73019, USA **Date of Birth:** September 23, 1941 **Education:** B.S. Chemical Engineering (1964), Washington State University; M.S. Engineering Administration (1971), Southern Methodist University; M.A. (1986)/Ph.D. History and Philosophy of Science (1989), Indiana University **Awards and Honors:** Received several awards including one from the Secretary of Defense **Previous Positions:** Worked in 3 different Government Laboratories (1964-75); Assistant Professor (1975-79), Air Force Institute of Technology; Associate Instructor (1985-89), Indiana University **Selected Memberships:** The History of Science Society; The British Society for the History of Science; The Society for the History of Technology **Discipline:** History and Philosophy of Science with a minor in Religious Studies **Related Areas of Interest:** Science, Technology, Religion, History, Philosophy, and their interactions.

Selected Publications:

_____. "A Barren Virgin? Teleology in the Scientific Revolution." Ph.D. diss. Indiana University, 1989.

McMullin, Ernan

Present Position and Address: Director Emeritus, Program in History and Philosophy of Science, Reilly Center for Science, Technology and Values, 309 O'Shaughnessy, University of Notre Dame, Notre Dame, IN 46556, USA **Work Phone:** (219) 239-5015 **Date of Birth:** October 13, 1924 **Education:** B.Sc. (1945)/B.D. Theology (1948), Maynooth College, Ireland; Fellowship in Theoretical Physics (1949-50), Institute for Advanced Studies, Dublin; Ph.D. Philosophy: "The Quantum Principle of Uncertainty" (1954), Louvain **Honorary Degrees:** Doctorate of Humane Letters (honoris causa), Loyola University (1969), National University of Ireland (1990) **Previous Positions:** Chairman (1965-72)/Lecturer (1954-72)/Professor (1972-84)/John Cardinal O'Hara Chair of Philosophy (1984-94), Department of Philosophy, University of Notre Dame; Visiting Professor: Center for the Philosophy of Science, University of Minnesota (1964-65)/University of California - Los Angeles (1977); Princeton University (Spring 1991); Yale University (Spring 1992)/Phi Beta; Kappa-Romanell Professor of Philosophy (1993-94) **Editorial Positions:** On editorial board over the years of 11 publications including *Faith and Philosophy*, *Isis*, *Philosophy of Science*, *Studies in the History and Philosophy of Science*; Editorial Consultant of 5 series **Selected Memberships:** President (1983-84), American Philosophical Association (Central Division); President (1980-82), Philosophy of Science Association; President (1973-74), Metaphysical Society of America; President (1966-67), American Catholic Philosophical Association (1966-67), American Catholic Philosophical Association; Chairman (1977-78), American Association for the Advancement of Science (Section L); Executive Council, Society of Christian Philosophers; Chairman (1982-84/86-88), US National Committee of the International Union of History and Philosophy of Science; Galileo Working Group (1982-93), Vatican Observatory; Fellow (since 1979), American Association for the Advancement of Science; Fellow (since 1986), American Academy of Arts and Sciences; Fellow (since 1988), International Academy of the History of Science **Discipline:** Philosophy; Theology; Physics; Philosophy of Science; Philosophy of Physics; History of the Philosophy of Science; Science and Religion **Related Areas of Interest:** Cosmology; Historical interactions of Science and Religion.

Selected Publications: His bibliography lists 9 books, 45 articles prior to 1968, and over 100 since then.

_____. "Natural Science and Belief in a Creator: Historical Notes." In *Physics, Philosophy and Theology: A Common Quest for Understanding*, ed. R. Russell et al., 49-79. University of Notre Dame Press, 1988.

_____. "The Impact of the Theory of Evolution on Western Religious Thought." In *Synthesis of Science and Religion*, ed. T.D. Singh, 75-86. Bhaktivedanta Institute: 1988.

_____. "A Common Quest for Understanding." *America* 160, 5 (1989): 100-4.

_____. Foreword to *Essays on the Trial of Galileo*, by Richard S. Westfall. Notre Dame: University of Notre Dame Press, 1989.

_____. "Galileo Heretic." *Physics Today* 42, 1 (1989): 76-8.

_____. "Plantinga's Defence of Special Creation." *Christian Scholar's Review* 21 (1991): 55-79.

_____. "Religion and Cosmology." In *Encyclopedia of Cosmology*, ed. N. Hetherington, 579-95. New York: Garland Press, 1993. Reprint, in *Cosmology*, ed. N. Hetherington, 581-606. New York: Garland Press, 1993.

_____. "Evolution and Special Creation." *Zygon* 28 (1993): 299-355.

_____. "Fine-tuning the Universe." In *Science, Technology, and Religious Ideas*, ed. G. Shields and M. Shale. Lanham, MD: University Press of America, 1994.

_____. "Indifference Principle and Anthropic Principle in Cosmology." *Studies in The History and Philosophy of Science* 24 (1993): 359-89.

McNally, Donald H.

Present Position and Address: Director of Research, NetAcess Systems Inc., (since 1993), 231 Main Street West, Suite E, Hamilton, ONT L8P 1J4, Canada; (Home) 59 Elizabeth Ct., Hamilton, ONT L8 S 2P5, Canada **Concurrent Positions:** Assistant Coordinator (since 1986), Christianity and Culture Programme: Christianity and Science Section and Instructor SMC 370, St. Michail's College, University of Toronto **E-mail:** dmcnally@epas.utoronto.ca *or* NetAcess, netaccess.on.ca **Work Phone:** NetAcess, (905) 524-2544 **Fax Number:** NetAcess, (905) 524-2544 **Home Phone:** (905) 526-6356 **Fax Number:** Home, (905) 526-9196 **Education:** B.A. History (Honors, 1972), McMaster University; Independent studies in history and philosophy (1972-73), Institute for Christian Studies, Toronto; M.A. History and Philosophy of Science and Tecshnology (1975)/Ph.D. History and Philosophy of Science (1982), University of Toronto **Previous Positions:** Co-founder and Assistant Director for Research Communications (1988-92), Pascal Centre, Ancaster, Canada **Selected Memberships:** American Scientific Affiliation; British Society for the History of Science; Canadian Scientific and Christian Affiliation; Canadian Society for the History and Philosophy of Science; Internet Society; Victorian Studies Association **Discipline:** History and Philosophy of Science; Early Victorian Science, Religion and Culture **Related Areas of Interest:** Historiography of Science and Religion; Intellectual Biography of William Whewell; Theology; Bioethics; Computer Communications, Information Science, and Scholarly Networking.

Selected Publications: His bibliography lists 4 publications and 16 unpublished papers.

_____. Review of *William Whewell: A Composite Portrait*, ed. Menachem Fisch and Simon Schaffer. Oxford: Clarendon Press, 1991. *British Journal for the History of Science* 25, Pt. 3, 86 (1992).

_____. Review of *William Whewell, Philosopher of Science*, ed. Menachem Fisch. Oxford University Press; Clarendon Press, 1991. *Isis* 84, 2 (1993).

Meador, Keith G.

Present Position and Address: Private Practice - Psychiatric Consultants in Nashville (since 1988), Suite 309, 310 25th Avenue North, Nashville, TN 37203, USA; (Home) 201 Leonard Avenue, Nashville, TN 37205, USA **Concurrent Positions:** Lecturer in Pastoral Theology and Counseling/Assistant Clinical Professor of Psychiatry (since 1988), Vanderbilt University Divinity School **Work**

Phone: (615) 340-2600 **Home Phone:** (615) 383-8694 **Date of Birth:** August 10, 1956 **Education:** B.A. (1978), Vanderbilt University; M.D. (1982), University of Louisville; Th.M. (1986), Duke University; M.P.H. (1988), University of North Carolina - Chapel Hill **Postgraduate Experience:** Resident in Psychiatry (1982-86), Department of Psychiatry, Duke University Medical Center; Chief Resident in Psychiatry (1985-86), Duke Veterans Administration Hospital; Fellow (1986-87)/Senior Fellow (1987-88) in Geropsychiatry, Center for the Study of Aging and Human Development, Duke University Medical Center **Awards and Honors:** Phi Beta Kappa **Previous Positions:** Psychiatric Director (1987-88)/Assistant Professor (1987-88)/Adjunct Assistant Professor of Psychiatry (since 1988), Duke University School of Medicine; Visiting Assistant Professor of Psychiatry and Pastoral Care (1987-88), Duke Divinity School **Selected Memberships:** Associate Clinical Member (since 1985), Association for Clinical Pastoral Education; American Psychiatric Association; American Geriatrics Society; Scientific Associate (since 1984), Association for Clinical Psychosocial Research; American Medical Association **Discipline:** Psychiatry; Theology **Related Areas of Interest:** Mental Health and Religion; Ethics and Medicine; Pastoral Care and Psychiatry.

Selected Publications:

_____. "Religious Beliefs: Fulfilling Legitimate Needs of Part of Psychosis?" Paper presented at the National Alliance for the Mentally Ill, Washington, DC, September 19, 1987.
_____. "Ethics and Aging." Paper presented at the Continuing Education Seminar, Duke Divinity School, March 18-19, 1987.
_____. "Pastoral Counselling and Mental Health." Paper presented at the Continuing Professional Education for Chaplains in the Seventh Army - Europe, Frankfurt, Germany, May 8-12, 1989.

Menninga, Clarence

Present Position and Address: Professor of Geology, Emeritus, Calvin College, Grand Rapids, MI 49546, USA **Work Phone:** (616) 957-7053 **Fax Number:** (616) 957-6501 **E-Mail:** menn@calvin.edu **Date of Birth:** April 6, 1928 **Education:** A.B. (1949), Calvin College; M.A.T. (1959), Western Michigan University; Ph.D. (1966), Purdue University **Previous Positions:** Chemist (1950-56), The Maytag Company; Teacher (1956-61), Grand Rapids Christian High School; Chemist (1965-67), Lawrence Radiation Laboratory, Livermore, CA **Selected Memberships:** American Scientific Affiliation; Affiliation of Christian Geologists **Discipline:** Geology; Chemistry **Related Areas of Interest:** Geology; Geologic History; Paleontology; Paleoanthropology; Creation and Geology; Radioactivity and the Ages of Things; Science and Christianity/Theology.

Selected Publications:

_____. "His Word and His World." *The Banner* (November 27, 1970).
_____. "Radioactivity and the Age of Things." *Christian Educators' Journal* (May 1973).
_____. "Floods of Lava." *Christian Educator's Journal* (September and October 1977).
_____. "Frozen Mammoths and Catastrophism." *Calvinist Contact* (April 7 1978).
_____. "Do We Idolize Science?" *The Banner* (February 23, 1979).
_____. "Creation and Geology, an Interview." *The Banner* (November 12, 1984).
_____. "A Christian Perspective on Science." *The Banner* (April 20, 1987).
_____. "Was the World Created with Appearance of Age?" *Calvinist Contact* (January 8, 1988); Reprint, in *Perspectives on Science and Christian Faith* (September 1988).
_____, coauthor. *Science Held Hostage.* Downers Grove, IL: InterVarsity Press, 1988.
_____. "A Legacy of Silence." *The Banner* (January 30, 1989).

Personal Notes: He is available to present talks to adult church groups and Christian teacher groups. Also available to conduct workshops on teaching science. He continues to write on issues in science and theology.

Mercier, André

Present Position and Address: Professor Emeritus, University of Berne; Institut für exakte Wissenschaften, Sidlerstrasse 5, CH - 3012 Berne, Switzerland; (Home) Bellevuestrasse 124, CH - 3095 Berne-Spiegel, Switzerland **Date of Birth:** April 15, 1913 **Languages Spoken:** French, English, German, Danish, Italian, Spanish **Education:** Lic. es. sc. Mathematics (1933)/Lic. és. sc. Physics (1934)/Dr. es. Science (1935), University of Geneva **Honorary Degrees:** Universidad Peruana Cayetano Heredia **Previous Positions:** Assistant à l'Institut de Geologie/Physique de l'Université de Genève; Assistant à la Chaire de Mécanique de l'Ecole Polytechnique Fédérale de Zurich; Privat-Docent a l'Université de Genève; Professeur de physique théorique à l'Université de Berne; Dean of Faculty of Science and Director/Professor de l'Institut de Physique théorique et de philosophie (Faculties of Science and Theology) de l'Université de Berne; Recteur de l'Université de Berne **Selected Memberships:** President and Member, Société Suisse de Physique/Philosophie; President and Founder, Société Suisse-Danemark; Vice President, Académie Internationale de Philosophie des Sciences; President and Member, Académie Int. de Philosophie de l'Art; Fellow, American Physical Society; Association of Members, Institute of Advanced Study, Princeton; Vice-president and Member, Institut International de Philosophie **Discipline:** Physical Science; Theoretical Physics; Philosophy of Science; Metaphysics **Related Areas of Interest:** Metaphysics, Cosmology, and the Christian Doctrine as well as the Problem of Proofs of God.

Selected Publications:

_____. *De la science à l'art et à la morale.* Neuchâtel, 1950.
_____. *De L'Amour et de l'Etre.* Louvain & Paris, 1960.
_____. "Mystik und Vernunft." In *Mystik und Wissenschaftlichkeit, "A Physicist's View on the Mind-Body Problem,"* hg. A. Mercier. *Epistemologia* 4: 21ff (Special Issue 1981).
_____. "Future of Religion in a Unified Civilization." In *Islam and Civilization. Proceedings of the 1st Islamic Philosophy Conference 19-22 November 1979, Cairo,* ed. M. Wahba, 117ff. Cairo: Ain Shams University Press, 1982.
_____. "The Metaphysical, the Mystical and the Religious Approach to Life." In *Philosophy and Cultures. Proceedings of the 2d Afro-Asian Philosophy Conference in Nairobi in 1981,* ed. H. Odera Oruka and D. A. Masolo, 75-85. Nairobi: Bookwise Ltd., 1983.
_____. "L'Avenir, où se cache le Dieu." In *Proceedings of the 21st Congress of the French Speaking Philosophical Societies, Athens 1986,* 38ff. Paris: J. Yoin Publishing Co., 1987.
_____. "El probleme de las pruebas de Dios Hoy." In *Proceedings of the Third World Congress of Christian Philosophy, 1990,* ed. The Pontifical University of Ecuador, 213ff.
_____. "The Problem of the Imperfection of a World, Itself Created by a Perfect God." *Foundations of Physics* 22 (1992): 205ff.
_____. *Roseau pensant.* Berne-Frankfurt/M.-New York-Paris: P. Lang Publishing Co., vol. 1, 1988; vol. 2, 1989; vol. 3, 1992.

Merrifield, S.J., Donald Paul

Present Position and Address: Chancellor, Loyola Marymount University, Loyola Boulevard at West 80th Street, Los Angeles, CA 90045-2699 USA **Work Phone:** (310) 338-3070 **Fax:** (310) 338-4450 **Date of Birth:** November 14, 1928 **Languages Spoken:** English, Spanish **Previous Positions:** President, Loyola Marymount University (1969-1984); Assistant Professor, Physics, University of San Francisco (1967-1969); Consultant, Theoretical Chemistry, Jet Propulsion Laboratory, California Institute of Technology (1962-1969); Lecturer, Engineering School, University of Santa Clara (1965, for one semester); Instructor, Physics, Loyola University of Los Angeles (1961-1962) **Honors:** S.T.D., University of Southern California (1969); Alumni Distinguished Service Award, California Institute of Technology (1971); D.H.L., University of Judaism (1984); D.H.L., Hebrew Union College, Jewish

Institute of Religion (1986) **Selected Memberships:** Society of Sigma Xi **Discipline:** Physics **Related Areas of Interest:** Religion and Science **Past Areas of Research:** Theoretical physics of molecular structure, inter-molecular forces, and interactions of molecules with surfaces. At JPL, this has been part of the scientific research program sponsored there as complementary to and supporting the lunar and planetary investigations which are the main task of the Laboratory.

Selected Publications: His bibliography includes 6 articles on science and religion.

_____, Russell M. Pitzer. "Minimum Basis Wave Function for Water," *J. Chem. Phys.,* 52, 4782 (1970).
_____. "Catholics and Israel: A Personal Reflection," *American,* Vol. 130, 322 (April 27, 1974).
_____. "I Beg to Differ!" *Catholic Mind,* LXXII, 1288 (December 1974).
_____. "'Heresy' in a Catholic University," *America,* Vol. 132, 51 (January 1975).
_____. "Hope for Tomorrow: Genuine Love Should Be the Moving Force," Loyola Marymount University, *Lion & Gryphon,* Vol. 9, No. 7, 2 (June 1975).
_____. "Catholicism: Its Place in the Contemporary University," *Evangelism in the American Context,* University of Notre Dame Press (1976).
_____. Forward to *The Abrahamic Connection.* Crossroads Books, 1994.

Mermann, Alan C.

Present Position and Address: Clinical Professor of Pediatrics (since 1979)/Chaplain (since 1982), Yale School of Medicine, 333 Cedar Street, Box 208000, New Haven, CT 06520-8000, USA **Work Phone:** (203) 785-2648 **Date of Birth:** June 23, 1923 **Education:** B.A. (1943), Lehigh University; M.D. (1947), Johns Hopkins University School of Medicine; M.Div. (1979)/S.T.M. (1988), Yale University Divinity School; Ordained to Christian Ministry (1979) **Previous Positions:** Private Practice, Pediatrics (1954-82), Guilford, CT; Research (1965-71), rural Alabama, Mississippi and Florida, Field Foundation; Lecturer in Pastoral Theology (1979-82), Yale Divinity School; Assistant Pastor (1979-82), First Congregational Church, Guilford, CT **Selected Memberships:** Fellow, Branford College (since 1975), Yale University; Fellow (since 1955), American Academy of Pediatrics; American Academy of Religion **Discipline:** Chaplain; Pediatrician and Professor **Related Areas of Interest:** Medical Ethics; Medicine and Christianity/Theology; Environmental Ethics.

Selected Publications:

_____. "A Medical School Chaplaincy." *The Journal of Pastoral Care,* 43, 3 (1989): 222-9.
_____. "The Doctor's Critic." *Pharos* 53, 1 (1990): 9-13.
_____. "Coping Strategies of Selected Physicians." *Perspectives in Biology and Medicine* 33, 2 (1990): 268-79.
_____. "Faith at the End of Life." Guest Editorial. *The Journal of Pastoral Care* 46, 4 (1992): 337-9.
_____. "Medicine and the Pilgrimage of the Spirit." *Humane Medicine* 8, 4 (1992): 294-9.
_____. "Reflection: Pastoral Prayer: Sacred or Profane." *Reflections* (Summer-Fall 1993): 24-5.
_____. "Love in the Clinical Setting." *Humane Medicine* 9, 4 (1993): 268-73.
_____, George E. Dickinson, and Michael R. Leming, eds. *Dying, Death, and Bereavement.* Annual Editions. The Dushkin Publishing Group, Inc., 1993.
_____. "The Whole Physician Divided in Three Parts: The Self as a Triptych." *The Pharos* (Summer 1994): 7-10.

Metzner, Helmut

Present Position and Address: Präsident, Europäische Akademie für Umweltfragen e. V., Derendinger Strasse 41-45, Tübingen 1, Germany. Professor Emeritus, University of Tübingen **Education:** Studies in Mathematics and Physics (1945-46), University of Münster; Studies in Physics, Chemistry and Biology (1946-1950), culminating in Dr. rer. nat. (1950), University of Göttingen; Rockefeller Fellow (1955-56), Department of Chemistry, University of California - Berkeley **Previous Positions:** Research Scientist (1950-51), Botanisches Institut, University of Münster; Assistant (1951-55)/Lecturer and Associate (1956-61), Pflanzenphysiologisches Institut, University of Göttingen; Habilitation (1955), Botanik und Pflanzenphysiologie, University of Göttingen **Editorial Positions:** Founding and Managing Editor (1980-1987), *Photobiochemistry and Photobiophysics*, Amsterdam. Coeditor (since 1967), *Photosynthetica*, Prague **Selected Memberships:** Vice President (since 1978), Studienzentrum Weikersheim e. V.; General Secretary (since 1984), Bioelectrochemical Society; Vice President (since 1985), Internationale Arbeitsgemeinschaft für Radioökologie, Berne **Discipline:** Photobiochemistry and Biophysics; Biochemical Engineering **Related Areas of Interest:** Environmental Ethics and Technological Progress.

Selected Publications: His *curriculum vitae* lists 151 publications in biology and biochemistry, many of which deal with photosynthesis.

_____. "Der Technologische Fortschritt - Chancen und Risiken." In *Fortschritt und Sicherheit*, ed. G. Rohrmoser and E. Lindenlaub, 47-59. Stuttgart: F.K. Schattauer Verlag, 1980.
_____. "Mensch und Umwelt im Spiegel gegenseitiger Abhängigkeiten." In *Verantwortung und Klarheit in bedrängter Zeit*, ed. H. Kremp and F.H. Fleck, 235-40. Würzburg: Creator-Verlag, 1988.

Metzner, Ralph

Present Position and Address: Professor of East-West Psychology, California Institute of Integral Studies, 765 Ashbury Street, San Francisco, CA 94117, USA; (Home) 18210 Robin Ave., Sonoma, CA 95476, USA **Concurrent Positions:** President, Green Earth Foundation, P.O. Box 327, Sonoma, CA 95433 **Date of Birth:** May 18, 1936 **Languages Spoken:** English, German, French **Education:** B.A. Psychology and Philosophy (1st Class, 1958), Queen's College, Oxford University; Ph.D. Clinical Psychology and Personality (1962), Harvard Graduate School of Arts and Sciences **Postgraduate Experience:** NIMH Postdoctoral Fellowship (1962-1963), Fellowship in Psychopharmacology, Harvard Medical School; Licensed Clinical Psychologist (1968) **Congresses and Conferences:** Organized major interdisciplinary conference on "Gaia Consciousness - The Goddess and the Living Earth" (1988) **Previous Positions:** Academic Dean (1979-1988), California Institute of Integral Studies **Editorial Positions:** Executive Editor (since 1987), *ReVision Magazine* **Selected Memberships:** American Psychological Association; Association for Humanistic Psychology; Association for Transpersonal Psychology; Executive Board (1982-1985), International Transpersonal Association; Founder/President, Green Earth Foundation **Discipline:** Psychotherapy; Mythology; Comparative Religion **Related Areas of Interest and Courses Taught:** East-West Religion; Ecology and Environmental Philosophy; Altered States of Consciousness; Asian Theories of Self; Metaphors of Transformation.

Selected Publications:

_____. *Maps of Consciousness.* New York: Macmillan, 1971.
_____. *Opening to Inner Light: The Transformation of Human Nature and Consciousness.* Los Angeles: J. P. Tarcher, St. Martin's Press, 1986. German ed. Freiburg: Verlag Hermann Bauer, 1987.
_____. "Gaia's Alchemy: Ruin and Renewal of the Elements." *ReVision* 9, 2 (1987): 41-51.
_____. "Molecular Mysticism: The Role of Psychoactive Substances in Shamanic Transformations of Consciousness." *Shaman's Drum* (Spring 1988).
_____. "The Mystical Symbolic Psychology of Hildegard von Bingen." *ReVision* 11, 2 (Fall 1988).
_____. "States of Consciousness and Transpersonal Psychology." In *Existential and Phenomenological Perspectives in Psychology*, ed. R. Vallee and S. Halling. New York: Plenum Press, 1989.
_____. "Spirit, Self and Nature." Essays in *Green Psychology*. Green Earth Foundation, 1993.
_____. *The Well of Remembrance.* Shambala Publications, 1994.

Meyerhoff, Gordon R.

Present Position and Address: Private Practice in Psychiatry, 19 Hillside Avenue, Roslyn Heights, NY 11577, USA **Date of Birth:** November 18, 1921 **Education:** B.A. (1943), Brooklyn College; M.A. (1946), Oberlin College; M.D. (1950), Columbia University **Previous Positions:** President (1976-1989), Roslyn Synagogue, Roslyn Heights, NY **Selected Memberships:** Fellow, American Psychiatric Association; Society for Psychophysiological Research; Member of National, State and County, Medical and Psychiatric Societies; Institute of Noetic Sciences **Discipline:** Psychiatry **Related Areas of Interest:** The Clergyman and the Psychiatrist **Current Areas of Research:** The Objective Measurement of Emotions.

Selected Publications:

_____. "The Psychiatrist and the Clergyman." *Journal of Religion and Health* 3, 3 (April 1964).

Meyers, Wayne Marvin

Present Position and Address: Chief, Mycobacteriology and Registrar, Leprosy Registry (since 1989), Armed Forces Institute of Pathology, Washington, DC 20306-6000, USA **Work Phone:** (202) 782-1873 **Home Phone:** (301) 490-4181 **Fax Number:** (202) 782-7161 **Date of Birth:** August 28, 1924 **Languages Spoken:** English, French **Education:** B.S. Chemistry (1947), Juniata College; Special Studies in Biology (1948-49), Northwestern University; Diploma (1950), Moody Bible Institute; M.S. Medical Microbiology (1953), University of Wisconsin; Ph.D. Medical Microbiology (1955), University of Wisconsin; MD (1959), Baylor College of Medicine; Special Studies in French (summer, 1964), Yale University; (1964-65), French, Alliance Francaise, Neuchatel, Switzerland **Honorary Degrees:** D.Sc. (1986), Juniata College, Huntingdon, PA **Congresses and Conferences:** Directed, 14th International Leprosy Congress, Orlando, FL; Participant, (1977), African-American Scholars Council, working conference; (1991), World Health Organization's Conference on Leprosy Control; (1993), President, 14th International Leprosy Congress, Orlando, FL **Awards and Honors:** Physician's Recognition Award (1993-96), American Medical Association; American Men and Women of Science; *Who's Who in the East*; *Who's Who in America*; *Who's Who in the World*; *Who's Who in Science and Engineering*; Men of Achievement; *Dictionary of International Biography*; Men and Women of Distinction; Biography International; *The International Who's Who of Contemporary Achievement* **Previous Positions:** Staff Physician (1960-61), Berrien General Hospital, Berrien Center, MI; /Medical Director (1961-62), Nyankanda Leprosarium, Ruyigi, Burundi (Africa); Staff Physician (1962-64), Oicha Hospital and Leprosarium, Oicha, Kivu province, Republic of Zaire (then Congo); Director (1965-68, 1969-73), Kivuvu Leprosy Service, Institut Medical Evangelique, Kimpese, Bas-Zaire province, Republic of Zaire; Visiting Professor, Biochemistry (1967-68), Universite Nationale (Kisangani campus), Republic of Zaire; Visiting Scientist (1968-69), Special Mycobacterial Diseases Branch, Armed Forces Institute of Pathology, Washington, DC, as National Institutes of Health/Leonard Wood Memorial Fellow in Research in Leprosy; Professor of Pathology (1973-75), Department of Pathology, University of Hawaii School of Medicine, Honolulu, HI; Chief, Division of Microbiology (1975-89), Department of Infectious and Parasitic Diseases Pathology, and Registrar, Leprosy Registry, Armed Forces Institute of Pathology, Washington, DC; Served 1961-73 as missionary appointee of ALM International (American Leprosy Missions, Inc.), Greenville, SC **Selected Memberships:** President, International Leprosy Association; International Society of Dermatology: Tropical Geographic, and Ecologic; International Academy of Pathology; American Society of Tropical Medicine and Hygiene; American Scientific Affiliation; American Society for Microbiology; American Association for the Advancement of Science; New York Academy of Science; President (1995-96), The Binford-Dammin Society of Infectious Disease Pathologists; Sigma Xi **Discipline:** Medicine and Microbiology **Related Areas of Interest:** Leprosy, Tropical Diseases; Medicine and Missions;

Medical Research; Lecturing; Scientific Writing **Current Areas of Research:** Leprosy in nonhuman primates; Mycobacterium ulcerans infections in West Africa; Leprosy and AIDS.

Selected Publications: His total bibliography contains 243 scientific publications, including chapters in medical textbooks and scientific journals and monographs, and 368 presentations (includes lectures, exhibits, illustrated talks, panel discussions). In addition, numerous talks to missionary circles and other church groups on missions, leprosy work, leprosy in the Bible, etc. The scientific meetings, mission or foundation board meetings, seminars, workshops etc. number 253.

_____, G. P. Walsh, et al. "Immunology, Epidemiology and Social Aspects of Leprosy." Monograph. Pontifical Academy of Sciences Document No. 10. Vatican City: Pontifical Academy of Sciences, 1984. In *The Proceedings of Working Group on Immunology, Epidemiology and Social Aspects of Leprosy, 28 May-1 June, 1984*, The Vatican.

_____, R. H. Wolf, B. J. Gormus, L. N. Martin, G. B. Baskin, G. P. Walsh, and C. H. Binford. "Experimental Leprosy in Three Species of Monkeys." *Science* 227 (1985): 529-31..

_____, G. P. Walsh, et. al. "Leprosy in a Mangabey Monkey — Naturally Acquired Infection." *International Journal of Leprosy* 53 (1985): 1-14.

_____, B. J. Gormus, M. Murphey-Corb, L. N. Martin, J. -Y. Zhang, G. B. Baskin, C. B. Trygg, and G. P. Walsh. "Interactions between Simian Immunodeficiency Virus and 'Mycobacterium Leprae' in Experimentally Inoculated Rhesus Monkeys." *Journal of Infectious Diseases* 160 (1989): 405-13.

_____, A. M. Marty. "Current Concepts in the Pathogenesis of Leprosy: Clinical, Pathological, Immunological and Chemotherapeutic Aspects." *Drugs* 41 (1991): 832-56.

_____. "Leprosy." In *Dermatology Clinics of North America*, ed. G. Lupton, 73-96. Philadelphia, PA: W. B. Saunders Co., 1992.

_____. B. J. Gormus, and G. P. Walsh. "Nonhuman Sources of Leprosy." International Journal of Leprosy 60 (1992): 477-81.

_____, S.-N. Cho, B. J. Gormus, K. Xu, R. P. Bohm Jr., G. P. Walsh, and J.-D. Kim. "Serologic Responses to Nerve Antigens in Sooty Mangabey Monkeys with Experimental Leprosy." *International Journal of Leprosy* 61 (1993): 236-44.

_____, P. E. M. Fine, C. K. Job, S. B. Lucas, J. M. Ponnighaus, and J. A. C. Sterne. "Extent, Origin and Implications of Observer Variation in the Histopathological Diagnosis of Suspected Leprosy." *International Journal of Leprosy* 61 (1993): 270-82.

_____, B. J. Gormus, and G. P. Walsh. "Experimental Leprosy." In *Leprosy*, ed. R. C. Hastings, 385-408. Edinburgh: Churchill-Livingstone, 2d. ed., 1994.

Miles, Sara Joan

Present Position and Address: Associate Professor of History and Biology (since 1994), Eastern College, 10 Fairview Drive, St. Davids, PA 19087; (Home) 3 David Lane, # 1-0, Yonkers, NY 10701, USA **Work Phone:** (610) 341-4389 **Home Phone:** (914) 963-0470 **Date of Birth:** June 26, 1938 **Languages Spoken:** English, French **Education:** B.A. Biology (1960), Ball State University; M.R.E. Christian Education (1963), Texas Christian University; Studied Anthropology (1963-1964), Hartford Seminary Foundation; Diplôme in African Studies (1965), École d'Administration, Brussels; M.S. Biology (1970), University of Illinois; Ph.D. History (1988), University of Chicago **Previous Positions:** High School Science Teacher (1960-61), Muncie Central High School, Muncie, IN; Missionary Teacher (1965-68), Institut Chrétien Congolais, Zaïre; Biology Teaching Assistant (1968-1989)/Counselor and Assistant Director of General Curriculum (1969-73), University of Illinois, Champaign IL; Junior High School Science Teacher (1973-74), Wheaton Christian Grammar School, IL; Health Professions Counselor (1974-77)/Assistant Professor of Biology (1977-88)/Associate Professor of History and Biology (1989-94), Wheaton College, Wheaton, IL **Selected Memberships:** History of Science Society; American Historical Association; American Scientific Affiliation; International Society for the Study of European Ideas; American Association for the Advancement of Science; Sigma Xi International Society for the History, Philosophy, and Social Studies of Biology **Discipline:** History; Biology; Anthropology; Christian Education **Related Areas of Interest:** Creation/Evolution; Demarcation of Science and Religion; Common Presuppositions of Science and Religion; Religious Influences on Science and Vice Versa; Biological Determinism and Human Behavior.

Selected Publications:

_____. "The Roots of the Scientific Revolution: Reformed Theology." *Journal of the American Scientific Affiliation (JASA)* 37, 3 (1985): 158-68.

_____. Review of *Trial and Error: The American Controversy over Creation and Evolution*, by E. J. Larson. *JASA* 38, 4 (1986): 271.

_____. "Conflict, Compartmentalization, and Complementarity: Three Models for Understanding the Relationship between Science and Religion." In *Conference Proceedings on the Religion/Science Controversy: The Use and Abuse of Science in the Defense of Religion.* Westville, IN: Purdue University North Central, 1986.

_____. "From Being to Becoming: Science and Theology in the Eighteenth Century." *Perspectives on Science and Christian Faith (PSCF)* 43, 4 (1991): 215-23.

_____. "My Genes Made Me Do It." Paper presented at a public forum sponsored by Immanuel Presbyterian Church, College of DuPage, February, 1993.

_____. "A Feminist Reading of Darwin: Clémence Royer and Evolutionary Theory in France." Paper presented at the Berkshire Conference on the History of Women, Vassar College, June 1993.

_____. Review of *Darwin: The Life of A Tormented Evolutionist*, by Adrian Desmond and James Moore. *PSCF* 45, 3 (1993): 191-5.

Miller, David Lee

Present Position and Address: Chair and Professor of Philosophy (since 1984), University of Wisconsin - La Crosse, 1725 State Street, La Crosse, WI 54601, USA **Date of Birth:** January 7, 1940 **Education:** B.A. (1962), West Virginia University; M.A. (1965)/Ph.D. (1969), Southern Illinois University - Carbondale **Previous Positions:** Assistant Professor of Philosophy and Religion (1967-70), Winthrop College, Rock Hill, SC; Philosopher/Research Assistant (Summers 1960/70), National Bureau of Standards, Washington, DC; Assistant Professor (1970-73)/Associate Professor of Philosophy (1973-1984), University of Wisconsin - La Crosse **Selected Memberships:** American Philosophical Association; Society for Philosophy of Creativity **Discipline:** Philosophy **Related Areas of Interest:** Metaphysics; Ethics; Philosophy of Religion. More specifically - Philosophy of Creativity; Philosophy as Meta-paradigm; Process Philosophy East and West; Philosophy of A. N. Whitehead.

Selected Publications:

_____. "The Experience of Creative Interchange." *The American Journal of Theology and Philosophy* (1986): 17-27.

_____. "Some Meanings of the Earth: A Process Perspective." *Journal of Value Inquiry* (The Netherlands: March 1987): 3-20.

_____. *Philosophy of Creativity.* New York; Bern: Peter Lang Publishing Inc., 1989.

_____. *Buddhism and the Emerging World Civilization.* Carbondale: Southern Illinois University Press, 1993.

Miller, James Bradley

Present Position and Address: Director (since 1984), United Campus Ministry of Pittsburgh, 100 N. Bellefield Avenue, Pittsburgh, PA 15213, USA; (Home) 917 Forest Avenue, Pittsburgh, PA 15202, USA **Work Phone:** (412) 682-1051 **Home Phone:** (412) 761-0971 **Date of Birth:** March 16, 1942 **Education:** B.A. American Studies (1965), University of Maryland; M.Div. (1968), Union Theological Seminary; Science, Technology and the University (1968-69), Interseminary Church and Society Internship; Ph.D. Religious Studies (1986), Marquette University; Ordained (June 1968), Presbyterian Church, USA **Previous Positions:** Teaching Technician (1969-73), Department of Engineering Mechanics, NC State University; Research Support Staff (1973-75), Synod of NC, Presbyterian Church,

USA; Campus Minister (1975-81), Portage Lake United Ministries in Higher Education:; Instructor, Department of Humanities (1978-79), Suomi College; Instructor, Department of Theology (1983-84), Marquette University; Executive Director, United Campus Ministry of Pittsburgh (1984-95); Pastoral Assistant (1986-88), Allegheny United Methodist Church; Adjunct Professor (1989-95), Carnegie Mellon University **Selected Memberships:** American Association for the Advancement of Science; American Academy of Religion; Center for Theology and the Natural Sciences; Institute on Religion in an Age of Science; National Association for Science, Technology and Society; Presbyterian Association on Science, Technology and the Christian Faith **Discipline:** Theology; Philosophy **Related Areas of Interest:** Historical and Cultural Interaction Between Science and Religion/Theology; Post-Critical Philosophy and Theology; Process Theology and Philosophy; Technology as an Ethical Engine for Theology; History and Philosophy of Science.

Selected Publications:

_____. "Humanity vs. Nature." *The Presbyterian Outlook* 153, 36 (1971).
_____. "Theological Modeling and Experimental Theology." *Zygon* 7, 1 (1972).
_____. "From Genesis to Genetics." Paper presented at the Grosse Pointe Winter Forum, 1 March 1981.
_____. "Knowing More Than We Can Say." Paper presented at the Midwest Regional American Academy of Religion meeting, 3 April 1982.
_____. "Revelation and Discovery: Cosmological Foundations for a Theological Epistemology." Paper presented at the Midwest Regional American Academy of Religion meeting, 9 April 1983.
_____. "In the Beginning was the World." Paper presented at the Midwest Regional American Academy of Religion meeting, 7 April 1984.
_____, D. Fowler. "What is Wrong with the Creation/Evolution Controversy." *Bulletin of the Center for Theology and the Natural Sciences* 4, 4 (1984).
_____. "The Emerging Post-Modern World." In *Post-modern Theology: Christian Faith in A Pluralistic World*, ed. Frederic B. Burnham, 1-19. San Francisco: Harper and Row, 1989.
_____. "From Organism to Mechanism to History: The Bifurcation and Reintegration of Western Culture." In *The Church and Contemporary Cosmology*, ed. James B. Miller and Kenneth E. McCall, 65-148. Pittsburgh: Carnegie Mellon University Press, 1990.

Miller, Keith Brady

Present Position and Address: Postdoctoral Fellow, Department of Geology, Kansas State University, Manhattan, KS 66506-3201, USA **Work Phone:** (913) 532-6724 **Fax Number:** (913) 532-5159 **Date of Birth:** December 23, 1955 **Education:** B.A. Geology (1978), Franklin and Marshall College, Lancaster, PA; M.A. Geology (1982), SUNY - Binghamton, Binghamton, NY; Ph.D. Geology (1988), University of Rochester, Rochester, NY **Awards and Honors:** Sigma Xi; Winning entry in the John Templeton Foundation's Call for Papers in Humility Theology Program (1993) **Previous Positions:** Visiting Assistant Professor (1989-90), Clemson University, Clemson, SC **Selected Memberships:** American Scientific Affiliation; Affiliation of Christian Geologists; Geological Society of America; SEPM (Society of Sedimentary Geology); Paleontological Society; International Paleontological Association; History of Earth Science Society **Discipline:** Paleoecology; Sedimentation and Stratigraphy **Related Areas of Interest:** "I am studying the implications of the developing scientific picture of the universe and its long creative history for our understanding of God's immanent and transcendent character. In particular I am seeking to explore the ways that the identity of God as Creator, Sustainer, and Redeemer is illuminated as we more fully comprehend His creation. Our perception of the character of the Creator and His creation also has significant implications for how we understand our position as God's image bearers and stewards of creation. I have also begun struggling with the meaning of pain and suffering in creation in light of God's revealed character."

Selected Publications: His total bibliography contains 8 journal articles, 4 field trip guidebook articles, and 19 abstracts.

_____, C. E. Brett and K. M. Parsons. "The Paleoecologic Significance of Storm-Generated Disturbance within a Middle Devonian Muddy Epeiric Sea." *Palaios* 3 (1988): 35-52.

_____, C. E. Brett and G. C. Baird. "A Temporal Hierarchy of Paleoecologic Processes within a Middle Devoian Epeiric Sea." In *Paleocommunity Temporal Dynamics: The Long-Term Development of Multispecies Assemblies,"* ed. W. Miller, III. *Paleontological Society. Special Publication* no. 5 (1990): 178-209.

_____. "'And God Saw That it was Good' - Death and Pain in the Created Order." Abstract in Forty-eighth Annual Meeting of the American Scientific Affiliation, Seattle, Washington, 1993.

_____. "Theological Implications of an Evolving Creation." Perspectives on Science and Christian Faith 45 (1993): 150-60.

_____. "Taxonomy, Transitional Forms and the Fossil Record." Abstract in Fortyninth Annual Meeting of the American Scientific Affiliation. St. Paul, MN, 1994.

Mills, Antonia

Present Position and Address: Associate Professor, First Nations Studies, University of Northern British Columbia, Prince George, BC V2N 429, Canada **Work Phone:** (609) 960-6690 **Date of Birth:** April 14, 1942 **Education:** B.A. Anthropology (*magna cum laude*, 1964), Radcliffe/Harvard Universities; Ph.D. Anthropology (1982), Harvard University **Postgraduate Experience:** Postdoctoral Fellow (1985-1987), Social Science and Humanities Research Council of Canada, affiliated with UBC, studying belief in and cases suggestive of reincarnation among the Gitksan, Wit'suwet'en and Beaver Indians; Research in Cases Suggestive of Reincarnation, Beaver Indian/Hindu and Half-Muslims **Awards and Honors:** NIMH Doctoral Fellowship **Previous Positions:** Instructor in Anthropology (1983), Simon Fraser University; Researcher (1985-87), the Gitksan-Wit'suwet'en Tribal Council, Hazelton, BC, Canada; Research Assistant Professor in the Division of Personality Studies, Department of Behavioral Medicine and Psychiatry/Lecturer, Department of Anthropology, University of Virginia, Charlottesville, VA **Editorial Positions:** Editorial Board (since 1988), *Anthropologica* **Selected Memberships:** American Anthropological Association; American Academy of the Advancement of Science; Canadian Anthropology Society; American Society for Psychical Research; Society for the Study of Native American Religious Traditions **Discipline:** Psychological Anthropology - specializing in Beaver, Wet'suwet'en and Gitksan Indians, Hindu and Indian Moslem Reincarnation **Related Areas of Interest:** Cosmology; Life after Death; Reincarnation; Cultural Construction.

Selected Publications:

_____. "The Meaningful Universe: Intersecting Forces in Beaver Indian Cosmology and Causality." *Culture* 6, 2 (1986): 81-91.

_____. "A Preliminary Investigation of Reincarnation among the Beaver and Gitksan Indians." *Anthropologica* 30, 1 (1988): 23-59.

_____. "A Replication Study: Three Cases of Children in Northern India Who Are Said to Remember a Previous Life." *Journal of Scientific Exploration* 3, 2 (1989): 133-84.

_____. *Eagle Down Is Our Law: Witsuwit'en Feasts, Laws and Land Claims.* Vancouver: University of British Columbia Press, 1994.

_____, Richard Slobodin, eds. *Amerindian Rebirth: Reincarnation Belief Among North American Indians and Inuit.* Toronto: University of Toronto Press, 1994.

_____, Erlendar Haroldsson, and H. H. Jürgen Keil. "Replication Studies of Cases Suggestive of Reincarnation by Three Independent Investigators." *Journal of the American Society for Psychical Research* 88 (1994): 207-19.

Mills, Gordon C.

Present Position and Address: Emeritus Professor of Biochemistry, University of Texas Medical Branch, Galveston, TX 77555, USA; (Home) 118 Barracuda Street, Galveston, TX 77550, USA **Home Phone:** (409) 762-6577 **Date of Birth:** February 13, 1924 **Education:** B.S. Chemistry (1946), University of Nevada - Reno; M.S. (1948)/Ph.D. (1951) Biochemistry, University of Michigan - Ann Arbor **Previous Positions:** Assistant (1955-61)/Associate (1961-67)/Professor (1967-89), Department of Human Biological Chemistry and Genetics and Research Associate Professor (1967-85), Department of Internal Medicine, University of Texas Medical Branch **Selected Memberships:** American Scientific Affiliation; Christian Medical and Dental Society **Discipline:** Biochemistry **Related Areas of Interest:** Chemical Evolution (origin of life); Evolution (macroevolution and microevolution); and other areas where science and theology interact.

Selected Publications:

_____. "Relation of Structure to Function for Mutant Hemoglobins." Part 1 of "Hemoglobin Structure and the Biogenesis of Proteins." *Journal of the American Scientific Affiliation (JASA)* 27 (1975): 33-8. "Significance of Protein Structure to the Biogenesis of Life." Part 2 of "Hemoglobin Structure and the Biogenesis of Proteins." *JASA* 27 (1975): 79-82.

_____. "Chemical Evolution." *JASA* 31 (1979): 193-4.

_____. Review of *Origins: A Skeptics Guide to the Creation of Life on Earth,* by Robert Shapiro. New York: Summit Books, 1986. *JASA* 39: 172-74 (1987).

_____. "Presuppositions of Science as Related to Origins." *Perspectives on Science and Christian Faith (PSCF)* 42 (1990): 153-61.

_____. "The Role of the Components of the Translation System in Information Transfer., In *Sources of Information Content of DNA: Proceedings of the Tacoma Conference, 1991,* 1-26.

_____. "Structure of Cytochrome c and c-like Genes: Significance for the Modification and Origin of Genes." *PSCF* 44 (1992): 236-45.

_____, M. Lancaster and W. L. Bradley. "Origin of Life and Evolution in Biology Textbooks - A Critique." *American Biology Teacher* 55 (1993): 78-83.

_____. "The Molecular Evolutionary Clock: A Critique." *PSCF* (1994): 159-68.

_____. "Theistic Evolution: A Design Theory at the Level of Genetic Information." Submitted to *Christian Scholar's Review* (1994).

_____. "A Theory of Theistic Evolution as an Alternative to the Naturalistic Theory." *PSCF* (1995). In press.

Milone, Eugene Frank

Present Position and Address: Professor (since 1981), Physics and Astronomy Department, The University of Calgary, 2500 University Drive, N.W., Calgary, ALB T2N 1N4, Canada **Date of Birth:** June 26, 1939 **Languages Spoken:** English, German, Spanish **Education:** A.B. Mathematics (1961), Columbia University; M.S. Astronomy (1963)/Ph.D. Astronomy (1967), Yale University **Congresses and Conferences:** Co-organizer and convenor, Conferences on "Science, Change, and Society" (1983); "Images of Humanity: The Implications of Contemporary Developments and Discoveries in Science for the Uniqueness of the Human Being" (1984); "Rapid Climate Change and Civilizations" (1987)**Previous Positions:** Assistant Professor (1969-71), Gettysburg College; Expert Consultant Astronomer (1967-1979), US Naval Research Laboratory; Assistant (1971-75)/Associate Professor (1975-81), University of Calgary **Selected Memberships:** Sigma Xi; Canadian Astronomical Society; American Astronomical Society and AAS Division (Dynamical Astronomy/History of Astronomy/Astronomy Software Groups); Astronomy Society of the Pacific International Astronomical Union; IAU Commissions, 25, 27, 37, 42; New York Academy of Science **Community Service and Religious Activities:** Member (since 1982), University of Calgary Lutheran Campus Ministry Committee; Member (since 1985), U. C., Chaplains' Advisory Council; Member (1985-87), U.C., Christian Thought Advisory Council; Member (1985-87), Christian Thought Chair Committee; Member,

Calgary Council of Lutheran Churches, Executive (1981-86); Member (1982-86), Theology Committee of C.C.L.C.; Member (1982-86), U. C. Humanities Institute, Executive Council; Member (1989-92), Evangelical Lutheran Church in Canada, College and University Services Committee; Member, ELCIC (1989), Ad Hoc Committee for Theological Education and Leadership **Discipline:** Astronomy; Astrophysics **Related Areas of Interest:** Archaeoastronomy; History of Astronomy; Ethnoastronomy; History of Philosophy; Theology.

Selected Publications:

_____. "Model Making and the Scientific Method." Chap. in *Science and Human Values*, 44-62. University of Calgary, 1981.
_____. "The Star of Bethlehem." Paper presented at Campus Ministry Breakfast Talk, University of Calgary, January 1983.
_____. "Life Beyond Earth." Paper presented at N.E. Rotary Club in Calgary, March 1988.
_____. "Cosmology." Paper presented at Campus Ministry Noon Seminars, University of Calgary, September 1990.

Mitcham, Carl

Present Position and Address: Director: Science, Technology, and Society Program/Associate Professor of Philosophy, Willard Bldg., Pennsylvania State University, University Park, PA 16802, USA **Work Phone:** (814) 865-9951 **Date of Birth:** September 20, 1941 **Languages Spoken:** English, Spanish **Education:** B.A. Philosophy/General Studies (*magna/summa cum laude*, 1967)/M.A. Philosophy (1969), University of Colorado; Ph.D. Philosophy (1988), Fordham University **Awards and Honors:** Abbot Payson Usher Prize (1974), Society for the History of Technology, for "Bibliography of the Philosophy of Technology"; Grant for research on "Engineering Ethics outside the USA," from National Science Foundation; MacArthur Foundation grant to organize, with the New York Academy of Science, a conference on "Ethical Issues Associated with the Military Support of Science of Technology" **Previous Positions:** Instructor in Philosophy (1970-72)Berea College, KY; Lecturer in Philosophy and Social Sciences (1972-1982), St. Catherine College, KY; Associate Professor of Humanities (1982-1989)/Director (1984-1990), Philosophy and Technology Studies Center, Polytechnic University, NY; Visiting Scholar (1988), Centro de Filosofía e Historia de la Ciencia y la Tecnología, Universidad de Puerto Rico, Mayagüez; Visiting Scholar (1993), Universidad de Oviedo, Spain **Editorial Positions:** Editor, *Research in Philosophy and Technology*; Editorial Boards: *Technology in Society* (since 1985); *Schopenhauer-Studien* (since 1986); *Design Issues* (since 1993) **Other Academic Experience:** Advisory Committee (1987-1991), National Network for Science, Technology, and Society Education; Member (1982-87), Columbia University Seminar on the History and Philosophy of Science **Selected Memberships:** American Catholic Philosophical Association; American Philosophical Association; American Association for the Advancement of Science; Humanities and Technology Association; Institute for the Theological Encounter with Science and Technology (ITEST); American Simone Weil Society; President (1980-82), Society for Philosophy and Technology; Society for Social Studies of Science; Society for the History of Technology; Agriculture, Food and Human Values Society **Discipline:** Philosophy **Related Areas of Interest:** Philosophy, Ethics, and Theology of Technology.

Selected Publications:

_____, R. Mackey, eds. *Philosophy and Technology: Readings in the Philosophical Problems of Technology.* New York: Free Press, 1972; Paperback 1983.
_____, Robert Mackey. *Bibliography of the Philosophy of Technology.* Chicago: University of Chicago Press, 1973. Reprint with index. Ann Arbor, MI: Books on Demand, 1985. Supplemented by numerous other bibliographies, including: with Jim Grote. "Current Bibliography of the Philosophy of Technology: 1975-1976." Special issue. *Research in Philosophy and Technology* 4 (1981): 1- 297. "Bibliography in the Philosophy of Technology: 1977-1978." *Research in Philosophy and Technology* 6 (1983): 231-96.

_____. "Philosophy of Technology." In *A Guide to the Culture of Science, Technology and Medicine*, ed. P. T. Durbin, 282-363. New York: Free Press, 1980.

_____. "The Religious and Political Origins of Modern Technology." In *Philosophy and Technology, Boston Studies in the Philosophy of Science 80*, ed. P. T. Durbin and F. Rapp, 267-73. Boston: D. Reidel, 1983.

_____, Jim Grote, eds. *Theology and Technology: Essays in Christian Analysis and Exegesis.* Lanham, MD: University Press of America, 1984.

_____. "Jacques Ellul." *Cross Currents* 35, 1 (Spring 1985): 1-108.

_____. *¿Qué es la filosofía de la tecnología?* Barcelona: Anthropos, 1989.

_____, P. Siekevitz, eds. "Ethical Issues Associated with Scientific and Technological Research for the Military." *Annals of the New York Academy of Sciences* 577 (December 29, 1989).

_____. *Philosophy of Technology in Spanish Speaking Countries, Philosophy and Technology.* Vol. 10. Boston: Kluwer, 1993.

_____. *Thinking Through Technology: The Path between Engineering and Philosophy.* Chicago: University of Chicago Press, 1994.

Mixter, Russell L.

Address: 120 Windsor Park Drive A206, Carol Stream, IL 60188, USA **Work Phone:** (708) 668-2032 **Date of Birth:** August 7, 1906 **Education:** A.B. (1928) Wheaton College; M.S. (1930), Michigan State University; Ph.D. (1939), University of Illinois **Previous Positions:** Instructor through Professor of Zoology (1928-79), Wheaton College; Instructor in Insects and Pond Life (1969-80), Audubon Camp in Wisconsin; Substitute Instructor (1980-84), Trinity/Barat/Judson Colleges **Selected Memberships:** American Scientific Affiliation; Association for Public Justice **Discipline:** Human Anatomy; Biology **Related Areas of Interest:** Creation and Evolution; Environmental Ethics.

Selected Publications: Book Reviews in *Journal of the American Scientific Affiliation* not listed.

_____. *Creation and Evolution.* American Scientific Affiliation, 1952.

_____, editor. *Evolution and Christian Thought Today.* Grand Rapids: Eerdmans, 1970.

_____. "Population Explosion." *Journal of American Scientific Affiliation (JASA)* 25 (March 1973): 9-13.

_____. "Your Lifespan: Can You Lengthen It?" *Christian Life* 35 (January 1974): 16-17.

_____. "Scriptures and Science with a Key to Health." *JASA* 28 (March 1976).

Moberg, David O.

Present Position and Address: Emeritus Professor of Sociology, Marquette University, Milwaukee, WI 53233, USA; (Home) 7120 W. Dove Ct., Milwaukee, WI 53223, USA **Work Phone:** (414) 357-7247 **Date of Birth:** February 13, 1922 **Education:** A.B. (1947), Seattle Pacific College; M.A. (1949), University of Washington; Ph.D. (1952), University of Minnesota **Postgraduate Experience:** Postdoctoral studies - State University of Groningen, The Netherlands (1957-58)/Münster University , Germany (1964-65) **Previous Positions:** Associate Instructor of Sociology (1948-49), University of Washington; Instructor to Professor of Sociology (1949-68)/Chairman, Department of Social Sciences (1952-68), Bethel College, St. Paul, MN; Sabbatical (1957-58), Fulbright Lecturer in Sociology, State University of Groningen, The Netherlands; Special Instructor of Sociology (1961-63), Mounds-Midway School of Nursing; Adjunct Professor (1964-1973), S.T.D. Program, San Francisco Theological Seminary; Sabbatical (1964-65), Fulbright Lecturer in Sociology of Religion, Münster University, Germany; Sociology Instructor (1965-66), Ancker School of Nursing, St. Paul, MN; Visiting and Adjunct Professorships (1970-1982), Regent College, Vancouver/McCormick Theological Seminary/Andrus Gerontology Center, University of S. California/Southern Baptist Theological Seminary, Louisville, KY/Princeton Theological Seminary **Editorial Positions:** Editor, *Adris Newsletter (*1971- 76), *Journal of the American Scientific Affiliation* (1962-64), *Review of Religious Research* (1969- 1973); Coeditor (since 1989), *Research in the Social Scientific Study of Religion* **Selected**

Memberships: American Scientific Affiliation; American Sociological Association; President (1976-77), Association for the Sociology of Religion; Christian Sociological Society; International Sociological Association; American Psychological Association, Psychologists Interested in Religious Issues; President (1981-82), Religious Research Association; Society for the Scientific Study of Religion **Discipline:** Sociology **Related Areas of Interest:** Social Indicators and Measures of Spiritual Well-being; Religion and Aging; Religious Hypocrisy; Sociology of Religion.

Selected Publications: He has written 213 articles in professional journals and books, 89 semi-popular articles and miscellaneous publication, and over 1,190 book reviews including about 980 for *Christian Sociological Society Newsletter*.

_____. *The Great Reversal: Evangelism and Social Concern*. Philadelphia: J. B. Lippincott Co., 1972, Rev. Ed. 1977.
_____, editor. *Spiritual Well-Being: Sociological Perspectives*. Washington, DC: University Press of America, 1979.
_____. *The Church as a Social Institution*. 2d ed. Grand Rapids: Baker Book House, 1984.
_____. *Wholistic Christianity: An Appeal for a Dynamic, Balanced Faith*. Elgin, IL: Brethren Press, 1985.

Molari, Carlo

Present Position and Address: Theological faculty member, Università Urbaniana di Propaganda Fide; Istituto di scienze religiose, Università Gregoriana **Date of Birth:** July 25, 1928 **Education:** B.A. Philosophy (1948)/Ph.D. Theology (1954)/Utroque Iure (1957), Pont. Università Lateranense, Rome **Selected Memberships:** Associazione teologica italiana; rivista internazionale *Consilium* **Discipline:** Theology; Dogmatics **Related Areas of Interest:** Evolution and Faith.

Selected Publications:

_____. *Darwinismo e teologia cattolica*. Roma: Boral, 1984.

Moltmann, Jürgen

Present Position and Address: Professor of Systematic Theology (since 1967) Universität Tübingen, Liebermeisterstr. 12, D - 7400 Tübingen, Germany **Concurrent Positions:** Teaching at Candler School of Theology, Emory University, Atlanta, GA **Date of Birth:** April 8, 1926 **Education:** Dr. theol. (1952)/Habilitation (1957), University of Göttingen **Lectures Presented:** Gifford Lecturer (1984-85), Edinburgh **Awards and Honors:** Literature Prize d'isola d'Elba (1971), for book *The Theology of Hope* **Previous Positions:** Professor of Theology (1958-63), University of Wuppertal; Professor (1963-67), University of Bonn; Visiting Professor (1967-68), USA **Discipline:** Systematic Theology **Related Areas of Interest:** Creation; Environmental Ethics and Ecology; Anthropology; Biomedical Ethics.

Selected Publications:

_____. "Theologie in der Welt der modernen Wissenschaften." In *Perspektiven der Theologie. Ges. Aufsätze*, by Jürgen Moltmann, 269-87. München/Mainz: Chr. Kaiser/Matthias-Grünewald, 1968.
_____. *Mensch. Christliche Anthropologie in den Konflikten der Gegenwart*. Stuttgart: Kreuz Verlag, 1971.
_____. *Zukunft der Schöpfung. Gesammelte Aufsätze*. München: Chr. Kaiser, 1977. English Translation: *The Future of Creation*. London; Philadelphia, 1979.
_____. *Gott in der Schöpfung: Ökologische Schöpfungslehre*. Munich: Christian Kaiser Verlag, 1985. English Translation: *God in Creation. A New Theology of Creation and the Spirit of God*. New York: Harper & Row, 1985. The 1984-85 Gifford Lectures.

Montefiore, Hugh

Present Position and Address: Right Reverend, Retired Bishop of Birmingham (since 1987); White Lodge, 23 Bellevue Road, Wandsworth Common, London SW7 7EB, UK **Work Phone:** 081-672 6697 **Date of Birth:** May 12, 1920 **Education:** M.A. (1947), Oxford University; M.A. (1950)/B.D. (1963), Cambridge University **Honorary Degrees:** Hon. D.D., Aberdeen and Birmingham Universities **Previous Positions:** Fellow and Dean (1954-63), Gonville and Caius Cottage, Cambridge; Lecturer in New Testament (1956-1963), Cambridge University; Vicar (1963-1970), University Church of UTS Mary's, Cambridge; Bishop of Kingston-on-Thames (1970-78); Bishop of Birmingham (1978-1987) **Selected Memberships:** Society for New Testament Studies **Discipline:** Theology **Related Areas of Interest:** Science and Theology.

Selected Publications: His selected bibliography lists over 30 monographs and 115 other publications.

_____. "Man's Dominion." In *The Responsible Church*, ed. Edwin Barker. Society for Promoting Christian Knowledge, 1966.
_____. *Can Man Survive?: The Question Mark and Other Essays*. Fontana, 1970.
_____. *Man and Nature*. Report with appended essays of working group appointed by the Archbishop of Canterbury in 1979 to work in connection with Doctrine Commission. Collins, 1975.
_____. *The Probability of God*. SCM, 1985.
_____. *So Near and Yet So Far*. Rome; Canterbury; SCM, 1986.
_____. "Communicating the Gospel in a Scientific Age." In *The Barclay Lectures in Glasgow, 1988*. St. Andrew Press, 1988.
_____. *Reclaiming the High Ground: A Christian Response to Secularism*. Macmillan, 1990.
_____. *Preaching for Our Planet*. Mowbray, 1992.
_____. *Credible Christianity*. Mowbray, 1993.

Monteiro, Hubert A.

Present Position and Address: Technical Director, CIBATUL, Ltd.; 53 Rebello House, 132 Hill Road, Bandra, Bombay-400 050, India **Work Phone:** (22) 643 63 41 **Date of Birth:** November 3, 1933 **Languages Spoken:** English, French **Education:** M.A. Chemistry (1955), University of Madras; M.Sc. Organic Chemistry (1956), University of Mysore; Doctorate Polymer Science (1961), University of Strasbourg, France **Postgraduate Experience:** Postdoctoral research, New York State University **Congresses and Conferences:** Member, National Advisory Council to Catholic Bishops Conference of India for 3 years **Lectures Presented:** Given lectures at various times at Institutes of Technology on various aspects of Polymer Science and Technology **Previous Positions:** Interviewed scientists of different religions on their attitude to religion; Twice elected Vice President, International Catholic Movement for Intellectual and Cultural Affairs (Pax Romana); Joint Secretary, International Secretariate for Scientific Questions (Pax Romana); President (8 years), Newman Association of India; Participated in 3 international seminars on Faith and Science; Participated in 3 seminars in India together with scientists of other religions on various aspects of Religion and Science; General Manager (1979-93), Additives, Plastics and Pigments Division, Hindustan Ciba-Geigy Limited **Discipline:** Chemistry; Commerce **Related Areas of Interest:** Science, Technology, Religion and Humanity; Human Environmental Ethics.

Selected Publications:

_____. "The Challenge of Secularization and the Apostolate of the Laity." *The Morning Star* (December 1971).
_____. "Science and Technology and Human Environment." *Convergence* (Pax Romana Journal, July 1971).
_____. "Religion, Science and Man." Paper presented at the World Conference of Religions on "Religion and Man," November 1981.
_____. "Attitudes of Indian Scientists to Religion." *Convergence* 1, 2 (1983). Article based on a survey.

_____. "Science, Technology and Religion: The Indian Situation." Report prepared for Asian Seminar of Catholic Scientists, Hong Kong, December, 1988.
_____. "Integral Education of Youth: Formal and Informal Setting." Paper presented at Federation of Asian Bishops' Conference Colloquium on Faith and Science, Tagaytay, Philippines, Jan. 31 - Feb. 6, 1993. *Vidyajyoti Journal of Theological Reflection* 58, 1 (1994).

Montgomery, John Warwick

Present Position and Address: Distinguished Professor of Theology and Law, Faith Evangelical Lutheran Seminary, P.O. Box 7186, Tacoma, WA 98407, USA; 4 Crane Court, No. 9, Fleet Street, London E.C. 4, UK **Concurrent Positions:** Professeur Honoraire de Theologie et Droit, 2 Rue de Rome, 67000 Strasbourg, France **Work Phone:** US: (206) 752-2020; France: 88.61.08.82; UK: 071 583-1210 **Date of Birth:** October 18, 1931 **Languages Spoken:** English, French **Education:** A.B. (with distinction, 1952), Cornell University; B.L.S. (1954)/M.A. (1958), University of California - Berkeley; M.Div (1958)/S.T.M. (1960), Wittenberg University; Ph.D. (1962), University of Chicago; Th.D. (1964), University of Strasbourg; LL.B. (1977), LaSalle Extension University: M.Phil. Law (1983), University of Essex **Previous Positions:** Librarian (1954-55), University of California Library; Instructor in Biblical Hebrew, Hellenistic Greek, Medieval Latin (1956-59), Wittenberg University and Hamma Divinity School; Ordained Minister, Lutheran Church; Head Librarian (1959-60), Swift Library of Divinity and Philosophy, University of Chicago; Associate Professor of History/Chairman (1960-64), History Department, Wilfred Lauriet University, ONT, Canada; Professor and Chairman (1964-74), Division of Church History and History of Christian Thought, Trinity Evangelical Divinity School/Director of European Program, University of Strasbourg, France; Professor of Law and Theology (1974-75), International School of Law, Washington, DC; Theological Consultant (1975-76), to Christian Legal Society; Director of Studies (1979-81), International Institute of Human Rights, Strasbourg; Dean/Director of Library/Professor of Jurisprudence (1980-88), Simon Greenleaf School of Law, Anaheim, CA **Other Academic Experience:** Admitted to Bar of Virginia (1978)/California (1979)/US Supreme Court (1981)/England and Wales (1984)/District of Columbia (1985)/Washington State (1990) **Selected Memberships:** International Bar Association; Fellow, American Scientific Affiliation; Fellow, Victoria Institute; Evangelical Theological Society **Discipline:** Law, Education, and Theology **Related Areas of Interest:** Christian Apologetics; Theology; Modern Culture and Science.

Selected Publications: Bibliography lists some 37 books and over 100 articles.

_____. "The Theologian's Craft: Theory Testing in Theology and Science." In *The Suicide of Christian Theology.* Minneapolis: Bethany, 1970.
_____. "Cross and Crucible." In *International Archives of the History of Ideas.* Vol. 55. The Hague: Nijhoff, 1973.

Montgomery, Robert Lancaster

Present Position and Address: Presbyterian Minister; Port Chaplain for the Seamen's Church Institute of New York and New Jersey, 118 Export Street, Port Newark, NJ 07114, USA; (Home) 384 Vesta Court, Ridgewood, NJ 07450, USA **Work Phone:** (201) 589-5828 **Home Phone:** (201) 445-9247 **Fax Number:** (201) 817-8565 **Date of Birth:** October 25, 1929 **Languages Spoken:** English, Mandarin Chinese, Amis, aboriginal language used on Taiwan **Education:** BA (1950), Rhodes College; BD (1953), Columbia Theological Seminary; Th.M. (1955), Princeton Theological Seminary; Ph.D. Religion, specializing in Social Scientific Studies (1976), Emory University **Previous Positions:** Pastorate, Spencer, WV; Presbyterian Missionary (1956-72), Taiwan; Pastorate, Bethany Presbyterian Church, Covington, GA; Assistant Pastor, First Chinese Presbyterian Church, NYC; Liaison to Churches, Federation of Protestant Welfare Agencies; Teacher, Yu-Shan Theological Institute and

Taiwan Theological College, Taiwan and Oglethorpe University, Atlanta, GA **Selected Memberships:** Society for the Scientific Study of Religion; Religious Research Association; Association for the Sociology of Religion; American Society of Missiology **Discipline:** Sociology of Religion with Specialization in Sociology of Missions **Related Areas of Interest:** Sociology of Science; To establish the Religious Basis for the Social Sciences and Science in General **Current Areas of Research:** His major focus has been on Sociological and Theological analysis of the spread of Religions.

Selected Publications: His bibliography contains 4 published articles.

_____. "Bias in Interpreting Social Facts: Is it a Sin?" *Journal for the Scientific Study of Religion* 23, 3 (1984).
_____. "Receptivity to an Outside Religion: Light from Interaction between Sociology and Missiology." *Missiology: An International Review* 4, 4 (1986).
_____. "Crosscutting Distinctions in Approaches to Meeting Human Needs." *Journal of Voluntary Action Research* 16, 4 (1987).
_____. "The Spread of Religions and Macro Social Relations." *Sociological Analysis* 52, 1 (1991).
Personal Notes: Dr. Montgomery retired from Port Chaplaincy at the end of 1994.

Moore, Brooke Noel

Present Position and Address: Professor of Philosophy (since 1979), California State University - Chico, Chico, CA 95929, USA; 1497 E. First Ave., Chico, CA 95926 **Work Phone:** (916) 345-9228 **Date of Birth:** December 2, 1943 **Education:** B.A. (1966), Antioch University; Ph.D. Philosophy (1972), University of Cincinnati **Previous Positions:** Assistant (1970-74)/Associate Professor (1974-79), California State University - Chico **Selected Memberships:** American Philosophical Association; American Association for the Advancement of Science **Discipline:** Philosophy **Related Areas of Interest:** Epistemology; Metaphysics.

Selected Publications:

_____. *The Philosophical Possibilities Beyond Death.* Springfield, IL: Charles Thomas, 1981.
_____. *The Cosmos, God and Philosophy.* New York: Peter Lang, 1989.

Moore, James R.

Present Position and Address: Lecturer (since 1975), Department of History of Science and Technology, Faculty of Arts, The Open University, Milton Keynes MK7 6AA, UK **Work Phone:** (0908) 652488 **Date of Birth:** March 13, 1947 **Languages Spoken:** English, French **Education:** B.S. Electrical Engineering (high honors, 1969), University of Illinois - Urbana; M.Div. (*summa cum laude*, 1972), Trinity Evangelical Divinity School, Deerfield, IL; Ph.D. Ecclesiastical History (1975), University of Manchester; Summer Institute of Linguistics (Summer 1968), University of North Dakota, Grand Forks; Faculté de Théologie Protestante (Spring 1972), University of Strasbourg **Previous Positions:** Adjunct Assistant Professor (1984-92), College of Arts and Letters London Program, University of Notre Dame, IN; Landon Clay Visiting Associate Professor of the History of Science (1992-93), Harvard University **Selected Memberships:** American Scientific Affiliation; Conference on Faith and History; British Society for the History of Science; British Society for Social Responsibility in Science; Science and Religion Forum **Discipline:** Theology; History of Science/Theology; Electrical Engineering **Related Areas of Interest:** Social History of Natural Theology, with special reference to Naturalism in the Biological and Human Sciences since 1800; Charles Darwin; Women in Nature and Science since 1800; Historical Hermeneutics of Genesis 1-11; Fundamentalism in American Culture; Bio-Bibliography of English-language literature on Science and Religion since 1860.

Selected Publications: His bibliography lists 7 books, 26 articles, 7 essay reviews, 9 chapters and 16 radio/TV works, plus 68 other items.

_____. "Darwin of Down: The Evolutionist as Squarson-Naturalist." In *The Darwinian Heritage*, ed. D. Kohn, 435-81. Princeton: Princeton University Press, 1985.

_____. "Darwin's Genesis and Revelations." Reviews of *A Calendar of the Correspondence of Charles Darwin, 1821-1882*, ed. F. Burkhardt et al. and *The Correspondence of Charles Darwin: Vol. 1, 1821-36*, ed. F. Burkhardt et. al. *Isis* 76 (1985): 570-80.

_____. "Evangelicals and Evolution: Henry Drummond, Herbert Spencer, and the Naturalization of the Spiritual World." *Scottish Journal of Theology* 38: 383-417 (1985).

_____. "Herbert Spencer's Henchmen: The Evolution of Protestant Liberals in Late Nineteenth-Century America." In *Darwinism and Divinity: Essays on Evolution and Religious Belief*, ed. J. R. Durant, 76-100. Oxford: Basil Blackwell, 1985.

_____. "Geologists and Interpreters of Genesis in the Nineteenth Century." In *God and Nature: Historical Essays on the Encounter between Christianity and Science*, ed. D. C. Lindberg and R. L. Numbers, 322-50. Berkeley: University of California Press, 1986.

_____. "Born-Again Social Darwinism." Review of *Taking Darwin Seriously: A Naturalistic Approach to Philosophy*, by M. Ruse. *Annals of Science* 44: 409-17 (1987).

_____, "Of Love and Death: 'Why Darwin 'gave up Christianity'." Chap. in *History, Humanity and Evolution: Essays for John C. Greene*, ed. James Moore, 195-229. Cambridge University Press, 1989.

_____. "Communications." In *Science, Technology and Everyday Life, 1870-1950*, ed. C. Chant, 200-49. London: Routledge in association with Open University Press, 1989.

_____. "Theodicy and Society: The Crisis of the Intelligentsia." In *Victorian Faith in Crisis: Essays on Continuity and Change in Nineteenth-Century Religious Belief*, ed. R. Helmstadter and B. Lightman, 153-86. Stanford University Press, 1991.

_____. "The Creationist Cosmos of Protestant Fundamentalism." In *Remaking the World: Fundamentalist Impact*, ed. M. Marty and S. Appleby. Princeton: Princeton University Press, 1991.

Morren, Lucien

Present Position and Address: Retired Professor, Catholic University of Louvain, Belgium; Avenue du Grand Cortil, 15A, B-1348 Louvain-la-Neuve, Belgium **Date of Birth:** May 20, 1906 **Languages Spoken:** French, English, Dutch **Education:** Civil Engineering (1928), University of Ghent; Mechanical/Electrical Engineering (1930), University of Brussels **Previous Positions:** Professor (1944-1976), Catholic University of Louvain; Director (1947-71), national laboratory for Measuring and Testing (Laboratoire Central d'Electricité) **Selected Memberships:** President, International Secretariat for Scientific Questions, Pax Romana - ICMICA; Member: ITEST (Institute for Theological Encounter with Science and Technology); ESSSAT (European Society for the Study of Science and Theology); laureate of the Royal Belgian Society of Electrical Engineers; Order of St. Gregorius the Great after 14 years as delegate of the Holy See to the Committee for Higher Education: and Research of the Council of Europe **Discipline:** Electrical Measurements; Photometry, Colorimetry and Lighting **Related Areas of Interest:** Science/Technology and Spiritual Values/Faith.

Selected Publications: The bibliography comprises over 120 titles, about half of which are technical and the other half spiritual. They are mostly in French, with a few in English .

_____. *Dieu est libre et lié - Le regard d'un scientifique sur la Foi*. Paris: Lethielleux, 1975. Translated into Dutch, Catalan, and Russian.

_____. "L'influence de la science et de la technologie sur l'image de l'homme et du monde." In *Science et Foi*, 71-86. Desclee International, 1982.

_____. De la loi d'entropie au Principe anthropique - Réflexions d'un chrétien sur la cosmologie." *Revue Théologique de Louvain* 15, 2 (1984): 160-83.

_____. "About Science in Modern Western Culture." Lecture delivered in symposium "Science, Technology and Spiritual Values" Tokyo, 1987. *Dialectics and Humanism* (The Polish Philosophical Quarterly) 14, 3 (1987): 39-47.

_____. "The Mission of the Catholic Scientist." Lecture delivered at seminar on "Science, High Technology and Faith" Hong Kong, 1988. In *Federation of Asian Bishops' Conferences Papers no. 51*, 54-69. Hong Kong: n.d.
_____. "A Scientific Bipolar Anthropology Completed by a Tripolar Theological Anthropology." In *Origins, Time & Complexity*, Part 2, 53-7. Geneva, Switzerland: Labor et Fides, 1994.

Mortensen, Viggo

Present Position and Address: Director for Theology and Studies/Secretary for the Church and Social Issues, The Lutheran World Federation, 150 Rt de Ferney, CH-1211 Geneva 2, Switzerland **Work Phone:** 4122 791 6161 **Fax Number:** 4122 798 8616 **Date of Birth:** May 15, 1942 **Languages Spoken:** Danish, English, German **Education:** Theology candidate (1969)/Ph.D. (1973)/Dr. Theol. (1988), University of Aarhus **Previous Positions:** Dean (1988-93)/Associate Professor (1973-93), Institute of Ethics and Philosophy of Religion, University of Aarhus, Denmark **Selected Memberships:** Wissenschaftliche Gesellschaft für Theologie; IRAS; Societas Ethica; Cofounder, Danish Forum Teologi Naturvidenskab; Member, Council for the European Society for the Study of Science and Theology **Discipline:** Theology; Ethics; Philosophy of Religion **Related Areas of Interest:** Models for relating Science and Religion; Biology and Ethics; Sociobiology.

Selected Publications:

_____. "Schöpfungstheologie und Anthropologie. Reflexionen eines Dänischen Theologen über Jürgen Moltmann: Gott in der Schöpfung." *Evangelische Theologie.* 5 (1987).
_____. "Free Will, Determinism and Responsibility." In *Free Will and Determinism*, ed. Viggo Mortensen and R. S. Sorensen. Aarhus: Aarhus University Press, 1987.
_____. "The Status of the Science-Religion Dialogue." In *Evolution and Creation*, ed. A. Peacocke and S. Andersen. Aarhus: Aarhus University Press, 1987.
_____. "Ethics and Medical Genetics in Denmark." In *Ethics and Human Genetics. A Cross Cultural Perspective*, ed. J. C. Fletcher. Heidelberg: Springer Verlag, 1988.
_____. "Theologie der Natur als natürliche Theologie?" In *Kann man Gott aus der Natur erkennen?*, ed. C. Bresch, S. M. Daecke, and H. Riedlinger. Freiburg, 1990.
_____, editor. *Gud og Naturen Kan der etableres en dialog mellem teologi og naturvidenskab?* (God and nature. Is it possible to establish a dialogue between theology and natural science?). Copenhagen: Munksgaard, 1990.
_____. *Gør livet fri. Om skaberværkets udlkrænkelighed* (Liberation of life. On the integrity of creation). Copenhagen, 1990.
_____. *Teologi og naturvidenskab. Hinsides restriktion og ekspansion* (Theology and science. Beyond restriction and expansion). Summary in English. Copenhagen: Munksgaard, 1989. German edition: Gütersloher Verlagrhaus, 1995.

Mosley, Glenn R.

Present Position and Address: Executive Director (since 1985), Association of Unity Churches, 401 S.W. Oldham Pkwy, Lee's Summit, MO 64081, USA **Work Phone:** (816) 524-7414 **Date of Birth:** May 23, 1935 **Languages Spoken:** English, Spanish **Education:** Science Teaching Certification (1954), Bowling Green of Ohio; Ordained Unity Minister (1961); A.A. (1973), State University of New York - Albany; B.A. (1974)/M.A. Mass Media Communications, Wayne State University, Detroit, MI; Ph.D. Interpersonal Communications (1976), Walden University, Naples, FL **Honorary Degrees:** D.D. (1976), Association of Unity Churches **Previous Positions:** Assistant to Personnel Director (1954-57), Babcock & Wilcox Company, Barberton, OH; Minister - Flushing (1959-1964)/Des Moines (1964-65)/New York City (1965-68, including services in Carnegie Hall)/Detroit Unity Temple (1968-1975)/Unity Church of Akron (1975-1985); Founding Director, The Foundation of Thanatology **Editorial Positions:** Editorial staff, *Journal of Thanatology* **Discipline:** Minister **Related Areas of Interest:** Staff Consultant of Dialogue House, NYC, an organization of clergy, physicians, and psychiatrists who recognize the essential meeting ground of modern depth psychology and creative religion and who conduct workshops and publish their research findings.

Selected Publications: His bibliography lists 4 books and two published cassette albums.

_____. *Secular and Religious Experiential Education Activities Compared.* Ohio State University, 1980.

Moss, Rowland Percy

Present Position and Address: Professor of Human Ecology (since 1979), University of Salford, Salford, Lancashire M5 4WT, UK; (Home) 154, Acre Lane, Cheadle Hulme, Cheadle, Cheshire SK8 7PD, UK **Date of Birth:** May 8, 1928 **Languages Spoken:** English, French **Education:** B.Sc. (1951), London University; Certificate in Soil Science (1952), Aberdeen University; Ph.D. (1961), London University **Postgraduate Experience:** Ordained Priest (1983), Church of England; General Ministerial Certificate of the Church of England (1984), St. Deiniol's Library, Hawarren, Clwyd, Wales (Theological Examination) **Previous Positions:** Soil Scientist (1952-62), Colonial Agricultural Service; Lecturer/Senior Lecturer/Reader/Professor of Biogeography (1962-79), University of Birmingham; Pro-Vice Chancellor (1982-86), University of Salford **Selected Memberships:** Former President/Honorary Member (since 1977), African Studies Association of the United Kingdom; Vice President (since 1978), International Association of African Studies; British Ecological Society; British Society of Soil Science; International Society of Soil Science; Christians in Science; Society of Ordained Scientists **Discipline:** Human Ecology; Agricultural Ecology; Theology **Related Areas of Interest:** Theology of Nature; Biblical Ethics applied to Technology; 3rd World Problems.

Selected Publications: His bibliography lists 3 books, 4 monographs and more than 100 papers on soil science and agricultural ecology plus 15 papers on the Philosophy of Science and Scientific Method.

_____. "Can Man Survive?" *Evangelical Magazine* (1972).
_____. "Responsibility in the Use of Nature." In *Christian Graduate.* Vol. 1 (1975), Vol. 2 (1976). Leicester, UK: IVP.
_____. "Environmental Problems and the Christian Ethic." In *Horizons of Science.* New York: Harper and Row, 1978.
_____. "God, Man and Nature: Contrasting Views in Christendom." *Teilhard Review* (University of Kent, 1978).
_____. *The Earth in our Hands.* Leicester: IVP, 1982.
_____. *Beyond the Treadmill.* London: S.U. Publishing, 1987.
_____. *How Green is the Gospel?* Leicester: IVP, in press.
_____. *The Healing of Nature: A Biblical Theology of Man and Environment.* Leicester: IVP, in press.

Müller, A. M. Klaus

Present Position and Address: Professor of Theoretical Physics (since 1972), Institut für Mathematische Physik, Technische Universität Carolo-Wilhelmina zu Braunschweig, Physikzentrum, Mendelssohnstrasse 3, D-38106 Braunschweig, Germany **Date of Birth:** February 20, 1931 **Languages Spoken:** German, English **Education:** Diplom-Hauptprüfung in Physik (1956); Dr. rer. nat. in Theoretical Physics (1960) **Previous Positions:** Assistant (1958-1968), Habilitation, Privatdozent (1968); Oberassistent (1968-1972); Universitätsdozent (1970) **Selected Memberships:** Forschungsstätte der Evangelischen Studiengemeinschaft, Heidelberg; Protestant Institute for Interdisciplinary Research (since 1974), Heidelberg **Discipline:** Theoretical Physics **Related Areas of Interest:** Mathematical Methods of Quantum Theory; Reflection on Time; Foundational Crises in the Sciences and Politics; Relationship of the Gospel and the Modern World.

Selected Publications:

_____. *Das unbekannte Land - Konflikt-Fall Natur. Erfahrungen und Visionen im Horizont der offenen Zeit.* Stuttgart: Radius, 1987.

_____. "Die Gefährdungen von Umwelt und Frieden im Atomzeitalter." In *Naturwissenschaft und Glaube. Natur- und Geisteswissenschaftler auf der Suche nach einem neuen Verständnis von Mensch und Technik, Gott und Welt,* ed. H. A. Müller, 270-301. Bern: Scherz, 1988.

_____. "Comments on the Oikos of Time." A Contribution to the Heidelberg Consultation on Theology and Science, May 1988, organized by the Center of Theological Inquiry, Princeton, NJ. *Panorama* (Braunschweig) 2 ,1 (1990): 41-7.

_____. "Chiffren eines dynamischen Gottes 'bildes' in der Schöpfung." In *Mein Gottesbild,* 221-37. München: Nymphenburger, 1990.

_____, G. Scharffenorth, eds. *Patientenorientierung als Aufgabe - Kritische Analyse der Krankenhaussituation und notwendige Neuorientierungen.* Heidelberg: Forschungsstätte der Evangelischen Studiengemeinschaft, 1990.

_____. "An der Schwelle zum Geheimnis der Zeit." *Mitteilungen der Technischen Universität Carolo-Wilhelmina zu Braunschweig* (Braunschweig) 257, 2 (1990): 28-38.

_____. "Interdisziplinäre Forschung als geschichtliche Herausforderung." *Mitteilungen der Technischen Universität Carolo-Wilhelmina zu Braunschweig* (Braunschweig) 26, 1 (1991): 37-44.

_____, H. Wismann and G. Scharffenorth. *Krankenhausseelsorge - eine vordringliche Aufgabe der Kirche?* Heidelberg: Forschungsstätte der Evangelischen Studiengemeinschaft, 1991.

_____. "Die ökonomische Totalmotivation - Verrat an der offenen Zeit?" A Contribution to the 4th International Rosenstock-Huessy-Conference, University of Twente, August 1992. *Mitteilungen der Technischen Universität Carolo-Wilhemina zu Braunschweig.* (Braunschweig) 29, 1 (1994): 71-83.

_____. *Diesseits und Jenseits der Wissenschaft* - Thesenreihe zu einer fächerübergreifenden Vorlesung, 1991/92 im Physikzentrum der Technischen Universität Braunschweig. (Braunschweig, in press).

Müller, Gert H.

Present Position and Address: Professor Emeritus of Mathematics and Logic (since 1973), Mathematisches Institut, Universität Heidelberg, D-69120 Heidelberg, Germany **Concurrent Positions:** Leader of Logic Group (since 1969), Heidelberg Academy of Sciences **Work Phone:** 0 62 21 56-5777 or 5766 **Date of Birth:** May 29, 1923 **Languages Spoken:** German, English, French **Education:** Ph.D. Philosophy, Astronomy, Mathematics (1947), University of Graz, Austria; Ph.D. Habilitation Mathematics (1962), University of Heidelberg **Previous Positions:** Scientific Assistant (1949-1960), Mathematics Institute of the Federal Institute of Technology (ETH), Zürich; Dozent (1963-65), Heidelberg; Associate Professor (1965-1973), University of Heidelberg; Director of Math Institute (1972-74), Heidelberg; Dean of Faculty of Mathematics (1977-79, 88-89), Heidelberg **Editorial Experience:** Editor in Chief of the international journal *Studium Generale* (Heidelberg: Springer Verlag); Consulting Editor (1958-1984), *Journal of Symbolic Logic; Zeitschrift für Mathematische Logik und Grundlagen der Mathematik* **Selected Memberships:** President (1976-1980), German Society for Mathematical Logic and Foundations of Mathematics; Vice President of the Division of Logic, Methodology and Philosophy of Science (1979-83), IUPHS; Member, Academie Internationale de Philosophie des Sciences (Bruxelles) **Discipline:** Mathematics **Related Areas of Interest:** Metaphysics and Mathematics.

Selected Publications:

_____. "Shadows of Infinity." Paper presented at Conference of the Academie Internationale de Philosophie des Sciences, Cesena, Italy, May 1988. *Epistemologia* 2 (1988): 157-209.

Mullins, Jeffrey Lynn

Present Position and Address: Senior Scientific Programmer, Hughes-STX, NASA Goddard Space-flight Center, Greenbelt, MD, USA; (Home) 7934 Quill Point Drive, Bowie, MD 20720-4372, USA **Concurrent Positions:** Doctoral Student, Committee on the History and Philosophy of Science, University of Maryland at College Park **Work Phone:** (301) 286-9152 **Home Phone:** (301) 805-4219 **Date of Birth:** August 9, 1956 **Education:** Master's Degree in Astronomy and Religion **Awards and Honors:** Hughes-STX Group Achievement Award for ROSAT; NASA Achievement Award for the Cosmic Background Explorer **Previous Positions:** Science Operations Specialist, Space Telescope Science Institute, Baltimore, MD; Senior Scientific Programmer ROSAT, NASA Goddard Spaceflight Center, Greenbelt, MD; Parallax Observer, University of Virginia; Senior Scientific Programmer, COBE, Cosmology Data Analysis Center, Greenbelt, MD **Selected Memberships:** American Scientific Affiliation **Discipline:** Astronomy; Philosophy of Science; Philosophy of Religion **Related Areas of Interest:** Cosmology; Philosophy of Science; Philosophy of Religion; Science and Religion Interaction; Christian Apologetics.

Selected Publications:

Hall, Edward Burke, Jr, Jeffrey Lynn Mullins. "A Distortion in the Light Curve of MM Herculis." IAU Bulletin of Variable Stars (1979).

Munday Jr., John Clingman

Present Position and Address: Interim Dean, School of Government/Professor of Natural Sciences, Regent University, 1000 Regent University Drive, Virginia Beach, VA 23464, USA **Work Phone:** (804) 579-4302 **Fax Number:** (804)579-4595 **E-mail:** jmunday@beacon.regent.edu **Date of Birth:** June 10, 1940 **Awards and Honors:** Americans in Science, *Who's Who*; Sigma Xi **Previous Positions:** Teaching Assistant, Department of Physiology and Biophysics, University of Illinois, Urbana, IL; Research Assistant, Marine Biological Laboratory, Wood Hole, MA; Research Assistant, Department of Botany, University of Illinois, Urbana, IL; Physicist, US Air Force, Holloman AFB, NM; Associate Marine Scientist, Virginia Institute of Marine Science, Gloucester, VA; Assistant Professor, University of Virginia, Charlottesville, VA; Assistant Professor, College of William and Mary, Williamsburg, VA; Assistant Professor, University of Toronto, Canada; Associate Professor through Professor, College of William and Mary, Williamsburg, VA **Selected Memberships:** American Society of Photogrammetry and Remote Sensing; Hydrospheric Sciences Committee; American Association for the Advancement of Science; Association of American Geographers; International Association for Energy Economics; Evangelicals for Social Action **Discipline:** Public Affairs: Christian Perspective on Science and Policy **Related Areas of Interest:** Biomedical and Environmental Issues **Current Areas of Research:** Manuscript — M. Stone. "Clergy Attitudes About Involvement in Pro-Life Activity." Book draft — "Natural Resources and Distributive Justice."

Selected Publications: His bibliography contains 16 journal publications, 3 book contributions, 18 symposia proceedings, 9 papers presented, 15 contract reports, 9 technical reports, 15 unpublished manuscripts, 1 magazine contribution, and 6 other oral presentations.

_____. "Creature Mortality: From Creation or the Fall?" *Journal of the Evangelical Theological Society* 35, 1 (1992): 51-68.
_____, Judith B. Munday. *Exploring creation: Life Science.* Vol. 1. Virginia Beach, VA: CBN Publishing, N.d.
_____, T. T. Alfoldi. "Landsat Test of Diffuse Reflectance Models for Aquatic Suspended Solids Measurement." *Remote Sensing of Environment* 8: 169-83.
_____, R. W. Johnson. "Remote Sensing of the Marine Environment." Chap 28 of *Manual of Remote Sensing*, 1371-1496. Falls Church, VA: American Society of Photogramm, N.d.
_____. "Eden's Geography Erodes Flood Geology." *Westminster Theological Journal* (Accepted).

Murdoch, Bernard Constantine

Present Position and Address: Private Practice as Psychologist/Psychotherapist; President, Fore (In) Sight Foundation, Inc., 1241 Adams Street, Macon, GA 31201, USA **Work Phone:** (912) 742-6017 **Date of Birth:** December 5, 1917 **Awards and Honors:** *Who's Who in America; Who's Who in the Southeast; American Men of Science*; Leaders in Education; Certificate of Merit, Georgia Psychological Association; Graduated *summa cum laude* **Previous Positions:** Dean (1946-48), Presbyterian College, Clinton, SC; Research Supervisor (1948-50), American Council on Education, Defense Department, Washington, DC; Dean (1950-54), Muskingum College, New Concord, OH; Head (1954-82)/Emeritus Professor (since 1982), Psychology/Behavioral Sciences Department, Wesleyan College, Macon, GA **Selected Memberships:** American Psychological Association; Southeastern Psychological Association; Georgia Psychological Association **Discipline:** Psychology **Related Areas of Interest:** Integration of Science, Psychology and Religion **Current Areas of Research:** Currently doing research for three books in Psychology, Education, and Religion.

Selected Publications: His total bibliography contains 4 books and 28 published articles.

_____. *Consistency of Test Responses*. Duke University, 1942.
_____. *Analysis of a Professional Organization: The American Educational Research Association*. Washington, DC, 1949.
_____. "Places of Birth and Training of Physicists." *Physics Today* 3, 12 (1950): 17-20.
_____. "The Adult Sunday Civic Club." *Earnest Worker* 81 (February 1950): 19-20.
_____. *The Production of Doctorates in the Sciences*. American Council on Education 1951.
_____. "Helping Your Young Adult Adjust to College." *The Christian Home* (September 1975).
_____. *Love and Problems of Living*. N.p., 1992. Based on a 4-factor theory of behavioral dynamics.

Murdy, William H.

Present Position and Address: Dean of Oxford College/Professor of Biology (since 1987), Emory University, Oxford, GA 30267, USA **Date of Birth:** December 25, 1928 **Education:** B.S. Biology (1956), University of Massachusetts; Ph.D. Botany (1959), Washington University **Previous Positions:** Assistant through Full Professor of Biology (since 1959), Emory University, Oxford, GA **Discipline:** Biology **Related Areas of Interest:** Religion and Science; Evolution Theory and Religion.

Selected Publications

_____. "Ethical and Philosophical Aspects of Biodiversity Conservation." In *Biological Diversity: Problems and Challenges*, by S. K. Majumbar, et. al., 199-208. Pennsylvania: The Pennsylvania Academy of Science, 1993.

Murphy, George L.

Present Position and Address: Pastor (since 1984), St. Mark Lutheran Church, 158 North Avenue, Box 201, Tallmadge, OH 44278, USA **Work Phone:** (216) 633-3718 **Date of Birth:** December 24, 1942 **Education:** B.S. Physics (*magna cum laude*, 1963), Ohio University; Ph.D. Physics (1972), Johns Hopkins University; M.Div. Thesis - "The Trademark of God: An Adult Curriculum on Creation, Evolution, and Christology" (1983), Wartburg Seminary **Awards and Honors:** (1993), Templeton Foundation Humility Theology paper award for "Chiasmic Cosmology: An Approach to the Science-Theology Dialogue" **Previous Positions:** Instructor and Assistant Professor of Physics (1968-1975), Westminster College, PA; Lecturer in Physics (1975-77), University of Western Australia; Assistant Professor of Physics (1977-79,80, 83), Luther College; Part-time Instructor (1979), Loras College/(1981-83), Wartburg Seminary/(1994), Trinity Seminary; Pastoral Intern (1981-82), St. Andrew's Lutheran Church, Ames, IA **Selected Memberships:** The American Physical Society; Fellow, American Scientific Affiliation; Member, The Center for Theology and the Natural Sciences; Steering Committee, ELCA Work Group on Science and Technology **Discipline:** Pastoral Ministry; Physics **Related Areas of Interest:** Cosmology/Astrophysics and Theology.

Selected Publications: His bibliography lists 24 articles in theoretical physics and 35 in science and theology.

_____. "Big Bang Model without Singularities." *Physical Review* D8 (1973): 4231ff.
_____. "A Positive Approach to Creation." *Journal of the American Scientific Affiliation (JASA)* 32 (1980): 230ff.
_____. *The Trademark of God.* Wilton, CT: Morehouse-Barlow, 1986.
_____. "A Theological Argument for Evolution." *JASA* 38 (1986): 19ff.
_____. "What Can We Learn from Einstein about Religious Language?" *Currents in Theology and Mission* 15 (1988): 342ff.
_____. "Chiasmic Cosmology as the Context for Bioethics." *Perspectives on Science and Christian Faith* 42 (1990): 94ff.
_____. "Cosmology as an Agenda Item for the Eighth Council." *Dialog* 30 (1991): 290ff.
_____. "Time, Thermodynamics, and Theology." *Zygon* 26 (1991): 359ff.
_____. "Chiasmic Cosmology: An Approach to the Science-Theology Dialogue." *Trinity Seminary Review* 13 (Fall 1991): 83ff.
_____. "The Incarnation as a Theanthropic Principle." *Word & World* 13 (1993): 256ff.

Murphy, Nancey C.

Present Position and Address: Associate Professor of Christian Philosophy, Fuller Theological Seminary, 135 N. Oakland Ave., Pasadena, CA, USA; 1494 E. Brae Burn Rd., Altadena, CA 91001, USA **Work Phone:** (818) 584-5253 **Date of Birth:** June 12, 1951 **Education:** B.A. Psychology and Philosophy (*summa cum laude*, 1973), Creighton University, Omaha, NE; Ph.D. Philosophy of Science (1980), University of California - Berkeley; Th.D. Theology and Philosophy of Religion - Thesis: "Theology in the Age of Probable Reasoning," (1987), Graduate Theological Union, Berkeley, CA **Awards and Honors:** American Academy of Religion Award for Excellence for *Theology in the Age of Scientific Reasoning* **Previous Positions:** Visiting Lecturer (1986), Lutheran School of Theology, Chicago; Lecturer in Philosophy (1987-88), Dominican School of Philosophy and Theology, Berkeley; Visiting Assistant Professor of Religion (1988-89), Whittier College **Selected Memberships:** Chair of Board of Directors, Center for Theology and the Natural Sciences **Discipline:** Philosophy of Religion; Theology **Related Areas of Interest:** Modern and Postmodern Philosophy; Philosophy of Science; Relation between Religion and Science.

Selected Publications:

_____. "Acceptability Criteria for Work in Theology and Science?" *Zygon* (September 1987).
_____. "Theology: An Experimental Science?" *Perspectives in Religious Studies* (Summer 1988).
_____. "Truth, Relativism, and Crossword Puzzles." *Zygon* (September 1989).
_____. "Another Look at Novel Facts." *Studies in History and Philosophy of Science* (1989).
_____. "Theology and the Social Sciences — Discipline and Antidiscipline." *Zygon* (1990).
_____. "Scientific Realism and Postmodern Philosophy." *British Journal for the Philosophy of Science* (1990).
_____. *Theology in the Age of Scientific Reasoning.* Cornell University Press, 1990.
_____, Robert Russell and C. J. Isham, eds. *Quantum Cosmology and the Laws of Nature: Scientific Perspectives on Divine Action.* Vatican Observatory, 1993; distributed in US by University of Notre Dame Press.
_____. "Philosophical Fractals; or, History as Metaphilosophy." *Studies in History and Philosophy of Science* 24, 3 (1993).
_____. "The Limits of Pragmatism and the Limits of Realism." *Zygon* (1993).

Musschenga, A. W.

Present Position and Address: Director (since 1979), Bezinningscentrum (Center for the study of Science, Society and Religion), Vrije Universiteit, P.O. Box 7161, 1007 MC Amsterdam, The Netherlands **Concurrent Positions:** Special Professor in Social Ethics, Department of Philosophy, Vrije Universiteit **Date of Birth:** June 6, 1950 **Languages Spoken:** Dutch, English, German **Education:** D.Theol. (1979), Vrije Universiteit **Discipline:** Theology; Ethics **Related Areas of Interest:** Science and Theology; Medical Ethics; Religion and Morality; Law and Morality.

Selected Publications:

_____, D. Gosling, eds. *Science Education and Ethical Values*. Geneva, 1985.
_____, C. Houtman, S. de Jong, and W. J. van der Steen. *Schepping en evolutie. Het creationisme een alternatief?* (Creation and evolution. Is creationism an alternative for evolution theory?). Kampen, 1986.
_____. "Boedelscheiding een noodzaak? (Is the separation of theology and science necessary?)" *Gereformeerd Theologisch Tijdschrift* 86 (1986): 131-55.

Musser, Donald W.

Present Position and Address: Professor of Religious Studies (since 1990), Stetson University, Campus Box 8351, DeLand, FL 32720, USA; (Home) 1521 Woodside Drive, DeLand, FL 32720, USA **Work Phone:** (904) 822-8930 **Home Phone:** (904) 736-7057 **Date of Birth:** June 8, 1942 **Education:** B.S. Chemical Engineering, Chemistry, Mathematics (1964), University of Pittsburgh; M.Div. Theology, Biblical Studies, History of Christianity (1968), Southern Baptist Theological Seminary; Ph.D. Theology, Philosophy of Religion, Religion and Culture (1981), University of Chicago Divinity School **Previous Positions:** Chemical Engineer: Hooker Corporation, Niagara Falls, NY (1963)/Exxon Corporation, Linden, NJ (1964-65); Pastor, Veale Creek Baptist Church (1966-68)/Emmanuel Baptist Church, Pittsburgh (1968-1974); Assistant Professor of Religion (1978-1984)/Associate Professor of Religion (1984-1990), Stetson University **Editorial Positions:** Book Review Editor (1977-78), *Zygon* **Selected Memberships:** American Academy of Religion; National Association of Baptist Professors of Religion; North American Paul Tillich Society; Society for the Study of Southern Literature; Michael Polanyi Society **Discipline:** Theology; Ministry; Chemical Engineering **Related Areas of Interest:** Science and Christianity; Philosophy of Religion; Scientific Theology.

Selected Publications:

_____. "Two Types of Scientific Theology: Burhoe and Nygren." *Zygon* 12 (March 1977): 72-87.
_____. "Foundations for Conversations between Science and Religion." Paper presented at the California State Polytechnic University, Pomona, April 1985; and College Theology Society, Florida Region, September 1985.
_____. "The Relevance of Science to Theology in Burhoe, Gilkey, and Polanyi." Paper presented at annual meeting of the American Academy of Religion, Atlanta, GA, 1986.
_____. "Tillich's Epistemology: An Assessment from a Post-Empiricist Standpoint." *Soundings* 69 (Winter 1986): 423-35.
_____. "Response to Darrell Fasching's, 'Technology Transcendence, and Public Policy.'" Paper Presented at College Theology Society, Florida Region, St. Petersburg, February 1987.
_____. "Creation Science." In *A New Handbook of Christian Theology*, ed. Joseph Price and Donald W. Musser. Nashville, TN: Abingdon, 1992.

Myers, David G.

Present Position and Address: John Dirk Werkman Professor of Psychology (since 1975), Hope College, Holland, MI 49422-9000, USA **Work Phone:** (616) 395-7730 **E-Mail:** myers@hope.edu **Date of Birth:** September 20, 1942 **Education:** B.A. Chemistry (*magna cum laude*, 1964), Whitworth

College; M.A. Psychology (1966)/Ph.D. Psychology (1967), University of Iowa **Honorary Degrees:** D. Human Letters (1987), Northwestern College/Whitworth College (1989) **Awards and Honors:** Allport Prize, Society for the Psychological Study of Social Issues (1978) **Previous Positions:** Assistant Professor (1967-70)/Associate Professor (1970-75), Hope College; Visiting Scholar (1985-86), University of St. Andrews, Scotland **Selected Memberships:** Fellow, American Psychological Association; American Psychological Society; Elder, Reformed Church in America **Discipline:** Psychology **Related Areas of Interest:** Social Psychology; Psychology and Christian Belief; American Social Trends.

Selected Publications: Scientific articles and chapters in 30 books and periodicals.

_____. *The Human Puzzle: Psychological Research and Christian Belief.* New York: Harper & Row, 1978.
_____. *The Inflated Self: Human Illusions and the Biblical Call to Hope.* Seabury/Winston, 1980; paperback, 1981.
_____, Ludwig, Westphal, and Klay. *Inflation, Poortalk and the Gospel.* Valley Forge, PA: Judson Press, 1981.
_____, M. Bolt. *The Human Connection.* Downers Grove, IL: InterVarsity, 1984; UK: Hodder/Stoughton, 1985.
_____, M. Jeeves. *Psychology Through the Eyes of Faith.* New York: Harper & Row, 1987.
_____. *Social Psychology.* 4th ed. New York: McGraw-Hill, 1993.
_____. *Exploring Psychology.* 2d ed. New York: Worth Publishers, 1993.
_____. *The Pursuit of Happiness: Who Is Happy-and Why.* New York: William Morrow, 1992; New York: Avon soft-cover, 1993.
_____. *Exploring Social Psychology.* New York: McGraw-Hill, 1994.
_____. *Psychology.* 4th ed. New York: Worth Publishers, 1995.

Needleman, Jacob

Present Position and Address: Professor of Philosophy, San Francisco State University, School of Humanities, 1600 Holloway Avenue, San Francisco, CA 94132, USA **Concurrent Positions:** In addition to his teaching and writing he serves as a consultant in the fields of Psychology, Education Medical Ethics, Philanthropy and Business **Date of Birth:** October 6, 1934 **Languages Spoken:** English, German, French **Education:** B.A. Philosophy (1956), Harvard University; Fullbright Scholarship (1957-58), University of Freiburg, Germany; Ph.D. Philosophy (1961), Yale University; Clinical Psychology Trainee (1960-61), West Haven VA Hospital, CT **Previous Positions:** Research Associate (1961-62), Rockefeller Institute, NYC; Taught in Department of Philosophy (since 1962), San Francisco State University; Director, Center for the Study of New Religious Movements/Visiting Professor of Comparative Religion (1977-83), Graduate Theological Union, Berkeley, CA; Adjunct Professor (1981-84), Department of Psychiatry, University of California Medical Center; Visiting Lecturer (1982-85), Pacific Medical Center, San Francisco; Adjunct Professor of Medical Ethics (since 1984), Institute for Health Policy Studies, School of Medicine, University of California - San Francisco **Editorial Positions:** General Editor, *The Penguin Metaphysical Library* - a collection of 16 texts in the area of ancient and modern mysticism, Religious metaphysics and traditional studies; Editorial Board, *The Macmillan Encyclopedia of Religion* **Discipline:** Philosophy **Related Areas of Interest:** Comparative Religion; Cultural Criticism; Ethics; The relationship between Philosophy, Psychology and Religion.

Selected Publications: His bibliography lists 16 books, and over 20 articles.

_____. *A Sense of the Cosmos*. New York: Doubleday, 1975.
_____. *Lost Christianity*. New York: Doubleday, 1980.
_____. *The Heart of Philosophy*. New York: Knopf, 1982.
_____. *The Way of the Physician*. New York: Harper and Row, 1985.
_____. *Money and the Meaning of Life*. New York: Doubleday, 1991.

Neidhardt, Walter Jim *(Deceased)*

Former Position and Address: Associate Professor of Physics (since 1967), Newark College of Engineering/New Jersey Institute of Technology (NJIT), Newark, NJ 07102, USA; (Home) 146 Park Avenue, Randolph, NJ 078869, USA **Work Phone:** (201) 596-3555 **Home Phone:** (201) 584-0436 **Date of Birth:** June 19, 1934 **Education:** M.E. Mechanical Engineering and Physics (1956)/M.S. Physics (1958)/Ph.D. Physics (1962), Stevens Institute of Technology **Previous Positions:** Research Associate (Summers 1958, 59), Brookhaven National Laboratory, NY; Research Assistant (1959-61)/Instructor in Physics (1961-62), Stevens Institute of Technology, NJ; Instructor in Physics (1962-63)/Assistant Professor (1963-67), Newark College of Engineering, Newark, NJ **Editorial Positions:** Consulting editor (since 1968), *Journal of the American Scientific Affiliation*, (*Perspectives on Science and Christian Faith*) **Selected Memberships:** Fellow, American Scientific Affiliation; American

Physical Society; American Association for the Advancement of Science; New York Academy of Science; Institute for Theological Encounter with Science and Technology (ITEST); The Center for Theology and the Natural Sciences (CTNS); Institute on Religion in an Age of Science (IRAS); The Victoria Institute; Interdisciplinary Biblical Research Institute (IBRI) **Discipline:** Physics - Quantum Physics and Systems Theory **Related Areas of Interest:** The integration of Scientific, Philosophical, and Religious Perspectives, all being forms of personal knowledge as ably pointed out by the scientist-philosopher, Michael Polanyi.

Selected Publications: He has published 48 professional papers.

_____. "Faith and Human Understanding." *Journal of the American Scientific Affiliation (JASA)* 21, 1 (1969): 9-15.
_____. "The Open-Endedness of Scientific Truth." IBRI Research Report No. 17 (1983).
_____. "Personal Knowledge: A Communication-Oriented Model of Exploration and Discovery." IBRI Research Report No. 18 (1983).
_____. "Realistic Faith Seeking Understanding - A Structured Model of Human Knowing." *JASA* 36, 1 (1984): 42-5.
_____. "The Anthropic Principle: A Religious Response." *JASA* (December 1984): 201-7.
_____. "The Creative Dialogue Between Human Intelligibility and Reality - Relational Aspects of Natural Science and Theology." *The Asbury Theological Journal* 41, 2 (1986): 59-83.
_____. "Thomas F. Torrance's Integration of Judeo-Christian Theology and Natural Science: Some Key Themes." *Perspectives on Science and Christian Faith (PSCF)* 41, 2 (1989): 87-98.
_____. Introduction to *The Christian Frame of Mind*, by T. F. Torrance. Colorado Springs: Helmers & Howard, 1989.
_____. "One Scientist's Reflections on the Contributions of Harold P. Nebelsick (1925-1989) to the Theology-Science Dialogue." In *Glaube und Denken, The 1990 Yearbook of the Karl Heim Society*, 20-47. Moers, Germany: Brendon Verlag, 1990.
_____, Lee Wyatt. "Judeo-Christian Theology and Natural Science: Analogies - Agenda for Future Research." *PSCF* 43, 1 (1991): 14-28.

Nelson, J. Robert

Present Position and Address: Senior Research Fellow (since 1992), Institute of Religion, Texas Medical Center, 1129 Wilkins Street, Houston, TX 77030, USA **Date of Birth:** August 21, 1920 **Languages Spoken:** English, French, German **Education:** A.B. (1941), DePauw University; B.D. (1944), Yale University; D.theol. (1951), Universität Zürich **Honorary Degrees:** LHD (1960), DePauw University; DD (1964), Ohio Wesleyan University; LLD (1969), Loyola, Chicago; DH (1985), Hellenic University **Awards and Honors:** Phi Beta Kappa **Previous Positions:** Executive Secretary (1953-57), Faith and Order Commission, World Council of Churches; Professor of Theology and Dean (1957-60), Vanderbilt Divinity School; Visiting Professor of Ecumenics (1960-61), Princeton Theological Seminary; Professor of Theology (1962-65), Oberlin Graduate School of Theology; Professor of Theology and Dean (1965-84), Boston University School of Theology; Director (1985-92), Institute of Religion, Texas Medical Center **Editorial Positions:** Editorial Board, *Human Gene Therapy*; *Journal of Ecumenical Studies* **Selected Memberships:** Fellow, American Academy of Arts and Sciences; American Theological Society (past President); North American Academy of Ecumenists (past President); Société Européenne de Culture, Venice (vice-president) Society of Health and Human Values; Institute on Religion in an Age of Science; National Council of Churches Faith and Order Commission **Discipline:** Systematic (ecumenical) Theology; Bioethics; Medical Humanities and Ethics **Related Areas of Interest:** All aspects of Ecumenism; Theological understanding of human life; Genetics.

Selected Publications: His selected bibliography lists over 50 publications since 1952, most of which are relevant to this area.

_____. "Mechanistic Mischief and Dualistic Dangers in a Scientific Society." Nobel Lecture. In *Responsible Science*, ed. K. Byrne, 93-120. San Francisco: Harper & Row, 1986.
_____. "Genetic Science for Human Benefit." Adopted policy statement of the National Council of Churches. Brochure (1986).
___ ___. "Organ Harvesting Creates a Moral Dilemma." *Newsday* (February 22, 1988).
_____. "Genetics and Theology: A Complementarity?" *The Christian Century* 105, 13 (1988): 188-9.
_____. "The Ecumenical Challenge of Ethical Issues." *Origins* 18, 25 (1989): 761-9.
_____. "The Role of Religion in the Analysis of Human Gene Therapy." *Human Gene Therapy* 1, 1 (1990).
_____, editor. *Life as Liberty, Life as Trust*. Grand Rapids: Eerdmans, 1992.
_____. *Human Life. A Biblical Basis for Bioethics*. Philadelphia: Fortress Press, 1984.
_____. *Science and Our Troubled Conscience*. Philadelphia: Fortress Press, 1980.
_____. *On the New Frontiers of Genetics and Religion*. Grand Rapids: Eerdmans, 1994.

Nelson, James S.

Present Position and Address: Associate Professor of Religion and Philosophy (since 1972), North Park College, 3225 W. Foster Avenue, Chicago, IL 60625, USA **Date of Birth:** June 10, 1937 **Education:** B.A. (1959), Bethel College, St. Paul, MN; Ph.D. (1968), Kings College, Aberdeen, UK **Editorial Positions:** Book Review Editor, *Zygon: A Journal of Science and Religion* **Selected Memberships:** Board Member, Chicago Center for Religion and Science **Discipline:** Systematic Theology **Related Areas of Interest:** Science and Religion.

Selected Publications:

_____. "Does Science Clarify God's Relation to the World?" *Zygon* (December 1991).
_____. "Questions for Theology Relating to Christian Love and Bio-Cultural Evolution." In *Bio-Cultural Evolution, Theology, and Evolution*. Loccum, Germany, 1994.
_____. "God's Action: Is it Credible?" *Zygon* (June 1995).

Nethöfel, Wolfgang

Present Position and Address: Professor of Social Ethics (since 1993), University of Marburg; Director of Institut für Wirbdrafts und Soriulethik, Rostock (since 1992) Hansastrasse 40, D-20144 Hamburg 13, Germany **Work Phone:** (040) 41 85 02 **Date of Birth:** May 26, 1946 **Languages Spoken:** German, French, some Spanish **Education:** Fakultätsexamen theol. (1973); Staatsexamen (Deutsch/Evangelische Religion, 1974); Dr. theol. (1982); Habilitation (1985); Gestalt-Therapist (1986) **Previous Positions:** Wissenschaftlicher Assistent (1977)/ Hochschulassistent (1980)/Privatdozent (1985)/Akademischer Oberrat (1989), Institut für Systematische Theologie und Sozialethik der Universität Kiel; In between: Lehrstuhlvertretungen, Universität Wuppertal (1986-87); Frankfurt (1988-89); Hamburg (1989-90) **Selected Memberships:** Deutsch-Skandinavische Gesellschaft für Religionsphilosophie **Discipline:** Systematic Theology (Dogmatics and Ethics) **Related Areas of Interest:** Theory of Science; Open Systems; Biology and Epistemology; Moral/Social/Technological Assessment of Science **Current Areas of Research:** Information-Ethics; Bioethics; Medical Ethics; Business Ethics.

Selected Publications:

_____. "Zwischen Ökonomie, Ökologie und Ökumene. Theologische Verantwortung für die Natur." *Ökumenische Rundschau* 36 (1987): 17-32.
_____. "Creatio, Creatura, Creativitas. Im Spannungsfeld zwischen Schöpfungslehre und Kreativitätsforschung." *Berliner Theologische Zeitschrift* 5 (1988): 68-84. "Creativity" in Science, Psychology and Theology.

_____. "Theologische Hermeneutik in der Postmoderne." *Neue Zeitschrift für Systematische Theologie* 29 (1987): 210-27. The impact of paradigm shifts in the media and science on Hermeneutics.

_____. "Vom Mythos zu den Medien. Christliche Identität im konsensuellen Wandel." In *Mythos und Rationalität*, ed. Hans Heinrich Schmid, 310-32. Gütersloh, 1988. Impact of paradigm shift in media and science on Christian identity.

_____. "Biotechnik zwischen Schöpferglauben und schöpferischem Handeln." *Evangelische Theologie* 49 (1989): 179-99. Bioethics in Christian perspective.

_____. "Dri Nerausforherung der Sdidpfungstheologie darzh die Praxis einen Sdiepfumpethink." In *Unsere Welt — Gottes Schöpfung*. Wilfred Härle, Manfred Marquardt, Wolfgang Nethöfel, Editors. 297-323. Marburg 1992. Impact of theology of creation on "ethics of creation."

_____. "Theologische Hermenutik. Vorn Mythos zie den Medien." (NBST9) *Neubiroher-Vluyn* 1992. Impact of paradigm shifts in the media and science on Christian identity.

Neuhouser, David L.

Present Position and Address: Professor of Mathematics (since 1971), Taylor University, Upland, IN; (Home) 910 S. Main, Upland, IN 46989, USA **Date of Birth:** March 28, 1933 **Education:** B.S. (1955), Manchester College, IN; M.S. (1959), University of Illinois; Ph.D. Mathematics (1966), Florida State University **Awards and Honors:** Distinguished Professor Award (1976)/Sears-Roebuck Foundation Teaching Excellence and Campus Leadership Award (1989), Taylor University **Previous Positions:** Teacher, Iowa Mennonite School, Kalona, Iowa (1955-57)/Huntertown High School in Indiana (1957-58); Mathematics Professor (1959-71)/Department Head (1966-71), Manchester College; Mathematics Department Head (1971-85)/Director of Honors Program (1978-83)Taylor University **Church and Community Service:** Member (since 1972), Upland Evangelical Mennonite Church, (served as Church Chairman, Deacon, Sunday School Teacher and on Manual Revision Committee); Sunday School Teacher, Trinity United Methodist Church (1978-79)/Upland United Methodist Church (since 1983); Has given many mathematics talks at High Schools in northeastern Indiana **Selected Memberships:** Mathematical Association of America; National Council of Teachers of Mathematics; Association of Christians in the Mathematical Sciences; American Scientific Affiliation (President, Indiana Section 1976-77); Kappa Mu Epsilon; Pi Mu Epsilon; Sigma Pi Sigma **Discipline:** Mathematics **Related Areas of Interest:** Mathematics and Faith/Theology; Reality and Truth in Mathematics and Religion.

Selected Publications: His bibliography lists 7 publications and 12 presented papers.

_____. "Understanding Proofs in Mathematics and Faith." *Universitas* (May 1973).

_____. "An Experiment in Individualization." *The Illinois Mathematics Teacher* (November 1974).

_____. Review of *Beyond Science*, by Denis Alexander. *Christian Scholar's Review* (November 1975).

_____. "Truth: Mathematical and Biblical." *Journal of American Scientific Affiliation* (March 1979).

_____. "Reality and Imagination in Mathematics and Religion." In *Proceedings of the Conference on Mathematics from a Christian Perspective, held at Wheaton College, June 3-6, 1981.*

_____. "Beauty in Mathematics: Some Theological Implications." In *Proceedings of the Seventh Conference on Mathematics from a Christian Perspective, held at Messiah College, May 31-June 3, 1989.*

Neuner, Peter

Present Position and Address: Professor of Dogmatics (since 1985), University of Munich; Grünwalderstrasse 103a, D-8000 München 90, Germany **Date of Birth:** March 23, 1941 **Education:** Grad. (1965)/Dr. theol. (1976)/Dr. theol. habil (1978), University of Munich **Previous Positions:** Professor of Fundamental Theology and Ecumenical Theology (1980-85), University of Passau **Discipline:** Dogmatics; Systematic Theology (Catholic) **Related Areas of Interest:** Catholic Modernism.

Selected Publications: His bibliography includes 145 entries.

_____. Rezension: K. E. Apfelbacher. *Frömmigkeit und Wissenschaft. Ernst Troeltsch und sein theologisches Programm*. München-Paderborn-Wien, 1978. Reprint, in *Ökumenische Rundschau* 28: 87-8 (1979).
_____. "Religion - Mystik - Wissenschaft." *Stimmen der Zeit* 197 (1979): 281-4.
_____. Rezension: J. Moltmann. *Gott in der Schöpfung. Ökologische Schöpfungslehre*. München, 1985. Reprint, in *Theologischer Literaturdienst* no. 2 (1986): 19.
_____. "Dialog als Methode der Ökumene." In *Vernunft des Glaubens. Wissenschaftliche Theologie und kirchliche Lehre*, ed. J. Rohls and G. Wenz, 670-87, Festschrift for W. Pannenberg. Göttingen: Vandenhoeck and Ruprecht, 1988.

Neville, Robert Cummings

Present Position and Address: Professor (since 1987), Departments of Religion and Philosophy; Dean (since 1988) Boston University, School of Theology, 745 Commonwealth Avenue, Boston, MA 02215, USA; (Home) 5 Cliff Road, Milton, MA 02186, USA **Concurrent Positions:** Ordained Elder, United Methodist Church **Home Phone:** (617) 698-4225 **Date of Birth:** May 1, 1939 **Education:** B.A. (*magna cum laude*, 1960)/M.A. (1962)/Ph.D. Philosophy (1963), Yale University **Previous Positions:** Instructor (1963-65), Department of Philosophy, Yale University; Visiting Lecturer in Education and Philosophy (1964-65), Wesleyan University, Middletown, CT; Assistant (1965-68)/Associate Professor (1968-73) of Philosophy, Fordham University, Bronx, NY; Associate for Behavioral Sciences (1971-73), Institute of Society, Ethics and the Life Sciences, Hastings, NY; Associate (1971-74)/Professor (1974-77) of Philosophy, State University of New York (SUNY) College - Purchase; Professor of Philosophy/Religious Studies (1978-87), SUNY - Stony Brook, NY **Editorial Positions:** Editorial Board member of among others, *Bioethics Newsletter / Social Philosophy Research Institute Book Series*; Associate Editor for *Behavioral and Neurological Sciences* in *The Encyclopedia of Bioethics*. NY: Macmillan-Free Press, 1978; Editor, SUNY Press series in Philosophy (1979-88)/Systematic Philosophy and Religious Studies (since 1979) **Selected Memberships:** American Philosophical Association; American Academy of Religion; American Theological Society; New Haven Theological Discussion Group; Society for the Study of Process Philosophy **Discipline:** Religion and Philosophy **Related Areas of Interest:** Metaphysics, Creation, Philosophy, Ethics, Theology and Society, and How They Relate.

Selected Publications: His bibliography lists over 95 articles and critical studies, 12 books and many reviews, most of which are relevant to this discussion.

_____. "Genetic Succession, Time, and Becoming." *Process Studies* 1, 3 (1971): 194-8.
_____. *The Cosmology of Freedom*. New Haven CT: Yale University Press, 1974.
_____. "Gene Therapy and the Ethics of Genetic Therapeutics." In *Proceedings of the New York Academy of Science, 1975*.
_____, associate editor. *The Behavioral and Neurological Sciences*. In *Encyclopedia of Bioethics*, ed. Warren Reich. New York: Macmillan-Free Press, 1978.
_____. *Creativity and God: A Challenge to Process Theology*. New York: Seabury Press, 1980.
_____. "From Nothing to Being: The Notion of Creation in Chinese and Western Thought." *Philosophy East and West* 30, 1 (1980): 21-34.
_____. "On the Relation of Christian to other Philosophies." In *Being and Truth: Essays in Honor of John Macquarrie*, ed. Alistair Kee and E. T. Long, 276-92. London: SCM Press, 1986.
_____. *Recovery of the Measure: Interpretation and Nature*. Albany, NY: SUNY Press, 1989.
_____. *God the Creator: On the Transcendence and Presence of God*. Chicago: University of Chicago Press, 1968. Reprint, with a new foreword, Albany, NY: SUNY Press, 1992.
_____. *Eternity and Time's Flow*. Albany, NY: SUNY Press

Newman, Robert Chapman

Present Position and Address: Director (since 1980), Interdisciplinary Biblical Research Institute; Professor of New Testament (since 1977), Biblical Theological Seminary, 200 N. Main Street, Hatfield, PA 19440, USA **Work Phone:** (215) 368-5000 **Fax Number:** (215) 368-7002 **Date of Birth:** April 2, 1941 **Education:** B.S. Physics (1963), Duke University; Ph.D. Astrophysics (1967), Cornell University; M.Div. (1970), Faith Theological Seminary; S.T.M. Old Testament (1975), Biblical Theological Seminary **Postgraduate Experience:** Postdoctoral Fellow (1967-68), Bartol Research Foundation **Previous Positions:** Physicist (GS-7, Summer 1963), US Weather Bureau; Associate Professor of Mathematics and Science (1968-71), Shelton College; Associate Professor of New Testament (1971-77), Biblical Theological Seminary **Selected Memberships:** Fellow, Interdisciplinary Biblical Research Institute (IBRI); Fellow, American Scientific Affiliation **Discipline:** Biblical Studies, New Testament; Christian Evidences; Interaction of Science and Christianity **Related Areas of Interest:** Origin of the Universe, Earth and Life; Mechanisms of Evolution; Cosmology and Quantum Theory.

Selected Publications:

_____. "Self-Reproducing Automata and the Origin of Life." *Perspectives on Science and Christian Faith* 40 (March 1988): 24-31.

_____, John A. Bloom, Perry G. Phillips, and John C. Studenroth. "The Status of Evolution as a Scientific Theory." *Origins Research* 12, 2 (1989): 8-9.

_____. "Are the Events in the Genesis Creation Account Set Forth in Chronological Order? Yes." In *The Genesis Debate: Persistent Questions About Creation and the Flood*, ed. R. Youngblood, 36-55. Nashville, TN: Thomas Nelson, 1986. Reprint, Grand Rapids: Baker, 1990.

_____. "Evangelicals and Modern Science." In *Evangelical Affirmations*, ed. Kenneth S. Kantzer and Carl F. H. Henry, 401-22. Grand Rapids: Zondervan/Academie, 1990.

_____, H. J. Eckelmann, Jr. *Genesis 1 and the Origin of the Earth*. Downers Grove, IL: InterVarsity, 1977. Reprint, Hatfield, PA: IBRI, 1991.

_____. "Inanimate Design as a Problem for Nontheistic Worldviews." "The Evidence of Cosmology." "Cosmogony, Genesis 1, and the Origin of the Earth." In *Evidence for Faith: Deciding the God Question*, ed. John W. Montgomery, 61-70, 71-91, 93-113. Dallas: Probe/Word, 1991.

_____. "An Ancient Historical Test of the Setterfield-Norman Hypothesis." *Creation Research Society Quarterly* 28 (September 1991): 77-8.

_____. "The Darwin Conversion Story: An Update." *Creation Research Society Quarterly* 29 (September 1992): 70-2.

Nicholi Jr., Armand Mayo

Present Position and Address: Clinical Associate in Psychiatry (since 1978), Massachusetts General Hospital; Associate Clinical Professor of Psychiatry (since 1987), Harvard Medical School; (Home) 209 Musterfield Road, Concord, MA 01742, USA **Education:** B.A. (1950), Cornell University; M.D. (1956), New York Medical College **Postgraduate Experience:** Intern in Surgery (1956-57), Cornell Surgical Division, Bellevue Hospital, NY; Psychiatric Resident (1957-58), Strong Memorial Hospital/Boston State Hospital (1958-59)/Massachusetts Mental Health Center (1959-60); Research Fellow (1960-62), Harvard University Health Services; American Board of Psychiatry and Neurology # 9812 (1968) **Previous Positions:** Assistant in Psychiatry (1964-73), Harvard Medical School; Lecturer in Social Relations (1969-71), Harvard University; Instructor in Psychiatry (1973-78), Massachusetts Mental Health Center; Clinical Instructor in Psychiatry (1978-84)/Assistant Clinical Professor of Psychiatry (1984-87), Harvard Medical School **Selected Memberships:** American Scientific Affiliation; American Association for the Advancement of Science; Fellow, American Psychiatric Association **Discipline:** Psychiatry and Neurology **Related Areas of Interest:** Relationship of Psychiatry and Theology.

Selected Publications:

_____. "Response to the Noble Lectures at Harvard University, by Robert N. Bellah." *Journal of Religious Intellect* 1, 2 (1984): 60.
_____. "Moral Maturity." *Journal of Pastoral Renewal* 10, 1 (1985): 12-15.
_____. "Moral Values and Mental Health." *Veritas Reconsidered* 3, 2 (1987): 1-15.

Nicholson, Philip

Present Position and Address: Part-time lecturer (since 1987), "Cross-Cultural Communication," at Showa Women's Institute, Boston (a Japanese-owned overseas campus); 52 Norfolk Road, Chestnut Hill, MA 02167, USA **Concurrent Positions:** Freelance writer and scholar (since 1976) **Work Phone:** (617) 566-7429 **Date of Birth:** October 26, 1944 **Education:** B.A. Philosophy (honors, 1966), Princeton University; J.D. (1969), Stanford University School of Law; M.S.P.H. (1973), Harvard School of Public Health **Previous Positions:** Administrative Officer (summers 1964, 65), St. John's Guild "Floating Hospital", NY; Community Organizer (summer 1968), Rural Legal-Medical Project, Tulare County, CA; Judge Advocate/Claims Officer/Base Labor Relations Specialist (1970-71), England AFB, LA; Legal Officer on multidisciplinary Social Actions Assistance Team (1971-73), AF/DPXST, HQ USAF, Pentagon, Washington, DC; Research Associate in Law and Psychiatry (1975-77), Harvard Mental Health Training Film Program, Harvard Medical School; Visiting Scholar (1984-85), Andover-Newton Theological School; Director (February 1988), Religious Futures Special Interest Subgroup, Church/Synagogue User Group, Boston Computer Society **Selected Memberships:** Dramatists Guild; National Writer's Union; Alliance of Independent Scholars; Institute on Religion in an Age of Science; Boston Computer Society; State Bar of California **Discipline:** Philosophy; Law; Public Health; Computers **Related Areas of Interest:** "Am working in a multidisciplinary field 'psychological and Religious futures' which asks the question - How are we, in the developed world, to live comfortably, work productively and share appropriately with the less fortunate, if we are stressed by the circumstances of life in the densely populated, fast-paced, technology-driven environments?" Also interested in the Neurological Correlates of Ecstatic Experiences; Society, Technology and Religion.

Selected Publications:

_____, M. Grace and D. Lipsett. *Your Self: An Introduction to Psychology.* New York: Hart Publishing Co., 1976.
_____. "Computer-Assisted Psychotherapy in Pastoral Contexts" and "Computers for Spiritual Growth: A Survey of Potential Application." Lecture presented at the 1st Annual Fair, Church and Synagogue Special Interest Group, Boston Computer Society, May 1988.
_____. "Technostress: An Emerging Opportunity for the Humanities." Lecture presented at Annual Meeting, Community College Humanities Association, Quincy, MA, November, 1988.
_____. "Conservation of Self in High-Tech Environments." Lecture presented at the 6th General Assembly of the World Future Society, Washington, DC, July, 1989.
_____. "The Cybernetics of Salvation: Systems Analysis, Computer Analogies, and Spiritual Insight." Unpublished article.

Nieznanski, Edward

Present Position and Address: Head of the Department of Logic (since 1982), Prorector (since 1990), Academy of Catholic Theology, Warsaw, Poland; ul. Capri 5 m. 42, PL-02-762 Warsaw, Poland **Date of Birth:** October 11, 1938 **Education:** Masters in Christian Philosophy, Aristotelian syllogistics (1962)/Ph.D. Philosophy and Logic (1969)/Habilitationsschrift, Dozent der Humanistischen Wissenschaften (1977); Professor of the humanities in domain of logic and methodology of science (1991), Academy of Catholic Theology in Warsaw **Previous Positions:** "Docent" Lecturer (appointed in 1979), Academy of Catholic Theology, Warsaw; Research Fellow (1979-1981), with Prof. Paul Weingartner, Institut für Wissenschaftstheorie des Internationalen Forschungszentrums für Grundlagen der Wissenschaften, Salzburg, Austria; Concurrently lectured at the University of Salzburg on "Spezielle Probleme der Logik (Logik der Gottesbeweise, Eine logische Theorie der Relationen; Logische Analyse Philosophischer Texte) **Discipline:** Philosophy **Related Areas of Interest:** Formal Logic; Semantics; Pragmatics; Theory and Logic of Models; Relational Theory, and Philosophy of Science.

Selected Publications: He has over 60 publications, and is the editor of the series *Miscellanea Logica* which is dedicated to applied logic.

_____. "Ein formalisierter Beweis für die Existenz eines ersten notwendigen Seienden." In *Philosophie als Wissenschaft*, ed. E. Morscher, 379-89. Bad Reichenhall: O. Neumaier, G. Zecha, 1981.

_____. "Logik und Gottesbeweise." In *Verantwortung, Wissenschaft, Fortschritt*, ed. M. Heitger, 75-82. Wien, 1981.

_____. "A Logical Analysis of Philosophical Arguments based on Leibniz's Principle of the Sufficient Reason of Existence." *Bulletin of the Section of Logic* 12 (1983): 188-93.

_____. "Logic of Belief and Faith of the 'Educated'" (in Polish). *Studia Philosophiae Christianae* 21, 1 (1985): 157-62.

_____. "Logical Analysis of Thomism. The Polish Programme that Originated in the 1930's." In *Initiatives in Logic*, ed. J. Srzednicki, 128-55. Dordrecht, 1987.

_____. "Einführung in die allgemein-polnische Philosophie. Der Thomismus." In *Christliche Philosophie im katholischen Denken des 19. und 20. Vol 2, Jahrhunderts*, ed. H. Schmidinger, 807-826. Graz, 1988.

_____. "Gründe, zureichende Gründe und Gottesbeweise ex contingentia mundi." In *Klassische Gottesbeweise in der Sieht der gegenwätigen Logic und Wissenschaftstheorie*, ed. F. Ricken, 124-39. Stuttgart, 1991.

_____. "Methoden - und Methodologiebegriffe in Auwendung auf die Pastoraltheologie." *Pastoraltheologische Informationen* no. 2 (1991): 189-200.

_____. "Axiologische Aspekte der autoritäten von Wissenschaftlern und der Wissenschaftler als Autoritäten." In *Werte in den Wissenschaften*, ed. F. M. Schmölz, 43-53. Innsbruck, 1991.

_____. "The Beginnings of Formalization in Theology." In *Advances in Scientific Philosophy*, ed. C. Schurz, 551-59. Amsterdam, 1991.

Nonneman, Arthur J.

Present Position and Address: Professor of Psychology and Director of Institutional Research and Planning (since 1991), Asbury College, 1 Macklem Drive, Wilmore, KY 40390, USA **Work Phone:** (606) 858-3511, ext. 2222 **Home Phone:** (606) 858-4563 **Fax Number:** (606) 858-3921 **Date of Birth:** January 17, 1943 **Languages Spoken:** English, some German **Education:** Graduated with honors (1965), Northwestern University **Awards and Honors:** Phi Beta Kappa; Phi Kappa Phi; Sigma Xi **Previous Positions:** Acting Director of Animal Behavior Research Laboratory (1972-73), Pennsylvania State University; Assistant Professor through Professor (1973-91)/Director of Behavioral and Neural Studies Program (1976-83)/Director of Graduate Studies (1983-89)/Chairman, Department of Psychology (1988-91), University of Kentucky **Selected Memberships:** American Psychological Association; American Psychological Society; Psychonomic Society; Society for Neuroscience; International Behavioral Neuroscience Society; International Society for Developmental Psychobiology; Society for the Scientific Study of Religion; American Scientific Affiliation; New York Academy of Science; Association for Supervision and Curriculum Development; Fellow, American Psychological Association (Division 6); Fellow, American Psychological Society **Discipline:** Physiological Psychology **Related Areas of Interest:** Neural and Behavioral Development; Age-Associated Neurodegenerative Diseases; Recovery from Brain Damage **Current Areas of Research:** Behavioral effects of impaired dopamine-system development; Behavioral effects of neural transplants in brain damaged adult and senescent rats.

Selected Publications: His total bibliography contains 1 book, 8 book chapters, 49 refereed journal articles, 6 published book reviews and 28 published abstracts.

_____, M. L. Woodruff, and R. H. Baisden. "Transplantation of Fetal Hippocampus May Prevent or Produce Behavioral Recovery from Hippocampal Lesions and Recovery Persists After Transplant Removal." In *Progress in Brain Research*. Vol. 86/87 of *Neural Transplantation: From Molecular Basis to Clinical Application*, ed. S. Dunnett and S. J. Richards, 367-76. Amsterdam: Elsevier, 1990.

_____. "Behavioral Effects of Selective and Nonselective Dopamine Agonists on Young Rats after Irreversible Antagonism of D-1 and/or D-2 Receptors." *Psychopharmacology* 3 (1993): 225-32.

_____, J. L. Neisewander, J. K. Rowlett, and M. T. Bardo. "Impaired Supersensitivity to Morphine Following Chronic Naltrexone Treatment in Senescent Rats." *Neurobiology of Aging* 15 (1994): 91-7.

_____, M. L. Woodruff, eds. *Toxin-Induced Models of Neurological Disorders.* New York: Plenum Press, 1994.

_____, M. L. Woodruff. "Animal Models and the Implications of Their Use." In *Toxin-Induced Models of Neurological Disorders*, ed., M. L. Woodruff and A. J. Nonneman. New York: Plenum Press, 1994.

_____, S. A. McDougall, and C. A. Crawford. "Age-Related Differences in Dopamine-Mediated Behaviors: Effects of Irreversible Antagonism." In *Neurobiological Plasticity: Learning, Development and Response to Brain Insult*, ed., N. Spear, L. Spear and M. Woodruff. New York: Erlbaum, 1995.

Personal Notes: His work is not an integration of science and theology but rather is "straight" or "mainline" science. He does, however, have an active interest in the interrelationships between, and the integration of science and theology, clearly evident in his teaching at a Christian liberal arts college rather than in his research.

Numbers, Ronald L.

Present Position and Address: William Coleman Professor of the History of Science and Medicine (since 1991), Department of the History of Medicine, University of Wisconsin, 1300 University Avenue, Madison, WI 53706, USA **Work Phone:** (608) 262-3701 **Date of Birth:** June 3, 1942 **Education:** B.A. Mathematics/Physics (1963), Southern College, TN; M.A. History (1965), Florida State University; Ph.D. History - History of Science (1969), University of California - Berkeley **Congresses and Conferences:** Organized: with D. C. Lindberg, "Christianity and Science," (April 23-25, 1981); with D. Amundsen, Historical Symposium on "Health/Medicine and the Faith Traditions," for Project X, Chicago, November 17-19, 1983 **Lectures Presented:** Invited lecturer to over 50 Colleges and Universities (since 1973) **Previous Positions:** Assistant Professor of History (1969-70), Andrews University; Assistant Professor of Humanities (1970-74), School of Medicine, Loma Linda University; Assistant (1974-76)/Associate Professor (1976-79)/Professor (1979-91) of the History of Medicine and the History of Science/Chairman (1977-81), Department of the History of Medicine, University of Wisconsin - Madison **Editorial Positions:** Editor, *Wisconsin Publications in the History of Science and Medicine* (since 1982); *Isis* (1989-93); Coeditor, *The Cambridge History of Science* (since 1994) **Selected Memberships:** Fellow (1983-85), Interdisciplinary Studies Program, The Menninger Foundation; Fellow (1973-74), Institute of the History of Medicine, Johns Hopkins University; American Society of Church History; History of Science Society; American Association for the History of Medicine; Fellow, Wesleyan/Holiness Studies Center (1987-90), Asbury Theological Seminary **Discipline:** History of Science/Medicine **Related Areas of Interest:** Christianity and Science; Religion and Medicine; Creationism.

Selected Publications:

_____. "Creationism in 20th-Century America." *Science* 217 (1982): 538-54.

_____. "The Dilemma of Evangelical Scientists." In *Evangelicalism and Modern America*, ed. George Marsden, 150-60. Grand Rapids: Eerdmans, 1984.

_____. "Science and Religion." *Osiris* 1 (1985): 59-80.

_____, David C. Lindberg, eds. *God and Nature: A History of the Encounter between Christianity and Science*. Berkeley and Los Angeles: University of California Press, 1986. Including chapter entitled "The Creationists." *Zygon* 22 (1987): 133-64.

_____, Darrel W. Amundsen, eds. *Caring and Curing: Health and Medicine in the Western Religious Traditions*. New York: Macmillan, 1986.

_____, J. S. Numbers. "Millerism and Madness: A Study of 'Religious Insanity' in Nineteenth-Century America." In *The Disappointed: Millerism and Millenarianism in the Nineteenth Century*, ed. R. L. Numbers and J. M. Butler, 92-117. Bloomington: Indiana University Press, 1987.

_____. "George Frederick Wright: From Christian Darwinist to Fundamentalist." *Isis* 79 (1988): 624-45.

_____. *The Creationists*. New York: Alfred A. Knopf, 1992. Paperback, Berkeley and Los Angeles: University of California Press, 1993.

_____, editor. *Creationism; in Twentieth-Century America*. 10 vols. Garland Publishing, 1995.

Oates, David D.

Present Position and Address: Assistant Professor of English (since 1985), Northrop University, Los Angeles, CA, USA; 3952 Albright Avenue, Los Angeles, CA 90066, USA **Date of Birth:** March 12, 1950 **Languages Spoken:** English, German **Education:** B.A. English (1972), Westmont College, Santa Barbara, CA; Ph.D. 19th Century British Literature (1978), Emory University **Previous Positions:** Assistant Professor of English (1978-80), Johnson C. Smith University, Charlotte, NC; Adjunct Professor of Communications and English (1980-84), Pepperdine University, Malibu, CA **Discipline:** English Literature and History of Ideas **Related Areas of Interest:** Nature Literature, Poetry, Environment.

Selected Publications:

_____. "Social Darwinism and Natural Theodicy." *Zygon* 23 (1988).
_____. *Earth Rising: Ecological Belief in an Age of Science*. Oregon State University Press, 1989.
_____. "Descendentalism: The Thoreauvian Inscape of the Environmental Movement." *Contemporary Philosophy* 12 (1989).
_____. "The Practice of the Presence of the Wild." *EarthLight: Spirituality and Ecology* 1 (1990).

Ogden, Philip M.

Present Position and Address: Professor of Physics (since 1976)/Chair (since 1974), Division of Natural Science and Mathematics, Roberts Wesleyan College, 2301 Westside Drive, Rochester, NY 14624-1997, USA **Work Phone:** (716) 594-6479 **Date of Birth:** February 3, 1938 **Education:** B.S. Physics and Mathematics (1959), Seattle Pacific University; Ph.D. Physics (1964), University of California - Berkeley **Postgraduate Experience:** Christian College Coalition Workshop (1986), Christianity and the History of Science, George Fox College; Christian College Coalition Workshop (1989), Christianity and the Technological Future, Seattle Pacific University **Awards and Honors:** *Who's Who in Frontiers of Science and Technology* **Previous Positions:** Assistant Professor (1964-66)/Associate Professor(1966-69)/Acting Chair (1968-69), Department of Physics, Seattle Pacific University; Associate Professor (1969-76), Roberts Wesleyan College **Selected Memberships:** Fellow and President-Elect (1973-75)/President (1975-77), Western New York Section, American Scientific Affiliation; Rochester Committee for Scientific Information; American Physical Society; American Association of Physics Teachers; North American Conference on Christianity and Ecology, World Future Society **Discipline:** Science - Physics; Mathematics **Related Areas of Interest:** Christianity and the History of Science; Christianity and Technology; Christianity and the Environment.

Selected Publications:

_____. "What Do You See?" *Light and Life* (July 8, 1975): 5-6.
_____. "The Christian and the Energy Crisis." *Prism* 3, 2 (Roberts Wesleyan College, March 1979): 3-4.

Ogden, Schubert Miles

Present Position and Address: Retired; 9652 West 89th Circle, Westminster, CO 80021-4406, USA
Date of Birth: March 2, 1928 **Languages Spoken:** English, German **Education:** A.B. (1950), Ohio
Wesleyan University; Johns Hopkins University (1950-51); B.D. (1954), The Divinity School, University of Chicago; Ph.D. (1958), Philipps Universität, Marburg, Germany (1962-63) **Honorary
Degrees:** Litt.D. (1965), Ohio Wesleyan University; L.H.D. (1983), University of Chicago **Lectures
Presented:** Sarum Lecturer (1980-81), Oxford University **Previous Positions:** University Professor
of Theology (1969-72), University of Chicago; Visiting Fellow (1977-78), Council of the Humanities,
Princeton University; Visiting Senior Fellow (1985-86), Institute for the Advanced Study of Religion,
University of Chicago; University Distinguished Professor of Theology/Director of the Graduate
Program in Religious Studies, Perkins School of Theology/Graduate Program in Religious Studies,
Southern Methodist University, TX; An ordained Methodist minister **Selected Memberships:** President (1976-77) and member (since 1957), American Academy of Religion; American Philosophical
Association (since 1959) ; American Theological Society (since 1968); Fellow (since 1985), American
Academy of Arts and Sciences **Discipline:** Theology **Related Areas of Interest:** Process Theology/Philosophy; Christian Faith in the Modern Scientific World.

Selected Publications:

_____. Review of *Modern Science and Christian Beliefs*, by Arthur F. Smethurst. *The Journal of Religion* 37 (1957):
267-8.
_____. "Theology and Philosophy: A New Phase of the Discussion." *Journal of Religion* 44 (1964): 1-16.
_____. Review of *The Phenomenon of Life: Toward a Philosophical Biology,* by Hans Jonas. *The Perkins School
of Theology Journal* 21, 2 and 3 (1968): 64-5.
_____. *The Reality of God and Other Essays*. 2d ed. New York: Harper & Row, 1977.
_____. "Linguistic Analysis and Theology." *Theologische Zeitschrift* 33 (1977): 318-25.
_____. "Ethical Queries about Modern Science." *Anticipation* 25 (1979): 15-17.
_____. "The Convergences of Science and Religion: A Response." *The Perkins School of Theology Journal* 36, 4
(1983): 15-20.

Oliver, Harold H.

Present Position and Address: Professor of Philosophical Theology (since 1986), Boston University,
School of Theology and Graduate School, Boston University School of Theology, 745 Commonwealth
Avenue, Boston, MA 02215, USA **Work Phone:** (617) 353-6493 **Home Phone:** (617) 729-8738 **Fax
Number:** (617) 353-3061 **E-Mail:** hholiver@bu.edu **Date of Birth:** October 9, 1930 **Education:** A.B.
(1952), Samford University; B.D. (1954), Southern Baptist Theological Seminary; Th.M. (1955),
Princeton Theological Seminary; Ph.D. (1961), The Graduate Institute of the Liberal Arts, Emory
University **Postgraduate Experience:** Faculty Fellowship (1963-64), Association of Theological
Schools, Tübingen University (Summer 1963)/Basel University (Fall 1963, Winter and Summer 1964);
Postdoctoral Fellowship for Cross-Disciplinary Study (Danforth Foundation, 1971-72) Visiting Fellow,
Institute for Theoretical Astronomy, Cambridge University; Studied philosophy with Ivor Leclerc
(1980), Emory University **Congresses and Conferences:** Commentator on a paper by Eric Chaisson,
a Harvard Astronomer (May 1-3, 1979), Unitarian-Universalist Advance Conference on Religion and
Science and the Sources of Ethical Motivation and Religious Experience, Harvard Divinity School;
Commentator on Noble Lectures by John Polkinghorne, (1992), Harvard University **Awards and
Honors:** Nominated for the Templeton Prize for Progress in Religion (1979) **Previous Positions:**
Instructor to Associate Professor (1957-65), Southeastern Baptist Theological Seminary, Wake Forest,
NC; Guest Professor (Summer 1965), Emory University; Associate Professor of New Testament
(1965-70)/Professor of New Testament and Theology (1970-86)/Acting Associate Dean (1984)/Director (1986-93) of D.Min. Program, Boston University, School of Theology; Theology; Chavanne

Visiting Professor of Religious Studies (1980-81), Rice University; Guest Professor (1993-94), Tufts University, MA **Editorial Positions:** Member of the Editorial Board (since 1979), *Zygon* **Selected Memberships:** American Theological Society; American Academy of Religion; American Association for the Advancement of Science; American Philosophical Association Metaphysical Society of America; International Society for Metaphysics; Fellow, The Royal Astronomical Society (London)**Discipline:** Theology; Philosophy **Related Areas of Interest:** Astronomy; Cosmology. Metaphysics as mediator of claims of Theology and Science.

Selected Publications:

_____. "The Complementarity of Theology and Cosmology." *Zygon* 13 (1978): 199-233. Reprint, in *Relatedness.* Macon, GA: Mercer University Press, 1984.
_____. "Karl Jaspers and Modern Physics." In *Karl Jaspers Today: Philosophy at the Threshold of the Future, Current Continental Research no. 010,* ed. L. H. Ehrlich and R. Wisser, 111-131. Washington, DC: Center for Advanced Research in Phenomenology and University Press of American, 1988.
_____. *Relatedness: Essays in Metaphysics and Theology.* Macon, GA: Mercer University Press, 1984.
_____. "The Neglect and Recovery of Nature in Twentieth Century Protestant Thought." *Journal of the American Academy of Religion* (1992): 60.

Olson, Everett C.

Present Position and Address: Professor Emeritus (since 1977), Zoology Department, University of California - Los Angeles, 405 Hilgard Avenue, Los Angeles, CA 90024-1606, USA **Date of Birth:** November 6, 1910 **Education:** B.S. Geology (1932)/M.S. Invertebrate Paleontology (1933)/Ph.D. Vertebrate Paleontology (1935), University of Chicago **Awards and Honors:** Paleontological Medal, 1980 **Previous Positions:** Professor of Vertebrate Paleontology and Chairman of Committee on Paleozoology, Department of Geology (Geophysical Sciences, 1935-69)/Associate Dean in Physical Sciences (1942-58) /Chairman (1958-62)/Head of College Program in Physical Sciences (1962-64), University of Chicago; Professor of Zoology (1969-77)/Chairman of Department of Zoology (1971-72), University of California - Los Angeles **Editorial Positions:** Editor (1952-58), *Evolution*; Editor (1962-67), *Journal of Geology*; Associate editor, *The Quarterly Review of Biology/Paleo. III*; On the editorial board of *Great Soviet Encyclopedia* - English Translation **Other Academic Experience:** Scientific governor (1958-69), Chicago Academy of Sciences; Member, International Committee for the First International Congress of Systematic and evolutionary Biology (Zoologists); Scientific Activities: Research Associate, Field Museum of Natural History and Los Angeles County Museum **Selected Memberships:** Subscribes to *Zygon*; Past President and member, Society of Vertebrate Paleontology (Distinguished Service Medal); Society for the Study of Evolution (past president); Fellow, Geological Society of America; Fellow, American Association for the Advancement Fellow, American Association for the Advancement of Science; Member, American Institute of Biological Sciences; Member, American Geological Institute; American Society of Zoologists; President (1979-81), Society of Systematic Zoology; Ecological Society; Society of Systematic Zoology; Ecological Society of America; Sigma XI; Paleonotology Society; Society of American Naturalists; National Academy of Sciences **Discipline:** Zoology; Biology; Geology **Related Areas of Interest:** The Evolution of Vertebrates, based mainly on Fish, Amphibians and Reptiles from the Permocarboniferous. The origin of Mammals. Biometrics in Paleontology; Comparative and Functional Morphology; The Correlation of Faunae of North America, Soviet Union and South Africa: Taxonomy, Biogeography and Evolution of Fossil Communities.

Selected Publications: His bibliography lists approximately 170 scientific papers in the field of vertebrate evolution.

_____, Agnes Whitmarsh. *Foreign Maps.* New York: Harper & Brothers, 1944.

_____, R. L. Miller. *Morphological Integration*. Chicago: University of Chicago Press, 1958.
_____. *The Evolution of Life*. London: Weidenfeld and Nicolson, 1965.
_____. "Dialectics in Evolutionary Studies." Review of *The Contemporary Status of Evolutionary Studies in the West*, by L. Davitashvili. *Evolution* 22 (1968): 426-36.
_____, Jane Robinson. *Concepts of Evolution*. Charles R. Merrill Publishing Company, 1975.
_____, M. Gordon, G. Bartholomew, and J. D. O'Connor, eds. *Zoology*. New York: Macmillan, 1976.
_____. "The Problem of Missing Links: Today and Yesterday." *Quarterly Review of Biology* 56 (1981): 405-42.
_____, Clifford Brunk. "The Evolutionary Synthesis Today: An Essay on Paleontology and Molecular Biology." In *Contributions to Geology, University of Wyoming*, Special Paper no. 3, ed. K. M. Flanagan and J. A. Lilligraven, 351-61. Laramie, WY, 1986.

Olson, Richard

Present Position and Address: Professor of History and Willard W. Keith Fellow in the Humanities (since 1976), Harvey Mudd College, Claremont, CA 91711, USA; (Home) 730 Lander Circle, Claremont, CA 91711, USA **Work Phone:** (714) 621-8000 ext. 4476 **Home Phone:** (909) 625-1279 **Date of Birth:** November 4, 1940 **Education:** B.S. Physics (1962), Harvey Mudd College, Claremont, CA; A.M. Physics (1963)/Ph.D. History of Science (1967), Harvard University **Previous Positions:** Instructor in History (1966-67)/Assistant to Associate Professor in History (1967-76), University of California - Santa Cruz **Discipline:** History of Science **Related Areas of Interest:** Anglican Natural Theology.

Selected Publications:

_____. "Sir John Leslie: 1766-1832, A Study of the Pursuit of the Exact Sciences in the Scottish Enlightenment." Ph.D. diss., Harvard University, 1967.
_____, editor. *Science as Metaphor: The Historical Roles of Scientific Theories in Forming Western Culture*. Belmont, CA: Wadsworth, 1971.
_____. *Scottish Philosophy and British Physics: 1750-1850; Foundations of the Victorian Scientific Style*. Princeton, NY: Princeton University Press, 1975. Italian trans. Bologna: Societa Editrice il Mulino, 1982.
_____. *Science Deified and Science Defied: The Historical Significance of Science in Western Culture: Vol. I, from the Bronze Age to c.1620*. University of California Press, 1982.
_____. "Tory-High Church Opposition to Scientism." In *The Uses of Science in the Age of Newton*, ed. John Burke, 171-204. University of California Press, 1983.
_____. "On the Nature of God's Existence, Wisdom, and Power: The Interplay of Organic and Mechanistic Imagery in Anglican Natural Theology: 1640-1740." In *Approaches to Organic Form*, ed. F. Burwick, 1-48. Boston Studies in the Philosophy of Science Series. Riedel, 1986.
_____. Introductory essays for 6 chapters in *Science and Culture in the Western Tradition*, ed. John Burke. Scottsdale, AZ: Gorsuch Scarisbrick Publishers, 1987.
_____. *Science Deified and Science Defied: The Historical Significance of Science in Western Culture: Vol. II, 1620-1820*. University of California Press, 1990.
_____. *The Emergence of the Social Sciences: 1642-1792*. Twayne, 1993.

Olson, Roger Eugene

Present Position and Address: Professor of Theology, Bethel College and Seminary, 3900 Bethel Drive, St. Paul, MN 55112, USA **Work Phone:** (612) 638-6210 **Date of Birth:** February 2, 1952 **Languages Spoken:** English, German **Previous Positions:** Assistant Professor of Theology (1982-84), Oral Roberts University, Tulsa, OK **Editorial Experience:** Editor, *Christian Scholar's Review*; Consulting editor, *Christianity Today* **Selected Memberships:** American Academy of Religion; Immediate Past President, Midwest Division, American Theological Society **Discipline:** Historical Theology **Related Areas of Interest:** Contemporary Theology; Evangelical-Liberal Dialogue; Narrative Theology **Current Areas of Research:** Postmodern Openings for Evangelical-Liberal Encounter and Dialogue; Textbook on History Theology.

Selected Publications: His bibliography contains 10 published articles; 5 book chapters and 1 coauthored book.

_____, Stanley J. Grenz. *Twentieth Century Theology: God and the World in a Transitional Age.* Grand Rapids: InterVarsity Press, 1992.
_____. "Trinity and Eschatology: The Historical Being of God in Jürgen Moltmann and Wolfhart Pannenberg." *Scottish Journal of Theology* 36, 2: 213-27.
_____. "Wolfhart Pannenberg's Doctrine of The Trinity." *Scottish Journal of Theology* 43: 175-206.

Osmond, Daniel Harcourt

Present Position and Address: Professor of Physiology, University of Toronto, Medical Sciences Building, Room 3334, 1 King's College Circle, Toronto, ONT M5S 1A8, Canada; (Home) 301 Rushton Road, Toronto, ONT M6C 2X8, Canada **Work Phone:** (416) 978-6048 **Home Phone:** (416) 653-5746 **Date of Birth:** August 22, 1934 **Languages Spoken:** English, French, Hebrew, Russian **Education** B.S.A. Animal Science (1958)/M.S.A. Endocrinology (1960), University of British Columbia; Ph.D. Path. Chem./Biochemistry and Physiology (1964), University of Toronto **Postgraduate Experience:** Fellow and Lecturer, Clinical Biochemistry (1964-66), University of Toronto; Research Fellow (1966-69), American Heart Association, Cleveland Clinic; Has received grants from Ontario Heart and Stroke Foundation since 1969 for continued research **Lectures Presented:** Five Lectures on Purpose and Meaning Sponsored by the Templeton Foundation and the American Scientific Affiliation given in Hollywood, CA, Oak Brook, IL, Seattle, WA, Atlanta, GA, and San Francisco, CA, Templeton Lecture Series (1994-95); Lecture/Discussion, "Creation ; and Evolution," Columbia Theological Seminary, Atlanta, GA/The Baptist Center, Georgia Institute of Technology, Atlanta, GA; "Teaching About Origins," Meeting with Faculty, University of Washington, Seattle, WA/Wheaton College, Wheaton, IL/Pepperdine University , Malibu, CA; "Science and Faith," Pepperdine University, Malibu, CA; From prorenin-renin to a "new pressor protein": an inter-disciplinary adventure. Seminar, Department of Pharmacology, University of Toronto; Renin-angiotensin system and the hypertensive renin-transgenic rat model, Cardiovascular Lecture Series (Collaborative Program), University of Toronto **Previous Positions:** Assistant (1964-74)/Associate (1974-80)/Full Professor of Physiology and Medicine/Member (since 1969), Graduate Faculty and the Institute of Medical Science, University of Toronto **Selected Memberships:** Canadian Biochemical/Physiological Societies; American Physiological Society; Elected Fellow, American Scientific Affiliation; American Societies of Hypertension/Nephrology International Hypertension Society; Elected fellow and past President, Canadian Scientific and Christian Affiliation; The Victoria Institute **Discipline:** Physiology and Medicine - with a specialty in Cardiovascular Disease, Hypertension **Related Areas of Interest:** Medicine/Science and Christian Ethics; Creation and Evolution; Use of Animals in Research.

Selected Publications:

_____. "Christian Witness and Influence in Health Science." *Ash Wednesday* 3, 1 (1981): 4-8.
_____. "Malice's Wonderland: Research Funding and Peer Review." *Canadian Association of University Teachers Bulletin* 31, 3 (1984): 31-7.
_____, J. De Koning, W. Graydon, A. Hedlin, D. Pierik, and D. Tinker. "University Malaise, or Who Was Martin Luther?" *University of Toronto Bulletin* (April 1986): 10p.
_____. "Animal Rights and Research," "Science and Ethics," "The Hippocratic Oath." In *Encyclopedia of Biblical and Christian Ethics,* ed. R. K. Harrison, 16-8, 365-7, 178-81. Nashville, TN: Thomas Nelson, 1987.
_____. "Traditional Values." University of Toronto Bulletin (April 1990): 8.
_____. "A Physiologist Looks at Purpose and Meaning in Life." Chap. in *Continuum,* ed. J. M. Templeton, 133-67. New York, 1994.

Oswald, Donald J.

Present Position and Address: Associate Professor of Economics, Department of Economics, California State University - Bakersfield, 9001 Stockdale Hwy, Bakersfield, CA 93311-1099, USA **Work Phone:** (805) 664-2465 **Fax Number:** (805) 664-2049 **Date of Birth:** October 15, 1946 **Languages Spoken:** English **Awards and Honors:** Omiron Delta Epsilon; Air Force Commendation Medal **Previous Positions:** Visiting Lecturer in Economics, Lincoln Christian College, Lincoln IL; Senior Consultant, Transportation Program, Ernst & Ernst, Washington, DC; Research Analyst, Office of the Assistant Secretary of Defense, Manpower and Reserve Affairs, Pentagon, Washington, DC; Major Command Economic analyst, Headquarters, Military Airlift Command, Scott Air Force Base, IL **Selected Memberships:** American Economic Association; Western Economic Association; Association of Social Economics; American Scientific Affiliation **Discipline:** Economics **Related Areas of Interest:** Economic Philosophy and Political Economy; Methodogy; Microeconomic Theory; Law and Economics **Current Areas of Research:** He is starting work on what may be the first of a series of books. The tentative Title: "The World View and Political of the Ancient World."

Selected Publications: His bibliography contains 3 articles in professional journals.

_____. "Metaphysical Beliefs and the Foundations of Modern Economics." *Review of Social Economy* 45 (December 1987): 276-97.
_____. "J. S. Mill's a priori Deductive Methodology: A Case Study in Post-Modern Philosophy of Science." *Review of Social Economy* 48 (Summer 1990): 172-97.
_____. "Metaphysical Beliefs and the Foundations of Smithian Political Economy." *History of Political Economy* 27, 3 (1995).

Pacholczyk, Andrzej G.

Present Position and Address: Professor, University of Arizona; Astronomer, Steward Observatory, Tucson, AZ 85721, USA **Phone:** (520) 297-6760 or (520) 621-6928 **Fax:** (520) 297-4797 or (520) 621-1532 **Concurrent Positions:** Director: Pachart Publishing House (since 1970)/Vatican Observatory Foundation (1986-89); Director and CEO (since 1984), Pachart Foundation (Non-Profit Organization) **Date of Birth:** September 23, 1935 **Languages Spoken:** English, Russian, Italian, Polish, French **Education:** Two master's degrees and a doctor's degree (1961), University of Warsaw, Poland **Congresses and Conferences:** Participant in seminars in the Apostolic Palace at Castel Gandolfo in the presence and with the participation of Pope John Paul II dealing with the relationship between Science, Religion and History (1982, 84, 86. 88) **Previous Positions:** Researched and/or lectured, Warsaw University; Astronomical Institute of the Polish Academy of Sciences; University of Turin, Italy; Institute of Physics of Earth of the USSR Academy of Science; Astronomical Institute; Institute of the Czechoslovak Academy of Science; Harvard College Observatory; Joint Institute for Laboratory Astrophysics, Boulder, CO; Arecibo Inonspheric Observatory, Puerto Rico; National Radio Astronomy Observatory; Istituto de Radioastronomia, Bologna, Italy; University of Sussex, England; University of Florence and the Vatican Observatory **Editorial Positions:** Director and Publisher (since 1982), *Philosophy in Science*; Publisher (since 1976), *The Astronomy Quarterly*; General Editor: *Astronomy and Astrophysics Series* (since 1972)/*History of Astronomy Series* (since 1984), both at Pachart Publishing House **Selected Memberships:** International Astronomical Union; Fellow, Royal Astronomical Society; American Astronomical Society; Acting Secretary (1960-62)/Secretary (1962-64), Polskie Towarzystwo Astronomiczne; Polskie Towarzystwo Fizyczne; Societa Astronomica Italiana **Discipline:** Astronomy and Physics **Related Areas of Interest:** Cosmology; The relationship between Science, Religion and History **Current Areas of Research:** His research initially included problems of gravitational instability, hydromagnetics and the interstellar medium, and later the physics of radio sources and nuclei of peculiar galaxies. With his research team, he discovered infrared radiation and optical variability in the nuclei of Seyfert galaxies. He is an originator and advocate of a model describing quasars and active galactic nuclei in terms of a dense cluster of many accreting black holes.

Selected Publications:

_____. "The Infinite Universe? III. Modern Science and the Beginning of the Universe." *The Astronomy Quarterly* 3 (1980): 127-35.
_____. *The Catastrophic Universe: An Essay in the Philosophy of Cosmology.* Vol 2 of *Philosophy in Science Library*, ed. M. Heller and J. Zycinski. Tucson: Pachart Publishing House, 1984.
_____, M. Heller and A. G. Pacholczyk. "Cosmology and Beyond." *The Astronomy Quarterly* 5 (1984): 43-51.

Page, William R.

Present Position and Address: Consultant to the Vermont Agency of Human Services and the Department of Corrections (on Long Range Planning); Fellow, Center for Psychology and Social

Change (Affiliate of Harvard Medical School); Box 482, RD-2, Orleans, VT **Work Phone:** (802) 525-3688 **Date of Birth:** October 5, 1920 **Education:** B.S. Chemical Engineering (1942), Tufts University; M.S. Chemical Engineering (1947)/Biology Courses (1982-84), Massachusetts Institute of Technology **Previous Positions:** Director (1960-85), Corporate Planning, Polaroid Corporation **Selected Memberships:** American Association for the Advancement of Science; Institute on Religion in an Age of Science; American Institute of Chemical Engineers **Discipline:** Chemical Engineering; Sociobiology **Related Areas of Interest:** Applications of Evolutionary Psychology to Religion and A New Understanding of Human Nature. (Book in process).

Selected Publications:

_____. "A Biological Perspective on Self-Responsibility and Global Survival." *Center for Psychology and Social Change* (1990).

Paloutzian, Raymond F.

Present Position and Address: Professor of Psychology, Westmont College, Santa Barbara, CA 93108, USA; (Home) 707 Palermo, Santa Barbara, CA 93105, USA **Work Phone:** (805) 565-6233 **Home Phone:** (805) 682-2888 **Fax Number:** (805) 565-6220 **E-Mail:** paloutz@westmont.edu **Date of Birth:** June 6, 1945 **Education:** B.A. Psychology (1968), California State University - Los Angeles; M.A. Experimental Psychology (1970)/Ph.D. Social Psychology (1972), Claremont Graduate School **Previous Positions:** Acting Assistant Professor (1972-73), Scripps College - The Claremont Colleges; Assistant to Associate Professor (1973-81), University of Idaho; Visiting Scholar (1979-80)/Visiting Associate Professor (Summer 1984), Stanford University; Associate to Full Professor (since 1981)/Department Chair (1984-89), Westmont College; Visiting Research Psychologist (1987-88), University of California - Santa Barbara **Selected Memberships:** Fellow, American Psychological Association; Fellow, American Psychological Society; Fellow, Western Psychological Association; Society for the Scientific Study of Religion; Society for Psychological Study of Social Issues; Society for the Advancement of Social Psychology **Discipline:** Psychology, Experimental and Social **Related Areas of Interest:** Psychology of Religion.

Selected Publications:

_____. "Purpose in Life and Value Changes Following Conversion." *Journal of Personality and Social Psychology* 41 (1981): 1153-60. Reprint, in *Psychology of Religion: Personalities, Problems, Possibilities*, ed. H. N. Malony, 479-90. Grand Rapids: Baker, 1991.
_____, C. W. Ellison. "Loneliness, Spiritual Well-Being, and the Quality of Life." In *Loneliness: A Sourcebook of Current Theory, Research and Therapy*, ed. L. A. Peplau and D. Perlman, 224-37. New York: Wiley-Interscience, 1982.
_____. *Invitation to the Psychology of Religion*. Glenview, IL: Scott, Foresman & Company, 1983. 2d ed. Needham Heights, MA: Allyn & Bacon, forthcoming.
_____, A. S. Janigian. "Interrelationship between Religiousness and Loneliness." *The Psychotherapy Patient* 2 (1986): 3-14. Reprint, in *Psychotherapy and the Lonely Patient*, ed. S. Natale, 3-14. New York: Haworth, 1986.
_____. "Relating Theologies and Belief Systems to Scientific Psychology: Recent Approaches and Perspectives." *Journal of Psychology and Theology* 17 (1989): 382-84.
_____. "Psychology of Religion as a Medium of Communication with General Psychology." *Journal of Psychology and Christianity* 5 (1986): 62-6. Reprint, in *Psychology of Religion: Personalities, Problems, Possibilities*, ed. H. N. Malony, 491-6. Grand Rapids: Baker, 1991.
_____, C. W. Ellison. *Manual for the Spiritual Well-Being Scale*. Nyack, NY: Life Advance, Inc., 1991.
_____, R. K. Bufford and C. W. Ellison. "Norms for the Spiritual Well-Being Scale." *Journal of Psychology and Theology* 19 (1991): 56-70.
_____. "Doing Psychology of Religion in Year APA 101." *Psychology of Religion* Newsletter 19, 1 (1994): 1-7.
_____, B. S. Smith. "The Utility of the Religion-as-Schema Model." *The International Journal for the Psychology of Religion* 5 (1995): 17-22.

Panitz, Michael E.

Present Position and Address: Rabbi (since 1982), Temple Beth Israel, Maywood, NJ; Assistant Professor of Jewish History (since 1989), Jewish Theological Seminary, Temple Beth Israel of Maywood, P.O. Box 782, Maywood, NJ 07607, USA **Date of Birth:** December 8, 1955 **Education:** B.A. (1977), University of Pennsylvania; M.A. (1981)/Rabbinic Ordination (1982)/Ph.D. (1989), Jewish Theological Seminary **Awards and Honors:** Awarded the Charles Revson Fellowship (1981-83) and the Memorial Foundation for Jewish Culture Fellowship **Previous Positions:** Lecturer (1985-89), Department of Theology, St. Peter's College; Lecturer (1988), Jewish History, Queens College; Associate Principal (July 1989), Jewish Theological Seminary **Selected Memberships:** Association of Jewish Studies; Medieval Academy of America; Rabbinical Assembly **Discipline:** Jewish History: Judaica **Related Areas of Interest:** Religion and Science; Intellectual History; Interreligious History.

Selected Publications:

_____. "New Heavens and a New Earth: Seventeenth to Nineteenth Century Jewish Responses to the New Astronomy." *Conservative Judaism* (Winter 1987/88).

Pannenberg, Wolfhart

Present Position and Address: Professor of Systematic Theology (since 1967)/Head of Institut für Fundamentaltheologie und Ökumene, FB Evangelische Theologie, Universität München, Schelling-strasse 3/III Vgb., D-8000 München 40, Germany **Work Phone:** 2180 3482 **Date of Birth:** October 2, 1928 **Education:** Doctorate in Theology (1953); Habilitation (1955) **Honorary Degrees:** D.D. - University of Glasgow, University of Manchester, Trinity College Dublin, and University of St. Andreias; Fellow, British Academy **Previous Positions:** Privatdozent (1955-58), Heidelberg; Professor of Systematic Theology (1958-61), Wuppertal; Professor (1961-67), University of Mainz **Selected Memberships:** Bavarian Academy of Sciences; Fellow, British Academy **Discipline:** Systematic Theology **Related Areas of Interest:** Philosophy of Science; History and Music; Hermeneutics and Modern Science.

Selected Publications:

_____, A. M. Klaus Müller. "Kontingenz und Naturgesetz." In *Erwägungen zu einer Theologie der Natur*, 33-80. Gütersloh, 1970.

_____. "Geist und Energie. Zur Phänomenologie Teilhards de Chardin." *Acta Teilhardiana* 8 (1971): 5-12.

_____. "The Doctrine of the Spirit and the Task of a Theology of Nature." *Theology* 75, 619 (1972): 8-21.

_____. *Theology and the Philosophy of Science*. London: Darton, Longman & Todd, 1976.

_____. "Christlicher Glaube und Naturverständnis." In *Gott - Geist - Materie. Theologie und Naturwissenschaft im Gespräch*, ed. J. Dietzfelbinger and L. Mohaupt, 11-13. Hamburg, 1980.

_____. "Theological Questions to Scientists." *Zygon* 16 (1981): 65-77. Reprint, in *The Sciences and Theology in the Twentieth Century*, ed. A. R. Peacocke, 297-9. Notre Dame, IN, 1981.

_____. "Gott und die Natur. Zur Geschichte der Auseinandersetzung zwischen Theologie und Wissenschaft." *Theologie und Philosophie* 58 (1983): 481-500.

_____. "The Doctrine of Creation and Modern Science." *East Asian Journal of Theology* 4 (1986): 33-46.

_____. *Systematische Theologie*. Vol. 2. Esp. 15-202. Göttingen: Vandenhoeck & Rupnecht, 1991. (F. Kapitsc: Dis Schöpfong der Welt). English Edition. Grand Rapids: Eerdmans, 1994.

_____. *Toward a Theology of Nature: Essays on Science and Faith*, ed. Theodore Peters. Louisville, KY: Westminster/John Knox Press, 1993.

Parenti, Sergio

Present Position and Address: Professor of Theology (since 1976), Studio Teologico Accademico Bolognese, Piazza S. Domenico 4, I-48018, Faenza Ra, Italy **Date of Birth:** June 22, 1947 **Languages Spoken:** Italian, French **Education:** Licenza in S. Teologia (1974)/Dottorato in S. Teologia (1986), Pontificia University S. Tommaso "Angelicum" - Roma **Discipline:** Theology **Related Areas of Interest:** Philosophy of Science; Rationality and Theology.

Selected Publications:

_____. "Il Senso Letterale della Scrittura secondo S. Tommaso." *Sacra Doctrina* (Bologna) 77 (1975): 69-97.
_____. "Sull'atto di fede." *Sacra Doctrina* (Bologna) 89 (1979): 5-78.
_____. "Segno, Senso e Significato." *Sacra Doctrina* (Bologna) 92 (1980): 83-119.
_____. "A Proposito del Problema Critico." *Sapienza* (Napoli) 1 (1986): 118-21.
_____. "Esperienze, Induzione, Deduzione." *Sapienza* (Napoli) 1 (1987): 107-14.
_____. *Comunicazione, Credibilita' De Cristo, Fede - La Conoscenza per Comunicazione de Notizia E La Credibilita' Umana Di Cristo in Rapporto All'atto Di Fede.* Bologna: Ediaioni Studio Domenicano, 1991.
_____. "Caso E Probabilita' - Suggerimenti Aristotelico-Tomisti." *Divus Thomas* (Bologna) 5 (1993): 91-126.

Parker, Thomas

Present Position and Address: Cyrus H. McCormick Professor in Systematic Theology (since 1975), McCormick Theological Seminary, 5555 S. Woodlawn Avenue, Chicago, IL 60637, USA **Work Phone:** (312) 947-6300 **Fax Number:** (312) 947-0376 **Date of Birth:** December 22, 1931 **Education:** A.B. (1954), California State College of Los Angeles; B.D. (1957), San Francisco Theological Seminary; Ph.D. (1965) Princeton Theological Seminary **Previous Positions:** Instructor through Associate Professor of Systematic Theology (1965-74), McCormick Theological Seminary **Selected Memberships:** American Theological Society; American Academy of Religion; Highlands Institute of American Religious Thought **Discipline:** Systematic Theology **Related Areas of Interest:** Empiricism/Pragmatism and Theological Method; Science and Religion.

Selected Publications:

_____, coeditor. *Peace, War and God's Justice.* Toronto: United Church Publishing Hse, 1989.
_____. "Immediacy and Interpretation." *American Journal of Theology and Philosophy* 12, 1 (1991).

Parrott III, Less

Present Position and Address: Associate Professor of Psychology; Director of the Center for Relationship Development, Seattle Pacific University, Seattle, WA 98119, USA **Work Phone:** (206) 281-2178 **Fax Number:** (206) 281-2500 **Date of Birth:** August 29, 1961 **Awards and Honors:** Trauis Award for Integration of Psychology and Theology, Fuller Theological Seminary **Previous Positions:** Medical Psychologist, University of Washington School of Medicine, WA **Selected Memberships:** American Psychological Association; American Association of Christian Counselors **Discipline:** Psychology **Related Areas of Interest:** Integration of Psychology and Theology **Current Areas of Research:** Impact of guilt on the ability to empathize.

Selected Publications: His bibliography contains 6 books and over 50 published articles.

_____. *How to Write Psychology Papers.* Harper Collins, 1993.
_____. *Helping the Struggling Adolescent: A Counseling Guide.* Zondervan Academic Books, 1993.
_____. *Helping the Struggling Adolescent: A Guide to Thirty Common Problems for Parents, Counselors, and Youthworkers.* Zondervan Academic Books, 1993.

_____. *Love's Unseen Enemy: How to Overcome Guilt to Build Healthy Relationships.* Zondervan Academic Books, 1994.

_____. "Stress in Children and Adolescents." *Journal of Psychology and Christianity* (1994).

_____. *Counseling and Psychotherapy: Theory, Skills and Practice.* McGraw-Hill, in press.

_____, L. Parrott. *Finding Meaning and Mission in the World of Work.* Contemporary Christian Counseling Series, ed. Gary Collins. Waco, TX: Word, in press.

_____, L. Parrott. "Approaches to Marriage Counseling." In *Christian Marriage Counseling: A Comparison of Approaches,* ed. Everett L. Worthington. Grand Rapids: Baker Book House, in press.

_____. "Pastoral Counseling and Teenagers." In *Leadership Handbook.* Vol. 2. Carol Stream, IL: Christianity Today Institute, in press.

_____. "Guilt and the Loving Person." In *The Psychology of Effective Functioning.* N.p., in press.

Paterson, John Leonard

Present Position and Address: Visiting Lecturer (1990), Geography Department, University of Waikato, Hamilton, New Zealand **Work Phone:** (64) 71-562889 **Date of Birth:** May 8, 1955 **Education:** B.A. Hons. (1977), Otago University; M.Phil. (1981), Waikato University; Currently enrolled in the Ph.D. program at the University of British Columbia **Previous Positions:** Temporary Lecturer in Geography (1987-89), Waikato University **Selected Memberships:** Association for Christian Scholarship; New Zealand Geographical Society **Discipline:** Human Geography **Related Areas of Interest:** Philosophy of Geography; Environmental Ethics; Religious Agricultural Groups; Regenerative Agriculture.

Selected Publications:

_____. "Transcendental Realism, Social Structures, and Human Geography: a Critical Review." Paper Presented at Conference of the Canadian Association of Geographers, Nanaimo, 1984. Available from the author.

_____. "The Two Dimensions of 'Religious Geography': The Dutch Reformational Tradition." Paper Presented at the Conference of the Canadian Association of Geographers, Trois Rivières, 1985. Available from the author.

_____. *Individuals, Societal Structures and Cultural Ideals: Methodological Individualism and Methodological Collectivism in the Social Sciences and Dooyeweerd's Social Theory.* Toronto: Institute for Christian Studies, 1986.

_____. "Religious Beliefs, Environmental Stewardship and Industrializing Agriculture: the Christian Farmers Federation of Alberta." In *Proceedings of the 15th Conference of the New Zealand Geographical Society.* Dunedin: New Zealand Geographical Society, 1990.

_____. "Stewards of the Land: the Religious Beliefs and the Institutional and Agricultural Practices of the Christian Farmers Federation of Alberta." Ph.D. diss. University of British Columbia (In progress).

Paul, Erich Robert *(Deceased)*

Former Position and Address: Professor of History of Science (since 1991), Dickinson College, Carlisle, PA 17013-2896, USA; (Home) 803 Wellington Drive, Carlisle, PA 17013, USA **Work Phone:** (717) 245-1400 **Fax Number:** (717) 245-1690 **E-Mail:** paulr@dickinson.edu **Date of Birth:** July 23, 1943 **Languages Spoken:** English, German **Education:** B.S. and M.S. Mathematics (1969), Brigham Young University, Provo, UT; M.A. History of Science (1974)/Ph.D. History and Philosophy of Science (1976), Indiana University - Bloomington, IN **Previous Positions:** Assistant (1976-82)/Associate Professor of History of Science (1982-91), Dickinson College; Adjunct Associate Professor (1983-84), American University, Washington, DC; Associate Professor of Philosophy (1989-90), Utah State University **Selected Memberships:** History of Science Society; Society for Scientific Exploration; Historical Astronomy Division (American Astron. Society); American History Association; Mormon History Association; Society for the History of Technology; Planetary Society **Discipline:** History of Science **Related Areas of Interest:** Cosmology; Science and Religion; Cosmology and Religious Worldviews; Cosmology and Cosmic Vision of Mormonism.

Selected Publications: His bibliography lists 30 publications.

_____. "Joseph Smith and the Plurality of Worlds Idea." *Dialogue* 19 (1986): 13-36.
_____. "J. C. Kapteyn and the Early Twentieth-Century Universe." *Journal for the History of Astronomy* 17 (1986): 155-82.
_____. *Science, Religion, and Mormon Cosmology.* University of Illinois Press, 1992.
_____. *The Milky Way Galaxy and Statistical Cosmology, 1890-1924.* Cambridge University Press, 1993.

Paul, Iain

Present Position and Address: Honorary Research Fellow, Trinity College, University of Glasgow; 116 Tryst Road, Stenhousemuir, Larbert FK5 4QJ, Central Region, UK **Home Phone:** (0324) 562641 **Date of Birth:** June 15, 1939 **Education:** B.Sc. Chemistry (1961), Royal College of Science and Technology, University of Strathclyde, Glasgow; Chemical Research (1961-63), University College of North Wales, Bangor; Ph.D. Chemistry (1967), University of Bristol; B.D. Christian Dogmatics (1974)/Part-time Ph.D. Christian Dogmatics, University of Edinburgh **Postgraduate Experience:** Postdoctoral Research (1967-69), University of Sheffield **Previous Positions:** Lecturer in Chemistry (1969-71), Queen Elizabeth College, University of London; Assistant Minister (1974-75), St. Conal's linked with St. Mark's, Kirkconnel; Minister (1976-88), Craigneuk and Belhaven Parish Church, Wishaw; Member (1979-80), Center of Theological Inquiry, Princeton, NJ; Guest Lecturer in Chemistry to postgraduate students (1988), Heriot-Watt University, Edinburgh **Selected Memberships:** Society of Ordained Scientists; The Scientific and Medical Network; European Society for the Study of Science and Theology; Member (1994), Center for Theology and the Natural Sciences, Berkeley, CA **Discipline:** Theology; Chemistry **Related Areas of Interest:** Theology and Science.

Selected Publications: His bibliography lists 26 scientific papers in Chemistry.

_____. *Science, Theology and Einstein.* Belfast: Christian Journals Ltd., 1982.
_____. *Science and Theology in Einstein's Perspective, Theology and Science at the Frontiers of Knowledge,* ed. T. F. Torrance, vol. 3. Edinburgh: Scottish Academic Press, 1986.
_____. *Knowledge of God: Calvin, Einstein and Polanyi.* Edinburgh: Scottish Academic Press, 1987.
_____, Jan Fennema, eds. *Science and Religion: One World - Changing Perspectives on Reality.* Plenary Lectures Presented at the Second European Conference on Science and Religion. Dordrect/Boston/London: Kluwer Academic Publishers, 1990.

Paul, William W.

Present Position and Address: Professor Emeritus, Department of Philosophy and Religion, Central College, Pella, IA 50219, USA; (Home) 1351 Broadway, Pella, IA 50219, USA **Work Phone:** (515) 628-5214 **Home Phone:** (515) 628-3442 **Education:** A.B. Philosophy and History (1944), Temple University; B.D. Theology (1947), Faith Theological Seminary; M.A. Philosophy (1949), University of Pennsylvania; Ph.D. Philosophy (1959), Columbia University **Previous Positions:** Instructor through Assistant Professor in Philosophy (1949-59), Shelton College, NYC and NJ; Visiting Professor (1959-60), Wheaton College, IL; Professor of Philosophy and Chair (since 1960), Central College; Visiting Professor (1971), Iowa State University; Exchange Professor (1983), Trinity College - Wales; Visiting Scholar, Princeton Theological Seminary; Chair, Department of Philosophy and Religion, Central College, Pella, IA **Selected Memberships:** Past-president and member, Iowa Philosophical Society; Institute for Comparative Philosophy; Philosophy of Science Association; American Scientific Affiliation; Society of Christian Philosophers **Discipline:** Philosophy; Theology **Related Areas of Interest:** Environmental Ethics; Genetic Engineering in Theological and Ethical Perspective; Ethics and Technology; Philosophy and Theology/Ethics.

Selected Publications:

_____. "Metaphysical Vision in Contemporary Naturalism." *Memorias: International Congress of Philosophy.* Vol. 9. Mexico City, 1964.

_____. "Philosophy of Science." In *Christianity and the World of Thought*, ed. H. Armerding. Grand Rapids: Eerdmans, 1968.

_____. Comparative review. "Earl MacCormac and Ian Barbour on Metaphor." *Christian Scholar's Review* 6, 2 (1978).

_____. "Time and Historical Significance." In *Interpretation and History*, ed. R. Laird Harris, 211-24. Singapore: Christian Life Publishers, 1986.

Peacocke, Arthur Robert

Address: Exeter College, Oxford OX1 3DD **Concurrent Positions:** Warden Emeritus, Society of Ordained Scientists; Hon. Chaplain (since 1988), and Honorary Canon (1994), Christ Church Cathedral, Oxford; Exeter College, Oxford OX1 3DD, UK **Work Phone:** (0865) 512041 **Fax Number:** (0865) 54791 **Date of Birth:** November 29, 1924 **Education:** B.A. (1st Class Hons, 1946)/B.Sc. (1946)/M.A. and D.Phil. (1948)/D.Sc. (1962)/all in Physical Biochemistry/D.D. Theology (1982), University of Oxford; Diploma in Theology (1960)/B.D. (1971), University of Birmingham; Sc.D. (1973), University of Cambridge **Honorary Degrees:** Hon. D.Sc. (1983), De Pauw University, IN ; D. Lit. Hum. (1991), Georgetown University, Washington, DC **Lectures Presented:** Bampton Lecturer (1978), Oxford University; Gifford Lecturer (1992-93), St. Andrew's University **Awards and Honors:** Le Conte Du Noüy Prize (1973); Academic Fellow (1986), Institute on Religion in an Age of Science; M.B.F. (1993) **Previous Positions:** Assistant through Senior Lecturer (1948-59), University of Birmingham, UK; Fellow and Tutor in Chemistry and then in Biochemistry (1959-73), St. Peter's College, Oxford; Dean and Fellow (1973-84), Clare College, Cambridge, UK; Director of the Ian Ramsey Centre (1985-88), Oxford; St. Cross College **Selected Memberships:** Vice President, Science and Religion Forum; Vice President, Modern Church People's Union; Council Member, ESSSAT; Previous Membership: Secretary/Chairman, British Biophysical Society (1965-69) **Discipline:** Physical Biochemistry; Theology, ordained 1971 as priest in the Church of England **Related Areas of Interest:** Physical Chemistry of Biological Systems; Interaction of Science and Theology and related philosophical issues; music.

Selected Publications:

_____, J. Dominian. *From Cosmos to Love*. Darton, Langman and Todd, 1977.

_____. *Creation and the World of Science*. Oxford University Press, 1979.

_____, editor. *The Sciences and Theology in the Twentieth Century*. Stocksfield UK: Oriel Press; Notre Dame: University of Notre Dame Press, 1982.

_____. *The Physical Chemistry of Biological Organization*. Oxford University Press, 1983. Reprint, 1989.

_____. *Intimations of Reality: Critical Realism in Science and Religion*. Notre Dame: University of Notre Dame Press, 1984.

_____, editor. *Reductionism in Academic Disciplines*. London: NFER-Nelson, 1985. Reprint,

_____. *God and the New Biology*. London: Dent, 1986; Gloucester, MA: Peter Smith, 1994.

_____, S. Andersen, eds. *Evolution and Creation*. Denmark: Aarhus University Press, 1987.

_____, G. Gillett, eds. *Persons and Personality*. Oxford: Blackwell, 1987.

_____. *Theology for a Scientific Age*. Oxford: Blackwell, 1990; 2nd enlarged edition, London: SCM Press; Minneapolis MN: Fortress Press (1993).

Pedersen, Olaf

Present Position and Address: Professor of History of Science (since 1967), Aarhus University, Ny Munkegade, DK-8000 Aarhus C, Denmark; (Home) 16 Elbaekvej, DK-8240 Risskov, Denmark **Date**

of Birth: April 8, 1920 **Languages Spoken:** Danish, English, French, German **Education:** B.Sc. (1940)/M.Sc. (1943)/Dr.Sci. (1956), Copenhagen University **Postgraduate Experience:** Postdoctoral studies with Gilson (1949-50), Paris **Previous Positions:** Science Master (1944-56), Public School; Associate Professor (1956)/Professor (1967), Aarhus University; Fellow (1969), St. Edmund's College, Cambridge; Visiting Professor (1971), Kiel University **Selected Memberships:** Associate, Royal Astronomical Society, London; Fellow, Royal Danish Academy; Council Member (1971)/Vice President (1981-85), International Union of History and Philosophy of Science; President (1985-89), International Academy of History of Science **Discipline:** History of Science **Related Areas of Interest:** Early and Medieval Science; History of Theology.

Selected Publications: His bibliography lists 9 books and many published papers in the field of history of science.

_____. *Early Physics and Astronomy*. London: MacDonald, 1974. Reprint, Cambridge, 1993.
_____. "The Corpus Astronomicum and the Traditions of Medieval Latin Astronomy." *Colloquia Copernicana* 3 (1975): 57-96.
_____. "Science and the Reformation." In *University and Reformation*, ed. L. Grane, 35-62. Leiden: Brill, 1981.
_____. "The God of Space and Time." *Concilium* (186) (1983): 14-20.
_____. "Galileo and the Council of Trent." *Specola Vaticana: Studi Galileiani* 1 (1983); Rev. ed. (1993).
_____. "Galileo's Religion." In *The Galileo Affair*, ed. G. V. Coyne, 75-102. Specola Vaticana, 1985.
_____. "Christian Belief and the Fascination of Science." In *Physics, Philosophy, and Theology: A Common Quest for Understanding*, ed. Robert J. Russell, William R. Stoeger, and George V. Coyne, 125-40. Vatican City State: Vatican Observatory, 1988; Notre Dame: University of Notre Dame Press, 1989.
_____. *The Book of Nature*. Vatican City State: Vatican Observatory; Notre Dame: University of Notre Dame Press, 1992.

Pellegrino, Edmund D.

Present Position and Address: John Carroll Professor of Medicine and Medical Humanities/Director, Center for Clinical Bioethics, Georgetown University, Washington, DC 20007, USA; (Home) Chalfont Court, Bethesda, MD 20816, USA **Work Phone:** (202) 687-8999 **Date of Birth:** June 22, 1920 **Languages Spoken:** English **Education:** B.S. (*summa cum laude*, 1937), St. John's University, Jamaica, NY; M.D. (1944), New York University **Honorary Degrees:** Recipient of 39 honorary doctoral degrees and numerous other awards **Previous Positions:** Professor/Chairman (1959-66), Department of Medicine, University of Kentucky Medical Center, Lexington, KY; Vice President for Health Sciences/Dean of School of Medicine/Director of Health Sciences Center/Professor of Medicine (1966-73), State University of New York - Stony Brook; Chancellor/Vice President for Health Affairs (1973-75), University of Tennessee; Professor of Medicine and Medical Humanities (1973-75), University of Tennessee Center for the Health Sciences; President/Chairman of Board of Directors/Professor of Medicine (1975-78), Yale-New Haven Medical Center and Yale University; President/Professor of Philosophy and Biology (1978-82), Catholic University of America, Washington, DC; Professor of Clinical Medicine and Community Medicine (1975-78), Georgetown University Medical School, Washington, DC; Director (1983-89), Kennedy Institute of Ethics, Georgetown University; Director (1989-94), Georgetown University Center for the Advanced Study of Ethics **Other Academic Experience:** Certified, American Board of Internal Medicine; Master, American College of Physicians **Selected Memberships:** Fellow or member of 20 Scientific, professional and honorary societies, including the Institute of Medicine of the National Academy of Sciences; Association of American Physicians; American Clinical and Climatological Association; American Osler Society **Discipline:** Medicine; Ethics **Related Areas of Interest:** Ethics and Medicine and Society.

Selected Publications: Author of approximately 400 publications, editorial contributions, articles, and reviews in scientific research, medical education and philosophy.

_____. *Humanism and the Physician.* University of Tennessee Press, 1979.
_____, David Thomasma. *A Philosophical Basis of Medical Practice.* New York: Oxford University Press, 1981.
_____, David Thomasma. *For the Patient's Good.* New York: Oxford University Press, 1988.
_____, David Thomasma. *Virtues in Medical Practice.* New York: Oxford University Press, 1993.

Peppin, John Francis

Present Position and Address: Internal Medicine Resident/Physician, Marshfield Clinic, Department of Internal Medicine, 3K2, 1000 N. Oak Avenue, Marshfield, WI 54449, USA; (Home) 814 E. 6th Street, Marshfield, WI 54449, USA **Concurrent Positions:** Adjunct Faculty (since 1991), Health Care Administration Department, University of Osteopathic Medicine and Health Sciences, Des Moines, IA **Work Phone:** (715) 387-5436 **Home Phone:** (715) 384-2838 **Fax Number:** (715) 387-5240 **Date of Birth:** May 8, 1950 **Languages Spoken:** English **Education:** B.A. Biology (1980), Skyline Community College, San Bruno, CA; B.S. Science of Physiology (1983), University of California - Davis; D.O. Osteopathy (1992), University of Osteopathic Medicine and Health Sciences, Des Moines, IA; Residency Program (since 1992), Marshfield Clinic/St. Joseph's Hospital Internal Medicine Residency Program **Awards and Honors:** Surgery Award (1992), Department of Surgery, University of Osteopathic Medicine and Health Services; President's Undergraduate Fellowship Grant (PUF) (1982-83), University of California - Davis for "Does Parathyroid Hormone Potentiate Glucose-Induced Insulin Secretion in the Perfused Rat Pancreas?"; Daly City Rotary Club Scholarship (1980) **Previous Positions:** Senior Research Associate (1984-88), University of California, School of Veterinary Medicine, Department of Physiological Sciences, Davis, CA; Assistant Research Associate (1983-84), Department of Internal Medicine, University of California, Veterans Administration Hospital, Marinez, CA; Co-professor (September 4-December 18, 1991), University of Medicine and Health Science, Des Moines, IA **Selected Memberships:** American College of Physicians; American Medical Association; Society of Christian Philosophers; Kennedy Institute of Ethics; Society for Health and Human Values; American Scientific Affiliation **Discipline:** Medicine; Medical Ethics **Related Areas of Interest:** Medicine; Medical Ethics; Philosophy; Theology **Current Areas of Research:** The question of Physician value neutrality in the practice of medicine; the interactions of pharmaceutical sales representatives and physicians; the importance of reinstating religious values back into the practice of medicine, specifically Judeo-Christian religious values.

Selected Publications: His bibliography contains 8 published articles, 2 presented papers, and 14 invited lectures on a variety of topics.

_____, S. J. Towner, and H. Tsukamoto. "Inhibitory Effects of Ethanol on Phosphatidylinositol Breakdown in Pancreatic Acini." *Fed. Proc.* 45 (1986): 567..
_____, H. Tsukamoto, G. Caballaro, et al. "Blood Ethanol Level Correlates with Liver Pathology and Gradient of Oxygen Tension from Postal to Hepatic Vein." *Hepatology* 6 (1986): 1189.
_____, H. Tsukamoto, S. J. Towner, and H. Sankaran. "Coordinated Breakdown of Phosphatidylinositol with CCK Binding and CCK-mediated Biological Responses in Rat Pancreatic Acini." *Dig. Dis. Sci.* 31 (1986): 1151.
_____, S. J. Towner, M. Matsuoka, et al. "Effects of Sustained Ethanol Intoxication and Optiman Nutrition on Free Amino Acid Levels in Plasma, Liver, and Muscle of the Rat." *Nutrition Research* 8 (1988): 65-71.
_____. "It's Still Not Over, Debbie." *AMSA: Standing Committee on Bioethics Newsletter* (December 1989).
_____. "Student Form Ethics Club." *Hawkeye Osteopathic Journal* 35 (September-October 1989).
_____. "The Osteopathic Distinction: Fact or Fancy?" *Journal of Medical Humanities* 14,4 (1993): 203-22.
_____. "Physician Neutrality and Patient Autonomy in Advanced Directive Decisions." *Issues in Law and Medicine* (Forthcoming 1995).

Percesepe, Gary John

Present Position and Address: Professor of Philosophy/Director of Honors Program, Cedarville College, Box 601, Cedarville, OH 45314, USA **Work Phone:** (513) 766-7980 **Fax Number:** (513) 766-2760 **Date of Birth:** February 9, 1954 **Languages Spoken:** French, Italian **Education:** MA Historical Theology, Denver Baptist Seminary; MA Philosophy, University of Denver; Ph.D. Philosophy, Saint Louis University **Postgraduate Experience:** Collegium Phaenonenologicum (1990), Perugia, Italy; American Institute at Mt. Zion (1994) **Congresses and Conferences:** Presentations: (1989) Radical Philosophy, NYC; (1985, 86, 90), Society for Phenomenology and Existential Philosophy; (1992), American Philosophical Association; (1988, 89), American Academy of Religion; (1988, 89, 90), Society of Christian Philosophers **Editorial Experience:** Fiction editor, *Antioch Review* **Selected Memberships:** American Philosophical Association; Society of Christian Philosophers; SPEP; Radical Philosophy Association; American Academy of Religion; National Collegiate Honors Council **Discipline:** Philosophy **Related Areas of Interest:** Literature **Current Areas of Research:** Postmodern Theorists: An Evangelical Perspective

Selected Publications: His bibliography contains 4 books, 10 published articles, and numerous poems.

_____. *Future(s) of Philosophy: The Thinking of Jacques Derrida.* N.p., 1988.
_____. *Philosophy: An Introduction to the Labor of Reason.* N.p., 1990,
_____. *Ethics of Inclusion.* Prentice-Hall, 1994.
_____, Kate Mehoran. *Free Spirits: Feminist Philosophers Diagnose Culture.* Prentice-Hall, 1994.

Perkins, Richard

Present Position and Address: Professor of Sociology (since 1988), Houghton College, Houghton, NY 14744, USA; (Home) Hazlett House, Houghton College, Houghton, NY 14744, USA **Work Phone:** (716) 567-4264 **Date of Birth:** March 20, 1943 **Education:** B.A. Psychology (1965), Wheaton College, IL; M.A. Sociology (1972)/Ph.D. Sociology (1977), University of Massachusetts - Amherst **Previous Positions:** Assistant Professor (1973-76), Department of Sociology, Washington and Jefferson College, Washington, PA; Assistant Professor of Sociology (1976-78), Westminster College, New Wilmington, PA; Associate Professor (1978-84)/Professor of Sociology/Head of Department (1983-88), Houghton College, Houghton, NY **Selected Memberships:** Associates for Religion and Intellectual Life; Association of Christians Teaching Sociology; American Sociological Association; Society for the Scientific Study of Religion **Discipline:** Sociology **Related Areas of Interest:** Sociology of Religion; Environmental Stewardship; Christianity and Sociology.

Selected Publications: His bibliography lists 13 publications.

_____. "The Orthodox Bigot: A Sociological Analysis." *Journal of the American Scientific Affiliation (JASA)* 28, 3 (1976): 116-22.
_____. "Sociology and the Christian Student: A Statement of the Problem." *JASA* 32, 2 (1980).
_____, Brian Sayers. "Between Alienation and Anomie: The Integration of Sociology and Christianity." *The Christian Scholar's Review* 17, 2 (1987): 122-42.
_____. *Looking Both Ways: Exploring the Interface Between Christianity and Sociology.* Grand Rapids: Baker Books, 1987.
_____. "Why Study Sociology?" Chap. 14 in *The Sociological Perspective: A Value-committed Approach*, ed. Michael Leming, Raymond DeVries, and Brendan Furnish. Grand Rapids: Zondervan, 1989.

Perry, David Kenneth

Present Position and Address: Postdoctoral fellow (since June, 1994), Departments of Medicine and Cell Biology, Duke University, Durham, NC 27710, USA **Home Phone:** (404) 633-0516 **Date of Birth:** October 31, 1962 **Languages Spoken:** English **Postgraduate Experience:** Postdoctoral fellow, Department of Biochemistry, Emory University, Atlanta, GA **Selected Memberships:** American Scientific Affiliation **Discipline:** Biochemistry **Related Areas of Interest:** Signal Transoluction **Current Areas of Research:** Regulation of Phospholipase D and Phosphatidic Acid Phosphohydrolase.

Selected Publications: His bibliography contains 4 published articles.

_____, D. J. Uhlinger. "A Carboxy-terminal Peptide from p47-phox is a Substrate for Phosphorylation by Protein Kinase C and by a Neutrophil Protein Kinase." *Biochemistry Biophysics Research Commission* 187 (1992): 940-8.
_____, W. L. Hard, D. E. Edmondson, J. D. Lamberh. "Role of Phospholipase D-derived Diradylglycerol in the Activation of the Human Neutrophil Respiratory Burst Oxidase." *Journal of Immunology* 149 (1992): 2749-58. 2749-58.
_____, V. L. Stevens, T. S. Widlanski, and J. D. Lambeth. "A Novel ecto-Phosphatidic Acid Phosphohydrolase Activity Mediates Activation of Neutrphil Superoxide Generation by Exogenous Phosphatidic Acid." *Journal Biol. Chemistry* 268 (1993): 25302-10.

Peters, Theodore Frank

Present Position and Address: Professor of Systematic Theology (since 1978), Pacific Lutheran Theological Seminary; 2770 Marin Avenue, Berkeley, CA 94708, USA **Work Phone:** (510) 524-5264 **Home Phone:** (510) 222-5596 **Date of Birth:** April 3, 1941 **Languages Spoken:** English, German **Education:** B.A. (1963), Michigan State University; M.Div. (1967), Trinity Lutheran Seminary, Columbus, OH; Studied (1967-68), University of Heidelberg, Germany; M.A. (1970)/Ph.D. (1973), University of Chicago **Previous Positions:** Pastor (1970-72), Trinity Lutheran Church, Chicago; Assistant Professor of Religion and Philosophy (1972-76), Newberry College, SC; Adjunct teaching responsibilities: Southern Seminary (1973-75)/Notre Dame School of Theology, New Orleans (1977); Associate Professor of Religious Studies (1976-78), Loyola University **Selected Memberships:** Evangelical Lutheran Church in America; Board member (since 1983), Center for Theology and the Natural Sciences **Discipline:** Theology; Pastoral Ministry **Related Areas of Interest:** The Modern Mind and Postmodern Religion; The Relationship of Physical Cosmology to the Doctrines of Creation and Eschatology; Genetics and Ethics; Pastoral Care and the Scientific Community.

Selected Publications: His *curriculum vitae* lists 7 books and 115 articles.

_____. "David Bohm. Postmodernism, and the Divine." *Zygon* 20, 2 (1985): 193-217.
_____, editor. *Cosmos as Creation*. Nashville, TN: Abingdon Press, 1989.
_____. "Genethics: Implications of the Human Genome Project." *The Christian Century* 107, 27 (1990): 868-72.
_____. *The Cosmic Self*. San Francisco: Harper, 1991.
_____. *God — The World's Future: Systematic Theology for a Postmodern Era*. Minneapolis: Fortress, 1992.
_____. "Intellectual Property and Human Dignity." In *The Genetic Frontier: Ethics, Law, Policy*, ed. Mark S. Frankel and Albert Teich. Washington, DC: AAAS Press, 1993.
_____. "Genome Project Forces New Look at Ethics." *Forum for Applied Research and Public Policy* 8, 3 (1993): 5-13.
_____, editor. *Toward a Theology of Nature: Essays on Science and Faith*, by Wolfhart Pannenberg. Louisville: Westminster/John Knox Press, 1993.
_____. *God as Trinity: Relationality and Temporality in Divine Life*. Louisville, KY: Westminster/John Knox, 1993.
_____. "Exo-Theology: Speculations on Extra-terrestrial Life." In *The Gods Have Landed*, ed. James R. Lewis. Albany, NY: SUNY, 1995.

Petersen, Rodney L.

Present Position and Address: Executive Director, Boston Theological Institute, 210 Herrick Road, Newton, MA 02159 **Phone:** (617) 527-4880, (617) 527-1073 (fax), E-Mail btirlp@harvarda.harvard.edu **Date of Birth:** January 17 1949 **Languages Spoken:** English, French, German **Education:** B.A (1971) Harvard University; M.Div (1974), Harvard Divinity School; Th.M. (1976), Harvard Divinity School; Ph.D. (1985) Princeton Theological Seminary **Previous Positions Held:** Professor (1987-90), Webster University, Geneva, Switzerland; Asst. Professor (1981-86), Trinity Evangelical Divinity School, Deerfield, ILL **Honors:** Boyden Scholarship (Harvard College); Rockefeller Theological Prize (National); Billings Preaching Prize (Harvard Divinity School); Issues Research Grant (Association of Theological Schools) **Discipline:** History

Selected Publications:

____. "Francis of Assisi and the Franciscan Ideal." In *Great Leaders of the Christian Church*, ed. J. H. Woodbridge. Chicago: Moody Press, 1988: 162-165.

____. "Continuity and Discontinuity: The Debate Through Church History." In *Continuity and Discontinuity. Perspectives on Relationships Between the Old and New Testaments,* ed. J. H. Woodbridge. Westchester, IL: Crossway Books, 1988: 17-34.

____. "People in Corporations: Ethical Responsibilities and Corporate Effectiveness." *Instituto de Estudios Superiores de la Empressa.* Barcelona, Spain, 1989; Webster University: Bellevue/Geneva, Switzerland.

____. "Bullinger's Prophets of the "*Restitutio*". In *Biblical Hermeneutics in Historical Perspective*, eds. M. S. Burrows and P. Rorem. Grand Rapids, MI: Eerdmans, 1991.

____. *Preaching in the Last Days. The Theme of "Two Witnesses" in the Sixteenth and Seventeenth Centuries.* New York: Oxford University Press, 1993.

____. "Perfectionism, Shame and Liberation." In *Finding God at Harvard*, ed. Kelly Monroe. Grand Rapids, MI: Zondervan, 1996.

____. "Local Ecumenism and the Neo-Patristic Synthesis of Father Georges Florovsky." In *Orthodoxy and the Ecumenical Movement (Essays in Honor of Father Georges Florovsky)*, ed. George Papademetriou. Brookline, MA: Holy Cross Greek Orthodox Press, 19946

____. "Hundred-handed, Argus-eyed' George H. Williams, Hollis Professor of Divinity, Emeritus, Celebrated on His 80th Birthday." *Harvard Divinity School Bulletin* (Summer, 1994).

____.ed and contributor. *Christianity and Civil Society: Theological Education for Public Life.* Maryknoll, NY: Orbis Books, 1995.

Peterson, James C.

Present Position and Address: C.C. Dickson Chair of Ethics, Director of the Program in Religion, Ethics, and Technology, Burris Hall, Wingate College, Charlotte, NC 28174, USA **Concurrent Positions:** Visiting Professor of Theology and Ethics, Gordon-Conwell Theological Seminary-Charlotte, Charlotte, NC, USA **Work Phone:** (704) 233-8071 **Fax:** (704) 233-8146 **E-mail:** peterson@wingate.edu **Date of Birth:** January 10, 1957 **Languages Spoken:** English **Awards and Honors:** Byington Fellow, 1980; Richard M. Weaver Fellow, 1983; Commonwealth Fellow, 1984; Dupont Fellow, 1985; Henry R. Luce Scholar, 1986; Davidge Fellow, 1987; Alpha Chi (WC) Teaching Award, 1990; Student Government Association (WC) Teaching Award, 1991; Phi Eta Sigma (Wingate College) Teaching Award, 1993; Elected to the Society of Christian Ethics, 1993; Endowed Chair, 1993; Jessie Ball duPont Research Fellow, 1995; Appointed 1996, Visiting Fellow in Molecular and Clinical Genetics (NIH ELSI program) **Previous Positions:** Faculty Member, University of Virginia Medical School; Adjunct at Virginia Commonwealth University; Visiting Professor, Ewha University, Seoul, Korea **Selected Memberships:** American Scientific Affiliation; Society of Christian Ethics; Park Ridge Center **Discipline:** Ethics **Related Interests:** Theology, Philosophy, Science, and Technology. **Current Research:** Ethics of Human Genetic Intervention.

Selected Publications:

_____. "Genetic Risk Prediction and Public Policy." *Bioethics Books* 2, 2 (Winter, 1991).
_____. *An Ethical Analysis and Proposal for the Direction of Human Genetic Intervention.* Ph.D. Dissertation, University of Virginia. Ann Arbor, MI: U.M.I. Dissertation Service, 1992.
_____. "A Good Death: Taking More Control at the End of Your Life." *Perspectives on Science and Christian Faith (PSCF)* 45, 4 (December, 1993).

Personal Notes: Chair of the Bioethics Commission of the American Scientific Affiliation and Serves on the Ethics Advisory Board of the Mercy Hospitals.

Philipchalk, Ronald Peter

Present Position and Address: Professor of Psychology (since 1989), Trinity Western University, Langley, BC V3A 6H4, Canada **Work Phone:** (604) 888-7511 **Date of Birth:** May 25, 1945 **Education:** B.A. (1967), University of Victoria; M.A. (1969), University of British Columbia; Ph.D. (1971), University of Western Ontario **Previous Positions:** Assistant Professor of Psychology (1971-74), St. Thomas University; Associate Professor (1982-88), Trinity Western University **Selected Memberships:** Canadian Psychological Association; Christian Association of Psychologists **Discipline:** Psychology **Related Areas of Interest:** Psychology of Religion; Integration of Psychology and Religion/Christianity; Social Psychology.

Selected Publications: His bibliography lists 10 publications.

_____. "Instrumentalism in Psychology: Some implications." *Perspectives on Science and Christian Faith* 39, 4 (1987): 198-202.
_____. *Psychology and Christianity: An Introduction to Controversial Issues.* Washington, DC: University Press of America, 1987.
_____. *Jesus Said.* Nashville, TN: Thomas Nelson, 1990.
_____, James McConnell. *Understanding Human Behavior.* 8th ed. Fort Worth, TX: Harcourt Brace College Publishers, n.d.
_____. *Invitation to Social Psychology.* Fort Worth, TX: Harcourt Brace College Publishers, n.d.

Pietrzak, Daniel M.

Present Position and Address: President, St. Hyacinth College and Seminary, 66 School Street, Granby, MA 01033, USA **Work Phone:** (413) 467-7191 **Fax Number:** (413) 467-9608 **Date of Birth:** March 12, 1939 **Languages Spoken:** Italian, Polish, French **Awards and Honors:** Fellowship, Fordham University; *Who's Who in Religion; International Who's Who* **Previous Positions:** Registrar (1968-76)/Academic Dean (1973-76), St. Hyacinth College and Seminary, Granby, MA; Assistant to Minister General, OFH Convention (1975-82), Rome, Italy; Rector, Seraphicum (1977-82), Rome, Italy; Minister Provincial (1982-91), St. Anthony Province **Selected Memberships:** American Psychological Association; National Catholic Education Association; Society for the Scientific Study of Religion; Fellowship of Catholic Scholars **Discipline:** Psychology **Related Areas of Interest:** Developmental (Life-Span); Psychology of the Religious Experience; Male Psychology/Spirituality **Current Areas of Research:** The study of what might constitute a masculine approach to spirituality.

Selected Publications: Most of his work has been published for private distribution on such areas as the adolescent faith-crisis, human development and authentic spirituality, and masculine approaches to spirituality.

_____. *The Masculine Approach to Spirituality.* Interprovince Publications, 1992.
_____. *Franciscan Formation and Human Development.* India: Franciscan Documentation, 1994.
_____. *Fundamentals of Community Building in the Franciscan Tradition.* Forthcoming.

Pike, Kenneth L.

Present Position and Address: Adjunct Professor (since 1979), University of Texas - Arlington; 7500 W. Camp Wisdom Road, Dallas, TX 75236-5628, USA **Concurrent Positions:** Member (Research and Translation, since 1935), The Summer Institute of Linguistics **E-Mail:** 73511.3566@compuserve.com **Date of Birth:** June 9, 1912 **Languages Spoken:** English, Spanish, Mixteco (of San Miguel y Grande, Mexico) **Education:** B.Th. (1933), Gordon College of Theology and Missions; Ph.D. Linguistics (1942), University of Michigan **Honorary Degrees:** Doctor of Humanities (1967), Huntington College; Doctor of Humane Letters (1973), Doctor of Letters, Houghton College (1977); University of Chicago; Docteur Honoris Causa (1978), University of Sorbonne; Doctor of Humane Letters, Gordon College (1982); Doctor of Humane Letters, Georgetown University (1984); Doctor of Philosophy Honoris Causa, Albert-Ludwigs University, Freiburg Germany (1993) **Awards and Honors:** Distinguished Faculty Achievement Award, University of Michigan (1966); Fellow of the Center for Advanced Study in the Behavioral Science (1968-69); Philippine government's Presidential Medal of Merit (1974); Nominated for Nobel Peace Prize (1983-94); Georgetown University's Dean's Medal (1992); Honorary Professorships: National University of Trujillo, Peru (1987); National University of Ucayali, Peru (1987); University of Lima, Peru (1991) **Previous Positions:** Faculty/Associate/Full Professor (1948-78), University of Michigan **Media Work:** Bibliography lists 5 Educational television programs **Selected Memberships:** Former President, Linguistic Association of Canada and the United States; Former President, Linguistic Society of America; National Academy of Sciences; President (1942-79), The Summer Institute of Linguistics; Permanent Council Member, International Phonetic Association (1942); Honorary member of International Association of Collective Contribution to Language Learning, Moscow (1990) **Discipline:** Linguistics; Bible Translator **Related Areas of Interest:** Christianity and Science/Culture/Language; The Relation of Philosophy to Science and Christianity.

Selected Publications: His printed bibliography lists 24 books and 151 articles and pamphlets in the field of Linguistics, and 11 books and 78 articles and pamphlets in Religion.

_____. *Language in Relation to a Unified Theory of the Structure of Human Behavior.* Glendale, CA: Summer Institute of Linguistics, Parts 1 and 2, 1955; Part 3, 1960. 2d rev. ed. The Hague: Mouton, Janua Linguarum Series maior 24, 1967.
_____. *With Heart and Mind: A Personal Synthesis of Scholarship and Devotion.* Grand Rapids: Eerdmans, 1962.
_____. "Christianity and Science." *The Church Herald* 22, 4 (1965): 4-6.
_____. "Christianity and Culture: Part 1 Conscience and Culture; Part 2 Incarnation in a Culture; Part 3 Biblical Absolutes and Certain Cultural Relativisms." *Journal of the American Scientific Affiliation* 31 (1979): 8-12; 92-6; 139-45.
_____. *Linguistic Concepts: An Introduction to Tagmemics.* Lincoln: University of Nebraska Press, 1982.
_____. *Talk, Thought and Thing: The Emic Road Toward Conscious Knowledge.* Dallas: Summer Institute of Linguistics (1993).

Pizzamiglio, Pierluigi

Present Position and Address: Curator of the Library for the History of Science "C. Vigano'"/Professor of Science and Theology (since 1995), Università Cattolica del Sacro Cuore, 25121 Brescia - Via Trieste, 17, Italy; Via Trebbia 34, 26100 Cremona, Italy **Work Phone:** (0372) 38086 or 27245 **Date of Birth:** May 26, 1945 **Languages Spoken:** Italian, English **Education:** Studies in Theology (1964-69), Seminary of Cremona; Laurea in Fisica (1975), Università di Bologna **Discipline:** History of Science; History of Physics and Mathematics; Philosophy of Science **Related Areas of Interest:** Religion and Science. Was in India from October 1990 through March 1991 researching the relationships between Indian thought and science. Was in Bangladesh from June 1991 through December 1994 teaching Philosophy of Science.

Selected Publications:

_____. "Una lettera del matematico protestante A. G. Kaestner al card. A. M. Querini sul rapporto che intercorre tra le scienze fisico-matematiche e la religione" (A letter from Protestant mathematician A. G. Kaestner to Cardinal A. M. Querini about the relationship existing between physico-mathematical sciences and religion). *Commentari dell'Ateneo di Brescia* (1983): 187-200.

_____. "Scienza e fede: questioni radicali e orientamenti metodologici" (Science and faith: radical problems and methodological directions). *Vita e Pensiero* 67 (1984): 47-54.

_____. "Ecclesiastici e scienza tra '700 e '800 in Italia" (Ecclesiastics and science between eighteenth and nineteenth centuries in Italy). Afterword to *Ottavio Ferrario: il Pasteur dei Fatebenefratelli*, by F. Molinari, 161-91. Milano: Ancora, 1988.

_____. "Le scienze e la patristica" (Sciences and patristics). In *Complementi Interdisciplinari di Patrologia*, ed. A. Quacquarelli, 185-221. Roma: Città Nuova, 1989.

_____. "Il senso comune in Asia" (Asian common sense). *Nuova Secondaria* 3 (1994): 52-4, 59.

Plantinga, Alvin C.

Present Position and Address: John A. O'Brien Professor of Philosophy (since 1982), University of Notre Dame, Notre Dame, IN 46556, USA **Date of Birth:** November 15, 1932 **Education:** A.B. (1954), Calvin College; M.A. (1955), University of Michigan; Ph.D. (1958), Yale University **Honorary Degrees:** D.D. (1982), Glasgow University **Lectures Presented:** Lecturer (20 times) in Council for Philosophical Studies Distinguished Visiting Philosopher Program **Awards and Honors:** Distinguished Alumni Award, Calvin College (1986) **Previous Positions:** Instructor (1957-58), Yale University; Assistant through Associate Professor (1958-63), Wayne State University; Associate Professor (1963-64)/Professor (1964-82), Calvin College; Visiting Professor - University of Illinois (1960)/Harvard (1964-65)/University of Chicago (1967)/University of Michigan (1967)/Boston University (1969)/Indiana University (1970)/UCLA (1977)/Syracuse University (1978)/University of Arizona (1980); Adjunct Professor (1973-81), University of Notre Dame; Named Lectureships at following Universities and Colleges: Arizona (1977); Marquette (1980); Loyola (1982); Glasgow (1982); Waterloo (1984); Wayne State (1984); Hillsdale College (1984); Hamilton College (1985); Wabash College (1985); Fordham (1986); Aberdeen (1987); Fuller Theological Seminary (1987); Belfast (1987); Oxford (1976, 80, 88); Southern Baptist Theological Seminary (1988) **Selected Memberships:** Fellow (1968-69), Center for Advanced Study in Behavioral Sciences; Council for Philosophical Studies (1968-74); Fellow (since 1975), American Academy of Arts and Sciences; Fellow, Calvin Center for Christian Scholarship; Fellowship (1980-81), American Council of Learned Societies; Former Vice President/President, American Philosophical Association; Former President, Society of Christian Philosophers; Director (since 1984), Christian Philosophers; Director (since 1984), Notre Dame Center for Philosophy of Religion **Discipline:** Philosophy; Philosophy of Religion **Related Areas of Interest:** Christianity and Evolutionary Biology.

Selected Publications: His bibliography lists 11 books and 100 articles.

_____. "The Reformed Objection to Natural Theology." In *Proceedings of the American Catholic Philosophical Association, 1980.*

_____. *Does God Have a Nature?* Milwaukee, WI: Marquette University Press, 1980.

_____, Nicholas Wolterstorff, eds. *Faith and Rationality*. Notre Dame: University of Notre Dame Press, 1984.

_____. "When Faith and Reason Clash: Evolution and the Bible." *Christian Scholar's Review* (September 1991).

_____. "Advice to Christian Philosophers." *Faith and Philosophy* (July 1984).

_____. "Evolution, Neutrality, and Antecedent Probability: A Reply to Van Till and McMullin." *Christian Scholar's Review* (September 1991).

_____. "Science: Augustian or Duhemian?" *Zygon* (Forthcoming).

_____. "Methodological Naturalism?" In *Proceedings of the Knowing God, Christ, and Nature in the Post-Positivistic Era Conference, April 1993.* Forthcoming.

Plendl, Hans S.

Present Position and Address: Professor (since 1974), Department of Physics, Florida State University, Tallahassee, FL 32306, USA **Work Phone:** (904) 644-2516 or -2724 **Date of Birth:** June 12, 1927 **Languages Spoken:** English, German, Italian **Education:** B.A. (1952), Harvard University; M.S. (1954)/Ph.D. (1958), Yale University **Previous Positions:** Assistant Professor of Physics (1956-64)/Associate Professor (1964-74), Florida State University; Researcher (1957-67), Physics Division, Oak Ridge National Laboratory; Visiting Scientist (1962-63), Nuclear Research Center, Karlsruhe and Max-Planck-Institute for Nuclear Physics - Heidelberg; Member of Program Advisory Committee (1969-78), Space Radiation Effects Laboratory, Newport News, VA; Visiting Staff Member (since 1969), Medium Energy Physics Division, Los Alamos Scientific Laboratory; Guest Senior Physicist (since 1982), Physics Department, Brookhaven National Laboratory; Guest Professor of Physics (1985-86), Technical University, Munich **Selected Memberships:** American Physical Society; APS Forum of Physics and Society; European Physical Society; Sigma Xi **Discipline:** Applied Physics; Nuclear and Particle Physics **Related Areas of Interest:** Interface between Theology, Philosophy and Science; Communication of Research Results and Implications to Non-scientists.

Selected Publications: His *curriculum vitae* lists 32 pages of publications and abstracts.

_____. "Das Heutige Weltbild der Physik." *Carolinum* (Göttingen) 35 (1969): 45.
_____. "Physics for Poets, Pianists, and Philosophers." *The Physics Teacher* 10 (1972): 273.
_____. "Mikrokosmos, Umwelt und Makrokosmos." *Carolinum* (Göttingen) 38 (1972): 29.
_____. "Philosophical Problems of Modern Physics." Parts 1- 3. *Synthese* 50, 1 and 3 (1982).
_____, editor. *Philosophical Problems of Modern Physics.* D. Reidel Publishing Co., 1982.
_____. "The Heisenberg Uncertainty Principle: Ambiguity and Precision in the Description of Nature." *North Dakota Quarterly* 51, 1 (1983): 82.
_____. "The Two-Cultures Revisited." *Research in Review* 35 (1982): 15.
_____. "Mirrors and our Understanding of Nature." *McDonald Observatory News* 13, 1 (1985): 4.

Polkinghorne, John Charlton

Present Position and Address: President (since 1989), Queens' College, Cambridge CB3 9ET, UK **Work Phone:** UK (0223) 335532 **Date of Birth:** October 16, 1930 **Education:** Ph.D. Theoretical Physics (1955)/M.A. Mathematics (1956)/Sc.D. Theoretical Physics (1974), Trinity College, Cambridge **Previous Positions:** Lecturer (1958-65)/Reader (1965-68)/Professor of Mathematics and Physics (1968-79), Cambridge University; Fellow, Dean and Chaplain (1986-89), Trinity Hall, Cambridge **Selected Memberships:** Fellow, Royal Society; Society of Ordained Scientists **Discipline:** Theoretical Elementary Particle Physics **Related Areas of Interest:** The interaction of Science and Theology.

Selected Publications: Many papers on theoretical elementary particle physics in learned journals.

_____. *The Way the World Is.* Triangle; Grand Rapids: Eerdmans, 1983.
_____. *The Quantum World.* Longman; Princeton: Princeton University Press, 1984.
_____. *One World.* SPCK; Princeton: Princeton University Press, 1986.
_____. *Science and Creation.* SPCK; New Science Library, Shambhala Press, 1988.
_____. *Science and Providence.* SPCK; New Science Library, Shambhala Press, 1989.
_____. *Reason and Reality.* SPCK; Trinity Press International, 1991.
_____. *The Faith of a Physicist.* Princeton: Princeton University, 1994; SPCK, 1994, as *Science and Christian Belief.*
_____. Quarks, Chaos and Christianity. SPCK, 1994.

Poloma, Margaret M.

Present Position and Address: Professor of Sociology (since 1982), University of Akron, Akron, OH 44325-1905, USA; (Home) 2872 Silver Lake Blvd., Silver Lake, OH 44224, USA **Work Phone:** (216) 972-6837 **Fax Number:** (216) 972-5377 **E-Mail:** Bitnet mpoloma@uakron.edu **Date of Birth:** August 27, 1943 **Education:** B.A. (1965), Notre Dame College of Ohio; M.A. Sociology (1967)/Ph.D. Sociology (1970), Case Western Reserve University, Cleveland, OH **Previous Positions:** Teaching (1967-69), Notre Dame College of Ohio/Case Western Reserve University/Cuyahoga Community College; Instructor of Sociology (1969-70), Cleveland State University; Assistant (1970-73)/Associate (1973-82)/Professor of Sociology (since 1982), University of Akron **Selected Memberships:** American Sociological Association; Association for the Sociology of Religion; Christian Sociological Society; Religious Research Association; Society for Pentecostal Studies; Secretary (1986-89), Society for Scientific Study of Religion **Discipline:** Sociology **Related Areas of Interest:** Christianity and Sociology/Social Science; Religious Tenets and Scientific Assumptions.

Selected Publications: Her bibliography lists some 6 books and 28 articles or other contributions.

_____. "Theoretical Models of Person in Contemporary Sociology: Towards Christian Sociological Theory." In *A Reader in Sociology: A Christian Perspective*, ed. De Santo, Smith-Hinds, and Redekap, 199-216. Harold Press, 1980.

_____. "Toward a Christian Sociological Perspective: Religious Values, Theory and Methodology." *Sociological Analysis* 43, 2 (1982): 95-108.

_____, Charles De Santo, eds. *Social Problems: Christian Perspectives*. Winston-Salem, NC: Hunter Textbooks, Inc. 1985.

_____. *The Assemblies of God at the Crossroads: Charisma and Institutional Dilemmas*. Knoxville: The University of Tennessee Press, 1989.

_____, George H. Gallup, Jr. *Varieties of Prayer: A Survey Report*. Philadelphia: Trinity Press International, 1991.

_____, Brian F. Pendleton. *Exploring Neglected Dimensions of Religion in Quality of Life Research*. Lewiston, NY: The Edwin Mellen Press, 1991.

_____, James L. Guth, John C. Green, and Corwin E. Smidt. "Pulpit and Politics: Protestant Clergy in the 1988 Elections." In *The Bible and the Ballot Box: Religion and Policies in the 1988 Election*, ed. John C. Green and James L. Guth, 73-93. Boulder, CO, 1991

_____. "Sociology of Religion." In *New Twentieth Century Encyclopedia of Religious Knowledge*, ed. J. D. Douglas, 2d ed., 765-67. Grand Rapids, MI: Baker Book House, 1991.

_____. "Pentecostal Pastor Blends Past and Present." In *Sources of Inspiration: 15 Modern Religious Leaders*, ed. Gene I. Maeroff, 222-38. Kansas City: Sheed & Ward, 1992.

_____, Charles P. DeSanto and Zondra G. Lindblade. *A Christian Perspective on Social Problems*. Indianapolis: Wesley Press, 1992.

Pon, Wing Y.

Present Position and Address: Chairman, Blue Diamond Technologies, Inc., 1707A Little Orchard Street, San Jose, CA. 95125, USA **Concurrent Positions:** President (since 1986), E-W Institute Inc., P. O. Box 32855, San Jose, CA 95152, research and experiments on non-local technologies, a byproduct from the synthetic integrations of the intuitive wisdom of the East and the intellectual constructs of the West **Work Phone:** (408) 975-1080 **E-Mail:** wpon@aol.com **Date of Birth:** January 15, 1939 **Education:** B.S. Physics and Mathematics (*magna cum laude*, 1964), California State University - San Francisco; M.S. Engineering Science (1968), Stanford University **Postgraduate Experience:** Graduate interdisciplinary studies on the invariant natures embedded in the complexity of Biological-Physical-Engineering systems **Awards and Honors:** *Who's Who in the West* (1982), *Who's Who in Theology and Science* (1992); *Who's Who in Leading American Executives* (1993), Special Adviser to the United States Congressional Advisory Board **Previous Positions:** Associate Professor of Physics (1970-71), California State University; Assistant Professor (1979-80), California Institute of Asian

Studies; Founder and President (1980-81), Dialectic Systems Corporation; Cofounder and Executive Vice President (1981-86), Applied Technology Associates, Inc. (the corporation won the small business prime contractor 1984 award from the United States Air Force Satellite Facility, and excellence award from Small Business Administrations) **Discipline:** Physics Professor; Businessman **Related Areas of Interest:** Integration of Eastern Philosophy and Western Science; Non-Local Science and Technology and Human Spirit.

Selected Publications:

_____. *Journey into a Science of Reality: An East West View of Reality*. San Jose, CA: East West Institute on Science and Philosophy, 1979.

_____. "Integration of Eastern (In Particular Chinese) Philosophy and Western Science: A Preliminary Introduction to A Theory of Everything." Paper presented at a week-long invited seminar, sponsored by the Chinese Academy of Science and Technology, Beijing, China, October 1989.

_____. "Information Medicine: Mathematics of Qi, An Analytical Integration on the Teachings of the Chinese, Hindu, Tibet, and Egyptian." Paper presented at the Qigong Institute, East West Academy of Healing Arts, February 27, 1994.

_____. "An East-West Mathematical Model on Body-Mind-Spirit Pathology and Model-Computer Demonstration." Paper presented at the 20th International Congress of The International Academy of Pathology and 11th World Congress of Academic and Environmental Pathology, Hong Kong, October 9-14, 1994.

_____. Two Volumes on the Theory of Everything: From God's Creation of the Big Bang to Elementary Particles; From Genesis to the Physics of Body-Mind-Spirit and Soul; From I-Ching to God's Non-Local Technology of Creation. Vol. 1, *Neo-Taoism: Putting God Back into Physics of the Theory of Everything*. San Jose, CA: E-W Institute, Ltd., 1995. Vol. 2, *Neo-Taoism: The Theory of Everything Applied to Each and Every Field of Knowledge*. San Jose, CA: E-W Institute, Ltd., 1995.

Poole, Jr. , Charles P.

Present Position and Address: Professor of Physics (since 1964), University of South Carolina, Columbia, SC 29208, USA **Date of Birth:** June 7, 1927 **Education:** B.S. Chemistry (1950)/M.S. Physics (1952), Fordham University; Ph.D. Physics (1958), University of Maryland **Previous Positions:** Westinghouse Electrical Corporation (1952-53); Gulf Research and Development (1958-64) **Selected Memberships:** Fellow, American Physical Society; Institute for Theological Encounter with Science and Technology (ITEST); Institute on Religion in an Age of Science (IRAS) Bishops Committee on Science and Technology **Discipline:** Physics **Related Areas of Interest:** How Science Supports Religion; Interactions between God and the World; Nature of the Soul **Current Areas of Research:** Solid State Physics; Superconductivity; Magnetic Resonance and Clifford Algebras.

Selected Publications:

_____, H. A. Farach. *Relaxation in Magnetic Resonance*. New York: Academic Press, 1971.

_____, Frank J. Owens, H. A. Farach. *Magnetic Resonance of Phase Transitions*. New York: Academic Press, 1979.

_____. *Electron Spin Resonance, A Comprehensive Treatment on Experimental Techniques*. New York: Interscience, 1967. Reprint (in Russian), Moscow: MIP Press, 1969.

_____. *Comprehensive Treatise on Experimental Techniques*. 2d. ed. New York: Wiley-Interscience, 1982.

_____, H. A. Farach. *Theory of Magnetic Resonance*. New York: Wiley, 1972. Reprint (in Spanish), Spain: Reverte. 1976. 2d. ed. New York: Wiley, 1987.

_____, T. Datta, and H. A. Farach. *Copper Oxide Superconductors*. New York: Wiley, 1988.

_____, R. J. Creswick, and H. A. Farach. Introduction to *Renormalization Group Methods in Physics*. New York: Wiley, 1991.

_____, H. F. Farach. *Handbook of Magnetic Resonance*. New York: American Institute of Physics Press, 1994.

_____, H. A. Farach, R. J. Creswick. *Textbook of Superconductivity*. Boston: Academic Press, 1994.

Poole, Michael William

Present Position and Address: Visiting Research Fellow, School of Education, King's College, London, Cornwall House Annex, Waterloo Road, London SE1 8WA, UK **Work Phone:** 0171-872 3097 **Fax Number:** 071-872 3182 **E-Mail:** Dialcom (TTNS) 01:YNS020 **Date of Birth:** February 14, 1936 **Education:** B.Sc. Physics (Hons, 1957)/M.Phil. (1983), King's College, London **Awards and Honors:** A.K.C. (Associate of King's College, 1957) **Previous Positions:** Director of Farmington Science and Religion in Schools Project (1986-88); Lecturer in Science Education (1973-91), King's College, London **Editorial Positions:** *Science and Christian Belief/Spectrum* **Selected Memberships:** F.R.S.A. (Fellow of the Royal Society of Arts); Christians in Science; Chairman, Christians in Science Education; Science and Religion Forum **Discipline:** Science Education **Related Areas of Interest:** The Interplay between Science and Religion with Special Reference to its Educational Context.

Selected Publications: His bibliography lists some 50 publications in science, religion and science Education.

_____. "An Investigation into Aspects of the Interplay between Science and Religion at Sixth Form Level." M.Phil. thesis., King's College, University of London, 1983.
_____. *Science and Religion in the Classroom.* Watford: Association of Christian Teachers, 1984. Reprint, in *God and Science, Farmington Papers on Science and Theology.* Oxford: Farmington Institute, 1988. *Christian Perspectives for* Education, ed. L. Francis and A. Thatcher. Leominster: Fowler Wright.
_____. "Science Education and the Interplay between Science and Religion." *School Science Review* 67, 239 (1985): 252-61.
_____, with a chap. by G. J. Wenham. *Creation or Evolution - A False Antithesis?* Latimer Studies 23/24. Oxford: Latimer House, 1987.
_____. "Science-and-religion: A Challenge for Secondary Education." *British Journal of Religious Education* 13, 1 (1990): 18-27.
_____. *A Guide to Science and Belief.* Vol. 128. Oxford: Lion Publishing, 1990.
_____. *Miracles: Science, the Bible and Experience.* London: Scripture Union, 1992.
_____. "Teaching About Issues of Science and Religion." In *Priorities in Religious* Education, ed. B. Watson, 144-64. London: Falmer Press, 1992.
_____. "Do We Teach Them Wrong? Teaching Young People About Science And Religion." In *Explorations in Science and Theology, Templeton London Lectures at the RSA,* 39-53. London: Royal Society Of Arts, 1993.
_____. *Beliefs and Values in Science Education.* Buckingham: Open University, 1995 (In press).

Post, Stephen G.

Present Position and Address: Associate Professor of Biomedical Ethics; School of Medicine, Center for Biomedical Ethics, Case Western Reserve University, Cleveland, OH 44106 **Work Phone:** (216) 368-6205 **Fax Number:** (216) 368-8713 **Date of Birth:** May 6, 1951 **Languages Spoken:** Spanish **Education:** B.S. Biology/Marine Science (1973), Long Island University; M.A. Religious Studies (1979), University of Chicago; Ph.D. Religion and Ethics (1983), University of Chicago, The Divinity School **Lectures Presented:** American Academy of Religion; American Philosophical Association; American Academy of Pediatrics; American Society of Neurosciences; International Conference on Alzheimer's Disease and Related Disorders; Society for Health and Human Values; Gerontological Society of America **Awards and Honors:** Elected Fellow, The Hastings Center, Briarcliff Manor, NY; Elected Senior Research Fellow, The Joseph and Rose Kennedy Institute of Ethics, Georgetown University; Elected Chair, American Academy of Religion Group on Ethics; Research Fellow, (1982-83), Institute for the Advanced Study of Religion, University of Chicago; Winner (1988), Rockefeller Institute of Government Working Papers Competition, State University of New York; Best article originating in a professional journal (1991), Catholic Press Association of the United States and Canada **Previous Position:** (1985-88), Division of Humanities, Marymount College, Tarrytown, NY; (1983-

85), Department of Religion, Mercy College of Detroit, MI **Discipline:** Religion; Ethics; Biology/Marine Science.

Selected Publications: His total bibliography contains 5 books, 2 edited books, 1 associate editorship of an encyclopedia, and 50 peer-reviewed articles.

_____. "Disinterested Benevolence: An American Debate Over the Nature of Christian Love." *Journal of Religious Ethics* 14, 2 (1986): 356-68.
_____. "Communion and True Self-Love." *Journal of Religious Ethics* 16, 2 (1988): 345-62.
_____. "The Inadequacy of Selflessness: God's Suffering and the Theory of Love." *Journal of the American Academy of Religion* 56, 2 (1988): 213-28.
_____. "Recent Works on Reproductive Technology." *Religious Studies Review* 15, 3 (1989): 210-13.
_____, Robert H. Binstock. "Rationing and Ethics in Health Care." *Christianity & Crisis* 51, 13 (1991): 290-2.
_____. "Ill and on the Street." *Christianity & Crisis* 52, 11 (1992): 248-50.
_____. "Love, Religion, and Sexual Revolution." Journal of Religion 72, 3 (1992): 403-16.
_____. "Psychiatry and Ethics: The Problematics of Respect for Religious Meanings." Culture, Medicine and Psychiatry: An International Journal of Comparative Cross-Cultural Research 17, 3 (1993): 363-83.
_____. Spheres of Love: Toward a New Ethics of the Family. Dallas: Southern Methodist University Press, 1994.
_____. "Religion, Medicine, and the Clinical Encounter." In Introduction to Religion: What Religions Do, ed. Jacob Neusner and William Scott Green. Louisville, KY: Westminster/John Knox Press, in press.

Poythress, Vern Sheridan

Present Position and Address: Professor of New Testament Interpretation (since 1987), Westminster Theological Seminary, P.O. Box 27009, Philadelphia, PA 19118, USA **Concurrent Positions:** Minister, Philadelphia Presbytery - Presbyterian Church in America **Date of Birth:** March 29, 1946 **Education:** B.S. Mathematics (with honor, 1966), California Institute of Technology, Pasadena; Ph.D. Mathematics (1970), Harvard University; M.Div. (1974)/Th.M. Apologetics (1974), Westminster Theological Seminary; M.Litt New Testament (1977), University of Cambridge; D.Th. New Testament (1981), University of Stellenbosch, South Africa **Previous Positions:** Assistant Professor of Mathematics (1970-71), Fresno State College; Assistant (1976-81)/Associate Professor of New Testament (1981-87), Westminster Theological Seminary **Editorial Positions:** Editorial Assistant (1973-74)/Book Review Editor (1978-79)/Associate Editor (since 1981), *Westminster Theological Journal* **Selected Memberships:** Linguistic Association of Canada and the United States **Discipline:** Mathematics; Pastoral Ministry; New Testament Interpretation **Related Areas of Interest:** Philosophy of Science; Christianity and Mathematics.

Selected Publications: His bibliography lists some 70 papers, reviews and other publications.

_____. "An Approach to Evangelical Philosophy of Science." Th.M. thesis, Westminster Theological Seminary, Philadelphia, PA, 1974.
_____. "Creation and Mathematics; or What Does God Have to Do with Numbers?" *The Journal of Christian Reconstruction* 1, 1 (1974): 128-40.
_____. "A Biblical View of Mathematics." In *Foundations of Christian Scholarship*, ed. Gary North, 159-88. Vallecito, CA: Ross House, 1976.
_____. *Philosophy, Science and the Sovereignty of God.* Nutley, NJ: Presbyterian and Reformed, 1976.
_____. "Science as Allegory,"; "Newton's Laws as Allegory,"; and "Mathematics as Rhyme." *Journal of the American Scientific Affiliation* 35, 2 (1983): 65-71; 35, 3 (1983): 156-61 and 35, 4 (1983): 296-303, respectively.
_____. *Science and Hermeneutics: Implications of Scientific Method for Biblical Interpretation.* Grand Rapids: Zondervan, 1988.

Prigogine, Ilya

Present Position and Address: Director (since 1959), Institut Internationaux de Physique et de Chimie, Brussels; Ashbel Smith Regental Professor (since 1984), University of Texas - Austin Service de Chimie Physique, Code Postal 231, Campus Plaine U.L.B., Boulevard du Triomphe, 1050, Bruxelles **Concurrent Positions:** Director (since 1967), Ilya Prigogine Center for Studies in Statistical Mechanics, Thermodynamics and Complex Systems, University of Texas - Austin **Date of Birth:** January 25, 1917 **Education:** Licencié en Sciences Chimiques/Physique (1939); Docteur (1941), Sciences Chimiques/Physique (1939); Docteur (1941), Sciences Chimiques; Agrégé de l'Enseignement Supérieur en Chimie Physique **Honorary Degrees:** Over 20 Honorary Doctorates from all over the world including France, USA, Belgium, Sweden, Brazil, Scotland, Spain, China, India, Argentina and Italy **Awards and Honors:** Nobel Prize in Chemistry (1977); Over 20 other scientific awards and prizes **Previous Positions:** Chargé de Course (1947)/Professeur extraordinaire à la Faculté des Sciences (1950)/Professeur ordinaire à la Faculté des Sciences (1951)/Professeur émérite (since 1987), l'Université Libre de Bruxelles; Chargé d'une chaire extraordinaire (1961-66), l'Université de Chicago, Department of Chemistry, Enrico Fermi Institute for Nuclear Studies and the Institute for the Study of Metals **Selected Memberships:** Previous Director, Correspondent, Member and President, l'Académie Royale des Sciences, Lettres et Beaux-Arts de Belgigue; Foreign Associate, National Academy of Sciences, Washington, DC; l'Académie des Sciences de l'URSS (1982); Honorary Foreign Member (1960), American Academy of Sciences and Arts, Boston, MA; Fellow (1962), New York Academy of Science; l'Académie de la République Roumanie; Society of Sciences, Sweden; Deutsche Akademie der Naturforscher Leopoldina; Östereichische Akademie der Wissenschaften; l'Acadmie Internationale de Philosophie des Sciences; American Chemical Society; Foreign Fellow, Indian National Science Academy; Society for Studies on Entropy, Japan; Past-President (1988), International Society for General Systems Research; World Academy of Art and Science; International Academy for Biomedical Drug Research **Discipline:** Chemistry; Biochemistry; Physics; Philosophy **Related Areas of Interest:** Time and Reality; Unification of Dynamics and Thermodynamics; Convergence of Science and Humanities.

Selected Publications: His bibliography lists over 16 works, many translated into English, Italian, Spanish, Portuguese, German, Dutch, Danish, Swedish, Rumanian, Russian, Japanese, Chinese, and Bulgarian.

_____, I. Stengers. *La Nouvelle Alliance, Les Métamorphoses de la Science.* Gallimard, Paris, France, 1979, 1981, 1986. English trans. *Order Out of Chaos.* New York: Bantam Books Inc., 1983; London: William Heinemann Ltd., 1984. Other languages: Italian, Serbo-Croatian, Spanish, Rumanian, Swedish, Dutch, Danish, Portuguese, German.
_____. *From Being to Becoming: Time and Complexity in the Physical Sciences.* San Francisco: W. H. Freeman & Company, 1980. Trans. into French, German, Japanese.
_____, I. Stengers. *Entre le temps et l'éternité.* Paris: Librairie Arthème Fayard, 1988. English translation planned.
_____, I. Stengers. *Das Paradoz der Zeit,* Piper, 1993.

Prosperi, Giovanni M.

Present Position and Address: Professore Ordinario (since 1968), Physics Department, University of Milano, via Celoria 16, I-20133, Milano, Italy; (Home) via Ampere 112 - I20131 Milano, Italy **Date of Birth:** March 15, 1931 **Education:** Laurea Physics (1956), University of Milano; Libera Docenza Theoretical Physics (1961), Italian Ministry of Education, Rome **Previous Positions:** Fellow, Assistant Professor and Associate Professor (1954-65), University of Milano; Full Professor (1965-67), University of Bari **Selected Memberships:** Societa Italiana di Fisica, Bologna; American Physical Society; Istituto Lombardo di Scienze e Lettere, Milano; Academie Internationale de Filosofie des Sciences,

Bruxelles **Discipline:** Theoretical Physics **Related Areas of Interest:** Theoretical Physics, Science and Philosophy; Science and Religion.

Selected Publications: His bibliography also lists some 66 papers in physics.

_____. "Determinismo e indeterminismo nella fisica moderna" (Determinism and indeterminism in modern physics). *Cultura e scuola* (Roma, 1964): 220-8.

_____. "Scienze Naturali ed esperienza religiosa" (Natural sciences and religious experience). *Scienza, Filosofia, Arte, Fede* (Centro Culturale S. Fedele, 1983): 21-7.

_____. "Cultura scientifica e magistero pontificio" (Scientific culture and papal teaching; with reference to John Paul II's teaching on culture and science). *Cultura, impegno per l'uomo*, Atti del IV Convegno sul magistero pontificio, suppl. a "La Traccia" 42-8. Milano: Coop. LCA, 1984.

_____. "L'immagine fisica del mondo" (The world picture in physics; research, methodology and the historical development and evolution of physical conceptions). *Per la Filosofia* (Milano: Massimo, 1984): 35-44.

_____. "Contribution to the Theme: Cultura religiosa e cultura degli scienziati" (Religious culture and scientific culture). *Valori, Scienza Trascendenza* (Values, Science and Transcendence). Volume 2. Torino: Fondzione Giovanni Agnelli, 1989.

_____. "The Evolution of Ideas in Physics, Their Cognitive Value and The Concept of Model." *Science et Sagesse*, ed. E. Agazzi. Fribourg, Switzerland: Editions Universitaires, 1991.

Proudfoot, Wayne

Present Position and Address: Professor of Religion (since 1972), Department of Religion, 506 Kent Hall, Columbia University, New York, NY 10027, USA **Date of Birth:** November 17, 1939 **Education:** B.S. Physics (1961), Yale University; B.D. (1964), Harvard Divinity School; Ph.D. Philosophy of Religion (1972), Harvard University **Discipline:** Philosophy of Religion **Related Areas of Interest:** Religious Experience, Science and Religion, Pragmatism.

Selected Publications:

_____. *Religious Experience*. Berkeley: University of California Press, 1985.

Provine, William B.

Present Position and Address: Professor (since 1969), Section of Ecology and Systematics, Cornell University, Corson Hall, Ithaca, NY 14853, USA **Date of Birth:** February 19, 1942 **Education:** B.S. Mathematics (1962)/M.A. History of Science (1965)/Ph.D. History of Science (1970), University of Chicago **Selected Memberships:** American Association for the Advancement of Science; History of Science Society; ASZ; AGA; GSA **Discipline:** History of Modern Biology, especially Genetics and Evolution **Related Areas of Interest:** Science and Religion; Foundations of Morality; Devout Rational Atheist.

Selected Publications:

_____. "Scientists, Face it, Science and Religion are Incompatible." Opinion Column. *The Scientist* (September 5, 1988): 10. Responses. *The Scientist* (October 17, 1988): 12; (November 14, 1988): Opinion section. *The Scientist* (December 26, 1988): 9, 10, 12.

_____. "Evolution and the Foundation of Ethics. A Cornell University Historian of Science Argues that the Implications of Evolutionary Biology are Clear: You Must Choose God or Darwin." *MBL Science* 3, 1 (1988): 25-9.

Puddefoot, John Charles

Present Position and Address: Head of Mathematics/Part-time Chaplain (since 1984), Eton College, Windsor, Berkshire, Benson House, Willowbrook, Eton, Windsor, Berks SL4 6HL, UK **Date of Birth:**

November 3, 1952 **Languages Spoken:** English, French **Education:** B.A. Hons (2nd Class, 1974)/M.A. (1978), Oxford University; B.D. Hons Theology (1st Class, 1978), Edinburgh University; Anglican (ordained 1978-79, Diocese of Durham) **Previous Positions:** Student Actuary (1974-75), Norwich Union Insurance Group; Assistant Curate (1978-81), Diocese of Durham; Industrial Chaplain (1981-84), Diocese of Chichester **Selected Memberships:** Center of Theological Inquiry, Princeton, NJ **Discipline:** Theology; Mathematics **Related Areas of Interest:** Mathematics and Theology; Theology and Science; Philosophy of Michael Polanyi; Modern Doctrine; Ecclesiology.

Selected Publications: His bibliography lists 23 publications.

_____. "A Christian Answer." In *In Defense of Freedom, the Ross McWhirter Memorial Essays*, ed. Lord Harris. N.p., 1978.
_____. "Indwelling: Formal and Non-formal Elements in Faith and Life." In *Belief in Science and in Christian Life*, ed. T. F. Torrance. Edinburgh: Handsel Press, 1980.
_____. "Michael Polanyi - His Aims and Methods." *Convivium* 21 (March, 1985).
_____. *Logic and Affirmation - Perspectives in Mathematics and Theology,* Theology at the Frontiers of Knowledge, ed. T. F. Torrance, vol. 6. Scottish Academic Press, 1987.
_____. "Information and Creation." In *Science and Theology of Information*, ed. Wassermann, Kirby and Rordorff. Geneva: Labor et Fides, 1992.
_____. "Complexity and Western Thought." *Journal of the European Society for the Study of Science and Theology* 1 (Geveva: Labor et Fides, 1993).
_____. "The Relationship of Natural Order to Divine Truth and Will." In Science and Theology: Questions at the Interface. Ed by M. Rae, H. Regan and J. Stenhouse. Edinburgh: T & T. Clark, 1994.
_____. "Faith's Third Age." In Colloquium. Brisbane, Australia: November, 1994.
_____. "Information Theory, Biology and Christology." In *Building Bridges Between Science and Theology*. Berkeley: CTNS, 1994.

Pun, Pattle P. T.

Present Position and Address: Professor of Biology (since 1988), Department of Biology, Wheaton College, Wheaton, IL 60187, USA; (Home) 727 Peter Road, Wheaton, IL 60187, USA **Current Positions:** Lay Preacher and Interpreter, Wheaton Chinese Alliance Church (since 1990) **Work Phone:** (708) 752-5303 **Home Phone:** (708) 668-0348 **Date of Birth:** September 30, 1946 **Languages Spoken:** English, Chinese (Mandarin, Cantonese) **Education:** B.S. Chemistry (1969), San Diego State University; M.A. (1972)/Ph.D. Biology (1974), State University of New York -Buffalo; M.A. Theology (1985), Wheaton College **Congresses and Conferences:** 3rd Quinquennial Chinese Congress of World Evangelism, Changli, Taiwan (August, 1986, by proxy); Invited participant (1987), Christianity Today Institute on Cosmology; Evangelical Affirmation (1989 - national and international conference of theologians held at Trinity Divinity School, Dearfield, IL, May 1989) **Lectures Presented:** Featured speaker on Evolution and Creation (since 1977) at many Universities and Churches including The Institute for Christian Studies, Toronto, Canada; University of California Medical Center, San Francisco; Virginia Polytechnic Institute and State University; China Evangelical Seminary, Taipei, Taiwan, China Graduate School of Theology, Hong Kong and Hong Kong Polytechnic **Previous Positions:** Resident Associate in Immunochemistry and Immunogenetics (1974-76), Argonne National Laboratory; Visiting Microbiologist (1980-81), University of Illinois at the Medial Center, Chicago; Visiting Scientist (Summer 1984), Department of Clinical Pharmacology and Drug Metabolism, American Hospital Supplies Company, McGraw Park, IL; Assistant and Associate Professor of Biology (1973-88), Wheaton College; Visiting Microbiologist (Summers 1985-88 and Fall 87)/Collaborative Research (Summers 1984-89) with Dr. Patricia Vary, Northern Illinois University; Visiting Pew Scientist (1990), Department of Biochemistry, Molecular and Cell Biology, Northwestern University, Evanston, IL; Research Associate, Department of Microbiology and Immunology, College of Medicine, University of Illinois-Chicago (summers, 1992-fall 1994); Leader in Chinese Christian Fellowship (1969-73),

State University of New York - Buffalo; Lay Preacher and member of Church Board (1981-87), Chinese Bible Church, Oak Park **Media Work:** Interviewed on radio for 2 hours (*Open Link*, a call-in program) by the Moody Broadcasting Network (1989) **Editorial Positions:** Coordinating Editor (1971-72), Chinese Bible Study Groups Bulletin of North America; Coordinating Editor (1973-74), *Ambassador* **Administrative Experience:** Member of Board of Directors (1976-80), Ambassadors for Christ, Inc. a non-profit missionary organization reaching Chinese intellectuals in North America; Secretary of the Board, Christian Communication Inc., Worldwide Literature Ministry Towards Chinese; President of the Board, Wheaton College Scholastic Honor Society (1987-88) **Selected Memberships:** Fellow, American Scientific Affiliation; Ambassadors for Christ, Inc.; American Society for Microbiology; New York Academy of Science **Discipline:** Microbiology; Molecular Genetics; Theology **Related Areas of Interest:** Creation and Evolution; Ethics and Genetic Engineering.

Selected Publications: His bibliography lists over 50 publications, many of which deal with the Creation and Evolution discussion, and many of which are in Chinese.

_____. "A Critical Evaluation of the Theory of Evolution." *Journal of the American Scientific Affiliation (JASA)* 29, 2 (1977): 84-91.
_____. *Evolution: Nature and Scripture in Conflict?* Grand Rapids: Zondervan, 1982.
_____. "Evolution." In *Evangelical Dictionary of Theology*, ed. W. Elwell, 388-92. Grand Rapids: Baker, 1984.
_____. "A Theology of Progressive Creationism." *JASA* 39, 1 (1987): 9-19.
_____. "How It All Began: Why Can't Evangelical Scientists Agree?" *Christianity Today* (August 12, 1988): 31-46.
_____. Response to Professor Plantinga's article on "When Faith and Reason Clash: Evolution and the Bible." *Christian Scholar's Review* 21, 1 (1991): 46-54.

Rahman, Abdul

Present Position and Address: Visiting Professor (since 1993), Birla Institute of Technology and Science, Pilani; Tower A-Flat 30, Zakir Bagh, Maulana Mohammad Ali Road, New Delhi-110025, India **Work Phone:** 684-1522 **Languages Spoken:** English, Hindi, Urdu **Education:** M.Sc. Biochemistry (1942), Aligarh Muslim University, Aligarh; A.I.I.Sc. (1945), Indian Institute of Science, Bangalore **Awards and Honors:** "Padma Shri" by Government of India for distinguished work in Science planning and Science and Society **Previous Positions:** Researcher (1949-56), Regional Research Laboratory, Hyderabad; Researcher (1957-60), Central Building Research Institute, Roorkee; Researcher (1960-62), Central Food Technological Research Institute, Mysore; Adviser for Planning (1962-82), Planning Group in Council of Scientific and Industrial Research (CSIR) Headquarters, New Delhi; Director and Founder (1982-84), Centre for the Study of Science, Technology and Development (later called National Institute of Science, Technology and Development Studies); Visiting Professor (1976-80), Birla Institute of Technology and Science, Pilani; Organizer, Centre for R&D Management, CSIR; Consultant for UNESCO, and other UN bodies and National Councils and academic bodies of different countries in area of History of Science, Science policy; R&D planning and management, science and social dynamics, and on problems connected with science, philosophy, ethics and culture; Consultant to Governments of Iraq, Kuwait and Brazil to prepare their plans and information systems; Visiting Professor to Chinese Academia of Management Sciences; French Government (and attached to CNRS for 2 months); Japan Society for the Promotion of Science (for 4 months); Project Director (1986-89), Indian National Science Academy, Project: Ion Science Atlas Project Director (1980-92), for National Institute for Research Advancement (Tokyo, Japan) on Science, Technology, Culture and Development **Selected Memberships:** Academy of Science, Berlin; International Science Policy Foundation (UK); Fellow, Operational Society of India; International Academy of History of Science, Paris; Vice President, Research Committee on Science and Politics of International Political Science Association; President, R&D Planning and Management Society of India; President, Forum for Science, Technology and Society; Former Director, National Institute and Society of India; Former President, International Council for Science Policy Studies of ICSU **Discipline:** Planning and Management; Social and Historical Problems of Science; Biochemistry **Related Areas of Interest:** Environmental Ethics; History of Science; Theology; Revaluation of Social, Ethical, and Philosophical problems of Science.

Selected Publications: He has written six books, about 10 monographs and over one hundred special papers, to be published as parts of books, for UN agencies and in special issues of journals. He has also coauthored four other books and edited six others books and edited six others.

_____. *Anatomy of Science*. New Delhi: National Publishing House, 1972.
_____. *Science and Technology in Medieval India*. Source Material in Sanskrit, Arabic and Persian. New Delhi: Indian National Science Academy, 1982.
_____, coeditor. *Science and Society*. New Delhi: People's Publishing House, 1982.
_____. *Trimurti: Science, Technology and Society*. New Delhi: People's Publishing House, 1983.

_____. *The Cultural and Philosophical Roots of Scientific Tradition.* New Delhi: National Institute of Science, Technology and Development Studies, CSIP, 1983.
_____. *Triveni - Science, Socialism and Democracy.* Indian Institute for Advanced Studies, Suita, n.d.
_____. *Maharaja Sewai Jai Snigh and Indian Renaissance.* New Delhi: Navrang Publishers, n.d.
_____. *Science, Technology, Culture and Development.* New Delhi: Wiley Eastern, 1995.

Ramm, Bernard

Address: 19191 Harvard #210, Irvine, CA 92715, USA **Education:** A.B., University of Washington; studied at University of Pennsylvania; B.D., Eastern Baptist Seminary; Ph.D. Philosophy, University of Southern California; Studies, Near East School of Theology, Beirut **Previous Positions:** Los Angeles Baptist Theological Seminary; Biola University; Bethel College and Seminary; Baylor University; California Baptist Seminary; Haigazian College (Beirut); Eastern Baptist Seminary, Philadelphia; American Baptist Seminary of the West; and Graduate Theological Union, Berkeley; Young Life Institute (summer school for 25 years); Adjunct Professor, Fuller Theological Seminary; Singapore Bible College; Sabbaticals in Basel (1957-58), Beirut (1966-67), Singapore (1984) **Discipline:** Philosophy; Theology **Related Areas of Interest:** Science and the Bible.

Selected Publications: His bibliography lists 23 books or chapters, and over 25 articles.

_____. *The Christian View of Science and Scripture.* White House Library. Trans. In Japanese, Korean, Spanish, Serbian and Chinese.

Ramsden, William E.

Present Position and Address: Executive Director, Religious Opportunities Institute, P.O. Box 507, Shawnee-on-Delaware, PA 18356, USA **Concurrent Positions:** Co-executive Director, Opportunity Associates; Secretary-Treasurer, Times Three **Work Phone:** (717) 421-4476 **Date of Birth:** September 6, 1932 **Languages Spoken:** English **Education:** B.A. (*summa cum laude*), University of Buffalo; S.T.B. (*magna cum laude*), Boston University **Previous Positions:** Metropolitan Coordinator, Methodist Board of Missions, Indianapolis, In; Pastor, Plymouth Methodist Church, Buffalo, NY; Pastor, Stanton Avenue Methodist Church, Boston, MA; Clinical Instructor, Boston University School of Theology; Adjunct Faculty: Christian Theological Seminary, Eastern Baptist Theological School, Lutheran Seminary of Philadelphia, Drew University Theological School, St. Joseph's University **Selected Memberships:** Phi Beta Kappa; Religious Research Association; Society for the Scientific Study of Religion **Discipline:** Clergy; Social Psychology **Related Areas of Interest:** Leading Edge of Science Developments and Potential Impacts on Society, Church, and Theology **Current Areas of Research:** New Paradigms for Church Life and Development, building on "modest" Stance Toward Abilities to Know and Control the Future.

Selected Publications: His bibliography contains 8 books, 19 published articles, and 4 articles accepted for publication.

_____. "Geographical vs. Functional Community." *Religion in Life* (1971).
_____. *The Church in a Changing Society.* Abingdon, 1979.
_____. *Inner Vitality, Outward Vigor.* Board of Global Ministries, 1986.
_____. "Raise Your Church's IQ." *Clergy Journal* (January 1990).
_____. "Building the Spiritual Foundation for Church Growth." *Clergy Journal* (September 1990).
_____. "Who Is Your Future?" *Clergy Journal* (March 1991).
_____. *Urban Cooperative Parishes.* Board of Global Ministries, 1991.

Rappaport, Roy A.

Present Position and Address: Professor (since 1972)/Walgreen Professor for the Study of Human Understanding (since 1991), Department of Anthropology; University of Michigan, Ann Arbor, MI 48709, USA **Date of Birth:** March 25, 1926 **Education:** B.S. Hotel Administration (1949), Cornell University; Ph.D. Anthropology (1966), Columbia University **Previous Positions:** US Army (1943-46); Owner-Operator (1951-59), Avoloch Inn, Lenox, MA; Assistant (1965-68)/Associate Professor (1968-72)/Chair of Department (1975-80), University of Michigan; Visiting Lecturer (1981), University of Adelaide **Selected Memberships:** President (1985-89), American Anthropological Association; Fellow (since 1987), American Association for the Advancement of Science; Board of Directors and Member (1985-87), Fellow (since 1991), American Academy of Arts and Sciences ; American Ethnological Society; Society for Cultural Anthropology; Society for Psychological Anthropology **Discipline:** Anthropology: Archaeology and Ethnology **Related Areas of Interest:** Ecological Anthropology; Anthropology of Religion.

Selected Publications: His bibliography lists 4 books, and over 45 articles, chapters and reviews.

_____. *Pigs for the Ancestors*. New Haven: Yale University Press, 1968; paperback, 1970. Italian edition. *Maiali per gli Antenati*. Milano: Franco Angeli Editore, 1980. Spanish edition. *Cerdos para los antepasados*. El ritual en la ecologia de un pueblo en Nueva Guinea. Cerro Del Agua, Mexico: Siglo veintiuno editors, 1987. 2d. rev. ed. New Haven: Yale University Press, 1984.

_____. "The Sacred in Human Evolution." *Annual Review of Ecology and Systematics* 2 (1971): 23-44.

_____. *Ecology, Meaning, and Religion*. Richmond, CA: North Atlantic Books, 1979.

_____. "Desecrating the Holy Woman: Derek Freeman's Attack on Margaret Mead." *American Scholar* 55, 3 (1986): 313-47. Selected portions reprinted in *The Samoa Reader*, ed. H. Caton. University Press of America, 1990.

_____. *The Construction of Time and Eternity in Ritual*. The Skomp Lecture, a Separate Publication. Indiana University Press, 1987.

_____. "Ritual as Communication." In *Annenberg Encyclopedia of Communication*. Oxford University Press, 1988.

_____. "Word, Words and the Problems of Language." In *The Word in Religious Thought*. University of Arizona Press, in press.

_____. "Law and Meaning, Discovery and Construction." In *Assessing Developments in Anthropology*, ed. R. Borofsky. New York: McGraw Hill, 1993.

Ratzsch, Del

Present Position and Address: Professor of Philosophy (since 1979); Calvin College, Grand Rapids, MI 49506, USA **Work Phone:** (616) 957-6415 **Home Phone:** (616) 451-4301 **Date of Birth:** April 22, 1945 **Education:** B.A. (1971), Western Washington State University; M.A. (1974)/Ph.D. (1975), University of Massachusetts - Amherst **Previous Positions:** Taught (1975-79), Franklin and Marshall College, Lancaster, PA **Discipline:** Philosophy; History/Philosophy of Science and Religion **Related Areas of Interest:** History of the Philosophy of Science; Creation and Evolution; Science and Religion; Philosophy of Religion and Science.

Selected Publications: His bibliography lists 1 book, 6 articles and 9 reviews, and over 10 papers presented.

_____. *Philosophy of Science, Contours of Christian Philosophy*, ed. C. Stephen Evans. Downers Grove, IL; Leicester, UK: InterVarsity Press, 1986; Portions excerpted in SDA *College and University Dialogue no. 1*, 1989.

_____. "Space Travel and Challenges to Religion." *Monist* 70, 4 (1987).

_____. "Nomo(theo)logical Necessity." *Faith and Philosophy* 4, 4 (1987). Reprint, in *Christian Theism and the Problems of Religion*, ed. Michael Beaty. Notre Dame, 1989.

_____. "Abraham Kuyper's Philosophy of Science." In the Papers from ICS Series.

Ravindra, Ravi

Present Position and Address: Professor of Comparative Religion (since 1979)/Chair(since 1983)/Adjunct Professor of Physics, Department of Comparative Religion, Dalhousie University, Halifax, NS, Canada; 12 Pottery Lane, Halifax, NS, B3P 2P5, Canada **Work Phone:** (902) 494-3578 **Home Phone:** (902) 477-1874 **Fax Number:** (902) 479-1070 **E-Mail:** ravi.ravindra@dal.ca **Date of Birth:** January 14, 1939 **Languages Spoken:** English, Hindi, Punjabi, French, Sanskrit, Urdu **Education:** B.Sc. Geology (1959)/Master of Technology in Exploration Geophysics (1961), Indian Institute of Technology, Kharagapur; M.Sc. Physics (1962)/Ph.D. Physics (1965), University of Toronto; M.A. Philosophy (1968), Dalhousie University **Postgraduate Experience:** Postdoctoral studies: Physics (1965), University of Toronto/Philosophy (1968-69), Princeton University/Religion (1973-74), Columbia University **Previous Positions:** Research Officer (1965-66), National Geophysical Research Institute, Hyderabad, India; Assistant Professor of Physics (1966-68)/Associate Professor of Physics and Philosophy (1969-73)/Associate Professor of Physics and Religion (1974-79); /Visiting Professor of Theatre (1979-80)/Adjunct Professor of Physics (since 1979), Dalhousie University, Canada; Visiting Member (1977), Institute of Advanced Study, Princeton; Visiting Member (1978), Indian Institute of Advanced Study, Simla; Founding Director and Chair (1978-80), Threshold Award for Integrative Knowledge **Selected Memberships:** American Academy of Religion; Canadian Society for the Study of Religion; International Society for the Comparative Study of Civilizations; American Society for the Study of Religion **Discipline:** Physics; Religion; Philosophy; Integrated Knowledge **Related Areas of Interest:** Science and Spirit - Metaphysical Consideration; Yoga and States of Attention; Time and Consciousness.

Selected Publications: His *curriculum vitae* lists 5 books, 5 book chapters and more than 70 articles in various journals dealing with physics, philosophy or religion.

_____. "Western Science and Technology and the Indian Intellectual Tradition." *Manthan* (September 1978): 8-16.
_____. "Science as a Spiritual Path." Journal of Religious Studies 7 (1979): 78-85.
_____. "Perception in Yoga and Physics." Re-Vision: Journal of Consciousness and Knowledge 3 (1980): 36-42.
_____. "Death and the Meaning of Life: a Hindu Response." In Mind and Brain: The Many-Faceted Problem, by John Eccles, 363-4. Paragon House Publishers, 1984.
_____. Whispers from the Other Shore. Wheaton, Il: Quest Books, 1984.
_____. "In the Beginning is the Dance of Love: Design in the Cosmos." *Studies in Religion/Sciences Religiuses* 16, 4 (1987): 449-58.
_____. "In the Beginning is the Dance of Love." In *The Origin and Evolution of the Universe: Evidence for Design?*, ed. John M. Robson, 259-79. Montreal: McGill-Queen's University Press, 1987.
_____, W. Metzger. "Science and Mystical Consciousness: An Interview with Ravi Ravindra." *The Quest* 1, 1 (1988): 59-65.
_____. *The Yoga of the Christ*. Shaftesbury, UK: Element Books, 1990.
_____, editor and main contributor. *Science and Spirit*. New York: Paragon House, 1991.

Reddington, Kenneth George

Present Position and Address: Instructor (since 1981), Psychology and Pastoral Counseling, Japan Central Bible School; 83 Miharashi Cho, Kumagaya Shi, Saitama Ken, Japan 360; (Home) 2340 NW 27th Street, Corvallis, OR 97330, USA **Date of Birth:** June 12, 1931 **Languages Spoken:** English, Japanese **Education:** B.A. Biblical Education (1962)/M.A. Biblical Education (1963), Columbia Bible College; M.S. Education and Psychology (1970), Oregon College of Education; Ph.D. Education and Psychology (1980), Oregon State University **Previous Positions:** Missionary (since 1956); Teacher (1970-77), Kochi Gaigo Junior and High School; Teacher (1977-80), Kochi Gakugei High School; Assistant Professor (1980-83), Kanto Gakuen University; Professor (1983-87), Kanto Junior College; Professor (1989-91), Saitama Junshin Junior College **Selected Memberships:** Japan Evangelical

Missionary Association; Japanese Psychological Association; American Scientific Affiliation **Discipline:** Psychology (human development and personality theory); Bible; Counseling **Related Areas of Interest:** Science and Bible teaching in general; Developing a Bible-based Personality Theory.

Selected Publications:

_____. *Ningen keisei to shite no Nihon no Kyoiku* (Japanese education as human development - towards reforming the cramming system of education). Saitama, Japan: Shinsei Undo Publishers, 1988.

Reich, K. Helmut

Present Position and Address: Research Associate (since 1984), Pädagogisches Institut (The Pedagogical Institute), Rue Faucigny 2, CH-1700 Fribourg, Switzerland; (Home) 29, rue de Bon-Port, CH-1820 Montreux, Switzerland **Work Phone:** (037) 297-560 **Fax:** (037) 299-711 **Email:** Helmut.Reich@unifr.ch **Home Phone:** (021) 963-0783 **Additional Position:** (since Fall 1994) Senior Professor (nonresidential), Senior University (Richmond, BC, Canada; Evanston, WY, USA) **Date of Birth:** May 7, 1923 **Education:** Physics and Electrical Engineering, Köln, Aachen, Braunschweig (Brunswick, Germany), Dipl.-Ing. (1951); Ph.D. Physics (1954), University of Paris/University of Nottingham, UK; Dr.-Ing. Microwave Engineering (1955), University of Braunschweig **Previous Positions:** Applied Physicist (1955-83), European Laboratory for Particle Physics (CERN), Geneva, Switzerland; Research Fellow at various times at Universities of Harvard/Dortmund/Tokyo **Past Editorial Positions:** Editorial Board, *The International Journal for the Psychology of Religion* **Selected Memberships:** International Seminar on Religious Education and Values (ISREV) **Discipline:** Presently: Cognitive-Developmental Constructivist Psychology and its application to Science/Religion; Previously: Physics and Electrical Engineering **Related Areas of Interest:** Cognitive development at the highest level; Religious Development; Relation between Science and Religion; Religious Education.

Selected Publications:

_____, A. Bucher. "Education scientifique et développement du jugement religieux: Dissonance ou harmonie?" In *Actes des 8èmes Journées Internationales sur l'éducation scientifique "Education scientifique et vie active"* (Chamonix), ed. A. Giordan and J. L. Martinand, vol. 3, 551-6. February 1986.
_____. "Religiöse und naturwissenschaftliche Weltbilder: Entwicklung einer komplementären Betrachtungsweise in der Adoleszenz." *Unterrichtswissenschaft* 15, 3 (1987): 321-31.
_____. "The Chalcedonian Definition, an Example of the Difficulties and the Usefulness of Thinking in Terms of Complementarity?" *Journal of Psychology and Theology* 18, 2 (1990): 148-57.
_____, F. Oser. "Moral Judgement, Religious Judgement, World View and Logical Thought: A Review of their Relationship." *British Journal of Religious Education* 12 (1990): 94-101. 172-81.
_____. "The Relation between Science and Theology: The Case for Complementarity Revisited." *Zygon* 25, 4 (1990): 369-90.
_____. "The Relation between Science and Theology: A Response to Critics of Complementarity." In *Origins, Time, and Complexity.* Vol. 2 of *Studies in Science and Religion. Yearbook of the European Society for the Study of Science and Religion (ESSSAT),* ed. G. V. Coyne, S. J and K. Schmitz-Moormann, 284-97. Part 2. Geneva: Labor et Fides, 1994.
_____. "Die Trinitätslehre als Modell für die Beziehungen zwischen Theologie und Naturwissenschaften." In *Glaube und Denken. Jahrbuch der Karl-Heim-Gesellschaft,* ed. H. Schwarz, vol. 7, 202-22. Moers, Germany: Brendow, 1994.
_____. "Can One Rationally Understand Christian Doctrines? An Empirical Study." *British Journal of Religious Education* 16, 2 (1994): 114-26.
_____. "The Doctrine of the Trinity as a Model for Structuring the Relations between Science and Theology." *Zygon: Journal of Religion and Science* 30, (3), 1995, 3833-405.

Reichenbach, Bruce R.

Present Position and Address: Professor of Philosophy (since 1968), Augsburg College, Minneapolis, MN 55454; (Home) 425 Maple Lane, Shoreview, MN 55126, USA **Work Phone:** (612) 330-1094 **Home Phone:** (612) 484-0876 **Date of Birth:** December 13, 1943 **Education:** B.A. Philosophy, Religion (1965), Wheaton College; M.A. Philosophy (1967)/Ph.D. Philosophy (1968), Northwestern University **Previous Positions:** Chairman of Philosophy Department (1969-76, 1980-83, 1989-92), Augsburg College; Visiting Professor of New Testament (1976-77), Morija Theological Seminary, Lesotho, Africa; J. Omar Good Visiting Distinguished Professor of Evangelical Christianity (1985-86), Juniata College, Huntingdon, PA; Part-time Professor of Theology, Bethel Theological Seminary, St. Paul, MN (1987) **Selected Memberships:** American Philosophical Association; Society of Christian Philosophers; Minnesota Philosophical Society **Discipline:** History of Philosophy; Bioethics; Philosophy of Religion **Related Areas of Interest:** Philosophy of Religion, Biology and Ethics.

Selected Publications: His bibliography lists 7 books, 37 articles, and 18 book reviews.

_____. "Natural Evils and Natural Laws: A Theodicy for Natural Evils." *International Philosophical Quarterly* 16, 2 (1976): 179-96.
_____. *The Cosmological Argument: A Reassessment.* Springfield, IL: Charles Thomas, 1972.
_____. *Evil and a Good God.* New York: Fordham University Press, 1982.
_____. "C. S. Lewis on the Desolation of De-Valued Science." *Christian Scholar's Review* 11, 2 (1982): 99-111.
_____. "Euthanasia and the Active-Passive Distinction." *Bioethics* 1, 1 (1987): 51-73.
_____, V. Elving Anderson. "Imaged Through the Lens Darkly: Human Personhood and the Sciences." *Journal of the Evangelical Theological Society* 33, 2 (1990): 197-213.
_____, V. Elving Anderson. *On Behalf of God: A Christian Ethic for Biology.* Grand Rapids: Eerdmans, 1995.

Reisz Jr., H. Frederick

Present Position and Address: President (since 1992), Lutheran Theological Southern Seminary, 4201 N. Main Street, Columbia, SC 29203 USA **Work Phone:** (803) 786-5150 **Date of Birth:** May 13, 1939 **Education:** A.B. (1961), Gettysburg College; B.D. (1965), Lutheran Theological Seminary, Gettysburg; A.M. (1967)/Ph.D. Contemporary, Systematic and Philosophical Theology (1977), The Divinity School, University of Chicago **Previous Positions:** Associate Lutheran Campus Pastor (1969-72), Penn State University; Pastor to the University (1973-78), Wittenberg University; Lutheran Denominational Counselor (1980-92), Harvard Divinity School; Senior Pastor (1978-92), University Lutheran Church, Cambridge, MA **Selected Memberships:** American Academy of Religion **Discipline:** Theology: Contemporary, Systematic and Philosophical **Related Areas of Interest:** Theology; Religious and Scientific Language and Models, World Views, Process Theology; Ethics.

Selected Publications: Some 40 publications listed.

_____. Reactor paragraphs to essay on "Theology and Technology." In *Faith, Science and Technology Forum III.* National Council of Churches, Education in the Society Unit, 1983.
_____. "Science and Religion: A Starter Bibliography." *Entree* (September 1984).
_____. "Knowing the Word and World?" (World Views in Science and Religion) *Word & World* (Summer 1993).

Reynolds, George T.

Present Position and Address: Class of 1909 Professor of Physics Emeritus (since 1987); Jadwin Hall, Princeton University, Princeton, NJ 08544-0708, USA **Concurrent Positions:** Radiation Monitoring Devices Inc. (since 1983); SPEX Industries (since 1986); National Science Foundation (since 1985) **Date of Birth:** May 27, 1917 **Education:** B.Sc. Physics and Mathematics (1939), Rutgers University; M.A. Physics (1942)/Ph.D. Physics (1943), Princeton University **Previous Positions:**

Research Physicist (1943-44), Princeton University; USNR (Lt.j.g.) Physicist (1944-46), Manhattan Project, Los Alamos and Tinian; Assistant (1946-51)/Associate (1951-59)/Professor (1959-78)/Class of 1909 Professor of Physics (1978-87), Princeton University; Visiting Professor (1955-56), Imperial College, University of London; Guggenheim Fellow (1955-56); Churchill Fellow (1973-74), Cambridge, UK; Visiting Professor (1981-82), Open University, UK; Visiting Fellow (1985), Royal Society, Oxford **Consultantships:** Atomic Power Division, Westinghouse Electric Corp (1952-70); Lockheed Missiles Space Co. (1960-76); Franklin CNO Corp (1960-77); Varian Associates (1968-70, 72); DuPont Corp (1970); Weston Instruments (EMR), 1970-78; FMC Corp (1972-81), Santa Clara, CA; Nesco Corp (1981-82) **Selected Memberships:** Fellow, American Physical Society; Biophysical Society; American Geophysical Society; Past local President, Sigma Xi; Institute of Electrical and Electronic Engineers (IEEE) American Society for Photobiology; Fellow, American Association for the Advancement of Science; New York Academy of Science **Discipline:** Physics **Related Areas of Interest:** The New Physics; Cosmology; God and Humanity's Place in the Universe.

Selected Publications: His bibliography lists 21 pages of publications.

_____. *The Implications of Physics for Man.* St. Louis, MO: United Campus Christian Fellowship Publications, 1964.
_____. "Institutional Response to Multidisciplinary Problems." Working Paper, W1, Center for Energy and Environmental Studies, Princeton University, January 28, 1972.
_____. "Teaching Remedies for an Old Disease: Hardening of the Categories." Working Paper, W2, Center for Energy and Environmental Studies, Princeton University, May 15, 1972.

Rice, Stanley Arthur

Present Position and Address: Assistant Professor (since 1993), Department of Biology, Southwest State University, Marshall, MN 56258, USA **Work Phone:** (507) 537-9838 **Date of Birth:** May 30, 1957 **Languages Spoken:** English, some Spanish, some Japanese **Education:** B.A. Environmental Biology (*summa cum laude*, 1979), University of California - Santa Barbara; Ph.D. Plant Biology (1987), University of Illinois, Urbana-Champaign **Previous Positions:** Teaching Assistant (1979-85)/Visiting Teaching Specialist (1986-87), University of Illinois; Assistant Professor (1987-90), Department of Biology, The King's College, Briarcliff Manor, NY; Assistant Professor (1990-93), Department of Biology, Huntington College, Huntington, IN **Selected Memberships:** American Scientific Affiliation; Ecological Society of America; British Ecological Society; Botanical Society of America **Discipline:** Plant Ecology; Teaching of General Biology **Related Areas of Interest:** Botany and Ecology; Plant Physiology; General Biology; Evolution; Natural Theology; Environmental Stewardship.

Selected Publications:

_____. "Botanical and Ecological Objections to a Pre-Flood Vapor Canopy." *Journal of American Scientific Affiliation* 37 (1985): 225-9.
_____. "Creationist Ecology?" *Bulletin, Ecological Society of America* 67 (1986): 8-10.
_____. "On the Problem of Apparent Evil in the Natural World." *Perspectives on Science and Christian Faith* (*PSCF*) 39 (1987): 150-7.
_____. "Scientific Creationism: Adding Imagination to Scripture." *Creation/Evolution* 24 (1988): 25-36.
_____. "Bringing Goodness out of Adversity: God's Activity in the World of Nature." *PSCF* 41 (March 1989): 2-9.
_____. "Faithful in the Little Things: Creationists and 'Operations Science.'" *Creation/Evolution* 25 (1989): 8-14.

Richards, Robert J.

Present Position and Address: Professor (since 1990), Social Sciences Building 205, University of Chicago, 1126 E. 59th Street, Chicago, IL 60637, USA; (Home) 2705 W. Fitch Avenue, Chicago, IL

60645, USA **Work Phone:** (312) 702-8348 **Home Phone:** (312) 743-8945 **Date of Birth:** November 14, 1950 **Education:** Ph.D. Philosophy (1971), St. Louis University; M.A. Biological Psychology (1974), University of Nebraska; Ph.D. History of Science (1978), University of Chicago **Previous Positions:** Assistant Professor (1978-84)/Director of B.A. Program in History, Philosophy and Social Studies of Science and Medicine/Chairman (since 1984), Conceptual Foundations of Science, University of Chicago; Visiting teacher (Spring 1983), Department of History of Science, Harvard University; Associate Professor (1984-90), University of Chicago **Selected Memberships:** Cheiron - The International Society for the History of Behavioral and Social Sciences; History of Science Society; Philosophy of Science Association; Society for History and Philosophy of Biology; Chicago Group for the History of Human Sciences **Discipline:** Philosophy; Biopsychology; History of Science **Related Areas of Interest:** Secularization in 19th Century Science; Evolution and Ethics; Role of God in 19th Century Biology.

Selected Publications: His bibliography lists some 31 publications.

_____. "Instinct and Intelligence in British Natural Theology: Some Contributions to Darwin's Theory of the Evolution of Behavior." *Journal of the History of Biology* 14 (1981): 193-230.
_____. "Emergence of Evolutionary Biology of Behavior in the Early Nineteenth Century." *British Journal for the History of Science* 15 (1982): 241-80.
_____. "Darwin and the Biologizing of Moral Behavior." In *The Problematic Science: Psychology in Nineteenth-Century Thought*, ed. W. Woodward and M. Ash, 43-64. New York: Praeger, 1982
_____. "The Personal Equation in Science: William James's Psychological and Moral Uses of Darwinian Theory." *A William James Renaissance. Harvard Library Bulletin* (special issue) 30 (1982): 387-425.
_____. "A Defense of Evolutionary Ethics," with replies by Cela-Conde, Gewirth, Hughes, Thomas, and Trigg, and rejoinder "Justification through Biological Faith." *Biology and Philosophy* 1, 3 (1986).
_____. *Darwin and the Emergence of Evolutionary Theories of Mind and Behavior*. Chicago: University of Chicago Press, 1987.
_____. "The Moral Foundations of the Idea of Evolutionary Progress: Darwin, Spencer, and the Neo-Darwinians." In *Ideas of Evolutionary Progress*, ed. Matthew Nitecki. Chicago: University of Chicago Press, 1988.
_____. *The Meaning of Evolution: The Morphological Construction and Ideological Reconstruction of Darwin's Theory*. Chicago: University of Chicago Press, 1992.

Riddiford, Alan Wistar

Present Position and Address: Engineering Physicist (since 1983), Fermi National Laboratory; (Home) 1590-D Burton Court, Aurora, IL 60505-1660, USA **Date of Birth:** March 27, 1937 **Languages Spoken:** English **Education:** Bachelor of Engineering Physics, (with distinction, 1961), Cornell University, Ithaca, NY; M.A., Applied Mathematics (1962), Harvard University **Awards and Honors:** Br. Yogindra (February 1974), Initiated by the President of the Ramakriehra Order of India at their HQ at Belur Math, north of Calcutta, India **Previous Positions:** Tutor in Applied Math (1963-66), Harvard University; Research and Development Engineer (1966-69), Beloit Corporation Research, South Beloit, IL; Senior Research Scientist (1969-72), Continental Can Company, Chicago, IL; Assistant Physicist (1972), Argonne Nation Labs; Instructor of Mathematics (1973), Chicago State University, Chicago, IL; Assistant Master of Math (1974-75), Trent College, England; Teacher of Physics, Calculus (1978-83), Marmion Military Academy **Selected Memberships:** Extern Oblate, Marmion Abbey (Roman Catholic Benedictines) **Discipline:** Applied Math; Benedictine Oblate; Vedanta **Related Areas of Interest:** Hindu - Christian Dialogue; Science and Religion (*Zygon*).

Selected Publications:

_____. "Air Entrainment Between an Impermeable Paper Web and a Dryer Surface of Infinite Width." Paper presented at the Second International Symposium on Water Removal at the Presses and Dryers, Mont Gabriel, Canada, October 1968. *Pulp and Paper Magazine of Canada* 53 (February 7, 1969).

_____. "Air Flow Between a Paper Web and a Dryer Surface, Finite Width Effects." Paper presented at the Twenty-third Engineering Conference of the Technical Association of the Pulp and Paper Industry, Houston, TX, November 1968. *Tappi* 52 (1969): 939.

_____, E. D. Cox. "One Dimensional Heat Conduction with Latent Heats of Melting and Vaporization." Continental Can Company Research Report 11-101-520 (August 1970).

_____. "On the Temperature Dependence of the Therman Diffusivity." *Polymer* 12 (1971): 146.

_____, D. Neuffer and A. G. Ruggiero. "A Model to Describe Diffusion Enhancement by the Beam - Beam Interaction." Fermilab TM - 1007 (August 1980).

_____, J. A. Carson, P. M. Mantsch and A. D. McInturff. "High Gradient Quadrupoles for DO Low Beta at F.N.A.L. Paper presented at the American Physical Society Meeting, April 1988.

_____, et. al. "The Fermilab Collider DO Low Beta System." Paper presented at the Particle Accelerator Conference, Rome, Italy, June, 1988.

_____. "Magnetic Designs of High Field Dipoles for a Tevatron Upgrade." Paper presented at the 1988 Summer Study on High Energy Physics in the 1990's, Snowmass, CO, June 1988.

_____, et al. "Design Considerations for a Large Aperture High Field Superconducting Dipole." Paper presented at the American Physical Society Meeting, March 1989.

_____. Endmatter in "Late Night Thoughts on the Cosmic Selt — New and Old." Reflections on *The Cosmic Self: A Penetrating Look at Today's New Age Movement*, by Ted Peters. *Zygon* (September 1994).

Riggan, George A.

Present Position and Address: Riley Professor Emeritus of Systematic Theology (since 1978), Hartford Seminary, 55 Elizabeth Street, Hartford, CT 06105, USA; (Home) HC 87, Box 37, Rowe, MA 01367, USA **Concurrent Positions:** Presently a retired minister of United Church of Christ, Connecticut Conference, Farmington Valley Association **Date of Birth:** December 20, 1909 **Education:** B.A. (*magna cum laude*, 1934), Oklahoma City University; B.D. (with distinction, 1938), Garrett Theological Seminary; Ph.D. (1949), Yale University; Ordained to the Methodist ministry (1938) **Previous Positions:** Held dual standing as a minister of the Congregational Churches from circa 1942 until withdrawal from the Methodist ministry (1951); Associate Professor of Systematic Theology and Ethics (1952-59)/Riley Professor of Systematic Theology (1959-78), Hartford Seminary, CT **Editorial Positions:** Board of Publication, *Zygon* **Selected Memberships:** Charter member and Fellow (1967-68), Center for Advanced Study of Theology and Science, Meadville-Lombard Theological School, Chicago; Academic Fellow (since 1988), former President and now Honorary Vice President, Institute on Religion in an Age of Science **Discipline:** Systematic Theology; Pastoral Ministry **Related Areas of Interest:** Science and Human Purpose; Science and Ethics; Physics and Freedom.

Selected Publications:

_____. "Testing of the Teilhardian Foundations." *Zygon* 3, 3 (1968): 259-312.
_____. "Epilogue to a Symposium on Science and Human Purpose." *Zygon* 8, 3 and 4 (1973): 443-80.
_____. "Mind in Nature." *Zygon* 16, 1 (1981): 79-94.
_____. "Quantum Physics and Freedom in a Whiteheadian Perspective." *Zygon* 17, 3 (1982): 255-65.
_____. "The Center for Advanced Study in Religion and Science: A Personal Perspective." *Zygon* 22 (Twentieth Anniversary Issue): 28-34.

Ritschl, Dietrich

Present Position and Address: Professor of Systematic Theology (since 1983), Ecumenical Institute, University of Heidelberg, Plankengasse 1, 69117 Heidelberg, Germany; (Home) 4418 Reigoldswil, BL. Switzerland **Concurrent Positions:** Director, International Wissenschaftsforum, Heidelberg, Germany **Work Phone:** (0049) 6221-543341 **Home Phone:** (0041) 61-961670 **Date of Birth:** January 17, 1929 **Languages Spoken:** English; German **Education:** Philosophy and Theology (1946-50), University Tübingen and Basel; Ph.D. (1958)/D.D. (1976), Edinburgh **Previous Positions:** Minister of German speaking churches in Scotland (1952-58); Associate Professor (1958-63), History of Dogma, Austin Presbyterian Theological Seminary/Episcopal Seminary; Professor (1963-69), Pittsburgh Theological Seminary; Adjunct Professor (1963-69), University of Pittsburgh; Harry Emerson Fosdick Professor (1969-70), Union Theological Seminary, NY; Professor of Systematic Theology (1970-83), University of Mainz; Guest Professor (8 x since 1970), United Theological Faculty, Melbourne/Pontifical University Gregoriana, Rome (1991-92) **Selected Memberships:** Commission on Faith and Order (WCC); Societas Ethica; International Association for Art and Therapy (IAACT) **Discipline:** Systematic Theology; Philosophy **Related Areas of Interest:** Philosophical Theology; Systematic Theology; Patristics; Medical Ethics; Psychotherapy in Teaching and Practice.

Selected Publications: Bibliography lists besides books about 50 scholarly articles in various journals in the USA, UK and Germany, as well as 100 other articles.

_____. *Theologie in den Neuen Welten.* Munich: Christian Kaiser Verlag, 1981.
_____. *Zur Logik der Theologie.* Munich: Christian Kaiser Verlag, 1984; English trans., *The Logic of Theology.* Philadelphia: Fortress Press, 1987.
_____. *Konzepte: Oekumene, Medizin, Ethik.* Munich: Christian Kaiser Verlag, 1986.
_____, coeditor. *Ethik in der Medizin.* Heidelberg/New York/Tokyo: Springer Verlag, 1989ff.
_____. *Ökumenische Theologie.* Kohlhammer Verlag, 1994.

Rivier, Dominique-Casimir

Present Position and Address: Professeur Honoraire (since 1988) à l'Université de Lausanne, l'oche 1008 Jouxtens, Switzerland; IPE/BSP, Faculté des Sciences, CH-1015, Lausanne-Dorigny, Switzerland **Date of Birth:** November 12, 1918 **Languages Spoken:** French, English, German **Education:** Bacculauréat ès lettres (1940), University of Lausanne; Studies in physics with Prof. Perrier and Stueckelberg (1941-1944); Assistant to Prof. Stueckelberg (1944-1949), the Institut de Physique théorique de l'Université de Genève; Doctorate in Physics (1948), Université de Lausanne **Postgraduate Experience:** Research Fellow (1951-52), Princeton University; Postdoctoral Fellow (1952-53), the National Research Council, Ottawa, Canada **Congresses and Conferences:** Treasurer (1969-1984), Conférence permanente des recteurs et vice-chanceliers européens; President (1973-1979)/Member (1979-1981), Commission de planification de la Conférence des rectuers suisses; President of the Conférence régulière sur les problèmes universitaires (1978-1980), Conseil de l'Europe, Strasbourg; Attended the Institut d'Education de la Foundation Européenne de la Culture (1980-81), Université de Paris, Dauphine **Previous Positions:** Professeur extraordinaire (chaire de physique expérimentale, 1953)/Director of the Physics Laboratory (1953-1968)/Professeur ordinaire in the Faculty of Science (1957-present)/Dean of the Faculty of Science (1964-1966)/Director of the Institute of Experimental Physics (1964-1968)/Rector (1968-1979), University of Lausanne **Selected Memberships:** Member (1960-1980), Commission fédérale pour l'encouragement de la Recherche, Berne; Member of the Conseil de l'Enseigement supérieur et de la Recherche (1968-1977), Conseil de l'Europe, Strasbourg; Member of "Science et Theologie" society which is being formed **Discipline:** Fundamental Physics, Theoretical Physics **Related Areas of Interest:** Science and Theology, and Science and Ethics.

Selected Publications: His *curriculum vitae* lists 79 publications.

_____. "Discours d'installation en qualité de professeur ordinaire." *P.U.L.* 19 (1958): 47-51.
_____. "La science à la recherche d'une conscience." *R.T.P.* 10 (1960): 42-57.
_____. "Guerre et paix à l'âge atomique. Un dialogue entre théologiens et savants." *R.T.P.* Sie III 12 (1962): 29-37.
_____. "La Physique et le Temps." *A.S.H.S.N.* 145 (1965): 214-37.
_____. "Science et foi chrétienne. Pour le renouvellement d'une confrontation." *Reformation* (Berne) 16, 3 (1967).
_____. "De la nécessité d'une formation éthique pour l'homme de science." In *L'Embryon, un homme.* Fribourg, 1987.

_____. L'Université de l'avenir. In *Actes du Colloque du 450e anniversaire de la Fondaton de l'Académie de Lausanne*, 121-7. Lausanne, 1988.
_____. "Le physicien et ses principes." *R.T.P.* 122 (1990): 15-32.

Roberts, Jon H.

Present Position and Address: Associate Professor of History, 416 COPS Bldg., University of Wisconsin - Stevens Point, WI 54481, USA; (Home) 1924 Ellis Street, Stevens Point, WI 54481, USA **Work Phone:** (715) 346-4479 **Home Phone:** (715) 345-2310 **Date of Birth:** November 7, 1947 **Education:** A.B. (1969), University of Missouri; A.M. (1970)/Ph.D. (1980), Harvard University **Selected Memberships:** American Historical Association; Organization of American Historians; American Society of Church History; History of Science Society **Discipline:** History **Related Areas of Interest:** Anglo-American Discussions of the Relationship between Science and Theology in the 19th and 20th Centuries; Protestant Apologetics (1800-present).

Selected Publications:

_____. "Science and American Protestant Theology, 1900-1950." Paper presented at the Craigville Conference on the History of the American Protestant Establishment in the Twentieth Century, June 28-30, 1985.
_____. *Darwinism and the Divine in America: Protestant Intellectuals and Organic Evolution, 1859-1900.* Madison, University of Wisconsin Press, 1988.

Roberts, Robert C.

Present Position and Address: Professor of Philosophy and Psychological Studies (since 1984), Wheaton College, 1013 E. Willow, Wheaton, IL 60187, USA **Work Phone:** (708) 752-5888 **Home Phone:** (312) 668-8536 **Languages Spoken:** English, Dutch **Education:** B.A. (1965)/M.A. (1970), Wichita State University; B.D. (1970)/Ph.D. (1974), Yale University **Previous Positions:** Instructor of Philosophy (1973)/Assistant (1974-79)/Associate (1979-83)/Professor of Philosophy (1983), Western Kentucky University **Selected Memberships:** American Philosophical Association; Society of Christian Philosophers **Discipline:** Ethics; Philosophy of Psychology; Kierkegaard, Philosophy of Religion **Related Areas of Interest:** (same as Discipline).

Selected Publications:

_____. "What an Emotion Is: A Sketch." *Philosophical Review* 97 (1988): 183-209.
_____. "Forgiveness as Therapy." *The Reformed Journal* 36, 7 (1986): 10-23.
_____. "Virtues and Rules." *Philosophy and Phenomenological Research* 51, 2 (1992): 325-43.
_____. "Emotions As Access to Religious Truths." *Faith and Philosophy* 9 (1992): 83-94.
_____. "Emotions Among the Virtues of the Christian Life." *Journal of Religious Ethics* 20 (1992): 201-32.
_____. "Thomas Aquinas on the Morality of Emotions." *History of Philosophy Quarterly* 9, 3 (1992): 287-304.
_____. "The Logic and Lyric of Contrition." *Theology Today* 50, 2 (1993): 193-207.
_____. *Taking the Word to Heart: Self and Other in an Age of Therapies.* Grand Rapids: Eerdmans, 1993.

Rockwell, Theodore

Present Position and Address: Engineer-Scientist in Private Practice; Author; 3403 Woolsey Drive, Chevy Chase, MD 20815, USA **Work Phone:** (301) 652-9509 **Fax Number:** (301) 652-0534 (call first) **E-Mail:** CompuServe 71524.1333 **Date of Birth:** June 26, 1922 **Education:** B.S. Engineering (1943)/M.S. Chemical Engineering (1945), Princeton University; Advanced Studies (1943-49), University of Tennessee, Oak Ridge Extension; Advance Studies (1947-48), Oak Ridge School of Reactor Technology; Sc.D. (with honors,1960), TriState University, IN **Previous Positions:** Process Improvement Engineer in the Electromagnetic Separation Pilot Plant (1944-45)/Head of Radiation Shielding Engineering (1945-49), Manhattan Project, Oak Ridge National Laboratory, TN; Director, Coolant Technology Div. (1949-54)/Technical Director (1954-64), Naval Reactors Headquarters; Founder and Principal Officer (1964-87), MPR Associates **Selected Memberships:** Cosmos Club (since 1967); Parapsychological Association (and for years was its representative to the AAAS); AAAS; Sigma Xi (Hon. research); National Press Club, Author's Guild; Vice President and Director, US Psychotronics Association (1989-92); Fellow, American Society for Psychical Research; American Society of Dowsers; Academy of Religion and Psychical Research; DC Steering Committee, Institute of Noetic Sciences **Discipline:** Nuclear Engineering **Related Areas of Interest:** Interaction between Scientific and Spiritual Communities **Current Areas of Research:** Current activities involve trying to make certain works on the scientific frontier known to mainstream scientists.

Selected Publications:

_____, coauthor. *Arms Control Agreements: Designs for Verification.* Baltimore, MD: Johns Hopkins Press, 1968.
_____. "Pseudoscience? or Pseudocriticsm?" *Journal Parapsychology* 43 (1979): 221-31.
_____, senior author. "Heresy, Excommunication, and Other Weeds in the Garden of Science." *New Realities* 4 (December 1981): 48ff.
_____, senior author. "Frames of Meaning: The Social Construction of Extraordinary Science." *Theta* 11 (April 1983): 69-71.
_____, senior author. "The Demarcation Between Science and Pseudoscience." *Journal American Society Psychical Research* 80 (January 1986): 105-12.
_____. "On Science and Religion." *The Scientist* 2, 1 (1988): 12.
_____. Review of *The Dove in the Stone: Finding the Sacred in the Commonplace. New Realities* 9, 5 (1989): 51.
_____, guest editorial. "Psi Is Not a Mere Anomaly." *Journal of the American Society of Psychical Research* 83, 3 (1989): 201-3. Reprinted, with commentary, in *Psi Review* 1 (1990).
_____. Review of *The Spindrift Papers. Journal American Society Psychical Research* 87 (October 1993).
_____. *Power to the People: Living with Technology on a Shrinking Planet.* In Progress.
_____. *The Rickover Effect: How One Man Made a Difference.* Naval Inst. Press, 1992. Paperback. John Wiley, 1995.

Rolston III, Holmes

Present Position and Address: Professor of Philosophy (since 1976), Colorado State University, Fort Collins, CO 80523, USA **Work Phone:** (303) 491-5328 **Home Phone:** (303) 484-5883 **Date of Birth:** November 19, 1932 **Education:** B.S. Physics (1953), Davidson College, NC; B.D. (1956), Union Theological Seminary; M.A. Philosophy of Science (1968), University of Pittsburgh, PA; Ph.D. Theology and Religious Studies (1958), University of Edinburgh; Sabbatical Year (1974-75), Center for the Study of World Religions, Harvard University **Previous Positions:** Instructor in Philosophy (1958), Hampden-Sydney College, VA; Assistant (1968-71)/Associate Professor (1971-76), Department of Philosophy, Colorado State University; Visiting Distinguished Scholar (Spring 1991), Center for Theology and the Natural Sciences, Berkeley **Editorial Positions:** Associate Editor, *Environmental Ethics*; Area Editor for environmental ethics and animal welfare, *Encyclopedia of Bioethics*, 2d ed.; Advisory Board, *Zygon* / Reidel Series, Environmental Ethics and Science Policy **Selected Memberships:** President (1987-88)/Member, American Academy of Religion; Past-President, Phi Beta Kappa; Past-President, American Association of University Professors; American Association for the Advancement of Science; Philosophy of Science Association; American Philosophical Association; United Presbyterian Church USA; Institute on Religion in an Age of Science; Center for the Study of Theology and the Natural Sciences **Discipline:** Theology; Philosophy of Science; Physics **Related Areas of Interest:** Science and Religion; Environmental Ethics.

Selected Publications: His bibliography lists 72 publications, many of them of direct relevance to the field.

_____. "The Preservation of Natural Value in the Solar System." In *Beyond Spaceship Earth: Environmental Ethics and the Solar System*, ed. Eugene C. Hargrove, 140-82. San Francisco: Sierra Club Books, 1986.

_____. "Science and the Ways to God: Stanley Jaki's Vision of Scientific Creativity." *Commonweal* 94, 10 (1987): 313-16.

_____. *Science and Religion: A Critical Survey*. New York: Random House, 1987.

_____. *Environmental Ethics: Values in and Duties to the Natural World*. Philadelphia: Temple University Press, 1988.

_____. "Wildlife and Wildlands: A Christian Perspective." *Church and Society* 80, 4 (1990): 16-40.

_____. "Disvalues in Nature." *The Monist* 75 (1992): 250-78.

_____. "Does Nature Need To Be Redeemed?" *Zygon* 29 (1994): 205-29. Also in *Horizons in Biblical Theology* 14, 2 (1993): 143-72.

_____. "Order and Disorder in Nature, Science, and Religion." In *Science, Technology and Religious Ideas: Proceedings of the Institute for Liberal Studies*, ed. George W. Shields, and Mark Shale, vol. 4, 1-14. Frankfort, KY: Institute for Liberal Studies, Kentucky State University, 1994.

_____. "Value in Nature and the Nature of Value." In *Philosophy and the Natural Environment*, ed. Robin Attfield and Andrew Belsey, 13-30. Cambridge: Cambridge University Press, 1994.

_____. *Conserving Natural Value*. New York: Columbia University Press, 1994.

Rossman, Parker

Present Position and Address: Writer; Vice President, Chair for Long Range Planning and Theological **Education:** Committee (since 1988), Global/Pacific (Electronic) University Consortium, Box 382, Niantic, CT 06357 USA **Work Phone:** (203) 739-5195 **E-Mail:** (Sprintmail) PROSSMAN **Date of Birth:** May 20, 1919 **Languages Spoken:** English, French **Education:** A.B. (1941), University of Oklahoma; B.D. (1944), University of Chicago; Ph.D. Religion in Education (1953), Yale University **Previous Positions:** Instructor, Columbia College (1945-48)/Yale Divinity School (1948-50); Campus Ministry Executive (1950-57), Board of Higher Education:, Disciples of Christ; Sabbatical year (1956), Geneva, Switzerland; Associate Professor of Religion in Higher Education: (1958-65), Yale Divinity School; William Henry Hoover Lecturer (1961), University of Chicago; Instructor (1965), Balamand Greek Orthodox Theological School, Lebanon; Dean (1966-72), Ecumenical Continuing Education Center, Yale University; Writer in Residence and Lecturer (1982-83), Central Philippines University **Selected Memberships:** Educom; ASIS, World Brain Group (Information Science Association); Glosas/USA (Global Systems Analysis and Simulation Association **Discipline:** Research Methods and Interdisciplinary Higher Education: **Related Areas of Interest:** Collective Intelligence; Technology and Education; World Brain.

Selected Publications:

_____. *Christians and the World of Computers*. Philadelphia: Trinity International Press, 1990.

Roth, Ariel Adrien

Present Position and Address: Senior Research Scientist (since 1994), Geoscience Research Institute, Loma Linda University, Loma Linda, CA 92350, USA **Work Phone:** (909) 824-4548 **Fax Number:** (909) 824-4314 **Date of Birth:** July 16, 1927 **Languages Spoken:** English; French **Education:** B.A (1948), Pacific Union College; M. S. (1949)/Ph.D. (1955), University of Michigan **Postgraduate Experience:** Training in radiation biology (1956-57), University of California - Berkeley; Training in geology and mathematics (1963-1969), University of California - Riverside **Awards and Honors:** Nominated to *Who's Who in America* (1974); Nominated to the Society of the Sigma Xi **Previous**

Positions: Instructor to Associate Professor of Biology (1950-57), Pacific Union College; Research Associate (1957-58), Loma Linda University; Professor and Chairman (1958-63), Department of Biology, Andrews University; Professor and Chairman (1963-71), Department of Biology, Loma Linda University; Research Scientist (1971-80)/Director, (1980-94), Geoscience Research Institute, Loma Linda University **Editorial Positions:** Editor, *Origins* (since 1974) **Selected Memberships:** Geological Society of America; Society for Sedimentary Geology; American Association of Petroleum Geologists **Discipline:** Biologist **Related Areas of Interest:** Theology; Geology; Philosophy of Science **Current Areas of Research:** Writing a book on Science and Scripture.

Selected Publications: His bibliography contains over 125 published articles.

_____, C. D. Clausen, P. Y. Yahiku, V. E. Clausen and W. W. Cox. "Some Effects of Light on Coral Growth." *Pacific Science* 36 (1982): 65-81.
_____. "Scientific Evidence of a Worldwide Flood." *Signs of the Times* 113, 1 (1986): 8-11; 20-1.
_____. "Catastrophism - Is It Scientific?" *Ministry* 59, 7 (1986): 24-6.
_____. "How to Invalidate the Bible - Unconsciously: Some Thoughts on Pluralism About Origins." *Adventist Perspectives* 2, 2 (1988): 12-27.
_____. "Science, A Good Place to Begin." *Signs of the Times* 115, 12 (1988): 19.
_____. "Those Gaps in the Sedimentary Layers." *Origins* 15 (1988): 75-92.
_____. "We Shall Behold Him in the Wonder of Creation." General Conference Bulletin 3. *Adventist Review* 167, 29 (1990): 741-3.
_____. "Life in the Deep Rocks and the Deep Fossil Record." *Origins* 19 (1992): 93-104.
_____. "Clash of the Titans." *Liberty* 88, 3 (1993): 19-25.

Rothenberg, David

Present Position and Address: Assistant Professor of Philosophy, Department of Humanities, New Jersey Institute of Technology, University Heights, Newark, NJ 07102, USA **Work Phone:** (201) 596-3289 **Fax Number:** (201) 565-0586 **Date of Birth:** July 8, 1962 **Languages Spoken:** English, French, Norwegian, Nepali **Education:** B.A. (*magna cum laude*, in Special Concentrations, 1984), Harvard University; Ph.D. Philosophy (1991),, Boston University **Congresses and Conferences:** Participant in many conferences including: Fifth World Wilderness Congress, Tromsø, Norway (1993); Delegate to United Nations Conference on the Ethical Implications of Agenda 21 **Lectures Presented:** Guest Lecturer at many colleges in the USA and other countries (1988-93) **Awards and Honors:** The Hoopes Prize (1984); Ira-Hiti Foundation Grant (1992); NJIT Separately Budgeted Research Grant (1993) **Previous Positions:** Teaching Assistant (1983), Harvard University; Intern (1985), Coolidge Center for the Environment; Research Assistant (1985-86), University of Oslo; Research Associate (1987), Harvard Law School, Human Rights Program; Teaching Fellow in Philosophy (1987-90), Boston University; Adjunct Professor, Antioch/New England Graduate School (1990-91); Consultant to the United Nations Environmental Program (UNEP) (1993); Adjunct Faculty, Union Institute graduate program (1994) **Media Work:** "The Age of Ecology" Interviewed by David Cayley, CBC Series Ideas, 1990; Consultant to BBC (1993) and Norwegian Broadcasting Company (NRK) (1992) **Editorial Positions:** Assistant editor and writer (1984), *The Ecologist*; Editor, *The Trumpeter: Journal of Ecology and Philosophy*; Consulting editor, *Orion*; Manuscript reader and consultant: Cambridge University Press, Routledge, MIT Press, University of California Press, Oxford University Press, University of Chicago Press **Other Academic Experience:** Consultant to the United Nations Environmental Program (UNEP), reviewing ethical implications of Agenda 21 (1993) **Selected Memberships:** American Philosophical Association (APA); Fellow, Institute for Human Ecology; International Society for Environmental Ethics; Orion Society American; Society for Forest History, referee; Society for Phenomenology and Existential Philosophy (SPEP); Ethics Advisory Committee, World Conservation Strategy (IUCN) **Discipline:** Philosophy; Music **Related Areas of Interest:** Ecosophy.

Selected Publications:

_____. *Arne Naess: Gjør det vondt å tenke?* Oslo: Grondahl-Dreyers Forlag, 1992.
_____, Peter Reed. *Wisdom in the Open Air: The Norwegian Roots of Deep Ecology.* Minneapolis: University of Minnesota Press, 1992.
_____. *Is It Painful to Think? Conversations with Arne Naess.* Minneapolis: University of Minnesota Press, 1992. Australia: Allen & Unvin, 1993.
_____. *Hand's End: Technology and the Limits of Nature.* Berkeley: University of California Press, 1993.
_____. "Deep Ecology." In *Encyclopedia of the Environment.* Boston: Houghton Mifflin, 1994.
_____. "Get Out of Whatever Cage: Avant-Garde in Nature." *Musicworks 58* (1994).
_____. "Sudden Music: Improvising across the Electronic Abyss." *Contemporary Music Review* (1994).
_____. "The Way of Pure Sound: Monastic Music of Tibet." *Himal* (1994).
_____. "Review of New Environmental Ethics Texts." *Environmental Ethics* (1994).
_____. "On the Impossibility of the Foremost Connection: The Work of Neil Evernden." *Orion* (Spring 1994).

Rothrock, Paul E.

Present Position and Address: Professor of Biology (since 1981), Taylor University, Upland, IN 46989, USA **Date of Birth:** October 17, 1948 **Education:** B.A. (1970), Rutgers University; M.S. (1973)/Ph.D. Plant Systematics (1976), Pennsylvania State University **Previous Positions:** Biology Professor (1976-81), Montreat-Anderson College **Selected Memberships:** American Scientific Affiliation **Discipline:** Plant Systematics **Related Areas of Interest:** Sociobiology; Evolutionary Biology; Environmental Ethics.

Selected Publications:

_____, M. E. Rothrock. "Christianity and E. O. Wilson's Mythology of Scientific Materialism." *Perspectives of Science and Christian Faith* 39, 2 (1987): 87-93.

Rottschaefer, William A.

Present Position and Address: Professor of Philosophy (since 1985), Lewis and Clark College, Portland, OR 97219, USA **Work Phone:** (503) 246-1473 or (503) 768-7479 **Fax Number:** (503) 768-3333 **E-Mail:** rotts@LClark.edu **Date of Birth:** June 20, 1933 **Education:** B.A. Philosophy and Letters (*cum laude*, 1957)/M.A. Philosophy (1960), St. Louis University; S.T.L. Licentiate in Sacred Theology (1966), St. Louis University; M.S. Physics (1969), University of Illinois; Ph.D. Philosophy (1973), Boston University **Previous Positions:** Visiting Assistant (1972-73)/Visiting Assistant Professor of Philosophy (1973-75), State University of NY; Assistant (1975-79)/Associate Professor of Philosophy (1979-85), Lewis and Clark College **Selected Memberships:** American Academy of Religion; American Philosophical Association; Center for Theology and the Natural Sciences; Institute on Religion in an Age of Science; International Society for the History, Philosophy and Social Study of Biology; Philosophy of Science Association **Discipline:** Philosophy of Science **Related Areas of Interest:** Philosophy of Religion; Epistemology; Metaphysics; Relationships between the Epistemic Structures of Scientific and Religious Cognition; Science and Values **Current Areas of Research:** He is currently working on a manuscript entitled, "The Biological and Psychological Bases or Moral Agency."

Selected Publications:

_____. "Religious Cognition as Interpreted Experience: An Examination of Ian Barbour's Comparison of the Epistemic Structures of Science and Religion." *Zygon* 20 (1985): 265-82.
_____. "Sociobiology, Religion and Values: The Case of E. O. Wilson." *Explorations* 4 (1985): 39-57.
_____. "The New Interactionism between Science and Religion." *Religious Studies Review* 14 (1988): 218-25.
_____. "Creation and Evolution: Some Epistemological Criteria for an Integration." *Explorations* 8 (1990): 29-42.

_____. "Really Taking Darwin Seriously: An Alternative to Michael Ruse's Darwinian Metaethics." *Biology and Philosophy* 5 (1990): 149-74.
_____. "Evolutionary Naturalistic Justifications of Morality: A Matter of Faith and Works." *Biology and Philosophy* 6 (1991): 341-49.
_____. "Some Philosophical Implications of Bandura's Social Cognitive Theory of Human Agency." *American Psychologist* 6 (1991): 153-5.
_____. "Philosophical and Religious Implications of Cognitive Social Learning Theories of Personality." *Zygon* 26 (1991): 137-48.
_____. "Social Learning Theories of Moral Agency." *Behavior and Philosophy* 19 (1991): 61-76.
_____. "What if the Universe is Fine-Tuned for Life." *Explorations* 11 (1993): 45-62.

Rubik, Beverly

Present Position and Address: Director, Center for Frontier Sciences, Temple University, Ritter Hall 003-00, Philadelphia, PA 19122, USA **Concurrent Positions:** Administration (since 1988), Temple University **Date of Birth:** January 12, 1951 **Education:** B.S. Chemistry (1972), Illinois Institute of Technology; Ph.D. Biophysics (1979), University of California **Previous Positions:** Senior Scientist (1983-84), Miles Laboratory, Berkeley, CA; Faculty (1985-88) Institute for Culture and Creation Spirituality, Holy Names College, Oakland, CA; Faculty (1979-82, 1985-88), San Francisco State University **Selected Memberships:** Center for Theology and the Natural Sciences, G.T.U., Berkeley, CA; Workshop leader, Friends of Creation Spirituality, Oakland, CA **Discipline:** Biophysics; Foundations of Science **Related Areas of Interest:** History and Philosophy of Science, Theology, Religion and Spirituality; Emerging paradigms in same; Ecology; Integration toward a Holistic World view; Faith Healing; Shamanism; Human Potential for Self-healing; Spontaneous Remission **Current Areas of Research:** Healers and the Healing Process; Working on a future book comprising lecture materials on "Healing the Rift between Science and Spirituality" (Matter and Spirit).

Selected Publications:

_____. "Called to Life by the Creative Cosmos." *Creation* 4, 4 (1988): 12.
_____. "The Quest of the Frontier Scientist." *Creation* 5, 5 (1989): 17-18.
_____. "Nature's Deep Wisdom." *Creation* 6, 3 (1989): 24-5.
_____. "Use of Ritual in Science: The Scientific Pow-Wow." In *Proceedings of the 7th International Conference on the Study of Shamanism and Alternate Modes of Healing*, ed. R. I. Heinze. Berkeley, CA: Independent Scholars of Asia, Inc., 1990.
_____, editor. *The Interrelationship Between Mind and Matter.* Philadelphia, PA: The Center for Frontier Sciences at Temple University, 1992.
_____, J. R. Havern. "Two Quantum Shamans: A Dialogue." In *The Reunion of Science and Spirit.* Cauldron Productions, Inc., 1992.
_____. "Reunion of Spirituality and Science." In *The Reunion of Science and Spirit.* New York: Cauldron Productions, Inc., 1992.
_____, B. D. Josephson. "The Challenge of Consciousness Research." *Frontier Perspectives* 3, 1 (1992): 15-19.
_____. "Energy Medicine: A Challenge for Science." *Noetic Sciences Review* (Winter 1993): 37-9. The Institute of Noetic Sciences, Sausalito, CA.
_____. "Shamanism and Spirits of Darkness." In *Evil, The Cosmic Shadow*, ed. L. Sherman, 29-40. New York: Cauldron Productions, 1994.
_____. "The Perennial Challenge of Anomalies at the Frontiers of Science." *British Homeopathic Journal* 83 (1994): 155-66.

Rupke, Nicolaas Adrianus

Present Position and Address: Professor of the History of the Bio-medical Sciences, and Director, Institute for the History of Medicine, University of Göttingen, Humboldtallee 36, 37073 Göttingen,

Germany **Date of Birth:** January 22, 1944 **Languages Spoken:** Dutch, English, German, French **Education:** B.A. Geology with Biology (1968), Groningen; M.A. Geology with History of Science (1970)/Ph.D. Geology and Geophysics (1972), Princeton University **Previous Positions:** Fellow in Geology (1972-73), Smithsonian Institution; Fellow in Geology (1973-76)/Fellow in the History of Science (1976-1981), University of Oxford; Visiting Lecturer (1978-79), Imperial College, London; Fellow in History of Science (1981-83, 1987), University of Tübingen; Fellow in History of Medicine (1983-87), Wellcome Institute, London; Fellow in History of Science (1985), Netherlands Institute for Advanced Study; Fellow in History of Science (1988-89), National Humanities Center, NC; Senior Fellow in History of Science, Institute of Advanced Studies, Australian National University, Canberra, Australia **Selected Memberships:** Fellow, Geological Society of America; Fellow, Royal Historical Society **Related Areas of Interest:** History of Science; Late-modern Earth and Life Sciences; Romantic Tradition in the Sciences; Science and Society; Genesis and Geology.

Selected Publications: His *curriculum vitae* lists 11 publications in geology, and 19 in the history of science.

_____. *The Great Chain of History: William Buckland and the English School of Geology, 1814-1849.* Oxford: Clarendon Press, 1983.
_____. "The Study of Fossils in the Romantic Philosophy of History and Nature." *History of Science* 21 (1983): 389-413.
_____. "The Apocalyptic Denominator in English Culture in the Early Nineteenth Century." In *Common Denominators in Art and Science*, ed. M. R. Pollock, 30-45. Aberdeen University Press, 1983.
_____. "Romanticism in The Netherlands." In *Romanticism in National Context*, ed. R. S. Porter and M. Teich, 191-216. Cambridge: Cambridge University Press, 1988.
_____. *Richard Owen: Victorian Naturalist.* London/New Haven, CT: Yale University Press, 1994.

Ruse, Michael

Present Position and Address: Professor of Philosophy (since 1974), University of Guelph, Guelph, ONT N1G 2WI, Canada **Date of Birth:** June 21, 1940 **Languages Spoken:** English, French, German **Education:** B.A. Philosophy and Mathematics (1962)/Ph.D. (1970), Bristol University; M.A. Philosophy (1964), McMaster University **Previous Positions:** Lecturer (1965-69)/Assistant Professor (1969-71)/Associate Professor (1971-74), University of Guelph; Associate (1972-73), Clare Hall, Cambridge **Selected Memberships:** Fellow, American Association for the Advancement of Science; Fellow, Royal Society of Canada; IRAS; Philosophy of Science Association **Discipline:** History and Philosophy of Biology **Related Areas of Interest:** Philosophical Questions on the Science-Religion Interface.

Selected Publications: His *curriculum vitae* lists 14 books, 43 articles in refereed journals, 31 contributions to discussions and articles in non-refereed journals and magazines, 37 contributions to books, and 116 reviews.

_____. "The Arkansas Creation Trial 1981: Is there a message for us all?" *History and Social Science Teacher* 17 (1982): 23-8.
_____. "Creation Science is not Science." *Science, Technology, and Human Values* (1982). Reprint, in *Creationism, Science, and the Law: The Arkansas Case*, ed. M. LaFollette. Cambridge, MA: MIT, 1983.
_____. "Genesis revised: Can We Do Better Than God?" *Zygon* 19 (1984): 297-316.
_____. *Taking Darwin Seriously: A Naturalistic Approach to Philosophy.* Oxford: Blackwell, 1986.
_____. "Evolutionary Ethics: A Phoenix Arisen." *Zygon* 21 (1986): 95-112.
_____. "Darwinism and Determinism." *Zygon* 22 (1987): 419-42.
_____, editor. *But is it Science? The Philosophical Question in the Evolution/Creation Controversy.* Buffalo, NY: Prometheus, 1988.
_____. *Philosophy of Biology Today.* Albany: SUNY Press, 1988.
_____. *The Darwinian Paradigm.* London: Routledge, 1989.

Russell, Colin Archibald

Present Position and Address: Research Professor in History of Science and Technology (since 1993), The Open University, UK; 64 Putnoe Lane, Bedford MK41 9AF, UK **Home Phone:** 0234-359695 **Date of Birth:** July 9, 1928 **Education:** B.Sc. Chemistry (1949), University College - Hull; M.Sc. (1958)/Ph.D. (1962)/D.Sc. History and Philosophy of Science (1978), University College - London **Lectures Presented:** Templeton Lectures (1993), "The Earth, Humanity and God," Cambridge, UK **Awards and Honors:** Dexter Award (1990), American Chemical Society, for "outstanding contributions to the history of chemistry." **Previous Positions:** Assistant Lecturer in Organic Chemistry (1950-59), Kingston Polytechnic; Lecturer, Senior Lecturer, Principal Lecturer (1959-70), Preston Polytechnic; Visiting Fellow (1985-86), Wolfson College, Cambridge; Senior Lecturer and Reader in History of Science and Technology (1972-81)/Chairman, History of Science and Technology (1981-93), The Open University **Media Work:** Several relevant television programmes for the BBC, such as "Astronomy before Copernicus," "The Heavens are Telling," "The Flood," etc. **Selected Memberships:** Fellow, Royal Society of Chemistry (FRSC); Royal Institution; President (1986-88), British Society for History of Science; Vice President (1987-92), Universities and Colleges Christian Fellowship; Chairman (1988-93), Christians in Science **Discipline:** History and Philosophy of Science; Chemistry **Related Areas of Interest:** Historical Studies in the Theology/Science Interface.

Selected Publications: Besides the publications listed below his bibliography contains numerous papers in heterocyclic chemistry, and about 100 articles and reviews, and 26 Open University Units in History of Science.

_____. "Noah and the Neptunists." *Faith and Thought* 100 (1972): 143-58.
_____. *Science and Belief: A Selection of Recent Historical Studies.* London: University of London Press, 1973.
_____. Three chaps. in *Wonders of Creation.* Lion Press, 1975.
_____. *Cross-Currents: Interactions Between Science and Faith.* UK: InterVarsity Press, 1985.
_____. "Some Founding Fathers of Physics." *Physics Education* 22 (1987): 27-33.
_____. "Science and Theology." In *New Dictionary of Theology.* UK: InterVarsity Press, 1988.
_____. "The Conflict Metaphor and its Social Origins." *Science and Christian Belief* 1 (1989): 3-26.
_____, coeditor and author. Four chaps. in *The Rise of Scientific Europe, 1500-1800.* Hodder & Stoughton, 1992.
_____, "Biological Science and Christian Thought." In *The Blackwell Encyclopedia of Modern Christian Thought.* Oxford, UK: Blackwell, 1993.
_____, *The Earth, Humanity and God.* London, UK: University College London Press, 1994.

Russell, Robert John

Present Position and Address: Professor of Theology and Science (since 1992), in Residence, The Graduate Theological Union, Berkeley; (Home) 111 Sea View Avenue, Piedmont, CA 94610, USA **Concurrent Positions:** Founder and Director (since 1981), The Center for Theology and the Natural Sciences, 2400 Ridge Road, Berkeley, CA 94709, USA; Ministry: Associate to Carleton College Chapel (1978-81)/Graduate Theological Union (since 1981) **Work Phone:** (510) 848-8152 **Home Phone:** (510) 645-7458 **Date of Birth:** August 23, 1946 **Languages Spoken:** English, French, Italian **Education:** B.S. Physics (1968), Stanford University; M.S. Physics (1970), University of California - Los Angeles; B.D. (*magna cum laude*, 1972)/M.A. Theology (1972), Pacific School of Religion, Berkeley; Ph.D. Physics (1978), University of California - Santa Cruz **Awards and Honors**: Three-time winner of Templeton Prize for Papers on Humility Theology; Judge (since 1994), Templeton Prize **Previous Positions:** Assistant Professor of Physics (1978-81), Carleton College, Northfield, MN; Visiting Adjunct Professor of Theology and Science (1981-82), Jesuit School of Theology, Berkeley; Assistant Professor of Theology and Science (1982-85); Associate Professor of Theology and Science (1985-91), Graduate Theological Union, Berkeley; Visiting Lecturer (Fall 1986), Lutheran School of Theology, Chicago; Ordained (June 1978), United Church of Christ - Congregational, to Ministry in

Higher Education: **Media Work:** 3 TV interviews, 2 radio presentations, and 10 articles in various Newspapers and 20 church related presentations; Featured in OMNI Magazine (October 1994) **Selected Memberships:** American Academy of Religion; American Association for the Advancement of Science; American Physical Society; Astronomical Society of the Pacific; Society of Ordained Scientists; Society for Values in Higher Education:; Sigma Xi - Scientific Research Society; Pacific Coast Theological Society **Discipline:** Physics; Theology **Related Areas of Interest:** Science; Cosmology; Thermodynamics; Chaos; Education; Human Genetics/Engineering; Theology; Trinity; Creation and Redemption; Resurrection, Christology and Eschatology; Relation of Theological and Scientific Methods and Language.

Selected Publications: His bibliography lists 3 books, 24 articles, over 33 papers, and 4 reviews all relevant to this area, plus 9 articles in science.

_____. "Entropy and Evil." *Zygon* 19, 4 (1984). Reprint, *CTNS Bulletin* 4, 2 (1984).

_____. "Contingency in Physics and Cosmology: A Critique of the Theology of Wolfhart Pannenberg." *Zygon* 23, 1 (1988).

_____. "Christian Discipleship and the Challenge of Physics: Formation, Flux and Focus." *CTNS Bulletin* 8, 4 (1988).

_____, William R. Stoeger, and George V. Coyne, eds. *Physics, Philosophy, and Theology: A Common Quest for Understanding.* Notre Dame, IN: University of Notre Dame Press, 1989.

_____. "Quantum Physics in Philosophical and Theological Perspective." In *Physics, Philosophy and Theology: A Common Quest for Understanding,* ed. R. J. Russell, W. R. Stoeger and G. V. Coyne. Notre Dame, IN: University of Notre Dame Press, 1989.

_____. "Agenda for the Twenty-first Century." In *The New Faith - Science Debate,* ed. John Mangum. Geneva: WCC Publications; Minneapolis: Fortress Press, 1989.

_____. "Cosmology, Creation and Contingency." In *Cosmos and Creation,* ed. Ted Peters. Nashville: Abingdon Press, 1989.

_____, W. R. Stoeger and G. V. Coyne. *John Paul II On Science and Religion: Reflections on the New View from Rome.* Vatican City State: Vatican Observatory, 1990.

_____, Nancey Murphy, and C. J. Isham, eds. *Quantum Cosmology and the Laws of Nature: Scientific Perspectives on Divine Action.* Copublished by Vatican City State: Vatican Observatory and Berkeley, CA: Center for Theology and the Natural Sciences, 1993.

Rüst, Peter

Present Position and Address: Research Associate Informatics (since 1974), Swiss Federal Dairy Research Station, Bern; Wagerten, CH-3148 Lanzenhäusern, Switzerland **Work Phone:** ++41-31-970'81'08 **Home Phone:** ++41-31-731'10'55 **Date of Birth:** August 7, 1934 **Languages Spoken:** German, English, some French **Education:** Ing. Chem. chemical engineering (1957)/Dr. Sc. tech. biochemistry (1961), Swiss Federal Institute of Technology, Zürich **Postgraduate Experience:** Research Fellow in Biochemistry (1958-61), Swiss Federal Institute of Technology, Zürich **Previous Positions:** Research Fellow through Associate (1961-63), Columbia University, NY; Research Associate (1963-64), University of Hawaii, Honolulu; Research Fellow (1964-67), California Institute of Technology, Pasadena; Research Fellow (1967-71), Swiss Institute Experimental Cancer Research, Lausanne; Head of Chemistry Section (1971-74), Swiss Federal Dairy Research Station, Bern **Discipline:** Chemistry; Biochemistry; Molecular Biology; Informatics **Related Areas of Interest:** Creation and Evolution; Science and Christian Faith; Epistemology of Science and Biblical Hermeneutics.

Selected Publications: He lists 43 articles dealing with topics concerning "Creation and Evolution" from 1980 to 1993.

_____. "Ist die Evolutionshypothese falsifizierbar?" *Factum* (July 1982): 24-6.

_____. "The Unbelievable Belief that almost any DNA Sequence will Specify Life." In *Proceedings of the Interdisciplinary Conference on "Sources of Information Content in DNA", Tacoma, WA, June 23-26, 1988.*

_____. "Una valutazione personale della creazione." (A personal assessment of creation). *Certezze* (GBU Italia, Roma) Nr.123-124 (1991): 5-31.

_____. "How Has Life and Its Diversity Been Produced?" *Perspectives on Science and Christian Faith* 44 (1992): 80-94.

_____. *Die Herkunft des Lebens - Wissen und Glauben.* Zürich: VBG-Verlag, 1994.

_____. "Spezielle und allgemeine Evolutionstheorie —Fakten und Spekulation." In *Zur Diskussion um Schöpfung und Evolution*, Porta-Studie no. 6, ed. E. Gutsche, P. C. Hägele and H. Hafner, 59-115. Marburg a. d. Lahn: Studentenmission in Deutschland, 1984; 4th. rev. ed., 1994.

Personal Notes: The following are representative of several unpublished manuscripts. "Modell 'Evolution' — ein kreationistischer Standpunkt." Paper presented at the Collegium Generale, Universität Bern, February 10, 1986. "Entstehung und Entwicklung des Lebens" (1986).

S

Sakimoto, Philip J.

Present Position and Address: Program Analyst for Evaluation and Assessment (since May, 1994), Minority University and Education Division, NASA Headquarters, Code EU, Washington, DC 20546 **Work Phone:** (202) 358-0949 **Home Phone:** (410) 799-7372 **Date of Birth:** January 21, 1954 **Languages Spoken:** English **Education:** B.A. Physics (*cum laude*, 1976), Pomona College; M.A. Astronomy (1977)/Ph.D. Astronomy (1985), University of California - Los Angeles **Postgraduate Experience:** Postgraduate Researcher (1979-85), Department of Astronomy, University of California - Los Angeles **Previous Positions:** Instructor in Astronomy (1977), Compton College; Planetarium Assistant (1975-78), Griffith Observatory; Instructor in Astronomy (1978-79), Terminal Island Federal Correctional Institution; Summer Faculty Fellow (Summer 1986), Laboratory for Astronomy and Solar Physics, NASA/Goddard Space Flight Center; Chair of Department of Astronomy (Fall 1986), Whitman College; Visiting Assistant Professor of Astronomy and Physics (1985-89), Whitman College; Assistant Director (1989-90), The Johns Hopkins Space Grant Consortium; Associate Research Scientist (1989-90), Department of Physics and Astronomy, The Johns Hopkins University; University Affairs Officer (1990-94), NASA/Goddard Space Flight Center, Greenbelt, MD **Selected Memberships:** Phi Beta Kappa; American Astronomical Society; American Association for the Advancement of Science; Astronomical Society of the Pacific; Center for Theology and the Natural Sciences; Cosmos and Creation **Discipline:** Astronomy, Physics **Related Areas of Interest:** Creation and Eschatology; Education, Ministry.

Selected Publications:

_____. "On Creationism in the Astronomy Classroom." In *I.A.U. Colloquium no. 105: The Teaching of Astronomy*, 243-6. Cambridge University Press, 1990.

Saler, Benson

Present Position and Address: Associate Professor (since 1968), Department of Anthropology, Brandeis University, Waltham, MA 02254, USA **Work Phone:** (617) 736-2221or -2210 **Home Phone:** (508) 369-0504 **E-Mail:** SALER@BINAH.CC.BRANDEIS.EDU **Date of Birth:** May 2, 1930 **Languages Spoken:** English, Spanish **Education:** B.A. (1952), Princeton University; M.A. (1957)/Ph.D. Anthropology (1960), University of Pennsylvania **Awards and Honors:** Sir Isaac Wolfson Foundation Prize (1978) **Previous Positions:** Instructor (1960-63), University of Connecticut; Assistant Professor (1963-68)/Associate Professor (since 1968)/Chairman of Anthropology Department (1975-78), Brandeis University **Selected Memberships:** Fellow, American Anthropological Association; North American Association for the Study of Religion **Discipline:** Anthropology **Related Areas of Interest:** Anthropology of Religion; World Religions; Analytical Categories and the Study of Religions.

Selected Publications: His bibliography lists 2 book and 21 articles.

_____. "Beliefs, Disbeliefs, and Unbeliefs." *Anthropological Quarterly* 41, 1 (1967): 29-33.
_____. "Supernatural as a Western Category." *Ethos* 5, 1 (1977): 31-53.
_____. "Religio and the Definition of Religion." *Cultural Anthropology* 2, 3 (1987): 395-9.
_____. *Conceptualizing Religion: Immanent Anthropologists, Transcendent Natives, and Unbounded Categories.* Leiden: E. J. Brill, 1993.

Salmon, James F.

Present Position and Address: Jesuit Priest; Retired Professor of Chemistry; Treasurer (since 1988), Corporation of the Roman Catholic Clergymen, Maryland Province of the Society of Jesus, 5704 Roland Avenue, Baltimore, MD 21210-1399, USA **Concurrent Positions:** Preached and directed Retreats (since 1966); Staff-member (1966-67), St. Thomas More Newman Center, Ohio State University **Work Phone:** (410) 532-1418 **Education:** B.S. Mechanical Engineering (1946)/M.E. (1947), Stevens Institute of Technology, Hoboken, NJ; M.A. Philosophy (1956), Boston College; Ph.D. Chemistry (1961), University of Pennsylvania; B.D. Theology (1965), Woodstock College **Postgraduate Experience:** Postdoctoral Fellow in Chemistry (1966-67), Ohio State University; Studies in Spiritual and Pastoral Theology (1965-66), Jesuit House of Studies -Auriesville, NY **Congresses and Conferences:** Codirector (since 1982), Annual "Cosmos and Creation" Conference, Loyola College; Consultant (since 1986), Committee on Human Values, National Conference of Catholic Bishops **Previous Positions:** Active Service in US Navy (1943-46); Ensign (1946), Line Officer aboard USS Denver; Engineering Trainee (1947)/Assistant Foreman (1947-49)/Assistant Foundry Superintendent (1949-50), International Nickel Company Inc., Bayonne, NJ; Assistant (1967-70)/Associate Professor of Chemistry (1970-73), Loyola College - Baltimore; President (1973-79), Loyola High School - Towson; Visiting Associate Professor of Theology (1980-81), Georgetown University, Washington, DC; Director (1970-71), Campus Ministry/Associate Professor of Chemistry and Theology (1981-84), Loyola College; Rector of Jesuit Community/Associate Professor of Chemistry and Theology (1981-84), Wheeling College **Other Academic Experience:** Ordained to Priesthood (1964). Studies in Spiritual Theology and Classical Languages (1950-53), Jesuit House of Studies - Wernersville, PA; Private Research 1979-80), Interrelation of Science and Theology, University of California/Graduate Theological Union, Berkeley **Selected Memberships:** Phi Lambda Upsilon; American Chemical Society; Sigma Xi; American Society of Mechanical Engineers **Discipline:** Chemistry; Theology; Philosophy **Related Areas of Interest:** The Interrelation between Theology/Philosophy/Ethics and Science/Chemistry.

Selected Publications: His bibliography lists 3 books and 11 articles.

_____, Thomas King, eds. *Teilhard and the Unity of Knowledge.* Mahwah, NJ: Paulist Press, 1983.
_____. *Teilhard and Prigogine.* American Teilhard Association for the Future of Man. Chambersburg, PA: Anima Books, 1986.
_____. Review of *A Theology for a Scientific Age*, by Arthur Peacocke. *Theological Studies* (*TS*) 53 (1992): 790-1.
_____. Review of *Religion in an Age of Science*, by Ian Barbour. *TS* 51 (1991): 168-9.

Salthe, Stanley N.

Present Position and Address: Professor of Biology (since 1973), Brooklyn College of the City University of New York (CUNY), Bedford Avenue and Avenue H, Brooklyn, NY 11210, USA **Date of Birth:** October 16, 1930 **Education:** B.S. Zoology (*cum laude*, 1959)/M.A. Zoology (1960)/Ph.D. Zoology (1963), Columbia University **Postgraduate Experience:** Postdoctoral Fellow (1963-65), American Cancer Society **Previous Positions:** Assistant through Professor of Biology (since 1965), Brooklyn College of CUNY **Selected Memberships:** American Society of Naturalists; New York

Academy of Science; Sigma Xi; American Association for the Advancement of Science; Society for the Study of the Origin of Life; Society for the Study of Evolution; American Society of Zoologists; Semeiotic Society of America; Society for Conservation Biology; Washington Evolutionary Systems Society; International Society for Systems Research **Discipline:** Evolutionary Biology **Related Areas of Interest:** The Emotional, Spiritual and Environmental Costs of Baconian/Newtonian/Darwinian/Comtean Science; Evolutionary Biology and Theology.

Selected Publications: His bibliography lists 4 books and 90 articles.

_____. "Original Life." *Nature* 295 (1982): 452.
_____. *Evolving Hierarchical Systems: Their Structure and Representation.* New York: Columbia University Press, 1985.
_____, B. M. Salthe. "Ecosystem Moral Considerability: A Reply to Cahen," *Environmental Ethics* 11 (1989): 355-61.
_____. "Self-organization of/in Hierarchically Structured Systems." *Systems Research* 6 (1989): 199-208.
_____. "The Evolution of the Biosphere: Towards a New Mythology." *World Futures: The Journal of General Evolution* 30 (1990): 1-15.
_____. *Complexity and Change in Biology: Development and Evolution.* Cambridge, MA: MIT Press, in press.

Sanguinetti, Francesco

Present Position and Address: Director of Private Research Laboratory, via Tommaso Gulli 28, 48100 Ravenna, Italy **Date of Birth:** August 19, 1927 **Languages Spoken:** Italian, English, French **Education:** M.D. (1953), University of Bologna; Ph.D. Biological Chemistry (1960), University of Pisa **Previous Positions:** Associate Professor (1960-65/73-74), University of Pisa **Selected Memberships:** Centro Internazionale di Studi di Filosofia della Religione, Università di Perugia, Italy **Discipline:** Medical doctor specializing in Environmental and Industrial Toxicology **Related Areas of Interest:** Philosophy of Science.

Selected Publications:

_____. "L'Immagine del Mondo di P. Teilhard de Chardin ed il Teilhardismo." *Vichiana* 6 (1969): 169-90.
_____. "L'Origine dell'Uomo secondo Xavier Zubiri." In *Filosofia e crisi della cultura*, ed. Albino Babolin, 151-90. Padova, 1974.
_____, Xavier Zubiri. *Pensiero filosofico e scienza moderna.* Padova, 1975.
_____. "Il metodo di ricerca delle scienze naturali." In *Il metodo della filosofia della religione*, ed. Albino Babolin, vol. 1, 321-58. Padova, 1975.
_____. "Quale evoluzione?" In *Xavier Zubiri*, ed. Albino Babolin, 117-32. Perugia, 1980.
_____. "L'umano e le scienze biologiche." *Antropologia e filosofia della religione* 1 (Perugia, 1982): 181-201.
_____. "Fede scientifica in M. Polanyi, W. A. Rottschaefer, J. Monod." In *Fede filosofica e filosofia della religione*, ed. Albino Babolin, vol. 2, 219-35. Perugia, 1989.
_____. "La testimonianza della scienza." In *Testimonianza religiosa e forme espressive*, ed. Albino Babolin, vol.2, 237-51. Perugia, 1990.
_____. "Scienza empirica e fede religiosa." Perugia, 1992.
_____. "Il problema dell'ateismo. Scienza e fede secondo W. Pannenberg." In *Ateismo e società*, ed. Albino Babolin, vol. 2. Perugia, 1993.

Santmire, H. Paul

Present Position and Address: Senior Pastor, Trinity Lutheran Church, Akron, OH, USA; 50 N. Prospect Street, Akron, OH 44304-1295, USA **Work Phone:** (216) 376-5154 **Date of Birth:** November 28, 1935 **Education:** B.A. (1957), Harvard College; B.D. (1960), Lutheran Theological Seminary, Philadelphia, PA; Th.D. (1966), Harvard Divinity School **Previous Positions:** Chaplain and

Lecturer in Religion (1969-80), Wellesley College; Pastor, Grace Lutheran Church, Hartford, CT **Discipline:** Historical and Systematic Theology **Related Areas of Interest:** Theology and Ecology.

Selected Publications:

_____. *Brother Earth: Nature, God, and Ecology in a Time of Crisis*. New York: Thomas Nelson, 1970.
_____. *The Travail of Nature: The Ambiguous Ecological Promise of Christian Theology*. Philadelphia: Fortress Press, 1985.

Sauter, Gerhard

Present Position and Address: Professor of Systematic and Ecumenical Theology/Director of Ecumenical Institute/Faculty of Protestant Theology, University of Bonn, Germany; Ökumenisches Institut der Evangelisch-Theologischen Fakultät, An der Schlosskirche 1, D-53113 Bonn, Germany; (Home) Lochnerstr. 76, D-53757 Sankt Augustin, Germany **Concurrent Positions:** External Member, Faculty of Theology, University of Oxford **Work Phone:** 0228-737669 **Home Phone:** 02241-337318 **Date of Birth:** May 4, 1935 **Languages Spoken:** German, English **Education:** Dr. theol., Theology and Philosophy (1954-59), Universities of Tübingen/Göttingen; Ordained Minister (1962), Evangelische Kirche of Kurhessen und Waldeck. Habilitation (1965), Göttingen **Previous Positions: Associate Professor of Systematic Theology (1965-68), University of Göttingen; Professor of Systematic Theology (1968-73), University of Mainz; Professor of Theology (since 1973)/Dean of Faculty (1976-77), University of Bonn; Chairman (1979-81), Wissenschaftliche Gesellschaft für Theologie, Section Systematic Theology; Visiting Professor (1979), Divinity School, Duke University; Visiting Professor of Theology (1983, 1986), Dormition Abbey, Jerusalem; Fellow (1988-89, 1991, 1993-94), Center of Theological Inquiry, Princeton, NJ Selected Memberships:** Gesellschaft für Evangelische Theologie; Wissenschaftliche Gesellschaft für Theologie **Discipline:** Systematic and Ecumenical Theology **Related Areas of Interest:** Foundations of Theology; Epistemology and Methodology; Anthropology.

Selected Publications: His bibliography lists 20 books and 220 articles.

_____. *Vor einem neuen Methodenstreit in der Theologie? Theologische Existenz heute, vol. 164*. München, 1970.
_____. "Theologie - eine kirchliche Wissenschaft." In *Jenseits vom Nullpunkt? Christsein im westlichen Deutschland*, Bischof D. Kurt Scharf zum 70, Geburtstag, 287-99. Stuttgart, 1972.
_____, Jürgen Courtin, Hans-Wilfried Haase, Gisbert König, Wolfgang Raddatz, Gerolf Schultzky and Hans Günter Ulrich. *Wissenschaftstheoretische Kritik der Theologie. Die Theologie und die neuere wissenschaftstheoretische Diskussion*. München, 1973.
_____, Wolfhart Pannenberg, Sigurd Martin Daecke, and Hans Norbert Janowski. *Grundlagen der Theologie - Ein Diskurs*. Urban Taschenbuch, 603. Stuttgart-Berlin-Köln-Mainz, 1974.
_____. "Der Wissenschaftsbegriff der Theologie." *Evangelische Theologie* 35: 283-309 (1975). Rev. ed., in *Der Wissenschaftsbegriff in den Natur - und in den Geisteswissenschaften*, Studia Leibnitiana, Sonderheft, by K. Müller, H. Schepers, and W. Totok, vol. 5, 165-95. Wiesbaden, 1975.
_____. "Überlegungen zu einem weiteren Gesprächsgang über 'Theologie und Wissenschaftstheorie'." *Evangelische Theologie* 40: 161-8 (1980).
_____. "Konsens als Ziel und Voraussetzung theologischer Wahrheitserkenntnis." In *Theologischer Konsens und Kirchenspaltung*, ed. P. Lengsfeld and H. G. Stobbe, 52-63; 162-4. Stuttgart-Berlin-Köln-Mainz, 1981.
_____. *Was heisst: nach Sinn fragen?: Eine theologischphilosophische Orientierung*. München, 1982.
_____. *In der Freiheit des Geistes*. Göttingen, 1988.
_____. *Eschatological Rationality: Essays*. Durham, NC: The Labyrinth Press, 1995.

Scadding, Steven R.

Present Position and Address: Associate Professor of Zoology (since 1984), University of Guelph, Guelph, ONT N1G 2W1 Canada **Work Phone:** (519) 824-4120 ext. 3334 **Home Phone:** (519) 823-8791 **Fax Number:** (519) 767-1656 **E-Mail:** scadding@uoguelph.ca **Date of Birth:** April 4, 1944 **Languages Spoken:** English, French **Education:** B.Sc. (1966)/M.Sc. (1968)/Ph.D. Developmental Biology (1973), University of Toronto; Certificate in Theology (1969), Cambridge **Previous Positions:** Medical Research Council Fellow (1973-74), University of Toronto; Assistant Professor (1974-84), University of Guelph **Selected Memberships:** Sigma Xi; Canadian Scientific and Christian Affiliation; Canadian Association of Anatomists; Canadian Society of Zoologists; Canadian Society for Cellular and Molecular Biology **Discipline:** Developmental Biology and Zoology **Related Areas of Interest:** The comparison of Scientific Theories (such as evolution) and Scientific ways of knowing with Theological Theories and ways of knowing; Limb Development and Regeneration.

Selected Publications: His bibliography lists over 45 articles and 20 book reviews.

_____. "Do 'Vestigial Organs' Provide Evidence for Evolution?" *Evolutionary Theory* 5 (1981): 173-6.
_____. "Vestigial Organs do not Provide Scientific Evidence for Evolution." *Evolutionary Theory* 6 (1982): 171-3.

Schaefer, Hans

Present Position and Address: Professor Emeritus, Physiology, University of Heidelberg, Karl-Christ Strasse 19, 69118 Heidelberg, Germany **Work Phone:** (06621) 80 02 70 **Date of Birth:** August 13, 1906 **Languages Spoken:** German, English, French **Education:** Dr. Medicine (1931), Bonn; Professor of Physiology (1940) **Previous Positions:** Head of Department of Physiology (1940), Kerckhoff-Institut, Bad Nauheim; Full Professor of Physiology (1950), Giessen; Director and Professor of Physiology (1951), Heidelberg **Selected Memberships:** Akademie für Ethik in der Medizin; Past-President, Paulus Gesellschaft (Wissenschaft/Theologie); Honorary Member: New York Academy of Science and Academia Scientiarum et Artium Europaea; Gesprächskreis Kirche-Wissenschaft, Katholische Akademie, Bayern **Discipline:** Physiology; Social Medicine **Related Areas of Interest:** Medical Ethics; Natural Science and Theology.

Selected Publications: His bibliography lists 850 publications, including over 20 on Science and Theology.

_____. "Über Analogien in der Situation der Theologie und der Naturwissenschaft." In *Gott in Welt. Festgabe für K. Rahner,* ed. J. B. Metz, vol. 2, 809-15. 1964.
_____. "Kann die Wissenschaft eine neue Ethik entwickeln?" *Internationale Dialog-Zeitschrift* 3 (1970): 300-16.
_____. "Naturwissenschaft und Wunder." In *Jenseits der Erkenntnis,* ed. L. Reinisch, 45-65. Suhrkamp, Frankfurt, 1977.
_____. *Tugenden, ein Weg zur Gesundheit.* Bad Mergentheim: Atrioc-Verlag, 1985.
_____. *Medizinische Ethik.* 2d ed. Heidelberg: Fischer Verlag, 1986.
_____. "Medizin und Theologie." In *Glaube, Wissen Zukunft,* ed. A. Kolb, 171-83. Graz: Styria, 1987.
_____. "Heilen und Heil." *Arzt und Christ* 34, 2 (1987).
_____. "Dein Glaube hat dich gesund gemacht" - Religion und Medizin im Wechselspiel. In *Humane Zukunft. Jahresband der Humboldt-Gesellschaft,* Hsg. H. Kessler. Mannheim, 1988.
_____. "Sexualität zwischen Trieb und Geist." *Focus MUL.* 9,4 (University of Lübeck, 1992).
_____. "Fundamentalismus." In *Gefahren und Chancen des Wertewandels. Jahresband der Humboldt-Gesellschaft,* Hsg. H. Kessler. Mannheim, 1993.

Scheffczyk, Leo

Present Position and Address: Retired Professor of Theology, Dall' Armistrasse 3a, 8000 München 19, Germany **Date of Birth:** February 21, 1920 **Education:** Dr. Theology (1950)/Dr. Theology habil. (1957), University of Munich **Previous Positions:** Professor in Dogmatics: Königstein (1951-59)/Tübingen (1959-65)/München (1965-85) **Editorial Positions:** Coeditor: *Münchener Theologische Zeitschrift* (1966-85); *Handbuch der Dogmengeschichte* (since 1968); *Forum Katholische Theologie* (since 1985) **Selected Memberships:** Bavarian Academy of Sciences **Discipline:** Catholic Dogmatics **Related Areas of Interest:** Creation and Science.

Selected Publications: His bibliography lists 61 publications.

_____. *Creation and Providence.* New York, 1970.
_____. *Einführung in die Schöpfungslehre.* Darmstadt,1975, 1982, 1988.
_____. *Die Theologie und die Wissenschaften.* Aschaffenburg, 1979.

Schenk, Richard

Present Position and Address: Professor for Philosophy and Systematic Theology, Graduate Theological Union at Berkeley (since 1990) , Roman Catholic Priest of the Dominican Order; Gerberstrasse 26, D-30169 Hannover, Germany **Date of Birth:** June 27, 1951 **Languages Spoken:** German, English **Education:** B.A. Philosophy (1974)/M.A. Philosophy (1977), Dominican School of Philosophy and Theology, Graduate Theological Union, Berkeley; Dr. theologiae (1986), University of Munich **Previous Positions:** Scientific Assistant (1983-85), University of Munich; Research Assistant of the Bavarian Academy of Sciences (1986-91); Visiting Professor of Dogmatics, University of Gribourg (1989-91) **Administrative Experience:** Managing Director of the Hannover Institute (since 1991) **Discipline:** Philosophy; Dogmatics; Medieval Studies **Related Areas of Interest:** History of Science, Philosophy, Psychology, Medicine and how they relate to Theology.

Selected Publications:

_____. *Die Gnade vollendeter Endlichkeit.* Friedberg: Herder, 1989.
_____. "Omnis Christ actio nostra est instructio." In *La doctrine de la révélation divine de saint Thomad d'Aquin, Studi Tomistici 37,* ed. L. Elders, 104-31. Vatican City State, 1990.
_____. "Tod und Auferstehung in christlicher Sicht." *Informationen und Berichte der Künstler-Union-Köln* 23 (May 1990): 9-36.
_____, P. Koslowski and R. Löw, eds. *Philosophie und Religion.* Schriftenreihe des Forschungsinstituts für Philosphie. Berlin (Morus), 1991.
_____. "Robert Kilwardby: Quaestiones in librum quartulm Sententiarum." Introduction to *Bayerische Akademie der Wissenschaften.* Veröffentlichungen der Kommission für die Herausgabe ungedruckter Texte aus der mittelalterlichen Geisteswelt, Band 17. München: Bayerische Akademie der Wissenschafdten, 1992.
_____. "Der Mensch-Krone der Schnpfung?" Internationale Katholische Zeitschrift. *Communio* 21 (1992): 397-418.
_____. "Theologische Überlegungen zum Sinn eines philosophischen Forschungsinstituts in kirchlicher Trägerschaft." *Jahrbuch des Forschungsinstituts für Philosophie Hannover 1992/93.* Hildesheim: Bernward , n.d.

Schmiedehausen, Hans

Present Position and Address: Kirchenrat (since 1987), Evangelische Kirche von Kurhessen-Waldeck, Der Beauftragte für Umweltfragen, Wolfhagerstrasse 268, 3500 Kassel, Germany **Concurrent Positions:** Pastor (since 1953) in several places of Hessia, in broadcasting and television; Pastor (since 1968), Kassel **Work Phone:** (0561) 882221 **Date of Birth:** October 10, 1927 **Languages Spoken:** German, English **Education:** Theology (1950, 1952), Universities of Marburg and Edinburgh **Selected**

Memberships: Konferenz der Umweltbeauftragten der Gliedkirchen der Evangelischen Kirche in Deutschland (EKD) **Discipline:** Church Dogmatics, Ecology **Related Areas of Interest:** Boundaries between Science and Theology; Environmentalism and Religion (protecting the Creation).

Selected Publications:

_____. "Menschen und Wäldern zuliebe, oder: Rettet das Auto, wir brauchen es noch." In *Schöpfungsverantwortung konkret*, ed. L. Barner and G. Liedke, 44-58. Kritische Auseinandersetzung mit dem Individualverkehr und seinen Umweltbelastungen
_____. *Den Kirschbaum blühen sehen, Wache Sinne für Gottes Schöpfung*. Stuttgart: Kreuz Verlag, 1988. Meditationen über das Leben mit der Natur in kritischer Auseinandersetzung mit einer sich "fortschriftlich" nennenden und im Mechanismus verharrenden Naturwissenschaft und Technik.

Schmitz-Moormann, Karl

Present Position and Address: Professor of Philosophical Anthropology and Ethics (since 1973), Department of Social Pedagogics, Fachhochschule Dortmund; Im Ostholz 160, D-4630 Bochum - Linden, Germany **Work Phone:** 0234 47 49 77 **Date of Birth:** March 14, 1928 **Languages Spoken:** German, French, English **Education:** Studied at Seminary (1945-48), Collegium Borromaeum, Münster; Theology, Philosophy and German Literature, (1948-49), University of Munich/(1949-52), University of Münster; Dr. Phil. (1957), University of Munich; Dr. Theol. (1969), Ruhr-Universität, Bochum **Congresses and Conferences:** Participant (September 1981), Colleque International UNESCO commemorating Centennial of Pierre Teilhard de Chardin; Participant (September 1983), 1st Colloquium by UN University for Peace, UN Headquarters, NY; Member of Organizing Committee, First European Conference on Science and Religion - Evolution and Creation (March 1986); Institute on Ultimate Reality and Meaning; Elected president, preparatory committee for next conferences on Science and Theology, newly founded European Society for Study of Science and Theology; Participant (December 1965), UNESCO-Colloquium "Science and Synthesis" in honor of Einstein and Teilhard de Chardin, Paris **Previous Positions:** Air Defense Service (1944-45, prisoner of war); Grammar School Teacher (1952-56); Professor (1957-58), École Saint Louis de Gonzague, Paris; Freelance writer and translator ((1957-62); Researcher (1962-66), Fondation Pierre Teilhard de Chardin, Paris; Since 1962 extensive lecturing in Germany and other countries; Scientific Assistant (1966-70) to Professor Dr. P. W. Scheele, Ruhr-Universität, Bochum; Lecturer (1970-73), Fachoberschule, Witten; Visiting Professor (1974), University of San Francisco/(1978), St. Andrew's College at University of Sydney/(1982), University of Wuppertal/(1985), Evolutionary Creation, St. Andrew's College, Sydney **Selected Memberships:** American Academy of Religion; Society for the Scientific Study of Religion; Corresponding Member, International Center for Integrative Studies, NY; Deutsche Gesellschaft Für Suchtforschung; Institute on Religion in an Age of Science; Scientific Committee Member, Association Internationale des Universités du Troisieme Age (AIUTA); **Discipline:** Theology; Philosophy; Teilhard de Chardin; Science and Theology **Related Areas of Interest:** For the past 20 years have principally worked in field of Science and Theology, mostly in line of Teilhard de Chardin centered around the concept of an Evolutionary Creation and the Notion of Redemption in an Evolving World.

Selected Publications: His bibliography lists 102 publications, including 19 editions of works of Teilhard de Chardin.

_____. "Pierre Teilhard de Chardin - 100 Years: Is There Anything He Has to Tell Us?" *The Teilhard Review* 16, 1-2 (1981): 78-83.
_____. "Pierre Teilhard de Chardin: 100 ans." *Les Cahiers fontenaisiens* no. 10 (1982): 1-10.
_____. "On the Need to Rewrite the Story of Creation." In *International Teilhard Compendium, The Desire to be Human, A Global Reconnaissance of Human Perspectives in an Age of Transformation*, ed. Leo Zonneveld and Robert Muller, 292-301. Wassenaar: Mirananda, 1983.

_____. "Evolution und Schöpfung, eine Konferenz über Naturwissenschaft und Religion." *Herderkorrespondenz* 40, Jg (Mai 1986): 247-9.
_____. "Philosophical and Theological Reflections on Recent Neurobiological Discoveries." *Zygon* 21, 2 (1986): 249-57,
_____. "Einleitung." In *Teilhard de Chardin in der Diskussion*, ed. Karl Schmitz-Moormann. Darmstadt: Wissenschaftliche Buchgesellschaft, 1986.
_____. "Theology's Relation to Science." "Evolution in the Catholic Theological Tradition." "Teilhard de Chardin's View on Evolution." In *Evolution and Creation, A European Perspective*, ed. S. Andersen and A. R. Peacocke, 27-34, 121-31, 162-8. Aarhus: Aarhus University Press, 1987.
_____. "On the Evolution of Human Freedom." *Zygon* 22, 4 (1987): 443-58.
_____. "Ein zu früh geborener Prophet? Weg und Werk des Teilhard de Chardin (1881-1955)." In *Gegenentwürfe, 24 Lebensläufe für eine andere Theologie*, ed. H. Häring und K. -J. Kuschel, 283-95. München-Zürich: Piper, 1988.
_____. "Concepts of Nature and God in the Middle Ages." In *Concepts of Nature and God, Resources for College and University Teaching*, ed Frederick Ferré, 38-46. Athens, GA: The University of Georgia, 1989.

Schoen, Edward L.

Present Position and Address: Professor of Philosophy (since 1985), Department of Philosophy and Religion, Western Kentucky University, Bowling Green, KY 42101, USA; (Home) WKU Box 8329, Bowling Green, KY 42101, USA **Work Phone:** (502) 745-3137 **Home Phone:** (502) 781-4676 **Date of Birth:** December 16, 1949 **Education:** B.A. (highest honors, 1971), Wheaton College; M.A. Philosophy (1974)/Ph.D. Philosophy (1976), University of Southern California, Los Angeles **Previous Positions:** Lecturer in Ethics (Fall 1975), University of Southern California; Lecturer (Summer, Spring 1975-76), California State University - Los Angeles; Lecturer (Spring 1975), California Lutheran College; Assistant Professor (1976-80)/Associate Professor of Philosophy (1980-85)/Tenured (1982), Western Kentucky University **Selected Memberships:** American Philosophical Association; Society of Christian Philosophers; Society for Philosophy of Religion **Discipline:** Philosophy **Related Areas of Interest:** Religion in Scientific Cultures; Epistemology of Religion.

Selected Publications: His bibliography lists 1 book and 30 articles.

_____. *Religious Explanations: A Model from the Sciences*. Durham, NC: Duke University Press, 1985.
_____. "Religious Explanations: A Reply to Professor McMullin." *Faith and Philosophy* 5, 3 (1988).
_____. Review of *Philosophy of Science*, by Del Ratzsch. *Faith and Philosophy* 5, 3 (1988).
_____. "Darwin and Darwinism." In *Concepts of Nature and God, Resources for College and University Teaching*, ed. Frederick Ferré. Athens, GA: The University of Georgia, 1989.
_____. "The Sensory Presentation of Divine Infinity." *Faith and Philosophy* 7, 1 (1990).
_____. "Anthropomorphic Concepts of God." *Religious Studies* 26, 1 (1990).
_____. "The Roles of Predictions in Science and Religion." *International Journal for Philosophy of Religion* 26, 1 (1991).
_____. "David Hume and the Mysterious Shroud of Turin." *Religious Studies* 27, 2 (1991).
_____. "Galileo and the Church." In *Proceedings of the Institute for Liberal Studies: Science, Technology and Religious Ideas*, vol. 3 (Fall).
_____. *Finding God: Places for the Divine in an Advanced Scientific Culture*. Forthcoming.

Schoepflin, Rennie B.

Present Position and Address: Coeditor (since 1980), book reviews for *Spectrum*; Assistant Professor of History (since 1983), Department of History and Political Science, Loma Linda University, Riverside, CA 92515, USA **Work Phone:** 714 785-2341 **Date of Birth:** 1952 **Education:** B.A. Religion/Pre-Med (1974), Walla Walla College; Attended Loma Linda University Medical School (1974-75); M.A. History (Church History, 1980), Loma Linda University; M.A. History of Science (1980) Ph.D. History of Science, University of Wisconsin - Madison **Selected Memberships:**

American Association for the History of Medicine; American Society of Church History; History of Science Society **Discipline:** History of Science; Medicine in America; Church History **Related Areas of Interest:** Religious and Mental Healing; Science, Medicine and Religion; Histories of Evolutionary/Christian Thought.

Selected Publications: His bibliography lists 7 articles.

_____. "The Christian Science Tradition." In *Caring and Curing: Historical Essays on Health, Medicine, and the Faith Traditions*, ed. Ronald L. Numbers and Darrel W. Amundsen, 421-46. New York: Macmillan, 1986.
_____. "Christian Science Healing in America." In *Other Healers: Unorthodox Medicine in America*, ed. Norman Gevitz, 192-214. Baltimore: The Johns Hopkins University Press, 1988.

Schrader, David Eugene

Present Position and Address: Chairman of Religion and Philosophy Department/Associate Professor of Philosophy (since 1984), Austin College, Sherman, TX 75090, USA; (Home) 2406 Rex Cruse Drive, Sherman, TX 75090, USA **Work Phone:** (214) 892-9101 ext. 242 **Home Phone:** (214) 893-3596 **Date of Birth:** October 1, 1947 **Education:** B.A. (1969), St. Olaf College; M.Th. (1971), Harvard University; M.A. (1974)/Ph.D. Philosophy (1975), University of Massachusetts **Previous Positions:** Instructor in Continuing **Education:** (1972)/Teaching Assistant in Philosophy (1972-73), University of Massachusetts; Instructor in Philosophy (1975-77)/Assistant Professor of Philosophy (1977-79), Loras College; Assistant Professor of Philosophy (1979-84), Austin College **Selected Memberships:** Society of Christian Philosophers; American Philosophical Association; Society for Business Ethics; Society for Philosophy and Public Affairs; Society for Philosophy of Religion; Philosophy of Science Association; American Secretary/Treasurer (since 1987), Association of University Professors **Discipline:** Philosophy: Ethics - Theoretical and Applied; Philosophy of Religion; History of Philosophy; Philosophy of Science/Law; Logic **Related Areas of Interest:** Ethics/Theology/Religion and Philosophy; Philosophy of Science/Religion.

Selected Publications: His bibliography lists 1 book and 10 articles.

_____. "Karl Popper as a Point of Departure for a Philosophy of Theology." *International Journal for Philosophy of Religion* 14 (1983): 193-201.
_____. "Frankfurt and Descartes: God and Logical Truth." *Sophia* 25, 1 (1986): 4-18.

Schroeder, W. Widick

Present Position and Address: Professor of Religion and Society (since 1971), Chicago Theological Seminary, 5757 S. University Avenue, Chicago, IL 60637-9990, USA **Date of Birth:** November 12, 1928 **Education:** B.A. (1949), Bethel College, KS; M.A. Sociology and Anthropology (1952), Michigan State University; B.D. (1955), University of Chicago Divinity School and Chicago Theological Seminary; Ph.D. Ethics and Society (1960), University of Chicago **Previous Positions:** Instructor (1953-54), Michigan State University; Research Associate (1955-58), Department of Research and Survey/Assistant (1960-64)/Associate Professor of Sociology of Religion (1964-71), Chicago Theological Seminary; Instructor in Ethics and Society (1958-60), Federated Theological Faculty, University of Chicago **Editorial Positions:** Editor (1964-69), *Review of Religious Research*; Coeditor (since 1968), Studies in Religion and Society series from Center for the Scientific Study of Religion; Coeditor (since 1975), at Exploration Press, Chicago Theological Seminary; Editorial Advisory Board (since 1979), *Zygon* **Other Academic Experience:** Ordained (since 1955), United Church of Christ **Selected Memberships:** American Academy of Religion; American Sociological Association; Center for Process Studies; IRAS; Religious Research Association Society of Christian Ethics; Society for the Scientific Study of Religion; United Church of Christ **Discipline:** Religion and

Society; Ethics; Ordained Minister **Related Areas of Interest:** Relation between Theology and the Human Sciences.

Selected Publications: His bibliography lists 11 books and 27 articles.

_____. *Cognitive Structures and Religious Research.* East Lansing: Michigan State University Press, 1970.
_____, Philip Hefner, eds. *Belonging and Alienation: Religious Foundations for the Human Future.* Chicago: Center for the Scientific Study of Religion, 1976.
_____. "Evolution, Human Values and Religious Experience: A Process Perspective." *Zygon* 17, 3 (1982).
_____, Franklin I. Gamwell, eds. *Economic Life.* Chicago: Center for the Scientific Study of Religion, 1988.
_____. *Flawed Process and Sectarian Substance: Analyticians Critical Perspectives on the United Church of Christ General Synod Pronouncement 'Christian Faith: Economic Life and Justice'.* Chicago: Exploration Press, 1990.

Schubert, Mathias

Present Position and Address: Consultant (since 1985), Theologische Studienabteilung beim Bund der Evangelischen Kirchen in der (ehemaligen) Deutschen Demokratischen Republik; 1040 Berlin, Auguststrasse 80, PF 222, Berlin, Germany; Markgrafenstrasse 41, D/O-1241 Markgrafpieske, Germany **Date of Birth:** July 26, 1952 **Education:** Dr. theol. (1985), Karl-Marx-Universität, Leipzig **Previous Positions:** Pastor (1980-85), Braunsbedra **Discipline:** Theology **Related Areas of Interest:** Creationism and Ethics; Science Ethics; Creation and Evolution; Genetic Engineering; Sociobiology; Ecology and Economy.

Selected Publications:

_____. *Schöpfungstheologie bei Kohelet.* Zürich/Paris/Frankfurt: Peter Lang Verlag, 1988.
_____. *Gentechnologie - die neue Macht des Menschen, Problemorientierungen, Informationen, theologisch-ethische Überlegungen.* Theologische Studienabteilung, 1988.
_____. *Soziobiologie und Menschenbild.* Theologische Studienabteilung, 1989.

Schütt, Hans-Werner

Present Position and Address: Full Professor of Technology, Technische Universität Berlin, Institut für Philosophie, Wissenschaftstheorie, Wissenschafts und Technikgeschichte, Ernst-Reuter-Platz 7, 10587 Berlin, Germany **Fax Number:** 7030-38006-258 **Date of Birth:** October 6, 1937 **Languages Spoken:** German, English **Education:** Ph.D. Physical Chemistry (1966), University of Kiel **Previous Positions:** Habilitation in History of Science (1975)/Assistant Professor (1977), University of Hamburg **Selected Memberships:** Former President, Gesellschaft für Wissenschaftsgeschichte **Discipline:** History of Exact Sciences and Technology **Related Areas of Interest:** Cultural Concepts of Nature and Science; Theology/Christianity and Science/Technology.

Selected Publications: His bibliography lists 3 books and 80 articles.

_____. "Zum Verhältnis von Naturwissenschaften, Technik und Theologie im 17. Jahrhundert." *Schriften der Georg-Agricola-Gesellschaft* 12 (1986): 108-18.
_____. "Theologische Weltsicht in Naturwissenschaft und Technik bis zum Barock." *Würzburger Medizinhistorische Mitteilungen* 4 (1986): 235-51.
_____. "Zwei Kulturen — zwei Wahrheiten? Galilei und die Römische Kirche." In *Wissenschaftsgeschichte Heute,* ed. Chr. Hünemöder, 47-68. Wiesbaden, 1987.
_____. "Naturverständnis und Naturwissenschaft im Biedermeier." *Jahrbuch der Droste-Gesellschaft* 2 (1988).
_____. "Die Kirchen des Westens und die Technik im Aufbruch zur Neuzeit." In *Technik und Relgion,* ed. A. Stöcklein u. M. Rassem, 181-95. Vol. 2 of *Technik und Kultur,* ed. W. Dettmering and A. Hermann. Düsseldorf, 1990.

_____. "Gott als Mechaniker. Zur Geschichte der naturphilosophischen Gottesdeutung." In *Wissenschaft und Transzendenz*, ed. G. Abel, 1-17. Berlin, 1992.
_____. "La vu du monde dans les sciences et lu technique." In *Science - Technology Relationships/Relations Sciences - Techniques*, ed. Alexander Herlea, 85-100. San Francisco, 1993.
_____. "Natur und Schöpfung." In Festschrift für Heribert Nobis, ed. x. Fricker, 93-118. In press.

Schuurman, Egbert

Present Position and Address: Professor in Reformational (Calvinistic or Christian) Philosophy at Universities of Delft (since 1972)/Eindhoven (since 1974)/Wageningen (since 1984); Karel Doorman-weg 7, 3621 JV Breukelen, The Netherlands **Concurrent Positions:** Senator in the Dutch Parliament (since 1983) **Date of Birth:** July 23, 1937 **Languages Spoken:** Dutch, English, German **Education:** Civil Engineering (1964), Technological University, Delft; Philosophy (1968), Free University, Amsterdam; Doctorate in Philosophy (1972), Free University **Other Academic Experience:** President, Prof. dr. G. A. Lindeboom-Institute, a center for Medical Ethics **Discipline:** Philosophy; Civil Engineering; Politics **Related Areas of Interest:** Ethics of Technology; Philosophy of Technology; Biotechnology; Genetic Manipulation.

Selected Publications:

_____. *Technology and the Future — a Philosophical Challenge*. Toronto: Wedge, 1980. Translated into Korean.
_____. *Reflections on the Technological Society*. Toronto: Wedge, 1983. Translated into Korean.
_____. "A Christian Philosophical Perspective on Technology." In *Theology and Technology*, ed. Carl Mitcham, 107-23. University Press of America, 1984.
_____. "From Systems Analysis via Systems Design to Systems Control." In *Social Science in a Christian Perspective*, ed. Paul A. Marshall, 343-57. University Press of America, 1988.
_____. *The Future: Our Choice or God's Gift*. Wellington, New Zealand: Exile Publications, 1990.
_____. *Christians in Babel*. Jordan Station, ONT, Canada: Paideia Press Ltd. Translated into Korean.
_____. *The Technological Paradise*. Toronto: Wedge, 1991.
_____. *Philosophy of Technology*. Toronto: Wedge, forthcoming.

Schwarz, Hans

Present Position and Address: Professor of Systematic Theology and Contemporary Theological Issues (since 1981), University of Regensburg, Universitätstrasse 31, D-93040 Regensburg, Germany **Work Phone:** (0941) 943-3683/4 **Date of Birth:** January 5, 1939 **Languages Spoken:** German, English **Education:** Dr. theol. Systematic Theology (1963), University of Erlangen **Previous Positions:** Instructor in Systematic Theology (1967/68)/Assistant (1968-71)/Associate Professor (1971-78)/Edward C. Fendt Professor of Systematic Theology (1968-81); Trinity Lutheran Seminary, Columbus, OH; Visiting Professor (1974), Pontifical Gregorian University, Rome; Adjunct Professor of Systematic Theology (since 1987), Lutheran Theological Southern Seminary, Columbia, SC **Editorial Positions:** Editor (since 1988), *Glaube und Denken, Jahrbuch der Karl-Heim-Gesellschaft* (Yearbook of the Karl Heim Society. Moers: Brendow Verlag) **Selected Memberships:** American Academy of Religion; Vice President, Karl-Heim-Gesellschaft **Discipline:** Systematic Theology **Related Areas of Interest:** Interface of Theology and Biology.

Selected Publications: His bibliography lists 25 books and 113 articles.

_____. "Darwinism between Kant and Haeckel." *Journal of the American Academy of Religion* 48, 4 (1980): 581-602.
_____. "On the Necessary Interdependence between the Natural Sciences and Theology." *Encounter* 42, 3 (1981): 207-23.

_____. "The Significance of Evolutionary Thought for American Protestant Theology: Late Nineteenth-Century Resolutions and Twentieth-Century Problems." *Zygon* 6, 3 (1981): 261-84.

_____. "God's Place in a Space Age," *Zygon* 21, 3 (1986): 353-68.

_____. "Manipulierte Fortpflanzung und Forschung an Embryonen." *Zeitwende. Die Neue Furche* 61, 2 (1990): 76-85.

_____. "The Flight From Creation: The Response of German Protestant Theology to the Onslaught of Materialism in the Latter Part of the Nineteenth Century." In *Papers of the Nineteenth Century Working Group, American Academy of Religion.* 1990.

_____. "The Re-emerging Dialogue between Theology and Science in Germany." *Panorama* (International Journal of Comparative Religious Education and Values) 3 (Winter 1991): 64-78.

_____. "The Interplay between Theology and Science in Uncovering the Matrix of Human Morality." *Zygon* 28, 1 (1993): 61-76.

_____. "Die Zeit vergeht — spurlos? Gottes Handeln im Kontext des naturwissenschaftlichen Zeitverständnisses." In *Glaube und Denken.*, Jahrbuch der Karl-Heim-Gesellschaft, 1994, 134-155.

_____. *Evil: A Historical and Theological Perspective,* Minneapolis, MN: Fortress Press, 1994.

Schwarzwäller, Klaus

Present Position and Address: Professor of Systematic Theology (since 1972), University of Göttingen; der Georg-August-Universität Göttingen, Platz der Göttichen Sieben 2, 37073 Göttingen, Germany **Work Phone:** 0551/39 71 50 **Date of Birth:** March 13, 1935 **Languages Spoken:** German, English, French **Education:** Dr. theol. (1963), University of Hamburg; Habilitation für Systematische Theologie (1969), University of Göttingen **Discipline:** Systematic Theology (Dogmatics and Ethics) **Related Areas of Interest:** Reformation Theology; Theological Anthropology, also with reference to Biology and Medicine; Problems and Ethics in Modern Church Life; Methodological Problems.

Selected Publications:

_____. *Theologia Crucis: Luther's Lehre von Prädestination nach De sevo arbitrio, 1525.* München: Kaiser, 1970.

_____. *Die Wissenschaft von der Torheit. Evangelische Theologie im Schnittpunkt von christlichem Glauben und kritischer Vernunft.* Stuttgart, Berlin: Kreuz, 1976.

_____. "Nun hat mein Auge dich gesheen" Leiden als Grundproblem de Theologie, in: *Einfach von Gott redem.* Festschrift for F. Mitdenbereger. Stuttgart: Kohlhammer, 1994. 190-225.

_____. Ed. (with Elke Axmacher), *Belehrter Glaube.* Festschrift for J. Wirsching. Frankfurt am Main: P. Lang. 1994.

_____. Ed. (with Dennis Bielfeldt), *Freiheit als Liebe be Luther (Freedom as Love in Luther).* Frankfurt am Main: P. Lang. 1995.

Sciegaj, Mark

Present Position and Address: Assistant to the Dean (since 1984)/Director of Academic Records (since 1986), Candler School of Theology, Suite 216, Emory University, Atlanta, GA 30322, USA; (Home) 510 Coventry Road, # 19-C, Decatur, GA 30030, USA **Concurrent Positions:** Consultant on Ethics and Public Health (since 1985), Administrative Services Section, Georgia Division of Public Health, Suite 200, 876 West Peachtree Street, Atlanta, GA 30309, USA **Work Phone:** (404) 727-6322 or (404) 894-6475 **Home Phone:** Home (404) 378-1033 **Date of Birth:** January 18, 1960 **Education:** B.A. Philosophy (1982), Bethany College; M.T.S. (1990)/M. Public Health (1990), Emory University **Awards and Honors:** Drotman Memorial Award (1988), American Public Health Association **Selected Memberships:** American Public Health Association **Discipline:** Theology; Public Health **Related Areas of Interest:** Theology and Public Health.

Selected Publications:

_____. "Public Health, Paideic Justice and Caring for the Earth." *Journal of Religion and Applied Behavioral Sciences* 10, 1 (1989): 2-5.

Seckler, Max

Present Position and Address: University Professor and Director (since 1964), Institut für Fundamentaltheologie, University Tübingen, Sommerhalde 5, D-72070, Tübingen, Germany **Date of Birth:** September 23, 1927 **Languages Spoken:** German, French **Education:** Dr. theol. (1959), University Tübingen; Habil. (1964), University München **Previous Positions:** Dozent (1962), University Passau; Dozent (1964), University München **Selected Memberships:** Academie International Society of Religion **Discipline:** Fundamental Theology **Related Areas of Interest:** Scientific Theory; Philosophy of Religion; Theory of Christendom.

Selected Publications:

_____. *Instinkt und Glaubenswille nach Thomas von Aquin.* N.p., 1959.
_____. *Das Heil in der Geschichte.* Geschichtsphilosophie. N.p., 1965.
_____. Theologie vor Gericht. N.p., 1972.
_____. Im Spannungsfeld von Wissenschaft und Kirche. N.p., 1980.
_____. Handbuch der Fundamentaltheologie. N.p., 1985-88.
_____. Die Schiefen Wände des Lehrhauses. N.p., 1988.
_____. *Teologia, Scienza, Chiesa.* N.p., 1988.

Seeger, Raymond John *(Deceased)*

Former Position and Address: Retired Physicist; 4507 Wetherill Road, Bethesda, MD 20816, USA **Date of Birth:** 1906 **Education:** B.A. Physics, Rutgers University; Ph.D. Theoretical Physics, Yale University **Postgraduate Experience:** Visiting Scholar (1961-62), Oxford University **Honorary Degrees:** D.Sc. Kent State University/University of Dubuque **Previous Positions:** National Science Foundation, Special Assistant to the Director/Deputy Assistant Director for the Mathematical, Physical, and Engineering Sciences/Executive Secretary, National Science Board Committee on Physical Sciences Report; Physical Sciences Report; First Director, University of Maryland Institute for Fluid Dynamics and Applied Mathematics; First Director, Catholic University of America Summer Institute on the History and Philosophy of Science; Visiting Professor of Science and Religion, Virginia Theological Seminary; Adjunct Professor of Applied Science/Associate Professor of Physics, George Washington University; Adjunct Professor of Scientific Thought, American University **Selected Memberships:** Omicron Delta Kappa; Phi Beta Kappa; Sigma Pi Sigma; Sigma Xi; Founder of Chesapeake Section, American Association of Physics Teachers First Chairman, Fluid Dynamics Division, American Physical Society; Past Chairman and Secretary, American Association for the Advancement of Science **Discipline:** Theoretical and Applied Physics **Related Areas of Interest:** The Humanistic aspects of the Development and Understanding of Physics together with its Literary and Social Interrelations, its Philosophical and Religious Implications **Current Areas of Research:** Research interest in the foundations of quantum mechanics, the electric breakdown of solids, and shockwave phenomena.

Selected Publications: His bibliography lists 7 books and technical articles.

_____. *Galileo Galilei.* N.p., 1966.
_____, coeditor. *Philosophical Foundations of Science.* N.p., 1974.

Segal, Robert A.

Present Position and Address: Lecturer in Religious Studies, Lancaster University, Lancaster LA1 4YG, UK **Work Phone:** 011 44 524 592414 **Home Phone:** 011 44 524 381751 **Date of Birth:** July 15, 1949 **Education:** B.A. (1970), Wesleyan University; M.A. (1974)/Ph.D. Religion (1983), Princeton University **Previous Positions:** Assistant Professor of Religion and Humanities (1975-82), Reed College; Visiting Associate Professor (Fall 1981), Centre for Religious Studies, University of Toronto; Lecturer in Western Culture Program (1982-84), Stanford University; Associate Professor through Full Professor (1984-94), Louisiana State University; Visiting Associate Professor of Religious Studies (Winter 1988), University of Pittsburgh; Visiting Professor of Jewish Studies (1993-94), Tulane University **Editorial Positions:** Editor, Theorists of Myth Series (Garland Publishing); Editor, *Encyclopedia of Myth Theory*; Associate North American Editor, *Religion*; Editorial Board, *Method and Theory in the Study of Religion*; Book editor, *Annals of Scholarship*; *Religion*; *Zygon*; Network editor, *Religious Studies Review*; Convener (1988-90), Group on the History of the Study of Religion, American Academy of Religion; Referee for Johns Hopkins University Press, Prentice-Hall, Harvard University Press, Yale University Press, Princeton University Press, Garland Publishing; Referee for *Journal of the American Academy of Religion*, *Journal for the Scientific Study of Religion*, *Zygon*, *Religion*, *Annals of Scholarship*, *Sociological Analysis*, and *Anthropology and Humanism Quarterly* **Selected Memberships:** Fellow, Institute for the Advanced Study of Religion; Society for the Scientific Study of Religion; American Academy of Religion; Association for the Sociology of Religion, North American Association for the Study of Religion **Discipline:** Religious Studies - especially Social Scientific Theories of Religion and Methodology and Gnosticism **Related Areas of Interest:** Social Scientific Theories of Religion; Methodology; Gnosticism.

Selected Publications: His bibliography lists over 70 publications and 50 presented papers.

_____. "In Defense of Reductionism." *Journal of the American Academy of Religion* 51 (March 1983): 97-124.
_____. "Have the Social Sciences Been Converted?" *Journal for the Scientific Study of Religion* 24 (September 1985): 321-4.
_____. *Joseph Campbell: An Introduction.* Theorists of Myth Series, No. 1. New York: Garland Publishing, 1987. Rev. ed. paperback. New York: New American Library Mentor Edition, 1990.
_____. *Religion and the Social Sciences: Essays on the Confrontation.* Brown Studies in Religion. Vol. 3. Atlanta: Scholars Press, 1989.
_____. "On Dogmas and Axioms in the Study of Religion." *Journal of the American Academy of Religion* 57 (Fall 1989): 591-605.
_____. "Misconceptions of the Social Sciences." *Zygon* 25 (September 1990): 263-78.
_____. Introduction to *In Quest of the Hero: Otto Rank, Lord Raglan, and Alan Dundes.* Mythos Series. Princeton: Princeton University Press, 1990.
_____, editor. *The Gnostic Jung.* Mythos Series. Princeton: Princeton University Press; London: Routledge and Kegan Paul, 1992.
_____. *Explaining and Interpreting Religion: Essays on the Issue.* Toronto Studies in Religion. Vol. 16. New York: Peter Lang, 1992.
_____, editor. *The Allure of Gnosticism: The Gnostic Experience in Jungian Psychology and Contemporary Culture.* Chicago: Open Court, 1995.

Seifert, Josef

Present Position and Address: Rector (since 1986)/Professor of Philosophy, Internationale Akademie für Philosophie (IAP), im Fürstentum Liechtenstein, Obergass 75, FL-9494 Schaan, Europe **Work Phone:** 075 232 86 75 **Languages Spoken:** German, English, Italian, French, Spanish **Education:** Doctorate in Philosophy (1969), University of Salzburg; Habilitation (1975), University of Munich **Previous Positions:** Assistant Professor of Philosophy (1972-76), University of Dallas; Director and

Professor (1973-80), Ph.D. program, University of Dallas, Institute of Philosophic Studies; Co-Director and Member of Faculty (1980-86) at the International Academy of Philosophy, Irving, TX **Memberships:** Aletheia OPPERTP (President); European Academy of Sciences and Arts; American Philosophical Association; Metaphysical Society of American; American Catholic Philosophical Association; Interamerican Philosophical Association, Dezitrich von Hildebrand Gesellschaft; Présence Gabriel Marcel **Discipline:** Philosophy with special emphasis on Epistemology, Metaphysics, and Philosophical Anthropology **Related Areas of Interest:** Value, Finality, and Meaning in the Biological Structure of Life; Bioethics.

Selected Publications: His bibliography lists 16 books and 250 articles.

____. "Intrinsic Right-Intrinsic Wrong? A Critical Examination of an Old Ethical Debate in Contemporary German Theology." In *Cogito*, University of Bristol, 1994: 255-264.

____. "Are There Timeless Falsities? On the Difference between Truth and Falsity with Respect to the Ideal Existence of Meaning-Units. A Reply to Mark Roberts." *Aletheia* VI (1993-94): 280-320 (Theory of Knowledge and Ethics).

____. "Is 'Brain Death' Actually Death?" *The Monist* 76 (1993): 175-202

____. "The Will." In *Handbook of Metaphysics and Ontology*, eds. H. Burkhardt and B. Smith. München: Philosophia Verlag, 1991:934-939.

____. *Back to Things in Themselves. A Phenomenological Foundation for Classical Realism.* Boston and London: Routledge and Kegan Paul, 1987.

____. "Genetischer Code und Teleologie. Information, Kausalität und Finalität." *Scheidewege* (1988).

____. *Essere e Persona. Verso una Foudazione Fenomenologica di una Metafisica classica e personalistics* (Being and Person. Towards a Phenomenological Foundation of a Classical and Personalistic Metaphysics). Milan: vita e Pensiero, 1988.

____. *Tgott als Gottesbeweis. Eine Phänomenologische Neubergründung des Ontologischen Arguments.* (God as Criterion of Himself. A Phenomenological Defense of the Ontological Argument.) Heidelberg: Univ. Winter, 1996.

Shacklett, Robert L.

Present Position and Address: Professor Emeritus of Physics (since 1979), California State University - Fresno; Vice President (since 1985), Foundation for Mind-Being Research, Los Altos, CA, USA; P.O. Box 2128, Aptos, CA 95001, USA **Work Phone:** (408) 722-6021 **Date of Birth:** April 5, 1926 **Education:** A.B. Physics (*summa cum laude*, 1949), California State University - Fresno; Ph.D. Physics (*cum laude*, 1956), California Institute of Technology **Previous Positions:** Assistant Professor through Professor of Physics (1955-79)/Assistant Academic Vice President and Assistant Dean and Dean of Graduate School (1967-76), California State University - Fresno **Selected Memberships:** American Physical Society; American Association of Physics Teachers; Sigma Xi; Foundation for Mind-Being Research; Wisdom Society **Discipline:** Physics **Related Areas of Interest:** Physics of Consciousness; Science and Religion; Models of Perception; Models of Reality; Whitehead's "Process."

Selected Publications:

____. "Christian Perspectives on Abortion." *Journal of the American Scientific Affiliation* 25, 2 (1973).

____. "Shaping Reality." *Newsletter of the Institute for Applied Intuition* (San Francisco, 1987).

____. "Information, Energy, and Meaning." *Foundation for Mind-Being Research Newsletter* (*FMBR Newsletter*) (September 1988).

____. "Chaos, Pattern, and Meaning." *FMBR Newsletter* (January 1989).

____. "Wholeness and the Missing Links." *FMBR Newsletter* (October 1989).

____. "Symmetry and the Golden Rule." *FMBR Newsletter* (January 1991).

____. "The Healing Context." *FMBR Newsletter* (September 1993).

____, W. C. Gough. "Physics, Parapsychology and Religion." *Journal of Religion and Psychical Research* 16 (1993): 2-4.

_____, W. C. Gough. "The Science of Connectiveness." *Subtle Energies*. Forthcoming Series of 3 Articles.

Shank, Michael H.

Present Position and Address: Associate Professor of the History of Science (since 1989), 4143 Helen C. White Hall, University of Wisconsin - Madison, 600 N. Park, Madison, WI 53706, USA; (Home) 2410 Chamberlain Avenue, Madison, WI 53705, USA **Work Phone:** (608) 262-3972 **Home Phone:** (608) 233-0679 **Date of Birth:** December 13, 1949 **Languages Spoken:** English, French, German **Education:** Diploma in Latin-Greek curriculum (1967), Athénée Royal de Rixensart, Belgium; B.A. Physics (with Honors, 1971), Goshen College; Associated Mennonite Biblical Seminaries (1971-72); M.A. History and Philosophy of Science (1975), University of Notre Dame; A.M. History of Science (1977)/Ph.D. History of Science (1983), Harvard University; University of Vienna (1979-81) **Previous Positions:** Assistant Professor of the History of Science and Assistant Head Tutor (1983-87)/Associate Professor of the History of Science (1987), Harvard University; Assistant Professor of Liberal Studies in the Graduate Institute of Liberal Arts and Coordinator of Liberal Studies program (1987-88), Emory University; Assistant Professor of the History of Science (1988), University of Wisconsin - Madison **Editorial Positions:** Associate Editor (1989-93), book reviews, *Isis* **Selected Memberships:** American Historical Association; History of Science Society; Medieval Academy of America; Society for the History of Technology; Renaissance Society of America **Discipline:** History/Philosophy of Science; Physics **Related Areas of Interest:** Relations of Science and Theology (Middle Ages and Early Modern Period).

Selected Publications: His bibliography lists 1 book and 7 articles.

_____. *"Unless You Believe, You Shall Not Understand:"* Logic, University, and Society in Late Medieval Vienna. Princeton, NJ: Princeton University Press, 1988.
_____. "Natural Sciences." In *The Mennonite Encyclopedia*. Vol. 5. Scottdale, PA, 1990.
_____. "The Notes on al-Bitruji Attributed to Regiomontanus: Second Thoughts." *Journal for the History of Astronomy* 23 (1992): 15-30.

Shank, Norman E.

Present Position and Address: Professor of Chemistry, Messiah College, Grantham, PA 17027, USA **Work Phone:** (717) 766-2511 **Home Phone:** (717) 766-7059 **Date of Birth:** June 7, 1943 **Education:** B.S. Chemistry (1965), Eastern Mennonite College; Ph.D. Physical Chemistry (1969), Ohio State University **Previous Positions:** Lecturer in Chemistry (1970-75), University of Zambia; Visiting Research Fellow (1974), University of Leeds; Assistant Professor through Professor of Chemistry (since 1975), Messiah College; Radiochemical Engineer (Summer 1986), TMI Nuclear Reactor **Selected Memberships:** Phi Lambda Upsilon (1966); Fellow, American Scientific Affiliation **Discipline:** Physical Chemistry **Related Areas of Interest:** Philosophical assumptions of Science and Christianity; God's activity in the world; What we can learn about origins from Scripture and Science.

Selected Publications:

_____. "Science and Finite Imagination." *Journal of the American Scientific Affiliation* 34 (1982): 99-100.

Sharpe, Kevin James

Present Position and Address: Professor (since 1987), Union Institute Graduate School; 65 Hoit Road, Concord, NH 03301, USA **Work Phone:** (603) 226-3328 **Fax Number:** (603) 226-3328 **Date of Birth:** January 23, 1950 **Languages Spoken:** English **Education:** B.Sc. Mathematics (Hons, 1971), University of Canterbury, Christchurch, New Zealand; Ph.D. Mathematics (1975), La Trobe University, Melbourne; Studies (1973), Princeton Theological Seminary; M.Div. (1976), Episcopal Divinity School, MA; Theol.M. (1979), Melbourne College of Divinity; Ph.D. Science, Philosophy and Religion (1987), Boston University **Awards and Honors:** Fulbright Graduate Travel Award **Previous Positions:** Mathematics Tutor (1971-72), La Trobe University; Theology Teacher (1976), Waikato Diocese, New Zealand; Tutor in Theology (1980), University of Otago; Taught in various departments (1980-84), University of Auckland - courses included Medical Ethics, Philosophy of Religion, Religious Dimensions of Evolution (taught in the Engineering School), Physics and Mysticism; Mysticism; Maclaurin Chaplain (1980-84), University of Auckland; Publisher (1983-90) of Australian and New Zealand theological and religious books (Interface Press) and distributor of Down Under religious books in UK and USA (Australian and NZ Religious Publications, became part of Meyer, Stone and Co.) **Editorial Positions:** Editor (1987-91), *Newsletter of IRAS*; Editorial Advisory Board (since 1989), *Zygon: Journal of Religion and Science;* Editor (since 1990), *Science & Religion News*; Editor, "Theology and The Sciences" Series, Fortress Press **Administrative Experience:** Vice President and Director of the International Division (1988-90), Meyer, Stone, & Co, Inc.; Administrative Assistant for D. Min. program (1985-86), Boston University; Executive Officer (1988-90), IRAS **Selected Memberships:** American Academy of Religion; Center for Theology and the Natural Sciences; Institute on Religion in an Age of Science; Victorian Institute; Science and Religion Forum; Australian Rock Art Research Association; Center for Advanced Study in Religion and Science; Society of Ordained Scientists **Discipline:** Theology; Science; Philosophy; Mathematics; Publisher; Administrator; Parish Minister **Related Areas of Interest:** Philosophy of Religion; Science and Ethics **Current Areas of Research:** Science and Religion in Dialogue/Action; Philosophy of Science, Systematic Theology; Anthropology of Religion.

Selected Publications: His bibliography lists 5 books and 25 articles.

_____. *From Science to an Adequate Mythology.* Auckland: Interface Press, 1983.
_____, John M. Kerr, eds. *Religion and Nature - Charles Birth and Others: Proceedings of the Eighth Auckland Religious Studies Colloquium, May 14-15, 1982.* Auckland: The University of Auckland Chaplaincy, 1983. Also contributed chapter, "Mysticism in Physics," 43-51.
_____. "Religion's Response to the Anthropic Principle of Physical Cosmology." In *Religion's Response to Change*, ed. J.M. Ker and K.J. Sharpe, 157-75. Auckland: Auckland University Chaplaincy Publishing Trust, 1985.
_____. *Christian Theology and the Physics, Metaphysics and Mathematics of David Bohm.* Ph.D. diss., Boston University, 1987.
_____. "Genesis: Fundamentalism and Liberalism are Both Inadequate." *Newsletter of the Institute on Religion in an Age of Science* 36 (1987): 18-20.
_____. "David Bohm's Physics and Religion." In *Science and Theology in Action*, ed. Chris Bloore and Peter Donovan, 72-8. Palmerston North, UK: The Dunmore Press Ltd, 1987.
_____. "Relating the Physics and Religion of David Bohm." *Zygon* 25 (1990): 105-22.
_____. "Biology Intersects Religion and Morality." *Biology and Philosophy* 5 (1990): 29-40.
_____. "Relating Science and Theology with Complementarity: A Caution." *Zygon* 26 (1991).
_____. *David Bohm's World: New Physics and New Religion.* Lewisburg, PA: Bucknell University Press, 1993.

Shaw, Marvin C.

Present Position and Address: Professor of Religious Studies (since 1978), Montana State University, Bozeman, MT 59717, USA; (Home) 604 South Black Avenue, Bozeman, MT 59715, USA **Work Phone:** (406) 994-5209 **Home Phone:** (406) 587-8805 **Date of Birth:** March 27, 1937 **Education:** B.A. (1959), Occidental College, Los Angeles; M.Div. (1962), Union Theological Seminary, NY; Ph.D. (1968), Columbia University, NY **Previous Positions:** Preceptor (1965-66), Columbia University; Lecturer (1966-67), Union Theological Seminary; Assistant (1968-72)/Associate (1972-78)/Professor (since 1978), Montana State University **Editorial Positions:** Editorial Board (since 1980), *American*

Journal of Theology and Philosophy; Editorial Consultant and Reviewer of *Zygon*/University Press of America/American Academy of Religion Studies in Religion Series/National Endowment for the Humanities Grants and Fellowships **Selected Memberships:** American Academy of Religion; Collegium - an Association of Liberal Religious Scholars; Society for Philosophy of Creativity (Wieman Studies); Society for Buddhist-Christian Studies; Highlands Institute for American Religious Thought; Phi Kappa Phi; Wesley Board, Methodist Campus Ministry **Discipline:** History and Philosophy of Western Religions **Related Areas of Interest:** Recent American Philosophy (pragmatism, naturalism, naturalistic theism, process philosophy) **Current Areas of Research:** Nineteenth and Twentieth Century Theology (the impact of modernity on religious tradition, science and religion); Philosophy of Religion.

Selected Publications: His bibliography lists 2 books and 18 articles.

_____. "Two Phases in Wieman's Thought: Wieman's Concept of the Divine." *Journal of Religion* 61, 1 (1981): 59-72.
_____. "Naturalism and the Christ: Wieman's Christology." *Encounter* 42, 4 (1981): 379-93.
_____. "Wieman's Misunderstanding of Dewy: The Christian Century Discussion." *Zygon* 22, 1 (1987): 7-19.
_____. *The Paradox of Intention: Reaching the Goal by Giving Up the Attempt to Reach It.* American Academy of Religion, Studies in Religion, no. 48. Atlanta, GA: Scholars Press, 1988.
_____. "The Moral Stance of Theism without the Transcendent God: Wieman and Heidegger." *Process Studies* 18, 3 (1989): 173-80.
_____. "Naturalistic Theism and the Chicago School." *Encounter* 49, 4 (1988): 297-319.
_____. "The Romantic Love of Evil: Loomer's Proposal of a Reorientation in Religious Naturalism." *American Journal of Theology and Philosophy* 10, 1 (1989): 33-42.
_____. "The Pastoral Theology of a Naturalist: Wieman on Prayer and Worship." *Encounter* 52, 3 (1991): 273-91.
_____. "Frankenberry's Critique and the Return to the Early Wieman." *American Journal of Theology and Philosophy* 13, 2 (1992): 105-16.
_____. *Nature's Grace: Essays on H. N. Wieman's Finite Theism.* Lewiston, NY: Edwin Mellen Press, in press.

Sheldon, Joseph K.

Present Position and Address: Professor of Biology (since 1992), Department of Natural Science, Messiah College, Grantham PA 17027, USA **Concurrent Position:** Summer Faculty Member, AuSable Institute of Environmental Studies, Mancelona, MI **Date of Birth:** November 11, 1943 **Education:** B.S. (1966), College of Idaho; Ph.D. Biology - Ecology/Entomology (1972), University of Illinois **Previous Positions:** Professor of Biology (1971-92), Department of Biology, Eastern College, St. Davids, PA 19087, USA **Selected Memberships:** American Institute of Biological Sciences; President, American Entomological Society (since 1991); Ecological Society of America; Society for Ecological Restoration; Fellow, American Scientific Affiliation **Discipline:** Biology - Ecology and Entomology **Related Areas of Interest:** Environmental Stewardship/Ethics.

Selected Publications: His bibliography lists 1 book and 18 articles.

_____. "Twenty-one Years After The Historical Roots of Our Ecologic Crisis: How Has the Church Responded?" *Perspectives on Science and Christian Faith* 41, 3 (1989): 152-8.
_____. "Another Hot Summer? The Greenhouse Effect, the Church, and You." *The ESA Advocate* (June 1989): 14-15.
_____. "Creation Rediscovered." *World Christian* 9, 4 (1990): 10-19.
_____. *Rediscovery of Creation: A Bibliographical Study of the Church's Response to the Environmental Crisis.* American Theological Library Association Bibliography Series. Metuchen, NJ: Scarecrow Press, 1992.

Sheldrake, Rupert

Address: 20 Willow Road, Hampstead, London NW3 1TJ, UK **Date of Birth:** June 28, 1942 **Languages Spoken:** English, French, Urdu **Education:** B.A. Natural Science (1963)/M.A. Biochemistry (1968)/Ph.D. Biochemistry (1968), Cambridge University Previous Positions: Research Fellow and Director of Studies in Biochemistry (1968-73), Clare College, Cambridge; Research Fellow of Royal Society (1970-73); Principal Plant Physiologist (1974-78), International Crops Research Institute, India; Fellow (1989), Institute of Noetic Sciences, Sausalito, CA **Selected Memberships:** Epiphany Philosophers, Cambridge; Society for Experimental Biology; Society for Psychical Research; Zoological Society Discipline: Biochemistry; Plant Physiology; Theoretical Biology **Related Areas of Interest:** Holistic Science, Eastern and Western Mysticism; Christian Theology.

Selected Publications:

_____. *A New Science of Life*. London: Blond and Briggs, 1981; Los Angeles: Tarcher, 1982.
_____. *The Presence of the Past: Morphic Resonance and the Habits of Nature*. New York: Times Books, 1988.
_____. *The Rebirth of Nature*. London: Century, 1990; New York: Bantam Books, 1991.
_____, R. Abraham and T. McKenna. *Trialogues at the Edge of the West*. Santa Fe, NM: Bear & Co., 1992.
_____. *Seven Experiments that Could Change the World*. London: Fourth Estate, 1994.

Shepard, Frederick Douglas

Present Position and Address: Adjunct Professor of Biology, Southern Oregon State College (Study and occasional teaching of Bioaesthetics); 995 Park Street, Ashland, OR 97520, USA **Date of Birth:** March 8, 1922 **Education:** B.A. Zoology (1943)/M.S. Zoology and Education (1948), Yale University; Ph.D., Evolutionary Biology (1968), Harvard University **Previous Positions:** High School Teacher/Vice-Principal (1948-54), Phoenix, OR; Missionary Educator/Administrator (1954-84), United Church Board for World Ministries, Middle East **Selected Memberships:** United Church of Christ **Discipline:** Zoology; Education; Evolutionary Biology; Administration **Related Areas of Interest:** Religion and Science and the role of Aesthetics (Bioaesthetics) in Ethical Issues and Confrontation; The Study of Opportunities for Integrated Formal and Informal Education.

Selected Publications:

_____. "Bioaesthetics, A Fresh Approach to Integrated Learning." *Journal of the University of the Bosphorus, Istanbul* 8-9 (1980-1981): 135-48.

Shewmon, D. Alan

Present Position and Address: Associate Clinical Professor (since 1981), Department of Pediatrics, Division of Neurology, Medical Center, University of California - Los Angeles, MDCC 22-464, 10833 Le Conte Avenue, Los Angeles, CA 90024, USA **Work Phone:** (213) 825-6196 **Date of Birth:** August 16, 1949 **Education:** B.A. Music (1971), Harvard College; M.D. (1975), NY University Medical School; Pediatric Residency (1975-77), Children's Hospital, San Francisco; Neurology Residency (1977-80), Loyola University Medical Center; Interdisciplinary Training in Mental Retardation and Developmental Disabilities (1980-81), UCLA Neuropsychiatric Institute **Previous Positions:** UCLA Neuropsychiatric Institute and Hospital (since 1980); UCLA Hospital and Clinics (since 1981) **Other Relevant Services:** Advisor (since 1987), The Human Dignity Institute; Consultant (December 1989), Pontifical Academy of Sciences session on the determination of the precise moment of death for purposes of organ transplantation; Ethics consultant (December 1987), California Nurses Association Executive Board **Selected Memberships:** American Academy of Neurology; American EEG Society; Child Neurology Society (Ethics Committee); American Epilepsy Society; Western EEG Society;

American Association for the Advancement of Science; American Association of Physicians and Surgeons **Discipline:** Neurology; Pediatrics **Related Areas of Interest:** Biomedical Ethics; Values in Society.

Selected Publications: His bibliography lists more than 33 articles and more than 5 chapters.

_____. "Ethics and Brain Death: A Response." *The New Scholasticism* 61, 3 (1987): 321-44.
_____. "The Probability of Inevitability: The Inherent Impossibility of Validating Criteria for Brain Death or 'Irreversibility' through Clinical Studies." *Statistics in Medicine* 6, 5 (1987): 535-53.
_____. "Active Voluntary Euthanasia: A Needless Pandora's Box." *Issues in Law and Medicine* 3, 3 (1987): 219-44.
_____. "Caution in the Definition and Diagnosis of Infant Brain Death." In *Medical Ethics: A Guide for Health Professionals*, ed. J. F. Monagle, and D. C. Thomasma, 38-57. Rockville, MD: Aspen, 1988.
_____, A. M. Capron, W. J. Peacock, and B. L. Schulman. "The Use of Anencephalic Infants as Organ Sources: A Critique." *Journal American Medical Association (JAMA)* 261, 2 (1989): 1773-81.
_____, C.M. DeGiorgio. "Early Prognosis in Anoxic Coma: Reliability and Rationale." In *Ethical Issues in Neurologic Practice*, ed. J. L. Bernat, vol. 7, no. 4, 823-43. Philadelphia: W. B. Saunders, Neurologic Clinics, 1989.

Shinn, Roger L.

Present Position and Address: Reinhold Niebuhr Professor of Social Ethics Emeritus (since 1985), Union Theological Seminary - New York, 3041 Broadway, New York, NY 10027, USA; (Home) 101 Birchwood, Southbury, CT 06488, USA **Work/Home Phone:** (203) 264-4753 **Fax Number:** (203) 264-6311 **Date of Birth:** January 6, 1917 **Education:** B.A. (1938), Heidelberg College, Tiffin, OH; M.Div. (*summa cum laude*, 1941), Union Theological Seminary; Ph.D. (1951), Columbia University **Honorary Degrees:** D.D. (1960), Mission House Theological Seminary; Litt.D. (1963), Heidelberg College; D.D. (1963), Franklin and Marshall College; L.H.D. (1984), Drury College; Humanities D. (1985), Blackburn University **Congresses and Conferences:** Cochair (with Margaret Mead, 1971-73), USA Task Force on the Future of Mankind and the Role of the Churches in a World of Science-Based Technology; Cochair (with Max Kohnstamm of Belgium, 1973), North American-European Conference on the Technological Future of the Industrialized Nations and the Quality of Life, Pont-a-Mousson, France; Chair (1974-77), National Council of Churches Task Force on Human Life and the New Genetics **Previous Positions:** Self-employed horticulturist and wholesale florist (1932-37); Student Assistant (1938-41), Second Presbyterian Church; US Army (1941-45); Ordained to ministry of Evangelical and Reformed Church (now United Church of Christ, 1946); Instructor in Philosophy of Religion (1947-49), Union Seminary; Chair (1949-54), Departments of Philosophy and Religion, Heidelberg College; Professor of Theology (1954-57)/Christian Ethics (1957-59), Vanderbilt University Divinity School; Professor of Christian Ethics/William E. Dodge, Jr. Professor of Applied Christianity (1960-70)/Dean of Instruction (1963-70)/Reinhold Niebuhr Professor of Social Ethics (1970-85)/Acting President (1974-75)/Counselor to Graduate Students (1975-85), Union Theological Seminary; Adjunct Professor of Religion and Society (1962-86), Columbia University; Adjunct Professor of Economics (1979), New York University Graduate School of Business Administration; Visiting Professor of Philosophies of Judaism (1982), Jewish Theological Seminary of America. Also lectureships in over 250 schools, colleges and universities in USA and overseas including William Belden Noble Lectures (1960), Harvard University; Visiting Lecturer (1971, 90), Princeton Theological Seminary; Visiting Lecturer (1971-74), Woodstock College; Visiting Professor: Pacific School of Religion (1986)/Vanderbilt University (1991)/Drew University (since 1987) **Editorial Positions:** Associate Editor, *The Bulletin of Science, Technology and Society*; Editorial Board, *Journal of Religious Ethics* **Other Academic Experience:** Council for Responsible Genetics (1983-90); World Council of Churches Committee on Church and Society; Member, Core Group of Center for Theology and the Natural Sciences- Human Genome Project (since 1992) **Selected Memberships:** Previous President, American Theological Society; Previous President, Society of Christian Ethics; American Academy of Religion; Science-Theology Discussion Group; American Association of University Professors **Discipline:** Theology; Ethics; Philosophy **Related Areas of Interest:** Religion and Society; Faith and Science and the Future.

Selected Publications: His bibliography lists 3 works of which he is editor or coeditor, 11 books he authored and over 60 chapters and essays, plus numerous scholarly articles and reviews. A 45-page bibliography of publications up to 1984 appears in *The Public Vocation of Christian Ethics*, by B. W. Harrison, R. L. Stivers and R. H. Stone. Pilgrim Press, 1986.

_____, editor. *Faith and Science in an Unjust World.* Vol. 1 of *Plenary Presentations, World Council of Churches Conference on Faith, Science and the Future.* Fortress Press and World Council of Churches, 1980.
_____. *Forced Options: Social Decisions for the Twenty-first Century.* Harper and Row, 1982; 2d ed. Pilgrim Press, 1985.

Shotwell, Thomas K.

Present Position and Address: President (since 1974), Shotwell & Carr, Inc. (Professional Services for the Pharmaceutical and Pesticide Industries), 3003 LBJ Freeway, Suite 100, Dallas, TX 75234, USA; (Home) 13243 Glenside Drive, Dallas, TX 75234, USA **Work Phone:** (214) 243-1634 **Fax Number:** (214) 243-3567 **Date of Birth:** May 31, 1934 **Languages Spoken:** English, German **Education:** A.S. (1953), Tarleton State University; B.S. (1955)/M.A. (1959), Texas A & M University; Ph.D. Agricultural and Extension Education (1965), Louisiana State University **Previous Positions:** Assistant County Agricultural Agent (1955-56), Van Zandt County, East Texas; US Army Artillery (1956-58); Biology Teacher (1961-62), Bryan, TX; Biological Sciences Section Head (1961-65), Allen College and Academy; Special Teacher (1965-66), creating model curriculum in agriculture; Science Writer (1966-67), Salsbury Laboratories; Government Relations Manager (1967-71), Salsbury Laboratories; Director of Regulatory Affairs (1971-74), Zoecon Industries Inc., Dallas, TX **Selected Memberships:** Regulatory Affairs Professionals Society; American Association for the Advancement of Science; New York Academy of Science; American Society of Agricultural Consultants; IRAS Isthmus Institute; American Association of Industrial Veterinarians; United States Animal Health Association **Discipline:** Biological Sciences; Managerial **Related Areas of Interest:** Biomedical Ethics; Philosophy and History of Science.

Selected Publications: His bibliography lists 7 books, 15 articles, and a newspaper column.

_____. "On the Probability of Our Demise." *The Humanist* 23, 5 (1963): 139-40.
_____. "The Problem of Evolution." *The American Biology Teacher* 27 (December 1965): 765-9.
_____. "Evolution and Evolutionism in America: A Report on the Opposition." Part 1. *The American Rationalist (AR)* 14, 4 (1970): 4-7; Part 2. *AR* 14, 5 (1970): 4-8.
_____. "On Tending the Fire that is Science." *AR* 16, 4 (1971): 5-6.
_____. "Regulatory Perspectives: An Industry View on Biotechnology in Animal Agriculture." In *Proceedings of Symposium on Biotechnology in Animal Health Sector: Scientific, Regulatory, and Ethical Implications,* 109-14. West Jefferson, OH: B & L Graphics, 1990.
_____. "An Essay on Beauty: Some Implications of Beauty in the Natural World." *Zygon* 27, 4 (1992): 479-90.
_____. "Compliance, Enforcement, Inspections: Industry Perspective of FDA Enforcement Actions." *Regulatory Affairs* 4 (Winter 1992): 423-8.
_____. "On Bringing Light Into a Dark Room: Some New Observations on C. P. Snow's Two Cultures." In *Ten Years With NPIRS: Conference Proceedings held in Savannah, GA, February 22-26, 1993,* 7-12.

Shull, Philip A.

Present Position and Address: Cofounder and Director (since 1979), Institute for Ethics and World Issue Awareness, 714 South Eighth, Bozeman, MT 59715, USA **Concurrent Positions:** Adjunct

Professor (since 1985), Montana State University; United Methodist Campus Pastor (since 1983), Montana State University **Date of Birth:** July 1, 1946 **Education:** Studies (1964-65), Baker University, Baldwin, KS; Studies (Winter and Spring 1966), University of Copenhagen, Denmark; B.A. Sociology (1968), Washburn University; M.Div. (1971), Iliff School of Theology, Denver **Previous Positions:** Minister to Youth (1969-71), St. Andrews UMC, Littleton, CO; Pastor (1971-76), Chinook UMC; Associate Pastor (1976-83), First UMC, Great Falls **Discipline:** Ethics and Public Policy; Theology; Pseudo-Science and Creationism **Related Areas of Interest:** Church-State Relations; Education and Science.

Selected Publications:

_____. "Technology and Production: Everyday Impacts." In *Technology and Politics: Who's in Control.* Kinko's Professional Pub., 1987.

Shults, F. LeRon

Present Position and Address: Assistant Dean for Academic Affairs, Walden University, 415 1st Ave. N., Minneapolis, MN 55401, USA; (Home) 2712 E. 125th St., Burnsville, MN 55337, USA **Work Phone:** (612) 338-7224 **Home Phone:** (612) 894-8726 **Education:** B.A. Religion/Philosophy, Roberts Wesleyan College; M.A. Theology, Fuller Theological Seminary; Ph.D. Education (1991), Walden University. Dissertation: "An Open Systems Model for Adult Learning in Theological Inquiry." **Discipline:** Adult Education **Related Areas of Interest:** Isomorphic Indicators in the Unitary Realist Epistemology of T. F. Torrance and the Integration of Reflection and Praxis in Interactive Adult Learning

Selected Publications:

_____. "Integrating the Arts and Sciences: An Experiment in Interdisciplinary Epistemology." Paper presented at the National Conference on Nontraditional/Interdisciplinary Programs, May 1991, George Mason University.
_____. "A Theology of Chaos: An Experiment in Postmodern Theological Science." *Scottish Journal of Theology* (Forthcoming).

Shweder, Richard Allan

Present Position and Address: Committee on Human Development; University of Chicago, 5730 South Woodlawn Avenue, Chicago, IL 60637, USA **Work Phone:** (312) 702-1524 **Home Phone:** (312) 947-9660 **Fax Number:** (312) 702-0320 **E-Mail:** rshd@quads.uchicago.edu **Date of Birth:** February 17, 1945 **Education:** B.A. Anthropology (*magna cum laude*, 1966), University of Pittsburgh; Ph.D. Social Relations/Anthropology (1972), Harvard University; Language Training in Oriya (1969), West Bengal, India **Awards and Honors:** AAAS Socio-Psychological Prize (1982) for publication, "Does the Concept of the Person Vary Cross-Culturally?" **Previous Positions:** Research Associate in Anthropology (1969-70), Bhubaneswar, Orissa, India; Research Fellow (1972-73), Department of Psychology and Social Relations, Harvard University; Lecturer in Sociology (1972-73), University of Nairobi, Kenya; Assistant Professor (1973-80)/Associate Professor (1980-85)/Chairman (1987-89), Committee on Human Development, University of Chicago; Research Associate of Psychology (1982-83), Utkal University, Bhubaneswar, Orissa, India **Editorial Positions:** Editorial Advisory Board (since 1989), *Moral Behavior and Development*; Series Editor (since 1989), *Society for Psychological Anthropology*, Cambridge University **Selected Memberships:** MacArthurFoundation Mid-Life Research Group (since 1989); Executive Council (since 1989), Society for the Advancement of Socio-Economics; American Anthropological Association; American Association for the Advancement of Science; The Classification Society; The Cognitive Science Society; Merrill-Palmer Society; Society for Cross-Cultural Research; Society for Psychological Anthropology; Society for Research on Child Development **Discipline:** Anthropology; Philosophy; Psychology **Related Areas of Interest:** Culture Theory; Comparative Ethics; Moral Development; Orders of reality presupposed by explanations of suffering **Current Areas of Research:** The study of cross-cultural variations in the concept of the person, and an examination of the role of conversational routines and tacit communications in the development of the self; Comparative Ethics, Mid-life Development.

Selected Publications: His bibliography lists 6 books and 53 articles.

_____, Robert A. LeVine, eds. *Culture Theory: Essays on Mind, Self and Emotions.* New York. Cambridge University Press, 1984.

_____, D. W. Fiske, eds. *Metatheory in Social Science: Pluralism and Subjectivities.* Chicago: University of Chicago Press, 1986.

_____, James Stigler and Gilbert Herdt, eds. *Cultural Psychology: Essays on Comparative Human Development.* New York: Cambridge University Press, 1990.

_____, M. Mahapatra and J. G. Miller. "Culture and Moral Development." In *The Emergence of Morality in Young Children,* ed. Jerome Kagan and Sharon Lamb, 1-83. Chicago: University of Chicago Press, 1987. Reprint, in *Cultural Psychology: Essays on Comparative Human Development,* ed. James Stigler, Richard A. Shweder and Gilbert Herdt. New York: Cambridge University Press, 1990.

_____. *Thinking Through Cultures: Expeditions in Cultural Psychology.* Cambridge, MA: Harvard University Press, 1991.

_____, Edmund J. Bourne. "Does the Concept of the Person Vary Cross-Culturally?" In *Cultural Conceptions of Mental Health and Therapy,* ed. A. J. Marsella and G. White" 97-137. Dordrecht, Holland: Reidel, 1982; Awarded 1982 AAAS Socio-Psychological Prize. Reprint, in *Culture Theory: Essays on Mind, Self and Emotion,* ed. R. A. Shweder and R. A. LeVine. New York: Cambridge University Press, 1984. Reprint, in *Thinking Through Cultures: Expeditions in Cultural Psychology,* by R. A. Shweder. Cambridge: Harvard University Press, 1991.

_____. '"Why Do Men Barbecue?" and Other Postmodern Ironies of Growing up in the Decade of Ethnicity.' *Daedalus,* Special Issue, "Children in America: Three to Eleven" 122, 1 (1993).

_____, Maria Sullivan. "Cultural Psychology: Who Needs It?" *Annual Review of Psychology* 44 (1993): 497-523.

_____. "The Cultural Psychology of the Emotions." In *The Handbook of Emotions,* ed. Michael Lewis and Jeannette Haviland. New York: Guilford Publications, 1993.

_____, Usha Menon. "Kali's Tongue: Cultural Psychology and the Power of 'Shame' in Orissa, India." In *Culture and the Emotions,* ed. Hazel Marus and Shinobu Kitayama. In press.

Siegel, Harvey

Present Position and Address: Professor of Philosophy (since 1988), University of Miami; P.O. Box 248054, Coral Gables, FL 33124, USA **Work Phone:** (305) 284-6109 **E-Mail:** hsiegel@umiami.ir.miami.edu **Date of Birth:** March 2, 1952 **Education:** B.A. (*cum laude,* 1974), Cornell University; Ed.M (1975)/Ed.D. Philosophy of Science/Science Education (1977), Harvard University **Congresses and Conferences:** Organizer and Chair (1983), symposium on "Philosophy of Science: Current Research and Implications for Science Education," AAAS **Previous Positions:** Instructor (1974-77), Northshore Community College; Assistant Professor of Philosophy of Education (1977-81), University of Nebraska; Assistant Professor of Philosophy (1981-83), Sonoma State University; Associate Professor of Philosophy (1983-84), Michigan Technological University; Associate Professor of Philosophy (1984-88), University of Miami; Visiting Positions -Arizona University (Summer 1981)/University of California - Berkeley (1980-82, Summer 1986)/Stanford University (Winter 1986)/University of Groninger, The Netherlands **Media Work:** Consultant and Participant (1981), California Public Radio - Creationism/Evolution controversy **Editorial Positions:** Editorial Board, *Philosophy and Education/Studies in Philosophy of Education* **Other Academic Experience:** Consultant and expert witness (1981), State of California suit concerning the teaching of evolution and creationism in California Public Schools **Selected Memberships:** American Philosophical Association; Philosophy of Science Association; British Society for the Philosophy of Science; Society for Philosophy and Psychology; Southern Society for Philosophy and Psychology; Philosophy of Education Society; Association for

Philosophy of Education Society; Association for Informal Logic and Critical Thinking; Sigma Xi; American Association for the Advancement of Science; American Educational Studies Association; California Association for Philosophy of Education; Association for Philosophy of Education; Florida Philosophical Association **Discipline:** Epistemology; Philosophy of Science; Philosophy of Education; Science Education **Related Areas of Interest:** Theology and Creation; Creation Science; Evolution and Creationism in Education; Rationality and Relativism in Religion, Ethics, Science and the Social Sciences; Rationality and Morality.

Selected Publications: His bibliography lists 2 books and 95 articles.

_____. "Creationism, Evolution, and The California Fiasco." *Phi Delta Kappan* 63, 2 (1981): 95-101.
_____. "The Response to Creationism." *Educational Studies* 15, 4 (1984): 349-63.
_____. "What Is the Question Concerning the Rationality of Science?" *Philosophy of Science* 52, 4 (1985): 517-37.
_____. *Relativism Refuted: A Critique of Contemporary Epistemological Relativism.* Synthese Library. Vol. 189. Dordrecht: D. Reidel, 1987.
_____. *Educating Reason: Rationality, Critical Thinking, and Education.* Philosophy of Education Research Library. London: Routledge, 1988.
_____. "The Rationality of Science, Critical Thinking, and Science Education." *Synthese* 80, 1 (1989): 9-41.
_____. "Philosophy of Science Naturalized?" *Studies in History and Philosophy of Science* 20, 3 (1989): 365-75.
_____. "Justification by Balance." *Philosophy and Phenomenology Research* 52, 1 (1992): 27-46.
_____. "Farewell to Feyerabend." *Inquiry* 32, 3 (1989): 343-69.
_____, A. Neiman. "Objectivity and Rationality in Epistemology and Education Scheffler's Middle Road." *Synthese* 94, 1 (1993): 55-83.

Siegwalt, Gérard

Present Position and Address: Professor of Systematic Theology (since 1964), Faculté de Théologie protestante, Université des Sciences Humaines, 67000 Strasbourg, France; (Home) 25, rue Sainte-Cécile, 67100 Strasbourg-Neudorf, France **Work Phone:** 88 44 37 99 **Date of Birth:** January 6, 1932 **Languages Spoken:** French, German, English **Education:** M.Div. (1949-53)/Doctoral Studies (1957-60)/Doctorat d'Etat en Théologie protestante (1967), Faculté de Théologie protestante de Strasbourg; M.Th. (1954), Princeton Theological Seminary **Previous Positions:** Pastor (1954-55), Lutheran Church; Military Service (1955-57); Lecturer in Biblical Languages (1960-64), Strasbourg **Discipline:** Systematic Theology **Related Areas of Interest:** Theological Cosmology; Theological Anthropology; Theological Theology.

Selected Publications:

_____, editor. *Nature menacée et responsabilté chrétienne.* Strasbourg: Oberlin, 1979.
_____, editor. *La nature a-t-elle un sens? Civilisation technologique et conscience chrétienne devant l'inquiétude écologique.* Association des Presses des Universités de Strasbourg, 1980.
_____. *La quête des fondements.* Vol. 1, no. 1, (1986); *Réalite et révélation.* Vol. 1, no. 2, (1987); *L'Eglise chrétienne dans la société humaine.* Vol. 2, no. 1, (1991); *Les médiations: L'Eglise et les moyens de grâce.* Vol. 2, no. 2, (1992) of *Dogmatique pour la catholicité évangélique.* Paris: Cerf; Geneva: Labor et Fides.

Siemens Jr., David F.

Address: 2703 E. Kenwood Street, Mesa, AZ 85213-2384, USA **Date of Birth:** September 18, 1925 **Languages Spoken:** English, Spanish **Education:** Diploma in Bible and Pastoral Training (1946), Fort Wayne Bible College; B.A. Bible and Greek (1947), Defiance College; M.A. Philosophy major and Science minor (1954), Indiana State University; Ph.D. Philosophy (1976), Claremont Graduate School **Previous Positions:** 5 years of High School Teaching; Taught Theology, Homiletics and Composition (1950-51), Rio Grande Bible Institute; Taught Zoology, Speech and Health (1954-55),

Central College, McPherson, KS; Taught History and Religion (1959-60), Pasadena City College; Taught Philosophy and Ethics (1959-65), Los Angeles City College; Taught Logic and Philosophy (1965-66), Riverside City College; Instructor through Professor of Philosophy (1966-86), Los Angeles Pierce College; Taught Logic (1985), Moorpark College; Taught Philosophy, Logic and Ethics (1988), Scottsdale Community College; Professor Emeritus, Los Angeles Pierce College **Selected Memberships:** Fellow, American Scientific Affiliation; Philosophy of Science Association; Association for Symbolic Logic; Society of Christian Philosophers; Evangelical Philosophical Society; American Association for the Advancement of Science **Discipline:** Philosophy; Science; Theology **Related Areas of Interest:** Science and Theology in Dialogue; Conflicts between Christianity and Physical Science/Biology; Creation.

Selected Publications: His bibliography lists 3 books and 16 articles.

_____. "Conflicts Between Christianity and Physical Science." *Journal of the American Scientific Affiliation (JASA)* 16 (1964): 12-15.
_____. "The Conflict Between Christianity and Biological Science." *JASA* 18 (1966): 5-7.
_____. "The Sources of Science." *JASA* 18 (1966): 84-6.
_____. "More Problems with Flood Geology." *Perspectives on Science and Christian Faith* 44 (1992): 228-35.

Siirala, Aarne *(Deceased)*

Former Position and Address: Retired Professor of Religion (1985), Wilfrid Laurier University; General Delivery, Carnarvon, ONT KOM 1JO, Canada **Date of Birth:** July 8, 1919 **Date of Death:** May 8, 1991 **Languages Spoken:** English, Finnish, Swedish, German **Education:** Candidate Theology (1943)/Dr. Theology (1956), University of Helsinki, Finland; Licentiate in Theology (Dogmatics and Ethics, 1950), Lund University, Sweden **Awards and Honors:** Nominated by the President of the Republic of Finland (1969) for the Professorship of Dogmatics (ordinarus) at the University of Finland **Previous Positions:** Soldier (1939-41)/Chaplain (1941-42)/Social Officer (1942-43), Finnish Army; Parish Pastor (1943-45)/Liason (1945-46) for Archbishop of Finland in Stockholm, The Church of Finland; Teacher through Vice-Principal (1946-52)/Principal (1952-60), Adult-Educational College and Evangelical Academy, Church of Finland; Docent (1962-64)/Research Fellow (1960-63), University of Helsinki; Professor of Systematic Theology (1963-1975), Waterloo Lutheran University and Seminary; Professor of Religion (1975-85), Wilfrid Laurier University **Selected Memberships:** Former President, Canadian Theological Society; American Academy of Religion; Canadian Society for the Study of Religion **Discipline:** Theology and Ethics **Related Areas of Interest:** Theology/Religion and Mental Health; Medical Ethics; Man, Medicine and Theology.

Selected Publications: His bibliography lists 5 books, 3 chapters, 40 articles in Finland, Scandinavia and Germany (1945-60), over 7 English articles, and 3 published papers.

_____. *The Voice of Illness.* Philadelphia, PA: N.p., 1964.
_____. *Divine Humanness.* Philadelphia, PA: N.p., 1970.

Simmons Jr., Ernest L.

Present Position and Address: Associate Professor (since 1987) Concordia College, Box 313, Moorhead, MN 56562, USA **Date of Birth:** September 19, 1947 **Languages Spoken:** English, Spanish **Education:** B.A. (1970), Colorado State University; M.Div (1973), Luther Northwestern Theological Seminary; Ph.D. Philosophy of Religion and Systematic Theology (1981), Claremont Graduate School **Previous Positions:** Instructor (1977-79), Great Plains Institute of Theology; Pastor (1977-79), Carpio Lutheran Church, ND; Assistant Professor (1979-87), Concordia College **Selected Memberships:** American Academy of Religion; Institute on Religion in an Age of Science **Discipline:** Philosophy of

Religion; Systematic Theology **Related Areas of Interest:** Theology and Space Development; Creation and Cosmology; Religious and Scientific Method.

Selected Publications:

_____. "Mystical Consciousness in a Process Perspective." *Process Studies* 14 (Spring 1984).
_____. "God and Space: Implications of Space Development for Theology." *Teaching at Concordia* (1989). Also under final review with *Zygon.*
_____. "Creation in Luther's Theology of the Cross." *Dialog* 30 , 1 (1991).

Simpkinson, Charles H.

Present Position and Address: Publisher (since 1980), *Common Boundary Magazine,* 5272 River Road, Suite 650, Bethesda, MD 20816, USA **Concurrent Positions:** Director (since 1985), Center for Advanced Study of Psychotherapy; Founder (1976-present), *The Family Therapy Networker Magazine* **Work Phone:** (301) 652-9495 **Date of Birth:** November 3, 1934 **Education:** B.A. (1957), Williams College; Studies (1960-61), Yale Divinity School; Ph.D. Clinical Psychology (1972), University of Tennessee **Awards and Honors:** Recipient (1978), Distinguished Service Award, Maryland Psychological Association; Psi Chi (National Honorary Society in Psychology); **Previous Positions:** Staff (1969-70), National Training Laboratory; Faculty (1970-72), Department of Psychiatry and Behavioral Science, Johns Hopkins Medical School; Staff (1972-85), Department of Health, Montgomery County, MD **Selected Memberships:** American Psychological Association; American Academy of Religion; Center for Advanced Study of Psychotherapy, held at College of Preachers, Washington National Cathedral (a biannual think tank on the interaction of Psychotherapy and Spirituality); Society for Psychotherapy Research; Society for Exploration of Psychotherapy Integration; Association of Transpersonal Psychology **Discipline:** Clinical Psychology **Related Areas of Interest:** Interaction of Spirituality and Psychotherapy.

Selected Publications: His bibliography lists 4 books and 10 articles.

_____. "Coming Home: The Spiritual Ends of Psychotherapy." *Common Boundary (CB)* 1, 5 (1983)
_____. "The Spiritual Transformation of Organizations." *CB* 2, 1 (1984).
_____. "Spirituality and the Inner Life of the Therapist." *CB* 2, 2 (1984).
_____. "Healing the Grief Our Fathers Lived: A Weekend with Robert Bly." *CB* 4, 4 (1986).
_____. "Is There Civilization Beyond Discontent." Review of *Transformations of Consciousness,* by Ken Wilbur, et al. CB 4, 4 (1986).
_____. "Alternative Psychology School Graduates Fight for Licensure." *CB* 8, 1 (1990).
_____. "Compassionate Living: Can We Integrate Healthy Narcissism and Social Responsibility?" *CB* 8, 4 (1990).
_____, Anne A. Simpkinson, eds. *Sacred Stories: A Celebration of the Power of Stories to Transform and Heal.* San Francisco: Harper, 1993.
_____, Douglas Wengell and M. J. A. Casavant. *Common Boundary Graduate Education Guide.* 2d ed. 1994.

Singh, Renuka

Present Position and Address: Freelance Researcher (since 1987), Integrated Human Development Services Foundation; K-24, Hauz Khas, New Delhi - 110016, India **Work Phone:** 668248 **Date of Birth:** August 23, 1952 **Languages Spoken:** English, Hindi, Punjabi, Urdu **Education:** B.A. (1973), Delhi University; M.A. (1975)/M.Phil. (1977)/Ph.D. (1986), Jawaharlal Nehru University **Previous Positions:** Freelance Researcher with various organizations: Vishva Yuvak Kendra (1980)/Centre for Social Research (1985-88); Family Counselor (1983) for Pragati **Discipline:** Sociology **Related Areas of Interest:** Women, Culture and Development; Religion and Society; Science, Technology, Culture and Development.

Selected Publications:

_____, coauthor. *Growing up in Rural India, Problems and Needs of Adolescent Girls*. Delhi: Radiant Publishers, 1989.
_____. *The Womb of Mind, A Sociological Exploration of the Status-experience of Women in Delhi*. Delhi: Vikas Publishing House, 1990. Deals with religion and society .

Sire, James W.

Present Position and Address: Senior Editor and Campus Lecturer (since 1984), InterVarsity Press, Box 1400, Downers Grove, IL 60515, USA **Work Phone:** (708) 964-5700 **Date of Birth:** October 17, 1933 **Education:** B.A. English and Chemistry (1955), University of Nebraska; M.A. English (1958), Washington State University; Ph.D. English (1964), University of Missouri **Previous Positions:** Instructor in English (1958-64), University of Missouri; Assistant (1964-66)/Associate Professor of English (1966-68), Nebraska Wesleyan University; Associate Professor of English (1969-70), Northern Illinois University **Editorial Positions:** Editor (1968-84), InterVarsity Press **Selected Memberships:** American Scientific Affiliation **Related Areas of Interest:** World View; Philosophy of Science; Apologetics.

Selected Publications: His bibliography lists 9 books and 2 articles.

_____. *The Universe Next Door: A Basic World View Catalogue*. 2d ed. Downer's Grove: InterVarsity Press, 1988.
_____. *Discipleship of the Mind*. Downer's Grove: InterVarsity Press, 1990.
_____. *Why Should Anyone Believe Anything at All?* Downers Grove: InterVarsity Press, 1994.

Skolimowski, Henryk

Present Position and Address: Head, Chair of Ecological Philosophy, Technical University of Lodz, Poland; Eco-Philosophy Center, 18500 Bowdish, Gregory, MI 48137, USA **Work Phone:** (313) 498-3016 **Date of Birth:** May 4, 1930 **Languages Spoken:** English, Polish, Russian **Education:** Warsaw College of Music (1948-52); M.Sc. (1956), Warsaw Institute of Technology; M.A. Philosophy (1959), Warsaw University; D.Phil. Philosophy (1964), New College - Oxford University **Postgraduate Experience:** Research Fellow: St. Antony's College (1959-64); Columbia University (1968); Linacre College, Oxford (1968-69); Clare Hall, Cambridge (1971-72) **Previous Positions:** Taught at following Institutions: Warsaw Institute of Technology (1956-59); Warsaw University (1958-59); University of Southern California - Los Angeles (1964-71); University of Michigan, Ann Arbor (1971-93); Philosopher in Residence (1979-83), Dartington Hall, Devon, UK; Philosopher in residence (1979-89), Arcosanti, AZ; University of Madras, India (1981); Member, Task Force on Appropriate Technology, US Congress; Consultant to UNESCO concerning the impact of science and technology on development and cultural values in Warsaw, Poland (1977), and Hyderabad, India (1978) **Selected Memberships:** Commission on Ecology, International Union for the Conservation of Nature; Vice President (since 1989), Teilhard Society in London; Director, Eco-Philosophy Center; President's Council on Ecology (Poland) **Discipline:** Philosophy; Music **Related Areas of Interest:** Eco-Theology; Eco-Ethics; Eco-Philosophy.

Selected Publications: Bibliography lists 17 books and over 400 articles.

_____. *Eco-Theology. Toward a Religion for our Times*. Ann Arbor: Eco-Philosophy Center, 1985.
_____. *Forests as Sanctuaries*. Ann Arbor: Eco-Philosophy Center, 1985.
_____. "Reverence for Life." In *Ethics of Environment and Development*, ed. J. Ronald Engel and Joan Gibb Engel. London: Belhaven Press, 1990.
_____. *Dancing Shiva in the Ecological Age*. New Delhi: Clarion Books, 1991.
_____. "Ecological Spirituality and Its Practical Consequences." *The Teilhard Review* (Summer 1992).

_____. *Ecology and the Sanctity of Life*. Ann Arbor: Eco-Philosophy Center, 1992.
_____. "Clinging to the Earth as an Ecological Prayer." *New Renaissance* 4, 1 (1993).
_____. "The Primacy of Hope." In *Voices on the Threshold of Tomorrow*, by Georg Feuerstein. Wheaton, IL: Quest Books, 1993. Reprint, *Quest Magazine* (Autumn 1993).
_____. *A Sacred Place to Dwell, Living with Reverence Upon the Earth*. Rockport, MA: Element Books, 1993.

Sleigh Jr., Robert Collins

Present Position and Address: Professor of Philosophy (since 1969), University of Massachusetts - Amherst, Amherst, MA 01003 USA **Date of Birth:** November 30, 1932 **Education:** B.A. (1954), Dartmouth College; M.A. (1957)/Ph.D. (1963), Brown University **Postgraduate Experience:** Faculty Research Fellow (1966), Wayne State University; Fellow (1967-68), Center for Advanced Study in Behavioral Sciences; Honorary Research Associate in Philosophy (1975-76), Harvard University; Visiting Fellow (1982-83), Princeton Theological Seminary; Fellow/Research Associate (1982-83, 86-87), Institute for Advanced Study, Princeton, NJ **Previous Positions:** Instructor (1958-61)/Assistant (1965-69)/Associate Professor (1965-69), Wayne State University; Visiting Professor - University of Illinois (summer 1963)/Dartmouth College (summer 1965)/Harvard University (1965)/University of Michigan (1973)/Brown University (1981)/Universidad Nacional Autonoma de Mexico (summer 1983)/University of Arizona (1984)/University of California - Irvine (1989)/University of Notre Dame (1990) **Selected Memberships:** American Philosophical Association; Leibniz Society of America; Council for Philosophical Studies; History of Science Society; American Council of Learned Societies; International Berkeley Society; American Historical Association **Discipline:** Philosophy **Related Areas of Interest:** Theodicy; Theological Foundations of Leibniz's Philosophy; Theology and Philosophy.

Selected Publications: His bibliography lists 4 books and 23 articles.

_____, coeditor. *The Yale Leibniz*. New Haven: Yale University Press, 1990.
_____. *Leibniz and Arnauld: A Commentary on their Correspondence*. New Haven: Yale University Press, 1990.

Smith, David H.

Present Position and Address: Professor of Religious Studies (since 1979)/Director (since 1982), Poynter Center for the Study of Ethics and American Institutions, Indiana University, 410 North Park Avenue, Bloomington, IN 47408, USA; (Home) 904 E. First Street, Bloomington, IN 47401, USA **Work Phone:** (812) 855-0261 **Home Phone:** (812) 336-2429 **Date of Birth:** April 28, 1939 **Education:** B.A. Philosophy (1961), Carleton College; B.D. (1964), Yale Divinity School; Ph.D., Princeton University **Previous Positions:** Assistant (1967-70)/Associate (1970-79)/Professor of Religious Studies (since 1979), Indiana University; Subject Matter (ethics) Expert (1985-86), Professional Development Training Conferences, Chaplain Corps, US Navy; Seminar Director, "Liberal Education and Moral Criticism" (1985-94), Workshop on the Liberal Arts **Discipline:** Theology; Philosophy **Related Areas of Interest:** Philosophy and Theology; Medical Ethics; Health, Medicine and Religion; Religious and Secular Morality.

Selected Publications: His bibliography lists 5 books and 23 articles.

_____. "Theological Reflection and the New Biology." *Indiana University Law Journal* 48 (Summer 1973): 607-22.
_____. "Scientific Knowledge and Forbidden Truths." *Hastings Center Report* 8, 6 (1978): 30-5.
_____. "Medical Loyalty: Dimensions and Problems of a Rich Idea." In *Theology and Bioethics*, ed. Earl L. Shelp, 267-82. Dordrecht: D. Reidel Publishing Co., 1985.
_____. *Health and Medicine in the Anglican Tradition. Conscience, Community and Compromise*. New York: Crossroads Publishing Co., 1986.

_____. "Suffering, Medicine, and Christian Theology." In *On Moral Medicine: Theological Perspectives in Medical Ethics*, ed. Stephen E. Lammers and Allen Verhey. Grand Rapids: Eerdmans, 1987.

Smith, Huston

Present Position and Address: Professor Emeritus of Philosophy and Religion (since 1983), Syracuse University; 130 Avenida Drive, Berkeley, CA 97408, USA **Date of Birth:** May 31, 1919 **Education:** A.B. (1940), Central Methodist College, Fayette, MO; Ph.D. Philosophy of Religion (1945), University of Chicago **Honorary Degrees:** Eight honorary degrees **Previous Positions:** Assistant through Associate Professor of Philosophy (1947-58), Washington University; Professor of Philosophy (1958-73), Massachusetts Institute of Technology; Thomas J. Watson Professor of Religion/Distinguished Adjunct Professor of Philosophy (1973-83), Syracuse University **Selected Memberships:** American Philosophical Association; American Academy of Religion; Center for Theology and the Natural Sciences **Discipline:** Comparative Philosophy and Religion **Related Areas of Interest:** Comparative Philosophy and Religion; Science and Theology interface.

Selected Publications: His bibliography lists 9 books and 67 articles.

_____. *Forgotten Truth: The Primordial Tradition*. New York: Harper & Row, 1976.
_____. "Excluded Knowledge: A Critique of the Modern Western Mind Set." *Teachers College Record* 80, 3 (1979). Reprint, in *Education and Values,* ed. Douglas Sloan. New York: Teachers College Press, 1980.
_____. "Beyond the Modern Western Mindset." *Teachers College Record* 32, 3 (1981).
_____. "Science and Theology: The Unstable Detente." *The Anglican Theological Review* 63, 4 (1981).
_____. "Evolution and Evolutionism." *The Christian Century* 99, 23 (1982).
_____. *Beyond the Post-Modern Mind*. Wheaton, IL: Quest Book, 1989.

Snoke, David Wayne

Present Position and Address: Alexander von Humboldt Fellow in Physics, Max-Planck-Institute - Stuttgart, Germany; Furtwänglerstrasse 95, 7000 Stuttgart 1, Germany **Date of Birth:** May 7, 1961 **Languages Spoken:** English, German **Education:** A.B. (*magna cum laude*, 1983), Cornell University; M.S. Physics (1984)/Ph.D. Physics (1990), University of Illinois **Awards and Honors:** Phi Beta Kappa **Previous Positions:** Research Engineer (1983), Westinghouse R&D, Pittsburgh, PA; Teaching and then Research Assistant (1983-90), University of Illinois **Selected Memberships:** APS; American Scientific Affiliation; Presbyterian Church in America; **Discipline:** Physics (solid state) **Related Areas of Interest:** Religious and Philosophical Beliefs of Physicists in America.

Selected Publications:

_____. "Star Wars - Looks More and More Politically Dead." *World* 4, 21 (1989).
_____. "God's Hand in Natural Disasters: Scientists Dabble with Theology." *World* 4, 22 (1989).
_____. "No 'Net Energy' from Fusion Says Energy Department Study." *World* 4, 26 (1989).
_____. "Shuttle Success Renews Question of Man's Future Role in Space." *World* 5, 32 (1990).
_____. "Supersecular Supercollider?" *World* 4, 37 (1990).
_____. "Superconducting Supercollider Might be in Trouble." *World* 4, 37 (1990).
_____. "Double Trouble: Hubble Flaw Follows Space Shuttle Grounding." *World* 5, 11 (1990).

Sollod, Robert N.

Present Position and Address: Professor of Psychology Cleveland State University, Cleveland, OH 44115, USA **Work Phone:** (216) 523-4266 **Home Phone:** (216) 231-2530 **Date of Birth:** February 20, 1942 **Languages Spoken:** French **Education:** B.A. *cum laude*, Harvard College (1965), Social

Relations; M.A. Duquesne University (1970), Clinical Psychology and Philosophy; Ph.D. Columbia University (1974), Clinical Psychology. **Awards and Honors:** Natural Merit Scholarship, 1960; Veteran's Administration Traineeship 1969-1973; Sigma Xi **Previous Positions:** Associate Professor of Psychology, Ferkauf Graduate School, Yeshiva University; Assistant Professor of Psychology, New York University **Selected Memberships:** Fellow, International Academy of Eclectic Psychotherapists; American Psychological Association, Divisions 29 and 36; Society for the Exploration of Psychotherapy Integration; Head of the Task Force for Undergraduate Education in Religion and Psychology **Discipline:** Psychology **Related Interests:** Spiritual approaches to psychotherapy; integration of religion and psychotherapy; Education about religion in colleges and universities **Current Research:** Psychotherapists integration of prayer and meditation.

Selected Publications: His bibliography includes 22 published articles, 12 chapters, 1 edited book, 2 study guides, and more than 60 presentations.

_____. "Carl Rogers and the Origins of Client Centered Therapy." *Professional Psychology* 9 (1978):93-104.
_____. "Non-Scientific Sources of Psychotherapeutic Approaches." In *Philosophy, Religion, and Psychotherapy*, ed. P. Sharkey. Washington, DC: University Press of America, 1982..
_____. "Behavioral Science and Illiteracy: Becoming Part of the Solution." *Behavioral Analysis and Social Action* 6, 1 (1987): 23-26.
_____. "Psychotherapy with Anomalous Experiences." In *Current Perspectives on Anomalous Experiences and Trauma*, eds. R. Laibow, R. Sollod, and J. Wilson. Dobbs Ferry, NY: Treat Publications, 1992.
_____. "The Hollow Curriculum: Our Oversight of Religion and Spirituality in Higher Education:." *Chronicle of Higher Education:* 38, 28 (1992): A60.
_____. "Integrating Spiritual Healing Approaches and Techniques into Psychotherapy." In *The Comprehensive Handbook of Psychotherapy Integration*, eds. G. Stricker and J. Gold. New York: Plenum, 1993.
_____. "Robert W. White and the Origins of the Concept of Competence: An Interview." *Archives of the History of American Psychology*. Akron, OH: University of Akron.

South, Oron P.

Present Position and Address: Consultant on Organization Change; Editor, *The Diversity Factor*; P.O. Box 11641, Green Lantern Station, Montgomery, AL 36111-0641, USA **Concurrent Positions:** Some Consulting Clients: Henry I Siegel Co., NY; Arnold Research Co, Tullahoma; USAF; Florida State Legislature Joint Committee on Education; Indiana Bell Telephone Co.; Westinghouse Learning Corp.; Florida International University; Atomedic Research Center; Montgomery AL; Girl Scouts of America; University of Miami Desegregation Center **Work Phone:** (205) 281-3819 **Date of Birth:** May 27, 1917 **Education:** B.S. (1939)/M.S. American History (1940), Auburn University; Ph.D. American History (1967), Vanderbilt University **Previous Positions:** Research Associate and Professor (1947-64), Aerospace Studies Institute, Air University, USAF; Associate Professor (1966-68), School of Engineering, Vanderbilt University; Director (1969-71), Midwest Division NTL Institute for Applied Behavioral Science; OD Team Leader and Resident Consultant (1972-75), Monroe County, Florida School District; President (1976-79), Center for Planned Change, St. Louis; Visiting Professor (1975-79), College of Education, Florida State University; Organization Development Team Leader and Resident Consultant (1979-83); Internal Revenue Service **Selected Memberships:** American Association for the Advancement of Science; Organization Development Network; Organization Behavior Teaching Society; Academy of Political Science; International Society for Planning and Strategic Management **Discipline:** Systematics **Related Areas of Interest:** How Dialogue is Organized.

Selected Publications:

_____. "Culture as a Target of Change." In *Corporate Cultures: Research Implications for Human Resource Development*, ed. John C. Glidewell, 67-85. Alexandria, VA: American Society for Training and Development, 1986.

_____. "The Resident Consultant-Entry Issues." *Organization Development Journal* 7, 2 (1989): 67-85.

_____, Jack Gant. "OD in Public Education Areas for Development." In *The Emerging Practice of Organization Development*, ed. Walter Sikes, Allan Drexler, and Jack Gant, 39-47. Alexandria VA: NTL Institute for Applied Behavioral Science and University Associates, 1989.

_____. "A Contextual Approach to Internal Consulting." In *Handbook of Organizational Consultation*, ed. Robert T. Golembiewski, 693-701. New York: Marcel Dekker, Inc., 1992.

Southgate, Beverley C.

Present Position and Address: Reader in History of Ideas (since 1967), School of Humanities and Education, University of Hertfordshire, Watford Campus, Aldenham, Herts WD2 8AT, UK **Work Phone:** (0707) 28 5650 **Date of Birth:** March 20, 1936 **Education:** B.A. (1961), University of Oxford; M.Sc. History of Finance(1970)/Ph.D. History of Science (1979), University of London **Previous Positions:** Part-time Tutor (1972-77), Open University; Panel Member (1977-85), CNAA History of Ideas Panel **Selected Memberships:** British Society for the History of Science; British Society for the History of Philosophy; International Society for the Study of European Ideas **Discipline:** Intellectual and Cultural History **Related Areas of Interest:** 17th Century Intellectual and Cultural History - including the relationship of Science and Religion.

Selected Publications:

_____. "'A Philosophical Divinity': Thomas White and an Aspect of Mid-seventeenth Century Science and Religion." *History of European Ideas* 8 (1987): 45-59.

_____. "Excluding Sceptics: The Case of Thomas White, 1593-1676." In *The Sceptical Mode in Modern Philosophy: Essays in Honor of Richard Popkin*, ed. R. A. Watson and J. E. Force. International Archives of the History of Ideas, vol. 117. Dordrecht, 1988.

_____. "'Forgotten and Lost': Some Reactions to Autonomous Science in the Seventeenth Century." *Journal of the History of Ideas* 50 (1989): 249-68.

_____. "'No other Wisdom'? Humanist Reactions to Science and Scientism in the Seventeenth Century." *The Seventeenth Century* 5 (1990): 71-92.

_____. "'The Power of Imagination': Psychological Explanations in Mid-seventeenth Century England." *History of Science* 30 (1992): 281-94.

_____. "'Cauterizing the Tumour of Pyrrhonism': Blackloism versus Scepticism." *Journal of the History of Ideas* 53 (1992): 631-45.

_____. "*Covetous of Truth": The Life and Work of Thomas White, 1593-1676*. International Archives of the History of Ideas, vol. 134. Dordrecht, 1993.

_____. "'Torn Between Two Obligations': The Compromise of Thomas White." In *The Rise of Modern Philosophy. The Tension Between the New and Traditional Philosophies from Machiavelli to Leibniz*, ed. T. Sorell. Oxford, 1993.

Spaemann, Robert

Present Position and Address: Professor of Philosophy (since 1971), Institut für Philosophie, University of München, Lehrstuhl für Philosophie I, Geschwister Scholl-Platz 1, 8000 München 22, Germany **Concurrent Positions:** Honorary Professor (since 1970), University of Salzburg, Austria **Date of Birth:** May 5, 1927 **Education:** Dr. phil (1952), University of Münster; Dr. phil. h.c. (1989), University of Fribourg, Switzerland **Awards and Honors:** Officier dans l'ordre des Palmes Académiques (French Government) **Previous Positions:** Professor (1952-69), University of Stuttgart; Professor (1969-71), University of Heidelberg; Visiting Professor Paris/Rio de Janeiro **Selected**

Memberships: Institut International de Philosophie Politique, Paris; Academia Scientiarium et Artium Europea, Salzburg **Discipline:** Philosophy **Related Areas of Interest:** Philosophy of Nature, Ethics, Political Philosophy, Philosophy of Religion, History of Ideas.

Selected Publications: His bibliography lists 8 books, and 27 articles.

_____. "Zur Frage der Notwendigkeit des Schöpfungswillens Gottes." *Philosophisches Jahrbuch* 60 (1950): 88-92.
_____, Reinhard Löw. *Die Frage Wozu? Geschichte und Wiederentdeckung des teleologischen Denkens.* München: R. Piper Verlag, 1981.
_____. "Ethische Aspekte der Energiepolitik." In *Energie und Gewissen*, ed. W. Heintzeler and H. J. Werhahn, 31-45. Stuttgart: Seewald Verlag, 1981.
_____. *Moralische Grundbegriffe.* München: C. H. Beck Verlag, 1982; 3d ed., 1986.
_____. *Das Natürliche und das Vernünftige. Aufsätze zur philosophischen Anthropologie.* München: R. Piper Verlag, 1987.
_____. *Glück und Wohlwollen. Versuch über Ethik.* Stuttgart: Klett-Cotta, 1989; 2d ed., 1990.

Spanner, Douglas C.

Present Position and Address: Professor Emeritus, University of London; "Ivy Cottage", Main Street, Grove, Wantage OX12 7JY, UK **Concurrent Positions:** Non-stipendiary priest (since 1973), Anglican Church **Work Phone:** 0235-7 66845 **Date of Birth:** October 30, 1916 **Education:** B.Sc. Botany (1946)/Ph.D. Plant Physiology (1951)/D.Sc. (1972), University of London **Honorary Degrees:** D.I.C. (Diploma of Imperial College, London); A.R.C.S. (Associateship of the Royal College of Science) **Previous Positions:** University Reader in Plant Physiology (1957-73)/Professor of Plant Biophysics (1973-78)/Director of Electron Microscope Unit, Bedford College, University of London **Selected Memberships:** Fellow, Institute of Biology; Fellow, Victoria Institute **Discipline:** Plant Physiology and Biophysics; Thermodynamics **Related Areas of Interest:** Creation and Evolution; Providence and God's Action in the World; Mind-Body Problem; Biblical Revelation.

Selected Publications: His bibliography lists 3 books and 53 technical articles.

_____. *Creation and Evolution.* London: Falcon Books, 1965.
_____. *Biblical Creation and the Theory of Evolution.* Exeter, UK: Paternoster Press, 1987.

Sperry, Roger W.

Present Position and Address: Professor Emeritus (since 1984), Division of Biology 156-29, California Institute of Technology, Pasadena, CA 91125, USA; (Home) 3625 Lombardy Road, Pasadena, CA 91108, USA **Work Phone:** (818) 356-4962 **Home Phone:** (818) 793-0117 **Date of Birth:** August 20, 1913 **Education:** A.B. English (1935)/M.A. Psychology (1937), Oberlin College; Ph.D. Zoology (1941), University of Chicago **Honorary Degrees:** Honorary Doctor of Science Degree, Cambridge University (1972)/University of Chicago (1976)/Kenyon College (1979)/Rockefeller University (1980)/Oberlin College (1982) **Awards and Honors:** Wolf Prize in Medicine (1979); Shared the Nobel Prize in Medicine/Physiology (1981) and many other awards **Previous Positions:** National Research Council Fellow (1941-42)/Biology Research Fellow (1942-46), Harvard University; Assistant Professor in Anatomy Department (1946-52)/Associate Professor of Psychology (1952-53), University of Chicago; Medical Research Project on Nerve Injuries (1942-45), OSRD, Military Service; Section Chief (1952-53), Neurological Diseases and Blindness, National Institutes of Health; Hixon Professor of Psychobiology (1954-84), California Institute of Technology **Editorial Positions:** Editorial Advisory Boards of *Experimental Neurology, Experimental Brain Research, Neuropsychologia, The International Journal of Neuroscience, Behavioral Biology, Zygon, Perspectives in Biology and Medicine* **Selected Memberships:** National Academy of Sciences; American Academy of Arts and Science; Society of Experimental Psychologists; American Psychological Association; American Neurological Association; American Philosophical Society; Royal Society; Pontifical Academy of Sciences; Society of Neuroscience; Institute for Advanced Philosophic Research; Mentor Society; Foreign Member, USSR Academy of Sciences **Discipline:** Religion-Science Tension and Transcendent Guidelines Consistent with Science **Related Areas of Interest:** Psychobiology; Neuropsychology; Neurobiology: Neural Plasticity tested by Nerve and Muscle Transplantation; Selective Patterning in Growth of Nerve Connections; Cytospecificity and Chemoaffinity Theory; Neural Mechanism in Perception and Memory; Split-Brain Approach to Cerebral Organization; Hemispheric Specialization; Mind-Brain Concepts and the Human Value Implications.

Selected Publications: His bibliography lists 3 books and 223 articles.

_____. "Absolute values: Problem of the Ultimate Frame of Reference." In *The Search for Absolute Values: Harmony Among the Sciences*, vol. 2, 689-95. New York: International Cultural Foundation Press, 1977.
_____. "Bridging Science and Values: A Unifying View of Mind and Brain." *Zygon* 14 (1979): 7-21.
_____. *Science and Moral Priority*. New York: Columbia University Press, 1983. Paperback ed. New York: Greenwood/Praeger Publishers, 1985.
_____, J. Eccles, I. Prigogine, and B. Josephson. *Nobel Prize Conversations*. With comments by Norman Cousins. Dallas: Saybrook Publishing Co., 1985.
_____. "Science, Values and Survival." *Journal of Humanistic Psychology* 26 (1986): 8-23.
_____. *Naturwissenschaft und Wertentscheidung*. München: R. Piper GmbH and Co. KG, 1986.
_____. "The Science-Values Relation: Impact of the Consciousness Revolution." In *Religion, Science and the Search for Wisdom, Proceedings of a Conference on Religion and Science*, ed. D. M. Byers, 110-33, September 1986. Washington, DC: United States Catholic Conference, Inc., 1987.
_____. "Psychology's Mentalist Paradigm and the Religion/Science Tension." *American Psychologist* 43 (1988): 607-13.

Spiro, Melford E.

Present Position and Address: Presidential Professor of Anthropology (since 1982), University of California - San Diego, La Jolla, CA 92093, USA **Concurrent Positions:** Professor and founder of Anthropology department (since 1968), University of California - San Diego **Education:** B.A. (1941), University of Minnesota; Ph.D. Anthropology (1950), Northwestern University **Previous Positions:** Assistant Professor (1948-52), Washington University; Assistant and Associate Professor (1952-57), University of Connecticut; Professor (1957-64), University of Washington; Professor (1964-68), University of Chicago; Research - Ojibwa Indians in Wisconsin (summer 1946)/Micronesia (1947-48)/Israel (1950-51 and intermittently 1975-84)/Burma (1961-62)/Thailand (Intermittently 1968-75), study of primary process thought and cultural symbolism in a psychoanalytic patient (1977-81) **Editorial Positions:** Editorial Boards of *The Journal of Sex Research*, *Israel Social Science Research*, *Journal of Psychoanalytic Anthropology*; Associate Editor of *Ethos*, *Psychoanalytic Study of Society*; Contributing Editor, *Zygon* **Selected Memberships:** American Ethnological Society; American Anthropological Association; Association of Asian Studies; American Psychoanalytic Association; Burma Research Society; Royal Anthropological Institute; Society for Psychological Anthropology; American Society for the Study of Religion; American Academy of Arts and Sciences; National Academy of Sciences **Discipline:** Anthropology **Related Areas of Interest:** Religion and Society; Religion and Psychology/Anthropology.

Selected Publications: His bibliography lists 10 books and 59 articles.

_____, Roy D'Andrade. "A Cross-Cultural Study of Some Supernatural Beliefs." *American Anthropologist* 60 (1958): 456-66.
_____. "Introduction" and "Religion and the Irrational." In *Symposium on New Approaches to the Study of Religion. American Ethnological Society, 1964.*

_____. "Symbolism and Functionalism in the Anthropological Study of Religion." In *Science of Religion: Studies in Methodology*, ed. Lauri Honko. Mouton, 1979.
_____. "Images of Man, Nature, and the Supernatural in the Buddhist Schema of Salvation." In *Images of Man*, ed. J. William Angel and E. Pendleton Banks. Macon, GA: Mercer University Press, 1984.

Spradley, Joseph L.

Present Position and Address: Professor of Physics and Astronomy (since 1972), Wheaton College, Wheaton, IL 60187, USA **Work Phone:** (708) 752-5895 **Date of Birth:** October 30, 1932 **Education:** B.S. (1954)/M.S. (1955)/Ph.D. Engineering Physics (1958), University of California - Los Angeles **Previous Positions:** Research Engineer (1954-58), Hughes Aircraft Company; Assistant Professor (1959-65)/Associate Professor (1968-70), Wheaton College; Acting President (1965-68), Haigazian College, Beirut; USAID Science Specialist (1970-72), Ahmadu Bello University, Nigeria; Visiting Professor (1988), Daystar University College, Kenya; Visiting Professor (1991-92), American University in Cairo, Egypt **Selected Memberships:** American Scientific Affiliation **Discipline:** Physics; Astronomy; History of Science **Related Areas of Interest:** History and Philosophy of Science and Christianity.

Selected Publications:

_____. "Christian Roots of Science." *Christianity Today* (March 13, 1970).
_____. "A Christian View of the Physical World." Chap. 3 in *The Making of a Christian Mind*, ed. Arthur Holmes. Downer's Grove, IL: InterVarsity Press, 1985.
_____. "The Abolition of Autonomous Science." *Perspectives on Science and Christian Faith* (*PSCF*) 39, 4 (1987): 204-11.
_____. "Tradition and Faith in the Copernican Revolution." *PSCF* 43, 1 (1991).
_____. "Changing Views of Science and Scripture: Bernard Ramm and the ASA." *PSCF* 44, 1 (1992).
_____. *Visions that Shaped the Universe*. Dubuque, IA: Wm. C. Brown, 1995.

Sprunger, Meredith Justin

Present Position and Address: Editor of *The Spiritual Fellowship Journal*, 4109 Plaza Drive, Fort Wayne, IN 46806 USA **Work Phone:** (219) 745-4363 **Date of Birth:** April 16, 1915 **Previous Positions:** Pastor (1941-50), United Church of Christ, Mulberry, IN; Teacher (1950-51), Department of Psychology, Elmhurst College; Pastor (1952-59), United Church of Christ, Culver, IN; Head, Department of Psychology/Chair, Division of Liberal Arts/President, (1959-77), Indiana Institute of Technology; Psychologist: Private Practice Certificate in State of Indiana; Testing and Consulting in Industry; Pastor (1964-79), United Church of Christ, Plum Tree, IN **Selected Memberships:** United Church of Christ **Related Areas of Interest:** The Growing Edge of Philosophy and Religion **Current Areas of Research:** Currently working on a critical evaluation of *The Urantia Book*.

Selected Publications:

_____. *Spiritual Psychology, A Primer*. Jemenon, Inc., 1992.

Sroufe, Joe Thomas

Present Position and Address: Senior Tutor in Religion and Society; Chaplain (since 1991); Family Life Educator (since 1987), Oxford Graduate School, 500 Oxford Drive, Crystal Springs, TN 37321, USA **Concurrent Positions:** Instructor in Family Life **Education:** and Sociology (since 1993); Oxford Graduate School; Pastoral Counselor (since 1980) **Work Phone:** (615) 775-6597 **Fax Number:** (615) 775-6599 **Date of Birth:** April 21, 1954 **Languages Spoken:** American Sign Language; Latin; Biblical

Greek **Previous Positions:** Administrator, (1981-86), Grace Christian School, Anadarko, OK; Director of Admissions (1991-93)/Assistant to the Chancellor for Institutional Advancement(1992-94), Oxford Graduate School **Selected Memberships:** Pi Dappa Delta; Delta Psi Omega; American Society of Christian Therapists; National Council on Family Relations **Discipline:** Social Science: Sociology - Family Life Education; Religion **Related Areas of Interest:** Psychology; Counseling; Theology **Current Areas of Research:** The affects of human relational intimacy in communication; A current review of the Educational and social model developed by Charlotte Mason; Social and emotional impact of vitiligo among African - Americans; Family life Education imperative goals.

Selected Publications:

_____, Kevin Leman, Randy Carlson and Barton Green. *Unlocking the Secrets of Your Childhood Memories Workbook.* Nashville: Thomas Nelson Publishers, 1994.
_____. *The Experiential Grieving Process of the Caucasian Vitiligo Patient.* Forthcoming.

Stahl, Rainer

Present Position and Address: Professor of Old Testament (since 1988), Kirchliche Hochschule Leipzig, Meusdorfer Strasse 47 b, D-7030 Leipzig, Germany **Work Phone:** Leipzig 32 60 47 **Date of Birth:** March 18, 1951 **Languages Spoken:** German, English **Education:** Diplom theologie (1974)/Dr. theol. (1978)/Dr. sc. theol. (1982), Theology Department, University of Jena **Previous Positions:** Assistant Professor in Old Testament (1977-82), Theology Department, University of Jena; Assistant to the General Secretary (1982-85), Lutheran World Federation, Geneva; Parish Pastor (1985-88), Altenburg, Ev.-Luth. Church, Thuringia **Selected Memberships:** National Committee of the Lutheran World Federation; Theologisches Seminar, Leipzig **Discipline:** Old Testament **Related Areas of Interest:** Old Testament Exegesis; Old Testament Hermeneutics; God as Creator; Theology of Nature; Ecumenism.

Selected Publications: His bibliography lists 15 publications.

_____. "Die neue technische Welt und die Kirchen" (The new technical world and the churches). Lutherische Welt-Information 2 (Geneva, 1988): 16-17.
_____. "Summary of Practical Discussion." In *The New Faith-Science Debate. Probing Cosmology, Technology, and Theology*, ed. J. M. Mangum, 157-9. Minneapolis/Geneva, 1989.

Stanciu, George

Present Position and Address: Academic Dean (since 1974), Magdalen College, 270 Daniel Webster Highway So., Bedford, NH 03102, USA **Work Phone:** (603) 669-7735 **Date of Birth:** March 7, 1937 **Education:** B.A. Physics (1958)/M.A. Physics (1960)/Ph.D. Physics (1964), University of Michigan **Postgraduate Experience:** Advanced Professional studies in the canonical texts of Western Civilization (Homer, Plato, Aristotle, Sophocles, Descartes, Bacon, Kant, Nietzsche, Darwin and others); Postdoctoral Research Fellow (1965-68, Los Alamos National Laboratory; special studies in theoretical physics; selected areas in biology **Previous Positions:** Research Assistant (1960-64), University of Michigan; Visiting Scientist (1964-65), University of Nijmegen; Tutor (1968-74), St. John's College - Santa Fe **Discipline:** Physics; History and Philosophy of Science **Related Areas of Interest:** Natural Theology.

Selected Publications: His bibliography lists 2 books and 5 articles.

_____, Robert Augros. *The New Story of Science*. Regnery/Gateway, 1984.
_____, Robert Augros. "Systematic Differentiation: A New Evolutionary Synthesis." *Biology Forum* (Winter 1986).

_____, Robert Augros. *The New Biology: Discovering the Wisdom in Nature.* New Science Library. New York: Shambhala/Random House, 1987.

Stanesby, Derek Malcolm

Present Position and Address: Canon of Windsor, 4 The Cloisters, Windsor Castle, Berkshire SL4 1NJ, UK **Date of Birth:** March 28, 1931 **Education:** B.A. (1956), University of Leeds; M.Ed. (1975)/Ph.D. Philosophy of Science (1984), University of Manchester **Previous Positions:** G.P.O. Radio Research (1947-51), Dollis Hill, London; Navigator (1951-53), Royal Air Force; Parish Priest (1958-85), Norwich, London, and Manchester, UK **Selected Memberships:** Society of Ordained Scientists; Science and Religion Forum **Discipline:** Philosophy of Science **Related Areas of Interest:** The interrelations between Science, Philosophy and Theology.

Selected Publications: Has written various articles on the subject in The Times and periodicals.

_____. *Science, Reason and Religion.* Croom Helm, 1985; Reprint, Routledge, 1988.

Stannard, Frank Russell

Present Position and Address: Professor of Physics, Science Faculty, Open University, Milton Keynes, MK7 6AA, UK **Date of Birth:** December 24, 1931 **Education:** B.Sc. Special Physics (1953)/Ph.D. Cosmic Ray Physics (1956), University College London (UCL) **Awards and Honors:** 1986 Templeton Project Trust Award "for his work within science and religion" **Previous Positions:** Research Assistant (1956-59), UCL; Physicist (1959-60), Lawrence Radiation Lab, Berkeley, CA; Lecturer (1960-63)/Honorary Research Fellow (1965-82), UCL; Reader (1969-71)/Pro-Vice-Chancellor of Planning (1975-77), Open University; Head of Department, Open University (1971-91), Vice President, Institute of Physics (1987-91); Visiting Fellow (1987-88), Center of Theological Inquiry, Princeton, NJ; Reader in the Church of England; Fellow, Institute of Physics and Chartered Physicist **Discipline:** Physics **Related Areas of Interest:** Science, Psychology and the Existence of God; Science and Christianity; Science and Religious Education.

Selected Publications: His bibliography lists 60 articles in Physics journals.

_____. *Science and the Renewal of Belief.* SCM Press, 1982.
_____. *Grounds for Reasonable Belief.* Scottish Academic Press, 1989.
_____. *The Time and Space of Uncle Albert.* London: Faber and Faber, 1989; Reprint, Henry Holt, 1990.
_____. *Black Holes and Uncle Albert.* London: Faber and Faber, 1991.
_____. *Here I Am!* London: Faber and Faber, 1992.
_____. *World of 1001 Mysteries.* London: Faber and Faber, 1993.
_____. *Doing Away with God?* Marshall Pickering, 1993.
_____. *Uncle Albert and the Quantum Quest.* London: Faber and Faber, 1994.

State, Stanley

Present Position and Address: Businessman; 720 Rodney Drive, San Leandro, CA 94577, USA **Date of Birth:** June 26, 1912 **Education:** A.B. (1934), Central College; Graduate work for 2 $\frac{1}{2}$ years at the Divinity School, The University of Chicago **Discipline:** Business **Related Areas of Interest:** Philosophy of Religion; The Relevance of Philosophy of History (mainly Oswald Spengler) to Modern Thought and Problems **Current Areas of Research:** God and the Question of Intentionality.

Selected Publications:

_____. "Cultural Relativity and the Search for Solutions." *Contemporary Philosophy* 11, 4 (1986).

_____. "The Hierarchy of Values Revisited." *Contemporary Philosophy* 13, 3 (1990).

Staudinger, Hugo

Present Position and Address: Member (since 1993), Institut für Wissenschaftstheoretische Grund-lagenforschung, Busdorfwall 16, D-4790 Paderborn, Germany **Date of Birth:** July 5, 1921 **Education:** Dr. phil. (1951); Professorship (1963) **Previous Positions:** Director (1958-66), Deutsches Institut für Bildung und Wissen **Selected Memberships:** Gemeinsame Synode der Bistümer der Bundesrepublik in Würzburg; Director (1970-93), Institut für Wissenschaftstheoretische Grundlagenforschung; Deutsches Institut für Bildung und Wissen **Discipline:** Intellectual History; Philosophy; Theory of Science **Related Areas of Interest:** Interdisciplinary and Integrative Studies and Methods.

Selected Publications: His bibliography lists 11 books.

_____, Wolfgang Behler. *Chance und Risiko der Gegenwart - Eine kritische Analyse der wissenschaftlich-technischen Welt.* 2d ed. Paderborn, 1976.
_____, Wolfgang Schlüter. *Wer ist der Mensch? Entwurf einer offenen und imperativen Anthropologie.* Stuttgart, 1981.
_____, Johannes Schlüeter. *An Wunder glauben? Gottes Allmacht und moderne Welterfahrung.* Freiburg, 1986.
_____, Johannes Schlüter. *Die Glaubwürdigkeit der Offenbarung und die Krise der modernen Welt - Überlegungen zu einer trinitarischen Metaphysik.* Stuttgart, 1987.
_____, Georg Masuch. *Geschöpfe ohne Schöpfer? Der Darwinismus als biologisches und theologisches Problem.* Wuppertal, 1987.

Stavenga, Gerben J.

Present Position and Address: Assistant Professor of Philosophy (since 1970), University of Groningen, A-weg 30, 9718 CW Groningen, The Netherlands; (Home), J Frisostraat 15, 9285 TS Buitenpost, The Netherlands **Work Phone:** 31 50 636161 **Home Phone:** 31 5115 42660 **Fax:** 31 50 63 6160 **Date of Birth:** June 20, 1938 **Languages Spoken:** Dutch, English, German **Education:** M.Sc. Physics (1959); M.Sc. Philosophy (1970); Ph.D. Philosophy (1991), University of Groningen **Discipline:** Philosophy of Science **Related Areas of Interest:** Foundations of Physics and Psychology; Theology and Science.

Selected Publications: His bibliography lists 13 publications.

_____. "The Fourth Structure of Physical Reality." *Journal for General Philosophy of Science* 14, 2 (1983): 354-67.
_____. "Wissenschaft von der Offenbarungswirklichkeit." *Zeitschrift für Dialektische Theologie* (*ZDT*) 2 (1986): 267-82.
_____. "Physik auf dem Wege zur Theologie." *ZDT* 3 (1987): 29-44.
_____. "Theologie als Wetenschap." *Kerk en Theologie* 40, 4 (1989): 268-79.
_____. *Science and Liberation: A Blind Spot in Scientific Research - Exploring a New Structure of Reality".* Amsterdam, 1991.

Stent, Gunther S.

Present Position and Address: Professor of Molecular Biology (since 1959); 201 Life Sciences Addition, Department of Molecular and Cell Biology, University of California - Berkeley, CA 94720, USA **Work Phone:** (510) 642-5214 **Date of Birth:** March 28, 1924 **Languages Spoken:** English, German, French **Education:** B.S. (1945)/Ph.D. Physical Chemistry (1948), University of Illinois **Honorary Degrees:** D.Sc. (1984), York University, Toronto **Previous Positions:** Fellow (1948-50), National Research Council, California Institute of Technology; American Cancer Society; Fellow: University of Copenhagen (1950-51)/Pasteur Institute, Paris (1951-52); Assistant Research Biochemist (1952-56)/Associate Professor of Bacteriology (1956-59)/Professor of Molecular Biology (since 1959)/Professor of Arts and Science/Director of Virus Laboratory (1980-86), University of California; Guggenheim Fellow (1969-70), Harvard Medical School; Fogarty Scholar in Residence (1990-91), National Institutes of Health, Bethesda; Chairman, Department of Molecular and Cell Biology (1987-93), University of California - Berkeley **Selected Memberships:** Fellow, Institute for Advanced Study - Berlin; National Academy of Sciences; American Philosophical Society; American Academy of Arts and Sciences; Fellow, American Society for the Advancement of Science; Society for Neuroscience; Akademie der Wissenschaften und der Literatur, Mainz; European Academy of the Sciences and the Arts; Max Planck Gesellsdraft **Discipline:** Molecular Biology/Genetics; Neurobiology; History and Philosophy of Science **Related Areas of Interest:** Genetics and Science; Ethics and Medical Science/Biology; Philosophy of Science and Morals.

Selected Publications: His bibliography lists over 200 publications, most of which are in molecular biology.

_____. "An Ode to Objectivity. Does God Play at Dice?" The Atlantic 228 (1971): 125-30.

_____. "The Dilemma of Science and Morals." Genetics 78 (1974): 41-51. Reprint, *Zygon* 10 (1975): 95-112.

_____. "Limits to the Scientific Understanding of Man." *Science* 187 (1975): 1052-7.

_____. "The Poverty of Scientism." In *Knowledge, Value and Belief*, ed. H. T. Engelhardt and D. Callahan, 225-46. Hastings-on-Hudson, NY: The Hastings Center, 1977.

_____, editor. *Morality as a Biological Phenomenon*. Berlin: Dahlem Konferenzen, 1978. Reprint, University of California Press, 1981.

_____. "Science and Morality as Paradoxical Aspects of Reason." In *Knowing and Valuing: The Search for Common Roots*, ed. H. T. Engelhardt and E. Callahan, 79-101. Hastings-on-Hudson, NY: The Hastings Center, 1979.

_____. "Does God Play Dice?" *The Sciences* (March 1979): 18-23.

_____. "Is Scientific Creationism the Nemesis of Sociobiology?" In *Science and Creationism*, by A. Montagu. New York: Oxford University Press; 1984.

_____. "Hermeneutics and the Analysis of Complex Biological Systems." In *Evolution at a Crossroads: The New Biology and the New Philosophy of Science,* ed. D. H. Depew and B. H. Weber, 209-25. Cambridge: M.I.T. Press, Bradford Books, 1984.

_____. "Hermeneutische Grundlagen des wissenschaftlichen Weltbildes." In *Weltbild und Weltgestaltung im Wandel der Zeit*, ed. W. Arber, 121-45. Basel: Helbing and Lichtenhahn, 1987.

Sternglass, Ernest J.

Present Position and Address: Professor Emeritus of Radiological Physics (since 1983), University of Pittsburgh, School of Medicine, 170 West End Avenue #274, New York, NY 10023, USA **Date of Birth:** October 24, 1923 **Education:** B.E.E. (1944)/M.S. Engineering Physics (1951)/Ph.D. Engineering Physics (1953), Cornell University **Previous Positions:** Advisory Physicist (1953-67), Westinghouse Research Lab; Professor of Radiological Physics (1967-83), University of Pittsburgh **Selected Memberships:** Fellow, American Physical Society; Philosophy of Science Association; Federation of American Scientists; American Astronomical Society; Radiological Society of North America; American Association for the Advancement of Science; Sigma Xi; Eta Kappa Nu **Discipline:** Physics; Philosophy of Science; Radiological Physics **Related Areas of Interest:** Science and Society; Ethical and Moral Responsibility of Scientists; Cosmology; Philosophy of Science and Religion.

Selected Publications:

_____. "The Origin of Black Holes in Active Galactic Nuclei." In *Testing the AGN Paradigm, American Institute of Physics Conference Proceedings*, ed. S. S. Holt, S. G. Neff, and C. M. Urry, no. 254. New York: American Institute of Physics, 1992.

_____, Jay M. Gould. "Breast Cancer: Evidence for a Relation to Fission Products in the Diet." *International Journal of Health Services* 23 (1993): 783-804.

Stevens Jr., Herbert Howe

Present Position and Address: Consulting Research and Development Engineer (since 1941); 218 Hix Bridge Road, Westport, MA 02790, USA **Concurrent Positions:** Independent Scholar, University of Massachusetts-Dartmouth **Work Phone:** (508) 636-2683 **Date of Birth:** May 12, 1913 **Education:** B.S. Mechanical Engineering (1936), Georgia Tech; M.A. Liberal Studies, Philosophy and the Arts (1969), New School, NYC; M.S. Physics (1986), Southeastern Massachusetts University; M.A. (1993), Professional Writing, University of Massachusetts-Dartmouth **Selected Memberships:** Institute on Religion in an Age of Science; Previous Participant, Quaker Theological Discussion Group **Discipline:** Speculative Philosophy (as defined by A. N. Whitehead, but different from his Organism - rather a Cartesian interactive dualism called Finitism) **Related Areas of Interest:** Introduction of Minds and a Creator into Physics, Healing the gap between the Humanities and Science.

Selected Publications:

_____. "Recentering Man." *Quaker Life* 14, 3 (1973): 8-9.
_____. "Two Realities, a Relating Principle: Finitism." *Speculations in Science and Technology* 1, 1 (1978):99-107.
_____. "Reality, Finitism, and Time." *Speculations in Science and Technology* 3, 5 (1980): 587-93.
_____. *Four Scientific Sonnets*. Privately published, 1988.
_____. "Evolution of Minds and Quantum Mechanical Fields." *Physics Essays* 3, 2 (1990).
_____. "The First Mind at Creation." *Physics Essays* 4, 2 (1991).
_____. "Least-Units and Big Bangs." *Physics Essays* 5, 4 (1992).
_____. *A View of the Universe from Westport, Massachusetts*. Privately Published, 1994.

Stines, James W.

Present Position and Address: Professor of Philosophy of Religion, Appalachian State University, Boone, NC 28608, USA **Date of Birth:** January 21, 1934 **Education:** B.A. (1954), Wake Forest University; B.D. (1957), Southern Baptist Theological Seminary; Ph.D. Religion/Philosophy of Religion (1970), Duke University **Previous Positions:** Part-time Instructor (1965-67), Duke University; Assistant Professor (1967-68), Campbell University; Assistant through Professor of Philosophy - Religion (since 1968), Appalachian State University **Selected Memberships:** Institute on Religion in an Age of Science; Polanyi Society; American Philosophical Association; American Academy of Religion **Discipline:** Religion; Philosophy of Religion **Related Areas of Interest:** Epistemology in Science and Religion; Teleology in Science and Religion; Relevance of Thought of Michael Polanyi to Philosophy of Science and Religion; Time and Chaos Theory.

Selected Publications:

_____. "Vocation Re-called: Personal Knowledge and Cosmic Re-enchantment." *Tradition and Discovery: The Polanyi Society Periodical* (Fall 1984-1985).
_____. "I Am the Way: Michael Polanyi's Taoism." *Zygon* (March 1985).
_____. "Time, Chaos Theory, and the Thought of Michael Polyani." *Perspectives on Science and the Christian Faith*. (December, 1992)
_____, James M. Mitchell, eds. *The Primacy of Persons and the Language of Culture: Essays by W.H. Poteal*. Columbia: University of Missouri Press, 1993.

Stoeger, William R.

Present Position and Address: Jesuit Priest; Staff Astronomer (since 1979), Vatican Observatory, Castel Gandolfo, Italy and Tucson, AZ; Vatican Observatory Research Group, Steward Observatory, University of Arizona, Tucson, AZ 85721, USA **Work Phone:** (602) 621-3225 **Home Phone:** (602) 795-986 **Date of Birth:** October 5, 1943 **Languages Spoken:** English, Italian **Education:** A.B.

Philosophy and Physics (*summa cum laude*, 1967), Spring Hill College; M.S. Physics (1969), University of California - Los Angeles; S.T.M. Theology (1972), Jesuit School of Theology, Berkeley, CA; Ph.D. Astrophysics (1979), University of Cambridge, UK **Previous Positions:** Lecturer in Physics (1969), University of San Francisco; Visiting Astronomer (1975), Vatican Observatory, Castel Gandolfo, Italy; Faculty Research Assistant in Physics and Astronomy (1977), University of Maryland; Sabbatical Research (1985-86), Department of Applied Mathematics, University of Cape Town, South Africa; J. K. Russell Fellowship (1988-89), Center for Theology and Natural Sciences, Berkeley, CA **Editorial Positions:** Coeditor, *Philosophy in Science*; Referee for several journals in Physics and Astrophysics **Selected Memberships:** Sigma Pi Sigma; American Physical Society; American Astronomical Society; International Astronomical Union; International Society on General Relativity and Gravitation; Astronomical Society of the Pacific; Italian Physical Society; Italian National Astronomical Society **Discipline:** Physics and Astrophysics; Philosophy and Theology **Related Areas of Interest:** Relationship and Dialogue between Science, Philosophy, Theology, and Cosmology **Current Areas of Research:** Issues related to divine action in the world, the interaction of science with other cultural components, the ontological status of theoretical entities, the use and import of teleological language in science.

Selected Publications: His bibliography lists 45 publications.

_____, M. Heller, and J. _yci_ski, eds. *Philosophy in Science.* Vols 1-5. Tucson, AZ: Pachart Publishing House, 1982-93. Includes his chapters, "The Evolving Interaction Between Philosophy and the Sciences: Towards a Self-Critical Philosophy," vol. 1, 21-44 and "A Causal Constraint on the Instraint on the Initial Singularity," with M. Heller, vol. 2, 61-5.

_____, editor. "Theory and Observational Limits in Cosmology." In *Proceedings of the Vatican Observatory Conference, July 1-9, 1985.* Vatican Observatory, 1987. Includes his article "Almost FLRW Observational Cosmologies," 275-305.

_____. "What Does Science Say About Creation?" *The Month* 249 (1988): 805-11.

_____, R. J. Russell and G. V. Coyne, eds. *Physics, Philosophy and Theology: A Common Quest for Understanding.* Vatican City State: Vatican Observatory; Notre Dame, IL: U. of Notre Dame Press, 1988. Includes his Chapter, "Contemporary Cosmology and Its Implications for the Science-Religion Dialogue," 219-247.

_____, R. J. Russell and G. V. Coyne, eds. *John Paul II on Science and Religion: Reflections on the New View from Rome.* Vatican City State: Vatican Observatory, 1990.

_____. "What Contemporary Cosmology and Theology Have to Say to One Another." *CTNS Bulletin* 9, 2 (1989): 1-15.

_____. "The Origin of the Universe in Science and Religion." In *Cosmos, Bios, Theos*, ed. Henry Margenau and Roy A Varghese, 254-69. La Salle, IL: Open Court, 1992.

_____. "Cosmologia e Teologia: Le Vie della Loro Mutua Interazione." *Giornale de Astronomia* nos. 1, 2 (1991): 15-19.

_____. "Theology and the Contemporary Challenge of the Natural Sciences." In *The Proceedings of the Catholic Theological Society of America, 1992,* vol. 46, 21-43.

_____. "Contemporary Physics and the Ontological Status of the Laws of Nature." In *Quantum Cosmology and the Laws of Nature: Scientific Perspectives on Divine Action*, ed. R. J. Russell, N. Murphy and C. J. Isham, 209-234. Vatican Observatory; University of Notre Dame Press, 1993.

Stol, John Henry

Present Position and Address: Executive Director, A.S.K., Inc., A professional counseling and Bible teaching organization; A.S.K., Inc., 1618 Amy Lane, Minneapolis, MN 55430, USA **Work Phone:** (612) 482-9888 **Home Phone:** (612) 561-3168 **Date of Birth:** February 22, 1925 **Languages Spoken:** English, studied French, Greek, Hebrew **Education:** Th.M. , Grace Theological Seminary; Ph.D., University of Notre Dame **Awards and Honors:** *Who's Who In American Education* (1961-63); Outstanding Educators of America (1972): *Who's Who In Religion* (1975); *Who's Who In Midwest*

(1976, 77, 92) **Previous Positions:** Chair, Department of Religion, Grace College, IN; Vice President, Academic Affairs, Calvary Bible College, Kansas City, MO; Registrar & Chair, Department of Religion, Cedarville College, OH; Teacher, Wheaton College, Wheaton, IL **Selected Memberships:** Evangelical Theological Society; American Scientific Association; American Association of Pastoral Counselors; Christian Association for Psychological Studies **Discipline:** Theology and Psychology **Related Areas of Interest:** Integration of Theology and Psychology; Biblical Archaeology; Philosophical Worldview **Current Areas of Research:** Currently writing a book on Biblical/Psychological principles for practical living.

Selected Publications: His total bibliography contains two published books and dozens of articles, written over forty years on Biblical/Philosophical/Psychological subjects.

_____. "Old Testament Survey." N.p.,1964.
_____. "The Book of Habbakuk." N.p., 1972.

Strobel, Henry W.

Present Position and Address: Ordained Priest, Episcopal Church, USA; Professor of Biochemistry and Molecular Biology (since 1982), University of Texas Medical School, P.O. Box 10708, Houston, TX 77225, USA **Concurrent Positions:** Visiting Professor (since 1986), Capital Institute of Medicine, Beijing China; Adjunct Fellow (since 1989), Institute of Religion, Texas Medical Center, Houston, TX **Work Phone:** (713) 792-5600 **Date of Birth:** February 19, 1943 **Education:** B.S. Chemistry (1964), College of Charleston, SC; N.I.H Traineeship (1964-69)/Ph.D. Biochemistry (1969), University of North Carolina - Chapel Hill **Previous Positions:** Assistant Research Biochemist (1969-70), University of Michigan; Instructor of Biological Chemistry (1970-72), University of Michigan; Assistant (1972-77)/Associate Professor of Biochemistry and Molecular Biology (1977-82)/Acting Department Chairman (1984-85), University of Texas Medical School, Houston **Selected Memberships:** Sigma Xi; Sigma Alpha Phi Honorary Fraternity; American Association for the Advancement of Science; American Chemical Society; American Society of Biological Chemists/Pharmacology and Experimental and Therapeutics; American Association for Cancer Research; Society of Toxicology **Discipline:** Biochemistry; Theology **Related Areas of Interest:** Biochemistry and Theology; Science and Religion.

Selected Publications: His bibliography lists 59 articles and 27 chapters.

_____, M. J. Coon, A. P. Autor, J. K. Heidema and W. Duppel. "Functional Components and Mechanism of Action of the Resolved Liver Microsomal Enzyme system, Catalyzing Fatty Acid, Hydrocarbon, and drug Hydroxylation." In *Biological Hydrozylation Mechanisms*, ed. G. S. Boyd and R. M. S. Smellie, 45-54. London: Academic Press, 1972.
_____, M. J. Coon, J. K. Heidema, R. M. Kaschnitz, A. P. Autor, and D. P. Ballou. "On the Mechanism of Hydroxylation Reactions in a Reconstituted Liver Microsomal Enzyme System Containing Cytochrome P450." In *The Molecular Basis of Electron Transport, Miami Winter Symposia*, vol. 4, 231-50. New York, London 1: Academic Press, 1972.
_____, W. F. Fang. "Role of Cytochrome P450 in the Response of the Colon to Xenobiotics." *Banbury Rep.* 7 (1981): 141-52.
_____, P. P. Lau. "Five Forms of Cytochrome P450 form Naphthoflavone-pretreated Rats." In *Microsomes, Drug Oxidations and Drug Toxicity*, ed. R. Sato and R. Kato, 91-92. Tokyo: Japan Scientific Societies Press; New York: Wiley-Interscience, 1982.
_____. "Recombinant DNA Technology and the Relationship of Humanity to God: A Plea for Thought about the Effects of Developments in Modern Molecular Biology on Theological Considerations." *St. Luke's Journal of Theology* 30 (1987): 265-71.
_____. "What is the Role for Law in the Decision-Making Process?" *St. Luke's Journal of Theology* 33 (1990): 289-96.

Stuhlhofer, Franz

Present Position and Address: freelance Author; Krottenbachstrasse 122/20/5, 1190 Vienna, Austria **Work Phone:** (0222) 44 10 434 **Date of Birth:** June 4, 1955 **Languages Spoken:** German, English **Education:** Dr. phil. History (1980), University of Vienna **Awards and Honors:** Kardinal-Innitzer-Förderungspreis for book *Lohn und Strafe in der Wissenschaft* **Discipline:** History of Science **Related Areas of Interest:** Reward System of Science; Darwinism in History; Religious Beliefs of past Scientists; History of Astrology; Scientometrics (on a historical basis).

Selected Publications: His bibliography lists 7 books and 15 articles.

_____. "Die Evolutionstheorie und die Frage nach dem Weltgrund." *Philosophia Naturalis* 20 (1982/1983): 492-505.
_____. *Lohn und Strafe in der Wissenschaft. Naturforscher im Urteil der Geschichte.* Wien/Köln/Graz: Böhlau Verlag, 1987.
_____. *Charles Darwin. Weltreise zum Agnostizismus.* Berneck, Suisse: Schwengeler Verlag, 1988.
_____. *Naturforscher und die Frage nach Gott.* Berneck, Suisse: Schwengeler Verlag, 1988. Translated into Italian as: *Vomini di scienza di fronte a Dio.* Isola del Gran Sasso, Italy: Diffusione Letteratura Cristiana, 1990.

Styczen, Tadeusz

Present Position and Address: Director (since 1983), John Paul II Institute, Catholic University, Lublin, Poland; Counselor of the Papal Commission for the Family Junoszy 7a, 20-057 Lublin, Poland **Languages Spoken:** Polish, German, Italian, English **Education:** M.A. (1955), Jagiellonian University, Cracow; Ph.D. (1963), Catholic University, Lublin **Previous Positions:** Head of Department of Ethics (1979), Catholic University, Lublin; Head of John Paul II Institute, Catholic University, Lublin (1983-) **Editorial Positions:** Editor in chief, *Ethos*; Editor, *The Philosophical Annals of the Catholic University of Lublin* **Selected Memberships:** International Academy for Philosophy, Liechtenstein; Learned Society of Catholic University of Lublin; Pontifical Academy for Life **Discipline:** Ethics **Related Areas of Interest:** Ethics; Metaethics; Philosophical and Theological Anthropology; The thought of John Paul II.

Selected Publications: His bibliography lists some 264 different publications in Polish and other languages. His main areas of publication are in the field of ethics, metaethics, philosophical and theological anthropology, and the thought of John Paul II.

_____. *Papieska Akademia Żaycia* (Z ks. Tadeuszem Styczniem rozmawia ks. Ireneusz Skubiś), "Niedziela" 37 (1994) nr 28, s. 1, 5.
_____. *Cztowiek drogą Boga Cztowieka czyi cztowiek widziany poprzez cayn cztowieka Boga,* "Przegląd Uniwersytecki" 6 (1994) nr 4, s. 7-9, 22.

_____. *Wolność z prawdy żyje. Wokót encykliki Veritas spendor,* "Ethos" 7 (1994) nr 25/26, s. 15-42.
_____. *Narodzić się, aby kochać,* w: WVII Miëdzynarodowy Knogres Rodziny, Warszawa 1994, S. 95-103.
_____. (Wraz z J. Merecki SDS), Un'Enciclica sulla libertą, w: Lettera enciclica Veritas splendor del sommo pontefice Giovanni Paolo II, Città del Vaticano 1994, s. 177-181.
_____. (Wraz z J. Merecki SDS), "Veritas splendor" — eine Enzyklika von der Freiheit, "Denkanstösse" 6(1994) z. 10, s. 42-49.
_____. Narodzić się, aby kochać, "Ethos" 7 (1994) nr 27, s. 37-44.

_____. Wolność z prawdy żyje. Wokót encykliki "Veritas spendor," w: Jan Paweł II. "Veritatis spledor." Tesk i komentarze, Lubin 1994, s. 127-168.
_____. Intorduzinone, w: Le encicliche di Giovanni Paolo II, Milano 1994, s. VII-XVIII.
_____. *Laudacja, w: Rocco Buttinglione. Doktorat honoris causa KUL, 18 maja 1994,* Lubin 1994, s. ... (Oprac. Marioa Filipiak.)

Sutherland, Brian P.

Present Position and Address: Retired Research Chemist (since 1966); 1577 Craigiewood Court, Victoria V8N 5Y3, BC, Canada **Work Phone:** (604) 477-9221 **Date of Birth:** July 25, 1904 **Education:** B.A. Sc. (1925), University of British Columbia; M.Sc. (1926)/Ph.D. Chemistry (1928), McGill University **Honorary Degrees:** D.D. (1983), Regent College, Vancouver, BC **Previous Positions:** Research Chemist (1929-51)/Board member (1948), Cominco Ltd.; Technical Assistant to Vice President (1951-60), Cominco - Western Region; Technical Assistant to President (1960-66), Cominco - Montreal **Selected Memberships:** Fellow (1941), Victoria Institute, London; Fellow (1946), American Scientific Affiliation; Fellow (1946), Chemical Institute of Canada **Discipline:** Chemistry **Related Areas of Interest:** Interrelations of Science and Theology.

Selected Publications:

_____. "Inanimate Nature, Its Evidence of Beneficent Design." In *Transactions of Victoria Institute*. N.p., 1941.

Suttle, Bruce B.

Present Position and Address: Professor of Philosophy, Religion and Liberal Arts and Sciences (since 1968), Parkland College, Champaign, IL 61821; (Home) 310 Flora Drive, Champaign, IL 61821, USA **Work Phone:** (217) 351-2526 **Home Phone:** (217) 373-3770 **Date of Birth:** January 12, 1935 **Education:** B.A. Philosophy (1961), Baldwin-Wallace College, Berea, OH; M.A. Philosophy (1963), Pennsylvania State University; Studied at the University of Rochester (1963-64); Ph.D. Phil. Education (1980), University of Illinois, Urbana **Previous Positions:** Instructor of Philosophy (1964-66), Baldwin-Wallace College; Instructor of Philosophy (Summers, 1967, 68), Ohio State University; Visiting Instructor of Philosophy (1970), Illinois State University; Assistant to the President (1987-90), Special Projects, Parkland College **Selected Memberships:** American Philosophical Association; Philosophy of Education Association; John Dewey Society; Society for the Advancement of American Philosophy; Society for Philosophy and Psychology; American Educational Studies Association; Association for the Development of Philosophy Teaching; American Association of Philosophy Teachers; Society of Professors of Education; Community College Humanities Association; Illinois Philosophical Association **Discipline:** Philosophy **Related Areas of Interest:** Moral Education in the Arts and Sciences; Philosophy of Religion.

Selected Publications: His bibliography lists 1 edited book and 28 articles.

_____. "Reason or/and Faith?" *Contemporary Philosophy* 9 (1983): 2.
_____. "On God Tolerating Evil." *Sophia* 26 (1987): 3.
_____. "Authority of Faith." In press.

Swift, David Leslie

Present Position and Address: Professor of Environmental Health Science, Johns Hopkins University School of Hygiene and Public Health, 615 N. Wolfe Street, Baltimore, MD 21205 USA **Work Phone:** (410) 955-3602 **Fax Number:** (410) 955-9334 **E-Mail:** swift@bigsis.sph.jhu.edu **Date of Birth:** August 7, 1935 **Languages Spoken:** English **Education:** B.S. Chemical Engineering (1957), Purdue University, Lafayette, IN; S.M. Chemical Engineering (1959), Massachusetts Institute of Technology, Cambridge, MA; Ph.D. Chemical Engineering (1973), Johns Hopkins University, Baltimore, MD **Postgraduate Experience:** Aerosol Physics (1966), London School of Hygiene, UK **Congresses and Conferences:** "The GAIA Hypothesis: Is It a Satisfactory View for Environmental Understanding and Regulation?" Paper presented at the Annual Meeting of American Scientific Affiliation, Seattle, WA, August, 1993 **Awards and Honors:** Tau Beta Pi, Engineering Honor Society; Delta Omega, Public

Health Honor Society; Thompson Visiting Lecturer, London School of Hygiene and Tropical Medicine **Previous Positions:** Assistant Chemical Engineer (1963-65), Division of Chemical Engineering, Argonne National Laboratory, Argonne, IL; Assistant Professor through Professor (since 1966), Department of Environmental Medicine, The Johns Hopkins University School of Hygiene and Public Health , Baltimore, MD; Visiting Professor (1986-87), Danish National Institute of Occupational Health, Copenhagen, Denmark; Director (1986-93), Industrial Hygiene and Safety Program, NIOSH Educational Resource Center, The Johns Hopkins School of Hygiene and Public Health, Baltimore, MD **Selected Memberships:** American Industrial Hygiene Association; British Occupational Hygiene Society; American Conference of Governmental Industrial Hygienists; Fellow, American Scientific Affiliation; Gesellschaft für Aerosolforschung - International Society for Aerosol Research; Sigma Xi - Research Society of America; American Association for Aerosol Research; British Aerosol Society; American Conference of Governmental Industrial Hygienists - Committee on Air Sampling instruments **Discipline:** Environmental Health Science; Biomedical Engineering **Related Areas of Interest:** Air Pollution; Occupational Health; Aerosol Science; Pharmaceutical Drug Delivery.

Selected Publications: His bibliography contains 18 book chapters and 82 published articles.

_____. "Experimental Studies of Inertial Aerosol Deposition in Human Upper Airway Casts: Implications for the Proposed NCRP lung Model." *Rad. Prot. Dos.* 38 (1991): 29-34.

_____, I. Gonda. "Losses of Gallium in Common Laboratory Ware and Ways to Minimize Them." *Eur. J. Nucl. Med.* 18 (1991): 511-13.

_____, Y.-S Chleng, Y.-F Su, and H.-C. Yeh. "Design, Characterization and Use of Replicate Human Upper Airways of Radon Dosimetry Studies." In *Indoor Radon and Lung Cancer: Reality or Myth, Proceedings of the 29th Hanford Symposium on Health and Environment, October 1990,* ed. R. T. Cross. 1992.

_____, J. C. Strong. "Deposition of Unattached Radon Daughters in Models of Human Nasal Airways." In *Indoor Radon and Lung Cancer: Reality or Myth, Proceedings of the 29th Hanford Symposium on Health and Environment,* October, 1990, ed. F. T. Cross. 1992.

_____, N. Montassier, K. Karpen-Hayes, and P. H. Hopke. "The Penetration of Ultrafine Particles of [218]Po Through Human Nasal and Oral Cast Models." *Rad. Prot. Dos.* 45 (1992): 665-7.

_____, N. Montassier, N. Hopke, K. Karpen-Hayes, Y.-S. Cheng, Y.-F. Yeh, H.-C. Yeh, and J. C. Strong. "Deposition of Ultrafine Particles in Human Nasal Replicate Casts". *Journal of Aerosol Science* 23 (1992): 65-72.

_____. "Apparatus and Method for Measuring Regional Distribution of Therapeutic Aerosols and Comparing Delivery Systems." *Journal of Aerosol Science* 23, suppl. 1 (1992): S495-8.

_____, Y.-S. Cheng, and Y.-F. Yeh. "Deposition of Thoron Progeny in the Human Head Airways." *Aerosol Science and Technology* 18 (1993): 359-75.

_____. "Dose Distribution of Pharmaceutical Aerosols." *Aerosol Science and Technology* 18 (1993): 272-8.

_____. "The GAIA Hypothesis: Is It a Satisfactory View for Environmental Understanding and Regulation?" Paper presented at the Annual Meeting of the American Scientific Affiliation, Seattle, WA, 1993.

Swinburne, Richard Granville

Present Position and Address: Nolloth Professor of the Philosophy of the Christian Religion (since 1985), University of Oxford; Oriel College, Oxford OX1 4EW, UK **Date of Birth:** December 26, 1934 **Languages Spoken:** English, Russian **Education:** B.A. Philosophy (1st Class, 1957)/Fereday Fellow (1958-61)/B.Phil. (1959)/Diploma in Theology (Distinction, 1960), Oxford University; Leverhulme Research Fellow in History and Philosophy of Science (1961-63), University of Leeds **Visiting Lectureships:** Universities of: Oxford (Natural and Comparative Religion, 1975-78)/Liverpool (History and Philosophy of Religion, 1977)/Exeter College, Oxford (1980); Adelaide (1982)/University College, Cardiff (Theology, 1983)/Aberdeen (1982-83 and 1983-84)/Birmingham (1987)/Syracuse (1987)/St. Louis (1990)/Penn State (1992) **Previous Positions:** Lecturer (1963-69)/Senior Lecturer in Philosophy (1969-72), University of Hull; Visiting Associate Professor of Philosophy (1969-70), University of Maryland; Professor of Philosophy (1972-84), University of Keele **Discipline:** Philoso-

phy; Theology; Philosophy and History of Science **Related Areas of Interest:** Philosophy/Science
and Theology; History/Philosophy of Science; Cosmology; Mind and Body.

Selected Publications: His bibliography lists 14 books and 79 articles.

_____. *The Existence of God.* Oxford: Clarendon Press, 1979; rev. ed., 1991.
_____. *Space and Time.* London: Macmillan and Co., 1981.
_____. *Faith and Reason.* Oxford: Clarendon Press, 1981.
_____. *The Evolution of the Soul.* Oxford: Clarendon Press, 1986.
_____. "The Argument from the Fine Tuning of the Universe." In *Physical Cosmology and Philosophy*, ed. J. Leslie.,
New York: Macmillan, 1989.
_____, editor. *Miracles.* New York: Macmillan Press, 1989.
_____. *Responsibility and Atonement.* Oxford: Clarendon Press, 1989.
_____. *The Coherence of Theism, Clarendon Library of Logic and Philosophy.* Oxford: Clarendon Press, 1977; rev.
ed., 1993.
_____. *Revelation.* Oxford: Clarendon Press, 1992.
_____. *The Christian God.* Oxford: Clarendon Press, 1994.

Swyhart, Barbara Ann DeMartino

Present Position and Address: Professor of Philosophy (since 1990), California University of
Pennsylvania; R.D. #1, Box 154-C, Leiber Manor, Hopwood, PA 15445, USA **Work Phone:** (412)
938-4429 **Home Phone:** (412) 437-1859 **Education:** B.A. Philosophy/Theology/Intellectual History
(1967)/M.A. History of Philosophy (1968), Marquette University; Ph.D. Philosophy and Religion
(1972), Temple University **Postgraduate Experience:** 25 hours in Ethics of Marital Therapy, University of Pennsylvania **Previous Positions:** Elementary and Secondary School Teacher (1960-68);
Itinerant Classics Teacher (1970-72), Philadelphia; Assistant Professor of Religious Studies (1972-
74)/Associate Professor (1976-80), San Diego State University; Visiting Lecturer and Director of
Religion and Public Education (1975-76), Harvard University (Divinity School); Professor of Philoso-
phy and Religion and Department Head (1980-86), James Madison University; Dean of College of
Liberal Arts (1986-90), California University of Pennsylvania **Selected Memberships:** National
Women's Studies Association; American Association for the Study of Professional and Applied Ethics;
American Academy of Religion; Phi Sigma Tau; Theta Alpha Kappa; Hastings Center for Society
Ethics and the Life Sciences; American Philosophy Association; American Academy of Religion;
National Association for Women in Higher Education:; American Association for Higher Education:
Discipline: Philosophy; Religious Ethics; Religious Education **Related Areas of Interest:** Ethics;
Medical Ethics; Science, Technology and Society; World Religions.

Selected Publications: Her bibliography lists 1 book and 14 articles, several monographs, book
reviews and essays.

_____. *Bioethical Decision Making: Releasing Religion from the Spiritual.* Philadelphia: Fortress Press, 1975.
_____. "Public Education Religion/Studies: Toward an Operation Process Methodology for Science, Religion and
Ethics." In *Public Schools Religion-Studies*, ed. Carr and Piediscalzi, 111-16. Scholars Press, 1975.
_____, editor, assisted by Mark Lester. *Narratives about Cosmic and Human Origins.* San Diego City Schools,
1976.
_____. "The Meeting of Science and Religion: Narratives about Origins." In *Teaching About Religion in Public
Schools*, ed. William Collie and Nicholas Piediscalzi, 233-44. UK: Argus Communications, 1977.
_____. "Paradigms-of-Reality in Process: The meeting of Religion and Science." *Religious Education* (July/August
1977).
_____. "Response to the Creation/Evolution Controversy in Public Education." In *Proceedings of South Atlantic
Philosophy of Education Society, October, 1981.*
_____. "A Philosophy of Parallelism and Metaphysical Mythology." *Contemporary Philosophy* (June 1984).

_____. "Jewish and Christian Reasoning About the Reproductive Process." *Contemporary Philosophy* (1987).
_____. *Woman's Self-Image and Reproductive Ethics: Epistemological Parameters*. Forthcoming.

$\mathcal{T}$

Tanner Jr., William F.

Present Position and Address: Regents Professor (since 1974), Geology Department, Florida State University, Tallahassee, FL 32306-3026, USA **Date of Birth:** February 4, 1917 **Languages Spoken:** English, Spanish, German **Education:** B.A. Geology (1937), Baylor University; M.A. Geology (1939), Texas Technological University; Ph.D. Geology (1953), Oklahoma University **Previous Positions:** US Navy (1941-45): active duty intelligence/weather school/meteorology; Commercial experience and consultant for many Universities and Oil Companies; Visiting Associate Professor through Professor (1954-present), Florida State University **Selected Memberships:** Fellow, American Association for the Advancement of Science; Fellow, Geological Society of America; Fellow, American Scientific Affiliation; Sigma Xi; Geological Society of America; American Meteorological Society; Die Geologische Vereinigung; Board of Directors, The Home Mission Board of Southern Baptist Convention/HMB Service Corporation **Discipline:** Geology **Related Areas of Interest:** Genesis and Geology; Scientific Thought in and underlying the New Testament; Creationist Misperceptions.

Selected Publications: His bibliography lists some 83 publications since 1978.

_____. "Time and the Rock Record." *Journal of the American Scientific Affiliation* 33, 2 (1981): 100-5.
_____. "Human and Not-So-Human Foot-Print Images on the Rocks." In *The Evolution-Creation Controversy*, ed. Robert Gastaldo and W. F. Tanner, 117-33. Paleontological Society Special Publication no. 1 (1984).

Tarli, Silvana Borgognini

Present Position and Address: Full Professor of Physical Anthropology (since 1980)/Chair (since 1985), Institute of Anthropology and Human Paleontology, University of Pisa, Via A. Volta 6, I-56100, Pisa, Italy **Work Phone:** 050 20255-21316 **Fax Number:** 050 24653 **Date of Birth:** June 8, 1940 **Languages Spoken:** Italian, English **Education:** M.S. Biological Sciences (full marks and honours, 1963), University of Florence; Ph.D. Anthropology (full marks, 1970), Scuola Normale Superiore of Pisa **Previous Positions:** Instructor of Physical Anthropology (1966-67)/Assistant Professor of Physical Anthropology (1967-80)/Contract Professor (1969-73)/Associate Professor (1973-77) of Biology of Human Populations/Associate Professor of Physical Anthropology (1977-80), University of Pisa; Lecturer of Anthropometry (1971-73), University of Milan; Coordinator of the Section "General Principles of Physical Anthropology" (1973-74), University of Turin; Professor of Human Paleontology (1986-88), Universita degli Anziani di Pisa **Editorial Positions:** Review Board: *Journal of Human Evolution* (1983-85)/*Human Evolution* (since 1986); Editorial Staff, *Antropologia contemporanea* **Selected Memberships:** Founding member, International Association of Human Biologists; Councillor (since 1985), Istituto Italiano di Antropologia; Unione Antropologica Italiana (Vice President, 1983-85); European Anthropological Association **Discipline:** Anthropology **Related Areas of Interest:** Evolutionary Biology/Anthropology.

Selected Publications: Her bibliography lists some 79 publications in refereed journals and edited books, 48 abstracts, book reviews and other publications, and 17 popular and creative writings.

_____. "L'evoluzione fisica dell'uomo e la sua posizione all'interno dell'ordine dei Primati," Atti del Convegno "Teilhard de Chardin, materia, evoluzione, speranza," Istituto Stensen, Firenze 25/4/81. Collana *Quale Società* diretta da A. Dall'Olio, L. Lombardo Radice, I. Mancini, A. Santini, 161-9. Borla, Roma, 1983.
_____. "Evoluzione e società," Scuola e Scienza - Incontri per le Scuole Superiori sull'Evoluzione. Rimini, Febbraio-Marzo 1982. Comune di Rimini, Assessorato alla Pubblica Istruzione: 1-25, 10 schemi f.t., 1983. In stampa.

Taylor, Howard G.

Present Position and Address: Minister (since 1986), St. David's Knightswood Church; c/o 60 Southbrae Drive, Glasgow G13 1QD, Scotland, UK **Work Phone:** 041 959-2904 **Date of Birth:** June 6, 1944 **Languages Spoken:** English, Chichewa (Malawi, Africa) **Education:** B.Sc. (Hons. 1965), Nottingham University; B.D. (Hons. 1970), Edinburgh University **Lectures Presented:** Public lectures in the Edinburgh University science faculty on "Fundamental Issues in Science and Theology" **Previous Positions:** Math and Physics Teacher (1965-67), University of Malawi, Africa; Ordained Missionary in Malawi, Africa (1971-81); Minister in Rural Argyll, Scotland (1981-86); Regular teaching of Apologetics course at the Glasgow Bible Training Institute **Discipline:** Parish Minister (interested in Dogmatic Theology); Physics and Mathematics **Related Areas of Interest:** Relativity and Quantum Theories - "Space and Time are not mere containers of nature. Natural existence is bound up with relationships. The structure of nature is fundamentally contingent. This leads to a deeper understanding not only of creation and providence but also of the theology of the Incarnation, Atonement, The Holy Spirit and The Doctrine of Man"; Christian Apologetics in the light of Science and Philosophy.

Selected Publications:

_____. *The Delusion of Unbelief in a Scientific Age.* Handsel Press, 1988.
_____. "The Gospel and the Open Frontiers of Science." Forthcoming.

Temple, Dennis Michael

Present Position and Address: Professor (since 1983), Department of Philosophy, Roosevelt University; 430 S. Michigan Avenue, Chicago, IL 60605, USA; (Home) 4532 Washington Street, Downers Grove, IL 60515, USA **Work Phone:** (312) 341-3734 **Home Phone:** (708) 241-3653 **Date of Birth:** July 25, 1941 **Languages Spoken:** English, German **Education:** B.A. (*cum laude*, 1963), Park College, Parkville, MO; M.A. (1965)/Ph.D. (1979), Washington University, St. Louis, MO **Previous Positions:** Assistant (1966-78)/Associate Professor (1978-83)/Department Chair (1987-93), Roosevelt University **Selected Memberships:** American Philosophical Association; Philosophy of Science Association; Society of Christian Philosophers; Illinois Philosophy Association; Association for the Development of Philosophy Teaching **Discipline:** Philosophy **Related Areas of Interest:** Philosophy of Religion/Science; Bioethics; Technology and Human Values.

Selected Publications: His bibliography lists some 10 publications and 6 presentations.

_____. "Can Science Know What's Necessary?" In *The Limits of Lawfulness*, ed. Nicholas Rescher. Washington, DC: University Press of America, 1983.
_____. "Discussion: The Contrast Theory of Explanation." *Philosophy of Science* 55, 1 (1988).
_____. "The New Design Argument: What Does It Prove?" In *Proceedings: Second Annual Conference on Science, Technology, and Religious Ideas, Kentucky State University, 1991.* Reprinted in *Science, Technology, and Religious Ideas*, eds. Mark H. Shale and George W. Shields. New York: University Press of America, 1994.

_____. "Hume's Logical Objection to the Argument From Design Based on the Uniqueness of the Universe." *Religious Studies* 28, 1 (1992).

Templeton, Sir John M.

Present Position and Address: President, First Trust Bank; (Office) Box N7776, Nassau, Bahamas; (Home) Lyford Cay Club, Nassau, Bahamas **Concurrent Positions:** Chairman, 1979-present, Templeton Foundation, Inc **Date of Birth:** November 29, 1912 **Education:** A.B. (1934), Yale University; M.A. Law (1936), Rhodes Scholar, Balliol College, Oxford University **Honorary Degrees:** LL.D. - (1968) Beaver College/(1980) Marquette University/(1983) Jamestown College/(1984) Maryville College/(1990) Manhattan College/(1992) Babson College/(1992) Rhode College/(1992) U. of Rochester/ (1993) LA College; D.Litt. (1974) Wilson College; D.D.: (1979) Buena Vista College; D.C.L.: (1984) University of the South; L.H.D.: (1992) U. of Dubuque/(1992) Fla. Southern Coll. **Awards and Honors:** Phi Beta Kappa; Zeta Psi **Previous Positions:** President and Director (1954-1975), Templeton Growth Fund Canada, Ltd., Toronto/Templeton World Fund, Inc. (1978-1995) **Selected Memberships:** American Scientific Affiliation; Board of Trustees - Wilson College (1941-73)/Center of Theological Inquiry, Princeton, NJ (1975-1993)/Princeton Theological Seminary (1950-1988) **Discipline:** Investment Counsel, Financial Analyst **Related Areas of Interest:** Pursuit of Integrative knowledge in Theology and the Natural Sciences; Values in Education; Templeton Prize for Progress in Religion.

Selected Publications:

_____. *The Humble Approach: Scientists Discover God*. New York: Seabury Press, 1981. With extensive 115 page bibliography of books and periodical articles in the area of theology and science.
_____. *The Templeton Plan: 21 Steps to Personal Success and Real Happiness*. Harper and Row, 1988.
_____, Robert L. Herrmann. *The God Who Would Be Known: Revelations of the Divine in Contemporary Science*. San Francisco: Harper and Row, 1989.
_____, Ed. *Riches for the Mind and Spirit*. San Francisco: HarperSanFrancisco1990.
_____, *Evidence of Purpose*. New York: Continuum Publishing Group, 1994.
_____, Robert L. Herrmann. *Is God the Only Reality?* New York: Continuum Publishing Group, 1994.
_____, *Discovering the Laws of Life*. New York: Continuum Publishing Group, 1994.

Teske, John A.

Present Position and Address: Associate Professor of Psychology (since 1990), Department of Psychology, Elizabethtown College, Elizabethtown, PA 17022, USA; (Home)58 Sycamore Lane, Palmyra, PA 17078, USA **Work Phone:** (717) 367-1151 ext 332 **Home Phone:** (717) 832-0542 **Fax Number:** (717) 361-1207 **E-Mail:** teskeja@vax.etown.edu **Date of Birth:** October 20, 1953 **Education:** B.A. Psychology (*magna cum laude*, 1974), Indiana University; M.A. (1978)/Ph.D. Psychology (1980), Clark University **Previous Positions:** Research Consultant: Department of Family Medicine, Hershey Medical Center (Summer 1982)/Philhaven Hospital, Mt Gretna, PA (Summer 1986); Assistant Professor of Psychology (1980-86), Division of Behavioral Science, Pennsylvania State University - Harrisburg; Textbook Reviewer (Fall 1986, 1990), Brooks/Cole Publishers; Assistant Professor of Psychology (1986-90), Elizabethtown College, PA **Selected Memberships:** American Psychological Society; International Society for Ecological Psychology; Society for Philosophy and Psychology; Society for the Advancement of Social Psychology; IRAS **Discipline:** Psychology: Philosophical, Social, Cognitive **Related Areas of Interest:** History/Philosophy of Science; Neurophilosophy; Philosophy of Mind; Psychology and Religion; Social Constructivism; Narrative.

Selected Publications: His bibliography lists 6 publications, and 21 presentations.

_____, R. D. Pea. "Metatheoretic Issues in Cognitive Science." *Journal of Mind and Behavior* 2 (1981): 123-78.

_____. "Conduit of Flesh." *Insights* 5, 1 (1993): 7-13.
_____. "Modularity of Mind and the Construction of Spirit." Paper presented at Fifth European Conference on Science and Theology, Munich, March 1994.
_____. "The Spiritual Limits of Neurocognitive Life." *Zygon* (In Preparation).

Thomson, Alexander

Present Position and Address: Minister of Religion (since 1973), Rutherglen Old Parish Church, Church of Scotland; 31 Highburgh Drive, Rutherglen, Glasgow, Scotland **Date of Birth:** April 25, 1947 **Education:** B.Sc. Biochemistry (with honors, 1970), Glasgow University; B.S. Dogmatics (with honors, 1973)/M.Phil. (1980), University of Edinburgh; Ph.D. Michael Polanyi (1985), University of Aberdeen **Previous Positions:** Chemist (1964-66), Dalziel Steel Works, Motherwell, Scotland **Discipline:** Minister of Religion (Church of Scotland) **Related Areas of Interest:** Relation of Science and Christianity in general.

Selected Publications:

_____. *Tradition and Authority in Science and Theology.* Theology and Science at the Frontiers of Knowledge Series, ed. Thomas F. Torrance, vol. 4. Scottish Academic Press, 1987.
_____. "A Comparison of Scientific Research with Worship." *The Bulletin of Science, Technology and Society* 9, 5 (N.d.).

Thorson, Walter Rollier

Present Position and Address: Professor of Chemistry, Emeritus, University of Alberta, Edmonton, ALB T6G 2G2, Canada; (Home) 4132 126th Street, Edmonton, ALB T6J 2A4, Canada **Work Phone:** (403) 492-3687 **Home Phone:** (403) 435-2412 **Date of Birth:** August 13, 1932 **Languages Spoken:** English, some German **Education:** B.S. Chemistry (with honors, 1953)/Ph.D. Physical Chemistry (1957), California Institute of Technology **Previous Positions:** Instructor in Chemistry (1957-58), Tufts University, Medford, MA; Assistant (1958-64)/Associate Professor of Chemistry (1964-68), Massachusetts Institute of Technology, Cambridge, MA; Adjunct Professor of Philosophy of Science, Regent College, Vancouver (frequent seminar course offered in Problems of Epistemology in Science and Religion) **Selected Memberships:** Fellow, American Physical Society; Canadian Association of Physicists; Theoretical Physics Institute, University of Alberta; American Scientific Affiliation **Discipline:** Physics; Chemistry **Related Areas of Interest:** Philosophy of Science/Religion; Christian Theology focusing on Epistemology.

Selected Publications: His bibliography lists over 60 scientific publications and 6 dealing with Science/Theology.

_____. "The Spiritual Dimensions of Science." In *Horizons of Science: Christian Scholars Speak Out*, ed. C. F. H. Henry. San Francisco: Harper and Row, 1975.
_____. "Reflections on the Practice of Outworn Creeds." *Journal of the American Scientific Affiliation* (*JASA*) 33 (1981): 3-11.
_____. "Science as the Natural Philosophy of a Christian." *JASA* 33 (1981).
_____. "The Biblical Insights of Michael Polanyi." *JASA* 33 (1981): 129-38.
_____. "Scientific Objectivity and the Word of God." *JASA* 36 (1984): 88-97. Reprint, "Scientific Objectivity and the Listening Attitude." In *Objective Knowledge: A Christian Perspective*, ed. Paul Helm. Leicester UK: InterVarsity Press, 1987.
_____. "Realism and Reverence." *JASA* 38 (1986): 75-86.
_____. "Constructing a Legitimate Natural Theology." Chap. 18 in *Alive to God: Studies in Spirituality*, by J. I. Packer and L. Wilkinson, 225-38. Downers Grove, IL: InterVarsity Press, 1992.

Personal Notes: For the period September 1, 1994 through June 30, 1995, Dr. Thorson will be a member in residence at the Center of Theological Inquiry, 50 Stockton Street, Princeton, NJ 08540. Phone: (609) 683-4797.

Thung, Mady A. *(married name M. A. Laeyendecker-Thung)*

Present Position and Address: Retired from Leadership of the Multidisciplinary Center for Church and Society (MCKS), but still conducting projects: "Economy and Ethics" and "The Need for Moral Discourse in the Churches"; (Home) Marskramersbaan 16, 3981 TK Bunnik, The Netherlands **Work Phone:** 03405- 67803 **Date of Birth:** November 17, 1926 **Languages Spoken:** Dutch, English, German, French **Education:** Gymnasium (1947); B.A. Law (1949); M.A. Sociology (1956); Ph.D. Sociology of Religion (1976) **Congresses and Conferences:** Coordinator (1975-78), Ecumenical Series of Conferences, "Reflections on the Future"; and Cofounder (1982) of its successor, the MCKS; Leader of MCKS **Previous Positions:** Investigation of the Social Impact of "Shift Labor" especially Sunday Labor (1956-1958); Assistant (1958-1960), Institute of Social Studies, The Hague; Advisor (1960-62), Protestant Welfare Work, Amsterdam; Study Secretary (1962-69), Dutch Missionary Council; Research Worker (1966-75), Sociological Institute, University of Amsterdam; Professor of Sociology of Religion (1978-83), University of Leyden; Participated in various study projects for the World Council of Churches (e.g. "Structures for Missionary Congregations"); Moderator, Foundation of Youth Work, Netherlands Reformed Church, Amsterdam; Advisory functions for various types of church work **Discipline:** Sociology; Sociology of Religion **Related Areas of Interest:** Relationship of Theory and Practice; Social Ethics; Methods of multidisciplinary exchange.

Selected Publications:

_____, Anneke Schipper-van Otterloo. *Change in the Church, a Sociological Design and an Exploration of Chances* (in Dutch). Alphen aan de Rijn, 1972.
_____. *The Precarious Organization. Sociological Explorations of the Church's Mission and Structure.* The Hague, 1976.
_____, together with a Working Group. *Exploring the New Religious Consciousness.* Amsterdam, 1985.
_____. *Technology as a Human Enterprise* (in Dutch). Driebergen: MCKS, 1985.
_____. *The Ecumenical Movement and the Technology Debate.* Driebergen: MCKS, 1985.
_____, editor. *Learning Mores Anew. Ideas about Moral Discourse in the Churches* (in Dutch). The Hague, 1986.
_____, editor. *Do We Keep Expanding Boundaries? A Basic Problem of Our Technological Age* (in Dutch). The Hague, 1991.
_____, B. Goudzwaard, et. al. *A Healthy Economy? Socio-cultural Dimensions of Economic Activity.* Kampen, 1994.

Thurman, L. Duane

Present Position and Address: Professor of Biology (since 1973), Oral Roberts University, Tulsa, OK 74171, USA **Date of Birth:** September 3, 1933 **Education:** B.S. Agriculture Education (1959)/M.S. Agronomy and Botany (1961), University of Nebraska - Lincoln; Ph.D. Botany (1966), University of California - Berkeley **Previous Positions:** Assistant Professor of Biology (1965-67), Southern California College, Costa Mesa, CA; Consultant (1986-87), Task Force for Biology book, Christian College Coalition **Selected Memberships:** American Scientific Affiliation; Association for Education of Teachers of Science; Sigma Xi; Society for College Science Teachers **Discipline:** Biology; Ecology **Related Areas of Interest:** Human Nutrition; Creation/Evolution **Current Areas of Research:** Ongoing work now centers on critical thinking about controversial Bible-science issues, especially in taking a broad, fair approach in seeing the whole problem and using a more mental (rather than emotional, one-sided) approach to problem solving.

Selected Publications: His bibliography lists 25 publications.

_____. *Creation and Evolution - the Renewed Controversy*. Minnesota: Burgess Publ. Co., 1977.

_____. *How to Think About Evolution*. Downers Grove, IL: InterVarsity Press, 1978.

_____. "A Grazing Ecotype in a Chlorophyllous Root-Parasite." *Orthocarpus faucibarbatus ssp. albidus* (Scrophulariaceae), Madrono 26 (1979): 13-21.

_____. Review of *Genesis and Development of Scientific Fact*, by Ludwig Fleck. *Journal of the American Scientific Affiliation* (*JASA*) 33 (1981): 125.

_____. Review of *Bent World: A Christian Response to Environmental Crisis*, by Ron Elsdon. *JASA* 35 (1983): 60.

_____. Review of *The Mystery of Life's Origin: Reassessing Current Theories*, by Thaxton, Bradley, and Olsen. *Journal of College Science Teaching* 15 (1986): 385-6.

_____. Review of *The Creation*, by Don Stewart. *Perspectives on Science and Christian Faith* (*PSCF*) 40 (1988): 56-7.

_____. Review of *The Genesis Solution*, by Ham and Taylor. *PSCF* 42 (1990): 256-65.

_____. Review of *Origin of Species Revisited*, by Wendell R. Bird, vol. 1. *PSCF* 44 (1992): 61-2.

_____. Review of *Darwin on Trial*, by Phillip Johnson. *PSCF* 44 (1992): 140-1.

Tierney, Nathan Llywellyn

Present Position and Address: Chair; Department of Philosophy, California Lutheran University, 60 West Olsen Road, Thousand Oaks, CA 91360 **Work Phone:** (805) 493-3232 **Fax Number:** (805) 493-3513 **E-Mail:** tierney@callutheran.edu **Date of Birth:** March 16, 1953 **Languages Spoken:** English **Education:** B.A. (with honors 1975), University of Melbourne, Australia; Ph.D. Philosophy (1989), Columbia University **Lectures Presented:** "By What Authority? The Moral Vacuum in Corporate Drug Testing Programs." Association for Practical and Professional Ethics, University of Maryland, March 6, 1993; "The Mean of Community in Confucius and Aristotle." East Meets West Conference, Long Beach, CA, April 4, 1993 **Awards and Honors:** New York University School of Continuing Education, Outstanding Service Award (1990) **Previous Positions:** Adjunct Assistant Professor (1984-90), New York University/SCE **Selected Memberships:** American Philosophical Association; National Association of Scholars; Society of Christian Philosophers; American Association for Practical and Professional Ethics **Discipline:** Philosophy **Related Areas of Interest:** Ethics Current Areas of Research: Selfhood and Service: The Communal Context of Moral Maturing.

Selected Publications: His bibliography contains 1 book and 1 article.

_____. "The Rights and Wrongs of Software Copying." *NYPC Magazine* (May 1991).

_____. *Imagination and Ethical Ideals*. New York: State University of New York Press, 1994.

Tilley, Terrence U.

Present Position and Address: Chair (since 1994), Department of Religious Studies, University of Dayton, Dayton, OH 45469, USA **Work Phone:** (513) 229-4321 **E-Mail:** ttilley@checkou.hm.udayton.edu **Date of Birth:** April 19, 1947 **Languages Spoken:** English **Awards and Honors:** Book of the Year Award (1976), College Theology Society for *Story Theology*; Teaching Excellence Awards (1991; 94), Florida State University **Previous Positions:** Assistant Professor of Theology (1976-79), Georgetown University; Assistant through Associate Professor of Religious Studies (1979-89), St. Michael's College, VT; Professor of Religion (1989-94), Florida State University **Selected Memberships:** AAR; College Theology Society; Catholic Theological Society of America; Society for Philosophy of Religion; Society of Christian Philosophers; ARIL; American Association of University Professors **Discipline:** Philosophical Theology **Related Areas of Interest:** Philosophy of Religion; Modern Roman Catholicism **Current Areas of Research:** A philosophy of religion.

Selected Publications: His bibliography contains 3 books, 2 books in process, 40 published articles, over 60 book reviews and 25 papers read to national conventions.

_____. *Talking of God: An Introduction to Philosophical Analysis of Religious Language.* New York: Paulist Press, 1978.

_____. "Philosophy of Science and Religion: Three Approaches." *Theological Studies* 45 (December 1984): 722-7.

_____. "Reformed Epistemology and Religious Fundamentalism: How Basic Are Our Basic Beliefs?" *Modern Theology* 6, 3 (1990): 237-57. Rev. ed. in *The Struggle Over the Past: Fundamentalism in the Modern World*, The Annual Volume of the College Theology Society, ed. William M. Shea, 181-206. Washington, DC: University Press of America, 1993.

_____. "Polemics and Politics in Explaining Religion." *The Journal of Religion* 71, 2 (1991): 242-54.

_____. *The Evils of Theodicy.* Washington, DC: Georgetown University Press, 1991.

_____. *Story Theology.* Wilmington: Michael Glazier, Inc., 1985. Reprint, Collegeville: Liturgical Press, 1991.

_____. "Religious Pluralism as a Problem for 'Practical' Religious Epistemology." *Religious Studies* 30, 2 (England).

_____. "Reformed Epistemology in a Jamesian Perspective." *Horizons* 19, 1 (1992): 84-98.

_____. "The Institutional Element in Religious Experience." *Modern Theology* 10, 2 (1994): 185-212.

_____. "In Favor of a 'Practical Theory' of Religion: Montaigne and Pascal." In *Theology without Foundations*, ed. Stanley Hauerwas, Nancey Murphy, and Mark Nation. Nashville, TN: Abingdon, 1994.

Timm, Roger E.

Present Position and Address: Pastor (since 1993), St. James Lutheran Church, P.O. Box 2317, Naperville, IL 60567-2317, USA **Work Phone:** (708) 357-8885 **Date of Birth:** April 2, 1945 **Education:** A.A. Pre-Theology (1964), Concordia College; B.A. English and Philosophy (1966), Concordia Senior College; M.Div. Systematic Theology (1970), Concordia Seminary; M.A. Philosophy (1970), Washington University; Ph.D. Religious Studies (1975), Columbia University and Union Theological Seminary, NY (Joint doctoral program) **Previous Positions:** Pastor (1970-73), St. John-Concordia Lutheran Church, Bronx, NY; Assistant Professor of Philosophy (1973-74), Concordia College; Pastor (1975-80), University Lutheran Chapel, Los Angeles, CA; Assistant and Acting Chaplain/Assistant Professor of Religion (1980-88), Muhlenberg College; College Pastor/Associate Professor of Religion (1989-92), Carthage College, Kenosha, WI **Selected Memberships:** Ordained (1971) and accepted (1980) into The Lutheran Church in America; Institute on Religion in an Age of Science; American Academy of Religion **Discipline:** Religious Studies; Philosophy of Religion **Related Areas of Interest:** Theology and Ecology; Religion and Science - Methodology, Cosmology, Creationism; Ethical issues raised in Science and Technology.

Selected Publications:

_____. "Faith, Science, and Ministry in the '80's." *Process* (Journal of the Catholic Campus Ministry Association) 6 (Summer 1980): 18-22.

_____. "Ecological Theology and the Bible." *Ecospirit Quarterly* 1, 3 (1985): 5-8.

_____. "Let's Not Miss the Theology of the Creation Accounts." *Currents in Theology and Mission* 13 (1986): 97-105.

_____. "The Complementarity of Science and Religion, Or, On Not Checking Your Brain at the Church Door." *Journal of Theta Alpha Kappa* 11 (Fall 1987): 2-15.

_____. "Scientific Creationism and Biblical Theology." In *Cosmos as Creation: Science and Theology in Consonance*, ed. Ted Peters. Nashville, TN: Abingdon Press, 1989.

_____. "Divine Majesty, Human Vicegerency, and the Fate of the Earth in Early Islam." *Hamdard Islamicus* 13 (1990): 47-57.

_____. "The Ecological Fallout of Islamic Creation Theology." *Bucknell Review* 37, 2 (1993): 83-95.

Tipler, Frank J.

Present Position and Address: Professor of Mathematics and Physics, Tulane University, New Orleans, LA 70118, USA **Work Phone:** (504) 865-5727 **Date of Birth:** February 1, 1947 **Education:** S.B. (1969), M.I.T.; Ph.D. (1976), University of Maryland **Previous Positions:** NSF Research Mathematician (1976-79), University of California - Berkeley; Senior Research Fellow (1979), Oxford University; Research Associate (1979-81), University of Texas - Austin; Associate Professor (1981-87), Tulane University; Visiting Fellow, University of Sussex (1985, 87); Visiting Senior Scientist (1987), Max-Planck-Institut für Physik und Astrophysik - München; Visiting Professor (1988), Universities of Liege/Bern; Invited to Colloquia internationally (since 1977), i.e. Oxford; Cambridge; Harvard; Munich; Darmstadt; Vienna; Cracow; Visiting Professor (1992), Universität Wien **Selected Memberships:** American Physical Society; Royal Astronomical Society; International Society on General Relativity and Gravitation; Sigma Xi **Discipline:** Mathematics; Physics; Astronomy **Related Areas of Interest:** Physics, Philosophy and Theology; Cosmology.

Selected Publications: His bibliography lists 55 papers in refereed journals and conference proceedings and 4 monographs and books.

_____. Review of *God and the New Physics*, by Paul Davies. *Foundations of Physics* 15 (1985): 989-92.
_____. "Cosmological Limits on Computation." *International Journal of Theoretical Physics* 25 (1986): 617-61.
_____, J. D. Barrow. *The Anthropic Cosmological Principle*. Oxford: Oxford University Press, 1986.
_____. "Olbers' Paradox, the Beginning of Creation, and Johann Mädler." *Journal for the History of Astronomy* 19 (1988): 45-8.
_____. "The Sensorium of God: Newton and Absolute Space." In *Newton and the New Directions in Science*, ed. Michael Heller and George Coyne. Rome: Vatican Observatory Press, 1988.
_____. "Johann Mädler's Resolution of Olbers' Paradox." *Quarterly Journal of the Royal Astronomical Society* (September 1988).
_____. "The Omega Point Theory." In *Physics, Philosophy, and Theology: A Common Quest for Understanding*, ed. Robert J. Russell, William R. Stoeger, and George V. Coyne. Vatican City State: Vatican Observatory, 1988; Notre Dame, IN: University of Notre Dame Press, 1989.
_____. "The Omega Point as Eschaton: Answers to Pannenberg's Questions for Scientists." *Zygon* (June 1989).
_____. Review of *The Emperor's New Mind*, by Roger Penrose. *Physics World* 2 (1989): 45-7.
_____. *The Physics of Immortality: Modern Cosmology, God and the Resurrection of the Dead*. New York: Doubleday, 1994.

Titanji, Vincent P. K.

Present Position and Address: Dean, Faculty of Science/Associate Professor of Biochemistry (since 1993), BP 63, Faculty of Science, University of Buea, Buea, Cameroon **Date of Birth:** February 19, 1947 **Languages Spoken:** English, French, Russian, Swedish **Education:** M.Sc. (1973), Lomonosov Moscow State University; Ph.D. (1978), University of Uppsala, Sweden **Previous Positions:** Senior Research Officer (1979-80), CUSS, Yaounde, Cameroon; Head of Biochemistry Section (1980-82), Medical Research Center, Yaounde; Director of Biotechnology Center (1988-93), University of Yaounde, Yaounde, Cameroon **Discipline:** Biochemistry (including immunology, molecular parasitology, enzymology) **Related Areas of Interest:** Ethics of Science Applications; Technology Exchange.

Selected Publications: His bibliography lists about 45 papers and 7 abstracts in biochemistry.

_____. "Research Misdirections: A Bird's-Eye view of Problems of Scientific Research in Black Africa." *Science and Public Policy* 12, 4 (1981): 207-10.
_____. "Scientific Collaboration Between Developed and Developing Countries: Its Implications and Modalities." *Annals of the Uppsala Royal Academy of Arts and Sciences* 27 (1987-1988): 8-12.
_____. "Scientific Research is my Christian Vocation." In *The New Faith-Science Debate*, ed. J. M. Mangum, 85-90. Minneapolis: Fortress Press, 1989.

Tjeltveit, Alan

Present Position and Address: Assistant Professor of Psychology (since 1989), Muhlenberg College, Allentown, PA; 2400 Chem Street, Allentown, PA 18104, USA **Work Phone:** (610) 821-3421 **Date of Birth:** November 1, 1954 **Education:** B.A. Psychology/Religion (1976), Saint Olaf College; M.A. Theology (1982), School of Theology/Ph.D. Clinical Psychology (1984), Graduate School of Psychology, Fuller Theological Seminary **Postgraduate Experience:** Clinical Psychology Internship, University of Minnesota **Previous Positions:** Group and Family Therapist (1984-1989), Mental Health Center and Counseling Center, Abbott Northwestern Hospital, Minneapolis; Psychotherapist - Institute for Psychological Therapies (1984-85)/Kiel Clinic, Minneapolis (1985-87)/Private Practice, Minneapolis (1987-88); Part-time Assistant Professor of Psychology (1985-88), St. Olaf College; Clinical Assistant Professor of Psychology (1987-1989), University of Minnesota **Selected Memberships:** American Psychological Association; American Academy of Religion; American Psychological Society; Christian Association for Psychological Studies; Professional Affiliate, American Association of Pastoral Counselors **Discipline:** Psychology; Theology **Related Areas of Interest:** Theology/Religion and Mental Health/Psychology.

Selected Publications: His bibliography lists some 11 published contributions.

_____. "The Impossibility of a Psychology of the Christian Religion: A Theological Perspective." *Journal of Psychology and Theology* 17, 3 (1989): 205-13.

Tobacyk, Jerome J.

Present Position and Address: Professor of Psychology (since 1977), Louisiana Tech University, Box 10048, Behavioral Sciences, Ruston, LA 71272, USA **Education:** B.A. Psychology (1970), SUNY - Oswego; M.A. Psychology (1975)/Ph.D. Personality Psychology (1977), University of Florida **Previous Positions:** Fulbright Lecturer in Psychology (1985-86), Catholic University, Lublin, Poland **Editorial Positions:** Manuscript Reviewer, *Journal for Scientific Study of Religion* **Selected Memberships:** American Psychological Association (including section 36, Psychologists Interested in Religious Issues); Society for Personality Assessment; Society for Scientific Study of Religion; Polish Institute of Arts and Sciences in America; Center for Scientific Anomaly Research; Louisiana Academy of Sciences; International Council of Psychologists **Discipline:** Psychology **Related Areas of Interest:** Religious Conversion and Personality Change/Personal Identity Development.

Selected Publications: His bibliography lists some 64 publications.

_____, G. Milford. "Belief in Paranormal Phenomena: Assessment Instrument Development and Implications for Personality Functioning." *Journal of Personality and Social Psychology* 44 (1983): 1029-37.
_____. "Religious Conversion Experience as a Mechanism of Personality Change and Development." *Materialy Wyklady z psychologii w KUL* (1987).

Tödt, Heinz Eduard *(Deceased)*

Former Position and Address: Professor of Systematic Theology and Ethics (since 1963), Universität Heidelberg, Schlosswolfsbrunnenweg 20, D-W6900 Heidelberg, Germany **Date of Birth:** May 4, 1918 **Education:** Dr. Theol. (1957), Universität Heidelberg **Selected Memberships:** Forschungsstätte der Evangelischen Studiengemeinschaft (F.E.ST. - Protestant Institute for Interdisciplinary Research, Heidelberg) **Discipline:** Systematic Theology and Ethics **Current Areas of Research:** See publications to follow.

Selected Publications: Small extract of publication list that deals with theology and science.

_____. Preface to *Glaube und Naturwissenschaft in der Theologie Karl Heims, Forschungen und Berichte der Evangelischen Studiengemeinschaft*, by Hermann Timm, vol. 23. Witten: Eckart-Verlag, 1968.
_____. Introduction to *Gott und die Technik*, by Günter Howe. Hamburg: Furche; Zürich: Theologischer Verlag, 1971.
_____. "Die Wirkungsgeschichte von 1. Mose 1, 28. Theologische Reflexionen zum Auftrag des Menschen, die Erde zu verwalten." In *Lese-Zeichen für Anneliese Findeiss zum 65. Geburtstag*, ed. Chr. Burchard and G. Theissen, 281-94. *Dielheimer Blätter zum Alten Testament, Beiheft* 3 (Heidelberg, 1984).
_____. "Säkularisierung." In *Evangelisches Staatslexikon,* vol. 2, 3037-45. 3d ed. Stuttgart: Kreuz Verlag, 1987.

Toolan, David

Present Position and Address: Associate Editor of America; 220 West 98th Street, New York, NY 10025, USA **Concurrent Positions:** Director, Catholic Book Club; Associate Editor, *The Way*, Heythrop College, University of London **Work Phone:** (212) 581-4640 **Home Phone:** (212) 866-6156 **Date of Birth:** August 11, 1935 **Education:** B.A. History (1957), Georgetown University; Ph.L. (1962), Loyola Seminary-Fordham; M.A. Philosophy (1964), Fordham University; S.T.B. (1967), Woodstock College; Ph.D. Philosophical Theology (1974), Southern Methodist University **Lectures Presented:** "Between Sky Gods and Earth Mothers," to The American Teilhard de Chardin Association, November 3, 1990; "America, Ethics and Ecology," at the University of New Mexico/Albuquerque, 1991; "The Benefits of the Conflict between Science and Religion in Western Culture," at the Parliament of the World's Religions, Chicago, IL, August 30, 1993 **Previous Positions:** Assistant Professor of Religious Studies (1970-79), Canisius College; Adjunct Professor of Theology (1981-82), St. Peter's College, Jersey City, NJ; Adjunct Professor of Religious Studies (1986)/Adjunct Associate Professor of Theology (1987-89), Fordham University; Pastoring (1965-79) **Editorial Experience:** National Book Critics Circle board of directors (1983-84); Associate Editor and Literary Editor, *Commonweal* (1979-89); Editorial Board, American Assistancy Seminar on Jesuit Spirituality, St. Louis, MO (1988-91); Contributing Editor, *New Realities*, Washington, DC (1988-90) **Selected Memberships:** Society of Jesus; Catholic Theological Society of America; American Academy of Religion **Discipline:** Philosophical Theology **Related Areas of Interest:** Psychology and Religion; Cosmology.

Selected Publications: His bibliography lists 44 publications.

_____. "Harmonic Convergence and All That: New Age Spirituality." *The Way* 32, 1 (London, 1992): 33-42. Reprint, "Le New Age aux Etats-Unis." *Christus* 39, 154 (Paris, 1992): 230-41.
_____. "The Male Agony: According to Walter J. Ong." *Commonweal* (November, 20, 1992): 13-18.
_____. "Nature Is a Heraclitean Fire: Reflections on Cosmology in an Ecological Age." *Studies in the Spirituality of Jesuits* 23, 5 (1991): 1-46. Reprint, *O Homen a Natureza a Nova era*. Brazil, Editora Saraiva, 1993.
_____. "Second Thoughts on the Population Bomb." *America* (February 13, 1993): 16-17.
_____. "Treasure Under Other Bridges: Alternative Spiritualities." In *Reading the Signs of the Times: Resources for Social and Cultural Analysis*, ed. T. Howland Sanks and John A. Coleman, 212-21. Paulist Press, 1993.
_____. "Reincarnation and Modern Gnosis." In *Reincarnation or Resurrection?*, ed. Herman Haring and Johann-Baptist Metz, 32-45. Concilium 1993, No. 5, Orbis Press, 1993.
_____. "What Makes a Man?" *Church* (Spring 1993): 55-8. The Catholic Press Association awarded this essay First Prize as "Best Review" (1994).
_____. "Jesuit Mission in a Divided Superpower." *The Way Supplement 79* (Spring 1994): 48-58.
_____. "Open to Life—and to Death: The Church on Population Issues." In *Embracing the Earth: Catholic Approaches to Ecology*, ed. John E. Carroll and Albert LaChance. Orbis Press, 1994.
_____."Cries and Whispers: Moscow." *America* (January 1, 1994): 3-4.

Torrance, Thomas F.

Present Position and Address: Emeritus Professor of Christian Dogmatics, University of Edinburgh; 37 Braid Farm Road, Edinburgh EH10 6LE, UK **Concurrent Positions:** Founder and Coeditor (since 1948), *Scottish Journal of Theology*, Edinburgh **Home Phone:** 031-447-3224 **Date of Birth:** August 30, 1913 **Languages Spoken**: English, German **Education:** M.A. Classical Languages and Philosophy (1934)/B.D. divinity-Systematic Theology (1937), Edinburgh University; Oriel College (1939-40), University of Oxford; Dr. Theology (1946), University of Basel; D. Litt. (on submission of 5 works on Theological Method, 1970), Edinburgh University. Also studied in Jerusalem and Athens (1936)/Berlin (1937) **Honorary Degrees:** D.D. (1950), Presbyterian College, Montreal; Dr. Théol. (1959), University of Geneva; Dr. Théol. (1959), Faculté Libre, Paris; D.D. (1960), St. Andrews University; Dr. Teol. (1961), Oslo University; D.Sc. (1983), Heriot-Watt University, Edinburgh; Dr. Th. (1988), Debrecen, Hungary **Congresses and Conferences:** Church of Scotland/Church of England Conversations (1950-58); Faith and Order Conference of the World Council of Churches (1952), World Council, Lund, Sweden; Faith and Order Commission on Christ and His Church (1952-62); World Alliance of Reformed Churches (1954), Princeton, NJ; World Council of Churches (1954), Evanston, IL; Church Leaders Conference (1972), British Council of Churches, Birmingham; Reformed/Roman Catholic Study Commission on the Eucharist (1974), Woudschoten, The Netherlands; Theological Dialogue between Orthodox and Reformed Churches, Istanbul and Geneva (1979-83); Geneva and Leuenberg (1986-88); Geneva and Minsk (1988-92) **Lectures Presented:** Hewett Lectures (1959), Union Theological Seminary, NY and Andover Newton Theological School, Newton Center, MA; Harris Lectures (1970), Queen's University, Dundee; Anderson Lectures (1971), Presbyterian College, Montreal, Canada; Taylor Lectures (1971), Yale University, CT; Keese Lecture (1971), University of Mississippi, MS; Cummings Lectures (1978), McGill University, Montreal, Canada; Richards Lectures (1978), University of Virginia/Charlottesville; Stanley Lectures (1978), Davidson College, NC; Queen's University Lectures on Theology (1980), Belfast; Warfield Lectures (1981), Princeton Theological Seminary, NJ; Payton Lectures (1981), Fuller Theological Seminary, CA; Didsbury Lectures (1982), Nazarene College, Manchester; Edmonton Lectures (1983), University of Alberta, Canada; Stanley Lectures (1983), Regent College, Vancouver, Canada; Hellenic Societies Lecture (1984), London **Awards and Honors:** Fellowships: FRSE (1979), Fellow of the Royal Society of Edinburgh; FBA (1982), Fellow of the British Academy, London; MBE (1944), Member of the British Empire, as Church of Scotland Chaplain with the British Army; Collins Religious Book Prize (1969), for *Theological Science*; Cross of St. Mark (1970), Patriarchate of Alexandria; Protopresbyter of the Greek Orthodox Church (1973), Patriarchate of Alexandria; Cross of Thyateira (1977); Templeton Prize for Progress in Religion (1978) **Previous Positions:** Professor of Systematic Theology (1938-39), Auburn Theological Seminary, NY; Ordained (1940), Parish Minister (1940-47), Alyth, Perthshire, Scotland; Chaplaincy Service with the Army (1943-45); Minister (1947-50), Beechgrove Parish Church; Professor of Church History (1950-52)/Professor of Christian Dogmatics (1952-79), Edinburgh University and New College; Convener (1954-62), Church of Scotland Commission on Baptism; Moderator of the General Assembly of the Church of Scotland (1976-77) **Selected Memberships:** Founder (1945), Scottish Church Theology Society; Member (1946), President (1970-71), Church Service Society of the Church of Scotland; Founder (1952), President (1966-68), Society for the Study of Theology; Foreign Member (1968), Société de l'Histoire du Protestantisme Français; Société Internationale pour l'Étude de la Philosophie Médiéval (1968); Member (1969), President (1972-81), Académie Internationale des Sciences Religieuses; Founding Member (1973), President (1976-77), Institute of Religion and Theology of Great Britain and Ireland; Académie Internationale de Philosophie des Sciences (1976); Advisory Board (since 1980), Center of Theological Inquiry, Princeton, NJ; Member of Kuratorium (since 1983), Das Deutsche Institut für Bildung und Wissen, Berlin and Paderborn; Committee member (1985), Royal Society of Edinburgh; Founder Member of Kuratorium (since 1986), Europäische Akademie für Umweltfraten, Tübingen **Discipline:** Christian Theology;

Theological Science; Philosophy of Science **Related Areas of Interest:** Reformed and Patristic Theology; Doctrine of the Trinity; Epistemological Foundations of Theology and Science. A primary concern is for rigorous Theological Formulation within the Inherent Intelligibility of the Created Universe Disclosed by Natural Science.

Selected Publications: A published bibliography (1941-89) of the writings of T. F. Torrance appeared in the *Scottish Journal of Theology* 43: 225-62. The bibliography lists some 473 publications, including 30 major books and several large editing projects.

_____. *Theological Science.* Oxford University Press, 1969.
_____. *The Hermeneutics of John Calvin.* Edinburgh: Scottish Academic Press, 1988.
_____. *The Christian Frame of Mind: Reason, Order and Openness in Theology and Natural Science,* introduction by W. Jim Neidhardt. Colorado Springs: Helmers & Howard, 1989.
_____. *Karl Barth, Biblical and Evangelical Theologian.* Edinburgh: T. & T. Clark, 1990.
_____. *Science Théologique* (tr. by J-Y Lacoste). 1990.
_____. *Senso del divino e scienza moderna* (tr by G. Del Re). 1992.
_____. *Trinitarian Perspectives.* Edinburgh: T. & T. Clark, 1994.
_____. *Preaching Christ Today, The Gospel and Scientific Thinking.* Grand Rapids: Eerdmans, 1994.
_____. *Divine Meaning, Studies in Patristic Hermeneutics.* Edinburgh: T. & T. Clark, 1995.
_____. *The Christian Doctrine of God, One Being, Three Persons.* Edinburgh: T. & T. Clark, 1995.

Tough, Allen MacNeill

Present Position and Address: Professor (since 1982), Ontario Institute for Studies in Education and the University of Toronto; Department of Adult Education. Ontario Institute for Studies in Education; 252 Bloor Street West, Toronto, ONT M5S 1V6, Canada **Work Phone:** (416) 444-3135 **Fax Number:** (416) 444-5538 **E-Mail:** atough@oise.on.ca **Date of Birth:** January 6, 1936 **Education:** B.A. Psychology (1958)/M.A. Education and Psychology (1962), University of Toronto; Ph.D. Adult Education (1965), University of Chicago **Awards and Honors:** Selected as one of the "most prolific and pre-eminent adult Education researchers in North America" in a study of the field's "most successful researchers" by M. Baskett and R. Garrison (1987); Listed in *American Men and Women of Science*; Certificate for Meritorious Service to the Field of Adult Education (1980), Adult Education Association of USA **Previous Positions:** Secondary School Teacher (English and Guidance), David and Mary Thomson Collegiate Institute, Scarborough, ONT; Staff Member (1962), Extension Division, University of Toronto; Assistant Professor of Psychology and Sociology (1964-66), Faculty of Education, University of Toronto; Instructor (1968), Postgraduate Diploma Course in Adult Education, University of Rajasthan, India; Assistant Professor (1966-69)/Associate Professor (1969-82), Department of Adult Education, Ontario Institute for Studies in Education; Visiting Instructor (1978), Department of Adult Education, North Carolina State University **Selected Memberships:** World Future Society; World Futures Studies Federation **Discipline:** Futures Studies; Adult Education; Psychology **Related Areas of Interest:** Religion and the Future; Reality sources of Meaning and Purpose; Cosmic Evolution and Humanity.

Selected Publications: His *curriculum vitae* lists 22 books, chapters in books and review articles, and 42 other publications.

_____. "Fundamental Priorities." *Futures* 18, 4 (1986): 536-42.
_____. "Gaining Meaning and Purpose from Seven Aspects of Reality." *Ultimate Reality and Meaning: Interdisciplinary Studies in the Philosophy of Understanding* 9, 4 (1986):291-300.
_____. "What Role Will Extraterrestrials Play in Humanity's Future?" *Interstellar Studies: Journal of the British Interplanetary Society* 39, 11 (1986): 491-8.

_____. "The Next Steps: 20 Possibilities." In *Bioastronomy — The Next Steps: Proceedings of the International Astronomical Union Colloquium 99, Balaton, Hungary, June 1987*, ed. George Marx, 397-404. Dordrecht: Kluwer, 1988.
_____. *Crucial Questions About the Future*. Lanham, MD: University Press of America, 1991.

Townes, Charles H.

Present Position and Address: Professor (since 1994), Graduate School, University of California - Berkeley; Professor Emeritus of Physics, University of California - Berkeley; 1988 San Antonio Avenue, Berkeley, CA 94707, USA **Date of Birth:** July 28, 1915 **Education:** B.A./B.S. (1935), Furman University; M.A. (1937), Duke University; Ph.D. (1939), California Institute of Technology **Honorary Degrees:** Various Honorary Degrees **Awards and Honors:** Nobel Prize in Physics; National Medal of Science **Previous Positions:** Staff Member (1939-47), Bell Telephone Laboratories; Associate Professor and Professor (1948-61), Columbia University; Vice President and Director of Research (1959-61), Institute for Defense Analysis; Provost (1961-66)/Institute Professor (1966-67), MIT; University Professor of Physics (1967-86), University of California - Berkeley **Selected Memberships:** National Academy of Sciences; American Philosophical Society; Foreign Member, Royal Society of London **Discipline:** Physics; Astronomy **Related Areas of Interest:** Philosophy and Comparison of Science and Religion.

Selected Publications: His bibliography lists over 300 publications, most of which are in the area of Physics and Astronomy.

_____. "The Convergence of Science and Religion." *Think* 32: 2 (March-April 1966). Reprint, *Technology Review* 68 (May 1966): 35. Reprint, *The Christian Science Monitor* 9 (May 7, 1966).
_____. "Quantum Electronics and Surprise in Development of Technology, The Problem of Research Planning." *Science* 159 (1968): 699. Reprint, *Science in America, Historical Selections*, ed. J. C. Burnham, 474. Holt, Rinehard and Winston Inc., 1971.
_____. "The Role of Science in Modern Education." *The Southern Baptist Educator* 33 (1969): 5.
_____. "How and Why did it All Begin?" *Journal of the American Scientific Affiliation* 24, 1 (1972): 1.
_____. "Science, Technology, and Invention: Their Progress and Interactions." In *Proceedings of National Academy of Science USA, vol. 80, December 1983.*
_____. "Technology and the Nuclear Weapons Impasse." Bohemian Club Library Notes 48 (1985).
_____. "On Science, and What It May Suggest About Us." Theological Education (a publication of the Association of Theological Schools) (December 1988).
_____. "Reflections on My Life as a Scientist." Center for Theology and Natural Sciences Bulletin 12, 3 (1993):1.

Trigg, Roger

Present Position and Address: Professor (since 1987), University of Warwick, Coventry CV4 7AL, UK **Work Phone:** (0203) 523421 **Fax Number:** (0203) 523019 **Date of Birth:** August 14, 1941 **Education:** M.A. (1967)/D.Phil. (1968), University of Oxford **Previous Positions:** Lecturer, Senior Lecturer, Reader (1966-87)/Chairman of Philosophy Department (1984-91, 1991-), University of Warwick; Visiting Fellow (1986-87/1991-92), St. Cross College, Oxford **Selected Memberships:** President, British Society for Philosophy of Religion; Member, British Society for the Philosophy of Science; British Science and Religion Forum; European Society for the Study of Science and Theology (ESSSAT); European Society for Philosophy of Religion **Discipline:** Philosophy **Related Areas of Interest:** Philosophy of Science, particularly the Metaphysical Presuppositions of Science; Philosophy of Social Science; Philosophy of Religion.

Selected Publications:

_____. Pain and Emotion. Oxford University Press, 1970.

_____. *Reason and Commitment.* Cambridge University Press, 1973.

_____. *Reality at Risk; A Defense of Realism in Philosophy and the Sciences.* Brighton: Harvester Press; New York: Barnes and Noble, 1980. 2d. enl. ed. London: Simon and Schuster, 1989.

_____. *The Shaping of Man: Philosophical Aspects of Sociobiology.* Oxford: Basil Blackwell; New York: Schocken Press, 1982.

_____. *Understanding Social Science.* Oxford/New York: Basil Blackwell, 1985.

_____. *Ideas of Human Nature: An Historical Introduction.* Oxford/New York: Basil Blackwell, 1988.

_____. *Rationality and Science: Can Science Explain Everything?* Oxford/Cambridge, MA: Basil Blackwell, 1993.

Trost, Lou Ann

Present Position and Address: Ph.D. student in Systematic and Philosophical Theology, Theology and Science, Graduate Theological Union; 1672 Oxford Street #5, Berkeley, CA 94709, USA **Work Phone:** (415) 848-1039 **Date of Birth:** February 2, 1951 **Languages Spoken:** English, German, Spanish **Education:** B.S. (1974), University of Michigan School of Natural Resources; M.P.H. (1977), University of Michigan School of Public Health; M.Div. (1983), Lutheran Theological Seminary - Gettysburg; Th.M. (1988), Lutheran School of Theology, Chicago **Field Work:** Field Assistant, Drinking Water Survey (1978), Department of Environmental Health, Wayne County Health Department, Detroit, MI **Previous Positions:** Environmental Education Director (1975-76), ALC Camps, Michigan District; Associate Pastor (1983-85), First Lutheran Church, Carlisle, PA; Interim supply Pastor (1987), Holy Trinity Lutheran Church, Chicago; Graduate Assistant (1988, 89, 90), Pacific School of Religion **Selected Memberships:** Center for Theology and the Natural Sciences; Institute on Religion in an Age of Science; American Academy of Religion; North American Conference on Christianity and Ecology **Discipline:** Theology; Theology and Science; Environmental Ethics; Philosophical Theology **Related Areas of Interest:** Physics and Theology; Eschatology and Cosmology; Environmental and Medical Ethics and Theology.

Selected Publications:

_____. "'The Future' in the Theology of Pannenberg, in the Light of Questions Arising from Contemporary Physics." *CTNS Bulletin* 8, 3 (1988): 1-9.

Troster, Lawrence

Present Position and Address: Rabbi, Oheb Shalom Congregation, South Orange, NJ, USA; 170 Scotland Rd., South Orange, NY 07079, USA **Work Phone:** (201) 762-7067 **Fax Number:** (201) 762-4591 **Date of Birth:** June 8, 1953 **Languages Spoken:** English, Hebrew **Education:** B.A. (1976), University College, University of Toronto (1974-5, Hebrew University of Jerusalem); M.A./M.Th. Rabbinical Ordination (1982), Jewish Theological Seminary of America, NYC **Previous Positions:** Assistant Rabbi (1982-86), Beth Tzedec Congregation, Toronto, ONT; Rabbi, Shaareh Haim Synagogue, Richmond Hill, ONT (1986-92); Research Associate, Centre for the Study of Religion in Canada, Emmanuel College, University of Toronto (1992-3); Scholar in Residence, Kehillat Ahavat Hesed Congregation, Toronto (1992-3) **Editorial Positions:** Editorial Board: *Conservative Judaism* **Selected Memberships:** Past President of Ontario Region of Rabbinical Assembly; Ideology and Social Action committees, Rabbinical Assembly **Discipline:** Jewish Rabbi **Related Areas of Interest:** Cosmology; Midrash, Problem of Evil; Bioethics; Interfaith Relations; Revelation; Environmental Theology.

Selected Publications:

_____. "Fragments of a Faith Remembered." *Conservative Judaism* 35, 2 (1982).

_____. "Therapy of Engineering: Jewish Responses to Genetic Research." *The Reconstructionist* 49, 6 (1984).

_____. "No Other God's Before Me." *Viewpoints* 13, 4 (1985).
_____. "Asymmetry, Negative Entropy and the Problem of Evil." *Conservative Judaism* 34, 4 (1985).
_____. "The Love of God and the Anthropic Principle." *Conservative Judaism* 39, 1 (1986).
_____. "Making Theological Room for Others: A Jewish Perspective." *Ecumenism* (June 1989).
_____. "To the Mountain: A Rationale for the Mitzvot in Three Parts." *Conservative Judaism* (Spring, 1989).
_____. "Chaos and Creation: A Review Essay." *The Reconstructionist* 57, 1 (1991).
_____. "Created in the Image of God: Humanity and Divinity in an Age of Environmentalism." *Conservative Judaism* 44, 1 (1991).
_____. "Kedushah as a Form of Environmental Awareness." In *Proceedings of the Rabbinical Assembly, vol. 54, 1992.*

Turner, Dean

Present Position and Address: Professor of Research, Evaluation and Development (since 1966), University of Northern Colorado; 1708 37th Avenue, Greeley, CO 80634, USA **Date of Birth:** May 24, 1927 **Education:** B.A. Psychology and Spanish (1955), Centro de Estudios Universitarios, Mexico City; M.Ed., Adams State College, Alamosa, CO; Ph.D. Philosophy of Education, University of Texas - Austin **Previous Positions:** Taught Sociology (1959-61), University of Maryland; Taught Spanish (1962-63), Sullins College **Selected Memberships:** American Scientific Affiliation; Society of Christian Philosophers; Society of Christian Ethics; Christian Educators Association International; Continuing Education Association **Discipline:** Ethics; Philosophy (including Philosophy of Education, Science and Religion); Spanish; Education **Related Areas of Interest:** Philosophy of Science/Religion/Morality; Physics, Math, Astronomy, Biology, Chemistry; Space-Time Theory.

Selected Publications: His bibliography lists 8 books and numerous book reviews and articles.

_____. *Lonely God, Lonely Man.* Philadelphia Library, 1960.
_____. *The Autonomous Man.* Bethany Press, 1970.
_____. *Commitment to Care.* Greenwich, CT: Devin-Adair, 1978.
_____. *The Einstein Myth and the Ives Papers.* Greenwich, CT: Devin-Adair, 1978.
_____. *Krinkle Nose: A Prayer of Thanks.* Greenwich, CT: Devin-Adair, 1978.
_____. *Classrooms in Crisis.* Accent, 1988.
_____. *Benevolent Living.* Carol Stream, IL: Hope Pub. Co., 1991.
_____. *Escape From God.* Carol Stream, IL: Hope Pub. Co., 1991.

Turner, Edith L. B.

Present Position and Address: Editor (since 1992), *Anthroplogy and Humanism*; Lecturer (since 1984), Department of Anthropology, University of Virginia, P.O. Box 9024, Charlottesville, VA 22906-9024, USA; (Home) 107 Carrsbrook Drive, Charlottesville, VA 22901, USA **Work Phone:** (804) 924-3536 **Home Phone:** (804) 973-6986 **Date of Birth:** June 17, 1921 **Languages Spoken:** English, French, Spanish, Ndembu **Education:** Diploma (1938), Alde House Domestic Science College; M.A. English (1980); Studies in Anthropology, Literature, and Language, Cape Town University/Princeton University/Smith College/University of Virginia **Field Work:** Field work in Anthropology: In collaboration with Victor Turner and solo (1951-94) in Africa, Mexico, Ireland, India, Brazil, Israel, Japan, Korea, and USA **Previous Positions:** Proof reader (1956-57), Manchester University Press; Teacher of Domestic Science (1957-58), Jewish High School, Manchester; Codirector (1971-83)/Director (1983-92), Comparative Symbology Inc. **Editorial Positions:** Coeditor (1974-76), *Primavera Women's Literary Magazine* **Selected Memberships:** American Anthropological Association; American Ethnological Society; Alaska Anthropological Association; Society for Humanistic Anthropology; Society for the Anthropology of Consciousness; Anthropology of Religion Interest

Group **Discipline:** Anthropology **Related Areas of Interest:** The Anthropological Study of Religious Experience; Forms of Non-medical Healing; Deep Participation for Field Workers.

Selected Publications: Her *curriculum vitae* lists around 60 publications.

_____. "Encounter with Neurobiology: The Response of Ritual Studies." *Zygon* 21 (June 1986): 219-32.
_____. *Experiencing Ritual: A New Interpretation of African Healing.* Philadelphia: University of Pennsylvania Press, 1992.
_____. "Psychology, Metaphor, or Actuality? A Probe into Inupiaq Healing." *The Anthropology of Consciousness* 3, 1 and 2 (1992): 1-8.
_____. "A Visible Spirit Form in Zambia." In *Being Changed by Cross-Cultural Encounters: The Anthropology of Extraordinary Experience*, ed. Jean-Guy Ganlet. Peterborough, ONT. Broadview, 1993.

Uhlig, Herbert H. *(Deceased)*

Former Position and Address: Professor Emeritus (since 1972), Department of Materials Science and Engineering, Massachusetts Institute of Technology (M.I.T.), Cambridge, MA 02139, USA; (Home) Duncan Road, P.O. Box 444, Hancock, NH 03449, USA **Work Phone:** (603) 525-3776 **Date of Birth:** March 3, 1907 **Education:** Sc.B. (1929), Brown University; Ph.D. Chemistry (1932), M.I.T **Awards and Honors:** Willis Whitney Award, National Association Corrosion Engineers; U.R. Evans Award, British Institution Corrosion Science and Technology; Guggenheim Fellow, Uhlig Corrosion lab at M.I.T. **Previous Positions:** Researcher (1940-46), General Electric Company Lab, Schenectady, NY; Professor (1946-72), M.I.T. **Selected Memberships:** Institute on Religion in an Age of Science; Meteoritical Society; Electrochemical Society (Palladium and Acheson Medals); National Association Corrosion Engineers; British Institution Corrosion Science and Technology; Fellow, American Academy Arts and Sciences **Discipline:** Materials Science and Engineering (Electrochemistry and Corrosion Science) **Related Areas of Interest:** Meteorites, Science and Religion.

Selected Publications:

_____. "On Life's Purpose, Scientific Contributions and Religious Goals." *Zygon* 2 (1967): 389-97.
_____. *Life, Science and Religious Concerns*. Rutland, VT: Academy Books, 1988.

Usandivaras, Raul J.

Present Position and Address: Private Practice; Director of two groups of research in Transpersonal Psychology and Useful Regression in Small Groups; La Pampa 3817-21, (1430) Buenos Aires, Argentina **Phone/Fax:** 00-54-1-551-7390 **Date of Birth:** January 28, 1924 **Education:** M.D. (1947), Universidad Nacional de Buenos Aires; Research in Psychiatry (1964-68) **Previous Positions:** First President (1954), Asociación Psicología y Psicoterapia de Grupo; Director of Clínica Racker of Asociación Psicoanalítica Argentina; Director, Department of Behaviourial Sciences of CEMIC (Centro de Educación Médica e Investigación Clínica); Professor of Social Psychology (1961-66), Universidad Catóica Argentina; Director (since 1954), Research in Human Relations, Instituto Catóico de Ciencias, La Pampa 3821, (1430) Buenos Aires, Republica Argentina **Selected Memberships:** Asociación Psicoanalítica Argentina; Asociación Argentina de Psicologia y Psicoterapia de Grupo; International Psychoanalytic Association; International Group Psychotherapy Association; American Group Psychotherapy Association; Group Analytic Society (London) **Discipline:** Psychiatry; Psychoanalysis; Group Analysis **Related Areas of Interest:** Group Psychology, Anthropology, Mythology, Ritual; Relations between Science and Religion.

Selected Publications:

_____. "De Lider a Chamán." Buenos Aires, 1992.
_____. "A New Perspective in Group Analysis." *Group Analysis* 26, 3 (1993): 269-76.

Utke, Allen R.

Present Position and Address: Professor of Chemistry, University of Wisconsin - Oshkosh, Oshkosh, WI 54901 **Date of Birth:** February 5, 1936 **Education:** B.A. Chemistry (1958), Augustana College, IL; M.S. Inorganic Chemistry (1961)/Ph.D. Inorganic Chemistry (1963), University of Iowa **Previous Positions:** Senior Research Chemist (1963-64), Pittsburgh Plate Glass Company; Assistant through Professor of Chemistry (since 1964), University of Wisconsin - Oshkosh; Visiting Professor (1987-90), various Universities in Malaysia **Selected Memberships:** International Society for the Study of Human Ideas on Ultimate Reality and Meaning (URAM); Institute on Religion in an Age of Science (IRAS); World Future Society **Discipline:** Chemistry, Interdisciplinary scholar **Related Areas of Interest:** The relationships of Science, Theology, Philosophy, and Futurism and how they can be used to save the future and the planet.

Selected Publications:

_____. *Bio-Babel: Can We Survive the New Biology?* Atlanta, GA: John Knox Press, 1978.
_____. *Playing God.* Amsterdam: Elmar Press, 1980.
_____. *Bio-Shock.* Munich: Kesel-Verlag Press, 1980.
_____. "Level Five Prognostication," and "Renaissance II: An Imperfect Blueprint for Saving the Future." In *Applied Systems and Cybernetics*, vol. 2, 548-53. New York: Pergamon Press, 1982.
_____. "The Cosmic Holism Concept: An Interdisciplinary Tool in the Quest for Ultimate Reality and Meaning." *Interdisciplinary Studies in the Philosophy of Understanding* 9, 2 (1986): 134-55.

Vahanian, Gabriel

Present Position and Address: Professor (since 1983), Université des Sciences Humaines - Strasbourg, 14 Palais Universitaire, 67084 Strasbourg Cedex, France **Concurrent Positions:** Visiting Professor (since 1993), Centre College **Date of Birth:** January 24, 1927 **Languages Spoken:** English, French, German **Education:** B.A. (1945), Grenoble; Diplome de l'Ecole des Hautes Etudes (1948), Sorbonne; Licence en Theologie (1949), Faculté de théologie protestante de Paris; Th.M. (1950)/Th.D. (1958), Princeton Theological Seminary; Docteur en Théologie (1978), Strasbourg Theological Seminary **Previous Positions:** Instructor (1955-58), Princeton University; Assistant through Professor (1958-73)/Director of Graduate Studies in Religion (1967-75)/Professor of Religion (1967-84), Syracuse University; Visiting Professor (1972-73, 75-76, 79-80), Université des Sciences Humaines de Strasbourg; Visiting Professor (1978), University of Toronto; Visiting Professor (1988-94), University of Metz **Selected Memberships:** World Council of Churches Scholar (1949-50); President (1969-70)/Board of Directors (1968-72)/Chairman (1968-72), American Academy of Religion; Consultant (1980-81), President's Commission for Ethical Problems in Medicine and Biomedical Research, Washington, DC; Society for the Arts, Religion and Contemporary Culture; American Association of University Professors; Societé des Professeurs Francais en Amérique; American Theological Society; President (1989), Société Française de Théologie; Corresponding Member, Académie de Marseille; Phi Eta Sigma; American Council of Learned Societies **Discipline:** Theology **Related Areas of Interest:** Ethics and Technology; Theology of Culture; Utopianism and the Christian Faith.

Selected Publications:

_____. "Theologische reikwijtde van de techniek." *Nexus* (1993): 6.
_____. "Démocratie, solidarité, utopie." In *Richard Rorty ambiguïtés et limites du postmodernisme.* Paris: Librairie Philosophique J. Vrin (Pour demain), 1994.
_____. "Democratie, solidariteit, utopie." In *Richard Rorty, ironie, politiek en postmodernisme,* ed G. Hottois, M. van den Bossche, and M. Weyembergh. Antwerpen-Baarn: Hadewijk, 1994.
_____. "Sacré, technique, et société." In *Sur Jacques Ellul,* ed. Patrick Troude-Chastenet. Bordeaux: L'Esprit du temps (diffusion P.U.F.), 1994.
_____. "Eschatologie et utopie." In *Temps et eschatologie,* ed. Jean-Louis Leuba. Paris: Éditions du Cerf (Académie internationale des sciences religieuses), 1994.
_____. "D'une approche naturaliste à une approche technicienne de la religion: Prolégomènes à une herméneutique de la révélation." In *filosofia della revelazione,* ed. Marco M. Olivetti. Padova: Cedam, 1994.
_____. "Environnement et développement." In *Materialità ecologica e sviluppo sostenibile,* ed. Nicolà Chiarappa and Nino Muzzi. Perugia: Istituto di Ricerche Exonomiche e Sociali, 1994.
_____. "Anarchy and Holiness." *The Ellul Forum* 13 (1994): 11-13.
_____, editor. *Le siècle de Jacques Ellul.* Paris: Foi et Vie, 1994..
_____. "Technique." In *Encyclopédie du Protestantisme Theologische* . Geneva: Labor et Fides, in press.

van de Beek, A.

Present Position and Address: Professor of Theology (since 1981), Faculteit der Godgeleerdheid, Leiden University, Matthias de Vrieshof 1, Postbus 9515, 2300 RA Leiden, The Netherlands; (Home) Hoofdstraat 32, 2235 CH Valkenburg, The Netherlands **Date of Birth:** October 9, 1946 **Languages Spoken:** Dutch, English, German, French **Education:** Dr. Biology (1974)/Dr. Theology (1980), Rijksuniversiteit, Utrecht, Leiden, The Netherlands **Discipline:** Biology and Theology **Related Areas of Interest:** Generally new Formulations of Faith; Creation with special respect to the relation of Theology and the Sciences; Sources of Knowledge, Possibility of Verification or Plausibility.

Selected Publications: His bibliography lists 25 publications in botany, and 136 articles in theology.

_____. "Rust is ver te zoeken" (Rest is far away). In *Gebrokenheid van de schepping* (Brokenness of creation), ed. H. van Erkelens, 42-52. Kampen, 1989.
_____. "Plantensystematiek en theologie. Analogieën en verschillen" (Systematic botany and theology. Analogies and differences)." *Kerk en Theologie* 41 (1989): 28-41.
_____. *Beelden van de Geest* (Symbols of the spirit). Meinema 's-gravenhage, 1989.
_____. *Why? On Suffering, Guilt, and God.* Grand Rapids: 1990.
_____. *Wonderen en wonderverhalen* (On miracles and miracle stories). Nijkerk, 1991.
_____. *Rechtvaardiger dan God. Gedachten bij het boek Job* (More righteous than God. Reflections on the Book of Hiob). Nijkerk, 1992.
_____. "Een jachtverbod op de snark" (A prohibition of snark-hunting)." In *Theologie en natuurwetenschap: op zoek naar een snark?* (Theology and Natural Sciences: Searching for a Snark?), ed. W.B. Drees, 19-28. Kok, Kampen, 1992.
_____. "De mens het beeld van God - of omgekeerd?" (The human being image of God - or the other way around?). *Kerk en theologie* 43, 4 (1992): 310-21.
_____. *Van verlichting tot verduistering? Theologen vanaf 1800* (From enlightenment to darkening? Theologians since 1800 AD). Nijkerk, 1993.
_____. "To Be Created Precedes Our Creativity." *Louvain Studies* 19 (1994): 34-45.

Vande Kemp, Hendrika

Present Position and Address: Professor of Psychology (since 1991), Graduate School of Psychology, Fuller Theological Seminary, 180 North Oakland Avenue, Pasadena, CA 91101; (Home) 219 N. Primrose, Monrovia, CA 91016, USA **Concurrent Positions:** Licensed Psychologist in CA PSY6311 (since 1980) **Work Phone:** (818) 584-5534 **Home Phone:** (818) 357-8983 **Date of Birth:** December 13, 1948 **Languages Spoken:** Dutch, English **Education:** B.A. Psychology (*magna cum laude* 1971), Hope College, Holland, MI; M.S. Clinical Psychology (1974)/Ph.D. Clinical Psychology (1977), University of Massachusetts - Amherst **Postgraduate Experience:** Fellow (1977), Case Study Institute, Cambridge, MA (Sponsored by the American Association of Theological Schools); Pre-doctoral Internship in Clinical Psychology (1975-76), Topeka State Hospital **Congresses and Conferences:** Chairperson (1983), Program Committee for the APA Convention, Anaheim, CA - Psychologists Interested in Religious Issues **Previous Positions:** Instructor for Psychology of Religion (1974), University of Massachusetts; Instructor through Tenured Associate Professor of Psychology (since 1976), Fuller Theological Seminary; Pasadena Community Counseling Clinic (1977-79) **Editorial Positions:** Reviews or editorial consultation for *The Journal of Psychology and Theology*; *The Journal of Psychology and Christianity*; *The Journal for the Scientific Study of Religion*; *American Psychologist* **Selected Memberships:** Society for the Scientific Study of Religion; American Academy of Religion; President (1988-89), Psychologists Interested in Religious Issues, American Psychological Association; American Family Therapy Academy **Discipline:** Clinical Psychology **Related Areas of Interest:** History of Psychology specializing in the relationship between Psychology and Religion/Theology.

Selected Publications:

_____, H. Malony. *Psychology and Theology in Western Thought, 1672-1965: A Historical and Annotated Bibliography*. Millwood, NY: Kraus International Publications, 1984.

_____. "Dangers of Psychologism: The Place of God in Psychology." *Journal of Psychology and Theology* 14, 2 (1986): 97-109.

_____. "Relational Ethics in the Novels of Charles Williams." *Family Process* 26, 2 (1987): 283-94.

_____. "Psychology and the Problem of Suffering in the 1980s." *Journal of Psychology and Christianity* 9, 1 (1990): 5-17.

_____. "Psychology and Religion." In *Dictionary of Christianity in America*, ed. D.G. Reid, R.D. Linder, B.L. Shelley and H.S. Stout, 953-55. Downers Grove, IL: InterVarsity Press, 1990.

_____. "Religion, Psychology of." In *Twentieth Century Encyclopedia of Religious Knowledge*, ed. J.D. Douglas, 706-9. Grand Rapids, MI: Baker, 1991.

_____. "G. Stanley Hall and the Clark School of Religious Psychology." *American Psychologist* 47, 2 (1992): 290-8.

_____. "The Family, Religion and Identity: A Reformed Perspective." In *Family Therapy: Christian Perspectives*, ed. H. Vande Kemp, 39-75. Grand Rapids, MI: Baker, 1992.

_____. "Psychotherapy and Redemption: A Tribute to a Dying Mom." *The Psychotherapy Patient* 8, 3 and 4 (1993): 93-112.

_____. "Adrift in Pain, Anchored by Grace." In *Storying Ourselves: A Narrative Perspective on Christians in Psychology*, ed. J. Lee, 261-91. Grand Rapids, MI: Baker, 1993.

van den Brom, Luco Johan

Present Position and Address: Professor of Systematic Theology and Christian Ethics (since 1993), Groningen University, Nieuwe Kijk in 't Jatstraat 104, 9712 SL Groningen, The Netherlands **Date of Birth:** November 14, 1946 **Education:** B.Sc. (1968)/B.D. Theology (1970)/Th.M. (1974)/Ph.D. Philosophy of Religion (1982), University of Utrecht **Congresses and Conferences:** 7th European Conference on Philosophy of Religion, Utrecht (1988), Münster (1988, 89), Trinity College, Dublin (1989, 92), Uppsala (1990, 91), Durham (1991-92); 4th Conference of the European Society for the Study of Science and Theology, Rome (1992), Cardiff (1993); Oxford (1994) **Lectures Presented:** Guest Lecturer: Groningen (1985, 87), Tilburg (1986), Amsterdam (1986), Delft (1986, 90), London (1988, 89) **Previous Positions:** Minister of the Dutch Reformed Church in Blokzijl (1975-82)/Soest (1982-87); Lecturer in Philosophy of Religion, University of Utrecht (1987-93) **Editorial Positions:** Editorial Board and General Secretary, *Nederlands Theologisch Tijdschrift*; editorial board, *Kerk en Theologie* **Selected Memberships:** British Society for Philosophy of Religion (UK); Society for the Study of Theology (UK); Dutch Association for Philosophy of Religion; Center for Theological Exploration Inc. (Florida); Association for the Study of Theology and Natural Science (Amsterdam, Free University) **Discipline:** Systematic Theology; Philosophy of Religion; Mathematics and Physics **Related Areas of Interest:** Philosophy, Science and Theology in Dialogue.

Selected Publications:

_____. "God's Omnipresent Agency." *Religious Studies* (1984).

_____. "God as a Person." In *Belief in God and Intellectual Honesty*, ed. A. F. Sanders and R. Veldhuis. Assen, 1990.

_____. *Creatieve Twijfel* (Creative doubt). Kampen, 1990.

_____."Gottes Welthandeln und die Schachmetapher." *Glaube und Denken/Jahrbuch der Karl-Heim-Gesellschaft* no. 3 (Moers 1990).

_____. "Interpreting the Doctrine of Creation." In *Interpreting the Universe as Creation*, ed. V. Brümmer. Kampen, 1991.

_____. "God, Gödel and Trinity." In *Christian Faith and Philosophical Theology*, ed. Gijsbert van den Brink, Luco J. van den Brom and Marcel Sarot. Kampen, 1992.

_____. "Is History a Domain of Divine Agency?" *Science and Religion Forum Reviews* 20 (February 1992).

_____. "The Conceivability of a Divine Act." *Svensk Teologisk Kvartalskrift* 69 (1993).
_____. *Divine Presence in the World.* Kampen, 1993.
_____. "Does God Act in History?" In *Origins, Time and Complexity,* ed. Christoph Wassermann, vol 2, part 2. Geneva, 1994.

Van der Meer, Jitse M.

Present Position and Address: Full Professor of Biology (since 1992)/Director, Pascal Centre for Advanced Studies in Faith and Science, Redeemer College, Ancaster, ONT L9K 1J4, Canada **Work Phone:** (905) 648-2131 ext.243 **Date of Birth:** October 3, 1947 **Languages Spoken:** English, German, Dutch **Education:** B.Sc. Biology (1969), State University of Groningen NL; M.Sc. Biology (1972), State University of Utrecht, NL; Ph.D. Biology (1978), Catholic University of Nijmegen, NL; M.A. Philosophy of Science (1993), University of Guelph, ONT **Postgraduate Experience:** Postdoctoral Research Fellow (1978-79), University of Heidelberg **Previous Positions:** Research Associate (1972-78), Catholic University of Nijmegen; Research Scientist (1979-80)/Visiting Assistant Professor of Biology (1981-82), Purdue University; Assistant through Associate Professor of Biology (1982-92), Redeemer College **Selected Memberships:** Society for Developmental Biology; Canadian Society for Theoretical Biology; Society for History, Philosophy and Social Studies of Biology **Discipline:** Biology; Philosophy of Science **Related Areas of Interest:** Developmental Biology; Philosophy of Science; Faith and Science **Current Areas of Research:** Contribution of the theory of level structures to an understanding of the interaction of religion and science; Theory of level structures, theory reduction; role of analogy and metaphor in science, in theology, and in their interaction; Modes of internal interaction of religion and science.

Selected Publications: His current bibliography lists over 25 publications.

_____. "Enkele Achtergronden van het Fundamentalistisch Creationisme" (Background of fundamentalistic creationism). *Beweging* 43, 4 (1979): 65-71.
_____. "Drie Studies over 'buitenwetenschappelijke' Invloeden in de Geschiedenis van Biologische en Astronomische Ideeen" (Three studies on 'extra-scientific' factors in the history of biological and astronomical ideas). *Radix* 7, 2 (1981): 80-100.
_____. Review of *The Experiment of Life. Science and Religion,* ed. F. Kenneth Hare. *Calvinist Contact* 39 (1982); 24 (1983).
_____. "Van Materie tot Mens: Creationisme en Evolutionisme in de Biologie en de Theologie" (Matter to man: creationism and evolutionism in biology and theology). *Radix* 12, 4 (1986): 188-214.
_____. "Hierarchy. Towards a Framework for the Coherence of Faith and Science." *Pro Rege* 17, 3 and 4 (1989): 19-33.
_____. "Beliefs in Science: Taking the Measure of Methodological Materialism." In *Proceedings of the Second Annual Wheaton Theology Conference on "The Relationship Between Theology and Science", Wheaton College, 1993.* Forthcoming. Rev. ver. published as Occasional Paper of the Pascal Centre, Ancaster, 1993.
_____. "The Belief Structure of Sociobiology: An Analysis of the Inclusion of Philosophical Materialism as a Background Belief in the Theory of Human Sociobiology via the Use of Physical Analogies." In *Facets of Faith and Science, Proceedings of the First International Pascal Centre Conference, Redeemer College, Ancaster, 1992,* ed. J. M. Van der Meer. Lanham: University Press of America, 1995.
_____. "The Concept of Human Nature in Science and Theology." In *Yearbook of the European Society for the Study of Science and Theology,* ed. N. Gregersen. Forthcoming, 1995 or 1996.

Van der Veken, Jan

Present Position and Address: Institute of Philosophy, Kard, Mercierpl. 2, 3000 Leuven, Belgium **Date of Birth:** November 4, 1932 **Education:** Doctorate in Philosophy (1965), Katholieke Universiteit, Leuven **Selected Memberships:** President, European Society of Process Thought; Center of Metaphysics and Philosophy of God **Discipline:** Metaphysics; Contemporary Philosophy; A. N.

Whitehead; M. Merleau-Ponty **Related Areas of Interest:** Metaphysics; A. N. Whitehead; Process Thought.

Selected Publications:

_____. "De spanning tussen de geesteshouding van de gelovige en die van de wetenschapsbeoefenaar. Nieuwe kansen voor een gesprek." In *Betrekkingen tussen geloof en wetenschap. Twee verkenningen*, 9-28. 's Hertogenbosch: Radboudstichting, 1981.

_____. "Faith and Science: Possibility for a New Dialogue?" *Tripod* 22 (1984): 55-72 (Engels); 12-21 (Chinese).

_____. "Kreativität als allgemeine Aktivität" (Creativity as universal activity). In *Whiteheads Metaphysik der Kreativität* (Whitehead's metaphysics of creativity), ed. F. Rapp and R. Wiehl. Freiburg/München: K. Alber, 1986; Reprint, in English, Albany: SUNY Press, 1986.

_____. *Kosmologie en geloof: kansen voor een nieuwe dialoog.* Vught, Radboudstichting, 1989.

_____. *Een kosmos om in te leven.* Kapellen/Kampen: DNB/Pelckmans-Kok Agora, 1990.

_____. "God en de natuur." In *God en de obsessies van de twintigste eeuw*, ed. F. Vosman, 103-16. Hilversum: Thomas More Academie/Gooi en Sticht, 1990.

_____. "Can Only a God Save Us?" In *Out of the Crucible: Science, Creativity and the Human Condition*, Acta van de conferentie, gehouden aan "The Centre for Human Aspects of Science and Technology," University of Sydney, op 12-14 December 1990. Sydney, 1991.

_____. "The Referent of the Word 'God'." In *Tradition and Renewal, Philosophical Essays Commemorating the Centennial of Louvain's Institute of Philosophy*, ed. D. Boileau and J. Dick, 153-65. Louvain Philosophical Studies 5. Vol. 1. Leuven University Press, 1992

_____. "Is onze wereld nog 'een wereld om in te liven'." In *Bevrijding of bedreiging door wetenschap en techniek*, by R. Weiler and D. Holemans, 93-109. Kapellen: Uitgeverij Pelckmans/Koninklijke Vlaamse Ingenieursvereniging, 1993.

Vander Vennen, Robert E.

Present Position and Address: Director of Educational Services (since 1974), Institute for Christian Studies; One Massey Square, Suite 1910, Toronto, ONT M4C 5L4, Canada **Concurrent Positions:** Assistant Editor (since 1986), *Christian Courier* **Date of Birth:** October 4, 1928 **Languages Spoken:** English **Education:** A.B. (1950), Calvin College; Ph.D. Physical Chemistry (1954), Michigan State University; Visiting Scholar in Chemistry (1972-74), University of Chicago **Selected Memberships:** Canadian Scientific and Christian Affiliation; Sigma Xi; American Association for Higher Education: **Discipline:** Physical Chemistry; Christian Higher Education: **Related Areas of Interest:** Christian Post-secondary Education; History and Philosophy of Science; Writing and Editing.

Selected Publications:

_____. "Is Science Value-Free?" *Journal of the American Scientific Affiliation* 27, 3 (1975): 107-11.

_____, Paul A. Marshall, eds. *Social Science in Christian Perspective.* Lanham MD: University Press of America, 1988.

_____. *Grace in Scarborough.* Toronto: Morning Star Press, 1989.

_____, editor. *Church and Canadian Culture.* Lanham, MD: University Press of America, 1991.

Vander Zee, Delmar

Present Position and Address: Professor (since 1981)/Chairman of Biology Department, Dordt College, Sioux Center, IA 51250, USA **Work Phone:** (712) 722-6280 **Date of Birth:** March 11, 1944 **Education:** A.B. Biology (1966), Dordt College; M.A. Biology (1968), Western Michigan University; M.S. Botany (1977), Iowa State University; Ph.D. Horticulture-Botany (1980), Washington State University **Previous Positions:** High School teacher in Mathematics and Biology (1968-69), Southwest Minnesota Christian High, Edgerton, MN; Instructor through Professor of Biology (since 1969), Dordt College; Summer Faculty (1981-90), AuSable Institute of Environmental Studies, Mancelona,

MI **Selected Memberships:** Iowa Academy of Sciences; Botanical Society of America; American Society of Plant Physiologists; The Nature Conservancy; Natural Resources Defense Council **Discipline:** Botany **Related Areas of Interest:** Theology and the Environment.

Selected Publications:

_____. "The Environmental Impact of Being Busy in the Creation." *Pro Rege* 13, 3 (1985): 12-20.
_____. "Gift of Grasp." *Christian Educators Journal* 27, 2 (1987): 15-17.
_____, Ron Vos. "Trends in Agriculture - Sustainability." *Pro Rege* 18, 3 (1990): 19-28.
_____. "Green Marketing: Real Change or Yuppie Fad." *The Banner* (December 30, 1991): 14-15.
_____. "The Environmental Pulse in Academia." *Pro Rege* 22, 3 (1994): 24-30.

van Dijk, Paul

Present Position and Address: Assistant Professor in Theology and Philosophical Ethics (since 1980), Department of Philosophy and Social Sciences, Twente University, Enschede, The Netherlands; Smuddeboshoek 10, 7546 GB Enschede, The Netherlands **Work Phone:** 053-893302 **Date of Birth:** July 11, 1933 **Languages Spoken:** Dutch, German, English **Education:** Theology and Philosophy (1959), Utrecht; Drs. degree in Theology and Moral Philosophy (1973), Enschede; Doctoral degree (1985), Enschede **Previous Positions:** Clergyman/Student Pastor (1959-80) **Selected Memberships:** Secretary of ATOMIUM - a group studying the problems facing theology and science, Technology and culture **Discipline:** Theology and Moral Philosophy (Ethics) **Related Areas of Interest:** Problems facing Science, Religion, and Natural Theology.

Selected Publications: Most of his works are in Dutch, some, in German.

_____. "Verzet tegen technocratie" (Opposition against technocracy). *Wending* 36 (1981): 482ff.
_____. "Geloof en Wetenschap, Evangelie en Techniek, een spanningsvolle relatie" (Faith and science, gospel and technology, a relation full of tension). In *Pastoraal Handboek*, 1-29. N.p., 1983.
_____. *Waar zijn we in vredesnaam mee bezig? Kernbewapening, kerk en cultuur bij C. J. Dippel* (Why on earth are we doing this? Nuclear armament, church and culture according to C. J. Dippel). 's-Gravenhage, 1985.
_____. *Op de grens van twee werelden. Een onderzoek naar het ethische denken van de natuurwetenschapper C. J. Dippel* (On the border of two worlds. An inquiry to the ethical way of thinking of the scientist C. J. Dippel). 's-Gravenhage, 1985.
_____. *Techniek, zegen of vloek?* (Technology, a blessing or a curse?). De techniek meester: 's-Gravenhage, 1985.
_____. "Eine neue Runde im Gespräch zwischen Theologie und Naturwissenschaft: I. Glaube und Wissenschaft in historischer Sicht. II. Dialektische Theologie und Naturwissenschaft. III. Die Theologie Karl Barths und die Krise der Wissenschaft des 20 Jahrhunderts." *Zeitschrift für Dialektische Theologie* (1987, 1988).
_____. *Schöpfung oder Natur? Zum Gespräch zwischen Theologie und Naturwissenschaft.* Arnoldshainer Heften, 1988.
_____. *Anders over de schepping denken. Theologisch-Antropologische overwegingen m.b.t. het milieuvraagstuk* (An alternative way of thinking about creation. Theological-anthropological reflections on the environmental problem). Kampen, 1988.
_____. Günther Anders: "di 'ginntiqueerd htid' van de mens." (The 'uniquatedness' of man). in Hans Achterhuis (ed.), *De many van de technich.* (The measure of technology) Baarn, 1992.

van Duijn, Pieter

Present Position and Address: Emeritus Professor of Cell Biology, Medical Faculty Rijksuniversiteit Leiden (Home) Jac. van Maerlantlaan 3, 2343 JX Oegstgeest, The Netherlands **Date of Birth:** July 22, 1921 **Education:** Doctorate in Organic Chemistry (1951), Free University of Amsterdam **Awards and Honors:** Pioneer Award, Histochemical Society, USA **Previous Positions:** Pathological Laboratory/Lecturer (1960-67)/Professor of Histochemistry, Medical Faculty, Leiden University **Selected Memberships:** Council for Church and Theology of the Dutch Reformed Church; Honorary Member,

American Association of Anatomists (1981); Honorary Member, Polish (1983) and Hungarian (1985) Histochemical Societies; Secretary General (1972)/President (1976), International Federation of Societies for Histochemistry and Cytochemistry; Member, Royal Dutch Academy of Sciences; Honorary Member, German Histochemical Society; Honorary Associate, Federation Societies Histochemistry **Discipline:** Cell Biology **Related Areas of Interest:** The interface between theology, natural science and society.

Selected Publications: Most of his works and research have been in the field of cell biology.

_____. "A Concentric University." Tranjural Lecture. Leiden, 1968.
_____. "Integrale ethiek, een verkenning" (Integral ethics, a reconnaissance). *Wending* 30, 11 (1976): 567-82.
_____. "Natuurwetenschap, Theologie en Maatschappij" (Natural science, theology and society). *Wending* 33, 9 (1978): 559-69.
_____. "Biotechnology between Science Push and Consumer Pull." *Bibliotheca Nutritio Dieta Kazger* (48) (1991): 1-16.

Van Dyke, Fred G.

Present Position and Address: Associate Professor of Natural History (since 1988), The AuSable Institute of Environmental Studies, Mancelona, MI, USA; Wildlife Biologist, Montana Department of Fish, Wildlife, and Parks; P.O. Box 1351, Red Lodge, MT 59068, USA **Date of Birth:** December 18, 1954 **Education:** B.S. (*summa cum laude*, 1976), Wildlife-fishery Resources, University of Idaho; M.S. Wildlife Ecology (1979), University of Wisconsin - Madison; Ph.D. Environmental and Forest Biology (1983), College of Environmental Science and Forestry, State University of New York-Syracuse **Lectures Presented:** Featured lecturer (February 1988), Science and Christian Thought Lecture Series, Grace College, Winona Lake, IN **Previous Positions:** Assistant Professor of Science (1983-87)/Administrative Assistant (1984-85), Fort Wayne Bible College; Assistant Professor (1984)/Associate Professor of Natural History (1987), The AuSable Institute of Environmental Studies **Selected Memberships:** Member (since 1985)/Chair (1988), Commission on the Global Environment; American Scientific Affiliation; Academic Council (1984), AuSable Institute of Environmental Studies **Discipline:** Wildlife Biology and Ecology **Related Areas of Interest:** Environmental Ethics; A Christian Approach to Evolution.

Selected Publications: His bibliography lists over 35 works much of which deals with the Environmental Ethics.

_____. "Beyond Sand County: A Christian Perspective on Environmental Ethics." *Perspectives on Science and Christian Faith* (*PSCF*) 37 (1985): 40-8.
_____. "Theological Problems of Theistic Evolution." *PSCF* 38 (1986): 11-18.
_____. "A Theological Argument for Evolution, A Response to George L. Murphy." *PSCF* 38 (1986): 126-8.
_____. "Planetary Economies and Ecologies: The Christian World View and Recent Literature." *PSCF* 40 (1988): 60-71.
_____. "'The Reality of Resource Scarcity.' A response to Herbert Schlossberg." *PSCF* 40 (1988): 255-6.
_____, A. J. Birkey and T. D. Nickel. "Integration and the Christian College: Reflection on the Nineteenth Psalm." *Faculty Dialogue* 9 (1988): 89-96. Reprint, in *The Best in Theology*, ed. M. L. White. 3d ed. Carol Stream, IL: Christianity Today, 1989.

Van Erkelens, Herbert

Present Position and Address: Research Scientist; (Home) Suzette Noiretstraat 36, 2033 AV Haarlem, The Netherlands **Date of Birth:** November 6, 1952 **Languages Spoken:** Dutch, English, German **Education:** Ph.D. Physics (1984), Institute of Theoretical Physics, University of Amsterdam **Previous Positions:** Research Scientist, Centrum Algemene Vorming, Faculty of Physics and Astronomy, Free

University, Amsterdam, The Netherlands **Discipline:** Theoretical Physics; Analytical Psychology **Related Areas of Interest:** Modern Physics and Analytical Psychology; Religious Experiences of Physicists.

Selected Publications:

_____. *Einstein, Jung en de Relativiteit van God* (Einstein, Jung and the relativity of God). Kampen, Holland: Kok Agora, 1988.

_____. "Wolfgang Pauli and the Spirit of Matter." In *Proceedings of the Symposium on the Foundations of Modern Physics, 1990.* Singapore: World Scientific Publishing Company, 1990.

_____. "Wolfgang Pauli's Dialogue with the Spirit of Matter." *Psychological Perspectives* 24 (Spring-Summer 1991). Los Angeles: C. G. Yung Institute of Los Angeles, 1991.

_____. "Modern Physics and Symbols of the Self." In *Proceedings of the Symposia on the Foundations of Modern Physics, 1992.* Singapore: World Scientific Publishing Company, 1993.

van Huyssteen, Jacobus Wentzel Vrede

Present Position and Address: James I. McCord Professor of Theology (from 1992), Princeton Theological Seminary, CN 821, Princeton, NJ 08542, USA **Date of Birth:** April 29, 1942 **Languages Spoken:** English, Afrikaans, German, Dutch **Education:** B.A. (*cum laude*, 1963)/Hons. B.A. Philosophy (*cum laude*, 1964)/B.Th (1966)/M.A. Philosophy (*cum laude*, 1966), University of Stellenbosch; Drs.Th (*cum laude*, 1968)/D.Th (1970), Free University, Amsterdam, The Netherlands; Part-time student (1969), Ludwig Maximillian University, Munich **Previous Positions:** Lecturer (1971), Huguenot College, Wellington, South Africa; Minister (1971-72), Dutch Reformed Church, Noorder-Paarl; Professor of Religious Studies (1972-1991)/Head of the Department for Religious Studies, University of Port Elizabeth, South Africa **Editorial Positions:** Editorial Committees: *Journal of Theology for Southern Africa*; *Scriptura: Journal for Biblical Studies; Skrif en Kerk: Tydskrif vir Teologie* **Selected Memberships:** Member of Advisory Panel (since 1988), Chicago Center for Religion and Science; American Academy of Religion; Center for Theology and Natural Sciences, Berkeley Ian Ramsey Centre, Oxford; Eastern Cape Theological Study Group; South African Dogmatological Society **Discipline:** Theology; Philosophy **Related Areas of Interest:** Science and Theology; Philosophy and Theology.

Selected Publications:

_____. "Thomas S. Kuhn en die Vraag na die Herkoms van ons Teologiese Denkmodelle" (T. S. Kuhn and the question of the origin of our theological 'thought-models'). *Ned. Geref. Teologiese Tydskrif* 24, 3 (1983).

_____. "Rationality and Creativity. A Design for a Critical, Constructive Theology." Academic Papers Series. Toronto, Canada: Institute for Christian Studies, April 1986.

_____. "Scientific Realism and Theology: A New Challenge." *S.A. Journal of Philosophy* 6, 4 (1987).

_____. "Evolution, Knowledge and Christian Faith: Gerd Theissen and the Credibility of Theology." *Hervormde Teologiese Studies* 44, 1 (1988).

_____. "Experience and Explanation. The Justification of Cognitive Claims in Theology." *Zygon* 23, 3 (1988).

_____. "Beyond Dogmatism: Rationality in Theology and Science." *Hervormde Teologiese Studies* 44, 2 (1988).

_____. "Inference to the Best Explanation? The Shaping of Rationality in Theology." In *Paradigms and Progress*, ed. J. Mouton. Pretoria: HSRC Publishers, 1988.

_____. "On Narrative and the Shaping of Rationality in Theological Reflection." Paper presented at Philosophy of Religion Section of American Academy of Religion, Annual Meeting, Chicago, November, 1988.

_____. "Truth and Commitment in Theology and Science." Paper presented at Pannenberg Symposium, Chicago Center for Religion and Science, November, 1988.

_____. *Theology and the Justification of Faith: The Construction of Theories in Systematic Theology.* Grand Rapids: Eerdmans, 1989.

Van Leeuwen, Mary Stewart

Present Position and Address: Senior Editor of *Christianity Today* (since 1987); Professor of Interdisciplinary Studies, Department of Philosophy, Calvin College, Grand Rapids, MI 49506, USA **Concurrent Positions:** Research Fellow (since 1985), Christianity Today Institute; Adjunct Professor (since 1985), Institute for Christian Studies, Toronto **Date of Birth:** May 29, 1943 **Languages Spoken:** English, French **Education:** B.A., Psychology (with honors, 1965), Queen's University, Kingston, ONT, Canada; M.A. Social Psychology (1970)/Ph.D. Social and Cross-Cultural Psychology (1971), Northwestern University, Evanston, IL **Field Work:** Dissertation field work in Zambia **Previous Positions:** Assistant through Associate Professor (1971-85), Department of Psychology and Division of Social Science, York University, Toronto, Canada; Visiting Professor of Psychology (1975-76)/Fellow (1981-82), Calvin Center for Christian Scholarship, Calvin College, Grand Rapids, MI; Visiting Professor (1976), Hope College, Holland, MI; Visiting Professor (1978), New College for Advanced Christian Studies, Berkeley, CA; Visiting Professor (1985), Trinity Christian College, Langley, BC **Editorial Positions:** *Radix* (since 1978); *Reformed Journal* (since 1984); Contributing Editor, *Journal of Psychology and Theology* (1974-79)/*Journal of the American Scientific Affiliation* (1977-85) **Selected Memberships:** Fellow, American Scientific Affiliation; Board Member, Christian Association for Psychological Studies; International Association for Cross-Cultural Psychology **Discipline:** Sociology and Psychology **Related Areas of Interest:** Sociology and Psychology within a Christian context.

Selected Publications: Her bibliography lists 4 books, 19 published academic articles, and 19 recent popular and semi-popular writings.

_____. "Cognitive Style, North American Values, and the Body of Christ." *Journal of Psychology and Theology* 2, 2 (1974):77-88. Reprint, *Journal of the American Scientific Affiliation* 27, 3 (1975): 3-13.
_____. "The View from the Lion's Den: Integrating Psychology and Christianity in the Secular University Classroom." *Christian Scholar's Review* 5 (1976): 364-73.
_____. *The Sorcerer's Apprentice: A Christian Looks at the Changing Face of Psychology*. Downers Grove, IL: InterVarsity Press, 1982.
_____. "The Missions of the Christian Liberal Arts College in Relation to the Social Sciences." *Center Journal* 2, 1 (1983): 95-113.
_____. *The Person in Psychology: A Contemporary Christian Appraisal*. Grand Rapids: Eerdmans, 1985.
_____. "Bringing Christian Criteria to Bear on Academic Work." In *Making Higher Education: Christian: The History and Mission of Evangelical Colleges in America*, ed. Kenneth W. Shipps and Joel A. Carpenter. Grand Rapids: Eerdmans, in press.
_____. "North American Evangelicalism and the Social Sciences: A Historical and Critical Appraisal." *Perspectives on Faith and Science* (In press).

Van Melsen, A. G. M. *(Deceased)*

Former Address: Adrianaweg 29, 6523 MV Nijmegen, The Netherlands **Date of Birth:** November 10, 1912 Date of Death: September 10, 1994 **Languages Spoken:** Dutch, English, German, French **Education:** Studied Chemistry and Philosophy (1930-37)/Dr. of Science (1941), University of Utrecht, The Netherlands **Honorary Degrees:** Doctor *honoris causa:* Duquesne University, Pittsburgh (1953)/Free University, Amsterdam (1980)/St. Thomas University, Manila (1984) **Awards and Honors:** A Knight of the Order of the Dutch Lion; Commander of the Order of St. Gregorius **Previous Positions**: Assistant Professor of Chemistry (1937-1945), University of Utrecht; Professor of Philosophy (1945-1985)/President (1969-1974), University of Nijmegen; Professor Extraordinarius of Philosophy, University of Groningen **Selected Memberships:** International Institute of Philosophy; Royal Netherlands Academy of Arts and Sciences **Discipline:** Philosophy of Science/Nature **Related Areas**

of Interest: Philosophy of Science and Religion; Ethical Problems Connected with the Development of Science.

Selected Publications:

_____. "Naturwissenschaft und Theologie, Zur Hermeneutik theologischer Erkenntnis." *Der Seelsorger* 37 (1967): 175-84.

_____. "Science and Christianity as Universals of Culture." *The Thomist* 31 (1967): 137-58.

_____. *Natuurwetenschap en ethiek. Een bezinning op het verband tussen natuur en zedelÿ kheid.* In Series *Filosofie en Kultuur*, vol. 8. Antwerpen, 1967. *Physical Science and Ethics.* Pittsburgh, Leuven, 1967. Translated into German, English, and Polish.

_____. *Geloof, wetenschap en maatschappel ijke omwentelingen. Wijsgerige beschouwingen over de crisis in de kultuur* (Faith, science and societal developments). Baarn, Nijmegen: Katholiek Studiecentrum, 1977.

_____. "Critical Reflections upon the Autonomy of Science." In *Proceedings of the Conference "Concern about Science," Conference on the Occasion of the Centennial of the Free University in Amsterdam, 11-24, 1982.*

_____. *Waar gaat het heen? Beschouwingen over geloof, wijsbegeerte en wetenschap* (Faith, philosophy, and science). Nijmegen, Baarn, 1985.

_____. "Ethische aspecten van de biotechnologie" (Ethical aspects of biotechnology). *Pharmaceutisch Weekblad* 121 (1986): 1198-1204.

_____. "Geloof en wetenschap (Faith and science)." In *Wetenschap en geloof. Verslag van een studiedag georganiseerd door het Katholiek Studiecentrum op 30 maart 1985*, 11-33. Nijmegen, 1987.

_____. *Geloof, rede en ervaring* (Faith, reason, and experience). Nijmegen-Kampen, 1989.

_____. "Science and Religion." In *Science and Religion*, 27-35. Dordrecht, 1990.

VanOstenburg, Donald O.

Present Position and Address: Professor of Physics (since 1974), Department of Physics, DePaul University, 2219 N. Kenmore Avenue, Chicago, IL 60614, USA **Work Phone:** (Voice) (312) 362-8659 **Fax Number:** (312) 362-5681 **Date of Birth:** July 19, 1929 **Languages Spoken:** English **Previous Positions:** Graduate Assistant and Graduate Instructor (1951-56), Michigan State University; Associate Physicist (1956-59), Armour Research Foundation (Now IITRI); Group Leader (1959-70), Argonne National Laboratory; Associate Professor of Physics (1970-74), DePaul University; Acting Chairman (March 1987-August 1987)/Chairman (September 1987-July 1993), Physics Department, DePaul University **Selected Memberships:** Fellow, American Physical Society; Fellow, American Scientific Affiliation **Discipline:** Solid State Physics **Related Areas of Interest:** Nuclear Magnetic Resonance **Current Areas of Research:** Developing Computer Simulations for Fourier Transform NMR

Selected Publications: He has published over 30 papers in major US and Foreign journals and delivered over 35 papers at technical meetings. Topics ranged from theory of static electrification, lattice dynamics of uranium to a study of the electronic structure of metals and alloys via nuclear magnetic resonance.

_____, D. J. Montgomery. "Charge Transfer Upon Contact Between Metals and Insulators." *Textile Research Journal* 28, 22 (1958).

_____. "Lattice Dynamics of Alpha Uranium." *Physical Review* 123 (1961): 1157.

_____, D. J. Lam, H. D. Trapp, and D. E. MacLeod. "Knight Shifts and Magnetic Susceptibilities in V Alloys with Ti, Cr and Tc." *Physical Review* 128 (1962): 1550.

_____, D. J. Lam, Masao Shimizu, and Atsushi Katsuki. "NMR Magnetic Susceptibilities and Electronic Specific Heat of Nb and Mo Metals and Nb-Tc and Nb-Mo Alloys." *Journal of the Physical Society* 18 (Japan 1963): 1744.

_____, C. H. Sowers and J. J. Spokas. "Nuclear - Spin - Lattice Relaxation of V^{51} in V-Fe Alloys." *Physical Review Letters* 20 (1966): 461.

_____, L. C. R. Alfred. "New Scheme for the Construction of Phase Shifts with Application to Nuclear Magnetic Resonance." *Physical Review* 161 (1967): 569.

_____, H. G. Hoeve. "High - Temperature Magnetic Susceptibility of Dilute CuCr Alloys." *Physical Review Letters* 26 (1971): 1020.

_____, R. L. Spiewak and S. S. Danyluk. "An NMR Relaxation Study of Polynucleotide - Nucleotide Interactions." *Bioinorganic Chemistry* 4 (1975): 225.
_____, Mark T. Ratajack. "Computer Simulation Teaches Fourier Transform NMR." *Computers in Physics* 8, 3 (1994): 279.

Van Till, Howard J.

Present Position and Address: Professor of Physics (since 1967), Calvin College, 3201 Burton SE, Grand Rapids, MI 49546, USA **Work Phone:** (616) 957-6341 **Home Phone:** (616) 949-6432 **Fax Number:** (616) 957-6501 **Date of Birth:** November 28, 1938 **Education:** B.S. (1960), Calvin College; Ph.D. Physics (1965), Michigan State University **Postgraduate Experience:** Postdoctoral Research: Solid State Physics (1965-66), University of California - Riverside; Millimeter wave astronomy (1974), University of Texas - Austin **Previous Positions:** Teacher (1966-67), University of Redlands; Coordinator (1984-85) of research team studying Creation and Cosmogony, Calvin Center for Christian Scholarship **Selected Memberships:** American Astronomical Society; American Scientific Affiliation **Discipline:** Physics; Astrophysics **Related Areas of Interest:** Creation Science and Evolutionism; Scientific Cosmology; Creation Theology.

Selected Publications:

_____. "The Cosmos: Nature or Creation?" *Occasional Papers from Calvin College* 3, 1 (1984).
_____. "Categorical Complementarity and The Creationomic Perspective." *Journal of the American Scientific Affiliation (JASA)* 37, 1 (1985): 149-57.
_____. "The Legend of the Shrinking Sun." *JASA* 38, 3 (1986): 164-74.
_____. *The Fourth Day; What the Bible and the Heavens are Telling Us about the Creation.* Grand Rapids: Eerdmans, 1986.
_____, Davis A. Young and Clarence Menninga. *Science Held Hostage; What's Wrong with Creation Science and Evolutionism?* Downers Grove: InterVarsity Press, 1988.
_____, Robert E. Snow, John H. Stek, and Davis A. Young. *Portraits of Creation: Biblical and Scientific Perspectives on the World's Formation.* Grand Rapids: Eerdmans, 1990.
_____. "When Faith and Reason Cooperate." *Christian Scholar's Review* 21, 1 (1991): 33-45.
_____. "Can the Creationist Tradition be Recovered?" An essay review of *Creation and History of Science*, by Christopher Kaiser. *Perspectives on Science and Christian Faith* 44, 3 (1992): 178-85.
_____. "Is Special Creationism a Heresy?" *Christian Scholar's Review* 22, 4 (1993): 380-95.
_____. "When Faith and Reason Meet." In *Man and Creation: Perspectives on Science and Theology*, 141-64. Hillsdale, MI: Hillsdale College Press, 1993.

Van Valen, Leigh M.

Present Position and Address: Professor of Biology, University of Chicago, Department of Ecology and Evolution, 1101 East 57th Street, Chicago, IL 60637-1573, USA; Research Associate (since 1971), Department of Geology, Field Museum - Chicago; **Work Phone:** (312) 702-9475 **Date of Birth:** August 12, 1935 **Education:** B.A. Zoology (1956), Miami University; M.A. Zoology (1957)/Ph.D. Zoology (1961), Columbia University **Postgraduate Experience:** Boese Postdoctoral Fellow (1961-62), Columbia; NATO and NIH Postdoctoral Fellow (1962-63), University College, London; Research Fellow (1963-66), American Museum of Natural History **Previous Positions:** Assistant Professor of Anatomy (1967-71); Associate Professor of Evolutionary Biology (1971-73)/Professor of Biology (since 1976)/Professor in Committees on Conceptual Foundations of Science, on Genetics, and on Evolutionary Biology, University of Chicago **Editorial Positions:** *Evolution* (1969-71); *Journal of Molecular Evolution* (1970-76); *Carnivore* (1977-80); *Behavioral and Brain Sciences* (since 1978); *Paleobiology* (1974-80); *Current Anthropology Associates* (since 1968); *Evolutionary Theory* (since 1973); *Evolutionary Monographs* (since 1977) **Selected Memberships:** Councillor (1970-72)/Vice

President (1973, 1980), Society for the Study of Evolution; Councillor (1980-82), Paleontological Society; Treasurer (1969-72)/Vice President (1974-75), American Society of Naturalists; Board of Directors (since 1981), International Society of Cryptozoology; National Advisory Board (since 1981), Voice of Reason **Discipline:** Biology **Related Areas of Interest:** Conflicts of Honesty, Originality, and Opportunity with Money, Power, and Tradition in Science; Gaia Hypothesis; Evolutionary Ethics; Bearing of Evolution on the Nature of God.

Selected Publications: His bibliography lists over 265 scientific publications.

_____. "On Discussing Human Races." *Perspectives in Biology and Medicine* 9 (1966): 377-83.
_____, Frank A. Pitelka. "Intellectual Censorship in Ecology." *Ecology* 55 (1974): 925-6.
_____. "Financial Discrimination by Journals — and What to do About it." *Evolutionary Theory* 1 (1975): 119-30.
_____. "Dishonesty and Grants." *Nature* 261 (1976): 1.
_____. "A Price for Progress in Paleobiology." Review of *Patterns of Evolution*, ed. A. Hallam. *Paleobiology* 4 and 7 (1978): 210-17 and 571 respectively .
_____. "Mendel was no Fraud." *Nature* 325 (1987): 395.
_____. "Originality and Acceptability." *British Ecological Society, Bulletin* 18 (1987): 78-9.
_____. "Evolution, Morality, and Historiographic Modes." *Evolutionary Theory* 8 (1988): 205-7.

Van Zytveld, John B.

Present Position and Address: Professor, Physics Department, Calvin College, Grand Rapids, MI 49546, USA **Fax Number:** (616) 957-6501 **E-Mail:** jvanzytv@calvin.edu **Date of Birth:** November 12, 1940 **Education:** A.B. (1962), Calvin College; M.S. Physics/Mathematics (1964)/Ph.D. Physics (1967), Michigan State University **Postgraduate Experience:** 2 postdoctoral fellowships in England (1967-68, 1974-75); Senior Fulbright-Hayes Scholar (1980-81), Yarmouk University, Jordan; (1990-91), Institute for Electronic Structure and Laser, F.O.R.T.H., Heraklion, Crete, Greece **Previous Positions:** Assistant through Professor of Physics (since 1967)/Department Chairman (1971-72, 1985-90), Calvin College; Program Director of Solid State Physics (1983-85), National Science Foundation, Washington, DC; Guest Professor (1991), Kyoto University, Kyoto, Japan **Selected Memberships:** Fellow, American Scientific Affiliation **Discipline:** Solid State Physics **Related Areas of Interest:** General interest in the Science/Religion dialogue.

Selected Publications:

_____. "Back from the Brink." *The Reformed Journal* 32, 7 (1982).
_____. Review of *Science and the Quest for Meaning*, by D. M. MacKay. *The Reformed Journal* 33, 3 (1983).

Varela, Francisco J.

Present Position and Address: Director of Research (since 1988), Institut des Neurosciences, Université de Paris-CNRS, 4 Place Jussieu, Paris 75005, France **Concurrent Positions:** Fondation de France Professor of Cognitive Science and Epistemology, CREA, Ecole Polytechnique, 1 rue Descartes, Paris 75005, France **Work Phone:** 331 49 27 34 13 **Date of Birth:** September 7, 1946 **Languages Spoken:** French, Spanish, English, German, Italian **Education:** German Lyceum (1951-63), Santiago, Chile; School of Medicine (1964-66), Catholic University of Chile; M.Sc. (Licenciatura) Biology (1965-67), University of Chile; Ph.D. Biology (1968-70), Harvard University **Previous Positions:** Assistant Professor (1970-73), Faculty of Sciences, University of Chile; Assistant Professor (1974-78), University of Colorado Medical School, Denver; Research Associate Professor (1979-80), Brain Research Laboratories, New York University Medical School; Professor of Biology (1980-85), University of Chile; Visiting Senior Researcher (1984), Max-Planck-Institute for Brain Research - Frankfurt, Germany; Professeur Associé (1986-88), Institut des Neurosciences, CNRS, Université de

Paris VI; Professor of Cognitive Science and Epistemology (1986-91), CREA, Ecole Polytechnique, Paris **Editorial Positions:** Associate Editor, *New Science Library* (Boston and London); Editorial/Advisory Boards: *Cybernetic, Zeitschrift für Systemische Therapie, ReVision, Revue Internationale de Systemique, Biology Forum* **Other Academic Experience:** Advisory Councils, Centre de Recherche Epistemologie, Ecole Polytechnique; The Lindisfarne Association, NY; Centri di Studi Epistemologie e Cognitivi, Italy; Scientific Consultant of Shell Corporation, London; Rouset-UCLAF, Paris; UN Global Learning Project **Discipline:** Biology **Related Areas of Interest:** Cognitive Science and Human Experience; Practices of Human Transformation.

Selected Publications: His bibliography lists some 130 published research papers, 9 books, and many abstracts, reviews, reports, videos, and other contributions.

_____, H. Maturana. *Autopoiesis and Cognition: The Realization of the Living.* Boston: D. Reidel, 1980.
_____, H. Maturana. *The Tree of Knowledge: A New Look at the Biological Roots of Human Understanding.* Boston: New Science Library, 1987.
_____. *Connaître: Les Sciences Cognitives, tendences et perspectives.* Paris: Editions du Seuil, 1988.
_____, editor. *Understanding Origin: Scientific Ideas on the Origin of Life, Mind, and Society, Stanford International Symposium.* Dordrecht: Kluwer Associates, 1990.
_____, E. Thompson and E. Rosch. *The Embodied Mind: Cognitive Science and Human Experience.* Cambridge, MA: MIT Press, 1991.
_____, editor. *Gentle Bridge: Conversations with the Dalai Lama on the Sciences of Mind.* Boston: Shambhala, 1992.

Venable III, William H.

Present Position and Address: Freelance writer; 114 Brunner Ct., Pittsburgh, PA 15214, USA **Concurrent Positions:** Codirector (since 1981), Rivertree Christian Ministries; Pastor (since 1961), Presbyterian Churches **Date of Birth:** June 6, 1933 **Languages Spoken:** English, French, German **Education:** B.S. (1954)/M.S. Physics (1955), Carnegie-Mellon University; S.T.B. Biblical Languages and Literature/Theology (1958), Harvard Divinity School **Previous Positions:** Interim Pastor (1958), Brentwood Presbyterian Church; Chaplain (1959-62), US Army **Selected Memberships:** American Scientific Affiliation; Evangelical Theological Society; Past-President, Greater Pittsburgh Association of Evangelicals (related to the N.A.E.) **Discipline:** Physics; Biblical Languages/Literature; Theology **Related Areas of Interest:** The Relationship of Natural Science and Theology; Philosophy of Science; Information Theory and Theology.

Selected Publications:

_____. "An Information-Theory look at Biblical Inerrancy." *Themelios* 5, 1 (1968).
_____. "Information Theory and Biblical Inerrancy." *Journal of the American Scientific Affiliation* (September 1987).

Verlinde, Jacques

Present Position and Address: Professor of Philosophy of Science, Faculté de Philosophie, Institut Catholique de Lyon, Chemin de la Petite Champague, 69340 - Franchville, France **Date of Birth:** August 5, 1947 **Education:** Docteur en Science (1972), Université Gand, Belgium; Maîtrise en Theologie (1985), Université Rome; Docteur en Philosophie (1988), Université Louvain, Belgium **Discipline:** Philosophy of Science; Theology of Science **Related Areas of Interest:** Philosophy/Theology of Science.

Selected Publications:

_____. "Physique et Metaphysique: Reflexion sur le concept de substance à la lumiére de la Physique classique et contemporaire." Unpublished Thesis.

_____. "La Révélation, fondement et esperance: eschatologiques de la science." *Revue des Questions Scientifique* 159, 1 (1988): 183-201.

Viladesau, Richard

Present Position and Address: Associate Professor of Theology and Assistant Chair for Undergraduate Studies, Department of Theology, Fordham University, Bronx, New York, USA; Our Lady of Blessed Sacrament Church, 34-24 203rd. Street, Bayside, NY 11361, USA **Work Phone:** (718) 817-3243 **Date of Birth:** December 24, 1944 **Languages Spoken:** Italian, Spanish, French, German, Russian **Selected Memberships:** Catholic Theological Society of America; College Theology Society; American Academy of Religion; North American Association of the Study of Religion; Society for the Scientific Study of Religion; Rahner Society of America **Discipline:** Systematic Theology; Philosophy of Religion **Related Areas of Interest:** God and Creation; Theology and Ecology; Theological Method **Current Areas of Research:** Investigation of the relationship of conceptual thought to imagination, and implications for theology.

Selected Publications: His total Bibliography includes 8 books and 10 published articles.

_____. *The Reason for Our Hope. An Introduction to Christian Anthropology.* New York: Paulist Press, 1984.

_____. *Answering for Faith. Christ and the Human Search for Salvation.* New York: Paulist Press, 1987.

_____, Mark Massa. *S. J. Foundations of Theological Study. A Sourcebook.* New York: Paulist Press, 1991.

_____. "How is Christ Absolute? Rahner's Christology and the Encounter of World Religions." *Philosophy and Theology* 2 (Spring 1988): 220-40.

_____. "The Trinity in Universal Revelation." *Philosophy and Theology* 4 (Summer 1990): 317-34.

Vincent, Merville O.

Present Position and Address: Private Psychiatry Practice (since 1986); Box 1202, Salmon Arm, BC V1E 4P3, Canada **Concurrent Positions:** Staff Psychiatrist (since 1986), Shuswap Lake General Hospital, Salmon Arm, BC, Canada **Date of Birth:** November 21, 1930 **Education:** B.A. (1950), Acadia University; M.D./C.M. (1955), Dalhousie University; Diploma in Community Mental Health (1972), Harvard Medical School **Specialty Qualifications:** Certificate in Internal Medicine R.C.P.S.(C) (1960); Certificate in Psychiatry R.C.P.S.(C) (1961); Fellowship in Psychiatry F.R.C.P.(C) (1962); Diplomate American Board of Internal Medicine (1962) **Previous Positions:** Staff Psychiatrist (1960-86)/Assistant Medical Superintendent (1962-72)/Executive Director (1972-86), The Homewood Sanitarium, Guelph; Consulting Staff (1960-86), Guelph General Hospital/St. Joseph's Hospital, Guelph; Field Surveyor (1975-86), Canadian Council on Hospital Accreditation; President of the Medical Staff (1989-91), Shuswap Lake General Hospital, Salmon Arm, BC, Canada **Editorial Positions:** Editorial Board, *Christian Medical Society Journal*; *Humane Medicine* **Selected Memberships:** Fellow, American Scientific Affiliation; Member, Aesculapian Society, University of Ottawa Medical School; International Research Council on Physician Impairment; Wellington County Medical Society; Ontario Psychiatric Association; Christian Medical-Dental Association of Canada; Christian Association of Psychological Studies; Royal College of Psychiatrists (UK); Canadian Medical/Psychiatric Associations **Discipline:** Psychiatry; Internal Medicine **Related Areas of Interest:** Christianity and Psychiatry; Medical Ethics, i.e. Abortion and Euthanasia; Sexual Conduct and Ethics.

Selected Publications: His bibliography lists over 130 articles, chapters and essays in medical, mental health and religious publications on a variety of topics including mental health, marriage, stress, mental illness, alcoholism, abortion, anxiety, suicide, Christianity and psychiatry, grief, manicdepressive illness.

_____. "Bibliography re Psychiatry and Christianity." *The Atlantic Baptist* 142 (September 1, 1968).
_____. "Psychiatric Indications for Therapeutic Abortion and Sterilization." In *Birth Control and the Christian*, ed. Walter O. Spitzer and Carlyle L. Saylor, 189-213. Wheaton, IL: Tyndale House Publishers, 1969.
_____. *God, Sex and You.* J.B. Lippincott Company, 1972; Reprint, 1975
_____. "Suicide, A Christian Perspective." In *Is It Moral To Modify Man?*, ed. Claude A. Frazier, 129-49. Springfield, IL: Charles C. Thomas, 1973.
_____. "Christianity and Psychiatry: Rivals or Allies?" *Canadian Psychiatric Association Journal* 20, 9 (1975): 527-32.

Vitz, Paul C.

Present Position and Address: Full Professor, Department of Psychology, New York University, 6 Washington Place, New York, NY 10003, USA **Work Phone:** (212) 998-7858 **Date of Birth:** August 27, 1935 **Education:** B.A. (1957), University of Michigan; Ph.D. (1962), Stanford University **Previous Positions:** Assistant through Full Professor of Psychology (since 1965), New York University **Selected Memberships:** Christianity Today Institute Research Scholar; Fellowship of Catholic Scholars **Discipline:** Psychology and its connection to Religion, especially Christianity **Related Areas of Interest:** Christian Interpretations of Psychology, especially Personality Theory, Counseling and Moral Development; Anti-religious Bias in textbooks; The Nature and Origin of Human Consciousness; Psychology and Art and Christian Thought.

Selected Publications: Listed below are only those relevant to theology and science written since 1983.

_____. "The Brain Hemispheres and Human Response to Art." *Dordt College Lecture Series,* 19-44. Sioux Center, Iowa: Dordt College Press, 1983.
_____, J. Gartner. "Jesus as the Anti-Oedipus." Part 1. "Jesus the Transformer of the Super-Ego." Part 2 of "Christianity and Psychoanalysis" *Journal of Psychology and Theology* 12 (1984): 4-14; 82-90.
_____. *Censorship: Evidence of Bias in our Childrens' Textbooks.* Ann Arbor, MI: Servant, 1986.
_____. "Secular Personality Theories: A Critical Analysis," and "A Christian Theory of Personality: A Covenant Theory." In *Man and Mind,* ed. T. J. Burke, 65-94 and 199-222. Hillsdale, MI: Hillsdale College Press, 1987.
_____. *Sigmund Freud's Christian Unconscious.* New York: Guilford, 1988.
_____. "God, the Body, and the Good Life." *This World* 25 (Spring 1989): 91-103.
_____. "The Use of Stories in Moral Development: New Psychological Reasons for an Old Educational Method." *American Psychologist* 45 (1990): 709-20.
_____. "From Analysis of the Past to Stories about It." Part 1. "From Stories of the Past to Stories for the Future." Part 2 of "Narratives and Counseling." *Journal of Psychology and Theology* 20 (1992):11-19; 20-7.

Vollmer, Gerhard

Present Position and Address: Professor of Philosophy (since 1991), Seminar für Philosophie der Technischen Universität, D-38106 Braunschweig, Germany; Zaunkönigweg 5, D-30826 Garbsen, Germany **Work Phone:** 0531-391-3452 **Home Phone:** 05031-7 15 64 **Date of Birth:** November 17, 1943 **Languages Spoken:** German, English, French; some Greek, Turkish, Italian, Polish **Education:** Ph.D. Physics (1971) Physikalisches Institut, Freiburg; Ph.D. Philosophy (1974), University of Freiburg **Postgraduate Experience:** Postgraduate studies, (1971-72), McGill University, Montreal **Previous Positions:** Assistant Professor of Physics (1971-75), Freiburg; Akademischer Rat Philosophy (1975-81), Hannover; Professor of Philosophy (1981-91), Justus-Liebig-Universität **Discipline:** Philosophy **Related Areas of Interest:** Philosophy of Science; Philosophy of Nature; Theory of Evolution; Self-Organization; Artificial Intelligence; Evolutionary Epistemology.

Selected Publications:

_____. *Evolutionäre Erkenntnistheorie*. Stuttgart: Hirzel, 1975; 6th ed. 1994.
_____. *Was können wir wissen? Vol. 1: Die Natur der Erkenntnis. Beiträge zur Evolutionären Erkenntnistheorie. Vol. 2: Die Erkenntnis der Natur. Beiträge zur modernen Naturphilosophie*. Stuttgart: Hirzel, 1985/86; 2d. ed. 1988.
_____, H.D. Ebbinghaus, eds. *Denken unterwegs. Fünfzehn metawissenschaftliche Exkursionen*. Stuttgart: Wiss. Verlagsgesellschaft, 1992.
_____. *Wissenschaftstheorie im Einsatz*. Stuttgart: Hirzel, 1993.
_____. *Biophilosophie*. Stuttgart: Reclam, 1995.
_____. *Auf der Suche nach der Ordnung. Beiträge zu einem naturalistischen Welt- und Menschenbild*. Stuttgart: Hirzel, 1995.

Vorster, Willem S.

Present Position and Address: Professor and Director (since 1975), Institute for Theological Research, University of South Africa, Box 392, 0001 Pretoria, South Africa **Work Phone:** 012 429-4369 **Home Phone:** International +27+12 429- **Fax Number:** 429-4000 **Date of Birth:** December 1, 1941 **Languages Spoken:** English, Afrikaans, German **Education:** B.A. Greek and Hebrew (*cum laude*, 1962)/B.A. Honours in Greek and Semitic Languages (*cum laude*, 1966)/M.A. Greek (*cum laude*, 1976)/B.D. (1966)/D.D. New Testament (1974), University of Pretoria, South Africa **Previous Positions:** Lecturer in Greek (1965-70), University of Pretoria; Senior Lecturer in New Testament and Biblical Studies (1971-75), University of South Africa **Selected Memberships:** Studiorum Novi Testamenti Societas; Society of Biblical Literature; Judaica Society of South Africa; Patristic Society of South Africa; Old/New Testament Societies of South Africa **Discipline:** New Testament; Greek **Related Areas of Interest:** Theory of Science and Theology.

Selected Publications: His bibliography lists 78 publications, 12 edited works, and 7 others that were coedited.

_____, J. Kilian and C. F. A. Borchardt. *South African Theological Bibliography*. 5 vols. Pretoria: University of South Africa (UNISA), Studia Composita, 1980-1990.
_____, editor. *Church and Industry*. Pretoria: UNISA, Miscellanea Congregalia 22, 1983.
_____, editor. *Reconciliation and Construction: Creative Options for a Rapidly Changing South Africa*. Pretoria: UNISA, Miscellanea Congregalia 27, 1986.
_____, editor. *Are We Killing God's Earth: Ecology and Theology*. Pretoria: UNISA, Miscellanea Congregalia 30, 1987.
_____, editor. *The Right to Life: Issues in Bioethics*. Pretoria: UNISA, Miscellanea Congregalia 34, 1988.
_____, J. Mouton and A. G. van Aarde. *Paradigms and Progress in Theology, HSRC Studies in Research Methodology*. Vol. 5. Pretoria: Human Sciences Research Council, 1988.

Vukanovic, Vladimir

Present Position and Address: Distinguished Professor Emeritus (since 1988), Rochester Institute of Technology, Rochester, NY; 66 Westland Ave., Rochester, NY 14618, USA **Work Phone:** (716) 461-0393 **Date of Birth:** July 16, 1923 **Languages Spoken:** English, Serbian, Russian, German **Education:** Studies in Physical Chemistry (1946-51), University of Belgrade, Yugoslavia; Ph.D. Physics, University of Münster, Germany **Awards and Honors:** October Prize for scientific research, City of Belgrade **Previous Positions:** Assistant (1951-56), Institute for Nuclear Science, Vinca, Nr. Belgrade; Assistant (1956-61)/Assistant Professor (1961-67)/Associate Professor (1967-75)/Full Professor (1975-79), Institute of Physical Chemistry, University of Belgrade; Experimental Work (1959-61), Institut für Spektrochemie und Angewandte Spectroskopie, Dortmund, Germany; Visiting Professor (1977-78), Columbia University, NY; Visiting Professor (1980-85)/Distinguished Professor of Physical Sciences (1985), College of Science, Rochester Institute of Technology; Advisory Board,

Spectrochimica Acta B - Atomic Spectroscopy **Selected Memberships:** American Scientific Affili-ation; IRAS; Center for Theology and the Natural Sciences, Berkeley, CA; World Institute for Scientific Humanism; Lowenstein Center, Fordham University, NY; Victoria Institute, London, UK **Discipline:** Physical Chemistry **Related Areas of Interest:** Relation between Science and Religion; Physical Chemistry: Atomic Spectroscopy, Plasma Chemistry.

Selected Publications: His *curriculum vitae* lists 123 scientific publications and 2 patents.

_____. "Opposite Directions." *Perspectives on Science and Christian Faith* 40 (1988): 84.
_____. *Science and Faith.* Submitted for publication

Wagner, Roy

Present Position and Address: Professor of Anthropology (since 1974), University of Virginia, Charlottesville, VA 22903, USA; (Home) RR#1, Box 1495, Keswick, VA 22947, USA **Date of Birth:** October 2, 1938 **Languages Spoken:** English, German **Education:** A.B. History (*cum laude*, 1961), Harvard College; A.M. Anthropology (1962)/Ph.D. Anthropology (1966), University of Chicago **Previous Positions:** Assistant Professor (1966-68), Southern Illinois University; Associate Professor (1968-74), Northwestern University; Chairman, Department of Anthropology (1974-79, 1982-86), University of Virginia **Selected Memberships:** Fellow, American Anthropological Association **Discipline:** Anthropology **Related Areas of Interest:** Relation of the Christian sacrament of Western cultural "core symbolism." In *Symbols that Stand for Themselves.* Chicago: University of Chicago Press, 1986. New Guinea Native Religions Project (1963-65), Bollingen Foundation and the University of Washington; "Generating Meanings for Rules: The Necessity of Contextual Contrast in Human Social Organization" (1979-80), national Science Foundation Grant.

Selected Publications: His *curriculum vitae* lists 27 books in the field of Anthropology.

_____. "Scientific and Indigenous Papuan Conceptualizations of the Innate: A Semiotic Critique of the Ecological Perspective." In *Subsistence and Survival: Rural Ecology in the Pacific*, ed. T. Bayliss-Smith and R. Feachem. London: Academic Press, 1977.

Wahlbeck, Phillip G.

Present Position and Address: Professor of Chemistry (1972-present), Wichita State University, Wichita, KS 67260-0051 USA **Work Phone:** 316/689-3120 **Fax:** 316/689-3431 **Date of Birth:** March 29, 1933 **Languages Spoken:** English **Previous Positions**: Instructor, Assistant Professor, Associate professor, Illinois Institute of Technology (Chicago) 1960-1972; Visiting Professor, Technical University of Norway (Trondheim); Visiting Scientist, Los Alamos National Laboratory **Honors:** Phi Lambda Upsilon (chem.), Pi Mu Epsilon (math), Sigma Xi **Memberships**: American Chemical Soc., Materials Research Soc., The Metallurgical Soc, American Scientific Affiliation **Discipline:** Chemistry **Related Areas of Interest:** Physical Chemistry, High Temperature Chemistry, High Temperature Superconductors **Current Areas of Research:** High Temperature Vaporization Processes, Vapor Pressure measurements, Thermal Decompositions.

Selected Publications: His bibliography contains 67 research papers.

_____, D.L Myers, and V.V. Troung. "Validity of the Ruff-MKW Boiling Point Method: Vapor Pressures, Diffusions Coefficients in Argon and Helium and Viscosity Coefficients for Gaseous Cadmium and Zinc.," *J. Chem. Phys.* 83: 5 (1985).
_____. "Comparison and Interrelations for Four Methods of Measurement of Equilibrium Vapor Pressures at High Temperatures," *High Tem. Sci.,* 21 (1986).
_____, D.L. Myers. "Activities of Copper in the Y-Ba-Cu-O System," *J. Chem. Phys.* 95: 7(1991).

_____, R.R. Richards, and D. L. Myers. "Vaporization of Thallium (III) Oxide and Thallium Activities in Thallium Superconductors, " *J. Chem. Phys.* 95:12 (1991).
_____. "TGA Experimental Data — Analysis Provided by Transpiration Theory," *Thermochimca Acta* 197 (1992).
_____, D.E. Peterson, M.P. Maley, J.O. Willis, P.J. Kung, J.Y. Coulter, K.V. Salazar, D.S. Phillips, J.F. Bingert, E.J. Peterson, and W.L. Hults. "Development of T1-1223 Superconducting Tapes," *Physica C* 199 (1992).

Walker, Laurence C.

Present Position and Address: Lacy Hunt Professor Emeritus of Forestry, Stephen F. Austin State University, Nacogdoches, TX ; (Home) 514 Millard Drive, Nacogdoches, TX 75961, USA **Home Phone:** (409) 569-9754 **Date of Birth:** September 8, 1924 **Education:** B.S. Forestry (1948), Penn State College; M.F. (1949), Yale University; Ph.D. Forestry (1953), SUNY - Syracuse **Previous Positions:** Administrative Forester (1949-51)/Research Forester (1953-54), US Forest Service; Assistant through Associate Professor (1954-63), School of Forestry, University of Georgia; Chief Forester (1958-59)/Consultant (1960-70), National Plant Food Institute; Dean, School of Forestry/Administrative-Technical Representative, Stephen F. Austin State University; University of Colorado Mountain Research Station (Summers 1988, 89); Foreign assignments to Mideast, Central America, Brazil, Indonesia and Europe; Presbyterian Minister of 2 rural churches in East Texas **Selected Memberships:** Past-President, Deep Texas Development Association; Environmental Steering Committee, Texas Utilities; Director, Governor's Goals for Texas Project; Fellow, Society of American Foresters; Fellow and former Council member, American Association for the Advancement of Science; Fellow, American Scientific Affiliation; Wm.T. Hornaday Conservation Gold Medalist, Boy Scouts of America **Discipline:** Forest Ecology, Forest Economics; Pastoral Ministry **Related Areas of Interest:** Current concern is the need to Recognize Environmental (natural resource) Issues in the Light of World Population Growth, Hunger, Homelessness, etc.

Selected Publications: His bibliography lists seven books on Forestry and over 100 other publications.

_____. "Ecological Concepts in Forest Management." *Journal of the American Scientific Affiliation* 32, 4 (1980): 207-14.
_____. "A Christian and the Environment." *Presbyterian Journal* 39 (July 30, 1980): 11.
_____. "Selfishness and the Environmental Ethic." In *The Environmental Crisis: An Ethical Dilemma*, 67-76. AuSable Trails Institute of Environmental Studies, 1982.
_____. "A Scientist and His Faith." *Cumberland Presbyterian.* Part 1. 155, 7 (1983): 20. Part 2 155, 10 (1983): 20.
_____. *Forests.* John Wiley Inc., 1990.
_____. *The Southern Forest: A Chronicle.* University of Texas Press, 1991.
_____. *Excelsior: The Higher Good: Memoirs of a Forester.* Stephen F. Austin State University, 1994.

Walker, Lawrence J.

Present Position and Address: Professor, Department of Psychology, University of British Columbia, 2136 West Mall, Vancouver, BC V6T 1Z4, Canada; (Home) 5386 Opal Place, Richmond, BC V7C 5B4, Canada **Work Phone:** (604) 822-3006 **Home Phone:** (604) 277-2682 **Fax Number:** (604) 822-6923 **E-Mail:** lwalker@cortex.psych.ubc.ca **Date of Birth:** January 7, 1953 **Education:** B.A. Psychology (First Class Honors, 1974)/M.A. Experimental Psychology (1976), University of New Brunswick; Ph.D. Developmental Psychology (1978), University of Toronto **Previous Positions:** Assistant Professor (1978-79), University of Winnipeg; Assistant through Full Professor (1979-present), University of British Columbia **Administration Experience:** Chairperson of the Board of Administration (1991-96), Carey Theological College **Selected Memberships:** American Psychological Association; American Scientific Affiliation; Association for Moral Education; Canadian Psychological Association; Society for Research in Child Development **Discipline:** Developmental Psychology **Related Areas of Interest:** Moral Reasoning; Morality and the Individual/Society.

Selected Publications: His bibliography lists over 37 publications, mostly in the area of moral reasoning and development.

_____. "Sex Differences in the Development of Moral Reasoning: A Critical Review." *Child Development* 55 (1984): 677-91.

_____. "Experiential and Cognitive Sources of Moral Development in Adulthood." *Human Development* 29 (1986): 113-24.

_____, B. de Vries and S. D. Trevethan. "Moral Stages and Moral Orientations in Real-life and Hypothetical Dilemmas." *Child Development* 58 (1987): 842-58.

_____. "The Development of Moral Reasoning." *Annals of Child Development* 5 (1988): 33-78.

_____. "A Longitudinal Study of Moral Reasoning." *Child Development* 60 (1989): 157-66.

_____, J. H. Taylor. "Stage Transitions in Moral Reasoning: A Longitudinal Study of Developmental Processes." *Developmental Psychology* 27 (1991): 330-7.

_____, J. H. Taylor. "Family Interactions and the Development of Moral Reasoning. *Child Development* 62 (1991): 264-83.

_____, T. J. Moran. "Moral Reasoning in a Communist Chinese Society." *Journal of Moral Education* 20 (1991): 139-55.

_____. "Sex Differences in Moral Reasoning." In *Handbook of Moral Behavior and Development: Research*, ed. W. M. Kurtines and J. L. Gewirtz, vol. 2, 333-64. Hillsdale, NJ: Erlbaum, 1991.

_____, R. C. Pitts, K. H. Hennig and M. K. Matusba. "Reasoning About Morality and Real-life Moral Problems." In *Morality in Everyday Life: Developmental Perspectives*, ed. M. Killen and D. Hart. Cambridge: Cambridge University Press, 1994.

Walker, Ralph C. S.

Present Position and Address: University Lecturer in Philosophy (C.U.F., since 1972), Magdalen College, Oxford OX1 4AU, UK **Concurrent Positions:** Fellow and Tutor in Philosophy (since 1972), Magdalen College, Oxford **Work Phone:** 0865-276073 **Date of Birth:** June 2, 1944 **Languages Spoken:** English, French **Education:** B.A. (1964), McGill University; B.Phil (1966)/D.Phil. (1970), Oxford University **Awards and Honors:** John Locke Prize in Mental Philosophy (Oxford, 1967) **Previous Positions:** Junior Research Fellow (1968-72), Merton College, Oxford **Discipline:** Philosophy **Related Areas of Interest:** Philosophy of Religion; Metaphysics; Epistemology.

Selected Publications:

_____. *Kant.* London: Routledge & Kegan Paul, 1978.

_____. *The Coherence Theory of Truth.* London: Routledge & Kegan Paul, 1988.

Wallwork, Ernest Edward

Present Position and Address: Professor of Ethics (since 1990), Syracuse University, Syracuse, NY, USA; (Home), 3021 Davenport Street N.W., Washington, DC 20008, USA **Concurrent Positions:** Adjunct Professor (since 1984), SUNY Health Science Center, Syracuse; Expert Bioethicist (since 1987), National Institutes of Health **Date of Birth:** October 6, 1937 **Education:** B.S. (1959), Bucknell University; B.D. (1964), Yale University; M.B.A. (1961)/Ph.D. (1971), Harvard University **Awards and Honors:** "Major Figure, (1975)" Society for the Scientific Study of Religion; *Durkheim: Morality and Milieu* nominated for National Book Award; Phi Beta Kappa **Previous Positions:** Assistant Professor (1968-72), Wellesley College; Assistant Professor (1973-74), Union Theological Seminary; Associate Professor (1965-79), Yale University; Visiting Fellow (1980-82), Kennedy Institute of Ethics, Georgetown; Associate Professor (1983-89), Syracuse University **Selected Memberships:** American Academy of Religion (Chair, Religion and Social Sciences Section); American Psychoanalytic Association; Washington Psychoanalytic Institute; American Society of Christian Ethics; Washington School of Psychiatry; Washington Philosophy Club; Society for the Scientific Study of

Religion; Society for Religion in Higher Education:; Society for Health and Human Values; Bioethics Program, National Institutes of Health **Discipline:** Ethics; Psychology of Religion and Morality; Sociology of Religion and Morality **Related Areas of Interest:** Psychoanalysis and Ethics; Sociology of Religion and Morals; Developmental Psychology and Morality; Bioethics; Business Ethics.

Selected Publications: His bibliography lists 3 books, 16 articles, 6 book reviews, 20 book notes, and 3 interviews.

_____. *Durkheim: Morality and Milieu.* Cambridge MA: Harvard University Press, 1972.
_____. "Durkheim's Early Sociology of Religion." Sociological Analysis 46 (Spring 1985): 201-18.
_____. "Moralentwicklung bei Durkheim und Kohlberg." In Gesellschaftlicher Zwang und moralische Autonomie, ed. Hans Bertram, 163-91. Frankfurt am Main: Suhrkamp Verlag, 1986.
_____. "A Constructive Freudian Alternative to Psychotherapeutic Egoism." Soundings 69 (Fall 1986): 145-64. Reprint, chap. 12 in Community in America: The Challenge of "Habits of the Heart", ed. Charles Reynolds and Ralph Norman, 202-14. Berkeley, CA: University of California Press, 1988.
_____, Anne Wallwork. "A Psychoanalytic Perspective on Religion." Chap. 9 in *Psychoanalysis and Religion.* Vol. 2 of Psychiatry and the Humanities Series, ed. Joseph E. Smith. Baltimore, MD: Johns Hopkins University Press, 1989.
_____. "Cognitive/Conative Problem in Psychology and Counseling." In *Dictionary of Pastoral Care and Counseling*, ed. Rodney J. Hunter, 185-6. Nashville, TN: Abingdon Press, 1990.
_____. "Moral Behavior and Religion." In *Dictionary of Pastoral Care and Counseling*, ed. Rodney J. Hunter, 749-50. Nashville, TN: Abingdon Press, 1990.
_____, coauthor. *Critical Issues in Modern Religion.* Prentice-Hall, 1973, 2d ed., 1990.
_____. *Psychoanalysis and Ethics.* New Haven, CT: Yale University Press, 1991.
_____. "Reconfiguring Ethics After Freud." *Criterion* 12 (1993): 24-32.

Walter, Christian

Address: 83 bis, rue de Courcelles, 75017 Paris, France **Work Phone:** (1) 43.80.45.76 **Date of Birth:** August 22, 1957 **Languages Spoken:** French, English **Education:** Essec (1983); Institute of Actuaries (1988); Ph.D. Economics (1994) **Previous Positions:** Professor at CESB Discipline: Finance, statistics **Related Areas of Interest:** Theology and Science; Probability and Statistics; Epistemology; Theory of Choices under Uncertainty.

Selected Publications:

_____. "Les physiciens et les théologiens parlent - ils du même Dieu?" *Foi et Vie* 84, 3 (April 1985).
_____. "Mythe de la Création et Modèle standard." *Foi et Vie* 86, 1 and 2 (1987).

Ward, Keith

Present Position and Address: Regius Professor of Divinity (1991), University of Oxford, Christ Church, Oxford OX1 1DP, UK **Work Phone:** (0865) 276 246 **Date of Birth:** August 22, 1938 **Education:** First Class Honours Degree in Philosophy (1962), University of Wales; B.Litt. and Ordination training for the Church of England (1962-64), University of Oxford **Lectures Presented:** Teape Lecturer (1989), in India; Cadbury Lecturer (1986), Birmingham; Gifford Lecturer (1993-94), Glasgow **Previous Positions:** Lecturer in Logic (1964-66)/Lecturer in Moral Philosophy (1966-69), University of Glasgow; Lecturer in Philosophy (1969-71), University of St. Andrews; Lecturer in Philosophy of Religion (1971-76), University of London, King's College; Fellow and Dean of Trinity Hall/Director of Studies in Philosophy and Theology/University Lecturer in Divinity (1976-83), Cambridge; Professor of Moral and Social Theology (1983-86)/Professor of the History and Philosophy of Religion (1986-1991), University of London, King's College; Visiting Professor - Drake University (Fall 1984)/Claremont Graduate School (1990) **Editorial Positions:** *Journal of Medical*

Ethics/King's Theological Review/Religious Studies **Administrative Experience:** Executive Committee, Board for Social Responsibility, Church of England; President, World Congress of Faiths **Selected Memberships:** Member, Council for National Academic Awards; Member of Council, Royal Institute of Philosophy; Member (1991), working group on Quantum Creation and the Origin of the Laws of Nature, Vatican Observatory Research Group **Discipline:** History and Philosophy of Religion **Related Areas of Interest:** Philosophy and Theology; Theology and Science; Medical Ethics.

Selected Publications: His bibliography lists 17 books, 13 chapters, 21 articles, and 2 contributions to official reports.

_____. "The Unity of Space and Time." *Philosophy* (January 1967).
_____. *Rational Theology and the Creativity of God.* Blackwell, 1982.
_____. *Battle for the Soul.* UK: Hodder & Stoughton, 1985.
_____. "Embryos and Persons." In *Lectures in Medical Ethics*, ed. P. Byrne. King's Fund. N.p., n.d.
_____. "Philosophical Issues about Embryos." In *Experiments on Embryos*, ed. A. Dyson and J. Harris. N.p., n.d.
_____. *Turn of the Tide.* BBC Publications, 1986.
_____. "God as Creator." In *The Philosophy in Christianity, Royal Institute of Philosophy Lectures for 1989*, ed. G. Vesey. Cambridge University Press, 1989.
_____. *Divine Action.* Collins, 1990.
_____. "God as a Principle of Cosmological Explanation." In *Quantum Cosmology and the Laws of Nature*, ed. Robert John Russell, Nancey Murphy and C. J. Isham. Notre Dame, IN: University of Notre Dame Press, 1993.
_____. "God, Time and the Creation of the Universe." In *Explanations in Science and Theology*. London: Royal Society of Arts, 1993.

Washburn, Michael

Present Position and Address: Professor of Philosophy (since 1989), Indiana University - South Bend, 1700 Mishawaka Avenue, P.O. Box 7111, South Bend, IN 46634, USA; (Home) 834 S. 31st Street, South Bend, IN 46615, USA **Work Phone:** (219) 237-4264 **Education:** B.A. (1964)/M.A. (1966), University of California - Riverside; C.Phil. (1969)/Ph.D. (1970), University of California - San Diego **Previous Positions:** Assistant (1970-76)/Associate (1976-89), Indiana University - South Bend **Editorial Positions:** Editor: SUNY Press's Series in The Philosophy of Psychology **Selected Memberships:** American Philosophical Association; Association for Transpersonal Psychology **Discipline:** Philosophy **Related Areas of Interest:** Philosophy/Psychology of Religious Experience; Transpersonal Psychology.

Selected Publications: His bibliography lists 13 publications.

_____. "Human Wholeness in Light of Five Types of Psychic Duality." *Zygon* 22, 1 (1987): 67-85.
_____. *The Ego and the Dynamic Ground: A Transpersonal Theory of Human Development.* SUNY Series in Transpersonal and Humanistic Psychology. Albany: SUNY Press, 1988. 2d. ed. Forthcoming.
_____. "Two Patterns of Transcendence." *Journal of Humanistic Psychology* 30 (Summer 1990): 84-112.
_____. *Transpersonal Psychology in Psychoanalytic Perspective.* SUNY Series in the Philosophy of Psychology. Albany: SUNY Press, 1994.
_____. "Reflections on a Psychoanalytic Theory of Gender Difference." *The Journal of the American Academy of Psychoanalysis* 22 (1994): 1-28.

Wason, Paul Kenneth

Present Position and Address: Foundations and Corporations Officer, Bates College, 306 Lane Hall, Lewiston, ME 04240, USA **Concurrent Positions:** freelance Writer (since 1984); Treasurer, The Children's Rainforest, USA **Work Phone:** (207) 786-6337 **Home Phone:** (207) 777-5033 **Fax Number:** (207) 786-8242 **E-Mail:** pwason@bates.edu **Date of Birth:** April 27, 1954 **Languages**

Spoken: English, Spanish **Education:** B.S., Biology (1976), Bates College, Lewiston, ME; M.A., Anthropology (1980), State University of New York - Stony Brook; Ph.D., Anthropology (1985), State University of New York - Stony Brook **Field Work:** Field Course in Archaeological Method, Bates College (1974); Field School in Long Island, SUNY - Stony Brook (1977); Programa Riego Antiguo (1979), North Costal Peru **Congresses and Conferences:** Conference Chair, SCAFRO (1995) **Lectures Presented:** "Crosscurrents Between Science and Christianity." (1991). Bates Christian Fellowship; "People and the Environment, Multicultural Perspectives." Bates College **Awards and Honors:** Phi Beta Kappa (1975); Rhodes Scholarship Semifinalist (1976); Graduate Council Fellowship (1976-79); Mildred and Herbert Weisinger Fellowship (1981); Sigma Xi (1991) **Previous Positions:** Instructor (1/1983-12/84; 1/86-12/87), Jefferson Community College, KY; Instructor (8/88-12/88), University of Louisville, KY **Editorial Positions:** Editorial Board: *Anthropology* (1980-86) **Selected Memberships:** American Anthropological Association; American Schools of Oriental Research; Northeast Anthropological Association; Paleoanthropology Society; Palestine Exploration Fund (London); Royal Anthropological Institute, Fellow (Great Britain and Ireland); Society for American Archaeology; Affiliation of Christian Biologists; American Scientific Affiliation; Christians in Science (Great Britain); Network of Christian Anthropologists; Victoria Institute (London) **Discipline:** Anthropology **Related Areas of Interest:** Human Biological, Social and Cultural Evolution; Social Archaeology; Archaeological Theory; Social Sciences and Theology; Christianity and Culture **Current Areas of Research:** The nature, consequences and early history of human social inequality; Naturalistic visions of religion and morality (and Christian Faith); The shadow history of Christianity: Objections to making good seem evil in revisionist Christian history; Social organization of the Upper Paleolithic and Neolithic.

Selected Publications: His total bibliography consists of 1 book, 1 published article, and 8 reviews.

_____. Review of *The Red Ape*, by Jeffrey H. Schwartz. *Perspectives on Science and the Christian Faith* (*PSCF*) 41, 1 (1989): 46-7.
_____. Review of *One World: The Interaction of Science and Theology*, by John Polkinghorne. *PSCF* 42, 2 (1989): 114-15.
_____. Review of *Darwin and the Emergence of Evolutionary Theories of Mind and Behavior*, by Robert J. Richards. *PSCF* 41, 4 (1989): 244-5.
_____. Review of *Did Darwin Get It Right?*, by John Maynard Smith. *PSCF* 43, 3 (1991): 201.
_____. Review of *Science and Providence*, by John Polkinghorne. *PSCF* 43, 3 (1991): 208-9.
_____. Review of *The Beginnings of Western Science*, by David Lindberg. *PSCF* 45, 3 (1993): 196-7.
_____, David J. Wood. "Watch My Lips." *Leading Light: Christian Faith and Contemporary Culture* (Quarterly Journal of the C. S. Lewis Centre, London) 1, 2 (1993): 5-7.
_____. *The Archaeology of Rank. New Studies in Archaeology*. Cambridge University Press, 1994.
_____. Review of *The Culture of Disbelief*, by Stephen Carter. *PSCF* 46, 3 (1994): 212-13.
_____. Review of *Theology for a Scientific Age: Being and Becoming—Natural, Divine, and Human*, 2d ed., by Arthur Peacocke. *PSCF* (In Press).

Wassermann, Christoph

Present Position and Address: Lecturer in Theology and Science at the Faculty of Theology (since 1992), University of Geneva; President of the Swiss Theological Society (since 1993), Breslauer Str. 7, D-79576 Weil am Phein, Germany **Concurrent Positions:** Vice-president of ESSSAT (The European Society for the Study of Science and Theology), (since 1994) **Work Phone:** (49) 7621-71753 **Date of Birth:** August 10, 1950 **Languages Spoken:** German, English, French, Arabic **Education:** B.Sc. (1967), American University of Beirut, Lebanon; Dipl. Phys. (1974)/Dr.rer.nat (1979), University of Hamburg; Dipl. Theol. (1985), University Tübingen **Previous Positions:** High school teacher in physics and mathematics (1974-76), Amt für Schule, Hamburg; Computer Programming (1985-87): multilingual text editing, computer concordance to the Arabic Bible, Tübingen, Germany; Director of the Physics-Theology Research Project of the faculty of Theology (1988-92), University of Geneva; Secretary of ESSSAT (1989-94) **Discipline:** Physics (specialization in Theoretical Astrophysics); Theology (specialization in Systematic Theology) **Related Areas of Interest:** The Interface between Science and Theology; Systems of Thought for the Interpretation of both Physics and Theology; Philosophical Implications of Modern Physics; Creative Theology.

Selected Publications:

_____. "The Relevance of 'An Introduction to Mathematics' to Whitehead's Philosophy." *Process Studies* 17 (1988): 181-92.

_____. "Evolutionary Understanding of Man and the Problem of Evil." In *Kooperation und Wettbewerb. Zu Ethik und Biologie menschlichen Sozialverhaltens, Loccumer Protokolle*, ed. H. May et al., vol. 75, 299-306. Rehburg-Loccum: Evangelische Akademie, 1989.

_____. "Mathematische Grundlagen von Whiteheads Religionsphilosophie." In *Natur, Subjektivität, Gott. Zur Prozessphilosophie Alfred N. Whiteheads*, ed. H. Holzhey et al., 240-61. Frankfurt am Main: Suhrkamp, 1990.

_____. *Struktur und Ereignis. Interdisziplinäre Studien in Physik, Theologie und Philosophie*. Geneva: Faculté autonome de théologie protestante, 1991.

_____. "Biblische Sühnetheologie im Kontext eines Weltbildes der modernen Physik." In *Altes Testament und christlicher Glaube*. Vol. 6 of *Jahrbuch für biblische Theologie*, ed. I. Baldermann et al., 195-211. Neukirchen-Vluyn: Neukirchener Verlag, 1991.

_____. "Reactions of Churches to Developments in Physics During the Nineteenth and Twentieth Centuries." In *Les Églises face aux sciences, du Moyen Age au XXe siécle*, ed. O. Fatio, 159-70. Actes du colloque de la Commission internationale d'histoire ecclésiastique comparée tenu à Genéve en aout 1989. Genéve: Droz, 1991.

_____, et al., eds. *The Science and Theology of Information. Proceedings of the Third European Conference on Science and Theology, Geneva, March, 1990*. Geneva: Labor et Fides, 1992.

_____. "Theological Remarks on C.F.v. Weizsäcker's Concept of an 'Information Stream' as an Interpretation of Quantum Reality." In *The Science and Theology of Information*, ed. C. Wassermann, et al., 97-102. Geneva: Labor et Fides, 1992.

_____, managing editor. *Studies in Science and Theology. Yearbook of the European Society for the Study of Science and Theology*. Geneva: Labor et Fides, 1993ff.

_____. "Individuality and Flux. Physical and Theological Remarks on the Complexity of Temporal Origination in Process Philosophy." Part 1 in *Studies in Science and Theology*. Vol. 1 of *Origins of Time and Complexity*, ed. G.V. Coyne et al., 141-58. Geneva: Labor et Fides, 1993.

Waters, Brent

Present Position and Address: Omer. E. Robbins Chaplain to the University and Director of the J.W. and Ida M. Jameson Center for the Study of Religion and Ethics; Office of the Chaplain, University of Redlands, Redlands, CA 92373- 0999, USA; (Home) 406 Eucalyptus Drive, Redlands, CA 92373, USA **Work Phone:** (909) 335-4006 ext. 2460 **Home Phone:** (909) 793-1824 **Date of Birth:** February 20, 1953 **Education:** B.A. (1975), University of Redlands; M.Div. (1979)/D.Min. (1984), School of Theology, Claremont; Ordained United Church of Christ **Previous Positions:** Youth Director (1977-79), 1st Christian Church, Glendora, CA; Campus Minister (1979-84), Iowa State University **Other Academic Experience:** Chair, Exploratory Committee on Science, Technology and the Christian Faith, United Ministries in Education; Participant, Project on Faith, Science and Technology, National Council of Churches **Selected Memberships:** American Academy of Religion; Association for College and University Religious Affairs; National Association for Science, Technology and Society; Association for Religion and Intellectual Life; American Association for the Advancement of Science; Victoria Institute **Discipline:** Chaplain **Related Areas of Interest:** Technology and Ethics; Science and Theology; Genetics and Pastoral Care.

Selected Publications: His bibliography lists 35 publications.

_____. "Christianity and Evolution." In *Did the Devil Make Darwin Do It?*, ed. David B. Wilson. Ames: Iowa State University Press, 1983.
_____, editor. *Science, Technology and the Christian Faith.* Dallas: United Ministries in Education, 1986.
_____. "Why Should the Church Support Scientific and Technological Education?" *Bulletin of Science, Technology and Society* (Winter and Spring 1987).
_____. "Technology as a Problem for Christian Ministry." *Word and World* (Fall 1987).
_____. "Faith and Knowledge: The Dialogue Between Science and Religion." In *Toward a Common Vision: Papers from the 1985 Conferences on Science and Religion*, ed. George Derfer and John Hatfield. Pomona: California State Polytechnic University, 1987.
_____. "Is technology Creating Us in its Own Image?" *WSCF Journal* (December 1989).
_____. "Pilgrims and Progress: Technology and Christian Ethics." In *Rediscovering Alexandria: Science, Technology and the Churches.* N.p., 1990.
_____, Verlyn L. Barker. *Science, Technology, and the Christian Faith: An Account of Some Pilgrims in Search of Progress.* Charlotte, NC: United Ministries in Higher Education, 1991.
_____. "Truth and Virtue in a Scientific and Technological Age." *Prism* (Fall 1991).
_____. "A Meditation on Fate and Destiny in a Technological Age." *Bulletin of Science, Technology and Society* (1992).

Watson, Paul Joseph

Present Position and Address: University of Chattanooga Foundation Professor of Psychology, University of Tennessee - Chattanooga, 350 Holt Hall, 615 McCallie, Chattanooga, TN 37403, USA **Work Phone:** (615) 755-4291 **E-Mail:** pwatson@utcvm.utc.edu **Date of Birth:** June 23, 1948 **Languages Spoken:** English **Editorial Positions:** Contributing Editor, *Journal of Psychology and Theology* **Selected Memberships:** Religious Research Association; Society for the Scientific Study of Religion **Discipline:** Psychology **Related Areas of Interest:** Religious Motivation; Social Construction of Religion and Social Science; Mental Health **Current Areas of Research:** Mental health of traditional religious commitments.

Selected Publications: His total bibliography contains 90 published articles, 2 book chapters, and 3 book reviews.

_____, R. J. Morris, J. E. Foster, and R. W. Hood, Jr. "Religiosity and Social Desirability." *Journal for the Scientific Study of Religion* 25 (1986): 215-32.
_____, R. J. Morris and R. W. Hood, Jr. "Antireligious Humanistic Values, Guilt, and Self Esteem." *Journal for the Scientific Study of Religion* 26 (1987): 535-46.
_____, R. W. Hood Jr., S. G. Foster, and R. J. Morris. "Sin, Depression, and Narcissism." *Review of Religious Research* 29 (1988): 295-305.
_____, R. W. Hood, Jr. and R. J. Morris. "Existential Confrontation and Religiosity." *Counseling and Values* 33 (1988): 47-54.
_____, R. J. Morris and R. W. Hood, Jr. "The Psychology and Ideology of Irrational Beliefs." Part 3 of "Sin and Self-Functioning." *Journal of Psychology and Theology* 16 (1988): 348-61.
_____, R. J. Morris and R. W. Hood, Jr. "Antireligious Humanistic Values, Individualism, and the Community." Part 5 of "Sin and Self-Functioning." *Journal of Psychology and Theology* 17 (1989): 157-72.
_____, R. J. Morris and R. W. Hood, Jr. "Interactional Factor Correlations with Means and End Religiousness." *Journal for the Scientific Study of Religion* 28 (1989): 337-47.
_____, R. J. Morris and R. W. Hood, Jr. "Quest and Identity within a Religious Ideological Surround." *Journal of Psychology and Theology* 20 (1992): 376-88.
_____, R. J. Morris and R. W. Hood, Jr. "Mental Health, Religion, and the Ideology of Irrationality." In *Research in the Social Scientific Study of Religion*, ed. D. O. Moberg and M. L Lynn, vol. 5, 53-88. Greenwich, CT: Jai Press, 1993.
_____. "Apologetics and Ethnocentrism: Psychology and Religion within an Ideological Surround." *International Journal for the Psychology of Religion* 3 (1993): 1-20.

Webster, John Wilfred

Present Position and Address: Professor of Theology (since 1992), Department of Religion, Helderberg College, P.O. Box 22, Somerset West 7130, Cape Province, South Africa **Work Phone:** 27 24 55-1210 **Fax Number:** 27 24 55-2917 **Date of Birth:** October 22, 1952 **Languages Spoken:** English, Afrikaans (Dutch) **Education:** B.A. (1973), University of South Africa; 4 yr. Theol. Diploma (1973), Helderberg College; B.Th. (with honors, 1978), University of South Africa; Graduate study in Theology, (1979-1983) University of South Africa/(1983-1985) Andrews University, MI; M.A. Religion (1985), Andrews University; Ph.D. (expected 1992), Princeton Theological Seminary, NJ **Previous Positions:** Associate Pastor (1974-1975), Cape Town, South Africa; Pastor (1976-1979), Durban, South Africa; Lecturer (1980-81), Department of Religion, Helderberg College; Computer Consultant (1984-1985), Berrien Springs, MI; Teaching Fellow (1987-90), Princeton Theological Seminary **Editorial Positions:** Coeditor (1989-90), *Koinonia: The Princeton Theological Seminary Graduate Forum*; Research, Project Director, and Editor (1989-1991), Center of Theological Inquiry, Princeton and the John Templeton Foundation **Selected Memberships and Other Relevant Experience:** Phi Kappa Phi; Member, Theology and Science Group, American Academy of Religion; Participant (October 1989), Princeton Consultation on Theology and Science; Andrews Society of Scholars; Karl Barth Society of North America; Dogmatologiese Werkgemeenskap van Suidelike Afrika - Theological Society of Southern Africa **Discipline:** Theology (and Ethics); Philosophy **Related Areas of Interest:** Issues in Philosophy of Science, Epistemology, Cosmology and Theological Method; A Post-Critical Theology of Revelation, God and Nature; Scientific Technology; Environmental, Educational and Ethical issues arising in 1st/3rd World interaction.

Selected Publications:

_____. "The Possibility and Place of Philosophy of Religion." M.A. thesis, Andrews University, 1984.
_____, editor. *Who's Who in Theology and Science*. Framingham, MA: Winthrop Publishing, 1991.
_____. "Theology After Method: The Problem of Realism and the Quest for a Realistic Theology." Ph.D. diss., Princeton Theological Seminary, expected 1992.

Weidemann, Volker

Present Position and Address: Professor of Astronomy and Astrophysics (since 1965), University of Kiel, Germany; Poeler Weg 3, D - 24107 Kiel 1, Germany **Date of Birth:** October 3, 1924 **Languages Spoken:** German, English **Education:** Dr. rer. nat. (1954), University of Kiel; Habilitation (1963), Braunschweig University **Selected Memberships:** Braunschweiger Kreis e. V. SMD (Student Missionary in Germany); International Astronomical Union; Astronomical Society of the Pacific; Deutsche Physikalische Gesellschaft; Astronomische Gesellschaft **Discipline:** Astronomy; Astrophysics **Related Areas of Interest:** Cosmology; Evolution; Reality; Theology.

Selected Publications: His bibliography includes 80 publications on Astronomy and Astrophysics.

_____. *Science and Theology: What do the stars teach us?* Lutheran Standard, N.d.
_____. "Grenzen naturwissenschaftlicher Erkenntnis." *Dynamis* 19 (N.d.).
_____. "Cosmology. Science or Speculation?" In *World Congress of Philosophy*, ed. A. Diemer and P. Lang, vol. 16, 1978. Frankfurt am Main, 1983.
_____. "Die Entstehung der Welt aus dem Nichts." In *Zur Kritik der wissenschaftlichen Vernunft.* Freiburg: Alber Verlag, 1986.
_____. "Das Inflationäre Universum - die Entstehung der Welt aus dem Nichts." In *Naturwissenschaft und Glaube*, ed. Helmut A. Muller. München: Scherz Verlag, 1988.
_____. "Die Frage nach dem Ursprung - der Mensch als Evolutionsprodukt." *Glaube und Denken. Jahrbuch der Karl-Heim-Gesellschaft* 2 (1989).
_____. "The Concept of the Universe and the Problem of Reality." *Mem. Soc. Astr. Ital.* 62, 3 (1991).

Weidlich, Wolfgang

Present Position and Address: Full Professor of Theoretical Physics (since 1966), University of Stuttgart, Pfaffenwaldring 57/III, D-70550 Stuttgart 80, Germany **Work Phone:** 0711-6854927 **Date of Birth:** April 14, 1931 **Languages Spoken:** German, English **Education:** Diploma Physics (1954)/Ph.D. Physics (1957)/Habilitation in Theoretical Physics (1963), Free University, Berlin **Honorary Degrees:** Ph.D. phil. honoris causa (1985), University of Umea for Merits in Interdisciplinary Research **Previous Positions:** Assistant Professor of Physics (1957-59), University of Erlangen; Assistant Professor (1959-63), Free University, Berlin; Associate Professor (1963-66), University of Stuttgart; Invited Guest Professor (1982-83), Case Western Reserve University, Cleveland, OH **Selected Memberships:** DPG; EPS; RSA **Discipline:** Theoretical Physics, Quantum Optics; Statistical Physics, Synergetics; Quantitative Social Science **Related Areas of Interest:** Compatibility and Reconciliation between Concepts of Science and Theology.

Selected Publications: His bibliography includes 2 books, 50 publications in Theoretical Physics and 30 publications in Interdisciplinary Research.

_____. "Zum Begriff Gottes im Felde zwischen Theologie, Philosophie und Naturwissenschaft." *Zeitschrift für Theologie und Kirche (ZThK)* 3 (1971): 381-94.
_____. "Befragung der philosophischen Theologie der radikalen Fraglichkeit." *ZThK* 2 (1973): 226-43.
_____. "Naturgesetz und Zufall, Sinnverwirklichung und Gebet." *Zeitwende* 5 (1975): 257-65.
_____. "Gefährdung und Berechtigung des Philosophierens zwischen Wissenschaft und Ideologie." In *Denken im Schatten des Nihilismus*, 293-309. Darmstadt: Wiss. Buchgesellschaft, 1975.
_____. "Die Theologie und die Einheit der Natur." *Naturwissenschaft und Theologie* 4 (1977): 274-83.
_____. "Der persönliche Gott und die Naturwissenschaft." In *Zukunft aus dem Wort*, 57-64. Calwer Verlag, 1978.
_____. "Naturwissenschaft, Gesellschaft und Kultur." *Brennpunkte der Forschung, DVA* (1981): 34-50.
_____. "Naturwissenschaft und Gottesbegriff." *Herrenalber Texte* 33 (1981): 78-92.
_____. "Reconciling Concepts between Natural Science and Theology." In *Science and Religion. One world, Changing Perspectives on Reality*, ed. Jan Fennema and Iain Paul, 73-86. Dordrecht: Kluwer Academic Publishers, 1990.
_____. "Physics and Social Science - The Approach of Synergetics." *Physics Reports* 204 (1991): 1-163.

Weil, Pierre

Present Position and Address: President, City of Peace Foundation, International Holistic University, Granja do ipê, CP 0521, CEP 71740-080 Brasília, Brazil **Date of Birth:** April 16, 1924 **Education:** Ph.D. Psychology, University of Paris **Previous Positions:** Professor of Psychology, University Federal Belo-Horizonte; UNESCO's Consultant for Peace Education **Selected Memberships:** Past Vice President, International Transpersonal Association (ITA); Former member, Council of the International Association of Group Psychotherapy; International Council of Planetary Citizens **Discipline:** Psychology **Related Areas of Interest:** Holistic Approach in Life; Transpersonal Psychology; Science and Mystical States of Consciousness.

Selected Publications: His bibliography lists 38 publications.

_____. *L'Homme Sans Frontieres.* Paris: L'Espace Bleu, 1991.
_____. *The Art of Living in Peace - Towards a New Peace Consciousness.* Scotland: Findhorn Press, 1994.

Weingartner, Paul

Present Position and Address: Full Professor of Philosophy (since 1971), Institut für Philosophie, Universität Salzburg, Franziskanergasse 1, A-5020 Salzburg, Austria **Concurrent Positions:** Chairman (since 1972), Institut für Wissenschaftstheorie **Date of Birth:** June 8, 1931 **Languages Spoken:**

German, English, Restricted knowledge of French and Russian **Education:** Studies in Philosophy, Mathematics, Theoretical Physics, Psychology (1956-61)/Doctor of Philosophy, minor Theoretical Physics (1961), University of Innsbruck, Austria **Previous Positions:** Research Assistant (1962-67), Institut für Wissenschaftstheorie, International Research Centre, Salzburg **Selected Memberships:** Académie Internationale de Philosophie des Sciences; Association of Symbolic Logic; International Union for the History and Philosophy of Science; Institut der Görres-Gesellschaft für Interdisziplinäre Forschung; Chairman (1971-79/88-90), Institut für Philosophie, Universität Salzburg **Discipline:** Philosophy (Logic, Philosophy of Science) **Related Areas of Interest:** Philosophy of Science; Problems of Metaphysics and Borderline Problems of Theology with the Help of Modern Means.

Selected Publications: His bibliography lists 4 books, 25 edited books, and 110 articles.

_____. "A Predicate Caldulus for Intensional Logic." *Journal of Philosophical Logic* 2 (1973): 220-303.
_____. "The Problem of the Universe of Discourse of Metaphysics." In *Science et Métaphysique.* Colleque of the l'Académie Internationale de Philosophie des Sciences, Fribourg, 1973, 207-54. Bruxelles: Office International de Librairie, 1976.
_____. "Kommentar zu Thomas von Aquin, Summa Theologica I, 19, 1 über den Willen Gottes." In *Kirche und Gesellschaft*, ed. E. Weinzierl, 167-87. Vienna/Salzburg: Geyer Edition, 1979.
_____. "Ens et Verum convertuntur?" *Freiburger Zeitschrift für Philosophie und Theologie* 26 (1979): 145-62.
_____. "Aquina's Theory of Conscience From a Logical Point of View." In *Conscience: An Interdisciplinary View*, ed. G. Zecha and P. Weingartner, 201-30. Dordrecht: Reidel, 1987.
_____. "Das größte und erste Gebot." In *Die eine Ethik in der pluralistischen Gesellschaft*, ed. P. Weingartner, 231-54. Innsbruck/Vienna: Tyrolia, 1987.
_____. "Wie schwach können die Beweismittel für Gottesbeweise sein?" In *Klassische Gottesbeweise in der Sicht der gegenwärtigen Logik und Wissenschaftstheorie*, ed. R. Ricken, 36-61. Stuttgart-Berlin-Köln: W. Kohlhammer, 1991.
_____. "Similarities and Differences between Scientific and Religious Belief." In *Scientific and Religious Belief. Proceedings of the International Conference on Belief at the Institut für Wissenschaftstheorie, Salzburg, 1991*, 105-42. Philosophical Studies Series 59. Dordrecht: Kluwer, 1994.
_____. *Basic Questions on the Problem of Truth.* Forthcoming.
_____. "Kann sich das natürliche Gesetz ändern?" *Kommentar zu Thomas van Aquin, Summa Theologica* I-II, 94, 5 (Forthcoming).

Weir, Jack L.

Present Position and Address: Professor of Philosophy (since 1990), Morehead State University, Morehead, KY 40351, USA **Concurrent Positions:** Adjunct Professor of Philosophy (since 1986), McMurry College, Abilene, TX **Work Phone:** (606) 783-2786 **Date of Birth:** June 21, 1950 **Education:** B.A. (1971), East Texas Baptist University; M.Div. (1975)/Ph.D. Theology (1978), Southwestern Seminary; M.A. (1984), University of Chicago **Previous Positions:** Visiting Professor of Philosophy of Religion and Theology (Fall 1983), Golden Gate Seminary; Associate Professor of Philosophy (Summer 1986), Texas Christian University, Fort Worth; Assistant (1977-82)/Associate (1982-87)/Professor (1987-90), Hardin-Simmons University **Selected Memberships:** American Philosophical Association; Southwestern Philosophical Society; Society for Philosophy of Religion **Discipline:** Philosophy; Theology, Ethics **Related Areas of Interest:** Newton and God; Ethics including Medical Ethics.

Selected Publications: His bibliography lists 11 papers.

_____. "Newton's Concept of God as Creator and Lawgiver: A Systematic Analysis." *Southwest Philosophical Studies* 9 (Spring 1984): 68-75.
_____. "Traditional Christianity and Biological Evolution." *Explorations: Journal for Adventurous Thought* 3 (March 1985): 25-36.

_____. "The Anthropic Argument for God's Existence." *Explorations: Journal for Adventurous Thought* 6 (Summer 1988): 53-61.
_____. "Kantian Wholism: Toward a Critical Environmental Ethic." *Southwest Philosophical Studies* 11 (Spring 1989).

Weiss, Arnold S.

Present Position and Address: Psychologist in Private Clinical Practice; Consultant to Psychologists and Sociologists in Research Design and Attorneys on Psycho-legal Issues; 1717 Stoner Avenue, #113, Los Angeles, CA 90025, USA **Work Phone:** (310) 478-8088 **Date of Birth:** September 7, 1934 **Education:** B.S. Physics & Electrical Engineering (*cum laude*, 1956), City College of New York; Graduate Program (Ph.D.) Physics ((1956-59), Columbia University, New York; M.A. (1983)/Ph.D. Psychology (1985), California School of Professional Psychology - Los Angeles **Previous Positions:** Senior Engineer (1959-61), Northrop Corp., Hawthorne, CA; Physicist (1961-62), Electro-Radiation, Inc., Los Angeles, CA; Project Engineer (1962-66), FMA, Inc., El Segundo, CA; Project Engineer (1966-68), TRW Systems, Manhattan Beach, CA; Senior Staff Scientist (1968-72), AIL Information Systems, A Cutler-Hammer Co., Los Angeles, CA; President (1972-74), Material Metrics Inc., Mountain View, CA; Systems Planning Manager (1974-76), Xerox Corp., El Segundo, CA; A founder, President, Chief Financial Officer (1976-80), Rheumatology Diagnostics Laboratory, Inc., Los Angeles, CA **Specialties:** Patients with life-threatening illnesses, the terminally ill, AIDS and cancer **Discipline:** Psychology **Related Areas of Interest:** Relationship between Religion and Psychology; Psychotherapy for Life-threatening Diseases and the Terminally Ill; Religious Issues (e.g., brainwashing, cults, new age religions); Industrial Psychology (utilizes my intimate knowledge of industry as a former technical, management, and business executive); Cross-cultural and Ethnic Issues **Current Areas of Research:** Mental Health and Personality Characteristics of Chassidic Jews as Related to Religiosity; Quantum Mechanics, The Mind, Consciousness, and Spirituality.

Selected Publications: In addition to the articles, papers presented, and book chapters listed below, he has written 50 technical papers in applied physics and engineering and produced four patents that are physics and engineering-related, and is co-inventor on one patent for a medical laboratory diagnostic test for rheumatological disease.

_____, A. L. Comrey. "Personality Factor Structure Among Hare Krishnas." *Educational and Psychological Measurement* 47 (1987): 317-28.
_____, A. L. Comrey. "Personality and Mental Health of Hare Krishnas Compared with Psychiatric Outpatients and 'Normals'." *Personality and Individual Differences* 8, 5 (1987): 721-30.
_____. "Shostrom's Personal Orientation Inventory: Arguments Against its Basic Validity." *Personality and Individual Differences* 8,6 (1987): 895-903.
_____. "Psychological Distress and Well-being in Hare Krishnas." *Psychological Reports* 61 (1987): 23-35.
_____, Richard H. Mendoza. "Effects of Acculturation into the Hare Krishna Movement on Mental Health and Personality." *Journal for the Scientific Study of Religion* 29, 2 (1990): 173-84.
_____. "A New Religious Movement and Spiritual Psychology Based on *A Course in Miracles*." Paper presented at the Annual Meeting of the Society for the Scientific Study of Religion, Virginia Beach, VA, November 1990.
_____. "The Measurement of Self-actualization: The Quest for the Test May be as Challenging as the Search for the Self." *Handbook of Self-actualization*. Special Issue. *Journal of Social Behavior and Personality* 6, 5 (1991): 265-90.
_____. "Personality and Mental Health of American Hare Krishnas." Paper presented at the Annual Meeting of the American Psychiatric Association, May 1991, New Orleans, LA.
_____. "A New Religious Movement and Spiritual Healing Psychology Based on A Course in Miracles." *Religion and the Social Order, (Association for the Sociology of Religion)* 4 (1994): 197-215.
_____. "Can Religion be Used as a Science in Psychotherapy?" *American Psychologist* (Forthcoming).

Weizsäcker, Carl Friedrich Freiherr von

Present Position and Address: Retired Physicist and Professor of Physics and Philosophy, currently involved in writing; Alpenstr, 15, D-82319, Söcking, Germany **Date of Birth:** June 28, 1912 **Education:** Studied Physics under both Heisenberg and Bohr (1929-33), Universities of Berlin, Göttingen, and Leipzig; Promot. (1933)/Habil. (1936), Leipzig **Awards and Honors:** Max-Planck Medal (1957); Goethe Prize (1958); Fed. Cross of Merit (1959); Peace Award of the Order Pour le Mérite (1961); Erasmus Prize (1969); Theodor Heuss-Prize (1989); Templeton Prize for Progress in Religion (1989) **Previous Positions:** Lecturer (1936-42), Kaiser-Wilhelm-Institut für Physik, Berlin; Lecturer in Theoretical Physics (1937-42), University of Berlin; Professor of Theoretical Physics (1942-44), University of Strasbourg; Chair of Department (1946-57), Max-Planck-Institut für Physik, Göttingen and Honorary Professor (1946-57)/Founder (with Günter Howe, 1949) Göttingen Physicists-Theologians Conversations, University of Göttingen; Full Professor of Philosophy (1957-69), University of Hamburg; Director (1970-80), Max-Planck-Institut zur Erforschung der Lebensbedingungen der wissenschaftlich-technischen Welt (Max Planck Institute for Research into the Prerequisites for Existence in the Scientific Technological Age), Starnberg, and concurrently Honorary Professor of Philosophy, University of Munich **Selected Memberships:** Max-Planck Society; German Academy of Scientific Researchers; Bavarian Academy of Science; Austrian Academy of Science; German Physical Society; American Physical Society; Academy of Moral and Political Sciences, Paris **Discipline:** Physics and Philosophy **Related Areas of Interest:** Conversations between Science and Religion and the Interrelationships of Physics, Cosmology, and Theology; Thought Structures of Quantum Physics and Relativity and of Religion.

Selected Publications: His works include some 160 articles, published lectures and contributions to collected works, along with over 40 volumes, books and manuscripts.

_____. *Die Geschichte der Natur. Zwölf Vorlesungen.* Göttingen: Vandenhoeck & Ruprecht, 1948.
_____. *Zum Weltbild der Physik.* Stuttgart: Hirzel, 1958. Particularly the section "Die Unendlichkeit der Welt. Eine Studie über das Symbolische in der Naturwissenschaft," 118-157.
_____. *Christlicher Glaube und Naturwissenschaft.* Berlin: Evang. Verlagsanstalt, 1959.
_____. *Die Tragweite der Wissenschaft. Vol. 1. Schöpfung und Weltentstehung. Die Geschichte zweier Begriffe.* Stuttgart: Hirzel V., 1964.
_____. *Der Garten des Menschlichen. Beiträge zur geschichtlichen Anthropologie.* München: Hanser, 1977.
_____. *Deutlichkeit. Beiträge zu politischen und religiösen Gegenwartsfragen.* München, 1978.
_____. "Bemerkungen zum Gespräch zwischen Naturwissenschaft und Theologie." In *Gott - Geist - Materie. Theologie und Naturwissenschaft im Gespräch,* ed. Hermann Dietzfelbinger and Lutz Mohaupt. Hamburg: Lutherisches Verlagshaus, 1980.
_____. *Die Zeit drängt. Eine Weltversammlung der Christen für Gerechtigkeit, Frieden und die Bewahrung der Schöpfung.* München: Hanser, 1986.
_____. *Bewußtseinswandel.* München: Hanser, 1988.
_____. *Zeit und Wissen.* München: Hanser, 1992.

Weizsäcker, Ernst von

Present Position and Address: President (since 1991), Wuppertal Institute for Climate, Environment and Energy; Döppersberg 19, D-42103 Wuppertal, Germany **Work Phone:** (49) 202-24920 **Fax Number:** (49) 202-2492108 **Date of Birth:** June 25, 1939 **Languages Spoken:** German, English, French **Education:** Diploma Physics (1965), Hamburg University; Dr. rer. nat. Biology (January 1969), Freiburg University **Previous Positions:** Past Fellow, Forschungsstätte der Evangelischen Studiengemeinschaft (F.E.ST.) (Protestant Interdisciplinary Research Institute), Heidelberg; Full Professor of Biology (1972-75), University of Essen; President (1975-80), University of Kassel; Director (1981-84), UN Centre for Science and Technology, NY; Director (1984-91), Institute for European

Environmental Policy **Selected Memberships:** Board member (1987-91), Vereinigung Deutscher Wissenschaftler; Club of Rome (since 1991) **Discipline:** Biology; Environmental Policy **Related Areas of Interest:** Theory of Open Systems; Environmental Policy; Global Responsibility.

Selected Publications: His bibliography includes many papers on environmental policy, genetic engineering, energy and technology policy, and the theory of open systems.

_____, editor. *Offene Systeme I.* 2d ed. Stuttgart, 1986.
_____, Jochen Jesinghaus. *Ecological Tax Reform: Policy Proposal for Sustainable Development.* London, 1992.
_____. *Earth Politics.* London, 1994.
_____. *Erdpolitik.* 4th ed. Darmstadt, 1994.

Welker, Michael

Present Position and Address: Professor of Systematic Theology (since April 1991), Theological Faculty, University of Heidelberg, Heidelberg, Germany **Date of Birth:** November 20, 1947 **Education:** Dr. theol. (1973), University of Tübingen; Dr. phil. (1978), University of Heidelberg; Habilitation in Systematic Theology (1980), University of Tübingen **Lectures Presented:** Warfield Lectures (March 1991), "Creation and Reality," Princeton Theological Seminary **Previous Positions:** Wissenschaftlicher Angestellter (1973-74)/Assistant Professor (Wissenschaftlicher Assistent, 1975-80)/Privatdozent (1981-83)/Professor of Systematic Theology (1983-87), University of Tübingen; Honorary Research Fellow (1984-85), Institute for the Advanced Study of Religion, Divinity School, University of Chicago; Visiting Professor (1985-1986), McMaster University, Hamilton, ONT, Canada; Chair for Reformed Theology (1987-1991), University of Münster; Visiting Professor (1988, 89), Princeton Theological Seminary, NJ **Editorial Positions:** Coeditor of *Jahrbuch für Biblische Theologie*; *Neukirchener Beiträge zur Systematischen Theologie; Verkündigung und Forschung; Soundings; Evangelische Theologie; Studies in Reformed Theology and History; Dialog* **Other Academic Experience:** Ordained Theologian of the Evangelische Kirche der Pfalz **Discipline:** Theology; Philosophy **Related Areas of Interest:** Theological Cosmology and Whitehead's Metaphysics; General Theory and Luhmann's Functional Systems Theory; Theology of Creation; The Doctrine of the Holy Spirit; Theology of the Law; The Church in Pluralistic Societies.

Selected Publications: His bibliography lists some 13 books and about 80 articles in journals and books.

_____. *Universalität Gottes und Relativität der Welt. Theologische Kosmologie im Dialog mit dem amerikanischen Prozessdenken nach Whitehead.* Neukirchen, 1981; 2d ed. 1988.
_____. *Theologie und funktionale Systemtheorie. Luhmanns Religionssoziologie in theologischer Diskussion.* Frankfurt, 1985.
_____. *Kritik der Theorie sozialer Systeme. Zur Struktur und Funktion von Theorietechnik, Erziehung, Religion und Recht.* Frankfurt, 1991.
_____. *Gottes Geist. Theologie des Heiligen Geistes.* 2. Aufl. 1993. American translation, 1994. Italian and Korean translations, 1995.
_____. *Kirche im Pluralismus.* Kaiser Verlag, Gütersloh, 1995.
_____. "What is Creation? Rereading Genesis 1 and 2." *Theology Today* 56-71 (April 1991).

West, Charles C.

Present Position and Address: Professor of Christian Ethics (1963-1991), Princeton Theological Seminary, NJ; 157 Mountain Road, Ringoes, NJ 08551, USA **Date of Birth:** February 3, 1921 **Languages Spoken:** English, German, French **Education:** B.A. (1942), Columbia University; B.D. (1945), Union Theological Seminary NY; Ph.D. Ethics (1955), Yale University **Previous Positions:** Instructor (1948), Peking National University; Instructor and Chaplain (1948-49), Cheeloo University,

Hangchow, China; Instructor in Christian Ethics (1949-50), Nanking Theological Seminary; Industrial Missioner (1950-51), Mainz-Kastel, Germany; Instructor (1950-53), Kirchliche Hochschule, Berlin; Associate Director (1956-61), Ecumenical Institute, Bossey, World Council of Churches; Theology Faculty (1956-61), Charge de cours, University of Geneva; Associate Professor (1961-63), Princeton Theological Seminary **Selected Memberships:** Past President and Vice President, Society of Christian Ethics; Past President, Christians Associated for Relations with Eastern Europe; Past President and Vice President, American Theological Society; International Bonhoeffer Society; Fellow, Center of Theological Inquiry, Princeton, NJ; American Society of Missiology; International Association for Mission Studies **Discipline:** Christian Ethics, with a special concern for Missiology, Ecumenics and Political Theory **Related Areas of Interest:** Christian Ethics: The Roots of Knowledge, Moral and Metaphysical; Faith, Philosophy and Science; Political Ethics; Ethics and Technology; The Mission of the Christian Church, and the Interaction of Evangelism with Social Action.

Selected Publications:

_____. *The Power to be Human*. Macmillan, 1970.
_____. "Status Quo, Evolution or Revolution?" In *Technology and Social Justice*, ed. Ronald Preston. SCM and Judson, 1971.
_____. "Justice Within the Limits of the Created World." *Ecumenical Review* 27 (January 1975): 57-64. Rev. ed. in *Justice: Interdisciplinary and Global Perspectives*, ed. T. M. Thomas and Jesse Levitt. Lamham University Press of America, 1988.
_____. "Facts, Morals, and the Bomb." In *To Avoid Catastrophe*, ed. Michael Hamilton. Grand Rapids: Eerdmans, 1977.
_____. "God, Man/Woman, Creation." *Ecumenical Review* 33 (January 1981): 13-28.

Westfall, Richard S.

Present Position and Address: Distinguished Professor Emeritus of History and Philosophy of Science (1976), Indiana University, Goodbody Hall 130, Bloomington, IN 47405, USA **Work Phone:** (812) 855-3622 **Date of Birth:** April 22, 1924 **Education:** B.A. (1948)/M.A. (1949)/Ph.D. (1955), Yale University; Studies (1951-52), University College London **Lectures Presented:** Sarton Lecturer (1981), American Association for the Advancement of Science; Kalb Lecturer (1982), Rice University; Sigma Xi Lecturer (1985," 1987), Green Distinguished Lecturer (1987), University of Texas - Dallas; Principal's Visiting Scholar (1987), Queen's University, Canada; Gross Memorial Lecturer (1988), Valparaiso University **Awards and Honors:** Pfizer Award (1972, 1983), History of Science Society; Leo Gershoy Award (1981), American Historical Association; Sarton Medal (1985), History of Science Society; Distinguished Faculty Research Lecture Award (1985), Indiana University; Wilbur L. Cross Medal (1988), Yale Graduate School **Previous Positions:** Service in US Navy (1944-46); Instructor of History (1952-53), California Institute of Technology; Instructor and Assistant Professor of History (1953-57), State University of Iowa; Assistant and Associate Professor of History (1957-63), Grinnell College; Professor of History of Science (1963-76)/Professor of History (1966), Indiana University; Distinguished Professor of History of Science (1976), Indiana University; Visiting Professor (1980), University of Melbourne; Henry R. Luce Visiting Professor of Cosmology (1981), Mount Holyoke College; Vernon Professor of Biography (Summer 1988), Dartmouth College; Visiting Professor (1990-91), Harvard University **Selected Memberships:** American Historical Association; American Association of University Professors; Sigma Xi; Membre effectif, Académie International d'Histoire des Sciences; Past President, History of Science Society; Council member and Fellow, American Academy of Arts and Sciences; Fellow, Royal Society of Literature; Fellow, Indiana University Institute of Advanced Study **Discipline:** History and Philosophy of Science **Related Areas of Interest:** Science and Christianity in the 17th Century.

Selected Publications: His bibliography lists 9 books and 104 articles.

_____. "Newton, Sir Isaac." In *The New Catholic Encyclopedia*, vol. 10, 424-8. Washington, DC, 1967.
_____. *Never at Rest. A Biography of Isaac Newton*. New York: Cambridge University Press, 1980.
_____. "Newton's theological manuscripts." In *Contemporary Newtonian Research*, ed. Z. Bechler, 129-43. Dordrecht, 1982.
_____. "Isaac Newton's Theologiae Gentilis Origines Philosophicae." In *The Secular Mind. Transformations of Faith in Modern Europe*, ed. W. Warren Wagar, 15-34. New York, 1982.
_____. "The Rise of Science and the Decline of Orthodox Christianity: A Study of Kepler, Descartes, and Newton." In *God and Nature. Historical Essays on the Encounter between Christianity and Science*, ed. David C. Lindberg and Ronald L. Numbers, 218-37. Berkeley, CA, 1986.
_____. "Newton and Christianity." In *Religion, Science, and Public Policy*, ed. Frank T. Birtel, 79-95. New York, 1987.
_____. "Newton's Scientific Personality." *Journal of the History of Ideas* 48 (1987): 551-70.
_____. "Galileo and the Jesuits." In *Metaphysics and Philosophy of Science in the Seventeenth and Eighteenth Centuries*, ed. R. S. Woodhouse, 45-72. Dordrecht, 1988.
_____. "The Trial of Galileo: Bellarmino, Galileo, and the Clash of Two Worlds." *Journal for the History of Astronomy* 20 (1989): 1-23.
_____. *Essays on the Trial of Galileo*. Vatican City State: Vatican Observatory Publications, 1989.

Westman, Robert

Present Position and Address: Professor (since 1988), Department of History/Science Studies Program, University of California - San Diego, CA 92093-0104, USA **Date of Birth:** October 21, 1941 **Languages Read and/or Spoken:** English, French, German, Spanish, Italian, Latin, Russian **Education:** B.A. History (Honors, 1963)/M.A. History (1965)/C.Phil. History (1966)/Ph.D. History of Science (1971), University of Michigan; Visiting Graduate Fellow (1967-69), Department of History of Science and Technology, Imperial College, University of London **Previous Positions:** Instructor (1965-66), Wayne State University; Acting Assistant Professor of History (1969-71)/Associate Professor of History (1974-80)/Professor (1980-88), University of California - Los Angeles; Visiting Fellow (1977-78), Department of History and Philosophy of Science, University of Cambridge **Editorial Positions:** Advisory Editor, *Isis* (1981-84); *The Conceptual Foundations of Science* (University of Chicago Press, since 1981); *Science in Context* **Selected Memberships:** History of Science Society; British Society for the History of Science; International Astronomical Union; 16th Century Studies Society; Renaissance Society of America; Corresponding Member, International Academy of the History of Science; Associate, UCLA Center for Medieval and Renaissance Studies **Discipline:** History; History of Science **Related Areas of Interest:** The Nature of Scientific Discovery; The Encounter of Christianity and Science.

Selected Publications: His bibliography lists 5 books, over 22 articles and more than 13 reviews.

_____. "The Wittenberg Interpretation of the Copernican Theory." In *The Nature of Scientific Discovery*, by O. Gingerich, 393-429; 430-57. Washington, DC: Smithsonian Institute, 1975.
_____. "Magical Reform and Astronomical Reform: The Yates Thesis Reconsidered." In *Hermeticism and the Scientific Revolution*, by Robert Westman and J. E. McGuire, 1-91. Los Angeles: William Andrews Clark Memorial Library, 1977.
_____. "Nature, Art, and Psyche: Jung, Pauli and the Kepler-Fludd Polemic." In *Occult and Scientific Mentalities in the Renaissance*, ed. Brian Vickers, 177-230. Cambridge: Cambridge University Press, 1984.
_____. "The Copernicans and the Churches." In *God and Nature: Historical Essays on the Encounter of Christianity and Science*, ed. D. C. Lindberg and R. L. Numbers, 76-113. Berkeley and Los Angeles: University of California Press, 1986.
_____. "La préface de Copernic au Pape: Esthétique Humaniste et Réforme de l'Eglise." *History and Technology* 4 (1987): 365-84.

_____, O. Gingerich. *The Wittich Connection: Conflict and Priority in Sixteenth Century Cosmology, Transactions of the American Philosophical Society*, vol. 78, no. 7. Philadelphia: The American Philosophical Society, 1988.

_____. "Proof, Poetics, and Patronage: Copernicus' Preface to De Revolutionibuss." In *Reappraisals of the Scientific Revolution*, ed. Robert Westman and David C. Lindberg, 167-205. Cambridge: Cambridge University Press, 1990.

_____. "The Duhemian Historiographical Project." *Synthese* 83, 2 (1990): 373-89.

_____. "Two Cultures or One? A Second Look at Kuhn's *The Copernican Revolution.*" *Isis* 85 (1994): 79-115.

_____. *Prophecy and Celestial Order. The Evolution of the Copernican Question.* Chicago: University of Chicago Press, forthcoming.

Wheeler, David L.

Present Position and Address: Professor of Theology, Central Baptist Theological Seminary, 741 N. 31 Street, Kansas City, KS 66102 **Work Phone:** (913) 371-5313 **Fax Number:** (913) 371-8110 **Date of Birth:** December 8, 1946 **Languages Spoken:** Spanish; Reading knowledge, French, German, Greek, Latin **Education:** BA (1968), Georgetown College, KY; M. Div. (1971), Yale Divinity School; Th. D. (1984), Graduate Theological Union **Postgraduate Experience:** Further studies in philosophy (since 1991), University of Kansas **Field Work:** Theologian in Residence (1991-94), Village Presbyterian Church, Prairie Village, KS **Congresses and** Conferences: Seminars on "Science and Faith" and related issues. Similar conferences in churches throughout the midwest **Lectures Presented:** Sessions of Central States SBL/AAR (1989-94), "Cosmic Christology," "Toward a Process-Relational Christian Soteriology," "Here and Hereafter," "The Theological Context of Francis Bacon's Revolution" **Awards and Honors:** "Luther Wesley Smith Citation for Christian Higher Education" (1989), American Baptist Churches Board of Educational Ministries **Previous Positions:** Baptist Church pastorates in Flushing, NY, San Francisco, CA, Elizabeth, NJ, Kansas City, KS; Adjunct or visiting professor, American Baptist Seminary of the West, Montclair State College, St. Mary College, Leavenworth, KS, Donnelly College, Kansas City, KS, Baker University, Baldwin City, KS, Nazarene Theological Seminary, Kansas City, MO, Northern Baptist Theological Seminary, Chicago, IL, Instituto Teológico Bautista, Santa Ana, El Salvador **Selected Memberships:** AAR; Baptist Association of Philosophy Teachers; Society of Christian Philosophers **Discipline:** Systematic Theology; Philosophical Theology **Related Areas of Interest:** Christology/Soteriology; Process-Relational Thought **Current Areas of Research:** Objective Effect(s) of Christian Redemptive Event(s) upon Humanity and Cosmos; Action of God in the World; Reciprocal Relationships between God and World.

Selected Publications: His bibliography contains 1 book, 11 published articles, and 2 articles forthcoming.

_____. "Toward a Process-Relational Christian Soteriology." *Process Studies* 18, 2 (1989).

_____. *A Relational View of the Atonement.* Peter Lang, 1989.

_____. "Cosmic Christology." *Explorations* 8, 3 (1990).

_____. "Is the Divine Gendered?" *Explorations* 12, 3 (1994).

_____. "Toward a Process-Relational Christian Eschatology." *Process Studies* 22, 2 (Forthcoming).

Whipple, Andrew P.

Present Position and Address: Professor of Biology (since 1991), Taylor University, Upland, IN 46989, USA; (Home) 9477 East 500 South, P.O. Box 448, Upland, IN 46989, USA **Work Phone:** (317) 998-5333 **Home Phone:** (317) 998-7992 **Fax Number:** (317) 998-4940 **Date of Birth:** February 12, 1949 **Education:** B.S. Microbiology/Biochemistry (1971), Ohio State University; M.S. Biochemistry (1974)/Ph.D. Cell Biology (1979), State University of New York - Albany **Postgraduate Experience:** Postdoctoral Research Fellow (1979-81), Sidney Farber Cancer Institute, Harvard Medical School; Participant (1980), National Cancer Institute Course, Histopathobiology of Cancer, Lake

Placid, NY **Previous Positions:** Research Assistant (1975-78)/University Fellow (1979), Biology Department/Instructor in the Biology of Cancer (graduate level course, 1979), State University of New York - Albany; Instructor in Microbiology (1979), Hudson Valley Community College; Instructor (1981-82), McDowell Technical College; Professor of Biology (1981-84), Montreat-Anderson College; Assistant through Associate Professor of Biology (1986-91), Taylor University; Summer Faculty Research Fellow (1987 and 88), Biochemistry Branch, Toxic Hazards Division, Aerospace Medical Research Lab., Wright-Patterson Air Force Base; Visiting Professor of Biology (1992-93), Tunghai University, Taichung, Taiwan, Republic of China **Selected Memberships:** American Association for the Advancement of Science; American Scientific Affiliation; American Society for Cell Biology; Society of Chinese Bioscientists in America; Tissue Culture Association **Discipline:** Cell Biology **Related Areas of Interest:** Harmonizing Revelation in the Word and in the World.

Selected Publications: His bibliography lists 9 articles and 13 abstracts.

_____. "Science and Creationism." *Nature* 333 (1988): 492.

Whipple, Elden C.

Present Position and Address: Center for Astrophysics and Space Sciences, C-011 (since 1975), University of California - San Diego, La Jolla, CA 92093, USA **Date of Birth:** January 17, 1931 **Education:** Diploma (1951), Multnomah Bible School, Portland, OR; Studies (1951-52), University of British Columbia, Vancouver, BC, Canada; B.S. (1955), Wheaton College; M.S. and Ph.D. Physics (1965), George Washington University **Awards and Honors:** NASA Award (1965), for patent **Previous Positions:** The Naval Research Laboratory (1955-58); Goddard Space Flight Center, Greenbelt, MD (1958-1965); National Oceanic and Atmospheric Administration, Boulder, CO (1965-1975) **Selected Memberships:** American Physical Society; American Geophysical Union; American Institute of Aeronautics and Astronautics; American Scientific Affiliation **Discipline:** Physics - especially the Physics of Plasmas in Space **Related Areas of Interest:** Fundamental Concepts of Physics and Theology.

Selected Publications: Most of his publications are technical works concerning the upper atmosphere and space.

_____. "Events as Fundamental Entities in Physics." *Il Nuovo Cimento* 92A (April 1986): 309-27.

White, David C.

Present Position and Address: Professor of Microbiology and Ecology/Distinguished Scientist and Research Scientist of Oak Ridge National Laboratory/Director (since 1986), Institute of Applied Microbiology, University of Tennessee, 10515 Research Drive, Suite 300, Knoxville, TN 37932-2575, USA **Work Phone:** (615) 974-8030 **E-Mail:** PA112238@utkvml.utk.edu **Date of Birth:** May 18, 1929 **Education:** A.B. (*magna cum laude*, 1951), Dartmouth College; M.D. (1955), Tufts University School of Medicine; Ph.D. (1962), Rockefeller University; Internship (1955-56), Internship Hospital, University of Pennsylvania **Previous Positions:** Military service (1956-58), research in aviation medicine, Aviation Medical Acceleration Laboratory, Naval Air Development Center; Assistant Professor through Professor of Biochemistry (1962-72), University of Kentucky Medical Center; Professor of Biological Sciences (1973-85)/Associate Director (1973-84), Program in Medical Sciences, Florida State University **Selected Memberships:** Society of Toxicology; American Chemical Society; American Society of Mass Spectroscopists; American Society of Microbiology; Society of General Microbiology; Society Limnology of Oceanography; Society of Organic Geochemistry; American Society of Biological Chemists and Molecular Biologists; Society of Industrial Microbiology **Discipline:** Medicine; Microbiology; Ecology **Related Areas of Interest:** Biotechnology and Its Implications to Theology.

Selected Publications: His bibliography lists 365 publications.

_____. *Sex, Drugs and Pollution: A Biological Basis for Human Decision.* Rev. ed. Raleigh NC: Contemporary Publishing Co., 1978.

White, Rhea A.

Present Position and Address: Director, Exceptional Human Experience Network, 2 Plane Tree Lane, Dix Hills, NY 11746, USA **Concurrent Positions:** Founder/Director (since 1981), Parapsychology Sources of Information Center, Dix Hills, NY; Founder/Producer (since 1983), Psiline Database; Half-time librarian, East Meadow Public Library (since 1965) **Work/Home Phone:** (516) 271-1243 **Date of Birth:** May 6, 1931 **Education:** B.A. (1953), Pennsylvania State University; M.L.S. (1965), Pratt Institute Library School **Previous Positions:** Research Fellow (1954-58), Parapsychology Laboratory, Duke University; Research Assistant (1959), Foundation for Integral Research, NYC; Research Fellow (1963-65), Menninger Foundation, Topeka, KS; Librarian (1965-67), Department of Psychiatry, Maimonides Medical Center, Brooklyn, NY; Director of Information (1965-80), American Society for Psychical Research, NYC **Editorial Positions:** Research and Editorial Associate (1959-62), American Society for Psychical Research, NYC; Founder/Editor (since 1983), *Exceptional Human Experience*; Editor, *Journal of the American Society for Psychical Research* (since 1984) **Discipline:** Librarian; Journal Editor; Parapsychologist; Author **Related Areas of Interest:** Parapsychology, Philosophy and Religious Concepts.

Selected Publications: Her bibliography lists 10 books, 20 chapters in books, and 33 articles.

_____. "The Future of Parapsychology." *Journal of Religion and Psychical Research* 6, 3 (1983): 220-6.
_____. "Parapsychology and the Transcendent." *Christian Parapsychologist* 5 (March 1984): 138-49. First published in *1983 Annual Proceedings of The Academy of Religion and Psychical Research*, 65-78. 1984.
_____. "Science, Mysticism, and Consciousness: Is There a Place for Parapsychology?" In *1985 Annual Conference Proceedings of the Academy of Religion and Psychical Research*, 56-71. 1986.
_____. "Meaning, Metanoia, and Psi." In *Parapsychology, Philosophy and Religious Concepts*, ed. B. Shapin and L. Coly, 167-89. New York: Parapsychology Foundation, 1987.
_____. "Exceptional Human Experience as Vehicles of Grace: Parapsychology, Faith , and the Outlier Mentality." In *1993 Proceedings of the Academy of Religion and Psychical Research*, 46-55.
_____. "Seek Ye First the Kingdom of Heaven: What are EHEs and What Can We Do About Them?" In *1992 Academy of Religion and Psychical Research Annual Conference Proceedings*, 1-42. Abridgment. *Spiritual Frontiers*, 25, 4 (1993): 155-60.
_____. "Exceptional Human Experiences and the More That We Are: EHEs and Identity. In *1994 Annual Academy of Religion and Psychical Research Conference Proceedings*, 77-88.
_____. "Psychic and Mystical Experiences and the Necessity to Proceed in a New Way." *Spiritual Frontiers* 26, 1-2 (1994): 3-6.
_____. "A Dynamic View of Psi Experience: By Their Fruits Ye Shall Know Them." In *Exceptional Human Experience: Background Papers*, by R. A. White. Dix Hills, NY: Exceptional Human Experience Network, 1994.
_____. "Exceptional Human Experiences as Vehicles of Grace: Parapsychology, Faith, and the Outlier Mentality." In Exceptional Human Experience: Background Papers, by R. A. White. Dix Hills, NY: Exceptional Human Experience Network, 1994.

Whitrow, Gerald James

Present Position and Address: Professor Emeritus/Senior Research Fellow (since 1979), Mathematics Department, Imperial College, London SW7 2AZ, UK; (Home) 41 Home Park Road, Wimbledon, London SW19 7HS, UK **Date of Birth:** June 9, 1912 **Education:** B.A. (1933)/M.A. (1937)/D.Phil.

(1939), Oxford University **Previous Positions:** Lecturer (1936-40), Christ Church, Oxford; Scientific Officer (1940-45), Ministry of Supply; Lecturer (1945-51)/Reader in Applied Mathematics (1951-71)/Professor of the History and Applications of Mathematics (1972-79), Imperial College, University of London; Robert Schlapp Lecturer (1970), University of Edinburgh; George Gibson Lecturer (1977), University of Glasgow **Selected Memberships:** Fellow (since 1940), Royal Astronomical Society; President (1967), British Society of the Philosophy of Science; President (1968-70), British Society of the History of Science; President (1971-73), British Society of the History of Mathematics **Discipline:** Mathematics; History of Mathematics **Related Areas of Interest:** Cosmology; Relativity; History of Science.

Selected Publications: His bibliography lists joint authorship for books on atoms, time, and Einstein, as well as the editing of Kant's *Cosmogony* and the inclusion of a long introductory essay.

_____. *The Structure of the Universe.* London: Hutchinson, 1949.
_____. *The Structure and Evolution of the Universe.* London: Hutchinson, 1959.
_____. *What Is Time?* London: Thames and Hudson, 1972.
_____. *The Natural Philosophy of Time.* 2d. rev. and enl. ed. Oxford University Press, 1980.
_____. *Time in History.* Oxford University Press, 1988.

Wicken, Jeffrey S.

Present Position and Address: Professor of Biochemistry, Penn State - Erie, The Behrend College, Division of Science, Engineering and Technology, Station Road, Erie, PA 16563-0203, USA **Editorial Positions:** Advisory Board, *Zygon*; Editorial Board, *Bridges* (a new journal in Science, Philosophy and Religion) **Selected Memberships:** Associate, Chicago Center for Theology and Science **Related Areas of Interest:** The Philosophical and Theological problems of an Evolutionary Cosmos.

Selected Publications: His bibliography lists 31 publications.

_____. "Chance, Necessity and Purpose: Toward a Philosophy of Evolution." *Zygon* 16 (1981): 303-22.
_____. "The Cosmic Breath: Reflections on the Thermodynamics of Creation." *Zygon* 19 (1984): 487-505.
_____. "On the Increase in Complexity in Evolution." In *Beyond Neo-Darwinism*, ed. M. W. Ho and P. T. Saunders, 89-112. London: Academic Press, 1984.
_____. *Evolution, Thermodynamics, and Information: Extending the Darwinian Program.* New York: Oxford University Press, 1987.
_____. "Thermodynamics, Information, and Emergence: Ingredients for a New Synthesis." In *Entropy, Information and Evolution*, ed. B. Weber, D. Depew, and J. Smith. Cambridge, MA: MIT Press, 1988.
_____. "Science and Religion in the Evolving Cosmos." *Zygon* 23 (1988): 45-55.
_____. "Toward an Ecology of Meaning." *Zygon* (Forthcoming).
_____. "Darwinism and the Humanities." *Bridges* (Forthcoming).

Wickler, Wolfgang

Present Position and Address: Professor of Zoology (since 1976), University of Munich; Director (since 1974), Max-Planck-Institut für Verhaltensphysiologie, D-82319 Seewiesen, Germany **Date of Birth:** November 18, 1931 **Languages Spoken:** German, English **Education:** Doctorate in Biology (1956), University of Münster **Previous Positions:** Researcher (1956-59); Staff Member (1960-1973), Max-Planck-Institut, Seewiesen **Editorial Positions:** Chief Editor, *Ethology* **Discipline:** Zoology; Administration **Related Areas of Interest:** Bioethics **Current Areas of Research:** Eco-sociology (impact of ecological factors on social behavior and social structures in animals) with special interest in the evolution of monogamy; Evolution and selective consequences of vocal dueting in birds; Traditive behavior in animals, especially its spreading through populations and its influence on genetically transmitted behavior traits. Interdisciplinary cooperation with archaeologists, linguists and moral philosophers.

Selected Publications:

_____. *The Biology of the Ten Commandments*. N.p., n.d.
_____. *Verhalten und Umwelt*. N.p., n.d.
_____, U. Seibt. *männlich weiblich. Der große Unterschied und seine Folgen*. München/Zürich: R. Piper & Co. Verlag, 1983.
_____. *Das Prinzip Eigennutz. Zur Evolution sozialen Verhaltens*. München/Zürich: R. Piper & Co. Verlag, 1991.

Wiebe, Donald

Present Position and Address: Professor (since 1987), Trinity College, University of Toronto, Toronto, ONT M5S 1A1, Canada **Date of Birth:** April 29, 1943 **Languages Spoken:** English **Education:** B.Th. Theology (1967), Mennonite Brethren College of Arts; B.A. (1967), Wilfred Laurier University; M.A. Philosophy (1970), University of Guelph; Ph.D. Religious Studies (1974), University of Lancaster, UK **Previous Positions:** Lecturer (1965-67), Canadian Nazarene College; Lecturer (1967-69), Winkler Bible Institute; Sessional Lecturer - University of Guelph (1969-70)/Winnipeg and Manitoba (1977-80); Lecturer (1973-74), Workers Educational Association; Assistant Professor (1975-77), Canadian Nazarene College; Assistant Professor (1980), Trinity College, University of Toronto; Appointed (1980), Advance Degree Faculty, Toronto School of Theology; Cross-appointed (1981), Centre of Religious Studies of School of Graduate Studies/Associate Professor of Trinity College (1982-92), University of Toronto **Selected Memberships:** North American Association for the Study of Religion; Canadian Society for the Study of Religion; American Academy of Religion; International Association for the History of Religions **Discipline:** Religious Studies; Philosophy **Related Areas of Interest:** Science and Religion in the Modern World; Science, Religion, and Rationality; Philosophy and Theology; Method in the Study of Religion.

Selected Publications: His bibliography lists 6 books, 63 articles, and 51 reviews.

_____. "Can Theology Withstand the Impact of Modern Science?" M.A. thesis, 1970, University of Guelph.
_____. "'Comprehensively Critical Rationalism' and Commitment." *Philosophical Studies* 21 (1973): 186-201.
_____. "Science, Religion, and Rationality: Problems of Method in Science and Religion." Ph.D. diss., University of Lancaster, 1974.
_____. "Explanation and Theological Method." *Zygon* 2 (1976): 35-49.
_____. "Science and Religion: Is Compatibility Possible?" *Journal of the American Scientific Affiliation* 30 (1978): 169-76.
_____. "Religion Transcending Science Transcending Religion." *The Dalhousie Review* 65 (1985): 196-206.
_____. "An Unholy Alliance? The Creationists' Quest for Scientific Legitimation." *Toronto Journal of Theology* 4 (1988): 162-77.
_____. "Is Science Really an Implicit Religion?" *Studies in Religion* 18 (1989): 171-83.
_____. "Religion, Science and the Transformation of 'Knowledge'." *Sophia* 32 (1993): 36-49.
_____. "Religion and the Scientific Impulse in the Nineteenth Century: Friedrich Max Müller and the Birth of the Science of Religion." *International Journal for Comparative Religions* (Forthcoming).

Wiebe, Phillip Howard

Present Position and Address: Professor of Philosophy (since 1988), Trinity Western University, Langley, BC V3A 6A9, Canada; (Home) 20015 50A Avenue, Langley, BC V3A 7HS, Canada **Work Phone:** (604) 888-7511 ext. 2334 **Home Phone:** (604) 533-2352 **Date of Birth:** August 23, 1945 **Languages Spoken:** English, German **Education:** B.A. Philosophy (1967)/M.A. Philosophy (1969), University of Manitoba; Ph.D. (1973), University of Adelaide, Australia **Previous Positions:** Sessional

Lecturer in Philosophy (1972-73), University of Manitoba; Assistant Professor of Philosophy (1973-78), Brandon University, Manitoba; Associate Professor of Philosophy (1978-88), Trinity Western University **Discipline:** Philosophy **Related Areas of Interest:** Philosophy of Science; Epistemology; Ethics; 20th Century Philosophy.

Selected Publications: His bibliography lists 1 book and 5 articles.

_____. *Theism in an Age of Science.* Lanham, MD: University Press of America, 1988.

Wiester, John L.

Present Position and Address: Chairman, Committee for Integrity in Science Education, American Scientific Affiliation; 7820 Santa Rosa Road, Buellton, CA 93427, USA **Date of Birth:** January 6, 1935 **Education:** B.S. Geology (1956)/M.B.A. (1958), Stanford University **Previous Positions:** Vice President Finance, Secretary Treasurer (1962-66)/Vice President Operations (1966-67), Redcor Corporation, Canoga Park, CA; President (1967-71), Astro Industries, Santa Barbara, CA **Selected Memberships:** Fellow, American Scientific Affiliation **Discipline:** Geology **Related Areas of Interest:** Science and Genesis 1; Science Education, especially High School.

Selected Publications:

_____. *The Genesis Connection.* Nashville: Thomas Nelson, 1983.
_____, Walter Russell Hearn, and D. Price. *Teaching Science in a Climate of Controversy.* Ipswich, MA: American Scientific Affiliation, 1986.
_____. "Teaching Evolution as Non-Science: Examples from California's 1990 *Science Framework.*" *Perspectives on Science and Christian Faith* (*PSCF*) 43, 3 (1991): 190-2.
_____. "How Science Works: The Views of Gingerich and Johnson." *PSCF* 44, 4 (1992): 249-52.
_____. "The Real Meaning of Evolution." *PSCF* 45, 3 (1993): 182-6.
_____. "Distorting for Darwinism: *NSTA Reports!*' Review of *Teaching Science in a Climate of Controversy.*" *PSCF* 46, 2 (1994): 128-32.

Wilbur, Frank H.

Present Position and Address: Professor of Biology/Head of Biology Department (since 1988), Asbury College, Wilmore, KY 40390, USA; (Home) 130 Cherrybrook Drive, Nicholasville, KY 40356, USA **Work Phone:** (606) 858-3511 ext 232 **Home Phone:** (606) 885-3024 **Date of Birth:** May 26, 1943 **Education:** B.S. Biology (1965), Washington and Lee University; Ph.D. Biology (1970), University of Virginia **Previous Positions:** Assistant Professor of Biology (1970-74), Mary Baldwin College; Assistant (1970-80)/Associate (1980-86)/Professor of Biology (1986-88), Oral Roberts University; Bacteriologist/Clinical Parasitologist/Mycologist (1974-77), King's Daughters' Hospital, VA; Guest Professor (1979-84)/Director of Nova Scotia Field Station, Canada (Summers 1980-84), Barrington College, RI **Selected Memberships:** Sigma Xi; American Scientific Affiliation; National Association of Biology Teachers **Discipline:** Biology **Related Areas of Interest:** Creation/Evolution; Role and Limitations of Scientific Inquiry; Scientific Integrity.

Selected Publications:

_____. *Horse Teeth and Heresy: Learning to Distinguish Among Science, Pseudoscience and Religion.* N.p., 1986.
_____. "Natural Science and the Supernatural." Forthcoming.
_____. "Learning to Differentiate Among Science, Pseudoscience, and Religion." Forthcoming.

Wilcox, David Linwood

Present Position and Address: Professor (since 1976), Eastern College; 412 Hillview Road, King of Prussia, PA 19406, USA **Work Phone:** (215) 341-5864 **Home Phone:** (215) 265-9011 **Date of Birth:** August 27, 1943 **Education:** B.S. Biology (1965), Geneva College; Studies in Medicine (1965-69), University of Colorado Medical School; Ph.D. Genetics (1981), Pennsylvania State University **Previous Positions:** Assistant Professor (1970-75), Edinboro State College **Selected Memberships:** Sigma Xi; Sigma Zeta; Chair of Creation Commission, American Scientific Affiliation; Society for the Study of Evolution **Discipline:** Genetics; Biology **Related Areas of Interest:** Theoretical Structure of Evolutionary Mechanisms; Theological and Historical Dimensions of Conflict (Evolution/Creation).

Selected Publications: His bibliography lists 13 publications.

_____. "A Christian Integrative Framework for Biology." *Christian Scholar's Review* 12 (1983): 339-48.
_____. "A Taxonomy of Creation." *Journal of the American Scientific Affiliation* (*JASA*) 38, 4 (1986): 244-50.
_____. "Three Models of Making: Prime Mover, Craftsman and King." *Perspectives on Science and Christian Faith* (*PSCF*) 39, 4 (1987): 212-20.
_____. "Let Science and Religion Disengage!" *The Scientist* 2 (1987).
_____. "Of Messages and Molecules; What is the Essence of Life?" *PSCF* 41, 4 (1989): 227-31.
_____. *The Creation: Spoken in Eternity, Established in Time.* Submitted to Duke, 1990.
_____. "Adam, where are You? A Paradigm Shift in Paleoanthropology." *Pascal Center Notebook* (1991).
_____. "Cohort Analysis of Human mtDNA Geneologies." Forthcoming.

Wilder-Smith, Arthur Ernest

Present Position and Address: Consultant/freelance Lecturer on Pharmacology and Drug Abuse, "Roggern", CH-3646, Einigen am Thunersee, Switzerland **Work Phone:** 033 545408 **Date of Birth:** December 22, 1915 **Languages Spoken:** English, French, German, Norwegian **Education:** 1st Public Exam in Natural Sciences (1935), Oxford University; B.Sc. (general) Botany, Zoology and Chemistry (1937)/B.Sc. (Hon. Chem., 1938)/Ph.D. Physical Organic Chemistry (1941), Reading University **Postgraduate Experience:** P.D. (Habil. med., 1956), École de Médecine, Genève; D.Sc. (1964), E.T.H., Zürich; Dr ès sciences (1964), Genéve **Lectures Presented:** Lecture tours on Drug Abuse and Biogenesis in most European universities (1971)/20 US and Canadian universities (1981, 1984, 1986)/Australia, New Zealand and Thailand (1987) **Previous Positions:** Associate (1943)/Fellow (1945), Royal Society of Chemistry, London; Consultant on Drug Abuse Prevention (1971-77), in Rank of General (3 star) to NATO Near East and Europe; Technical Assistant (1940-45), I.C.I. Ltd.; Fellow in Cancer Research (1945-49), Middlesex Hospital, London; Chief of Research (1951-55), Geistlich Soehne Ltd., Lucerne; Privat Docent (1956-64), École de Médecine; Visiting Assistant Professor (1957-58)/Professor of Pharmacology (1964-70), University of Illinois Medical Center, Chicago; Visiting Professor of Pharmacology (1960-62), University of Bergen, Norway **Consultancies:** Chemotherapy (1955-60), Chemical Industry in Basel; Pharmacology (1958-60), British Pharmaceutical Firm; Drug Abuse (1970-77), US Army and Air Force in Europe; Pharmacological Research in Europe (1958-60); Consultant (1946-47), BAOR on German Affairs with rank equivalent to Lt. Colonel (1958-60), Armour Pharmaceutical Corp., Kalamazoo; (1956-58), Leprostatics and tuberculostatics, Bengué Pharmaceuticals, England; (1955-64), Sapos S. A., Geneva; President (1979-87), Pro Universitate Student and Academic Seminars in Germany and Denmark **Media Work:** TV videotapes and interviews **Selected Memberships:** Sigma Xi; Rho Chi; American Association for the Advancement of Science; Fellow, Royal Society of Chemistry **Discipline:** Pharmaceutics; Drug Abuse Awareness **Related Areas of Interest:** Creation/Evolution.

Selected Publications: His bibliography lists 34 books and 54 articles.

_____. *Man's Origin, Man's Destiny.* Wheaton, IL: Harold Shaw Publishers, 1968.
_____. *The Creation of Life, A Cabernetic Approach to Evolution.* Wheaton, IL: Harold Shaw Publishers, 1970.
_____. *Basis for a New Biology, An Alternative Biological Perception.* Stuttgart: Telos Verlag, 1974.
_____. *The Natural Sciences Know Nothing of Evolution.* San Diego: Creation-Life Publishers, 1981.
_____. *He Who Thinks Has to Believe.* San Diego: Master Books, 1982.
_____. *Ein Naturwissenschaftler auf der Kanzel.* Berneck, Switzerland: Schwengeler Verlag, 1983.
_____. *The Scientific Alternative to Evolutionary Theory.* Costa Mesa, CA: TWFT, 1988.

Wildiers, Max

Present Position and Address: Retired Professor of Theology (since 1974); 44 Kerklei, Brecht 2960, Belgium **Date of Birth:** July 29, 1904 **Languages Spoken:** Dutch, English, French, German, Italian **Education:** Humanities, Philosophy, Theology, Biology. Ph.D. Theology (1932), Gregorian University, Rome **Previous Positions:** (1932-40), Seminary S. Bonaventure; (1940-64), K.V. Hogeschool, Antwerp; (1940-64), Higher Institute for Social Work, Louvain; (1964-74), University of San Francisco; (1965-74), University of Louvain; (1975), University of Alberta, Canada; Visiting Lecturer - University of California - Berkeley/G.T.U., Berkeley/Newman Theological College, Edmonton, Canada; G.T.U. Dubuque, IA; several universities in Europe **Discipline:** Theology; Philosophy; Biology; Humanities **Related Areas of Interest:** Philosophy of Science; History of Cosmology; Biological Evolution.

Selected Publications: His bibliography includes 14 books.

_____. *Evolutionisme en Wereldbeschouwing* (Evolution and world picture). N.p., 1952.
_____. *Teilhard de Chardin: Een Enleiding in zijn Denken.* N.p.,1960. Translated into French, German, Italian, Spanish, Portuguese, Polish, Japanese, Serbo-Croatian and English: *An Introduction to Teilhard de Chardin*, trans. Hubert Hoskins. New York: Harper & Row, 1968.
_____. *Theologie en Wereldbeeld.* N.p., 1973. Translated into German, Polish and English: *The Theologian and His Universe: Theology and Cosmology from the Middle Ages to the Present.* New York: The Seabury Press, 1982.
_____. *De Muziek der Sferen* (The music of the spheres). Essays. N.p., 1983.
_____. *Theologie op nieuwe wegen* (New roads in theology). N.p., 1985.
_____. *Kosmologie in de Westerse Cultuur* (Cosmology in western culture). N.p., 1988.

Wilkins III, Walter J.

Present Position and Address: Assistant Professor of History/Philosophy (since 1985), Virginia Wesleyan College, Wesleyan Drive, Norfolk, VA 23502, USA **Work Phone:** (804) 455-3235 **Date of Birth:** November 30, 1950 **Education:** B.S. (1973), Washington and Lee University; M.Div. (1978), Austin Presbyterian Theological Seminary; Ph.D. (1985), Florida State University **Previous Positions:** Teaching Assistant (1982-85), Humanities Program, Florida State University **Selected Memberships:** American Academy of Religion; American Historical Association; American Society of Church History; Institute on Religion in an Age of Science; Center for Theology and the Natural Sciences **Discipline:** Interdisciplinary teaching of History and Philosophy courses focusing on cultural history **Related Areas of Interest:** Darwinism and Christian thought; Contemporary Physics and Theological Construction; Medieval Science and Sexuality.

Selected Publications:

_____. *Science and Religious Thought: A Darwinism Case Study.* Ann Arbor: University of Michigan Research Press, 1987.

Williams, George C.

Present Position and Address: Professor Emeritus of Ecology and Evolution, State University of New York (SUNY) - Stony Brook, NY 11794, USA **Date of Birth:** May 12, 1926 **Languages Spoken:** English, Icelandic **Education:** A.B. (1949), University of California - Berkeley; Ph.D. Zoology (1955), University of California - Los Angeles **Previous Positions:** Teaching (1955-60), Michigan State University **Selected Memberships:** Society for the Study of Evolution; American Society of Naturalists; American Association for the Advancement Science **Discipline:** Biology **Related Areas of Interest:** Evolutionary Theory; Evolution and Ethics.

Selected Publications: His bibliography lists 19 publications since 1980.

James Paradis and G. C. Williams, eds. *Evolution and Ethics: T. H. Huxley's "Evolution and Ethics" with New Essays on its Victorian and Sociobiological Context.* Princeton: Princeton University Press, 1989.
_____. "Ruminations on Ruse and Religion." *Zygon* 29 (1994): 37-43.

Willis, David L.

Present Position and Address: Professor Emeritus of Radiation Biology (since 1987), Oregon State University - Corvallis, OR, USA; 3135 NW McKinley Drive, Corvallis, OR 97330, USA **Date of Birth:** March 15, 1927 **Education:** B.Th. (1949), Biola Seminary, LA; B.A. Bible (1951), Biola University; A.A. Science (1951), Pasadena City College; B.S. General Science (1952), Wheaton College; M.A. Biology (1954), California State University - Long Beach; Ph.D. Radiation Biology (1963), Oregon State **Previous Positions:** Science teacher (1952-54), Brethren High School, Paramount, CA; Science teacher and Department Chairman (1954-57), Anaheim Union High School District; State Park Naturalist (summers 1954-56), California State Park System; Biology Instructor (1957-61), Fullerton College, CA; Visiting Investigator (1968-69), Radiation Ecology Section, Oak Ridge National Laboratory, TN; NSF Science Faculty Fellow (1961-62); Assistant (1962-65); Associate Professor of Biology (1965-71); Professor of Radiation Biology (1971-87)/Acting (1967-68) and Department Chairman (1969-85)/Special Assistant to Dean of Science (1986-87), Oregon State University **Selected Memberships:** Fellow, American Scientific Affiliation; Radiation Research Society; Health Physics Society **Discipline:** Radiation Biology with emphasis on Radionuclide Metabolism and Environmental Radioactivity **Related Areas of Interest:** Creation/Evolution; Origins and Change.

Selected Publications: His bibliography lists 12 books and manuals and 16 articles.

_____, editor. *Origins and Change: Selected Readings from the Journal of the American Scientific Affiliation.* Elgin, IL: American Scientific Affiliation, 1978.
_____. "Alternative Views of Evolution." *Journal of the American Scientific Affiliation (JASA)* 27, 1 (1975): 2-7.
_____. "Creation and/or Evolution." *JASA* 29, 2 (1977): 68-72.
_____. "Nukes or no Nukes: Absolute Thinking in a Relative World." *JASA* 32, 2 (1980): 102-8.

Wilson, Edward Osborne

Present Position and Address: Pellegrino University Professor (since 1994)/Curator in Entomology (since 1972) of the Museum of Comparative Zoology/Mellon Professor of the Sciences (1990-93), Harvard University, Cambridge, MA 02138, USA **Date of Birth:** June 10, 1929 **Education:** B.S. Biology (1949)/M.S. Biology (1950), University of Alabama; Ph.D. Biology (1955), Harvard University **Awards and Honors:** National Medal of Science (1977); Pulitzer Prize in General Non-fiction (1979/91); Tyler Prize for Environmental Achievement (1984); Medal of the National Zoological Park (1987); Craford Prize of the Royal Swedish Academy of Sciences (1990); Prix du l'Institut de la Vie

(1990); International Prize for Biology, Government of Japan (1993) **Previous Positions:** Assistant Professor of Biology (1956-58)/Associate Professor (1958-64)/Professor of Zoology (1964-76), Baird Professor of Science (1976-94) Harvard University **Discipline:** Zoology; Sociobiology; Ecology **Related Areas of Interest:** Sociobiology of Religion; The Relation between Science and Theology.

Selected Publications:

_____. *Sociobiology: the New Synthesis*. Cambridge, MA: Harvard University Press, 1975.
_____. *On Human Nature*. Cambridge, MA: Harvard University Press, 1978.
_____, Charles J. Lumsden. *Promethean Fire*. Cambridge, MA: Harvard University Press, 1983.
_____. *Biophilia*. Cambridge, MA: Harvard University Press, 1984.
_____, Bert Hölldobler. *The Ants*. Cambridge, MA: Harvard University Press, 1990.
_____. *Success and Dominance in Ecosystems*. Germany: Ecological Institute, 1990.
_____. *The Diversity of Life*. Cambridge, UK: Cambridge University Press, 1993.
_____, Bert Hölldobler. *Journey to the Ants*. Cambridge, MA: Harvard University Press, 1994.
_____. *Naturalist*. Washington, DC: Island Press, 1994.

Wilson, R. Ward

Present Position and Address: Professor and Chair (since 1986), Psychology Department, King College, Bristol, TN 37620, USA; (Home) 141 Hermitage Drive, Bristol, TN 37620, USA **Work Phone:** (615) 878-4340 **Date of Birth:** May 17, 1930 **Education:** B.A. (1953), Wheaton College; M.A. Christian Education and Biblical Literature (1958), Wheaton Graduate School; Part-time graduate study - University of California at Berkeley/University of Michigan/Nova University, FL; M.Sc. Experimental Psychology (1969), Eastern Michigan University; Ph.D. Social Psychology (1976), University of Florida **Previous Positions:** Director of Christian Education and Youth Work (1958-1962), Lakeside Baptist Church, Oakland, CA; Campus Staff Member (1962-67), InterVarsity Christian Fellowship; Graduate Teaching and Research Assistant (1967-69), Eastern Michigan University; Volunteer Assistant Chaplain and Fellow (1969-72), University of Florida; Instructor in Psychology (1975-78), University of Wisconsin; Assistant Professor of Psychology and Theology (1972-79)/Chair (1973-77), Viterbo College, WI; Associate Professor of Christian Ministries (1979-80), Wheaton Graduate School; Associate Professor and Chair (1980-83), Psychology Department, Greenville College **Selected Memberships:** American Association for the Advancement of Science; American Psychological Association, Psychologists interested in Religious Issues; Society for the Scientific Study of Religion; Society for the Psychological Study of Social Issues; National Association of Evangelicals; Baptist General Conference/American Baptist Convention **Discipline:** Social Psychology **Related Areas of Interest:** Integrating the Social Sciences with Biblical Theology. This includes studying cross-cultural values in relation to God's image in all humanity.

Selected Publications: His bibliography lists 11 articles.

_____. *A Social-Psychological Study of Religious Experience with Special Emphasis on Christian Conversion*. Ph.D. diss., University of Florida. Ann Arbor, MI: University Microfilms, 1977.
_____. "Integrating Christianity and Personality Theory." *Journal of Psychology and Theology* (1985).

Wiltsher, Christopher D.

Present Position and Address: University of Leeds Adult Education Centre, 37 Harrow Road, Middlesbrough TS5 5HT UK. **Work Phone:** (0642) 814987 **Date of Birth:** December 1, 1947 **Languages Spoken:** English, French, German **Education:** B.Sc. Mathematics (1968), University of London; B.A. Philosophy and Theology (1976), University of Bristol; M.Litt. Systematic Theology/Biblical Studies (1981), Durham **Previous Positions:** Tutor in Systematic Theology, Philosophy and Ethics (1981-88), Wesley College, Bristol; Part-time Lecturer (1982-88), University of Bristol; Part-time Lecturer (1989), University of Durham and Sunderland Polytechnic **Selected Memberships:** Science and Religion Forum, UK; Society for the Study of Theology, UK; Society of Ordained Scientists; European Society for the Study of Science and Theology **Discipline:** Theology and Philosophy; Mathematics, Computer Science **Related Areas of Interest:** Relationship of Science and Theology; Doctrine of Creation; Cosmology; Science and Popular Religious Beliefs.

Selected Publications:

_____. *Everyday Science, Everyday God*. Epworth Press, 1986.
_____. "Science and Theology from an Arminian Perspective." In *Freedom and Grace*, ed. Ivor H. Jones and Kenneth B. Wilson. Epworth Press, 1988.

Wolsky, Alexander

Present Position and Address: Retired Professor of Biology; 4800 Maisonneuve Blvd. #510, Montreal Westmount, PQ H3Z 1M2, Canada **Date of Birth:** August 12, 1902 **Languages Spoken:** English, German, Hungarian **Education:** Doctor of Philosophy in Zoology (1928), University of Budapest; Honorary Reader (Docent, 1935), Experimental Animal Morphology, University of Budapest **Postgraduate Experience:** Zoology (1931-32), King's College, University of London; Zoological Laboratory (1934), University of Cambridge; Experimental Zoology with Rockefeller Fellowship (1935-36, 47), University of Stockholm **Previous Positions:** Assistant Lecturer in Zoology (1925-29), University of Budapest; Research Assistant (1929-34)/Associate (1934-39)/Acting Director (1939-45), Hungarian State Biological Research Institute, Tihany; Professor of General Zoology/Chairman of Department of General Zoology (1945-48), University of Budapest; Principal Scientific Officer and Director of regional offices of scientific cooperation (1948-54), UNESCO; Professor of Experimental Embryology and Genetics (1954-66), Fordham University, NY; Professor of Biology and Chairman of Departments of Science (1966-72), Marymount College, Tarrytown, NY; Adjunct Professor of Radiation Biology (1973-86), New York University Medical; UNESCO consultant to University of Teheran (1960)/Government of Pakistan (1962) **Editorial Positions:** Section Editor, *Oncology* (1968-76)/*Experimental Cell Biology* (1977-86); Editor in chief, *Monographs in Developmental Biology*. Basel: Karger, 1976-83; Editor, *Experimental Biology and Medicine*. Basel: Karger, 1976-86 **Selected Memberships:** American Association for the Advancement of Science; Hungarian Academy of Sciences; Indian Zoological Society; Zoological Society, Calcutta; Fellow (1961), New York Academy of Science; American Society of Zoologists; Deutsche Zoologische Gesellschaft; International Institute of Developmental Biologists; Society of Experimental Biology and Medicine; British Society of Experimental Biology; International Society of Cell Biology; American Teilhard Association; Society of Developmental Biology **Discipline:** Philosophy of Science; Zoology **Related Areas of Interest:** Teilhard de Chardin; Evolutionary Biology.

Selected Publications: His bibliography includes over 130 articles.

_____. "A Hundred Years of Darwinism in Biology." In *Darwin's Vision and Christian Perspectives*, ed. W. J. Ong. New York: Macmillan, 1961.
_____, M. de I. Wolsky. *The Mechanism of Evolution: A New Look at Old Ideas*. Basel: Karger, 1976.
_____. *Teilhard de Chardin's Biological Ideas*. Teilhard Studies, no. 4. White Plains, NY: American Teilhard de Chardin Association, 1981.
_____. "Progress in Evolutionary Thinking. Teilhard de Chardin's Biological Ideas in Historical Perspective." *Teilhard Perspective* 18, 1 (1985): 9-10.
_____, M. de I. Wolsky. "The Evolution of Evolution: Theory in Search of a New Paradigm." In *Behavior as a Main Factor of Evolution*, ed. V. Leonovicova and V. J. A. Novak, 33-42. Praha: Czechoslovak Academy of Sciences, 1987.

Wolsky, Maria de Issekutz

Present Position and Address: Retired Professor of Biology (since 1978), Manhattanville College, Purchase, NY; (Home) 4800 Maisonneuve Blvd. W, Apt. 510, Montreal Westmount, PQ H3Z 1M2, Canada **Work Phone:** (514) 932-9477 **Date of Birth:** June 16, 1916 **Education:** Doctor of Medicine (*summa cum laude*, 1942), University of Budapest **Previous Positions:** Research Associate in Pharmacology (1937-38), University of Budapest; Assistant (1956-60)/Associate (1960-68)/Professor of Biology (1968-78), Manhattanville College; Visiting Professor (1969), University of Addis Ababa, Ethiopia; Professor of Preventive Medicine (1975-76), University of Jeddah, Saudi Arabia **Selected Memberships:** American Association for the Advancement of Science **Discipline:** Theoretical Biology; Cell Biology **Related Areas of Interest:** Evolutionary Biology; Biology and Philosophy.

Selected Publications: Her bibliography lists 30 relevant research papers in journals and collections.

_____, A. Wolsky. *The Mechanism of Evolution: A New Look at Old Ideas*. Basel: Karger, 1976.
_____. "Reflections on the 'Anthropic Principle'." *Manhattanville* (Spring 1982): 10-14.
_____, A. Wolsky. "The Evolution of Evolution: Theory in Search of a New Paradigm." In *Behavior as a Main Factor of Evolution*, ed. V. Leonovicova and V. J. A. Novak, 33-42. Praha: Czechoslovak Academy of Sciences, 1987.

Wolterstorff, Nicholas

Present Position and Address: Noah Porter Professor of Philosophical Theology (since 1989), Yale University Divinity School, Yale University, New Haven, CT, 06520, USA **Date of Birth:** January 21, 1932 **Education:** A.B. (1953), Calvin College; M.A. (1954)/Ph.D. (1957), Harvard University **Previous Positions:** Instructor in Philosophy (1957-59), Yale University; Professor of Philosophy (1959-89), Calvin College; Professor of Philosophy (1986-89), Free University, Amsterdam; Visiting Professor - (Spring 1961), Haverford College/(Fall 1964), University of Chicago/(Summer 1969), University of Texas/(Summer 1973), University of Michigan/(Fall 1977), Temple University/(Fall 1981), Free University, Amsterdam/(Spring 1985), Princeton University/(1986-87), University of Notre Dame; Adjunct Professor (1976), University of Notre Dame; Member (since 1971), panels of evaluation, NEH **Editorial Positions:** Editorial Board, *Faith and Philosophy/Topics in Philosophy*; General Editor, Supplementary Textbook Project, Christian College Coalition **Selected Memberships:** President, American Philosophical Association, Central Div. (1992); President, Society of Christian Philosophers (1992-); American Society for Aesthetics **Discipline:** Philosophy **Related Areas of Interest:** Epistemology; Philosophy of Religion; Aesthetics.

Selected Publications: His bibliography lists 11 books, 59 professional articles, and 99 popular and semi-popular articles.

_____. *Reason within the Bounds of Religion*. Grand Rapids: Eerdmans, 1976.
_____, Hendrik Hart, and Johan VanderHoeven. *Rationality in the Calvinian Tradition*. University Press of America, 1983.
_____, Alvin Plantinga. *Faith and Rationality*. Notre Dame: Notre Dame Press, 1984.
_____. "Integration of Faith and Science — The Very Idea." *Journal of Psychology and Christianity* 3 (1984): 2.
_____. "Realism vs. Anti-Realism: How to Feel at Home in the World." In *Proceedings of the American Catholic Philosophical Association, 1985*.
_____. "The Migration of the Theistic Arguments From Natural Theology to Evidentialist Apologetics." In *Rationality, Religious Belief, and Moral Commitment*, ed. R. Audi and W. J. Wainwright. Ithaca: Cornell University Press, 1986.

Wonderly, Daniel E.

Present Position and Address: Semiretired, independent consultant; Rt. 2, Box 808, Oakland, MD 21550, USA **Work Phone:** (301) 334-3762 **Date of Birth:** April 21, 1922 **Education:** A.B. Anthropology (1949), Wheaton College; B.D. (1952)/Th.M. (1955), Central Baptist Seminary, Kansas City; M.S. Zoology/Botany (1961), Ohio University, Athens **Postgraduate Experience:** Also further work in geology and paleontology at Indiana University and the Bermuda Biological Station **Previous Positions:** Instructor in Bible and Anthropology et al. (1952-55), Southeastern Bible College; Assistant Professor of Biological Sciences (1961-66), Wingate College, Wingate, NC; Assistant Professor in Biological Sciences (1966-73), Grace College, Winona Lake, IN **Selected Memberships:** Geological Society of America; Fellow, American Scientific Affiliation; West Virginia Academy of Science; Interdisciplinary Biblical Research Institute **Discipline:** Theology; Biology; Geology **Related Areas of Interest:** The History of Creation Doctrine; Participation in Professional Geology meetings and organized field trips; The Alleviation of Misunderstandings Regarding Paleontology and Geology among Conservative Evangelicals.

Selected Publications: His bibliography lists 7 publications.

_____. "Non-radiometric data relevant to the question of age." *Journal of the American Scientific Affiliation (JASA)* 27, 4 (1975): 145-53. Reprint, Appendix to *Genesis One and the Origin of the Earth*, by Robert Newman and Herman Eckelman, Jr. Grand Rapids: Baker Book House, 1981.
_____. *God's Time-records in Ancient Sediments: Evidences of Long Time Spans in Earth's History*. Flint, MI: Crystal Press Publishers, 1977.
_____. "Scientific Truth: Is It Transient or Enduring?" *JASA* 33, 3 (1981): 142-45.
_____. "Coral Reefs and Related Carbonate Structures as Indicators of Great Age." Research Report no. 16. Hatfield, PA: Interdisciplinary Biblical Research Institute, 1983.
_____. *Neglect of Geologic Data: Sedimentary Strata Compared with Young-Earth Creationist Writings*. Hatfield, PA: Interdisciplinary Biblical Research Institute, 1987.

Wong, Wing-Hong

Present Position and Address: Ph.D. student in Systematic Theology (1987-1991), Faculty of Divinity, King's College, University of Aberdeen, Aberdeen AB9 2UB, Scotland, UK; (Home) 5C Seaton Avenue, Aberdeen AB2 1XB, Scotland, UK **Date of Birth:** August 8, 1944 **Languages Spoken:** English, Cantonese, Mandarin **Education:** Ph.D. Physics (1973), University of Hong Kong; M.Div. student (1973-76)/Th.M. (1978), Westminster Theological Seminary. Currently Ph.D. student (1987-91), University of Aberdeen, dissertation: "An Appraisal of the Interpretation of Einsteinian Physics in T.F. Torrance's Scientific Theology" **Previous Positions:** Assistant Professor of Systematic Theology and Apologetics (1978-87), China Evangelical Seminary, Taipei **Discipline:** Systematic Theology; Apologetics; Physics **Related Areas of Interest:** Science and Theology in Dialogue - especially New Physics and the Theology of Torrance.

Selected Publications: His bibliography lists 34 articles.

_____. "A Christian Approach to the Foundations of Physics." Th.M. Thesis, Westminster Theological Seminary, 1978.
_____. "The God of the Bible in Secular and Industrialized Contexts." In *God in Asian Contexts*, ed. Bong Rin Ro and Mark Albrecht, 227-35. Taichung: Asia Theological Association, 1988.

Worthington Jr., Everett Lee

Present Position and Address: Professor Psychology; Virginia Commonwealth University, Box 842018, Richmond, VA 23284-2018 **Work Phone:** (804) 828-6251 **Fax Number:** (804) 828-2237

E-Mail: eworth@cabell.vcu.edu **Date of Birth:** September 19, 1946 **Languages Spoken:** English
Education: B.S.N.E. Nuclear Engineering, University of Tennessee/Knoxville; S.M.N.E. Nuclear
Engineering, Massachusetts Institute of Technology; M.A. Psychology, University of Missouri/Co-
lumbia; Ph.D. Psychology, University of Missouri/Columbia **Field Work:** Counseling Internship,
University of Missouri/Columbia Counseling Services (American Psychological Association accred-
ited) **Lectures Presented:** Scandrette Lectures, Wheaton College, Wheaton, IL **Awards and Honors:**
Templeton Humility Theology Award (1991), for "Psychotherapy and Religious Values: An Update."
Journal of Psychology and Christianity; Pines-Briggs Award for outstanding scholarly article (1991),
Association for Research on Values in Counseling for "Marriage Counseling: A Christian Approach.
Counseling and Values (1990) **Previous Positions:** Military Service, U.S. Navy; Nuclear Engineer,
Stone and Webster Engineering Corporation **Discipline:** Psychology; Marriage Counseling.

Selected Publications: His total bibliography contains 10 books, over 100 journal articles or chapters,
5 articles in popular magazines, 9 video or audiotapes, and over 75 convention presentations.

C. A. Clark and Everett Lee Worthington, Jr. "Family Variables Affecting the Transmission of Religious Values
from Parents to Adolescents: A Review." *Family Perspective* 21 (1987): 1-21.
_____. "Understanding the Values of Religious Clients: A Model and its Application to Counseling." *Journal of
Counseling Psychology* 35 (1988): 166-74.
_____. *Marriage Counseling: A Christian Approach to Counseling Couples.* Downers Grove, IL: InterVarsity Press,
1989.
_____. "Marriage Counseling: A Christian Approach to Counseling Couples." *Counseling and Values* 35 (1990):
3-15.
_____, editor. "Psychotherapy and Religious Values: An Update." *Journal of Psychology and Christianity* 10
(1991): 211-23.
_____. *Psychotherapy and Religious Values.* Grand Rapids, MI: Baker Book House, 1993.
_____. *I Care About Your Marriage: Helping Friends or Family Members with Marital Difficulties.* Chicago, IL:
Moody, 1994.
_____, Douglas McMurry. *Marriage Conflicts: Resources for Strategic Pastoral Counseling.* Grand Rapids, MI:
Baker book House, 1994.
_____. "Marriage Counseling: A Christian Approach." *Journal of Psychology and Christianity* 13 (1994): 166-73.
M. E. McCullough and Everett Lee Worthington, Jr. "Encouraging Clients to Forgive People Who have Hurt Them:
Review, Critique, and Research Prospectus." *Journal of Psychology and Theology* 22 (1994): 3-20.

Wright, Richard T.

Present Position and Address: Professor of Biology, Gordon College, Wenham, MA; (Home) 7
Whipple Road, S. Hamilton, MA 01982, USA **Date of Birth:** June 28, 1933 **Education:** A.B. Natural
Science (1959), Rutgers University; A.M Biology (1960)/Ph.D. Biology (1963), Harvard University
Postgraduate Experience: NSF Postdoctoral (1963-65), Institute of Limnology, Uppsala University
Previous Positions: Assistant (1965)/Associate (1968)/Professor (1971)/Chairman of Department of
Biology (1968-71, 1976, 1984), Gordon College, Wenham, MA; NSF Science Faculty Fellow and
Visiting Associate Professor (1969-70), Oregon State University; Visiting Scientist (summer 1974),
Bigelow Laboratory for Ocean Science; Academic Chairman (since 1981), AuSable Institute for
Environmental Studies, MI **Selected Memberships:** American Society of Limnology and Oceanog-
raphy; American Association for the Advancement of Science; American Scientific Affiliation **Disci-
pline:** Biology; Oceanography; Microbiology; Environmental Science **Related Areas of Interest:**
Christian Environmental Stewardship; Biological Origins.

Selected Publications: His bibliography lists 33 publications.

_____. Review of *Genesis and Scientific Inquiry*, by Albert van der Ziel. *Journal of the American Scientific
Affiliation* 19 (1967): 31-2.

_____. "Hunger, Malnutrition, and Famine: the World Food Problem." In *Our Society in Turmoil: Society, Christianity, and Social Issues*, ed. G. Collins, 25-150. Tyndale Press, 1970.
_____. "Responsibility for the Ecological Crisis." *Bioscience* 20 (1970): 851-3.
_____. *Biology Through the Eyes of Faith*. San Francisco: Harper & Row Publishers, 1989.
_____, Bernard J. Nebel. *Environmental Science: The Way the World Works*. Englewood Cliffs, NJ: Prentice Hall, 1993.

Wu, Kathleen Johnson

Present Position and Address: Professor (since 1994), Department of Philosophy, University of Alabama, P.O. Box 870218, Tuscaloosa, AL 35487-0218, USA; (Home) 3332 Arcadia Drive, Tuscaloosa, AL 35404, USA **Work Phone:** (205) 348-1910 **Home Phone:** (205) 553-5719 **Date of Birth:** June 17, 1940 **Education:** A.B. Philosophy (*cum laude*, 1963), Bryn Mawr College; M.A. Philosophy (1967)/Ph.D. Philosophy (1970), Yale University **Previous Positions:** Part-time Lecturer (1970-71), Suffolk University; Assistant through Professor of Philosophy (since 1972), University of Alabama **Selected Memberships:** American Philosophical Association **Discipline:** Philosophy **Related Areas of Interest:** Self and Society.

Selected Publications: Her bibliography lists 1 book, 11 articles and 7 abstracts.

_____. "A Formalization of the Logic of Knowledge and Belief." Abstract. *The Journal of Symbolic Logic* 33 (1968): 641-2.
_____. "A New Approach to Formalization of A Logic of Knowledge and Belief." *Logique et Analyse* 16 (1973): 513-25.
_____. "Believing and Disbelieving." In *The Logical Enterprise*, ed. A. R. Anderson, R. B. Marcus, and R. M. Martin, 211-19. New Haven: Yale University Press, 1975.
_____. "On Lao Tzu's Idea of the Self." *Zygon* 16 (1981): 165-80.

Wulff, David M.

Present Position and Address: Professor of Psychology (since 1986), Wheaton College, Norton, MA 02766, USA **Home Phone:** (401) 751-4631 **Date of Birth:** November 7, 1940 **Languages Spoken:** English, German **Education:** B.A. (1961), Wittenberg University; M.A. (1963)/Ph.D. (1969), University of Michigan **Honorary Degrees:** Th. D. (1993), University of Lund, Sweden **Previous Positions:** Assistant (1969-77)/Associate Professor of Psychology (1977-86), Wheaton College, Norton, MA **Selected Memberships:** Fellow, American Psychological Association; Fellow, Society for the Scientific Study of Religion; Society for Values in Higher Education **Discipline:** Psychology: Psychology of Religion, Personality, History and Systems **Related Areas of Interest:** Psychology of Religion and History of Religions.

Selected Publications: His bibliography lists 4 publications.

_____. "Psychological Approaches." In *Contemporary Approaches to the Study of Religion*, ed. F. Whaling, 21-88. Vol. 2 of *The Social Sciences*. The Hague: Mouton, 1985.
_____. *Psychology of Religion: Classic and Contemporary Views*. New York: John Wiley & Sons, 1991. Swedish translation, 2 vols., 1993.
_____. "Reality, Illusion, or Metaphor? Reflections on the Conduct and Object of the Psychology of Religion." *Journal of the Psychology of Religion* 1 (1992): 25-51.
_____. "On the Origin and Goals of Religions Development." *International Journal for the Psychology of Religion* 3 (1993): 181-6.

Yamauchi, Edwin M.

Present Position and Address: Professor of History (since 1973), Miami University, Oxford, OH 45056, USA **Languages Spoken:** English, Japanese, Spanish **Education:** B.A. Hebrew and Hellenistics (1960), Shelton College; M.A. Mediterranean Studies (1962)/Ph.D. Mediterranean Studies (1964), Brandeis University **Lectures Presented:** Papers presented to over 60 learned societies, and over 80 lectures at Universities and Seminaries throughout USA **Previous Positions:** Instructor in Greek (1960-61), Shelton College; Assistant Professor of History (1964-69), Rutgers University; Associate Professor (1969-73)/Director of Graduate Studies in History Department (1978-82), Miami University **Editorial Positions:** Editor-at-Large (1972-79), Senior Editor (1992-) *Christianity Today*; Editorial Board (since 1981), *Fides et Historia*; Editorial Committee (since 1983), *Journal of the Evangelical Theological Society*; Consulting editor on *History* (1970-83)/Editorial Board (since 1983), *Journal of American Scientific Affiliation*; Editorial Board (since 1991), *Bulletin for Biblical Research*; Manuscript Consultant for Baker Book House, Broadman Press, Itolman Press, InterVarsity Press, Moody Press, Rutgers University Press, Scholars Press, Zondervan **Selected Memberships:** Chairman (1965-66), Eastern Section of Evangelical Theological Society; President (1973-74), Archaeological Institute of America - Oxford Chapter; Board of Directors (since 1973)/Vice President (1978-79), Near East Archaeological Society; President (1974-76), Conference on Faith and History; President (1983), American Scientific Affiliation; Chairman (1984-86)/President (1986-89), Institute for Biblical Research **Discipline:** Ancient Near Eastern History, Languages, and Archaeology **Related Areas of Interest:** Creation, Evolution, Anthropology and Archaeology.

Selected Publications: His bibliography lists 14 books in Archaeology and Ancient History, 16 chapters in edited works, and over 300 articles and reviews.

_____. "Immanuel Velikovsky's Catastrophic History." *Journal of American Scientific Affiliation (JASA)* 25 (1973): 134-9.
_____. "Problems of Radiocarbon Dating and of Cultural Diffusion in Pre-History." *JASA* 27 (1975): 25-31.
_____. "Ancient Ecologies and the Biblical Perspective." *JASA* 32 (1980): 193-203.
_____. "Magic in the Biblical World." *Tyndale Bulletin* 34 (1983): 169-200.
_____. "Sociology, Scripture and the Supernatural." *Journal of Evangelical Theological Society* 27 (1984): 169-92.
_____. "Magic or Miracle? Demons, Diseases and Exorcisms." In *The Miracles of Jesus*, ed. D. Wenham and C. Blomberg, 89-183. Sheffield, UK: JSOT Press, 1986.
_____. "The Magi Episode." In *Chronos, Kairos, Christos*, ed. J. Vardaman and E. Yamauchi, 15-39. Winona Lake, IN: Eisenbrauns, 1989.

Yockey, Hubert P.

Present Position and Address: Author of Scientific Books and Wilderness Exploration in northern Quebec, Canada; 1507 Balmoral Drive, Bel Air, MD 21014, USA **Work Phone:** (410) 879-0477 **Home Phone:** (410) 879-2329 **Date of Birth:** April 15, 1916 **Education:** B.A. Physics (Honors, 1938)/Ph.D.

Radiation Laboratory (1942), University of California - Berkeley **Previous Positions:** Manhattan Project during WW2, Radiation Laboratory - Berkeley/Oak Ridge, TN; Cofounder of Atomics International (1946-52), North American Aviation Inc., El Segundo, CA; Employed (1952-53) at Convair Inc. (now GE), Fort Worth, TX; Assistant Director of Health Physics Division (1953-59), Oak Ridge National Laboratory; Assistant Technical Director (1959-62), Aerojet-General Nucleonics, San Ramon, CA; Senior Scientist (1962-64), Hughes Research Laboratories, Malibu, CA **Selected Memberships:** Fellow, American Physical Society; Fellow, Explorers Club of New York; Charter Member, Health Physics Society; Certified Health Physicist (Emeritus); Charter Member, American Nuclear Society **Discipline:** Molecular Biology; Hazard Management **Related Areas of Interest:** Origin of Life.

Selected Publications:

_____. "A Calculation of the Probability of Spontaneous Biogenesis by Information Theory." *Journal of Theoretical Biology (JTB)* 67 (1977): 377-98.
_____. "Can the Central Dogma be Derived from Information Theory." *JTB* 74 (1978): 149-52.
_____. "Self-Organization Origin of Life Scenarios and Information Theory." *JTB* 91 (1981): 13-31.
_____. "First Down Québec's Whole River." *The Explorers Journal* (September 1989).
_____. "Les Voyageur Moderne on Québec's Swampy Bay River." *The Explorer's Journal* (Winter 1990).
_____. "Did the Norsemen Sail from Greenland to Ungava Bay for Lumber?" *The Explorers Journal* (Fall 1992).
_____. *Information Theory and Molecular Biology.* Cambridge University Press, 1992.

Yonge, Keith Arnold

Present Position and Address: Emeritus Professor of Psychiatry (since 1975), University of Alberta, Canada; (Home) "Mevagissey", 4345 Kingscote Road, R.R.#3, Cobble Hill, BC V0R IL0, Canada **Date of Birth:** June 22, 1910 **Languages Spoken:** English, French **Education:** M.D., C.M. (1948), McGill University; D.P.M. (1952), University of London, UK; C.R.C.P.(C) (1953); F.R.C.P.(C) (1972) **Previous Positions:** Assistant (1954-55)/Associate Professor of Psychiatry (1955-56), University of Saskatchewan; Professor and Head of Psychiatry (1957-75), University of Alberta **Selected Memberships:** Fellow (since 1960), American Psychiatric Association (Committee on Religion and Psychiatry, 1960-64); President (1969-70), Canadian Psychiatric Association; Fellow (since 1970), American College of Psychiatry; Founding Fellow (1973), Royal College of Psychiatrists; President (1973, 77), Inter-American Council of Psychiatric Associations **Discipline:** Medicine/Psychiatry **Related Areas of Interest:** Philosophy of Medical Science; Medical Ethics.

Selected Publications:

_____. "The Mind-Body Relationship: Proceedings of the 3rd World Congress on Mental Health." *Canadian Psychiatric Association Journal (CPAJ)* 7, 2 (1962).
_____. "Towards an Integration of Psychodynamic and Psychophysiological Concepts." *CPAJ* 10, 4 (1965).
_____. "The Theoretical Basis of the Psychosomatic Approach in Psychiatry." *Neurologica-Neurocirugia-Psychitria* (Mexico) 2, 1 (1971).
_____. "The Moral Imperative in Mental Health." In *Proceedings of the 1978 Congress of the World Federation for Mental Health, 1978.*
_____. "Body and Mind." Part 1. "Science and Philosophy." Part 2 of "The Philosophic Basis of Medical Practice." *Humane Medicine* 1, 1 (1985); 2, 1 (1986).
_____. "Reflections on the Epistemology of Psychiatry." *Canadian Journal of Psychiatry* 33 (November 1988).

Young, Davis A.

Present Position and Address: Department Chair and Professor of Geology, Calvin College, Grand Rapids, MI 49546, USA; (Home) 2215 Plymouth Avenue S.E., Grand Rapids, MI 49506, USA **Work**

Phone: (616) 957-6374 **Home Phone:** (616) 245-0378 **Fax Number:** (616) 957-8551 **E-Mail:** youn@legacy.calvin.edu **Date of Birth:** March 5, 1941 **Education:** B.S.E. Geological Engineering (honors, 1962), Princeton University; M.S. Geochemistry and Mineralogy (1965), Pennsylvania State University; Ph.D. Geological Sciences (1969), Brown University **Awards and Honors:** Sigma Xi **Previous Positions:** Assistant Professor of Geology (1968-73), New York University; Associate Professor of Geology (1973-78), University of North Carolina - Wilmington; Associate Professor (1978-82)/Professor of Geology (since 1982), Calvin College; Fellow (1984-85), Calvin Center for Christian Scholarship **Administrative Experience:** Member of Board of Trustees (1978-87), Westminster Theological Seminary; Chair, Department of Geology, Geography and Environmental Studies (since 1990), Calvin College **Selected Memberships:** Christian Reformed Church; Geological Society of America; Mineralogical Society of America; American Scientific Affiliation; Affiliation of Christian Geologists **Discipline:** Geology **Related Areas of Interest:** Geology, Creation and the Flood; The Age of the Earth; Scripture and Geology; History of Science/Theology Discussion.

Selected Publications:

_____. "Is 'Creation Science' Science or Religion? - a response." Journal of American Scientific Affiliation 36 (1984): 156-8.

_____. "Was the Earth Created a Few Thousand Years Ago? - No." In *The Genesis Debate*, ed. Ronald Youngblood, 56-85. Nashville, TN: Thomas Nelson, 1986.

_____. "Scripture in the Hands of Geologists." Parts 1 and 2. *Westminster Theological Journal* 49 (1987): 1-34, 257-304.

_____. "The Contemporary Relevance of Augustine's View of Creation." *Perspectives on Science and Christian Faith* 40 (1988): 42-5.

_____. "Theology and Natural Science." *Reformed Journal* 38 (1988): 10-16.

_____. Chap. 6, "Making Mysteries out of Missing Rock"; Chap. 7, "Popular Portraits of Science: Focused or Fuzzy? In *Science Held Hostage; What's Wrong with Creation Science and Evolutionism?*, by Davis A. Young, Howard Van Till, and Clarence Menninga. Downers Grove: InterVarsity Press, 1988.

_____. Chap. 1, "Where are We?"; Chap. 3, "The Discovery of Terrestrial History. In *Portraits of Creation: Biblical and Scientific Perspectives on the World's Formation*, by Davis A Young, Howard J. Van Till, Robert E. Snow and John H. Stek. Grand Rapids: Eerdmans, 1990.

_____. Review of *The Creationists: The Evolution of Scientific Creationism*, by Ronald L. Numbers. *Fides et Historia* 24: 100-10.

_____. *The Biblical Flood: A Case Study of the Church's Response to Extra-Biblical Knowledge*. Grand Rapids: Eerdmans, 1995.

Yu, Carver Tatsum

Present Position and Address: Principal Lecturer (since 1987); Director of Postgraduate Studies (since 1989), China Graduate School of Theology, Hong Kong Baptist College, 224 Waterloo Rd., Kowloon, Hong Kong **Date of Birth:** February 14, 1949 **Languages Spoken:** English, Chinese (Mandarin and Cantonese) **Education:** Diploma in Biology (1969), Hong Kong Baptist College; M.Div. (1975)/Th.M. (1976), Fuller Theological Seminary; D.Phil. (1981), Oxford University **Previous Positions:** Lecturer (1975-77, 81-84), China Graduate School of Theology; Senior Lecturer (1984-87)/Head of Religion and Philosophy Department (since 1985), Hong Kong Baptist College **Editorial Positions:** Editorial member, *Wen Yi* (1982-85)/*Chinese Theological Journal* (1985); Editor, *Nahan Magazine* (since 1984) **Selected Memberships:** Chinese Theological Society; Hong Kong Philosophy Society; Academic Advisory Committee, International Society of Chinese Philosophy **Discipline:** Systematic Theology; Historical Theology; Christianity and Chinese Culture; History of Philosophy (particularly in relation to the metaphysical foundation of modern science) **Related Areas of Interest:** Metaphysical Foundation of Science; Socio-cultural Impacts of Science and Technology; Field Theory and the Doctrine of God; The Concept of Time.

Selected Publications:

_____. "The Stratification of the Meaning of Time." *Scottish Journal of Theology* 33 (1979): 13-34.

_____. *Being and Relation - A Theological Critique of Western Dualism and Individualism, Theology and Science at the Frontiers of Knowledge*, ed. T. F. Torrance, vol. 8. Edinburgh: Scottish Academic Press, 1987.

_____. "Being and Existence—The Crisis of Scientistic Culture." In *Proceedings of International Conference on Tang Chun-i's Thought*, vol. 4, 86-112. Hong Kong: Dharmastiti Press, 1991.

_____. "Modern Christian Thought: China." In *Blackwell Encyclopaedia of Modern Christian Thought*, 15-20. Oxford: Blackwell, 1993.

_____. "The Principle of Relativity in Theology." In *Proceedings of the Symposium on Science and Theology. Otago Theological Foundation, 1994.*

Zajonc, Arthur G.

Present Position and Address: Professor of Physics (since 1991), Amherst College, Amherst, MA 01002, USA; (Home) 22 Orchard Street, Amherst, MA 01002, USA **Work Phone:** (413) 542-2033 **Home Phone:** (413) 256-0655 **Date of Birth:** October 11, 1949 **Languages Spoken:** English, German **Education:** B.S.E. Engineering Physics (1971)/M.S. Physics (1973)/Ph.D. Physics (1976), University of Michigan **Postgraduate Experience:** Postdoctoral Research Associate (1976-78), Joint Institute for Laboratory Astrophysics, University of Colorado/National Bureau of Standards, Boulder **Previous Positions:** Assistant Professor of Physics (1976-84)/Associate Professor of Physics (1984-91), Amherst College; Visiting Professor (1981-82), Ecole Normale Superieure, Paris, France; Visiting Scientist (1985, 86), Max-Planck-Institute for Quantum Optics/University of Hannover; Fulbright Professor (1993), University of Innsbruck, Austria **Selected Memberships:** Fellow, Fetzer Institute; Fellow, Lindisfarne Association; Society for Literature and Science; Anthroposophical Society; American Physical Society; History of Science Society **Discipline:** Physics - Atomic and Laser Studies, Quantum Optics; The Foundations of Science/Technology and Spirituality **Related Areas of Interest:** Goethe's Scientific Studies and the Relationships between the Humanities and Science; Rudolf Steiner.

Selected Publications: His bibliography lists 14 publications in physics, and 12 in science and the humanities.

_____. "Facts as Theory: Aspects of Goethe's Philosophy of Science." In *Goethe and the Sciences: a Reappraisal*, ed. F. Amrine, F. Zucker and H. Wheeler. Boston: Reidel, 1986.
_____. "Light and Cognition: The Imperatives of Science." In *Gaia: A Way of Knowing: Part 2*, ed. W. I. Thompson. Italy: Lindisfarne Press, 1992.
_____. *Catching the Light, The Entwined History of Light and Mind.* Bantam Books, 1993.
_____. "New Wine in what Kind of Wineskins? Metaphysics in the Twenty-first Century." In *New Metaphysical Foundations of Modern Science.* Institute of Noetic Sciences, 1994.
_____, editor. *The Eye's Mind: Cognitive Studies in the Light of Goethe's Scientific Work.* A Collection of essays. Forthcoming.

Zeh, H. Dieter

Present Position and Address: Retired Professor of Theoretical Physics, University of Heidelberg, Germany; Gaiberger Str. 38, D-6903 Waldhilsbach, Germany **Work Phone:** (06223) 3150 **Date of Birth:** August 5, 1932 **Languages Spoken:** German, English **Education:** Dr. rer. nat. (1961), University of Heidelberg **Previous Positions:** Research Assistant (1964-65), California Institute of Technology; University Dozent (1966), University of Heidelberg; Research Assistant (1965; 67-68), University of California - San Diego **Selected Memberships:** American Physics Society; New York Academy of Science **Discipline:** Theoretical Physics **Related Areas of Interest:** Foundations of Quantum Theory; Element synthesis; Direction of Time; Cosmology.

Selected Publications:

_____. "On the Interpretation of Measurement in Quantum Theory." *Foundations of Physics* 1 (1970): 69-76.
_____. "Emergence of Classical Time from a Universal Wave Function." *Physics* 116 (1986): 9-12.
_____. *The Physical Basis of the Direction of Time*. Springer Verlag, 1989.

Zhang, Hwe Ik

Present Position and Address: Professor, Department of Physics, Seoul National University, Seoul 151-742, Korea; (Home) Moonchon 304-801, Ju-Yup-Dong, Ko-Yang-Si, Kyong-Gi-Do, Korea **Work Phone:** Korea 02-880-6602 **Home Phone:** 0344-911-4849 **Date of Birth:** May 14, 1938 **Languages Spoken:** Korean, English **Education:** B.S. Physics (1961), Seoul National University; Ph.D. Physics (1969), Louisiana State University **Previous Positions:** Research Scientist Associate (1969-70), University of Texas; Assistant Professor through Full Professor (since 1971), Seoul National University **Selected Memberships:** Physical Society of Korea; Korean History of Science Society; Korean Society of Science and Philosophy **Discipline:** Physics **Related Areas of Interest:** Condensed Matter Physics; Foundation of Physics; Philosophy of Science; Relation between Science and Theology.

Selected Publications: Over 50 scientific papers published.

_____. "Human Being in Cosmogenesis." *Hyunsang Kwa Insik* 3 (1979): 107-26.
_____. "Human Being as a Model for Cosmic Reality." In *Sial, Man and History*, 257-80. Seoul: Han-Gil-Sa, 1982.
_____. "Worldview of Natural Science and Worldview of Scripture." *The Theological Thought* (Korean) 42 (1983): 471-91.
_____. "The Structural Relation Between Science and Ethics." In *Modern Science and Ethics*, 89-138, (in Korean). MinUmSa, Seoul: 1988.
_____. "On Ontological Consideration Concerning the Units of Life" (in Korean). *Philosophical Studies* 23 (1988): 89-105.
_____. "Humanity in the World of Life." *Zygon* 24 (1989): 447-57.
_____. *Science and Metascience* (in Korean). Seoul: Jisiksanup-Sa, 1990.

Zimmerman, Michael E.

Present Position and Address: Professor and Chair, Department of Philosophy, Tulane University, New Orleans, LA 70118, USA; (Home) 921 Fern Street, New Orleans, LA 70118, USA **Work Phone:** (504) 865-5702 **Home Phone:** (504) 891-1029 **Date of Birth:** July 7, 1946 **Languages Spoken:** English, French, Spanish, German **Education:** B.A. Philosophy (1968), Louisiana State University; M.A. (1972)/Ph.D. Philosophy (1974), Tulane University; Fulbright-Hays Fellow (1972-73), l'Université Catholique de Louvain **Congresses and Conferences:** An invited participant at a conference on the new cosmic narrative led by Thomas Berry and Brian Swimme in the Bay Area, January 1990 **Lectures Presented:** A 13-part lecture series on Science and Theology given at Trinity Episcopal Church in 1988 **Previous Positions:** Assistant Professor (1974-75), Denison University; Assistant (1975-78)/Associate (1978-83)/Full Professor (since 1983)/Chair (since 1989), Tulane University; Visiting Professor (1982), California School of Professional Psychology, Berkeley; Clinical Professor of Psychiatry (since 1983), LSU School of Medicine; Clinical Professor of Psychology (since 1984), Tulane School of Medicine **Discipline:** Philosophy - Modern German Philosophy (Heidegger, Nietzsche, Hegel, Marx); Philosophy, Science, and Technology; Philosophy, Medicine and Psychiatry; Social and Political Philosophy; Philosophy and Gender; Environmental Philosophy; Eastern Religions; Ethics **Related Areas of Interest:** Raised a Roman Catholic. Theology/Philosophy/Ethics and Environment/Ecology - "Humanity's Relation to Nature" (radical environmentalism and deep ecology as seen in Heidegger's thought); Cosmic narrative in Science and Theology; Jewish and Christian attitudes toward Creation and Nature; Process Theology and the origin and evolution of the universe.

Selected Publications:

_____. "Contemporary Developments in Science and their Effect on our Understanding of Creation and the Divine." Unpublished paper, 1985.
_____. "Implications of Heidegger's Thought for Deep Ecology." *The Modern Schoolman* 64 (November 1986): 10-43.
_____. "Quantum Theory, Intrinsic Value, and Pantheism." *Environmental Ethics* 10 (Spring 1988): 3-30.
_____. "On Autonomy and Humanity's Relation to Nature." *Tikkun* 4 (March-April 1989): 102-4.

Zycinski, Józef

Present Position and Address: Professor of Philosophy of Science (since 1988); Pontifical Academy of Cracow, Bernardynska 3, 31 069 Kraków, Poland; (Home), Moscickiegs 9, 33 100 Tarnów, Poland **Concurrent Positions:** Bishop at Tarnów (since 1990) **Home Phone:** (4814) 222501 **Date of Birth:** September 1, 1948 **Languages Spoken:** Polish, English, French, Russian, Italian **Education:** Master in Theology (1974)/Doctorate in Philosophy (1978), Academy of Catholic Theology, Warsaw; Master in Philosophy (1972)/Doctorate in Theology (1976)/Habilitation in Philosophy (1981), Pontifical Academy of Cracow. Also studied at Catholic University of Leuven, Belgium (1980-81) **Previous Positions:** Assistant Professor (1979-81)/Adjoined Professor (1981-88)/Associate Dean of Faculty of Philosophy (since 1982)/Full Professor (since 1988)/Associate Director of the Institute for Interdisciplinary Research (since 1984), Pontifical Academy of Cracow **Editorial Positions:** Editor (since 1980), *Philosophy in Science* (Tucson, AZ); *Philosophical Problems of Science* (Cracow) **Selected Memberships:** Polish Philosophical Society; American Catholic Philosophical Association; Polish Theological Society; European Academy for Arts and Sciences **Discipline:** Philosophy of Science; Relativistic Cosmology; Metalogic **Related Areas of Interest:** History of Science and Relationships between the Natural Sciences and Christian Faith.

Selected Publications: Besides what is listed below, over 50 papers dealing with process philosophy, artificial intelligence, post-positivist philosophy of science, published in English and Polish in the *British Journal for the Philosophy of Science, The New Scholastic Science, The New Scholasticism, Znak, Przeglad Powszechny, Analecta Cracoviensia,* and *Studia Philosophiae Christianae.*

_____. *The Dilemas of Evolution* (in Polish). Krakow: Polish Theological Society, 1990.
_____. Socratean Meditations (in Polish). Roma Czestochowa: Edizioni Pauline, 1991.
_____. The Problem of Universals in the Context of Modern Science (in Polish). Krakow: PAT, 1991.
_____. God of Abraham and Whitehead (in Polish). Tarnów: Biblos, 1992.
_____. To Disclose Grace in Nature (in Polish). Krakow: Znak, 1992.
_____. *The Frontiers of Rationality* (in Polish). Warsaw: PWN, 1993.
_____. "Donnès scientifiques on verité?" *L'Enseignement Philosophique* 41, 1 (1990): 26-36.
_____. "The Role of Religious and Intellectual Elements in Overcoming Marxism in Poland." *Studies in Soviet Thought* 43 (1992): 139-57.
_____. "The Nontrivial Character of the Weak Anthropic Principle." *Theoria et Ilistoria Scientiarum* 2 (1992): 77-9.
_____. "Quantum Cosmology, Possible Worlds, and Modal Actualism." *Theoria et Ilistoria Scientiarum* 3 (1993): 45-58.

Zylstra, Uko

Present Position and Address: Professor of Biology (since 1976), Calvin College, Grand Rapids, MI 49546, USA **Date of Birth:** March 29, 1943 **Languages Spoken:** English, Dutch **Education:** A.B.

Biology and Greek (1965), Calvin College; M.S. Botany (1968), University of Michigan; Ph.D. Zoology (1972), Free University of Amsterdam **Previous Positions:** Teaching Assistant (1966-68), University of Michigan; Teaching Assistant (1972), Free University of Amsterdam **Selected Memberships:** American Society for Cell Biology; American Scientific Affiliation; Electron Microscopy Society of America; International Society for the History, Philosophy and Social Studies of Biology (ISHPSSB) **Discipline:** Cell Biology, Zoology **Related Areas of Interest:** Ecology and Ethics/Religion; Hierarchy Theory, Philosophy of Biology.

Selected Publications:

_____. "Biology." In *Shaping School Curriculum*, ed. G. J. Steensma and H. W. Van Brummelen, 120-9. Terre Haute, IN: Signal Publishing Company, 1977.

_____. "Tending God's Garden: The Christian in Agriculture Today." *Reformed Journal* 28, 7 (1978): 9-11.

_____. "Dooyeweerd's Concept of Classification in Biology." In *Life is Religion*, ed. H. van der Goot, 234-48. St. Catherine's, ONT: Paedeia Press, 1981.

_____. "Ecological Aspects of Food Production: Biblical Directives for Agriculture." In *The Environmental Crisis: The Ethical Dilemma*, ed. E. R. Squires, 135-50. AuSable Trails Institute of Environmental Studies, 1982.

_____. "Toward a Sustainable Agriculture: Biblical, Ecological and Resource Perspectives." *The Christian Farmer* 16, 1 (1983): 7-12.

_____. "Living Things as Hierarchically Organized Structures." *Synthese* 91, 1-2 (1992): 111-33.

_____. "The Influence of Evolutionary Biology on Hierarchical Theory in Biology, with Special Reference to the Problem of Individuality." In Press.

Directory B

Individuals Actively Interested in the Field

Adams, Dawn A.

Present Position and Address: Assistant Professor of Biology, Baylor University, P. O. Box 97388, Waco, TX 76798-7388 **Phone:** (817) 755-2911; **Fax:** (817) 755-2969 **E-Mail:** Dawn_Adams@baylor.edu **Date of Birth:** June 30, 1952 **Languages Spoken:** English, French **Education:** Ph.D., University of California at Berkeley **Previous Positions:** Assistant Professor of Biology, Presbyterian College, Clinton, SC; Instructor, Dept. of Physical Science, Mt. Diablo Community College, Pleasanton, CA; Instructor, Dept. of Vertebrate Paleontology, University of California, Berkeley **Honors:** National Science Foundation Grant (DUE-9254171 June 1993-Sept 1995, approx. $270,000) **Memberships:** Center for Theology & Natural Science, American Association for the Advancement of Science, American Indian Science & Engineering Society, Society of Vertebrate Paleontology, Sigma Xi **Discipline:** Vertebrate Paleontology **Relevant Area of Interest:** Evolutionary theory, biological determinism, philosophy of science, use of phenomenological methodology in science, spirituality, ritual **Current Project:** Mechanics of ceratopsid dinosaurs, development of "post-modern science" via science education reform movement

Personal Notes: Her bibliography contains 2 published journal papers regarding Ceratopsian dinosaurs, her dissertation, thesis and numerous presentation abstracts. She is a member of the Choctaw Nation of Oklahoma.

Adler, Thomas C.

Present Position and Address: Senior Research Associate (since 1982), Lawrence Berkeley Laboratory, Berkeley, CA 94720, USA; (Home) 1307 Bonita Avenue, Berkeley, CA 94709, USA **Work Phone:** (415) 524-2256 **Date of Birth:** May 14, 1943 **Education:** B.S. Chemistry (1969), University of Toledo **Previous Positions:** Senior Research Associate (1970-82), School of Public Health, University of California; **Selected Memberships:** American Association for the Advancement of Science; American Chemical Society; Astronomical Society of the Pacific **Discipline:** Electrochemistry **Related Areas of Interest:** Evolutionary Psychology and Psychobiology; Lucid Dreaming and Spiritual Evolution.

Albertsen, Andres Roberto

Present Position and Address: Pastor (since 1992), Lutheran-Danish Church, Buenos Aires; Iglesia Dinamarquesa en Buenos Aires, Carlos Calvo 257, 1102 Buenos Aires, Argentina **Work Phone:** (541) 3629154 **Fax:** (541) 3614727 **Date of Birth:** May 13, 1964 **Languages Spoken:** Spanish, English, Danish **Education:** M.Th. (1990), Instituto Superior Evangelico de Estudios Teologicos, Buenos Aires; Studies at the Faculty of Theology of the University of Aarhus, Denmark (1990-91) **Previous Positions:** Lay Pastor (1988-90), Lutheran-Danish Church, Buenos Aires; Temporary Pastor (1991), Parish of

Haarslev of the Church of Denmark **Discipline:** Systematic Theology **Related Areas of Interest:** Scientific Theology.

Allen, George W. J.

Present Position and Address: Graduate student, Cornell University; Research Assistant in Steve Zinder's lab, Cornell University, currently isolating carbon nonoxide dehydrogerase from Methanathrix; CALS-1 201 Wing Hall, Cornell University, Ithaca, NY 14850, USA **Date of Birth:** September 1, 1963 **Education:** B.S. Moravian College (1986) **Selected Memberships:** Organization: American Society of Microbiology **Discipline:** Microbiology **Related Areas of Interest:** Bacterial Evolution.

Ambrosino, Salvatore V.

Present Position and Address: Medical Director of the Children's Developmental Center, St. Andrew's School, Flushing, NY; Clinical Associate Professor in Psychiatry, NY University School of Medicine; 164-03 33rd Avenue, Flushing, NY 11358 **Concurrent Positions:** Psychiatric Expert (1972-79), Tribunal of Diocese of Brooklyn **Date of Birth:** April 17, 1926 **Education:** A.B. Degree (*magna cum laude,* 1949), Washington Square College, NY University; M.D. (1953)/Fellowship in Neurology, NY University School of Medicine **Postgraduate Studies:** Intern in Psychiatry (1953-54), Kings County Hospital, Brooklyn, NY **Field Work:** Resident in Psychiatry (1954-57), Bellevue Hospital, NY **Previous Positions:** Clinical Assistant/Visiting Neuropsychiatrist (1959-72), Bellevue Hospital NY; Clinical Instructor in Psychiatry (1959-71), New York University School of Medicine; Assistant Attending in Psychiatry (1960-62, 1976-85), Flushing Hospital NY; Assistant Attending in Psychiatry (1960-77), Kew Gardens General Hospital, Elmhurst NY; Director (1965-77), Children's Developmental Center, Woodhaven NY; Assistant Attending in Psychiatry (1968-72, 1978-present), New York University Medical Center NY; Lectures in Psychiatry to Residents (1974-76), Creedmoor State Hospital NY; Clinical Assistant (1977-79)/Clinical Associate Professor in Psychiatry (since 1979), NY University School of Medicine; Assistant Physician in Psychiatry (1964-68)/Associate Attending in Psychiatry (1969-73), St. John's Queens Hospital, Elmhurst NY; Staff Psychiatrist (1970-76), Long Island Jewish-Hillside Medical Center, New Hyde Park, NY; Assistant Professor of Clinical Psychiatry (1973-76), SUNY; Medical Director (1979-81), Children's Developmental Center, Bellevue Hospital **Editorial Work:** Contributing Editor (1972-79), Medical Times; Editor (1973-77), Children's Developmental Center - Psychoeducational Journal for the Treatment of Children **Selected Memberships:** Fellow, American Psychiatric Association; American Association for the Advancement of Science; International College of Psychosomatic Medicine; American Medical Association **Discipline:** Psychiatry **Related Areas of Interest:** During the past ten years working on a book concerning neuropsychiatric syncretic approach to consciousness, evolution, affect, the man and woman and the destiny of the human soul.

Ansbacher, Stefan

Present Position and Address: Freelancer; 2505 "D" Lowson Blvd., Delray Beach, FL 33445, USA **Date of Birth:** January 27, 1905 **Languages Spoken:** English, German **Education:** B.S. (1923), Frankfurt; M.S. (1929)/Bio M.D. (1933), University of Geneva **Previous Positions:** Science and Religion teacher (1976-90), Palm Beach Co. School System **Selected Memberships:** Futurist Society; American Humanist Association; Institute for Theological Encounter with Science and Technology (ITEST) **Discipline:** Biomedicine **Related Areas of Interest:** What can be done to make the religious establishment aware of scientific progress.

Arvedson, Peter Fredrick

Present Position and Address: Rector (since 1992), St. Andrew's Episcopal Church, 3105 Masin Street, Buffalo, NY 14214, USA **Work Phone:** (716) 834-9337 **Date of Birth:** April 15, 1937 **Education:** B.S. Chemistry (1959), University of Illinois; Ph.D. Inorganic Chemistry (1964), University of Wisconsin; M.Div. (1967), Theological Seminary, New York City **Previous Positions:** Vicar (1967-72), St Laurence Episcopal Church, Effingham IL; Rector (1972-78), All Souls' Episcopal Church, Okinawa in Japan; Rector (1978-88), St. Andrew's Episcopal Church, Madison WI; Interim Rector (1988-89), Grace Episcopal Church, Lockport NY; Senior Canon (1989-92) St. Paul's Episcopal Cathedral, Buffalo, NY **Selected Memberships:** Society of Ordained Scientists **Discipline:** Pastoral Ministry; Inorganic Chemistry **Related Areas of Interest:** Science and Faith; Theology and the Natural Sciences.

Ayers, David John

Present Position and Address: Assistant Professor Department of Sociology, The King's College, Briarcliff Manor, NY 10510 **Work Phone:** (914) 941-7200 **Home Phone:** (914) 631-6679 **Date of Birth:** May 30, 1956 **Education:** B.A. Psychology (1982), Edinboro, PA; M.A. Sociology (1985), American University; Ph.D. student (currently) at N.Y. University **Previous Positions:** Childcare Worker and Supervisor (1980-82), Heritage House Group Homes; Psychiatric Associate (1982-84), Psychiatric Institute of America; Research Associate (1984-85), Dept. of H.U.D.; Research Associate at Health Systems Technology (1985-86) **Selected Memberships:** American Sociological Association; Society for the Study of Social Problems; Law and Society Association; Family Research Council; Christian Sociological Association **Discipline:** Sociology and Psychology **Related Areas of Interest:** Deviance and Stigma; Law/Social Control; Social Movements (especially violent, ethnic, the feminist movement and right wing).

Baclig, Paulita Villegas

Present Position and Address: Project Development Specialist (since 1990), Alger Foundation, Hawaii #22 K-8 Street, 1102 Kamias, Quezon City, Philippines **Date of Birth:** June 29, 1955 **Languages Spoken:** English, Tagalog, Cebuano **Education:** B.Sc. Zoology (cum laude, 1976)/M.D. (1980)/Residency in Family Practice (1985), University of the Philippines; M.Public Health (Pauline Stitt Outstanding Graduate, 1989), University of Hawaii **Previous Positions:** Medical Director (1986-88), Home for the Abandoned, Philippines; National Trainer, Natural Family Planning Catholic Bishop's Conference of the Philippines (1984-88); Faculty (1987-88), Ateneo de Cagayan College of Medicine; Consultant (1988-90), University of Hawaii School of Public Health **Selected Memberships:** ITEST; Delta Omega; Phi Beta Delta; Phil. Society of Family Medicine Graduates **Discipline:** Family Medicine; Public Health - preventative and community medicine/international health **Related Areas of Interest:** Health Care and Ethical Societal Issues; Family Planning; Abortion; Health Aid to Developing Countries and Disadvantaged Groups; Care of "Terminally Ill" and Dying and of Homeless.

Baer, Donald R.

Present Position and Address: Staff Scientist (since 1976), Battelle Pacific Northwest Laboratories, Interphase Chemistry Group Leader, Molecular Science Research Center, Richland, WA 99352, USA; (Home) 2035 Howell Avenue, Richland, WA 99352, USA **Date of Birth:** November 12, 1947 **Education:** B.S. in Physics (1969), Carnegie-Mellon University, Pittsburgh, PA; Ph.D., Experimental Solid State Physics (1974), Cornell University, New York **Previous Positions:** Research Associate (1974-1976), University of Illinois; Visiting Research Fellow (1974-1985), University of Surrey, England **Selected Memberships:** American Scientific Affiliation **Discipline:** Physics, surface science, materials science **Related Areas of Interest:** Theology and Technology.

Barclay, Peter R.

Present Position and Address: Student Employee, Boston University, Boston, MA; (Home) P.O. Box 43, Unit 3-3, Norfolk, MA 02056-0043, USA **Home Phone:** (617) 878-6381 **Date of Birth:** September 24, 1963 **Languages Spoken:** Spanish **Education:** B.S. (Summa Cum Laude, 1991), Boston University; MLA (1994), Boston University **Selected Memberships:** Religious Research Association; American Sociological Association; SSSR; Association for Sociology of Religion **Discipline:** Under: Sociology; Grad: Inter-disciplinary; Post-grad: Christian Social Ethics **Related Areas of Interest:** Theological Ethics; Sociology of Religion; Ecumenism; Process Theology.

Barker, Verlyn L.

Present Position and Address: Minister for Ministries in Higher Education (since 1961), United Church Board for Homeland Ministries; 700 Prospect Ave., Cleveland, OH 44115, USA **Work Phone:** (216) 736-3797 **Date of Birth:** July 25, 1931 **Education:** A.B. (1952), Doane College; B.D. (1956)/S.T.M. (1960) Yale University Divinity School; Ph.D. (1970), St. Louis University **Honorary Degrees:** Honorary Degree: D.D. (1977), Doane College **Awards and Honors:** Society for Health and Human Values Annual Award (1987) **Previous Positions:** University Pastor (1956-59), University of Nebraska **Selected Memberships:** Society for Health and Human Values; Institute for Study of Religion in an Age of Science; United Ministries in Higher Education; New York Academy of Sciences; American Association for the Advancement of Science; National Association for Science; Technology, and Society; Center for Theology and the Natural Sciences **Discipline:** American Studies **Related Areas of Interest:** Genetic Engineering; Theological/Ethical Issues of Contemporary Science and Technology.

Barrett, Peter J.

Present Position and Address: Research Fellow (1994-95), Department of Church History, Unisa, Pretoria, South Africa **Date of Birth:** January 1, 1934 **Education:** B.Sc. Engineering (1954), University of Cape Town; M.A. Physics (1961), Oxford University; Ph.D. Physics (1966), Imperial College, University of London **Awards and Honors:** Rhodes Scholarship, Rhodesia (1955-1958) **Previous Positions:** Lecturer (1958-1961), University of Cape Town; Research Associate (1965-1969), Culham Lab, UK Atomic Energy Authority; Adjunct Assistant Professor (1969-1971), University of California - Los Angeles; Senior Lecturer (1972-79)/Associate Professor of Physics (1980-94), University of Natal; Research (summers 1987, 89) Plasma Physics Lab, Princeton University **Selected Memberships:** Anglican Church; S. A. Science & Religion Forum **Discipline:** Physics **Related Areas of Interest:** Church Mission; Gospel and Culture; Natural Theology **Current Research:** History of Science and Theology.

Bauman, Michael E.

Present Position and Address: Director of Christian Studies/Associate Professor of Theology and Culture (since 1988), Hillsdale College, Hillsdale, MI; Associate Dean of the Summer School (since 1990) Centre for Medieval and Renaissance Studies, Oxford, England; (Home) 4202 W. Hallett Road, Hillsdale, MI 49242, USA **Work Phone:** (517) 437-4990 **Date of Birth:** February 14, 1950 **Education:** B.A. Biblical Studies O.T. (1977), Trinity College; M.A. New Testament/Church History (1979), McCormick Seminary; Ph.D. interdisciplinary program in Theology and History (1983), Fordham University **Postgraduate Studies:** National Endowment for the Humanities Visiting Research Fellow (1988), Department of English, Princeton University **Previous Positions:** Lecturer in Church History (1985-86), Regional Seminary of the Northeast, Basking Ridge NJ; Adjunct Professor (1982-83)/Associate Professor (1986-87) of History of Christianity, Fordham University, Bronx, NY; Chairman, Division of General Education/Assistant Professor of History and Church History (1983-88), Northeastern Bible College, Essex Falls NJ; Also 7 years of Pastoral experience **Selected Memberships:** Evangelical Theological Society; American Academy of Religion **Discipline:** Theology, History and Language **Related Areas of Interest:** Theological Beliefs of Isaac Newton, Galileo, Michael Servetus, and John Locke.

Bell Jr., Reuben Paul

Present Position and Address: Owner and director of two centers: Western Maine Outpatient Center (since 1984); and Conatus Counseling Service (since 1988), both in Fryeburg, ME, USA; (Home) Highland House, Highland Park, Fryeburg, ME 04037; (Work) Western Maine Outpatient Center, 114 Main Street, Fryeburg, ME 04037, USA **Concurrent Positions:** Also currently enrolled as an M.Div student in the Swedenborg School of Religion, Newton, MA **Work Phone:** (207) 935-3383 **Home Phone:** (207) 935-2434 **Date of Birth:** November 23, 1948 **Education:** B.S. (1972)/M.S. (1977) Zoology, University of Tulsa, OK; D.O. Doctor of Osteopathy (1979), Oklahoma College of Osteopathic Medicine, Tulsa; M.Div (hopefully 1991), Swedenborg School of Religion, Newton, MA **Discipline:** Osteopathic General Practitioner **Related Areas of Interest:** Morphogenic Fields/Electromagnetic Properties of Living Organisms; Soul/Body Interaction **Current Research:** The 'New Science' with Respect to the Ideas of Emanuel Swedenborg (1688-1772); Spiritual Considerations in Health and Disease.

Bellini, Gianpaolo

Present Position and Address: Professor of Physics, Physics Department University of Milan, Via G. Celoria 16, Milano 20133, Italy **Work Phone:** (02) 2392.370 **Fax:** (02) 2392617 **E-Mail/Telex:** 334687 INFN MI **Previous Positions:** Experimental researcher in Elementary Particle Physics, responsible for a group of researchers at Milan University and at the Institute for Nuclear Physics; Visiting scientist, European Center for Nuclear Research (CERN-Geneva), at Fermi National Laboratory (FNAL-Chicago) and at Experimental activities, Serpukhov accelerator (USSR) **Selected Memberships:** National Institute for Nuclear Physics, board of Directors (1973-present); Executive Committee of the National Institute for Nuclear Physics (1983-90); Council of the European Physical Society (1980-83); European Committee for Future Accelerators (ECFA) and of Restricted ECFA (RECFA) (1983-86) **Discipline:** Elementary Particle Physics **Related Areas of Interest:** Cultural aspects of physics and, more generally, of science. Cofounder of 35 cultural centers in Italy which concentrate on the relation between the different sciences, the relation between scientific knowledge and reality and between science and religion. He is also the author of seven volumes on elementary particle physics and is the author of more than 150 publications in international scientific journals, in which original results are presented **Current Research:** Most important and original research results concern the physics of the excited states of the elementary particle; of the resonances; of the "heavy quarks" and in particular of "charm and beauty;" of the interactions between particles and nuclei obtained with completely new experimental methods as the Silicon active targets.

Bennett, J. W.

Present Position and Address: Professor, Department of Cell and Molecular Biology, Tulane University, New Orleans, LA 70118, USA **Work Phone:** (504) 865-5546 or (504) 862-8101 **Fax:** (504) 865-6756 or (504) 865-6785 **Date of Birth:** September 15, 1942 **Education:** B.S. Biology and History, Upsala College, East Orange, NJ; M.S./Ph.D. Genetics, University of Chicago **Previous Positions:** Assistant/Associate/Full Professor (1971-present), Department of Biology, Tulane University **Selected Memberships:** President (1990-91), American Society for Microbiology; American Association for the Advancement of Science; British Mycological Society; Louisiana Academy of Science; Mycological Society of America; Society for General Microbiology; Society for Industrial Microbiology; Torrey Botanical Club **Discipline:** Fungal Genetics **Related Areas of Interest:** Science and Literature; Bioethics. A basic scientist who likes to teach, read, and publish outside of the basic sciences.

Benninghoff, Jean

Present Position and Address: Retired but giving short seminars on science and religion for my Quaker Meeting; (Home) 3 Broad Path West, Lloyd Neck, Huntington, NY 11743, USA **Home Phone:** (516) 271-8045 **Date of Birth:** May 15, 1927 **Education:** B.A. Mathematics and Physics (1948), Barnard College of Columbia University; M.S. Physics (1950), Indiana University; M.Div. (1986), Union Theological Seminary **Previous Positions:** Assistant Professor Radiology (1950-55), Temple University Hospital and Medical School, Philadelphia; Assistant Professor Physics (1955-56), Philadelphia Textile Institute, Philadelphia; Physicist (1956-57), NASA Lewis Flight Propulsion Laboratory, Cleveland OH; Assistant/Adjunct Assistant Professor of Physics, Nassau Community College, Garden City, NY **Selected Memberships:** Institute on Religion in an Age of Science **Discipline:** Religion; Physics including Radiation Physics **Related Areas of Interest:** M.Div. Thesis on Science and Religion.

Berry Jr., Maxwell R.

Address: No. 1 Magnolia Point, Panama City, FL 32408, USA **Date of Birth:** June 7, 1910 **Education:** B.A. (1931), VMI, Cornell; M.D. (1935), Cornell; Ph.D. Med. (1941), Mayo Clinic, University of Minnesota **Previous Positions:** Assistant Professor of Medicine (1942-45), Medical College VA; Founder of St. Joseph's Tumor Clinic (non-profit)/HCA West Faces Ferry Hospital/Annandale Village for Retarded Adults (non-profit) **Selected Memberships:** Fellow, and President of Gastroenterology (1965-66), American College of Physicians; Elder, Presbyterian Church **Discipline:** Medicine **Related Areas of Interest:** Combating Atheism

Bettencourt, Estêvão Tavares

Present Position and Address: Catholic Priest Mosteiro de Sao Bento, Rua Dom Gerardo 68, Caixa Postal 2666, 20001 Rio de Janeiro RJ, Brazil **Date of Birth:** September 16, 1919 **Languages Spoken:** Portuguese, French, German, Italian **Education:** Licentiate in Philosophy (1942)/Doctorate in Theology (1945), Pontifical Institute of Saint Anselm, Rome **Previous Positions:** Biblical Studies at the Pontifical Bible Institute of Rome and at the Ecole Biblique of Jerusalem; **Selected Memberships:** Founding member of the Sociedade Brasileira de Parapsicologia, Academia Brasileira de Filosofia; **Discipline:** Systematic Theology and Biblical Studies; Philosophy **Related Areas of Interest:** Theology and Philosophy; Biblical Sciences; Interreligious Dialogue; Atheism. Has a publication entitled Ciência e Fé (Science and Faith).

Biesele, John Julius

Present Position and Address: Professor Emeritus in Zoology (since 1978), University of Texas - Austin (Home) 2500 Great Oaks Parkway, Austin, TX 78756, USA **Work Phone:** (512) 452-2670 **Date of Birth:** March 24, 1918 **Education:** B.A. with highest honors (1939)/Ph.D. Zoology (1942), University of Texas - Austin **Previous Positions:** Fellow (1942-44), International Cancer Research Foundation; Associate in Genetics (1944-46), Carnegie Institution; Assistant (1946)/Associate (1947-55)/Member (1955-58), Sloan-Kettering Institute for Cancer Research, NY; Assistant/Associate/Full Professor of Biology (1950-58), Cornell University Graduate School Medical Science; Professor of Zoology/Member of Graduate Faculty (1958-78)/Professor of Education (1973-78), University of Texas - Austin **Selected Memberships:** American Association Advancement of Science; American Association Cancer Research (director, 1960-63); Sigma Xi; A number of professional biology, conservation, health, consumerism and peace organizations **Discipline:** Cell Biology (cytogenetics, cancer research, cellular fine structure) **Related Areas of Interest:** Maintenance of Earth's Habitability, and Reverence for Life; Evolution; Chromosomal and Nutritional Basis of Retardation, Malbehavior, and Disease.

Bingemer, Maria Clara Lucchetti

Present Position and Address: Associate Professor of Theological and Human Sciences Center, Theological Department of the Pontificia Universidade Catolica Rio de Janeiro, Brazil; (Home) Rua Almirante Salgado, 51, Laranjeiras, RJ-22240-170, Rio de Janeiro, Brazil **Concurrent Positions:** Assistant Professor in Theology, Santa Ursula University; Academic Assistant at the Instituto Brasileiro de Desenvolvimento (Faith-Culture work group); Coordinator of Loyola Center of Faith and Culture, Center for Formation of the Laity **Work Phone:** 021-225 0874 **Fax:** 00-55-21-2452458 or 00-55-21-2666157 **Date of Birth:** May 19, 1949 **Languages Spoken:** Portuguese, French, English, Spanish, Italian **Education:** B.A. Journalism (1975)/M.Th. Theology (1982), Pontificia Universidade Catolica, Rio de Janeiro; Ph.D. Theology (1989), Pontificia Universidade Gregoriana, Rome **Editorial Work:** Responsible for several publications at the Instito Superior de Estudos de Religiao **Discipline:** Systematic Theology **Current Areas of Research:** Ethical "Exemplarity" and Holiness in Late Modernity with some Female "Case Studies": Edith Stein, Simone Weil, Etty Hillesum.

Bjork, Russell C.

Present Position and Address: Professor of Computer Science (since 1978) Department of Mathematics and Computer Science, Gordon College, 255 Grapevine Road, Wenham MA 01948, USA **Date of Birth:** July 1, 1948 **Education:** BSEE, MSEE (1969), Massachusetts Institute of Technology; M.Div. (1982), Gordon Conwell Theological Seminary **Previous Positions:** Campus Staff (1969-78), Campus Crusade for Christ **Selected Memberships:** American Scientific Affiliation; Association of Christians in the Mathematical Sciences; Association for Computing Machinery; Institute of Electrical and Electronic Engineers (IEEE) - Computer Society **Discipline:** Computer Science **Related Areas of Interest:** Theological and Social Implications of Computing.

Blaising, Craig A.

Present Position and Address: Professor, Systematic Theology, Dallas Theological Seminary, Dallas, TX; (Work) 3909 Swiss Avenue, Dallas, TX 75204, USA **Work Phone:** (214) 824-3094 **Date of Birth:** September 28, 1949 **Education:** B.S. Aerospace Engineering (1971), University of Texas - Austin; Th.M. (1976) and Th.D. (1979), Dallas Theological Seminary; Ph.D. Theology (1988), University of Aberdeen, Scotland **Previous Positions:** Adjunct Instructor (Spring 1978), University of Texas - Arlington; Assistant/Associate Professor (1980-89)/Acting Department Chair, Systematic Theology (1988-89), Dallas Theological Seminary **Selected Memberships:** American Academy of Religion; Evangelical Theological Society; American Association for the Advancement of Science **Discipline:** Systematic Theology **Related Areas of Interest:** Theological Method; Contemporary Religious Thought; Philosophy of Science; History of Science.

Booher, Bruce

Present Position and Address: Pastor (since 1992), Bethlehem Lutheran Church, 777 N. 4th St. Beaumont, TX 77701, USA **Date of Birth:** July 5, 1950 **Education:** attended M.I.T. (1968-70); B.A. History (1972), Ohio State University; M.Div. (1981), Trinity Lutheran Seminary, Columbus OH

Previous Positions: Programmer (1972-81), Monroe Div. of Litton Industries; Pastor (1982-84), First Lutheran Church, Floresville, TX; Pastor (1984-92), Christ Lutheran Church, La Porte, TX **Selected Memberships:** Steering Committee, Evangelical Lutheran Church in America Work Group on Science and Technology; Member, Center for Theology and the Natural Sciences, Berkeley CA; General Affiliate, Chicago Center for Religion and Science; Member, Institute on Religion in an Age of Science **Discipline:** Theology; Pastoral Ministry **Related Areas of Interest:** Theology and Science.

Boutinon, Jean Claude

Present Position and Address: Currently studying Theology; (Home) 14 bis rue des rossignols, 95 380 Puiseux, France **Work Phone:** 1 34 72 44 29 **Date of Birth:** February 3, 1945 **Languages Spoken:** French, English **Education:** Licence de Sciences Naturelles (1967), Poitiers; Maîtrise de Théologie (1985), Vaux sur Seine; DEA (1994), Sorbonne, Paris **Discipline:** Professeur de Théologie **Related Areas of Interest:** Relation between Biology and Theology.

Braganza, Karuna Mary

Address: St. Joseph's College, P.O. Turpa 835227, Dist. Ranchi - Bihar, India 835227 **Date of Birth:** October 23, 1923 **Education:** B.A. Honors English Literature (1944), St. Xavier's College Bombay; M.A. Honors, English Literature (1946), University of Bombay; LL.D. Hon. (1976), University of San Diego, USA **Postgraduate Studies:** Postdoctoral visiting fellowship (1973-74), Harvard University **Previous Positions:** Principal Sophia College, Bombay; Member of Senate, Academic Council of the University of Bombay; General Secretary of Aiache; Member of the Pontifical Council for Culture; **Discipline:** English Language and Literature; Developmental Education **Related Areas of Interest:** Developmental Education; Women's Concerns; Culture.

Brennan, John Lester

Present Position and Address: Retired Pathologist; now Priest in charge of Holy Trinity Church in Chrishall 5 Engleric, Chrishall, Royston, Herts SG8 8QZ, England **Date of Birth:** April 30, 1920 **Education:** MBBS (1944)/Diploma in Theology/MD (1952)/MRCP Internal Medicine (1951), University of London; MRCPath (1965)/FRCPath (1977); Barrister of the Middle Temple (1971); LLM. (1986), University of Keele **Previous Positions:** Forensic Pathology with part-time work for the police Internship and Army Service (1944-48); Junior Pathology appointments in London (1949-53); Clinical Pathologist and Assistant Professor (1954-62), Christian Medical College, Ludhiana, India; Deacon (1955) and Priest (1956) in the Church of India; Professor of Pathology and Chairman of Department (1962-64); Junior Appointment (1965-69), University College; Consultant Pathologist (1969-86), Robert Jones and Agnes Hunt Orthopaedic Hospital, Oswestry **Selected Memberships:** Society of Ordained Scientists; Ecclesiastical Law Society; Royal Society of Medicine **Discipline:** Medicine and Pathology. Haematology, Histopathology and Bone Pathology **Related Areas of Interest:** Medical Science and Faith; Medicolegal and Medical Ethical Problems.

Bridges Jr., Carl B.

Present Position and Address: Professor of New Testament, Johnson Bible College, Knoxville, TN 37998, USA **Work Phone:** (615) 573-4517 **Fax:** (615) 579-2337 **Date of Birth:** February 3, 1951 **Languages:** English **Previous Positions:** Lecturer and Principal (1976-83), Ghana Christian College; Adjunct Professor (1991-92), Milligan College, TN; **Selected Memberships:** Society of Biblical

Literative **Discipline:** New Testament; Greek Language **Related Interests:** New Testament; Greek; Linguistics; Cultural Anthropology **Current Area of Research:** Working as exegetical consultant for scripture translation in the Crimean Tatar Language.

Personal Notes: His bibliography contains 35 popular articles published in Christian periodicals.

Brigham, Joseph John

Present Position and Address: Retired, 313 Coriander Drive, New Bern, NC 28562, USA **Home Phone:** (919) 633-2627 **Date of Birth:** December 8, 1923 **Languages:** English; Portuguese; some French **Previous Positions:** International Data Processing Manager, 3M Company; Industrial Engineering Manager, 3M Company; **Selected Memberships:** American Association for the Advancement of Science; Professional Engineering - Ontario **Discipline:** Engineering **Related Interests:** General Science; Genetics.

Brobeck, John R.

Present Position and Address: Professor Emeritus, University of Pennsylvania, School of Medicine Department of Physiology, Philadelphia, PA 19104-6085, USA; (Home) 224 Vassar Avenue, Swarthmore, PA 19081 **Date of Birth:** April 12, 1914 **Education:** B.S. (1936), Wheaton College IL; M.S. (1937)/Ph.D. (1939), Northwestern University, Chicago; M.D. (1943), Yale University **Honorary Degrees:** LL.D (1960), Wheaton College **Conferences and Congresses:** Addresses to the Christian Medical Society, International Conference of Christian Physicians, British Christian Medical Fellowship **Previous Positions:** Faculty (1943-52), Yale University School of Medicine; Chairman (1952-70), Department Physiology/Herbert C. Rorer Professor of Medical Science (1970-84), School of Medicine, University of Pennsylvania; Secretary, Board of Managers of the American Missionary Fellowship; Board of Trustees, Lancaster Bible College **Editorial Work:** *Yale Journal of Biology and Medicine* (1949-52); *Physiological Reviews* (1963-72); *History of American Physiological Society* (1987) **Selected Memberships:** Member, American Scientific Affiliation; Member, Christian Medical Society; Member, National Academy of Sciences; Fellow, American Academy of Arts and Sciences; President (1971-72), American Physiological Society **Discipline:** Physiology, Specifically Physiological Control Systems Especially for Food Intake, Body Temperature, Energy Balance **Related Areas of Interest:** Medicine, Physiology and their Relation to Christianity.

Brooks, George Gordon

Present Position and Address: Minister, UU Fellowship of Charlotte County, FL, USA P.O. Box 694, Enfield, NH 03748; (During Winter) Box 5321, SLR, Lake Wales, FL 33853 **Date of Birth:** December 14, 1922 **Education:** A.B. Physics (1944), Amherst College; S.M. Physics (1947), Massachusetts Institute of Technology (MIT); S.T.B. (1951), Harvard Divinity School **Postgraduate Studies:** NSF Summer Institutes (1964-1972). Chatauqua Short Courses (at least six, 1970-1985) **Field Work:** Astronomy and Geology Courses (2 quarter sabbatical) Michigan State (1976-1977) **Previous Positions:** UU Ministry (full-time, 1951-1968); Physics Professor (1968-1986), Lorain County Community College, OH **Discipline:** Physics and Theology; Pastoral Ministry **Related Areas of Interest:** Origins; Cosmology; Relating Physical Knowledge to Life and Values; The Place of Chaos Theory in Origins and Development; Is Entropy related to Complexity?

Bunnell, Adam Eugene

Present Position and Address: Professor of History, Department of History, Bellarmine College, 2001 Newburg Road, Louisville, KY 40205, USA **Date of Birth:** August 1, 1946 **Education:** B.A. (1969)/M.A. History (1970), St. Louis University; Theological Studies (1970-1973), Universities of Wuerzburg and Vienna; Ph.D. History and Religious Studies (1985) **Previous Positions:** Professor (1976-1983), Church History, St. Paul Seminary, St. Paul, MN; Adjunct Professor (1987), Humanities, Continuing Education Division, St. Francis College, Joliet, IL; Tenured Assistant Professor of History (1985-1990), Regis College, Denver **Discipline:** History, Religious Studies and Religious History **Current Research:** Philosophy and Modern Society; Christian Theology in the 19th Century; History of the Family; Anti-Semitism.

Burns Sr., John Lanier

Present Position and Address: Chair/Professor, Systematic Theology, Dallas Theological Seminary, 3909 Swiss Avenue, Dallas, TX 75204, USA; (Home), 3505 Wentwood, Dallas, TX 75225, USA **Work Phone:** (214) 369-7940 **Date of Birth:** November 8, 1943 **Education:** B.A. Davidson College; Th.M. (1972)/Th.D. (1979), Dallas Theological Seminary; Ph.D., Humanities (1993), University of Texas **Field Work:** A substantial amount of training in the History of Science as it relates to Philosophy **Relevant Congresses or Conferences:** The Science and Religion Colloquy of the American Academy of Religion **Previous Positions:** Professor and Chairman of Systematic Theology (1982-present) **Selected Memberships:** Various Philosophical Societies; Christian Medical Society; American Scientific Affiliation **Discipline:** Systematic Theology and Philosophy **Related Areas of Interest:** History of Ideas and Ethics; Artificial Intelligence; Ethics in Biomedical Research; Specialty in the Social Sciences; Presently synthesizing 20 years of research on "The City and Social Justice."

C

Capart, Laurent J. N.

Present Position and Address: Lecturer at "institut Gramme," Quai Du Condroz, 28, B-4031 Angleur, Belgium **Work Phone:** (32) 41/42.82.91 **Fax:** (32) 41/23.30.28 **Date of Birth:** August 27, 1957 **Languages Spoken:** French, English, Dutch **Discipline:** Engineering **Related Areas of Interest:** Relations Between Science, Technology, Ethics, and Theology.

Carlson, Richard F.

Present Position and Address: Professor of Physics, Department of Physics, University of Redlands, P.O. Box 3080, Redlands, CA 92373-0999 **Work Phone:** (909) 793-2121, ext. 2931 **Date of Birth:** June 19, 1936 **Languages:** English; German; Hebrew; Greek **Education:** M.A. Theology and Liberal Studies, Fuller Theological Seminary; Ph.D. Physics, University of Minnesota **Awards and Honors:** 14 Research Grants; Faculty Research Lecturer, University of Redlands **Previous Positions:** Acting Assistant Professor (1964-67), Department of Physics, University of California - Los Angeles; through Professor (since 1967), Department of Physics, University of Redlands, CA **Selected Memberships:** American Physical Society; American Scientific Affiliation **Discipline:** Physics (Experimental Nuclear Physics) **Related Interests:** Nuclear Physics Research; Theology; Philosophy of Science **Current Area of Research:** Total reaction studies (with alpha particles, deuterms, and (3)He), Svedberg Lab, Uppsala University, Sweden; Nuclear size determinations for a number of Sn Isotops, Crocker Lab., University of California - Davis.

Personal Notes: His bibliography contains 42 published nuclear physics research studies.

Casanova, José V.

Present Position and Address: Assistant Professor (since 1987), Graduate Faculty of Political and Social Science, New School for Social Research 65 Fifth Avenue, New York, NY 10003, USA; (Home) 12 Haussler Terrace, Clifton, NJ 07013, USA **Work Phone:** (212) 741-5316 **Home Phone:** (201) 473-4360 **Date of Birth:** January 29, 1951 **Languages Spoken:** English, German, Spanish, Ukrainian **Education:** B.A. Philosophy (1969), Seminario Metropolitano, Saragossa, Spain; M.A. Theology (1973), University of Innsbruck, Austria; M.A. Sociology (1977), New School for Social Research; Ph.D. Sociology (1982) **Postgraduate Studies:** (Dissertation title: "The Opus Dei Ethic and the Modernization of Spain"), Graduate Faculty of the New School for Social Research, New York **Previous Positions:** Adjunct Instructor, Seton Hall University/Montclair State College/The Cooper Union (during the period 1979-81); Bilingual Assistant Professor in Social Studies (1982-87), Passaic County College, New Jersey; Adjunct Professor (Spring 1985), Department of Sociology, New York University; Adjunct Professor (1985-87), Department of Sociology, New School for Social Research, New York **Selected Memberships:** Associate Member (1981-present), "Content and Methods of the

Social Sciences", Columbia University Seminar; Associate editor (1982-87), Telos; Associate Editor (1983-86), Current Perspectives in Social Theory **Discipline:** Sociology **Related Areas of Interest:** Sociological Theory: Classical and Contemporary; Social Change and Modernization; Political Sociology; Hispanic Studies; Sociology of Religion.

Cereti, Giovanni

Present Position and Address: Professor of Ecumenical Theology (since 1985), Istituto di Studi Ecumenici, Venise, Italy via Traspontina 18, I-00193, Rome, Italy **Work Phone:** (6) 68826612 **Home Phone:** (336) 732734 **Date of Birth:** December 1, 1933 **Languages Spoken:** Italian, English, French **Education:** Doctorate in Civil Law (1956), Genoa; Licence in Dogmatic Theology (1975)/Doctor in Theology (1981), Gregorian University, Rome **Selected Memberships:** President, Italian section of "World Conference on Religion and Peace"; Advisory Committee, Concilium reviewing Church Law **Discipline:** Ecumenical Theology **Related Areas of Interest:** Marriage: History of Christian Marriage; Dialogue between Christians and other Religions; Religion/ethics and the Social Sciences.

Church, F. Forrester

Present Position and Address: Senior Minister, Unitarian Church of All Souls, New York City, NY USA. Columnist, a weekly op-ed column for the *New York Post*; (Home) 7 Gracie Square, No. 6A, New York, NY 10028; (Work) Unitarian Church of All Souls, 1157 Lexington Avenue, New York, NY 10021, USA **Work Phone:** (212) 535-5530 **Home Phone:** (212) 879-0096 **Education:** A.B. (1970), Stanford University; M.Div. (1974), Harvard Divinity School; Ph.D. Early Church History (1978), Harvard University **Previous Positions:** Columnist (1987-88), Chicago Tribune; Written or edited 15 books; Bill Moyer's interview (1988) **Discipline:** Writer and Pastor.

Clarke, Charles L.

Present Position and Address: Retired; 4165 Park Avenue, Memphis, TN 38117-4620, USA **Home Phone:** (901) 685-7101 **Date of Birth:** February 13, 1912 **Education:** B.S. (1937), University of Tennessee, Knoxville, TN; M.D. (1937), University of Tennessee, Memphis, TN **Postgraduate Experience:** Internship, Knoxville General Hospital (1937-39); Residency, Internal Medicine (1940-43), Walter Reed General Hospital **Field Work:** LECT: Panel participant, Rhodes College, Memphis, "Death and Dying"; Lectured to clergy training for Hospital Chaplaincy **Awards and honors:** Tennessee Department of Human Services - Volunteer Support Awards (1984-86); City of Memphis Award of Merit (1984); Active Living Award - Senior Citizen Services - Memphis (1984); Memphis Outstanding Senior Citizen - Kiwanis Club (1985); Memphis City Council Certificate of Recognition for Outstanding Contribution to Community (1987); L. M. Graves Memorial Health Award for outstanding contribution to Community Health (1987); State of Tennessee - Governor's Award: Outstanding Professional Care of Elderly, Dist. 9 (1991) **Previous Positions:** Private Practice (1939-40, 45-78); General Staff (1939-40), Memorial Hospital, Johnson City, TN; General Staff (1940-41), Huntsville General Hospital; Military service, Chief of Cardiovascular Renal Section, Walter Reed Hospital (1943)/Northington General Hospital (1943-45), Tuscaloosa, AL; Instructor through Associate Professor (1945-retirement), University of Tennessee; Chief of Cardiovascular Renal Section (1943-45), Northington General Hospital, Tuscaloosa, AL; Secretary of Staff, Chairman of various committee, including executive committee several times, President of Staff (1945-retirement), Methodist Hospital, Memphis, TN; Courtesy Staff (1945-retirement), Baptist Memorial Hospital, Memphis, TN; Courtesy Staff (1945) St. Joseph Hospital, Memphis, TN; Internal Medicine Staff (1945-retirement), City of Memphis and U.T. Hospitals; **Administrative Experience:** Medical Director, Trezevant

Manor and Allen Morgan Nursing Home (until 1990); Medical Director and Director, Lincoln American Life Insurance Company (1959-85); Member, Board of Directors, St. Peters Villa/Samaritan Counseling Center/Church Health Center **Selected Memberships:** Memphis and Shelby County Medical Society; Tennessee State Medical Society; American College of Physicians; Memphis Academy of Internal Medicine; American Geriatric Society; International Society of Internal Medicine; Association of Life Insurance Medical Directors of America; Center for Theology and the Natural Sciences; past member, Institute of Medicine and Religion **Discipline:** Medicine.

Cloutier, Stephen

Present Position and Address: Process Design Coordinator (since 1981), UOP 1175 Ivy Hall Lane, Buffalo Grove, IL 60089, USA **Date of Birth:** September 25, 1949 **Education:** BS.Ch E, Chemical Engineering (1972), Michigan Technological University; M.Div. (1980), Trinity Evangelical Divinity School; M.Ch E, Chemical Engineering (1987), Illinois Institute of Technology **Previous Positions:** Development Engineer (1972-74)/Safety Analyst (1975-80) **Selected Memberships:** American Scientific Affiliation **Discipline:** Chemical Engineering **Related Areas of Interest:** Integrating personal faith with science.

Cobb, Larry R.

Present Position and Address: Professor (since 1967), Department of Government, Slippery Rock University (SRU) Slippery Rock, PA 16057; (Home) 250 Slippery Rock Road, Slippery Rock, PA 16057, USA **Work Phone:** (412) 738-2416 **Home Phone:** (412) 794-2938 **Education:** A.B. Economics (1961), West Virginia University; M.A. Philosophy and Government (1964)/Ph.D. Government (1967), Southern Illinois University - Carbondale **Previous Positions:** Instructor (1964-65), Glenville State College WV; Instructor in Government (1965-67), Southern Illinois University; Teaching (1967-81), Department of Political Science/Graduate Faculty Appointment (1970-present)/Director (1978-85), Human Inquiry Interdisciplinary Program/Director (1984-86), University Honors Program, Slippery Rock University; Visiting Lecturer (1985), Southern Illinois University; Teacher (1986), Humanities, Governor's School, Mary Baldwin College; Visiting Professor (1988), Allegheny College **Selected Memberships:** Newsletter Editor and member of the Board (1977-present), Society for Philosophy of Creativity; Secretary-Treasurer (1982-87), Foundation for Philosophy of Creativity; Chair (1983-88), APSCUF Committee on Quality in Higher Education; Member (1984-85), "Task Force on the Future," Pennsylvania AAUP; Executive Committee Member (1985-present), Institute for Values Inquiry **Discipline:** Public Administration **Related Areas of Interest:** Education and values.

Cole, R. David

Present Position and Addresses: Professor Emeritus, Department of Molecular and Cell Biology, University of California - Berkeley, Berkeley, CA; (Home) 1147 Park Hills Road, Berkeley, CA 94708, USA **Home Phone:** (510) 845-3885 **Date of Birth:** November 17, 1924 **Education:** B.S. Chemistry (1948)/Ph.D. Biochemistry (1954), University of California, Berkeley **Previous Positions:** Chemist (1949-1951), Tidewater Oil Company, Avon CA; Postdoctoral Fellowship (Foundation for Infantile Paralysis), National Institute Medical Research (1955), London; Rockefeller University Research Associate (1956-1958); Assistant Professor (1958)/Associate Professor (1962)/Professor (1964)/Chairman (1967-1972), Department of Biochemistry, University of California - Berkeley **Selected Memberships:** American Association for the Advancement of Science; American Chemistry Society; American Society of Biochemistry and Molecular Biology; Center for Theology and the

Natural Sciences; American Scientific Affiliation **Discipline:** Biochemistry **Related Areas of Interest:** Nuclear Proteins, Cytoskeletal Proteins; Theological Implications of Human Genome Project.

Colvis, John Paris

Present Position and Address: Senior Engineer (since 1987), Space Launch Systems - Guidance and Navigation Analysis, Martin Marietta Astronautics Group, Denver CO, 4978 South Hoyt Street, Littleton, CO 80123-1988, USA **Work Phone:** (303) 973-9687 **Date of Birth:** June 30, 1946 **Languages Spoken:** English, French **Education:** B.S. Mathematics (1977), Washington University, St. Louis **Previous Positions:** Associate System Safety Engineer (1978-1981), McDonnell Douglas Astronautics Company, St. Louis; Senior System Safety Engineer (1981-1987), Strategic Systems, Martin Marietta Astronautics Group, Denver **Selected Memberships:** Mathematical Association of America; American Association for the Advancement of Science **Discipline:** Aerospace Engineer **Related Areas of Interest:** Biblical foundations of Science and Mathematics; Quantum Postulate; Quantum Philosophy of Science and Mathematics; United Field, Quantum Mathematics.

Crutcher, Keith A.

Present Position and Address: Professor (since 1991), Department of Neurosurgery, Mail Loc. #515, University of Cincinnati, College of Medicine, 231 Bethesda Avenue, Cincinnati, OH 45267-0515, USA **Work Phone:** (513) 558-3552 **E-mail:** crutcher@ucbeh.san.uc.edu **Education:** B.A. Biology (1974), Point Loma College, San Diego; Ph.D. Anatomy (1977), Ohio State University, Columbus **Postgraduate Studies:** Postdoctoral studies (1980), Duke University, Durham **Previous Positions:** Research Associate, Neurology (1977-80), Department of Medicine, Duke University; Assistant Professor (1980-85)/Associate Professor, Department of Anatomy, University of Utah (1980-1987) **Selected Memberships:** Society for Neuroscience; AAAS **Discipline:** Neuroscience **Related Areas of Interest:** Neuroscience; Theology; Medical Ethics; Currently Involved in the Debate on "The Use of Human Fetal Tissue for Medical Research and Treatment" and the Human Genome Project.

Cudworth, Kyle M.

Present Position and Address: Associate Professor (since 1981), Yerkes Observatory, University of Chicago Yerkes Observatory, Box 258, Williams Bay, WI 53191 USA **Work Phone:** (414) 245-5555 **Fax:** (414) 245-9805 **E-Mail:** KMC@YERKES.UCHICAGO.EDU **Date of Birth:** June 7, 1947 **Education:** B.Phys. (1969), University of Minnesota, Minneapolis; Ph.D. Astronomy (1974), University of California - Santa Cruz **Previous Positions:** Assistant Professor (1974-81), Yerkes Observatory, University of Chicago **Selected Memberships**: Astronomical Society of the Pacific; American Astronomical Society; American Scientific Affiliation; International Astronomical Union **Discipline:** Astronomy **Related Areas of Interest:** Star clusters; Stellar Proper Motions, Kinematics and Parallaxes; Galactic Structure; Planetary Nebulae.

Dagnall, Bernard

Present Position and Address: Parish Minister (since 1975) St. Nicolas Vicarage, 53 Sutcliffe Avenue, Reading, RG6 2JN, UK **Work Phone:** 0734 663563 **Date of Birth:** August 19, 1944 **Education:** B.Sc. Chemistry (1965)/M.R.S.C. Chemistry (1972), King's College, London; M.A. Theology (1978), Oxford University **Previous Positions:** Research Chemist (1965-70), King's College, London and Head of NMR Department; Czechoslovak Academy of Science (1970-71); Research Chemist (1971-72), May and Baker **Selected Memberships:** Society of Ordained Scientists (editor of its Bulletin) **Discipline:** Organic Chemistry; Parish Ministry **Related Areas of Interest:** Industrial Mission; Spirituality/Theology and Science.

Davis, Lloyd J.

Present Position and Address: Professor of Physics and Math (since 1979), Montreat-Anderson College 708 Ninth Street, Black Mountain, NC 28711, USA **Date of Birth:** May 27, 1945 **Education:** A.B. Physics (1967), M.S. Physics (1969), Miami University **Previous Positions:** Physics Instructor (1969-71), Asbury College; Physics Instructor (1971-76), Kent State University, Regional Campuses; Dayton Christian H.S. (1976-79) **Selected Memberships:** American Scientific Affiliation; Association of Christians in Mathematical Sciences; American Association of Physics Teachers **Discipline:** Physics **Related Areas of Interest:** Integration of Christian Faith and Science and Mathematics.

Deckert, Curtis Kenneth

Present Position and Address: Technical and Management Consultant, Curt Deckert Associates Inc., 18061 Darmel Place, Santa Ana, CA 92705-1923 (since 1976) **Phone:** (714) 639-0746 **Date of Birth:** January 3, 1939 **Languages Spoken:** English **Education:** AA (1958) Fullerton College; BSME (1960) University of Arizona; MSME (1962) University of So. California/MBA (1968); Ph.D. (1989) California Coast University /Certified Management Consultant (1981) **Previous Positions Held:** Senior Engineer (1960-66) Nortronics, Anaheim, CA; Technical Staff (1966-70) California Computer Products, Anaheim, CA; Manager, Research and Development (1971) Universal Graphics, Irvine, CA; Private Practice (1971-72); Research and Development Engineer (1972-75) Ford Aerospace, Newport Beach, CA; Sr. Development Engineer (1975-76) Abbott Labs, Cerritos, CA **Memberships:** American Scientific Affiliation; I.S.A; S.P.I.E.; I.M.C.; I.E.E.E.; O.S.A. **Discipline:** Management and Development of Optical Technology **Relevant Areas of Interest:** Optical and Image Processing as related to our creation and that of all God has made for us to enjoy **Current Project:** Evidence for creation in vision, optics and image processing.

DeGraaf, Donald E.

Present Position and Address: Professor Emeritus of Physics (since 1990), University of Michigan - Flint (Home) 1008 Fremont Street, Flint MI 48504, USA **Date of Birth:** June 17, 1926 **Education:** A.B. Mathematics (1948), Calvin College; B.S.E. (1947)/M.S. Physics (1950)/Ph.D. Physics (1957), University of Michigan **Previous Positions:** Assistant (1957-61)/Associate (1961-67)/Professor (1967-1990), University of Michigan - Flint **Selected Memberships:** American Scientific Affiliation **Discipline:** Physics **Related Areas of Interest:** Broad Interest in Science and Christian Faith.

Denues, A. R. Taylor

Present Position and Address: Retired Rev. Dr. and President Emeritus, CANCIRCO; Advisory Boards , the Albert Schweitzer Memorial Foundation and Institute; RD 3 Box 199, York, PA 17402, USA **Work Phone:** (717) 757-1422 **Date of Birth:** August 16, 1914 **Languages Spoken:** English, French, German **Education:** Peabody Conservatory of Music, Prep. Dept. (1922-30); B.E. (1935)/M.G.E. (1937), School of Engineering, Johns Hopkins University; Ph.D. (1939), University of Maryland; M.P.H. Biology (1973), Yale University School of Medicine **Postgraduate Studies:** Berkeley Divinity School Special Study (1955/73), Yale University; Union Theological Seminary (Summer 1967); Albert Schweitzer College (1967-68), Switzerland **Awards and Honors:** Legion of Merit (1946), US Army; National Research Council Fellow/American Cancer Society Fellow in Biology (1947-8), MIT **Previous Positions:** Research Chemical Engineer (US Bureau of Mines) and Munitions Development Officer (1935-47), US Army; Researcher in Cancer Cytology and Epidemiology (1947-90) and corporate Administrator (1953-90); Research Member (from 1948)/Deputy Director (1953-59)/Vice President and Acting Director (1959-62), The Sloan-Kettering Institute for Cancer Research; Professor/Chairman/Adjunct Professor of Life Sciences (1968-73), New York Institute Technology; Director (1975-78), Allegheny Hospital Center for Cancer Planning; Founding Director/President/Program Director of CANCIRCO, the Cancer International Research Co-Operative; Also part-time Church Organist (1982-87) and Supply Minister (1981-87) **Discipline:** Chemical Engineering - Safety in Mines and Mining/Flames and Explosives Ballistics and Munitions Development; Cancer: Research and Administration in Cytology, Chemotherapy and Epidemiology, and Corporate Executive. Also a licensed (Episcopal) Lay Reader, Preacher, Ordained Deacon and Priest (1982/84) **Related Areas of Interest:** Theology, Medicine and Society. Has written a paper and some relevant letters included in *Seabury Journal* and in *Christian Challenge*.

Dierick, G. P. A.

Address: Katholiek Studiecentrum, Katholieke Universiteit Nijmegen, Thomas van Aquinostraat 5, 6525 G Nijmegen, Netherlands **Date of Birth:** March 27, 1941 **Education:** Studied Philosophy and Theology, Seminary of Missionaries of the Holy Family, Kaatsheuvel, Netherlands; History (doctorandus drs.), Catholic University, Nijmegen **Discipline:** History; Philosophy; Theology **Related Areas of Interest:** The Interrelation of Faith and Science.

Dittes, James E.

Present Position and Address: Professor of Psychology of Religion (since 1968), Yale University 409 Prospect Street, New Haven, CT 06511, USA **Work Phone:** (203) 432-5316 **Fax:** (203) 432-5756 **Date of Birth:** December 26, 1926 **Education:** B.A. (1949), Oberlin; B.D. (1954)/M.S. (1955)/Ph.D. Psychology (1958), Yale University **Awards and Honors:** Guggenheim Fellow (1965-6); N.E.H. Senior Fellow; Fulbright Research Fellow, Rome; Guggenheim, NEH Senior Faculty Fellowship

Previous Positions: Instructor (1950-52), American School in Talas Turkey; Ordained to ministry, United Church of Christ (1954); Chairman of Council on Graduate Studies in Religion in US and Canada (1970-71); Instructor through Professor (1955-68)/Chairman of Department of Religious Studies (1975-82), Yale University; **Selected Memberships:** Society for Scientific Study of Religion **Discipline:** Ordained Minister; Psychology of Religion **Related Areas of Interest:** Psychology and Religion/Theology

Dols Jr., William L.

Present Position and Address: Executive Director (since 1987), The Educational Center , 6357 Clayton Road, St. Louis, MO 63117, USA; (Home) 5 Benton Place, St. Louis, MO 63104, USA **Work Phone:** (314) 721-7604 **Home Phone:** (314) 771-9455 **Date of Birth:** April 17, 1933 **Education:** B.A. (cum laude, 1955), Washington and Lee University, Lexington VA; M.Div. (1958), Virginia Theological Seminary, Alexandria; Ph.D. in Biblical Studies and Psychology (1988), Graduate Theological Union and University of California - Berkeley **Previous Positions:** Assistant to the Rector (1958-61), St. Thomas' Church, Owings Mills, Maryland; Vicar (1961-65), St. John's Church, Glencarlyn Arlington, VA; Rector (1965-72), St. James' Church, Wilmington, NC; Rector (1972-83), Immanuel Church-on-the-Hill, Alexandria, VA **Discipline:** Theology; Psychology **Related Areas of Interest:** The Relationships Between Biblical Studies, Theology and Psychology.

Dormer, Kenneth J.

Present Position and Address: Professor, Department of Physiology, College of Medicine, University of Oklahoma, P.O. Box 26901, Biomedical Sciences Building Rm 653, Oklahoma City, OK 73190, USA **Work Phone:** (405) 271-2226 **Date of Birth:** March 10, 1944 **Education:** B.S. Marine Biology (1966), Cornell University; M.S. Physiology/Ph.D. Biology, University of California - Los Angeles **Postgraduate Studies:** Postdoctoral Fellowship, Neural Control of Circulation, University of Texas Medical Branch, Galveston **Previous Positions:** Vice President and Director of Research, Hough Ear Institute, Baptist Medical Center, Oklahoma City; Lecturer (since 1978), College of Medicine, University of Oklahoma **Selected Memberships:** Christian Medical and Dental Society (Student Chapter); Ethics in Research (Biomedical); American Scientific Affiliation; Christian Fellowship Coordinator for F.A.S.E.B./Society for Neuroscience Annual meetings **Discipline:** Neural Control of Cardiovascular Function; Implantable Auditory Prostheses (Human) **Related Areas of Interest:** Biomedical Ethics; Science/Medicine and Theology/Religion.

Duguay, Michel A.

Present Position and Address: Professor of Physics and Engineering (since 1988), Departement Genie Electrique Université Laval, Sainte-Foy, Quebec, G1K 7P4 Canada **Date of Birth:** September 12, 1939 **Education:** B.S. Physics (1961), University of Montreal; Ph.D. Physics (1966), Yale University **Previous Positions:** Member of Technical Staff (1966-87), Bell Telephone Laboratories **Selected Memberships:** International Society for the Study of Time; IRAS **Discipline:** Physics and Engineering **Related Areas of Interest:** Science and Religious Thought, Especially from the Point of View of our Conceptions of Time.

DuMaine, R. Pierre

Present Position and Address: Bishop of San Jose in California, 900 Lafayette Street, Ste. 301, Santa Clara, CA 95050-4966, USA **Work Phone:** (408) 983-0171 **Fax Number:** (408) 983-0295 **Date of Birth:** August 2, 1931 **Languages Spoken:** English, Spanish **Education:** BA (1953), St. Patrick's College; Graduate Studies in Education (1958-61), The Catholic University of America; (summer), University of California - Berkeley; Ph.D. (1962), The Catholic University of America **Congresses and Conferences:** (1968-71), USCC Committee on Education; (1978-86), Committee on Communications, (Chair, 1983-86); (1979-86, 87-90), NCCB/USCC Administrative Committee; (1984-89), Pontifical Commission for Social Communications, Vatican; (1987-present), NCCB Committee on Science and Human Values (chair, 1987-90); (1987-92), Advisor, NCCB Committee on Doctrine; (1987-92), Chair, Commission of Bishops and Scholars; (1992-present), NCCB Committee on Migration Refugee Services; (1992), NCCB Committee on Women in Society and the Church **Previous Positions:** Assistant Pastor (1957-58), Immaculate Heart Parish, Belmont, CA; Assistant Professor (1961-63), The Catholic University of America; Faculty (1963-65), Serra High School, San Mateo, CA; Assistant Superintendent of Catholic Schools (1965-74), Archdiocese of San Francisco; Superintendent (1974-78), Archdiocese of San Francisco, CA; General Director (1968-81), Archdiocesan Educational Television Network, Menlo Park, CA **Media:** Board of Directors (1968-present), Catholic Television Network (CTN); President (1975-77), CTN; Board of Directors (1975-80), Public Service Satellite Consortium; US Department of State Advisory Committee (1978-79), 1979 World Administrative Radio Conference **Discipline:** Theology Related Areas of Interest: Communications, Administration.

Edgar, William

Present Position and Address: Professor of Apologetics (since 1993) Westminster Theological Seminary, Church Road and Willow Grove Avenue, Philadelphia, PA 19118, USA **Work Phone:** (215) 887-5511 **Home Phone:** (215) 884-6334 **Date of Birth:** October 11, 1944 **Languages Spoken:** English, French **Education:** B.A. Music (with Honors, 1966), Harvard University; M.Div. (1966-69), Westminster Theological Seminary, Philadelphia; Graduate Studies in Ethnomusicology, Columbia University NY; D. Th. (1993), Université Genevé, Switzerland **Previous Positions:** Teacher Philosophy/Music (1970-78), Brunswick School, Greenwich CT; Secretary (1973-78)/Board of Trustees (1971-78, 91-), Fellowship of Christians in Universities and Schools (FOCUS); Instructor (1979-81)/Professeur d'Apologétique (1981-1989)/Comité Directeur (1988-1989), Faculté Libre de Théologie Réformée, Aix-en-Provence, France **Selected Memberships:** Served 5 years as president/ex officio member, Comité de Réflexion sur l'Ethique Médicale (C.E.R.E.M.), France; President, Huguenot Fellowship (since 1989); President, Chestnut Hill Hospital Medical Ethics Committee **Discipline:** Apologetics, Theology, Ethics and Musicology **Related Areas of Interest:** Cultural Analysis; Music, Art, Modern Culture and Christian Theology.

Eicher, Andreas Daud

Present Position and Address: Graduate Student, Yale School of Forestry and Environmental Studies and Yale School of Public Health, 205 Prospect Street, New Haven, CT 06511 USA **Phone:** (203) 562-7851, (203) 432-5942 (fax), E-Mail: Andi@minerva.ycc.yale.edu **Date of Birth:** April 2, 1969 **Languages Spoken:** English, German, some Hindi **Previous Positions:** Researcher, Social Ecology/Forestry Study, Central Himalaya, N. India (May-Nov. 1993); Field Assistant, Fire Ecology Study, Oregon State University, H.J. Andrews Exp. Forest (summer 1992); Research Assistant, Weed Seedbank Ecology Study, Taylor University, IN (summer 1991); Volunteer, Mussoorie Gramin Vikas Samiti (Indian Development Agency) (Mar-April 1990). **Honors:** Harvey Fellow, 1994-95 **Memberships:** Society of American Foresters, International Society of Tropical Foresters, Chi Alpha Omega. **Discipline:** Community Forestry, Community Health **Relevant Areas of Interest:** Silviculture, Rural Sociology, Political Economy, Epidemiology **Current Area of Research:** Aspects of change in forest protection in a Himalayan village. **Personal Notes:** Indian Citizen, missionary parents.

Elliott, John Eric

Present Position and Address: Ph.D. candidate (May 1991), Department of History and Sociology of Science, University of Pennsylvania 2504-D Miller Park Circle, Winston-Salem, NC 27103, USA **Work Phone:** (919) 721-1685 **Date of Birth:** July 30, 1960 **Languages Spoken:** English, German **Education:** A.B. History of Science (highest honors, 1982), University of North Carolina; M.A. (1985), University of Pennsylvania; J.D. (1988), School of Law, Villanova University **Previous**

Positions: Teaching Assistant (1983-84), University of Pennsylvania; Graduate Intern (1984-87), Center for History of Chemistry; Youth Coordinator (1986-87), Wayne United Methodist Church PA; Principal Organizer (with Peter Morris, Open University UK) of symposium "Die IG Farben und der Staat" at the XVIII International Congress of the History of Science, Hamburg, Germany; Exhibit Designer (Fall 1989), National Plastics Center and Museum, Leominster, MA **Discipline:** History and Sociology of Science **Related Areas of Interest:** Science, Technology and Religion.

Evans, C. A.

Present Position and Address: Professor/Chairman of Religious Studies (since 1981) Trinity Western University, 7600 Glover Road, Langley, BC V3A 6H4, Canada **Date of Birth:** January 21, 1952 **Education:** B.A. (1974), Claremont McKenna College, CA; M.Div. (1977), Western Baptist Seminary, OR; M.A. (1980)/Ph.D. (1983), Claremont Graduate School, CA **Previous Positions:** Assistant Professor of Religious Studies, McMaster University (1980-81); Sessional Lecturer, Regent College (1985-87)/University of British Columbia (1988-89); Visiting Fellow (1987-88), Princeton Theological Seminary **Discipline:** Religious Studies **Related Areas of Interest:** Ethics.

Fairchild, Roy W.

Present Position and Address: Professor Emeritus of Spiritual Life and Psychology, San Francisco Theological Seminary, San Anselmo, CA 1 Idalia Road, San Anselmo, CA 94960, USA **Concurrent Positions:** Accreditation Team (1974), Western Association of Schools and Colleges **Date of Birth:** September 9, 1921 **Education:** A.B. (1943), University of California - Berkeley; B.D. (1946) San Francisco Theological Seminary; M.A. (1947), University of Chicago; Ph.D. (1956), University of Southern California **Postgraduate Studies:** Postdoctoral training in Conjoint Family Therapy (1962-63), Mental Research Institute, Palo Alto, CA; Lilly Foundation Postdoctoral fellowship in Empirical Research in Religious Education at Western Behavioral Sciences Institute and the University of California (1965-66) **Conferences and Congresses:** Professional Seminars at C. G. Jung Institute, San Francisco (since 1973) **Previous Positions:** Assistant Pastor, First Presbyterian Church, San Anselmo, CA (1943-46)/Wheaton, IL (1946-47); State Certified Teacher (1944-46), San Quentin Prison; University Pastor and Staff Counselor (1948-50), University of Southern California; Assistant Professor of Psychology (1950-56), Occidental College, Los Angeles; Associate Director (1956-59), Office of Family Research, United Presbyterian Church; Professor of Education and Social Psychology (1959-81), San Francisco Theological Seminary; Visiting Fellow (1966), Western Behavioral Sciences Institute, La Jolla, CA; US Air Force Leadership Training Seminar Leader in Alaska, Japan and Philippines (1968); Consultant and Seminar Director (1972-74), World Council of Churches **Selected Memberships:** American Psychological Association; Psi Chi, National Honorary Society in Psychology; Society for the Scientific Study of Religion **Discipline:** Theology; Psychology; Sociology **Related Areas of Interest:** Psychology and Religion/Spiritual life; Theology and Sociology.

Fast, Edwin

Present Position and Address: Retired (since 1993); 1549 Beverly Road, Idaho Falls, ID 83402, USA **Home Phone:** (208) 524-2627 **Date of Birth:** July 2, 1914 **Languages Spoken:** English, German, Low-German **Previous Positions:** Teaching, University of Oklahoma, University of Idaho, Extension/Idaho State University, Missouri Baptist College; Spectrographic Analysis, Phillips Petroleum, Bartlesville, OK; Health Physics, Phillips Petroleum, Idaho Falls, ID; Head, Reactor Experiments Section, Phillips Petroleum and Idaho Nuclear Co., Idaho Falls, ID; Nuclear Reactor and Critically Safety Engineer, E G &G, and Westinghouse Idaho Nuclear Co., Idaho Falls, ID **Selected Memberships:** American Physical Society; American Nuclear Society; American Scientific Affiliation; Former member: American Chemical Society; Optical Society of America **Discipline:** Physics; Chemistry; Math **Related Areas of Interest:** Nuclear Criticality Safety; Nuclear Reactor Physics.

Faulkner Jr., George R.

Present Position and Address: Managing Consultant, A. Foster Higgins & Company Inc., Philadelphia, PA; (Home) 105 Vernon Lane, Yardley, PA 19067, USA **Work Phone:** (215) 246-1448 **Home Phone:** (215) 295-2328 **Date of Birth:** May 6, 1947 **Education:** B.A. English (1969), Lafayette College; M.Phil. Religious Studies (1978), Syracuse University **Discipline:** Employee Benefits Consulting **Related Areas of Interest**: Religion and Science and Philosophy **Current Research:** Occasionally teach and speak at the Unitarian-Universalist Church.

Feil, Dirk

Present Position and Address: Professor of Chemistry and Physics (since 1966) Twente University, Enschede, Netherlands; (Home) Langenkampweg 97, 7522 LL Enschede, Netherlands **Date of Birth:** February 17, 1933 **Languages Spoken:** Languages Spoken: Dutch, English, German **Education:** Physics and Chemistry, Utrecht; M.Sc. (1958), Utrecht; Ph.D. (1961), Pittsburgh, PA, USA/Utrecht, Netherlands **Previous Positions:** Research Associate (1958-60), Pittsburgh, USA; Lecturer (1960-61), Utrecht; Lecturer (1961-64), Cape Town, South Africa; Reader (1964-66), Twente University, Netherlands **Discipline:** Chemistry and Physics **Related Areas of Interest:** Science - Theology; Science and the Third World.

Ferrell, Ginnie

Present Position and Address: Associate Minister (since 1987) 203 Main Street, Sanford, ME 04073, USA **Work Phone:** (207) 324-3524 **Date of Birth:** April 29, 1953 **Education:** Education B.A. Geology (1975), Hampshire College, Amherst, MA; B.S. Chemistry (1983), University of Alaska - Fairbanks; M.Div. (1987), Bangor Theological Seminary, ME **Previous Positions:** Geologist, Geophysics Technician (1975-81) **Discipline:** Ordained Minister (United Church of Christ, 1988); Geology and Chemistry **Related Areas of Interest:** Environmental Ethics; Science, Technology and the Church.

Firestone, Homer Loon

Address: 57610 Crestview Drive, Yucca Valley, CA 92284, USA; CaSilla 4773, Cochabamba, Bolivia **Work Phone:** (619) 365-3747 **Date of Birth:** December 10, 1921 **Education:** B.Th. (1944), Kansas City College and Bible School; B.A. (1946), University of Kansas City; M.A. (1956), University of Chicago; Ph.D. (1963), University of New Mexico **Previous Positions:** University of Redlands (1965-70); Azusa Pacific University (1970-71); Missionary in Bolivia (1946-present), presently a retired research volunteer **Discipline:** Theology (Missions); Marriage and Family Therapy; Anthropology; Linguistics **Related Areas of Interest:** Religion and Marriage; Family and Child Therapy; Anthropology in the Context of Missions.

Ford, Mary Anne Kehoe

Present Position and Address: Director, Rhone-Poulenc, 349 Westport Turnpike, Fairfield, CT 06430, USA; (Home) P. O. Box 881, Shelton, CT 06484, USA **Work Phone:** 9203) 925-3574 **Home Phone:** (203) 454-1433 **Date of Birth:** June 24, 1941 **Languages:** English, German, French **Congresses:** Delegate, Earth summit, Rio de Janeiro (1992) **Lectures:** Grower Talks (1977-81) **Previous Positions:** Vice-President, John Volk Co.; Manager, Public Affairs, Rhone-Poulene; Manager, Public Affairs, Union Carbide; Director, Public Relations, Geo. J. Bau Inc.; **Media Experience:** Feature writer, *New*

York Times (1979) **Editorial Experience:** Writer, *Ohio State Florist Bulletin* (1992) **Selected Memberships:** Institute for Science and Theology; Society for Health & Human Values **Discipline:** Communications **Related Interests:** Bioethics; Environmental Ethics.

Forman, Frank

Address: 6923 Clarendon Road, Bethesda, MD 20814, USA **Work Phone:** (202) 401-0182 **Home Phone:** (301) 652-5792 **Date of Birth:** October 28, 1944 **Education:** B.A. Mathematics (1966)/M.A. Economics (1968), University of Virginia; Ph.D. Economics (1985), George Mason University **Previous Positions:** Research Economist (1969-84), Civil Aeronautics Board; Economist (since 1985), US Department of Education **Selected Memberships:** Institute on Religion in an Age of Science; Public Choice Society; The Mencken Society **Discipline:** Economics **Related Areas of Interest:** Ethics; the Metaphysics of Political Philosophy.

Fuchs, Peter C.

Present Position and Address: Pathologist and Hospital Epidemiologist (since 1968)/Chairman of Medical Morals Committee (since 1975) St. Vincent Hospital and Medical Center, 9205 SW Barnes Road, Portland, OR 97225, USA **Date of Birth:** May 16, 1936 **Education:** B.S. (1957), Georgetown University; Ph.D. Anatomy (1961)/M.D. (1963), University of Maryland **Discipline:** Pathology and Epidemiology **Related Areas of Interest:** Medical Ethics and Medical Morals.

Furtado, Daphne

Present Position and Address: Lecturer and Head of Department in Biochemistry Sophia College, Bhulabhai Desai Road, Bombay, 400 026, India **Work Phone:** 8221601; 8221642 **Date of Birth:** September 2, 1939 **Languages Spoken:** English, French, Hindi **Education:** Doctorate in Biochemistry (1982), London; Research and study (1979, 1982), Bioethics, Kennedy Institute of Ethics, Georgetown University, Washington D.C. USA **Selected Memberships:** Society of the Sacred Heart of Jesus, University of Bombay; Member of Medical Bioethics Group, Archdiocese of Bombay **Discipline:** Biochemistry/Chemistry **Related Areas of Interest:** Bioethics.

Gailey, Franklin B.

Address: Berea College, C.P.O. Box 795, Department of Biology, Berea, KY 40404, USA **Date of Birth:** October 18, 1918 **Education:** B.S. Chemistry (1940), Georgia Institute of Technology; M.S. (1942)/Ph.D. Biochemistry (1946), University of Wisconsin **Previous Positions:** Instructor (1946-48), Biology and Chemistry, Lees Junior College; Assistant Professor through Chairman (1948-82), Emeritus Professor (since 1989), Biology Department, Berea College **Selected Memberships:** Institute on Religion in an Age of Science **Discipline:** Physiology and Biochemistry **Related Areas of Interest:** Courses taught include: science and Christian faith; Brain/Mind Phenomena; Creation, Evolution and Humanization of Life; Holistic Health.

Gardipee, Steven M.

Present Position and Address: Currently a Ph.D. candidate in Theology, Marquette University; (Home) N81 W15111 Appleton Avenue #8, Menomonee Falls, WI 53051, USA **Date of Birth:** September 19, 1955 **Education:** Marian College of Fond du lac (1973-76); B.A. (1978)/M.A. candidate (1978-82), Marquette University, Milwaukee, WI **Selected Memberships:** Center for Process Studies, Claremont Graduate School, CA **Discipline:** Theology/Philosophy **Related Areas of Interest:** Contemporary American Theology/Philosophy; Metaphysics; Process Theology; Theological Implications of Whiteheadian Cosmology.

Gill, Stephen P.

Present Position and Address: Founder and Chief Scientist Magnetic Pulse Inc. (since 1986), Volan Division of MOSCOM, Inc. (since 1979); 32 Flood Circle, Atherton, CA 94025, USA **Date of Birth:** November 13, 1938 **Education:** B.S. (1960), Massachusetts Institute of Technology; M.A. (1961)/Ph.D. (1964), Harvard University **Previous Positions:** Votan-Voice Recognition; MPI - Oil Well Logging **Discipline:** Applied Mathematics and Physics **Related Areas of Interest:** Science and Theology.

Gillette, P. Roger

Present Position and Address: Senior Research Physicist (since 1950, but only part-time since 1986), SRI International P.O. Box 908, Half Moon Bay, CA 94019, USA **Work Phone:** (415) 726-5741 **Date of Birth:** May 12, 1917 **Education:** B.A. Physics (1937), Cornell College; B.S. Engineering Physics (1938)/M.S. Physics (1939)/Ph.D. Physics (1942), University of Illinois **Postgraduate Studies:** Postgraduate studies in Philosophy (1986-88), College of Notre Dame, Belmont, CA **Previous Positions:** Professor of Philosophy (1987-88); Lecture Series on Science, Religion and Ethics

(April-May 1990) **Selected Memberships:** Institute on Religion in an Age of Science; Center for Theology and the Natural Sciences; The Hastings Center **Discipline:** Engineering Physics (Systems Development); Ethics in Technology, Medicine and Business **Related Areas of Interest:** Interrelationships among the following: Science, Art and Technology; Theology and Religion; Human Values and Ethics.

Giulianelli, James L.

Present Position and Address: Professor of Chemistry (since 1985) Regis College, W. 50th Blvd. and Lowell Blvd., Denver, CO 80221, USA **Work Phone:** (303) 458-4045 **Date of Birth:** August 7, 1940 **Education:** B.S. Chemistry (1962), University of Massachusetts; Ph.D. Physical Chemistry (1969), University of Wisconsin **Previous Positions:** Postdoctoral Research Fellow (1969-71), University of Texas; Assistant Professor of Chemistry (1971-77), Universidad de Los Andes, Venezuela; Visiting Assistant Professor (1977-79)/Assistant Professor (1979-85), Colorado School of Mines **Selected Memberships:** American Chemical Society; Sigma Xi; NSTA **Discipline:** Chemistry **Related Areas of Interest:** Teaching Science in a Jesuit College.

Gosden, Roger G.

Present Position and Address: Professor of Reproductive Biology (since 1994), School of Medicine, University of Leeds, Clavendon Wing, Leeds General Infirmary, Leeds 2S2 9NS, UK **Work Phone:** 113 292 3157 **Date of Birth:** September 23, 1948 **Education:** B.Sc. (1970), University of Bristol; Ph.D. (1974), Cambridge University; D.Sc. (1989), Edinburgh University **Previous Positions:** Population Council Fellow (1974-75), Duke University; MRC Fellow (1973-74, 1975-76), Cambridge University; Lecturer/Senior Lecturer in Physiology (1976-94), Medical School - Teviot Place, University of Edinburgh, Scotland; Guest Scientist (1979, 1981, 1987), University of Southern California **Selected Memberships:** Fellow, Institute of Biology, London **Discipline:** Physiology of Reproduction and Ageing **Related Areas of Interest:** Human Embryology and Ageing; Biomedical Science and Christian Theology **Current Research:** Has spoken on these topics to academic and theological groups.

Gouldstone, Tim

Present Position and Address: Vicar of St Keverne (since 1985), The Vicarage, Helston, St. Keverne, Cornwall, TR12 6NG, UK **Date of Birth:** February 7, 1946 **Education:** B.Sc. Geology (Hons, 1968)/M.Sc. Geology (1976), Exeter University; Bristol Certificate in Theological Studies (1978); BD (External), (1994), London University **Selected Memberships:** Society of Ordained Scientists; British Astronomical Association **Discipline:** Geology; Pastoral Ministry **Related Areas of Interest:** Science, Liturgy and Prayer; Holistic View of Science and Theology.

Gowenlock, Brian G.

Present Position and Address: Emeritus Professor of Chemistry (since 1990), Heriot-Watt University, Edinburgh; Honorary Research Fellow, Department of Chemistry, University of Exeter, Exeter EX4 4QJ, UK; (Home), 5 Roselands, Sidmouth EX10 8PB, UK **Date of Birth:** February 9, 1926 **Education:** B.Sc. (1946)/M.Sc. (1947), Ph.D. (1949), University of Manchester; D.Sc. (1962), University of Birmingham **Awards and Honors:** C.B.E. (Commander of the Most Excellent Order of the British Empire, 1986); FRSE (Fellow of the Royal Society of Edinburgh, 1969) **Previous Positions:** Assistant and Lecturer (1948-55), University College of Swansea; Lecturer and Senior Lecturer in Chemistry (1955-66), University of Birmingham; Professor of Chemistry (1966-90), Heriot-Watt University, Edinburgh **Discipline:** Chemistry **Related Areas of Interest:** Contribution of Michael Polanyi to Science/Theology Dialogue; Science and National Policy Interplay with Particular Reference to Higher Education Institutions; Exploration of the Doctrine of Creation.

Gregory, William Edgar (Edgar)

Present Position and Address: Professor Emeritus of Psychology, University of the Pacific, Stockton, CA 95211 USA (Home) 976 West Mendocio, Stockton, CA 95204 USA **Home Phone:** (209) 463-0982 **Date of Birth:** November 13, 1910 **Languages Spoken:** English, French **Education:** A.B. Colorado College (cum laude), 1933; B.D. Chicago Theological Seminary (Univ. of Chicago) 1936 **Awards and Honors:** Psi Chi; Sigma Xi **Previous Positions:** Chair, Psychology Department, University of the Pacific; Director, Honors Program, University of the Pacific; Professor, Abroad, University of Maryland; Director of Research, Northern California Council of Churches; Army Chaplain; Acting Superintendent, Fort Berthold Indian Mission; Pastor, West Congregational Church, Concord, NH; Editorial Associate of Advance, published by the Congregational Church; Associate Student Pastor, Jefferson Park Congregational Church, Chicago **Selected Memberships:** American Psychological Association; American Sociological Association **Discipline:** Psychology **Related Areas of Interest:** Religion **Current Areas of Research:** Personality (Adaptability).

Griffin, Douglas L.

Present Position and Address: Coordinator of Chaplaincy Service (since 1985) Wilson Health Care Center of Asbury Methodist Village, 201 Russell Avenue, Gaithersburg, MD 20877, USA **Work Phone:** (301) 330-3000 **Date of Birth:** July 19, 1952 **Education:** B.A. (1975), Columbia Union College; M.Div. (1979), Andrews University; Ph.D. (currently), Catholic University **Previous Positions:** Chaplain (1979-80), Leland Memorial Hospital, MD; Director, Chaplaincy Services (1981-85), Shady Grove Adventist Hospital, MD **Selected Memberships:** Society for the Scientific Study of Religion; Institute on Religion in an Age of Science; Association for Clinical Pastoral Education **Discipline:** Pastoral Care; Institutional Chaplain **Related Areas of Interest:** Medicine and Religion; Medical Anthropology; Psychology and Religion; Neuropsychological Processes in Religious Cognition.

Haas III, John W.

Present Position and Address: EIC Laboratories, Inc., 111 Downey Street, Norwood, MA. 02062 USA (Home) 3 Thomas Drive, Franklin, MA 02038 USA **Home phone:** (508) 520-9737 **Date of Birth:** March 27, 1959 **Education:** B.A. Chemistry (1981), Dartmouth College; Ph.D. Analytical Chemistry (1986), University of Massachusetts **Previous Position:** Researcher, Oak Ridge National Laboratory, Operated by Martin Marietta Energy Systems, Inc., P. O. Box 2008, Oak Ridge, TN 37831-6113 **Selected Memberships:** American Scientific Affiliation; American Chemical Society **Discipline:** Analytical Chemistry **Related Areas of Interest:** Ethics and science.

Haba, Hanako

Present Position and Address: Research Officer, IBJ International PLC, Bracken House, One Friday Street, London EC4M 9JA; (Home) 115 Lockesley Drive, Petts Wood, Kent BR5 2AD, UK **Work Phone:** (071) 236-1090 **Home Phone:** 0689-873772 **Date of Birth:** February 5, 1945 **Education:** B.Sc. (1967)/M.Sc. (1969), Tokyo University, Japan **Selected Memberships:** Soka Gakkai International; **Discipline:** Philosophy of Science and Religion **Related Areas of Interest:** Philosophy, Natural and Social Sciences and Religion.

Hall, Forrest G.

Present Position and Address: Staff Scientist, Laboratory for Terrestrial Physics NASA Goddard Spaceflight Center (Code 623), Greenbelt, MD 20771, USA **Work Phone:** (301) 286-2974 **Education:** B.S. Mechanical Engineering (1963), University of Texas - Austin; M.S. Physics (1967)/Ph.D. Physics (1970), University of Houston **Previous Positions:** Johnson Space Center (1964-80); Chief, Scene Analysis Branch, Earth Resource Research Division, Johnson Space Center; Ordained Church Elder, Brown Memorial Church in Baltimore; Consultant to National Geographic **Discipline:** Terrestrial Physics.

Harman, William K.

Present Position and Address: Pastor (since 1982) Bethlehem Lutheran Church, 925 Balour Drive, Encinitas, CA 92024, USA **Work Phone:** (617) 753-1026 **Date of Birth:** July 22, 1939 **Education:** A.B. (1961), Wittenberg University OH; B.D. (1965), Lutheran School of Theology at Chicago; Th.M. (1967), Graduate Theological Union, Berkeley, CA **Conferences and Congresses:** Attended a conference in Germany in 1988 on science and theology which was sponsored by Vesper Society and the Chicago Center for Theology and Science **Previous Positions:** Professor/Tutor (1967-70), Makumira Theological College, Arusha, Tanzania; Tutor (1975-1979), St. Andrews Theological College,

Trinidad; Executive (1979-1982), Lutheran World Federation, Geneva, Switzerland; Inter-Conference Coordinator (1985-1988), Vesper International, San Leandro, CA **Selected Memberships:** Vesper Society, 311 MacArthur Blvd., San Leandro, CA 94577 **Discipline:** USA Church History **Related Areas of Interest:** Application of Science to International Development and Contribution of Science to International Relations - North-South Dialogue **Current Research:** Presented a Paper on Science/theology for a Conference in Mexico City in 1973; Author, *Paths to Peace*, Vesper Society Conferences, Summary, 1988.

Hartwig, Edward Clayton

Present Position and Address: Staff Senior Scientist Emeritus, Lawrence Berkeley Laboratory, University of California, Berkeley, 100 Santa Rita Drive, Walnut Creek, CA 94596 **Work Phone:** (510) 486-5584 **Home Phone:** (520) 935-0319 **Date of Birth:** February 21, 1917 **Languages Spoken:** English **Awards and Honors:** Staff Senior Scientist Emeritus **Previous Positions:** Control Engineer, Westinghouse Electric (1943-52); Various Positions, Univ. of Calif., Lawrence Livermore Lab and Lawrence Berkeley Lab (1953-86); Dept Head of Electronic Engineering, Lawrence Berkeley Lab **Selected Memberships:** The Center for Theology and Natural Science **Discipline:** Physics and Engineering **Related Interests:** The creation, discovery, and probable end of the cosmos as we know it **Current Research:** His research consists of an attempt at self-education in understanding our origins and purpose (if any).

Selected Publications: He has written perhaps two dozen articles about control theory and the design of particle accelerators, all before 1980.

Haury, David L.

Present Position and Address: Associate Professor (since 1990), College of Education University of Lowell, One College Avenue, Lowell, MA 01854, USA **Date of Birth:** September 17, 1947 **Languages Spoken:** English, German **Education:** B.A. (1974)/M.A. Biology (1978), University of Oregon; Ph.D. Science Education (1983), University of Washington **Previous Positions:** High School Science teacher (1974-77), South Australia; Assistant Professor of Biology (1982-84), Judson Baptist College; Assistant Professor of Science Education (1984-90), Tufts University **Selected Memberships:** National Association for Research in Science Teaching; Association for the Education of Teachers in Science; National Science Teachers Association; American Association for the Advancement of Science; American Scientific Affiliation **Discipline:** Science Education; Biology **Related Areas of Interest:** Public Perceptions of Science; Communicating Scientific Epistemology; Science and Faith - as a Science Educator with Strong Religious Convictions, I am most interested in promoting an intellectually honest view of science as a way of knowing, as a way of understanding both the substances and processes of the material universe.

Hefley, James C.

Present Position and Address: Adjunct Professor, Hannibal-LaGrange College, Hannibal, MO 63401, USA **Concurrent Positions:** CEO, Hefley Communications, Inc., Publisher of Hannibal Books **Work Phone:** (314) 221-2462 **Date of Birth:** June 2, 1930 **Education:** B.A. Bible/Literature (1950), Ouachita Baptist University; M.Div. (1953), New Orleans Baptist Theological Seminary; Ph.D. Broadcasting/Journalism (1982), University of Tennessee **Honorary Degrees:** D.Let. (1981), Ouachita Baptist University **Previous Positions:** Pastor (1953-1961), Southern Baptist Churches in New Orleans; Accredited Staley Foundation Lecturer for Christian Colleges and Universities; Director of annual Mark Twain Writers Conference in Hannibal, MO; Teacher of "Writing for Publication"; Scripted, produced, directed religious dramas, over 20 radio stations (4 years)/Evangelistic Youth Broadcast (1 year); Pioneered Broadcast-telephone counseling ministry, New Orleans (2 years); Correspondent of Christianity Today (11 years); Contributing editor of Christian Life (12 years) **Selected Memberships:** Immanuel Baptist Church in Hannibal; Kappa Tau Alpha **Discipline:** Journalism; Publishing **Related Areas of Interest:** Theology/Ethics and Science/Technology.

Heim, S. Mark

Present Position and Address: Professor of Christian Theology (since 1993), Andover Newton Theological School 210 Herrick Road, Newton Center, MA 02154, USA **Date of Birth:** March 14, 1950 **Education:** B.A. (1972), Amherst College; M.Div. (1976), Andover Newton Theological School; Ph.D. (1982), Boston College **Previous Positions:** Assistant (1982-86)/Associate (1987-92) Professor, Andover Newton Theological School **Selected Memberships:** Faith and Science Exchange, (Boston Theological Institute); American Academy of Religion; **Discipline:** Systematic Theology **Related Areas of Interest:** Cosmology; Philosophy of Science; History of Science/Theology.

Heron, Alasdair Iain Campbell

Present Position and Address: Professor Ordinarius for Reformed Theology, Theological Faculty University of Erlangen-Nürnberg, Kochstrasse 6, D-91054 Erlangen, Germany **Date of Birth:** July 24, 1942 **Languages Spoken:** English, German **Education:** B.A. (1965)/M.A. (Classical Tripos/Moral Sciences Tripos, 1968), Sidney Sussex College, Cambridge; B.D. (1968), University of Edinburgh; D.Th. (summa cum laude, 1973), University of Tübingen, Germany **Previous Positions:** Assistant Minister (1969-1971), St. Michael's Parish Church in Linlithgow, Scotland; Assistant to Professor Dr. Ulrich Wickert (1971-73), Church History, University of Tübingen; Research Lecturer in Systematic Theology (1973-74), Irish School of Ecumenics, Dublin; Lecturer in Christian Dogmatics (1974-1981), New College, Edinburgh; Editor of Scottish Journal of Theology (since 1974); Kerr Lecturer in Trinity College, Glasgow (1976-1979); Active in WCC/WARC (since 1978); Co-editor of *Heinrich Bullinger, Theologische Werke* (since 1983) **Selected Memberships:** Academie Internationale des Sciences Religieuses; Society for the Study of Theology; Wissenschaftliche Gesellschaft für Theologie; Association Internationale d'Études Patristiques; Ökumenischer Arbeitskreis Evangelischer und Katholischer Theologen **Discipline:** Theology.

Hess, Gerald D.

Present Position and Address: Professor of Biology (since 1983), Messiah College, Grantham, PA 17027-0800, USA; (Home) 227 N. Grantham Road, Dillsburg, PA 17019, USA **Work Phone:** (717) 766-2511 **Date of Birth:** March 13, 1943 **Education:** B.A. Biology (cum laude, 1965), Messiah College; M.S. Physiology (1968)/Ph.D. Physiology (1970), Michigan State University **Previous Positions:** Assistant through Full Professor of Biology (since 1970), Messiah College; Research Assistant (Summers 1985-88), Pennsylvania State University **Selected Memberships:** American Association for the Advancement of Science; American Physiological Society; American Scientific Affiliation; Sigma Xi **Discipline:** Biology **Related Areas of Interest:** Bioethics and Ethics of Technology.

Hess, Peter M.

Present Position and Address: Adjunct Faculty (instructor in Ethics, since 1984), University of San Francisco; Teaching, Santa Clara University, Santa Clara, CA, USA; (Home) 317 Twenty-Fourth Avenue, San Francisco, CA 94121, USA **Date of Birth:** June 14, 1956 **Languages Spoken:** English, French, German **Education:** B.A. Theology, Philosophy and French (summa cum laude, 1978), University of San Francisco; B.A. (1981)/M.A. Philosophy and Theology (1984), Oxford University; Ph.D. Social Ethics and Early Modern Intellectual History (1993), Graduate Theological Union, Berkeley, CA **Previous Positions:** High School Teacher in World History, Ethics and Theology (1980-84), St. John Ursuline High School, San Francisco, CA; Lecturer in Philosophy (1983), Holy Family College in Fremont, CA **Selected Memberships:** Center for Ethics and Social Policy in Berkeley; Center for Theology and the Natural Sciences, Berkeley; American Academy of Religion; American Society of Church History; Society of Christian Ethics **Discipline:** Philosophy; Theology **Related Areas of Interest:** The Relationship Between Science and Religion in 17th-19th Century England; Environmental Ethics.

Hilden, Kurt Mark

Present Position and Address: Current applicant for Post M.A. Studies P.O. Box 70185, Pasadena, CA 91117-7185, USA **Date of Birth:** June 24, 1951 **Languages Spoken:** English, German **Education:** A.A. (1971), Suomi College; A.B. (1973), Carthage College; Lutheran N.W. Theological Seminary (1973-75); M.A. (1985), Fuller Theological Seminary; Pacific Lutheran Theological Seminary (1986) **Previous Positions:** Hospital Support Services; Municipal Government/Professional Association; High School Registrar; High School Lecturer **Selected Memberships:** Institute on Religion in an Age of Science; Park Ridge Center for the Study of Ethics **Discipline:** Theology; Philosophy **Related Areas of Interest:** Ethics; Biological Scientific Study in the Light of Biblical Studies.

Hinkle, John E.

Present Position and Address: Professor of Pastoral Counseling (since 1978) Garrett-Evangelical Theological Seminary, 2121 Sheridan Road, Evanston, IL 60201, USA **Date of Birth:** October 14, 1933 **Education:** B.A. (1955), Taylor University; B.D. (1959), Garrett-Evang. Theological Seminary; M.A. (1960)/Ph.D. (1970), Northwestern University. Licensed Clinical Psychologist (1970), Indiana; Licensed Marriage and Family Therapist (1994), ILL; National Registry of Certified Group Psychotherapists **Previous Positions:** Worked as missionary and Pastor (1960-1972), United Methodist Church, Director of Clergy Career Candidate Assessment Services (since 1972); Training Director (since 1984), Asian American Pastoral Counseling Center in Chicago; Senior Staff Psychotherapist (since 1972), Pastoral Psychotherapy Institute, Parkside Human Services, Inc., Park Ridge, IL; Associate Professor of Pastoral Psychology and Counseling (1972-77)/Chairman (1979-82), Garrett-Evangelical Theological Seminary; Affiliate Professor of Pastoral Counseling (1969-1972), Christian Theological Seminary **Selected Memberships:** American Academy of Psychotherapists; American Association of Group Psychotherapists; Fellow, American Association of Pastoral Counselors **Discipline:** Psychology; Pastoral Counseling **Related Areas of Interest:** Pastoral Psychology; Psychological Anthropology (cult and personality); Cross-cultural Pastoral Counseling.

Hoggatt, Austin Curwood

Present Position and Address: Professor of Business, Emeritus (since 1991), University of California - Berkeley 4601 Grass Valley Road, Oakland, CA 94605, USA **Date of Birth:** August 31, 1929 **Education:** B.S. (1950), Northwestern University; M.A. (1952)/Ph.D. (1957), University of Minnesota **Previous Positions:** Assistant (1958)/Associate (1962)/Professor of Business Administration (1967-91)/Emeritus (since 1991), University of California - Berkeley **Selected Memberships:** Montclair Presbyterian Church; Fellow, American Association for the Advancement of Science; Supporter of the Center for Theology and the Natural Sciences, GTU, Berkeley **Discipline:** Economics **Related Areas of Interest:** Information in the Management of Resources to Control Pollution and Protect the Environment, Particularly with Energy Management in the Emerging Economies in Post-communist Europe. Environmental Ethics.

Holmes, H. Rodney

Present Position and Address: Senior Lecturer in Biological Sciences Collegiate Division (since 1989)/Staff Member in Basic Program, Office of Continuing Education (since 1989) University of Chicago, 1116 East 59th Street, Chicago, IL 60637, USA; (Home) 6 Danube Way, Olympia Fields, IL 60461, USA **Work Phone:** (312) 702-8587 **Date of Birth:** November 1, 1952 **Education:** B.S. Psychology (*magna cum laude* 1978), Abilene Christian University TX; M.S. Veterinary Physiology and Pharmacology (1979), Purdue University; Ph.D. Physiology and Biophysics (1984), University of Oklahoma Health Sciences Center **Previous Positions:** Postdoctoral Fellow (1984-85), University of Oklahoma; Postdoctoral Fellow (1985-86), University of Calgary; Postdoctoral Fellow and Lecturer (1986-89), University of Chicago **Selected Memberships:** American Association for the Advancement of Science; American Physiological Society; Society for Neuroscience; Associate of the Chicago Center for Religion and Science; Institute on Religion in an Age of Science (IRAS, affiliate of AAAS); Chicago Advanced Seminar on Religion in an Age of Science (CASIRAS) **Discipline:** Biological Science - Physiology and Biophysics (Biomedical Engineering, Medical Ethics); Psychology **Related Areas of Interest:** Medicine; Biomedical Engineering; Science and Ethics; Taught a course on Science, Technology and Human Values, Physical, Genetic and Religious Perspectives **Current Research:** A publication entitled, "What is the ethical context of the neurosciences?" is forthcoming.

Hoppin, Marion C.

Present Position and Address: Professor Emeritus (1977), New College in Sarasota, FL; (Home) 1212 Center Place, Sarasota, FL 34236, USA **Date of Birth:** December 23, 1905 **Languages Spoken:** English, French, German **Education:** B.A. (1932), Bates College; A.M. (1936)/Ph.D. Psychology (1950), Columbia University; C. G. Jung Institute in Zürich (1951) **Previous Positions:** Private Practice in psychotherapy; Professor of Psychology (1965-77), New College in Sarasota, FL **Selected Memberships:** American Psychological Association; Florida Psychological Association; Jung Foundation **Discipline:** Psychology **Related Areas of Interest:** Psychology and Religion.

Horswell, Kevin

Present Position and Address: Present Position Chaplain (since 1986), Lady Margaret Hall, Oxford OX2 6QA, UK (Home) 19 Hayfield Road, Oxford OX2 6TX, UK **Work Phone:** (0865) 274386 **Home Phone:** (0865) 56802 **Date of Birth:** April 8, 1955 **Education:** B.A. Mathematics (1977), Jesus College, Cambridge; B.A. Theology (1981), Nottingham University **Selected Memberships:** Memberships: Society of Ordained Scientists; Science and Religion Forum; Center for Theology and the

Natural Sciences; Theology; Mathematics; Physics **Discipline:** Cosmology; Logic in Theology, Mathematics, and Science.

Hoshiko, Tomuo

Present Position and Address: Professor in Physiology (since 1969), Case Western Reserve University School of Medicine, Cleveland, OH 44106, USA **Date of Birth:** October 5, 1927 **Education:** B.S. Zoology (1949), Kent State University; Ph.D. Physiology (1953), University of Minnesota **Previous Positions:** Instructor in Physiology (1953-55), University of Utah; Research Fellow (1955-57), American Heart Association at Zoophysiological laboratory, University of Copenhagen; Senior Instructor (1957-59)/Assistant Professor (1959-66)/Associate Professor (1966-69)/Professor in Physiology, Case Western Reserve University; Visiting Assistant Professor (1964-65), Tokyo Medical and Dental University, Tokyo; Visiting Professor (1971-72), Institute of Technology in Chicago; Guest Professor (1980-81), Laboratorium voor Fysiologie, Katholieke Universiteit Leuven, Belgium **Selected Memberships:** American Association for the Advancement of Science (since 1951); American Physiological Society (since 1958); Society of General Physiologists (since 1967, Secretary 1973-75/President 1981/Council 1981-1983); Biophysical Society (since 1958); American Scientific Affiliation; Council of Scientific Society Presidents; C.W.R.U. Center for Biomedical Ethics, Professional Advisory Committee, (since 1985) **Discipline:** Physiology; Biophysics **Related Areas of Interest:** Bioethics, Natural Theology, Animal Experiments, Theonomy.

Hulme, Norman A.

Present Position and Address: Retired Clinical Project Director, Clinical Research Department, Sterling-Winthrop Research Institute 50 Sunset Drive, Delmar, NY 12054, USA **Date of Birth:** June 9, 1924 **Education:** M.A. Biochemistry (1953), Johns Hopkins University; Ph.D. Pharmacology (1957), University of Maryland **Previous Positions:** Research Coordinator (1954-62), Sterling-Winthrop Research Institute; Clinical Pharmacologist (1962-67)/Senior Clinical Pharmacologist (1967-68)/Research Project Director (1969-78)/Clinical Research Associate (1978-80), Clinical Research Department, Sterling-Winthrop Research Institute **Selected Memberships:** Subscriber to *Zygon* **Discipline:** Pharmacology **Related Areas of Interest:** Scientific Justification for Christianity.

Hunter, Lloyd P.

Present Position and Address: Professor Emeritus, Department of Electrical Engineering University of Rochester, Rochester, NY 14627, USA **Work Phone:** (716) 442-1493 **Date of Birth:** February 11, 1916 **Education:** B.A. (1939), College of Wooster; B.S. (1939), Massachusetts Institute of Technology; M.S. (1940)/D.Sc. (1942), Carnegie Institute of Technology **Previous Positions:** Researcher (1939-51), Westinghouse Research Laboratories; Researcher (1951-1963)/Director of Component Engineering (1960), International Business Machines Corporation; Professor of Electrical Engineering (1963-81), University of Rochester, NY **Selected Memberships:** Fellow, American Physical Society; Fellow, Institute of Electrical and Electronic Engineers (IEEE); American Association of University Professors; Sigma Xi **Discipline:** Electrical Engineering **Related Areas of Interest:** Reducing Technological Illiteracy Among Clergy and Theologians; the Problem of Evil; Discerning Harmony Between Science and Faith.

J

Jackelén, Antje

Present Position and Address: Ordained pastor, currently doing postgraduate studies in Dogmatics at Lund University, Sweden; General Secretary of The European Society for the Study of Science and Theology (ESSSAT); Högseröds Prästgard, S-240 33 Löberöd, Sweden **Phone:** +46 413 30398 **Date of Birth:** June 4, 1955 **Education:** Kirchliche Hochschule Bethel (1974-76), Germany; Universität Tübingen (1976-77); Swedish Teol. Kand (1977-80), Uppsala University. Scholarship "Studienstiftung des deutschen Volkes" **Conferences and Congresses:** Cyprus Consultation on Science and Faith (1987); 2nd -5th European Conference on Science and Theology (1988, 90, 92, 94) **Discipline:** Philosophy of Religion; Dogmatics **Related Areas of Interest:** The Concept of Time in Theology and Science.

Jang, Allen Wai

Present Position and Address: Science/Psychology Teacher and College Advisement Counselor, Blair High School - Health Academy, 1201 S. Marengo Avenue, Pasadena, CA 91106, USA; Core Adjunct Faculty, Department of Natural Science; Department of Psychology, National University, 9920 La Cienega Blvd., Inglewood, CA 90301, USA **Work Phone:** (818) 441-2201, ext. C-29 **Home Phone:** (818) 281-6180 **Date of Birth:** August 18, 1950 **Languages:** English; Cantonese Chinese **Lectures:** Frequent speaker at churches, camps, workshops. etc. on the subject of Christian apologetics, creation-evolution, etc. **Awards and Honors:** M.E.S.A. Advisor of the Year (1992); (Mathematics, Engineering, Science Achievement), California State University - Los Angeles; National Honor Roll Science Teacher (1993), Association of Science Technology Centers **Concurrent Positions:** Local Leader, National Science Teachers Association, Pasadena - Alhambra Areas; M.E.S.A. Advisor (Mathematics, Engineering, Science Achievement), California State University - Los Angeles, 5151 State College Drive, Los Angeles, CA 90032, USA **Selected Memberships:** National Science Teacher's Association; South California Academy of Sciences; American Scientific Affiliation; American Psychological Association; Christian Association for Psychological Studies; American Association of Christian Counselors; National Association of College Admission Counselors; Associates for Biblical Research **Discipline:** Psychology and Natural Sciences **Related Interests:** Science Education; Psychology Instruction: Christian Apologetics.

Personal Notes: He has 3 extensive published "letters to the editor" and 2 published book reviews dealing with creation-evolution.

Jappe, Fred

Present Position and Address: Professor (since 1968), Chemistry, Science and Religion, New Testament, Mesa College; (Home) 10205 Vista de la Cruz, La Mesa, CA 92041, USA **Date of Birth:**

February 17, 1932 **Education:** B.A. Education (1953)/B.S. Chemistry (1953), University of Washington; Southwestern Baptist Theological Seminary (1956-57); M.A. (1961), San Diego State University; M.S. Chemistry (1966), Seattle University **Previous Positions:** Quality Control (1953-54), Boeing Aircraft Company; Panther Oil and Grease in Fort Worth (1956-57) **Selected Memberships:** American Scientific Affiliation; American Chemical Society; Jesus Seminar **Discipline:** Chemistry; New Testament **Related Areas of Interest:** Evolution; Biblical Studies.

Johnson, Anthony P.

Present Position and Address: Executive Director (since 1989), It's Time. . . Inc., New York, NY; Adjunct Faculty in Non-Profit Management, New School for Social Research, 1993; (Home) 202 N. Brook Drive, Milltown, NJ 08850 USA **Work Phone:** (212) 962-3069 **Home Phone:** (908) 247-8864 **Fax:** (212) 406-5879 **Education:** B.A. (*cum laude,* 1971), Boston University; M.Div. (1977), Harvard University; M.S. in Urban Affairs and Policy Analysis (1990), New School for Social Research NY **Previous Positions:** Minister (1977-80), Unitarian Fellowship, Burbank, CA; Minister (1981-86), Unitarian Society New Brunswick, NJ; Coordinator (1986-87), Ozanam Shelter for Homeless Men, New Brunswick, NJ; Consultant (1988), Trust for Public Land - New York City Land Project **Selected Memberships:** Institute on Religion in an Age of Science (IRAS); *Zygon* **Discipline:** Social Science; Pastoral Ministry; Non-Profit Management **Related Areas of Interest:** Social Sciences, Ethics, Theory and History of Philanthropy.

Johnston, G. Archie

Present Position and Address: Marriage/Family/Child Counselor, CA. Lic. No. MW009326 Post Office Box 9066, Eureka, CA 95502, USA **Work Phone:** (707) 441-1271 **Date of Birth:** July 10, 1940 **Education:** B.A. Psychology/Social Welfare (1971), California State University - Long Beach; M.A. Behavioral Science (1973), California State University - Dominguez Hills; Ph.D. Psychology (1976), California Coast University - Santa Ana; Ph.D. Human Behavior (1980), Newport University; D.Min. Pastoral Care/Counseling (1987), California Graduate School of Theology - Glendale; M.S. Clinical Nutrition (1988), International College for Nutrition Education, Newport Beach **Previous Positions:** 15 years of food service management/culinary arts experience before 1973; Drug-Alcohol/Rehabilitation Psychologist (1972-78), Federal Correctional Institute; Behavioral Scientist/Educational Consultant (1975-85), Alcoholism Council of Greater Long Beach; Professor of Behavioral Sciences/Vice President (1977-88), Newport University; Executive Director (1977-82), California Behavioral Science Institute; Marriage/Family/Child Counselor/Nutritionist Private Practice (1982-present); Internship Supervisor/Supervising Clinician (1984-85), Simpson College; Adjunct Faculty Professor (1987-89), International University for Nutrition Education; Staff Therapist (1988), Los Altos Mental Health Hospital - Long Beach **Selected Memberships:** American College of Forensic Psychology; Fellow, American Scientific Affiliation; Christian Medical Society; Christian Association for Psychological Studies; First Covenant Church - AIDS Research, Addiction **Discipline:** Psychology; Nutrition; Counseling and Therapy **Related Areas of Interest:** Pastoral Care of Society; Psychology and Christian Faith.

Jones, Jack R.

Address: 4715 Rittenhouse Street, Riverdale, MD 20737, USA **Home Phone:** (301) 277-2242 **Date of Birth:** April 16, 1941 **Education:** B.S. General Science (1964), Virginia Polytechnic Institute and State University, Blacksburg VA; Social Ecology (1974), Goddard College, VT **Selected Member-**

ships: Baltimore Green Party; Maryland Libertarian Party; **Discipline:** Social Ecology; Agricultural Systems/Cities **Related Areas of Interest:** Applied Science and Applied Religion.

Junkin III, William F.

Present Position and Address: Professor of Physics (since 1974), Erskine College Due West, SC 29639, USA; P.O. Box 184, Due West, SC 29639, USA **Work Phone:** (803) 379-8822 **Home Phone:** (803) 379-2245 **Date of Birth:** February 15, 1942 **Education:** B.A. Physics and Math (summa cum laude, 1963), King College, Bristol, TN; Ph.D. Theoretical Nuclear Physics (1967), M.I.T. **Previous Positions:** Assistant Professor (1967-70, 1973-74), University of Richmond; Associate Professor (1970-73), Tunghai University, Taiwan; Elder of PC USA (currently), Greenville Presbyterian Church, Donalds, SC **Discipline:** Physics **Related Areas of Interest:** Theology and Physics; Cosmology; Quantum Mechanics.

Kalthoff, Mark A.

Present Position and Address: Instructor (since 1989), Department of History Hillsdale College, Hillsdale MI 49242; (Home) 163 Oak Street, Hillsdale, MI 49242, USA **Work Phone:** (517) 439-0186 **Date of Birth:** August 29, 1962 **Education:** B.S. History, Math, Biology (1984), Hillsdale College; M.A. History and Philosophy of Science (1987)/Ph.D. History and Philosophy of Science (currently), Indiana University **Previous Positions:** Associate Instructor of Math (1985-86)/Associate Instructor of History and Philosophy of Science (1986-87), Indiana University **Selected Memberships:** History of Science Society; American Historical Association; American Scientific Affiliation **Discipline:** History and Philosophy of Science **Related Areas of Interest:** American Science; Science and Religion; American Social and Intellectual History; Philosophy of Science.

Kassel, Victor

Present Position and Address: Private Practice of Geriatrics, Medical, Psychiatric and Social Problems of Aging (1951); 721 16th Avenue, Salt Lake City, UT 84103-3706, USA **Work Phone:** (801) 359-8245 **Date of Birth:** August 18, 1920 **Education:** B.S. (1941), University of Maryland; M.D. (1944), Long Island College of Medicine **Discipline:** Geriatrics **Related Areas of Interest:** Relevant Area of Interest: The Role of Religion (i.e. Judaism) in Healing and Health. Encouraging Clerics and Patients to Look on Religion as the Best Medicine to Solving Many Problems Facing Society Today.

Keggi, J. John

Present Position and Address: Interim, Trinity Church, Bridgewater, MA 02146, USA (Home) 62 Crest Road, Wellesley, MA 02181, USA **E-mail:** (Internet) ekggi@delphi.com **Date of Birth:** August 24, 1932 **Languages Spoken:** English, French, German, Spanish, Latvian **Education:** B.S. (1954), Brooklyn College; M.S. (1958)/Ph.D. Organic Chemistry (1962), Yale University **Previous Positions:** Research Chemist (1961-66), American Cyanamid; Coordinator Technical Education (1966-70), Sun Oil; Training Manager (1970-71), American Hoechst; Director (1973-76), Management Programming, ILE School - Cornell; Director, Continuing Education and Associate Professor (1976-81), Institute of Paper Chemistry; Training Consultant (1981-82), KC of Mexico; Dean (1984-87), St. Andrews Center for Theological Studies; Rector (1986-87), St. Mark's Guadalajara; Interim Priest, Diocese of Massachusetts **Selected Memberships:** Society of Ordained Scientists **Discipline:** Organic Chemistry **Related Areas of Interest:** Faith and Science; Spirituality in a Post-Technological World; Entropy and Spirit.

Keiper Sr., Glenn L.

Present Position and Address: Currently a Graduate Student in Philosophy and Medical Ethics Cleveland State University; Oral and Maxillofacial Surgery, 733 West Street, Suite 107, Akron, OH 44303, USA **Date of Birth:** March 23, 1937 **Education:** B.S. (1958), University of Pittsburgh; D.D.S. (1962), Case Western Reserve University, Cleveland, OH **Previous Positions:** Assistant Professor (1985-87), Department Community Dentistry, CURU; Instructor (1986-87), Department of Human Values in Medicine, Northeast Ohio University College of Medicine **Selected Memberships:** Society for Health and Human Values **Discipline:** Oral and Maxillofacial Surgery **Related Areas of Interest:** Health Profession Ethics.

Kent, Raymond D.

Present Position and Address: Professor (since 1977) Department of Communicative Disorders, College of Letters and Science, University of Wisconsin - Madison, 1975 Willow Drive, Madison, WI 53706, USA **Date of Birth:** December 21, 1942 **Education:** B.A. Speech Pathology and Audiology (1965), University of Montana, Missoula; M.A. (1969)/Ph.D. Speech Pathology and Audiology (1970), University of Iowa **Postgraduate Studies:** Postdoctoral work in Speech Communication (1970-71), Massachusetts Institute of Technology, MA **Previous Positions:** Assistant through Professor (1971-present), Department of Communicative Disorders, University of Wisconsin - Madison; Staff Scientist (1977-79), Clinical Research Center for Neurogenic Speech Disorders, Waisman Center on Mental Retardation and Human Development, Madison; Principal Investigator, Public Health Service Research Grant No's. NS-11022, NS-ND-12881, NS-16763, NS-22458; Co-Principal Investigator (currently) in 2 areas **Selected Memberships:** Institute on Religion in an Age of Science; New York Academy of Sciences; American Association of Phonetic Sciences; Speech Pathology **Discipline:** Religion in the Age of Science.

Kern, John C.

Present Position and Address: Directing Trustee (since 1966), The Kern Foundation 3712 Adams Road, Oak Brook, IL 60521, USA **Work Phone:** (312) 654-3678 **Home Phone:** (708) 654-3678 **Fax:** (708) 654-3694 **Date of Birth:** May 22, 1925 **Education:** S.B. (1950), Massachusetts Institute of Technology (MIT); Harvard Business School/Northwestern University, Staff Transfer from MIT (1951-53); Organ. Theory (1969-71) **Previous Positions:** Technical Director (1964-69), Coleman Instruments, Division of Perkin-Elmer **Selected Memberships:** Vice Chair, Theosophical Investment Trust, Happy Valley Foundation, Ojai, CA; Executive Committee/Trustee, Museum of Contemporary Art, Chicago; Council for the Arts at MIT; Visiting Com. for Regenstein and other Libraries, University of Chicago **Discipline:** Research Management; Foundation Management **Related Areas of Interest:** Interrelation of Arts and Science.

Kerr, John Maxwell

Present Position and Address: Chemistry/Logic Teacher; Winchester College, Winchester, Hampshire SO23 9NA UK **Current Positions:** Tutor in Theology (since 1993), Oxford University Summer School **Work Phone:** (0962) 862317 **Date of Birth:** April 19, 1943 **Education:** BA Sc. Chemical Engineering (1966), University of Toronto; M.Sc. Tribology (1970), University of Leeds; Dip. Theol (1976), Nottingham University **Previous Positions:** Professional Engineer (1966-69), Shell Canada; Athlone Research Fellow (1969-71), Leeds; Lecturer in Chemical Engineering (1971-77), Nottingham; Curate (1977-80), Windsor; Chaplain (1980-82), Cheltenham; Visiting Research Fellow (for 1990),

Merton College, Oxford **Selected Memberships:** Science and Religion Forum (Secretary 1984-88); Warden (since 1992), Society of Ordained Scientists; Warden (since 1991), Scientific and Medical Network **Discipline:** Theology; Biomedical Engineering; History and Philosophy of Science **Related Areas of Interest:** Philosophical Theology; Cosmology; Models and Metaphors in Science and Religion; Ethics; Education in Science and Religion.

Kim, Stephen S.

Present Position and Address: Associate Professor/Associate Dean (since 1987) School of Theology, Claremont, 1325 N. College Avenue, Claremont, CA 91711, USA **Date of Birth:** March 29, 1943 **Languages Spoken:** English, Korean **Education:** B.A. (1969), Yonsei University; M.Div. (1972), University of Dubuque; Ph.D. (1987), Drew University **Selected Memberships:** American Academy of Religion; History of Science Society **Discipline:** Historical Theology; Religion and Science (19th Century); World Religions **Related Areas of Interest:** Natural theology; Darwin and Tyndall; Thermodynamics; Quantum Physics; Nature of Reality.

Kirby, Richard

Present Position and Address: Occupant of Stuart C. Dodd Chair in Social Innovation, The Forum Foundation, Seattle, WA, USA; Pastor (since 1978), Order of the Academy of Christ; 3 Victoria Terrace, Ealing Green, London W5 5QS, UK; 4427 2nd Avenue NE, Seattle, WA 98105-6191, USA **Date of Birth:** July 16, 1949 **Education:** B.A. Hons. (1st Class, 1973), London University; M.Div. (Hons., 1985), General Theological Seminary, Episcopal Church USA; Ph.D. Theology (1992) King's College, London **Selected Memberships:** Society of Authors (UK); Religious Futurists Network; World Network of Religious Futurists; Mensa, World Future Society **Discipline:** Theology **Related Areas of Interest:** Cosmology and Eschatology; Astronautics; Computer Science and Artificial Intelligence; Social Science.

Kirchoff, Bruce K.

Present Position and Address: Associate Professor of Biology (since 1990) University of North Carolina - Greensboro, NC 27412-5001; (Home) 1315 Oak Lane, Hillsborough, NC 27278, USA **Work Phone:** (910) 334-5391, ext. 37 **Home Phone:** (919) 732-5369 **E-Mail:** kirchoff@goodall.uncg.edu **Date of Birth:** November 26, 1952 **Education:** B.G.S. (Bachelor of General Studies, with distinction, 1975)/M.S. Biology (1977), University of Michigan, Ann Arbor; Ph.D. Botany (1981), Duke University NC **Previous Positions:** Visiting Assistant Professor of Botany (1981-82), Louisiana State University; Postdoctoral Fellowship at the Hebrew University of Jerusalem (1982-84); Research Associate (1984-86), Fairchild Tropical Garden, Miami, FL **Selected Memberships:** American Association for the Advancement of Science; Society for the Evolution of Science; Society for Scientific Exploration **Discipline:** Botany - flower development/systematics/genetics **Related Areas of Interest:** Unifying Art and Science; Learning to See Spirit Manifest in Nature.

Kuharetz, Boris

Present Position and Address: Associate Professor of Physics New Jersey Institute of Technology (NJIT), Newark, NJ 07102, USA **Date of Birth:** March 3, 1921 **Education:** B.S. Physics (1951)/A.M. Physics (1961), Columbia University NYC; Ph.D. Physics (1980), Stevens Institute of Technology **Previous Positions:** Lecturer in Physics (1956-62)/Assistant (1962-65)/Associate Professor of Physics

(1967-84)/Associate Chair (1984-85), New Jersey Institute of Technology **Selected Memberships:** American Physical Society; American Association for the Advancement of Science; NY Academy of Science; American Scientific Affiliation; Fellow, World Academy of Art and Science; President, Sigma Xi Chapter, NJIT **Discipline:** Astrophysics **Related Areas of Interest:** Connections between Developments in Modern Physics and Theology.

Lamoureux, Denis Oswald

Present Position and Address: Doctoral Student, University of Alberta, Faculty of Dentistry, Department of Oral Biology; #1908 8515-112 Street, Edmonton, Alberta T6G 1K7, Canada **Education:** B.S. (1976), University of Alberta; Doctor of Dental Surgery (1978), University of Alberta; Diploma of Christian Studies (1986), Regent College; M.D. (1987), Regent College and Carey Hall; Master of Christian Studies Old Testament (1987), Regent College; Ph.D. (1991), University of St. Michael's College/Wycliffe College, Toronto School of Theology, University of Toronto.

Landess, Marcia McBroom

Present Position and Address: Lecturer. Founder/President (since 1986), For Our Children's Sake Foundation; New York representative African Commentary Magazine 60 East 42nd Street, Suite 1310, New York, NY 10017, USA **Date of Birth:** August 6, 1947 **Education:** B.A. (1973), Hunter College, NY; Joint studies at New York Theological Seminary/New York University (1980) **Previous Positions:** Director of Religious Education (1975-85), Community Church of New York; Cultural coordinator (1986), Week of Special Session on Africa at the United Nations; Started first Human Rights Committee on a Community Board in the history of NY City; Created breast feeding poster which was distributed globally; originated Apartheid Awareness Project for High School students; Presently a board member of U.N.A. NY/Metro Comm. UNICEF/REA/Community Bd #6 Manhattan NYC/Rod Rodgers; Dance Company/member Latin American Advisory Council LaLeche League International; Wrote for Study Guide which accompanies Old Tales for a New Day, edited by S. Lyon Fahs and Alice Cobb **Selected Memberships:** Unitarian Universalist, NY; Ethical Culture Society, NY **Discipline:** Social Action, Education and Religion **Related Areas of Interest:** Global Citizenship; The Use of Language in Shaping World Views, and the Use of Science and Religion in Obtaining World Peace.

Larsen, Judith K.

Present Position and Address: Vice-President, Worldwide Research Dataquest (Microelectronics) 3790 La Selva, Palo Alto, CA 94306, USA **Date of Birth:** November 23, 1942 **Education:** B.A. (1964), Gustavus Adolphus College; M.A. (1965), Syracuse University; Ph.D. (1980), University of California **Previous Positions:** Engineer (1964-67), Philco-Ford; Senior Research Scientist (1967-82), American Institutes for Research; President (1982-87), Cognos Associates **Discipline:** Microelectronics.

Legrain, Michel

Present Position and Address: Professor á l' U. E. R. of Theology and Sciences and Religious (since 1972), á l'Institut Catholique de Paris 24 rue Cassette, 75006 Paris, France **Work Phone:** 42 22 76 00

Date of Birth: January 5, 1929 **Education:** Licence de théologie (1957), Gregorian University, Rome; Doctorate in Canon Law (1965(, á l'Institut Catholique de Paris **Previous Positions:** Professor of Moral Theology, Pastoral Care and Canon Law (1960-74), au Séminaire des Pères du Saint-Esprit á Chevilly-Larue; Professor of Canon Law (1965-94), á l'Institut Catholique de Paris **Discipline:** Canon Law and Ethics **Related Areas of Interest:** Theology and Culture.

Libanio, João Batista

Present Position and Address: Professor of Fundamental Theology, Faculty of Theology, Ingnatius Institute (since 1987) Av. Cristiano Guimarães 2127, caixa postal 5047, 3i.710 Belo Horizonte, Brazil **Date of Birth:** February 19, 1932 **Languages Spoken:** Portuguese, English, Spanish, French, German, Latin, Italian **Education:** Philosophy LE (1955-57), Jesuit Faculty of Philosophy in Nova Friburgo, RJ Brazil; LLA (1955-58), PUC of Rio, Brazil; STL (1959-62), Theological Jesuit School of Frankfurt, Germany; D.D. (1963-68), Pontifical Gregorian University of Rome **Previous Positions:** Dean of PUC (1972-73), Faculty of Theology, Rio; Dean of Faculty of Theology, Saint Ignatius Institute in Brazil (1988-93); Dean of Ignatius Institute, Faculty of Theology (1987-94) **Selected Memberships:** President (1985-97), Theological Association of Brazil; Member of the Priests Council of the Archdiocese of BH (1987-88) **Discipline:** Philosophy; Liberal Arts (New Latin Languages); Theology (including Liberation Theology) **Related Areas of Interest:** Theology (fundamental, eschatological, liberation) and Social Science (analytical, economics, political).

Liljas, Anders

Present Position and Address: Professor (since 1988), Department of Molecular Biophysics Lund University, Box 124, S-221 00 Lund, Sweden **Work Phone:** (046) 104681 **Date of Birth:** May 9, 1939 **Languages Spoken:** Swedish, English, German **Education:** B.Sc. Mathematics/Chemistry (1964)/M.Sc. Chemistry (1966)/D.Sc. Chemistry (1971), Uppsala University **Previous Positions:** Research Assistant in Biological Structure (1964-71), under Prof. B. Strandberg, Uppsala University; Postdoctoral research associate (1971-73), Department of Biological Sciences, Purdue University, W. Lafayette, IN; Research Associate (1973-79)/Scientist at the natural science council (1979-86)/Lecturer (1986-88), Department of Molecular Biology, Uppsala University **Discipline:** Molecular Biophysics.

Lindenblad, Irving W.

Present Position and Address: Retired Astronomer (since 1989), US Naval Observatory, Washington D.C.; Associate Pastor, Palisades Community Church, Washington, DC; (Home), 4507 MacArthur Blvd., NW, Washington, DC 20007-4201, USA **Home Phone:** (202) 333-2245 **Date of Birth:** July 31, 1929 **Education:** A.B. (1950), Wesleyan University; M.Div. (1956), Colgate Rochester Divinity School; M.A. Religion (1963), George Washington University; Chaplain Intern, Washington Hospital Center, (1990-92) **Previous Positions:** Pastor of the following congregations -Savannah Congregational Church, Savannah, NY (1954-55)/Market Street Baptist Church, Harrisburg, PA (1957)/Montowese Baptist Church, North Haven, CT (1961-62); Astronomer (1953, 1958-60, 1963-89), US Naval Observatory, Washington DC **Selected Memberships:** Fellow, Royal Astronomical Society (UK); American Astronomical Society; Institute on Religion in an Age of Science; Advisory Committee, Northern Virginia Mental Health Institute; Religious Outreach Network, National Alliance for the Mentally Ill; International Council of Community Churches **Discipline:** Astrometric and Geodetic Astronomy; Parish Ministry **Related Areas of Interest:** Relationships Between Christian Mysticism, Science and Religion; Spirituality and Mental Health.

Ling, Vincent

Present Position and Address: Postdoctoral Research Associate Harvard University, 16 Divinity Ave, Cambridge, MA 02138, USA **Education:** B.A. Molecular Biology (1984), University of California - Berkeley; M.S. Plant Biology (1987)/Ph.D (1990), University of Illinois at Urbana-Champaign **Previous Positions:** Research Associate (1984-85), Lawrence Berkeley Laboratory, Berkeley; **Discipline:** Plant Biology.

Lovett Doust, Jonathan Nicolas de Grave

Present Position and Address: Professor (since 1993), Biological Sciences University of Windsor, Windsor, Ontario, N9B 3P4 Canada **Work Phone:** (519) 253-4232 ext 2699 **Home Phone:** (519) 322-0541 **Date of Birth:** November 5, 1950 **Education:** B.Sc. Hons. Biology (1973), Queen's University, Canada; Ph.D. (1978), University of Wales **Previous Positions:** Postdoctoral Teaching Fellow (1978-79), University of Western Ontario/University of British Columbia (1979-81); Assistant Professor (1981-87), Amherst College; Associate Professor (1987-88), Hartford College **Selected Memberships:** American Association for the Advancement of Science; Society for the Study of Evolution; Botanical/Ecological Societies of America; British Ecological Society **Discipline:** Biology, reproductive ecology **Related Areas of Interest:** Religion and Science Interaction **Current Research:** Sexuality and gender; Plant Population Biology and Demography; Biology of Umbelliferae and Araceae; Plant-animal Interactions; Clonal Growth and Evolutionary Ecology.

Lynden-Bell, Donald

Present Position and Address: Astronomer, Institute of Astronomy, University of Cambridge The Observatories, Madingley Road, Cambridge CB3 0HA, England **Work Phone:** (0223) 337525 **Discipline:** Astronomy **Related Areas of Interest:** Cosmology; big bang theory. "I have spent time, as have many other good Christian scientists, thinking about the contrast between faith and revelation and the scientific method, and the contrast between the degree of determinism contained in the known physical world and the concept that God works in the world, and not merely through the cracks of in determinism left by quantum mechanics."

$$\mathcal{M}$$

Macior, Lazarus Walter

Present Position and Address: Franciscan Priest; Distinguished Professor of Biology (since 1994), University of Akron, Akron, OH 44325-3908, USA **Work Phone:** (216) 972-7163 **Fax Phone:** (216) 972-8445 **Date of Birth:** August 26, 1926 **Education:** A.B. (1948)/M.A. (1950), Columbia University; Ph.D. University of Wisconsin - Madison **Postgraduate Experience:** Postgraduate studies in Philosophy (1951-53), St. Francis College, Burlington, WI/Theology (1953-57), Christ the King Seminary, West Chicago, IL **Previous Positions:** Instructor in Biology (1960-62), St. Francis College; Lecturer (1962-64), Marquette University, WI; Assistant Professor (1965-67), Loras College, Dubuque, WI; Project Director (1966-68), Institute of Arctic and Alpine Research, University of Colorado, Boulder; Assistant Professor (1967-68)/Associate Professor (1968-1972)/ Professor of Biology (1972-94), University of Biology of Akron, OH; Project Director (1971-73), Ohio State University Institute of Polar Studies, Columbus; Honorary Research Associate (1988-1990), New York Botanical Garden **Editorial Positions:** Editorial Reviewer and Referee of 13 journals **Other Academic Experience:** Courses taught include bioethics and evolutionary biology **Selected Memberships:** Fellow, American Association for the Advancement of Science; Fellow, Ohio Academy of Science; Society for the Study of Evolution **Discipline:** Franciscan Priest; Biology **Related Areas of Interest:** "As a Franciscan padre I try to integrate my work with my personal philosophy of an appreciation of nature as a continuing phenomenon of Divine creation." **Current Areas of Research:** The co-evolution of floral form and insect pollinator behavior especially at high altitude stress environments. Research (summer 1990), centered on the Western Himalaya region (previously worked in Japan, North America and Europe).

Mackler, Aaron L.

Present Position and Address: Assistant Professor, Department of Theology, Duquesne University, Pittsburgh, PA 15282, USA **Date of Birth:** December 9, 1958 **Education:** B.A. Religion, Biochemistry (summa *cum laude*, 1980), Yale University; M.A. Rabbi (1985), Jewish Theological Seminary; Ph.D. Philosophy, Georgetown University (1992) **Previous Positions:** Staff Ethicist, New York State Task Force for Life and the Law; Visiting Assistant Professor of Jewish Philosophy, Jewish Theological Seminary of America, NYC **Discipline:** Jewish Theology; Bioethics; Religion; Philosophy **Related Areas of Interest:** Jewish Thought; Bioethics.

Maduro L., Otto A.

Present Position and Address: Visiting Professor (since 1987), Maryknoll School of Theology, Maryknoll, NY 10545, USA; (Home) 27 Upper Croton Avenue, Apt. # 3, Ossining, NY 10562-3842, USA **Work Phone:** (914) 941 7590, ext. 533 **Home Phone:** (914) 762-1733 **Date of Birth:** April 14, 1945 **Languages Spoken:** English, French, Italian, Portuguese, German **Education:** Licentiate in Philosophy (1968), Universidad Central de Venezuela; M.Phil. (*magna cum laude*, 1973)/Ph.D. (*magna* *cum laude,* 1977)/M.A. Sociology of Religion (1978), Universite Catholique de Louvain, Belgium **Previous Positions:** Social Worker (1967-69), Consejo Venezolano del Nino; University Professor de Los Andes (1969-85); Visiting Professor for Undergraduate studies in Venezuela, Universidad Central de Venezuela (1983-85)/Instituto Juan German Roscio (1983)/Pontificia Universidad Catolica Andres Bello (1983-86); Visiting Professor for Graduate Studies in Venezuela, Universidad Central de Venezuela (1977, 1981)/Universidad de Los Andes (1978, 1980)/Universidad Nacional Experimental Simon Rodriguez (1983); Visiting Professor in USA, University of Notre Dame (1982)/Maryknoll School of Theology (Semesters in 1982, 1985, 1986)/University of Southern California (Summer 1988); Research Director (1984-86), Center for Latin American Studies Romulo Gallegos **Selected Memberships:** International Sociological Association; International Conference on the Sociology of Religion; Society for the Scientific Study of Religion; Association for the Sociology of Religion; International Catholic Movement for Intellectual and Cultural Affairs **Discipline:** Philosophy; Sociology of Religion **Related Areas of Interest:** Social Theory of Religion.

Malino, Jerome R.

Present Position and Address: Rabbi Emeritus, The United Jewish Center, 141 Deer Hill Avenue, Danbury, CT 06810, USA; Adjunct lecturer in Homiletics, Hebrew Union College, Jewish Institute of Religion, New York, NY, USA **Date of Birth:** June 7, 1911 **Languages Spoken:** English, Hebrew, Yiddish, French, German **Education:** B.A. (1931), College of the City of New York; Ordained as Rabbi (1935)/M.A. Hebrew Literature, Jewish Institute of Religion **Postgraduate Experience:** Postgraduate study in Europe and Israel (1955-56)/Hebrew Union College - Biblical and Archaeological School in Jerusalem (1965); Studied Jewish communities in Hungary, Austria, Germany, Iran, Czechoslovakia, and South Africa **Honorary Degrees:** D. of Humane Letters (1958), Alfred University; D.D. (1960), Hebrew Union College, Jewish Institute of Religion **Previous Positions:** Rabbi of the United Jewish Center (1935-1981), Danbury, CT; Lectured at Colleges and Universities throughout Eastern USA and taught at Western Connecticut State University (1982, 1984) **Selected Memberships:** Former President of Danbury Ministerial Association; Served on Executive Board/President/Vice President of Association of Religious Communities (ARC); Member of and former President of the Central Conference of American Rabbis; Former President and member of Advisory Board of Institute on Religion in an Age of Science **Discipline:** Rabbi **Related Areas of Interest:** Biblical Archaeology; Value Systems in Social Biology.

Marshall, Jr., John Harris

Present Position and Address: Geologist (since 1982), Marshall Energetics, Inc., 8001 LBJ Freeway, Suite 450, Dallas, TX 75251, USA **Concurrent Positions:** President (since 1992), Madera Production Co., Dallas, TX; President (since 1993), Summit Oil and Gas Worldwide Company, Dallas, TX; Chairperson, The Foundation for Evangelism of the United Methodist Church, Lake Junaluska, NC **Work Phone:** (214) 907-8001 **Date of Birth:** March 12, 1924 **Languages Spoken:** English **Education:** B.A. Geology (1949)/M.A. Geology (1950), University of Missouri **Selected Conferences and Congresses:** Delegate to the World Methodist Council (1991), Singapore **Awards and Honors:** Sigma Xi; *Who's Who in the South and Southwest, Finance and Engineering* **Previous Positions:** Geology Lab Instructor (1948-50), University of Missouri-Columbia; Geologist (1950-82), Mobil Corp.; Director Exploration (1985-91), Anschutz Corp., Dallas, TX/Denver, CO **Administrative Experience:** Chief Executive Officer (since 1982), Marshall Energetics, Inc., Dallas, TX **Selected Memberships:** Past President, Los Angeles Basin Geological Society; American Association Petroleum Geologists; Petroleum Exploration Society of New York; Dallas Geological Society; Rocky Mountain Association of Geologists; Alaska Geological Society; Pacific Section, American Association Petroleum Geologists; Oklahoma City Geological Society; American Geological Institute; New York Academy of Science; American Scientific Affiliation; Affiliation of Christian Geologists **Discipline:** Geology **Related Areas of Interest:** Applied research in the search for Oil and Gas; Evangelism in the United Methodist Church **Current Research:** 3-D Seismic project in Nigeria; Geologic Subsurface study of West Texas, Loving County and East Texas, Gregg and Rusk County.

Marshner, William

Present Position and Address: Associate Professor of Theology (since 1990), Christendom College, 2101 Shenandoah Shores Rd., Front Royal, VA 22630, USA; (Home) 19600 Enterprise Way, Gaithersburg, MD 20879, USA **Concurrent Positions:** Editor, *HLI Reports, Human Life International*, Gaithersburg, MD **Work Phone:** (703) 636-2900 **Home Phone:** (301) 330-8346 **Date of Birth:** August 14, 1943 **Education:** B.A. Classics (*magna cum laude*, 1964), Gettysburg College; Graduate Studies (1964-68)/Ph.D. Candidate, Near Eastern Languages and Literature (1968), Yale University; M.A. Philosophy (1977), University of Dallas; STL (1992), John Paul II Institute for Studies on Marriage and Family; STD Candidate, John Paul II Institute for Studies on Marriage and Family **Previous Positions:** Lecturer (1971-72), Universidad de Maria Cristina, Spain; Lecturer (1976-77), Departments of Theology and Philosophy, University of Dallas; Professor and Chairman (1977-85)/Adjunct Professor (1986-90), Department of Theology, Christendom College; Senior Scholar (1986-90), Institute for Cultural Conservatism, Free Congress Foundation, Washington, DC **Selected Memberships:** American Catholic Philosophical Association; Mariological Society of America (President 1981-84); American Oriental Society **Discipline:** Theology; Philosophy **Related Areas of Interest:** Bioethics; Symbolic Logic.

Martin, Robert K.

Present Position and Address: Assistant Professor of Christian Education, Yale University Divinity School, 409 Prospect St., New Haven, CT 06511, USA **Date of Birth:** August 12, 1959 **Selected Memberships:** Association of Professors and Researchers in Religious Education, AAR **Discipline:** Christian Education **Related Interests:** Theology and Science Dialogue, Including Both Human and Natural Sciences; Theological Orientation of Education in the Church; Philosophical Clarification of Christian Education; Political and Social Implications of Christian Education.

Martino, Rocco Leonard

Present Position and Address: Board of Directors, XRT, Inc.; (Home) 512 Watch Hill Rd., Villanova, PA 19087, USA **Work Phone:** (215) 254-0300 **Date of Birth:** June 25, 1929 **Education:** B.Sc. Applied Mathematics (1951)/M.A. Applied Mathematics/Ph.D. Institute of Aerospace Studies (1955), University of Toronto **Previous Positions:** Adjunct Professor of Mathematics (1961-65), New York University; Professor of Engineering and Department Head (1964-65), University of Waterloo **Administrative Experience:** Member of the Board, St. Joseph's University/Gregorian University-Foundation;ChairmanoftheBoard,MBFCenterforDisabledChildren **Selected Memberships:** Catholic Academy of Sciences in the United States of America; Board of Directors, ITEST; Pontifical Gregorian Circle; Founder, Vatican Observatory; Knight Commander of Eastern Lieutenancy and Member of the Council of the Eastern Order of the Holy Sepulchre; Member, Knights of Malta; **Discipline:** Computer Science; Finance; Technology; Applied Mathematics; Aerospace **Related Areas of Interest:** Theology and science and their applications to life.

Mauser, Ulrich Wilhelm

Present Position and Address: Helen P. Manson Professor of New Testament Literature and Exegesis (since 1990), Princeton Theological Seminary, CN821, Princeton, NJ 08542; USA; (Home) 52 Mercer Street, Princeton, NJ 08540 **Work Phone:** (609) 497-7762 **Date of Birth:** October 3, 1926 **Languages Spoken:** German, English **Education:** University of Tübingen (1946-1951); University of St. Andrews (1952); Ph.D. (1957), University of Tübingen, Germany **Previous Positions:** Pastor (1956-1959), Auferstehungskirche Ludwigsburg, Germany; University Pastor (1959-1964), Corvallis, OR; Associate (1964-1967)/Professor (1967-1977), Biblical Studies, Louisville Presbyterian Theological Seminary; Errett M. Grable Professor of New Testament (1977-1990)/Dean of the Seminary (1981-1990), Pittsburgh Theological Seminary, Pittsburgh, PA **Selected Memberships:** American Academy of Religion **Discipline:** Biblical Theology **Related Areas of Interest:** Ancient Cosmology and Science as it Relates to Theology.

McClellan, William T.

Present Position and Address: Ph.D. Candidate in Philosophy of Religion and Theology, Claremont Graduate School; (Home) Box 1315, Claremont, CA 91711, USA **Date of Birth:** April 15, 1945 **Education:** B.A. (1968), Goddard College; M.A. Religion (1982), Yale Divinity School; Ph.D. candidate, Claremont Graduate School, CA **Related Areas of Interest:** Philosophical-Theological Anthropology; Mind-Body Issues; Comparative Mystical Physiology; Aesthetics; Process thought.

McCormack, Elizabeth J.

Present Position and Address: Rockefeller Family and Associates, Advisor to the Rockefeller family (since 1974); 245 E. 58 Street Apt. # 23F, New York, NY 10022, USA **Concurrent Positions:** Director of General Foods Corp., Champion International Corporation, Stamford, CT **Date of Birth:** March 7, 1922 **Education:** B.A. (1944), Manhattanville College; M.A. (1957), Providence College; Ph.D. (1966), Fordham University **Honorary Degrees:** LL.D. Brandeis University (1972)/Princeton University (1974)/Marlboro College **Previous Positions:** Assistant to President through Academic Dean (1958-66)/Professor of Philosophy and President (1966-74), Manhattanville College **Selected Memberships:** Trustee of American Savings Bank, NYC; Member of Faculty Fellowship Program of United Negro College Fund/Council on Foreign Relations; Trustee of Spelman College, Atlanta/Hamilton College, Clinton, NY; Whitney Museum of American Art, NYC (since 1982); Board of Directors, American Ditchley Foundation/Swarthmore College, PA (since 1980)/Memorial Sloan-Kettering Cancer Center, NYC **Discipline:** Philosophy **Related Areas of Interest:** Philosophy; Relationship of History of Religions and Theology to the other Sciences.

McCrea, Sir William (Hunter)

Present Position and Address: Emeritus Professor of Astronomy (since 1972), Astronomy Centre, University of Sussex, Brighton BN1 9QH, UK **Date of Birth:** December 13, 1904 **Education:** M.A. (1931)/Ph.D. (1929)/Sc.D. (1958), Cambridge University **Honorary Degrees:** Honorary Degrees from National University of Ireland, and the Universities of Cordoba (Argentina), Belfast, Dublin, Sussex **Awards and Honors:** Gold Medal of the Royal Astronomical Society; Keith Prize of the Royal Society of Edinburgh **Previous Positions:** Professor of Mathematics (1936-1944), Queen's University, Belfast; Professor of Mathematics (1944-1966), Royal Holloway College, University of London; Professor of Astronomy (1966-1972), University of Sussex **Selected Memberships:** Fellow of Royal Society **Discipline:** Theoretical Astronomy **Related Areas of Interest:** Astronomy and Cosmology **Personal**

Notes: All of his publications are in mathematics and astronomy, however he is deeply interested in this field.

McFeeley, Daniel

Present Position and Address: Assistant Director of Security, Olivet Nazarene University, Kankakee, IL 60901-0592, USA; (Home) 575 S. Alma, Apt. #3, Kankakee, IL 60901, USA **Date of Birth:** June 19, 1955 **Education:** B.A. Religion/Psychology (1985)/M.A. Religion (1993), Olivet Nazarene University; M.A. Thesis, "An Interdisciplinary Study of Psychology and Religion: Elements of Spirituality in the Literature of the Recovery Movement" **Selected Memberships:** Episcopal Church; Subscriber, *Zygon*; Institute on Religion in an Age of Science **Related Areas of Interest:** Philosophy; Philosophy of Science; Contemporary Psychoanalysis.

McGrath, Alister E.

Present Position and Address: Lecturer in Historical and Systematic Theology (since 1983), Wycliffe Hall, Oxford OX2 6PW, UK **Work Phone:** (Oxford) 865-274209 **Home Phone:** 865-244658 **Date of Birth:** January 23, 1953 **Education:** B.A. Final Honour School of Natural Sciences (1st Class, 1975)/M.A. (1978)/D.Phil. Molecular Biology (1978)/B.A. Honour School of Theology (1st Class Honours, 1978)/B.D. Medieval Theology (1983), Wadham College (1971-75)/Linacre College (1975-76)/Merton College (1976-78), Oxford University and St. John's College (1978-80), Cambridge University **Previous Positions:** Curate (1980-83), St. Leonard's Parish Church, Wollaton; Examiner/Chairman of Examiners (1983-86)/Secretary (since 1987), Oxford University Certificate in Theology; Lecturer in Systematic Theology (since 1984), Oxford University Certificate in Theology; Lecturer in Systematic Theology (1984), Oxford Diocesan Non-Stipendiary Ministerial Training Scheme; Secretary and Convenor (1984-85), Oxford Diocesan Anglican-Lutheran Dialogue Group; Examiner in Ecclesiastical History (since 1988), Final Honour School of Theology; Bampton Lecturer (1990), Oxford University; Tipple Visiting Professor (Fall, 1990), Drew University, NJ, USA **Discipline:** Biology; Theology **Related Areas of Interest:** The Interaction of Theological and Scientific Methodology; Scientific Theories as Models for Doctrinal Statements.

McKowen, Paul M.

Present Position and Address: Retired Pastor (since 1990), Irvington Presbyterian Church, P.O. Box 1336, Fremont, CA 94538, USA; (Home) 733 Iroquois Way, Fremont CA 94539, USA **Date of Birth:** January 17, 1931 **Languages Spoken:** English, Spanish **Education:** B.A. Physics, Mathematics, and History (1952), University of California - Berkeley; San Francisco Theological Seminary (1952-53); M.Div. (1955), Princeton Theological Seminary; Instituto de Espanol (1962), Costa Rica **Previous Positions:** Assistant Pastor (1956-59), First Presbyterian Church, Hayward, CA; Pastor (1959-62), Cannon Beach Presbyterian Church; Venezuelan Fraternal Worker missionary (1962-67); Associate Pastor (1967-77), First Presbyterian Church, Richmond, CA; Pastor (1977-90), Irvington Presbyterian Church, Fremont, CA **Selected Memberships:** American Scientific Affiliation; American Romanian Academy **Discipline:** Philosophy; Spanish **Related Areas of Interest:** The American Romanian Academy Papers of Christology of Miguel de Unamuno and the Christology of Mircea Eliade.

Medgyesi, György

Present Position and Address: Head of Quality Control Division (since 1981), National Institute of Haematology and Blood Transfusion, H-1502 Budapest, Hungary; (Home) Szamoca utca 3, H-1125 Budapest, Hungary **Work Phone:** 166-62-15 **Date of Birth:** March 7, 1936 **Languages Spoken:** Hungarian, English, Italian **Education:** Diploma in Chemistry (1959)/Ph.D. Natural Sciences (1971) and Biological Science (1983), Eötvös Lorand University, Budapest **Previous Positions:** Junior Research Associate in Protein Research (1959-1965)/Research Associate in Immunochemistry (1965-1981), National Institute of Haematology and Blood Transfusion **Selected Memberships:** Hungarian Societies of Immunology/Haematology/Biochemistry **Discipline:** Biochemistry; Haematology; Immunology **Related Areas of Interest:** Evolution and Theology; Ethics of Scientific Research; Role of Research in Society.

Miles, Caroline Mary

Present Position and Address: Chairperson (since 1984), Oxfordshire Health Authority; Director (since 1988), Ian Ramsey Centre, and Ian Ramsey Fellow, St. Cross College, Oxford, UK; (Home) Millbrook, Brookend, Chadlington, Oxford OX7 3NF, UK **Concurrent Positions:** Governor: Ditchley Foundation (since 1983) and Oxford Polytechnic (since 1988) **Date of Birth:** April 30, 1929 **Education:** Somerville College, Oxford **Previous Positions:** HM Treasury (1953-54); NIESR (1954-56,64-67); Attached to UN Secretariat (1956-63), NY; Member (1968-71), Textile Council; Associate Member (1972-74), Nuffield College, Oxford; Inflation Accounting Committee (1974-75); Monopolies and Mergers Commission (1975-84); NEB (1976-79) **Discipline:** Administration; Commerce.

Mills, Joy

Present Position and Address: Director (since 1980), Krotona School of Theosophy, 46 Krotona Hill, Ojai, CA 93023, USA **Date of Birth:** October 9, 1920 **Education:** B.S. (1941), University of Wisconsin-Milwaukee **Postgraduate Experience:** Postgraduate work in English Literature (1941-42), University of Chicago; Postgraduate work in American History (1948-55), University of Washington **Previous Positions:** High School teacher (1948-55), Seattle, WA **Selected Memberships:** National President (1965-74), The Theosophical Society in America; International Vice President (1974-80), The Theosophical Society **Discipline:** Initial work in English; Later studies in American History; Religious and Psychological Studies Independently **Related Areas of Interest:** Religious Studies; Jungian Psychology; Contemporary Science.

Mills, Stephen A.

Present Position and Address: Graduate Student, University of California - Berkeley; c/o P. A. Bartlett, Department of Chemistry, University of California - Berkeley, Berkeley, CA 94720, USA; (Home) 1810 Parker Street, Berkeley, CA 94703, USA **Work Phone:** (510) 642-7076 **Home Phone:** (510) 649-8658 **E-Mail:** steve@fire.cchem.berkeley.edu **Date of Birth:** May 23, 1970 **Languages Spoken:** English **Selected Memberships:** American Chemical Society, American Scientific Affiliation; InterVarsity Christian Fellowship **Discipline:** Bioorganic Chemistry **Related Areas of Interest:** Organic Synthesis; Biological Chemistry **Current Areas of Research:** Synthesis and Evaluation of Phosphorus-based protease inhibitors.

Mitchell, Robert P.

Present Position and Address: Manager, Marketing Support for Scholastic, Inc; Seminarian, New Brunswick Theological Seminary; (Home) 54 Stillman Avenue, Bergenfield, NJ 07621, USA **Work Phone:** (201) 939-8050, ext. 306 **Home Phone:** (201) 384-0951 **Fax Number:** (201) 939-1455 **Date of Birth:** July 15, 1939 **Languages Spoken:** Italian, French, German, English **Media:** Consultant: TV Series, *Space, Time, and God*, being produced by the American Scientific Affiliation **Selected Memberships:** Associate Member, American Scientific Affiliation **Discipline:** Divinity, I.E. Preparation for Pulpit Ministry **Related Areas of Interest:** Jewish/Christian Relations; Origin Science in Relation to Theology and Christian Teaching.

Mohrenweiser, Harvey W.

Present Position and Address: Senior Biomedical Scientist (since 1987), Molecular Biology Section, Biomedical Sciences Division L-452, Lawrence Livermore National Laboratory, Livermore, CA 94550, USA **Work Phone:** (415) 423-0534 **Fax Phone:** (415) 422-2282 **Date of Birth:** October 12, 1940 **Education:** B.S. (1962)/M.S. (1966), University of Minnesota; Ph.D. (1970), Michigan State University **Previous Positions:** Research Associate (1970-1973), McArdle Laboratory for Cancer Research, University of Wisconsin - Madison; Research Chemist (1973-1976), Division of Mutagenic Research, National Center for Toxicological Research, Jefferson, AR; Assistant Professor (1976-1984)/Associate Research Scientist (1984-1987), Department of Human Genetics, University of Michigan Medical School **Selected Memberships:** Center for Theology and the Natural Sciences, Berkeley, CA; Center for Advanced Study in Religion and Science, Chicago **Discipline:** Human Genetics; Molecular Biology **Related Areas of Interest:** Biomedical Ethics; Role of Church in Scientific/Medical Decisions.

Moldoff, Sol

Present Position and Address: Retired Electrical Engineer, 44 Ferguson Avenue, Broomall, PA 19008, USA **Education:** MSEE (1967), University of Pennsylvania **Discipline:** Electrical Engineering **Related Areas of Interest:** Jewish History/Theology and Science.

Monse, Ernst U.

Present Position and Address: Professor of Chemistry (since 1974), Rutgers University - Newark, University Heights, Olson Laboratories, Newark, NJ 07102, USA; (Home) 3 Eileen Court, Wharton, NJ 07885, USA **Date of Birth:** January 10, 1927 **Languages Spoken:** English, German **Education:** M.S. (1952)/Ph.D. (1957), University of Mainz, Germany **Postgraduate Experience:** Postdoctoral studies (1957), Max-Planck-Institute-Mainz; Postdoctoral Studies (1957-59), Columbia University, NY **Previous Positions:** Associate Professor of Chemistry (1965-74), Rutgers University **Selected Memberships:** American Chemical Society; Fellow, American Scientific Affiliation **Discipline:** Theoretical Chemistry **Related Areas of Interest:** Promoting the Integration of Christian Faith and Science.

Moore, Thomas J.

Present Position and Address: SE Manager (since 1985), Electronic Data Systems; (Home) 2285 Golfview Drive, Apt. #205, Troy, MI 48084, USA **Date of Birth:** November 3, 1942 **Education:** B.S.

Accounting (1964)/M.B.A. Administrative Sciences (1967), Wayne State University, Detroit, MI **Previous Positions:** Management Consultant (1966-72), Arthur Andersen & Company; Project Leader (1972-74), J. L. Hudsons; Systems Project Manager (1974-79), National Bank of Detroit; Computer Systems Manager (1979-81), Michigan Cancer Foundation; Manager of Systems Development (1981-85), Harper/Grace Hospitals **Selected Memberships:** Unitarian Universalist Association; Fellowship of Religious Humanists; American Humanist Association; Association of Systems Management; Data Processing Management Association **Discipline:** Management; Data Processing **Related Areas of Interest:** Philosophy; Humanism; Naturalism; Theology; Music; Art.

Morgan, Peter F.

Present Position and Address: Professor of English (since 1974), University College, Toronto M5S 1A1, ONT, Canada **Work Phone:** (416) 978-8152 **Date of Birth:** January 9, 1930 **Languages Spoken:** English, French **Education:** B.A. (1951), University of Birmingham; M.A. (1955)/Ph.D. (1957), University of London **Previous Positions:** Taught at the University of Toronto since 1960 **Selected Memberships:** Society for the Study of Ultimate Reality and Meaning; International Society for Phenomenology and Literature; International Imagery Association **Discipline:** English; Philosophy **Related Areas of Interest:** A Literary Contribution to the Unity of Knowledge; Study of Ultimate Reality and Meaning; Phenomenology; Heidegger and English Poetry; McLuhan's View of Ultimate Reality and Meaning.

Morton, Donald C.

Present Position and Address: Director General (since 1986), Herzberg Institute of Astrophysics, National Research Council of Canada, 5071 W. Saanich Road, Victoria V8X 4M6, BC, Canada **Work Phone:** (604) 363-0040 **Date of Birth:** June 12, 1933 **Education:** B.A. (1956), University of Toronto; Ph.D. Astrophysics (1959), Princeton University **Previous Positions:** Astronomer (1959-1961), US Naval Research Laboratory; Research Associate through Senior Research Astronomer with rank of Professor (1961-1976), Princeton University; Director (1976-1986), Anglo-Australian Observatory **Selected Memberships:** Fellow, Australian Academy of Science **Discipline:** Astrophysics **Related Areas of Interest:** Interstellar Medium; Quasi-stellar Objects; Space Observations; Astronomical Instrumentation.

Muck, Terry C.

Present Position and Address: Senior Vice President (since 1985), Christianity Today/Executive Director, Christianity Today Institute, *Christianity Today,* 465 Gundersen Drive, Carol Stream, IL 60188, USA; (Home) 602 South Gables Boulevard, Wheaton, IL 60187, USA **Concurrent Positions:** Adjunct Professor in Religious Studies (1987-present), Wheaton College, IL **Date of Birth:** June 14, 1947 **Languages Spoken:** English, German, Sinhalese, Pali **Education:** B.A. Philosophy/Psychology (1969), Bethel College; M.Div. Pastoral Care/New Testament (1972), Bethel Theological Seminary; Ph.D. Comparative Religion (1977), Northwestern University; Ordained to Baptist Ministry (1982) **Previous Positions:** Instructor in General Psychology (1969-1971), St. Paul Bible College/Bethel College **Editorial Positions:** Executive Editor, *Christianity Today Magazine* **Selected Memberships:** American Academy of Religion; Evangelical Theological Society; Society for the Scientific Study of Religion; Society of Buddhist-Christian Studies **Discipline:** Theology **Related Areas of Interest:** Relation between Scientific World View and Religious World View; Criteria of Truth in Science and Religion.

Mullen, Pierce C.

Present Position and Address: Professor of History (since 1972), Department of History and Philosophy, College of Letters and Science, Montana State University, Bozeman, MT 59717, USA **Languages Spoken:** English, German, French **Education:** A.B. Math (1957), Hastings College; M.A. History (1958), University of Nebraska; Ph.D. History, University of California -Berkeley **Previous Positions:** Assistant Professor, San Francisco State University **Selected Memberships:** History of Science Society **Discipline:** History **Related Areas of Interest:** History of Science (Biomedical Science); 19th Century German Developmental Biology.

Mullins, Carl Phillips (Phil)

Present Position and Address: Professor of Humanities (since 1978), Missouri Western State College, St. Joseph, MO 64507, USA; (Home) 2512 Francis, St. Joseph, MO 64501, USA **Work Phone:** (816) 271-4386 **Home Phone:** (816) 233-8301 **Date of Birth:** May 20, 1947 **Education:** A.B. English (1969), Vanderbilt University; M.A. Theology (1971)/M.Div. (1972), Pacific School of Religion, Berkeley, CA; Ph.D. Theology, Thesis "Hermeneutical and Aesthetic Applications of the Thought of Michael Polanyi" (1976), Graduate Theological Union at Berkeley, CA **Editorial Positions:** General Editor: *Tradition and Discovery: The Polanyi Society Periodical* **Selected Memberships:** American Academy of Religion; The Polanyi Society; Society for Values in Higher Education **Related Areas of Interest:** Theology; Philosophy **Current Areas of Research:** Modern Philosophical and Religious Thought; Policy Ethics; Hermeneutical Issues in Art and Literature; Interdisciplinary Studies.

Mwenegoha, Amani

Present Position and Address: Executive Secretary (since 1987), Evangelical Lutheran Church in Tanzania, P.O. Box 3033, Arusha, Tanzania **Work Phone:** Arusha 3221 **Date of Birth:** December 25, 1954 **Education:** LL.B. (Honors, 1982), University of Dar-es-Salaam, Tanzania **Previous Positions:** Foreign Service Officer (1982-83); Assistant Executive Secretary (1984-87), Evangelical Lutheran Church in Tanzania **Discipline:** Administration **Related Areas of Interest:** "There is an absence of many well-trained African theologians with specializations in theology and science, however I would be very interested in organizing (if funds became available) consultations in this area, like the one I attended in Cyprus organized by Dr. John Mangum."

Nasimiyu, Anne

Present Position and Address: Senior Lecturer (since 1988), Department of Philosophy and Religious Studies, Kenyatta University, P.O. Box 43844, Nairobi, Kenya **Date of Birth:** November 6, 1949 **Languages Spoken:** Kiluyha, English, Kiswahili, Luganda **Education:** B.A. Liberal Arts (*magna cum laude*, 1981), Magdalen College, Bedford, NH; Advanced Catechetical Diploma (1982), Gannon University, PA; Ph.D. Religion (honors, 1986), Duquesne University, PA **Previous Positions:** Confraternity of Catholic Doctrine Teacher, St. Elizabeth Seton Parish, Manchester, NH (1979-81)/St. Anne's Parish and Sacred Heart School, Erie, PA (1981-82); Guest Lecturer on Feminism in Third World Countries (1984-86), Duquesne University, Pittsburgh, PA; Lectures on Peace and Justice (1982-84), Central Catholic High School, Pittsburgh, PA; Part-time lecturer in African Traditional Religion (1985), Fall Carlow College, Pittsburgh, PA; Lecturer (1987), Religious Liberation in Africa, CHIEA; Consultant for Apostolate to the Nomads of AMECEA's polygamy Consultation (1988) **Discipline:** Religious Studies **Related Areas of Interest:** Church and Society in an African Context; Philosophy and Theology; Women in Africa.

Ndumbe, Peter Martins

Present Position and Address: Associate Professor in Virus Immunology (since 1992), Faculty of Medicine and Biomedical Sciences (FMBS), University of Yaounde 1, BP 8445, Yauonde, Cameroon **Work Phone:** (237) 31 20 51/31 51 04 **Fax Phone:** (237) 31 51 78/31 12 24 **Date of Birth:** December 1, 1954 **Languages Spoken:** English, French **Education:** M.D. (1979), CUSS University of Yaounde; M.Sc., Medical Microbiology (1982)/Ph.D. Immunology (1985), University of London **Previous Positions:** Doctor (1979-80), Central Hospital, Yaounde; Doctor (1980-81), General Hospital Nkambe, Cameroon; Doctor (1982), Hammersmith Hospital, London; Doctor (1982-85), Hospital for Sick Children, London, UK; Senior Lecturer in Immunology (1986-92), Centre Universitaire des Sciences de la Santé (CUSS), University of Yaounde, Cameroon **Selected Memberships:** British Society of Immunology; New York Academy of Science; Royal College of Pathologists, UK **Discipline:** Medicine; Immunology **Related Areas of Interest:** Ethics; Care of Dying; Faith Healing.

Nelson, Paul Alfred

Present Position and Address: Ph.D. student, Department of Philosophy, University of Chicago, 1050 East 59th Street, Chicago, IL 60637, USA **Concurrent Positions:** Tutor (since 1986), Philosophy and Writing, University of Chicago **E-Mail:** 5825514@mcimail.com **Date of Birth:** September 14, 1958 **Education:** B.A. Philosophy (1984), University of Pittsburgh, PA **Selected Memberships:** International Society for the History, Philosophy, and Social Studies of Biology (ISHPSSB); Staff, Students for Origins Research (since 1983) **Discipline:** Philosophy **Related Areas of Interest:** Creationism; History and Philosophy of Biology; Nature of Scientific Explanation; the Design Argument.

Nelson, Robert T.

Present Position and Address: Priest-in-Charge (since 1983), St. Thomas/Liscard/Wallasey; Diocesan Industrial Missioner for Wirral (since 1987), Diocese of Chester, 5 Sedbergh Road, Wallasey, Merseyside L44 2BR, UK **Work Phone:** (051) 630-2830 **Date of Birth:** May 30, 1943 **Education:** B.Sc. Hons (1965), Liverpool Regional College of Technology; Qualified for Ordination on North-West Ordination Course (1979) **Previous Positions:** Scientist (1965-87), Unilever Research; Assistant Curate (1979-83), Our Lady and St. Nicholas, Liverpool **Selected Memberships:** Founder member/Assistant Secretary (since 1989), Society of Ordained Scientists **Discipline:** Anglican Priest; Scientist (Detergent/Textile Science) **Related Areas of Interest:** Ethics and Society; Liturgy and Science; Science and Spirituality.

Neubauer, Thomas

Present Position and Address: Currently in Phase III of Clinical Studies, Human Medicine, at University of Tübingen; (Home) Viktor-Renner Strasse 17, 7400 Tübingen, Germany **Date of Birth:** August 9, 1963 **Languages Spoken:** German, English **Education:** B.S. Biochemistry (1986); B.S. Basic Medical Science (1987) **Selected Conferences and Congresses:** Visited 2 symposiums on this subject - Enschede, The Netherlands (March 1988), and at Loccum, Germany (October 1988) **Other Academic Experience:** Throughout studies has taken some theological courses i.e. "H. Jonas - Prinzip Verantwortung" by E. Jüngel; Currently participating in a circle of philosophers studying Hegel and Whitehead **Discipline:** Medicine and Biochemistry **Related Areas of Interest:** Medical Ethics and Responsibility; Process Theology and Reality; Theology and its Relationship to the Sciences.

Nickel Jr., Gerhard *(Registered pseudonyms are Gerard Nichol, G. Nichol)*

Present Position and Address: Freelance Carpenter and Sheet Metal Technician (since 1990); 501 S.W. 11th Street, Newton, KS 67114, USA **Concurrent Positions:** Teaching elder (since 1970), Mennonite Brethren Church **Date of Birth:** June 9, 1928 **Languages Spoken:** English, German **Education:** B.A. Bible and Mission (1953), Grace College of the Bible, Omaha; B.A. Secondary Education and Biology, German and French (1963); NSF Institute in German (1964); M.S. Physical Science Teaching and Earth Science (1972), Emporia State University, KS; NSF Institute in Earth Science (1972) **Previous Positions:** S. S. Missioner (1953-55), 'Go Ye' Mission, Tahlequah, OK; Self Employed Carpenter and Sheet Metal Technician (1957-63); High School Teacher, Wichita, KS Public Schools (1963-72)/Berean Academy, Elbing (1972-77) **Selected Memberships:** National Science Teachers Association; Kansas Association of Teachers of Science; Bible-Science Association; Creation Research Society; American Scientific Affiliation **Discipline:** General Science; Physics; Chemistry; Geology; Earth Science; German **Related Areas of Interest:** Correlation of Scientifically Testable Statements in the Hebrew-Christian Scriptures; Creation Research; Bible and Science.

Nordgren, Richard

Present Position and Address: Chaplain, Tri-Cities Chaplaincy, 7525 W. Deschutes Pl. Kennewick, WA 99336 USA; (Home) 1105 Putnam Street, Richland, WA 99352, USA **Date of Birth:** March 26, 1939 **Education:** B.S. Chemistry (1962), St. John's University; M.Div. (1975), San Francisco Theological Seminary **Previous Positions:** Research Chemist (1963-72), Veterans Administration Hospital Aging Research Laboratory, Baltimore, MD **Discipline:** Pastoral Care; Previously a Research Chemist **Related Areas of Interest:** Personal Interest in the Dialogue between Science and Religion.

Onimus, Jean

Present Position and Address: Full Professor (since 1958), Universities of Aix-en-Provence, Nice, 746 Chemin du Taméyé, 06560 Valbonne, France **Date of Birth:** September 1, 1909 **Languages Spoken:** French, English **Education:** Agrégé des Lettres (1934); Doctorate in French Modern Literature (1950) **Awards and Honors:** Chevalier, Légion d'Honneur; Chevalier, Lettres et Arts; Officier, Mérite national **Previous Positions:** Successively Professor at Lycée de Tunis, l'Institut francais de Bucarest, la Faculté des Lettres d'Aix; Professeur honoraire de littérature francaise contemporaine à l'Université de Nice **Discipline:** French Modern Literature **Related Areas of Interest:** Modern Poetry and Art; Epistemology (Evolution of Science); Evolution of Religious Feeling **Personal Notes:** He has published 5 works on art and poetry and 3 works on pedagogy and education, 6 works on the modern world, and 3 works dealing with religious questions. He has also published 5 works on Charles Péguy, as well as Teilhard de Chardin, Camus, Samuel Beckett, Philippe Jaccottet and Jean Tardieu.

Oorjitham, Santha

Present Position and Address: Staff Correspondent with *Asiaweek* (since 1985), Asiaweek Kuala Lumpur Bureau, 12/F Plaza MBF, Jln. Ampang, 50450 Kuala Lumpur, Malaysia **Date of Birth:** May 2, 1959 **Languages Spoken:** English, Malay, German **Education:** B.A. Communication Arts (1981), Pacific Lutheran University, Tacoma, WA, USA **Previous Positions:** Journalist (1982-85), *New Straits Times* (Malaysia); "Together with other journalists in this region, I have been attending a series of workshops on environmental reporting organized by the Carl Duisberg Gesellschaft (Germany) and together with several others am one of the founding members of COMCON (Communicators for Conservation)." **Discipline:** Communication Arts **Related Areas of Interest:** Environmental Protection. "As you will see from the biodata I am neither a scientist nor a theologian. I was invited to the Lutheran conference in Cyprus in December 1987 (on Science and Theology) as a communicator. As such, I would be happy to help in any way in the area of communication/liason. My special area of interest is environmental protection, and I have published a number of articles on environmental concerns in Malaysia, both in the *New Straits Times* and in *Asiaweek*."

Overman, Richard H.

Present Position and Address: Professor of Religion Emeritus (since 1993), University of Puget Sound, WA, 2336 Sunset Drive W., Tacoma, WA 98466, USA **Date of Birth:** January 20, 1929 **Education:** B.A. (1950)/M.D. (1954), Stanford University; M.Th. (1961), School of Theology, Claremont; Ph.D. (1966), Claremont Graduate School **Previous Positions:** Assistant (1965-68)/Associate Professor of Religion (1968-75), University of Puget Sound; United Methodist Minister;

Professor of Religion (1975-93), University of Puget Sound, WA **Discipline:** Religion **Related Areas of Interest:** Science; Medicine; Traditional and Esoteric Spirituality.

Owens, Joseph V.

Present Position and Address: Catholic Priest in pastoral work (since 1983) in Honduras; Apartado 37, El Progreso, Yoro, Honduras **Date of Birth:** December 21, 1940 **Languages Spoken:** English, Spanish **Education:** B.A. Philosophy (1964)/M.A. Philosophy (1965), Boston College; M.Div. (1971), Weston School of Theology **Previous Positions:** Catholic Priest working in grass-roots organizing in Jamaica (1970-78) **Selected Memberships:** Subscribes to *Zygon* **Discipline:** Catholic Priest; Philosophy **Related Areas of Interest:** The work of Ralph Burhoe, Bernard Lonergan and others.

Parks, Lyle Fredrick

Present Position and Address: Private Practice in Springfield, IL; 800 S. Durkin Drive #414, Springfield, IL 62704, USA **Date of Birth:** April 25, 1956 **Education:** A.S. Life Science (1979), Lincoln Land Community College; B.S. Biology (1982), University of Illinois, Champagne; M.D. (1987), University of Illinois, Chicago College of Medicine **Postgraduate Experience:** Three years of residency training in psychiatry, Southern Illinois University College of Medicine, Springfield; one year residency training in psychiatry, Illinois State Psychiatric Institute, Chicago **Discipline:** Psychiatry; Psychoanalysis **Related Areas of Interest:** Psychoanalysis and Religion.

Patrick, Thomas E.

Present Position and Address: Adjunct Professor (since 1981), University of St. Thomas, St. Paul, MN; 1648 Scheffer Avenue, St. Paul, MN 55116, USA **Date of Birth:** January 15, 1933 **Languages Spoken:** English, Dutch, French, German **Education:** B.A. Philosophy (1956), Assumption Seminary and College; M.A. Liberal Arts (1959)/Th.D. Theology (1964), Universite de Louvain, Belgium; M.H.A. Hospital Administration (1972), University of Minnesota **Previous Positions:** Lecturer through Professor of Theology (1933-69), Assumption Seminary and College/Saint Paul Seminary/College of Saint Catherine; Hospital Administrator (1969-81), Anoka State Hospital/Norton Children's Hospitals//Catawba State Hospital/Western State Hospital/Hennepin County Community Services/American Hospital Association/United States Veterans Administration; Instructor (1982-87) in Business Mathematics/Management, Philosophy and Psychology, Ethics and Morality, Minnesota School of Business/National College of Business/College of Saint Francis **Selected Memberships:** Catholic Biblical Association; Society of Biblical Literature **Discipline:** Theology; Hospital Administration **Related Areas of Interest:** Biblical Studies; Law and New Testament; Philosophical Systems; Planetary Science: Earth and Environs.

Patton, John H.

Present Position and Address: Professor of Pastoral Theology, Columbia Theological Seminary, 701 Columbia Drive, Box 520, Decatur, GA 30031, USA; (Home) 1329 Springdale Road NE, Atlanta, GA 30306, USA **Concurrent Positions:** Director, Th.D. Program in Pastoral Counseling, Atlanta Theological Association; Adjunct Professor of Pastoral Care, Candler School of Theology, Emory University; Member and Past President, International Council on Pastoral Care and Counseling **Work Phone:** (404) 378-8821 **Home Phone:** (404) 378-6827 **Date of Birth:** August 4, 1930 **Education:** B.A. (1951)/B.D. (1953), Emory University; Ph.D. (1968), University of Chicago **Previous Positions:** United Methodist Pastor in VA, IL, GA (1955-61); Director of Chaplaincy Services (1961-67), Emory University Hospital, Henrietta Egleston Hospital for Children and Wesley Homes Inc.; Director of Pastoral Counseling (1968-70), Georgia Association for Pastoral Care; Executive Director (1970-89),

Georgia Association for Pastoral Care; Visiting Professor of Pastoral Theology (Spring 1988, 89), Vanderbilt University **Editorial Positions:** Associate Editor, *Dictionary of Pastoral Care and Counseling* (Abingdon, 1990); Editorial Advisory Committee, *Journal of Pastoral Care* **Selected Memberships:** American Association of Pastoral Counselors; American Association of Marriage and Family Therapists; American Academy of Psychotherapists **Discipline:** Pastoral Counseling; Psychotherapy **Related Areas of Interest:** Mental Health and Religion; Psychology and Christianity.

Payton, Robert L.

Present Position and Address: Director, Indiana University Center on Philanthropy, University Place, Suite 200, 850 W. Michigan Street, Indianapolis, IN 46202, USA **Date of Birth:** August 23, 1926 **Education:** M.A. History, University of Chicago; Doctorate in Literature (1975), Adelphi University **Awards and Honors:** Distinguished Service to Education Award (1975), from CASE **Previous Positions:** Vice Chancellor of Washington University, St. Louis, MO; US ambassador to Cameroon (1967-69); President, Hofstra University, Hempstead, NY; President, C. W. Post College, Brookville, Long Island, NY; President (1977-87), Exxon Education Foundation; Scholar-in-Residence, Philanthropic Studies, University of Virginia **Editorial Positions:** Editor, *Herald,* Burlington, IA **Selected Memberships:** Boards of Independent Sector/Technoserve/Cultural Literacy Foundations; Advisory Board, Mandel Center for Non-Profit Organizations at Case Western Reserve University; Fellow, American Academy of Pediatrics; Chair, Partnership for Child Health **Discipline:** Philanthropic Studies **Related Areas of Interest:** Religion, Science, and Society.

Pazan, Stephen

Present Position and Address: TRANSPAC Data Analyst/Data Manager (since 1982), Scripps Institution of Oceanography, University of California - San Diego, Ocean Research Division, A-030, La Jolla, CA 92093, USA **Date of Birth:** October 18, 1943 **Education:** B.S. Physics (1966), University of California - Berkeley; M.A. Physics (1975)/Ph.D. Physical Oceanography (1975), University of California -San Diego **Postgraduate Experience:** Student Researcher (1967-69), University of California - San Diego; Student, Researcher (1970-75)/NORPAX Data Management Operations (1976-82), Scripps Institution of Oceanography **Previous Positions:** Researcher (1966-67), General Atomics, San Diego, CA; Pilot Ocean Data System Oceanographer (1981-83), Jet Propulsion Laboratory, California Institute of Technology (Cal Tech), Pasadena **Selected Memberships:** American Geophysical Union; American Meteorological Society **Discipline:** Physics; Physical Oceanography.

Pearson III, Daniel B.

Present Position and Address: Private Practice in Psychiatry (since 1989), 836 N. Zang Blvd., Dallas, TX 75208, USA **Work Phone:** (214) 943-1310 **Date of Birth:** May 25, 1949 **Education:** B.A. Geology (1971)/M.A. Geology (1973)/Ph.D. Geochemistry (1981), Rice University, Houston, TX; M.S. Geochemistry (1974), California Institute of Technology; M.D. (1985), University of Texas Health Science Center - San Antonio **Previous Positions:** Resident (1985-1989), University of Texas Health Science Center - San Antonio **Selected Memberships:** Episcopal Church **Discipline:** Psychiatrist; Geochemist; Geologist **Related Areas of Interest:** Relationship of Spiritualism to Psychiatry; Organizational and Occupational Psychiatry, Executive Coaching.

Peat, David

Present Position and Address: Research Fellow in Astrophysics, University of Leeds; 12 North Grange Mews, Headingley, Leeds LS6 2EW, UK **Work Phone:** (0113)- 243 1751 **Date of Birth:** December 18, 1937 **Education:** B.A. (1959)/Ph.D. Astrophysics (1962), Cambridge University **Previous Positions:** Senior Lecturer in Astrophysics (1964-77), University of Cambridge; College Chaplain (1977-83); Vicar of East Ardsley, West Yorkshire (1983-87); Adult Education Officer (1987-94), Diocese of London **Selected Memberships:** Society of Ordained Scientists **Discipline:** Ordained Astrophysicist **Related Areas of Interest:** Doctrine of Creation in Christian Tradition and Spirituality; Science and Theological Education.

Perry, David L.

Present Position and Address: Associate Consultant (since 1989), Ethics Resource Center, Washington, DC; Currently Ph.D. candidate (expected degree in 1991), Ethics and Society, University of Chicago Divinity School; 2730 Wisconsin #84, Washington, DC 20007, USA **Date of Birth:** April 9, 1959 **Education:** B.A. Religion (1981), Pacific Lutheran University; A.M.Div. (1982), University of Chicago Divinity School **Previous Positions:** Preceptor in Clinical Ethics (1986), University of Chicago Pritzger School of Medicine; Planning Commission on Scientific/Intellectual Change, Lutheran Church in America Division for World Mission and Ecumenism (1984-87); Research Intern (1987), Center for Strategic and International Studies; Task Force on Science and Technology, Evangelical Lutheran Church in America (since 1988) **Discipline:** Moral and Political Philosophy **Related Areas of Interest:** Evolutionary Theory and Sources of Moral Character; Fetal Brain Development and Abortion; Cosmology and Theodicy.

Petras, David M.

Present Position and Address: Pastor (since 1990), St. Nicholas Church, Cleveland; Director of Seminary Education (since 1988), Diocese of Parma, OH, USA; 3431 Superior Avenue, Cleveland, OH 44114, USA **Date of Birth:** August 28, 1941 **Education:** S.T.Lic. (1967), Pontifical Gregorian University; S.E.O.D. (Doctor of Sacred Eastern Ecclesiology, 1982), Pontifical Oriental Institute, Rome **Previous Positions:** Pastor, (1970-72; 1980-90), Dormiton Church, Akron, OH; Pastor (1972-78), Christ the King Church, Taylor, MI; Professor of Liturgy (1978-80), Byzantine Catholic Seminary, Pittsburgh, PA **Selected Memberships:** Catholic Theological Society of America; North American Academy of Liturgy and Societas Liturgica; Orthodox/Catholic Theological Dialogue (since 1983) **Discipline:** Liturgy (Eastern Christian Churches) **Related Areas of Interest:** Human Ritual; Cosmology.

Petzoldt, Matthias

Present Position and Address: Professor of Fundamental Theology and Hermeneutics (since 1994), Theologische Fakultät der Universität Leipzig: Poetenweg 16, D-04155 Leipzig, Germany **Date of Birth:** June 10, 1948 **Languages Spoken:** German, English **Education:** Dr. Theology (1984), Theologische Fakultät Leipzig; Dr. theol. habil. (1992), Augustana-Hochschule Neuendettelsau **Previous Positions:** Parish minister (1977-85), Bautzen; Assistant (1985-87)/Lecturer in Theology (1987-90), Theologisches Seminar Leipzig; Professor of Theology (1990-93), Kirchliche Hochschule Leipzig; apl. Professor of Theology (1993-94), Theologische Fakultät der Universität Leipzig **Selected Memberships:** Arbeitskreis von Theologen für den Dialog mit den Naturwissenschaften, Wittenberg; The European Society for the Study of Science and Theology (ESSSAT) **Discipline:** Systematic

Theology, especially Fundamental Theology and Hermeneutics **Related Areas of Interest:** Theory of Science and Theology.

Pilchik, Ely E.

Present Position and Address: Retired Rabbi, 5 Cherrywood Circle, West Orange, NJ 09052, USA, **Date of Birth:** June 12, 1913 **Languages Spoken:** English, Yiddish, Hebrew **Education:** A.B. (1935), University of Cincinnati; M. Hebrew Lit. (1936), Hebrew Union College; D.D. (1964); Ordained Rabbi (1939) **Previous Positions:** Founder and Director (1939-40), Hillel Foundation; Assistant Rabbi (1940-41), Har Sinai Temple, Baltimore; Rabbi (1942-47), Temple Israel, Tulsa; Chaplain (1944-46), USNR; Rabbi (1947-81), Temple B'nai Jeshurun, Short Hills, NJ; Professor of Jewish Thought (since 1969), Uppsala College **Selected Memberships:** President (1977-79), Central Conference American Rabbis; President (1957-58), Jewish Book Council America Board of Directors, Newark Museum; Member, Ethics Committee, NJ Bar Association; American Association for the Advancement of Science; New York Academy of Science **Discipline:** Jewish Rabbi and Professor of Jewish Thought **Related Areas of Interest:** Science and Religion.

Porter, Andrew P.

Present Position and Address: Physicist (since 1968); Special Studies Group, Lawrence Livermore National Laboratory, P.O. Box 800, Livermore, CA 94550, USA **Work Phone:** (415) 443-4041 **Date of Birth:** October 5, 1946 **Education:** B.A. Physics and Chemistry (1968), Harvard College; M.S. Applied Science (1968)/Ph.D. Applied Science (1976), University of California - Davis; MTS, Church Divinity School, Berkeley, CA; Ph.D. (1991), Graduate Theological Union, Berkeley; Ph.D. thesis (1976), "The Method of Independent Timesteps in the Numerical Solution of Initial Value Problems"; MTS thesis (1980), "Meeting God in History, Relativity and Pluralism"; Ph.D. (1991) thesis, "H. Richard Niebuhr's Doctrine of Providence in the Light of Martin Heidegger's Philosophy" **Previous Positions:** Instructor in Theology (1980-90), School for Deacons of the Episcopal Church, Diocese of California **Selected Memberships:** Catholic Theological Society of America; American Academy of Religion; Mathematical Association of America **Discipline:** Physics; Numerical Methods; Systematic and Philosophical Theology **Related Areas of Interest:** Shock Hydrodynamics, Celestial Mechanics; The Thought of H. R. Niebuhr, M. Heidegger; Analogy; Phenomenology of Monotheism.

Porter, Kenneth W.

Present Position and Address: President, Pulse Turbines Ltd., 4440, 92nd Avenue SE, Mercer Island, WA 98040, USA **Date of Birth:** August 23, 1925 **Languages Spoken:** English, French **Education:** Higher National Certificate in Mechanical Engineering (1951), Derby Technical College, UK; Graduate (1956), Institution of Mechanical Engineers **Previous Positions:** Assistant Project Engineer (1947-56), Rolls Royce Ltd.; Gas Turbine Design Engineer (1956-59), Orenda Engines; Project Engineer, Curtiss-Wright Corp. (1959-60)/Fairchild-Stratos Corp. (1960-64)/The Boeing Company (1964-85); Chairman (1985-87), Mission Strategy Committee, Presbytery of Seattle, WA **Selected Memberships:** President (1987-88), Puget Sound Engineering Council; Commissioner (1984), General Assembly PC. USA; Institution of Mechanical Engineers; American Institute of Aeronautics and Astronautics Society of Automotive Engineers; American Scientific Affiliation **Discipline:** Thermodynamics; Heat Engines **Related Areas of Interest:** Cosmology; Bioengineering.

Price, Daniel J.

Present Position and Address: Pastor, International Protestant Church of Zürich, Switzerland; Eierbrechtstrasse 55, 8053 Zürich, Switzerland **Work Phone:** (01) 262-5525 **Date of Birth:** May 15, 1952 **Languages Spoken:** English, some German **Education:** B.A. (1974), Westmont College; M.Div. (1978), Fuller Seminary; Ph.D. candidate, Aberdeen University **Previous Positions:** Associate Pastor, Easton Presbyterian Church of Fresno, CA **Selected Memberships:** Affiliate Member, American Scientific Affiliation **Discipline:** Systematic Theology; Parish Ministry **Related Areas of Interest:** Relation between Theology and Philosophy of Science, Especially Barth-Torrance as they Relate to Contemporary Philosophy of Social Science; The Philosophy of John MacMurray and His Philosophy of Science.

Prodi, Giovanni

Present Position and Address: Institute of Mathematics, University of Pisa, Via Derna, 1, 56100 Pisa, Italy; (Home) Via Pisanello 33, I-56123, Pisa, Italy **Work Phone:** 24.550 - 26.350 **Selected Memberships:** Secretary, Scienza e fede **Discipline:** Theology and Science.

Puckett, Laura E.

Present Position and Address: Professor of Psychology (since 1975), Department of Psychology, North Hennepin Community College, 7411 85th Avenue N., Minneapolis, MN 55445, USA **Education:** Ph.D. Veterinary Physiology and Pharmacology (1968)/Ph.D. Clinical Psychology (1978), University of Minnesota **Previous Positions:** Licensed Consulting Psychologist in Private Practice; Adjunct Professor, St. Cloud State University **Selected Memberships:** Society for Scientific Exploration; American Association for the Advancement of Science; American Psychological Association **Discipline:** Clinical Psychology; Physiology and Pharmacology **Related Areas of Interest:** Psychology and Religion.

Pullinger, David J.

Present Position and Address: Director (since 1986), Society, Religion and Technology Project (SRT), Church of Scotland, 23 Magdala Crescent, Edinburgh EH12 5BD, UK **Work Phone:** (031) 313-3040 **Date of Birth:** June 30, 1951 **Education:** B.A. Hons Mathematics (1972)/M.Phil in Difference, Fuzzy Geometry (1975), University of York; M.Sc. Quantum Theory (1973), Mathematical Institute, University of Oxford; M.Sc. Ergonomics (distinctions, 1980), University of London. Awarded a Ph.D. for thesis in Human Computer Interaction (1988), University of Technology, Loughborough **Awards and Honors:** Research Fellow (1980-87), University of Technology, Loughborough **Previous Positions:** Assistant Master in Mathematics (1975-79), Dulwich College **Discipline:** Mathematics; Ergonomics; Computer Science **Related Areas of Interest:** Society, Religion and Technology.

Q

Queen, Christopher S.

Present Position and Address: Lecturer in Religion (since 1990), Harvard University, 14 Stoneleigh Road, West Newton, MA 02165, USA **Date of Birth:** April 22, 1945 **Languages Spoken:** English, French, Hindi **Education:** B.A. (1967), Oberlin College; M.Div. (1972), Union Theological Seminary, New York City; Ph.D. (1986), Boston University **Previous Positions:** Adjunct Assistant Professor (1982-1989), Boston University **Selected Memberships:** American Academy of Religion **Discipline:** Philosophy; Phenomenology of Religion **Related Areas of Interest:** Science and Religion; Religion and Culture; Systems Theory; Buddhism.

Rangel, Paschoal Sellitti

Present Position and Address: Director da Editora, "O Lutador," Rua Irmâ Celeste, 185, Bairro Planalto, 31710, Belo Horizonte, Mg, Brasil, Caixa Postal 2428 (CEP 30161) **Date of Birth:** May 17, 1922 **Education:** Curso de Filosofia (1941-42), Seminário do Instituto dos Missionários Sacramentinos de N. Sra.; Curso de Teologia (1943-46), Seminário Arquidiocesano de Belo Horizonte, MG; Licenciatura am Filosofia (1970-71), Ciências e Letras Dom Bosco, Sâo João del Rei, MG; Bachelato em Comunicação Social (1978-81), PUV/MG **Previous Positions:** Professor of Philosophy and History of Philosophy (1951-83), Seminário do Instituto dos Missionários de N. Sra. and Smo. Sacramento PUV/MG No Seminário; Professor (1968-71)/Professor de Deontologia da Medicina e Enferemagem (1969-83)/Ética da Communicaçâo Social (1981-83), PUC/MG **Selected Memberships:** Founder and Director (since 1969), Atualização - Revista de Teologia; Academia Municipalista de Letras de MG Sociedade de Teologia e Ciências da Religiâo (SOTER) **Discipline:** Philosophy; Theology; Social Communication; Literature **Related Areas of Interest:** The relation of Philosophy, Theology, and Brazilian Literature to Science.

Reding, Georges R.

Present Position and Address: Chief Psychiatric Officer, Kalamazoo County Human Services Department, 953 North 35th Street, Galesburg, MI 49053, USA **Concurrent Positions:** Private Practice in New York (since 1977) **Date of Birth:** April 9, 1925 **Languages Spoken:** English, French **Education:** Medical Degree (*magna cum laude*, 1950), Brussels University; Student (1951-52), Columbia University Psychoanalytic Clinic for Training and Research, and Psychiatric Residency at New York State Psychiatric Institute and Hospital **Previous Positions:** Founder and Director (1952-56), Dept. of Psychosomatic Medicine, University of Geneva Hospital, Switzerland; Private Practice in Psychiatry (1956-62), Brussels; Assistant Professor of Psychiatry (1962-68) University of Chicago; Consulting Psychiatrist (1962-68), State of Illinois Department of Mental Health; Director of Community Mental Health Services (1968-72), County of Franklin, Malone, NY; Director (1972-74), Dept. of Community Mental Health, Charles Cole Memorial Hospital in Coudersport, PA; Medical Director (1974-86), Monmouth Center for Vocational Rehabilitation in Tinton Falls, NJ; Medical Director (1978-85), Brooklyn School for Special Children, Brooklyn, NY; Private Practice (1974-87), Red Bank, NJ; Psychiatrist (1986-87), Mobile Crisis Intervention Team, Visiting Nurse Service of NY; Psychiatrist (1987-90), Dutchess Mobile Crisis Intervention Team, Hudson River Psychiatric Center **Certifications:** Diplomate in Psychiatry, American Board of Psychiatry and Neurology; Certified for the practice of Psychoanalysis by the American Psychoanalytic Association. Medical Licensures for NY, NJ, PA, IL, and the European Common Market Member Countries **Discipline:** Psychiatry; Psychoanalysis **Related Areas of Interest:** Evolutionary History of Consciousness; Teilhard de Chardin; Michael Polanyi.

Rees, Martin J.

Present Position and Address: Royal Society Research Professor (since 1993), Cambridge University; Plumian Professor of Astronomy and Experimental Philosophy (since 1973), King's College, Cambridge CB2 151, UK **Date of Birth:** June 23, 1942 **Education:** M.A./Ph.D. (1967), Cambridge University **Awards and Honors:** Balzan Prize (1989) **Selected Memberships:** Fellow of the Royal Society; National Academy of Science; Foreign Honorary Member, American Association of Arts and Sciences; Member of Pontifical Academy of Sciences **Discipline:** Astrophysics **Related Areas of Interest:** Astronomy; Cosmology; Theoretical Physics.

Richardson, W. Mark

Present Position and Address: Director of Program (since 1990), Center for Theology and the Natural Sciences, 2400 Ridge Road, Berkeley, CA 94709, USA **Date of Birth:** May 28, 1949 **Education:** B.A. (1971), University of Oregon; M.Div. (1975), Princeton Theological Seminary; Ph.D. (1991), Graduate Theological Union, Berkeley **Awards and Honors:** Episcopal Church Fellow (1990); Sir John Templeton Postdoctoral Fellowship (1993) **Previous Positions:** Associate Pastor (1978-81), Church of Ascension, NYC; Visiting Scholar (1984-85), Trinity Church, Menlo Park; Associate Director (1986-90), Trinity Institute, NYC **Editorial Positions:** Editor: *The CTWS Bulletin* (1990-94), a publication of scholarly articles and book reviews **Selected Memberships:** Center for Theology and the Natural Sciences; Episcopal Church **Discipline:** Philosophical Theology **Related Areas of Interest:** Philosophy of Mind; Theology in Dialogue with the Natural Sciences.

Riegel Jr., Theodore

Present Position and Address: Director (since 1982), Riegel Mobility, Inc., 985 West Broad Street, Athens, GA 30601, USA **Date of Birth:** September 1, 1934 **Languages Spoken:** English, German **Education:** B.A. American Studies (1956)/M.A. Philosophy (1959), Yale University; Ph.D. Educational Psychology (1979), University of Georgia **Postgraduate Experience:** Postdoctoral studies in Gerontology and Health Education, University of Georgia **Awards and Honors:** Certified Teacher. Life Certificate in Mathematics at T-5 level/Gifted Education at T-5 level, State of Georgia **Previous Positions:** Mathematics Teacher (1959-60), Westminster Schools, Atlanta, GA; Special Education Teacher (1960-62), Northside School, Inc., Atlanta, GA; Teacher-Trainer (1962), Goodwill Industries, Atlanta, GA; Psychology Teacher (1962), Georgia State College, Atlanta; Mathematics Teacher (1962-65), Briarcliff High School, Atlanta, GA; Vocational Rehabilitation Counselor (1966-68), Central State Hospital, Milledgeville, GA; Intern (1973), US Dept. of Education, Office of Gifted and Talented, Washington, DC; Teacher/Tutor (1974)/Counselor (1975), Empire State College, NY **Selected Memberships:** Phi Delta Kappa Educational Fraternity; Council for Exceptional Children - Gifted; National Mathematics Teachers Association; National Education Association; Georgia Education Association; American Educational Research Association **Discipline:** Educational Psychology; Mathematics; Philosophy **Related Areas of Interest:** Perception of Time.

Rios, Cesar A.

Present Position and Address: Psychiatrist in Private Practice; Arcos 1102, 1426 Buenos Aires, Argentina **Date of Birth:** October 4, 1943 **Languages Spoken:** Spanish, English, French, Portuguese **Education:** M.D. (1968), Cordoba University, Argentina **Selected Memberships:** Asociacion Gestaltica de Buenos Aires **Discipline:** Psychiatry **Related Areas of Interest:** Transpersonal Psychology.

Roberts, Kenneth L.

Present Position and Address: Retired Professional Engineer and Forester, 3328 Highland Lane, Fairfax, VA 22031, USA **Date of Birth:** December 15, 1901 **Education:** B.S. Forestry (1923)/Civil Engineering (1933), Cornell University **Previous Positions:** Worked for 50 years mostly on projects to conserve natural resources and to find wise ways to manage and use land, forest, water and to use renewable resources for continuing productivity **Selected Memberships:** Institute on Religion in an Age of Science; American Humanist Association; Cedar Lane Unitarian Church; National Capital Area Skeptics; American Society of Civil Engineers; National Society of Professional Engineers; Society of American Foresters **Discipline:** Civil Engineering; Forestry **Related Areas of Interest:** Biology; Ecology; Cosmology; Science as it Illuminates Religious Belief and Life.

Robertson, John H.

Present Position and Address: Retired Lecturer, University of Leeds, UK; 5 Ancaster Road, Leeds LS16 5HH, UK **Date of Birth:** May 18, 1923 **Languages Spoken:** English and some German **Education:** B.Sc. Chemistry (1944)/Ph.D. X-ray Crystallography (1949), University of Edinburgh, Scotland **Previous Positions:** Lecturer (1954-88), University of Leeds, England **Selected Memberships:** Science and Religion Forum (UK); The Research Scientists' Christian Fellowship (RSCF) now renamed Christians in Science **Discipline:** Structural Chemistry; X-Ray Crystallography **Related Areas of Interest:** Philosophy of Scientific Method; Nature of Thought; All Topics Related in any way to Science and Faith.

Roche, Barbara A.

Present Position and Address: Editor (since 1988), *Horizons*; 5525 Forest Lake Drive, Prospect, KY 40059, USA **Education:** B.A. (1956), Stanford University; M.Div (1960), Princeton Theological Seminary; D.Min (1984), San Francisco Theological Seminary **Previous Positions:** Director of Student Services (1973-76)/Dean of Students (1976-84), Pacific School of Religion **Editorial Positions:** Editor (1984-88), *Concern* **Discipline:** History; Religious Education.

Rockefeller, Laurance S.

Present Position and Address: Honorary Chairman, Memorial Sloan-Kettering Cancer Center, Room 5600, 30 Rockefeller Plaza, New York, NY 10112, USA **Date of Birth:** May 26, 1910 **Education:** B.A. Philosophy (1932), Princeton University **Honorary Degrees:** LHD (hon., 1981), Duke University, Brown University, Princeton University, Syracuse University, Texas Tech, Georgetown University **Awards and Honors:** Decorated Commandeur de L'Ordre Royal du Lion, Belgium (1950); National Institute of Social Sciences Gold Medal Award (1959-67); Alfred P. Sloan, Jr., Memorial Award, American Cancer Society (1969); Medal of Freedom (1969); James Ewing Layman's Award, Society of Surgical Oncology (1980); Commander, Order of the British Empire; Congressional Gold Medal (1991) **Discipline:** Philanthropy and Business **Related Areas of Interest:** Promotion of Scientific Research for the Purpose of Improving Human Life and the Enhancement of the Human Spirit.

Rogers, Norma Prichard

Address: 1277 Dexter Lane, Cordova, TN 38018, USA **Date of Birth:** November 24, 1920 **Education:** B.A. (1941), Vassar College; Montessori Diploma (1968), St. Nicholas, London; M.A. (1973),

Memphis State University; Ph.D. (1986), University of Mississippi **Previous Positions:** Teaching English, Latin, American History, choral music, Great Books in public and private schools in Birmingham, AL and Memphis, TN; early childhood classes in several Montessori schools; English Composition, University of Mississippi **Discipline:** Classics and English literature; Psychology via Montessori teaching **Related Areas of Interest:** "Three research trips to UK to investigate the career of John Sherman, first in print with the tenets of Cambridge Platonism (17th century), which established modern theological and philosophical attitudes, the late C. Attfield Brooks, O.B.E., author of *The Dedham Lectureship in Nonconformist Essex,* providing assistance."

Romagosa, Alfredo A.

Present Position and Address: Chief Scientist, Harris Computer Systems; 3400 N.W. 68 Ct., Ft. Lauderdale, FL 33309, USA **Date of Birth:** January 17, 1945 **Education:** B.S. Electrical Engineering (1965), Marquette University, Milwaukee WS; M.S. Electrical Engineering (1974), University of Miami, FL; M.A. Religious Studies (1983), Barry University, FL **Previous Positions:** Engineer (1965-67), Allis-Chalmers Corporation; Engineer (1967-71), Milgo Electronics; Adjunct Professor (1984), Religious Studies, St. Thomas University **Selected Memberships:** Institute of Electrical and Electronic Engineering; Association for Computing Machinery; American Teilhard Association **Discipline:** Computer Scientist **Related Areas of Interest:** Religion and Technical Progress.

Rónay, Géza S.

Present Position and Address: Retired Chemist, Shell Development Company; 1 Osborne Court, Oakland, CA 94611, USA **Work Phone:** (414) 531-4669 **Date of Birth:** May 5, 1911 **Languages Spoken:** English, Hungarian, German, Serbo-Croatian **Education:** A.B. (1945), University of California - Berkeley **Selected Memberships:** American Chemical Society (ACS), Colloid and Surface Chem. Sec. of ACS; Center for Theology and the Natural Sciences, Berkeley **Discipline:** Colloid and Surface Chemistry **Related Areas of Interest:** Science and Theology in Dialogue.

Ross, H. Miriam

Present Position and Address: Associate Professor of Christian Missions and Social Issues (since 1990), Acadia Divinity College affiliated with Acadia University, Wolfville, NS B0P 1X0, Canada **Work Phone:** (902) 542-2285 **Home Phone:** (902) 542-9523 **Languages Spoken:** English, French **Education:** R.N. Nursing (1951), Victoria General Hospital; B.A. Bible and Greek (*magna cum laude,* 1955), Gordon College; M.S. Nursing (1958), Boston University; Ph.D. Sociocultural Anthropology (1981), University of Washington, Seattle **Previous Positions:** Staff Nurse (1951-58), New England Baptist Hospital; Nursing Instructor (1958-59), Victoria General Hospital School of Nursing; Staff Nurse of rural hospitals (1961-64), Bas-Zaire, Zaire; French (1965-66), Laval University; Instructor (1967-70)/Assistant Director (1971-74), School of Nursing at Institut Medical Evangelique, Zaire; Consultant in Anthropology (1979), MEDCAM, University of Hawaii; Assistant Professor (1982-85), School of Nursing at University of Ottawa; Assistant Professor (1985-90), Acadia Divinity College **Other Academic Experience:** State Certified Midwife (1961), Maternity Hospital, Bellshill, Lanarkshire, Scotland **Discipline:** Nursing; Sociocultural Anthropology; Missions **Related Areas of Interest:** Christian Missions (including Medical Missionaries) and Social Issues; Women in Church/Mission and Society; Christian Values and Social Mores **Current Areas of Research:** Women and Social Issues like World Hunger, Poverty, Ecology; The Church and the World.

Ross, Norman Albert

Present Position and Address: President, RosDat, Inc., 593 N. Main Street, Brewer, ME 04412-1219, USA **Work Phone:** (207) 989-3397 **Home Phone:** (207) 989-1004 **Date of Birth:** February 6, 1935 **Languages Spoken:** English, Russian **Education:** B.MEg. (5 years), Cornell University; B.S. Agriculture, University of Maine; M.S. Astronomy, University of Maryland; Master's Thesis: "The Moons of Mars," University of Maryland **Previous Positions:** Faculty (Physics and Astronomy), U.S. Naval Academy; Assistant Professor, Maine Maritime Academy; Executive Officer, Naval Space Surveillance System; Faculty, Naval War College, War Gaming Center **Selected Memberships:** American Scientific Affiliation **Discipline:** Astronomy **Related Areas of Interest:** Computers **Current Areas of Research:** Software Development.

Ross, Robert S.

Present Position and Address: Professor of Meteorology, Department of Earth Sciences, Millersville University, Millersville, PA 17551, USA **Work Phone:** (717) 872-3289 **Date of Birth:** February 25, 1943 **Education:** B.S. Natural Sciences (1966), Mercer University; M.S. Meteorology (1970)/Ph.D. Meteorology (1977), Florida State University **Selected Memberships:** American Meteorological Society; Institute on Religion in an Age of Science **Discipline:** Meteorology **Related Areas of Interest:** Tropical Meteorology; Interaction of Science and Religion.

Roukens de Lange, A.

Present Position and Address: Senior Research Associate (since 1983), Institute for Futures Research, University of Stellenbosch, South Africa; P.O. Box 2010, Bellville 7535, RSA; 183A Campground Road, Newlands 7700, South Africa **Work Phone:** 021-642718 **Date of Birth:** October 11, 1940 **Languages Spoken:** English, Afrikaans, Dutch **Education:** B.Sc. Chemical Engineering (1961), University of Cape Town; Ph.D. Chemical Engineering (1976), University of Witwatersrand **Previous Positions:** Research Officer (1963-67), AECI in Johannesburg; Lecturer in Chemical Engineering (1968-75)/Senior Research Fellow (1976-82), Department of Applied Mathematics, University of Witwatersrand **Discipline:** Futures Research **Related Areas of Interest:** Future of Mankind and the World; Interface between Science and Religion; First/Third World Interaction.

Routh, Donald K.

Present Position and Address: Professor (since 1985), University of Miami; (Home) 9394 S.W. 77th Avenue, F7, Miami, FL 33156, USA **Work Phone:** (305) 284-5208 **Fax Phone:** (305) 284-4795 **Date of Birth:** March 3, 1937 **Education:** B.A. English (1962), University of Oklahoma; M.S. Psychology (1965)/Ph.D. Clinical Psychology (1967), University of Pittsburgh **Previous Positions:** Assistant Professor (1967-70) University of Iowa; Associate Professor (1970-71), Bowling Green State University, OH; Associate Professor (1971-77), University of North Carolina; Professor (1977-85), University of Iowa **Selected Memberships:** American Psychological Association; Society for Research in Child Development **Discipline:** Clinical Psychology **Related Areas of Interest:** Psychology and Religion.

Rowatt, Wade Clinton

Present Position and Address: Graduate Teaching Assistant, Department of Psychology, University of Louisville; (Home) 3511 Forest Brook Drive, Louisville, KY 40207-4320, USA **Work Phone:** (502)

852-6775 **E-Mail:**wcrowao1@ulkyvm.Louisville.edu **Date of Birth:** September 3, 1969 **Awards and Honors:** *Who's Who Among American Colleges and Universities* (1991); Letter of Commendation (1993), Department of Psychology, University of Louisville **Previous Positions:** Consortium Research Fellow, U.S. Army Research Institute for the Behavioral and Social Sciences, Fort Knox, KY; Undergraduate Teaching Assistant, Department of Philosophy/Department of Psychology, William Jewell College, Liberty, MO **Selected Memberships:** APA - Student Affiliate; Lambda Chi Alpha Fraternity; Society for Personality in Social Psychology **Discipline:** Social - Personality Psychology **Related Areas of Interest:** Deceptive Self-Presentation; Five-Factor Model of Personality; Behavioral Genetics; Measures of Religious Orientation **Current Areas of Research:** Individual and Collective Impression Management. **Personal Notes:** His bibliography contains 1 book, 3 articles, and 2 conference papers.

Ruark, James Ellwood

Present Position and Address: Senior Editor, Zondervan Publishing House, 5300 Patterson Ave., SE, Grand Rapids, MI 49530 USA **Work Phone:** (616) 698-3450 **Fax:** (616) 698-3454 **Date of Birth:** January 30, 1941 **Previous Positions:** Senior Editor, Academic and Professional Books, Zondervan Publishing House; Junior High Editor, David C. Cook Publishing Co., Elgin IL; News Editor, Bucks Country Courier Times, Levittown, PA **Selected Memberships:** American Scientific Affiliation **Discipline:** English and Literature **Related Areas of Interest:** Cosmology, Origin Issues, Astronomy, Integration of Science and Faith, Medical Ethics.

$$S$$

Saltzman, Judy D.

Present Position and Address: Professor of Philosophy (since 1985), California Polytechnic State University, San Luis Obispo, CA 93407, USA **Date of Birth:** February 2, 1942 **Education:** B.A. (*cum laude*, 1963), San Jose State University; M.A. Philosophy (1965), University of California - Berkeley; M.A. Religious Studies (1973)/Ph.D. Religious Studies (1977), University of California - Santa Barbara **Previous Positions:** Instructor in Philosophy (1966-67), Santa Barbara City College; Instructor (1973-75), Ventura College; Lecturer (1975)/Assistant and Associate Professor of Philosophy (1978-85), California Polytechnic State University **Selected Memberships:** American Academy of Religion; Society for the Scientific Study of Religion; German Studies Association **Discipline:** Religious Studies; Religion **Related Areas of Interest:** Philosophy of Religion; German Idealism; Neo-Kantianism.

Sardana, Lal

Address: 4537 Larch, Bellaire, TX 77401, USA **Work Phone:** (713) 666-2225 **Date of Birth:** October 1, 1926 **Education:** B.S. Science (1948), India; M.E. Engineering (1967), Southern Methodist University, Dallas; M.B.A. (1967)/Ph.D. (1969), University of California - Los Angeles **Selected Memberships:** American Humanist Organization **Related Areas of Interest:** Creationism versus Evolution; Comparative Theology; Promotion of East-West understanding.

Schaefer III, Henry F.

Present Position and Address: Graham Perdue Professor of Chemistry/Director (since 1987), Center for Computational Quantum Chemistry, University of Georgia, Athens, GA 30602, USA **Work Phone:** (706) 542-2067 **Fax:** (706) 542-0406 **Date of Birth:** June 8, 1944 **Education:** S.B. Chemical Physics (1966), Massachusetts Institute of Technology; Ph.D. (1969), Stanford University **Awards and Honors:** American Chemical Society Award in Pure Chemistry (1979); Leo Hendrik Baekeland Award (1983); Centenary Medal, Royal Society of Chemistry, London (1993); Third Most Highly Cited Chemist in the World (1984-91) **Previous Positions:** Assistant Professor (1969-74)/Associate (1974-78)/Full Professor (1978-87), University of California - Berkeley; Wilfred T. Doherty Professor of Chemistry/Director of Institute for Theoretical Chemistry (1979-80), University of Texas - Austin **Selected Memberships:** American Chemical Society; American Physical Society; International Academy of Quantum Molecular Sciences; American Scientific Affiliation; Victoria Institute **Discipline:** Chemical Physics; Theoretical Chemistry **Related Areas of Interest:** Bible and Science; Creation/Evolution; Cosmology; Apologetics.

Scheie, Paul

Present Position and Address: Professor of Physics, Texas Lutheran College, Seguin, TX 78155, USA
Date of Birth: June 24, 1933 **Education:** B.A. Physics (1955), St. Olaf College; M.S. Physics (1957), University of New Mexico; Ph.D. Biophysics (1965), Pennsylvania State University (Penn State) **Previous Positions:** Assistant Professor of Physics (1958-63), Oklahoma City University; Assistant Professor of Biophysics (1966-73), Penn State University; Assistant through Professor of Physics (since 1973), Texas Lutheran College; Visiting Professor (1980-81/1990-91), University of Bergen, Norway **Selected Memberships:** Committee on the Christian Faith and the Liberal Arts (1980-87), Division of College and University Services, American Lutheran Church **Discipline:** Physics; Biophysics **Related Areas of Interest:** Conflicts between Science and Religion.

Schmitt, Francis O.

Present Position and Address: Foundation Scientist, Neurosciences Research Foundation, Inc.; Institute Professor Emeritus, Massachusetts Institute of Technology, Department of Biology, Room 16-512, 77 Massachusetts Avenue, Cambridge, MA 02139, USA **Work Phone:** (617) 253-5015 **Date of Birth:** November 23, 1903 **Education:** A.B. (1924)/Ph.D. (1927), Washington University **Postgraduate Experience:** Postdoctoral Studies, University of California (1927-28)/University College, London (1928)/Kaiser Wilhelm Institute, Berlin-Dahlem (1928-29) **Honorary Degrees:** D.Sc., Johns Hopkins (1950), Washington University (1952), University of Chicago (1957), Valparaiso University (1959), Michigan State University (1968), NY State Medical College (1971); M.D. honoris causa, University of Gothenburg, Sweden(1964); LL.D. honoris cause, Wittenberg University (1966), Juniata College (1968) **Previous Positions:** Assistant through Professor of Zoology (1929-41)/Head (1941), Washington University; Professor of Biology (1941)/Head (1942-55)/Institute Professor (1955-69)/Emeritus (since 1973), Massachusetts Institute of Technology **Selected Memberships:** National Academy of Sciences; Member Board of Trustees, Massachusetts General Hospital; American Association for the Advancement of Science; New York Academy of Science; Fellow, American Academy Arts and Sciences; American Physiological Society; American Society of Zoologists; Society for Experimental Biology and Medicine; Society for Neuroscience; Society Philomathique de Paris; Swedish Royal Academy Sciences; Phi Beta Kappa; Sigma Xi; Previous Member of Board of Scientific Counselors NINCDS, NIH; Former National Advisor General Medical Sciences Council **Discipline:** Neuroscience **Related Areas of Interest:** Medical Ethics **Current Research:** Research in area of Neuroscience.

Schneider, Hans-Georg

Present Position and Address: Research Fellow (since 1984), St. Cross College, Oxford OX1 3LZ, UK **Date of Birth:** August 6, 1945 **Languages Spoken:** English, German **Education:** M.A. (1976)/Dr. phil. (1981), University of Heidelberg **Selected Memberships:** History of Science Society; British Society for the History of Science; Society for the History of Alchemy and Chemistry **Discipline:** History and Sociology of Science **Related Areas of Interest:** Physico-theology; Emergence of the Concept of the Laws of Nature in Early Modern Europe.

Schocher, Arno Johannes

Present Position and Address: Reverend on sabbatical leave; Casa al Funtania, Strada Canzonale, 6981 Banco, Switzerland **Date of Birth:** October 5, 1932 **Education:** Engineer (1956), Swiss Federal Institute of Technology, Zürich; Dr. Sc. Tech. (1959), Technical University, Delft, The Netherlands;

Study of Theology, University Basel, Ordination (1986) **Previous Positions:** Scientific Research Officer (1959-61), National Research Council, Ottawa, Canada; Group Leader Antibiotics Research (1961-65), Hoffmann-La Roche (HLR), Nutley, USA; Chief Microbiological Researcher (1965-74), Department of HLR Basel, Switzerland; Staff Member of General Management (1974-78), Biotechnology, HLR Basel; General Manager (1979-81), Citrique Belge of HLR, Belgium; Head Ecology and Waste Management (1981-82), HLR, Switzerland **Discipline:** Technology; Microbiology; Theology **Related Areas of Interest:** Science and Theology; Church and Industrial Society.

Scholz, Günter

Present Position and Address: Research Scientist (since 1955), Institute of Genetics and Crop Plant Research, 06466 Gatersleben, Germany; Schmiedestrasse 1, 06466 Gatersleben, Germany **Work Phone:** 49-03948-5345 **Home Phone:** 49-03948-5476 **Date of Birth:** July 9, 1931 **Education:** Agriculture and Chemistry (1951-55), Martin-Luther University of Halle; Dr. agr. (1960)/Dr. habil. (1970), Halle **Selected Memberships:** Member (1968-75), Central Committee of World Council of Churches (WCC); Member (1975-82), WCC Working Committee on Church and Society Council of Evangelical Churches in Eastern Germany (formerly the GDR); European Conference on Science and Theology **Discipline:** Plant Physiology; Plant Biochemistry **Related Areas of Interest:** Science Ethics; Science and Theology Dialogue.

Schotman-Veldman, Judith L.

Address: Oranje Nassaulaan 41, 3708 GC Zeist, The Netherlands **Date of Birth:** July 19, 1944 **Languages Spoken:** Dutch, English, German, French **Education:** Drs. of Chemistry (1969), Rijksuniversiteit, Utrecht **Previous Positions:** Staffmember (1982-85), MCK (Multidisciplinair Centrum voor Kerk en Samenleving), Driebergen **Selected Memberships:** ATOMIUM **Discipline:** Physical Chemistry; History of Science; Applied Physics **Related Areas of Interest:** Science and Theology; Social responsibility of Scientists and Technologists.

Schubert, Klaus R. von

Present Position and Address: Ordinarius Professor of Experimental High-Energy Physics; University of Karlsruhe, am Pferchelhang 33, 6900 Heidelberg 1, Germany, **Date of Birth:** December 28, 1939 **Languages Spoken:** German, English, French **Education:** Studied Physics at Karlsruhe, Berlin, and Heidelberg: Dipl. (1963); Promot. (1966); Dr.rer.nat **Previous Positions:** Research work at Heidelberg, Geneva (CERN), Hamburg (DESY), and Karlsruhe **Selected Memberships:** Director, Forschungsstätte der Evangelischen Studiengemeinschaft (F.E.ST.) **Discipline:** Physics.

Scott, Philip Maxwell

Present Position and Address: Vicar of Hillsborough (since 1987); 102 Hillsborough Road, Hillsborough, Auckland 1004, New Zealand **Work Phone:** (9) 659-604 **Date of Birth:** June 28, 1949 **Education:** B.Sc. (1970)/M.Sc. Mathematics (Class I Honours), 1971, Auckland University; Diploma in Teaching (1974), Auckland Teachers College; B.D. Theology (1978), Otago University **Previous Positions:** Temporary Junior Lecturer in Mathematics (1971); Commonwealth Scholar in Mathematics (1971/72), Sheffield University, UK; Secondary School Teacher (1972), Auckland Grammar School; Assistant Curate (1978-80), Manurewa; Assistant Curate (1980-82), Henderson; Vicar (1982-87),

Bucklands Beach **Selected Memberships:** Diocesan Council, Diocese of Auckland **Discipline:** Mathematics; Theology **Related Areas of Interest:** Logic; Worship; Systems Theory; Cosmology.

Sevenhoven, J. C. A. M.

Present Position and Address: Doctoral student, Philosophical Theology; Stoutenburgerlaan 5 NL-3835 PB Stoutenburg, The Netherlands **Date of Birth:** July 13, 1946 **Education:** Currently preparing a dissertation on paradigm theories in scientific practice and reformations in traditions of views of life, under the supervision of Prof. V. Brümmer **Discipline:** Philosophical Theology **Related Areas of Interest:** Science, Philosophy and Theology in Dialogue.

Sheldon, John M.

Present Position and Address: M.D. student, Johns Hopkins University; and Ph.D. student at University of Chicago Divinity School; 32510 Creekside Drive, Pepper Pike, OH 44124, USA **Date of Birth:** July 9, 1965 **Education:** A.B. (*magna cum laude*, 1987), Dartmouth College **Awards and Honors:** Phi Beta Kappa **Discipline:** Medical Ethics; Medicine **Related Areas of Interest:** Medical Ethics; Medicine and Philosophy; Medicine and Religion; Science and Religion.

Sheppard, Norman

Present Position and Address: Emeritus Professor of Chemistry (since 1986), University of East Anglia, Norwich, UK; 5 Hornor Close, Norwich NR2 2LY, England, UK **Date of Birth:** May 16, 1921 **Languages Spoken:** English, French **Education:** B.A. Chemistry (1st Class Honors, 1943)/Ph.D. Chemistry (1947), Cambridge University **Previous Positions:** Various Research Fellowships (to 1955); Assistant Director of Research in Spectroscopy (1955-64), Cambridge University; Fellow of Trinity College; Professor of Chemistry (1964-86), University of East Anglia **Selected Memberships:** Science and Religion Forum, UK; Convivium (a British group concerned with the life and thought of Michael Polanyi); Fellow, Royal Society **Discipline:** Physical Chemistry; Chemical Spectroscopy **Related Areas of Interest:** Philosophy of Science; Science and Religion Relationships.

Shropshire Jr., W.

Present Position and Address: Biophysicist Emeritus; Pastor, Foundry United Methodist Church, Washington, DC; (Office) Omega Laboratory, P.O. Box 189, Cabin John, MD 20818-0189; (Home) 4816 Flower Valley Drive, Rockville, MD 20853-1627, USA **Concurrent Positions:** Adjunct Faculty, Congregational Based Ministries, Wesley Theological Seminary (since 1990) **Date of Birth:** September 4, 1932 **Education:** B.S. Physics (1954)/M.S. Botany (1956)/Ph.D. Plant Physiology (1958), George Washington University; Postdoctoral Fellow in Biophysics (1957-59), California Institute of Technology; M.Div. (*summa cum laude*, 1990), Wesley Theological Seminary **Awards and Honors:** Smithsonian Outstanding Performance Award (1967); Smithsonian Research Award (1968) **Previous Positions:** Physicist (1954-57/1959-63), Smithsonian Institution; Assistant Director (1963-86), Smithsonian Radiation Biology Lab and Environmental Research Center; Visiting Professor: University Freiburg, Germany (1968-69)/University Zürich, Switzerland (1985-86); Botany Adjunct Professor (1960-85), George Washington University **Selected Memberships:** Fellow, American Association for the Advancement of Science; Biophysical Society; Past President, International Solar Energy Society; Explorer's Club; Past-President, Washington Society for Jungian Psychology; Past-President, American Society Photobiology **Discipline:** Minister; Biophysicist **Related Areas of Interest:** "The world is an incredible place, rich with unexplored and unexplained interconnections between the biological and physical parts. . . I also have benefited from mystical religious experiences of others and my own that enable me to work at the interface between science and religion. My belief is that the pursuit of both subjective and objective knowledge of ourselves and the universe we live in is necessary to enable humanity to develop to its fullest potential."

Smith-Moran, Barbara Putney

Present Position and Address: Associate Rector (since 1991), St. Andrew's Episcopal Church Framingham, MA 01742, USA **Concurrent Positions:** Coordinator of Campus Ministry and Protestant Chaplain (since 1993), Framingham State College, Concord, MA; Director (since 1989), Center for Faith and Science Exchange (F.A.S.E) **Date of Birth:** July 15, 1945 **Education:** A.B. (1967), Randolph-Macon Woman's College; M.A.T. (1969), Johns Hopkins University; M.A. (1974), Harvard University; M.Div. (1989), Episcopal Divinity School; Ordination to Priesthood (1990), Episcopal Church **Previous Positions:** Chair (1989-90), Task Force for Cultural Exchange between Faith and Science, Episcopal Diocese of Massachusetts; Priest Associate, St. Paul's Episcopal Church in Bedford, MA **Selected Memberships:** American Association for the Advancement of Science; Astronomical Society of the Pacific; Center for Theology and the Natural Sciences; Faith and Science Exchange; Society of Ordained Scientists **Discipline:** Chemistry; Astronomy; Theology **Related Areas of Interest:** The Scientific Community; Exchange of Critiques, Metaphors, Ideas between the Faith Culture and the Scientific Culture; Ministry with a view to the Spirituality of Scientists, and a Theology Responsive to American Scientific Culture.

Smith, Ronald N.

Present Position and Address: Retired Aerospace Engineer (since 1974), The Boeing Company; 10220 SE 21st, Bellevue, WA 98004, USA **Date of Birth:** June 6, 1911 **Education:** B.A. Physics (1931)/M.A. (1933), University of British Columbia; Ph.D. Physics (1941), Purdue University **Previous Positions:** Instructor through Assistant Professor (1941-46), Physics Department, Purdue University **Selected Memberships:** American Association for the Advancement of Science; Presbyterian Church Elder (since 1950) **Related Areas of Interest:** Cosmology; Molecular Biology; Writing - Science and Religion.

Smucker, Silas J.

Present Position and Address: Retired; 1801 Greencroft Blvd., Apt. 215, Goshen, IN 46526, USA **Home Phone:** (219) 537-4592 **Date of Birth:** December 31, 1904 **Languages Spoken:** English, German **Education:** A.B. (1930), Goshen College, IN; M.S. Agriculture (1932), Purdue University **Previous Positions:** Plant Pathologist (1935-45)/Soil Conservationist (1946-59), US Department Agriculture; Community Development Advisor (1960-69), U. S. State Department, Laos **Selected Memberships:** Soil Conservation Society of America; Indiana Academy of Science; American Scientific Affiliation **Discipline:** Agriculture **Related Areas of Interest:** Stewardship of God's Creation.

Spak, K. Edmund

Present Position and Address: Private Practice in Ophthalmology (since 1973); 8830 Long Point #405, Houston, TX 77055, USA **Date of Birth:** November 8, 1925 **Languages Spoken:** English,

French, German, Polish, Russian, Swedish **Education:** Medical Diploma (1951)/Residency in Ophthalmology (1951-55), College of Medicine, Poznan, Poland; Board Certified in Ophthalmology (1955), Poznan, Poland; Doctor of Medical Science (1960-62), Wroclaw, Poland; Preceptorship in Ophthalmology (1970-71), Baylor College of Medicine, TX; Basic and Clinical Science Course (1971-73), American Academy of Ophthalmology and Otolaryngology. License in Sweden (1968) **Previous Positions:** Clinical Instructor (1951-55)/Senior Clinical Instructor (1956-57), College of Medicine, Poznan, Poland; Chief of Ophthalmology Service (1955-56), Polish Red Cross Hospital, Korea; Head of Eye Department (1957-67), District Hospital, Wroclaw, Poland; Assistant Head of Eye Department (1968-69), District Hospital, Växjö, Sweden; Ophthalmology Associate (1971-74), Louis J. Girard, Houston, TX **Selected Memberships:** American Academy of Ophthalmology; Association for Research in Vision and Ophthalmology; American Intra-Ocular Implant Society; International Corneal Society Société Francaise d'Ophtalmologie in Paris; American Academy of Medical Ethics **Discipline:** Medicine; Ophthalmology **Related Areas of Interest:** General Interest in Science and Theology Interaction.

Stahl, C. Larry

Present Position and Address: Retired; 3355 N. Delta Hwy # 123, Eugene, OR 97408, USA **Home Phone:** (503) 344-4568 **Date of Birth:** January 19, 1932 **Languages Spoken:** English, some German **Education:** M.A. English (1967), California State University - Los Angeles **Previous Positions:** Minister; Educator, High School English; Business and Related **Discipline:** Linguistics **Related Areas of Interest:** Education **Current Areas of Research:** Identifying the Beginning of Language(s) in Indo-European; Reconciling Science and Religion.

Stein, Sharon A.

Present Position and Address: Currently Ed.D. candidate in Human Development and Psychology, Harvard University; Counseling (since 1988), Center for Addiction Studies, Department of Psychiatry, Harvard Medical School and The Cambridge Hospital; 88 Endicott Street, Boston, MA 02113, USA **Date of Birth:** July 28, 1959 **Education:** B.A. Philosophy and English Literature (1981), University of Minnesota; Ed.M. Counseling and Consulting Psychology (1986), Harvard University; M.A. English Language and Literature (1987), University of Minnesota **Previous Positions:** Research Assistant for Hypertension Study (1980-82)/Teaching Assistant (1983-84), University of Minnesota; Teacher in Language Skills (1982-84), Macalester College, St. Paul, MN/(1985-87), Katherine Gibbs School, Boston; Field Research Coordinator (1985-87), Dare Institute, Cambridge; Teaching Fellow (Fall 1986), Harvard University; Clinical Fellow in Psychiatry (1987-88)/Lecturer in Psychology (1988-89), Harvard Medical School **Selected Memberships:** Society for Research in Child Development; Jean Piaget Society; Institute on Religion in an Age of Science **Discipline:** Developmental Psychology; Philosophy; Education **Related Areas of Interest:** Addiction; Human Development; Psychology and Spirituality.

Stewart, John Frederick Hudson

Present Position and Address: Bible and Latin Teacher (since 1979); Grenville Christian College, Box 610, Brockville, ONT K6V 5V8, Canada **Date of Birth:** March 23, 1917 **Languages Spoken:** English **Education:** B.A. (1938)/M.D. (1950), University of Toronto; Licentiate in Theology (1941)/Bachelor of Divinity (1958), Wycliffe College; Diploma in Tropical Medicine and Hygiene (1955), London School of Tropical Medicine and Hygiene; Certificand (1959) and Fellow (1971), Royal College of Surgeons of Canada **Previous Positions:** Medical Missionary (1955-65), Liberia;

Medical Staff (1965-78), Rideau Regional Center (for mentally retarded) **Selected Memberships:** Fellow, American Scientific Affiliation; Canadian Scientific and Christian Affiliation **Discipline:** Medicine; Theology **Related Areas of Interest:** African Tribal Medicine; West African History.

Stulman, Julius

Present Position and Address: Lumber Executive; 603 Longboat Club Road, Longboat Key, FL 34228, USA **Date of Birth:** April 11, 1906 **Previous Positions:** Chairman of Board of Lumber Industries Inc. NYC/Lumber Exchange Terminal Inc., NYC; President of Green Street Terminal Corp., NYC; Director of Foundation Life Insurance Company of America/World-Wide Press Company (1953-60) **Selected Memberships:** President, World Institute Council, NYC; Vice President, Center Integrative Education, NYC; Advisory Council member, Society of General Systems Research, Washington; Consortium on Peace Research, Education and Development, Institute Behavioral Sciences, Boulder, CO; Advanced Board, California Institute Asian Studies; International Cooperation Council; Fellow, World Academy of Arts and Sciences; Poetry Society of America; World Medical Association; American Cycle Association Club; Masons **Discipline:** Commerce **Related Areas of Interest:** World Economic Development, World Peace and Emergence.

Sturm, Mary J.

Present Position and Address: Currently a Ph.D. student in Theology, University of Chicago; Assistant to Director (since 1988), Legislative Coordinating Commission; 1759 White Bear Avenue, Maplewood, MN 55109, USA **Date of Birth:** March 2, 1956 **Education:** B.A. Theology (1978), College of St. Catherine; M.A. Divinity (1979), University of Chicago **Previous Positions:** Research Assistant (1982-84)/Lecturer in Science and Theology (in the extension program, 1983), University of Chicago; Visiting Instructor of Religious Studies (1984-85), Iowa State University; Instructor of Religion (1985), Saint Olaf College; Administrative Assistant to Minister (1987-88), Unity Church-Unitarian **Selected Memberships:** American Academy of Religion; Catholic Theological Society **Discipline:** Theology, with emphasis on Religion and Science **Related Areas of Interest:** Science and Religion; Metaphysics; Philosophy of Religion; Process Philosophy; Philosophy of Science.

Sutherland, Jr., Malcolm Read

Present Position and Address: Minister Emeritus (since 1994), Harvard Unitarian Church, P.O. Box 217, Harvard, MA 01451, USA; (Home) 21 Woodside Rd., Harvard, MA 01451, USA **Date of Birth:** November 11, 1916 **Education:** A.B. (1938), Miami University, OH; M.S. (1941), Case Western Reserve University, Cleveland, OH; B.D. (1945), Federated Theological Faculty, University of Chicago; Ordination (1945), Unitarian Church **Honorary Degrees:** LL.D. (1963), Emerson College, L.H.D. (1975), Meadville-Lombard Theological School **Lectures Presented:** Thomas Minns Lectures (1955, 1979), Warner Free Lectures (1985, 1993) **Awards and Honors:** Honorary Fellow, Manchester College, Oxford University (1973); Distinguished Service Award (1975), International Association Religious Freedom **Previous Positions:** Regional Housing Supervisor (1941-42), Farm Security Administration; Housing Management Supervisor (1942-43), FPHA; Pastor (1944-60), churches in IL, VA, MA; Robert Collier Professor of Church and Society, President, and Dean of Faculty (1960-75), Meadville Theological School, Lombard College, Chicago; Executive Director of US Committee (1980-83)/ International Council (since 1984)/Honorary President (since 1994), World Conference on Religion and Peace **Editorial Positions:** Chair, Editorial Board (1955-60), *Christian Register*; Editorial Advisory Committee (since 1965), and Co-chair, Publications Board (since 1965), *Zygon* **Selected Memberships:** Co-founder, Board of Directors, and Secretary (since 1965), Center for Advanced

Study in Religion and Science; President (1969,75-77)/Hon. Vice President (since 1980)/Fellow (1988), Institute on Religion in an Age of Science **Discipline:** Pastoral Ministry; Administration; Education **Related Areas of Interest:** Church; Science and Society.

$\mathcal{T}$

Tayler, Roger J.

Present Position and Address: Professor of Astronomy (since 1967), Astronomy Centre, University of Sussex, Falmer, Brighton BN1 9QH, UK **Work Phone:** (0273) 678118 **Date of Birth:** October 25, 1929 **Education:** B.A. (1950)/M.A. and Ph.D. (1954), University of Cambridge **Previous Positions:** Staff Member (1955-61), Harwell and Culham Laboratories, UK Atomic Energy Authority; Senior Research Astrophysicist (1961-64)/Lecturer in Applied Mathematics (1965-67), Cambridge University **Selected Memberships:** Secretary (1971-79)/Treasurer (1979-87)/President (1989-90), Royal Astronomical Society; Churchwarden, St. Anne's Church Lewes, East Sussex **Discipline:** Astronomy and Cosmology (Theoretical) **Related Areas of Interest:** Cosmology and Religion - Creation; Christian approach to the use of science.

Taylor, Jon

Present Position and Address: Associate Professor of Religion (since 1985), College of Great Falls, MT; 1301 20th Street South, Great Falls, MT, 59405, USA **Fax Phone:** (406) 761-8210 **E-Mail:** jontaylor@ATTMAIL.COM **Date of Birth:** June 30, 1938 **Education:** S.T.L. (1967), Pontifical University of St. Thomas; S.S.L. (1970), Pontifical Biblical Institute **Previous Positions:** Professor of Sacred Scripture (1969-71), St. John Seminary, Plymouth, MI; Professor of Sacred Scripture (1971-73), St. Patrick Seminary, Menlo Park, CA; Visiting Associate Professor of Religion (1973-74), Gonzaga University, Spokane, WA; Assistant Professor of Religion (1978-85), Siena Heights College, Adrian, MI **Selected Memberships:** Institute on Religion in an Age of Science; American Academy of Religion **Discipline:** Old Testament **Related Areas of Interest:** Computer analysis of texts; Theology and Science.

Tester, Leonard W.

Present Position and Address: Director, Department of Human Relations and Clinical Professor, New York Institute of Technology; Practice of Group and Individual Psychotherapy (since 1983); Psychologist, New York State, 115 E. 93rd, Street, 2G, New York, NY 10036, USA **Concurrent Positions:** Supervisor, American Institute for Hypnosis and Psychotherapy **Date of Birth:** August 21, 1933 **Languages Spoken:** English, some Spanish **Education:** S.T.B. (1965), Harvard University Divinity School; Ed.D. (1976), Teachers College, Columbia University; Ph.D. Psychology (1981), Columbia University **Postgraduate Experience:** Clinical Training: Massachusetts Mental Health Center; Peter Bent Brigham Hospital **Previous Positions:** Former minister (not now a Christian); Presently teaching a seminar on Religion and Psychotherapy **Editorial Positions:** Op-Ed. Columnist (1987-89), *The Korea Times, New York*, English Edition **Discipline:** Psychologist; Psychotherapist **Related Areas of Interest:** Religion and Psychotherapy.

Toledo, J. Rafael

Present Position and Address: Assistant Professor of Psychology, Psychology Department, University of North Texas, Denton, TX 76226, USA **Work Phone:** (817) 565-2671 **Date of Birth:** July 23, 1939 **Languages Spoken:** English, Spanish, French **Education:** M.D. (1963), Universidad Autonoma, Guadalajara, Mexico; Pediatrics (1969), University of Texas Medical Branch, Galveston, TX **Previous Positions:** Private Practice (1971-72), Mexico; Children's Unit (1972-73), Kalamazoo State Hospital, MI; Director (1973-75), Maverick County Child Health Care Center; Assistant Professor of Pediatrics (1975-76), University of Texas Southwestern Medical School, Dallas; Consultant (1974-77), Children's Heart Program, Driscoll Hospital; Physician, Student Health Center (1977-84)/Director of Behavioral Medicine Clinic (1981-84), North Texas State University; Pediatric training of medical students (1978-80), Southwestern Medical School, Dallas; Adjunct Professor, Medical Anthropology Program, Anthropology Department, Southern Methodist University, Dallas, TX; Pediatric Private Practice, TX **Selected Memberships:** Fellow, American Academy of Pediatrics; Texas Pediatric Society **Discipline:** Pediatrics **Related Areas of Interest:** Interaction of Belief Systems; Cognitive Functions; Neurophysiology; Health and Health Practices including Religious Healing.

Trautteur, Giuseppe

Present Position and Address: Professor of Cybernetics (since 1980), Department of Physical Science, Mostra D'Oltremare, Pad. 19, I-80125, Napoli, Italy; (Home) Via Monte di Dio 5, I-80132, Napoli, Italy **Work Phone:** (081) 725-3413 **Home Phone:** (081) 764-1758 **Date of Birth:** December 5, 1936 **Languages Spoken:** Italian, French, English **Education:** Maturità Classica (1954), Rome; Laurea in Fisica (1959), Università di Roma; M.S. Communication Sciences (1967), University of Michigan; Candidate in Computer and Communication Science (1970), University of Michigan **Previous Positions:** Researcher (1959-60), Laboratorio Gas ionizzati, INFN Frascati; Assistant to Chair of Spectroscopy (1960), Università di Roma; Assistant (1960-65), Istituto di Fisica Teorica/Associate Professor (1968-80), Università di Napoli; Research Assistant (1965-68), Systems Engineering Lab, University of Michigan; Visiting Research Associate, University of British Columbia (1971)/ISSCO at University of Geneva (1976-78) **Discipline:** Computer Science - Cybernetics **Related Areas of Interest:** Theories of Meaning; Epistemology of Miracles.

Trook, Douglas A.

Present Position and Address: Psychotherapist, Pocono Neuropsychiatric Center, Stroudsburg, PA; Rd. 3, Box 3300, Dove Lane, E. Stroudsburg, PA 18301, USA **Concurrent Positions:** Program Coordinator, Carbon-Monroe-Pike Mental Health/Mental Retardation, Stroudsburg, PA **Work Phone:** (717) 424-2175 **Date of Birth:** June 16, 1950 **Languages Spoken:** English, Spanish **Education:** B.A. Psychology (1972), Wheaton College; M.A. Clinical Psychology (1974), Duquesne University; M.A.R. Systematic Theology (1976), Westminster Theological Seminary; M.Phil (1981)/Ph.D. (1986), Theological and Religious Studies, Drew University Graduate School **Previous Positions:** Youth Pastor (1974-76), Third Reformed Presbyterian Church, Philadelphia; Psychotherapist (1974-76), Christian Counseling and Education Foundation; Youth Pastor (1977-82), Bethany Evangelical Free Church, West Orange, NJ; Intern Pastor (1983-84), Emmanuel Orthodox Presbyterian Church, Whippany, NJ; Psychotherapist (1988-90), Lutheran Welfare Services, Stroudsburg, PA **Selected Memberships:** Evangelical Theological Society **Discipline:** Hermeneutics (Theological, Philosophical and Scientific); Systematic Theology; Theological Foundations of Psychology **Related Areas of Interest:** Integration of personality theory and Christology; Space-time Relativity and Theological Hermeneutics; Scientific Theology of T. F. Torrance.

Truog, Dean-Daniel W.

Present Position and Address: Founding President and Life Management Consultant/Counselor, The Counerstone Institute for Values and Relationships (since 1990); 15 Sheridan Road, Swampscott, MA 01907, USA **Concurrent Positions:** Special Consultant to members of U.S. Congress (since 1993); Vice President, U.S.—Bulgaria Institute (since 1991); Tutor and Lecturer in Biblical Studies and Practical Christianity (since 1965), The Navigators International; Boston Area Representative and Lecturer at Large (since 1985), The Navigators USA **Work Phone:** (617) 581-9412 **Date of Birth:** April 1, 1938 **Languages Spoken:** English, French **Education:** Studies in Philosophy (1961), Bethel College, MN and in Philosophical Theology (1968), L'Abri Fellowship Foundation, Switzerland; Diploma in Bible and Leadership Development (1968), The Navigators International Training Institute; B.A. European History (1971), University of Colorado, Boulder; DEUG French Civilization (1977), Université de Strasbourg; M.A. Liberal Education (1986), St. John's College Graduate Institute, Annapolis/Santa Fe; ALM History of Science (1987), Harvard University **Postgraduate Experience:** Interdisciplinary Studies: Philosophy of Science/Religion (1987-93), Boston University **Field Work:** Research trips to Brazil (1985)/China (1989) **Previous Positions:** Vice President, National Board of Directors, Les Navigateurs en France (1984-87); President and Founding Director, Les Navigateurs en France; Chairman of Advisory Board, Navpresse, France;Tutor in Great Books Seminars (1988), C.S. Lewis Institute, Oxford University, UK; Teaching at student and professional conferences and training programs in USA, most countries of Western Europe, and in Eastern Europe, Quebec, and Brazil; Designing and directing leadership development programs in the Washington, DC area, Colorado, Austria, France, and Switzerland; Senior Teaching Fellow in Non-Departmental Studies (1987-90, certificate of Distinction in Teaching in 1990), Harvard University; North House Tutor in Philosophy of Science/Religion (1987-91), Harvard College, Cambridge, MA; Founding Chairman, Harvard Christian Associates(1987-92) **Selected Memberships:** American Scientific Affiliation; Society of Christian Philosophers; Associates for Religion and Intellectual Life; Institute on Religion in an Age of Science; History of Science Society; Center for Theology and the Natural Sciences **Discipline: Education:**; Religion; Philosophy of Science/Religion; History of Science/Religion; French Civilization **Related Areas of Interest:** History/Philosophy of Science/Religion; Relationship of Scientific and Religious Knowledge (Epistemology); Psychology of Religion; Origins and Evolutionary Theory.

Selected Publications: So far he has not published in this area although he has been active in speaking engagements and presenting papers and in research.

_____. "The Din Over Darwin: An Assessment of the Scientific and Philosophical Dimensions of the Conflict Over the Theory of Evolution During the Generation since the Centennial of the Publication of Darwin's Origin of Species (1959-87)." A.L.M. thesis, Harvard University, 1987.

Turner, Robert Eugene

Present Position and Address: Professor (since 1983), Department of Oceanography and Coastal Sciences, and, Coastal Ecology Institute, Louisiana State University, Baton Rouge, LA 70803 USA **Concurrent Positions**: Intecol Working Group on Wetlands (since 1979), Chairperson (since 1984) **Work Phone:** (504) 388-6454 **Fax Number:** (504) 388-6326 **Date of Birth:** April 7, 1945 **Education:** B.A. Zoology (1967), Monmouth College, IL; M.A. Zoology (1969), Drake University; Ph.D. Ecology (1974), University of Georgia **Previous Positions:** Research Associate (1974)/Assistant (1975-78)/Associate Professor (1978-83), Louisiana State University; Consultant to Ministry of Public Works (1974), Indonesia; Chairman (1989-1992), Marine Sciences; Center for Wetland Resources, Louisiana State University, Baton Rouge, LA **Selected Memberships:** American Association for the Advancement of Science; American Fisheries Society; American Society of Limnology and Oceanography;

Association of Wetland Scientists; Ecological Society of America; Federation of American Scientists; INTECOL; International Estuarine Research Federation; International Society of Tropical Ecology **Discipline:** Zoology; Ecology.

Ulbrich, Paul W.

Present Position and Address: Assistant Professor of Emergency Medicine, Midwestern University; 5132 S. Dorchester, Chicago, IL 60615-4188 USA **Date of Birth:** May 17, 1941 **Education:** B.S. Zoology, Michigan State University; D.O. (1970), Chicago Osteopathic College of Medicine; Fellow, American College of Emergency Physicians **Selected Memberships:** Chicago Center for Religion and Science **Discipline:** Emergency Medicine **Related Areas of Interest:** Operational Scientific Definitions of Theological Concepts; Functional Concepts of Ethics.

Ulrickson, Brian Lee

Present Position and Address: Ordained Catholic Priest; Assistant Professor (since 1989), Physics Department, Gonzaga University, Spokane, WA 99258, USA **Work Phone:** (509) 328-4220 ext. 3357 **Date of Birth:** November 18, 1949 **Education:** B.A. Philosophy (1973), Gonzaga University; M.Div. Theology (1978), Weston School of Theology, Cambridge, MA; B.S. Physics (1982)/Ph.D. Atmospheric Sciences (1988), University of Washington, Seattle; Ordained Catholic Priest (1978), Society of Jesus **Postgraduate Experience:** Graduate Research Assistant (1982-88), Department of Atmospheric Sciences, University of Washington **Previous Positions:** High School Instructor (1973-75), Sciences/Mathematics/Religion, Bellarmine Preparatory School, Tacoma, WA; Hospital Chaplain (1978-80), St. Elizabeth's Hospital, Yakima, WA **Selected Memberships:** American Meteorological Society; American Association for the Advancement of Science **Discipline:** Atmospheric/Earth Sciences; Theology **Related Areas of Interest:** Cosmology and Religious Beliefs; Biological Evolution and Concepts of God; Religious knowing in relation to Scientific Knowing; the Religious Experience of the Scientist; Creation-centered Theology and Beliefs based on Revelation.

Underkofler, Leland A.

Present Position and Address: Retired Director of Molecular Biology Research Laboratory (since 1971), 2002 Westridge Road, #507, Carlsbad, NM 88220, USA **Work Phone:** (505) 885-6943 **Date of Birth:** April 24, 1906 **Education:** A.B. Chemistry (1928), Nebraska Wesleyan University; Ph.D. Biophysical Chemistry (1934), Iowa State College **Postgraduate Experience:** Postdoctoral studies (1940), University of Wisconsin **Honorary Degrees:** Honorary D.Sc. (1953), Nebraska Wesleyan University **Previous Positions:** Professor of Chemistry (1933-35), Westminster College; Instructor through Professor of Chemistry (1935-55), Iowa State College; Director of Research (1955-59), Takamine Laboratory/Director of Enzymology Research Laboratory (1959-67)/Director of Molecular Biology Research Laboratory (1968-71), Miles Laboratories, Inc; Distinguished Visiting Professor (1978), Memphis State University **Selected Memberships:** American Chemical Society; American Society of Biological Chemists; American Association of Cereal Chemists; American Academy of Microbiology; Fellow and National President (1967-68)/Editor (1974-85), Society for Industrial

Microbiology; Sigma Xi **Discipline:** Biophysical Chemistry **Related Areas of Interest:** Theology and Science in Dialogue.

Van Arsdel, III, William Campbell

Present Position and Address: Pharmacologist (since 1963), Center for Drug Evaluation and Research (CDER), Food and Drug Administration; 1000 6th Street, S.W., Apt. 301, Washington, DC 20024, USA **Education:** B.S. Zoology (1949)/M.S. Zoology (1951)/Ph.D. Physiology and Zoology (1959), Oregon State College; M.S. Pharmacology (1954), University of Oregon Medical School **Selected Memberships:** American Academy for the Advancement of Science; New York Academy of Science; Washington Academy of Science; Sigma XI; Society of Experimental Biology and Medicine; Undersea and Hyperbaric Medical Society; American Chemical Society **Related Areas of Interest:** Pharmacology **Current Areas of Research:** Toxicology; Teratology; Electrocardiology; Physiology; Marine Biology; Anthropometry; Science and Theology.

Vance, Forrest L.

Present Position and Address: Retired Dean of College of Arts and Sciences and Professor Emeritus of Psychology, Valparaiso University, Valparaiso, IN 46383, USA **Date of Birth:** October 26, 1929 **Education:** Study (1947-50), Bethel College/Bethel Theological Seminary (1951-52), St. Paul, MN; B.A. (1952)/Ph.D. Psychology and Education (1958), University of Minnesota **Previous Positions:** Assistant to Director (1952-53), Institute of Child Welfare, University of Minnesota; Instructor (1957-65), University of Minnesota; Psychology Consultant to VA Hospitals in Minneapolis and St. Cloud (1957-65); Associate Dean of Students (1965-66)/Director of Counseling and Special Services (1965-74)/Chairman (1974-79), and Associate Professor through Full Professor of Psychology (1965-1981), University of Rochester **Selected Memberships:** American Psychological Association; Licensed Psychologist in New York and Indiana **Discipline:** Clinical Psychology **Related Areas of Interest:** Science and Ethics.

van Kouwenhoven, Willem F.

Present Position and Address: Pastor, Adama van Scheltemastraat 17, 6824 NL Arnhem, Nederland **Work Phone:** 85-64 52 81 (after 10/10/95, 26-464 52 81) **Languages Spoken:** Dutch, English **Education:** A.B. History (1965), University of Chicago; M.Div. (1970), McCormick Theological Seminary, Chicago; Kerkelijk Examen (1987), Rijksuniversiteit, Utrecht **Previous Positions:** Math teacher (1970-76), Board of Education, Chicago; Pastor (1976-82), Pierceton Presbyterian Church, Pierceton, IN; Pastor (1987-92), Hervormde Gemeente Hoenderloo, The Netherlands **Selected Memberships:** Association for Clinical Pastoral Education **Discipline:** Theology **Related Areas of Interest:** Psychology and Theology; Pastoral Care and Counseling; Biochemistry; Archeology.

Van Ness, William

Present Position and Address: Campus Pastor (since 1967), University of California - Santa Barbara; (Home) 777 Camino Pescadero, Goleta, CA 93117, USA **Date of Birth:** April 7, 1927 **Education:** B.A. (1948), Occidental College; B.D. (1951), San Francisco Theological Seminary; M.A. (1970)/Ph.D. (1975), University of California - Santa Barbara **Previous Positions:** Parish ministries (1951-67), Presbyterian Church, USA **Selected Memberships:** American Academy of Religion; Presbyterian Ministers in Higher Education **Discipline:** Religion and Higher Education **Related Areas of Interest:** Religion and Science; Religion and Society; Religion and Environment.

Van Vliet, Carolyne M.

Present Position and Address: Professor (since 1969), Centre de Recherches Mathématiques, Université de Montréal, CP 6128 CentreVille, Montréal PQ H3C3J7, Canada **Concurrent Positions:** Visiting Professor (since 1974), University of Florida; Gainesville and Florida International University, Miami **Date of Birth:** December 29, 1929 **Languages Spoken:** English, French, German, Dutch **Education:** Ph.D. (1956), Free University, Amsterdam **Previous Positions:** Professor (1956-69), University of Minnesota **Selected Memberships:** American Physical Society; European Physical Society; Canadian Association of Physicists; Fellow, American Scientific Affiliation; Institute of Electrical and Electronic Engineers (IEEE); Anglican (Episcopal) Church **Discipline:** Theoretical Physics **Related Areas of Interest:** New Testament Theology; Canon; Pseudepigrapha; Extra Canonical Gospels; Dead Sea Scrolls **Personal Notes:** A full bibliographical list would include about 200 papers in Scientific Journals, including articles in the *ASA Journal* ("The Meaning of Soul"), *The Banner* (On Election as taught by the Canons of Dordt).

Varadarajan, Lotika

Present Position and Address: Associate Professor (since 1986), School of Arts and Aesthetics, Jawaharial Nehru University, New Delhi; Apt. 4A, Girdhar Apartments, 28 Feroze Shah Road, New Delhi 110 001, India **Work Phone:** 371 2512 **Date of Birth:** May 28, 1934 **Languages Spoken:** English, Bengali, Hindi, French **Education:** B.A. Hons. History (1954)/M.A. History (1956), Miranda House, University of Delhi; Historical Tripos (1956-58), Newnham College, University of Cambridge, UK; M.A. History (1962), University of Cambridge; Ph.D. History (1965), Heras Institute of Indian History and Culture, St. Xavier's College, University of Bombay **Previous Positions:** Lecturer (1964-71)/Senior Lecturer in History (1971-74)/Honorary Professor for Research (1976-82), Sophia College, Bombay; Visiting Lecturer (June 1980), Department of History, University of Sydney, Australia; Assistant Professor (1982-86), Centre for Historical Studies, Jawaharial Nehru University, New Delhi **Selected Memberships:** Asiatic Society of Bombay; Fellow, Heras Institute of Indian History and Culture, University of Bombay; Société Asiatique, Paris; Royal Asiatic Society, London **Discipline:** History **Related Areas of Interest:** Earth Science; Commerce; Environment; Technology; Education; Anthropology and Religion/Ethics.

Vayhinger, John M.

Present Position and Address: Professor Emeritus (since 1981), Anderson University, IN; Clinical Psychologist, 420 N. Nevada Avenue, Colorado Springs, CO 80903, USA **Concurrent Positions:** Private Practice in Psychotherapy (since 1958) **Work Phone:** (719) 471-8522 **Date of Birth:** January 27, 1916 **Education:** A.B. (1937), Taylor University, IN; Asbury Theological Seminary (1937-39); Butler University School of Religion, IN (1939); B.D. Theology (*cum laude*, 1940), Drew Theological

Seminary; M.A. Experimental and Abnormal Psychology (1948), Columbia University; M.A. Philosophy (1951), Drew University; Ph.D. Clinical Psychology (1956), Columbia University **Previous Positions:** Pastor for over 15 years; Instructor (1948-49), Drew Theological Seminary; Associate Professor of Psychology/Dept. Head (1949-51), West Virginia Wesleyan University; Chief Clinical Psychologist (1951-58), St. Joseph County Adult and Child Guidance Clinic, IN; University Lecturer (1953-58), Indiana University - South Bend; Professor of Pastoral Psychology and Counseling (1958-64), Garrett Theological Seminary; Professor of Psychology of Religion and Pastoral Counseling (1964-67), Iliff School of Theology, University of Denver; Minister of Pastoral Counseling (1967-68), Park Hill United Methodist Church, Denver; Lecturer in Psychology (1967-68), Graduate School, University of Colorado; Clinical Consultant (1967-68), Onondaga Pastoral Counseling-Psychiatric Center, Syracuse, NY; Professor of Psychology and Pastoral Care (1968-81)/Department Head (1981), Anderson School of Theology, Anderson University; Director (1968-81), NIMH workshops in Mental Health for Clergy, Anderson, IN; Professor of Pastoral Care (1981-84), Asbury Theological Seminary; Executive Director (1985-86), Colorado Interfaith Counseling Center, Colorado Springs, CO; National Chair (1989), Pastoral Counseling Institute Board; Vice President (1986), Greater Colorado Springs Association of Evangelicals **Selected Memberships:** United Methodist Church; American Psychological Association; Fellow, American Orthopsychiatric Association; American Association of Marital and Family Therapists; Fellow, Society for the Scientific Study of Religion; Religious Research Association; Fellow, American Scientific Affiliation; Christian Association for Psychological Studies; Diplomate, American Association of Pastoral Counselors; American Association of University Professors; Academy of Religion and Mental health; American Association for the Advancement of Science; Association of Military Chaplains of the United States; American Forestry Association; National Audubon Society **Discipline:** Clinical Psychology/Pastoral Therapy; Psychotherapy; Psychology **Related Areas of Interest:** Psychology and Theology.

Waldenfels, Hans

Present Position and Address: Professor (since 1977), Bonn University, Grenzweg 2, D-40489 Düsseldorf y, Germany **Date of Birth:** October 20, 1931 **Languages Spoken:** German, English, Japanese, Italian **Education:** Lic. Phil. (1956), Pullach, München; Lic. theol. (1964), Sophia University, Tokyo; Dr. theol. (1968), Gregoriana University, Rome; Dr. theol. habil. (1976), Würzburg University; Dr. theol. k. c. ATK Warszawa (1993) **Previous Positions:** Lecturer in Religious Science and Missiology (1970-75), Phil.-Theol. Hochschule, St. Georgen/University, Innsbruck; Professor of Fundamental Theology, Theology of non-Christian Religions and Philosophy of Religion (since 1977), Bonn University; Dean of Faculty of Roman Catholic Theology (1979-80, 1988-90) **Selected Memberships:** Chairman (since 1978), Internationales Institut für missionswissenschaftliche Forschungen e.V.; International Association for Mission Studies; Deutsche Vereinigung für Religionsgeschichte; Deutsche Gesellschaft für Missionswissenschaft; Member of the Society of Jesus **Discipline:** Theology; Religious Studies; Philosophy; Missiology **Related Areas of Interest:** Cross-cultural Research; Interreligious Dialogue; Buddhism/Christianity; Modern Theology since 1945.

Washburn, Marilyn

Present Position and Address: Assistant Professor, Community Health, Emory University; President, Presbyterian Health Network; 5 Lakeview Pl., Avondale Estate, GA 30002, USA **Date of Birth:** October 28, 1951 **Education:** B.A. Chemistry (1972)/M.D. (1976), Emory University; M.Div. (1981), Columbia Theological Seminary **Selected Memberships:** Presbyterian Health Network, Task Forces of PCUSA: Health Costs, Policies/Sexuality/Nestlé Monitoring; American Academy of Family Physicians **Discipline:** Medicine: Family Medicine; Ministry **Related Areas of Interest:** Biomedical Ethics; Death and Dying; Family Systems Theory; Political Theology.

Wathen-Dunn, Weiant

Present Position and Address: Retired Scientist, who has served (since 1976) as Secretary of The Institute on Religion in an Age of Science (IRAS); 552-C, Brookhaven, Lexington, MA 02173-8044, USA **Date of Birth:** April 12, 1912 **Languages Spoken:** English, German, French, Turkish **Education:** B.A. Physics (1934)/M.A. Physics (1936), Wesleyan University **Previous Positions:** Instructor in Physics and Mathematics (1936-40), Robert College, Istanbul, Turkey; Teacher in Physics (1940-41), Williston Academy; Physicist (1941-51), Sound Div., Naval Research Laboratory; Research in Speech Processing (1951-72), Air Force Cambridge Research Lab **Selected Memberships:** IRAS **Discipline:** Physics and Communication Engineering **Related Areas of Interest:** Interaction between Religion and Science.

Watson, John Robert

Present Position and Address: Emeritus Professor of Public Health; Senior Medical Director (part-time, since 1980), Hawaii Medical Services Association; 4707 Aukai Avenue, Honolulu, HI 96816, USA **Work Phone:** (808) 734-8141 **Date of Birth:** January 31, 1925 **Languages Spoken:** English, French **Education:** M.B.B.S. (1949), University of London, St. Bartholomew's Hospital Medical College; M.P.H. (1976), School of Public Health, University of Hawaii; M.A. (1989), South Asian Studies/Certificate in French Language, University of Hawaii **Postgraduate Experience:** Internship and Residency: Chesterfield Royal Hospital (1947-48), UK; Queen Alexandra Military Hospital/Victoria Hospital for Children/St. Bartholomew's Hospital (1949-52, in London) **Previous Positions:** Private Practice: Singapore (1954-56)/Honolulu Medical Group (1959-70)/Hawaii Ear, Nose and Throat Group (1970-77); Clinical Associate Professor of Surgery (1966-74), John A. Burns School of Medicine; Professor of Surgery/Chairman (1974-77), Division of Otolaryngology; Director (1975-77), Continuing Medical Education, School of Medicine; Chief-of-Party (1977-79), MEDEX/Pakistan, School of Medicine; Professor of Public Health/Chairman of Department of International Health (1979-83), School of Public Health **Consultant Positions:** Ministry of Health, Government of Western Samoa (1963)/Government of Fiji (1970-73); Government of American Samoa/US Department of Interior (1963, 1964); US Agency for International Development (1976), Thailand/Pakistan **Selected Memberships:** Fellow, American College of Surgeons; Royal College of Surgeons, Edinburgh/England; Hawaii Medical Library; Institute on Religion in an Age of Science **Discipline:** Surgery; Medicine **Related Areas of Interest:** Medical aspects of classic Hindu texts; Psychological aspects of early Buddhism.

Wattles, Jeffrey Hamilton

Present Position and Address: Assistant Professor of Philosophy, Kent State University, Kent, OH 44242-0001, USA; (Home) 2465 E. Norman Drive, Stow, OH 44242, USA **Work Phone:** (216) 672-2315 **Home Phone:** (216) 688-9659 **Date of Birth:** February 10, 1945 **Languages Spoken:** English, French **Education:** B.A. Philosophy (1966), Stanford University; M.A. (1970)/Ph.D. Philosophy (1973), Northwestern University **Postgraduate Experience:** Postgraduate studies in Philosophy of Science and History of Philosophy (1967-68), University of Louvain, Belgium; Postgraduate study in Religion and Social Science (1973-74), Fuller Theological Seminary; Research Reader, Centre for Religious Studies, University of Toronto (1989-90) **Previous Positions:** Assistant Professor of Humanities (1977-83), Armstrong University, Berkeley; Lecturer then Visiting Assistant Professor (1984-86), Santa Clara University; Director (1986-88), The Boulder School, Boulder, CO **Selected Memberships:** American Philosophical Association; American Academy of Religion; International Society for Chinese Philosophy **Discipline:** Philosophy **Related Areas of Interest:** Constructing a Philosophy of Living from Concepts of Truth (in Science, Philosophy, and Spiritual Experience), Beauty (in Nature and the arts), and Goodness; The Psychology of Altruism, The Neurophysiology of Spiritual Experience, and Scientific Perspectives on Regarding Humankind as One Family.

Weaver, Glenn David

Present Position and Address: Professor of Psychology (since 1975), Calvin College, Grand Rapids, MI 49546, USA **Date of Birth:** July 30, 1947 **Languages Spoken:** English, German **Education:** A.B. (1969), Wheaton College; M.Div. (1972), Princeton Theological Seminary; M.A. (1974)/Ph.D. Psychology (1978), Princeton University **Discipline:** Psychology **Related Areas of Interest:** Psychology and Religion; Psychopathology (moral issues in diagnosis, addiction); Psychology of Motivation/Religion.

Webster, Frederic A.

Present Position and Address: Retired; Box 35, So. Pomfret, VT 05067, USA **Concurrent Positions:** Standby preacher (since 1978), UU Church, Woodstock, VT **Date of Birth:** April 3, 1912 **Languages Spoken:** English, French **Education:** B.S. (1935), Harvard College; Medical Science Courses (1938), Harvard Medical School **Previous Positions:** Research Staff (1936-39), Harvard Fatigue Laboratory; Commander, Naval Aviation Training Program (Naval Reserve 1940-45); Research Staff (1947-50), Harvard Psycho-acoustic Lab.; Staff (1951-54)/Research Director (1958-70), MIT-Lincoln Lab.; Coordinator (1954-58), N. Wiener Cybernetics Group; Miscellaneous writing (1971-77); Consultant (1960-70), American Foundation for the Blind; Consultant (1970), National Geographic Society **Discipline:** Medical Science; Sensory and Brain Science **Related Areas of Interest:** Interface of Science and Religion. Sermons focus mostly on aspects of science that are relevant to science-religion interactions and most of published material deals with human and animal echolocation, much of it going into blind-guidance sources.

Welch, Claude

Present Position and Address: Professor of Historical Theology (since 1971) and Dean Emeritus; Graduate Theological Union, 2400 Ridge Road, Berkeley, CA 94709, USA; (Home) 123 Fairlawn Drive, Berkeley, CA 94708, USA **Concurrent Positions:** Core Group (since 1989), Vatican Observatory conference on "Quantum Creation of the Universe and the Origin of the Laws of Nature." **Work Phone:** (510) 649-2455 **Home Phone:** (510) 548-9236 **Date of Birth:** March 10, 1922 **Education:** A.B. (*summa cum laude*, 1942), Upper Iowa University; Studied Theology at Garrett-Evangelical Theological Seminary (1942-43); B.D. (*cum laude*, 1945), Yale Divinity School; Ph.D. Historical Theology (1950), Yale University; Ordained (1947), United Methodist Church **Honorary Degrees:** DD. (1973), Church Divinity School of the Pacific; L.H.D. (1976), University of Judaism; D.D. (1982), Jesuit School of Theology at Berkeley **Selected Lectures:** Lectures in the USA, UK, Germany and Switzerland **Previous Positions:** Instructor (1947-50)/Assistant Professor (1950-51), Department of Religion, Princeton University; Assistant Professor (1951-54)/Associate Professor (1954-60)/Director of Graduate Studies in Religion (1954-55)/Chairman of Department of Religion (1954-56)/Presiding Officer of Graduate Faculty in Religion (1958-60), Yale University; Berg Professor of Religious Thought Chairman of the Department (1960-71)/Associate Dean of College of Arts and Sciences (1964-68), University of Pennsylvania; Director (1969-71), ACLS Study of Graduate Education in Religion; Dean (1971-87) and President (1972-82), Graduate Theological Union; Pastorates, Myrtle Beach Methodist Church in Milford, CT (1945-47)/Cheshire Methodist Church, CT (1953-56)/various interim pastorates **Major Consulting and Advising Activities:** Numerous consultations with USA and Canadian Universities, Colleges and Theological Schools; Chairman of Advisory Council (1969-72), Princeton University Department of Religion; Religious Studies Consultant, Florida State University system; Consultant and Researcher on faculty and scholarship issues (1989-90), Presbyterian Church USA General Assembly Special Committee to Study Theological Institutions; Frequent Review Panelist, Philosophy and/or Religion: Fulbright Commission/National Endowment for the Humanities/Guggenheim Foundation **Selected Memberships:** Secretary (1954-63), North American Section, Theological Commission on Christ and the Church; Joint Catholic-Protestant Theological Commission on Apostolicity and Catholicity (1964-66), World Council of Churches; Chairman (1969-75, 85-90), Council of Societies for the Study of Religion; Society for Values in Higher Education Religion; Pacific Coast Theological Society; American Theological Society; American Church History Society; American Academy of Religion (Founder of 19th Century Theology Working Group in 1972; Vice President, 1968-69; President, 1969-70) **Discipline**: History of Religion; Religion in Education **Related Areas**

of Interest: Cosmology; History of Theology and Science; Quantum Creation of the Universe and the Origin of the Laws of Nature; Theology and Science in the 19th Century.

West, Richard B.

Present Position and Address: Retired Research Statistician for State Board of Equalization; 4818 Schuyler Drive, Carmichael, CA 95608, USA Work Phone: (916) 961-7592 **Date of Birth:** February 5, 1920 **Education:** B.A. History/English (1947), Atlantic Union College; M.A. Secondary Education/History (1955), Pacific Union College **Postgraduate Experience;** Postgraduate studies in Psychology, University of California **Previous Positions:** Taught grades 5-10 for 6 years; Health research for several years before working as research statistician for state **Discipline:** Teacher; Research Statistician **Related Areas of Interest:** Biblical Creation; The Flood; Geology and Dating.

Wetherbee, James M. (Jimm)

Present Position and Address: Reference Librarian (since 1988), Ethel K. Smith Library; P.O. Box 217, Wingate College, NC 28174-0219, USA; (Home) 411 Victoria Avenue, Monroe, NC, USA **Date of Birth:** June 13, 1959 **Education:** B.A. Philosophy of Religion (*cum laude*, 1981), Taylor University; M.Div. (1987), Louisville Presbyterian Theological Seminary; M.A. Philosophy of Religion (1987), Trinity Evangelical Divinity School; M.S.L.S. (1988), University of Kentucky, College of Library and Information Science **Previous Positions:** Graduate Assistant Librarian (1987-88), Lexington Theological Seminary **Selected Memberships:** Society of Christian Philosophers; Evangelical Theological Society; American Library Association; North Carolina Library Association **Discipline:** Reference Librarian **Related Areas of Interest:** Philosophy of Religion; Philosophy of Science; Ethics.

Whitehead, Clay C.

Present Position and Address: Private Practice in Psychiatry (since 1974); Medical Director, Samaritan Counseling Center (since 1988); (Office) 1014 West St. Maartens Drive, St. Joseph, MO 64506, USA; (Home) 2903 Ashland Avenue, St. Joseph, MO 64506, USA **Concurrent Positions:** Associate Clinical Professor of Psychiatry (since 1983), UCLA **Work Phone:** (816) 232-7711 **Home Phone:** (816) 279-5797 **Date of Birth:** December 12, 1942 **Education:** B.A. (1964), University of California - Berkeley; M.D. (1968), University of California - Los Angeles (UCLA); Board of Psychiatry and Neurology (1974) **Previous Positions:** Chief of Mental Health Services (1972-74), McClellan AFB; Coordinator and Originator (1969-72), UCLA/NPI Methadone Maintenance Research Programs; Assistant Chief of Psychiatry Service (1974-78); Chief of Psychoenvironmental Program (1973-88), Sepulveda Veterans Administration Medical Center, Sepulveda, CA **Selected Memberships:** Former President, Los Angeles Psychoanalytic Clinical Associates Organization (1975-76); Associate Faculty (since 1986), Los Angeles Psychoanalytic Society; Fellow (since 1986), American Psychiatric Association; Chairman (since 1986), Committee on Psychiatry and Religion, Southern California Psychiatric Society **Discipline:** Psychiatry; Psychoanalysis **Related Areas of Interest:** Psychiatry and Religion.

Whittaker-Johns, Barbara A.

Present Position and Address: Minister (since 1975), Unitarian Universalist Society of Amherst, 121 North Pleasant Street, P.O. Box 502, Amherst, MA 01004, USA **Work Phone:** (413) 549-4741 **Date of Birth:** October 8, 1943 **Education:** B.S. Social Sciences (1964), Simmons College, Boston, MA;

M.S. Special Education (1967), Ferkauf Graduate School, Yeshiva University, NYC; M.Div. (1984), Harvard Divinity School **Postgraduate Studies:** Continuing Ordained Minister (1984), Unitarian Universalist, First Parish Brewster; Final Fellowship (1988), Unitarian Universalist Ministry; Clinical Pastoral Education (1984), Basic Unit, R.I. Hospital **Previous Positions:** Teaching, Special Education (1963-76); Director of Group Services Program (1975-79), Cape Cod Family and Children's Service, Hyannis; Student Minister (1982-84), Brewster, MA/Nauset Fellowship, Eastham, MA **Selected Memberships:** Clerk (1985-87)/Co-Good Offices Person (since 1987), CVD Chapter, Unitarian Universalist Minister's Association; Vice President for conferences, speaker, Institute on Religion in an Age of Science; American Academy of Religion; Society for the Scientific Study of Religion **Discipline:** Minister; Social Science **Related Areas of Interest:** Philosophy of Religion and Philosophy of Science; Religion in an Age of Science.

Whitten, Robert C.

Present Position and Address: Research Scientist (Retired, working part-time in technical documentation and research on planetary atmospheres), NASA, American Research Center, Meffett Field, CA 94035; 1117 Yorkshire Drive, Cupertino, CA 95014, USA **Work Phone:** (408) 252-9213 **Date of Birth:** December 6, 1926 **Education:** B.S. (1947), US Merchant Marine Academy; B.A. (1955), State University of New York - Buffalo; M.A. Physics (1958), Duke University; Ph.D. Physics (1959), Duke University; M.S. Meteorology (1971), San Jose State University **Awards and Honors:** NASA Group Achievement Awards (Environmental Effects Team, Space Shuttle and Pioneer Venus Orbiter Science Team) **Previous Positions:** Physicist and Sr. Physicist (1959-67), SRI International, Menlo Park, CA **Selected Memberships:** Associate Fellow, American Institute of Aeronautics and Astronautics; Center for Theology and the Natural Sciences, Berkeley **Discipline:** Astrophysics (most recent work on the Upper Ionospheres or Plasmaspheres of Venus and Mars); Earth Science (until 1985 worked in the field of Atmospheric Science) **Related Areas of Interest:** Chaos and Nonlinear Mechanics; Defense Technology.

Widmer, Gabriel-Philippe

Present Position and Address: Ordinarius Professor of Systematic Theology, Faculté Autonome de Théologie (Prot.); Université de Genéve, Place de l'Université 3, 1211 Geneva 4, Switzerland; (Home) rue Michéli-du-Crest 2, Geneva, Switzerland **Date of Birth:** 1923.

Winkeler, L. G. M.

Present Position and Address: Member of the Graduate Staff (since 1985), Catholic Documentation Centre, Nijmegen, Rembrandtstraat 73, 6521 MD, Nijmegen, The Netherlands **Date of Birth:** July 18, 1951 **Languages Spoken:** Dutch, English, German **Education:** Master's degree (1979), R.C. Theological University, Utrecht; Doctoral Degree (1987), Catholic University, Nijmegen **Previous Positions:** Researcher (1979-85), Catholic Documentation Centre, Nijmegen **Discipline:** Theology (Church History) **Related Areas of Interest:** Dutch Catholicism, 19th/20th century.

Winkler, Hans-Joachim

Present Position and Address: Principal of Intern Clinic (since 1979), Königin Elisabeth (Evangelical Hospital), Eginhardstrasse 19, 10318 Berlin, Germany **Date of Birth:** March 22, 1931 **Languages Spoken:** German, English **Education:** M.D. (1955), Humboldt University, Berlin; Later qualified as specialist in Internal Medicine **Previous Positions:** Assistant (1955-60) in district Hospital Bernau, near Berlin; Assistant (1960-62), city Hospital Kaulsdorf; First Assistant (1962-79), Queen Elisabeth Hospital **Selected Memberships:** Member of Research, Academy in Evangelical Church of Union, Berlin **Discipline:** Internal Medicine; Specializing in Gastroenterological Disease **Related Areas of Interest:** Ethical Problems in Science and Medicine and the Connection between Soul and Body, i.e. Psychosomatic Diseases.

Witherspoon, William

Present Position and Address: Investment Analyst (since 1928); Witherspoon Investment Counsel (since 1981); 6401 Ellenwood, St. Louis, MO 63105-2228, USA **Work Phone:** (314) 727-0804 **Home Phone:** Summer (616) 547-6793 **Date of Birth:** November 21, 1909 **Education:** "Studied subjects in Science and Theology and Technology that interested me, a number of which I did not have the prerequisites for and therefore received no College credit (evening school 1928-38, 46-48), Washington University, St. Louis." **Previous Positions:** A. G. Edwards and Sons (1928-31), Head of Research (1930-31); President (1931-34), Witherspoon Investment Co.; Head of Research (1934-43), Newhard Cook and Co; Chief Price Analysis Division (1943-45), St. Louis Ordnance Dist. (Civilian); Head of Research (1945-53), Newhard Cook and Co; Owner (1953-64, 81-present), Witherspoon Investment Counsel; Limited Partner in Research (1964-68), Newhard Cook and Co.; Vice President and Research (1968-81), Stifel Nicolaus and Co.; Lecturer on Investments (1948-67), evening school at Washington University; Ordained Ruling Elder (1939), Presbyterian Church; Has served on following General Assembly Committees: Investment Committee (1976-79), Committee to Write Ordination Exams (1979-85) **Other Academic Experience:** Independent study in Theology and Science (since 1931) **Selected Memberships:** Founder and first President (1948-50), St. Louis Financial Analyst Society; Financial Analyst Federation; Institute Chartered Financial Analysts, University of Virginia **Discipline:** Investment Analysis, Economics **Related Areas of Interest:** Regression Analysis Model of the Stock Market and Related System of Common Stock Analysis; Central Banking Economics **Current Areas of Research:** Theology and Science in Dialogue **Personal Notes:** He has written 4 unpublished papers dealing with the higher dimensions of the brain, mind, and spirit, the trinity, christology, and salvation. He has also written many shorter articles.

Wolf, Jakob

Present Position and Address: Minister (since 1983), the Lutheran Church of Denmark, Lumsås; Stenstrupvej 69, Lumsås, DK-4500 Nykobing Sj., Denmark **Work Phone:** (03) 42-1072 **Date of Birth:** January 22, 1952 **Languages Spoken:** Danish, English, German **Education:** Ph.D. Theology (1984), University of Copenhagen **Previous Positions:** Assistant Professor (1980-82), University of Copenhagen **Discipline:** Theology **Related Areas of Interest:** Morphology; Phenomenology.

Wood, Frederic C.

Present Position and Address: Retired Consulting Engineer to Colleges and Universities and major Hospitals; 167 Cat Rock Road, Cos Cob, CT 06807, USA **Date of Birth:** March 1, 1903 **Education:** C.E. (1924), Cornell University **Previous Positions:** General Operations Manager (1932-40), Montgomery Ward; Vice President (1940-50), W. T. Grant Company; Trustee of Cornell University (1946-56) **Discipline:** Civil Engineer who Departed from the Path of Pure Engineering to Apply Engineering Principles to the Manifold, Auxiliary Functions of Business Management **Related Areas of Interest:** Religion and God **Current Areas of Research:** Currently writing a book called *With God in Mind.*

Wood III, William A.

Present Position and Address: Associate Pastor, First Presbyterian Church, 2001 El Camino Real, Oceanside, CA 92054, USA **Work Phone:** (619) 757-3560 **Fax Phone:** (619) 439-5355 **Date of Birth:** October 3, 1951 **Languages Spoken:** German **Education:** Ph.D. Organic Chemistry (1977), University of California - Berkeley; Ordained Minister, Presbyterian Church (1983) **Awards and Honors:** Phi Beta Kappa (1973) **Previous Positions:** Research Scientist (1977-79), Eastman Kodak Company, Rochester, NY; Lecturer (1980-83), Department of Chemistry, University of Southern California, Los Angeles, CA **Selected Memberships:** Center for Theology and the Natural Sciences, Berkeley **Discipline:** Pastoral Ministry and Teaching in the Local Church **Related Areas of Interest:** Cosmology; Biblical Interpretation; Mutual Interaction of Science and Theology **Current Areas of Research:** Interpretation of the Interaction of Science and Theology in the Local Church **Personal Notes:** His bibliography contains a variety of sermons and lecture/discussions on Science and Theology.

Woodward, J. Guy

Present Position and Address: Retired Fellow (since 1979), Technical Staff, RCA Laboratories, Princeton, NJ; 208 Laurel Circle, Princeton, NJ 08540, USA **Work Phone:** (609) 924-1331 **Date of Birth:** November 19, 1914 **Education:** A.B. (1936), North Central College; M.S. Physics (1938), Michigan State College; Ph.D. Physics (1942), Ohio State University **Previous Positions:** Engaged in research at the RCA Laboratories, Princeton, NJ (1942-82) until retirement **Selected Memberships:** Life Member Sigma Xi; Life Member, American Association for the Advancement of Science; Fellow, Acoustical Society of America; Institute of Electrical and Electronic Engineers; Honorary member and past President, Audio Engineering Society **Discipline:** Physics **Related Areas of Interest:** Has a strong abiding interest in the relations between Religion, Theology and Science.

York, Donald G.

Present Position and Address: Horace B. Horton Professor of Astrophysics and Astronomy (since 1992), University of Chicago, 1205 E. Madison Park, Chicago, IL 60615, USA **Date of Birth:** October 28, 1944 **Education:** B.S. (1966), Massachusetts Institute of Technology; Ph.D. (1971), University of Chicago **Previous Positions:** Research Associate (1970-76)/Research Astronomer (1976-82), Princeton University; Associate Professor (1982-85)/Professor (1985-92), University of Chicago **Selected Memberships:** American Astronomical Society; International Astronomical Union **Discipline:** Astronomy and Astrophysics **Related Areas of Interest:** History of the conflict between Science and Religion; History of Western Science; "Truth" in Science; Biblical Archeology.

Yoshikawa, Shoichi

Present Position and Address: Principal Research Physicist (since 1966)/Professor (since 1969), Princeton Plasma Physics Laboratory, P.O. Box 451, Princeton, NJ 08543, USA, **Work Phone:** (609) 243-2497 **Home Phone:** (609) 921-1723 **Fax Phone:** (609) 243-2874 **Date of Birth:** April 9, 1935 **Languages Spoken:** English, Japanese **Education:** B.S. Physics (1958), University of Tokyo; Ph.D. Nuclear Engineering (1961), Massachusetts Institute of Technology (MIT) **Awards and Honors:** Mainichi Publication Award, Challenge to Nuclear Fusion **Previous Positions:** Professor (1973-75), University of Tokyo **Discipline:** Physics - Nuclear Engineering **Related Areas of Interest:** Society and Ethics; Cosmology; Energy.

Young, David Nigel de Lorentz

Present Position and Address: Bishop Mount (since 1977); Ripon, N. Yorics, HG4 5DP, UK **Date of Birth:** February 9, 1931 **Education:** B.A. Mathematics (1st class Hons., 1954)/Diploma in Mathematical Statistics (1955)/Qualifying Exam for BD (equivalent to a 2nd in the Hon. School of Theology, 1958), Oxford University **Previous Positions:** Research Mathematician (1955-59), Plessey Company; Director (1963-67), Department of Buddhist Studies, Theological College; Lecturer in Buddhist Studies (1967-70), Manchester University; Vicar of Burwell, Cambridgeshire (1970-75); Archdeacon of Huntingdon (1975-77) **Discipline:** Interfaith Encounter; Theology; Mathematical Statistics **Related Areas of Interest:** Cosmology.

Yuguchi, Takashi

Present Position and Address: Assistant Director (since 1989), The Japan Lutheran Hour, Room 201, Belvedere Kudan, 15-5, Fujimi 2-Chome, Chiyoda-ku, Tokyo 102, Japan; (Home) 11-10 Shirokane-dai 4-chome, Minato-du, Tokyo 108, Japan **Work Phone:** (03) 473-9249 **Fax Phone:** (03) 261-6033 **Date**

of Birth: July 14, 1952 **Languages Spoken:** Japanese, English **Education:** M.Sc. Physics (1979), Aoyama Gakuin University; M.A. Journalism (1988), Sophia University; Currently Doctoral candidate, Department of Journalism, Sophia University **Previous Positions:** Public Relations (1981-89), The Japan Lutheran Hour; Chief of History Compilation Committee of Japan Lutheran Church (1988) **Selected Memberships:** The Japan Society for Studies in Journalism and Mass Communication; Shukyo Shakaigaku Kenkyukai (Society of Sociology of Religion); World Association for Christian Communication; Lutheran Communication in Asia; Japan Lutheran College and Seminary **Discipline:** Physics; Journalism **Related Areas of Interest:** History of Christian Journalism in Asia; Religious Sociology in Mass Communication; Physics and Religion.

Directory C

Organizations

Organizations

Affiliation of Christian Geologists

Brief Description: The Affiliation of Christian Geologists (a division of the American Scientific Affiliation) is a fellowship of approximately 150 members working to integrate faith and the study of geology. **Contact Person:** Dr. Jeffrey K. Greenberg **Address:** Department of Geology, Wheaton College, Wheaton, IL 60187, USA. **Telephone:** (708) 752-5063 **Date of Founding:** August 1989. **Purpose:** To promote fellowship among Christian geologists, to promote the integrity of geology as a scientific discipline, to investigate the ways in which Christian faith and geology bear upon one another, to educate the Christian public about geology, to develop avenues of witness to non-Christian geologists, to promote Christian stewardship and service in the geological sphere, and to provide intellectual leadership at the interface between Christian and geologic thought. **Membership:** Regular membership is open to individuals with at least a bachelor's degree in geology. Student membership shall be open to individuals who are presently enrolled in an undergraduate degree program in geology. Associate membership shall be open to individuals who have degrees or experience in allied sciences such as oceanography or planetary science. Membership shall be international and is open only to those who can assent to the purpose and statement of principles whether or not they are members of ASA. Annual Dues are $10. **Organizational Structure:** Officers: President, Past President, Vice President, Secretary—Newsletter Editor, and Treasurer. The officers compose the Executive Committee. Officers are elected by mail ballot of regular members, and may be reelected to successive three-year terms. **Current Officers:** President, Jeffrey K. Greenberg (Wheaton College); Vice President, Paul Ribbe (Virginia Polytechnic Institute); Secretary, David Dathe (Alverno College); Treasurer, Kenneth Van Dellen (Macomb Community College). **Meetings:** The Affiliation convenes whenever possible at annual meetings of the Geological Society of America and is attempting to sponsor a formal program each year. Also planned are informal meetings with groups of theologians and Christian leaders. **Publication:** *The News*, a small newsletter, about 2-3 times per year.

The Alister Hardy Research Centre

Brief Description: The late Sir Alister Hardy, FRS, was an eminent bilogist, who received the Templeton Prize in 1985 for Progress in Religion, having founded the "Religious Experience Research Unit" in 1969 to pursue his lifetime's interest, and his conviction that studies of religious experience are "a true study of life as a whole." The Alister Hardy Society has now been set up to examine, and develop the perspectives that he stood for. Membership of that Society is open to all and the members receive a regular newsletter about the Society and the work of the Religious Experience Research Centre. There are also regular meetings at which current research findings and other issues of interest are discussed. Members have access to Sir Alister's library. The Religious Experience Research Centre offers advice about research procedures, findings, and related issues concerning religious and other experiences, across individuals, institutions, and traditions, including the social or personal characterists of those likely to report religious and other experiences, and how they can be used. It is hoped that the results of research into whatever questions are raised may clarify the place and the relevance of religion in life, education, welfare, and other concerns. In general terms, the Centre's research lies at the intersection of social science and religion. **Director:** Dr. Laurence Brown **Address:** Westminster College, Oxford, OX2 9AT, UK. **Phone:** (0865) 243006 **Fax:** (0865) 251-847 **Founding:** 1969 **Publications:** *De Numinis* is the newsletter of the Alister Hardy Society, and we have an occasional *Journal of Religious Experience* that publishes scientific papers. Books available from the Centre include Alister Hardy's (1979) *The Spiritual Nature of Man*, David Hay's *Religious Experience Today* and *Exploring Inner Space: Scientists and Religious Experience*. Mowbray, 1982; Meg Maxwell and Verena Tschudin, ed. *Seeing the Invisible: Modern Religious and Transcendent Experiences*. Penguin Arkana Press, an anthology from the Archives of the A.H.R.C.; and Laurence Brown's (1994) *The Human Side of Prayer*. **Memberships:** Full membership £25; Family membership £30; Reduced rate for unwaged and senior citizens £17; Reduced rate for students £5. These dues help to fund the Centre's research activities, and to develop the Archive of around 6,000 accounts that have been sent in to us, the earliest being in response to Hardy's request for accounts of "life-shaping religious experiences." **Current Officers:** Director, Dr. Laurence Brown; Administrative Secretary, Mrs. Polly Wheway.

The American Scientific Affiliation (ASA)

Brief Description: The American Scientific Affiliation is a fellowship of over 2,000 Christians in the sciences organized in 18 local sections in most of the fifty states (with additional members in 46 other countries), committed to understanding the relationship of science to the Christian faith. The stated purposes of the ASA are "to investigate any area relating Christian faith and science" and "to make known the results of such investigations for comment and criticism by the Christian community and by the scientific community." **Executive Director:** Dr. Donald W. Munro. **Address:** The American Scientific Affiliation, P. O. Box 668, Ipswich, MA 01938. **Telephone:** (508) 356-5656. **Fax Number:** (508) 356-4375. **Date of Founding:** September 1941, in Chicago. **Goals and Objectives:** ASA lists three specific objectives for itself: 1. To develop ASA as an instrument to integrate and interpret the discoveries of natural and social science with the insights which can be derived from the total message of Scripture and our Christian faith. 2. To share our scientific knowledge and ethical concerns as fellow believers in a Christian context in order to help the Church better understand science and the good technical gifts that God gives us. 3. To share our faith with our fellow scientists. To this end specific goals include the stimulation and encouragement of efforts at integration of science and faith; to help the Christian public better understand how technology can be used for the good or ill of society; to cooperate with other Evangelical parachurch groups in projects of mutual benefit; to aid young persons beginning the study of science in their intellectual and spiritual pursuits, and particularly to encourage scientists in the developing world. **Organizational Structure:** The American Scientific Affiliation is an incorporated non-profit organization governed according to its constitution and bylaws. The affairs of the Affiliation are directed by a five-member Executive Council elected by Fellows and Members. At present there are 18 local sections which further promote the objectives of the Affiliation through regional meetings and activities. **Membership:** Anyone interested in the objectives of the Affiliation may have a part in the ASA. There are five membership categories: 1) Full, voting membership is open to all persons with at least a bachelor's degree in science who can give assent to our statement of faith. Science is interpreted broadly to include the social and human sciences. Full member dues are $45/year. 2) Associate membership is available to anyone interested in science who can give assent to our statement of faith. Associates receive all member's benefits and publications and take part in all the affairs of the ASA except voting and holding office. Associate member dues are $40/year. 3) Full-time students may join as Student Members (science majors) or Student Associates (non-science majors) for discounted dues of $20/year. Retired individuals, parachurch staff, and spouses may also qualify for a reduced rate. Full-time missionaries are entitled to a complimentary Associate membership in the ASA. 4) An individual wishing to participate in the ASA without joining as a member or giving assent to our statement of faith, may become a Friend of ASA. Payment of a yearly fee of $45 entitles them to receive all ASA publications and to be informed about ASA activities. 5) Finally, anyone who has been a member for at least five years and who fulfills at least two of the following criteria may be elected Fellow — a) active and sustained participation in the affairs of the Affiliation, b) publication or lecturing on the interrelationship of Science and Faith, or c) distinction in one or more fields of specialization. Election as a Fellow is carried out by the body of Fellows upon recommendation of the Executive Council. **Statement of Faith:** Four basic points spell out the distinctive character of the ASA: First, we affirm the "divine inspiration, trustworthiness and authority of the Bible in matters of faith and conduct." Second, we "confess the Triune God affirmed in the Nicene and the Apostle's creeds which we accept as brief, faithful statements of Christian doctrine based upon Scripture." Third, we affirm that "in creating and preserving the universe God has endowed it with contingent order and intelligibility, the basis of scientific investigation." Finally, we "recognize our responsibility, as stewards of God's creation, to use science and technology for the good of humanity and the whole world." Note: As an organization the ASA has not taken a strict position on controversial issues when there is honest disagreement between Christians, but is committed to providing an open forum where such controversies can be discussed without fear of unjust condemnation. Biological evolution is an example of an issue in which Affiliation members will be found on different sides of the issues. **Publications:** *Perspectives on Science and Christian Faith*, the quarterly journal of the Affiliation (see separate entry). A bimonthly *Newsletter* for members. A *Directory* of the entire membership is provided all members. *Contemporary Issues in Science and Christian Faith: A Resource Book,* offers an expanded, annotated book list providing key books on science/faith issues, a Speaker's Bureau, rentals of video and audio/slide presentations, and other science/faith resources ($10.50). *Teaching Science in a Climate of Controversy* (4th revision): a book published by the ASA to help teachers cope with the array of complex and contradictory issues surrounding contemporary teaching of science and evolution in the classroom ($7.00). Available from the national office (quantity discounts available). **Current Projects:** Commissions for the study and preparation of symposia and published papers are presently working in the following areas: Biomedical Ethics; Creation; Global Resources; Industrial/Engineering Ethics; Science Education. Committees are at work in the following areas: Computer Applications; Integrity in Science Education; Long-Range Planning; Publications. **Local Sections of the ASA:** Local sections hold meetings and provide an interchange of ideas at the regional level. For specific information on an individual section contact the ASA national office. Current sections include: Central California; Chicago-Wheaton; Delaware Valley; Indiana-Ohio; Los Angeles; New England; New York-New Jersey; North Central; Houston-Galveston; Oregon-Washington; Rockey Mountain; San Diego; San Francisco Bay; So. California; Southwest; Washington-Baltimore; Western New York. **Divisions and Affiliations:** Divisions provide for individual scientific disciplines to function with a degree of autonomy with the ASA. Divisions are open to both members and non-members of the Affiliation. See the Affiliation of Christian Geologists and Affiliation of Christian Biologists. The Canadian Scientific & Christian Affiliation was incorporated in 1973 as a direct affiliate of the ASA with a distinctly Canadian orientation (see separate entry). **Annual Meeting Schedule:** 1996, Toronto, Canada. 1997, Westmont, Santa Barbara, CA; 1998, England. **Contact Persons of the ASA:** Current Executive Council: Fred Hickernell, Motorola Co.; Raymond Brand, Wheaton College; David Wilcox, Eastern College; Kenneth Olson, Genentech Corp.; Elizabeth Zipf, Biosis Corp. Key Personnel: Donald W. Munro, Executive Director; J. W. Haas, Jr., Editor, *Perspectives on Science & Christian Faith;* Dennis Fencht, *Newsletter* Editor; Richard Ruble, Book Review Editor; Carol Aiken, Executive Assistant; Frances C. Polischuk, Financial/List Manager; Lyn Berg, Managing Editor; all at the following address: P.O. Box 668, Ipswich, MA 01938.

Applied Christian Theology Unit for Scientists, Engineers and Technologists (ACTUSET)

Brief Description: ACTUSET was founded in response to perceived needs recognized during ministry among scientists, engineers and technologists, and their families. These needs related to pastoral and prophetic concerns associated with work done by practicing Christians in the chemical and nuclear industries. **Founder:** Rev. Dr. Peter Levitt. **Address:** Church House, 50 Deepdale, Hollinswood, Telford, Shropshire, TF3 2EJ, UK. **Telephone:** 0952 200546 **Date of Founding:** 1985. **Aims and Objectives:** ACTUSET's first aim was to inquire of scientists, engineers and technologists (SETs) who were also practicing Christians what they had found helpful in the churches' teaching and discussion documents on the roles of God and human beings in the natural world viewed as God's creation. Considerable efforts have been made in recent years, by individuals and groups within the churches, to relate Christian thinking about the creation to human activities in science, engineering and technology. The collecting and analyzing of the views of as many SETs as possible is considered to be valuable in order to develop a better working understanding of Christian thinking about the roles of God and human beings in creation. Following such a study, ACTUSET aims to work interactively with SETs toward providing further resources for study and action, prayer and worship, that will help them serve God and their neighbors more effectively, if possible. A third aim is to help provide better pastoral care for SETs and their families by making insights provided by SETs into their spiritual needs and resources available to Christians, ordained and lay, serving in scientific, technological and industrial communities so that they may all work together more effectively for the Kingdom of God on earth. **Special Projects:** The first aim has been pursued in a research project involving 78 SETs in Britain and presented in a thesis entitled "Interpreting the Christian Doctrine of Creation: An Investigation of the Thinking of Scientists, Engineers and Technologists in Contemporary Britain" (1989).

The Association of Christians in the Mathematical Sciences (ACMS)

Brief Description: The Association of Christians in the Mathematical Sciences is a group of about 300 members seeking to integrate faith and the full spectrum of the mathematical sciences. **Address:** 1006 N. Washington Street, Wheaton, IL 60187, USA. **Phone:** Executive Secretary (708) 752-5869 **Founding:** 1985 **Current Officers:** President, Russell Howell (Westmont College); Vice President, David Lay (Univ. of Maryland); Executive Secretary, Robert Brabenec (Wheaton College). **Purpose:** 1. To encourage Christians in the mathematical sciences to explore the relationship of their faith to their discipline. 2. To promote interaction among Christians in the mathematical sciences. 3. To encourage research and writing by Christians, especially on topics interrelating their faith and their discipline. 4. To promote innovative and effective teaching. **Conferences:** A conference is sponsored every two years and the Proceedings are published. The 9th conference was held at Westmont College from June 2-5, 1993. The next conference will be at Taylor University from May 31 to June 3, 1995. **Publications:** Copies of Proceedings of past conferences are available. An *Annotated Bibliography of Christianity and Mathematics* was published in 1983, with an updated version planned for 1996. Copies are available from Dordt College Press. **Membership:** Dues for membership are $15, for a two year membership. There is a short statement of faith required: "God is the creator and faithful sustainer of His creation. Jesus Christ is the Son of God, fully God and fully man, and through His atonement is the mediator between God and man. The Old and New Testaments are the Word of God, the Christian's authoritative guide for faith and conduct." **Board Members:** Carol Harrison (Susquehanna Univ.); Richard Stout (Gordon College); Dale Varberg (Hamline Univ.); Paul Zwier (Calvin College).

Associazione Teilhard de Chardin - Centro di ricerca per il futuro dell'uomo

[See under Il Futuro dell'Uomo in the directory of Journals]

ATOMIUM, Working Group for the Study of Theology and Science

Brief Description: ATOMIUM is an informal group of theologians and scientists. Its aim is to provide information concerning theology-science problems on an academic level, and to discuss problems which are relevant to the participants in their own working fields. ATOMIUM presently has 45 members. Address: c/o Dr. P. van Dijk, Twente University, Department of Philosophy and Social Sciences, P.O. Box 217, NL 7500 Enschede, The Netherlands. **Telephone:** (053) 893302 **Date of Founding:** May 1959 **Current Officers:** President, Prof. Dr. H. W. de Knijff; Secretaries, Dr. P. van Dijk; Dr. J. Mooij; Dr. G. W. Oosterwegel. **Conferences:** Twice a year for two days in January and in August. **Membership Criteria:** An academic degree.

Au Sable Institute of Environmental Studies

Brief Description: Au Sable is a Christian environmental stewardship Institute whose mission is to bring healing and wholeness to the biosphere and the whole of Creation. Au Sable offers programs and courses of study for college students, for evangelical Christian colleges, denominations and churches, and the broader world community. In a setting of northern lower Michigan forests, wetlands, lakes, and wild rivers, students at Au Sable take college courses, gain field experience, and develop practical tools for environmental stewardship. **Director:** Dr. Calvin B. DeWitt. **Address:** 7526 Sunset Trail N.E., Mancelona, MI 49659. **Telephone:** (616) 587-8686 **Date of Founding:** 1980. **Purpose and Activities:** The mission of Au Sable is the integration of knowledge of creation with biblical principles for the purpose of bringing the Christian community and the general public to a better understanding of the Creator and the stewardship of God's creation. In pursuing its professional and vocational mission, the Institute: 1) provides courses and programs in environmental stewardship for 90 Christian colleges and seminaries in the United States and Canada; 2) provides courses and programs for all college and university students with professional, vocational and/or academic interests in developing an understanding of Christian environmental stewardship; 3) provides environmental education, information, and analytical services to school systems and governmental agencies; 4) provides services to evangelical Christian colleges for nurture and development of their environmental curriculum and stewardship goals; and 5) cooperates with and assists churches and denominations, educational institutions, and environmental stewardship organizations in responding to environmental needs and issues in a manner consistent with the proper care, keeping and restoration of the Creation. As a catalyst for the development of Christian ecology, the Institute offers the Au Sable Forum. Through the nearly annual forum, many scientists and theologians have had the opportunity to develop thinking, writing, and action on Christian ecological theology, missionary earthkeeping, Christian land ethics, economics, and restoration stewardship. **Organizational Structure:** The Institute has an administrative staff and Board of Trustees. The administration is: Calvin B. DeWitt (Director); David C. Mahan (Associate Director); Robert Barr (Coordinator of Support Services); Patricia Fagg (Coordinator of School Programs); Peter Bakken (Coordinator of Outreach and International Relations); and Richard T. Wright (Academic Chair). The members of the Board of Trustees are: Orin G. Gelderloos (Chair); John D. Loeks (Vice-Chair); Bertel Froysland (Treasurer); Rolf Bouma (Secretary); Susan Drake; Job Ebenezer; Jocele Meyer; John Olmstead; Ghillean T. Prance; and Harold Z. Snyder. **Publications:** The Au Sable Official Bulletin provides further information on Au Sable courses, fora and activities. For group presentations, the Institute makes available a slide-tape program and a mini-pack. The mini-pack consists of a set of 36 slides and a typed narrative. The Institute produces a newsletter for all who wish to keep informed about Institute programs and Christian environmental stewardship. One may contact the Institute office for placement on its mailing list. **Facilities:** The Institute is located in the Great Lakes Forest on a crystal clear lake. Motel-type rooms, rustic dormitories, and log cabins serve as living accommodations. Dining facilities look out on surrounding forest flora, and a lodge with fireplace, lounge, library, and auditorium provide for classes, relaxation, and study. Earth Hall, an earth-bermed and solar assisted laboratory, supports field study. A recreation building provides for indoor recreation, and trails lead to the lake shore, a nearby beaver pond and more distant bogs, lakes and marshes.

Het Bezinningscentrum (Interdisciplinary Center for the Study of Science, Society and Religion)

Brief Description: Het Bezinningscentrum, a center at the Vrije Universiteit (Amsterdam), is to stimulate research on the relation between science (including humanities) and religion, both theoretically and with an eye on social aspects. The center also organizes public events, like lectures, and bears the editorial responsibility for monographs, published with Kok, Kampen, The Netherlands. **Director:** Prof. Dr. A. W. Musschenga. **Address:** Bezinningscentrum, Vrije Universiteit, De Boelelaan 1115, 1081 HV Amsterdam, The Netherlands. **Telephone:** +31-20-4445670 **Fax:** +31-20-4445680 **Date of Founding:** 1979. **Purpose:** The Vrije Universiteit was established in 1880 as a University rooted in the Reformed tradition in the Netherlands. Almost a century later, the "Bezinningscentrum" was established to stimulate reflection on the identity of the Vrije Universiteit. A new vision on the relation between Christian faith and scientific research was needed. At the same time, the social functioning of science had come under critique. "Concern for identity" and "concern about science" are the two motives that led to the establishment of the Center. **Projects:** Members of the staff of the Center collaborate with faculty on a variety of topics, including ethics (A. W. Musschenga), secularization, public religion, relativism in religion and in the social sciences (A. van Harskamp), theology and the natural sciences (W. B. Drees). The center has a staff member who works on new developments in liturgy. The center also intends to serve the churches by bringing together people from the academic scene to reflect on issues of interest to the churches. **Organizational Structure:** The center has a small staff, which cooperates with academics from the Free University and other universities on interdisciplinary research projects. The board of the center appoints the members of the staff; the board consists of faculty of the Free University as well as a few students and staff members. **Conferences and Lectures:** The center organizes conferences and symposia. In the past it has organized in collaboration with the World Council of Churches a conference on science education and values, and with the local Council of Churches a series of six symposia on Justice, Peace and the Integrity of Creation, and one on secularization, confronting perspectives from theology with approaches from the social sciences. A wide variety of other topics have been addressed and will be addressed in the future. Invited speakers for the annual "BC-lectures" have included Gerhard Liedke, Alvin Plantinga, Anton Vergoote, Norman Kretzmann, Hans Küng, Jan van der Veken, and A. R. Peacocke. **Publications:** 1) In English: David Gosling and Bert Musschenga, eds. *Science Education and Ethical Values: Introducing Ethics into the Science Classroom and Laboratory.* Geneva: WCC, 1985. 2) A series of over twenty monographs in Dutch, partly popular, partly academic, has been published with Ten Have (Baarn), and as of 1985, Kok, Kampen. Among the titles are: C. Houtman. *Wereld en tegenwereld: mens en milieu in de Bijbel.* (1982); A. W. Musschenga, ed. *Onderwijs in de natuurwetenschappen en morele vorming.* (1984); C. Houtman, et al. *Schepping en evolutie: het creationisme een alternatief?* (1986); J. W. Hovenier, et al. *De plaats van aarde en mens in het heelal.* (1987); M. C. Doeser, A. W. Musschenga, eds. *De werkelijkheid van de wetenschappen.* (1989); H. J. Boersma, et al. *Aspecten van tijd.* (1991). 3) An academic, series of *Studies* also with Kok, Kampen, includes among other titles: Hans Küng, et al. *Godsdienst op een keerpunt.* (1990); Anton van Harskamp, ed. *Verborgen God of lege kerk? Theologen* *en sociologen over secularisatie.* (1991), W. B. Drees, ed. *Theologie en Natuurwetenshcap: Op zoek naar een Snark?* (1992); W. B. Drees, ed. *Denken over God en Wereld.* (1994); H. Looren de Long. *Naturalism and Psychology.* 4) In the new popular series, *Interacties:* C. Sanders. *Geloof - zin en on zin: over geloofskennis en werkelijkheid.* (1990); W. B. Drees. *Heelal, mens en God.* (1991). 5) Six proceedings of "hearings" on the JPIC-program have been edited by H. van Erkelens (1989, all with Kok, Kampen). 6) Eighteen smaller publications in two series, *Reflekties*, and *Kahiers* (with Free University Press).

Center for Advanced Study in Religion and Science (CASIRAS)

Description: The Center for Advanced Study in Religion and Science is an independent, non-sectarian, not-for-profit corporation of 25 members seeking to achieve a greater integration between the scientific and religious models or images concerning the nature and destiny of human beings. **Address:** 1100 E. 55th Street, Chicago, IL 60615-5199, USA. **Phone:** (312) 753-0670; (215) 898-6059 **Date of Founding:** 1964 by Ralph Burhoe and Meadville/Lombard Theological School. **Organizational Structure:** Board of Directors elects officers; Board is self-perpetuating and seeks to gain members from among scientists and theologians. **Current Officers:** President, Prof. Solomon Katz (Anthropology, University of Pennsylvania); Vice President, Dr. Donald Z. Harrington (Minister Emeritus, NY); Secretary, Carol Rausch Gorski (Associate for Programs, Chicago Center for Religion and Science [CCRS, see separate entry]); Treasurer, Thomas L. Gilbert (Associate Director, CCRS); Chicago contact, Philip Hefner at above address. **Special Projects:** Cofounded, and cosponsors, Chicago Center for Religion and Science; Copublishes *Zygon: Journal of Religion and Science*; Sponsors conferences; Offers courses in Chicago, through the Association of Chicago Theological Schools; Sponsors annual series of Seminars, "Chicago Advanced Seminar in Religion and Science" [see separate entry]; Offers occasional grants to Fellows.

Center for Faith and Science Exchange (FASE)

Brief Description: The Center for Faith and Science Exchange, an interfaith organization, was organized in 1989 for the purpose of encouraging interdisciplinary dialogue, with the sharing of knowledge, metaphors, and values. Crucial to such cooperation is the resolution of historical misunderstandings between the two communities which have resulted in cultural division. Since 1990, FASE has coordinated the Science and Religion Program of the Boston Theological Institute (BTI), a consortium of nine seminaries, schools and departments of theology in the greater Boston area. FASE is the only faith-and-science organization with its center of activity and influence in New England. **Director:** The Reverend Barbara Smith-Moran **Address:** 93 Anson Road, Concord, MA 01742. **Purpose:** FASE promotes a prophetic vision of change: religious leaders who are better informed about science and more responsive to the challenges of faithful living in a technological age, and a scientific community that recognizes the spiritual reality apprehended in the experience of being fully human. **Programs:** FASE currently maintains four activity areas. 1) A public lecture series that invites theologians to speak at scientific institutions and scientists to speak at the BTI member schools. 2) An eight-part discussion series for adult Christian education groups. 3) An Ignatian-type spiritual retreat for scientists and engineers, based largely upon the writings of geologist-priest Pierre Teilhard de Chardin. 4) A fifth-anniversary symposium entitled "Religion & Genetics: Science in Dialogue with Belief," planned for the fall of 1994, with educational materials to be published. **Publications:** FASE publishes a monthly newsletter, *Bicultural Times.* Subscription price is a donation of at least $10, made payable to the Boston Theological Institute, with a notation for support of FASE. Subscription address: Center for Faith and Science Exchange, c/o Boston Theological Institute, 210 Herrick Road, Newton Centre, MA 02159. **Membership Categories:** Newsletter Subscriber, $10; Contributing Member, $25;

Supporting Member, $50; Sustaining Member, $100; Sponsor, $200 and above **Organizational Structure:** The Advisory Board is an interfaith group of clergy and laypeople, most of them trained as scientists and engineers. Some are academic scientists and theologians, and some are industrial scientists and pastors of congregations. **Current Board Members:** the Rev. Barbara Smith-Moran, S.O.Sc., Director (astronomy; Episcopal parish priest); Ms. Elizabeth Bjorkman (physics); the Rev. Roger Brown (biophysics; United Church of Christ congregational pastor); Dr. Gail Bucher (chemistry, Gilette Co.); the Rev Demetri Demopulos (genetics, Greek Orthodox parish priest); Dr. Mary Louise Dolan, C.S.J. (biology, Roman Catholic religious); the Rev. Dr. Norman Faramelli (chemical engineering, Massachusetts Port Authority); the Rev. Dr. Meredith Handspicker (theologian, Andover Newton Theological School); the Rev. Dr. Mark Heim (theologian, Andover Newton Theological School); Mr. William B. Jones (earth and planetary science; seminarian, Andover Newton Theological School); Dr. Alan Kafka (geophysicists, Boston College); the Rev. Dr. Gordon Kaufman (theologian, Harvard Divinity School); the Rev. Dr. John Keggi, S.O.Sc. (chemistry, Episcopal parish priest); the Rev. Dr. Judith Kohatsu (materials scientists, United Methodist pastor); Dr. Margaret Lidback (geologist, Framingham State College); the Rev. Dr. Harold Oliver (theology, Boston University School of Theology); Rabbi Dr. Joshua Segal (computer science, congregational rabbi); Dr. Eric Shank (physicist, MIT Lincoln Laboratories)l the Rev. Dr. James Skehan, S.J. (geologist, Boston college)l the Rev. Dr. Owen Thomas (physics; theologian, Episcopal Divinity School); and Mr. Steven Walker (biology; librarian, Harvard Divinity School).

The Center for Frontier Sciences

Brief Description: The Center for Frontier Sciences was established in 1987 to coordinate globally, information exchange, networking, and education on the frontier issues of science, technology, and medicine. The Center assists in bridging gaps in human knowledge by bringing together both specialists and interdisciplinarians to probe the puzzles of frontier issues in open dialogue. **Director:** Dr. Beverly Rubik **Address:** Temple University, Ritter Hall 003-00, Philadelphia, PA 19122 **Telephone:** (215) 204-8487 **Fax:** (215) 204-5553 **Purpose:** History has repeatedly shown that new ideas or discoveries that were once disregarded or even scorned by the scientific establishment were later accepted as mainstream. The Center for Frontier Sciences engenders greater openness tempered by a healthy level of skepticism toward novel ideas ranging from tributaries of mainstream science to the unorthodox. As an integral part of Temple University, the Center maintains high academic standards in reviewing novel discoveries toward which it initially holds a neutral profile. By creating a forum of open discussion with the goal of identifying the most significant questions for further research, the Center helps facilitate progress and understanding on the furthest horizons of human knowledge. **Activities:** The Center hosts roundtable meetings with invited scientists and scholars of various disciplines to clarify specific frontier issues. Previous themes include: fields and living systems; the relationship of mind and matter; the frontiers of the philosophy of quantum mechanics; houeopathy; geobiology; pleormorphism in biology and medicine; and issues involving quantum theory, biology, and cognition. Throughout the academic year, the Center sponsors a number of colloquia at Temple University. A global database of over 3000 associated researchers, scholars, educators, and affiliated institutions exists. **Publications:** *The Interrelationship Between Mind and Matter*, book, with 15 contributing authors, edited by Rubik, B., 1992, Philadelphia: Center for Frontier Sciences at Temple University, 281 pp. *Frontier Perspectives*, a journal detailing Center activities includes articles contributed by its affiliates and is published and distributed by the Center. **Membership:** Qualified scientists, scholars, medical doctors, and other professionals with a commitment to frontier sciences are eligible for affiliation with the Center, whether they work in academia, industry, government, or private institutes. Affiliates will receive the newsletter and other official mailings of the Center and are requested to assist the Center in its networking and database efforts by informing the Center of new research findings and potential affiliates. Applicants for Affiliate status should include with their application a resume, list of publications, and $25.

Center for Theology and the Natural Sciences (CTNS)

Brief Description: The Center for Theology and the Natural Sciences is an ecumenical organization of more than 500 members committed to the fruitful interaction of science and religion. The CTNS program includes fundamental research, doctoral and seminary courses, international conferences, public forums, and church programs. The Center is an Affiliate of the Graduate Theological Union, Berkeley and is located just north of the University of California - Berkeley campus. **Founder and Director:** Robert John Russell **Address:** 2400 Ridge Road, Berkeley, CA 94709. **Telephone:** (510) 848-8152 **Fax:** (510) 848-2535 **Date of Founding:** 1981. **Purpose and Activities:** From its inception the program of the Center has been organized around three objectives (research, education, public service), incorporating sixteen programs: 1) To reshape the future of theological scholarship and education by including the natural sciences and technology within the theological agenda; 2) To provide resources to the church, enabling it to rediscover its vision and prophetic ministry in an age of science and technology; and 3) To engage the general public in a responsible discussion of moral and spiritual issues raised by science and technology. The character of CTNS is open and inclusive. The Center has been structured as an open forum for mutual dialogue, growth, and transformation among scientists, clergy, technologists, faculty and students, and the general public. Currently the CTNS program involves the following activities: 1) The annual J. K. Russell Fellowship in Religion and Science bringing internationally distinguished senior scholars to the Graduate Theological Union (GTU) for an extended period of research, conferences, teaching, and public events; 2) International Research Conferences; 3) Courses for doctoral and seminary students; 4) Location for visiting scholars; 5) Offering local churches and denominational structures, workshops, preaching, weekend events and summer programs, continuing education courses, seminars, and participation in denominational task forces; 6) Public lectures, public forums, and other events designed for scientists, clergy, technologists, and the general public, as well as lectures at scientific, philosophical, and religious studies professional meetings; 7) Continuing Education courses for clergy; 8) Publication of the *CTNS Bulletin*, a journal of scholarly articles in the interdisciplinary field, and the *CTNS Newsletter*. 9) CTNS membership. **Future Goals:** The Center has begun to expand its program by moving toward a broader vision for the future focused on these additional long-term goals: 1) Building a Bay Area research group of scientists, philosophers, and theologians who will regularly discuss their research in theology and science and whose working papers will be published; 2) Increasing the involvement of GTU doctoral candidates with the science programs of area institutions; 3) Offering financial support for promising graduate students; 4) Diversifying the CTNS by adding emphasis on the biological sciences, while continuing work with cosmology, astrophysics, quantum physics, thermodynamics, and mathematics; 5) Offering an extended summer institute for theologians for the purpose of equipping them with a working understanding of natural sciences; 6) Offering an extended summer institute for scientists to equip them with a working understanding of systematic theology, historical theology, philosophy of religion, and Biblical hermeneutics, as well as history and philosophy of science; 7) Organizing CTNS membership in terms of local and regional groups with their own programs and events, and providing increased networking; 8) Developing an extensive computerized bibliography of texts, articles, and lectures in theology and science. **Organizational Structure:** The Center is an incorporated nonprofit organization led by a Director and Board of Directors. The current CTNS Board of Directors are: Ian Barbour (Carleton College); Bishop Mark Hurley (Vatican Secretariat for Non-Believers); Robert Barr (businessman); R. David Cole (professor emeritus, biochemistry); Dr. Judith Larsen (businesswoman); William R. Stoeger, S.J. (Cosmologist and professor); Nancey Murphy (Fuller Theological Seminary); Ted Peters (Pacific Lutheran Seminary); Charlotte Ann Russell (Piedmont Community Church);

Robert John Russell (GTU and Director of the Center); Charles Townes (Emeritus, University of California - Berkeley); Claude Welch (GTU); and Carl York (Physicist and Chair of Development). Members of the CTNS Board of Advisors are: Michael Buckley, SJ; John B. Cobb, Jr.; Andrew Dufner, SJ; Freeman Dyson; Durwood Foster; Langdon Gilkey; Philip Hefner; Chris J. Isham; Nicholas Lash; Guy Fitch Lytle; Charles McCoy; Sallie McFague; Ernan McMullin; Wolfhart Pannenberg; Arthur Peacocke, SOSc.; John Polkinghorne; Karl Peters; Benjamen Reist; Rustum Roy; Robert Schimke; Janet Martin Soskice; and David Tracy. Bonnie Johnston is Administrative Associate. **Publications:** The Center publishes a quarterly *CTNS Bulletin*, with scholarly articles and book reviews, and a monthly *CTNS Newsletter*, with local and international news on conferences and programs. Audio Tapes of recent CTNS Public Forums and Lectures are available to CTNS members for $5. Among tapes offered are Bill Stoeger, "Science and Religion: a New View From Rome," Nancey Murphy, "Can Atoms Explain the World?" and John Polkinghorne, "God's Action in the World." **Membership:** CTNS membership includes clergy, laypersons, theologians of many faiths, students, and scientists. Membership is available in general and student categories. Fees: $25 per year, general; $15 per year, student; $10 per year, international postage. Members receive the *CTNS Bulletin* and the *CTNS Newsletter*, as well as news of special events and course offerings.

The Center of Theological Inquiry (CTI)

Brief Description: The Center of Theological Inquiry is dedicated to developing advanced research in Christian theology as a means of renewing faith through its convergence with the disciplines of modern critical understanding. The Center is an independent institution devoted exclusively to both theoretical and practical research. Promising and outstanding scholars with such concerns are brought together through conferences, consultations, and periods of residential scholarhsip. Those associated with its work need not have theology or religion as their primary field, but represent many fields of modern intellectual endeavor. The Center is ecumenical, interreligious and international in scope. **Director:** The Rev. Professor Daniel W. Hardy. **Address:** 50 Stockton Street, Princeton, NJ 08540 **Telephone:** (609) 683-4797 **Fax:** (609) 683-4030 **Purpose and Goals:** The Center of Theological Inquiry is strongly committed to: (1) the reshaping of theological inquiry for its future public role by establishing its convergence with the disciplines of modern understanding, (2) the development of sustained, concentrated research of this kind, (3) the activation of critical discussion to renew the responsiveness of theology to the issues of cosmology and ecology, social institutions, biology and personal ethics, culture and the religions. It seeks thereby to resource those who are concerned with these matters in the academy, the churches and the public sphere. The center fulfills these aims through programs of (a) regular and occasional inter-disciplinary conferences and (b) collegial scholarship by twelve fellows selected for periods of residential membership of up to two years' duration. In both cases, the Center initiates a new vision of the scope, resources and responsibilities of theological inquiry today. In the future, it will expand its work to include a wider range of conferences and consultations, concentrated research by teams of scholars at the Center and the development of ongoing mutual cooperation amongst those associated with the Center. **Organizational Structure:** The Center is incorporated as a non-profit organization guided by its Board of Trustees and Director, who are aided also by an Advisory Committee. The Board of Trustees consists of the following members: James F. Armstrong (Secretary); Robert M. Ayres, Jr.; James H. Billington; Richard M. Cromie; John H. Donelik; Harold B. Erdman (Treasurer); James Fitzpatrick (Emeritus); James E. Fogartie (Emeritus); Roland M. Frye; Thomas W. Gillespie (Chairman); Daniel W. Hardy (Director); Margaret W. Harmon (Emerita); W. Frank Harrington; Bryant M. Kirkland ((Vice-Chairman); Henryk R. de Kwiatkowski; William E. Lawder (Emeritus); William H. Lazareth; Henry Luce III; George T. Piercy; Frank P. Reiche; William H. Scheide; William Sword; John M. Templeton (Emeritus); David B. Watermulder. The Advisory Committee includes the following members: Diogenes Allen (Princeton Theological Seminary); Michael J. Buckley (Boston College); Ellen T. Charry (Perkins School of Theology); Roland M. Frye, ex officio (Emeritus, University of Pennsylvania); Daniel W. Hardy (Director); John H. Leith (Emeritus, Union Theological Seminary, Richmond); Thomas C. Oden (Drew University); Gerhard Sauter (University of Bonn); Walter R. Thorson (University of Alberta); and Robert L. Wilken (University of Virginia). **Publications:** In addition to an Annual Report which explores the nature and significance of theological inquiry today, the Center publishes *Centerings*, a twice-yearly journal of its life and work, and a series of Center Reports about the work of its conferences and residential members. There are many books whose origin lies in the work of its members in residence; a list may be obtained from the Center. **Facilities:** Conferences are arranged a thte Center and accommodated nearby in Princeton. Residential scholars are provided with studies in Luce Hall, a Georgian building constructed in 1984 in the heart of Princeton. They also have access to the libraries of Princeton Theological Seminary and Princeton University. Furnished accommodation suitable for families is provided rent-free in new townhouses three miles away from Princeton. Where necessary, financial assistance is granted on a case-by-case basis.

The Centre for Advanced Religious and Theological Studies

Brief Description: The Faculty of Divinity at Cambridge, with the backing of the University, intends to establish a Centre for Advanced Religious and Theological Studies. This Centre will provide a forum where the best Christian scholars in Europe and the United States can work together on the contemporary ethical and human questions which puzzle society. Where appropriate, they will be joined by scholars from other religious traditions and cultures who bring their insights to a common search for ethical and moral structures that do justice to the religious aspect of human experience. **Purpose and Objectives:** The central purpose of the Centre is to develop two types of discourse: the first is across disciplinary boundaries, especially between theologians and scientists — medical, physical and social; the second is across national boundaries — European, American, and where appropriate, Asian and African. The Centre's work will be carried on in several ways. 1) There will be a small group of Visiting Fellows, for periods between six months and a year, who will be involved in collaborative projects or related work of their own; some will be from participating American Universities, and others will be supported directly by the Centre. 2) There will be a program of colloquia, seminars, and lectures, which will enable other overseas scholars to visit for shorter periods, and contribute to the work of the Centre in that way. 3) Members of the Cambridge Theology Faculty and other related Faculties in the University, will be involved in research projects to further the objectives of the Centre. The Centre will have three "audiences." The first will be the worldwide community of scholars. The second will be the Churches, and especially church leaders, who increasingly need to be aware of detailed research materials as they offer guidance on contemporary issues. The third will be those who form policy and implement it, who often have the greatest influence in setting the social values of their societies. The work of the Centre will be communicated through a publication and the holding of short courses or colloquia. **Projects:** Five areas for collaborative investigation and action have been initially suggested. 1) The religious exploration of social and political relationships, particularly in context of events in Eastern Europe. 2) The relationship between the rich, developed countries and the poor, drawing on the existing interdisciplinary study of social change in developing countries in Cambridge. 3) A Christian response to current research on the geophysics and geopolitics of the environment. 4) Sexual ethics and the ethics of gender. 5) The ethics of genetic engineering. **Organizational Structure:** The Centre will be an integral part of the University of Cambridge, under the supervision of the General Board of the Faculties. It will have a Director, and a Committee of Management who will be responsible for electing Visiting Fellows, determining the program and administering the funds.

The Chicago Advanced Seminar on Religion in an Age of Science

Brief Description: The Chicago Advanced Seminar in Religion and Science seeks to advance research on Religion in an Age of Science, particularly focusing on values, through an annual series of 10 sessions each year (usually consecutive weeks in the Spring). **Address:** 1100 E. 55th Street, Chicago, IL 60615-5199, USA. **Telephone:** Requirements, registration and questions should be discussed with Professors Hefner or Gilbert at 753-0670 or 643-6031 **Date of Founding:** 1965, by Ralph Wendell Burhoe and Meadville/Lombard Theological School. **Current Chairpersons:** Philip Hefner, Thomas Gilbert, Ralph Burhoe. **Description:** Since 1965 an inter-school advanced seminar on religion in the context of the sciences has been offered for faculty, students, and professionals in the Chicago area. The seminars developed under Ralph Wendell Burhoe, Director of the Center for Advanced Study in Religion and Science (CASIRAS) at Meadville/Lombard Theological School. CASIRAS traces its origins to the scientists who comprised the Committee on Science and Human Values of the American Academy of Arts and Sciences, begun in 1952, when Burhoe was Executive Officer of the Academy. This group worked on the significance of religion within the processes of genetic and socio-cultural evolution. In 1970, CASIRAS and its courses were affiliated with the Chicago Cluster of Theological Schools. Philip Hefner, Professor of Systematic Theology at the Lutheran School of Theology at Chicago (LSTC) became program Cochair of CASIRAS. In 1988 the Chicago Center for Religion and Science (CCRS) was founded by LSTC and CASIRAS. This new center became a cosponsor of the Advanced Seminar, along with its Associate Director, physicist Thomas Gilbert. From this tradition, the Seminar arose as part of a multidisciplinary network of persons seeking to interpret the long-evolved heritages of religion credibly in the context of modern science. The goal is that religion might become more compellingly credible, better appreciated and more effective in its critical functions for human life as the prime cultural bearer of ultimate values or concerns today. **Membership:** The seminar is a voluntary association with no fees, open to scientists, theologians, students at M.Div., M.A. and Ph.D. level, and professionals from any field. The number of participants fluctuates between 15 and 35. **Academic Credit:** The seminar series is also available for course credit for students, through the LSTC and Meadville/Lombard Theological School. There are special 1-hour sessions each week for credit-seeking persons.

The Chicago Center for Religion and Science (CCRS)

Brief Description: The Chicago Center for Religion and Science is a program of the Lutheran School of Theology at Chicago, operated in collaboration with the Center for Advanced Study in Religion and Science. It is dedicated to relating religious traditions and scientific knowledge in order to gain insight into the origins, nature and destiny of humans and their environment, and to realize the common goal of a world in which love, justice, and ecologically responsible styles of living prevail. **Director:** Philip Hefner **Address:** 1100 East 55th Street, Chicago, IL 60615-5199. **Telephone:** (312) 753-0670 **Fax:** (312) 702-1225 **Date of Founding:** January 4, 1988. **Purpose and Activities:** The purpose of CCRS is to provide a place of research and discussion between scientists, theologians, and other scholars on the most basic issues pertaining to 1) how we understand the world in which we live and our place in the world, 2) how traditional concerns and beliefs of religion can be related to scientific understandings, and 3) how the joint reflection of scientists, theologians, and other scholars can contribute to the welfare of the human community. The overall program of the Center takes shape in research, teaching and outreach. The research program is interested in interpreting classic Christian faith in ways that are credible in the context of contemporary scientific understanding. Research program activities include 1) supporting the research of resident scholars, including doctoral candidates, 2) organizing conferences and seminars on topics of current interest, and 3) providing support for topical research workshops proposed by Center Associates. The teaching program includes teaching courses at all levels for seminary students and cooperating in doctoral programs in the field of religion and science. The outreach program makes the insights gained from Center activities available to a wider audience and includes 1) organizing public lectures, workshops, and continuing education courses, 2) attracting pastors, scientists and laity for periods of study at the Center, and 3) publishing a newsletter, research summaries and Center reports. **Organizational Structure:** The Center is accountable to the administration and the Board of Directors of the Lutheran School of Theology at Chicago. Policies are formulated by a Board of Governors of the Center. Leadership and direction are provided by a director, who is a theologian and chairperson of the Board of Governors, and an associate director, who is a scientist and an ex officio member of the Board. There is further an Advisory Committee made up of Center Associates, those scientists, theologians, and other scholars who participate actively in initiating and implementing the research, teaching, and outreach programs of the Center. The leadership is constituted by the following: Philip Hefner, Theology (Director); Thomas L. Gilbert, Physics (Associate Director); Carol Rausch Gorski (Associate for Programs). The Board of Governors includes the following: William Broman, Geophysics (Shell Offshore Exploration, Inc.); Mihaly Csikszentmihalyi, Psychology (University of Chicago); Harold Lohr, Chemistry (Bishop, Northwestern Minnesota Evangelical Lutheran Church in America); Solomon H. Katz, Anthropology (University of Pennsylvania); and Karl E. Peters, Philosophy, Religion (Rollins College). Senior Associates are Ralph W. Burhoe, Science and Theology (Emeritus, Meadville/Lombard School of Theology) and Langdon Gilkey, Theology (Emeritus, University of Chicago Divinity School). Associates of the Center include the following members: Gerald O. Barney, Physics, Environment (Institute for 21st Century Studies); Don Browning, Religion and Psychological Studies (University of Chicago Divinity School); Richard Busse, Religion and Philosophy (Indiana University - Northwest); Willem B. Drees, Theology, Physics (Free University Amsterdam); Lindon G. Eaves, Genetics (Virginia Commonwealth University); Charles Ehret, Biology (Argonne National Laboratory); Robert Glassman, Psychology (Lake Forest College); Paul Heltne, Primatology (Chicago Academy of Sciences); H. Rodney Holmes, Neurophysiology (University of Chicago); Paul E. Lutz, Biology (University of North Carolina - Greensboro); Linda McDonald, Physics (North Park College); William E. Lesher (President, Lutheran School of Theology at Chicago); Walter L. Michel, Old Testament (Lutheran School of Theology at Chicago); Nancey Murphy, Philosophy, Theology (Fuller Theological Seminary); James Nelson, Theology (North Park College); Arthur R. Peacocke, Theology, Biochemistry (St. Cross College, Oxford); David Rhoads, New Testament (Lutheran School of Theology at Chicago); G. Roy Ringo, Physics (Argonne National Laboratory); Michael Ruse, History, Philosophy (University of Guelph); Robert J. Russell, Physics, Theology (Center for Theology and the Natural Sciences, GTU); Karl Schmitz-Moormann, Theology (Fachhochschule Dortmund); Wentzel van Huyssteen, Theology (Princeton Theological Seminary); Jeffrey S. Wicken, Physical Biochemistry (Behrend College, Pennsylvania State University); and Donald G. York, Astronomy and Astrophysics (University of Chicago). **Membership:** Individuals may affiliate with the Center through one or more of the following categories: 1) Associates - scientists, theologians, and other scholars who participate actively in initiating and implementing the programs of the Center and constitute an advisory committee. Names are added to this group by invitation. 2) Professional Affiliates - scientists, theologians, and other scholars who support the purposes of the Center and provide occasional advice and assistance but are unable to make the time commitment for the ongoing, active participation of an Associate. This category is open to applications. 3) General Affiliates - Pastors, laity, and groups who have an interest in the work of the Center and wish to serve as a resource for advice to the Center and its programs. This category is open to applications. 4) Sponsors - individuals and groups who provide financial support for the Center by continuing annual contributions. **Publications:** CCRS publishes a newsletter in May, October, and February called, *Insights*. The Editor for *Insights* is Richard Busse; Production Manager is Kristi Bangert. The leadership and staff of CCRS also help edit and produce, *Zygon: Journal of Religion and Science*. The meeting of CCRS together with the Evangelischen Akademie Loccum, September 14-17, 1989 has been published in *Loccumer Protokolle* 78/'89 and is entitled *Menschliche Natur und*

Moralische Paradoxa (Human Nature and Moral Paradox), edited by Hans May, Meinfried Striegnitz, and Philip Hefner.

Christians in Science (CIS)

Brief Description: Christians in Science (formerly the Research Scientist's Christian Fellowship) is one of many professional study groups formed under the Universities and Colleges Christian Fellowship (UCCF). Among its 750 members are scientists together with philosophers, theologians, ministers and others with an interest in science-religion questions. **Address:** c/o UCCF, 38 De Montfort Street, Leicester, LE1 7PG, England. **Telephone:** (0533) 551700 **Fax:** 445-3355 5672 **Date of Founding:** 1942 as The Research Scientist's Christian Fellowship. **Purpose:** To promote a positive Christian view of the nature, scope and limitations of science in the modern world. To develop clearly thought out Christian views of the changing interactions between science and faith. To encourage Christians who are involved with science to maintain a lively faith and apply it to their discipline. To present a Christian viewpoint in the world of science and the wider community. **Organizational Structure:** An Executive Committee is elected by the Professional Groups Committee of Universities and Colleges Christian Fellowship from nominations by the Executive Committee. Sub-committees are appointed by the Executive for Christians in Science Education, Research in the Third World, Contacts in Eastern Europe, and specialist groups in Geology, etc. **Current Officers:** Chairman, Professor Colin A. Russell; Secretary, Mr. Bennet McInner; Publications Secretary, Dr. Oliver Barclay; UCCF Office Liaison, Mr. David Thistlewaite. **Special Projects and Conferences:** An annual Conference is held in London. Study groups have been set up to write on: The Environment; The Use of Animals; Miracles; Scientists in Industry. Occasionally other meetings and conferences are held. **Membership:** Full membership is open to all those with a professional interest in science who assent to the membership declaration: "I declare my faith in Jesus Christ as my Saviour, my Lord and my God, whose atoning sacrifice is the only and all-sufficient ground of my salvation, and I will seek both in life and thought to be ruled by the clear teaching of the Bible, believing it to be the inspired Word of God." Others are welcome as Associate members on payment of the same subscription, with the opportunity to receive the literature, including the journal, and to take part in meetings. Annual fees are £10 (£5 for students or research students); £4 for one year's subscription to UCCF's quarterly magazine *Christian Arena* (an extra £4 for air mail outside Europe, if required). **Publications:** Since 1989 a Journal, *Science and Christian Belief* (see separate entry). CIS also publishes occasional books or booklets, such as the articles in O. R. Barclay, editor, *Christian Faith and Science.*

Christians in Science Education (CISE)

Brief Description: Christians in Science Education is an organization set up to help people involved or interested in Science Education from a Christian viewpoint, mainly in the UK. Subscribers are mainly teachers at school level, but also include advisers and inspectors, university teachers and teacher trainers. **Address:** 5 Longcrofte Road, Edgware, Middlesex HA8 6RR, UK. **Phone:** (44) 181 952 5349 **Founding:** 1989 **Current Officers:** Chairman: Michael W. Poole; Secretary: John Bausor. **Purpose:** To provide a service to Christians who are involved in science education; CISE aims to keep people in touch with developments in this field and to help them to brings a Christian perspective to their work. **Conferences:** A display stand and symposium are mounted at the Annual Meeting each January of the Association for Science Education. **Publications:** The CISE Newsletter is published twice a year. **Membership:** The annual subscription is £5 including two issues of the Newsletter. Anyone intereste may subscribe. CISE is sponsored by the Association of Christian Teachers and Christians in Science (q.v.).

Committee on Human Values of the National Conference of Catholic Bishops

Brief Description: The primary goal of the Committee on Human Values of the National Conference of Catholic Bishops is to establish ongoing discussion between the bishops and the American scientific community. The Committee seeks to probe the ramifications of the relationship between religion and science and to help clear the air so that neither the religious nor the scientific communities are uncomfortable in the presence of the other. **Chairman:** Most Rev. James A. Hickey **Address:** National Conference of Catholic Bishops, Committee on Human Values, 1312 Massachusetts Avenue, N.W., Washington, DC 20005. **Telephone:** (202) 659-6838 **Purpose and Activities:** The Committee on Human Values promotes a dialogue which tries 1) to clarify problems in question and 2) to discover a possible convergence of the various truths involved. It holds that Catholic theology must confront the spirit of scientific humanism in contemporary American culture, and that Catholic moral values must be brought to bear on issues in science and technology. Wisdom lies where the truths of religion and science conjoin. The Committee achieves its purpose by establishing and maintaining ongoing dialogue groups concerned with issues of theological and philosophical interest. It also refers scientific/technological advances to outside groups for study of their theological implications. Where appropriate, it uses the results of such consultation to comment on selected questions in association with other NCCB/USCC committees. In addition, the Committee sponsors an annual Conference on Religion and Science with speakers and respondents from the scientific and theological communities. **The Current Membership of the Committee on Human Values:** Most Rev. James A. Hickey (Chairman); Most Rev. Edward M. Egan; Most Rev. Howard J. Hubbard; Most Rev. Mark J. Hurley; Bernard Cardinal Law; Most Rev. Dale J. Melczek; Most Rev. A. James Quinn. **Consultants are:** Rev. Robert Brungs, S.J.; Rev. Enrico Cantore, S.J.; John Collins Harvey, M.D.; Rev. Albert S. Moraczewski, O.P.; Edmund D. Pellegrino, M.D.; Rev. James Salmon, S.J.; Robert J. White, M.D., Ph.D.

The Common Boundary Between Spirituality and Psychotherapy

[See entry under the same title in Directory D]

Cosmos and Creation

Brief Description: Cosmos and Creation is a group whose function consists of an annual conference of scientists, who engage in a three day intensive dialogue with an invited speaker who has done creative and significant work in theology and science integration. **General Coordinators:** James Salmon and Francis McGuire. **Address:** Loyola College in Maryland, 4501 N. Charles Street, Baltimore, MD 21210. **Telephone:** (301) 323-1010 Ext. 2261 **Date of Founding:** 1981. **Purpose:** The purpose of the consultation is to further the creative efforts of the individual participants in their own work in relating their scientific understanding with their religious faith. **Organizational Structure:** The consultation is coordinated by an executive committee, including James Salmon, Thomas King, and Francis McGuire. **Participation:** Working scientists with religious concerns may contact Francis McGuire for more information. **Conference Topics:** Conference topics and speakers have included: "The History of Science and the Dogma of Creation" (Stanley Jaki), "The Dice-Playing God" (Rustum Roy), "The Anthropic Principle" (Ernan McMullin), "God and Contemporary Physics" (Geoffrey Chew), "God and the Scientific Culture" (Langdon Gilkey), "Cosmos: Child of Science, and Science: Child of Technology" (Frederick Ferré), "God and the New Physics" (Michael Buckley), "God and Evolution" (Karl Schmitz-Moormann), and "Cosmology and Creation" (Ian Barbour).

The European Society for the Study of Science and Theology (ESSSAT)

Brief Description: ESSSAT was established in 1990 in response to the growing sense of a change of climate in the relationship between science and theology. For the last 200 years this relationship was mostly marked by reciprocal distrust and conflict. But in more recent times there has been a growing interest among scientists to understand what transcends the boundaries of their research, and among theologians a desire to get a better grasp of the world they speak of as creation. It appears obvious that this situation calls for an open dialogue between scientists and theologians. **ESSSAT Secretary:** For more information on the Society, or for application for membership, write to; The Secretary of ESSSAT, Revd. Antje Jackelén **Address:**Högseröds prästgård, S-240 33 Löberöd, Sweden. **Telephone:** +46 413 30398 **Purpose of the Society:** The European Society for the Study of Science and Theology seeks to answer the growing demand for a dialogue between science and theology. Its aims are: a) to advance the open and critical communication between theology and science; b) to mutually appropriate their respective knowledge for each other; and c) to work on the solution of interdisciplinary problems. In this task the Society regards itself as committed to the Judaeo-Christian tradition in its different occidental expressions. **Conferences:** When the Society was still in *statu nascendi*, two European Conferences on Science and Theology were organized: 1986 in Loccum, Germany on "Evolution and Creation"; 1988 in Twente, Holland on "One World — Changing Perspectives on Reality"; and 1990 in Geneva, Switzerland on "Information and Knowledge in Science and Theology." In continuation of this biannual tradition, conferences were held in 1992 in Rocca di Papa near Rome, Italy on "Origins, Time and Complexity", and in 1994 in Freising and Munich, Germany on "The Concept of Nature in Science and Theology". The proceedings of these conferences are available in print. The Sixth European Conference on Science and Theology is planned to be held in Cracow, Poland in 1996 on "The Interplay of Scientific and Theological World Views". Yearbooks: The first two yearbooks "Studies in Science and Theology" appeared in 1993 and 1994, edited by G. V. Coyne, K. Schmitz-Moormann and C. Wassermann. **Other Activities:** Over and above this form of dialogue and cooperation between academic scientists and theologians, the Society aims: a) to establish interdisciplinary research projects in the field of science and theology; b) to further the study of historical and present relationships between science and theology; and c) to develop integrative university curricula on theology and science. To facilitate such efforts a communication network will be set up among the members of the Society. Since the Society is committed to its Judaeo-Christian heritage and is open towards the different churches that embody this tradition, it is at the disposition of responsible church representatives to cooperate with them on the solution of present and future problems related to developments in science that are of significance for the church. In 1996 two ESSSAT-Prizes for Studies in Science and Theology will be awarded to younger scholars for outstanding reflection bearing on the relationship between theology and natural sciences in contemporary culture. **Membership and Fees:** All those working in the different academic fields of science and theology and all those who wish to participate in or support the work of the Society are invited to become members of ESSSAT. The members of the Society will be informed on upcoming conferences and will be granted priority with regards to participation. The membership categories and minimum annual membership fees are currently fixed as follows: a) Student member — candidates, DM (Deutsche Mark) 40; b) Personal members, DM 75; c) Membership of Voluntary Societies, DM 200; d) Membership of Public and International Institutions, DM 400. The fees for personal members include the ESSSAT yearbook and a subscription to *Science & Religion News* published by the Institute on Religion in an Age of Science (IRAS), USA. These fees are to be considered the minimum rates and all members are encouraged to donate more towards the advancement of the goals of the Society. This is especially anticipated from associate members who, though they might not be directly involved in interdisciplinary research, nevertheless want to be informed and to financially support the Society to the benefit of full members actually engaged in interdisciplinary research. Contributors should note that donations are to a nonprofit professional society. Payment of membership fees must be in German currency, and can be transferred to the following account: Postgirobank Dortmund, P.O. Box 10 60 50, D-4600 Dortmund 9, Germany; Account Number 654-460, to the benefit of ESSSAT. (Interested persons from former East-Block countries with financial difficulties can be sponsored by members of the Society from other countries. Contact the Secretary for details). **Organization:** The council of the Society is elected by the general assembly that is held during the biannual conferences of the Society. The current council members are: Friedrich Gramer (Germany); Willem B. Frees (publication of ESSSAT-newsletter, Holland); Botond Gaal (Hungary); Ulf Görman (Sweden); Michael Heller (Poland); Jürgen Hübner (Germany); Michael Parsons (Great Britian); Arthur Peacock (Great Britian); Xavier Salantin (France); Karl Schmitz-Moormann (Germany); Jacqueline Stewart (Great Britian). The council elects the executive officers of the Society. They are currently: President, Karl Schmitz-Moormann; Vice-president for conferences, Michael Heller; Vice-president for publications, Christoph Wassermann (Germany); Scientific Program Officer, Niels Henrik Gregersen (Denmark); Treasurer: Charlotte Methuen (Germany/Great Britian); Secretary, Antje Jackelén (Sweden).

Evangelische Akademie Loccum (The Protestant Academy at Loccum)

Brief Description: The Protestant Academy at Loccum is a place dedicated to open debate on any matters relating to the furtherance of a responsible approach to future directions in society. The Academy is an institution of the Hanover Province of the Lutheran Church. It is run by thirteen academical and sixteen administrative staff plus five freelancers. **Date of Founding:** 1946. **Address:** Postfach 2158 31545 Rehburg-Loccum, Germany. **Telephone:** +49 05766-81-0 **Fax:** +49 05766-81-188 **Purpose and Objectives:** The main emphasis of the Protestant Academy at Loccum concerns the fields of East-West and North-South relationships and security policy, issues of migration, economic and social policy, environmental policy, educational and cultural policy; patterns of living, and of social and psychological identity, interreligious dialogue, and theology in the modern world. By organizing conferences, workshops, and seminars the Academy makes it possible for people from different backgrounds and with differing points of view to meet and discuss problems, to explain and mediate between opposing interests and thus to be engaged in the process of problem solving. The Academy is a forum open to all who are divided from each other by being on opposite sides of a conflict but also united by their involvement with the common issue. The Academy itself does not take sides between the disputed positions. Among those who take part in the events organized by the Academy are representatives, opinion-formers, and decision-makers from administration, politics, business, the academic world, professional associations, and non-governmental organizations. In the Protestant Academy at Loccum, the Protestant Church's commitment to its social co-responsibility manifests itself in the form of a service institution, based on the spirit of Christian charity and existing to promote the development of a democratic spirit in society and the community. **Special Projects:** Main topics of discussion at the Academy include Theology in the Modern World; Religion and Science; Interreligious/Intercultural Dialogue; Fundamental Theology; Ethics; Meditation; International Relations; Peace Research; Economics/Economy; History; Technology; Ecology; Medicine and Health, and Ethics in Medicine. **Organizational Structure:** The Academy's program of events is decided upon by the "Konvent" or Board of Governors, an independent body consisting of representatives of public life. **Current Academical Staff:** Dr. Fritz-Erich Anhelm, Director; Dr. Beate Blatz; Dr. Hans-Peter Burmeister; Dr. Jörg Calliess; Dr. Andreas Dally; Kurt Dantzer; Sybille Fritsch-Oppermann; Dr. Wolfgang Greive; Andrea Grimm; Dr. Christoph Hüttig; Jörg Mayer. **Organizational Management:** Ernst Bohnenkamp. **Freelancers:** Otto Lange; Dr. Karl Ermert; Prof. Dr. Detlef Hoffmann; Prof. Dr. Jan Jarre; Udo Schlaudraff; Andrea Weinert. **Publications:** Twice per annum the Academy publishes *Forum Loccum*, the journal of the Academy with news on the Academy's conferences, comments, events, etc. At various times the Academy publishes *Forum Loccum Extra*, including extracts from conferences, conference papers, and *Loccumer Protokolle*, conference documentation. Meetings of the Evangelischen Akademie Loccum together with the Chicago Center for Religion and Science are published in the following *Loccumer Protokolle*: *Loccumer Protokolle* 78/'89. *Menschliche Natur und Moralische Paradoxa* (Human Nature and Moral Paradox), edited by Hans May, Meinfried Striegnitz, and Philip Hefner. *Loccumer Protokolle* 75/'88 *Kooperation und Wettbewerb. Zu Ethik und Biologie menschlichen Sozialverhaltens, 1988* (Cooperation and Competition. The Ethics and Biology of Human Social Attitude), ed. Hans May, Meinfried Striegnitz, and Philip Hefner. The Documentation of the Conference "Altruismus - aus Sicht von Evolutionsbiologie und Theologie" (Altruism - from the Point of View of Evolutionary Biology and Theology). Forthcoming. **Physical Assets:** The Academy has 2 lecture halls, 11 rooms for groups from 10 to 40 participants, a day room, a library, 105 single rooms, and 30 double rooms.

Forschungsinstitut für Philosophie Hannover

Brief Description: The Forschungsinstitut für Philosophie Hannover (Hannover Institute of Philosophical Research) seeks to encourage thought within the horizon and spirit of Roman Catholic belief. The Forschungsinstitut promotes concentrated study in philosophy including metaphysics, humanities, philosophy of nature, philosophy of society, and industrial ethics. **Directors:** Prof. Dr. Peter Koslowski; Prof. Drs. Reinhard Löw; Prof. Dr. Richard Schenk. **Address:** Gerberstrasse 26, 30169 Hannover, Germany. **Telephone:** (0511) 1 64 09-0 **Telex:** (0511) 1640935. **Date of Founding:** September 8, 1988 by the Bishop of Hildesheim, Dr. Josef Homeyer. **Purpose and Activities:** The Forschungsinstitut is a registered non-profit church foundation. It advises and supports foundational study of issues involving ecumenical and interdisciplinary exchange. The Forschungsinstitut sponsors the following areas of work: 1) Guest professors and Fellows are invited to conduct and discuss research. 2) Lectures, seminars, and colloquia are organized by the institute, which offers the possibility of postgraduate study. 3) The work of the institute is extended through books and journals and public discussions.

Forschungsstätte der Evangelischen Studiengemeinschaft (F.E.ST.) in Heidelberg

Brief Description: F.E.ST. is a Protestant Institute for Interdisciplinary Research at Heidelberg. It is sponsored by the Protestant Research Group (Evangelische Studiengemeinschaft e. V.). The Protestant Church in Germany (EKD) and its regional Churches, the directors of the Protestant Academies and the German Protestant Church Congress (Deutscher Evangelischer Kirchentag) support this Institute. **Director:** Klaus von Schubert. **Address:** Schmeilweg 5, D-6900 Heidelberg, Germany. **Background:** One of the stimuli leading to the establishment of F.E.ST. was the dialogue between physicists and theologians founded in Göttingen by Carl Friedrich von Weizsäcker and Günter Howe in the late 1940's and 1950's. **Activities:** The Institute supports research, consultations and publications that deal with issues arising in the interface between the Church and Society, including such areas as the Social and Natural Sciences, Law, Ecology, and Politics. **Members Include:** Ulrich Duchrow, Jürgen Hübner, Christian Link, Klaus M. Meyer-Abich, Klaus Müller, Georg Picht, Ulrich Ratsch, Heinz Eduard Tödt. **Publications:** *Glaube und Forschung.* F.E.ST. has also sponsored a major contribution to the dialogue between Theology and Science in the form of the publication of Jürgen Hübner's, editor. *Der Dialog zwischen Theologie und Naturwissenschaft. Ein bibliographischer Bericht*, Forschungen und Berichte der Evangelischen Studiengemeinschaft 41 (München: Chr. Kaiser, 1987).

The Geoscience Research Institute

Brief Description: The Geoscience Research Institute, founded in 1958, was established to address questions of beginnings by looking at the scientific evidence concerning origins. The Institute uses both science and revelation to study the question of origins because it considers the exclusive use of science as too narrow an approach. **Director:** Ariel A. Roth **Address:** GRI, Loma Linda University, Loma Linda, CA 92350 USA. **Telephone:** (909) 824-4548 **Fax:** (909) 824-4314 **Purpose and Objectives:** The Geophysical Research Institute was established by the Seventh-day Adventist Church to gather information regarding the origin and past history of the natural world and correlate this research with biblical concepts of origins. The Institute has two major foci — research and communication. 1) Research is conducted by the Institute's five research scientists: Benjamin L. Clausen is a nuclear physicist who studies the action of subatomic particles; M. Elaine Kennedy specializes in the study of sediments; L. James Gibson, trained in speciation and biogeography, concentrates his studies on the patterns of distribution of animals over the earth; Ariel A. Roth, the Director of the Institute, is researching both fossil and living coral reefs, and also works on issues in philosophy of science; Clyde L. Webster has been using trace-element analysis to characterize ejection patterns of volcanoes in Hawaii and Yellowstone. Special research topics center mostly around the question of time, particularly time for life on earth. The Institute also supervises a modest research grant program providing help for other investigators studying questions related to the purposes of the Institute. 2) The staff of the Institute communicates the results of its research and study in numerous lectures to general and church audiences and in the teaching of classes at educational institutions. Extended field conferences have been conducted for students, educators, and administrators in Europe, the Caribbean, the South Pacific, South America, and several parts of North America. Research results are reported professionally through the scientific literature and society meetings. In addition, the Institute publishes three periodicals. **Publications:** The Institute publishes *Geoscience Reports*, (subscription rate: $3.00/year), a triannual newsletter designed for popular readership. *Ciencia de los Origenes* is a triannual Spanish publication covering the broad issues of origins. The biannual scholarly journal of the Institute that deals with the broad issues of the past history of the earth is *Origins*. Subscription inquiries should be made to the Institute. The rate for *Origins* is $8 per year. **Facilities:** The Institute's facilities, located at Loma Linda University, include office space, laboratories, computers for data analysis and a 18,000 volume science library including 100 journal subscriptions.

The Institute for Scientific Humanism (ISH)

Brief Description: The Institute for Scientific Humanism is an autonomous and nonsectarian international association of scientists and other scholars who work to overcome the split between the so-called two cultures. The Institute involves a theoretical concentration on human life in the age of science. **Director:** Enrico Cantore. **Address:** Lowenstein Center at Fordham University, New York, NY 10023, USA. **Date of Founding:** Established and incorporated in New York City as a nonprofit organization in 1974. **Purpose and Goals:** ISH is interested in humanism in the traditional sense of the term - it aims to comprehensively understand the human not only as a factual being but also as a value-oriented person. The humanism it strives for is scientific in that it should fit the needs of the scientific age by integrating the new perspectives disclosed by science with the perennial insights of the humanities. ISH pursues its goal by means of a dialogical-catalytic procedure. It fosters research by encouraging reflection and dialogue among experts. It then acts as a catalyst with regard to education and the public welfare by placing this information at the disposal of all interested persons, especially students. **Publications:** The Institute plans a series of books collectively entitled *Introduction to Scientific Humanism*. The first volume of the series appeared in 1977 and is entitled *Scientific Man*, by Enrico Cantore. The book is distributed by International Scholarly Book Services, Inc., P.O. Box 555, Forest Grove OR, 97116, USA.

Institute for Theological Encounter with Science and Technology (ITEST)

Brief Description: The Institute for Theological Encounter with Science and Technology is an international, interdisciplinary, interfaith community of Christians concerned with the revolutionary advance in scientific and technological capability, particularly as it is being directed toward living systems. ITEST involves over 600 members in 30 countries. **Director:** Robert A. Brungs, S.J. **Address:** 221 North Grand, St. Louis, MO 63103, USA. **Telephone:** (314) 658-2703 **Date of Founding:** 1968. **Description**: ITEST addresses itself primarily to the scientist and technologist. It also invites the integrating participation of economists, lawyers, social and behavioral scientists, physicians, philosophers, theologians and those concerned with the opportunities and challenges of contemporary and future scientific development. ITEST is concerned with the *meaning* of scientific and technological advance as that relates to the Christian understanding of the human and of creation. The Institute functions in the spirit expressed by the U.S. Catholic Bishops at the 1977 Synod of Bishops in Rome: "If the gospel is to . . . bring about a transformation of 'humanity's criteria of judgment, determining values, points of interest, lines of thought, sources of inspiration and models of life,' the world of science cannot be ignored." **Purpose:** To act as an "early-warning system" for the churches on work being done in the scientific laboratories. To translate this information into a theological/ecclesial vocabulary. To identify those scientific and technological developments affecting Christian *belief* and to promote Christian teaching in these matters. To work to build a community of scientists who are dedicated both to the advancement of scientific understanding as well as to the growth of the churches. **Membership:** Dues-paid members receive Conference Proceedings, a Bulletin and an occasional Monograph or paper. Annual dues are $35. **Conferences and Special Projects:** ITEST has sponsored 40 conferences on issues of science and technology which concern the church and which demand an informed response. Twice yearly conferences/ workshops on topics of science and Christian faith are offered. **Publications:** ITEST publishes a quarterly Bulletin on Science/Theology issues; The ITEST Faith/Science Press offers over 40 publications. Among recent titles are *The Inner Environment*; *The Human Genome Project*; *Transfiguration: Elements of Science and Christian Faith*; *The Vineyard - Scientists in the Church*; *Some Christian and Jewish Perspectives on the Creation* and *You See Lights Breaking Upon Us: Doctrinal Perspectives on Biological Advance*. **Organization:** Two full-time personnel: Director, and Director of Communications. **Current Officers:** Director, Robert A. Brungs, S.J.; Vice-Director, Robert Bertram; Treasurer, Thad Niemira; Secretary and Director of Communications, Marianne Postiglione, RSM. **Board of Directors:** Robert W. Bertram, Robert J. Collier, John Cross, Armgard Everett, Charles Ford, Peggy Keilholz, John Matschiner, Robert Morey, Thad Niemira, Marie C. Sherman, Helen Mandeville.

Institute for the Study of Christianity in an Age of Science and Technology (ISCAST)

Brief Description: The Institute for the Study of Christianity in an Age of Science and Technology has been set up to aid the study of the interaction between science and the Christian faith, and the assessment of modern technological advances in terms of the insights of that faith. The Institute is registered in New South Wales as a nonprofit company. It is governed by a Board of Directors elected at an annual general meeting of Fellows (members). Fellows have been invited by the Directors to apply for election in consequence of being persons of academic standing who have declared themselves in agreement with the aims and objectives of ISCAST as set out in its Articles of Association. **Address:** P.O. Box 483, Lindfield NSW 2070, Australia. **Telephone:**61-2-498-2710 **Date of Founding:** 1987. **Secretary:** R.J. Sterling, Ph.D. **Principles of ISCAST:** Fellows of ISCAST take a theological stance which is based upon a belief that God is the Author of all truth and in particular that Jesus the Living Word of God is revealed in the Holy Scriptures. The statements of the Apostles' Creed would be warmly affirmed by all Fellows. Fellows of ISCAST affirm the general objectives of scientific research, which aims at increasing our understanding of the universe, and take the view that scientific research should be employed for the benefit of all. ISCAST Fellows believe that the Christian faith makes an essential contribution to the study and resolution of contemporary issues. They believe that the investigation of the natural world by the methods of science affords valid and useful information because the universe is rational, the creation of God who is the source of reason. No satisfactory world view can therefore be developed unless it takes into account the universal activity of God in creating and sustaining the material universe. We are challenged by the nature of phenomena to investigate complementarity theories which seek to bring order and meaning to varying theories of knowing. **Logistics:** The activities by which ISCAST carries out its aims and objectives include: The arrangement of seminars and conferences for the discussion of topics relevant to its objectives; The publication and circulation of ISCAST bulletins; and the invitation to Australia of distinguished scholars who can bring their own experience and insights to bear on matters related to science, technology and the Christian faith. **Membership:** By invitation. There is no subscription, but Fellows are elected on the basis of their academic record and Christian activities. **Organization:** Board of Directors (7) elected annually. The current President of the Board is Professor J.W. White, FAA, FRS. The organization of local groups (chapters) is encouraged where there are Fellows who are able and willing to take responsibility for the conduct of its affairs. Such local groups are responsible to the Institute as a whole. The activities of ISCAST are supported by the Hugh Lyons Memorial Fund, but it is intended that as far as possible all activities will be self-supporting. **Professional Relationships:** Cooperation with other organizations with similar aims such as the American Scientific Affiliation, Christians in Science (UK) and the Victoria Institute (UK) is encouraged and their publications will be promoted. ISCAST already has established informal links with these bodies. ISCAST seeks cordial relationships with such bodies in Australia as the Zadok Centre, the Australian Fellowship of Evangelical Students, Christian Medical Fellowship, and the Australian Teachers' Christian Fellowship. ISCAST also recognizes the value of longer established, similar institutes such as the Center for Theology and the Natural Sciences, Berkeley, USA and the Ian Ramsey Centre, Oxford, UK. **Information Service:** The Institute provides a service whereby persons who would like advice on, and as far as possible answers to, questions in the general area of science and Christianity, may have such an opportunity by putting any such questions to informed Christian scholars. **Conferences:** 1989 visit by Prof. M. A. Jeeves, FRSE (Psychology, St. Andrews, Scotland); 1991 (August) visit by Prof. Gareth Jones (Anatomy, Dunedin, New Zealand) who discussed issues relating to biomedical technology; 1993 visit by Professor John Polkinghorne, FRS.

The Institute of Religion at Texas Medical Center

Brief Description: The Institute of Religion is dedicated to service, education and research in relating the concerns of religious ministry to those of health and medicine. **Address:** P.O. Box 20569, Houston TX 77225, USA. **Telephone:** (713) 797-0600 **Fax:** 797-9199 **Date of Founding:** 1955. **Current Officers:** President of Board of Trustees, Jan van Eys, Ph.D., M.D.; Director, J. Robert Nelson, D.Theol. **Purpose:** The Institute seeks to relate the insights of religious faith to medical education, patient care, and biomedical issues. It seeks to train persons of all community and religious organizations to become better leaders in the field of religion and medicine, including ethical issues in health care. **Organizational Structure:** The Board of Trustees includes 30 members, representing medical, civic and religious communities. The trustees elect their members. They are independent of any religious body. The trustees also appoint the Director and such faculty members as deemed needed. Faculty are chosen for their competence in dealing with matters of theology, ethics, medicine and pastoral care. In addition to the Director and two faculty, there is a development coordinator, a controller, and an office manager. **Special Projects and Conferences:** "Genetics, Religion and Ethics" is a three-year project associated with the Human Genome Research Project. It is of international scope. A conference was held in 1990, and one is planned for 1992. The Institute also offers seminars and workshops, as well as The Parker Memorial Lectures since 1984. In 1990 the lectures were on basic insights about human life as informed by religious faith. This year the theme is "Religion, Morality and Sexuality." **Physical Assets:** The Institute owns a four-story building, constructed in 1960. One floor is used by the Center for Ethics, Medicine and Public Issues, which the Institute cosponsors with Rice University and Baylor College of Medicine.

Institute on Religion in an Age of Science (IRAS)

Brief Description and Background: IRAS is an interdisciplinary group of scientists, theologians and others who are interested in exploring how to make religion more meaningful in a civilization dominated by sciences and their technologies. It has 310 members, widely distributed geographically, with international representation. IRAS arose from the mid-twentieth century initiatives of two pioneer groups. The first was a group of scientists from the Committee on Science and Values of the American Academy of Arts and Sciences. The second was a post-World War II interfaith, religious coalition, disappointed that religion was so weak in motivating justice and peace. It sought to reform and revitalize religion for today's needs. In 1954 the scientists accepted an invitation to present their views to the religious group at a seven-day conference on religion in an age of science. Ten scientists explained how they thought scientific and religious knowledge could be integrated. While a number of both scientists and clergy held that religious truth can hardly be approached by scientific beliefs, there was a strong recognition that today we can increase our understanding of our destiny and of our relationship to that "in which we live and move and have our being," not only by reading ancient texts, but also by building up the science of theology in harmony with other science. **President:** Ursula Goodenough. **Date of Founding:** November 9, 1954. **Purposes and Objectives:** The purposes of IRAS as stated in its Constitution are: 1) To promote creative efforts leading to the formulation, in the light of contemporary knowledge, of effective doctrines and practices for human welfare; 2) To formulate dynamic and positive relationships between the concepts developed by science and the goals and hopes of humanity expressed through religion; and 3) To state human values in such universal and valid terms that they may be understood by all peoples, whatever their cultural background or experience, in such a way as to provide a basis for world-wide cooperation. **Organizational Structure:** IRAS is a volunteer membership organization which is incorporated and nonprofit. It is governed according to its Constitution and Bylaws. There is an annual meeting of the membership. The IRAS Council is its decision-making body. It consists of fifteen elected members (five elected each year for 3-year terms) and the following ex officio members: Immediate Past President, Vice President for Conferences, Vice President for Development, Secretary, Treasurer, Editor of *Zygon*, and a representative of CASIRAS (Center for Advanced Study in Religion and Science). Meetings of the Council are customarily held twice a year, in January and July. The Council appoints program and conference committees and their chairs. Criteria for selection includes maintaining a balance of theologians and scientists on its council and committees and in conference programs. **Current Officers:** President, Ursula Goodenough; Vice President for Religion, Karl E. Peters; Vice President for Science, Rodney Holmes; Vice President for Interdisciplinary Affairs, Chris Corbally; Vice President for Conferences, Barbara Whittaker-Johns; Vice President for Development, Thomas L. Gilbert; Secretary, Paul Rasor; Treasurer, Thomas Fangman. **Special Projects and Conferences:** IRAS programs and activities include an annual summer conference since 1954, on Star Island (ten miles off Portsmouth, New Hampshire), IRAS-sponsored sessions and banquet at AAAS (American Association for the Advancement of Science, of which IRAS is an Affiliate), a reception at AAR (American Academy of Religion) organized by IRAS and co-sponsored with other Theology and Science groups, and occasional other conferences. Over the years IRAS has sponsored more than 250 meetings in conjunction with its affiliates and with various universities, colleges, and theological schools. **Publications:** IRAS is a copublisher of the quarterly journal *Zygon: Journal of Religion and Science.* It also publishes the *IRAS Newsletter,* which comes out three times a year; and *Science and Religion News,* published four times a year. **Awards:** IRAS gives 1) an Academic Fellow Award, an act of recognition for scholarly activity, research and/or teaching in the disciplines covered by the Institute's purpose and span of activities; 2) IRAS Service Award, an act of recognition for major service with respect to time, effort, ingenuity or monies given to the operation of the Institute and/or the implementation of the Institute's program; and 3) IRAS Institutional Service Award, an act of recognition to an organization which has performed meritorious service in helping the Institute achieve its objectives. **Membership:** IRAS membership is open to all who are interested in supporting its purposes. It does not represent any particular community of faith or political orientation. Categories of membership with annual dues are: Individual Member, $50 (outside US and Canada £37.50). Joint Member (two memberships but one set of publications), $55 (outside US and Canada £42.50). Student Member, $30 (outside US and Canada £22.50). Institutional Member, $100 (outside US and Canada £75). Application for membership may be made to Dr. Thomas Gilbert, IRAS Membership Committee, 1100 E. 55th St., Chicago, IL 60615-5199. **Affiliations:** IRAS is affiliated with the American Association for the Advancement of Science (AAAS); the Council of Societies for the Study of Religion (CSSR); and the Center for Advanced Study in Religion and Science (CASIRAS).

Institut für Wissenschaftstheoretische Grundlagenforschung

Description: The Institut für Wissenschaftstheoretische Grundlagenforschung (Institute for Investigation into the Foundations of Theoretical Knowledge) is a special department of the Deutsches Institut für Bildung und Wissen E. V. Berlin which, according to its statutes, attempts to ensure "that the knowledge available in our time is conveyed to people in a meaningful order, that man's view is opened to universal reality, and that thereby comprehensive cultural learning is promoted. . . All this is intended in full commitment to the Christian message. . . Within the compass of these aims the Institute carries out its research." Some 100 scholars from various disciplines work on behalf of the Institute, on a voluntary basis. **Date Founded:** The Institute was established in 1970. **Founding director:** Hugo Staudinger. **Officers:** Director (since 1993), Carsten Peter Thiede. **Address:** 33098 Paderborn, Busdorfwall 16, Germany. **Telephone:** (5251) 24905 **Fax:** (5251) 28 00 11 **Major Projects:** The department began with two major, fundamental projects, the first of which has now been successfully completed. Its central theme was "to work out the intellectual and spiritual trends of the present age and to analyze them as a challenge of belief to one-dimensional rationality." The four volumes pertaining to this project are: 1. Hugo Staudinger and Wolfgang Behler, *Chance und Risiko der Gegenwart - Eine kritische Analyse der wissenschaftlich-technischen Welt,* 2nd Edition (Paderborn, 1976). 2. Hugo Staudinger and Johannes Schlüter, *Wer ist der Mensch? Entwurf einer offenen und imperativen Anthropologie.* 2nd. Edition. Stuttgart, 1991. 3. Ludwig Kerstiens, *Verbindliche Perspektiven menschlichen Handelns - Zum Problem der Gültigkeit, Anerkennung und Vermittlung von Werten und Normen.* Stuttgart, 1983. Reprint, "Wie sollen wir handeln?" BzD 8, Wuppertal/Zürich, 1990. 4. Hugo Staudinger and Johannes Schlüter, *Die Glaubwürdigkeit der Offenbarung und die Krise der modernen Welt - Überlegungen zu einer trinitarischen Metaphysik.* Stuttgart, 1987. The second major project, "The Ethics of Science and Technology," is being carried out under the chairmanship of Professor Dr. Johannes Schlüter. Several symposia have taken place so far, some of them in cooperation with the Ministry of Research and Technology in Bonn. In addition a number of workshops have been organized, and they meet at regular intervals. **Other Monographs Published:** Apart from the two major projects, a good number of various problems have been studied and discussed. The following are some of the books that have resulted: 1. Hugo Staudinger and Max Horkheimer. *Um die Zukunft von Aufklärung und Religion. Briefwechsel und Gespräch.* Wuppertal/Zürich, 1991, BzD 11. 2. Hugo Staudinger, *Die historische Glaubwürdigkeit der Evangelien.* 6th edition. Wuppertal, 1994; English edition, 1981; Italian edition, 1992. 3. Hugo Staudinger and Wolfgang Behler, *Grundprobleme menschlichen Nachdenkens - Eine Einführung in modernes Philosophieren* (Freiburg, 1984; Spanish edition 1987). 4. Georg Masuch and Hugo Staudinger, *Geschöpfe ohne Schöpfer? Der Darwinismus als biologisches und theologisches Problem*. Wuppertal, 1987. 5. Hugo Staudinger and Johannes Schlüter, *An Wunder glauben? Gottes Allmacht und moderne Welterfahrung*. Freiburg, 1986. 6. Carsten Peter Thiede. *Funde, Fakten, Fährtensuche. Spuren des frühen Christentums in Europa*. Wuppertal/Zürich 1992; English edition 1992. 7. Carsten Peter Thiede. *Die älteste Evangelien-Handschrift? Ein Qumran-Fragment wird entschlüsselt*. Wuppertal/Zürich 1994; Italian edition 1987; Dutch edition 1988; Spanish edition 1989; English edition 1992. **Tape Recordings of Symposia:** The following symposia initiated and organized under the direction of the Deutsches Institut für Bildung und Wissen were recorded on tape and published as transcripts: 1. Reinhard Wegner, editor, "Das Problem der Zeit." Paderborn 1982. 2. Reinhard Wegner, editor, "Die Datierung der Evangelien." Paderborn, 1986. 3. Martin Petzolt, editor, "Die Zukunft der Metaphysik." Paderborn, 1985. 4. Martin Petzolt, editor, "Ethik der Wissenschaft und der Technologie." Paderborn, 1988. 5. Martin Petzolt, ed. "Konzeption und Aufgabe künftiger Metaphysik." Paderborn 1989. 6. Ulrich Niemann, ed. "Zum Problem der Selbstorganisation der materie." Paderborn 1991. 7. Ludger Verst, ed. "Glaubenswissen und Glaubenserfahrung." Paderborn 1989. 8. Patricia Indiesteln, ed. "Ethik des Journalismus in den Printmedien." Paderborn 1992. 9. Martin Petzolt, ed. "Das Problem der kerygmatischen Wahrheit." Paderborn 1992. 10. Hugo Staudinger, ed., Richard Ph. Krenzer. "Personverständnis und demokratische Gesellschaft." Paderborn 1993. 11. Georg Masuch, Johannes Schlüter, and Carsten Peter Thiede, eds. "Das Problem der Identität." Paderborn 1993. 12. Carsten Peter thiede, ed. "Bibelübersetzung zwischen Inkulturation und Manipulation." Paderborn 1993. 13. Ulrich Niemann, ed. "Information und informationsträger." Paderborn 1993. **Periodical:** The Deutsches Institut für Bildung und Wissen publishes *ibw-Journal* which is issued six times a year by the Burg-Verlag, Sachsenheim. Its chief editor is Hermann-Joseph Rick. The Journal contains interim results and shorter contributions on various topics. Since 1992, the Institute publishes a monthly information service, *WND*.

Instituut voor Ethiek aan de Vrije Universiteit (IEVU)

Description: The Instituut voor Ethiek aan de Vrije Universiteit (Institute of Ethics at the Free University) is an interdisciplinary institute, with 22 part-time participants, at the Free University of Amsterdam, The Netherlands. **Address:** Faculteit Wijsbegeerte, Vrije Universiteit, De Boelelaan 1105, 1081 HV Amsterdam, The Netherlands. **Date of Founding:** June 28, 1989. **Current Officers:** Professor Dr. A. W. Musschenga; Dr. J. S. Reinders; Professor Dr. W. J. van der Steen. **Goals and Objectives:** Interdisciplinary research. The Institute has a research program entitled Ethics in a Pluralistic Society, in which ethicists with a background in philosophy, theology, law, medicine and the natural sciences participate. The program has two main themes: a) the relation between worldview, morality and law; b) and the relation between theory and practice in ethics, and its consequences for several fields of "applied ethics." There will be a strong emphasis on a methodological analysis of current debates. **Organizational Structure:** All 22 participants are members (faculty or doctoral students) of the various departments within the Vrije Universiteit who invest part of their research effort in the Institute's program. The Institute has a staff of one full-time coordinator and a part-time secretary. The Institute's coordinator has an office at the department of philosophy, which is used for staff meetings as well. The Institute's Board consists of all senior members of the Faculty and two elected representatives of Ph.D. students, and it is financed almost completely by the University. **Membership:** Full membership is open to any staff member of the Vrije Universiteit, and to researchers from other universities whose research project can be incorporated in the Institute's research program (under the provisions of the Dutch system of "voorwaardelijke financiering" or "conditional state funding"). **Special Projects:** The Institute organized a two day conference on Ethics between Theory and Practice in November 1990, with invited lectures by Stanley Hauerwas and Gerald Postema, and workshops on medical ethics, business ethics, environmental ethics, ethics and technology, moral education, worldview and morality, and morality and law. **Publications:** A selection of 30 papers presented at the above mentioned conference is in press with the title *Morality, World View and Law*, edited by A. W. Musschenga, A. Soeteman and B. Voorzanger. The papers were refereed and edited after the conference.

Interdisciplinary Biblical Research Institute (IBRI)

Brief Description: IBRI is an organization of some 100 members, mostly in the U.S., informally associated with Biblical Theological Seminary, and self-described as "Christians who see a desperate need for men and women who believe in the complete reliability of the Bible to: (1) get training both in biblical studies and in some other academic discipline, and (2) to use this training to help other Christians deal with the many areas in which non-Christian teaching is so dominant today." Historically, IBRI has devoted much of its effort to the interaction of Christianity with science. **Director:** Dr. Robert C. Newman. **Address:** P.O. Box 423, Hatfield, PA 19440-0423. **Telephone:** (215) 368-5000 **Fax Number:** (215) 368-7002 **Date of Founding:** Fall, 1979, at Hatfield, Pennsylvania. **Objectives:** IBRI has several objectives: 1. To strengthen the Christian church in evangelism and academic competence. 2. To defend Christianity against intellectual attacks and to attack anti-Christian views. 3. To prepare and distribute educational materials supporting these objectives. 4. To encourage and support research in areas related to these objectives. 5. To encourage the development of distinctively Christian approaches to various academic disciplines, emphasizing biblical exegesis. 6. To help prepare Christian scholars who will strengthen the faculties of Christian institutions of higher education and provide a strong Christian presence in secular institutions. **Organization:** IBRI is a nonprofit association governed by a constitution and bylaws. Day-to-day operation is carried out by the Director under the oversight of a three-person Executive Committee. Final authority is vested in a twelve-member Board of Control which is self-perpetuating. **Membership:** There are three categories of membership in IBRI: 1) Friends, who agree with the objectives and doctrinal statement of IBRI, and who will support the organization with their prayers and, as finances permit, with donations. 2) Associates, selected from among the Friends by the Board of Control, who must have either an earned academic doctorate in some field, or a Masters degree in a seminary program emphasizing biblical exegesis. 3) Fellows, elected from among the Associates by the existing Fellows, who must have both of the academic qualifications listed for Associates. **Doctrinal Statement:** 1. The Bible alone, and the Bible in its entirety is the written Word of God, our absolute authority, inerrant in the autographs. 2. There is only one God, eternally existing in three persons, Father, Son and Holy Spirit, who created all things by His power. He is a spirit, infinite, eternal and unchangeable in His being, wisdom, power, holiness, justice, goodness and truth. 3. Jesus Christ is God the Son, coequal and coeternal with the Father and the Holy Spirit. He became man through a virginal conception and birth, lived a life of perfect righteousness, performed miracles, and died on the cross as a substitute to pay for the sins of all who trust in Him. He rose physically from the dead, ascended to heaven, and will one day return to rescue His own and put an end to sin. 4. All people are sinners as a result of Adam's fall and their own disobedience. Only through repentance from sin and dependence on Christ's work alone may they return to a right relationship with God. Those who return will one day be delivered from sin and death to spend an eternity of blessing enjoying and serving God. Those who continue in sin will one day face God's judgment, after which they will forever experience His wrath. **Publications:** An annual *Catalog* describing IBRI and listing its publications, audio and video cassettes, and speakers bureau. A semiannual *Newsletter* to update members. A series of *Research Reports* (41 to date, 15 in science), which are individual articles 10-35 pages in length. Several books, of which two, *Genesis One and the Origin of the Earth* by Robert C. Newman and Herman J. Eckelmann, *Neglect of Geologic Data:*

Sedimentary Strata Compared with Young-Earth Creationist Writings by Daniel E. Wonderly, and *The Genesis Connection* by John L. Wiester, relate to science. Numerous audio cassettes, including the Summer Theological Institutes at Biblical Seminary, the IBRI Colloquium presentations, the "Dice or Deity" Seminar on Creation and Evolution, and "Models of Special Creation," a seminar debating the age of the earth with representatives of the Institute for Creation Research. IBRI also distributes a number of books, booklets and tracts published by others. **Other Activities:** IBRI sponsors a monthly colloquium series held at Biblical Theological Seminary during the school year, occasional seminars on origins and Christian evidences, and provides a speakers bureau for presentations to churches, colleges and other interested groups. IBRI also makes limited donations of its literature to groups engaged in evangelism and apologetics.

Internationales Wissenschaftsforum der Universität Heidelberg (IWH)

Brief Description: The Internationales Wissenschaftsforum der Universität Heidelberg is a center for intradisciplinary and interdisciplinary exchange of knowledge through symposia and discussion groups. The IWH is particularly concerned with furthering the discussion of new research and perspectives. **Director:** Professor Drs. Dietrich Ritschl **Address:** Internationales Wissenschaftsforum, Hauptstrasse 242, 69117 Heidelberg, Germany. **Telephone:** 06221-165833 **Fax:** 06221-165896 **Date of Founding:** 1986 **Purpose:** The IWH is a center for international conferences in the sciences and humanities. Approximately 12 symposia and colloquia are held on specific themes per year. There are also approximately 30 interdisciplinary colloquia per year. **Organizational Structure:** The officers are appointed by the University; The officers are also paid by the University (the director operates on an honorary basis without salary). **Current Officers:** Director, Professor Dietrich Ritschl, Ph.D., D.D.; Manager, Theresa Reiter, Dr.rer.nat.; Secretary, Mrs. Gudrun Strehlow; Mrs. Doris Hirsch. **Special Projects and Conferences:** Any faculty member is entitled to organize a symposium. The application is examined by a board of 12 professors (of various disciplines) and the Rector of the University. For instance, the Center of Theological Inquiry in Princeton held a symposium with Prof. Torrance and scientists at the Heidelberg Wissenschaftsforum in 1987. **Number of Resident Fellows:** Guest lecturers and participants are in residence during symposia only (room for 19). **Publications:** Most of the proceedings of the symposia are published in book form. **Physical Assets:** 1 large building: 3 office rooms, 4 seminar rooms, bedrooms for 11; and as part of another building there are bedrooms for 8.

The International Society for the Study of Human Ideas on Ultimate Reality and Meaning (ISSURAM or simply URAM)

Brief Description and Background: URAM is an international and interdisciplinary association of professors and experts involved in scientific research with an interest in scrutinizing axiomatic presuppositions operating in various sciences, philosophies, religions and value systems as well as in individuals' personal lives. The URAM assumption is that each science as well as each individual human being: 1) has an ultimate - that to which the human mind reduces and relates everything and that which one does not relate or reduce to anything else; 2) posits a final hermeneutical principle which is not interpreted any further yet in the light of which everything else is interpreted; and 3) accepts a supreme value for which one would sacrifice everything and which one would not lose for anything else, at least for the time being. This is what the idea of ultimate reality and meaning, URAM, means. By studying human ideas on ultimate reality and meaning we touch the deepest mystery, yet the most common constituent of each human being, which differentiates us as well as joins us together. It was in 1967 that the idea was conceived. In 1970 the Institute for Encyclopedia of Human Ideas on Ultimate Reality and Meaning was formed with scholars from numerous fields. In 1976 the Association of Concern for Ultimate Reality and Meaning was incorporated and registered by the Ontario

Government of Canada as a philanthropic, educational and charitable organization. It is a union of men and women who support the URAM project. The International Society was founded in 1985 as an umbrella organization for the Institute, for the Association, and for Regional and Local Divisions. **URAM Headquarters and Information:** Prof. Tibor Horvath, S.J., URAM General Editor, Regis College, 15 St. Mary Street, Toronto, Ontario, M5Y 2R5, Canada. *Prof. Horvath's address for 1994-95 is Fényi Gyula tér 10. Miskilc, 3523- Hungary **Telephone:** (416) 922-2476, or 922-5474 and leave a message. **Fax:** (416) 922-2898 **Purpose of the Society:** The purpose of the Society is to promote interdisciplinary studies and research on human ideas on ultimate reality and on the human effort to find meaning in our world by: 1) Publishing a journal for scholarly studies of human ideas on ultimate reality and meaning; 2) Publishing a newsletter to disseminate information on activities of the Society, to prepare and conduct elections by ballots and to facilitate discussions and less formal exchange of ideas on topics and issues related to URAM questions; 3) Organizing biennial meetings (uneven years in Toronto, Canada, even years in Leuven, Belgium) for the presentation of papers which may be published in the URAM journal and discussing methodological and structural questions in the form of symposia; 4) Collecting, organizing and updating journal articles for publication in an *Encyclopedia of Human Ideas on URAM* and undertaking subsequent periodic revisions thereof; 5) Prompting reflective, structural and systematic research on the ideas presented in the URAM journal and *Encyclopedia*; 6) Establishing and maintaining suitable centers with conferences, halls, library and book collections, to be affiliated with major universities, that shall provide facilities for scholars from different disciplines to meet and work together on projects within the scope of the research program; 7) Developing a model syllabus and introducing URAM Courses for colleges and universities. **Publications:** The first issue of the refereed scholarly journal, *Ultimate Reality and Meaning, Interdisciplinary Studies in the Philosophy of Understanding* was launched in 1978. Since that time the journal appears regularly four times a year. It is administered by the University of Toronto Press, Journals Department, 5201 Dufferin Street, M3H 5TS, Canada. The board of editors is listed on the inside cover of each issue of the URAM journal. **Subscriptions:** In Canada: (individual) $25 + GST Tax; (institutional) $43 + GST Tax; Foreign: (individual) $25 Canadian + $5 for postage and handling; (Institutional) $43 Canadian + $5 for postage and handling. Subscription includes URAM membership. URAM Monographs No. 1. *American Philosophers Ideas of Ultimate Reality and Meaning.* No. 2. *Jesus Christ as Ultimate Reality and Meaning. A Contribution to the Hermeneutics of Counciliar Theology Eternity and Eternal Life. Speculative Theology and Science in Discourse.* Wilfrid Laurier University Press. **Membership:** Membership is open to all who support the purpose of the Society, and is maintained by subscribing to *Ultimate Reality and Meaning*, the journal of the Society. Scholars financially less advantaged, can maintain membership simply by their scholarly contribution. The members of the Board of Directors make a yearly donation of Canadian $100, and the members of the Board of Trustees make a one-time gift of Canadian $5,000. **Organization:** The Society is organized into four research divisions: Humanities and the Arts, Philosophy, Religion, and Science. There are two support divisions - individual and corporate. Supporting university members are Case Western Reserve University, Cleveland, OH, U.S.A.; Concordia University, Montreal, P.Q., Canada; Fordham University, New York, N.Y., U.S.A.; Marquette University, Milwaukee, WI, U.S.A.; Regis College, Federated College of the University of Toronto, Toronto, Ont., Canada; Santa Clara University, Santa Clara, CA, U.S.A.; University of Bonn, Faculty of Catholic Theology, Fundamentaltheologisches Seminar, Bonn, Germany. The governing council consists of elected officers: President, Vice President, President-elect, Secretary, Treasurer, Chairperson of the Board of Trustees, Chairperson of the Board of Directors, and the General Editor. **Regional and Local Divisions:** Among the regional and local divisions are the following: the URAM Committee for Europe (Dr. Raymond Macken, Institute of Philosophy, University of Leuven, Kardinal Mercierplein 2, B-300, Leuven); for Asia (Dr. Gerhold K. Becker, Hong Kong Baptist College, 224 Waterloo Rd., Kowloon, Hong Kong); for Africa (Dr. Olusegun Gbadegesin, Obafemi Awolowo University, Ile-Ife, Nigeria); for South America (Dr.

Yamandu Acosta Roncagliolo, Alarcón 1573, Montevideo, Uruguay); and the local Toronto URAM group (Prof. T. Horvath (1994-95), Fényi Gyula Tér 10. Miskolc, 3523- Hungary).

The Isthmus Institute

Brief Description: The Isthmus Institute mission is to provide a forum for participants to explore the interactions between religious and scientific approaches to reality, so that an increased understanding among people who use these ways of knowing can improve the quality of life for individuals and communities. **Address:** 5956 Sherry Lane, Suite 1221, Dallas, TX 75225, USA. **Telephone:** (214) 987-0795 **Fax:** (214) 987-0796 **Date of Founding:** 1980. **Current Officers:** President, Ruth Tiffany Barnhouse, M.D., Th.M; Secretary/Treasurer, Robert E. Price. (There are slots for 2 vice presidents, but both are vacant at this time). **Organizational Structure:** President, Secretary/Treasurer, 2 vice presidents. Board size varies from 10 to 20 members, meeting monthly. Various committees deal with specific tasks, such as program and speaker selection, but the entire board votes on any decision. Members are chosen for their ability to contribute either to the intellectual and spiritual portion of the Institute's activities, or for their ability to help with fund-raising and other practical matters. An Honorary Advisory Board is chosen mainly from previous speakers. **Special Projects:** For the last 5 years, and for the foreseeable future a theme is chosen for the year. A major weekend conference with 7-9 speakers is held in late April. Speakers are selected partly from among scientists, and partly from among theologians/philosophers. In addition, 3 meetings are held during the year prior to the April conference. These are lectures or workshops, and are on the general theme for the year. Conference themes for past years have been as follows: "The Convergences of Science and Religion" (1983); "Struggles for Order and Freedom" (1984); "The Reach of the Mind" (1985); "Cosmology: Order of the Universe?" (1986); "Free Will vs. Determinism" (1987); "The Universe Within: Consciousness and the Physical World" (1988); "The Dynamics of Harmony: Cooperation and Aggression in Nature and Society" (1989); "Earth Alive: A Gaia View of Earth, Nature and Humankind" (1990); "Can Consciousness Survive Physical Death?" (1991). **Publications:** For the first five years, many lectures were published in *The Perkins Journal* (Southern Methodist University, Perkins School of Theology publication). A collection of the 1982 Isthmus lectures are published as the book: *Nobel Prize Conversations* with Sir John Eccles, Roger Sperry, Ilya Prigogine, and Brian Josephson, with a commentary by Norman Cousins (Dallas: Saybrook Publishing Co., 1985). Audiotapes of most lectures are also available. Among the audiotapes offered are: "The New Dialogue of Man with Nature" (Ilya Prigogine); "Voluntary Movement, Free Will and Moral Responsibility" (Sir John Eccles); "Psychic Research: New Dimensions or Old Delusions?" (Robert G. Jahn); "Cosmology and Creation" (A. R. Peacocke); "The Biology of Being Appropriate" (Lyall Watson); "Creation and Cosmology" (Ian Barbour); "Science and Religion: What Lies Ahead?" (William Harman and Larry Dossey); and "Dialogues with Scientists and Sages: The Search for Unity" (Renee Weber). **Membership:** Basic membership is $100. The Institute has about 150 members, some of whom are not local. Its mailing list is about 3500. Major conferences draw 200-400 people, occasionally more, and many come from out of state.

Karl-Heim-Gesellschaft

Brief Description: The Karl-Heim-Gesellschaft is a society of approximately 80 members and 550 friends who promote the legacy of Karl Heim and hence a Christian orientation within a scientific-technological world through publications, seminars, and lectures. **Address:** Unter den Eichen 13, D-3504 Marburg, Germany. **Phone:** 06421/83129 **Date of Founding:** 1974. **Purpose:** To promote the legacy of Karl Heim and thereby "further a biblical-Christian orientation in a scientific-technological world." The society wants to express Karl Heim's concerns in modern idiom, confronting contemporary issues as they relate to the modern scientific and secular worldview. **Organizational Structure:** The up to 11 members of the Governing Board including a president, two vice presidents, secretary, and treasurer are elected at the membership meeting for an initial 4-year term. Their elections can be renewed. Every two years there is a membership meeting to which the members are invited in writing by the president. The Yearbook is edited by Prof. Dr. Hans Schwarz (Regensburg), in conjunction with an advisory board consisting of Prof. Dr. Peter Cornelius Hägele (Pfaffenhofen/Roth), Prof. Drs. Rainer Mayer (Stuttgart), and Dr. Christoph Wassermann (Weil am Rhein). The editorial board of the semiannual *Evangelium und Wissenschaft* consists of StD i. K. OStR Wolfgang Doerk (Pforzheim), Dr. Erastos Filos (Brussels), The Rev. Hermann Hafner (Marburg), and OStR Oskar Kalisch (Villingen-Schwenningen). **Current Officers:** President, Wolfgang Doerk (Pforzheim); Vice Presidents: Prof. Dr. Hans Schwarz (Regensburg) and Dr. Reinhard Küspert (Rheinstetten); Treasurer, The Rev. Reinhard Wettach (Pforzheim); Secretary, The Rev. Hermann Hafner (Marburg). **Special Projects and Conferences:** The Society maintains the archives of Karl Heim's writings and related literature; publishes the Yearbook of the Karl-Heim-Gesellschaft, *Glaube und Denken*; publishes *Evangelium und Wissenschaft* (usually a semiannual publication for friends and members); disseminates Heim's works; conducts seminars on topics relating to theology and science for both lay persons and experts. Lectures by members are conducted on demand. **Membership:** Annual membership dues are DM 50. Friends are encouraged to contribute voluntarily. Membership will be extended on application. **Publications:** Yearbook, *Glaube und Denken*, Vol. 1- (Moers: Brendow, since 1988); *Evangelium und Wissenschaft* (Marburg: Karl-Heim-Gesellschaft, since 1980); Video movie: *Karl Heim. Denker evangelischen Glaubens* (Marburg: Karl-Heim-Gesellschaft, 1988) with a printed booklet. **Physical Assets:** The Karl Heim archive is located in the Albrecht-Bengel-Haus (Dr. Rolf Hille), Ludwig-Krapf-Str. 5, D-72072 Tübingen; Secretariat, Unter den Eichen 13, D-3504 Marburg.

Katholiek Studiecentrum (KSC) (Catholic Study Center of the Catholic University of Nijmegen)

Brief Description: The task of the KSC is to promote within the Catholic University of Nijmegen the study of subjects in which the relation between science and Christian inspiration is relevant. Also it is a task of the KSC to promote the study of subjects that relate to the catholic part of the nation. KSC organizes several study groups, congresses, and symposia. **Officers:** Prof. Dr. B. M. F. van Iersel, President of the Steering Committee; Drs. G. P. A. Dierick, Secretary of the Steering Committee. **Address:** University Nijmegen, Erasmuslaan 36, 6525 GG Nijmegen, The Netherlands. **Telephone:** 09-31-80-612414 **Date of Founding:** February 1977 **Publications:** KSC has overseen the publication of 44 books, including *Kunstmatige voortplanting en de status van het embryo* (Artificial Insemination and the Status of the Embryo), (Nijmegen, 1988), and *Aids. Medische, ethinsche en maatschappelijke aspecten* (Aids. Medical, Ethical and Social Aspects), (Nijmegen-Kampen, 1989). KSC also publishes a periodical (Quarterly) *Erasmusplein* since 1990.

Nova Spes

Brief Description: Nova Spes is an international foundation whose aim is the promotion of qualitative human development realized on the basis of fundamental values. Nova Spes seeks to overcome the problem of cultural fragmentation by means of an operative alliance of the four forces that animate the human personality: belief, knowledge, production, and communication. **Founder and President:** Cardinal Franz König, Archbishop emeritus of Vienna. **Address:** Nova Spes General Secretariat, Via Di Villa Emiliani 10, 00197 Rome, Italy. **Telephone:** 06/804369 **Purpose and Objectives:** Nova Spes is a cultural action aimed at activating a process of transformation of contemporary life through the elaboration five alternative proposals: 1) The Humanism of New Hope which is based on the "unity of the person"; 2) The Operational Alliance of Religion, Science, Communication, and Economy as a new method for interpreting and tackling, in a global approach, the problems of the development of the person and of society; 3) The ethical recomposition of the individual and society around fundamental human values; 4) A new order of interpersonal and social relationships based on the "co-possibility of differences"; and 5) A culture based on the primacy of "being." Nova Spes is a meeting point for the representatives of the forces of Religion, of Science, of Communication, and of Economics, with whom it intends to promote this new development. The Foundation is also an organization which operates on a central and territorial level with the collaboration of those people who identify with its aims and with the cooperation of other Organizations, for the attainment of common aims. In June 1986, Nova Spes sponsored "An Alliance for Man" conference in Rome marking the dawn of an operative phase for the Foundation. At that time initiatives were outlined to promote the recovery of global man through the interaction between religion, science, communication, and economy. **Publications:** The Foundation publishes a quarterly periodical of cultural information entitled, *Nova Spes Letter*. A number of studies, research, presentations, and addresses connected with the Foundation are also available. A catalogue may be obtained from the above address.

The Park Ridge Center

Brief Description: The Park Ridge Center For the Study of Health, Faith, and Ethics is an interreligious, multidisciplinary institute for research, discovery and publication. The Center functions as an international forum for experts in health care, religion and ethics, and as a resource for information on religion and bioethics. **Address:** 676 N. St. Clair, Suite 450, Chicago, IL 60611. **Organizational Structure:** The Park Ridge Center has a Board of Directors and a Council of Academic Advisors. The Board of Directors is constituted by the following: George B. Caldwell; Michael D. Carver; Candida Lund (Chair); Martin E. Marty; Laurence J. O'Connell (ex officio); Daniel S. Schechter (Vice Chair); Robert A. Stein; and Stephen L. Ummel (ex officio). The Council of Academic Advisors consists of Don S. Browning (Chair); Karen A. Lebacqz; Richard A. McCormick; and Daniel Rudman. **Publications and Membership:** The Park Ridge Center entitles its journal, *Second Opinion*. As its name implies, the complexities of modern health care make it increasingly difficult to find the single "correct" action, thought, or method. Each situation is open to a variety of apparently legitimate and appropriate interpretations and applications. By inviting contributions from a wide range of perspectives, *Second Opinion* stimulates interdisciplinary conversations between members of fields relating to health, faith, and ethics. While other publications deal with one or two of these concerns, *Second Opinion* distinctively seeks to address all three. The Center created the journal in the hope that it will help form one public out of a number of related constituencies. *Second Opinion* is published every March, July, and November. The membership/subscription fee is $35 for one year, $65 for two years, and $95 for three years. Subscribers also receive the *Bulletin of the Park Ridge Center* (published three times a year) and discounts on selected Center books and periodicals. The editor of *Second Opinion* is Martin E. Marty.

The Pascal Centre for Advanced Studies in Faith and Science

Brief Description of Objectives: The Pascal Centre has several objectives: 1) To study and develop the implications of the Biblical teaching on creation for understanding the origin and nature of the physical and biological worlds. 2) To express, in the light of Scripture, the relationships between theology, philosophy and the natural sciences. 3) To conduct research in line with the Pascal Centre's goals, in the fields of philosophy, theology, history of science, mathematics, psychology, anthropology, and the natural sciences, both theoretical and experimental. 4) To promote an awareness among Christians that a Biblical approach to scholarship in the natural sciences goes beyond the examination of ethical and social issues to include bringing our knowledge of the subject matter itself under the lordship of Christ. 5) To serve like-minded Christians worldwide by communicating the work of the Pascal Centre through various publications. **Director:** Dr. Jitse van der Meer **Address:** Redeemer College, 777 Highway 53 East, Ancaster, Ontario, L9K 1J4, Canada. **Telephone:** (905) 648-2131 **Fax:** (905) 648-2134 **E-mail:** erewhon!JMVDM@maccs.dcss.mcmaster.ca (or) ere-whon%JMVDM@maccs.dcss.mcmaster.ca **Date of Founding:** June 1, 1988. **Special Projects and Conferences:** 1) Pascal Centre Academic Seminar Series features scholars each year on a variety of topics. 2) A philosophy of science research project analyzing the levels of complexity model for the relation between belief and the natural sciences (Dr. J. van der Meer). 3) A philosophy of science research project developing a formal vocabulary for identifying artifacts of design and distinguishing them from the products of natural science, and justifying the design hypothesis both as a scientifically acceptable theory and as the best scientific explanation of biological complexity (Drs. Stephen Meyer, William Dembski and Paul Nelson). 4) A history of science and hermeneutics research project analyzing the interaction of cosmology and the Bible in early modern Protestant Europe using original data and analyses of prominent Dutch and German scientists and theologians (Dr. Kenneth Howell).**Publications:** The Pascal Centre publishes a quarterly newsletter, *Pascal Centre Notebook*, which began publication in July 1990. The Pascal Centre is currently preparing a three-volume edited book manuscript *Facets of Faith and Science* (anticipated publication in 1995) by the University Press of America. **Physical Assets:** The Pascal Centre is affiliated with Redeemer College and shares its facilities. **Organizational Structure:** The Pascal Centre for Advanced Studies in Faith and Science is administered by its Advisory Council. Ordinary membership on the Advisory Council is by nomination, interview and appointment for a three-year term with possibility of renewal. **Advisory Council:** The Pascal Centre is administered by its advisory council consisting of: Ms. Lynda J. Cockroft, Administrative Assistant, Secretary of the Advisory Council and Managing Editor of the *Notebook*; Mr. Lloyd Hack, vice president (administration and finance), Redeemer College; Mr. Clarence Joldersma, Smithville Christian High School, Smithville, Ontario and Ph.D. candidate at the Ontario Institute for Studies in Education, Toronto, Ontario; Dr. Jitse M. van der Meer, Director, Chair of Advisory Council (Professor of Biology, Redeemer College); Dr. Wytse van Dijk, acting vice president (academic) and professor of Physics and Mathematics, Redeemer College. **Administrative Officers:** Dr. Jitse van der Meer, Director; Ms. Lynda J. Cockroft, Administrative Assistant.

Person, Culture and Religion (a group of the American Academy of Religion)

Brief Description: Person, Culture and Religion (PCR) is an affiliated scholarly society of the American Academy of Religion (AAR). PCR is an international network of over 200 scholars working in the fields of religion and psychology, broadly defined, who share common interests in the relationship between religion, psychology and contemporary culture. **Secretary:** Professor John McDargh **Address:** Department of Theology, Boston College, Chestnut Hill, MA 02167 **Telephone:** (617) 552-3880 **Date of Founding:** 1986 **Purpose and Activities:** The primary purpose of PCR is to foster creative research in the fields of the Group's interest, both academic and applied, to encourage the creative exchange of ideas and to provide within the AAR a forum for the discussion of the issues raised by these intellectual projects. The Group meets officially once a year at the annual meeting of the AAR. In addition to a session arranged within the Religion and Social Sciences unit of the AAR, for the last six years the PCR has also conducted a Pre-Session program meeting the day before the beginning of the AAR proper. **Organizational Structure:** The work of maintaining PCR, coordinating with the AAR, selecting conference papers, setting an agenda and mailing its newsletter is done by a steering committee whose members serve for terms of two years. **Publications and Dues:** Between yearly meetings PCR members maintain contact with one another through a newsletter published three times a year. Annual dues that cover the mailing of the newsletter and a premailing of conference papers are $10 a year ($12 Canadian). For further information one may contact the PCR Secretary.

The Polanyi Society

Brief Description: *The Polanyi Society* of North America is an association of persons interested in pursuing solutions or approaches to the crisis of culture precipitated by the objectivist outlook of the modern mind. It aims to encourage and to promote original research into the nature of knowing as it affects all areas of human endeavor and especially as it is understood in the fields of disciplined inquiry. It seeks particularly to further exploration and development of the direction of thought, toward a post-critical philosophy, suggested in the writing of Michael Polanyi (scientist, philosopher, and educator, 1891-1976). In the spirit of Polanyi's concept of "a society of explorers," it seeks more to work for the discovery of ways beyond the dichotomies of body and mind, spirit and matter, and faith and reason than to limit itself to one person's thought. **Director:** Richard Gelwick, Th.D. **Address:** University of New England, 11 Hills Beach Road, Biddeford, Maine 04005-9599, USA. **Phone:** (207) 283-0171; Fax # (207) 283-3249. **Date of Founding:** 1972 **Goals and Objectives:** Exploration of the thought of Michael Polanyi and its implications for our time; Development of interchange with others pursuing similar inquiry towards a post-critical philosophy. The Polanyi Society functions primarily as an information network for persons sharing in these aims, and as a way for conferences, gatherings at professional meetings, and publications to be furthered. **Current Officers:** General coordinator, Richard Gelwick; Religious studies coordinator, David Rutledge, Art studies coordinator, Douglas Adams; Education Studies coordinator, Ray Wilkin; Philosophical studies coordinator, Martha Crunkleton; Rhetorical studies coordinator, Sam Watson; Medical studies coordinator, Allen Dyer. **Organizational Structure:** Officers are selected by a conference of members, and appointed by the General Committee of the Society. **Membership Classifications and Dues:** Regular members, dues $20 per year; Student members, dues $10 per year. Currently the Society has 350 members. **Activities:** 1. Satellite meetings are held at various professional conferences, such as the American Academy of Religion, and the Modern Language Association meetings, etc. 2. Occasional National Conferences. 3. Occasional Summer Seminars. **Publications:** The 40 page periodical *Tradition and Discovery* is published twice a year in the Winter and Spring [see separate entry]. Occasional Newsletters are also circulated. Besides the association in North America, there is an association in Great Britain which also publishes its articles and news in *Tradition and Discovery.*

Pope John XXIII Medical-Moral Research and Education Center

Brief Description: The Pope John Center was established as an independent organization to identify, study and respond to the moral and ethical issues confronting health care in the fast developing sciences and technology. The Center's responses are based on traditional Judeo-Christian values and Catholic teaching. **Address:** 186 Forbes Road, Braintree, MA 02184, USA. **Phone:** (617) 848-6965 **Fax:** (617) 849-1309 **Date of Founding:** 1972 **Chief Executive Officer:** Fr. Russell E. Smith, S. T. D., President **Projects and Activities:** The Pope John XXIII Center sponsors workshops for clergy, health care workers, physicians, nurses, and teachers. Consultation service is offered to clergy, physicians, hospitals, clinics and nursing homes. Visiting scholars, fellows and interns are in residence at the Center offices for various lengths of time throughout the year. Program length and course content is on an individual basis with the staff, and through grand-rounds in local universities and hospitals. **Publication:** *Ethics & Medics* is a monthly newsletter, with guest and staff contributors under the direction of the Editor, Fr. David Beauregard, O. T. V. The Center also publishes books related to the field of medicine and health care ethics, and also publishes the proceedings of an annual Bishops' Workshop. **Organizational Structure:** A board of directors establishes policy and reviews finances. The Center is headed by a President, CEO who is responsible to the board of directors. The President is selected through a board appointed search committee, interviewed and selected by the board of trustees. The main office of the Pope John XXIII Center is located in Braintree, MA with 6 staff members and one or two interns. For Harvard University Divinity students and, through the Harvard program, for other students enrolled in Boston Theological Institute schools, the Pope John Center serves as an accredited field education site. **Membership:** Yearly Institutional Membership - $350, entitles a member to copies of books published that year and multiple copies of the newsletter *Ethics & Medics*, as well as consultation services; Yearly Individual Membership - $100, entitles a member to copies of books published that year, a subscription to the *Ethics & Medics* newsletter, and Consultation services for one year; Individual subscriptions to the monthly newsletter *Ethics & Medics* are available for $15.00 per year, $28.00 for 2 years and $41.00 for 3 years. Subscriptions outside the USA are $18.00 for 1 year, $33.00 for 2 years and $48.00 for 3 years.

Psychological Centre for Comparative Mysticism (PSYCOM)

Brief Description: PSYCOM is an organization registered under the Government of India's Act for Registration of Societies, XXI of 1860. The basic consideration in establishing the PSYCOM has been the conviction that through the comparative study of morality and of religious themes across societies and cultures, it is possible to appreciate the interrelatedness of human values and discern new directions for change in technologically-dominated and consumption-oriented societies. **President:** Professor (Dr.) H. C. Ganguli, Fellow, Indian National Science Academy. **Address:** PSYCOM, F 8/13 Model Town, Delhi - 110 009, India. **Telephone:** (011) 7226080 **Date and Place of Founding:** August, 1988, Delhi. **Purpose and Objectives:** When first established the emphasis of PSYCOM was on studies of the psychological dimensions of mystical experience and meditation. However, the PSYCOM is gradually shifting more toward studies on moral values and moral order. **Organizational Structure:** PSYCOM has an Executive Committee and a Council. The Executive Committee consists of three to seven members. The Council consists of Founding Members and Honorary Members who have voting rights. Besides these, there is provision for Patrons, Members and Affiliate Members. Patrons can be persons or organizations. The Honorary Secretary is: Ms. Manju Banerjee, M.A., B.Ed. (Psychologist). PSYCOM is a new and dynamic organization and is still evolving. **Publications:** PSYCOM has no journal of its own. It publishes its research papers in scientific journals in India and abroad. Over the last ten years, the current president of PSYCOM has published articles on the following: meditation programs in Canada; motivation of members and drug use (in *Human Relations* of London); values and moral education (in *UNESCO Handbook for the Teaching of Social Studies)*; non-violence as an attitude-behavior principle (in *Social Change*, New Delhi); considerations for the development of a moral order (in the *Indian Journal of Social Work*, Bombay); religion and contraception (Chapter in his book, *Behavioral Research in Sexuality*, New Delhi, 1988); and teaching about values (in the *Indian Journal of Social Work*, 1990). The last conference the president attended was a Workshop on Research in Sexuality at Ottawa and the 5th International AIDS Conference at Montreal (1989). PSYCOM currently publishes two books: *Job Satisfaction: Scales for Effective Management* and *Industrial Worker: Psychological Studies*. **Current Project:** Moral Persuasion: Conditions of Success and Failure. (An Analysis of Gandhi's Actions for Improving Hindu-Muslim Relations).

The Reilly Center for Science, Technology, and Values

Brief Description: The University of Notre Dame's Center for Science, Technology and Values (The Reilly Center) is an endowed program of the University with two major emphases. First, it provides material resources and administrative support for three interdisciplinary academic programs: an undergraduate Concentration Program in Science, Technology, and Values; a Ph.D. Program in History and Philosophy of Science; and a Five Year Double Degree Program in Arts and Letters & Engineering. Secondly, it provides a focus for faculty research in the various fields of "science studies" through support of frequent visiting speakers, conferences and symposia, a publication series in Science and the Humanities that appears from the Notre Dame Press, and through the hosting of visiting scholars at the Center. **Director:** Rev. Ernan McMullin, O'Hara Professor of Philosophy. **Address:** 309 O'Shaughnessy Hall, University of Notre Dame, Notre Dame, IN 46556. **Telephone:** (219) 239-5015 **Date of Founding:** June 13, 1985. **Purpose of the Center:** The Center seeks to contribute through research and teaching to the improved understanding of science and technology as complex human practices and powerful social institutions in the modern world, with particular emphasis on their social, historical and philosophical dimensions. In each of these areas significant value questions quickly come to the fore, and the term 'Values' is incorporated into the Center's name to give proper recognition to this fact. The range of relevant value concerns is broad, including religious, theological, aesthetic, and sociopolitical issues, as well as properly ethical ones. Through teaching, publications, and its other public activities the Center seeks to give prominence to the multifaceted value dimensions of science and technology. Current information about the activities of the Center is disseminated through the *Reilly Center Newsletter* sent annually to nearly a thousand faculty, alumni, students and colleagues in other institutions. **Conferences:** To date the Center has hosted four major research conferences, "The Shaping of Scientific Rationality" (1986), "Philosophical Lessons from Quantum Mechanics?" (1987), and "The Social Dimensions of Science" (1989), and "The Origins of the Human Sciences" (1991). **Publications:** All conference proceedings are available as volumes in the series: Studies in Science and the Humanities from the Reilly Center for Science, Technology and Values, published through the University of Notre Dame Press.

Science and Religion Forum

Brief Description: Was founded in 1972 to enable conversations between scientists, theologians and clergy who wished to relate their scientific knowledge and methods of study to religious faith and practice. The Forum itself was formally inaugurated at a meeting in Durham in 1975. **Address:** 155 Almond Street, Derby, DE23 6LY, UK. **Phone:** Derby (01332) 766603 **Fax:** Derby (01332) 270837 **Current Officers:** President, The Archbishop of York, The Most Revd. & Rt. Hon. Dr. J. S. Habgood; Vice President, Dr. Arthur Peacocke; Chairman, Professor Russell Stannard, The Open University; Secretary, The Revd. Dr. Michael W. S. Parsons; Treasurer and Membership Secretary, The Revd. Phillip Edwards, St. Albans Vicarage, Mercer Avenue, Coventry CV2 4PQ; Editor of *Reviews*, Dr. Peter E. Hodgson, Corpus Christi College, Oxford OX1 4JF. **Date of Founding:** 1972, 1975. **Activities of the Forum:** The Forum organizes an annual conference for the exchange of ideas between members and invited speakers. Papers from these conferences are usually published (see below). There is also opportunity at the conference for members to present their own short papers. The Forum also publishes a journal, *Reviews*, twice a year, which includes reviews of recent literature of interest in the field. **Membership:** Membership of the Forum is open to all interested in relating scientific knowledge and religious faith and practice and the membership currently stands at about 300, around half of whom are scientists. To join please send your subscription to the Membership Secretary and Treasurer. The annual subscription is £7, £3.50 for fulltime students, or £10 outside of UK. The membership year runs from January to December. **Some Details of Past Conferences of the Forum (plus publication information where provided):** 1976 (Windsor), "Man's Responsibility for Nature." *Zygon* 13, 3 (1977); 1977 (Leeds), "Science and Religion, Partners in Education." *Crucible* (Spring 1978); 1978 (Bristol), "God's Action in the World." *Epworth Review* (Sept., 1978 and later issues); 1979 (Cambridge), "Technology was made for Man — and Man for?" *Crucible* (April/June 1980), and *Epworth Review* (Sept. 1980); 1980 (Manchester), "New Perspectives on Man." 1981 (Oxford), "The Theologians take Account of Developments in Science." *Epworth Review* (Sept., 1982); 1982 (Guildford),

"Cosmos and Creation - the Physicists View." *Irish Astronomical Journal* 15, 3 (March, 1982); 1983 (Durham), "The Challenge of Sociobiology to Ethics and Theology." *Zygon* 19, 2 (1984); 1984 (Canterbury), "From Artificial Intelligence to Human Consciousness." *Zygon* 20, 4 (1985); 1985 (Oxford), "In the Beginning: the Science and Pseudo-science of Creation." *Zygon* 22, 2 (1987); 1986 (Nottingham),"Science & Religion: Philosophical and Historical Aspects of the Dialogue." 1987 (Winchester), "Wholeness and Holiness: Freud, Jung and God." 1988 (Liverpool), "Tradition and Authority in Science and Religion." 1989 (Hoddesdon), " 'Could do Better' Educational Perspectives on Science and Religion." 1990 (Hoddesdon), "God, Time and the New Physics." 1991 (Durham), "God's Action in the World." 1992 (Durham), "Science and Religion from Feud to Reconciliation." 1993 (Hoddesden), "Questions about Ecology."

Scienza e Fede

Brief Description: The association aims: a) at furthering the knowledge and discussion among its members, who mainly are scientists, on theoretical and cultural issues which have some relevance for a religious world view; b) at providing its members with opportunities for meditation and spiritual growth. **Address:** Via Antonio Pisano 33, 56123 Pisa, Italia. **Telephone:** 050/560588 **Date of Founding:** 197.7 **Current officers:** Giovanni Prodi. **Organizational Structure:** The association, according to its "amateurish" nature, is purposely lacking an official structure. Typically its activity hinges on a collective decision at each periodic meeting about the agenda of the next one, followed by the organizational work done by a small group of members, who fix the program and contact possible speakers, often not members of the association. **Conferences:** The association meets every six months for a weekend. The association takes no part in external or extra activities, though many of its members are engaged in similar local activities in their own cities. **Membership:** There is no official membership to the association. It rests on a network of private communications, and participation in the meetings is open to any interested person. Most of the members are university professors. **Size of Organization:** The association numbers about 100 members, among them a core of about 30 long-time members.

Society for Health and Human Values (SHHV)

Brief Description: The Society for Health and Human Values is an international organization of over 800 members dedicated to promoting the inclusion of humanities disciplines in the curricula and educational ambiance of health professional schools. This is cultivated through such activities as publications and national meetings of the Society, which offer formal programs, workshops, and the opportunity for informal interdisciplinary consultations and discussions. **Address:** 6728 Old McLean Village Drive, McLean, VA 22101, USA. **Date of Founding:** 1969 from an ad hoc committee formed in 1963 to explore questions of human values in medical education. **Current Officers:** President, Rita Charon, MD; President-elect, David Barnard, PhD; Treasurer, Robert Arnold, MD; Past President, Ruth Purtilo, PhD. **Purpose:** The purposes of SHHV are to encourage consideration of issues in human values as they relate to health services, the education of health care professionals, and research; to conduct educational meetings dealing with such issues; and to stimulate research in areas of such concern. **Organizational Structure:** General supervision, control and direction of the affairs of the Society are the responsibility of the Council which consists of between 7 and 9 members of the Society, plus the officers of the Society and other elected members. **Council Members include:** Warren Reich, STD; Joy D. Skeel, MDiv; Julia E. Connely, MD; George A Kanoti, STD. **Special Activities and Conferences:** Annual Society Award, Annual Meeting each fall, Spring National Meeting; devising a computer system for the networking of members; liaison with other organizations; involving students; developing handbooks in history, humanities, religion, literature, dentistry, social work, evaluation, allied health, funding, tenure issues, clinical ethics, and research; cataloging curriculum resources; and identifying foreign travel support. The Society also includes the following sections and interest groups: Directors of Humanities/Human Values Programs in Medical Education; Association for Faculty in the Medical Humanities; Residency Interest Group; Ministry in Health Care Education; Nursing and Humanities Section; Dentistry Interest Group; Allied Health Interest Group; Student Interest Group. **Publications:** *The Bulletin*, the newsletter of the Society, is published 5 times per year. *Medical Humanities Review* is the official journal of the Society. SHHV offers its own publications and a selection of other publications at a discount to its members. Among the titles available are: William R. Rogers and David Barnard, eds. *Nourishing the Humanities in Medicine: Interactions with the Social Sciences.* University of Pittsburgh Press, 1979. Donald W. Shriver, Jr., ed. *Medicine & Religion: Strategies of Care.* University of Pittsburgh Press, 1980. Geri Berg, ed. *The Visual Arts and Medical Education.* Southern Illinois University Press, 1983. J. Ivey Boufford, MD, and R. A. Carson, MD, et al. *The Teaching of Humanities and Human Values in Primary Care Residency Training.* SHHV, 1984. D. C. Duncombe. *Ministers in Medical Education.* 5th ed. SHHV and The United Ministries in Higher Education. Delese Wear, Martin Kohn and Susan Stocker, eds. *Literature and Medicine: A Claim for a Discipline.* SHHV, 1987. Eric T. Juengst and Barbara A. Koenig, eds. *Studies in Health and Human Values Vol. 1: The Meaning of AIDS: Implications for Medical Science, Clinical Practice and Public Health Policy.* Praeger Press, 1989. Chris Hackler, R. Moseley and Dorothy E. Vawter, eds. *Studies in Health and Human Values Vol. 2: Advance Directives in Medicine.* Praeger Press, 1989. Available on videocassette: *CBS News, Face the Nation* on "Baby Jane Doe," 3/4" color videocassette format only; *Hospital Ethics Committee*, 3/4" color videocassette format only. **Membership:** SHHV is composed of persons having a substantial interest in human values issues as these relate to the education and practice of the health professions and to health science research. Membership is initiated by the individual and is contingent on payment of annual membership dues.

The Society of Christian Philosophers

Brief Description: The Society of Christian Philosophers is an association of nearly 1100 members representing a wide variety of denominations, theological perspectives, and philosophical orientations. **Address:** c/o Kelly J. Clark, Secretary, Department of Philosophy, Calvin College, 3201 Burton Street SE, Grand Rapids, MI 49546-4388, USA. **Date of Founding:** 1978 **Purpose:** The purpose of the Society is to promote fellowship among Christian philosophers and to stimulate study and discussion of issues which arise from their joint Christian and philosophical commitments. The Society seeks to achieve this by publishing a journal, *Faith and Philosophy*, holding meetings in conjunction with professional societies, and sponsoring workshops and conferences. **Organizational Structure:** The Society is governed by a President, a Secretary-Treasurer, and an Executive Committee consisting of 12 elected members, the retired President, and the Editor of *Faith and Philosophy*. **Current Officers:** President, Nicholas Wolterstorff; Secretary-Treasurer, Kelly J. Clark. Officers and Executive Committee members must be members in good standing of the Society and are elected to three-year terms. Candidates are chosen by a Nominating Committee, selected annually by the President. **Special Projects:** The Society sponsors regular meetings in conjunction with the Eastern, Central and Pacific Divisions of the American Philosophical Association, the Canadian Philosophical Association, and, less regularly, with the American Catholic Philosophical Association. There is a Pacific Regional Conference during the winter, and Eastern Regional Conference in the spring, and a Midwestern Regional Conference in the fall. A number of workshops have been sponsored or cosponsored by the Society. **Membership:** Membership is open to any person who classifies himself/herself as both a philosopher and a Christian; membership is not restricted to professional philosophers. Regular membership, $25 per year; Student or unemployed, $15 per year. Dues include a subscription to *Faith and Philosophy*. **Publications:** The Society publishes a quarterly journal called *Faith and Philosophy* which commenced in 1984. Philip L. Quinn (Notre Dame) is Editor, assisted by Alfred Freddoso (Notre

Dame). Michael Peterson (Asbury College) is Managing Editor. The journal is designed primarily for articles which address philosophical issues from a Christian perspective, for discussions of philosophical issues which arise within the Christian faith, and for articles from any perspective which deal critically with the philosophical credentials of the Christian faith. **Executive Committee:** C. Stephan Evans, David Basinger, Peg Falls-Corbitt, Jane Mary Trau, Lynn Rudden Baker, Jean Hampton, Arthur F. Holmes, William J. Wainwright, Thomas P. Flint, Julius M. Moraucsik, Patricia Sayre, Frederick Suppe.

Society of Ordained Scientists

Brief Description: The Society of Ordained Scientists is a fellowship of scientists within the ordained ministry who meet for support and the furtherance of service in their scientific and spiritual endeavor. **Secretary:** The Rev. Dr. Richard L. Hills **Address:** Stamford Cottage, 47 Old Rd., Mottram Hyde, Cheshire SK14 GLW, UK **Date of Founding:** 1987 **Purpose and Rule:** The five aims of the Society of Ordained Scientists are: 1) To offer to God in their ordained role the work of science in the exploration and stewardship of creation; 2) To express both the commitment of the Church to the scientific enterprise and concern for its impact on the world; 3) To develop a fellowship of prayer for ordained scientists by the following of a common Rule; 4) To support each other in their vocation; and 5) To serve the Church in its relation to science and technology. The Rule is as follows: 1) To pray for the aims of the Society and for its members; 2) To remember the Society and its members monthly at public worship; and 3) To endeavour to attend the annual gathering and retreat of the Society. **Organizational Structure:** The Society has three officers. The Visitor is a bishop in the Anglican Communion who admits members to the Society and who makes a final decision in matters of the interpretation or application of the rules of the Society. The Warden of the Society exercises pastoral oversight over the members, convenes and chairs meetings, consults with members, and initiates actions with members' consent. The Secretary of the Society facilitates communication between members and handles all finances. **Membership:** The Society originates as a community of scientists within the ordained ministry (men and women) of the Anglican Communion but membership is open to ordained members of any other church willing, if they are permitted, to further the Aims of the Society and to obey its Rule and Constitution. The designation "scientist" is intended to refer to those who have some measure of experience of science and technology at a professional level. Members make a commitment in the form of an avowal to pursue the Aims of the Society and to obey its Rule and Constitution, before, if possible, the Visitor in the context of a Eucharist at which the Visitor presides during the annual gathering of the Society. **Finances:** There is a minimum annual subscription paid to the Secretary of £20.

Society, Religion and Technology Project (SRT)

Description: The Society, Religion and Technology Project is a project of the Church of Scotland which exists to open up the processes of technical and social change to Christian scrutiny. It seeks an informed understanding of the technical and social forces which both shape the future and are shaped by the future. Its goal is primarily to contribute to society and its processes, in particular in the technological areas of expertise of the current director. It has a further objective which is to develop a theology for a technological society. It contributes to the work of the churches by participating in their main committees and acting as a technological think-tank for the church. **Director:** Dr. David J. Pullinger, BA MSc, PhD, MErgS. **Address:** 121 George Street, Edinburgh, Scotland EH2 4YN, UK. **Phone:** +31 225 5722 **Fax:** +31 220 3113 **Date of Founding:** 1970. **Organizational Structure:** The SRT Project has a Director, appointed for between 3-6 years, who is expected to be at the cutting edge of some technological discipline. It has secretarial support within the Church of Scotland and a budget whereby to commission books, papers and work necessary to fulfil its objectives. SRT has an advisory committee with Dr. John Francis as its Chairman. It reports to its funding body, the Church of Scotland, through the Board of National Mission. **Physical Assets:** At present the Project forms part of the headquarters of the Church of Scotland in Edinburgh. But in 1991 a move is planned to John Knox House, where there will be rooms for conferences and additional research fellows and staffing. **Membership:** Anyone interested in the work of the Project is encouraged to contact the Project and participate in whatever way is mutually agreed upon. **Major Projects:** There have been five main strands in the 20 years of work: a) energy issues; b) environmental issues, including pollution; c) social issues such as changing work patterns and an ethical guide to social security; d) defence and disarmament; e) and general technological and ethical values. **Selection of SRT Project Publications:** (Available from SRT) John Francis and Paul Abrecht, editors, *Facing up to Nuclear Power* (Saint Andrew Press, 1976), preparatory papers and report of the WCC's hearing on Nuclear Power at Sigtuna, Sweden, 1975 (£0.25); *Faslane - Facts and Feelings* (SRT, 1981), a study and record of people's attitudes and feelings with regard to nuclear arms and defence policies, presented to the 1981 WCC public hearings on Nuclear Weapons and Disarmament (£1.25); *Against the Grain* (SRT, 1982), a pamphlet which raises questions about the methods and purposes of our agriculture and its effects on other parts of the world (£0.50); Howard Davis and David Gosling, editors, *Will the Future Work?* (SRT/WCC Church & Society, 1985), exploring ways in which the church can make an informed and practical response in a time of rapid change, focussing on declining industrial areas as well as new industries like micro-electronics (£3.75); *While the Earth Endures*. SRT, 1986, a theological view of how we consider the difficult questions in afforestation, pollution and agriculture today (£2.95); Howard Davis, ed. *Ethics and Defence*. Basil Blackwell, 1986, an integrated collection of essays by an ecumenical and multidisciplinary study group, available from the publisher (£7.95); David J. Pullinger, ed. *With Scorching Heat and Drought?* SRT/ Saint Andrew Press, 1989, a set of essays on the Greenhouse Effect, introducing the scientific background and assumptions that have led to the predictions of atmospheric warming and containing policy and theological responses, available from Saint Andrew Press (£2.95); Helen Alexander. *Genetic Engineering*. SRT, 1989, a discussion paper summarizing what others have written on the problems of manipulation of DNA and the current legislation being considered in Europe and the UK (£1.50). **Audio Visual Materials:** *Not in my Back Yard*, A video on pollution and a call to prevent unnecessary damage to the environment; *While the Earth Endures*, A video split into two halves, the first on visual presentation of a poem on Decreation, following Genesis Creation, and the second on illustration of how it is possible to have responsible and interesting afforestation. Both available for sale or hire from, Sound and Vision Department, Church of Scotland Bookshop, 119 George Street, Edinburgh.

St. George's House, Windsor Castle

Brief Description: St. George's House is a small residential conference centre located within the walls of Windsor Castle. It occupies a large Queen Anne house to the north of St. George's Chapel, in the Lower Ward of the Castle. The House has 24 bedrooms (8 twin, 16 single), a dining room, seating 36, and 3 sitting rooms used for discussions and group work. The principal meeting room is the 15th century Chapter Library. St. George's House is established on the ancient foundations of both State and Church, yet seeks to be a resource for meeting contemporary needs in a rapidly changing world. Windsor Castle was originally built by William the Conqueror in 1070, and has been a Royal residence ever since. The College of St. George (a community of clergy and laity set apart for prayer, worship and study) was founded by Edward III alongside the Order of the Garter in 1348. Its present Chapel was begun by Edward IV in 1475, and many of its buildings are of medieval origin. The choir has a nearly unbroken tradition of singing Chapel Services on a regular basis since the foundation. Conscious of its history of service to the spiritual, intellectual, and social needs of the Nation, the College founded

St. George's House as a continuing commitment to these ends and a response to present day needs. **Warden:** Prof. Richard Whitfield. **Address:** Windsor Castle, Berkshire SL4 1NJ, UK. **Telephone:** (0753) 861341 **Fax:** (0753) 832115 **Purpose and Objectives:** The purpose of St. George's House is to provide an opportunity for men and women of responsibility and influence from all walks of life and society to meet in order to discuss frankly in an atmosphere of confidentiality the problems confronting society, and to exchange and develop their ideas about possible solutions. The connection of the House with the College of St. George guarantees it to be a place where the fundamental values and ethical and spiritual standards of individuals and institutions can be brought into sharp focus. It allows current political, social, industrial and religious problems and opportunities to be explored, in a spirit of open and free debate. St. George's House also provides an opportunity for clergy to come together for ecumenical courses, consultations and workshops adapted to meet the needs of career in ministry at various stages. The clergy in-service work draws on the experience and understanding provided by the work of the House seen as a whole, so that ministerial responsibilities and functions are presented in the context of contemporary society and modern social conditions. Almost half of the House's programme is devoted to running ecumenical courses, consultations, and workshops for ordained ministers. For most of the remainder of the Programme, under the direction of the Staff and guidance of the Council of the House, consultations are held throughout the year on topics considered to be of major concern to society. These topics are reviewed each year, but the following current examples give a sense of the scope of House Consultations: "Science and Religion," "Family Policy and Values," "Education and Culture," "European Society and Religion," "Investing in Skills," "Ethical Standards in the Professions," "Christianity and Wealth Creation." What begins as a topic for a single consultation may promote a theme for linked consultations stretching over several years. The House provides the background staff work to the consultations, identifying and defining as best it can the prise nature of the questions and challenges to be faced, and inviting as participants people who represent a diversity of informed viewpoints on a topic and who can be expected to be effective implementing insights and conclusions emerging from the consultation. There are also opportunities each year for outside organizations to use the unique facilities of the House for their own consultations. Applications from organizations are always welcome, and whenever possible bookings will be accepted from those whose aims and purposes are in broad sympathy with those of the House. Although outside organizations are responsible for devising and planning their own consultations, advice will always be provided, when required, by the Staff of the House. **Publications:** The House publishes an *Annual Review* which includes selected speeches and articles from the activities of the year. Leave to publish some of the material prepared for consultations has been given to the Leadership Development Group, the British and Foreign Bible Society, and the Epworth Press of the Methodist Church. **Organization:** St. George's House is advised by the Council of the House which includes representative knights of the Order of the Garter, the Dean and Canons of Windsor, and the Staff of the House. The Staff of St. George's House is as follows: Prof. Richard Whitfield, Warden; Mr. Dominick Harrod, Programme Director; Mrs. Sylvia Stephens, Domestic Bursar.

Stiftung "Theologie und Natur" beim Stifterverband für die Deutsche Wissenschaft ("Theology and Nature" Foundation)

Brief Description: Stiftung "Theologie und Natur" beim Stifterverband für die Deutsche Wissenschaft ("Theology and Nature" Foundation) promotes research in the field of Theology of Nature and of Natural Theology. This purpose is realized by holding symposia and conferences, giving allowances for publications, and awarding prizes for excellent publications in this field. **Address:** Morbacher Strasse 53, W-5000 Köln 41, Germany. **Telephone:** 0221-43 75 09 **Date of Founding:** 1984. **Special Projects and Conferences:** Past Conferences/symposia: November 16-17, 1985 in Freiburg/Breisgau (Germany); March 9-12, 1989 in Goldegg near Salzburg (Austria). **Publications:** Carsten Bresch,

Sigurd M. Daecke, Helmut Riedlinger, eds. *Kann man Gott aus der Natur erkennen? Evolution als Offenbarung*. Freiburg: Herder Verlag, 1990. **Advisory Board:** Founder, Dr. Hans Martin Schmidt (Köln); Erich Steinsdörfer (Stifterverband für die Deutsche Wissenschaft); Professor Dr. Carsten Bresch (Freiburg); Professor Dr. Sigurd M. Daecke (Aachen).

Techniek, Beroep, Geloof (Technology, Profession and Faith Foundation)

Brief Description: Techniek, Beroep, Geloof seeks to create a meaningful relation between Technology, Profession and Faith by promoting discussions between people from different areas of expertise and experience and of various faiths and views. **Address:** Oude Delft 18, 2611 PE Delft, The Netherlands. **Date of Founding:** 1988. **Organizational Structure:** The Foundation is a voluntary organization of 50 to 200 members, building upon students from the University of Technologies, an ecumenical (Protestant and Catholic) student and university chaplaincy, and engineers and scientists in Government and Industry. **Current Officers:** Dr. T. Meijknecht (Roman Catholic Priest); Dr. M. T. Hilhorst (Medical Ethics, Erasmus University, Rotterdam). **Special Projects and Conferences:** Annual seminars on the Profession, symposia on Faith and Technology and the editing and publication of a Dutch *Delfts Cahier*. **Membership:** Dues 50 Dutch Guilders. **Publications:** *Delfts Cahier* 1 (1990) on Faith and Information Technology and Profession; *Delfts Cahier* 2 (1991) on Faith, Profession and Product-development; *Delfts Cahier* 3 (1991) on Faith, Profession and Regional Planning. **Office Space:** House of Ecumenical Student Chaplaincy (and facilities).

Theology and Science Group of the American Academy of Religion

Brief Description: The Theology and Science Group of the AAR is a working group of scholars in the American Academy of Religion who meet during the annual meeting of the AAR to explore both topical and methodological issues in the relationship of theology and science. **Date of Founding:** 1986, first as a consultation and now as a working group. **Goals and Objectives:** This group explores the possibility for theology to fashion a new critical and constructive linkage with the sciences which can contribute to a revitalized theological enterprise and enhance the understanding between theological and scientific disciplines. It attempts to address: the disciplinary status of theology and science as a field of study; the current state of studies in the relationship of theology and science; what challenges or issues such a field of study faces and to what extent the credibility of theology depends upon its ability to relate itself convincingly to the sciences and their achievements. **Publications:** Although not guaranteed, many of the papers presented at these working sessions are later published in the journal, *Zygon*. **Organization:** Cochairs: Karl Peters, Rollins College, Winter Park, FL 32789-4496 and Ernest Simmons, Concordia College, Moorhead, MN 56562. Steering Committee: Ian Barbour, David Breed, Don Browning, Marjorie Davis, Mary Gerhart, Langdon Gilkey, Philip Hefner, Nancey Murphy, and Robert Russell. **Membership:** Membership is open to any member of the American Academy of Religion and there are no fees except for duplication costs for papers presented at the meetings.

Thijmgenootschap

Brief Description: Thijmgenootschap is an interdisciplinary learned society for Catholic scholars in the Netherlands. Currently there are some 1500 members from Dutch speaking communities (especially the Netherlands and Belgium). **Address:** Huygensweg 14, 6522 HL Nijmegen, The Netherlands. **Telephone:** 080-232122 **Date of Founding:** 1904 **Current Officers:** Chairman: Prof. Dr. R. A. de Moor (Tilburg); Treasurer: Mr. A. Hammerstein (Arnhem); Secretary-General: Dr. G. A. M. Beekelaar (Nijmegen). **Goals and Objectives:** Promotion of interdisciplinary contact between Catholic scholars in the areas where religion and other forms of ideology touch on the problems of society. Also the promotion of studies in these areas, particularly choosing for an interdisciplinary approach to these problems. **Organizational Structure:** The Thijmgenootschap is a nonprofit organization governed according to its statutes. The Executive Board consisting of five members is elected by the members of the Thijmgenootschap. Membership is open to scholars of all fields. The Thijmgenootschap has two subdivisions, one for medical doctors and one for lawyers. The association is run by volunteers, and the annual budget is about 100,000 Dutch guilders. **Membership Classifications and Dues:** Membership is open to scholars of all faculties. Each individual who is interested in the aims of the Thijmgenootschap, will be accepted as a member. The membership dues are 50 Dutch guilders a year. For medical doctors the fee is 60 Dutch guilders. **Special Conferences:** Each year there is a general meeting devoted to a special topic, with lectures and discussion. Besides the subdivisions for medical doctors and lawyers each have their own annual meetings. **Publications:** Three to four times a year *Annalen van het Thijmgenootschap* is published by AMBO publishers at Baarn in the Netherlands. Each issue is devoted to a special theme which is approached by scholars from different fields.

The Victoria Institute

[See *Science and Christian Belief* in Directory D]

Additional Organizations

NOTE: This section includes the names and contact information for organizations concerned with the interaction of theology and science. Although we were unable to provide full entries for these groups, we hope this information may be helpful.

American Academy of Religion
1703 Cliffton Road NE
Suite G5
Altanta, GA 30339-4075
(404) 727-7920
(404) 727-7959
E-Mail: AAR@Emory.edu

American Society of Law, Medicine and Ethics
765 Commonwealth Avenue
Boston, MA 02215
(617) 262-4990
(617) 437-7596 (fax)

Association of Christian Economists
c/o Dr. John Mason
Gordon College
255 Grapevine Road
Wenham, MA 01984
(508) 927-2300 ext. 4390

Association of Christian Engineers and Scientists
P. O. Box 244
Vernomia, OR 97064

Association of Christian Librarians
P. O. Box 4
Cedarville, OH 45314

Association of Unity Churches
P. O. Box 610
401 SW Oldham Parkway, Suite 210
Lee's Summit, MO 64081
(816) 524-7414
(816) 525-4020 (fax)

Australian Theological Foundation
c/o OTIRA College
73 Walpole Street
Kew, 3101 Australia
(03) 853-2000
(03) 853-5263 (fax)

Center for Process Studies
1325 North College Avenue
Claremont, CA 91711
(909) 626-3521, ext. 288
(909) 626-7062
E-mail: process@cgs.edu

Center for Theological Exploration
Mr. Craig M. Massey, Secretary
P. O. Box 2787
Lakeland, FL 33806

Christian Association for Psychological Studies, Inc.
P. O. Box 890279
Temecula, CA 92589-0279

Christian Career Women
4235 Coe Avenue, North
Olmstead, OH 44070

Christian Educators Association
P. O. Box 50025
Pasadena, CA 91115
(818)798-1124

Christian Foresters' Fellowship
c/o Prof. Dennis Lynch
School of Natural Resources
Colorado State University
Ft. Collins, CO 80521

Christian Medical & Dental Society
1616 Gateway Blvd.
P. O. Box 830689
Richardson, TX 75083
(214) 783-8385

Christian Sociological Society
c/o Prof. Larry Ingram
Department of Sociology
University of Tennessee
Martin, TN 38238
(901) 587-7515/(901) 587-7520

Christian Veterinary Mission
19303 Fremont Avenue N.
Seattle, WA 98133

Coalition for Christian Colleges and Universities
329 Eighth Street, NE
Washington, DC 2002-6158
(202) 546-8713
(202) 546-8913 (fax)

Conference on Faith and History
c/o Dr. Jewel Spears Brooker
Collegium of Letters
Eckerd College
St. Petersburg, FL 33711
(813) 867-1166

Das Deutshe Institut fur Bildung und Wissen
Institu fur Wissenschaftstheoretische Grundlagenforschung
Busdorfwall 16
4790 Paderborn
Germany

Evangelical Philosophical Society
c/o Bethel College and Theological Seminary
3949 Bethel Drive
St. Paul, MN 55112
(612) 638-6167

Evangelical Philosophical Society
5422 Clinton Boulevard
Jackson, MS 39209

Fellowship of Christian Librarians and Information Services
The Christian Broadcasting Network, Inc.
CBN Center
Virginia Beach, VA 23463

Gespr chskreis Kirche und Wissenschaft
Katholische Akademie in Bayern
Mandlstrasse 23, Postfach 40 10 08
8000 Munchen
Germany

Institute for Christian Studies
229 College Street
Toronto, ONT M5T 1R4 Canada
(416) 979-2330
(416) 979-2332 (fax)

Institute for Advanced Study
Olden Lane
Princeton, NJ 08540
(609) 734-8055
(609) 924-8399 (fax)

Institute for Interdisciplinary Research
2828 3rd Street #11
Santa Monica, CA 90405-4150
(310) 396-0517

Institute of Noetic Sciences
475 Gate Five Road, Suite 300
Sausalito, CA 94965
(415) 331-5650
(415) 331-5673 (fax)

International New Thought Alliance
5003 E. Broadway Rd.
Mesa, AZ 85206
(602) 830-2461

John E. Fetzer Institute, Inc.
9292 West KL Avenue
Kalamazoo, MI 4909-9398
(616)375-2000
(616) 372-2163 (fax)

National Institute for Healthcare Research
6110 Executive Boulevard, Suite 908
Rockville, MD 20852
(301) 984-7162
(301) 984-8143 (fax)

Directory C: Additional Organizations

Mind/Body Medical Institute
New England Deaconess Hospital
110 Frances Street, Suite 1A
Boston, MA 02215
(617) 632-9530
(617) 632-7383 (fax)

Philosophy & Technology Studies Center
Polytechnic Institute of New York
333 Jay Street
Brooklyn, NY 11201
(718) 260-3200

Reasons to Believe
P. O. Box 5978
Pasadena, CA 91117
(818) 335-1480
(818) 852-0178 (fax)

Science and Theology Group of AAR
(American Academy of Religion)
Pacific Luthern University
Dept. of Religion
Tacoma, WA 98447
(206) 535-7238

Society for the Scientific Study of Religion
Pierce Hall #193
Purdue University
West Lafayette, IN 47907
(317) 494-1231

The Travis Institute
Fuller Theological Seminary
135 North Oakland Avenue
Pasadena, CA 91182
(818) 584-5300
(818) 584-5321 (fax)

Trinity Institute
74 Trinity Place
New York, NY 10006-2088
(212) 602-0870
(212) 602-0717 (fax)

Vatican Observatory
(Castel Gandolfo)
V-00120 Città del Vaticano
Rome, Italy
39 6 698-3411 5266
39-6-698-4671 (fax)

Vatican Observatory
Research Group
Steward Observatory
University of Arizona
Tuscon, AZ 85721
(602) 621-3225
(602) 621-1532 (fax)

Directory D

Journals and Newsletters

Journals & Newsletters

Bridges: An Interdisciplinary Journal of Theology, Philosophy, History, and Science

Brief Description: *Bridges* was an independent publication that focuses on contemporary social and human issues from a scholarly perspective. Each issue was devoted to a specific theme. (Published 1988-1991, publishing currently suspended). **Date of Founding:** 1988. Vol. 1, 1989 **ISSN#:** 1042-2234 **Editor:** Robert S. Frey **Address:** P.O. Box 850, Columbia, MD 21044-0850, USA; or contact Nancy Thompson-Frey, 5702 Yellow Rose Court, Columbia MD 21045, USA.

Common Boundary Between Spirituality and Psychotherapy

Brief Description: The Common Boundary, Inc., a non-profit organization founded in 1980, publishes the bimonthly magazine *Common Boundary* and holds an annual conference for those interested in exploring the relationship of psychology, spirituality, and creativity. **President and Editor:** Anne Simpkinson **Address:** 5272 River Road, Bethesda, MD 20816, USA. **Phone:** (301) 652-9495 **Date of Founding:** 1980 **ISSN #:** 0885-8500 **Advisory Board:** Daniel Goleman, John McDargh, Edith Sullwold, Frances Vaughan, and Roger Walsh. **Background and Activities:** *Common Boundary* is specifically aimed at psychologists, psychiatrists, pastoral counselors, social workers, psychiatric nurses, etc., who are interested in the spiritual aspects of psychotherapy and the psychological dimensions of spiritual growth. The bimonthly magazine has over 20,000 subscribers. The organization also gives an annual $1,000 award to the most outstanding psychospiritual thesis or dissertation. The magazine and conferences have featured Robert Bly, Ram Dass, James Hillman, Stephen Levine, Thich Nhat Hanh, Alice Walker, Matthew Fox, and Marion Woodman, and have discussed topics such as Shamanism, expressive arts, meditation, contemplation, ecofeminism, co-dependency, bodywork, and dreams. The annual conferences are held in the Washington DC area with typically over 2,000 participants. The yearly budget is approximately $1,000,000. **Subscriptions:** $22 per year. **Other Publications:** Common Boundary, Inc. also publishes a Graduate Education Guide.

Il Futuro dell'Uomo

Basic Description: *Il Futuro dell'Uomo* is a biannual journal concerned with the interactions of Science and Theology and with the works and thoughts of Pierre Teilhard de Chardin. **Sponsoring Bodies:** The owner and publisher of the Journal is the Istituto Niels Stensen of Florence. Linked to the journal is the Associazione Teilhard de Chardin - Centro di ricerca per il futuro dell'uomo. **Addresses:** Istituto Niels Stensen - Viale Don Minzoni 25/a I-50129 FIRENZE. The same address for the "Association Teilhard de Chardin." **Telephone:** (055) 576551 **Owner and Publisher:** L. Galleni, Editor, telephone: (050) 578154 **ISSN #:** 0390-217X **Date of Founding:** 1974. **Editor:** Lodovico Galleni, Professor of General Zoology, University of Pisa, Via San Michele degli Scalzi 2 I 56124 Pisa, Italy. Assistant to the Editor: Silvio Cazzante, Istituto Niels Stensen. **Editorial Advisory Board:** Dario

Beruto (Genova), Silvana Borgognini (Pisa), Annetta Daverio (Torino), Carlo De Filippi (Firenze), Paolo Giannoni (Firenze), Rosino Gibellini (Brescia), Fabio Mantovani (Verona), Luciano Martini (Firenze), Alceste Santini (Roma). **Editorial Panel of Reference:** Marcel Bourg (Francia), Ennio Brovedani (Milano), Marcello Buiatti (Firenze), Brunetto Chiarelli (Firenze), Marcello Ciafaloni (Firenze), Gianni Colzani (Milano), Yves Coppens (Francia), Giuseppe Del Re (Napoli), Edward O. Dodson (Canada), Fiorenao Facchini (Bologna), Guglielmo Forni (Bologna), Pierluigi Fortini (Ferrara), Ursula King (UK), Italo Mancini (Urbino), Giuseppe Minelli (Bologna), Pietro Omodeo (Siena), Giovanni Prodi (Pisa), Silvio Ravera (Savona), Tarcisse Tshibangu (Zaire), Phillip V. Tobias (Republic of South Africa), Bernard Vinaty (Roma). **Content:** Each issue contains five papers of a research nature and a "forum" section devoted to the discussion of main topics. Finally there is also a book review section. The language of the journal is Italian but books in other languages are reviewed. Early issues contained articles on theories of evolution and theology, the anthropic principle, environmental ethics, bioethics, the scientific papers of Pierre Teilhard de Chardin, the Doctrine of Creation, etc. **Subscription Rates:** The journal appears twice a year. Rates: 1 year, Lire 20.000 (Italy), Lire 30.000 (abroad).

Isis (Journal of the History of Science Society)

Brief Description: ISIS is an international review devoted to the history of science and its cultural influences. **Editorship:** Margaret W. Rossiter (Editor); John Neu and Peter Dear (Associate Editors); Jon M. Harkness (Managing Editor). **Address:** Department of Science and Technology Studies, Cornell University, 726 University Avenue, Ithaca, NY 14850, USA. **Telephone:** (607) 254-4747 **Fax:** Isis@Cornell.edu. **Date of Founding:** 1912 by George Sarton.

Journal of Interdisciplinary Studies (JIS)

Brief Description: *The Journal of Interdisciplinary Studies: An International Journal of Interdisciplinary and Interfaith Dialogue* is the official journal of the International Christian Studies Association, cosponsored and published by the Institute for Interdisciplinary Research. JIS seeks to uncover the lost unity of Renaissance learning while affirming transcendental values and faith. **Address:** 2828 Third Street, Suite 11, Santa Monica, CA 90405, USA. **Telephone:** (310) 396-0517 **ISSN#:** 0890-0132 **Date of Founding:** Fall 1989 **Current Officers:** Editor, Oskar Gruenwald (Institute for Interdisciplinary Research); Associate Editor, William R. Marty (University of Memphis); Book Review Editor, Terence J. Smith (Science Applications International). **Description and Purpose:** It is becoming increasingly clear that the narrow compartmentalization of knowledge, and its insulation from transcendental values and faith, acts as a barrier to new scientific discoveries as well as human self-discovery. JIS offers an interdisciplinary forum for the exploration of the human condition in the light of Christian understanding. It welcomes manuscripts from both those who do and those who do not share the journal's Christian commitment, yet seek vital new insights, into, and/or a reconceptualization of, the interfaces and linkages between facts and values, knowledge and faith, science and religion. Thus *JIS* hopes to encourage both excellence of scholarship and openness to dialogue across geographical, disciplinary, and denominational boundaries. *JIS* is trilingual: English, German and French. Most articles are in English. Other-language articles carry a 500-word English summary. *JIS* International Editorial Board members represent Canada, Germany, Mexico, Switzerland, and the USA in the social sciences and humanities. All article manuscripts undergo peer review. **Subscription:** *JIS* is published in a double thematic issue once a year (Sept. release), and features 10-12 articles on 1-2 major themes, plus book reviews (ca. 224 pp., 6"x9" trim, 2-color cover). Individual $15; Student $10; Institutional $25 (Overseas airmail add $5). (U.S. funds drawn on a U.S. bank).

Perspectives on Science and Christian Faith

Basic Description: *Perspectives on Science and Christian Faith* is the quarterly Journal of the American Scientific Affiliation, and has become an important forum for discussion of key issues at the interface of science and Christian thought. It also contains news of current trends in science and reviews of important books on science/faith issues. **Address:** American Scientific Affiliation, P.O. Box 668, Ipswich, MA 01938. **Phone:** (508) 356-5656 **ISSN #:** 0892-2675 **Date of Founding:** Volume 1 was published in 1949 and the June 1991 issue was Volume 43, number 2. (Formally it was simply called the *Journal of the American Scientific Affiliation or JASA*). **Editors:** J. W. Haas, Jr., Editor, P.O. Box 668, Ipswich, MA 01938; Lyn Berg, Managing Editor, P.O. Box 668, Ipswich, MA 01938; Richard Ruble, Book Review Editor, 212 Western Hills Drive, Siloam Springs, AR 72761. **Editorial Board:** Jerry D. Albert (Mesa College), Stephen Bell (University of Dundee, Scotland), Richard H. Bube (Stanford University), Wilbur L. Bullock (University of New Hampshire), Dewey K. Carpenter (Louisiana State University), Gary R. Collins (Trinity Evangelical Divinity School), Edward B. Davis (Messiah College), Owen Gingerich (Harvard-Smithsonian Center for Astrophysics), Herrmann Hafner (Marburg, Germany), Walter R. Hearn (Berkeley, California), Russell Heddendorf (Covenant College), Charles Hummel (Inter-Varsity Christian Fellowship), D. Gareth Jones (University of Otago, New Zealand), Christopher Kaiser (Western Theological Seminary), Robert D. Knudsen (Westminster Theological Seminary), Gordon R. Lewthwaite (California State University), Russell Maatman (Dordt College), H. Newton Maloney (Fuller Theological Seminary), John A. McIntyre (Texas A&M University), David Moberg (Marquette University), Stanley W. Moore (Pepperdine University), Evelina Orteza y Miranda (University of Calgary, Canada), Claude E. Stipe (Escondido, California), Walter R. Thorson (University of Alberta, Canada), Edwin M. Yamauchi (Miami University - Ohio), Davis A. Young (Calvin College). **Manuscript Guidelines:** The pages of *Perspectives* are open to any contribution dealing with the interaction between science and Christian faith in a manner consistent with scientific and theological integrity. Papers published do not necessarily reflect any official position of the ASA. All manuscripts (except Book Reviews) should be addressed to the Editor, P.O. Box 668, Ipswich MA 01938. Authors of Papers and Communications must submit *3 typed double-spaced copies* of their paper on good quality 8½ x 11 inch paper, for review purposes. Regular papers should be accompanied by an *Abstract* of not more than 100 words. References and footnotes should be collected at the end. Figures or diagrams should be clear, black and white, line ink drawings or glossy photographs suitable for direct reproduction. Captions should be provided separately. "Regular Papers" are major treatments of a particular subject relating to science and the Christian position. Such papers should be at least 10 pages in length, but not more than 20 pages. Publication for such papers normally take 12 to 18 months from the time of acceptance. "Communications" are brief treatments of a wide range of subjects of interest to readers, not longer than 9 pages. Accepted Communications should normally be published in 9 to 12 months. "Book Reviews" are an important part of the Journal. They serve to alert the readership to books of interest and provide a valuable source for reference. Readers are encouraged to review books in their scientific fields which have implications for the Christian faith. Prospective reviewers should notify the Book Review editor of their intentions, and obtain the guidelines for book reviews. "Letters" to the Editor may be published, subject to editorial review, unless marked not for publication. Letters selected for publication will be published within 6 months. "Advertising" is accepted in *Perspectives*, subject to editorial approval. The Managing Editor can provide rates and further information. **Subscription Rate:** $30 per year.

Progress in Theology

Basic Description: *Progress in Theology* is the quarterly newsletter of the John Templeton Foundation's Humility Theology Information Center. It provides updates on Templeton Foundation activities and explores issues involved with humility theology. **Addresses:** A free subscription is available by writing to P.O. Box 429, Topsfield, MA 01983-0629 USA. Editorial matters should be addressed to : P.O. Box 797, Ipswich, MA 01938, (508) 356-1971; Fax: (508) 356-7775. **Date of Founding:** First issue was March 1993. **Editorial Coordinator:** Robert L. Herrmann, Ph.D. **Managing Editor:** Patricia Ames. **Format and Content:** Each issue is 8 pages long. Generally, each one contains news of Templeton Foundation activities, brief sketches of two or three Humility Theology Information Center Advisory Board Members, information about current and upcoming Templeton Foundation award and other programs, and abstracts of award winning papers on humility theology. Occasionally a reprinted book review is also included. **Subscription:** Subscriptions are *free*. They may be requested by writing to the subscription office listed above.

Science and Christian Belief

Basic Description: *Science and Christian Belief* is a biannual journal concerned with the interactions of science and religion, with particular reference to Christianity. Two former periodicals, *Faith and Thought* (the journal of The Victoria Institute) and *Science and Faith* (the newsletter of Christians in Science, formerly the Research Scientist's Christian Fellowship) which were concerned with similar topics, have now been merged to form the more ambitious journal *Science and Christian Belief*. **Sponsoring Bodies:** Christians in Science (formerly known as the Research Scientists' Christian Fellowship), which is one of a considerable number of Christian Professional Groups linked with the Universities and Colleges Christian Fellowship (UCCF). The Victoria Institute. **Addresses:** Publisher: Paternoster Press, Paternoster House, 3 Mount Radford Crescent, Exeter, EX2 4JW, UK. Christians in Science, UCCF, 38 De Montfort Street, Leicester, LE1 7GP, UK. The Victoria Institute, P.O. Box 216, Welling, Kent, DA16 2ED, UK. **ISSN #:** 0954 4194 **Date of Founding:** Spring 1989. **Editors:** Oliver R. Barclay, MA, PhD; A. Brian Robins, BSc, PhD. **Panel of Reference:** A Panel of Reference, including the following people, will advise the editors: Professor R. J. Berry, FRSE (University College, London); Professor M. H. P. Bott, FRS (University of Durham); Sir Robert Boyd, FBA (formerly University College, London); Professor D. C. Burke (Vice Chancellor, University of East Anglia); Dr. J. T. Houghton, FRS (Meteorological Office); Professor C. J. Humphreys, FIM, FInstP (University of Liverpool); Dr. D. J. E. Ingram, FInstP (Vice Chancellor, University of Kent); Professor M. A. Jeeves, FRSE (University of St. Andrews); Professor O. M. T. O'Donovan (University of Oxford); Rev. Dr. A. E. McGrath (University of Oxford); Professor C. A. Russell, FRSC (The Open University); Professor D. J. Wiseman, FBA (formerly University of London). **Content:** Each issue contains two or three major papers or research articles which will have been refereed by the panel of reference or those delegated by it. Typically, several shorter articles are also included, as well as notices of forthcoming meetings and brief reports of meetings in the recent past both nationally and internationally, plus other notes, comments and abstracts of relevant material from other journals, scientific and theological. In addition to book reviews, which are a significant feature, there are also occasional 'update' articles reviewing the recent literature on a specific topic. Early issues contained articles on the following topics: Chance, randomness and design; The impact of the 'new physics' on the science and religion debate; The social origins of the science/religion 'conflict hypothesis'; Reductionism in science and theology; The ethical use of animals; A critique of F. Capra's *The Tao of Physics*; The abuse of the environment; Miracles; Objective knowledge in science; A Christian approach to the allocation of financial resources for research. **Subscription:** Members of Christians in Science or The Victoria Institute (including corresponding members), receive the journal *free* in virtue of their membership. Those wishing to enquire about membership should contact the organization concerned: CIS (RSCF), Secretary, UCCF, 38 De Montfort Street, Leicester LE1 7GP; The Victoria Institute, P.O. Box 216, Welling, Kent, DA16 2ED. Others should subscribe direct to the *publisher* (Paternoster Press, Paternoster House, 3 Mount Radford Crescent, Exeter EX2 4JW). **Subscription Rates:** The journal appears twice a year. Rates (which include mailing costs) are as follows: 1 year UK £9.40, USA $28.20; 2 years UK £17.85, USA $53.55; 3 years UK £26.10, USA $78.30. Overseas subscribers who cannot easily transmit funds should correspond with the *Christians in Science* office.

Science and Religion News

Description: *Science and Religion News* is a quarterly newsletter published by the Institute on Religion in an Age of Science. Its purpose is to provide a vehicle for an ongoing interchange of news and ideas relevant to the dialogue of Science and Religion. *Science and Religion News* welcomes comments, announcements, and resources. **Editor:** Kevin Sharpe; Associate Editors, Virginia Slayton and Tom Slayton. **Address:** 65 Hoit Rd, Concord, NH 03301, USA. **Phone:** (603) 226-3328 **Fax:** (603) 226-3328 **ISSN #:** 1048-8642 **Format and Content:** Each issue is in brochure format (12 pages) with the following sections: a) A Calendar giving upcoming events of interest to the readership; b) A News column giving a wide range of information on conferences, calls for papers, activities of organizations and centers, and other items of news; c) A review of Periodicals listing relevant articles by author and title under each Periodical reviewed; d) A brief review of recently published books dealing with relevant topics; e) A listing of Books received but not commented on (In all cases full publication details are given for Journals and Books); f) An Editorial, either by the editors or a guest individual. **Annual Subscription Rates:** For USA, $9.50; For Canada or Mexico, $11.50; For elsewhere, $13.50 (by air). Remit in US funds; VISA and MasterCard are also accepted.

Second Opinion

Brief Description: *Second Opinion* is the journal of the Park Ridge Center, an Institute for the Study of Health, Faith, and Ethics [See separate entry under Organizations]. As its name implies, the complexities of modern health care make it increasingly difficult to find the single "correct" action, thought, or method. Each situation is open to a variety of apparently legitimate and appropriate interpretations and applications. By inviting contributions from a wide range of perspectives, *Second Opinion* stimulates interdisciplinary conversations between members of fields relating to health, faith, and ethics. While other publications deal with one or two of these concerns, *Second Opinion* distinctively seeks to address all three. The Center created the journal in the hope that it will help form one public out of a number of related constituencies. **Editors and Assistants:** Executive Editor, Laurence J. O'Connell; Editor, Martin E. Marty; Associate Editor, Barbara Hofmaier; Managing Editor, Sandy Pittman; Editorial Assistant, Donna Ray; Text Processor, Rose A. Luciano; Designer, Micah Marty. **Board of Editorial Advisors:** Robert N. Bellah, Daniel J. Callahan, Jimmy Carter, James F. Childress, Robert Coles, Arthur J. Dyck, H. Tristram Engelhardt, Jr., E. Duane Engstrom, William H. Foege, Jeffrey K. Hadden, Stanley S. Harakas, Jay Katz, F. Dean Lueking, Richard A. McCormick, William F. May, Ronald L. Numbers, Edmund D. Pellegrino, Ruth B. Purtilo, Sidney A. Rand, Dietrich Ritschl, Judith A. Ryan, Donald W. Shriver, Lewis Thomas, Edwin R. Wallace IV, William J. Winslade, Gerald Winslow, Philip Woollcott, Jr., Ernst L. Wynder. **Subscription:** *Second Opinion* is published every March, July, and November. Subscription fee is $35 for one year, $65 for two years, and $95 for three years. All inquiries should be sent to the Park Ridge Center, 676 N. St. Clair, Suite 450, Chicago IL 60611.

Tradition and Discovery: The Polanyi Society Periodical

Brief Description: *Tradition and Discovery* is an indexed, peer reviewed journal with two or three numbers each academic year. Each 40 page issue contains articles, reviews, and news of interest to members of the Polanyi Society. *Tradition and Discovery* promotes interest in, and creative use of, the philosophical work of Michael Polanyi. Most articles are concerned with topics in philosophy, religious studies, and education, although essays treating other subjects also appear. *Tradition and Discovery* incorporates material from the former United Kingdom Polanyi group that published *Convivium*. **Editors:** General Editor: Phil Mullins, Missouri Western State College, St. Joseph, MO 64507; Fax: (816) 271-4386; Phone: (816) 271-4386; E-mail: mullins@griffon.mwsc.edu. Book Review Editor: Walter Gulick, Montana State University at Billings, Billings, MT 59101-0298; Fax: (406) 657-2037. **Subscription:** *Tradition and Discovery* is distributed to all members of the Polanyi Society. Regular membership (due at the beginning of the fall semester) is $20/academic year (student membership is $10/academic year). Checks and money orders payable to the Polanyi Society should be sent to Richard Gelwick, General Coordinator for the Polanyi Society, University of New England, Biddeford, ME 04005.

Ultimate Reality and Meaning, Interdisciplinary Studies in the Philosophy of Understanding

[See entry under **The International Society for the Study of Human Ideas on Ultimate Reality and Meaning** (ISSURAM or URAM) in the Organizations Directory]

Zygon: Journal of Religion and Science

Brief Description: *Zygon: Journal of Religion and Science* is a quarterly journal which explores the relationship between religious beliefs and philosophies and the theories and findings of modern-day science in order to illuminate issues of human purpose and moral direction in contemporary life. It is published by the Joint Publication Board. **Sponsoring Organizations:** *Zygon's* three sponsoring organizations, which appoint the Joint Publication Board, are: 1) The Institute on Religion in an Age of Science (IRAS). Founded in 1954, IRAS is an independent society of natural scientists, social scientists, philosophers, religion scholars, theologians, and others who seek to understand and reformulate the theory and practice of religion in the light of contemporary scientific knowledge. It is both an affiliate society of the American Association for the Advancement of Science and a member of the Council of Societies for the Study of Religion. 2) The Center for Advanced Study in Religion and Science (CASIRAS). Founded in 1972, CASIRAS is an independent society of scholars and scientists from various fields who pursue critical, interdisciplinary studies of the possibilities for constructively relating religion and science. In affiliation with the Association of Chicago Theological Schools it offers instruction and research opportunities in the implications of science for religion to seminarians, graduate students, visiting scholars, and faculty. 3) Rollins College, Winter Park, Florida. Founded in 1885, Rollins is a private, nonsectarian liberal arts college. **Joint Publication Board Members:** Founding Editor, Ralph Wendell Burhoe; Editor, Philip Hefner (ex officio); representatives of the Institute on Religion in an Age of Science: Solomon H. Katz (cochair), Karl E. Peters, and Robert C. Sorensen; representatives of the Center for Advanced Study in Religion and Science: Malcolm R. Sutherland, Jr. (cochair), Jeffrey S. Wicken, and Donald Szantho Harrington; representative of Rollins College: Daniel R. DeNicola. **Founding Editor:** Ralph Wendell Burhoe **Editorship:** Editor, Philip Hefner; Editor for Development, Karl D. Peters; Executive Editor, Carol Rausch (Gorski) Albright; Assistant Editor, Diane Goodman. **Editorial and Book Review Office:** Chicago Center for Religion and Science (CCRS), 1100 E. 55th St., Chicago, IL 60615-5199 **Telephone:** (312) 753-0671 **Fax:** (312) 753-0782 **Book Review Council:** James Nelson, Chair (Religious Studies); Philip Clayton (Philosophy); William Irons (Anthropology); Marian Kaehler (Biological Sciences); Robert Segal (Social Sciences). **Associate Editors:** John Bowker, Don Browning, Bernard D. Davis, Solomon H. Katz, A. R. Peacocke, Robert C. Sorensen. **Advisory Board:** Ian G. Barbour; Charles L. Birch; Robert Brungs; Donald T. Campbell; Kenneth Cauthen; Eric J. Chaisson; John B. Cobb, Jr.; Mihaly Csikszentmihalyi; Eugene G. d'Aquili; Jose M. R. Delgado; Irven Devore; Lindon Eaves; John C. Eccles; James W. Fowler; Mary Gerhart; John C. Godbey; Ward H. Goodenough; Garrett Hardin; Nancy Houk; Sarah Blaffer Hrdy; James E. Huchingson; Ervin Laszlo; Paul D. MacLean; Viggo Mortensen; Nancey C. Murphy; Howard T. Odum; Harold H. Oliver; Wolfhart Pannenberg; George Edgin Pugh; George A. Riggan; Holmes Rolston, III; Michael Ruse; Robert John Russell; Karl Schmitz-Moormann; W. Widick Schroeder; Kevin Sharpe; R. W. Sperry; Malcolm R. Sutherland, Jr.; Winnifred A. Tomm; Jeffrey S. Wicken; Edward O. Wilson. **Publishing Agent:** Basil Blackwell, Inc., Colleen Doyle, 3 Cambridge Center, Cambridge, MA 02141 (Phone: 617-225-0430); and Basil Blackwell Ltd., 108 Crowley Road, Oxford, OX4 1JF, England. **Subscription Rates:** *Zygon* is published quarterly. Rates include postage. All orders must be prepaid. As of Volume 26, 1991, *Individuals*: $30 (North America), £19.50 (UK and Europe), £21 (Rest of World). *Institutions*: $42.50 (North America), £34 (UK and Europe), £36 (Rest of World). *Students* $22 (North America), £16.50 (UK and Europe), £16.50 (Rest of World). Subscription orders should be sent to the relevant Publishing Agent.

Additional Journals and Newsletters

NOTE: This section includes the names and contact information for journals and newsletters concerned with the interaction of theology and science. Although we were unable to provide full entries for these publications, we hope this information may be helpful.

ADVANCES: The Journal of Mind-Body Health
c/o The Fetzer Institute
9292 West KL Avenue
Kalamazoo, MI 49009-9398
(616) 375-2000

Journal for the Scientific Study of Religion
1365 Stone Hall, Sociology Dept
Purdue University
West Lafayette, IN 47907
(317) 494-6286
(317) 496-1476 (fax)
E-Mail: SSSR@SRI.SOC.PURDUE.EDU

CTNS Bulletin, CTNS Newsletter
Center for Theology and the Natural Sciences
2400 Ridge Road
Berkeley, CA 94709
(510) 848-8152
(510) 848-2535 (fax)

ESSSAT Newsletter
Bezinningscentrum Vrije Universiteit
DeBoelelaan 1115
1081 HV Amsterdam
The Netherlands
31 20 444 5675
31 20 6429634 (fax)

FASE Notices
Center for Faith and Science Exchange
The Boston Theological Institute
210 Herrick Road
Newton Centre, MA 02159
(617) 527-4880
(617) 527-1073 (fax)

ITEST Bulletin
Institute for Theological Encounter with Science and Technology
221 North Grand Boulevard
St. Louis, MO 63103
(314) 977-2703
(314) 977-7211 (fax)

Newsletter of the Center for Process Studies
1325 North College Avenue
Claremont, CA 91711
(909) 626-3521, ext. 288
(909) 627-7062 (fax)

Ethics and Medics
Pope John XXIII Medical/Moral Research & Education Center
186 Forbes Road
Braintree, MA 02184
(617) 848-6965
(617) 849-1309 (fax)

Hodoi: The Journal of Inquiry
Sponsored by the American Humanist Association
9330 Bankside
Houston, TX 77031

How to Use the Indexes

There are five indexes. The first is an alphabetical listing of individuals, the second lists all individuals by country (or in the case of the USA by state), and the third lists individuals by discipline (i.e. by subject area). An index of organizations and another of journals follows. These latter two indexes are quite straightforward and need no special instructions save to say that they are listed alphabetically (ignoring leading articles), with all organizations on one page, and journals on another.

In the three indexes of individuals a few common conventions are followed that need some explanation. The first is the use of a contrast between bold and normal type. This convention is consistently used in all three indexes to indicate in which Directory (A or B) you can find a specific individual. See, for example, these two names taken from the Alphabetical Index:

Adler, Thomas C. *(Chemistry)* California   Normal type-- Directory B

Ajakaiye, Deborah Enilo *(Physics,* **Earth Science)** Nigeria   **Bold type**-- Directory A

The second convention is the use of italicized print to distinguish a primary from among one or more secondary categories or locations. So, in the first example given below, the subject category *Philosophy* is italicized to distinguish it as the primary discipline from among other cross-reference fields (in this case, Theology and Physics). The same applies to *Theology* in the next two examples. The same concept applies to geographical locations: the primary country or state is italicized (in this case, California). The two examples that follow are taken from the Geographical Index listing:

Felt, James W. *(Philisophy,* **Theology/Religion, Physics)** *California*   *Philosophy* is the primary subject category

Firestone, Homer Loon *(Theology/Religion,* Psychology/Counseling) *California,* also Bolivia   *California,* not Bolivia, is his prime location

The third convention is the use of subject categories (i.e. one or more codes given in parentheses after the individual's name), to indicate his or her primary and secondary fields of study or professional fields. Although these categories are used mainly in the Subject Index, they are also included in the other indexes for convenience's sake, and, therefore, a list with the complete range of areas included in a category is given at the beginning of each index. In the Subject Index the individual is listed under only the primary subject area applicable in his or her case.

Alphabetical Index

This index is organized alphabetically by name. Names in **bold** type indicate an entry in Directory A, while normal type indicates the entry is in Directory B. Subject categories which indicate an individual's primary and secondary fields of study or professional fields and geographical locations are also included with each entry. (Subject categories are listed below.) *Italicized* print indicates a "primary" area, be it an italicized state or country or subject category.

Subject Categories

Administration
Anthropology
Astronomy/Astrophysics (Physical Cosmology)
Biochemistry/Biophysics
Biology (Botany, Zoology, etc)
Chemistry
Commerce
Communications
Computer and Information Sciences
Earth Science (Geology, Mineralogy, Meteorology, Geography, Agriculture, etc)
Ecology/Environment (Environmental Ethics, Conservation and Preservation)
Economics
Education
Engineering
Ethics
Finance
Genetics

History
History and Philosophy of Science
Interdisciplinary Studies
Jurisprudence/Law
Languages
Literature
Management
Mathematics
Medical Science
Molecular Biology (Microbiology)
Philosophy
Physics
Political Science/Politics
Psychiatry
Psychology/Counseling
Sociobiology
Sociology
Technology
Theology/Religion

A

Adams, Dawn A. (*Biology*) *Texas*

Adler, Thomas C. (*Chemistry*) *California*

Ajakaiye, Deborah Enilo (*Physics*, also Earth Science) *Nigeria*

Albertsen, Andres Roberto (*Theology/Religion*) *Argentina*

Albright, Carol Rausch (*Communications*) *Illinois*

Albright, John R. (*Physics*) *Illinois*

Allen, Diogenes (*Philosophy*, also Theology/Religion) *New Jersey*

Allen, George W. J. (*Biology*) *New York*

Allert, Gebhard (*Medical Science*, also Psychiatry, Theology/Religion) *Germany*

Alley, James W. (*Medical Science*) *Georgia*

Alston, William (*Philosophy*) *New York*

Altner, Günter (*Theology/Religion*, also Biology) *Germany*

Ambrose, Edmund Jack (*Biology*, also Medical Science) *United Kingdom*

Ambrosino, Salvatore V. (*Psychiatry*) *New York*

Ammerman, Nancy Tatom (*Sociology*, also Theology/Religion) *Georgia*

Amrhein, Eva Maria (*Physics*, also Theology/Religion) *Wisconsin*, also Germany

Anch, A. Michael (*Psychology/Counseling*, also Theology/Religion) *Missouri*

Anderson, Odin W. (*Sociology*) *Wisconsin*

Ansbacher, Stefan (*Medical Science*) *Florida*

Apyczynski, John V. (*Theology/Religion*, also Philosophy) *New York*

Armogathe, Jean-Robert (*Philosophy*, also Theology/Religion, History and Philosophy of Science) *France*

Armstrong, John Reginald (*Theology/Religion*, also Earth Science, History and Philosophy of Science) *Canada*

Artigas, Mariano (*Physics*, also Philosophy) *Spain*

Arvedson, Peter Fredrick (*Theology/Religion*, also Chemistry) *New York*

Ashbrook, James B. (*Theology/Religion*, also Psychology/Counseling, Psychiatry) *Illinois*

Ashley, Benedict M. (*Ethics*, also Political Science/Politics, Theology/Religion, Philosophy) *Washington, D.C.*

Atkinson, David John (*Theology/Religion*, also Chemistry, Psychology/Counseling) *United Kingdom*

Augros, Robert M. (*Philosophy*) *New Hampshire*

Aurenche, Christian (*Theology/Religion*, also Medical Science) *Cameroon*

Austin, William H. (*Philosophy*, also Theology/Religion) *Texas*

Ayala, Francisco J. (*Biology*, also Genetics, Philosophy) *California*

Ayers, David John (*Sociology*, also Psychology/Counseling) *New York*

ℬ

Baclig, Paulita Villegs (*Medical Science*) *Philippines*

Baer, Donald R. (*Physics*) *Washington*

Bag, A. K. (*History and Philosophy of Science*, also Mathematics) *India*

Balslev, Anindita Niyogi (*Philosophy*, also Theology/Religion) *Virginia*

Balswick, Jack Orville (*Sociology*, also Theology/Religion) *California*

Bame, Michael (*Theology/Religion*) *Cameroon*

Banco, Eugene C. (*Theology/Religion*) *Georgia*

Banner, Michael Charles (*Philosophy*, also Theology/Religion) *United Kingdom*

Barbour, Ian G. (*Theology/Religion*, also Physics, Philosophy) *Minnesota*

Barclay, Oliver Rainsford (*Biology*, also Theology/Religion) *United Kingdom*

Barclay, Peter R. (*Sociology*, also Ethics) *Massachusetts*

Bargatzky, Thomas (*Anthropology*) *Germany*

Barker, Eileen (*Sociology*, also Theology/Religion) *United Kingdom*

Barker, Verlyn L. (*Political Science/Politics*) *Ohio*

Barkman, Paul F. (*Psychology/Counseling*, also Theology/Religion) *California*

Barnes, Michael H. (*Theology/Religion*, also History and Philosophy of Science) *Ohio*

Barnhouse, Ruth Tiffany (*Psychiatry*, also Medical Science, Theology/Religion) *Texas*

Barrett, Peter J. (*Physics*) *South Africa*

Barrow, John D. (*Astronomy/Astrophysics*, also Physics, Philosophy, Mathematics) *United Kingdom*

Bartek, Edward J. (*Philosophy*, also Psychology/Counseling) *Connecticut*

Bartholomew, Gilbert A. (*Physics*) *Canada*

Bassett, Rodney L. (*Psychology/Counseling*) *New York*

Batson, C. Daniel (*Psychology/Counseling*, also Theology/Religion, Education) *Kansas*

Bauman, Michael E. (*Theology/Religion*, also History, Languages) *Michigan*, also United Kingdom

Beck, Horst Waldemar (*Theology/Religion*, also Technology, Philosophy) *Germany*

Beck, Malcolm Nestor (*Psychiatry*, also Medical Science) *Canada*

Becker, Gerhold K. (*Theology/Religion*, also Philosophy) *Hong Kong*

Becker, Thomas (*Biology*, also Theology/Religion) *Germany*

Becker, Werner (*Philosophy*, also Political Science/Politics, Ethics) *Germany*

Begzos, Marios (*Theology/Religion*, also Philosophy) *Greece*

Beinert, Wolfgang (*Theology/Religion*, also Philosophy) *Germany*

Bell Jr., Reuben Paul (*Medical Science*) *Maine*

Bellini, Gianpaolo (*Physics*) *Italy*

Bennema, P. (*Chemistry*, also Physics) *The Netherlands*

Benner, David G. (*Psychology/Counseling*) *Canada*

Bennett, J. W. (*Genetics*) *Louisiana*

Benninghoff, Jean (*Theology/Religion*, also Physics) *New York*

Benson, Purnel H. (*Psychology/Counseling*, also Sociology, Economics) *New Jersey*

Benvenuto, Edoardo (*Technology*, also Theology/Religion, Physics, History and Philosophy of Science) *Italy*

Berg, Myles Renver (*Engineering*, also Physics, Mathematics) *California*

Bergh, Bob (*Genetics*) *California*

Bergman, Jerry (*Biology*, also Physics, Chemistry, Psychology/Counseling) *Ohio*

Berry Jr., Maxwell R. (*Medical Science*) *Florida*

Berry, Robert James (*Genetics*, also Molecular Biology, Ecology/Environment) *United Kingdom*

Berry, Thomas (*History*, also Theology/Religion) *New York*

Bertsch, Hans (*Biology*, also Theology/Religion, Philosophy) *California*

Bettencourt, Estêvão Tavares (*Theology/Religion*, also Philosophy) *Brazil*

Biesele, John Julius (*Biology*) *Texas*

Bingemer, Maria Clara Lucchetti (*Theology/Religion*) *Brazil*

Birch, L. Charles (*Biology*, also Theology/Religion) *Australia*

Bishop, Robert C. (*Physics*) *Texas*

Bjork, Russell C. (*Computer and Information Sciences*) *Massachusetts*

Blaising, Craig A. (*Theology/Religion*) *Texas*

Blake, Deborah D. (*Theology/Religion*, also Philosophy, Ethics) *Colorado*

Blankenburg, Wolfgang (*Psychiatry*, also Philosophy) *Germany*

Blasi, Paolo (*Physics*, also Theology/Religion) *Italy*

Bloemendal, Michael (*Biochemistry/Biophysics*, also Chemistry) *United Kingdom*

Bloom, John A. (*Physics*, also Theology/Religion, Computer and Information Sciences, History) *Pennsylvania*

Böckman, Peter Wilhelm (*Ethics*, also Theology/Religion, Philosophy) *Norway*

Bohon, Robert L (*Chemistry*, also Technology, Earth Science, Management) *Minnesota*

Böhringer, Siegfried (*Theology/Religion*) *Germany*

Bolt, Martin (*Psychology/Counseling*) *Michigan*

Bolyki, János (*Theology/Religion*, also History) *Hungary*

Bonting, Sjoerd L. (*Biochemistry/Biophysics*, also Biology, Chemistry, Theology/Religion) *The Netherlands*

Booher, Bruce (*Theology/Religion*) *Texas*

Boon, Rudolf (*Theology/Religion*, also Philosophy, History and Philosophy of Science) *The Netherlands*

Bouma III, Hessel (*Biology*, also Genetics) *Michigan*

Bourne, Malcolm C. (*Chemistry*) *New York*

Boutinon, Jean Claude (*Theology/Religion*) *France*

Boyd, Sir Robert Lewis Fullarton (*Physics*, also Chemistry, Astronomy/Astrophysics, Technology) *United Kingdom*

Bradley, Walter L. (*Physics*, also Technology) *Texas*

Braganza, Karuna Mary (*Literature*, also Education) *India*

Brand, Raymond. H. (*Biology*, also Ecology/Environment) *Illinois*

Branson, Roy (*Ethics*, also Theology/Religion) *Washington, D.C.*

Bratton, Susan P. (*Ecology/Environment*, also Ethics) *Georgia*

Breed, David R. (*Theology/Religion*, also Philosophy) *Illinois*

Breed, James Lincoln (*Theology/Religion*, also Philosophy) *Illinois*

Bregman, Lucy (*Theology/Religion*, also Psychology/Counseling) *Pennsylvania*

Brennan, John Lester (*Medical Science*) *United Kingdom*

Bridges Jr., Carl B. (*Theology/Religion*, also Languages) *Tennessee*

Brigham, Joseph John (*Engineering*) *North Carolina*

Brobeck, John R. (*Medical Science*) *Pennsylvania*

Brooke, John Hedley (*History and Philosophy of Science*, also Chemistry, Theology/Religion, Philosophy) *United Kingdom*

Brooks, George Gordon (*Physics*, also Theology/Religion) *New Hampshire*, also Florida

Brown, Robert Hanbury (*Philosophy*, also Astronomy/Astrophysics) *United Kingdom*

Brown, Warren S. (*Medical Science*, also Psychology/Counseling) *California*

Browning, Don S. (*Ethics*, also Theology/Religion) *Illinois*

Brück, Hermann Alexander (*Astronomy/Astrophysics*, also History and Philosophy of Science) *United Kingdom*

Brugger, Hans Rudolf (*Physics*, also Astronomy/Astrophysics) *Switzerland*

Brun, Rudolf B. (*Biology*) *Texas*

Brungs, Robert (*Theology/Religion*, also Physics, Ethics) *Missouri*

Bube, Richard H. (*Physics*, also Theology/Religion) *California*

Buckley, Michael J. (*Theology/Religion*, also Philosophy) *Indiana*

Budenholzer, Frank (*Chemistry*, also Physics, Theology/Religion) *Taiwan*

Buehler, David A. (*Theology/Religion*, also Ethics, Computer and Information Sciences) *Massachusetts*

Bulka, Reuven P. (*Theology/Religion*, also Philosophy, Psychology/Counseling) *Canada*

Bunnell, Adam Eugene (*History*, also Theology/Religion) *Kentucky*

Burhoe, Ralph Wendell (*Theology/Religion*) *Illinois*

Burke, Derek C. (*Molecular Biology*, also Theology/Religion) *United Kingdom*

Burke, Thomas J. (*Theology/Religion*, also Philosophy, History and Philosophy of Science) *Michigan*

Burneko, Guy C. (*Interdisciplinary Studies*) *Alaska*

Burnham, Frederic B. (*History and Philosophy of Science*, also Theology/Religion) *New York*

Burns Sr., John Lanier (*Theology/Religion*, also Philosophy) *Texas*

Busse, Richard Paul (*Theology/Religion*, also Philosophy) *Indiana*

Buswell III, James O. (*Anthropology*) *California*

Buttiglione, Rocco (*Philosophy*, also Political Science/Politics, Ethics) *Liechtenstein*

Byers, David M. (*Theology/Religion*) *Washington, D.C.*

Byrne, Patrick H. (*Philosophy*) *Massachusetts*

C

Cahill, Lisa Sowle (*Theology/Religion*, also Ethics) *Massachusetts*

Cain, Dallas E. (*Engineering*) *New York*

Cantor, Geoffrey (*History and Philosophy of Science*, also Philosophy) *United Kingdom*

Cantore, Enrico (*Philosophy*, also Physics, Theology/Religion) *New York*

Capart, Laurent J. N. (*Engineering*) *Belgium*

Carey, Patrick W. (*Theology/Religion*, also History and Philosophy of Science) *Michigan*

Carlson, Richard F. (*Physics*) *California*

Carvallo, Marc E. (*Philosophy*, also Education, Theology/Religion) *The Netherlands*

Casanova, José V. (*Sociology*) *New York*

Casebolt, James R. (*Psychology/Counseling*) *Virginia*

Casey, Thomas Michael (*Theology/Religion*, also Psychology/Counseling) *Massachusetts*

Cauthen, W. Kenneth (*Theology/Religion*) *New York*

Cereti, Giovanni (*Theology/Religion*) *Italy*

Chadha, N. K. (*Psychology/Counseling*) *India*

Challice, Cyril Eugene (*Biochemistry/Biophysics*, also Theology/Religion) *Canada*

Chase, Gene Barry (*Mathematics*, also Computer and Information Sciences) *Pennsylvania*

Childs, Brian H. (*Psychology/Counseling*) *Georgia*

Chirico-Rosenberg, Donna (*Psychology/Counseling*) *New York*

Church, F. Forrester (*Communications*, also Theology/Religion) *New York*

Clark, Kelly James (*Philosophy*, also Theology/Religion, History and Philosophy of Science) *Michigan*

Clarke, Charles L. (*Medical Science*) *Tennessee*

Clarke, Christopher James Seaton (*Philosophy*, also Mathematics) *United Kingdom*

Clayton, Philip (*Philosophy*, also Theology/Religion, History and Philosophy of Science) *Massachusetts*

Clifton, Robert K. (*History and Philosophy of Science*, also Philosophy, Physics) *Canada*

Cloots, André (*Philosophy*, also History and Philosophy of Science) *Belgium*

Cloutier, Stephen (*Chemistry*, also Engineering) *Illinois*

Cobb Jr., John B. (*Theology/Religion*, also Philosophy) *California*

Cobb, Larry R. (*Administration*) *Pennsylvania*

Cohen, Ernest B. (*Engineering*, also Technology, Psychology/Counseling) *Pennsylvania*

Cole, David R. (*Biochemistry/Biophysics*) *California*

Cole-Turner, Ronald S. (*Theology/Religion*, also Ethics) *Tennessee*

Collins, Gary R. (*Psychology/Counseling*) *Illinois*

Colvis, John Paris (*Engineering*, also Astronomy/Astrophysics) *Colorado*

Colzani, Gianni (*Theology/Religion*) *Italy*

Combs, Allan L. (*Psychology/Counseling*) *North Carolina*

Conrad, Constance C. (*Medical Science*, also Education) *Georgia*

Cook, Sir Alan Hugh (*Physics*, also Astronomy/Astrophysics) *United Kingdom*

Copenhaver, Brian P. (*History*, also Physics) *California*

Copestake, David R. (*Theology/Religion*, also Psychology/Counseling) *United Kingdom*

Corbally, Christopher J. (*Astronomy/Astrophysics*, also Theology/Religion) *Arizona*

Corsi, Pietro (*History and Philosophy of Science*, also Philosophy) *Italy*

Cotter, Graham (*Theology/Religion*, also Literature, History and Philosophy of Science) *Canada*

Count, Earl W. (*Sociology*, also Theology/Religion) *California*

Coyne, George V. (*Astronomy/Astrophysics*) *Italy*

Cramer, John Allen (*Physics*) *Georgia*

Crippen, Timothy (*Sociology*, also Sociobiology) *Virginia*

Crombie, Alistair Cameron (*History and Philosophy of Science*, also Biology) *United Kingdom*

Crosby, Donald Allen (*Philosophy*, also Theology/Religion) *Colorado*

Crosby, John F. (*Philosophy*, also Theology/Religion) *Ohio*

Crowe, Michael J. (*History and Philosophy of Science*, also Physics, Astronomy/Astrophysics) *Indiana*

Crutcher, Keith A. (*Medical Science*) *Ohio*

Cudworth, Kyle M. (*Astronomy/Astrophysics*) *Wisconsin*

Curry, John F. (*Psychology/Counseling*, also Medical Science) *North Carolina*

𝒟

D'Ambrosio, Ubiratan (*History and Philosophy of Science*, also Mathematics, Philosophy) *Brazil*

d'Aquili, Eugene G, (*Psychiatry*, also Medical Science, Anthropology) *Pennsylvania*

da Cruz, Eduardo Rodrigues (*Theology/Religion*, also Physics) *Brazil*

Daecke, Sigurd (*Theology/Religion*) *Germany*

Dagnall, Bernard (*Chemistry*, also Theology/Religion) *United Kingdom*

Dalferth, Ingolf Ulrich (*Theology/Religion*, also Philosophy) *Germany*, also Switzerland

Dallaporta, Nicolo (*Physics*) *Italy*

Dally, Andreas Michael (*Biology*) *Germany*

Davies, Paul Charles William (*Physics*) *Australia*

Davis, Edward B. (*History and Philosophy of Science*, also Philosophy) *Pennsylvania*

Davis, Lloyd J. (*Physics*) *North Carolina*

Davis, Marjorie Hall (*Theology/Religion*, also Psychology/Counseling) *Connecticut*

de Beauregard, O. Costa (*Physics*, also Philosophy) *France*

de Knijff, Henri Wijnandus (*Theology/Religion*) *The Netherlands*

Deason, Gary Bruce (*Theology/Religion*, also History and Philosophy of Science) *Minnesota*

Deckert, Curtis Kenneth (*Management*, also Technology) *California*

DeGraaf, Donald E. (*Physics*) *Michigan*

DeHaan, Robert F. (*Psychology/Counseling*) *Pennsylvania*

Del Re, Giuseppe (*Chemistry*, also Physics, Philosophy) *Italy*

Denues, A. R. Taylor (*Chemistry*, also Engineering, Medical Science, Theology/Religion) *Pennsylvania*

Deuser, Hermann (*Theology/Religion*) *Germany*

DeWitt, Calvin B. (*Biology*, also Ecology/Environment, Ethics) *Wisconsin*

Di Bernardo, Giuliano (*History and Philosophy of Science*, also Philosophy) *Italy*

Dierick, G.P.A. (*History*, also Philosophy, Theology/Religion) *The Netherlands*

Dillenberger, John (*Theology/Religion*) *California*

Dilworth, Craig (*Philosophy*, also History and Philosophy of Science) *Sweden*

Dittes, James E. (*Theology/Religion*, also Psychology/Counseling) *Connecticut*

Dobbs, Betty Jo Teeter (*History and Philosophy of Science*) *Illinois*

Dodson, Edward O. (*Biology*, also Genetics) *Canada*

Dols Jr., William L. (*Theology/Religion*, also Psychology/Counseling) *Missouri*

Dormer, Kenneth J. (*Medical Science*) *Oklahoma*

Downing, Barry H. (*Theology/Religion*, also Technology) *New York*

Drago, Antonino (*History and Philosophy of Science*, also Physics) *Italy*

Drees, Willem B. (*Theology/Religion*, also Physics) *The Netherlands*

Drozdek, Adam (*Computer and Information Sciences*) *Pennsylvania*

Duchrow, Ulrich (*Theology/Religion*) *Germany*

Dufner, Andrew J. (*Theology/Religion*, also Philosophy, Physics) *Oregon*

Duguay, Michel A. (*Physics*, also Engineering) *Canada*

DuMaine, R. Pierre (*Theology/Religion*) *California*

Dundon, Stanislaus J. (*Philosophy*, also Theology/Religion, History and Philosophy of Science) *California*

Durant, John Robert (*History and Philosophy of Science*, also Biology) *United Kingdom*

Durbin Jr., William A. (*History and Philosophy of Science*, also Communications) *North Carolina*

Dye, David L. (*Physics*, also Technology) *Washington*

Dyson, Freeman J. (*Physics*) *New Jersey*

E

Eaves, Lindon John (*Genetics*, also Theology/Religion, Mathematics) *Virginia*

Eccles, Sir John C. (*Medical Science*, also History and Philosophy of Science, Philosophy) *Switzerland*

Eckstrom, Vance L. (*Theology/Religion*) *Kansas*

Eder, Gernot (*Physics*) *Austria*

Edgar, William (*Theology/Religion*) *Pennsylvania*

Ehlers, Vernon J. (*Psychology/Counseling*, also Physics, Ethics) *Michigan*

Ehrenfeld, David W. (*Ecology/Environment*, also Biology, Medical Science) *New Jersey*

Eicher, Andreas D. (*Ecology/Environment*, also Medical Science) *Connecticut*

Eiff von, August Wilhelm (*Medical Science*, also Ethics) *Germany*

Eigen, Manfred (*Biochemistry/Biophysics*, also Chemistry) *Germany*

Elgee, Neil J. (*Medical Science*) *Washington*

Elkins, Thomas Edward (*Medical Science*) *Louisiana*

Ellens, J. Harold (*Psychology/Counseling*, also Theology/Religion) *Michigan*

Elliott, John Eric (*History and Philosophy of Science*, also Mathematics) *North Carolina*

Ellis, George F. R. (*Mathematics*, also Philosophy) *South Africa*

Emerton, Norma Elizabeth (*History and Philosophy of Science*) *United Kingdom*

Engels, Eve-Marie (*Philosophy*, also History and Philosophy of Science, Ethics) *Germany*

Erbich, Paul (*Philosophy*, also Biology, Theology/Religion) *Germany*

Erdmann, Erika (*Interdisciplinary Studies*, also Philosophy) *Canada*

Euvé, François (*Theology/Religion*, also Physics, Philosophy) *France*

Evans, Abigail Rian (*Ethics*, also Philosophy, Theology/Religion, Medical Science) *Washington, D.C.*

Evans, C. A. (*Theology/Religion*) *Canada*

Evans, C. Stephen (*Philosophy*, also Psychology/Counseling) *Minnesota*

Everest, F. Alton (*Engineering*, also Technology) *California*

Ewald, Günter (*Mathematics*, also History and Philosophy of Science) *Germany*

F

Faber, Roger J. (*Physics*, also Philosophy, Chemistry) *Illinois*

Facchini, Fiorenzo (*Anthropology*) *Italy*

Fagg, Lawrence W. (*Physics*, also Theology/Religion) *Virginia*

Fairchild, Roy W. (*Theology/Religion*, also Psychology/Counseling, Sociology) *California*

Falla Jr., William S. (*Theology/Religion*, also Earth Science) *Pennsylvania*

Farnsworth, Kirk E. (*Psychology/Counseling*, also Theology/Religion) *Washington*

Fasching, Darrell J. (*Theology/Religion*, also Ethics, Philosophy) *Florida*

Fast, Edwin (*Physics*, also Chemistry, Mathematics) *Idaho*

Faulkner Jr., George R. (*Management*) *Idaho*

Fayter, The Rev. Paul (*History and Philosophy of Science*, also Theology/Religion, Interdisciplinary Studies) *Canada*

Feifel, Herman (*Psychology/Counseling*) *California*

Feil, Dirk (*Chemistry*, also Physics) *The Netherlands*

Felt, James W. (*Philosophy*, also Theology/Religion, Physics) *California*

Fennema, Jan W. R. (*Physics*, also Philosophy, Theology/Religion) *The Netherlands*

Ferré, Frederick (*Philosophy*, also Theology/Religion, Ethics, Technology) *Georgia*

Ferrell, Ginnie (*Theology/Religion*, also Earth Science, Chemistry) *Maine*

Feucht, Dennis L. (*Technology*, also Computer and Information Sciences) *Oregon*

Fiddes, Victor H. (*Theology/Religion*) *Canada*

Finney, Joseph Claude Jeans (*Psychology/Counseling*, also Psychiatry, Theology/Religion) *California*

Firestone, Homer Loon (*Theology/Religion*, also Psychology/Counseling, Languages) *California, also Bolivia*

Fischer, Dick (*Theology/Religion*) *Virginia*

Fischer, Robert B. (*Chemistry*, also Theology/Religion, Education) *California*

Fleming, Fraser Fergusson (*Chemistry*) *Pennsylvania*

Fokker, Adriaan D. (*Astronomy/Astrophysics*) *The Netherlands*

Force, James E. (*Philosophy*, also History and Philosophy of Science) *Kentucky*

Ford, Charles E. (*Mathematics*, also Computer and Information Sciences) *Missouri*

Ford, Mary Anne Kehoe (*Communications*) *Connecticut*

Forman, Frank (*Economics*) *Maryland*

Forster, Peter R. (*Theology/Religion*, also History) *United Kingdom*

Foster, Mark A. (*Sociology*) *Georgia*

Fowler III, James W. (*Theology/Religion*, also Ethics, Education, Psychology/Counseling) *Georgia*

Fowler, Thomas B. (*Engineering*, also Computer and Information Sciences, Philosophy) *Washington, D.C.*

Frair, Wayne (*Biology*, also Genetics) *New York*

Frecska, Ede (*Psychiatry*, also Biochemistry/Biophysics) *New York*

Freire-Maia, Newton (*Genetics*, also Biology) *Brazil*

Frey, Christofer (*Theology/Religion*, also Sociology, Ethics) *Germany*

Frye, Roland Mushat (*Literature*, also Theology/Religion) *Pennsylvania*

Fuchs, Peter C. (*Medical Science*) *Oregon*

Furtado, Daphne (*Biochemistry/Biophysics*, also Chemistry) *India*

G

Gaál, Botond (*Theology/Religion*, also Physics, Mathematics) *Hungary*

Gaede, S. D. (*Sociology*, also History and Philosophy of Science) *Massachusetts*

Gailey, Franklin B. (*Medical Science*, also Biochemistry/Biophysics) *Kentucky*

Galleni, Lodovico (*Biology*) *Italy*

Ganguli, H. C. (*Psychology/Counseling*, also Philosophy) *India*

Gardipee, Steven M. (*Theology/Religion*, also Philosophy) *Wisconsin*

Gay, Volney P. (*Psychology/Counseling*, also Theology/Religion, Anthropology) *Tennessee*

Geisler, Norman L. (*Philosophy*, also Theology/Religion) *Texas*

Gelwick, Richard (*Theology/Religion*, also Philosophy, History and Philosophy of Science, Interdisciplinary Studies) *Maine*

Germine, Mark (*Psychiatry*, also Medical Science) *Connecticut*

Giannoni, Paolo (*Theology/Religion*) *Italy*

Giberson, Karl Willard (*Physics*) *Massachusetts*

Gibson, Arthur (*Philosophy*, also Literature, Astronomy/Astrophysics, Political Science/Politics) *United Kingdom*

Gilbert, Thomas L. (*Physics*, also Chemistry, Theology/Religion) *Illinois*

Gilkey, Langdon (*Theology/Religion*, also Philosophy) *Illinois*

Gill, Anthony J. (*Political Science/Politics*) *Washington*

Gill, Stephen P. (*Mathematics*, also Physics) *California*

Gillespie, Neal C. (*History and Philosophy of Science*, also History) *Georgia*

Gillette, P. Roger (*Engineering*, also Physics, Technology, Ethics) *California*

Gingerich, Owen (*Astronomy/Astrophysics*, also History and Philosophy of Science, Philosophy) *Massachusetts*

Giulianelli, James L. (*Chemistry*) *Colorado*

Glassman, Robert B. (*Psychology/Counseling*, also Sociobiology) *Illinois*

Glódz, Malgorzata (*Physics*) *Poland*

Goldsmith, W. (Walter) Mack (*Psychology/Counseling*, also Theology/Religion) *California*

Golshani, Mehdi (*Physics*, also Theology/Religion, Philosophy, History and Philosophy of Science) *Iran*

Goodenough, Ward H. (*Anthropology*) *Pennsylvania*

Gorsuch, Richard L. (*Psychology/Counseling*, also Theology/Religion) *California*

Gosden, Roger G. (*Medical Science*) *United Kingdom*

Gouldstone, Tim (*Genetics*, also Theology/Religion) *United Kingdom*

Gowenlock, Brian G. (*Chemistry*) *United Kingdom*

Gracely, Brett W. (*Engineering*) *Colorado*

Grant, Theodore F. (*Psychology/Counseling*) *Washington, D.C.*, also Maryland

Green, Thomas F. (*Education*, also Sociology, Philosophy) *New York*

Greenhow, Donald Eric Fraser (*Medical Science*) *Pennsylvania*

Gregersen, Niels Henrik (*Theology/Religion*, also History and Philosophy of Science, Ethics) *Denmark*

Gregorios, Paulos Mar (*Theology/Religion*, also Administration, History and Philosophy of Science, Philosophy) *India*

Gregory, Frederick (*History and Philosophy of Science*) *Florida*

Gregory, William Edgar (*Psychology/Counseling*) *California*

Griffin, David Ray (*Theology/Religion*, also Philosophy, History and Philosophy of Science) *California*

Griffin, Douglas L. (*Theology/Religion*) *Maryland*

Griffiths, Robert B. (*Physics*, also Mathematics) *Pennsylvania*

Grizzle, Raymond Edward (*Ecology/Environment*) *Indiana*

Gromacki, Robert Glenn (*Theology/Religion*) *Ohio*

Gruenwald, Oskar (*Communications*, also Psychology/Counseling, Interdisciplinary Studies, Philosophy) *California*

Grzegorczyk, Andrzej (*Philosophy*, also Mathematics, Ethics) *Poland*

Gumlich, Hans-Eckhart (*Physics*, also Technology) *Germany*

ℋ

Haas Jr., John W. (*Chemistry*, also History and Philosophy of Science) *Massachusetts*

Haas III, John W. (*Chemistry*) *Massachusetts*

Haba, Hanako (*Philosophy*, also Theology/Religion) *United Kingdom*

Habgood, John S. (*Theology/Religion*, also Biochemistry/Biophysics) *United Kingdom*

Hafner, Hermann Friedrich (*Theology/Religion*, also History and Philosophy of Science) *Germany*

Haikola, Lars T. J. (*Theology/Religion*, also Philosophy) *Sweden*

Hall, Forrest G. (*Physics*) *Maryland*

Hallberg, Fred W. (*Philosophy*, also Psychology/Counseling) *Iowa*

Hancock Jr., Monte F. (*Mathematics*) *Florida*

Handspickel, Meredith Brook (*Theology/Religion*) *Massachusetts*

Hanford, Jack T. (*Theology/Religion*, also Philosophy, Ethics) *Michigan*

Hankins, Thomas L. (*History and Philosophy of Science*, also History, Education) *Washington*

Hannon, Ralph H. (*Chemistry*, also Physics, Mathematics) *Illinois*

Happel, Stephen (*Theology/Religion*) *Washington, D.C.*

Hardy, Daniel W. (*Theology/Religion*) *New Jersey*

Harman, William K. (*History*, also Theology/Religion) *California*

Harper, Charles L. (*Earth Science*, also Theology/Religion, Philosophy, Technology) *United Kingdom*

Harré, Rom (*History and Philosophy of Science*, also Philosophy) *United Kingdom*

Harrington, Donald S. (*Theology/Religion*) *New York*

Harris, E. Lynn (*Theology/Religion*, also Literature, Psychology/Counseling) *Illinois*

Hart, John (*Theology/Religion*, also Philosophy, Commerce, Ethics) *Montana*

Hartwig, Edward Clayton (*Physics*, also Engineering) *California*

Hartzell, Karl Drew (*Administration*, also History, Education, Ethics) *New York*

Hartzler, H. Harold (*Mathematics*, also Physics, Astronomy/Astrophysics) *Indiana*

Hasel, Frank Michael (*Theology/Religion*) *Michigan*

Haught, John F. (*Theology/Religion*) *Washington, D.C.*

Haury, David L. (*Education*, also Biology) *Massachusetts*

Hay, David (*Biology*, also Theology/Religion, Sociology) *United Kingdom*

Hayward, Jeremy (*Physics*, also History and Philosophy of Science, Theology/Religion) *Canada*

Hazard, Evan Brandao (*Biology*) *Minnesota*

Hazelett, Samuel Richard (*Philosophy*, also Engineering) *Vermont*

Hazen, Craig J. (*Biology*, also Theology/Religion, Jurisprudence/Law) *California*

Heaney, John J. (*Theology/Religion*, also Psychology/Counseling) *New York*

Hearn, Walter Russell (*Biochemistry/Biophysics*, also Communications, Theology/Religion) *California*

Heckenlively, Donald B. (*Biology*, also Computer and Information Sciences) *Michigan*

Hedman, Bruce A. (*Theology/Religion*, also Mathematics) *Connecticut*

Heelan, Patrick A. (*Philosophy*, also Physics, Earth Science, Theology/Religion) *New York*

Hefley, James C. (*Communications*) *Missouri*

Hefner, Philip (*Theology/Religion*, also Interdisciplinary Studies, Philosophy) *Illinois*

Heim, S. Mark (*Theology/Religion*) *Massachusetts*

Heller, Michael (*Philosophy*, also Astronomy/Astrophysics, History and Philosophy of Science) *Poland*

Hemminger, Hansjörg (*Biology*, also Philosophy) *Germany*

Henry, Carl F. H. (*Theology/Religion*, also Philosophy, Ethics) *Virginia*

Henry, James P. (*Psychiatry*, also Medical Science, Biochemistry/Biophysics) *California*

Hermann, Robert A. (*Mathematics*, also Physics, Philosophy) *Maryland*

Hernandez, Edwin Ivan (*Sociology*) *Michigan*

Heron, Alasdair Iain Campbell (*Theology/Religion*) *Germany*

Herrmann, Robert L. (*Biochemistry/Biophysics*, also Chemistry, Molecular Biology) *Massachusetts*

Hess, Gerald D. (*Biology*) *Pennsylvania*

Hess, Peter M. (*Philosophy*, also Theology/Religion) *California*

Hesse, Mary Brenda (*History and Philosophy of Science*, also Physics, Philosophy, Mathematics) *United Kingdom*

Hickernell, Fred S. (*Engineering*, also Technology) *Arizona*

Hiebert, Erwin Nick (*History and Philosophy of Science*, also Chemistry, Physics) *Massachusetts*

Hiebert, Paul G. (*Anthropology*, also Theology/Religion) *Illinois*

Hilden, Kurt Mark (*Theology/Religion*, also Philosophy) *California*

Hilhorst, Medard T. (*Ethics*, also Theology/Religion, Technology) *The Netherlands*

Hill, David R. (*Computer and Information Sciences*, also Psychology/Counseling, Engineering) *Canada*

Hillar, Marian (*Molecular Biology*, also Biochemistry/Biophysics, Medical Science, History) *Texas*

Hillery Jr., George A. (*Sociology*, also Anthropology) *Virginia*

Hinkle, John E. (*Psychology/Counseling*) *Illinois*

Hird, John Francis (*Technology*, also Engineering, Theology/Religion) *Delaware*

Hodges, Bert H. (*Psychology/Counseling*, also Philosophy) *Massachusetts*

Hodgson, Peter E. (*Physics*) *United Kingdom*

Hoge, Dean Richard (*Sociology*) *Washington, D.C.*

Hogenhuis, C. T. (*Physics*) *The Netherlands*

Hoggatt, Austin Curwood (*Economics*) *California*

Holmes, Arthur F. (*Philosophy*, also Theology/Religion) *Illinois*

Holmes, H. Rodney (*Biology*, also Psychology/Counseling) *Illinois*

Hood, Randall (*Sociobiology*, also Theology/Religion) *California*

Hood, Thomas Charles (*Sociology*, also AT) *Tennessee*

Hoppin, Marion C. (*Psychology/Counseling*) *Florida*

Horswell, Kevin (*Philosophy*, also Theology/Religion) *United Kingdom*

Horvath, Tibor (*Theology/Religion*, also Philosophy, Interdisciplinary Studies) *Canada*

Hoshiko, Tomuo (*Biochemistry/Biophysics*, also Medical Science) *Ohio*

Houghton, John T. (*Physics*) *United Kingdom*

Howe, George Franklin (*Biology*) *California*

Hübner, Jürgen (*Theology/Religion*, also Molecular Biology, Ecology/Environment, History and Philosophy of Science) *Germany*

Hugenberger, Gordon P. (*Theology/Religion*) *Massachusetts*

Hughes, Cecil Forrest (*Theology/Religion*) *California*

Hull, John M. (*Education*, also Theology/Religion) *United Kingdom*

Hulme, Norman A. (*Biochemistry/Biophysics*, also Medical Science) *New York*

Humbert, Jean (*Biology*, also Earth Science) *France*

Hummel, Charles E. (*Theology/Religion*, also Chemistry, Technology) *Massachusetts*

Humphreys, Colin John (*Technology*, also Physics) *United Kingdom*

Hunt, Mary E. (*Theology/Religion*, also Ethics) *Maryland*

Huntemann, Georg (*Theology/Religion*, also Philosophy, Ethics) *Germany*

Hunter, Lloyd P. (*Engineering*) *New York*

Hutch, Richard A. (*Theology/Religion*, also Psychology/Counseling, History) *Australia*

Hyers, Conrad (*Theology/Religion*) *Minnesota*

I

Ice, Jackson Lee (*Theology/Religion*, also Philosophy) *Florida*

Ice, Rodney D. (*Physics*) *Georgia*

Ingram, David J. E. (*Physics*) *United Kingdom*

Ingram, Larry C. (*Sociology*) *Tennessee*

Isaak, Paul John (*Theology/Religion*) *Namibia*

Isak, Rainer (*Theology/Religion*, also Biology, Philosophy) *Germany*

Isham, Christopher J. (*Physics*) *United Kingdom*

J

Jackelén, Antje (*Philosophy*, also Theology/Religion) *Sweden*

Jackson, Wes (*Biology*, also Genetics, Ecology/Environment, Ethics) *Kansas*

Jain, Devaki (*Sociology*, also Ethics) *India*

Jaki, Stanley L. (*Theology/Religion*, also Physics, History and Philosophy of Science) *New Jersey*

Jang, Allen Wai (*Psychology/Counseling*) *California*

Jappe, Fred (*Chemistry*, also Theology/Religion) *California*

Jasso, Guillermina (*Sociology*) *New York*

Jeeves, Malcolm A. (*Psychology/Counseling*, also Theology/Religion) *United Kingdom*

Jenkins, Eric Neil (*Chemistry*, also Theology/Religion, Ethics) *United Kingdom*

Jervis, R. E. (*Technology*, also Chemistry, Physics) *Canada*

Johnson, Anthony P. (*Management*, also Theology/Religion) *New York*

Johnson, Delmer A. (*Theology/Religion*) *Colorado*

Johnson, Doyle Paul (*Sociology*) *Texas*

Johnson, Rodney W. (*Technology*, also Physics) *Virginia*, also Maryland

Johnson, Walter Colin (*Psychiatry*, also Psychology/Counseling, Medical Science) *Massachusetts*

Johnston, G. Archie (*Psychology/Counseling*, also Biology) *California*

Jones, D. Gareth (*Medical Science*, also Biology, Ethics) *New Zealand*

Jones, Jack R. (*Ecology/Environment*) *Maryland*

Jones, James W. (*Psychology/Counseling*, also Theology/Religion) *New Jersey*

Jones, Stanton Louis (*Psychology/Counseling*) *Illinois*

Juergensmeyer, Mark (*Ethics*, also Sociology, Philosophy, Theology/Religion) *California*

Junkin III, William F. (*Physics*) *South Carolina*

𝒦

Kahoe, Richard Dean (*Psychology/Counseling*) *Oklahoma*

Kaiser, Christopher B. (*Theology/Religion*, also Physics, History and Philosophy of Science) *Michigan*

Kaita, Robert (*Physics*) *New Jersey*

Kalthoff, Mark A. (*History and Philosophy of Science*, also Philosophy) *Michigan*

Kanagy, Sherman P. (*Astronomy/Astrophysics*, also Philosophy, Physics) *Indiana*

Kang, Phee Seng (*Philosophy*, also Theology/Religion, Mathematics) *Hong Kong*

Karkalits Jr., Olin Carroll (*Chemistry*, also Engineering) *Louisiana*

Kassel, Victor (*Medical Science*) *Utah*

Keggi, J John (*Chemistry*, also Theology/Religion) *Massachusetts*

Keilholz, Peggy J. (*Psychology/Counseling*, also Theology/Religion) *Missouri*

Keiper Sr., Glenn L. (*Medical Science*) *Ohio*

Kelly, Dr. William L. (*Chemistry*) *Ohio*

Kent, Raymond D. (*Theology/Religion*) *Wisconsin*

Kern, John C. (*Management*) *Illinois*

Kerr, John Maxwell (*Theology/Religion*, also Engineering, Biology, History and Philosophy of Science) *United Kingdom*

Kerze, Michael A.. (*Theology/Religion*, also History and Philosophy of Science) *California*

Key, Thomas D. S. (*Biology*, also Theology/Religion) *Mississippi*

Kim, Stephen S. (*Theology/Religion*, also History and Philosophy of Science) *California*

King Jr., Morton B. (*Sociology*) *Texas*

Kirby, Richard (*Theology/Religion*) *Washington*

Kirchoff, Bruce K. (*Ecology/Environment*, also Genetics) *North Carolina*

Kirkpatrick, Lee Alan (*Psychology/Counseling*) *South Carolina*

Klaaren, Eugene M. (*Theology/Religion*, also History and Philosophy of Science) *Connecticut*

Klaus, Hanna (*Medical Science*, also Theology/Religion) *Maryland*

Klotz, John W. (*Ecology/Environment*, also Theology/Religion, Ethics) *Missouri*

Knapp, Andreas (*Theology/Religion*, also Ethics) *Germany*

Knapp II, John Allen (*Literature*, also Education, Theology/Religion) *New York*

Knight, Christopher C. (*Theology/Religion*, also Astronomy/Astrophysics, Physics) *United Kingdom*

Knight, David Marcus (*History and Philosophy of Science*) *United Kingdom*

Knight, Douglas A. (*Theology/Religion*) *Tennessee*

Knight, James Allen (*Psychology/Counseling*, also Theology/Religion, Medical Science) *Texas*

Knobloch, Irving William (*Biology*) *Michigan*

Koenig, Harold G. (*Medical Science*, also Psychology/Counseling) *North Carolina*

Koenigsberger, Dorothy (*History*, also History and Philosophy of Science) *United Kingdom*

Kohn, David (*History and Philosophy of Science*) *New Jersey*

Kolega, D. G. A. (*Theology/Religion*, also Philosophy, Ethics) *The Netherlands*

Koltermann, Rainer (*Biology*, also Philosophy, Theology/Religion) *Germany*

Korsmeyer, Jerry (*Physics*, also Theology/Religion) *Pennsylvania*

Koteskey, Ronald L. (*Psychology/Counseling*) *Kentucky*

Kovel, Joel (*Psychiatry*, also Sociology, Psychology/Counseling) *New York*

Kracher, Alfred (*Chemistry*, also Earth Science) *Iowa*

Kraft, R. Wayne (*Technology*, also Physics) *Pennsylvania*

Krolzik, Udo (*Theology/Religion*) *Germany*

Kropf, Richard W. (*Theology/Religion*, also Philosophy, Psychology/Counseling) *Michigan*

Kuharetz, Boris (*Astronomy/Astrophysics*) *New Jersey*

Külling, Samuel (*Theology/Religion*) *Switzerland*

Kupke, Donald Walter (*Biochemistry/Biophysics*) *Virginia*

Küppers, Bernd-Olaf (*History and Philosophy of Science*, also Molecular Biology, Interdisciplinary Studies) *Germany*

L

LaBar, Martin (*Biology*, also Ethics) *South Carolina*

Laeyendecker, L. (*Sociology*, also Theology/Religion) *The Netherlands*

LaFargue, Michael (*Theology/Religion*, also History and Philosophy of Science, Interdisciplinary Studies) *Massachusetts*

Lamoureux, Denis Oswald (*Medical Science*) *Canada*

Landess, Marcia McBroom (*Political Science/Politics*, also Education, Theology/Religion) *New York*

Landsberg, Peter T. (*Mathematics*, also Philosophy, History and Philosophy of Science) *United Kingdom*

Lantum, Noni Daniel (*Medical Science*, also Sociology, Administration) *Cameroon*

Larsen, Judith K. (*Technology*) *California*

Larson, David Bruce (*Medical Science*, also Psychiatry, Administration) *Maryland*

Larson, Duane H. (*Theology/Religion*, also Administration) *Pennsylvania*

Larson, Edward J. (*Jurisprudence/Law*, also History and Philosophy of Science) *Georgia*

Larson, Laurence A. (*Biology*, also Interdisciplinary Studies) *Ohio*

Larzelere, Robert Earl (*Psychology/Counseling*) *Nebraska*

Lategan, Bernard C. (*Theology/Religion*) *South Africa*

Laughlin, Charles D. (*Anthropology*, also Medical Science) *Canada*

Laurikainen, Kalervo Vihtori (*History and Philosophy of Science*, also Physics, Theology/Religion, Philosophy) *Finland*

Legrain, Michel (*Jurisprudence/Law*, also Ethics) *France*

Lejeune, Jérôme Jean Louis Marie (*Genetics*, also Medical Science) *France*

Leming, Michael Richard (*Sociology*) *Minnesota*

Lenz, Hermann (*Psychiatry*) *Austria*

Leslie, John (*Philosophy*, also Astronomy/Astrophysics, History and Philosophy of Science, Theology/Religion) *Canada*

Levitt, J. Peter Fletcher (*Theology/Religion*, also Physics) *United Kingdom*

Lewthwaite, Gordon R. (*Earth Science*, also History) *California*

Libanio, João Batista (*Philosophy*, also Languages, Theology/Religion) *Brazil*

Liedke, Gerhard (*Theology/Religion*) *Germany*

Lifton, Robert Jay (*Psychiatry*, also Psychology/Counseling, Medical Science, Ethics) *New York*

Liljas, Anders (*Biochemistry/Biophysics*) *Sweden*

Lindberg, David C. (*History and Philosophy of Science*, also Physics, Philosophy) *Wisconsin*

Lindenbald, Irving W. (*Astronomy/Astrophysics*, also Theology/Religion) *Washington, D.C.*

Lindquist, Stanley E. (*Psychology/Counseling*) *California*

Ling, Vincent (*Biology*) *Massachusetts*

Link, Christian (*Theology/Religion*, also Physics) *Germany*

Lipinski, Boguslaw (*Biochemistry/Biophysics*) *Massachusetts*

Livingstone, David Noel (*Earth Science*, also Philosophy, Sociology) *North Ireland*

Loder, James Edwin (*Theology/Religion*, also Psychology/Counseling, Philosophy) *New Jersey*

Lovell, Sir Bernard (*Physics*, also Astronomy/Astrophysics) *United Kingdom*

Lovett Doust, Jonathan Nicolas de Grave (*Biology*, also Ecology/Environment) *Canada*

Löw, Reinhard (*Philosophy*, also History and Philosophy of Science, Ethics) *Germany*

Lucas, J. R. (*Philosophy*) *United Kingdom*

Lumsden, Charles J. (*Physics*, also Biology, Medical Science) *Canada*

Lynden-Bell, Donald (*Astronomy/Astrophysics*) *United Kingdom*

ℳ

Maatman, Russell W. (*Chemistry*) *Iowa*

MacCready, Paul B. (*Astronomy/Astrophysics*, also Physics, Commerce) *California*

Maciel, Paulo Frederico do Rĕgo (*Economics*, also Philosophy) *Brazil*

Macior, Lazarus Walter (*Theology/Religion*, also Biology) *Ohio*

MacKay, David B. (*Commerce*, also Earth Science) *Indiana*

Mackler, Aaron L. (*Theology/Religion*, also Ethics, Philosophy) *Pennsylvania*

Macy, Joanna R. (*Theology/Religion*) *California*

Maduro, L. Otto A. (*Philosophy*, also Sociology) *New York*

Magnuson, Norris A. (*Theology/Religion*, also History) *Minnesota*

Mailloux, Noël (*Psychology/Counseling*, also Theology/Religion) *Canada*

Malino, Jerome R. (*Theology/Religion*) *New York*

Mallove, Eugene F. (*Communications*, also Astronomy/Astrophysics) *New Hampshire*

Malony, H. Newton (*Psychology/Counseling*, also Theology/Religion) *California*

Manenschijn, Gerrit (*Ethics*, also Theology/Religion) *The Netherlands*

Manganello, James A. (*Psychology/Counseling*) *Massachusetts*

Mangum, John M. (*Theology/Religion*, also Communications, Administration) *Illinois*, also Pennsylvania

Marc, Alexandre (*Philosophy*) *France*

Margulis, Lynn (*Biology*) *Massachusetts*

Marshall Jr., John Harris (*Earth Science*) *Texas*

Marshner, William (*Theology/Religion*, also Philosophy) *Virginia*

Martin, Daniel (*Mathematics*) *United Kingdom*

Martin, David Alfred (*Sociology*) *United Kingdom*

Martin, Helen Elizabeth (*Mathematics*) *Pennsylvania*

Martin, James P. (*Theology/Religion*) *Canada*

Martin, Robert K. (*Education*) *Connecticut*

Martino, Rocco Leonard (*Computer and Information Sciences*, also Finance, Mathematics, Physics) *Pennsylvania*

Marty, Martin E. (*Theology/Religion*, also Communications) *Illinois*

Masani, Pesi R. (*Mathematics*) *Pennsylvania*

Mason, John Martin (*Theology/Religion*) *Minnesota*

Matsen, Fredrick A. (*Philosophy*, also Chemistry) *Texas*

Matthews, Dale A. (*Medical Science*) *Washington, D.C.*, also Virginia

Mauser, Ulrich Wilheilm (*Theology/Religion*) *New Jersey*

May, Hans (*Theology/Religion*) *Germany*

May, John Y. (*Philosophy*) *Pennsylvania*

Maziarz, Edward Anthony (*Theology/Religion*, also Philosophy, Mathematics, Physics) *Illinois*

McClellan, William T. (*Theology/Religion*) *California*

McCone, R. Clyde (*Anthropology*, also Literature, Theology/Religion) *California*

McCormack, Elizabeth J. (*Philosophy*) *New York*

McCrea, Sir William (Hunter) (*Astronomy/Astrophysics*) *United Kingdom*

McDargh, John (*Theology/Religion*, also Psychology/Counseling) *Massachusetts*

McDonald, Harry S. (*Biology*) *Texas*

McFague, Sallie (*Theology/Religion*) *Tennessee*

McFeeley, Daniel (*Philosophy*, also Psychology/Counseling) *Illinois*

McGrath, Alister E. (*Biology*, also Theology/Religion) *United Kingdom*

McIntyre, John A. (*Physics*) *Texas*

McKenna, John E. (*Theology/Religion*, also Chemistry) *California*

McKowen, Paul M. (*Philosophy*, also Languages) *California*

McMullen, Emerson Thomas (*History and Philosophy of Science*) *Oklahoma*

McMullin, Ernan (*Philosophy*, also Theology/Religion, Physics, History and Philosophy of Science) *Indiana*

McNally, Donald H. (*History and Philosophy of Science*, also Theology/Religion) *Canada*

Meador, Keith G. (*Psychiatry*, also Theology/Religion) *Tennessee*

Medgyesi, György (*Biochemistry/Biophysics*, also Medical Science) *Hungary*

Menninga, Clarence (*Earth Science*, also Chemistry) *Michigan*

Mercier, André (*Physics*, also History and Philosophy of Science) *Switzerland*

Mermann, Alan C. (*Medical Science*, also Theology/Religion) *Connecticut*

Merrifield S.J., Donald Paul (*Physics*) *California*

Metzner, Helmut (*Biochemistry/Biophysics*, also Philosophy, Ethics) *Germany*

Metzner, Ralph (*Psychology/Counseling*, also Theology/Religion) *California*

Meyerhoff, Gordon R. (*Psychiatry*, also Theology/Religion) *New York*

Meyers, Wayne Marvin (*Medical Science*) *Washington, D.C.*

Miles, Caroline Mary (*Administration*, also Commerce) *United Kingdom*

Miles, Sara Joan (*History and Philosophy of Science*, also Biology, Anthropology, Education) *Pennsylvania*

Miller, David Lee (*Philosophy*) *Wisconsin*

Miller, James Bradley (*Theology/Religion*, also Philosophy) *Pennsylvania*

Miller, Keith Brady (*Earth Science*) *Kansas*

Mills, Antonia (*Anthropology*) *Canada*

Mills, Gordon C. (*Biochemistry/Biophysics*, also Genetics) *Texas*

Mills, Joy (*Theology/Religion*, also Psychology/Counseling, History, Literature) *California*

Mills, Stephen A. (*Biochemistry/Biophysics*) *California*

Milone, Eugene Frank (*Astronomy/Astrophysics*) *Canada*

Mitcham, Carl (*Philosophy*) *Pennsylvania*

Mitchell, Robert P. (*Theology/Religion*) *New Jersey*

Mixter, Russell L. (*Biology*) *Illinois*

Moberg, David O. (*Sociology*) *Wisconsin*

Mohrenweiser, Harvey W. (*Genetics*, also Molecular Biology) *California*

Molari, Carlo (*Theology/Religion*) *Italy*

Moldoff, Sol (*Engineering*) *Pennsylvania*

Moltmann, Jürgen (*Theology/Religion*) *Germany*

Monse, Ernst U. (*Chemistry*) *New Jersey*

Montefiore, Hugh (*Theology/Religion*) *United Kingdom*

Monteiro, Hubert A. (*Chemistry*, also Commerce) *India*

Montgomery, John Warwick (*Jurisprudence/Law*, also Education, Theology/Religion) *Washington*

Montgomery, Robert Lancaster (*Theology/Religion*, also Sociology) *New Jersey*

Moore, Brooke Noel (*Philosophy*) *California*

Moore, James R. (*Theology/Religion*, also History and Philosophy of Science) *United Kingdom*

Moore, Thomas J. (*Management*, also Computer and Information Sciences) *Michigan*

Morgan, Peter F. (*Literature*, also Philosophy) *Canada*

Morren, Lucien (*Technology*) *Belgium*

Mortensen, Viggo (*Theology/Religion*, also Ethics, Philosophy) *Switzerland*

Morton, Donald C. (*Astronomy/Astrophysics*) *Canada*

Mosley, Glenn R. (*Theology/Religion*) *Missouri*

Moss, Rowland Percy (*Ecology/Environment*, also Theology/Religion) *United Kingdom*

Muck, Terry C. (*Theology/Religion*) *Illinois*

Mullen, Pierce C. (*History*) *Montana*

Müller, A. M. Klaus (*Physics*) *Germany*

Müller, Gert H. (*Mathematics*) *Germany*

Mullins, Carl Phillips (Phil) (*Theology/Religion*, also Literature) *Missouri*

Mullins, Jeffrey Lynn (*Astronomy/Astrophysics*, also Philosophy) *Maryland*

Munday Jr., John Clingman (*Political Science/Politics*, also Ethics, Theology/Religion) *Virginia*

Murdoch, Bernard Constantine (*Psychology/Counseling*) *Georgia*

Murdy, William H. (*Biology*) *Georgia*

Murphy, George L. (*Theology/Religion*, also Physics) *Ohio*

Murphy, Nancey C. (*Philosophy*, also Theology/Religion) *California*

Musschenga, A. W. (*Theology/Religion*, also Ethics) *The Netherlands*

Musser, Donald W. (*Theology/Religion*, also Chemistry, Engineering) *Florida*

Mwenegoha, Amani (*Administration*) *Tanzania*

Myers, David G. (*Psychology/Counseling*) *Michigan*

𝒩

Nasimiyu, Anne (*Theology/Religion*) *Kenya*

Ndumbe, Peter Martins (*Medical Science*) *Cameroon*

Needleman, Jacob (*Philosophy*, also Psychology/Counseling, Theology/Religion) *California*

Neidhardt, Walter Jim (*Physics*, also Theology/Religion) *New Jersey*

Nelson, J. Robert (*Theology/Religion*, also Ethics) *Texas*

Nelson, James S. (*Theology/Religion*) *Illinois*

Nelson, Paul Alfred (*Philosophy*) *Illinois*

Nelson, Robert T. (*Theology/Religion*, also Biochemistry/Biophysics) *United Kingdom*

Nethöfel, Wolfgang (*Theology/Religion*, also Ethics) *Germany*

Neubauer, Thomas (*Medical Science*, also Biochemistry/Biophysics) *Germany*

Neuhouser, David L. (*Mathematics*) *Indiana*

Neuner, Peter (*Theology/Religion*) *Germany*

Neville, Robert Cummings (*Theology/Religion*, also Philosophy) *Massachusetts*

Newman, Robert Chapman (*Theology/Religion*) *Pennsylvania*

Nicholi Jr., Armand Mayo (*Psychiatry*, also Theology/Religion) *Massachusetts*

Nicholson, Philip (*Philosophy*, also Jurisprudence/Law, Medical Science, Computer and Information Sciences) *Massachusetts*

Nickel Jr., Gerhard (*Physics*, also Chemistry, Earth Science, Languages) *Kansas*

Nieznaski, Edward (*Philosophy*) *Poland*

Nonneman, Arthur J. (*Psychology/Counseling*) *Kentucky*

Nordgren, Richard (*Theology/Religion*, also Chemistry) *Washington*

Numbers, Ronald L. (*History and Philosophy of Science*, also Medical Science) *Wisconsin*

𝒪

Oates, David D. (*Literature*, also History) *California*

Ogden, Philip M. (*Physics*, also Mathematics) *New York*

Ogden, Schubert Miles (*Theology/Religion*) *Colorado*

Oliver, Harold H. (*Theology/Religion*, also Philosophy) *Massachusetts*

Olson, Everett C. (*Biology*, also Earth Science) *California*

Olson, Richard (*History and Philosophy of Science*) *California*

Olson, Roger Eugene (*Theology/Religion*) *Minnesota*

Onimus, Jean (*Literature*) *France*

Oorjitham, Santha (*Communications*) *Malaysia*

Osmond, Daniel Harcourt (*Medical Science*) *Canada*

Oswald, Donald J. (*Economics*) *California*

Overman, Richard H. (*Theology/Religion*) *Washington*

Owens, Joseph V. (*Theology/Religion*, also Philosophy) *Honduras*

𝒫

Pacholczyk, Andrzej G. (*Astronomy/Astrophysics*, also Physics) *Arizona*

Page, William R. (*Chemistry*, also Engineering, Biology, Sociology) *Vermont*

Paloutzian, Raymond F. (*Psychology/Counseling*) *California*

Panitz, Michael E. (*Theology/Religion*, also History) *New Jersey*

Pannenberg, Wolfhart (*Theology/Religion*) *Germany*

Parenti, Sergio (*Theology/Religion*) *Italy*

Parker, Thomas (*Theology/Religion*) *Illinois*

Parks, Lyle Fredrick (*Psychiatry*, also Psychology/Counseling) *Illinois*

Parrott III, Less (*Psychology/Counseling*) *Washington*

Paterson, John Leonard (*Earth Science*) *New Zealand*

Patrick, Thomas E, (*Theology/Religion*, also Administration) *Minnesota*

Patton, John H. (*Psychology/Counseling*) *Georgia*

Paul, Erich Robert (*History and Philosophy of Science*) *Pennsylvania*

Paul, Iain (*Theology/Religion*, also Chemistry) *United Kingdom*

Paul, William W. (*Philosophy*, also Theology/Religion) *Iowa*

Payton, Robert L. (*Ethics*) *Indiana*

Pazan, Stephen (*Physics*, also Earth Science) *California*

Peacocke, Arthur Robert (*Biochemistry/Biophysics*, also Theology/Religion) *United Kingdom*

Pearson III, Daniel B. (*Psychiatry*, also Earth Science) *Texas*

Peat, David (*Astronomy/Astrophysics*, also Theology/Religion) *United Kingdom*

Pedersen, Olaf (*History and Philosophy of Science*) *Denmark*

Pellegrino, Edmund D. (*Medical Science*, also Ethics) *Washington, D.C.*, also Maryland

Peppin, John Francis (*Medical Science*, also Ethics) *Wisconsin*

Percesepe, Gary John (*Philosophy*) *Ohio*

Perkins, Richard (*Sociology*) *New York*

Perry, David Kenneth (*Biochemistry/Biophysics*) *North Carolina*

Perry, David L. (*Philosophy*) *Washington, D.C.*

Peters, Theodore Frank (*Theology/Religion*) *California*

Petersen, Rodney L. (*History*) *Massachusetts*

Peterson, James C. (*Ethics*) *North Carolina*

Petras, David M. (*Theology/Religion*) *Ohio*

Petzoldt, Matthias (*Theology/Religion*) *Germany*

Philipchalk, Ronald Peter (*Psychology/Counseling*) *Canada*

Pietrzak, Daniel M. (*Psychology/Counseling*) *Massachusetts*

Pike, Kenneth L. (*Languages*, also Theology/Religion) *Texas*

Pilchik, Ely E. (*Theology/Religion*) *New Jersey*

Pizzamiglio, Pierluigi (*History and Philosophy of Science*) *Italy*

Plantinga, Alvin C. (*Philosophy*, also Theology/Religion) *Indiana*

Plendl, Hans S. (*Physics*) *Florida*

Polkinghorne, John Charlton (*Physics*) *United Kingdom*

Poloma, Margaret M. (*Sociology*) *Ohio*

Pon, Wing Y. (*Physics*, also Commerce) *California*

Poole Jr., Charles P. (*Physics*) *South Carolina*

Poole, Michael William (*Education*) *United Kingdom*

Porter, Andrew P. (*Physics*, also Mathematics, Theology/Religion) *California*

Porter, Kenneth W. (*Engineering*) *Washington*

Post, Stephen G. (*Theology/Religion*, also Biology, Ethics) *Ohio*

Poythress, Vern Sheridan (*Mathematics*, also Theology/Religion) *Pennsylvania*

Price, Daniel J. (*Theology/Religion*) *Switzerland*

Prigogine, Ilya (*Chemistry*, also Biochemistry/Biophysics, Physics, Philosophy) *Belgium*

Prodi, Giovanni (*Theology/Religion*) *Italy*

Prosperi, Giovanni M. (*Physics*) *Italy*

Proudfoot, Wayne (*Theology/Religion*, also Philosophy) *New York*

Provine, William B. (*History and Philosophy of Science*, also Genetics) *New York*

Puckett, Laura E. (*Psychology/Counseling*, also Biochemistry/Biophysics) *Minnesota*

Puddefoot, John Charles (*Theology/Religion*, also Mathematics) *United Kingdom*

Pullinger, David J. (*Mathematics*, also Biochemistry/Biophysics, Computer and Information Sciences) *United Kingdom*

Pun, Pattle P.T. (*Molecular Biology*, also Genetics, Theology/Religion) *Illinois*

Q

Queen, Christopher S. (*Philosophy*, also Theology/Religion) *Massachusetts*

R

Rahman, Abdul (*Management*, also History and Philosophy of Science, Biochemistry/Biophysics, Theology/Religion) *India*

Ramm, Bernard (*Philosophy*, also Theology/Religion) *California*

Ramsden, William E. (*Theology/Religion*, also Psychology/Counseling) *Pennsylvania*

Rangel, Paschoal Sellitti (*Philosophy*, also Theology/Religion, Communications, Literature) *Brazil*

Rappaport, Roy A. (*Anthropology*) *Michigan*

Ratzsch, Del (*Philosophy*, also History and Philosophy of Science) *Michigan*

Ravindra, Ravi (*Physics*, also Theology/Religion, Philosophy) *Canada*

Reddington, Kenneth George (*Psychology/Counseling*, also Theology/Religion) *Japan*

Reding, Georges R. (*Psychiatry*) *Michigan*

Rees, Martin J. (*Astronomy/Astrophysics*) *United Kingdom*

Reich, K. Helmut (*Psychology/Counseling*, also Physics, Engineering, Theology/Religion) *Switzerland*

Reichenbach, Bruce R. (*Philosophy*, also Ethics, Theology/Religion) *Minnesota*

Reisz Jr., H. Frederick (*Theology/Religion*, also Ethics) *South Carolina*

Reynolds, George T. (*Physics*) *New Jersey*

Rice, Stanley Arthur (*Ecology/Environment*, also Biology, Education) *Minnesota*

Richards, Robert J. (*Philosophy*, also History and Philosophy of Science, Psychology/Counseling) *Illinois*

Richardson, W. Mark (*Theology/Religion*) *California*

Riddiford, Alan Wistar (*Mathematics*, also Theology/Religion) *Illinois*

Riegel Jr., Theodore (*Psychology/Counseling*, also Education, Mathematics, Philosophy) *Georgia*

Riggan, George A. (*Theology/Religion*) *Connecticut*

Rios, Cesar A. (*Psychiatry*) *Argentina*

Ritschl, Dietrich (*Theology/Religion*, also Philosophy) *Germany*

Rivier, Dominique-Casimir (*Physics*) *Switzerland*

Roberts, Jon H. (*History*) *Wisconsin*

Roberts, Kenneth L. (*Engineering*, also Ecology/Environment) *Virginia*

Roberts, Robert C. (*Ethics*, also Psychology/Counseling, Philosophy, Theology/Religion) *Illinois*

Robertson, John H. (*Chemistry*) *United Kingdom*

Roche, Barbara A. (*History*, also Education, Theology/Religion) *Kentucky*

Rockefeller, Laurance S. (*Ethics*, also Commerce) *New York*

Rockwell, Theodore (*Engineering*, also Technology) *Maryland*

Rogers, Norma Prichard (*Engineering*, also Literature, Psychology/Counseling) *Tennessee*

Rolston III, Holmes (*Theology/Religion*, also Philosophy, Physics) *Colorado*

Romagosa, Alfredo A. (*Computer and Information Sciences*) *Florida*

Rónay, Géza S. (*Chemistry*) *California*

Ross, H. Miriam (*Medical Science*, also Sociology) *Canada*

Ross, Norman Albert (*Astronomy/Astrophysics*) *Maine*

Ross, Robert S. (*Physics*) *Pennsylvania*

Rossman, Parker (*Interdisciplinary Studies*) *Connecticut*

Roth, Ariel Adrien (*Biology*) *California*

Rothenberg, David (*Philosophy*) *New Jersey*

Rothrock, Paul E. (*Biology*, also Earth Science) *Indiana*

Rottschaefer, William A. (*Philosophy*, also History and Philosophy of Science) *Oregon*

Roukens de Lange, A. (*Commerce*, also Engineering, Chemistry, Mathematics) *South Africa*

Routh, Donald K. (*Psychology/Counseling*) *Florida*

Rowatt, Wade Clinton (*Psychology/Counseling*) *Kentucky*

Ruark, James Ellwood (*Literature*) *Michigan*

Rubik, Beverly (*Biochemistry/Biophysics*) *Pennsylvania*

Rupke, Nicolaas Adrianus (*History and Philosophy of Science*, also Earth Science) *Germany*

Ruse, Michael (*History and Philosophy of Science*, also Biology) *Canada*

Russell, Colin Archibald (*History and Philosophy of Science*, also Chemistry) *United Kingdom*

Russell, Robert John (*Physics*, also Chemistry, Theology/Religion) *California*

Rüst, Peter (*Chemistry*, also Biochemistry/Biophysics) *Switzerland*

S

Sakimoto, Philip J. (*Astronomy/Astrophysics*, also Physics) *Washington, D.C.*

Saler, Benson (*Anthropology*) *Massachusetts*

Salmon, James F. (*Chemistry*, also Theology/Religion, Philosophy) *Maryland*

Salthe, Stanley N. (*Biology*) *New York*

Saltzman, Judy D. (*Theology/Religion*) *California*

Sanguinetti, Francesco (*Medical Science*, also Ecology/Environment) *Italy*

Santmire, H. Paul (*Theology/Religion*, also History) *Ohio*

Sardana, Lal (*Engineering*) *Texas*

Sauter, Gerhard (*Theology/Religion*) *Germany*

Scadding, Steven R. (*Biology*) *Canada*

Schaefer, Hans (*Medical Science*, also Sociology) *Germany*

Schaefer III, Henry F. (*Physics*, also Chemistry) *Georgia*

Scheffczyk, Leo (*Theology/Religion*) *Germany*

Scheie, Paul (*Physics*, also Biochemistry/Biophysics) *Texas*

Schenk, Richard (*Philosophy*, also History) *Germany*, also *California*

Schmiedehausen, Hans (*Theology/Religion*, also Ecology/Environment) *Germany*

Schmitt, Francis O. (*Medical Science*) *Massachusetts*

Schmitz-Moormann, Karl (*Theology/Religion*, also Philosophy, History) *Germany*

Schneider, Hans-Georg (*History and Philosophy of Science*, also Sociology) *United Kingdom*

Schocher, Arno Johannes (*Technology*, also Biology, Theology/Religion) *Switzerland*

Schoen, Edward L. (*Philosophy*) *Kentucky*

Schoepflin, Rennie B. (*History and Philosophy of Science*, also Medical Science, Theology/Religion) *California*

Scholz, Günter (*Biochemistry/Biophysics*) *Germany*

Schotman-Veldman, Judith L. (*Chemistry*, also History and Philosophy of Science, Physics) *The Netherlands*

Schrader, David Eugene (*Philosophy*, also Ethics) *Texas*

Schroeder, W. Widick (*Theology/Religion*, also Ethics) *Illinois*

Schubert von, Klaus R. (*Physics*) *Germany*

Schubert, Mathias (*Theology/Religion*) *Germany*

Schütt, Hans-Werner (*History and Philosophy of Science*) *Germany*

Schuurman, Egbert (*Philosophy*, also Engineering, Political Science/Politics) *The Netherlands*

Schwarz, Hans (*Theology/Religion*) *Germany*

Schwarzwäller, Klaus (*Theology/Religion*, also Ethics) *Germany*

Sciegaj, Mark (*Theology/Religion*) *Georgia*

Scott, Philip Maxwell (*Mathematics*, also Theology/Religion) *New Zealand*

Seckler, Max (*Theology/Religion*) *Germany*

Seeger, Raymond John (*Physics*) *Maryland*

Segal, Robert A. (*Theology/Religion*) *United Kingdom*

Seifert, Josef (*Philosophy*) *Liechtenstein*

Sevenhoven, J. C. A. M. (*Theology/Religion*, also Philosophy) *The Netherlands*

Shacklett, Robert L. (*Physics*) *California*

Shank, Michael H. (*History and Philosophy of Science*, also Physics) *Wisconsin*

Shank, Norman E. (*Chemistry*) *Pennsylvania*

Sharpe, Kevin James (*Theology/Religion*, also Philosophy, Mathematics, Communications) *New Hampshire*

Shaw, Marvin C. (*History and Philosophy of Science*, also Philosophy) *Montana*

Sheldon, John M. (*Ethics*, also Medical Science) *Ohio*

Sheldon, Joseph K. (*Biology*, also Ecology/Environment) *Pennsylvania*

Sheldrake, Rupert (*Biochemistry/Biophysics*) *United Kingdom*

Shepard, Frederick Douglas (*Biology*, also Education, Administration) *Oregon*

Sheppard, Norman (*Chemistry*) *United Kingdom*

Shewmon, D. Alan (*Medical Science*) *California*

Shinn, Roger L. (*Theology/Religion*, also Ethics, Philosophy) *New York*

Shotwell, Thomas K. (*Biology*, also Management) *Texas*

Shropshire Jr., W. (*Theology/Religion*, also Biochemistry/Biophysics) *Washington, D.C.*, also Maryland

Shull, Philip A. (*Ethics*, also Theology/Religion) *Montana*

Shults, F. LeRon (*Education*) *Minnesota*

Shweder, Richard Allan (*Anthropology*, also Philosophy, Psychology/Counseling) *Illinois*

Siegel, Harvey (*Philosophy*, also Education) *Florida*

Siegwalt, Gérard (*Theology/Religion*) *France*

Siemens Jr., David F. (*Philosophy*, also Theology/Religion) *Arizona*

Siirala, Aarne (*Theology/Religion*, also Ethics) *Canada*

Simmons Jr., Ernest L. (*Philosophy*, also Theology/Religion) *Minnesota*

Simpkinson, Charles H. (*Psychology/Counseling*) *Maryland*

Singh, Renuka (*Sociology*) *India*

Sire, James W. (*Communications*, also History and Philosophy of Science) *Illinois*

Skolimowski, Henryk (*Philosophy*) *Michigan*

Sleigh Jr., Robert Colins (*Philosophy*) *Massachusetts*

Smith, David H. (*Theology/Religion*, also Philosophy) *Indiana*

Smith, Huston (*Philosophy*, also Theology/Religion) *California*

Smith, Ronald N. (*Engineering*, also Physics) *Washington*

Smith-Moran, Barbara Putney (*Chemistry*, also Astronomy/Astrophysics, Theology/Religion) *Massachusetts*

Smucker, Silas J. (*Ecology/Environment*) *Indiana*

Snoke, David Wayne (*Physics*) *Germany*

Sollod, Robert N. (*Psychology/Counseling*, also Theology/Religion) *Ohio*

South, Oron P. (*Management*) *Alabama*

Southgate, Beverley C. (*History*) *United Kingdom*

Spaemann, Robert (*Philosophy*) *Germany*

Spak, K. Edmund (*Medical Science*) *Texas*

Spanner, Douglas C. (*Biochemistry/Biophysics*) *United Kingdom*

Sperry, Roger W. (*Theology/Religion*) *California*

Spiro, Melford E. (*Anthropology*) *California*

Spradley, Joseph L. (*Physics*, also Astronomy/Astrophysics, History and Philosophy of Science) *Illinois*

Sprunger, Meredith Justin (*Philosophy*, also Theology/Religion) *Indiana*

Sroufe, Joe Thomas (*Sociology*, also Theology/Religion) *Tennessee*

Stahl, C. Larry (*Languages*) *Oregon*

Stahl, Rainer (*Theology/Religion*) *Germany*

Stanciu, George (*Physics*) *New Hampshire*

Stanesby, Derek Malcolm (*History and Philosophy of Science*, also Theology/Religion) *United Kingdom*

Stannard, Frank Russell (*Physics*) *United Kingdom*

State, Stanley (*Commerce*, also History and Philosophy of Science) *California*

Staudinger, Hugo (*History and Philosophy of Science*, also Philosophy) *Germany*

Stavenga, Gerben J. (*History and Philosophy of Science*) *The Netherlands*

Stein, Sharon A. (*Psychology/Counseling*, also Philosophy, Education) *Massachusetts*

Stent, Gunther S. (*Biology*, also Genetics, History and Philosophy of Science) *California*

Sternglass, Ernest J. (*Physics*, also History and Philosophy of Science) *New York*

Stevens Jr., Herbert Howe (*Philosophy*) *Massachusetts*

Stewart, John Frederick Hudson (*Medical Science*, also Theology/Religion) *Canada*

Stines, James W. (*Theology/Religion*, also Philosophy) *North Carolina*

Stoeger, William R. (*Physics*, also Astronomy/Astrophysics, Philosophy) *Arizona*

Stoll, John Henry (*Theology/Religion*, also Psychology/Counseling) *Minnesota*

Strobel, Henry W. (*Biochemistry/Biophysics*, also Theology/Religion) *Texas*

Stuhlhofer, Franz (*History and Philosophy of Science*) *Austria*

Stulman, Julius (*Commerce*) *Florida*

Sturm, Mary J. (*Theology/Religion*) *Minnesota*

Styczen, Tadeusz (*Ethics*) *Poland*

Sutherland, Brian P. (*Chemistry*) *Canada*

Sutherland Jr., Malcolm Read (*Theology/Religion*, also Administration, Education) *Massachusetts*

Suttle, Bruce B. (*Philosophy*) *Illinois*

Swift, David Leslie (*Medical Science*, also Ecology/Environment, Engineering) *Maryland*

Swinburne, Richard Granville (*Philosophy*, also Theology/Religion) *United Kingdom*

Swyhart, Barbara Ann DeMartino (*Philosophy*, also Ethics, Theology/Religion, Education) *Pennsylvania*

$\mathcal{T}$

Tanner Jr., William F. (*Earth Science*) *Florida*

Tarli, Silvana Borgognini (*Anthropology*) *Italy*

Tayler, Roger J. (*Astronomy/Astrophysics*) *United Kingdom*

Taylor, Howard G. (*Theology/Religion*, also Physics, Mathematics) *United Kingdom*

Taylor, Jon (*Theology/Religion*) *Montana*

Temple, Dennis Michael (*Philosophy*) *Illinois*

Templeton, Sir John M. (*Economics*, also Finance, Theology/Religion, Management) *Bahamas*

Teske, John A. (*Psychology/Counseling*) *Pennsylvania*

Tester, Leonard W. (*Psychology/Counseling*) *New York*

Thomson, Alexander (*Theology/Religion*) *United Kingdom*

Thorson, Walter Rollier (*Physics*, also Chemistry) *Canada*

Thung, Mady A. (*Sociology*, also Theology/Religion) *The Netherlands*

Thurman, L. Duane (*Biology*, also Ecology/Environment) *Oklahoma*

Tierney, Nathan Llywellyn (*Philosophy*) *California*

Tilley, Terrence U. (*Theology/Religion*, also Philosophy) *Ohio*

Timm, Roger E. (*Theology/Religion*, also Philosophy) *Illinois*

Tipler, Frank J. (*Mathematics*, also Physics, Astronomy/Astrophysics) *Louisiana*

Titanji, Vincent P.K. (*Biochemistry/Biophysics*) *Cameroon*

Tjeltveit, Alan (*Psychology/Counseling*, also Theology/Religion) *Pennsylvania*

Tobacyk, Jerome J. (*Psychology/Counseling*) *Louisiana*

Tödt, Heinz Eduard (*Theology/Religion*, also Ethics) *Germany*

Toledo, J. Rafael (*Medical Science*) *Texas*

Toolan, David (*Theology/Religion*, also Philosophy) *New York*

Torrance, Thomas F. (*Theology/Religion*, also History and Philosophy of Science) *United Kingdom*

Tough, Allen MacNeill (*Education*, also Psychology/Counseling) *Canada*

Townes, Charles H. (*Physics*, also Astronomy/Astrophysics) *California*

Trautteur, Giuseppe (*Computer and Information Sciences*) *Italy*

Trigg, Roger (*Philosophy*) *United Kingdom*

Trook, Douglas A. (*Psychology/Counseling*, also Theology/Religion) *Pennsylvania*

Trost, LouAnn (*Theology/Religion*, also Ecology/Environment, Philosophy) *California*

Troster, Lawrence (*Theology/Religion*) *New Jersey*, also New York

Truog, Dean-Daniel W. (*Education*, also Theology/Religion, History and Philosophy of Science) *Massachusetts*

Turner, Dean (*Ethics*, also Philosophy, Languages, Education) *Colorado*

Turner, Edith L. B. (*Anthropology*) *Virginia*

Turner, Robert Eugene (*Biology*, also Ecology/Environment) *Louisiana*

𝒰

Uhlig, Herbert H. (*Engineering*, also Technology) *Massachusetts*

Ulbrich, Paul W. (*Medical Science*) *Illinois*

Ulrickson, Brian Lee (*Earth Science*, also Theology/Religion) *Washington*

Underkofler, Leland A. (*Biochemistry/Biophysics*) *New Mexico*

Usandivaras, Raul J. (*Psychiatry*) *Argentina*

Utke, Allen R. (*Chemistry*, also Interdisciplinary Studies) *Wisconsin*

𝒱

Vahanian, Gabriel (*Theology/Religion*) *France*

Van Arsdel III, William Campbell (*Biochemistry/Biophysics*, also Medical Science) *Washington, D.C.*

van de Beek, A. (*Biology*, also Theology/Religion) *The Netherlands*

van den Brom, Luco Johan (*Theology/Religion*, also Mathematics, Physics) *The Netherlands*

Van der Meer, Jitse M. (*Biology*, also Astronomy/Astrophysics) *Canada*

Van der Veken, Jan (*Physics*, also Philosophy) *Belgium*

van Dijk, Paul (*Theology/Religion*, also Ethics) *The Netherlands*

van Duijin, Pieter (*Biology*) *The Netherlands*

Van Dyke, Fred G. (*Biology*, also Ecology/Environment) *Michigan*, also Montana

Van Erkelens, Herbert (*Physics*, also Psychology/Counseling) *The Netherlands*

van Huyssteen, Jacobus Wentzel Vrede (*Theology/Religion*, also Philosophy) *New Jersey*

van Kouwenhoven, Willem F. (*Theology/Religion*) *The Netherlands*

Van Leeuwen, Mary Stewart (*Sociology*, also Psychology/Counseling) *Michigan*

Van Melsen, A. G. M. (*History and Philosophy of Science*) *The Netherlands*

Van Ness, William (*Theology/Religion*, also Education) *California*

Van Till, Howard J. (*Physics*, also Astronomy/Astrophysics) *Michigan*

Van Valen, Leigh M. (*Biology*) *Illinois*

Van Vliet, Carolyne M. (*Physics*) *Canada*

Van Zytveld, John B. (*Physics*) *Michigan*

Vance, Forrest L. (*Psychology/Counseling*) *Indiana*

Vande Kemp, Hendrika (*Psychology/Counseling*, also Education) *California*

Vander Vennen, Robert E. (*Chemistry*) *Canada*

Vander Zee, Delmar (*Biology*) *Iowa*

VanOstenburg, Donald O. (*Physics*) *Illinois*

Varadarajan, Lotika (*History*) *India*

Varela, Francisco J. (*Biology*) *France*

Vayhinger, John M. (*Psychology/Counseling*) *Colorado*

Venable III, William H. (*Physics*, also Theology/Religion) *Pennsylvania*

Verlinde, Jacques (*History and Philosophy of Science*, also Theology/Religion) *France*

Viladesau, Richard (*Theology/Religion*, also Philosophy) *New York*

Vincent, Merville O. (*Psychiatry*, also Medical Science) *Canada*

Vitz, Paul C. (*Psychology/Counseling*, also Theology/Religion) *New York*

Vollmer, Gerhard (*Philosophy*) *Germany*

Vorster, Willem S. (*Theology/Religion*) *South Africa*

Vukanovic, Vladimir (*Chemistry*) *New York*

𝒲

Wagner, Roy (*Anthropology*) *Virginia*

Wahlbeck, Phillip G. (*Chemistry*) *Kansas*

Waldenfels, Hans (*Theology/Religion*, also Philosophy) *Germany*

Walker, Laurence C. (*Earth Science*, also Theology/Religion) *Texas*

Walker, Lawrence J. (*Psychology/Counseling*) *Canada*

Walker, Ralph C. S. (*Philosophy*) *United Kingdom*

Wallwork, Ernest Edward (*Ethics*, also Psychology/Counseling, Sociology) *New York*, also Washington, D.C.

Walter, Christian (*Economics*) *France*

Ward, Keith (*Theology/Religion*, also Philosophy) *United Kingdom*

Washburn, Marilyn (*Medical Science*, also Theology/Religion) *Georgia*

Washburn, Michael (*Philosophy*) *Indiana*

Wason, Paul Kenneth (*Anthropology*) *Maine*

Wassermann, Christoph (*Physics*, also Theology/Religion) *Germany*

Waters, Brent (*Theology/Religion*) *California*

Wathen-Dunn, Weiant (*Physics*, also Communications, Engineering) *Massachusetts*

Watson, John Robert (*Medical Science*) *Hawaii*

Watson, Paul Joseph (*Psychology/Counseling*) *Tennessee*

Wattles, Jeffrey Hamilton (*Philosophy*) *Ohio*

Weaver, Glenn David (*Psychology/Counseling*) *Michigan*

Webster, Frederic A. (*Medical Science*) *Vermont*

Webster, John Wilfred (*Theology/Religion*, also Ethics, Philosophy) *South Africa*

Weidemann, Volker (*Astronomy/Astrophysics*) *Germany*

Weidlich, Wolfgang (*Physics*) *Germany*

Weil, Pierre (*Psychology/Counseling*) *Brazil*

Weingartner, Paul (*Philosophy*, also History and Philosophy of Science) *Australia*

Weir, Jack L. (*Philosophy*, also Theology/Religion, Ethics) *Kentucky*

Weiss, Arnold S. (*Psychology/Counseling*) *California*

Weizsäcker von, Carl Friedrich Freiherr (*Physics*, also Philosophy) *Germany*

Weizsäcker von, Ernst (*Biology*, also Ecology/Environment, Political Science/Politics) *Germany*

Welch, Claude (*History*, also Theology/Religion, Education) *California*

Welker, Michael (*Theology/Religion*, also Philosophy) *Germany*

West, Charles C. (*Ethics*, also Political Science/Politics) *New Jersey*

West, Richard B. (*Education*, also Mathematics) *California*

Westfall, Richard S. (*History and Philosophy of Science*) *Indiana*

Westman, Robert (*History*, also History and Philosophy of Science) *California*

Wetherbee, James M. (*Literature*) *North Carolina*

Wheeler, David L. (*Theology/Religion*, also Philosophy) *Kansas*

Whipple, Andrew P. (*Biology*) *Indiana*

Whipple, Elden C. (*Physics*) *California*

White, David C. (*Medical Science*, also Biology, Ecology/Environment) *Tennessee*

White, Rhea A. (*Administration*, also Communications, Theology/Religion, Philosophy) *New York*

Whitehead, Clay C. (*Psychiatry*) *Missouri*, also California

Whitrow, Gerald James (*Mathematics*, also History and Philosophy of Science) *United Kingdom*

Whittaker-Johns, Barbara A. (*Theology/Religion*, also Education) *Massachusetts*

Whitten, Robert C. (*Astronomy/Astrophysics*, also Earth Science) *California*

Wicken, Jeffrey S. (*Biochemistry/Biophysics*, also Philosophy, Theology/Religion) *Pennsylvania*

Wickler, Wolfgang (*Biology*, also Administration) *Germany*

Widmer, Gabriel-Philippe (*Theology/Religion*) *Switzerland*

Wiebe, Donald (*Theology/Religion*, also Philosophy) *Canada*

Wiebe, Phillip Howard (*History and Philosophy of Science*, also Ethics, Philosophy) *Canada*

Wiester, John L. (*Earth Science*) *California*

Wilbur, Frank H. (*Biology*) *Kentucky*

Wilcox, David Linwood (*Genetics*, also Biology) *Pennsylvania*

Wilder-Smith, Arthur Ernest (*Biochemistry/Biophysics*) *Switzerland*

Wildiers, Max (*Theology/Religion*, also Philosophy, Biology) *Belgium*

Wilkins III, Walter J. (*Interdisciplinary Studies*, also History, Philosophy) *Virginia*

Williams, George C. (*Biology*) *New York*

Willis, David L. (*Biology*) *Oregon*

Wilson, Edward Osborne (*Biology*, also Ecology/Environment) *Massachusetts*

Wilson, R. Ward (*Psychology/Counseling*) *Tennessee*

Wiltsher, Christopher D. (*Theology/Religion*, also Philosophy, Mathematics, Computer and Information Sciences) *United Kingdom*

Winkeler, L. G. M. (*Theology/Religion*) *The Netherlands*

Winkler, Hans-Joachim (*Medical Science*) *Germany*

Witherspoon, William (*Commerce*, also Economics) *Missouri*

Wolf, Jakob (*Theology/Religion*) *Denmark*

Wolsky, Alexander (*History and Philosophy of Science*, also Biology) *Canada*

Wolsky, Maria de Issekutz (*Biology*, also Philosophy) *Canada*, also New York

Wolterstorff, Nicholas (*Philosophy*) *Connecticut*

Wonderly, Daniel E. (*Theology/Religion*, also Biology, Earth Science) *Maryland*

Wong, Wing-Hong (*Theology/Religion*, also Physics) *United Kingdom*

Wood, Frederic C. (*Engineering*, also Commerce) *Connecticut*

Wood, William A. (*Theology/Religion*) *California*

Woodward, J. Guy (*Physics*) *New Jersey*

Worthington Jr., Everett L. (*Psychology/Counseling*) *Virginia*

Wright, Richard T. (*Biology*, also Ecology/Environment) *Massachusetts*

Wu, Kathleen Johnson (*Philosophy*) *Alabama*

Wulff, David M. (*Psychology/Counseling*, also Theology/Religion, History) *Massachusetts*

γ

Yamauchi, Edwin M. (*History*, also Languages) *Ohio*

Yockey, Hubert P. (*Biology*, also Management) *Maryland*

Yonge, Keith Arnold (*Psychiatry*) *Canada*

York, Donald G. (*Astronomy/Astrophysics*) *Illinois*

Yoshikawa, Shoichi (*Physics*) *New Jersey*

Young, David Nigel de Lorentz (*Theology/Religion*, also Mathematics) *United Kingdom*

Young, Davis A. (*Earth Science*) *Michigan*

Yu, Carver Tatsum (*Theology/Religion*, also History, Philosophy) *Hong Kong*

Yuguchi, Takashi (*Physics*, also Communications) *Japan*

Z

Zajonc, Arthur G. (*Physics*) *Massachusetts*

Zeh, H. Dieter (*Physics*) *Germany*

Zhang, Hwe Ik (*Physics*) *Korea*

Zimmerman, Michael E. (*Philosophy*) *Louisiana*

Zycinski, Jósef (*History and Philosophy of Science*, also Ecology/Environment, Theology/Religion, Ethics) *Poland*

Zylstra, Uko (*Biology*) *Michigan*

Geographical Index

This index is organized alphabetically by geographical location. Each person is listed under *each* geographical area which applies to him or her. Names in **bold** type indicate an entry in Directory A, while normal type indicates the entry is in Directory B. Subject categories which indicate an individual's primary and secondary fields of study or professional fields and geographical locations are also included with each entry. (Subject categories are listed below.) *Italicized* print indicates a "primary" area, be it an italicized state or country or subject category.

Subject Categories

Administration
Anthropology
Astronomy/Astrophysics (Physical Cosmology)
Biochemistry/Biophysics
Biology (Botany, Zoology, etc)
Chemistry
Commerce
Communications
Computer and Information Sciences
Earth Science (Geology, Mineralogy, Meteorology, Geography, Agriculture, etc)
Ecology/Environment (Environmental Ethics, Conservation and Preservation)
Economics
Education
Engineering
Ethics
Finance
Genetics

History
History and Philosophy of Science
Interdisciplinary Studies
Jurisprudence/Law
Languages
Literature
Management
Mathematics
Medical Science
Molecular Biology (Microbiology)
Philosophy
Physics
Political Science/Politics
Psychiatry
Psychology/Counseling
Sociobiology
Sociology
Technology
Theology/Religion

Alabama

South, Oron P. (*Management*)
Wu, Kathleen Johnson (*Philosophy*)

Alaska

Burneko, Guy C. (*Interdisciplinary Studies*)

Argentina

Albertsen, Andres Roberto (*Theology/Religion*)

Rios, Cesar A. (*Psychiatry*)

Usandivaras, Raul J. (*Psychiatry*)

Arizona

Corbally, Christopher J. (*Astronomy/Astrophysics*, also Theology/Religion)

Hickernell, Fred S. (*Engineering*, also Technology)

Pacholczyk, Andrzej G. (*Astronomy/Astrophysics*, also Physics)

Siemens Jr., David F. (*Philosophy*, also Theology/Religion)

Stoeger, William R. (*Physics*, also Astronomy/Astrophysics, Philosophy)

Australia

Birch, L. Charles (*Biology*, also Theology/Religion)

Davies, Paul Charles William (*Physics*)

Hutch, Richard A. (*Theology/Religion*, also Psychology/Counseling, History)

Weingartner, Paul (*Philosophy*, also History and Philosophy of Science)

Bahamas

Templeton, Sir John M. (*Economics*, also Finance, Theology/Religion, Management)

Belgium

Capart, Laurent J. N. (*Engineering*)

Cloots, André (*Philosophy*, also History and Philosophy of Science)

Morren, Lucien (*Technology*)

Prigogine, Ilya (*Chemistry*, also Biochemistry/Biophysics, Physics, Philosophy)

Van der Veken, Jan (*Physics*, also Philosophy)

Wildiers, Max (*Theology/Religion*, also Philosophy, Biology)

Bolivia

Firestone, Homer Loon (*Theology/Religion*, also Psychology/Counseling, Languages) Also *California*

Brazil

Bettencourt, Estêvão Tavares (*Theology/Religion*, also Philosophy)

Bingemer, Maria Clara Lucchetti (*Theology/Religion*)

D'Ambrosio, Ubiratan (*History and Philosophy of Science*, also Mathematics, Philosophy)

da Cruz, Eduardo Rodrigues (*Theology/Religion*, also Physics)

Freire-Maia, Newton (*Genetics*, also Biology)

Libanio, João Batista (*Philosophy*, also Languages, Theology/Religion)

Maciel, Paulo Frederico do Rêgo (*Economics*, also Philosophy)

Rangel, Paschoal Sellitti (*Philosophy*, also Theology/Religion, Communications, Literature)

Weil, Pierre (*Psychology/Counseling*)

California

Adler, Thomas C. (*Chemistry*)

Ayala, Francisco J. (*Biology*, also Genetics, Philosophy)

Balswick, Jack Orville (*Sociology*, also Theology/Religion)

Barkman, Paul F. (*Psychology/Counseling*, also Theology/Religion)

Berg, Myles Renver (*Engineering*, also Physics, Mathematics)

Bergh, Bob (*Genetics*)

Bertsch, Hans (*Biology*, also Theology/Religion, Philosophy)

Brown, Warren S. (*Medical Science*, also Psychology/Counseling)

Bube, Richard H. (*Physics*, also Theology/Religion)

Buswell III, James O. (*Anthropology*)

Carlson, Richard F. (*Physics*)

Cobb Jr., John B. (*Theology/Religion*, also Philosophy)

Cole, David R. (*Biochemistry/Biophysics*)

Copenhaver, Brian P. (*History*, also Physics)

Count, Earl W. (*Sociology*, also Theology/Religion)

Deckert, Curtis Kenneth (*Management*, also Technology)

Dillenberger, John (*Theology/Religion*)

DuMaine, R. Pierre (*Theology/Religion*)

Dundon, Stanislaus J. (*Philosophy*, also Theology/Religion, History and Philosophy of Science)

Everest, F. Alton (*Engineering*, also Technology)

Fairchild, Roy W. (*Theology/Religion*, also Psychology/Counseling, Sociology)

Feifel, Herman (*Psychology/Counseling*)

Felt, James W. (*Philosophy*, also Theology/Religion, Physics)

Finney, Joseph Claude Jeans (*Psychology/Counseling*, also Psychiatry, Theology/Religion)

Firestone, Homer Loon (*Theology/Religion*, also Psychology/Counseling, Languages) Also Bolivia

Fischer, Robert B. (*Chemistry*, also Theology/Religion, Education)

Gill, Stephen P. (*Mathematics*, also Physics)

Gillette, P. Roger (*Engineering*, also Physics, Technology, Ethics)

Goldsmith, W. (Walter) Mack (*Psychology/Counseling*, also Theology/Religion)

Gorsuch, Richard L. (*Psychology/Counseling*, also Theology/Religion)

Gregory, William Edgar (*Psychology/Counseling*)

Griffin, David Ray (*Theology/Religion*, also Philosophy, History and Philosophy of Science)

Gruenwald, Oskar (*Communications*, also Psychology/Counseling, Interdisciplinary Studies, Philosophy)

Harman, William K. (*History*, also Theology/Religion)

Hartwig, Edward Clayton (*Physics*, also Engineering)

Hazen, Craig J. (*Biology*, also Theology/Religion, Jurisprudence/Law)

Hearn, Walter Russell (*Biochemistry/Biophysics*, also Communications, Theology/Religion)

Henry, James P. (*Psychiatry*, also Medical Science, Biochemistry/Biophysics)

Hess, Peter M. (*Philosophy*, also Theology/Religion)

Hilden, Kurt Mark (*Theology/Religion*, also Philosophy)

Hoggatt, Austin Curwood (*Economics*)

Hood, Randall (*Sociobiology*, also Theology/Religion)

Howe, George Franklin (*Biology*)

Hughes, Cecil Forrest (*Theology/Religion*)

Jang, Allen Wai (*Psychology/Counseling*)

Jappe, Fred (*Chemistry*, also Theology/Religion)

Johnston, G. Archie (*Psychology/Counseling*, also Biology)

Juergensmeyer, Mark (*Ethics*, also Sociology, Philosophy, Theology/Religion)

Kerze, Michael A.. (*Theology/Religion*, also History and Philosophy of Science)

Kim, Stephen S. (*Theology/Religion*, also History and Philosophy of Science)

Larsen, Judith K. (*Technology*)

Lewthwaite, Gordon R. (*Earth Science*, also History)

Lindquist, Stanley E. (*Psychology/Counseling*)

MacCready, Paul B. (*Astronomy/Astrophysics*, also Physics, Commerce)

Macy, Joanna R. (*Theology/Religion*)

Malony, H. Newton (*Psychology/Counseling*, also Theology/Religion)

McClellan, William T. (*Theology/Religion*)

McCone, R. Clyde (*Anthropology*, also Literature, Theology/Religion)

McKenna, John E. (*Theology/Religion*, also Chemistry)

McKowen, Paul M. (*Philosophy*, also Languages)

Merrifield S.J., Donald Paul (*Physics*)

Metzner, Ralph (*Psychology/Counseling*, also Theology/Religion)

Mills, Joy (*Theology/Religion*, also Psychology/Counseling, History, Literature)

Mills, Stephen A. (*Biochemistry/Biophysics*)

Mohrenweiser, Harvey W. (*Genetics*, also Molecular Biology)

Moore, Brooke Noel (*Philosophy*)

Murphy, Nancey C. (*Philosophy*, also Theology/Religion)

Needleman, Jacob (*Philosophy*, also Psychology/Counseling, Theology/Religion)

Oates, David D. (*Literature*, also History)

Olson, Everett C. (*Biology*, also Earth Science)

Olson, Richard (*History and Philosophy of Science*)

Oswald, Donald J. (*Economics*)

Paloutzian, Raymond F. (*Psychology/Counseling*)

Pazan, Stephen (*Physics*, also Earth Science)

Peters, Theodore Frank (*Theology/Religion*)

Pon, Wing Y. (*Physics*, also Commerce)

Porter, Andrew P. (*Physics*, also Mathematics, Theology/Religion)

Ramm, Bernard (*Philosophy*, also Theology/Religion)

Richardson, W. Mark (*Theology/Religion*)

Rónay, Géza S. (*Chemistry*)

Roth, Ariel Adrien (*Biology*)

Russell, Robert John (*Physics*, also Chemistry, Theology/Religion)

Saltzman, Judy D. (*Theology/Religion*)

Schenk, Richard (*Philosophy*, also History) Also *Germany*

Schoepflin, Rennie B. (*History and Philosophy of Science*, also Medical Science, Theology/Religion)

Shacklett, Robert L. (*Physics*)

Shewmon, D. Alan (*Medical Science*)

Smith, Huston (*Philosophy*, also Theology/Religion)

Sperry, Roger W. (*Theology/Religion*)

Spiro, Melford E. (*Anthropology*)

State, Stanley (*Commerce*, also History and Philosophy of Science)

Stent, Gunther S. (*Biology*, also Genetics, History and Philosophy of Science)

Tierney, Nathan Llywellyn (*Philosophy*)

Townes, Charles H. (*Physics*, also Astronomy/Astrophysics)

Trost, LouAnn (*Theology/Religion*, also Ecology/Environment, Philosophy)

Van Ness, William (*Theology/Religion*, also Education)

Vande Kemp, Hendrika (*Psychology/Counseling*, also Education)

Waters, Brent (*Theology/Religion*)

Weiss, Arnold S. (*Psychology/Counseling*)

Welch, Claude (*History*, also Theology/Religion, Education)

West, Richard B. (*Education*, also Mathematics)

Westman, Robert (*History*, also History and Philosophy of Science)

Whipple, Elden C. (*Physics*)

Whitehead, Clay C. (*Psychiatry*) Also *Missouri*

Whitten, Robert C. (*Astronomy/Astrophysics*, also Earth Science)

Wiester, John L. (*Earth Science*)

Wood, William A. (*Theology/Religion*)

Cameroon

Aurenche, Christian (*Theology/Religion*, also Medical Science)

Bame, Michael (*Theology/Religion*)

Lantum, Noni Daniel (*Medical Science*, also Sociology, Administration)

Ndumbe, Peter Martins (*Medical Science*)

Titanji, Vincent P.K. (*Biochemistry/Biophysics*)

Canada

Armstrong, John Reginald (*Theology/Religion*, also Earth Science, History and Philosophy of Science)

Bartholomew, Gilbert A. (*Physics*)

Beck, Malcolm Nestor (*Psychiatry*, also Medical Science)

Benner, David G. (*Psychology/Counseling*)

Bulka, Reuven P. (*Theology/Religion*, also Philosophy, Psychology/Counseling)

Challice, Cyril Eugene (*Biochemistry/Biophysics*, also Theology/Religion)

Clifton, Robert K. (*History and Philosophy of Science*, also Philosophy, Physics)

Cotter, Graham (*Theology/Religion*, also Literature, History and Philosophy of Science)

Dodson, Edward O. (*Biology*, also Genetics)

Duguay, Michel A. (*Physics*, also Engineering)

Erdmann, Erika (*Interdisciplinary Studies*, also Philosophy)

Evans, C. A. (*Theology/Religion*)

Fayter, The Rev. Paul (*History and Philosophy of Science*, also Theology/Religion, Interdisciplinary Studies)

Fiddes, Victor H. (*Theology/Religion*)

Hayward, Jeremy (*Physics*, also History and Philosophy of Science, Theology/Religion)

Hill, David R. (*Computer and Information Sciences*, also Psychology/Counseling, Engineering)

Horvath, Tibor (*Theology/Religion*, also Philosophy, Interdisciplinary Studies)

Jervis, R. E. (*Technology*, also Chemistry, Physics)

Lamoureux, Denis Oswald (*Medical Science*)

Laughlin, Charles D. (*Anthropology*, also Medical Science)

Leslie, John (*Philosophy*, also Astronomy/Astrophysics, History and Philosophy of Science, Theology/Religion)

Lovett Doust, Jonathan Nicolas de Grave (*Biology*, also Ecology/Environment)

Lumsden, Charles J. (*Physics*, also Biology, Medical Science)

Mailloux, Noël (*Psychology/Counseling*, also Theology/Religion)

Martin, James P. (*Theology/Religion*)

McNally, Donald H. (*History and Philosophy of Science*, also Theology/Religion)

Mills, Antonia (*Anthropology*)

Milone, Eugene Frank (*Astronomy/Astrophysics*)

Morgan, Peter F. (*Literature*, also Philosophy)

Morton, Donald C. (*Astronomy/Astrophysics*)

Osmond, Daniel Harcourt (*Medical Science*)

Philipchalk, Ronald Peter (*Psychology/Counseling*)

Ravindra, Ravi (*Physics*, also Theology/Religion, Philosophy)

Ross, H. Miriam (*Medical Science*, also Sociology)

Ruse, Michael (*History and Philosophy of Science*, also Biology)

Scadding, Steven R. (*Biology*)

Siirala, Aarne (*Theology/Religion*, also Ethics)

Stewart, John Frederick Hudson (*Medical Science*, also Theology/Religion)

Sutherland, Brian P. (*Chemistry*)

Thorson, Walter Rollier (*Physics*, also Chemistry)

Tough, Allen MacNeill (*Education*, also Psychology/Counseling)

Van der Meer, Jitse M. (*Biology*, also Astronomy/Astrophysics)

Van Vliet, Carolyne M. (*Physics*)

Vander Vennen, Robert E. (*Chemistry*)

Vincent, Merville O. (*Psychiatry*, also Medical Science)

Walker, Lawrence J. (*Psychology/Counseling*)

Wiebe, Donald (*Theology/Religion*, also Philosophy)

Wiebe, Phillip Howard (*History and Philosophy of Science*, also Ethics, Philosophy)

Wolsky, Alexander (*History and Philosophy of Science*, also Biology)

Wolsky, Maria de Issekutz (*Biology*, also Philosophy) Also New York

Yonge, Keith Arnold (*Psychiatry*)

Colorado

Blake, Deborah D. (*Theology/Religion*, also Philosophy, Ethics)

Colvis, John Paris (*Engineering*, also Astronomy/Astrophysics)

Crosby, Donald Allen (*Philosophy*, also Theology/Religion)

Giulianelli, James L. (*Chemistry*)

Gracely, Brett W. (*Engineering*)

Johnson, Delmer A. (*Theology/Religion*)

Ogden, Schubert Miles (*Theology/Religion*)

Rolston III, Holmes (*Theology/Religion*, also Philosophy, Physics)

Turner, Dean (*Ethics*, also Philosophy, Languages, Education)

Vayhinger, John M. (*Psychology/Counseling*)

Connecticut

Bartek, Edward J. (*Philosophy*, also Psychology/Counseling)

Davis, Marjorie Hall (*Theology/Religion*, also Psychology/Counseling)

Dittes, James E. (*Theology/Religion*, also Psychology/Counseling)

Eicher, Andreas D. (*Ecology/Environment*, also Medical Science)

Ford, Mary Anne Kehoe (*Communications*)

Germine, Mark (*Psychiatry*, also Medical Science)

Hedman, Bruce A. (*Theology/Religion*, also Mathematics)

Klaaren, Eugene M. (*Theology/Religion*, also History and Philosophy of Science)

Martin, Robert K. (*Education*)

Mermann, Alan C. (*Medical Science*, also Theology/Religion)

Riggan, George A. (*Theology/Religion*)

Rossman, Parker (*Interdisciplinary Studies*)

Wolterstorff, Nicholas (*Philosophy*)

Wood, Frederic C. (*Engineering*, also Commerce)

Delaware

Hird, John Francis (*Technology*, also Engineering, Theology/Religion)

Denmark

Gregersen, Niels Henrik (*Theology/Religion*, also History and Philosophy of Science, Ethics)

Pedersen, Olaf (*History and Philosophy of Science*)

Wolf, Jakob (*Theology/Religion*)

District of Columbia (Washington)

Ashley, Benedict M. (*Ethics*, also Political Science/Politics, Theology/Religion, Philosophy)

Branson, Roy (*Ethics*, also Theology/Religion)

Byers, David M. (*Theology/Religion*)

Evans, Abigail Rian (*Ethics*, also Philosophy, Theology/Religion, Medical Science)

Fowler, Thomas B. (*Engineering*, also Computer and Information Sciences, Philosophy)

Grant, Theodore F. (*Psychology/Counseling*) Also Maryland

Happel, Stephen (*Theology/Religion*)

Haught, John F. (*Theology/Religion*)

Hoge, Dean Richard (*Sociology*)

Lindenbald, Irving W. (*Astronomy/Astrophysics*, also Theology/Religion)

Matthews, Dale A. (*Medical Science*) Also Virginia

Meyers, Wayne Marvin (*Medical Science*)

Pellegrino, Edmund D. (*Medical Science*, also Ethics) Also Maryland

Perry, David L. (*Philosophy*)

Sakimoto, Philip J. (*Astronomy/Astrophysics*, also Physics)

Shropshire Jr., W. (*Theology/Religion*, also Biochemistry/Biophysics) Also Maryland

Van Arsdel III, William Campbell (*Biochemistry/Biophysics*, also Medical Science)

Wallwork, Ernest Edward (*Ethics*, also Psychology/Counseling, Sociology) Also *New York*

Finland

Laurikainen, Kalervo Vihtori (*History and Philosophy of Science*, also Physics, Theology/Religion, Philosophy)

Florida

Ansbacher, Stefan (*Medical Science*)

Berry Jr., Maxwell R. (*Medical Science*)

Brooks, George Gordon (*Physics*, also Theology/Religion) Also *New Hampshire*

Fasching, Darrell J. (*Theology/Religion*, also Ethics, Philosophy)

Gregory, Frederick (*History and Philosophy of Science*)

Hancock Jr., Monte F. (*Mathematics*)

Hoppin, Marion C. (*Psychology/Counseling*)

Ice, Jackson Lee (*Theology/Religion*, also Philosophy)

Musser, Donald W. (*Theology/Religion*, also Chemistry, Engineering)

Plendl, Hans S. (*Physics*)

Romagosa, Alfredo A. (*Computer and Information Sciences*)

Routh, Donald K. (*Psychology/Counseling*)

Siegel, Harvey (*Philosophy*, also Education)

Stulman, Julius (*Commerce*)

Tanner Jr., William F. (*Earth Science*)

France

Armogathe, Jean-Robert (*Philosophy*, also Theology/Religion, History and Philosophy of Science)

Boutinon, Jean Claude (*Theology/Religion*)

de Beauregard, O. Costa (*Physics*, also Philosophy)

Euvé, François (*Theology/Religion*, also Physics, Philosophy)

Humbert, Jean (*Biology*, also Earth Science)

Legrain, Michel (*Jurisprudence/Law*, also Ethics)

Lejeune, Jérôme Jean Louis Marie (*Genetics*, also Medical Science)

Marc, Alexandre (*Philosophy*)

Onimus, Jean (*Literature*)

Siegwalt, Gérard (*Theology/Religion*)

Vahanian, Gabriel (*Theology/Religion*)

Varela, Francisco J. (*Biology*)

Verlinde, Jacques (*History and Philosophy of Science*, also Theology/Religion)

Walter, Christian (*Economics*)

Georgia

Alley, James W. (*Medical Science*)

Ammerman, Nancy Tatom (*Sociology*, also Theology/Religion)

Banco, Eugene C. (*Theology/Religion*)

Bratton, Susan P. (*Ecology/Environment*, also Ethics)

Childs, Brian H. (*Psychology/Counseling*)

Conrad, Constance C. (*Medical Science*, also Education)

Cramer, John Allen (*Physics*)

Ferré, Frederick (*Philosophy*, also Theology/Religion, Ethics, Technology)

Foster, Mark A. (*Sociology*)

Fowler III, James W. (*Theology/Religion*, also Ethics, Education, Psychology/Counseling)

Gillespie, Neal C. (*History and Philosophy of Science*, also History)

Ice, Rodney D. (*Physics*)

Larson, Edward J. (*Jurisprudence/Law*, also History and Philosophy of Science)

Murdoch, Bernard Constantine (*Psychology/Counseling*)

Murdy, William H. (*Biology*)

Patton, John H. (*Psychology/Counseling*)

Riegel Jr., Theodore (*Psychology/Counseling*, also Education, Mathematics, Philosophy)

Schaefer III, Henry F. (*Physics*, also Chemistry)

Sciegaj, Mark (*Theology/Religion*)

Washburn, Marilyn (*Medical Science*, also Theology/Religion)

Germany

Allert, Gebhard (*Medical Science*, also Psychiatry, Theology/Religion)

Altner, Günter (*Theology/Religion*, also Biology)

Amrhein, Eva Maria (*Physics*, also Theology/Religion) Also *Wisconsin*

Bargatzky, Thomas (*Anthropology*)

Beck, Horst Waldemar (*Theology/Religion*, also Technology, Philosophy)

Becker, Thomas (*Biology*, also Theology/Religion)

Becker, Werner (*Philosophy*, also Political Science/Politics, Ethics)

Beinert, Wolfgang (*Theology/Religion*, also Philosophy)

Blankenburg, Wolfgang (*Psychiatry*, also Philosophy)

Böhringer, Siegfried (*Theology/Religion*)

Daecke, Sigurd (*Theology/Religion*)

Dalferth, Ingolf Ulrich (*Theology/Religion*, also Philosophy) Also Switzerland

Dally, Andreas Michael (*Biology*)

Deuser, Hermann (*Theology/Religion*)

Duchrow, Ulrich (*Theology/Religion*)

Eiff von, August Wilhelm (*Medical Science*, also Ethics)

Eigen, Manfred (*Biochemistry/Biophysics*, also Chemistry)

Engels, Eve-Marie (*Philosophy*, also History and Philosophy of Science, Ethics)

Erbich, Paul (*Philosophy*, also Biology, Theology/Religion)

Ewald, Günter (*Mathematics*, also History and Philosophy of Science)

Frey, Christofer (*Theology/Religion*, also Sociology, Ethics)

Gumlich, Hans-Eckhart (*Physics*, also Technology)

Hafner, Hermann Friedrich (*Theology/Religion*, also History and Philosophy of Science)

Hemminger, Hansjörg (*Biology*, also Philosophy)

Heron, Alasdair Iain Campbell (*Theology/Religion*)

Hübner, Jürgen (*Theology/Religion*, also Molecular Biology, Ecology/Environment, History and Philosophy of Science)

Huntemann, Georg (*Theology/Religion*, also Philosophy, Ethics)

Isak, Rainer (*Theology/Religion*, also Biology, Philosophy)

Knapp, Andreas (*Theology/Religion*, also Ethics)

Koltermann, Rainer (*Biology*, also Philosophy, Theology/Religion)

Krolzik, Udo (*Theology/Religion*)

Küppers, Bernd-Olaf (*History and Philosophy of Science*, also Molecular Biology, Interdisciplinary Studies)

Liedke, Gerhard (*Theology/Religion*)

Link, Christian (*Theology/Religion*, also Physics)

Löw, Reinhard (*Philosophy*, also History and Philosophy of Science, Ethics)

May, Hans (*Theology/Religion*)

Metzner, Helmut (*Biochemistry/Biophysics*, also Philosophy, Ethics)

Moltmann, Jürgen (*Theology/Religion*)

Müller, A. M. Klaus (*Physics*)

Müller, Gert H. (*Mathematics*)

Nethöfel, Wolfgang (*Theology/Religion*, also Ethics)

Neubauer, Thomas (*Medical Science*, also Biochemistry/Biophysics)

Neuner, Peter (*Theology/Religion*)

Pannenberg, Wolfhart (*Theology/Religion*)

Petzoldt, Matthias (*Theology/Religion*)

Ritschl, Dietrich (*Theology/Religion*, also Philosophy)

Rupke, Nicolaas Adrianus (*History and Philosophy of Science*, also Earth Science)

Sauter, Gerhard (*Theology/Religion*)

Schaefer, Hans (*Medical Science*, also Sociology)

Scheffczyk, Leo (*Theology/Religion*)

Schenk, Richard (*Philosophy*, also History) Also California

Schmiedehausen, Hans (*Theology/Religion*, also Ecology/Environment)

Schmitz-Moormann, Karl (*Theology/Religion*, also Philosophy, History)

Scholz, Günter (*Biochemistry/Biophysics*)

Schubert von, Klaus R. (*Physics*)

Schubert, Mathias (*Theology/Religion*)

Schütt, Hans-Werner (*History and Philosophy of Science*)

Schwarz, Hans (*Theology/Religion*)

Schwarzwäller, Klaus (*Theology/Religion*, also Ethics)

Seckler, Max (*Theology/Religion*)

Snoke, David Wayne (*Physics*)

Spaemann, Robert (*Philosophy*)

Stahl, Rainer (*Theology/Religion*)

Staudinger, Hugo (*History and Philosophy of Science*, also Philosophy)

Tödt, Heinz Eduard (*Theology/Religion*, also Ethics)

Vollmer, Gerhard (*Philosophy*)

Waldenfels, Hans (*Theology/Religion*, also Philosophy)

Wassermann, Christoph (*Physics*, also Theology/Religion)

Weidemann, Volker (*Astronomy/Astrophysics*)

Weidlich, Wolfgang (*Physics*)

Weizsäcker von, Carl Friedrich Freiherr (*Physics*, also Philosophy)

Weizsäcker von, Ernst (*Biology*, also Ecology/Environment, Political Science/Politics)

Welker, Michael (*Theology/Religion*, also Philosophy)

Wickler, Wolfgang (*Biology*, also Administration)

Winkler, Hans-Joachim (*Medical Science*)

Zeh, H. Dieter (*Physics*)

Greece

Begzos, Marios (*Theology/Religion*, also Philosophy)

Hawaii

Watson, John Robert (*Medical Science*)

Honduras

Owens, Joseph V. (*Theology/Religion*, also Philosophy)

Hong Kong

Becker, Gerhold K. (*Theology/Religion*, also Philosophy)

Kang, Phee Seng (*Philosophy*, also Theology/Religion, Mathematics)

Yu, Carver Tatsum (*Theology/Religion*, also History, Philosophy)

Hungary

Bolyki, János (*Theology/Religion*, also History)

Gaál, Botond (*Theology/Religion*, also Physics, Mathematics)

Medgyesi, György (*Biochemistry/Biophysics*, also Medical Science)

Idaho

Fast, Edwin (*Physics*, also Chemistry, Mathematics)

Faulkner Jr., George R. (*Management*)

Illinois

Albright, Carol Rausch (*Communications*)

Albright, John R. (*Physics*)

Ashbrook, James B. (*Theology/Religion*, also Psychology/Counseling, Psychiatry)

Brand, Raymond. H. (*Biology*, also Ecology/Environment)

Breed, David R. (*Theology/Religion*, also Philosophy)

Breed, James Lincoln (*Theology/Religion*, also Philosophy)

Browning, Don S. (*Ethics*, also Theology/Religion)

Burhoe, Ralph Wendell (*Theology/Religion*)

Cloutier, Stephen (*Chemistry*, also Engineering)

Collins, Gary R. (*Psychology/Counseling*)

Dobbs, Betty Jo Teeter (*History and Philosophy of Science*)

Faber, Roger J. (*Physics*, also Philosophy, Chemistry)

Gilbert, Thomas L. (*Physics*, also Chemistry, Theology/Religion)

Gilkey, Langdon (*Theology/Religion*, also Philosophy)

Glassman, Robert B. (*Psychology/Counseling*, also Sociobiology)

Hannon, Ralph H. (*Chemistry*, also Physics, Mathematics)

Harris, E. Lynn (*Theology/Religion*, also Literature, Psychology/Counseling)

Hefner, Philip (*Theology/Religion*, also Interdisciplinary Studies, Philosophy)

Hiebert, Paul G. (*Anthropology*, also Theology/Religion)

Hinkle, John E. (*Psychology/Counseling*)

Holmes, Arthur F. (*Philosophy*, also Theology/Religion)

Holmes, H. Rodney (*Biology*, also Psychology/Counseling)

Jones, Stanton Louis (*Psychology/Counseling*)

Kern, John C. (*Management*)

Mangum, John M. (*Theology/Religion*, also Communications, Administration) Also Pennsylvania

Marty, Martin E. (*Theology/Religion*, also Communications)

Maziarz, Edward Anthony (*Theology/Religion*, also Philosophy, Mathematics, Physics)

McFeeley, Daniel (*Philosophy*, also Psychology/Counseling)

Mixter, Russell L. (*Biology*)

Muck, Terry C. (*Theology/Religion*)

Nelson, James S. (*Theology/Religion*)

Nelson, Paul Alfred (*Philosophy*)

Parker, Thomas (*Theology/Religion*)

Parks, Lyle Fredrick (*Psychiatry*, also Psychology/Counseling)

Pun, Pattle P.T. (*Molecular Biology*, also Genetics, Theology/Religion)

Richards, Robert J. (*Philosophy*, also History and Philosophy of Science, Psychology/Counseling)

Riddiford, Alan Wistar (*Mathematics*, also Theology/Religion)

Roberts, Robert C. (*Ethics*, also Psychology/Counseling, Philosophy, Theology/Religion)

Schroeder, W. Widick (*Theology/Religion*, also Ethics)

Shweder, Richard Allan (*Anthropology*, also Philosophy, Psychology/Counseling)

Sire, James W. (*Communications*, also History and Philosophy of Science)

Spradley, Joseph L. (*Physics*, also Astronomy/Astrophysics, History and Philosophy of Science)

Suttle, Bruce B. (*Philosophy*)

Temple, Dennis Michael (*Philosophy*)

Timm, Roger E. (*Theology/Religion*, also Philosophy)

Ulbrich, Paul W. (*Medical Science*)

Van Valen, Leigh M. (*Biology*)

VanOstenburg, Donald O. (*Physics*)

York, Donald G. (*Astronomy/Astrophysics*)

India

Bag, A. K. (*History and Philosophy of Science*, also Mathematics)

Braganza, Karuna Mary (*Literature*, also Education)

Chadha, N. K. (*Psychology/Counseling*)

Furtado, Daphne (*Biochemistry/Biophysics*, also Chemistry)

Ganguli, H. C. (*Psychology/Counseling*, also Philosophy)

Gregorios, Paulos Mar (*Theology/Religion*, also Administration, History and Philosophy of Science, Philosophy)

Jain, Devaki (*Sociology*, also Ethics)

Monteiro, Hubert A. (*Chemistry*, also Commerce)

Rahman, Abdul (*Management*, also History and Philosophy of Science, Biochemistry/Biophysics, Theology/Religion)

Singh, Renuka (*Sociology*)

Varadarajan, Lotika (*History*)

Indiana

Buckley, Michael J. (*Theology/Religion*, also Philosophy)

Busse, Richard Paul (*Theology/Religion*, also Philosophy)

Crowe, Michael J. (*History and Philosophy of Science*, also Physics, Astronomy/Astrophysics)

Grizzle, Raymond Edward (*Ecology/Environment*)

Hartzler, H. Harold (*Mathematics*, also Physics, Astronomy/Astrophysics)

Kanagy, Sherman P. (*Astronomy/Astrophysics*, also Philosophy, Physics)

MacKay, David B. (*Commerce*, also Earth Science)

McMullin, Ernan (*Philosophy*, also Theology/Religion, Physics, History and Philosophy of Science)

Neuhouser, David L. (*Mathematics*)

Payton, Robert L. (*Ethics*)

Plantinga, Alvin C. (*Philosophy*, also Theology/Religion)

Rothrock, Paul E. (*Biology*, also Earth Science)

Smith, David H. (*Theology/Religion*, also Philosophy)

Smucker, Silas J. (*Ecology/Environment*)

Sprunger, Meredith Justin (*Philosophy*, also Theology/Religion)

Vance, Forrest L. (*Psychology/Counseling*)

Washburn, Michael (*Philosophy*)

Westfall, Richard S. (*History and Philosophy of Science*)

Whipple, Andrew P. (*Biology*)

Iowa

Hallberg, Fred W. (*Philosophy*, also Psychology/Counseling)

Kracher, Alfred (*Chemistry*, also Earth Science)

Maatman, Russell W. (*Chemistry*)

Paul, William W. (*Philosophy*, also Theology/Religion)

Vander Zee, Delmar (*Biology*)

Iran

Golshani, Mehdi (*Physics*, also Theology/Religion, Philosophy, History and Philosophy of Science*)

Italy

Bellini, Gianpaolo (*Physics*)

Benvenuto, Edoardo (*Technology*, also Theology/Religion, Physics, History and Philosophy of Science)

Blasi, Paolo (*Physics*, also Theology/Religion)

Cereti, Giovanni (*Theology/Religion*)

Colzani, Gianni (*Theology/Religion*)

Corsi, Pietro (*History and Philosophy of Science*, also Philosophy)

Coyne, George V. (*Astronomy/Astrophysics*)

Dallaporta, Nicolo (*Physics*)

Del Re, Giuseppe (*Chemistry*, also Physics, Philosophy)

Di Bernardo, Giuliano (*History and Philosophy of Science*, also Philosophy)

Drago, Antonino (*History and Philosophy of Science*, also Physics)

Facchini, Fiorenzo (*Anthropology*)

Galleni, Lodovico (*Biology*)

Giannoni, Paolo (*Theology/Religion*)

Molari, Carlo (*Theology/Religion*)

Parenti, Sergio (*Theology/Religion*)

Pizzamiglio, Pierluigi (*History and Philosophy of Science*)

Prodi, Giovanni (*Theology/Religion*)

Prosperi, Giovanni M. (*Physics*)

Sanguinetti, Francesco (*Medical Science*, also Ecology/Environment)

Tarli, Silvana Borgognini (*Anthropology*)

Trautteur, Giuseppe (*Computer and Information Sciences*)

Japan

Reddington, Kenneth George (*Psychology/Counseling*, also Theology/Religion)

Yuguchi, Takashi (*Physics*, also Communications)

Kansas

Batson, C. Daniel (*Psychology/Counseling*, also Theology/Religion, Education)

Eckstrom, Vance L. (*Theology/Religion*)

Jackson, Wes (*Biology*, also Genetics, Ecology/Environment, Ethics)

Miller, Keith Brady (*Earth Science*)

Nickel Jr., Gerhard (*Physics*, also Chemistry, Earth Science, Languages)

Wahlbeck, Phillip G. (*Chemistry*)

Wheeler, David L. (*Theology/Religion*, also Philosophy)

Kansas

Batson, C. Daniel (*Psychology/Counseling*, also Theology/Religion, Education)

Eckstrom, Vance L. (*Theology/Religion*)

Jackson, Wes (*Biology*, also Genetics, Ecology/Environment, Ethics)

Miller, Keith Brady (*Earth Science*)

Nickel Jr., Gerhard (*Physics*, also Chemistry, Earth Science, Languages)

Wahlbeck, Phillip G. (*Chemistry*)

Wheeler, David L. (*Theology/Religion*, also Philosophy)

Kentucky

Bunnell, Adam Eugene (*History*, also Theology/Religion)

Force, James E. (*Philosophy*, also History and Philosophy of Science)

Gailey, Franklin B. (*Medical Science*, also Biochemistry/Biophysics)

Koteskey, Ronald L. (*Psychology/Counseling*)

Nonneman, Arthur J. (*Psychology/Counseling*)

Roche, Barbara A. (*History*, also Education, Theology/Religion)

Rowatt, Wade Clinton (*Psychology/Counseling*)

Schoen, Edward L. (*Philosophy*)

Weir, Jack L. (*Philosophy*, also Theology/Religion, Ethics)

Wilbur, Frank H. (*Biology*)

Kenya

Nasimiyu, Anne (*Theology/Religion*)

Korea

Zhang, Hwe Ik (*Physics*)

Liechtenstein

Buttiglione, Rocco (*Philosophy*, also Political Science/Politics, Ethics)

Seifert, Josef (*Philosophy*)

Louisiana

Bennett, J. W. (*Genetics*)

Elkins, Thomas Edward (*Medical Science*)

Karkalits Jr., Olin Carroll (*Chemistry*, also Engineering)

Tipler, Frank J. (*Mathematics*, also Physics, Astronomy/Astrophysics)

Tobacyk, Jerome J. (*Psychology/Counseling*)

Turner, Robert Eugene (*Biology*, also Ecology/Environment)

Zimmerman, Michael E. (*Philosophy*)

Maine

Bell Jr., Reuben Paul (*Medical Science*)

Ferrell, Ginnie (*Theology/Religion*, also Earth Science, Chemistry)

Gelwick, Richard (*Theology/Religion*, also Philosophy, History and Philosophy of Science, Interdisciplinary Studies)

Ross, Norman Albert (*Astronomy/Astrophysics*)

Wason, Paul Kenneth (*Anthropology*)

Malaysia

Oorjitham, Santha (*Communications*)

Maryland

Forman, Frank (*Economics*)

Grant, Theodore F. (*Psychology/Counseling*)
Also *District of Columbia*

Griffin, Douglas L. (*Theology/Religion*)

Hall, Forrest G. (*Physics*)

Hermann, Robert A. (*Mathematics*, also Physics, Philosophy)

Hunt, Mary E. (*Theology/Religion*, also Ethics)

Johnson, Rodney W. (*Technology*, also Physics)
Also *Virginia*

Jones, Jack R. (*Ecology/Environment*)

Klaus, Hanna (*Medical Science*, also Theology/Religion)

Larson, David Bruce (*Medical Science*, also Psychiatry, Administration)

Mullins, Jeffrey Lynn (*Astronomy/Astrophysics*, also Philosophy)

Pellegrino, Edmund D. (*Medical Science*, also Ethics) Also *District of Columbia*

Rockwell, Theodore (*Engineering*, also Technology)

Salmon, James F. (*Chemistry*, also Theology/Religion, Philosophy)

Seeger, Raymond John (*Physics*)

Shropshire Jr., W. (*Theology/Religion*, also Biochemistry/Biophysics) Also *District of Columbia*

Simpkinson, Charles H. (*Psychology/Counseling*)

Swift, David Leslie (*Medical Science*, also Ecology/Environment, Engineering)

Wonderly, Daniel E. (*Theology/Religion*, also Biology, Earth Science)

Yockey, Hubert P. (*Biology*, also Management)

Massachusetts

Barclay, Peter R. (*Sociology*, also Ethics)

Bjork, Russell C. (*Computer and Information Sciences*)

Buehler, David A. (*Theology/Religion*, also Ethics, Computer and Information Sciences)

Byrne, Patrick H. (*Philosophy*)

Cahill, Lisa Sowle (*Theology/Religion*, also Ethics)

Casey, Thomas Michael (*Theology/Religion*, also Psychology/Counseling)

Clayton, Philip (*Philosophy*, also Theology/Religion, History and Philosophy of Science)

Gaede, S. D. (*Sociology*, also History and Philosophy of Science)

Giberson, Karl Willard (*Physics*)

Gingerich, Owen (*Astronomy/Astrophysics*, also History and Philosophy of Science, Philosophy)

Haas Jr., John W. (*Chemistry*, also History and Philosophy of Science)

Haas III, John W. (*Chemistry*)

Handspickel, Meredith Brook (*Theology/Religion*)

Haury, David L. (*Education*, also Biology)

Heim, S. Mark (*Theology/Religion*)

Herrmann, Robert L. (*Biochemistry/Biophysics*, also Chemistry, Molecular Biology)

Hiebert, Erwin Nick (*History and Philosophy of Science*, also Chemistry, Physics)

Hodges, Bert H. (*Psychology/Counseling*, also Philosophy)

Hugenberger, Gordon P. (*Theology/Religion*)

Hummel, Charles E. (*Theology/Religion*, also Chemistry, Technology)

Johnson, Walter Colin (*Psychiatry*, also Psychology/Counseling, Medical Science)

Keggi, J John (*Chemistry*, also Theology/Religion)

LaFargue, Michael (*Theology/Religion*, also History and Philosophy of Science, Interdisciplinary Studies)

Ling, Vincent (*Biology*)

Lipinski, Boguslaw (*Biochemistry/Biophysics*)

Manganello, James A. (*Psychology/Counseling*)

Margulis, Lynn (*Biology*)

McDargh, John (*Theology/Religion*, also Psychology/Counseling)

Neville, Robert Cummings (*Theology/Religion*, also Philosophy)

Nicholi Jr., Armand Mayo (*Psychiatry*, also Theology/Religion)

Nicholson, Philip (*Philosophy*, also Jurisprudence/Law, Medical Science, Computer and Information Sciences)

Oliver, Harold H. (*Theology/Religion*, also Philosophy)

Petersen, Rodney L. (*History*)

Pietrzak, Daniel M. (*Psychology/Counseling*)

Queen, Christopher S. (*Philosophy*, also Theology/Religion)

Saler, Benson (*Anthropology*)

Schmitt, Francis O. (*Medical Science*)

Sleigh Jr., Robert Colins (*Philosophy*)

Smith-Moran, Barbara Putney (*Chemistry*, also Astronomy/Astrophysics, Theology/Religion)

Stein, Sharon A. (*Psychology/Counseling*, also Philosophy, Education)

Stevens Jr., Herbert Howe (*Philosophy*)

Sutherland Jr., Malcolm Read (*Theology/Religion*, also Administration, Education)

Truog, Dean-Daniel W. (*Education*, also Theology/Religion, History and Philosophy of Science)

Uhlig, Herbert H. (*Engineering*, also Technology)

Wathen-Dunn, Weiant (*Physics*, also Communications, Engineering)

Whittaker-Johns, Barbara A. (*Theology/Religion*, also Education)

Wilson, Edward Osborne (*Biology*, also Ecology/Environment)

Wright, Richard T. (*Biology*, also Ecology/Environment)

Wulff, David M. (*Psychology/Counseling*, also Theology/Religion, History)

Zajonc, Arthur G. (*Physics*)

Michigan

Bauman, Michael E. (*Theology/Religion*, also History, Languages) Also United Kingdom

Bolt, Martin (*Psychology/Counseling*)

Bouma III, Hessel (*Biology*, also Genetics)

Burke, Thomas J. (*Theology/Religion*, also Philosophy, History and Philosophy of Science)

Carey, Patrick W. (*Theology/Religion*, also History and Philosophy of Science)

Clark, Kelly James (*Philosophy*, also Theology/Religion, History and Philosophy of Science)

DeGraaf, Donald E. (*Physics*)

Ehlers, Vernon J. (*Psychology/Counseling*, also Physics, Ethics)

Ellens, J. Harold (*Psychology/Counseling*, also Theology/Religion)

Hanford, Jack T. (*Theology/Religion*, also Philosophy, Ethics)

Hasel, Frank Michael (*Theology/Religion*)

Heckenlively, Donald B. (*Biology*, also Computer and Information Sciences)

Hernandez, Edwin Ivan (*Sociology*)

Kaiser, Christopher B. (*Theology/Religion*, also Physics, History and Philosophy of Science)

Kalthoff, Mark A. (*History and Philosophy of Science*, also Philosophy)

Knobloch, Irving William (*Biology*)

Kropf, Richard W. (*Theology/Religion*, also Philosophy, Psychology/Counseling)

Menninga, Clarence (*Earth Science*, also Chemistry)

Moore, Thomas J. (*Management*, also Computer and Information Sciences)

Myers, David G. (*Psychology/Counseling*)

Rappaport, Roy A. (*Anthropology*)

Ratzsch, Del (*Philosophy*, also History and Philosophy of Science)

Reding, Georges R. (*Psychiatry*)

Ruark, James Ellwood (*Literature*)

Skolimowski, Henryk (*Philosophy*)

Van Dyke, Fred G. (*Biology*, also Ecology/Environment) Also Montana

Van Leeuwen, Mary Stewart (*Sociology*, also Psychology/Counseling)

Van Till, Howard J. (*Physics*, also Astronomy/Astrophysics)

Van Zytveld, John B. (*Physics*)

Weaver, Glenn David (*Psychology/Counseling*)

Young, Davis A. (*Earth Science*)

Zylstra, Uko (*Biology*)

Minnesota

Barbour, Ian G. (*Theology/Religion*, also Physics, Philosophy)

Bohon, Robert L (*Chemistry*, also Technology, Earth Science, Management)

Deason, Gary Bruce (*Theology/Religion*, also History and Philosophy of Science)

Evans, C. Stephen (*Philosophy*, also Psychology/Counseling)

Hazard, Evan Brandao (*Biology*)

Hyers, Conrad (*Theology/Religion*)

Leming, Michael Richard (*Sociology*)

Magnuson, Norris A. (*Theology/Religion*, also History)

Mason, John Martin (*Theology/Religion*)

Olson, Roger Eugene (*Theology/Religion*)

Patrick, Thomas E, (*Theology/Religion*, also Administration)

Puckett, Laura E. (*Psychology/Counseling*, also Biochemistry/Biophysics)

Reichenbach, Bruce R. (*Philosophy*, also Ethics, Theology/Religion)

Rice, Stanley Arthur (*Ecology/Environment*, also Biology, Education)

Shults, F. LeRon (*Education*)

Simmons Jr., Ernest L. (*Philosophy*, also Theology/Religion)

Stoll, John Henry (*Theology/Religion*, also Psychology/Counseling)

Sturm, Mary J. (*Theology/Religion*)

Mississippi

Key, Thomas D. S. (*Biology*, also Theology/Religion)

Montana

Hart, John (*Theology/Religion*, also Philosophy, Commerce, Ethics)

Mullen, Pierce C. (*History*)

Shaw, Marvin C. (*History and Philosophy of Science*, also Philosophy)

Shull, Philip A. (*Ethics*, also Theology/Religion)

Taylor, Jon (*Theology/Religion*)

Van Dyke, Fred G. (*Biology*, also Ecology/Environment) Also *Michigan*

Missouri

Anch, A. Michael (*Psychology/Counseling*, also Theology/Religion)

Brungs, Robert (*Theology/Religion*, also Physics, Ethics)

Dols Jr., William L. (*Theology/Religion*, also Psychology/Counseling)

Ford, Charles E. (*Mathematics*, also Computer and Information Sciences)

Hefley, James C. (*Communications*)

Keilholz, Peggy J. (*Psychology/Counseling*, also Theology/Religion)

Klotz, John W. (*Ecology/Environment*, also Theology/Religion, Ethics)

Mosley, Glenn R. (*Theology/Religion*)

Mullins, Carl Phillips (Phil) (*Theology/Religion*, also Literature)

Whitehead, Clay C. (*Psychiatry*) Also California

Witherspoon, William (*Commerce*, also Economics)

Namibia

Isaak, Paul John (*Theology/Religion*)

Nebraska

Larzelere, Robert Earl (*Psychology/Counseling*)

The Netherlands

Bennema, P. (*Chemistry*, also Physics)

Bonting, Sjoerd L. (*Biochemistry/Biophysics*, also Biology, Chemistry, Theology/Religion)

Boon, Rudolf (*Theology/Religion*, also Philosophy, History and Philosophy of Science)

Carvallo, Marc E. (*Philosophy*, also Education, Theology/Religion)

de Knijff, Henri Wijnandus (*Theology/Religion*)

Dierick, G.P.A. (*History*, also Philosophy, Theology/Religion)

Drees, Willem B. (*Theology/Religion*, also Physics)

Feil, Dirk (*Chemistry*, also Physics)

Fennema, Jan W. R. (*Physics*, also Philosophy, Theology/Religion)

Fokker, Adriaan D. (*Astronomy/Astrophysics*)

Hilhorst, Medard T. (*Ethics*, also Theology/Religion, Technology)

Hogenhuis, C. T. (*Physics*)

Kolega, D. G. A. (*Theology/Religion*, also Philosophy, Ethics)

Laeyendecker, L. (*Sociology*, also Theology/Religion)

Manenschijn, Gerrit (*Ethics*, also Theology/Religion)

Musschenga, A. W. (*Theology/Religion*, also Ethics)

Schotman-Veldman, Judith L. (*Chemistry*, also History and Philosophy of Science, Physics)

Schuurman, Egbert (*Philosophy*, also Engineering, Political Science/Politics)

Sevenhoven, J. C. A. M. (*Theology/Religion*, also Philosophy)

Stavenga, Gerben J. (*History and Philosophy of Science*)

Thung, Mady A. (*Sociology*, also Theology/Religion)

van de Beek, A. (*Biology*, also Theology/Religion)

van den Brom, Luco Johan (*Theology/Religion*, also Mathematics, Physics)

van Dijk, Paul (*Theology/Religion*, also Ethics)

van Duijin, Pieter (*Biology*)

Van Erkelens, Herbert (*Physics*, also Psychology/Counseling)

van Kouwenhoven, Willem F. (*Theology/Religion*)

Van Melsen, A. G. M. (*History and Philosophy of Science*)

Winkeler, L. G. M. (*Theology/Religion*)

New Hampshire

Augros, Robert M. (*Philosophy*)

Brooks, George Gordon (*Physics*, also Theology/Religion) Also Florida

Mallove, Eugene F. (*Communications*, also Astronomy/Astrophysics)

Sharpe, Kevin James (*Theology/Religion*, also Philosophy, Mathematics, Communications)

Stanciu, George (*Physics*)

New Jersey

Allen, Diogenes (*Philosophy*, also Theology/Religion)

Benson, Purnel H. (*Psychology/Counseling*, also Sociology, Economics)

Dyson, Freeman J. (*Physics*)

Ehrenfeld, David W. (*Ecology/Environment*, also Biology, Medical Science)

Hardy, Daniel W. (*Theology/Religion*)

Jaki, Stanley L. (*Theology/Religion*, also Physics, History and Philosophy of Science)

Jones, James W. (*Psychology/Counseling*, also Theology/Religion)

Kaita, Robert (*Physics*)

Kohn, David (*History and Philosophy of Science*)

Kuharetz, Boris (*Astronomy/Astrophysics*)

Loder, James Edwin (*Theology/Religion*, also Psychology/Counseling, Philosophy)

Mauser, Ulrich Wilheilm (*Theology/Religion*)

Mitchell, Robert P. (*Theology/Religion*)

Monse, Ernst U. (*Chemistry*)

Montgomery, Robert Lancaster (*Theology/Religion*, also Sociology)

Neidhardt, Walter Jim (*Physics*, also Theology/Religion)

Panitz, Michael E. (*Theology/Religion*, also History)

Pilchik, Ely E. (*Theology/Religion*)

Reynolds, George T. (*Physics*)

Rothenberg, David (*Philosophy*)

Troster, Lawrence (*Theology/Religion*) Also New York

van Huyssteen, Jacobus Wentzel Vrede (*Theology/Religion*, also Philosophy)

West, Charles C. (*Ethics*, also Political Science/Politics)

Woodward, J. Guy (*Physics*)

Yoshikawa, Shoichi (*Physics*)

New Mexico

Underkofler, Leland A. (*Biochemistry/Biophysics*)

New York

Allen, George W. J. (*Biology*)

Alston, William (*Philosophy*)

Ambrosino, Salvatore V. (*Psychiatry*)

Apyczynski, John V. (*Theology/Religion*, also Philosophy)

Arvedson, Peter Fredrick (*Theology/Religion*, also Chemistry)

Ayers, David John (*Sociology*, also Psychology/Counseling)

Bassett, Rodney L. (*Psychology/Counseling*)

Benninghoff, Jean (*Theology/Religion*, also Physics)

Berry, Thomas (*History*, also Theology/Religion)

Bourne, Malcolm C. (*Chemistry*)

Burnham, Frederic B. (*History and Philosophy of Science*, also Theology/Religion)

Cain, Dallas E. (*Engineering*)

Cantore, Enrico (*Philosophy*, also Physics, Theology/Religion)

Casanova, José V. (*Sociology*)

Cauthen, W. Kenneth (*Theology/Religion*)

Chirico-Rosenberg, Donna (*Psychology/Counseling*)

Church, F. Forrester (*Communications*, also Theology/Religion)

Downing, Barry H. (*Theology/Religion*, also Technology)

Frair, Wayne (*Biology*, also Genetics)

Frecska, Ede (*Psychiatry*, also Biochemistry/Biophysics)

Green, Thomas F. (*Education*, also Sociology, Philosophy)

Harrington, Donald S. (*Theology/Religion*)

Hartzell, Karl Drew (*Administration*, also History, Education, Ethics)

Heaney, John J. (*Theology/Religion*, also Psychology/Counseling)

Heelan, Patrick A. (*Philosophy*, also Physics, Earth Science, Theology/Religion)

Hulme, Norman A. (*Biochemistry/Biophysics*, also Medical Science)

Hunter, Lloyd P. (*Engineering*)

Jasso, Guillermina (*Sociology*)

Johnson, Anthony P. (*Management*, also Theology/Religion)

Knapp II, John Allen (*Literature*, also Education, Theology/Religion)

Kovel, Joel (*Psychiatry*, also Sociology, Psychology/Counseling)

Landess, Marcia McBroom (*Political Science/Politics*, also Education, Theology/Religion)

Lifton, Robert Jay (*Psychiatry*, also Psychology/Counseling, Medical Science, Ethics)

Maduro, L. Otto A. (*Philosophy*, also Sociology)

Malino, Jerome R. (*Theology/Religion*)

McCormack, Elizabeth J. (*Philosophy*)

Meyerhoff, Gordon R. (*Psychiatry*, also Theology/Religion)

Ogden, Philip M. (*Physics*, also Mathematics)

Perkins, Richard (*Sociology*)

Proudfoot, Wayne (*Theology/Religion*, also Philosophy)

Provine, William B. (*History and Philosophy of Science*, also Genetics)

Rockefeller, Laurance S. (*Ethics*, also Commerce)

Salthe, Stanley N. (*Biology*)

Shinn, Roger L. (*Theology/Religion*, also Ethics, Philosophy)

Sternglass, Ernest J. (*Physics*, also History and Philosophy of Science)

Tester, Leonard W. (*Psychology/Counseling*)

Toolan, David (*Theology/Religion*, also Philosophy)

Troster, Lawrence (*Theology/Religion*) Also *New Jersey*

Viladesau, Richard (*Theology/Religion*, also Philosophy)

Vitz, Paul C. (*Psychology/Counseling*, also Theology/Religion)

Vukanovic, Vladimir (*Chemistry*)

Wallwork, Ernest Edward (*Ethics*, also Psychology/Counseling, Sociology) Also District of Columbia

Wolsky, Maria de Issekutz (*Biology*, also Philosophy) Also *Canada*

White, Rhea A. (*Administration*, also Communications, Theology/Religion, Philosophy)

Williams, George C. (*Biology*)

New Zealand

Jones, D. Gareth (*Medical Science*, also Biology, Ethics)

Paterson, John Leonard (*Earth Science*)

Scott, Philip Maxwell (*Mathematics*, also Theology/Religion)

Nigeria

Ajakaiye, Deborah Enilo (*Physics*, also Earth Science)

North Carolina

Brigham, Joseph John (*Engineering*)

Combs, Allan L. (*Psychology/Counseling*)

Curry, John F. (*Psychology/Counseling*, also Medical Science)

Davis, Lloyd J. (*Physics*)

Durbin Jr., William A. (*History and Philosophy of Science*, also Communications)

Elliott, John Eric (*History and Philosophy of Science*, also Mathematics)

Kirchoff, Bruce K. (*Ecology/Environment*, also Genetics)

Koenig, Harold G. (*Medical Science*, also Psychology/Counseling)

Perry, David Kenneth (*Biochemistry/Biophysics*)

Peterson, James C. (*Ethics*)

Stines, James W. (*Theology/Religion*, also Philosophy)

Wetherbee, James M. (*Literature*)

North Ireland

Livingstone, David Noel (*Earth Science*, also Philosophy, Sociology)

Norway

Böckman, Peter Wilhelm (*Ethics*, also Theology/Religion, Philosophy)

Ohio

Barker, Verlyn L. (*Political Science/Politics*)

Barnes, Michael H. (*Theology/Religion*, also History and Philosophy of Science)

Bergman, Jerry (*Biology*, also Physics, Chemistry, Psychology/Counseling)

Crosby, John F. (*Philosophy*, also Theology/Religion)

Crutcher, Keith A. (*Medical Science*)

Gromacki, Robert Glenn (*Theology/Religion*)

Hoshiko, Tomuo (*Biochemistry/Biophysics*, also Medical Science)

Keiper Sr., Glenn L. (*Medical Science*)

Kelly, Dr. William L. (*Chemistry*)

Larson, Laurence A. (*Biology*, also Interdisciplinary Studies)

Macior, Lazarus Walter (*Theology/Religion*, also Biology)

Murphy, George L. (*Theology/Religion*, also Physics)

Percesepe, Gary John (*Philosophy*)

Petras, David M. (*Theology/Religion*)

Poloma, Margaret M. (*Sociology*)

Post, Stephen G. (*Theology/Religion*, also Biology, Ethics)

Santmire, H. Paul (*Theology/Religion*, also History)

Sheldon, John M. (*Ethics*, also Medical Science)

Sollod, Robert N. (*Psychology/Counseling*, also Theology/Religion)

Tilley, Terrence U. (*Theology/Religion*, also Philosophy)

Wattles, Jeffrey Hamilton (*Philosophy*)

Yamauchi, Edwin M. (*History*, also Languages)

Oklahoma

Dormer, Kenneth J. (*Medical Science*)

Kahoe, Richard Dean (*Psychology/Counseling*)

McMullen, Emerson Thomas (*History and Philosophy of Science*)

Thurman, L. Duane (*Biology*, also Ecology/Environment)

Oregon

Dufner, Andrew J. (*Theology/Religion*, also Philosophy, Physics)

Feucht, Dennis L. (*Technology*, also Computer and Information Sciences)

Fuchs, Peter C. (*Medical Science*)

Rottschaefer, William A. (*Philosophy*, also History and Philosophy of Science)

Shepard, Frederick Douglas (*Biology*, also Education, Administration)

Stahl, C. Larry (*Languages*)

Willis, David L. (*Biology*)

Pennsylvania

Bloom, John A. (*Physics*, also Theology/Religion, Computer and Information Sciences, History)

Bregman, Lucy (*Theology/Religion*, also Psychology/Counseling)

Brobeck, John R. (*Medical Science*)

Chase, Gene Barry (*Mathematics*, also Computer and Information Sciences)

Cobb, Larry R. (*Administration*)

Cohen, Ernest B. (*Engineering*, also Technology, Psychology/Counseling)

d'Aquili, Eugene G, (*Psychiatry*, also Medical Science, Anthropology)

Davis, Edward B. (*History and Philosophy of Science*, also Philosophy)

DeHaan, Robert F. (*Psychology/Counseling*)

Denues, A. R. Taylor (*Chemistry*, also Engineering, Medical Science, Theology/Religion)

Drozdek, Adam (*Computer and Information Sciences*)

Edgar, William (*Theology/Religion*)

Falla Jr., William S. (*Theology/Religion*, also Earth Science)

Fleming, Fraser Fergusson (*Chemistry*)

Frye, Roland Mushat (*Literature*, also Theology/Religion)

Goodenough, Ward H. (*Anthropology*)

Greenhow, Donald Eric Fraser (*Medical Science*)

Griffiths, Robert B. (*Physics*, also Mathematics)

Hess, Gerald D. (*Biology*)

Korsmeyer, Jerry (*Physics*, also Theology/Religion)

Kraft, R. Wayne (*Technology*, also Physics)

Larson, Duane H. (*Theology/Religion*, also Administration)

Mackler, Aaron L. (*Theology/Religion*, also Ethics, Philosophy)

Mangum, John M. (*Theology/Religion*, also Communications, Administration) Also *Illinois*

Martin, Helen Elizabeth (*Mathematics*)

Martino, Rocco Leonard (*Computer and Information Sciences*, also Finance, Mathematics, Physics)

Masani, Pesi R. (*Mathematics*)

May, John Y. (*Philosophy*)

Miles, Sara Joan (*History and Philosophy of Science*, also Biology, Anthropology, Education)

Miller, James Bradley (*Theology/Religion*, also Philosophy)

Mitcham, Carl (*Philosophy*)

Moldoff, Sol (*Engineering*)

Newman, Robert Chapman (*Theology/Religion*)

Paul, Erich Robert (*History and Philosophy of Science*)

Poythress, Vern Sheridan (*Mathematics*, also Theology/Religion)

Ramsden, William E. (*Theology/Religion*, also Psychology/Counseling)

Ross, Robert S. (*Physics*)

Rubik, Beverly (*Biochemistry/Biophysics*)

Shank, Norman E. (*Chemistry*)

Sheldon, Joseph K. (*Biology*, also Ecology/Environment)

Swyhart, Barbara Ann DeMartino (*Philosophy*, also Ethics, Theology/Religion, Education)

Teske, John A. (*Psychology/Counseling*)

Tjeltveit, Alan (*Psychology/Counseling*, also Theology/Religion)

Trook, Douglas A. (*Psychology/Counseling*, also Theology/Religion)

Venable III, William H. (*Physics*, also Theology/Religion)

Wicken, Jeffrey S. (*Biochemistry/Biophysics*, also Philosophy, Theology/Religion)

Wilcox, David Linwood (*Genetics*, also Biology)

Philippines

Baclig, Paulita Villegs (*Medical Science*)

Poland

Glódz, **Malgorzata** (*Physics*)

Grzegorczyk, Andrzej (*Philosophy*, also Mathematics, Ethics)

Heller, Michael (*Philosophy*, also Astronomy/Astrophysics, History and Philosophy of Science)

Nieznaski, Edward (*Philosophy*)

Styczen, Tadeusz (*Ethics*)

Zycinski, Jósef (*History and Philosophy of Science*, also Ecology/Environment, Theology/Religion, Ethics)

South Africa

Barrett, Peter J. (*Physics*)

Ellis, George F. R. (*Mathematics*, also Philosophy)

Lategan, Bernard C. (*Theology/Religion*)

Roukens de Lange, A. (*Commerce*, also Engineering, Chemistry, Mathematics)

Vorster, Willem S. (*Theology/Religion*)

Webster, John Wilfred (*Theology/Religion*, also Ethics, Philosophy)

South Carolina

Junkin III, William F. (*Physics*)

Kirkpatrick, Lee Alan (*Psychology/Counseling*)

LaBar, Martin (*Biology*, also Ethics)

Poole Jr., Charles P. (*Physics*)

Reisz Jr., H. Frederick (*Theology/Religion*, also Ethics)

Spain

Artigas, Mariano (*Physics*, also Philosophy)

Sweden

Dilworth, Craig (*Philosophy*, also History and Philosophy of Science)

Haikola, Lars T. J. (*Theology/Religion*, also Philosophy)

Jackelén, Antje (*Philosophy*, also Theology/Religion)

Liljas, Anders (*Biochemistry/Biophysics*)

Switzerland

Brugger, Hans Rudolf (*Physics*, also Astronomy/Astrophysics)

Dalferth, Ingolf Ulrich (*Theology/Religion*, also Philosophy) Also *Germany*

Eccles, Sir John C. (*Medical Science*, also History and Philosophy of Science, Philosophy)

Külling, Samuel (*Theology/Religion*)

Mercier, André (*Physics*, also History and Philosophy of Science)

Mortensen, Viggo (*Theology/Religion*, also Ethics, Philosophy)

Price, Daniel J. (*Theology/Religion*)

Reich, K. Helmut (*Psychology/Counseling*, also Physics, Engineering, Theology/Religion)

Rivier, Dominique-Casimir (*Physics*)

Rüst, Peter (*Chemistry*, also Biochemistry/Biophysics)

Schocher, Arno Johannes (*Technology*, also Biology, Theology/Religion)

Widmer, Gabriel-Philippe (*Theology/Religion*)

Wilder-Smith, Arthur Ernest (*Biochemistry/Biophysics*)

Taiwan

Budenholzer, Frank (*Chemistry*, also Physics, Theology/Religion)

Tanzania

Mwenegoha, Amani (*Administration*)

Tennessee

Bridges Jr., Carl B. (*Theology/Religion*, also Languages)

Clarke, Charles L. (*Medical Science*)

Cole-Turner, Ronald S. (*Theology/Religion*, also Ethics)

Gay, Volney P. (*Psychology/Counseling*, also Theology/Religion, Anthropology)

Hood, Thomas Charles (*Sociology*, also AT)

Ingram, Larry C. (*Sociology*)

Knight, Douglas A. (*Theology/Religion*)

McFague, Sallie (*Theology/Religion*)

Meador, Keith G. (*Psychiatry*, also Theology/Religion)

Rogers, Norma Prichard (*Engineering*, also Literature, Psychology/Counseling)

Sroufe, Joe Thomas (*Sociology*, also Theology/Religion)

Watson, Paul Joseph (*Psychology/Counseling*)

White, David C. (*Medical Science*, also Biology, Ecology/Environment)

Wilson, R. Ward (*Psychology/Counseling*)

Texas

Adams, Dawn A. (*Biology*)

Austin, William H. (*Philosophy*, also Theology/Religion)

Barnhouse, Ruth Tiffany (*Psychiatry*, also Medical Science, Theology/Religion)

Biesele, John Julius (*Biology*)

Bishop, Robert C. (*Physics*)

Blaising, Craig A. (*Theology/Religion*)

Booher, Bruce (*Theology/Religion*)

Bradley, Walter L. (*Physics*, also Technology)

Brun, Rudolf B. (*Biology*)

Burns Sr., John Lanier (*Theology/Religion*, also Philosophy)

Geisler, Norman L. (*Philosophy*, also Theology/Religion)

Hillar, Marian (*Molecular Biology*, also Biochemistry/Biophysics, Medical Science, History)

Johnson, Doyle Paul (*Sociology*)

King Jr., Morton B. (*Sociology*)

Knight, James Allen (*Psychology/Counseling*, also Theology/Religion, Medical Science)

Marshall Jr., John Harris (*Earth Science*)

Matsen, Fredrick A. (*Philosophy*, also Chemistry)

McDonald, Harry S. (*Biology*)

McIntyre, John A. (*Physics*)

Mills, Gordon C. (*Biochemistry/Biophysics*, also Genetics)

Nelson, J. Robert (*Theology/Religion*, also Ethics)

Pearson III, Daniel B. (*Psychiatry*, also Earth Science)

Pike, Kenneth L. (*Languages*, also Theology/Religion)

Sardana, Lal (*Engineering*)

Scheie, Paul (*Physics*, also Biochemistry/Biophysics)

Schrader, David Eugene (*Philosophy*, also Ethics)

Shotwell, Thomas K. (*Biology*, also Management)

Spak, K. Edmund (*Medical Science*)

Strobel, Henry W. (*Biochemistry/Biophysics*, also Theology/Religion)

Toledo, J. Rafael (*Medical Science*)

Walker, Laurence C. (*Earth Science*, also Theology/Religion)

United Kingdom

Ambrose, Edmund Jack (*Biology*, also Medical Science)

Atkinson, David John (*Theology/Religion*, also Chemistry, Psychology/Counseling)

Banner, Michael Charles (*Philosophy*, also Theology/Religion)

Barclay, Oliver Rainsford (*Biology*, also Theology/Religion)

Barker, Eileen (*Sociology*, also Theology/Religion)

Barrow, John D. (*Astronomy/Astrophysics*, also Physics, Philosophy, Mathematics)

Bauman, Michael E. (*Theology/Religion*, also History, Languages) Also *Michigan*

Berry, Robert James (*Genetics*, also Molecular Biology, Ecology/Environment)

Bloemendal, Michael (*Biochemistry/Biophysics*, also Chemistry)

Boyd, Sir Robert Lewis Fullarton (*Physics*, also Chemistry, Astronomy/Astrophysics, Technology)

Brennan, John Lester (*Medical Science*)

Brooke, John Hedley (*History and Philosophy of Science*, also Chemistry, Theology/Religion, Philosophy)

Brown, Robert Hanbury (*Philosophy*, also Astronomy/Astrophysics)

Brück, Hermann Alexander (*Astronomy/Astrophysics*, also History and Philosophy of Science)

Burke, Derek C. (*Molecular Biology*, also Theology/Religion)

Cantor, Geoffrey (*History and Philosophy of Science*, also Philosophy)

Clarke, Christopher James Seaton (*Philosophy*, also Mathematics)

Cook, Sir Alan Hugh (*Physics*, also Astronomy/Astrophysics)

Copestake, David R. (*Theology/Religion*, also Psychology/Counseling)

Crombie, Alistair Cameron (*History and Philosophy of Science*, also Biology)

Dagnall, Bernard (*Chemistry*, also Theology/Religion)

Durant, John Robert (*History and Philosophy of Science*, also Biology)

Emerton, Norma Elizabeth (*History and Philosophy of Science*)

Forster, Peter R. (*Theology/Religion*, also History)

Gibson, Arthur (*Philosophy*, also Literature, Astronomy/Astrophysics, Political Science/Politics)

Gosden, Roger G. (*Medical Science*)

Gouldstone, Tim (*Genetics*, also Theology/Religion)

Gowenlock, Brian G. (*Chemistry*)

Haba, Hanako (*Philosophy*, also Theology/Religion)

Habgood, John S. (*Theology/Religion*, also Biochemistry/Biophysics)

Harper, Charles L. (*Earth Science*, also Theology/Religion, Philosophy, Technology)

Harré, Rom (*History and Philosophy of Science*, also Philosophy)

Hay, David (*Biology*, also Theology/Religion, Sociology)

Hesse, Mary Brenda (*History and Philosophy of Science*, also Physics, Philosophy, Mathematics)

Hodgson, Peter E. (*Physics*)

Horswell, Kevin (*Philosophy*, also Theology/Religion)

Houghton, John T. (*Physics*)

Hull, John M. (*Education*, also Theology/Religion)

Humphreys, Colin John (*Technology*, also Physics)

Ingram, David J. E. (*Physics*)

Isham, Christopher J. (*Physics*)

Jeeves, Malcolm A. (*Psychology/Counseling*, also Theology/Religion)

Jenkins, Eric Neil (*Chemistry*, also Theology/Religion, Ethics)

Kerr, John Maxwell (*Theology/Religion*, also Engineering, Biology, History and Philosophy of Science)

Knight, Christopher C. (*Theology/Religion*, also Astronomy/Astrophysics, Physics)

Knight, David Marcus (*History and Philosophy of Science*)

Koenigsberger, Dorothy (*History*, also History and Philosophy of Science)

Landsberg, Peter T. (*Mathematics*, also Philosophy, History and Philosophy of Science)

Levitt, J. Peter Fletcher (*Theology/Religion*, also Physics)

Lovell, Sir Bernard (*Physics*, also Astronomy/Astrophysics)

Lucas, J. R. (*Philosophy*)

Lynden-Bell, Donald (*Astronomy/Astrophysics*)

Martin, Daniel (*Mathematics*)

Martin, David Alfred (*Sociology*)

McCrea, Sir William (Hunter) (*Astronomy/Astrophysics*)

McGrath, Alister E. (*Biology*, also Theology/Religion)

Miles, Caroline Mary (*Administration*, also Commerce)

Montefiore, Hugh (*Theology/Religion*)

Moore, James R. (*Theology/Religion*, also History and Philosophy of Science)

Moss, Rowland Percy (*Ecology/Environment*, also Theology/Religion)

Nelson, Robert T. (*Theology/Religion*, also Biochemistry/Biophysics)

Paul, Iain (*Theology/Religion*, also Chemistry)

Peacocke, Arthur Robert (*Biochemistry/Biophysics*, also Theology/Religion)

Peat, David (*Astronomy/Astrophysics*, also Theology/Religion)

Polkinghorne, John Charlton (*Physics*)

Poole, Michael William (*Education*)

Puddefoot, John Charles (*Theology/Religion*, also Mathematics)

Pullinger, David J. (*Mathematics*, also Biochemistry/Biophysics, Computer and Information Sciences)

Rees, Martin J. (*Astronomy/Astrophysics*)

Robertson, John H. (*Chemistry*)

Russell, Colin Archibald (*History and Philosophy of Science*, also Chemistry)

Schneider, Hans-Georg (*History and Philosophy of Science*, also Sociology)

Segal, Robert A. (*Theology/Religion*)

Sheldrake, Rupert (*Biochemistry/Biophysics*)

Sheppard, Norman (*Chemistry*)

Southgate, Beverley C. (*History*)

Spanner, Douglas C. (*Biochemistry/Biophysics*)

Stanesby, Derek Malcolm (*History and Philosophy of Science*, also Theology/Religion)

Stannard, Frank Russell (*Physics*)

Swinburne, Richard Granville (*Philosophy*, also Theology/Religion)

Tayler, Roger J. (*Astronomy/Astrophysics*)

Taylor, Howard G. (*Theology/Religion*, also Physics, Mathematics)

Thomson, Alexander (*Theology/Religion*)

Torrance, Thomas F. (*Theology/Religion*, also History and Philosophy of Science)

Trigg, Roger (*Philosophy*)

Walker, Ralph C. S. (*Philosophy*)

Ward, Keith (*Theology/Religion*, also Philosophy)

Whitrow, Gerald James (*Mathematics*, also History and Philosophy of Science)

Wiltsher, Christopher D. (*Theology/Religion*, also Philosophy, Mathematics, Computer and Information Sciences)

Wong, Wing-Hong (*Theology/Religion*, also Physics)

Young, David Nigel de Lorentz (*Theology/Religion*, also Mathematics)

Utah

Kassel, Victor (*Medical Science*)

Vermont

Hazelett, Samuel Richard (*Philosophy*, also Engineering)

Page, William R. (*Chemistry*, also Engineering, Biology, Sociology)

Webster, Frederic A. (*Medical Science*)

Virginia

Balslev, Anindita Niyogi (*Philosophy*, also Theology/Religion)

Casebolt, James R. (*Psychology/Counseling*)

Crippen, Timothy (*Sociology*, also Sociobiology)

Eaves, Lindon John (*Genetics*, also Theology/Religion, Mathematics)

Fagg, Lawrence W. (*Physics*, also Theology/Religion)

Fischer, Dick (*Theology/Religion*)

Henry, Carl F. H. (*Theology/Religion*, also Philosophy, Ethics)

Hillery Jr., George A. (*Sociology*, also Anthropology)

Johnson, Rodney W. (*Technology*, also Physics) Also Maryland

Kupke, Donald Walter (*Biochemistry/Biophysics*)

Marshner, William (*Theology/Religion*, also Philosophy)

Matthews, Dale A. (*Medical Science*) Also *District of Columbia*

Munday Jr., John Clingman (*Political Science/Politics*, also Ethics, Theology/Religion)

Roberts, Kenneth L. (*Engineering*, also Ecology/Environment)

Turner, Edith L. B. (*Anthropology*)

Wagner, Roy (*Anthropology*)

Wilkins III, Walter J. (*Interdisciplinary Studies*, also History, Philosophy)

Worthington Jr., Everett L. (*Psychology/Counseling*)

Washington

Baer, Donald R. (*Physics*)

Dye, David L. (*Physics*, also Technology)

Elgee, Neil J. (*Medical Science*)

Farnsworth, Kirk E. (*Psychology/Counseling*, also Theology/Religion)

Gill, Anthony J. (*Political Science/Politics*)

Hankins, Thomas L. (*History and Philosophy of Science*, also History, Education)

Kirby, Richard (*Theology/Religion*)

Montgomery, John Warwick (*Jurisprudence/Law*, also Education, Theology/Religion)

Nordgren, Richard (*Theology/Religion*, also Chemistry)

Overman, Richard H. (*Theology/Religion*)

Parrott III, Less (*Psychology/Counseling*)

Porter, Kenneth W. (*Engineering*)

Smith, Ronald N. (*Engineering*, also Physics)

Ulrickson, Brian Lee (*Earth Science*, also Theology/Religion)

Wisconsin

Amrhein, Eva Maria (*Physics*, also Theology/Religion) Also Germany

Anderson, Odin W. (*Sociology*)

Cudworth, Kyle M. (*Astronomy/Astrophysics*)

DeWitt, Calvin B. (*Biology*, also Ecology/Environment, Ethics)

Gardipee, Steven M. (*Theology/Religion*, also Philosophy)

Kent, Raymond D. (*Theology/Religion*)

Lindberg, David C. (*History and Philosophy of Science*, also Physics, Philosophy)

Miller, David Lee (*Philosophy*)

Moberg, David O. (*Sociology*)

Numbers, Ronald L. (*History and Philosophy of Science*, also Medical Science)

Peppin, John Francis (*Medical Science*, also Ethics)

Roberts, Jon H. (*History*)

Shank, Michael H. (*History and Philosophy of Science*, also Physics)

Utke, Allen R. (*Chemistry*, also Interdisciplinary Studies)

Primary Subject Index

This index is organized alphabetically by groups of individuals listed by their *primary* field of study/professional field. Secondary fields are listed under each individual, but are not indexed. Names in **bold** type indicate an entry in Directory A, while normal type indicates the entry is in Directory B. Subject categories which indicate an individual's primary and secondary fields of study or professional fields and geographical locations are also included with each entry. (Subject categories are listed below.) *Italicized* print indicates a "primary" area, be it an italicized state or country or subject category.

Subject Categories

Administration
Anthropology
Astronomy/Astrophysics (Physical Cosmology)
Biochemistry/Biophysics
Biology (Botany, Zoology, etc)
Chemistry
Commerce
Communications
Computer and Information Sciences
Earth Science (Geology, Mineralogy, Meteorology, Geography, Agriculture, etc)
Ecology/Environment (Environmental Ethics, Conservation and Preservation)
Economics
Education
Engineering
Ethics
Finance
Genetics

History
History and Philosophy of Science
Interdisciplinary Studies
Jurisprudence/Law
Languages
Literature
Management
Mathematics
Medical Science
Molecular Biology (Microbiology)
Philosophy
Physics
Political Science/Politics
Psychiatry
Psychology/Counseling
Sociobiology
Sociology
Technology
Theology/Religion

Administration

Cobb, Larry R. (*Administration*) *Pennsylvania*

Hartzell, Karl Drew (*Administration*, also History, Education, Ethics) *New York*

Miles, Caroline Mary (*Administration*, also Commerce) *United Kingdom*

Mwenegoha, Amani (*Administration*) *Tanzania*

White, Rhea A. (*Administration*, also Communications, Theology/Religion, Philosophy) *New York*

Anthropology

Bargatzky, Thomas (*Anthropology*) *Germany*

Buswell III, James O. (*Anthropology*) *California*

Facchini, Fiorenzo (*Anthropology*) *Italy*

Goodenough, Ward H. (*Anthropology*) *Pennsylvania*

Hiebert, Paul G. (*Anthropology*, also Theology/Religion) *Illinois*

Laughlin, Charles D. (*Anthropology*, also Medical Science) *Canada*

McCone, R. Clyde (*Anthropology*, also Literature, Theology/Religion) *California*

Mills, Antonia (*Anthropology*) *Canada*

Rappaport, Roy A. (*Anthropology*) *Michigan*

Saler, Benson (*Anthropology*) *Massachusetts*

Shweder, Richard Allan (*Anthropology*, also Philosophy, Psychology/Counseling) *Illinois*

Spiro, Melford E. (*Anthropology*) *California*

Tarli, Silvana Borgognini (*Anthropology*) *Italy*

Turner, Edith L. B. (*Anthropology*) *Virginia*

Wagner, Roy (*Anthropology*) *Virginia*

Wason, Paul Kenneth (*Anthropology*) *Maine*

Astronomy/Astrophysics

Barrow, John D. (*Astronomy/Astrophysics*, also Physics, Philosophy, Mathematics) *United Kingdom*

Brück, Hermann Alexander (*Astronomy/Astrophysics*, also History and Philosophy of Science) *United Kingdom*

Corbally, Christopher J. (*Astronomy/Astrophysics*, also Theology/Religion) *Arizona*

Coyne, George V. (*Astronomy/Astrophysics*) *Italy*

Cudworth, Kyle M. (*Astronomy/Astrophysics*) *Wisconsin*

Fokker, Adriaan D. (*Astronomy/Astrophysics*) *The Netherlands*

Gingerich, Owen (*Astronomy/Astrophysics*, also History and Philosophy of Science, Philosophy) *Massachusetts*

Kanagy, Sherman P. (*Astronomy/Astrophysics*, also Philosophy, Physics) *Indiana*

Kuharetz, Boris (*Astronomy/Astrophysics*) *New Jersey*

Lindenbald, Irving W. (*Astronomy/Astrophysics*, also Theology/Religion) *Washington, D.C.*

Lynden-Bell, Donald (*Astronomy/Astrophysics*) *United Kingdom*

MacCready, Paul B. (*Astronomy/Astrophysics*, also Physics, Commerce) *California*

McCrea, Sir William (Hunter) (*Astronomy/Astrophysics*) *United Kingdom*

Milone, Eugene Frank (*Astronomy/Astrophysics*) *Canada*

Morton, Donald C. (*Astronomy/Astrophysics*) *Canada*

Mullins, Jeffrey Lynn (*Astronomy/Astrophysics*, also Philosophy) *Maryland*

Pacholczyk, Andrzej G. (*Astronomy/Astrophysics*, also Physics) *Arizona*

Peat, David (*Astronomy/Astrophysics*, also Theology/Religion) *United Kingdom*

Rees, Martin J. (*Astronomy/Astrophysics*) *United Kingdom*

Ross, Norman Albert (*Astronomy/Astrophysics*) *Maine*

Sakimoto, Philip J. (*Astronomy/Astrophysics*, also Physics) *Washington, D.C.*

Tayler, Roger J. (*Astronomy/Astrophysics*) *United Kingdom*

Weidemann, Volker (*Astronomy/Astrophysics*) *Germany*

Whitten, Robert C. (*Astronomy/Astrophysics*, also Earth Science) *California*

York, Donald G. (*Astronomy/Astrophysics*) *Illinois*

Biochemistry/Biophysics

Bloemendal, Michael (*Biochemistry/Biophysics*, also Chemistry) *United Kingdom*

Bonting, Sjoerd L. (*Biochemistry/Biophysics*, also Biology, Chemistry, Theology/Religion) *The Netherlands*

Challice, Cyril Eugene (*Biochemistry/Biophysics*, also Theology/Religion) *Canada*

Cole, David R. (*Biochemistry/Biophysics*) *California*

Eigen, Manfred (*Biochemistry/Biophysics*, also Chemistry) *Germany*

Furtado, Daphne (*Biochemistry/Biophysics*, also Chemistry) *India*

Hearn, Walter Russell (*Biochemistry/Biophysics*, also Communications, Theology/Religion) *California*

Herrmann, Robert L. (*Biochemistry/Biophysics*, also Chemistry, Molecular Biology) *Massachusetts*

Hoshiko, Tomuo (*Biochemistry/Biophysics*, also Medical Science) *Ohio*

Hulme, Norman A. (*Biochemistry/Biophysics*, also Medical Science) *New York*

Kupke, Donald Walter (*Biochemistry/Biophysics*) *Virginia*

Liljas, Anders (*Biochemistry/Biophysics*) *Sweden*

Lipinski, Boguslaw (*Biochemistry/Biophysics*) *Massachusetts*

Medgyesi, György (*Biochemistry/Biophysics*, also Medical Science) *Hungary*

Metzner, Helmut (*Biochemistry/Biophysics*, also Philosophy, Ethics) *Germany*

Mills, Gordon C. (*Biochemistry/Biophysics*, also Genetics) *Texas*

Mills, Stephen A. (*Biochemistry/Biophysics*) *California*

Peacocke, Arthur Robert (*Biochemistry/Biophysics*, also Theology/Religion) *United Kingdom*

Perry, David Kenneth (*Biochemistry/Biophysics*) *North Carolina*

Rubik, Beverly (*Biochemistry/Biophysics*) *Pennsylvania*

Scholz, Günter (*Biochemistry/Biophysics*) *Germany*

Sheldrake, Rupert (*Biochemistry/Biophysics*) *United Kingdom*

Spanner, Douglas C. (*Biochemistry/Biophysics*) *United Kingdom*

Strobel, Henry W. (*Biochemistry/Biophysics*, also Theology/Religion) *Texas*

Titanji, Vincent P.K. (*Biochemistry/Biophysics*) *Cameroon*

Underkofler, Leland A. (*Biochemistry/Biophysics*) *New Mexico*

Van Arsdel III, William Campbell (*Biochemistry/Biophysics*, also Medical Science) *Washington, D.C.*

Wicken, Jeffrey S. (*Biochemistry/Biophysics*, also Philosophy, Theology/Religion) *Pennsylvania*

Wilder-Smith, Arthur Ernest (*Biochemistry/Biophysics*) *Switzerland*

Biology

Adams, Dawn A. (*Biology*) *Texas*

Allen, George W. J. (*Biology*) *New York*

Ambrose, Edmund Jack (*Biology*, also Medical Science) *United Kingdom*

Ayala, Francisco J. (*Biology*, also Genetics, Philosophy) *California*

Barclay, Oliver Rainsford (*Biology*, also Theology/Religion) *United Kingdom*

Becker, Thomas (*Biology*, also Theology/Religion) *Germany*

Bergman, Jerry (*Biology*, also Physics, Chemistry, Psychology/Counseling) *Ohio*

Bertsch, Hans (*Biology*, also Theology/Religion, Philosophy) *California*

Biesele, John Julius (*Biology*) *Texas*

Birch, L. Charles (*Biology*, also Theology/Religion) *Australia*

Bouma III, Hessel (*Biology*, also Genetics) *Michigan*

Brand, Raymond. H. (*Biology*, also Ecology/Environment) *Illinois*

Brun, Rudolf B. (*Biology*) *Texas*

Dally, Andreas Michael (*Biology*) *Germany*

DeWitt, Calvin B. (*Biology*, also Ecology/Environment, Ethics) *Wisconsin*

Dodson, Edward O. (*Biology*, also Genetics) *Canada*

Frair, Wayne (*Biology*, also Genetics) *New York*

Galleni, Lodovico (*Biology Italy*

Hay, David (*Biology*, also Theology/Religion, Sociology) *United Kingdom*

Hazard, Evan Brandao (*Biology*) *Minnesota*

Hazen, Craig J. (*Biology*, also Theology/Religion, Jurisprudence/Law) *California*

Heckenlively, Donald B. (*Biology*, also Computer and Information Sciences) *Michigan*

Hemminger, Hansjörg (*Biology*, also Philosophy) *Germany*

Hess, Gerald D. (*Biology*) *Pennsylvania*

Holmes, H. Rodney (*Biology*, also Psychology/Counseling) *Illinois*

Howe, George Franklin (*Biology*) *California*

Humbert, Jean (*Biology*, also Earth Science) *France*

Jackson, Wes (*Biology*, also Genetics, Ecology/Environment, Ethics) *Kansas*

Key, Thomas D. S. (*Biology*, also Theology/Religion) *Mississippi*

Knobloch, Irving William (*Biology*) *Michigan*

Koltermann, Rainer (*Biology*, also Philosophy, Theology/Religion) *Germany*

LaBar, Martin (*Biology*, also Ethics) *South Carolina*

Larson, Laurence A. (*Biology*, also Interdisciplinary Studies) *Ohio*

Ling, Vincent (*Biology*) *Massachusetts*

Lovett Doust, Jonathan Nicolas de Grave (*Biology*, also Ecology/Environment) *Canada*

Margulis, Lynn (*Biology*) *Massachusetts*

McDonald, Harry S. (*Biology*) *Texas*

McGrath, Alister E. (*Biology*, also Theology/Religion) *United Kingdom*

Mixter, Russell L. (*Biology*) *Illinois*

Murdy, William H. (*Biology*) *Georgia*

Olson, Everett C. (*Biology*, also Earth Science) *California*

Roth, Ariel Adrien (*Biology*) *California*

Rothrock, Paul E. (*Biology*, also Earth Science) *Indiana*

Salthe, Stanley N. (*Biology*) *New York*

Scadding, Steven R. (*Biology*) *Canada*

Sheldon, Joseph K. (*Biology*, also Ecology/Environment) *Pennsylvania*

Shepard, Frederick Douglas (*Biology*, also Education, Administration) *Oregon*

Shotwell, Thomas K. (*Biology*, also Management) *Texas*

Stent, Gunther S. (*Biology*, also Genetics, History and Philosophy of Science) *California*

Thurman, L. Duane (*Biology*, also Ecology/Environment) *Oklahoma*

Turner, Robert Eugene (*Biology*, also Ecology/Environment) *Louisiana*

van de Beek, A. (*Biology*, also Theology/Religion) *The Netherlands*

Van der Meer, Jitse M. (*Biology*, also Astronomy/Astrophysics) *Canada*

van Duijin, Pieter (*Biology*) *The Netherlands*

Van Dyke, Fred G. (*Biology*, also Ecology/Environment) *Michigan*, also Montana

Van Valen, Leigh M. (*Biology*) *Illinois*

Vander Zee, Delmar (*Biology*) *Iowa*

Varela, Francisco J. (*Biology*) *France*

Weizsäcker von, Ernst (*Biology*, also Ecology/Environment, Political Science/Politics) *Germany*

Whipple, Andrew P. (*Biology*) *Indiana*

Wickler, Wolfgang (*Biology*, also Administration) *Germany*

Wilbur, Frank H. (*Biology*) *Kentucky*

Williams, George C. (*Biology*) *New York*

Willis, David L. (*Biology*) *Oregon*

Wilson, Edward Osborne (*Biology*, also Ecology/Environment) *Massachusetts*

Wolsky, Maria de Issekutz (*Biology*, also Philosophy) *Canada*, also New York

Wright, Richard T. (*Biology*, also Ecology/Environment) *Massachusetts*

Yockey, Hubert P. (*Biology*, also Management) *Maryland*

Zylstra, Uko (*Biology*) *Michigan*

Chemistry

Adler, Thomas C. (*Chemistry*) *California*

Bennema, P. (*Chemistry*, also Physics) *The Netherlands*

Bohon, Robert L (*Chemistry*, also Technology, Earth Science, Management) *Minnesota*

Bourne, Malcolm C. (*Chemistry*) *New York*

Budenholzer, Frank (*Chemistry*, also Physics, Theology/Religion) *Taiwan*

Cloutier, Stephen (*Chemistry*, also Engineering) *Illinois*

Dagnall, Bernard (*Chemistry*, also Theology/Religion) *United Kingdom*

Del Re, Giuseppe (*Chemistry*, also Physics, Philosophy) *Italy*

Denues, A. R. Taylor (*Chemistry*, also Engineering, Medical Science, Theology/Religion) *Pennsylvania*

Feil, Dirk (*Chemistry*, also Physics) *The Netherlands*

Fischer, Robert B. (*Chemistry*, also Theology/Religion, Education) *California*

Fleming, Fraser Fergusson (*Chemistry*) *Pennsylvania*

Giulianelli, James L. (*Chemistry*) *Colorado*

Gowenlock, Brian G. (*Chemistry*) *United Kingdom*

Haas Jr., John W. (*Chemistry*, also History and Philosophy of Science) *Massachusetts*

Haas III, John W. (*Chemistry*) *Massachusetts*

Hannon, Ralph H. (*Chemistry*, also Physics, Mathematics) *Illinois*

Jappe, Fred (*Chemistry*, also Theology/Religion) *California*

Jenkins, Eric Neil (*Chemistry*, also Theology/Religion, Ethics) *United Kingdom*

Karkalits Jr., Olin Carroll (*Chemistry*, also Engineering) *Louisiana*

Keggi, J John (*Chemistry*, also Theology/Religion) *Massachusetts*

Kelly, Dr. William L. (*Chemistry*) *Ohio*

Kracher, Alfred (*Chemistry*, also Earth Science) *Iowa*

Maatman, Russell W. (*Chemistry*) *Iowa*

Monse, Ernst U. (*Chemistry*) *New Jersey*

Monteiro, Hubert A. (*Chemistry*, also Commerce) *India*

Page, William R. (*Chemistry*, also Engineering, Biology, Sociology) *Vermont*

Prigogine, Ilya (*Chemistry*, also Biochemistry/Biophysics, Physics, Philosophy) *Belgium*

Robertson, John H. (*Chemistry*) *United Kingdom*

Rónay, Géza S. (*Chemistry*) *California*

Rüst, Peter (*Chemistry*, also Biochemistry/Biophysics) *Switzerland*

Salmon, James F. (*Chemistry*, also Theology/Religion, Philosophy) *Maryland*

Schotman-Veldman, Judith L. (*Chemistry*, also History and Philosophy of Science, Physics) *The Netherlands*

Shank, Norman E. (*Chemistry*) *Pennsylvania*

Sheppard, Norman (*Chemistry*) *United Kingdom*

Smith-Moran, Barbara Putney (*Chemistry*, also Astronomy/Astrophysics, Theology/Religion) *Massachusetts*

Sutherland, Brian P. (*Chemistry*) *Canada*

Utke, Allen R. (*Chemistry*, also Interdisciplinary Studies) *Wisconsin*

Vander Vennen, Robert E. (*Chemistry*) *Canada*

Vukanovic, Vladimir (*Chemistry*) *New York*

Wahlbeck, Phillip G. (*Chemistry*) *Kansas*

Commerce

MacKay, David B. (*Commerce*, also Earth Science) *Indiana*

Roukens de Lange, A. (*Commerce*, also Engineering, Chemistry, Mathematics) *South Africa*

State, Stanley (*Commerce*, also History and Philosophy of Science) *California*

Stulman, Julius (*Commerce*) *Florida*

Witherspoon, William (*Commerce*, also Economics) *Missouri*

Communications

Albright, Carol Rausch (*Communications*) *Illinois*

Church, F. Forrester (*Communications*, also Theology/Religion) *New York*

Ford, Mary Anne Kehoe (*Communications*) *Connecticut*

Gruenwald, Oskar (*Communications*, also Psychology/Counseling, Interdisciplinary Studies, Philosophy) *California*

Hefley, James C. (*Communications*) *Missouri*

Mallove, Eugene F. (*Communications*, also Astronomy/Astrophysics) *New Hampshire*

Oorjitham, Santha (*Communications*) *Malaysia*

Sire, James W. (*Communications*, also History and Philosophy of Science) *Illinois*

Computer and Information Sciences

Bjork, Russell C. (*Computer and Information Sciences*) *Massachusetts*

Drozdek, Adam (*Computer and Information Sciences*) *Pennsylvania*

Hill, David R. (*Computer and Information Sciences*, also Psychology/Counseling, Engineering) *Canada*

Martino, Rocco Leonard (*Computer and Information Sciences*, also Finance, Mathematics, Physics) *Pennsylvania*

Romagosa, Alfredo A. (*Computer and Information Sciences*) *Florida*

Trautteur, Giuseppe (*Computer and Information Sciences*) *Italy*

Earth Science

Harper, Charles L. (*Earth Science*, also Theology/Religion, Philosophy, Technology) *United Kingdom*

Lewthwaite, Gordon R. (*Earth Science*, also History) *California*

Livingstone, David Noel (*Earth Science*, also Philosophy, Sociology) *North Ireland*

Marshall Jr., John Harris (*Earth Science*) *Texas*

Menninga, Clarence (*Earth Science*, also Chemistry) *Michigan*

Miller, Keith Brady (*Earth Science*) *Kansas*

Paterson, John Leonard (*Earth Science*) *New Zealand*

Tanner Jr., William F. (*Earth Science*) *Florida*

Ulrickson, Brian Lee (*Earth Science*, also Theology/Religion) *Washington*

Walker, Laurence C. (*Earth Science*, also Theology/Religion) *Texas*

Wiester, John L. (*Earth Science*) *California*

Young, Davis A. (*Earth Science*) *Michigan*

Ecology/Environment

Bratton, Susan P. (*Ecology/Environment*, also Ethics) *Georgia*

Ehrenfeld, David W. (*Ecology/Environment*, also Biology, Medical Science) *New Jersey*

Eicher, Andreas D. (*Ecology/Environment*, also Medical Science) *Connecticut*

Grizzle, Raymond Edward (*Ecology/Environment*) *Indiana*

Jones, Jack R. (*Ecology/Environment*) *Maryland*

Kirchoff, Bruce K. (*Ecology/Environment*, also Genetics) *North Carolina*

Klotz, John W. (*Ecology/Environment*, also Theology/Religion, Ethics) *Missouri*

Moss, Rowland Percy (*Ecology/Environment*, also Theology/Religion) *United Kingdom*

Rice, Stanley Arthur (*Ecology/Environment*, also Biology, Education) *Minnesota*

Smucker, Silas J. (*Ecology/Environment*) *Indiana*

Economics

Forman, Frank (*Economics*) *Maryland*

Hoggatt, Austin Curwood (*Economics*) *California*

Maciel, Paulo Frederico do Rêgo (*Economics*, also Philosophy) *Brazil*

Oswald, Donald J. (*Economics*) *California*

Templeton, Sir John M. (*Economics*, also Finance, Theology/Religion, Management) *Bahamas*

Walter, Christian (*Economics*) *France*

Education

Green, Thomas F. (*Education*, also Sociology, Philosophy) *New York*

Haury, David L. (*Education*, also Biology) *Massachusetts*

Hull, John M. (*Education*, also Theology/Religion) *United Kingdom*

Martin, Robert K. (*Education*) *Connecticut*

Poole, Michael William (*Education*) *United Kingdom*

Shults, F. LeRon (*Education*) *Minnesota*

Tough, Allen MacNeill (*Education*, also Psychology/Counseling) *Canada*

Truog, Dean-Daniel W. (*Education*, also Theology/Religion, History and Philosophy of Science) *Massachusetts*

West, Richard B. (*Education*, also Mathematics) *California*

Engineering

Berg, Myles Renver (*Engineering*, also Physics, Mathematics) *California*

Brigham, Joseph John (*Engineering*) *North Carolina*

Cain, Dallas E. (*Engineering*) *New York*

Capart, Laurent J. N. (*Engineering*) *Belgium*

Cohen, Ernest B. (*Engineering*, also Technology, Psychology/Counseling) *Pennsylvania*

Colvis, John Paris (*Engineering*, also Astronomy/Astrophysics) *Colorado*

Everest, F. Alton (*Engineering*, also Technology) *California*

Fowler, Thomas B. (*Engineering*, also Computer and Information Sciences, Philosophy) *Washington, D.C.*

Gillette, P. Roger (*Engineering*, also Physics, Technology, Ethics) *California*

Gracely, Brett W. (*Engineering*) *Colorado*

Hickernell, Fred S. (*Engineering*, also Technology) *Arizona*

Hunter, Lloyd P. (*Engineering*) *New York*

Moldoff, Sol (*Engineering*) *Pennsylvania*

Porter, Kenneth W. (*Engineering*) *Washington*

Roberts, Kenneth L. (*Engineering*, also Ecology/Environment) *Virginia*

Rockwell, Theodore (*Engineering*, also Technology) *Maryland*

Rogers, Norma Prichard (*Engineering*, also Literature, Psychology/Counseling) *Tennessee*

Sardana, Lal (*Engineering*) *Texas*

Smith, Ronald N. (*Engineering*, also Physics) *Washington*

Uhlig, Herbert H. (*Engineering*, also Technology) *Massachusetts*

Wood, Frederic C. (*Engineering*, also Commerce) *Connecticut*

Ethics

Ashley, Benedict M. (*Ethics*, also Political Science/Politics, Theology/Religion, Philosophy) *Washington, D.C.*

Böckman, Peter Wilhelm (*Ethics*, also Theology/Religion, Philosophy) *Norway*

Branson, Roy (*Ethics*, also Theology/Religion) *Washington, D.C.*

Browning, Don S. (*Ethics*, also Theology/Religion) *Illinois*

Evans, Abigail Rian (*Ethics*, also Philosophy, Theology/Religion, Medical Science) *Washington, D.C.*

Hilhorst, Medard T. (*Ethics*, also Theology/Religion, Technology) *The Netherlands*

Juergensmeyer, Mark (*Ethics*, also Sociology, Philosophy, Theology/Religion) *California*

Manenschijn, Gerrit (*Ethics*, also Theology/Religion) *The Netherlands*

Payton, Robert L. (*Ethics*) *Indiana*

Peterson, James C. (*Ethics*) *North Carolina*

Roberts, Robert C. (*Ethics*, also Psychology/Counseling, Philosophy, Theology/Religion) *Illinois*

Rockefeller, Laurance S. (*Ethics*, also Commerce) *New York*

Sheldon, John M. (*Ethics*, also Medical Science) *Ohio*

Shull, Philip A. (*Ethics*, also Theology/Religion) *Montana*

Styczen, Tadeusz (*Ethics*) *Poland*

Turner, Dean (*Ethics*, also Philosophy, Languages, Education) *Colorado*

Wallwork, Ernest Edward (*Ethics*, also Psychology/Counseling, Sociology) *New York*, also Washington, D.C.

West, Charles C. (*Ethics*, also Political Science/Politics) *New Jersey*

Genetics

Bennett, J. W. (*Genetics*) *Louisiana*

Bergh, Bob (*Genetics*) *California*

Berry, Robert James (*Genetics*, also Molecular Biology, Ecology/Environment) *United Kingdom*

Eaves, Lindon John (*Genetics*, also Theology/Religion, Mathematics) *Virginia*

Freire-Maia, Newton (*Genetics*, also Biology) *Brazil*

Gouldstone, Tim (*Genetics*, also Theology/Religion) *United Kingdom*

Lejeune, Jérôme Jean Louis Marie (*Genetics*, also Medical Science) *France*

Mohrenweiser, Harvey W. (*Genetics*, also Molecular Biology) *California*

Wilcox, David Linwood (*Genetics*, also Biology) *Pennsylvania*

History

Berry, Thomas (*History*, also Theology/Religion) *New York*

Bunnell, Adam Eugene (*History*, also Theology/Religion) *Kentucky*

Copenhaver, Brian P. (*History*, also Physics) *California*

Dierick, G.P.A. (*History*, also Philosophy, Theology/Religion) *The Netherlands*

Harman, William K. (*History*, also Theology/Religion) *California*

Koenigsberger, Dorothy (*History*, also History and Philosophy of Science) *United Kingdom*

Mullen, Pierce C. (*History*) *Montana*

Petersen, Rodney L. (*History*) *Massachusetts*

Roberts, Jon H. (*History*) *Wisconsin*

Roche, Barbara A. (*History*, also Education, Theology/Religion) *Kentucky*

Southgate, Beverley C. (*History*) *United Kingdom*

Varadarajan, Lotika (*History*) *India*

Welch, Claude (*History*, also Theology/Religion, Education) *California*

Westman, Robert (*History*, also History and Philosophy of Science) *California*

Yamauchi, Edwin M. (*History*, also Languages) *Ohio*

History and Philosophy of Science

Bag, A. K. (*History and Philosophy of Science*, also Mathematics) *India*

Brooke, John Hedley (*History and Philosophy of Science*, also Chemistry, Theology/Religion, Philosophy) *United Kingdom*

Burnham, Frederic B. (*History and Philosophy of Science*, also Theology/Religion) *New York*

Cantor, Geoffrey (*History and Philosophy of Science*, also Philosophy) *United Kingdom*

Clifton, Robert K. (*History and Philosophy of Science*, also Philosophy, Physics) *Canada*

Corsi, Pietro (*History and Philosophy of Science*, also Philosophy) *Italy*

Crombie, Alistair Cameron (*History and Philosophy of Science*, also Biology) *United Kingdom*

Crowe, Michael J. (*History and Philosophy of Science*, also Physics, Astronomy/Astrophysics) *Indiana*

D'Ambrosio, Ubiratan (*History and Philosophy of Science*, also Mathematics, Philosophy) *Brazil*

Davis, Edward B. (*History and Philosophy of Science*, also Philosophy) *Pennsylvania*

Di Bernardo, Giuliano (*History and Philosophy of Science*, also Philosophy) *Italy*

Dobbs, Betty Jo Teeter (*History and Philosophy of Science*) *Illinois*

Drago, Antonino (*History and Philosophy of Science*, also Physics) *Italy*

Durant, John Robert (*History and Philosophy of Science*, also Biology) *United Kingdom*

Durbin Jr., William A. (*History and Philosophy of Science*, also Communications) *North Carolina*

Elliott, John Eric (*History and Philosophy of Science*, also Mathematics) *North Carolina*

Emerton, Norma Elizabeth (*History and Philosophy of Science*) *United Kingdom*

Fayter, The Rev. Paul (*History and Philosophy of Science*, also Theology/Religion, Interdisciplinary Studies) *Canada*

Gillespie, Neal C. (*History and Philosophy of Science*, also History) *Georgia*

Gregory, Frederick (*History and Philosophy of Science*) *Florida*

Hankins, Thomas L. (*History and Philosophy of Science*, also History, Education) *Washington*

Harré, Rom (*History and Philosophy of Science*, also Philosophy) *United Kingdom*

Hesse, Mary Brenda (*History and Philosophy of Science*, also Physics, Philosophy, Mathematics) *United Kingdom*

Hiebert, Erwin Nick (*History and Philosophy of Science*, also Chemistry, Physics) *Massachusetts*

Kalthoff, Mark A. (*History and Philosophy of Science*, also Philosophy) *Michigan*

Knight, David Marcus (*History and Philosophy of Science*) *United Kingdom*

Kohn, David (*History and Philosophy of Science*) *New Jersey*

Küppers, Bernd-Olaf (*History and Philosophy of Science*, also Molecular Biology, Interdisciplinary Studies) *Germany*

Laurikainen, Kalervo Vihtori (*History and Philosophy of Science*, also Physics, Theology/Religion, Philosophy) *Finland*

Lindberg, David C. (*History and Philosophy of Science*, also Physics, Philosophy) *Wisconsin*

McMullen, Emerson Thomas (*History and Philosophy of Science*) *Oklahoma*

McNally, Donald H. (*History and Philosophy of Science*, also Theology/Religion) *Canada*

Miles, Sara Joan (*History and Philosophy of Science*, also Biology, Anthropology, Education) *Pennsylvania*

Numbers, Ronald L. (*History and Philosophy of Science*, also Medical Science) *Wisconsin*

Olson, Richard (*History and Philosophy of Science*) *California*

Paul, Erich Robert (*History and Philosophy of Science*) *Pennsylvania*

Pedersen, Olaf (*History and Philosophy of Science Denmark*

Pizzamiglio, Pierluigi (*History and Philosophy of Science*) *Italy*

Provine, William B. (*History and Philosophy of Science, also Genetics*) *New York*

Rupke, Nicolaas Adrianus (*History and Philosophy of Science, also Earth Science*) *Germany*

Ruse, Michael (*History and Philosophy of Science, also Biology*) *Canada*

Russell, Colin Archibald (*History and Philosophy of Science, also Chemistry*) *United Kingdom*

Schneider, Hans-Georg (*History and Philosophy of Science, also Sociology*) *United Kingdom*

Schoepflin, Rennie B. (*History and Philosophy of Science, also Medical Science, Theology/Religion*) *California*

Schütt, Hans-Werner (*History and Philosophy of Science*) *Germany*

Shank, Michael H. (*History and Philosophy of Science, also Physics*) *Wisconsin*

Shaw, Marvin C. (*History and Philosophy of Science, also Philosophy*) *Montana*

Stanesby, Derek Malcolm (*History and Philosophy of Science, also Theology/Religion*) *United Kingdom*

Staudinger, Hugo (*History and Philosophy of Science, also Philosophy*) *Germany*

Stavenga, Gerben J. (*History and Philosophy of Science*) *The Netherlands*

Stuhlhofer, Franz (*History and Philosophy of Science*) *Austria*

Van Melsen, A. G. M. (*History and Philosophy of Science*) *The Netherlands*

Verlinde, Jacques (*History and Philosophy of Science, also Theology/Religion*) *France*

Westfall, Richard S. (*History and Philosophy of Science*) *Indiana*

Wiebe, Phillip Howard (*History and Philosophy of Science, also Ethics, Philosophy*) *Canada*

Wolsky, Alexander (*History and Philosophy of Science, also Biology*) *Canada*

Zycinski, Jósef (*History and Philosophy of Science, also Ecology/Environment, Theology/Religion, Ethics*) *Poland*

Interdisciplinary Studies

Burneko, Guy C. (*Interdisciplinary Studies Alaska*

Erdmann, Erika (*Interdisciplinary Studies, also Philosophy*) *Canada*

Rossman, Parker (*Interdisciplinary Studies Connecticut*

Wilkins III, Walter J. (*Interdisciplinary Studies, also History, Philosophy*) *Virginia*

Jurisprudence/Law

Larson, Edward J. (*Jurisprudence/Law, also History and Philosophy of Science*) *Georgia*

Legrain, Michel (*Jurisprudence/Law, also Ethics*) *France*

Montgomery, John Warwick (*Jurisprudence/Law, also Education, Theology/Religion*) *Washington*

Languages

Pike, Kenneth L. (*Languages, also Theology/Religion*) *Texas*

Stahl, C. Larry (*Languages Oregon*

Literature

Braganza, Karuna Mary (*Literature, also Education*) *India*

Frye, Roland Mushat (*Literature, also Theology/Religion*) *Pennsylvania*

Knapp II, John Allen (*Literature*, also Education, Theology/Religion) *New York*

Morgan, Peter F. (*Literature*, also Philosophy) *Canada*

Oates, David D. (*Literature*, also History) *California*

Onimus, Jean (*Literature*) *France*

Ruark, James Ellwood (*Literature*) *Michigan*

Wetherbee, James M. (*Literature*) *North Carolina*

Management

Deckert, Curtis Kenneth (*Management*, also Technology) *California*

Faulkner Jr., George R. (*Management*) *Idaho*

Johnson, Anthony P. (*Management*, also Theology/Religion) *New York*

Kern, John C. (*Management*) *Illinois*

Moore, Thomas J. (*Management*, also Computer and Information Sciences) *Michigan*

Rahman, Abdul (*Management*, also History and Philosophy of Science, Biochemistry/Biophysics, Theology/Religion) *India*

South, Oron P. (*Management*) *Alabama*

Mathematics

Chase, Gene Barry (*Mathematics*, also Computer and Information Sciences) *Pennsylvania*

Ellis, George F. R. (*Mathematics*, also Philosophy) *South Africa*

Ewald, Günter (*Mathematics*, also History and Philosophy of Science) *Germany*

Ford, Charles E. (*Mathematics*, also Computer and Information Sciences) *Missouri*

Gill, Stephen P. (*Mathematics*, also Physics) *California*

Hancock Jr., Monte F. (*Mathematics*) *Florida*

Hartzler, H. Harold (*Mathematics*, also Physics, Astronomy/Astrophysics) *Indiana*

Hermann, Robert A. (*Mathematics*, also Physics, Philosophy) *Maryland*

Landsberg, Peter T. (*Mathematics*, also Philosophy, History and Philosophy of Science) *United Kingdom*

Martin, Daniel (*Mathematics*) *United Kingdom*

Martin, Helen Elizabeth (*Mathematics*) *Pennsylvania*

Masani, Pesi R. (*Mathematics*) *Pennsylvania*

Müller, Gert H. (*Mathematics*) *Germany*

Neuhouser, David L. (*Mathematics*) *Indiana*

Poythress, Vern Sheridan (*Mathematics*, also Theology/Religion) *Pennsylvania*

Pullinger, David J. (*Mathematics*, also Biochemistry/Biophysics, Computer and Information Sciences) *United Kingdom*

Riddiford, Alan Wistar (*Mathematics*, also Theology/Religion) *Illinois*

Scott, Philip Maxwell (*Mathematics*, also Theology/Religion) *New Zealand*

Tipler, Frank J. (*Mathematics*, also Physics, Astronomy/Astrophysics) *Louisiana*

Whitrow, Gerald James (*Mathematics*, also History and Philosophy of Science) *United Kingdom*

Medical Science

Allert, Gebhard (*Medical Science*, also Psychiatry, Theology/Religion) *Germany*

Alley, James W. (*Medical Science*) *Georgia*

Ansbacher, Stefan (*Medical Science*) *Florida*

Baclig, Paulita Villegs (*Medical Science*) *Philippines*

Bell Jr., Reuben Paul (*Medical Science*) *Maine*

Berry Jr., Maxwell R. (*Medical Science*) *Florida*

Brennan, John Lester (*Medical Science*) *United Kingdom*

Brobeck, John R. (*Medical Science*) *Pennsylvania*

Brown, Warren S. (*Medical Science*, also Psychology/Counseling) *California*

Clarke, Charles L. (*Medical Science*) *Tennessee*

Conrad, Constance C. (*Medical Science*, also Education) *Georgia*

Crutcher, Keith A. (*Medical Science*) *Ohio*

Dormer, Kenneth J. (*Medical Science*) *Oklahoma*

Eccles, Sir John C. (*Medical Science*, also History and Philosophy of Science, Philosophy) *Switzerland*

Eiff von, August Wilhelm (*Medical Science*, also Ethics) *Germany*

Elgee, Neil J. (*Medical Science*) *Washington*

Elkins, Thomas Edward (*Medical Science*) *Louisiana*

Fuchs, Peter C. (*Medical Science*) *Oregon*

Gailey, Franklin B. (*Medical Science*, also Biochemistry/Biophysics) *Kentucky*

Gosden, Roger G. (*Medical Science*) *United Kingdom*

Greenhow, Donald Eric Fraser (*Medical Science*) *Pennsylvania*

Jones, D. Gareth (*Medical Science*, also Biology, Ethics) *New Zealand*

Kassel, Victor (*Medical Science*) *Utah*

Keiper Sr., Glenn L. (*Medical Science*) *Ohio*

Klaus, Hanna (*Medical Science*, also Theology/Religion) *Maryland*

Koenig, Harold G. (*Medical Science*, also Psychology/Counseling) *North Carolina*

Lamoureux, Denis Oswald (*Medical Science*) *Canada*

Lantum, Noni Daniel (*Medical Science*, also Sociology, Administration) *Cameroon*

Larson, David Bruce (*Medical Science*, also Psychiatry, Administration) *Maryland*

Matthews, Dale A. (*Medical Science*) *Washington, D.C.*, also Virginia

Mermann, Alan C. (*Medical Science*, also Theology/Religion) *Connecticut*

Meyers, Wayne Marvin (*Medical Science*) *Washington, D.C.*

Ndumbe, Peter Martins (*Medical Science*) *Cameroon*

Neubauer, Thomas (*Medical Science*, also Biochemistry/Biophysics) *Germany*

Osmond, Daniel Harcourt (*Medical Science*) *Canada*

Pellegrino, Edmund D. (*Medical Science*, also Ethics) *Washington, D.C.*, also Maryland

Peppin, John Francis (*Medical Science*, also Ethics) *Wisconsin*

Ross, H. Miriam (*Medical Science*, also Sociology) *Canada*

Sanguinetti, Francesco (*Medical Science*, also Ecology/Environment) *Italy*

Schaefer, Hans (*Medical Science*, also Sociology) *Germany*

Schmitt, Francis O. (*Medical Science*) *Massachusetts*

Shewmon, D. Alan (*Medical Science*) *California*

Spak, K. Edmund (*Medical Science*) *Texas*

Stewart, John Frederick Hudson (*Medical Science*, also Theology/Religion) *Canada*

Swift, David Leslie (*Medical Science*, also Ecology/Environment, Engineering) *Maryland*

Toledo, J. Rafael (*Medical Science*) *Texas*

Ulbrich, Paul W. (*Medical Science*) *Illinois*

Washburn, Marilyn (*Medical Science*, also Theology/Religion) *Georgia*

Watson, John Robert (*Medical Science*) *Hawaii*

Webster, Frederic A. (*Medical Science*) *Vermont*

White, David C. (*Medical Science*, also Biology, Ecology/Environment) *Tennessee*

Winkler, Hans-Joachim (*Medical Science*) *Germany*

Molecular Biology

Burke, Derek C. (*Molecular Biology*, also Theology/Religion) *United Kingdom*

Hillar, Marian (*Molecular Biology*, also Biochemistry/Biophysics, Medical Science, History) *Texas*

Pun, Pattle P.T. (*Molecular Biology*, also Genetics, Theology/Religion) *Illinois*

Philosophy

Leslie, John (*Philosophy*, also Astronomy/Astrophysics, History and Philosophy of Science, Theology/Religion) *Canada*

Libanio, João Batista (*Philosophy*, also Languages, Theology/Religion) *Brazil*

Löw, Reinhard (*Philosophy*, also History and Philosophy of Science, Ethics) *Germany*

Lucas, J. R. (*Philosophy*) *United Kingdom*

Maduro, L. Otto A. (*Philosophy*, also Sociology) *New York*

Marc, Alexandre (*Philosophy*) *France*

Matsen, Fredrick A. (*Philosophy*, also Chemistry) *Texas*

May, John Y. (*Philosophy*) *Pennsylvania*

McCormack, Elizabeth J. (*Philosophy*) *New York*

McFeeley, Daniel (*Philosophy*, also Psychology/Counseling) *Illinois*

McKowen, Paul M. (*Philosophy*, also Languages) *California*

McMullin, Ernan (*Philosophy*, also Theology/Religion, Physics, History and Philosophy of Science) *Indiana*

Miller, David Lee (*Philosophy*) *Wisconsin*

Mitcham, Carl (*Philosophy*) *Pennsylvania*

Moore, Brooke Noel (*Philosophy*) *California*

Murphy, Nancey C. (*Philosophy*, also Theology/Religion) *California*

Needleman, Jacob (*Philosophy*, also Psychology/Counseling, Theology/Religion) *California*

Nelson, Paul Alfred (*Philosophy*) *Illinois*

Nicholson, Philip (*Philosophy*, also Jurisprudence/Law, Medical Science, Computer and Information Sciences) *Massachusetts*

Nieznaski, Edward (*Philosophy*) *Poland*

Paul, William W. (*Philosophy*, also Theology/Religion) *Iowa*

Percesepe, Gary John (*Philosophy*) *Ohio*

Perry, David L. (*Philosophy*) *Washington, D.C.*

Plantinga, Alvin C. (*Philosophy*, also Theology/Religion) *Indiana*

Queen, Christopher S. (*Philosophy*, also Theology/Religion) *Massachusetts*

Ramm, Bernard (*Philosophy*, also Theology/Religion) *California*

Rangel, Paschoal Sellitti (*Philosophy*, also Theology/Religion, Communications, Literature) *Brazil*

Ratzsch, Del (*Philosophy*, also History and Philosophy of Science) *Michigan*

Reichenbach, Bruce R. (*Philosophy*, also Ethics, Theology/Religion) *Minnesota*

Richards, Robert J. (*Philosophy*, also History and Philosophy of Science, Psychology/Counseling) *Illinois*

Rothenberg, David (*Philosophy*) *New Jersey*

Rottschaefer, William A. (*Philosophy*, also History and Philosophy of Science) *Oregon*

Schenk, Richard (*Philosophy*, also History) *Germany*, also California

Schoen, Edward L. (*Philosophy*) *Kentucky*

Schrader, David Eugene (*Philosophy*, also Ethics) *Texas*

Schuurman, Egbert (*Philosophy*, also Engineering, Political Science/Politics) *The Netherlands*

Seifert, Josef (*Philosophy*) *Liechtenstein*

Siegel, Harvey (*Philosophy*, also Education) *Florida*

Siemens Jr., David F. (*Philosophy*, also Theology/Religion) *Arizona*

Simmons Jr., Ernest L. (*Philosophy*, also Theology/Religion) *Minnesota*

Skolimowski, Henryk (*Philosophy*) *Michigan*

Sleigh Jr., Robert Colins (*Philosophy*) *Massachusetts*

Smith, Huston (*Philosophy*, also Theology/Religion) *California*

Spaemann, Robert (*Philosophy*) *Germany*

Sprunger, Meredith Justin (*Philosophy*, also Theology/Religion) *Indiana*

Stevens Jr., Herbert Howe (*Philosophy*) *Massachusetts*

Suttle, Bruce B. (*Philosophy*) *Illinois*

Swinburne, Richard Granville (*Philosophy*, also Theology/Religion) *United Kingdom*

Swyhart, Barbara Ann DeMartino (*Philosophy*, also Ethics, Theology/Religion, Education) *Pennsylvania*

Temple, Dennis Michael (*Philosophy*) *Illinois*

Tierney, Nathan Llywellyn (*Philosophy*) *California*

Trigg, Roger (*Philosophy*) *United Kingdom*

Vollmer, Gerhard (*Philosophy*) *Germany*

Walker, Ralph C. S. (*Philosophy*) *United Kingdom*

Washburn, Michael (*Philosophy*) *Indiana*

Wattles, Jeffrey Hamilton (*Philosophy*) *Ohio*

Weingartner, Paul (*Philosophy*, also History and Philosophy of Science) *Australia*

Weir, Jack L. (*Philosophy*, also Theology/Religion, Ethics) *Kentucky*

Wolterstorff, Nicholas (*Philosophy*) *Connecticut*

Wu, Kathleen Johnson (*Philosophy*) *Alabama*

Zimmerman, Michael E. (*Philosophy*) *Louisiana*

Physics

Ajakaiye, Deborah Enilo (*Physics*, also Earth Science) *Nigeria*

Albright, John R. (*Physics*) *Illinois*

Amrhein, Eva Maria (*Physics*, also Theology/Religion) *Wisconsin*, also Germany

Artigas, Mariano (*Physics*, also Philosophy) *Spain*

Baer, Donald R. (*Physics*) *Washington*

Barrett, Peter J. (*Physics*) *South Africa*

Bartholomew, Gilbert A. (*Physics*) *Canada*

Bellini, Gianpaolo (*Physics*) *Italy*

Bishop, Robert C. (*Physics*) *Texas*

Blasi, Paolo (*Physics*, also Theology/Religion) *Italy*

Bloom, John A. (*Physics*, also Theology/Religion, Computer and Information Sciences, History) *Pennsylvania*

Boyd, Sir Robert Lewis Fullarton (*Physics*, also Chemistry, Astronomy/Astrophysics, Technology) *United Kingdom*

Bradley, Walter L. (*Physics*, also Technology) *Texas*

Brooks, George Gordon (*Physics*, also Theology/Religion) *New Hampshire*, also Florida

Brugger, Hans Rudolf (*Physics*, also Astronomy/Astrophysics) *Switzerland*

Bube, Richard H. (*Physics*, also Theology/Religion) *California*

Carlson, Richard F. (*Physics*) *California*

Cook, Sir Alan Hugh (*Physics*, also Astronomy/Astrophysics) *United Kingdom*

Cramer, John Allen (*Physics*) *Georgia*

Dallaporta, Nicolo (*Physics*) *Italy*

Davies, Paul Charles William (*Physics*) *Australia*

Davis, Lloyd J. (*Physics*) *North Carolina*

de Beauregard, O. Costa (*Physics*, also Philosophy) *France*

DeGraaf, Donald E. (*Physics*) *Michigan*

Duguay, Michel A. (*Physics*, also Engineering) *Canada*

Dye, David L. (*Physics*, also Technology) *Washington*

Dyson, Freeman J. (*Physics*) *New Jersey*

Eder, Gernot (*Physics*) *Austria*

Faber, Roger J. (*Physics*, also Philosophy, Chemistry) *Illinois*

Fagg, Lawrence W. (*Physics*, also Theology/Religion) *Virginia*

Fast, Edwin (*Physics*, also Chemistry, Mathematics) *Idaho*

Fennema, Jan W. R. (*Physics*, also Philosophy, Theology/Religion) *The Netherlands*

Giberson, Karl Willard (*Physics*) *Massachusetts*

Gilbert, Thomas L. (*Physics*, also Chemistry, Theology/Religion) *Illinois*

Glódz, Malgorzata (*Physics*) *Poland*

Golshani, Mehdi (*Physics*, also Theology/Religion, Philosophy, History and Philosophy of Science) *Iran*

Griffiths, Robert B. (*Physics*, also Mathematics) *Pennsylvania*

Gumlich, Hans-Eckhart (*Physics*, also Technology) *Germany*

Hall, Forrest G. (*Physics*) *Maryland*

Hartwig, Edward Clayton (*Physics*, also Engineering) *California*

Hayward, Jeremy (*Physics*, also History and Philosophy of Science, Theology/Religion) *Canada*

Hodgson, Peter E. (*Physics*) *United Kingdom*

Hogenhuis, C. T. (*Physics*) *The Netherlands*

Houghton, John T. (*Physics*) *United Kingdom*

Ice, Rodney D. (*Physics*) *Georgia*

Ingram, David J. E. (*Physics*) *United Kingdom*

Isham, Christopher J. (*Physics*) *United Kingdom*

Junkin III, William F. (*Physics*) *South Carolina*

Kaita, Robert (*Physics*) *New Jersey*

Korsmeyer, Jerry (*Physics*, also Theology/Religion) *Pennsylvania*

Lovell, Sir Bernard (*Physics*, also Astronomy/Astrophysics) *United Kingdom*

Lumsden, Charles J. (*Physics*, also Biology, Medical Science) *Canada*

McIntyre, John A. (*Physics*) *Texas*

Mercier, André (*Physics*, also History and Philosophy of Science) *Switzerland*

Merrifield S.J., Donald Paul (*Physics*) *California*

Müller, A. M. Klaus (*Physics*) *Germany*

Neidhardt, Walter Jim (*Physics*, also Theology/Religion) *New Jersey*

Nickel Jr., Gerhard (*Physics*, also Chemistry, Earth Science, Languages) *Kansas*

Ogden, Philip M. (*Physics*, also Mathematics) *New York*

Pazan, Stephen (*Physics*, also Earth Science) *California*

Plendl, Hans S. (*Physics*) *Florida*

Polkinghorne, John Charlton (*Physics*) *United Kingdom*

Pon, Wing Y. (*Physics*, also Commerce) *California*

Poole Jr., Charles P. (*Physics*) *South Carolina*

Porter, Andrew P. (*Physics*, also Mathematics, Theology/Religion) *California*

Prosperi, Giovanni M. (*Physics*) *Italy*

Ravindra, Ravi (*Physics*, also Theology/Religion, Philosophy) *Canada*

Reynolds, George T. (*Physics*) *New Jersey*

Rivier, Dominique-Casimir (*Physics*) *Switzerland*

Ross, Robert S. (*Physics*) *Pennsylvania*

Russell, Robert John (*Physics*, also Chemistry, Theology/Religion) *California*

Schaefer III, Henry F. (*Physics*, also Chemistry) *Georgia*

Scheie, Paul (*Physics*, also Biochemistry/Biophysics) *Texas*

Schubert von, Klaus R. (*Physics*) *Germany*

Seeger, Raymond John (*Physics*) *Maryland*

Shacklett, Robert L. (*Physics*) *California*

Snoke, David Wayne (*Physics*) *Germany*

Spradley, Joseph L. (*Physics*, also Astronomy/Astrophysics, History and Philosophy of Science) *Illinois*

Stanciu, George (*Physics*) *New Hampshire*

Stannard, Frank Russell (*Physics*) *United Kingdom*

Sternglass, Ernest J. (*Physics*, also History and Philosophy of Science) *New York*

Stoeger, William R. (*Physics*, also Astronomy/Astrophysics, Philosophy) *Arizona*

Thorson, Walter Rollier (*Physics*, also Chemistry) *Canada*

Townes, Charles H. (*Physics*, also Astronomy/Astrophysics) *California*

Van der Veken, Jan (*Physics*, also Philosophy) *Belgium*

Van Erkelens, Herbert (*Physics*, also Psychology/Counseling) *The Netherlands*

Van Till, Howard J. (*Physics*, also Astronomy/Astrophysics) *Michigan*

Van Vliet, Carolyne M. (*Physics*) *Canada*

Van Zytveld, John B. (*Physics*) *Michigan*

VanOstenburg, Donald O. (*Physics*) *Illinois*

Venable III, William H. (*Physics*, also Theology/Religion) *Pennsylvania*

Wassermann, Christoph (*Physics*, also Theology/Religion) *Germany*

Wathen-Dunn, Weiant (*Physics*, also Communications, Engineering) *Massachusetts*

Weidlich, Wolfgang (*Physics*) *Germany*

Weizsäcker von, Carl Friedrich Freiherr (*Physics*, also Philosophy) *Germany*

Whipple, Elden C. (*Physics*) *California*

Woodward, J. Guy (*Physics*) *New Jersey*

Yoshikawa, Shoichi (*Physics*) *New Jersey*

Yuguchi, Takashi (*Physics*, also Communications) *Japan*

Zajonc, Arthur G. (*Physics*) *Massachusetts*

Zeh, H. Dieter (*Physics*) *Germany*

Zhang, Hwe Ik (*Physics*) *Korea*

Political Science/Politics

Barker, Verlyn L. (*Political Science/Politics*) *Ohio*

Gill, Anthony J. (*Political Science/Politics*) *Washington*

Landess, Marcia McBroom (*Political Science/Politics*, also Education, Theology/Religion) *New York*

Munday Jr., John Clingman (*Political Science/Politics*, also Ethics, Theology/Religion) *Virginia*

Psychiatry

Ambrosino, Salvatore V. (*Psychiatry*) *New York*

Barnhouse, Ruth Tiffany (*Psychiatry*, also Medical Science, Theology/Religion) *Texas*

Beck, Malcolm Nestor (*Psychiatry*, also Medical Science) *Canada*

Blankenburg, Wolfgang (*Psychiatry*, also Philosophy) *Germany*

d'Aquili, Eugene G, (*Psychiatry*, also Medical Science, Anthropology) *Pennsylvania*

Frecska, Ede (*Psychiatry*, also Biochemistry/Biophysics) *New York*

Germine, Mark (*Psychiatry*, also Medical Science) *Connecticut*

Henry, James P. (*Psychiatry*, also Medical Science, Biochemistry/Biophysics) *California*

Johnson, Walter Colin (*Psychiatry*, also Psychology/Counseling, Medical Science) *Massachusetts*

Kovel, Joel (*Psychiatry*, also Sociology, Psychology/Counseling) *New York*

Lenz, Hermann (*Psychiatry*) *Austria*

Lifton, Robert Jay (*Psychiatry*, also Psychology/Counseling, Medical Science, Ethics) *New York*

Meador, Keith G. (*Psychiatry*, also Theology/Religion) *Tennessee*

Meyerhoff, Gordon R. (*Psychiatry*, also Theology/Religion) *New York*

Nicholi Jr., Armand Mayo (*Psychiatry*, also Theology/Religion) *Massachusetts*

Parks, Lyle Fredrick (*Psychiatry*, also Psychology/Counseling) *Illinois*

Pearson III, Daniel B. (*Psychiatry*, also Earth Science) *Texas*

Reding, Georges R. (*Psychiatry*) *Michigan*

Rios, Cesar A. (*Psychiatry*) *Argentina*

Usandivaras, Raul J. (*Psychiatry*) *Argentina*

Vincent, Merville O. (*Psychiatry*, also Medical Science) *Canada*

Whitehead, Clay C. (*Psychiatry*) *Missouri*, also California

Yonge, Keith Arnold (*Psychiatry*) *Canada*

Psychology/Counseling

Anch, A. Michael (*Psychology/Counseling*, also Theology/Religion) *Missouri*

Barkman, Paul F. (*Psychology/Counseling*, also Theology/Religion) *California*

Bassett, Rodney L. (*Psychology/Counseling*) *New York*

Batson, C. Daniel (*Psychology/Counseling*, also Theology/Religion, Education) *Kansas*

Benner, David G. (*Psychology/Counseling*) *Canada*

Benson, Purnel H. (*Psychology/Counseling*, also Sociology, Economics) *New Jersey*

Bolt, Martin (*Psychology/Counseling*) *Michigan*

Casebolt, James R. (*Psychology/Counseling*) *Virginia*

Chadha, N. K. (*Psychology/Counseling*) *India*

Childs, Brian H. (*Psychology/Counseling*) *Georgia*

Chirico-Rosenberg, Donna (*Psychology/Counseling*) *New York*

Collins, Gary R. (*Psychology/Counseling*) *Illinois*

Combs, Allan L. (*Psychology/Counseling*) *North Carolina*

Curry, John F. (*Psychology/Counseling*, also Medical Science) *North Carolina*

DeHaan, Robert F. (*Psychology/Counseling*) *Pennsylvania*

Ehlers, Vernon J. (*Psychology/Counseling*, also Physics, Ethics) *Michigan*

Ellens, J. Harold (*Psychology/Counseling*, also Theology/Religion) *Michigan*

Farnsworth, Kirk E. (*Psychology/Counseling*, also Theology/Religion) *Washington*

Feifel, Herman (*Psychology/Counseling*) *California*

Finney, Joseph Claude Jeans (*Psychology/Counseling*, also Psychiatry, Theology/Religion) *California*

Ganguli, H. C. (*Psychology/Counseling*, also Philosophy) *India*

Gay, Volney P. (*Psychology/Counseling*, also Theology/Religion, Anthropology) *Tennessee*

Glassman, Robert B. (*Psychology/Counseling*, also Sociobiology) *Illinois*

Goldsmith, W. (Walter) Mack (*Psychology/Counseling*, also Theology/Religion) *California*

Gorsuch, Richard L. (*Psychology/Counseling*, also Theology/Religion) *California*

Grant, Theodore F. (*Psychology/Counseling*) *Washington, D.C.*, also Maryland

Gregory, William Edgar (*Psychology/Counseling*) *California*

Hinkle, John E. (*Psychology/Counseling*) *Illinois*

Hodges, Bert H. (*Psychology/Counseling*, also Philosophy) *Massachusetts*

Hoppin, Marion C. (*Psychology/Counseling*) *Florida*

Jang, Allen Wai (*Psychology/Counseling*) *California*

Jeeves, Malcolm A. (*Psychology/Counseling*, also Theology/Religion) *United Kingdom*

Johnston, G. Archie (*Psychology/Counseling*, also Biology) *California*

Jones, James W. (*Psychology/Counseling*, also Theology/Religion) *New Jersey*

Jones, Stanton Louis (*Psychology/Counseling*) *Illinois*

Kahoe, Richard Dean (*Psychology/Counseling*) *Oklahoma*

Keilholz, Peggy J. (*Psychology/Counseling*, also Theology/Religion) *Missouri*

Kirkpatrick, Lee Alan (*Psychology/Counseling*) *South Carolina*

Knight, James Allen (*Psychology/Counseling*, also Theology/Religion, Medical Science) *Texas*

Koteskey, Ronald L. (*Psychology/Counseling*) *Kentucky*

Larzelere, Robert Earl (*Psychology/Counseling*) *Nebraska*

Lindquist, Stanley E. (*Psychology/Counseling*) *California*

Mailloux, Noël (*Psychology/Counseling*, also Theology/Religion) *Canada*

Malony, H. Newton (*Psychology/Counseling*, also Theology/Religion) *California*

Manganello, James A. (*Psychology/Counseling*) *Massachusetts*

Metzner, Ralph (*Psychology/Counseling*, also Theology/Religion) *California*

Murdoch, Bernard Constantine (*Psychology/Counseling*) *Georgia*

Myers, David G. (*Psychology/Counseling*) *Michigan*

Nonneman, Arthur J. (*Psychology/Counseling*) *Kentucky*

Paloutzian, Raymond F. (*Psychology/Counseling*) *California*

Parrott III, Less (*Psychology/Counseling*) *Washington*

Patton, John H. (*Psychology/Counseling*) *Georgia*

Philipchalk, Ronald Peter (*Psychology/Counseling*) *Canada*

Pietrzak, Daniel M. (*Psychology/Counseling*) *Massachusetts*

Puckett, Laura E. (*Psychology/Counseling*, also Biochemistry/Biophysics) *Minnesota*

Reddington, Kenneth George (*Psychology/Counseling*, also Theology/Religion) *Japan*

Reich, K. Helmut (*Psychology/Counseling*, also Physics, Engineering, Theology/Religion) *Switzerland*

Riegel Jr., Theodore (*Psychology/Counseling*, also Education, Mathematics, Philosophy) *Georgia*

Routh, Donald K. (*Psychology/Counseling*) *Florida*

Rowatt, Wade Clinton (*Psychology/Counseling*) *Kentucky*

Simpkinson, Charles H. (*Psychology/Counseling*) *Maryland*

Sollod, Robert N. (*Psychology/Counseling*, also Theology/Religion) *Ohio*

Stein, Sharon A. (*Psychology/Counseling*, also Philosophy, Education) *Massachusetts*

Teske, John A. (*Psychology/Counseling*) *Pennsylvania*

Tester, Leonard W. (*Psychology/Counseling*) *New York*

Tjeltveit, Alan (*Psychology/Counseling*, also Theology/Religion) *Pennsylvania*

Tobacyk, Jerome J. (*Psychology/Counseling*) *Louisiana*

Trook, Douglas A. (*Psychology/Counseling*, also Theology/Religion) *Pennsylvania*

Vance, Forrest L. (*Psychology/Counseling*) *Indiana*

Vande Kemp, Hendrika (*Psychology/Counseling*, also Education) *California*

Vayhinger, John M. (*Psychology/Counseling*) *Colorado*

Vitz, Paul C. (*Psychology/Counseling*, also Theology/Religion) *New York*

Walker, Lawrence J. (*Psychology/Counseling*) *Canada*

Watson, Paul Joseph (*Psychology/Counseling*) *Tennessee*

Weaver, Glenn David (*Psychology/Counseling*) *Michigan*

Weil, Pierre (*Psychology/Counseling*) *Brazil*

Weiss, Arnold S. (*Psychology/Counseling*) *California*

Wilson, R. Ward (*Psychology/Counseling*) *Tennessee*

Worthington Jr., Everett L. (*Psychology/Counseling*) *Virginia*

Wulff, David M. (*Psychology/Counseling*, also Theology/Religion, History) *Massachusetts*

Sociobiology

Hood, Randall (*Sociobiology*, also Theology/Religion) *California*

Sociology

Ammerman, Nancy Tatom (*Sociology*, also Theology/Religion) *Georgia*

Anderson, Odin W. (*Sociology*) *Wisconsin*

Ayers, David John (*Sociology*, also Psychology/Counseling) *New York*

Balswick, Jack Orville (*Sociology*, also Theology/Religion) *California*

Barclay, Peter R. (*Sociology*, also Ethics) *Massachusetts*

Barker, Eileen (*Sociology*, also Theology/Religion) *United Kingdom*

Casanova, José V. (*Sociology*) *New York*

Count, Earl W. (*Sociology*, also Theology/Religion) *California*

Crippen, Timothy (*Sociology*, also Sociobiology) *Virginia*

Foster, Mark A. (*Sociology*) *Georgia*

Gaede, S. D. (*Sociology*, also History and Philosophy of Science) *Massachusetts*

Hernandez, Edwin Ivan (*Sociology*) *Michigan*

Hillery Jr., George A. (*Sociology*, also Anthropology) *Virginia*

Hoge, Dean Richard (*Sociology*) *Washington, D.C.*

Technology

Theology/Religion

Bettencourt, Estěvăo Tavares (*Theology/Religion*, also Philosophy) *Brazil*

Bingemer, Maria Clara Lucchetti (*Theology/Religion*) *Brazil*

Blaising, Craig A. (*Theology/Religion*) *Texas*

Blake, Deborah D. (*Theology/Religion*, also Philosophy, Ethics) *Colorado*

Böhringer, Siegfried (*Theology/Religion*) *Germany*

Bolyki, János (*Theology/Religion*, also History *Hungary*

Booher, Bruce (*Theology/Religion*) *Texas*

Boon, Rudolf (*Theology/Religion*, also Philosophy, History and Philosophy of Science) *The Netherlands*

Boutinon, Jean Claude (*Theology/Religion*) *France*

Breed, David R. (*Theology/Religion*, also Philosophy) *Illinois*

Breed, James Lincoln (*Theology/Religion*, also Philosophy) *Illinois*

Bregman, Lucy (*Theology/Religion*, also Psychology/Counseling) *Pennsylvania*

Bridges Jr., Carl B. (*Theology/Religion*, also Languages) *Tennessee*

Brungs, Robert (*Theology/Religion*, also Physics, Ethics) *Missouri*

Buckley, Michael J. (*Theology/Religion*, also Philosophy) *Indiana*

Buehler, David A. (*Theology/Religion*, also Ethics, Computer and Information Sciences) *Massachusetts*

Bulka, Reuven P. (*Theology/Religion*, also Philosophy, Psychology/Counseling) *Canada*

Burhoe, Ralph Wendell (*Theology/Religion*) *Illinois*

Burke, Thomas J. (*Theology/Religion*, also Philosophy, History and Philosophy of Science) *Michigan*

Burns Sr., John Lanier (*Theology/Religion*, also Philosophy) *Texas*

Busse, Richard Paul (*Theology/Religion*, also Philosophy) *Indiana*

Byers, David M. (*Theology/Religion*) *Washington, D.C.*

Cahill, Lisa Sowle (*Theology/Religion*, also Ethics) *Massachusetts*

Carey, Patrick W. (*Theology/Religion*, also History and Philosophy of Science) *Michigan*

Casey, Thomas Michael (*Theology/Religion*, also Psychology/Counseling) *Massachusetts*

Cauthen, W. Kenneth (*Theology/Religion*) *New York*

Cereti, Giovanni (*Theology/Religion*) *Italy*

Cobb Jr., John B. (*Theology/Religion*, also Philosophy) *California*

Cole-Turner, Ronald S. (*Theology/Religion*, also Ethics) *Tennessee*

Colzani, Gianni (*Theology/Religion*) *Italy*

Copestake, David R. (*Theology/Religion*, also Psychology/Counseling) *United Kingdom*

Cotter, Graham (*Theology/Religion*, also Literature, History and Philosophy of Science) *Canada*

da Cruz, Eduardo Rodrigues (*Theology/Religion*, also Physics) *Brazil*

Daecke, Sigurd (*Theology/Religion*) *Germany*

Dalferth, Ingolf Ulrich (*Theology/Religion*, also Philosophy) *Germany*, also Switzerland

Davis, Marjorie Hall (*Theology/Religion*, also Psychology/Counseling) *Connecticut*

de Knijff, Henri Wijnandus (*Theology/Religion*) *The Netherlands*

Deason, Gary Bruce (*Theology/Religion*, also History and Philosophy of Science) *Minnesota*

Deuser, Hermann (*Theology/Religion*) *Germany*

Dillenberger, John (*Theology/Religion*) *California*

Dittes, James E. (*Theology/Religion*, also Psychology/Counseling) *Connecticut*

Dols Jr., William L. (*Theology/Religion*, also Psychology/Counseling) *Missouri*

Downing, Barry H. (*Theology/Religion*, also Technology) *New York*

Drees, Willem B. (*Theology/Religion*, also Physics) *The Netherlands*

Duchrow, Ulrich (*Theology/Religion*) *Germany*

Dufner, Andrew J. (*Theology/Religion*, also Philosophy, Physics) *Oregon*

DuMaine, R. Pierre (*Theology/Religion*) *California*

Eckstrom, Vance L. (*Theology/Religion*) *Kansas*

Edgar, William (*Theology/Religion*) *Pennsylvania*

Euvé, François (*Theology/Religion*, also Physics, Philosophy) *France*

Evans, C. A. (*Theology/Religion*) *Canada*

Fairchild, Roy W. (*Theology/Religion*, also Psychology/Counseling, Sociology) *California*

Falla Jr., William S. (*Theology/Religion*, also Earth Science) *Pennsylvania*

Fasching, Darrell J. (*Theology/Religion*, also Ethics, Philosophy) *Florida*

Ferrell, Ginnie (*Theology/Religion*, also Earth Science, Chemistry) *Maine*

Fiddes, Victor H. (*Theology/Religion*) *Canada*

Firestone, Homer Loon (*Theology/Religion*, also Psychology/Counseling, Languages) *California*, also *Bolivia*

Fischer, Dick (*Theology/Religion*) *Virginia*

Forster, Peter R. (*Theology/Religion*, also History *United Kingdom*

Fowler III, James W. (*Theology/Religion*, also Ethics, Education, Psychology/Counseling) *Georgia*

Frey, Christofer (*Theology/Religion*, also Sociology, Ethics) *Germany*

Gaál, Botond (*Theology/Religion*, also Physics, Mathematics) *Hungary*

Gardipee, Steven M. (*Theology/Religion*, also Philosophy) *Wisconsin*

Gelwick, Richard (*Theology/Religion*, also Philosophy, History and Philosophy of Science, Interdisciplinary Studies) *Maine*

Giannoni, Paolo (*Theology/Religion*) *Italy*

Gilkey, Langdon (*Theology/Religion*, also Philosophy) *Illinois*

Gregersen, Niels Henrik (*Theology/Religion*, also History and Philosophy of Science, Ethics) *Denmark*

Gregorios, Paulos Mar (*Theology/Religion*, also Administration, History and Philosophy of Science, Philosophy) *India*

Griffin, David Ray (*Theology/Religion*, also Philosophy, History and Philosophy of Science) *California*

Griffin, Douglas L. (*Theology/Religion*) *Maryland*

Gromacki, Robert Glenn (*Theology/Religion*) *Ohio*

Habgood, John S. (*Theology/Religion*, also Biochemistry/Biophysics) *United Kingdom*

Hafner, Hermann Friedrich (*Theology/Religion*, also History and Philosophy of Science) *Germany*

Haikola, Lars T. J. (*Theology/Religion*, also Philosophy) *Sweden*

Handspickel, Meredith Brook (*Theology/Religion*) *Massachusetts*

Hanford, Jack T. (*Theology/Religion*, also Philosophy, Ethics) *Michigan*

Happel, Stephen (*Theology/Religion*) *Washington, D.C.*

Hardy, Daniel W. (*Theology/Religion*) *New Jersey*

Harrington, Donald S. (*Theology/Religion*) *New York*

Harris, E. Lynn (*Theology/Religion*, also Literature, Psychology/Counseling) *Illinois*

Hart, John (*Theology/Religion*, also Philosophy, Commerce, Ethics) *Montana*

Hasel, Frank Michael (*Theology/Religion*) *Michigan*

Haught, John F. (*Theology/Religion*) *Washington, D.C.*

Heaney, John J. (*Theology/Religion*, also Psychology/Counseling) *New York*

Hedman, Bruce A. (*Theology/Religion*, also Mathematics) *Connecticut*

Hefner, Philip (*Theology/Religion*, also Interdisciplinary Studies, Philosophy) *Illinois*

Heim, S. Mark (*Theology/Religion*) *Massachusetts*

Henry, Carl F. H. (*Theology/Religion*, also Philosophy, Ethics) *Virginia*

Heron, Alasdair Iain Campbell (*Theology/Religion*) *Germany*

Hilden, Kurt Mark (*Theology/Religion*, also Philosophy) *California*

Horvath, Tibor (*Theology/Religion*, also Philosophy, Interdisciplinary Studies) *Canada*

Hübner, Jürgen (*Theology/Religion*, also Molecular Biology, Ecology/Environment, History and Philosophy of Science) *Germany*

McFague, Sallie (*Theology/Religion*) *Tennessee*

McKenna, John E. (*Theology/Religion*, also Chemistry) *California*

Miller, James Bradley (*Theology/Religion*, also Philosophy) *Pennsylvania*

Mills, Joy (*Theology/Religion*, also Psychology/Counseling, History, Literature) *California*

Mitchell, Robert P. (*Theology/Religion*) *New Jersey*

Molari, Carlo (*Theology/Religion*) *Italy*

Moltmann, Jürgen (*Theology/Religion*) *Germany*

Montefiore, Hugh (*Theology/Religion*) *United Kingdom*

Montgomery, Robert Lancaster (*Theology/Religion*, also Sociology) *New Jersey*

Moore, James R. (*Theology/Religion*, also History and Philosophy of Science) *United Kingdom*

Mortensen, Viggo (*Theology/Religion*, also Ethics, Philosophy) *Switzerland*

Mosley, Glenn R. (*Theology/Religion*) *Missouri*

Muck, Terry C. (*Theology/Religion*) *Illinois*

Mullins, Carl Phillips (Phil) (*Theology/Religion*, also Literature) *Missouri*

Murphy, George L. (*Theology/Religion*, also Physics) *Ohio*

Musschenga, A. W. (*Theology/Religion*, also Ethics) *The Netherlands*

Musser, Donald W. (*Theology/Religion*, also Chemistry, Engineering) *Florida*

Nasimiyu, Anne (*Theology/Religion*) *Kenya*

Nelson, J. Robert (*Theology/Religion*, also Ethics) *Texas*

Nelson, James S. (*Theology/Religion*) *Illinois*

Nelson, Robert T. (*Theology/Religion*, also Biochemistry/Biophysics) *United Kingdom*

Nethöfel, Wolfgang (*Theology/Religion*, also Ethics) *Germany*

Neuner, Peter (*Theology/Religion*) *Germany*

Neville, Robert Cummings (*Theology/Religion*, also Philosophy) *Massachusetts*

Newman, Robert Chapman (*Theology/Religion*) *Pennsylvania*

Nordgren, Richard (*Theology/Religion*, also Chemistry) *Washington*

Ogden, Schubert Miles (*Theology/Religion*) *Colorado*

Oliver, Harold H. (*Theology/Religion*, also Philosophy) *Massachusetts*

Olson, Roger Eugene (*Theology/Religion*) *Minnesota*

Overman, Richard H. (*Theology/Religion*) *Washington*

Owens, Joseph V. (*Theology/Religion*, also Philosophy) *Honduras*

Panitz, Michael E. (*Theology/Religion*, also History) *New Jersey*

Pannenberg, Wolfhart (*Theology/Religion*) *Germany*

Parenti, Sergio (*Theology/Religion*) *Italy*

Parker, Thomas (*Theology/Religion*) *Illinois*

Patrick, Thomas E, (*Theology/Religion*, also Administration) *Minnesota*

Paul, Iain (*Theology/Religion*, also Chemistry) *United Kingdom*

Peters, Theodore Frank (*Theology/Religion*) *California*

Petras, David M. (*Theology/Religion*) *Ohio*

Petzoldt, Matthias (*Theology/Religion*) *Germany*

Pilchik, Ely E. (*Theology/Religion*) *New Jersey*

Post, Stephen G. (*Theology/Religion*, also Biology, Ethics) *Ohio*

Price, Daniel J. (*Theology/Religion*) *Switzerland*

Prodi, Giovanni (*Theology/Religion*) *Italy*

Proudfoot, Wayne (*Theology/Religion*, also Philosophy) *New York*

Puddefoot, John Charles (*Theology/Religion*, also Mathematics) *United Kingdom*

Ramsden, William E. (*Theology/Religion*, also Psychology/Counseling) *Pennsylvania*

Reisz Jr., H. Frederick (*Theology/Religion*, also Ethics) *South Carolina*

Richardson, W. Mark (*Theology/Religion*) *California*

Riggan, George A. (*Theology/Religion*) *Connecticut*

Ritschl, Dietrich (*Theology/Religion*, also Philosophy) *Germany*

Rolston III, Holmes (*Theology/Religion*, also Philosophy, Physics) *Colorado*

Saltzman, Judy D. (*Theology/Religion*) *California*

Santmire, H. Paul (*Theology/Religion*, also History *Ohio*

Sauter, Gerhard (*Theology/Religion*) *Germany*

Scheffczyk, Leo (*Theology/Religion*) *Germany*

Schmiedehausen, Hans (*Theology/Religion*, also Ecology/Environment) *Germany*

Schmitz-Moormann, Karl (*Theology/Religion*, also Philosophy, History *Germany*

Schroeder, W. Widick (*Theology/Religion*, also Ethics) *Illinois*

Schubert, Mathias (*Theology/Religion*) *Germany*

Schwarz, Hans (*Theology/Religion*) *Germany*

Schwarzwäller, Klaus (*Theology/Religion*, also Ethics) *Germany*

Sciegaj, Mark (*Theology/Religion*) *Georgia*

Seckler, Max (*Theology/Religion*) *Germany*

Segal, Robert A. (*Theology/Religion*) *United Kingdom*

Sevenhoven, J. C. A. M. (*Theology/Religion*, also Philosophy) *The Netherlands*

Sharpe, Kevin James (*Theology/Religion*, also Philosophy, Mathematics, Communications) *New Hampshire*

Shinn, Roger L. (*Theology/Religion*, also Ethics, Philosophy) *New York*

Shropshire Jr., W. (*Theology/Religion*, also Biochemistry/Biophysics) *Washington, D.C.*, also Maryland

Siegwalt, Gérard (*Theology/Religion*) *France*

Siirala, Aarne (*Theology/Religion*, also Ethics) *Canada*

Smith, David H. (*Theology/Religion*, also Philosophy) *Indiana*

Sperry, Roger W. (*Theology/Religion*) *California*

Stahl, Rainer (*Theology/Religion*) *Germany*

Stines, James W. (*Theology/Religion*, also Philosophy) *North Carolina*

Stoll, John Henry (*Theology/Religion*, also Psychology/Counseling) *Minnesota*

Sturm, Mary J. (*Theology/Religion*) *Minnesota*

Sutherland Jr., Malcolm Read (*Theology/Religion*, also Administration, Education) *Massachusetts*

Taylor, Howard G. (*Theology/Religion*, also Physics, Mathematics) *United Kingdom*

Taylor, Jon (*Theology/Religion*) *Montana*

Thomson, Alexander (*Theology/Religion*) *United Kingdom*

Tilley, Terrence U. (*Theology/Religion*, also Philosophy) *Ohio*

Timm, Roger E. (*Theology/Religion*, also Philosophy) *Illinois*

Tödt, Heinz Eduard (*Theology/Religion*, also Ethics) *Germany*

Toolan, David (*Theology/Religion*, also Philosophy) *New York*

Torrance, Thomas F. (*Theology/Religion*, also History and Philosophy of Science) *United Kingdom*

Trost, LouAnn (*Theology/Religion*, also Ecology/Environment, Philosophy) *California*

Troster, Lawrence (*Theology/Religion*) *New Jersey*, also New York

Vahanian, Gabriel (*Theology/Religion*) *France*

van den Brom, Luco Johan (*Theology/Religion*, also Mathematics, Physics) *The Netherlands*

van Dijk, Paul (*Theology/Religion*, also Ethics) *The Netherlands*

van Huyssteen, Jacobus Wentzel Vrede (*Theology/Religion*, also Philosophy) *New Jersey*

van Kouwenhoven, Willem F. (*Theology/Religion*) *The Netherlands*

Van Ness, William (*Theology/Religion*, also Education) *California*

Viladesau, Richard (*Theology/Religion*, also Philosophy) *New York*

Vorster, Willem S. (*Theology/Religion*) *South Africa*

Waldenfels, Hans (*Theology/Religion*, also Philosophy) *Germany*

Ward, Keith (*Theology/Religion*, also Philosophy) *United Kingdom*

Waters, Brent (*Theology/Religion*) *California*

Webster, John Wilfred (*Theology/Religion*, also Ethics, Philosophy) *South Africa*

Welker, Michael (*Theology/Religion*, also Philosophy) *Germany*

Wheeler, David L. (*Theology/Religion*, also Philosophy) *Kansas*

Whittaker-Johns, Barbara A. (*Theology/Religion*, also Education) *Massachusetts*

Widmer, Gabriel-Philippe (*Theology/Religion*) *Switzerland*

Wiebe, Donald (*Theology/Religion*, also Philosophy) *Canada*

Wildiers, Max (*Theology/Religion*, also Philosophy, Biology) *Belgium*

Wiltsher, Christopher D. (*Theology/Religion*, also Philosophy, Mathematics, Computer and Information Sciences) *United Kingdom*

Winkeler, L. G. M. (*Theology/Religion*) *The Netherlands*

Wolf, Jakob (*Theology/Religion*) *Denmark*

Wonderly, Daniel E. (*Theology/Religion*, also Biology, Earth Science) *Maryland*

Wong, Wing-Hong (*Theology/Religion*, also Physics) *United Kingdom*

Wood, William A. (*Theology/Religion*) *California*

Young, David Nigel de Lorentz (*Theology/Religion*, also Mathematics) *United Kingdom*

Yu, Carver Tatsum (*Theology/Religion*, also History, Philosophy) *Hong Kong*

Organizations Index

Affiliation of Christian Geologists

The Alister Hardy Research Centre

The American Scientific Affiliation (ASA)

Applied Christian Theology Unit for Scientists, Engineers and Technologists (ACTUSET)

The Association of Christians in the Mathematical Sciences (ACMS)

Associazione Teilhard de Chardin - Centro di ricerca per il futuro dell'uomo

ATOMIUM, Working Group for the Study of Theology and Science

Au Sable Institute of Environmental Studies

Het Bezinningscentrum (Interdisciplinary Center for the Study of Science, Society and Religion)

Center for Advanced Study in Religion and Science (CASIRAS)

Center for Faith and Science Exchange (FASE)

The Center for Frontier Sciences

Center for Theology and the Natural Sciences (CTNS)

The Center of Theological Inquiry (CTI)

The Centre for Advanced Religious and Theological Studies

The Chicago Advanced Seminar on Religion in an Age of Science

The Chicago Center for Religion and Science (CCRS)

Christians in Science (CIS)

Christians in Science Education (CISE)

Committee on Human Values of the National Conference of Catholic Bishops

The Common Boundary Between Spirituality and Psychotherapy

Cosmos and Creation

The European Society for the Study of Science and Theology (ESSSAT)

Evangelische Akademie Loccum (The Protestant Academy at Loccum)

Forschungsinstitut für Philosophie Hannover

Organizations Index

Forschungsstätte der Evangelischen Studiengemeinschaft (F.E.ST.) in Heidelberg

The Geoscience Research Institute

The Institute for Scientific Humanism (ISH)

Institute for Theological Encounter with Science and Technology (ITEST)

Institute for the Study of Christianity in an Age of Science and Technology (ISCAST)

The Institute of Religion at Texas Medical Center

Institute on Religion in an Age of Science (IRAS)

Institut für Wissenschaftstheoretische Grundlagenforschung

Instituut voor Ethiek aan de Vrije Universiteit (IEVU)

Interdisciplinary Biblical Research Institute (IBRI)

Internationales Wissenschaftsforum der Universität Heidelberg (IWH)

The International Society for the Study of Human Ideas on Ultimate Reality and Meaning (ISSURAM or simply URAM)

The Isthmus Institute

Karl-Heim-Gesellschaft

Katholiek Studiecentrum (KSC) (Catholic Study Center of the Catholic University of Nijmegen)

Nova Spes

The Park Ridge Center

The Pascal Centre for Advanced Studies in Faith and Science

Person, Culture and Religion (a group of the American Academy of Religion)

The Polanyi Society

Pope John XXIII Medical-Moral Research and Education Center

Psychological Centre for Comparative Mysticism (PSYCOM)

The Reilly Center for Science, Technology, and Values

Science and Religion Forum

Scienza e Fede

Society for Health and Human Values (SHHV)

The Society of Christian Philosophers

Society of Ordained Scientists

Society, Religion and Technology Project (SRT)

St. George's House, Windsor Castle

Stiftung "Theologie und Natur" beim Stifterverband für die Deutsche Wissenschaft ("Theology and Nature" Foundation)

Techniek, Beroep, Geloof (Technology, Profession and Faith Foundation)

Theology and Science Group of the American Academy of Religion

Thijmgenootschap

The Victoria Institute

Journal Index

Bridges: An Interdisciplinary Journal of Theology, Philosophy, History, and Science

Common Boundary Between Spirituality and Psychotherapy

Il Futuro dell'Uomo

Isis (Journal of the History of Science Society)

Journal of Interdisciplinary Studies (JIS)

Perspectives on Science and Christian Faith

Progress in Theology

Science and Christian Belief

Science and Religion News

Second Opinion

Tradition and Discovery: The Polanyi Society Periodical

Ultimate Reality and Meaning, Interdisciplinary Studies in the Philosophy of Understanding

Zygon: Journal of Religion and Science

About Sir John Marks Templeton

Sir John Marks Templeton, the sponsor of this book and whose staff compiled this reference book, was chairman of Templeton, Galbraith and Hansberger, Ltd., an investment counsel firm, until 1992.

He established the well-known international Templeton Foundation Prize for Progress in Religion to call attention to a variety of persons who have found new ways "to increase man's love of God or man's understanding of God." The award has been presented annually since 1973.

Sir John serves on the management council of Templeton College, Oxford University, and is trustee and founder of the John Templeton Foundation. He was on the board of Princeton Theological Seminary for thirty-nine years, serving as chairman for fifteen of those years. He has been a trustee for the restoration of Westminster Abbey since 1991, and a founding member of the Chief Executives organization.

The following statement — The Theology of Humility — was written by Sir John Templeton in March of 1990. Presented here by Sir Templeton as a document to stimulate thought and discussion, it has no relation of any kind to the compilation of data in *Who's Who in Theology and Science.*

The Theology of Humility

Centered in an Infinite God

The Theology of Humility means we know so little and need to learn so much and to devote resources to research. The Theology of Humility is not man-centered but God-centered. It proposes that the infinite God may not even be describable adequately in human words and concepts and may not be limited by human rationality. Perhaps God is not limited by our five senses and our perceptions of three dimensions in space and one dimension in time. Perhaps there was no absolute beginning and there will be no absolute end, but only everlasting change and variety in the unlimited purposes, freedom and creativity of God.

Maybe God is all of time and space — and much more. The appearance of humankind on this planet may be said to have heralded the coming of a new quality encircling the earth, the sphere of the intellect. Then, as we have used our intellects to investigate this mysterious universe, accumulating knowledge at an ever-increasing rate, there has come a growing awareness that material things are not what they seem; that maybe thoughts are more real and lasting than matter and energy.

Perhaps this heralds a new quality, the sphere of the spirit. God may be creating not only the infinitely large, but also the infinitely small; not only the outward, but also the inward; not only the tangible, but also the intangible. Thoughts, mind, soul, wisdom, love, originality, inspiration and enthusiasm may be little manifestations of a Creator who is omniscient, omnipotent, eternal and infinite. The things that we see, hear and touch may be only appearances. They may be only manifestations of underlying forces, including spiritual forces, which may persist throughout all the transience of physical existence. Perhaps the spiritual world, and the benevolent Creator whom it reflects, may be the only reality.

Presumably the sphere of the spirit may enclose not only this planet but the entire universe, and so God is all of Nature, is inseparable from it, and yet exceeds it. Perhaps it is mankind's own ego which leads us to think that we are at the center, rather than merely one tiny temporal outward manifestation of a vast universe of being which subsists in an eternal and infinite reality which some call God. Maybe all of nature is only a transient wave on the ocean of all that God eternally is. Maybe time, space and energy provide no limit to the Being which is God.

Creative, Progressive

The Theology of Humility encourages change and progress. Science is revealing to us an exciting world in dynamic flux, whose mechanisms are ever more baffling and staggering in their beauty and complexity. Scientists are learning to live and work with quantum uncertainty and complementarily, major discontinuities in evolution and baffling complexity in cellular differentiation. Yet scientists have turned these and other discoveries into opportunities, and many of them have expressed a new openness to philosophical and religious questions about life and the universe.

While science has generally responded favorably to change, the long history of religion is filled with the failures of thousand of religions. Perhaps these religions disappeared partly because their conceptions of God were too small or their practitioners were too inflexible to receive new revelations. A Theology of Humility proposes that maybe God is now providing new revelations in ways which go beyond any religion, to those who welcome the originality of the Creation and its continual surprises. For example, some theologians and scientists see tremendous possibilities for our future understanding of ourselves and our Creator through an integration of the new discoveries of science with many religious traditions — a new "theology of science."

Perhaps our human concepts of God are still tied to a previous century. the twenty-first Century after Christ may well represent a new Renaissance in human knowledge, a new embarkation into the concepts of the future. Persons now living can hardly imagine the small amount of knowledge and the limited concepts of the cosmos which man had when the scriptures of the five major religions were written. Perhaps old scriptures need new interpretations. The Theology of Humility seeks to build on the great theologies of the past and present and does not oppose any other theology. It welcomes the ideas and inspiring literature of all religions. But perhaps we should be open to the possibility of various new unprecedented religions where the revolutions in our conceptions of time, space and matter significantly shape our theology. Perhaps, while recognizing that God should not be thought of as impersonal, our names for God should be less heavily focused on personhood, since their usage favors man-centered concepts. The Creator seems to be both transcendent and immanent, accessible both by science and by prayer, ready to transform the lives of those who invite him in.

The Theology of Humility encourages thinking which is open-minded and conclusions which are qualified with the tentative world "maybe." It encourages change and progress and does not resist any advance in the knowledge of God or of nature, but is always ready to rethink what is known and to revise the assumptions and preconceptions behind our knowledge. It is possible that, through the gift of free will, God allows us to participate in this ongoing creative process. Perhaps prerequisite on our part is to look beyond our biases and our fears, our personal hopes and aspirations, to see the glorious planning and the infinite majesty of the Planner. Maybe we should also ask ourselves —whether we are students of the natural or spiritual worlds — to study and experience the intimate relationships between physical and spiritual realities in our own lives.

Diversity

The Theology of Humility does not encourage syncretism but rather an understanding of the benefits of diversity. Constant change would seem to be the character of our universe. Despite the cycles of day and night and the seasons, we may be learning that nothing really repeats. The pattern that unfolds with time may not close back upon itself. Maybe it moves ahead, upward a little at each turn. The evolution of our universe would seem to be vast in its conception, yet curiously experimental and tentative, a truly creative work in progress. Perhaps human beings, so late an appearance in this evolutionary process, have been given some creative role in seeking to understand and interpret awesome and mysterious processes which science only now begins to fathom. We suppose that our part might be likewise to conceptualize and experiment over a wise diversity of possibilities in the physical and spiritual worlds.

In the physical world, perhaps we should reexamine the arrow of time. Thermodynamics has tended to provide a picture of irreversible movement from order to randomness as the universe "runs down." But this is the antithesis of what appears to happen in the evolution from simplicity to complexity which has occurred in the evolution of the universe and of life. It is as though apparently self-integrated units of the simplest matter exhibit powers which successfully oppose the trend to randomness and produce instead orderly events and structures. Where man-made structures decay, natural systems seem driven toward growth and toward greater diversity and complexity. Here perhaps we have one of the greater laws describing the nature of the cosmos. If only blind chance were involved in evolution, we might expect decay and disorder. Yet the end-product of evolution, up to this point, is a conscious being endowed with a remarkable brain and dominated by purpose. Perhaps the physical world can only be understood as the expression of the purposes of the Creator.

In the spiritual world, perhaps diversity is also reflected in the variety of religions and in the multiplicity of denominations. It may be that this increasing diversity provides for a freedom and a loving and healthy competition without which there might be only lesser progress. Perhaps we should applaud the new research programs and the new organizations arising in each of the world's religions.

Encouraging Progress

The Theology of Humility does not rely on man-made institutions or governments, nor does it seek to influence them. Perhaps one of the greatest developments in human history has been the increasing possibility for the freedom of each individual to learn and grow and develop. The Theology of Humility seeks to improve the human condition by internal and spiritual sources rather than by external human governments or institutions.

It encourages worship of the Creator rather than dependence upon government, and spiritual growth rather than human, social and political activities.

The Theology of Humility suggests that tremendous benefits could accrue from our greater understanding of spiritual subjects such as love, prayer, meditation, thanksgiving, giving, forgiving and surrender to the Divine will. It further suggests that, since science is opening our eyes to the vast works of an Infinite Creator, science may also be applied to varieties of experimental and statistical study of these spiritual entities. It may be that we shall see the beginning of a new age of "experimental theology," wherein studies may reveal that there are spiritual laws, universal principles which operate in the spiritual domain, just as some natural laws function in the physical realm. Perhaps we will discover that the sphere of the spirit is intensifying as God's evolving plans unfold and accelerate.

Perhaps research foundations and religious institutions should devote vast resources and manpower to these scientific studies in the spiritual realm, equal or greater in magnitude to those currently expended on studies in the physical realm. There could be enormous rewards in terms of increased human peace, harmony, happiness and productivity if we collected more evidence that the God of the universe had put us here on this planet to learn from and challenge each other and to act as channels to radiate God's love, wisdom and joy.

John Marks Templeton

The John Templeton Foundation

March 1, 1990